West Africa

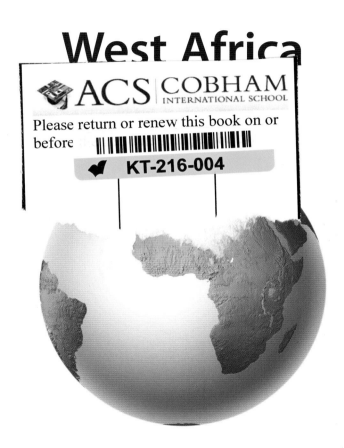

Anthony Ham

Tim Bewer, Stuart Butler, Jean-Bernard Carillet,
Paul Clammer, Emilie Filou, Katharina Kane, Adam Karlin,
Tom Masters, Kate Thomas

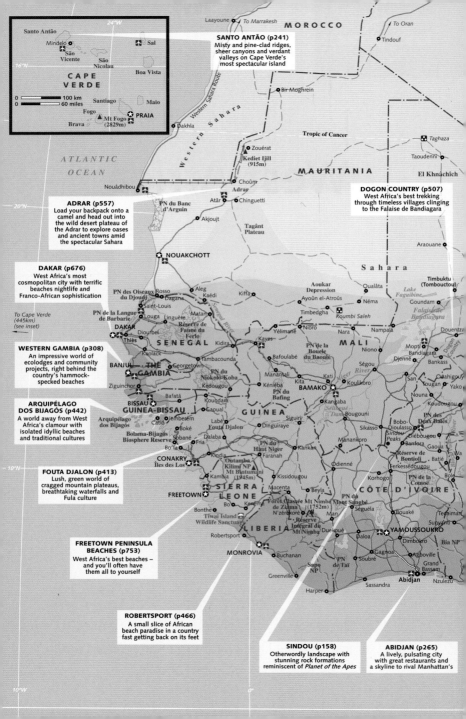

CAPE VERDE

Santo Antão
Mindelo ● São Vicente ● ■ Sal
São Nicolau
Boa Vista

0 —— 100 km
0 —— 60 miles

Santiago ● Maio
Fogo ▲ Mt Fogo ☆ PRAIA
Brava (2829m)

SANTO ANTÃO (p241)
Misty and pine-clad ridges, sheer canyons and verdant valleys on Cape Verde's most spectacular island

DOGON COUNTRY (p507)
West Africa's best trekking through timeless villages clinging to the Falaise de Bandiagara

ADRAR (p557)
Load your backpack onto a camel and head out into the wild desert plateau of the Adrar to explore oases and ancient towns amid the spectacular Sahara

DAKAR (p676)
West Africa's most cosmopolitan city with terrific beaches nightlife and Franco-African sophistication

WESTERN GAMBIA (p308)
An impressive world of ecolodges and community projects, right behind the country's hammock-speckled beaches

ARQUIPÉLAGO DOS BIJAGÓS (p442)
A world away from West Africa's clamour with isolated idyllic beaches and traditional cultures

FOUTA DJALON (p413)
Lush, green world of cragged mountain plateaus, breathtaking waterfalls and Fula culture

FREETOWN PENINSULA BEACHES (p753)
West Africa's best beaches – and you'll often have them all to yourself

ROBERTSPORT (p466)
A small slice of African beach paradise in a country fast getting back on its feet

SINDOU (p158)
Otherworldly landscape with stunning rock formations reminiscent of *Planet of the Apes*

ABIDJAN (p265)
A lively, pulsating city with great restaurants and a skyline to rival Manhattan's

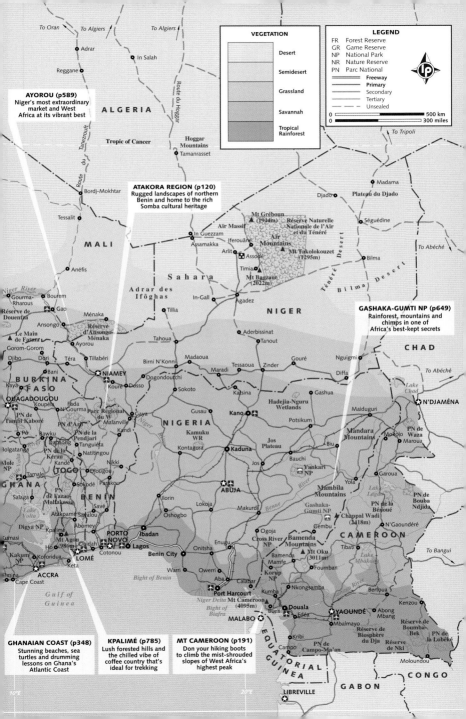

VEGETATION

Desert
Semidesert
Grassland
Savannah
Tropical Rainforest

LEGEND

FR Forest Reserve
GR Game Reserve
NP National Park
NR Nature Reserve
PN Parc National

━━━ Freeway
━━━ Primary
━━━ Secondary
┄┄┄ Tertiary
─ ─ ─ Unsealed

0 ────── 500 km
0 ────── 300 miles

AYOROU (p589)
Niger's most extraordinary market and West Africa at its vibrant best

ATAKORA REGION (p120)
Rugged landscapes of northern Benin and home to the rich Somba cultural heritage

GASHAKA-GUMTI NP (p649)
Rainforest, mountains and chimps in one of Africa's best-kept secrets

GHANAIAN COAST (p348)
Stunning beaches, sea turtles and drumming lessons on Ghana's Atlantic Coast

KPALIMÉ (p785)
Lush forested hills and the chilled vibe of coffee country that's ideal for trekking

MT CAMEROON (p191)
Don your hiking boots to climb the mist-shrouded slopes of West Africa's highest peak

West Africa Highlights

West Africa covers a wide swathe of the continent, from steamy tropical forest to the quiet dignity of the desert regions, areas peopled by many distinct groups, and held together by a sense of tribes, cultures and music. We asked our authors to share their favourite activities, impressions and experiences of this seductive region. Do you agree with their choices, or have we missed your favourites? Go to lonelyplanet.com/thorntree and tell us your highlights.

DAVID EL

1 TREKKING THROUGH MALI'S DOGON COUNTRY

Villages colonising the cliff face. Intricate cultural traditions that survived the onslaughts of the modern world. A landscape of rare beauty that rises from the plains of the Sahel like an apparition. Welcome to Mali's Dogon Country (p507), an extraordinary outpost of Old Africa.

Anthony Ham, Coordinating Author, West Africa

2 RANCH DE NAZINGA, BURKINA FASO

Elephants galore! In Serengeti National Park? No, in the humble Ranch de Nazinga (p161), near the Ghanaian border. At certain times of the year, you're almost guaranteed to get up close and personal with herds of truck-sized elephants. We saw them grazing foliage just in front of our bungalow!

Jean-Bernard Carillet, Lonely Planet Author, West Africa

STUART BUTLER

3 MINDELO'S CARNIVAL, CAPE VERDE

I'd heard all about Mindelo's Carnival (p239) but didn't really expect much from it. Hours after arriving in the city though and I was enveloped in clouds of colour and noise as hundreds of beautiful people tarted up like spring butterflies danced through the sweaty streets of Africa's sexiest festival.

Stuart Butler, Lonely Planet Author, West Africa

CHRISTOPHER HERV

4 **MONROVIA, LIBERIA**

Liberia's capital, Monrovia (p460), seethes in the heat, relishing its dramatic position on a hilly spit of land between the Atlantic beaches and the 'swamp' – the marshy Mersurado River. The buildings may be in large part burnt-out ruins, and a collapsed bridge may be the city's most iconic emblem, but there's still an undeniable energy and optimism rising from the street. Despite the shanty towns and the UN military presence, Monrovia is undeniably one of the great African cities and deserves to be seen.

Tom Masters, Lonely Planet Author, West Africa

CHRISTOPHER HERV

5 **SLEEP ON THE BEACH, SIERRA LEONE**

Whether you pitch a tent or let locals string a mozzie net under a thatch roof on a local beach (p753), a night that begins with a bonfire and a barracuda dinner often becomes a magical moment.

Tim Bewer, Lonely Planet Author, West Africa

ARIADNE VAN ZANDBERGEN

6 ⓺ GAMBIA RIVER NATIONAL PARK, THE GAMBIA

The first flicker of sunlight sparks a symphony of baboon barks, birdcall and the morning shrieks of the chimps on the river in Gambia River National Park (p317). The cool water of the outdoor shower trickles down my spine, and as I walk across the platform for my morning coffee, I'm convinced that those cheeky red colobus monkeys are debating that curious creature who has come to join their treetop haven.

Katharina Kane, Lonely Planet Author, West Africa

JANE SWEEP

7 FROM TOGO TO BENIN ON THE ROAD LESS TRAVELLED

There is something exciting about crossing a border without going through a check-point: bureaucratic hassle aside, it's a reminder of how arbitrary borders can be when everything in the landscape, the people and the culture talks of continuity. Driving along the Atakora mountains' red tracks, surrounded by majestic beauty and unique *tata* architecture, is a fine example of that. Just get your passport stamped at the police station in Nadoba or Kandé in Togo (p795) and Boukoumbé in Benin (p120), and away you go.

Emilie Filou, Lonely Planet Author, West Africa

CHRISTINE SCHROE

8 BEN AMIRA MONOLITH, MAURITANIA

I didn't expect to find the second biggest monolith in the world standing in the empty Mauritanian desert, but it was even more of a surprise to find at its base an open-air sculpture exhibition. At Ben Amira (p560), granite boulders had been carved into animals, faces and abstract shapes to commemorate the year 2000, and then virtually forgotten about and left for travellers to chance upon by accident. Wild camping at this surreal art gallery remains one of my favourite memories of Mauritania.

Paul Clammer, Lonely Planet Author, West Africa

Contents

Regional Map Contents

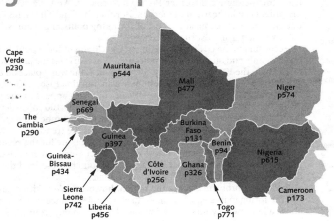

Cape Verde p230

Mauritania p544

Mali p477

Niger p574

Senegal p669

The Gambia p290

Guinea p397

Burkina Faso p131

Benin p94

Nigeria p615

Guinea-Bissau p434

Côte d'Ivoire p256

Ghana p326

Sierra Leone p742

Liberia p456

Togo p771

Cameroon p173

Destination West Africa

West Africa has cachet and soul in equal measure. Home to the signature African landscapes of our imaginations and inhabited by an astonishing diversity of peoples who still hold fast to their traditions, this is Africa as it used to be.

Here, elephants share the desert sands with indigo-clad Tuareg nomads, while the otherworldly animist traditions of the Dogon cling to the cliff faces. Elsewhere, extraordinarily rich musical traditions animate an already epic landscape, from the peoples along the shore of Niger River which labours through the Sahel like an evocation of a fairytale, to the melancholy soundtrack of Cape Verde in the shadow of its austerely beautiful volcanos. Or perhaps you'll best understand West Africa's allure amid the verdant rainforests of Cameroon, contemplating an Atlantic sunset alongside swaying palm trees, or with the red Sahel dust beneath your feet.

West Africa is in-your-face, full-volume Lagos, or the silent steps of a camel caravan silhouetted against a blood-red Saharan sunset. It's a smile of friendship from some of the world's poorest people. It's a beat, a rhythm, an idea of Africa that has somehow survived the ravages of time.

Good news about Africa can be hard to find, but West Africa has much to be proud of. Peace has returned to Côte d'Ivoire, Liberia and Sierra Leone and in a region where military rule was once the norm, Guinea and Mauritania now look like the odd ones out. In Mali, the Tuareg rebellion that began in 2006 seems to have almost run its course, while Benin has won plaudits for its press freedom and general economic progress. Senegal and Cape Verde rarely make the news, but continue to exhibit the stability and good governance which are their trademark. Ghana has been the star performer with another successful democratic transition in the 2008 elections, and its citizens riding a wave of optimism thanks to the discovery of offshore oil.

Of course, it's not all good news. Nigeria, that behemoth of disappointed hopes and seemingly perpetual unrest, continues to lumber and lurch, forward and back. In Niger and Mauritania, vast tracts of the Saharan north remain off-limits, home to bandits and rebels, while the assassination of Guinea-Bissau's president in March 2009 was the latest grim news to emerge from this beleaguered former Portuguese colony. And the rumblings of discontent can be heard in Cameroon, Burkina Faso and The Gambia where one-man rule has come at the cost of shrinking political freedoms. Togo is still emerging from just such a scenario.

According to the UN's annual Human Development Index, which is based on economic and quality-of-life indicators, West Africa is the poorest region on earth. In the 177-country study, Sierra Leone is the worst place on earth in which to live. Rounding out the bottom five are Burkina Faso, Guinea-Bissau, Niger and Mali. Five other West African countries appear in the bottom 20 and not one West African country appears in the 100 most-developed countries in the world. Only Cape Verde, which has climbed to a creditable 102nd despite negligible natural resources, bucks the trend.

Environmental degradation is another massive issue for the region. The Sahel in particular is facing a host of big-ticket environmental issues. So precarious is the outlook that one senior UN official described the region as the world's 'ground zero' for climate change.

For all the problems facing the region, however, West Africa has never lost the spring in its step. Dive in. Return the smiles. Dance to the music. But above all, immerse yourself in a journey that will change your life forever.

FAST FACTS

Number of West African countries: 17

Most common unit of currency: Euro (€)

Estimated total population: 297.7 million (half of whom are Nigerians)

Number of Unesco World Heritage–listed sites: 24

Longest/shortest life expectancy at birth: Cape Verde (71)/Sierra Leone (41.8)

Highest/lowest adult literacy rates: Cape Verde (81.2%)/Burkina Faso (23.6%)

Highest/lowest per capita annual incomes: Cape Verde (US$1940)/Liberia (US$167)

West Africa's highest point: Mount Cameroon (4095m)

Length of Niger River (Africa's third-longest): 4100km

The Sahara covers more than half of: Mali, Mauritania and Niger

Getting Started

Welcome to one of the least-known corners of the earth. In many cases, half-remembered fragments represent the sum total of Western knowledge about West Africa: the shadowy presence of Timbuktu, the sculpted perfection of a Saharan sand dune, the memory of a song by Youssou N'Dour. This lack of knowledge, this sense of entering into a realm remote from the world's consciousness, is what makes planning a trip to the region all the more rewarding. By visiting West Africa, you're embarking on a major expedition that requires careful planning and, for many travellers, setting out into the unknown. Addressing both elements – the practical and the stuff of dreams – should occupy most of your pre-departure planning.

For all but French-speaking travellers, finding good information on West Africa can be a challenge. What follows in this chapter is a distillation of the most useful and inspiring resources to help in your preparation, from the travel literature that captures the region's unmistakable whiff of the exotic to a host of unique festivals that can act as your route planner to the region. The region's world-renowned music, which will provide a stirring soundtrack for your visit, deserves a chapter of its own: see p57.

How you get around the region is an important question to consider before you touch down in Dakar, Bamako or Accra. Most travellers use buses, bush taxis and trains; although slower than travelling with a private vehicle, and you probably won't reach as many places, it's cheap and a great way to experience local life. If you've never travelled in Africa before, you may want to consider an organised tour (p838). For a range of possible itineraries to whet your appetite, see p20.

WHEN TO GO

Tourist seasons vary across the region, although high season generally runs from October or November through to March or April, with low season running from May to September. Exceptions include the beach resorts of Cape Verde, The Gambia and Senegal which are often packed to the rafters during the European summer.

See p810 for climate charts for major regional centres.

The best time to visit West Africa is during the drier and generally cooler months of November to February, although the dusty harmattan winds of the Sahel, which can reduce visibility and cause respiratory complaints, often begin in January and blow on and off through to May. Any time up to April is also dry; from then on it gets progressively hotter and more humid and May can be unbearably hot in the Sahel. Hotels along the coasts of Senegal and The Gambia are packed with European sunbathers on package tours from December to March. The Dogon Country, Timbuktu and Djenné in Mali can be very crowded, especially in December and January.

Unless you've no other option, the rain, heat and humidity of the rainy season, from May/June to September/October, is best avoided. The wettest areas are Guinea, Sierra Leone and Liberia, where annual rainfall often tops 4000mm and the humidity can be unbearable anywhere along the coast during this period. In all areas, rainy periods get shorter and rainfall decreases as you move further north and away from the ocean; in the Sahel, rain falls for a few hours per day, keeping the skies clear of dust and temperatures down. In a region where most minor roads are dirt, many roads can become impassable after heavy rains. Many wildlife reserves also close from June to November.

Another consideration for planning when to go are the major festivals that enliven travel in the region. Our pick of the festivals worth changing your

---

DON'T LEAVE HOME WITHOUT...

- sealable plastic bags – to protect your belongings from moisture and dust
- the requisite vaccinations (p851) and proof of yellow fever vaccination (most countries won't let you in without it)
- travel insurance (p816) – accidents do happen
- one smart set of clothes – advisable for visa applications, crossing borders or if you're invited to somebody's house
- basic medical kit (see p851)
- mosquito net and repellent
- light sleeping bag (for cold desert nights) or a sleeping sheet (for less-than-clean hotels)
- sunglasses, hat and sunscreen (as essential in the Sahara as on the beach)
- torch (flashlight) and spare batteries – electricity can be a stop-start affair
- sturdy water bottle, water purifier and filter
- universal washbasin plug and length of cord for drying clothes
- sanitary towels or tampons
- condoms
- an emergency stash of toilet paper
- photocopies of your important documents (and leave a copy somewhere safe back home)
- English-language books – they're rarely available in West Africa
- a Frisbee or small (size-three) football – a great way to meet local kids
- contact-lens-cleaning-and-soaking solutions and a pair of prescription glasses as a back-up
- patience – most transport does leave eventually

---

itinerary for are covered in the boxed text on p19. For a wider selection, you'll find the major festivals in each country in the Directory for each individual country chapter. Region-wide holidays, such as Ramadan and other major Islamic holidays (see p815) are also worth keeping an eye on, especially in the Sahel countries where everything can grind to a halt for a few days.

COSTS & MONEY

Just because West Africa is one of the poorest regions on earth doesn't mean that travelling here is cheap. Petrol can cost the same as it does in the West, with obvious implications for the cost of transport. For everything else, expect to pay between 50% and 75% of what you'd pay back home; Mali and Senegal are particularly expensive. Exceptions to the generally high prices include local food and beer. When crafting an overall budget for your trip, remember to include visa fees and the cost of hiring local guides.

If you're staying in the most basic accommodation (from US$5 a night), eating only local food (as little as US$2 a day), getting around on local transport (around US$3 per 100km), taking no tours and buying few souvenirs you can count on spending a minimum of US$15 per day, although US$20 to US$25 is more manageable. Those looking for more comfort (midrange hotels can range from US$20 to US$75 per night) and preferring to eat in reasonable restaurants (from US$4 to US$15 for a sit-down meal) could get by on US$35, but US$60 is a more reasonable budget. At the upper end, the sky's the limit. Top-end hotels start at around US$80 and can be three times that, organised tours are scarcely cheaper than taking a tour in Europe and car rental averages at least US$100 per day and sometimes more, plus petrol.

For advice on local accommodation costs, see the Accommodation section in each individual country's Directory.

TRAVELLING RESPONSIBLY

In West Africa, where the global inequities of wealth distribution are so pronounced, it's particularly important to ensure that your travel enjoyment is not at the expense of locals and their environment.

At one level, the impact of tourism can be positive: it can provide an incentive for locals to preserve environments and wildlife by generating employment, while enabling them to maintain their traditional lifestyles. However, the negative impacts of tourism can be substantial and contribute to the gradual erosion of traditional life. Please try to keep your impact as low as possible by considering the following tips

- Try to give people a balanced perspective of life in developed countries and point out the strong points of local culture (eg strong family ties, openness to outsiders).
- Make yourself aware of the human-rights situation, history and current affairs in the countries you travel through.
- Try not to waste water. Switch off lights and air-conditioning when you go out.
- When visiting historical sites, consider the irreparable damage you inflict upon them by taking home unattached artefacts (eg pottery shards or arrowheads).
- Many precious cultural objects are sold to tourists – you should only buy newly carved pieces to preserve West Africa's history and stimulate the carving industry.
- Question any so-called eco-tourism operators for specifics about what they're really doing to protect the environment and the people who live there.
- Support local enterprise. Use locally owned hotels and restaurants and support trade and craft workers by buying locally made souvenirs.
- Resist the local tendency of indifference to littering.

UK-based organisation **Tourism Concern** (☎ 020-7133 3800; www.tourismconcern.org .uk; Stapleton House, 277-281 Holloway Rd, London N7 8HN) is primarily concerned with tourism and its impact upon local cultures and the environment. It has a range of publications and contacts for community organisations, as well as further advice on minimising the impact of your travels.

WEST AFRICA'S WORLD HERITAGE SITES

Benin Royal palaces of Abomey (p112)

Cameroon Réserve de Biosphère du Dja (p215)

Côte d'Ivoire Parc National de Taï (p278) and Parc National de la Comoé (p264)

The Gambia James Island (p314)

Ghana Coastal forts and castles (see the boxed text, p354) and Ashanti traditional buildings in Kumasi (p369)

Guinea Nimba Mountains (see the boxed text, p425)

Mali Djenné old town (p499), Timbuktu (p516), Tomb of the Askia (Gao; p526) and Falaise de Bandiagara (Dogon Country; p507)

Mauritania Parc National du Banc d'Arguin (p556) and the *ksour* (fortified areas, or old quarters) of Ouadâne (p562), Chinguetti (p561), Tichit (p564) and Oualâta (p566)

Niger Réserve Naturelle Nationale de l'Aïr et du Ténéré (p578) and Parc Regional du W (p592)

Nigeria Osun Sacred Forest & Groves (p634) and Sukur Cultural Landscape

Senegal Île de Gorée (p693), Saint Louis (p707), Parc National des Oiseaux du Djoudj (p712), Parc National de Niokolo-Koba (p716) and the Stone Circles of Senegambia

Togo Koutammakou, the Land of the Batammariba (p795)

To see our list of businesses and activities committed to environmentally, socially, culturally or economically sustainable travel, turn to p910.

For advice on how to handle requests for gifts from everyone from beggars to slick-fingered policemen, see the boxed text, p37. Tips for travelling in Islamic areas are covered in the box on p43, for eating etiquette on p53 and for meeting locals on p40.

TRAVEL LITERATURE

The following inspirational titles all range across more than one West African country. For travel literature about individual countries, please see the Directory section of each country chapter.

The Lost Kingdoms of Africa, by Jeffrey Taylor, is a highly readable account of a modern journey through the Sahel, especially northern Nigeria, Niger and Mali; it was published in the US as *Angry Wind*.

The Shadow of the Sun, by Ryszard Kapuściński, is a masterpiece by one of Africa's most insightful observers with Africans always taking centre stage. Ghana, Nigeria, Mauritania, Senegal, Liberia, Cameroon and Mali all make an appearance.

Journey Without Maps, by Graham Greene, is a wonderful narrative by one of the 20th century's best writers as he travelled through the forests of Liberia and Sierra Leone in 1935.

Travels in the White Man's Grave, by Donald MacIntosh, is a little-known classic by a writer who spent much of his working life in the forests of Liberia, Nigeria, Côte d'Ivoire and Cameroon.

Travels in the Interior of Africa, by Mungo Park, recounts the troubled expeditions of one of Europe's most intrepid early-19th-century explorers; it's a fascinating window onto West Africa on the cusp of colonialism.

To Timbuktu, by Mark Jenkins, follows in the paddle-strokes of Mungo Park down the Niger River from its source on the Sierra Leone–Guinea border into Mali. It's great writing, if a little testosterone-fuelled in parts.

Sahara Unveiled, by William Langewiesche, takes you from Algiers to Dakar via the Sahara Desert. The prose can be as spare as the desert itself, which makes it a classic of Saharan travel literature.

French Lessons in Africa, by Peter Biddlecombe, skips lightly through the region, but it's one of few travel narratives to bring such a breadth of West African countries to an English-speaking audience.

'The prose can be as spare as the desert itself, which makes it a classic of Saharan travel literature.'

INTERNET RESOURCES

For specific country overviews and hundreds of useful links, head to Lonely Planet's website (www.lonelyplanet.com), including the Thorn Tree, Lonely Planet's online forum.

Background information on West Africa can also be found at the following websites:

Africa Centre (www.africacentre.org) US-based portal that's good for African events in the states with a handful of useful links.

African Studies Center (www.africa.upenn.edu//Home_Page/Country.html) Extensive links from the University of Pennsylvania's Africa program.

Ecowas (www.ecowas.info/index.htm) The official site of the Economic Community of West African States (Ecowas) with a few useful links.

Norwegian Council for Africa (www.afrika.no) A comprehensive site with extensive information and links for each country, chat forums and more.

Sahara Overland (www.sahara-overland.com) The best practical guide for travellers to the Sahara, with useful forums, route information and book reviews.

The Africa Guide (www.africaguide.com) An all-purpose, all-Africa site with everything from extensive background information to NGOs and travel links.

FAVOURITE FESTIVALS & EVENTS

- Festival in the Desert (p521; early January; Mali) Exceptional music festival amid Saharan sand dunes
- Voodoo Festival (p109; 10 January; Benin) Much merriment and voodoo celebration in Ouidah
- Festival Sur Le Niger (p494; late January–early February; Mali) Performances along the Niger riverbank in Ségou by Mali's leading musicians
- Grand Magal in Touba (p705; 48 days after Islamic New Year; Senegal) Spiritually charged annual pilgrimage that draws over two million followers of the Mouride Sufi brotherhood
- Carnival (p440; February; Guinea-Bissau) Latin-style street festival in Bissau with masks, parties and parades
- Fêtes des Masques (p284; February; Côte d'Ivoire) Man hosts West Africa's most important mask festival
- Fespaco (see the boxed text, p135; February-March in odd years; Burkina Faso) Africa's world-renowned film festival, held in Ouagadougou
- Argungu Fishing Festival (see the boxed text, p658; February-March) A fantastic fishing and culture festival on the banks of the Sokoto River in Nigeria's north
- Mardi Gras (see the boxed text, p239; 40 days before Easter; Cape Verde) Spectacular carnival-type celebration with street parades, especially in Mindelo
- Saint-Louis International Jazz Festival (p708; May; Senegal) West Africa's premier jazz festival that attracts big-name African and international artists
- Dak'Art Biennale (p734; May/June every even year; Senegal) West Africa's premier arts festival is held in Dakar
- Fetu Afahye Festival (p354; first Saturday in September; Ghana) Colourful carnival, dances and sacrifices to the gods
- La Cure Salée (see the boxed text, p604; usually first half of September; Niger) World-famous annual celebration by Fula herders featuring a male beauty contest and camel races, near In-Gall
- Igue Festival (Ewere Festival; p635; first half of December; Nigeria) Colourful seven-day festival with traditional dances, mock battle and procession to the palace to reaffirm loyalty to the *oba* (king) in Benin City
- Festival Kora & Cordes (p405; December; Guinea) A terrific music festival in Conakry with acoustic music groups from all over Guinea
- Cattle Crossing (see the boxed text, p497; December or January; Mali) Spectacular annual festival of Fula cattle herders around Mali's Inland Delta, especially Diafarabé
- Kano Durbar (p655; during Tabaski, 69 days after Ramadan; Nigeria) Colourful cavalry processions and high ceremony to honour West Africa's most important Islamic festival

Travel Africa (www.travelafricamag.com) The best print magazine on Africa; articles on West Africa are scattered amid the mainly East and Southern African subject matter.
West Africa Review (www.westafricareview.com) A scholarly journal with in-depth articles on West African countries and region-wide issues.

For good news sites on the region, try **AllAfrica.com** (www.allafrica.com), **Reuters Africa** (http://af.reuters.com), **Afrol News** (www.afrol.com), **BBC** (www.bbcnews.com/africa), **IRINNews** (www.irinnews.org/IRIN-Africa.aspx), **West Africa News** (www.westafricanews.com) and **Media Foundation for West Africa** (www.mediafound.org). In French, try **Jeune Afrique** (www.jeuneafrique.com, in French), **APA** (www.apanews.net), **Afrik** (www.afrik.com, in French) and **Afrique Index** (www.afriqueindex.com, in French). For country-specific websites, see the individual country chapters.

Itineraries
CLASSIC ROUTES

From Dakar to Agadez (around 4800km) can be reasonably done in six weeks (a week in Senegal, two to three weeks in Mali, a week in Burkina Faso and another week for Niger) using public transport. Two months would, be ideal.

THROUGH THE HEART OF THE SAHEL   Six to Eight Weeks / Dakar to Agadez

If you're wondering why Africa gets under the skin, begin in cosmopolitan **Dakar** (p676), leaving time for an offshore excursion to tranquil **Île de Gorée** (p693). Jump aboard the train to **Bamako** (p482) with its world-class nightlife and unmistakably African feel. Travelling northeast, pause in **Djenné** (p497) for its beautiful mud-brick mosque and clamorous Monday market, en route to the **Dogon Country** (p507) with its outstanding trekking and intriguing cultural traditions. No trip to West Africa is complete without an excursion to **Timbuktu** (Tombouctou; p516) on the Sahara's fringe. Timbuktu is on the road to nowhere so retrace your steps to the lovely, riverside town of **Ségou** (p493). From there make for Burkina Faso and **Bobo-Dioulasso** (p149), an infectiously languid town, then continue on to gloriously named **Ouagadougou** (p136) with a vibrant arts scene. After a detour to Togo's otherworldly **Tamberma Valley** (p795), head for Niger's riverbank capital, **Niamey** (p579), then on to **Agadez** (p599), an evocative former caravan town of the Sahara.

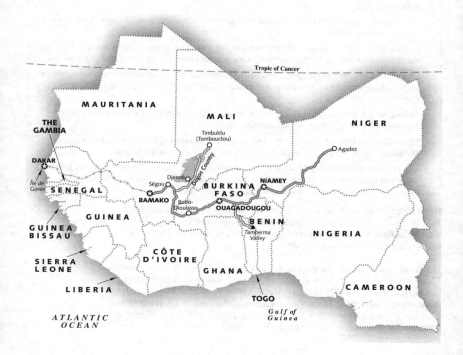

ATLANTIC ODYSSEY
Six Weeks / Dakar to Limbe

From the arid coastlines of the northwest to the palm-fringed tropics of Cameroon, West Africa's coastline has it all. Senegal's capital **Dakar** (p676), with its African sophistication and role as regional air hub, serves both as a starting point and a base for the first part of your journey. To the north, **Saint-Louis** (p707) is like stepping back into pre-colonial Africa. From Dakar, fly to the Cape Verde Islands with their soulful musical soundtrack, unspoiled beaches, mountainous interior and laid-back locals; **Santiago** (p234), **São Vicente** (p238), and **Santo Antão** (p241) are particularly beautiful. Returning to Dakar, head south to The Gambia which may be small, but its beaches, especially those around **Serekunda** (p298), make a good (English-speaking) rest stop for taking time out from the African road. From **Banjul** (p294), consider flying to agreeable **Accra** (p335) in Ghana, from where excursions to the old **coastal forts** (see the boxed text, p354), **Cape Coast Castle** (p352) and stunning beaches at **Kokrobite** (p348) and **Busua** and **Dixcove** (p360) never disappoint. Don't fail to detour north to **Kumasi** (p369) in the Ashanti heartland. There's plenty of onward transport to the fascinating markets and fine museum of **Lomé** (p776) and don't miss an inland hiking detour around **Kpalimé** (see the boxed text, p786). Not far away is Benin, with **Ouidah** (p107), the evocative former slaving port and home of voodoo, the history-rich town of **Abomey** (p111) and the stilt-villages of **Ganvié** (p104). **Cotonou** (p97) has all the steamy appeal of the tropics; from here fly to **Yaoundé** (p178) in Cameroon, which has a distinctive Central African feel. **Kribi** (p216) and **Limbe** (p187) are places to laze on the sand and consider just how far you've travelled.

Dakar to Limbe (around 2500km by land, plus flights) should take about six weeks (one week in Senegal, two in Cape Verde, two travelling from Ghana to Benin and a further week in Cameroon).

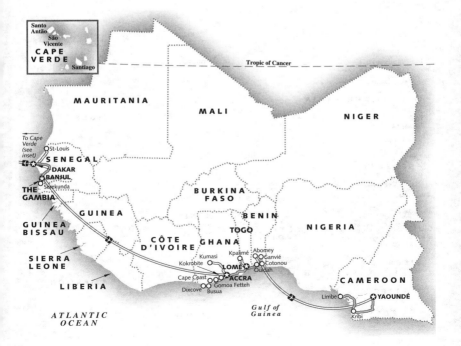

ROADS LESS TRAVELLED

UNKNOWN WEST AFRICA   One Month to Forever / Dakar to Sassandra

The westernmost extremity of Africa's bulge has, until recently, been off-limits to travellers. But while peace has come, the same can't be said for tourists – you could have these destinations all to yourself. Begin in **Dakar** (p676) and catch the ferry to **Ziguinchor** (p721), capital of **Casamance** (p719), home to fine beaches, labyrinthine river systems and lush forests. Guinea-Bissau is distinguished by the architectural remnants of Portugal's colonial occupation, some of West Africa's friendliest people, and a village-like capital, **Bissau** (p437). The **Arquipélago dos Bijagós** (p442) is isolated, rich in wildlife and like nowhere else on the coast. Continuing south, the excellent **Parque Nacional do Catanhez** (p450) is worth a detour. Across the border into Guinea, **Conakry** (p401), with good nightlife, is your gateway to the country's lush and beautiful interior; the stunning **Fouta Djalon highlands** (p413) offers good trekking and **Mali-Yemberem** (p418) is stunning. Head into the forests of Guinea's **Forest Region** (p423). Sierra Leone is another country on the up, with stunning beaches and **Freetown** (p746), the oddly beautiful capital that seems to contain all the country's optimism and drive. The truly adventurous may want to dip into **Liberia** (p454), but consider flying to **Abidjan** (p265), the still-sophisticated one-time 'Paris of Africa'. Head for **Yamoussoukro** (p279) and its improbable basilica, then, if the interior's safe, on to **Man** (p280) in the heart of Dan country. En route to the coast, stop off in the **Parc National de Taï** (p278) as you head for **Sassandra** (p277), a glorious fishing village with great beaches.

> Getting as far as Freetown involves around 3300km of dodgy roads and infrequent transport – count on anywhere between a month and forever. Transport is generally better in Côte d'Ivoire, where you'll cover an extra 1000km.

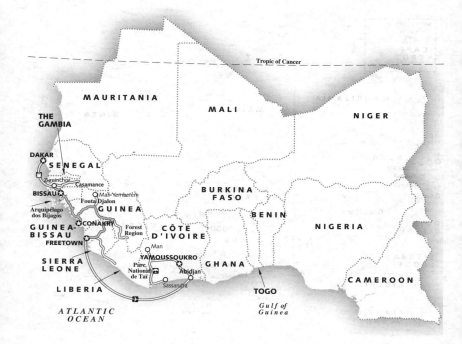

NIGERIA & CAMEROON   Two Months / Lagos to Ring Road

Nigeria is one of those destinations that suffers from bad press, although it must be said that most of the horror stories are told by those who've never set foot in the country. **Lagos** (p622) may be in-your-face, high volume and logistically confronting, but it's also Africa's most energetic city, awash with pulsating nightlife, clamorous markets and a terrific museum. **Osun Sacred Forest** (p634) in Okumu Sanctuary, and the Oba's Palace in **Benin City** (p636) are worthwhile stopovers as you head across the south en route to **Calabar** (p639), which is likeable for its old colonial buildings, fish market and lovely setting. Close to Calabar, don't miss **Afi Mountain Drill Ranch** (p643), the focus of an outstanding primate project, and then continue northeast to the remote but terrific **Gashaka-Gumti National Park** (p649) for some of Nigeria's best wildlife-watching. On your way north, stop off in **Zaria** (p651), then on to **Kano** (p653), West Africa's oldest city and one of the Sahel's most significant cultural centres.

The long journey east takes you across the border to **Maroua** (p208), a pleasant base for exploring the weird-and-wonderful landscapes of the **Mandara Mountains** (p210) and **Parc National de Waza** (p212). From **N'Gaoundéré** (p205), you can either head deep into the utterly untouristed rainforests (p213) of the southeast, which offer a verdant taste of Central Africa, or take the train through the country's heart, all the way to **Yaoundé** (p178). After longish detours to see the sea turtles at **Ebodjé** (p219), and to climb **Mt Cameroon** (p191), West Africa's highest peak, head for **Bamenda** (p195), your gateway to the villages of the **Ring Road** (p197), a deeply traditional area of Cameroon that feels untouched by time.

This route will see you covering at least 5500km (much more if you detour down into Cameroon's remote southeast) and will take a minimum of two months by public transport.

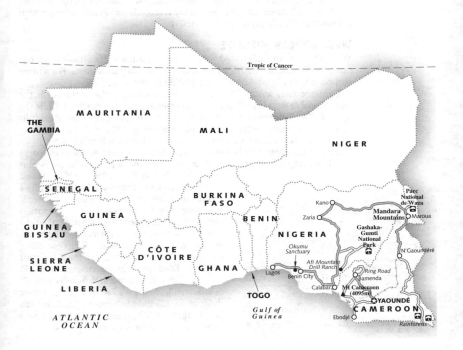

TAILORED TRIPS

INTO THE SAHARA

The sculpted perfection of seas of sand dunes. The timeless serenity of former caravan towns. The solitude of a vast land without horizons. If you're drawn by the call of these unmistakeable signposts of the world's largest desert, this itin-

erary is for you, although you'll either need your own or a rented 4WD. There's only one problem: at the time of writing, much of the Sahara is in rebellion (see the boxed texts, p525 and p606) and some destinations may be off-limits. Check the latest travel advice before setting out.

The safest route for crossing the Sahara is via its easternmost extremity, entering West Africa from the Western Sahara (p836). **Nouâdhibou** (p554) in Mauritania is a jumping-off point for the dramatic landform of **Ben Amira** (see the boxed text, p560), and for the wonderful oasis towns of **Chinguetti** (p561), surrounded by sand dunes, and **Ouadâne** (p562) with its stone-ruin sense of abandonment. Mauritania's **Tidjikja** (p564), **Tichit** (p564) and **Oualâta** (p566) all have beautifully painted houses deep in the desert. In Mali, **Timbuktu** (Tombouctou; p516), perhaps the greatest of all desert cities, is a gateway to lonely **Araouane** (p524). Evocative **Agadez** (p599) in Niger enables you to explore the other-worldly **Aïr Mountains** (p603), a desert home of the Tuareg, and the exquisitely remote **Ténéré Desert** (p603), which is known as the 'desert beyond the desert'.

WEST AFRICAN WILDLIFE

West Africa is an underrated wildlife destination and its little-known national parks host more African mega-fauna than they do tourists. For a more complete list of West Africa's best wildlife reserves, see p85.

Cameroon has some of West Africa's best national parks. In the north, the **Parc National de Waza** (p212), is home to elephants, giraffes and lions, while the southern **Parc National de Campo-Ma'an** (p220) hosts buffalos, elephants, mandrills and a nascent ecotourism project. **Korup National Park** (p194) is also outstanding, while on no account miss the chance to see sea turtles at **Ebodjé** (p219).

Benin's **Parc National de la Pendjari** (p121) is one of West Africa's best parks with lions, leopards, elephants and hippos. The same can be said for the Benin-

Niger cross-border **Parc Regional du W** (p592 and p123). Ghana's **Mole National Park** (p380), with 94 mammal species, including elephants, baboons, and antelopes, is that country's conservation showpiece. The **Réserve de Douentza** (p530) in Mali, home to Africa's northernmost elephants, is one of West Africa's best wildlife-watching experiences, as is tracking down the Sahel's last giraffes at **Kouré** (p589) in Niger. Senegal's World Heritage–listed **Parc National de Niokolo-Koba** (p716) is also terrific. Senegal's **Parc National des Oiseaux du Djoudj** (p712) and Mauritania's **Parc National du Banc D'Arguin** (p556) are among the best birding sites in the world for migratory species.

WEST AFRICA'S BEST MARKETS

West Africa's markets are where the peoples of the region meet and trade, where music blaring from speakers competes for attention with aromas fair and foul and where all the colours of Africa will brighten your day.

In Ghana, Kumasi's **Kejetia Market** (p369) is awash with the colours of Ashanti culture, while **Makola Market** (p339) in Accra is a wonderful slice of functioning chaos. In neighbouring Togo, the **Marché des Féticheurs** (p777) in Lomé will appeal if you need a monkey's skull. In Benin, Cotonou's huge **Grand Marché du Dantokpa** (p100) is similarly for those who get turned on by talismans. Lagos' **Balogun Market** (p626) is the best of many in Nigeria's capital. To the north, Kano's **Kurmi Market** (p653) is one of the largest markets in Africa. In Niger, the **Tuareg camel market** (p600) in Agadez is full of Tuareg men in turbans, while **Ayorou's Sunday Market** (p589) and **Gorom-Gorom's Thursday spectacular** (p163) in Burkina Faso are a who's who of the Sahel's ethnic groups. In Mali, Djenné's **Monday market** (p498) has the town's extraordinary mud-built mosque as a backdrop. **Bamako market** (p485), Bobo-Dioulasso's **Grand Marché** (p151) in Burkina Faso, Nouakchott's **Port de Pêche** (p551) in Mauritania, Dakar's **Marché Sandaga** (p691) and the massive market in **Kaolack** (p706), also in Senegal, are all also outstanding.

IN SLAVERY'S FOOTSTEPS

A visit to the sites where West Africa's slaves left the continent's shores for the last time is one of the region's most poignant experiences.

Ghana is home to the greatest concentration of slavery sites. Accra's **National Museum** (p339) has an evocative exhibition that sets the scene as you head for the many forts and castles where slaves were held in dire conditions and then loaded onto equally dire ships. They're all worth visiting, but **Cape Coast Castle** (p352), Elmina's **St George's Castle** (p357) and **Fort Amsterdam** (p351) are the showpieces. East along the coast, **Ouidah** (p107) in Benin is another emotion-filled reminder of slavery's horrors with a well-marked **Route des Esclaves** (p108) and a moving 'Point of No Return' memorial. **Badagry** (p630), in neighbouring Nigeria, was another major slaving centre with a good museum and coastal monument.

The ports of Senegal were also used by slaving ships, with slaves from the interior brought to the coast. Île de Gorée's **La Maison des Esclaves** (see the boxed text, p692), a grim former holding centre for slaves, is perhaps the most famous. Across the border in The Gambia, **Jufureh and Albreda** (p314), of *Roots* fame, and **James Island** (p314) are hugely significant sites. In Guinea is the lesser-known **Îles de Los** (p410) where countless Africans saw their last view of their continent. In Sierra Leone, **Bunce Island** (see the boxed text, p755) was a major shipping port for slaves, while **Freetown** (p746) was originally founded as a refuge for ex-slaves.

History

West Africa's story is one of history's grand epics. This is a place where the great issues and contradictions of Africa's past resonate through the present: from ancient empires of unrivalled extravagance to the ravages of slavery, from the region's fabulous natural resources to the destruction wrought by climate change, from proud independence and the colonial yolk to the more complicated sovereignty of the present. This is a tale that encompasses the stirring emptiness of the Sahara, the fluid interaction of trade and cultures along the Niger River and the clamour of the region's humid, tropical coasts. Above all, history West African–style is about an astonishing patchwork of peoples (see p71) trying to write their own history against all the odds.

For the colonial and postcolonial history of the 17 countries covered in this book, see the History sections of each individual country chapter.

African Rock Art, by David Coulson and Alec Campbell, is definitive and beautifully illustrated. It's one to keep on your coffee table, not carry in your backpack.

FIRST FOOTPRINTS ON THE SAHEL

West Africa's earliest history is shrouded in mystery, its archaeological evidence either residing in the belly of a termite or consumed by tropical climates and the shifting sands of the Sahara.

The first meaningful signposts to West Africa's past appeared around 10,000 years ago in the Sahara, especially the Aïr Mountains of northern Niger (p603) and the Adrar des Ifôghas in Mali (p529), where nomads roamed across a very different West Africa from what you see today. Rivers, forests, vast lakes and savannah occupied much of what is now the Sahara, the human population was small and widely dispersed, and animals such as elephants, giraffes and the great cats were plentiful.

Opinion among historians is divided as to whether knowledge of iron-working was introduced to the region from Egypt or actually originated in West Africa.

Around 5000 BC, domesticated cattle replaced elephants and giraffes in the carvings and finely rendered rock paintings left by hunter-gatherer peoples. This rock art, which serves as the Sahara's history books of the time, marks the moment when West Africans began to tame their natural environment as water became scarcer.

The earliest signs of organised society in West Africa date from around 1500 BC, in present-day Mauritania and northern Nigeria, where the remains of stone villages and domestic animals have been found. As settlements spread, two dominant groups emerged, the first along the Niger River, and the second around Lake Chad – both areas where soils were fertile and well-suited to agriculture. These groups built large stone villages and even towns. The first urban settlement of note was Jenné-Jeno, in present-day Mali (p500), which was established around 300 BC and is often considered the father of West African cities. By AD 500, towns and villages were dotted across the region.

Empires of Medieval West Africa: Ghana, Mali, and Songhay, by David Conrad, covers the sweep of West Africa's three greatest historical empires in one accessible tome.

TIMELINE

200,000 BC	From 5000 BC	450 BC
Homo erectus, the predecessor of *Homo sapiens* (modern humans), occupies much of West Africa, as suggested by the region's archaeological evidence: tools and other artefacts found in Senegal, Guinea, Mali, Mauritania and elsewhere.	Rains become infrequent and the Sahara begins to become a desert. Most of West Africa's peoples forsake transient life and settle in communities around water-holes, begin to rely on agriculture, and begin to move south.	The appearance of iron-working in central Nigeria enables the clearing of forests which expands agricultural land and commences the process of denuding West Africa's landscape that has never really abated in the centuries since.

WEST AFRICA'S GOLDEN EMPIRES

Hard as it is to believe now, two thirds of the world's gold once came from West Africa and the indigenous empires that controlled the West African interior, and hence the lucrative trans-Saharan trade routes were among the richest in the world.

Empire of Ghana

The Empire of Ghana was the first major state of its kind established in West Africa. It was founded in AD 300 with its capital at Koumbi Saleh, in present-day Mauritania, about 200km north of modern Bamako (Mali). By Ghana's 8th-century heyday, the empire covered much of present-day Mali and parts of eastern Senegal. Although smaller than the empires that followed it, Ghana was extremely wealthy and powerful, controlling not just trans-Saharan trade, but also massive gold deposits; rumour had it that the streets were paved with gold and that the emperor of Ghana routinely tied his horse to a nugget of pure gold.

Islam was introduced by traders from the north, but it couldn't save Ghana – the empire was destroyed in the late 11th century by the better-armed Muslim Berbers of the Almoravid Empire from Mauritania and Morocco. The Almoravids justified their invasion by pointing to Ghana's half-hearted adoption of Islam, but many historians believe that it had more to do with the Almoravid desire for Ghana's gold and control of trade routes.

Into Africa: A Journey through the Ancient Empires, by Marq de Villiers and Sheila Hirtle, looks at Africa's past through the prism of modern journeys through the region.

Empire of Mali

The Empire of Mali, founded in the middle of the 13th century by Sundiata Keita, leader of the Malinké people, was perhaps the most legendary of West African empires. Such was its wealth and prestige that it, more than any other African empire, was to spark the outside world's interest in the continent.

Mali's heyday was the 14th century. Mali's kings controlled not only Saharan trade and the gold mines that had fuelled the prosperity of the Empire of Ghana, but also a swath of territory that stretched from modern-day Senegal in the west to Niger in the east. Their ambition was matched only by the extravagance of their rule.

One such monarch, King Abubakari II, sent an expedition across the Atlantic in an attempt to discover the Americas almost two centuries before Christopher Columbus. Only one ship returned, with stories of a great river running through the ocean's heart. Abubakari II himself led a second expedition of 200 ships. Not a single ship returned.

King Abubakari's anointed successor, King Kankan Musa (the grand-nephew of Sundiata Keita), would prove to be one of the most extraordinary of all African kings. Like all of Mali's rulers, Musa was a devout Muslim and, in 1324, he made his pilgrimage to Mecca, accompanied by an entourage of more than 60,000 people and needing 500 slaves to carry all the gold. Along

Sundiata: An Epic of Old Mali, by DT Niane, is the most accessible English-language version of Mali's founding epic; it's like listening to the *griots* (praise singers attached to the royal court), during West Africa's glory days.

Timbuktu: The Sahara's Fabled City of Gold, by Marq de Villiers and Sheila Hirtle, provides a detailed look at Timbuktu, and the Songhaï capital Gao, during the Mali and Songhaï empires.

300 BC	AD 300	900
Jenné-Jeno is founded in what is now Mali and is recognised as West Africa's first-known urban settlement. It proves remarkably enduring – by AD 800, Jenné-Jeno is home to an estimated 27,000 people.	The Empire of Ghana is founded in what is now the barren badlands of the western Sahel. The first of the great West African empires, it holds sway over the region for 800 years.	Islam first reaches the Sahel, almost 250 years after it swept across the Sahara. It arrives as part of the trans-Saharan caravan trade and later becomes the predominant religion throughout much of West Africa.

THE EPIC OF SUNDIATA

In the annals of West African history, few tales have endured quite like the story of Sundiata Keita. In the 13th century, a sacred hunter prophesied to a minor Malinké king known as 'Maghan the Handsome', that if he married an ugly woman, she would one day bear him a son who would become a great and powerful king, known to all the world. Maghan followed the seer's advice, but when his son Sundiata was born, he was disabled and unable to walk. When Maghan's successors battled for the throne, Sundiata was bypassed and forced into exile, only to return one day as king. When he defeated his more powerful Sosso rivals in 1240, he was crowned 'Mansa', or 'King of Kings', whereafter he founded the Empire of Mali, with its capital at his village of Niani, close to the Guinea–Mali border. He drowned in 1255 but his legend lives on in the tales of *griots* (praise singers) and in songs that drew heavily on his story.

the way he gave away so much of his gold as gifts that the world gold price did not recover for 12 years, some say a generation. His actions attracted the attention of European merchants in Cairo and news spread quickly about a fabulously wealthy land in the desert's heart.

Under Malian sovereignty, trans-Saharan trade reached its peak, and the wealth created meant that Mali's main cities became major centres of finance and culture. The most notable was Timbuktu, where two Islamic universities were founded, and Arab architects from Granada (in modern-day Spain) were employed to design new mosques, such as Timbuktu's Dyingerey Ber mosque (p518).

> Some historians believe that the Gambia River's name (and indeed the name of the country) derives from the Portuguese word *cambio*, meaning 'exchange' or 'trade'.

Empire of Songhaï

While Mali was at the height of its powers, the Songhaï people had established their own city-state to the east, around Gao in present-day Mali. As Mali descended into decadence and royal squabbles, Gao became powerful and well organised. At its height, the Songhaï Empire stretched from close to Lake Chad in the east to the hinterland of the Atlantic Coast in the west. Its emperors were reported to have travelled to Mecca with 300,000 gold pieces.

A hallmark of the Empire of Songhaï was the creation of a professional army and a civil service with provincial governors. The state even subsidised Muslim scholars, judges and doctors. By the mid-15th century, the Empire of Songhaï was at its most powerful and presided over most of West Africa, and by the 16th century, Timbuktu was an important commercial city with about 100,000 inhabitants and a great seat of learning with its Sankore University home to 25,000 scholars.

> Until the Portuguese dispelled the myths, Cape Bojador was considered among sailors as the point of no return, beyond which lay monstrous sea-creatures, whirlpools, boiling waters and waterless coastlines.

But the Songhaï Empire would prove to be the last of West Africa's great empires. The golden period ended with an audacious invasion by Berber armies crossing the Sahara from Morocco in 1591.

Around 1000	Late 11th century	1240
Timbuktu is founded, near where the Niger River enters the Sahara Desert as a seasonal encampment for Tuareg nomads. It later becomes a great centre of scholarship and wealth, home to 100,000 people.	Not for the last time, one of West Africa's empires of the Sahel is overthrown by armies crossing the Sahara as the Empire of Ghana is destroyed by the Berber armies of the Almoravid Empire.	Sundiata Keita founds the Empire of Mali with its capital at Niani. The empire rules the Sahel for two centuries and presides over what many consider to be West Africa's golden age.

RECLAIMING WEST AFRICA'S HISTORY

West African history was, for centuries, assumed to be a solely oral tradition, the preserve of *griots* who kept alive the legends of the past; Mali's greatest 20th-century writer, Amadou Hampaté Bâ, summarised the strength of the tradition best: 'the death of an old man is like the burning down of a library'. Later, non-African historians interpreted the absence of written records as indicating an absence of civilisation; H Trevor Roper wrote in 1963 that 'Perhaps in the future there will be some African history to teach. But at present there is none. There is only the history of Europeans in Africa. The rest is darkness'.

That changed in the 1990s when an astonishing storehouse of manuscripts – up to five million across the Sahara by some estimates – was 'discovered' in Timbuktu and surrounding regions. The manuscripts contained scholarly works of poetry, philosophy, astronomy, mathematics, geography, physics, optics and medicine, including some that dated to the 13th century.

The manuscripts also included detailed histories of the region written by Africans, as well as the first-known examples of local languages in their written form, thereby suggesting that Africans could read and write long before Europeans arrived. Timbuktu also had a book-making tradition far more advanced than anything that Europe could muster until the invention of movable type in the 15th century and many books were printed on European-manufactured paper which had reached Timbuktu long before any explorers completed the journey.

According to Dr John Hunwick, a leading expert on Africa's written history: 'Africa has for too long been stereotyped as the continent of song and dance, where knowledge is only transmitted orally. We want to demonstrate that Africans think and write and have done so for centuries'. In short, the manuscripts could change forever the way we see West African history.

To learn more about the manuscripts of Timbuktu, turn to p518. The oases of the Adrar region of Mauritania also have rich manuscript collections, especially Chinguetti (p561) and Ouadâne (p563).

Later States & Empires

As the Empire of Mali declined, the Wolof people established the Empire of Jolof (also spelt Yollof) in 1360 near the site of present-day Dakar in Senegal. Meanwhile, on the southeastern fringe of the Songhaï realm, the Hausa created several powerful city-states, such as Katsina, Kano and Zinder (still important trading towns today), but they never amalgamated into a single empire.

Further east again, on the shores of Lake Chad, the Kanem-Borno Empire was founded in the early 14th century. At its height it covered a vast area including parts of present-day Niger, Nigeria, Chad and Cameroon, before being loosely incorporated into the Songhaï sphere of influence; it nonetheless remained a powerful force until the 19th century.

To the south, between the 13th and 16th centuries, several smaller but locally powerful states arose in gold-producing areas: the kingdoms of Benin (in present-day Nigeria), Dahomey (Benin), Mossi (Burkina Faso)

Although among the least-known European explorers, the English brothers Richard and John Lander outdid their better-known counterparts by establishing that the Niger River flowed into the Atlantic in the 1830s.

1351	**1375**	**1434**
Ibn Battuta leaves Fez to cross the Sahara, whereafter he travels extensively throughout the Empire of Mali. His later book is one of the earliest and most detailed accounts of life in the region.	Mali's King Kankan Musa is depicted on a 1375 European map of Africa holding a gold nugget. The caption reads: 'So abundant is the gold found in his country that he is the richest and most noble king in all the land'.	Portuguese ships become the first to round Cape Bojador in almost two millennia and begin the era of European trade along West Africa's coast. Nine years later, they reach the mouth of the Senegal River.

and Akan-Ashanti (Ghana); see the individual country chapters for more information.

COLONIAL WEST AFRICA

The appearance of Europeans on the Atlantic Coast of West Africa in the 15th century marked the beginning of the end of West African independence and would forever change the region in ways that still ripple down through history today.

European Footholds

By the 13th century the financial stability of several major European powers depended largely on the supply of West African gold. With gold and intriguing tales of limitless wealth making their way across the Sahara and Mediterranean, European royalty became obsessed with West Africa. Thus it was that, at the precise moment when West Africa's empires went into decline and began to fragment, Europe began to turn its attention to West Africa.

Prince Henry of Portugal (Henry the Navigator, 1394–1460) was the first to act, encouraging explorers to sail down the coast of West Africa, which soon became known as Guinea. In 1434, a Portuguese ship rounded the infamous Cape Bojador (in present-day Morocco), the first seagoing vessel to do so since the Phoenicians in 613 BC. Prince Henry convinced his reluctant seamen with the words: 'You cannot find a peril so great that the hope of reward will not be greater'.

The legendary Sundiata Keita, founder of the Empire of Mali in the 13th century, included a clause prohibiting slavery in his Charter of Kurukanfuga.

Bury the Chains: The First International Human Rights Movement, by Adam Hochschild, is masterful in its treatment of the British campaign to abolish slavery in the 18th century.

EUROPEAN EXPLORERS IN WEST AFRICA

The following first-hand accounts and later reconstructions capture the fevered spirit of exploration that drove Europe's encounter with West Africa in the 19th century.

- *Travels in the Interior of Africa,* by Mungo Park, is an epic tale of exploration on the Niger River in the late 18th and early 19th centuries.

- *Difficult & Dangerous Roads,* by Hugh Clapperton, is a vivid portrait of the Sahara, Niger and Nigeria in the 1820s by this haughty but ever-observant traveller.

- *Travels Through Central Africa to Timbuktu,* by Réné Caillié, is the first account of Europe's first encounter with Timbuktu in 1828.

- *Travels & Discoveries in North and Central Africa 1849-1855,* by Heinrich Barth, is a fascinating insight into what is now Niger, Nigeria and Mali, from arguably West Africa's greatest explorer.

- *The Gates of Africa – Death, Discovery and the Search for Timbuktu,* by Anthony Sattin, is a stirring account of Europe's fascination with Timbuktu and West Africa.

- *The Race for Timbuktu – In Search of Africa's City of Gold,* by Frank T Kryza, covers similar terrain and is another great read.

1482	Late 15th century	1512
Portugal constructs the first European structure on West African soil, the warehouse-fortress of Sao Jorge de la Mina in what is now Ghana, providing confirmation of increasingly prosperous trade between Portugal and West Africa.	The Kingdom of Benin helps Portugal to capture and export slaves, thereby transforming the slave trade from a small-scale African concern to a much larger trade that sends millions of West Africans into exile.	Leo Africanus visits West Africa and writes that 'The rich king of Tombuto keeps a splendid and well-furnished court…a great store of doctors, judges, priests and other learned men, that are bountifully maintained at the king's expense.'

In 1443 Portuguese ships reached the mouth of the Senegal River. Later voyages reached Sierra Leone (1462) and Fernando Po (now Bioko in Equatorial Guinea, off the coast of Nigeria; 1472), while the first Portuguese settlers arrived on Cape Verde in 1462. As the Portuguese made contact with local chiefs

SLAVERY IN WEST AFRICA

Slavery had existed in West Africa for centuries, but it gained momentum with the arrival of Islam, opening the region as it did to more far-reaching trade networks and to distant empires where slave-trading was widespread. The Moors, Tuareg and Soninke in particular were known as slave traders. Later, the Portuguese took the trade to a whole new level, transporting slaves en masse to work on the large sugar plantations in Portuguese colonies across the Atlantic (including present-day Brazil) between 1575 and 1600.

By the 17th and 18th centuries, other European nations (particularly England, Spain, France and Holland) had established colonies in the Americas, and were growing sugar, tobacco, cotton and other crops. Huge profits depended on slave labour and the demand for African slaves was insatiable, not least because conditions on the plantations were so bad that life expectancy after arriving in the Americas was often no more than a few years.

In most cases, European traders encouraged Africans on the coast to attack neighbouring tribes and take captives. These were brought to coastal slaving stations and exchanged for European goods such as cloth and guns. A triangular trans-Atlantic trade route developed – the slaves were loaded onto ships and transported to the Americas, the raw materials they produced were transported to Europe, and the finished goods were transported from Europe to Africa once again, to be exchanged for slaves and to keep the whole system moving. Exact figures are impossible to come by, but it is estimated that from the end of the 15th century until around 1870, when the slave trade was abolished, as many as 20 million Africans were captured. Up to half of these died, mostly while being transported in horribly overcrowded and unhealthy conditions.

But more than a century after the slave trade was abolished, slavery has yet to be consigned to history in West Africa where people continue to be born into, and live their whole lives, in slavery. In Niger, the local anti-slavery NGO Timidria estimated in 2003 that 7% of Niger's population was living in conditions of forced labour, while **Anti-Slavery International** (☎ 020 7501 8920; www.antislavery.org; The Stableyard, Broomgrove Rd, London SW9 9TL, UK) estimates that an unknown number of Malians, and an extraordinary 18% of Mauritania's more than three million people, live in slavery; Mauritania finally criminalised slavery in August 2007.

The governments of the region dispute these figures as gross exaggerations. Such denials notwithstanding, the issue was brought dramatically into the international spotlight when, in October 2008, Hadijatou Mani, an escaped slave, took Niger's government before the Court of Justice of the West African regional body Ecowas (Economic Community of West African States). The court upheld her argument that Niger's government had failed to protect her by not implementing Niger's own anti-slavery legislation and awarded her substantial compensation. The decision set a legal precedent which applies in all West African countries. For more information on slavery in Niger, see the boxed text, p576, while the situation in Mauritania is covered in the boxed text, p547.

1591	1659	1796
The Empire of Songhaï, the last and most extensive of the Sahel's empires, falls to the armies of al-Mansur, ruler of Marrakesh. The Songhaï political capital Gao, and its commercial and cultural capital Timbuktu, fall into Moroccan hands.	The French set up their first permanent trading post in West Africa, at St Louis, in modern Senegal in 1638. Twenty-two years later, the British establish a base at the mouth of the Gambia River.	The Scottish explorer Mungo Park arrives at the Niger River near Ségou and solves one of the great unanswered questions of African geography: the Niger flows east, not west as had previously been reported.

and began to trade for gold and ivory, West Africa turned on its axis and the focus of its trade (and power) began shifting from the Sahara to the coast.

In 1482 the Portuguese built a fortified trading post at Elmina (p357), on today's Ghanaian coast. It was the earliest European structure in sub-Saharan Africa. At around the same time, Portuguese traders and emissaries made their first contact with the Kingdom of Benin (in modern-day Nigeria), an advanced, stable state whose artisans had mastered highly skilled bronze- and brass-casting as early as the 13th century. The cordial relations and resulting trade between Portugal and Benin proved highly profitable.

By the early 16th century, with the Songhaï Empire still ruling much of the West African interior, French, British and Dutch ships had joined the Portuguese in making regular visits along the coast, building forts as they went. But with few large rivers that allowed access to the interior, the European presence in West Africa was confined to the coast and its immediate hinterland. The prolific gold mines that had first captured the attention of Europe remained in African hands.

Europe Ventures Inland

The inability to penetrate the West African interior haunted the great powers of Europe. In 1788, a group of influential Englishmen, led by Sir Joseph Banks, founded the Africa Association to promote African exploration. The French soon followed suit. Although questions of commerce and national prestige played an important role, the august men of the Africa Association and their French counterparts were driven by a burning desire to solve the great geographical questions of the age. In 1796, more than 300 years after Europeans had first begun scouting the West African coast, Mungo Park finally determined that the Niger River flowed east, while it was not until 1828 that the Frenchman René Caillié became the first European to reach Timbuktu and return safely.

West Africans were by no means passive bystanders and local resistance was fierce. The most notable leader of the time was Omar Tall (also spelled Umar Taal), who led a major campaign against the French in the interior of Senegal from around 1850. After his death, the jihads known as the 'Marabout Wars' persisted in Senegal until the 1880s.

For all their progress, the European powers were largely confined to pockets of territory on the coast, among them the French enclave of Dakar (Senegal), and the British ports of Freetown (Sierra Leone) and Lagos (Nigeria). Portugal, no longer a major force, retained some territory, notably, Bissau, capital of today's Guinea-Bissau. The relentless European pursuit of territory nonetheless continued with brutal military expeditions into the interior increasingly the norm. Minor treaties were made with local chiefs, but the lives of ordinary West Africans were more often determined by unspoken understandings between European powers.

Someone Knows My Name (also called *The Book of Negroes*), by Lawrence Hill, follows Aminatta, a slave abducted from Mali in 1755 who later helps to compile a list of freed slaves. It won the Commonwealth Writers' Prize in 2008.

The Scramble for Africa, by Thomas Packenham, can be a bit dry in patches, but it's a seminal text on the 1884-85 Berlin Conference and the European lust for African territory.

Britain's Lord Salisbury told the House of Commons after the Berlin Conference that 'the Gallic rooster, who likes to scratch the earth, will wear down his claws, while the fertile region remains in our hands'.

1828	1870	1884-85
Frenchman René Caillié becomes the first European to reach the fabled city of Timbuktu and return home alive. Two years earlier, the Scotsman Alexander Gordon Laing reached Timbuktu but was murdered on the return journey.	The slave trade is officially abolished, but not before up to 20 million Africans were transported to the Americas, never to return. Around one half of those loaded onto ships died en route.	The Berlin Conference divides Africa into colonial spheres of influence. France is awarded almost one third of the entire continent and 10 West African countries in what becomes known as Afrique Occidentale Française (French West Africa).

The Scramble for Africa

Europe's wholesale colonisation of Africa was triggered in 1879 by King Leopold of Belgium's claim to the Congo. The feeding frenzy that followed saw Africa parcelled out among the European powers. Africans had no say in the matter.

Togo and parts of Cameroon fell under German rule, Portugal held fast to Guinea-Bissau and Cape Verde, Britain staked its claim to The Gambia, Sierra Leone, the Gold Coast (Ghana) and Nigeria, while the Sahel (and much of Cameroon) was the preserve of the French. These claims, at once military realities and colonial fantasies as many Africans had not seen a European from the country to whom his or her land now supposedly belonged, were confirmed at the Berlin Conference of 1884–85. The final adjustments to the colonial map were made after Germany's defeat in WWI: Togo went to the French and Cameroon was divided between France and Britain.

Introducing 'civilisation' to the 'natives' officially replaced trade as the *raison d'être* of the colonial mission, but the primary aim of European governments was to exploit the colonies for raw materials. In West Africa, gem and gold mining was developed, but the once gold-rich region disappointed the occupiers. Consequently, labour-intensive plantations were established, and cash crops such as coffee, cocoa, rubber, cotton and groundnuts (peanuts) came to dominate the economies of the fledgling colonies. Such infrastructure as was built in West Africa (the Dakar–Bamako rail line, for example) was designed primarily to benefit the colonial economy. Little or no attempt was made to improve living standards or expand education for West Africans, let alone build the institutions on which their future depended.

During the first half of the 20th century, France controlled its West African colonies with a firm hand, and through a policy of 'assimilation' allowed Africans to become French citizens if they virtually abandoned their African identity. Britain made no pretence of assimilation and was slightly more liberal in its approach towards its colonies. Portugal ruled its empire in Africa with a rod of iron.

INDEPENDENCE

Although nationalism and calls for independence grew in West Africa throughout the first half of the 20th century, it was not until after WWII that the winds of real change began to sweep the region.

In 1957 Ghana became the first country in West Africa to gain independence, with the reluctant blessing of Britain. In September 1958, the French government of Charles de Gaulle held a referendum in its African colonies in which Africans were asked to choose between immediate independence and remaining under French control. All chose the latter, except Guinea, which was to pay dearly for its independence. Affronted by Guinea's perceived lack of gratitude, the French, whose bureaucrats effectively ran Guinea

> After the Berlin Conference, Britain's Lord Salisbury said: 'We have been giving away mountains and rivers and lakes to each other, only hindered by the small impediment that we never knew exactly where the mountains and rivers and lakes were'.

> Up to 200,000 African soldiers served in the French army during WWI and a further 200,000 in WWII when at least 50,000 were killed defending France, many on French soil.

1957	**1958**	**1973**
Ghana is the first West African country to gain independence after a long campaign entitled 'Self Government Now'. The campaign's leader Kwame Nkrumah becomes Ghana's post-independence leader and a hero to millions of West Africans.	Guinea opts to go it alone, rejecting ongoing French rule in favour of immediate independence. France takes revenge by withdrawing all assistance to the country.	Guinea-Bissau, a long-time Portuguese colony, becomes the last West African country to achieve independence. Unlike former French and British colonies, Guinea-Bissau has to fight for its freedom in a bloody war that devastates the country.

Africa: Altered States, Ordinary Miracles, by Richard Dowden, is a nuanced work with detailed sections on Senegal, Sierra Leone, Nigeria and the transition from colonialism to independence.

and who had trained very few locals to a level capable of running the country, took revenge by removing its administrative staff and all financial assistance from Guinea, leaving its former colony to fend for itself. In 1960 Benin, Côte d'Ivoire, Nigeria, Togo, Senegal and several other countries won their independence. Most other countries in the region became independent in the following few years. Only recidivist Portugal held firm, not granting independence to Guinea-Bissau until 1973 and only then with great reluctance.

France encouraged its former colonies to remain closely tied in a trade-based 'community', and most did; Guinea was a notable exception, while Senegal and Côte d'Ivoire were the darlings of Franco–West African relations. In contrast, Britain reduced its power and influence in the region. The French maintained battalions of its own army in several former colonies, while the British preferred more discreet military assistance.

The period immediately following independence was a time of unbridled optimism in West Africa. For the first time in centuries, political power was in the hands of Africans themselves. Inspirational figures such as Kwame Nkrumah in Ghana and Léopold Senghor in Senegal spoke of a new African dawn, while Guinea's Sekou Touré was lauded for having thumbed his nose at the French.

Wonders of the African World, by Henry Louis Gates Jr, is an at once scholarly and enthusiastic re-evaluation of African history before colonialism; its section on Timbuktu is fascinating.

Then reality set in. Without exception, the newly minted countries of West Africa were ill-equipped for independence. Colonialism had created fragile economies based on cash crops which were prone to huge price fluctuations, while artificial boundaries and divide-and-rule policies that had favoured one ethnic group over others quickly created tensions. Education for Africans had never been a priority for the colonial overlords and few members of the new ruling class and bureaucrats had the necessary training or experience to tackle the massive challenges faced by the new states. The catchcry of Sekou Touré – who would prove to be a particularly nasty dictator – of preferring 'freedom in poverty to prosperity in chains' soon became horribly true. Poor governance, coups d'état and massive economic problems increasingly became the norm, with civil wars, border disputes and dictatorship often thrown in for good measure. When Côte d'Ivoire – for so long an exception and a byword for West Africa's post-independence progress and optimism – descended into civil war after 2000, it was a massive blow to the region's self image. For more on the conflict in Côte d'Ivoire, see p257.

WEST AFRICA TODAY

The end of the Cold War led to dramatic changes throughout West Africa, as the popular demand for democracy gathered strength and multiparty elections were held in several countries. But even as democracy spread, West Africa's hopes of a new dawn were tempered by the scale of the challenges it faced, not least among them environmental degradation on a massive scale,

1982	**1997**	**2000**
Paul Biya comes to power in Cameroon. At the time of writing, he is West Africa's longest-serving president, with Burkina Faso's Blaise Compaoré (1987) waiting in the wings to claim the title.	Sierra Leone erupts in a brutal civil war in which hundreds of thousands are killed or maimed. Conflict in neighbouring Liberia and massive refugee camps in Guinea add up to a regional humanitarian catastrophe.	Côte d'Ivoire, the former poster child for West African development, begins its descent into anarchy. Within years, the country is divided in two and immigrants who helped build the country's economic miracle are made scapegoats.

widespread and worsening poverty across the region and the ailing economic health of the two regional powerhouses, Nigeria and Côte d'Ivoire.

There *has* been some good news: Ghana, Benin and Mali have made largely successful transitions to democracy; Senegal remains a beacon of stability; Cape Verde became the first West African nation to be reclassified by the UN as a 'Medium-Developed Country'; and Liberia and Sierra Leone have made an impressive return to peace after decades of civil war. Such positive news is not to be underestimated.

But simmering unrest from Guinea to Niger and from Cameroon to Mauritania, not to mention Nigeria, continues to cloud the horizon. And the fact remains that many West Africans have as little control over their own destinies and economic wellbeing as they did at independence.

After WWII, one French writer wrote that 'West Africa is a French land, its inhabitants are as French as those of Romorantin or Pézenas'.

2005	2007	2008
Ellen Johnson-Sirleaf is elected president in Liberia, ending decades of civil war and in the process becoming Africa's first elected female president.	Tuareg rebels launch rebellion in northern Niger and the conflict soon spills over into Mali. Much of the Sahara becomes the domain of rebels and government soldiers.	Ghana wins plaudits for its peaceful democratic transition. With the discovery of offshore oil and a proven track record of democracy, Ghana is widely seen as West Africa's shining light.

The Culture

The profound depth and variety of West African cultural life animates just about every encounter you'll have in the region. Here, strong traditions of literature, architecture and cinematography rub shoulders with the complicated roles of religion and gender relations. The altogether pleasurable questions of regional food and drink and West Africa's obsession with sport also take centre stage. Underlying it all is the complex interplay between tradition and the assaults and innovations of the modern world.

For more on the major ethnic groups in West Africa and their traditions, see p71. West African music, that standard bearer of West African culture to the outside world, is so important that we've given it its own chapter: see p57.

Remotely Global: Village Modernity in West Africa, by Charles Piot, is a somewhat dense but illuminating study of how a village in northern Togo handles the daily struggles between tradition and modernity.

LIFESTYLE

Family life is the bedrock for most West Africans. In traditional society, especially in villages, homes are arranged around a family compound and life is a communal affair – the family eats, takes important decisions, celebrates and mourns together in a space that is identifiably theirs and in a family group that spans generations. Such family structures remain strongly evident in many villages and rural areas, and family remains a critical source of support for many West Africans, not least because government welfare is largely non-existent.

But things are changing. Vast numbers of Africans have migrated to cities, where ethnic identity takes on added significance, as recent arrivals in cities gravitate towards those with whom they share an ethnic tradition. Most (but by no means all) form friendships with people from their own ethnic groups. This is particularly true of minorities.

Despite rapid urbanisation, only in Cape Verde (62%) and Benin (52%) does more than half of the population live in cities. West Africa's least urbanised countries are Burkina Faso (9%), Mali (19%), Niger (20%) and Guinea-Bissau (20%).

If family and ethnic identity are the fundamental foundations of a West African's existence, the nation to which they belong serves to announce who they are to the rest of the world. Most West Africans proudly identify themselves as being, for example, Malian or Nigerian, suggesting that one success of post-colonial West Africa has been the building of national identity in countries whose borders often cut across longer-standing ethnic boundaries. That said, the tragic descent into conflict in Côte d'Ivoire suggests that ethnic origins remain hugely significant and a never-forgotten calling card.

Traditional Culture

Before the arrival of colonialism, West African society was, in most cultures, organised along hierarchical lines: each person's place in society was determined by birth and the family's social status. At the top were traditional noble and warrior families, followed by farmers, traders and persons of lower caste, such as blacksmiths (see p69), leather workers, woodcarvers, weavers and musicians. Slaves were at the bottom of the social hierarchy. Difficult economic circumstances and urbanisation have reduced the importance of these traditional roles to some degree, but they remain important for many West Africans. For example, although slavery no longer officially exists (see the boxed text, p31), many descendants of former slaves still work as tenant farmers for the descendants of their former masters. Another surviving practice in traditional societies is that older people (especially men) are treated with deference, while teachers, doctors and other professionals (usually men) often receive similar treatment.

According to the UN Environment Programme, more than half of West Africa's urban population lives in slums in every country of the region. The highest proportions are in Niger (96.2%) and Sierra Leone (95.8%).

In urban areas in particular, modernity is increasingly eroding traditional hierarchies. The government official who shows contempt for a rural chief may actually be a member of a lower caste.

DO YOU HAVE SOMETHING FOR ME?

Begging

There's no government welfare cheque for the unemployed, crippled, homeless, sick or old in Africa, and the only social-security system is the extended family, meaning that many people are forced to beg. Because helping the needy is part of traditional African culture, and one of the pillars of Islam, you'll see even relatively poor people giving to beggars. If you want to give, even a small coin is appreciated. If you don't have any change, just say 'next time' and at least greet the person and acknowledge their presence. Please don't give cash, sweets, pens etc to children. It encourages begging and undermines existing social structures. Also, doling out medicines can encourage people not to seek proper medical advice. A donation to a recognised project or NGO is more constructive.

Cadeau

Far more pervasive than begging are the endless requests of '*Donnez-moi un cadeau*' (literally 'Give me a gift'), usually from children, but also from youths and adults. Part of this expectation comes from a belief that anyone to whom God has been good (and all foreigners are thought to be rich by local standards – even a shoestring traveller's daily budget of US$15 a day is more than the average local labourer makes in a month) should be willing to spread the wealth around.

It is sometimes appropriate to give a small gift in return for a service. Simply being pointed in the right direction is not a significant service, whereas being helped for 10 minutes to find a hotel probably is. If you're not prepared to offer a tip, don't ask for significant favours. Do remember, however, that some people will help you out of genuine kindness and will not expect anything in return.

Things sometimes work the other way. West Africans are frequently very friendly towards foreigners and, after just a few minutes of talking, may offer you food or a bed for the night. You may want to repay such kindness with a small gift.

Bribery

A gift or tip becomes a different matter when you have to pay an official to get something done (also called a *cadeau* in Francophone countries, or a 'dash' in English-speaking countries). The best approach is to feign ignorance, smile a lot, be patient and simply bluff your way through. Be personable and calm, and give the official plenty of room to back down and save face. Never simply offer to pay, and remember that threats or shows of anger won't get you anywhere.

There are occasionally cases where a small dash or *cadeau* is unavoidable. If you really have no choice, remember that the 'fee' is always negotiable.

Some things don't change, however. At the other end of the spectrum, children rate very low on the social scale and are expected to defer to adults in all situations. Unfortunately, for half the region's population, the status of women is only slightly higher.

But traditional culture is not just about immutable social roles and, as it most often manifests itself in public these days, it can often be a celebration of what binds communities together. Village festivals (*fêtes* in French), which are fundamental to traditional life, are held to honour dead ancestors, local traditional deities and to celebrate the end of the harvest. Some festivals include singing and dancing; some favour parades, sports or wrestling matches. In some areas you may see elaborate performances with masks, which play an important part in traditional life. For more information on festivals, see the boxed text, p19.

Monique and the Mango Rains: Two Years with a Midwife in Mali, by Kris Holloway, gives a human face to statistics detailing the difficulties faced by women in traditional, rural West Africa. It's a great, sobering read.

ECONOMY

Nigeria, the economic powerhouse of West Africa, is an important case study in the problems blighting the region. Nigeria has received more than US$325 billion in oil revenues over 30 years, yet the per capita income

WEST AFRICA IN ECONOMIC DATA

Country	Life expectancy (years)	Literacy (%)	GDP per capita (US$)	Population living on less than $2 a day (%)	Under-five mortality rate (per 1000 live births)
Benin	55.4	34.7	508	73.7	150
Burkina Faso	51.4	23.6	391	71.8	191
Cameroon	49.8	67.9	1034	50.6	149
Cape Verde	71	81.2	1940	-	35
Côte d'Ivoire	47.4	48.7	900	48.8	195
The Gambia	58.8	42.5	304	82.9	137
Ghana	59.1	57.9	485	78.5	112
Guinea	54.8	29.5	350	-	150
Guinea-Bissau	45.8	44.8	190	-	200
Liberia	44.7	51.9	167	-	235
Mali	53.1	24	392	72.1	218
Mauritania	63.2	51.2	603	63.1	125
Niger	55.8	28.7	244	85.8	256
Nigeria	46.5	69.1	752	92.4	194
Senegal	62.3	39.3	707	56.2	136
Sierra Leone	41.8	34.8	216	74.5	282
Togo	57.8	53.2	358	-	139
UK	79	99	36,509	-	6
USA	77.9	99	41,890	-	7

All data from UN Development Programme (www. undp.org)

For an exhaustive list of UN socio-economic data for the 17 West African countries, visit the website of the UNDP (http://hdrstats.undp .org/countries/).

of its citizens is less than US$2 per day; the average Nigerian now earns less than in 1960, before oil was discovered. Rampant corruption exists alongside simmering civil conflict and massive environmental damage in Nigeria's oil-rich but desperately poor Niger Delta. For more on Nigeria's oil dilemma, see the boxed text, p639.

With Nigeria having failed so spectacularly to improve the lives of its people through oil revenues, all eyes have turned to Ghana, which has discovered commercial quantities of offshore oil. Its government has promised to learn from the mistakes of other resource-rich countries in the region. Time will tell.

SPORT

To find out more about corruption levels in the region, visit the website of the respected anti-corruption watchdog Transparency International (www.trans parency.org). Their Corruption Perception Index and Global Corruption Barometer are particularly enlightening.

Sport in West Africa means one thing: football (soccer). Football owes its popularity to two important factors: the national teams of West African countries are the footballing powerhouses of the continent, and the success of West African footballers in Europe.

Ever since Cameroon stormed the 1990 World Cup finals in Italy, defeating the reigning champions Argentina in the opening match of the tournament and going on to become the first African team to reach the quarter finals, West Africa has been touted as an emerging world power in the sport. For a decade or so, the optimism seemed well placed: Senegal defeated the defending champions France in 2002 and reached the quarter finals, while Cameroon won the football gold medal at the 2000 Sydney Olympics. But Cameroon, Nigeria and Senegal dramatically failed to qualify for the 2006 World Cup, where West Africa was represented by Ghana, Togo and Côte d'Ivoire; only Ghana made it to the second round where they were knocked out by Brazil. For the moment, all hopes are directed towards the 2010 World

Cup, to be held in South Africa. Perhaps, the argument goes, an African crowd can lift an African team to victory.

The African Cup of Nations, held every two years in January, also stirs great passions across the continent. Almost two years of qualifying rounds culminate in the 16 best teams playing it out for the crown of Africa's champions. Although Cameroon won the 2002 event in Mali, North African sides (Tunisia in 2004 and Egypt in 2006 and 2008, when they defeated Côte d'Ivoire and Cameroon, respectively) have dominated the event ever since. Egypt's 2008 victory in Ghana raised their tally to an unequalled six titles; Ghana and Cameroon (four titles), Nigeria (two) and Côte d'Ivoire (one) are West Africa's most successful teams in the tournament.

But the success or otherwise of national teams is only part of the story. Impromptu football games on just about any patch of open ground will be a recurring sight on your travels through the region, with every participant dreaming of becoming the next Samuel Eto'o (Cameroon and Barcelona), Didier Drogba (Côte d'Ivoire and Chelsea), Emmanuel Adebayor (Togo and Arsenal), Michael Essien (Ghana and Chelsea) or Frédéric Kanouté (Mali and Sevilla). West Africa's footballers have enjoyed phenomenal success in European leagues, in the process becoming the focal point for the aspirations of a generation of West African youngsters. And it's not just the kids: every weekend from September to May, West Africans crowd around communal TV sets to follow the fortunes of teams in Spain, Italy, the UK and France, especially those games involving West African players. There is a sense that the success of West Africans in Europe is something in which they can all share with pride, something that reflects well on the region as a whole.

All West African countries have football leagues and tournaments in which teams from different towns and cities compete on a national or regional basis, although their popularity is significantly less than European leagues. The winners of local league and cup competitions qualify for continent-wide club competitions, which include the African Champions League and the Confédération Africaine de Football (CAF) Cup, both held annually. Both

For the latest results and news on African football, fans can check out the (somewhat chaotic) website of the Confédération Africaine de Football (CAF; www.cafonline .com), Africa's football governing body.

The Belly of the Atlantic, the first novel by Senegalese writer Fatou Diome, poignantly captures the dreams of West Africans hoping to make it as professional footballers in France.

'LE DAKAR' IN NAME ONLY

It began in 1979 as the Paris–Dakar, a trans-Saharan epic considered to be one of the world's longest (10,000km), hardest and most dangerous driving events. Then it became simply **Le Dakar** (www.dakar .com), starting not from Paris, but from a handful of other European cities. But one thing was constant – the grand entrance of dusty motorcycles, cars or trucks into an African capital, usually Dakar. Throughout its history, Le Dakar had faced threats from bandits, rebellion and terrorist groups, but the race had always been rerouted and had survived. Then the unthinkable happened: on the eve of the 2008 Dakar Rally, citing French intelligence reports of direct threats to the race and following the killing of four French tourists and three soldiers in Mauritania in an apparent terrorist attack, organisers suddenly cancelled the race for the first time in its history. With most north–south trans-Saharan routes plagued by rebellion and general uncertainty, organisers saw no alternative but to relocate the 'Dakar' Rally to South America: after no race in 2008, the 2009 event traversed Argentina and Chile.

With Le Dakar's future so uncertain, many fear that the world's most famous rally may have left Africa forever. The race clings to the Dakar name and organisers haven't ruled out returning the race to its roots in years to come should the security situation improve in West Africa. Check out the race's official website for the latest news. But the air of invincibility that always surrounded the race, and its inextricable link with Africa, has been shattered, ending an era of glamorous European adventurism in West Africa.

For a less-glamorous West African alternative to Le Dakar that's for amateur drivers, see the boxed text, p837.

TIPS ON MEETING LOCALS

Greetings

There are few more important elements in person-to-person encounters in West Africa than greetings. In villages, highly ritualised greetings can seem to last an eternity. In cities, the traditional greetings may give way to shorter ones in French or English, but they're never forgotten. Muslims usually start with the traditional Islamic greetings, *Salaam aleikum* and *Aleikum asalaam* ('Peace be unto you', 'And peace be unto you'). This is followed by more questions, such as 'How are you?', 'How is the family?' and 'How are the people of your village?' The reply is usually *Al humdul'allah* (meaning 'Thanks be to God'). While language constraints may mean that your ability to greet West African–style is limited, launching straight into business is considered rude. Learning some greetings in the local language (see p860 for some useful phrases) will smooth the way considerably in just about every circumstance.

Hand shaking is also an important part of greetings. Use a soft – rather than overly firm – handshake. Some Muslim men prefer not to shake hands with women, and West African women don't usually shake hands with their male counterparts.

Deference

Another consideration is eye contact, which is usually avoided, especially between men and women in the Sahel. If a West African doesn't look you in the eye during a conversation, remember that they're being polite, not cold. When visiting rural settlements it's a good idea to request to see the chief to announce your arrival and request permission before wandering through a village. You'll rarely be refused.

Conduct

Although West Africa is changing, social mores remain conservative, so please keep in mind the following guidelines:

- If you're in a frustrating situation, be patient, friendly and considerate. A confrontational attitude can easily inflame the situation (especially when dealing with police officers and immigration officials) and offend local sensibilities.
- Be respectful of Islamic traditions and don't wear revealing clothing; loose, lightweight clothing is preferable.
- Public displays of affection are usually inappropriate, especially in Muslim areas.
- Ask permission to photograph people and always respect the wishes of those who decline.
- If you promise to send someone a photo, make sure you do so.
- Avoid vocal criticism of the government or country; the former could get your friends in trouble and many West Africans take the latter personally.

competitions have been dominated by North African club sides in recent years, although teams from Ghana, Cameroon, Nigeria and Côte d'Ivoire traditionally put on a strong show.

MULTICULTURALISM

West Africans know a thing or two about living side by side with people from different cultures. For a start, West Africa as you see it today is the result of centuries of population shifts and mass migrations that have created a patchwork of diverse but largely cohabiting cultures (for more on the major ethnic groups in West Africa see p71). After the colonial period and independence, most groups found themselves being asked to share a new national identity with other cultures that were, in some cases, wholly different from their own. Later, widespread urbanisation produced polyglot West African cities that are among the most multicultural on earth. And then there are the twin issues of immigration and emigration – millions of West Africans live in Europe and elsewhere, creating new levels of multiculturalism in the Western countries they now inhabit.

The majority of immigrants trying to enter Europe illegally in recent years come from West Africa. Most are driven to emigrate by dire economic conditions, authoritarian governments and/or conflict, and their departure leaves gaping holes in the structure of traditional societies, not to mention local economies. Some West African countries face a critical shortage of skilled labour, especially doctors and nurses. In particular, doctors and nurses from Ghana and Nigeria help to keep the UK health system operational, while back home health services are crying out for skilled staff.

On the other side of the equation, the benefits derived from those who do reach Europe and find employment are considerable, with remittances from Europe playing an important role for many West African economies. Some traditional chiefs (especially in eastern Mali) actually gather funds to pay for the fittest young man to try his luck, in the hope that those who stay behind will profit significantly from remittances he sends home.

The movement of people in search of opportunity within West Africa is less widely reported in the international media, but operates on a much larger scale than emigration to Europe. Côte d'Ivoire's one-time economic miracle drew immigrants from across the region, providing much-needed labour for a booming economy and a livelihood for millions of citizens of neighbouring countries. However, after political instability began in 2000, the economy slumped and the country descended into a conflict that exposed the thin veneer of tolerance with which many Ivorians viewed the immigrants. Second-generation immigrants – some of whom had known no country but Côte d'Ivoire – were told that they were no longer welcome and blamed for all the country's ills.

Emigration has also had an important impact upon the communities that immigrants leave behind. Among the Tuareg of northern Niger and Mali, for example, entire villages have emptied of young men who have been driven by drought and rebellion to cities and neighbouring countries in search of subsistence. In the process many have left behind, probably forever, the nomadic lifestyle that once defined their people and which now struggles to survive.

> Cameroon alone has around 280 ethnic groups; tiny Togo counts 40 ethnic groups among its five million people, while Guinea-Bissau, a country of less than one million people, has 23.

MEDIA

Although TV is a largely state-run enterprise in West Africa (and is generally pretty dire), West Africa has a surprising proliferation of private and community radio stations and newspapers. Even so, many of these media outlets are extremely vulnerable to changes in the political wind and many dare not criticise governments for fear of retribution. In recent years, for example, numerous journalists and editors in Niger have been imprisoned on charges of criticising the government or interviewing rebel representatives in the north of the country, while journalists have been murdered with impunity in Burkina Faso. Even in Sierra Leone, a community radio station was attacked by an angry mob and its broadcasting equipment destroyed in November 2008 after it broadcast an unpopular press release from the local authorities. Journalists reporting in the troubled political spheres of Côte d'Ivoire, Mauritania and Nigeria also face a particularly difficult task. According to Reporters Without Borders, journalists in The Gambia live in fear of unlawful detention, repression and possibly even of losing their lives.

A good barometer of press freedom in the region is to be found in the annual Press Freedom Index compiled by **Reporters Without Borders** (www.rsf .org), which ranks 167 countries according to the freedoms enjoyed by the

> According to the World Bank, in 2007 Nigeria received US$3.3 billion in remittances from Nigerians living abroad, the highest in Africa. Senegal came in third with US$0.9 billion.

independent media. In the 2008 version, the usual suspects fared badly: Côte d'Ivoire (149th), Mauritania (138th), Liberia (123rd) and Nigeria (117th). But it wasn't all bad news: Benin was the highest-ranked West African country (27th) and second on the continent only to South Africa (26th). Benin even ranked higher than many Western countries, including the UK. The same can be said for Cape Verde, which came in at an impressive 38th, ahead of Australia, Italy and Spain.

RELIGION

Roughly half of all West Africans are Muslim and it's very much a north–south divide: the countries of the Sahel and Sahara are predominantly Muslim, while Christianity is more widespread in the southern coastal countries. That said, in almost every country of the region, traditional or animist beliefs retain a significant hold over the population. For information on the religious make-up of individual countries, see the relevant country chapters.

Traditional Religions

Before the arrival of Islam and Christianity, every race, tribe or clan in West Africa practised its own traditional religion. While many in the Sahel converted to Islam, and those in the south converted to Christianity, traditional religions remained strong and still retain a powerful hold over the consciousness of West Africans, even coexisting with established aspects of Islam or Christianity. When discussing traditional beliefs, terms such as 'juju', 'voodoo' and 'witchcraft' are frequently employed. In certain specific contexts these may be correct, but these are much misunderstood terms; for more information see the boxed text, p109.

There are hundreds of traditional religions in West Africa, with considerable areas of overlap. What you won't find are any great temples (more modest local shrines often served the same purpose) or written scriptures (in keeping with West Africa's largely oral tradition). Beliefs and traditions can be complex and difficult to understand, but several common factors are found again and again. The following description provides an overview only, and is necessarily very simplified.

Almost all traditional religions are animist, meaning that they are based on the attribution of life or consciousness to natural objects or phenomena. Thus a certain tree, mountain, river or stone may be sacred (such as among the Lobi of southwestern Burkina Faso; see p75) because it represents, is home to, or simply *is* a spirit or deity. The number of deities of each religion varies, as does the phenomena that represents them. The Ewe of Togo and Ghana, for example, have more than 600 deities, including one that represents the disease smallpox.

Several traditional religions accept the existence of a supreme being or creator, alongside spirits and deities. This being usually figures in creation myths and is considered too exalted to be concerned with humans – see, for example, the Bobo people (p72) of Burkina Faso and Mali. In many cultures, communication with the creator is possible only through lesser deities or through the intercession of ancestors.

Thus, in many African religions, ancestors play a particularly strong role; two powerful examples of this are found among the Igbo (see p75) and Yoruba (p78) of Nigeria. The principal function of ancestors is usually to protect the tribe or family, and they may on occasion show their ancestral pleasure or displeasure (eg in the form of bad weather, a bad harvest, or when a living member of the family becomes sick). There are almost as many variations on the theme as there are distinct cultural groups in West Africa. The Baoulé people of Côte d'Ivoire, for example, believe in a parallel world to our

Media Foundation for West Africa (www .mediafound.org) is a terrific Ghanaian-based website that monitors the state of the media and press freedom in West Africa. Although it does cover Francophone countries, its focus is Anglophone West Africa.

The Way of the Elders: West African Spirituality & Tradition, by Adama and Naomi Doumbia, is one of surprisingly few books to provide an overview of the foundations of traditional West African religions.

TIPS FOR TRAVELLERS IN ISLAMIC AREAS

When you visit a mosque, take off your shoes; women should cover their heads and shoulders with scarves. In some mosques, women are not allowed to enter if prayers are in progress or if the imam (prayer leader) is present; in others, there may be separate entrances for men and women. In others still, non-Muslims are not allowed to enter at all.

If you've hired a guide or taxi driver for the day, remember that he'll want to say his prayers at the right times, so look out for signs that he wants a few moments off, particularly around noon, late afternoon and sunset. Travellers on buses and bush taxis should also be prepared for prayer stops at these times.

Despite the Islamic proscription against alcohol, some Muslims may enjoy a quiet drink. Even so, it's impolite to drink alcohol in their presence unless they show approval.

During Islamic holidays, shops and offices may close. Even if the offices are officially open, during the Ramadan period of fasting, people become soporific (especially when Ramadan falls in the hot season) and very little gets done.

own where parallel relatives can have an important influence over the 'real' world (see p72). Many traditional religions also hold that the ancestors are the real owners of the land and, while it can be enjoyed and used during the lifetime of their descendants, it cannot be sold and must be cared for.

Communication with ancestors or deities may take the form of prayer, offerings (possibly with the assistance of a holy man, or occasionally a holy woman) or sacrifice. Requests may include good health, bountiful harvests and numerous children. Many village celebrations are held to ask for help from, or in honour of, ancestors and deities. The Dogon people in Mali, for instance, have celebrations before planting (to ensure good crops) and after harvest (to give thanks); for more on traditional Dogon religion see the boxed text, p508.

Totems, fetishes (talismans) and charms are also important features of traditional religions (see p68). Among the Senoufo (p76), for example, the dead take on the form of the clan's animal totem. Masks (p65) also play a significant role.

Muslims form a majority in The Gambia, Guinea, Mali, Mauritania, Niger, Senegal and Sierra Leone, and 50% of the inhabitants of Burkina Faso and Nigeria. Only Cape Verde and Ghana have Christian majorities.

Islam & West Africa

Between AD 610 and 620 in the city of Mecca, Saudi Arabia, the Prophet Mohammed, after a series of revelations from Allah, called on the people to turn away from pagan worship and submit to Allah, the one true god. As such, Islam provided a simpler alternative to the established faiths, which had become complicated by hierarchical orders, sects and complex rituals, offering instead a direct relationship with God based only on the believer's submission to God ('Islam' means submission). The Prophet Mohammed's teachings appealed to poorer levels of society and angered the wealthy merchant class. In 622 Mohammed and his followers were forced to flee to Medina. This migration, the Hejira, marks the beginning of the Islamic calendar, year 1 AH (anno Hegirae). By 630 (8 AH), Mohammed had gained a large following and returned to Mecca. Mohammed died in 632 but within two decades most of Arabia was converted to Islam; within a century it was the dominant religion as far west as Morocco.

The natural barrier formed by the Sahara meant that Islam took longer to trickle down into West Africa than elsewhere. It first reached the Sahel around 900, via trans-Saharan traders from present-day Morocco and Algeria. Although ordinary people generally preferred to retain their traditional beliefs, Islam quickly became the state religion in many West African kingdoms and empires, where rulers skilfully combined aspects of Islam with traditional religions in the administration of the state. The result was a fusion of beliefs that remains a feature of West African life today.

Marabouts – holy men who act as a cross between priest, doctor and adviser for local people – are one example of this hybrid form. In some countries, especially Senegal (see the boxed text, p673), marabouts wield considerable political power. Sufism, which emphasises mystical and spiritual attributes, was one of the more popular Islamic forms in West Africa; some scholars speculate that the importance that Sufis ascribe to religious teachers may have found favour in West Africa as it mirrored existing hierarchical social structures.

Islam cemented its position as the dominant religion in the Sahel in the 17th and 18th centuries, filling the vacuum left by the then-defunct Sahelian empires. Spiritual power was fused with political and economic hegemony, and Islamic jihads (holy wars) were declared on non-believers and backed by the powers of the state. In time, several Muslim states were established, including Futa Toro (in northern Senegal), Futa Djalon (Guinea), Masina (Mali) and the Sokoto state of Hausaland (Niger and Nigeria).

Islam: A Short History, by Karen Armstrong, is a first-rate primer on the world's fastest-growing religion; it's distinguished by a fair-minded approach and language that makes it all sound so clear.

THE FIVE PILLARS OF ISLAM

The five pillars of Islam (the basic tenets that guide Muslims in their daily lives) are as follows:

Shahada (the profession of faith) 'There is no god but Allah, and Mohammed is his Prophet' is the fundamental tenet of Islam.

Salat (prayer) Muslims must face Mecca and pray at dawn, noon, mid-afternoon, sunset and nightfall. Prayer times are marked by the call to prayer, which rings out across the towns and villages of the Sahel.

Zakat (alms) Muslims must give a portion of their income to the poor and needy.

Sawm (fasting) Ramadan commemorates Mohammed's first revelation, and is the month when all Muslims fast from dawn to dusk.

Haj (pilgrimage, usually written hadj in West Africa) Every Muslim capable of affording it should perform the haj, or pilgrimage, to the holiest of cities, Mecca, at least once in his or her lifetime. The reward is considerable: the forgiving of all past sins. This can involve a lifetime of saving money, and it's not unusual for families to save up and send one member. Before the advent of air travel, the pilgrimage often involved an overland journey of a year or more. In West Africa, those who complete the pilgrimage receive the honorific title of Hadj for men, and Hadjia for women.

SONY & THE QURAN

West African Islam is generally regarded as more liberal than the practises espoused by Islamic purists in Cairo or Mecca. In October 2008, that diversity of opinion was thrust into the international spotlight in a realm not usually associated with debates over Islamic orthodoxy. A Sony video game, 'LittleBigPlanet', was withdrawn from sale after a Muslim playing a trial version of the game alerted Sony that a piece of background music included two phrases from the Quran. It could, he said, be considered blasphemous by Muslims for its combination of music and sacred words from Islam's holy book. Fearful of alienating Muslim gamers, Sony recalled the game and removed the song in question before releasing it back onto the market. For this, Sony was praised for its cultural sensitivity by the influential Muslim Forum think tank.

But the decision was viewed somewhat differently in West Africa. The offending song was 'Tapha Niang', recorded by Mali's master kora player Toumani Diabaté and which had appeared on his acclaimed 2006 album *Boulevard de l'Independence*. Diabaté, a devout Muslim whose favourite live-music venue in Bamako was recently transformed into an Islamic cultural centre, denied that the song was in any way blasphemous. 'In my family there are only two things we know,' he told the BBC, 'the Quran and the kora'. Expressing his disappointment, he went on to say that it was entirely acceptable in Mali for Islamic tenets to be put to music as a way of glorifying Islam.

ISLAMIC CUSTOMS

In everyday life, Muslims are prohibited from drinking alcohol and eating carrion, blood products or pork, which are considered unclean, the meat of animals not killed in the prescribed manner and food over which the name of Allah has not been said. Adultery, theft and gambling are also prohibited.

Islam is not just about prohibitions but also marks the important events of a Muslim's life. When a baby is born, the first words uttered to it are, in many places, the call to prayer. A week later there is a ceremony in which the baby's head is shaved and an animal sacrificed in remembrance of Abraham's willingness to sacrifice his son to Allah. The major event of a boy's childhood is circumcision, which normally takes place between the ages of seven and 12. When a person dies, a burial service is held at the mosque and the body is buried with the feet facing Mecca.

For information on Islamic holidays, including a table of dates, see p816.

> In only three West African countries is the female adult literacy rate above 50%: Cape Verde (75.5%), Nigeria (60.1%) and Cameroon (59.8%). Women fare worst in Niger (15.1%), Mali (15.9%), Burkina Faso (16.6%) and Guinea (18.1%).

WOMEN IN WEST AFRICA

West African women face a formidable array of barriers to their participation in public life on an equal footing with men. In much of the region, social mores demand that a women is responsible for domestic work (cooking, pounding millet, child rearing, gathering firewood), while many women also work (often as market or street vendors) to supplement meagre family incomes. Indeed, it's a depressingly common sight to see women pounding millet or otherwise working hard while men lounge in the shade 'working' on their social relationships. Education of girls also lags significantly behind men, as evidenced by often appalling female literacy rates. Little wonder, therefore, that West African women are greatly under-represented in most professions – of the hundreds of accredited guides working with tourists in Mali, for example, less than five are women – let alone in government or at the upper levels of industry.

> Musow (www.musow .com, in French) is a slick and thoroughly modern online women's lifestyle magazine that offers a mainly Malian antidote to the grim struggles faced by most West African women.

Marriage & Polygamy

In many parts of West Africa, marriage is an expensive affair. Gifts from the groom to the bride's family can easily cost several hundred dollars in a region where annual incomes of US$200 are typical. In traditional societies, marriage often took place among teenagers, but financial constraints and the growing demands for lavish weddings mean that many men cannot afford to get married until their late 20s or 30s.

Despite such restrictions, polygamy is reasonably widespread in West Africa. The practice, which pre-dates the arrival of Islam (the Quran allows up to four wives, provided the husband can provide for them all), is particularly strong in rural and predominantly Islamic areas; according to one study, half of all marriages in Senegal are polygamous. You will be told (by men) that women are not averse to polygamy, and that the wives become like sisters, helping each other with domestic and child-rearing duties. In reality, however, fighting and mistrust between wives is more common than marital bliss. However, as few if any countries in the region have outlawed polygamy, there's not much women can do. Leaving a marriage simply because a husband takes another wife can bring shame to the woman and her family. She might be cast out of the family home or even physically beaten as punishment by her own father or brothers.

> In 2008, an 84-year-old Nigerian man was arrested, charged with insulting Islam and imprisoned for 59 days. His crime? He was married to 86 women (with whom he had fathered 170 children).

Female Genital Mutilation

Female genital mutilation (FGM), often euphemistically termed 'female circumcision' or 'genital alteration', is widespread throughout West

FEMALE GENITAL MUTILATION – AN INTERVIEW *Anthony Ham*

In January 2009, I interviewed Menidiou Kodio who, along with his wife Maryam Dougnon, works in Mali's Dogon Country to end the practice of female genital mutilation.

Anthony Ham (AH): What proportion of young girls undergo female genital mutilation?
Menidiou Kodio (MK): In some traditional Dogon villages, it is every girl.
AH: What made you start this work?
MK: At the beginning, we were working with two NGOs, but now we work alone. We do it because we have six daughters.
AH: Do you meet much resistance when trying to stop the practice?
MK: It is very difficult to convert people, so when I visit a village I make a free concert and the lyrics of the songs speak against FGM, and then I make a speech. I tell people that I respect traditional culture, but that not everything in tradition is good. As one of my songs says, 'You don't have to listen to everything that the Ana Sara [Europeans] say and you shouldn't change all of your traditions for them. But in this case, we should listen to them'.
AH: What reasons do you give for stopping the practice?
MK: First we explain to them that their daughters run a very high risk of contracting HIV, because the knife they use in some places is 40 years old. Tetanus is another risk, a disease that only came to the Dogon Country from knives like this. Then we tell them that it is a very risky procedure and that if the girls lose too much blood, they can die. We also tell them that childbirth is more difficult for a woman who has been cut. And finally we tell them that they are cutting the bodies of their daughters, the bodies that God gave to them.
AH: And do people listen?
MK: Many people don't. Many men also still believe that it is bad to marry a woman who has not been cut, because they worry that the woman will be stronger than him. But some people are starting to listen and some villages have promised to stop the practice. The truth is, we won't know whether they have kept their promise until 15 years from now, when these girls start to have children.
AH: What will it take for this practice to end?
MK: FGM will continue until all the old people, especially the old women, have died.

Gogo Mama: A Journey into the Lives of Twelve African Women, by Sally Sara, includes illuminating chapters on a Liberian former child soldier, Ghanaian former slave and a Malian midwife.

The Female Genital Cutting Education and Networking Project (www.fgmnetwork .org/index.php) is an excellent resource on female genital mutilation (FMG), including statistics for many West African countries.

Africa. The term covers a wide range of procedures, from a small, mainly symbolic, cut, to the total removal of the external genitalia (known as infibulation). In West Africa, the procedure usually involves removal of the entire clitoris.

Although outsiders often believe that FGM is associated with Islam, it actually pre-dates the religion (historical records of infibulation date back 6000 years) and has far more to do with long-standing cultural traditions than religious doctrine; in predominantly Muslim northern Mali, FGM prevalence rates are less than 10%. The procedure is usually performed by midwives on girls and young women. They sometimes use modern surgical instruments, but more often it's done with a razor blade or even a piece of glass. If the procedure is done in a traditional setting the girl will not be anaesthetised, although nowadays many families take their daughters to clinics to have the procedure performed by a trained doctor. Complications, especially in the traditional setting, include infection of the wound, leading to death, or scarring, which makes childbirth and urination difficult.

In West Africa, FGM is seen among traditionalists as important for maintaining traditional society. An unaltered woman would dishonour her family and lower its position in society, as well as ruining her own chances for marriage – a circumcised woman is thought to be a moral woman, and more likely a virgin. Many believe that if left, the clitoris can make a woman infertile or damage, and even kill, her unborn children.

This issue excites strong emotions in some countries. In Sierra Leone in February 2009, four female journalists were stripped and marched through the streets of Kenema as punishment for their perceived criticisms of FGM.

Some West African countries have enacted laws outlawing FGM, but poor enforcement means that, even where FGM is illegal, the practice continues as before. Practitioners may fear legal sanction but find it hard to resist the social pressures of going against tradition. FGM is illegal in Guinea, for example, and punishable in some cases by life imprisonment with hard labour, yet an estimated 98% of women still undergo the procedure. Laws against FGM are also on the books in Burkina Faso, which nonetheless has a 71% prevalence rate, and in Côte d'Ivoire (44.5%). The practice is also extremely common in Mali (93%), Sierra Leone (80-90%), The Gambia (60-90%) and Nigeria (25%), none of whom have laws outlawing FGM. FGM is a particularly common practice among the Fulani.

ARTS

West Africa has a rich artistic heritage that extends from arts and handicrafts (see p65) and music (p57) to literature, architecture and a thriving film industry.

Literature

Stories, usually in oral or musical form, have always played an important role in West African life. This is how cultural traditions and the great events of the day were chronicled and, in the frequent absence of written histories, such tales catalogued the collective memory of the region's peoples. The greatest and most famous historical tale is the Epic of Sundiata (see the boxed text, p28), the story of the founder of the Empire of Mali whose story is still recounted by modern *griots* (musician caste), musicians and writers.

Modern-day West African writers have adapted this tradition, weaving compelling tales around the great issues facing modern West Africa, most notably the arrival and legacy of colonial powers, and the role of women within traditional society.

Nigeria dominates West Africa's Anglophone literary scene, while some of the best novels in Francophone West African literature have also been translated into English. Listed here are the major West African authors who have achieved international renown, along with a brief selection of their works.

Apart from those Anglophone writers covered at length below, other names to watch out for include: Aminatta Forna (Sierra Leone; *Ancestor Stones* and the memoir *The Devil that Danced on the Water*); Ghana's foremost writer, Ayi Kwei Armah (*The Beautiful Ones Are Not Yet Born*; 1969); Ama Ata Aidoo (Ghana; *Changes: A Love Story* and *Our Sister Killjoy*); Kojo Laing (Ghana; *Woman of the Aeroplanes, Search Sweet Country* and *Major Gentl and the Achimota Wars*); and William Conton (The Gambia) whose 1960s classic *The African* is a semi-autobiographical tale of an African student in Britain who later returns to his homeland and becomes president.

For more titles by regional authors see the individual country chapters.

NIGERIA

Nigeria is credited with producing the first African novels of international quality. Amos Tutuola's *The Palm-Wine Drunkard,* about an insatiable drunkard who seeks his palm-wine tapster in the world of the dead, was the first African writer to catch the world's attention by providing a link between traditional storytelling and the modern novel. If Tutuola made the world sit

A particularly incisive account of the clash between modern and traditional views on polygamy is given in *So Long a Letter,* an especially fine novel written in the voice of a widow by Senegalese author Miriama Bâ.

Moolade, the powerful 2004 film by the Senegalese director Ousmane Sembène, is one of the few mass-release artistic endeavours to tackle head-on the taboo issue of female genital mutilation.

WEST AFRICAN ARCHITECTURE - TOP PICKS

Mudbrick Mosques

- Djenné Mosque (Mali; p498)
- Dyingerey Ber Mosque and Sankoré Mosque, Timbuktu (Mali; p518)
- Grande Mosquée, Bobo-Dioulasso (Burkina Faso; p151)
- The seven mosques of Bani (Burkina Faso; p163)
- Grande Mosquée, Agadez (Niger; p599)

Fortified Villages

- Dogon Country (Mali; p507)
- Tamberma Valley (Togo; see the boxed text, p797)
- Lobi family compounds (Burkina Faso; see the boxed text, p160)

Painted Facades

- Gourounsi homes, Tiébélé (Burkina Faso; p161)
- Tichit (Mauritania; p564)
- Oualâta (Mauritania; p566)

Saharan Architecture

- Ouadâne (Mauritania; p562)
- Chinguetti (Mauritania; p561)
- Timbuktu (Mali; p516)
- Agadez (Mali; p599)

Traditional Palaces & Forts

- Foumban (Cameroon; p203)
- Bafut (Cameroon; p200)
- Bafoussam (Cameroon; p201)
- Abomey (Benin; p112)
- Ashanti buildings, Kumasi (Ghana; p369)
- Ghana's colonial-era forts (see the boxed text, p354)

Stilt Villages

- Ganvié (Benin; p104)
- Nzulezu (Ghana; p364)

up and take notice, Chinua Achebe won for African literature the international acclaim it still enjoys to this day. His classic work, *Things Fall Apart* (1958), has sold over eight million copies in 30 languages, more than any other African work. Set in the mid-19th century, this novel charts the collision between pre-colonial Ibo society and European missionaries. Achebe's more recent work, *Anthills of the Savannah*, is a satirical study of political disorder and corruption. It was a finalist for the 1987 Booker Prize.

Building on the work of these early pioneers, Wole Soyinka has built up an extraordinary body of work, which includes plays (*A Dance of the Forest, The Man Died, Opera Wonyosi* and *A Play of Giants*), poetry (including

Idane & Other Poems), novels (including *The Interpreters*), political essays and the fantastical childhood memoir *Ake*. Praised for his complex writing style, Soyinka won the Nobel Prize for Literature in 1986 (the first author from Africa to achieve this accolade).

The exceptionally talented Ben Okri is a thoughtful essayist *(A Way of Being Free)* and an accomplished poet *(An African Elegy)*, but his magical realist novels have seen him labelled the Nigerian Gabriel García Márquez. His novel *The Famished Road*, which follows Azaro, a spirit-child, won the Booker Prize in 1991. When critics grumbled that to appreciate the book's style and symbolism the reader had to 'understand Africa', Okri recalled reading Victorian novelists such as Dickens as a schoolboy in Nigeria. His *Songs of Enchantment* (1993) and *Infinite Riches* (1998) completed his Azaro trilogy. He continues to fuse modern style with traditional mythological themes in his later novels *Dangerous Love, Astonishing the Gods* and, most recently, *Starbook*.

Buchi Emecheta is one of Africa's most successful female authors. Her novels include *Slave Girl, The Joys of Motherhood, Rape of Shavi* and *Kehinde,* and focus with humour and irrepressible irony on the struggles of African women to overcome their second-class treatment by society.

Two young Nigerian writers – Chimamanda Ngozi Adichie and Helon Habila – have successfully made the leap from promising talents to skilled novelists with a growing international following. Adichie in particular followed up her impressive first novel *Purple Hibiscus* (2004) with the exceptional *Half of a Yellow Sun* (2006), which is set in Nigeria during the Biafra War. Helon Habila, too, managed to build on the success of his first novel *Waiting for an Angel* (2004) with an acclaimed follow-up, *Measuring Time* (2007), the stirring story of twins in a Nigerian village.

Other young Nigerian novelists to watch out for include Helen Oyeyemi (*The Icarus Girl*) and Uzodinma Iweala (*Beasts of No Nation*).

FRANCOPHONE WEST AFRICA

Until recently, Francophone West African writers were little known beyond France, but a flurry of translations into English has brought them the international readership they richly deserve.

Until his death in 1991, Amadou Hampaté Bâ, Mali's most prolific novelist, was one of the most significant figures in West African literature, as well as a leading linguist, ethnographer and religious scholar. Three of his books – *The Fortunes of Wangrin* (which won the 1976 'Grand Prix litéraire de l'Afrique noire'), *Kaidara* and *Radiance of the Great Star* – are available in English.

The late Ousmane Sembène, from Senegal, is better known as an acclaimed movie director (see p673), but he has also published short-story collections and *God's Bits of Wood*, an accomplished novel set in colonial Mali and Senegal. Two female Senegalese writers worth tracking down are Mariama Bâ, whose novel *So Long a Letter* won the Noma Award for publishing in Africa, and Fatou Diome, whose first novel, *The Belly of the Atlantic* (2003), suggests that she has a promising future. Nafissatou Dia Diouf is also attracting attention although her *Retour d'Un Long Exil et Autres Nouvelles* (2001) and *Sables Mouvants* (2000) are still available only in French. The late Leopold Senghor, former Senegalese president and a literary figure of international note, is the author of several collections of poetry and writings. For more information on Senegalese writers, see p672.

Côte d'Ivoire's finest novelist, Ahmadou Kourouma, is widely available in English. His *Waiting for the Wild Beasts to Vote* is a masterpiece that evocatively captures both the transition to colonial rule and the subsequent corruption of power by Africa's leaders. *The Suns of Independence, Monnew*

Butabu: Adobe Architecture of West Africa, by James Morris, is a stunning photographic study of West Africa's traditional architecture with informative text; a great reminder of your visit.

In 1952, Dylan Thomas described Amos Tutuola's *The Palm-Wine Drunkard* as 'brief, thronged, grisly and bewitching' and a 'nightmare of indescribable adventures'.

The annual Caine Prize for African Writing (www.caineprize.com), which is awarded for the best published short story by an African writer, is one of Africa's most prestigious literary awards. Previous West African winners include Helon Habila (2001) and SA Afolabi (2005).

TOP 10 WEST AFRICAN NOVELS

- Chinua Achebe, *Things Fall Apart*
- Ben Okri, *The Famished Road*
- Chimamanda Ngozi Adichie, *Half of a Yellow Sun*
- Helon Habila, *Measuring Time*
- Aminatta Forna, *Ancestor Stones*
- Ahmadou Kourouma, *Waiting for the Wild Beasts to Vote*
- Ousmane Sembène, *God's Bits of Wood*
- Amadou Hampaté Bâ, *The Fortunes of Wangrin*
- Mongo Beti, *The Poor Christ of Bomba*
- Ayi Kwei Armah, *The Beautiful Ones Are Not Yet Born*

---

and *Allah Is Not Obliged* are also great reads. For more on Côte d'Ivoirean literature, see p262.

Cameroon's best-known literary figure is the late Mongo Beti. *The Poor Christ of Bomba* is Beti's cynical recounting of the failure of a missionary to convert the people of a small village. Other works by Beti include *Mission to Kala* and *Remember Ruben*.

Camara Laye (Guinea) wrote *The African Child* (also called *The Dark Child*), which was first published in 1954 and is one of the most widely printed works by an African.

Cinema

West Africa rarely makes an appearance in cinemas beyond the region – *Blood Diamond*, set (but not filmed) in 1990s Sierra Leone, is a rare exception – and most West African films can be difficult for travellers to track down. But, despite limited resources, West African film is high quality, a regular presence at the world's best film festivals and has, for decades, been quietly gathering plaudits from critics. West Africa also has a respected film festival of its own, Fespaco (see the boxed text, p135), which takes place biannually in Ouagadougou in Burkina Faso and has placed quality filmmaking at the centre of modern West African cultural life.

The international availability of works by African novelists owes much to the Heinemann African Writers Series (www.africanwriters.com), which publishes 68 novels that would otherwise be out of print or hard to find.

A handful of themes resonate through post-colonial West African cinema, among them: the exploitation of the masses by colonialists; corrupt and inefficient independent governments; the clash between tradition and modernity; and traditional African values (usually in a rural setting) portrayed as suffering from Western cultural influence. As such, the region's films act like a mirror to West African society and history.

The 1970s was the zenith of African film making, and many films from this era still inspire the new generation of directors working today. From the 1980s onwards, however, directors have found it increasingly difficult to find the necessary finance, production facilities and – most crucially – distribution that would give West African directors the wider recognition they deserve.

West African film is dominated by three countries: Senegal, Mali and Burkina Faso.

Ousmane Sembène from Senegal is arguably West Africa's best-known director. His body of work includes *Borom Sarret* (1963), the first commercial film to be made in post-independence Africa, *Xala*, *Camp Thiaroye* and, most recently, the critically acclaimed *Moolade*. For more information on Senegalese films, see p673.

Mali's leading director is Souleymane Cissé, whose 1970s films include *Baara* and *Cinq Jours d'Une Vie*. Later films include the wonderful *Yeelen*, a prize winner at the 1987 Cannes festival, a lavish generational tale set in 13th-century Mali, and *Waati*. Cheick Oumar Sissoko has won prizes at Cannes and his *Guimba, un Tyran, une Epoque Guimba*, won the Étalon d'Or de Yennega, Africa's 'Oscar', at the 1995 Fespaco. For more information on Malian films, see p481.

From Burkina Faso, Idrissa Ouédraogo won the 1990 Grand Prix at Cannes for *Tilä*, an exceptional cinematic portrayal of life in a traditional African village. He is one of very few West African film makers to find genuine commercial success in the West. His other movies include *Yaaba*, *Samba Traoré*, *Kini* and *Adams*. Gaston Kaboré is another fine director whose film *Buud Yam*, a tale of childhood identity, superstition and a 19th-century African world about to change forever, was the 1997 winner of the Étalon d'Or de Yennenga. For more information on films from Burkina Faso, see p134.

Other important films include: *Dakan*, by Mohamed Camara of Guinea, which daringly uses the issue of homosexuality to challenge prevailing social and religious taboos; *Clando*, by the Cameroonian director Jean-Marie Teno, which addresses the timely issue of Africans choosing between fighting corrupt regimes at home and seeking a better life in Europe; and *The Blue Eyes of Yonta*, by Flora Gomes, one of few feature films ever made in Guinea-Bissau – it captures the disillusionment of young Africans who've grown up in the post-independence era.

The 18th edition of Fespaco in 2003 was an especially successful one for West African films. The Étalon d'Or de Yennenga went to the little-known Mauritanian director, Abderrahmane Sissako, for *Heremakono*, while Mali's Assane Kouyaté picked up the Jury Prize and Best Screenplay awards for *Kabala*. Four years later, the Étalon d'Or de Yennenga went to Nigeria's Newton Aduaka for *Ezra* (which also made a rare West African appearance at the Sundance Film Festival), while the runner-up award went to *Les Saignantes* by Cameroonian director Jean Pierre Bekolo.

And, as much as we'd like to forget the fact, Nigeria is home to the world's third-largest film industry. Going by the name of 'Nollywood', it turns out massive numbers of low-budget, high-energy films that are widely popular on DVD, but which won't win any critics' awards. For more, see p621.

FOOD & DRINK

For most West Africans, food is a question of survival rather than enjoyment and, as a result, is often monotonous. But for most travellers, the combination of unfamiliar tastes and the range of influences – including local, French and even Lebanese – results in some fine cuisine. The key is knowing where to find it (you won't find much variety outside larger cities), trying not to let the rather generous amounts of oil used in cooking bother you and learning to appreciate the atmosphere – an essential ingredient in the region's cooking – as much as the food. The quality of food varies considerably from country to country: culinary highlights of the region include Côte d'Ivoire and Senegal, while in desert countries such as Mauritania or Niger, ingredients are limited.

Staples & Specialties

Rice, rice and more rice is the West African staple that you'll eat again and again on your travels. Millet is also common, although this grain is usually pounded into flour before it's cooked. The millet flour is steamed

California Newsreel (www.newsreel.org) is a terrific resource on African film with extensive reviews and a Library of African Cinema, where you can order many of the best West African films, especially Fespaco prize winners.

South of the Sahara: Traditional Cooking from the Lands of West Africa, by Elizabeth A Jackson, brings the flavours of West Africa to your kitchen; the writer lived in Africa for a time and loves her food.

KOLA NUTS

Kola nuts are yellow or purple nuts, about half the size of a golf ball, which are sold in streets and markets everywhere in West Africa and are known for their mildly hallucinogenic effects. West Africans traditionally give kola nuts as gifts, and they're also a good option for travellers to carry and give to people in exchange for their kindness (or if you want to endear yourself to your fellow passengers in a bush taxi). The nuts last longer if you keep them moist but will become mouldy in a day or two if kept in a plastic bag. Despite the nuts' popularity among West Africans, most foreigners find them too bitter to chew and anyone looking for a high is usually disappointed.

---

then moistened with water until it thickens into a stiff porridge that can be eaten with the fingers. In the Sahel, couscous (semolina or millet grains) is always on the menu.

In coastal countries, staples may be root crops such as yam or cassava (also called manioc), which are pounded or grated before being cooked. They're served as a near-solid glob called *fufu* or *foufou* (which morphs into *foutou* further north) – kind of like mashed potatoes mixed with gelatine and very sticky. You grab a portion (with your right hand), form a ball, dip it in the sauce and enjoy. In the coastal countries, plantain (green banana) is also common.

If all that sounds a little uninspiring, remember that the secret's often in the sauce, which usually goes by the name of *riz sauce*. In some Sahel countries, groundnuts (peanuts) are common, and a thick, brown groundnut sauce (usually called *arachide*) is often served, either on its own or with meat or vegetables mixed in with the nuts. When groundnut sauce is used in a stew, it's called *domodah* or *mafé*. Sometimes deep-orange palm oil is also added. Sauces are also made with vegetables or the leaves of staple food plants such as cassava. Stock cubes or sachets of flavouring are ubiquitous across the region (Maggi is the most common trade name) and are often thrown into the pot as well. Where it can be afforded, or on special occasions, meat or fish is added to the sauce; sometimes succulent slices, sometimes grimly unattractive heads, tails and bones.

Cooking the West African Way, by Bertha Vining Montgomery and Constance Nabwire, is another fine cookbook and one of only a handful that dedicates itself solely to West Africa.

Okra is popular, particularly in coastal countries – the result is a slimy green concoction that tastes infinitely better than it looks. Other vegetables used in meals include *pommes de terre* (potatoes), *patates* (sweet potatoes), *oignons* (onions), *haricots verte* (green beans) and *tomates* (tomatoes). For flavouring, chillies may be used, or *jaxatu* (ja-ka-too) – similar to a green or yellow tomato but extremely bitter.

Some of the most memorable regional specialties include: the ubiquitous *jollof rice* (rice and vegetables with meat or fish and called 'riz yollof' in Francophone countries); *kedjenou* (Côte d'Ivoire's national dish of slowly simmered chicken or fish with peppers and tomatoes); *poulet yassa* (a Senegalese dish consisting of grilled chicken in an onion-and-lemon sauce) the sauce is also used to make *poisson yassa* (fish), *viande yassa* (meat) and just plain old *yassa*; and *tiéboudienne* (Senegal's national dish of rice baked in a thick sauce of fish and vegetables).

The availability of fruit depends on the season, but choice always increases as you head south from the Sahel into the coastal countries. Fruits you're likely to see include oranges, mandarins and grapefruits (often with green skin despite being ready to eat), bananas, mangoes, papayas, pineapples, guavas and passionfruits.

See individual country chapters for more details on regional specialities, while for other dishes you'll come frequently come across, turn to p54.

Drinks

NON-ALCOHOLIC DRINKS

International and local brands of soft drinks are sold virtually everywhere. A tiny shop in a remote village may sell little food but chances are they'll have a few dusty bottles of Coca-Cola or Pepsi for sale. (Coke is called 'Coca' in Francophone countries.) Bottled mineral water is widely available.

Homemade drinks include ginger beer and *bissap*, a purple mixture made from water and hibiscus leaves. Although they are refreshing, the water may not be clean, so they're usually best avoided.

In the Sahel countries, tea comes in two sorts: made with a tea bag ('Lipton tea', even if the brand is actually something else) and tea drunk by the local population. The latter is made with green leaves (often imported from China) and served with loads of sugar in small glasses. Half the fun of drinking local-style tea is the ritual that goes with it, taking at least an hour. Traditionally, the tea is brewed three times and poured from a small pot high above the glass.

Coffee is almost exclusively instant coffee (Nescafé is the usual brand). One of the region's finest institutions (found mainly in French-speaking countries) are the coffee stalls where clients sit on small benches around a table and drink glasses of Nescafé mixed with sweetened condensed milk. In some areas the water may be infused with a local leaf called *kinkiliba*, which gives it a woody tang – unusual but not unpleasant once you get over the shock.

ALCOHOLIC DRINKS

You can sometimes find imported beers from Europe and the USA, but about 45 brands of beer are brewed in West Africa, with Nigeria alone producing about 30. Some beers are European brands, brewed locally, others are specific to the region. The quality is often very good. Brands to look out for include: Club (Ghana, Nigeria and Liberia), Flag (Côte d'Ivoire, Mali and Senegal), Castel (Mali), Star (Sierra Leone, Ghana and Nigeria), Harp and Gulder (Nigeria and Ghana). Guinness, too, is found in several countries.

In the Sahel a rough, brown and gritty beer made from millet (called *chakalow* or *kojo*) is common, but West Africa's most-popular brew is palm wine. The tree is tapped and the sap comes out mildly fermented. Sometimes yeast is added and the brew is allowed to ferment overnight, which makes it much stronger.

Celebrations

Ceremonies are very important in traditional societies as they reinforce social structures, connect people to their traditions, mark important rites of passage (baptisms or naming ceremonies, circumcisions, weddings and funerals) and generally provide an excuse for a big feed. Most of these family

A Slice of Africa: Exotic West African Cuisines, by Chidi Asika-Enahoro, is written by a Nigerian who has lived for decades in the West - the perfect combination of insider's perspective aimed at an international audience.

The Africa Guide's cooking webpage (www .africaguide.com/cooking .htm) is not as detailed as most cookbooks but it's good on basic ingredients and does have some tasty West African recipes.

MINDING YOUR MANNERS

If you're invited to share a meal with locals, there are a few customs to observe. You'll probably sit with your hosts on the floor and it's usually polite to take off your shoes. It may be impolite, however, to show the soles of your feet, so observe closely what your hosts do.

The food, normally eaten by hand (remember to use only the right hand and don't be embarrassed to ask for a spoon), is served in one or two large dishes. Beginners will just pick out manageable portions with their fingers, but experts dig deep, forming a ball of rice and sauce with the fingers. Everybody washes their hands before and after eating. As an honoured guest you might be passed choice morsels by your hosts, and it's usually polite to finish eating while there's still food in the bowl to show you've had enough.

or village ceremonies involve gifts and, invariably once the formal rituals are completed, a meal of slaughtered sheep or goat.

Some travellers have been lucky enough to stay with local people, where a great way to repay their hospitality is to pay for a special meal for the entire family. This way you'll also be able to see how meals are put together. For the full picture, visit the market with the lady of the house (it's always the women who do the cooking in domestic situations) and see the various ingredients being bought.

Where to Eat & Drink

The best place to eat, if you're lucky enough to be invited, is at somebody's house. Most days, though, you'll be heading for a restaurant or eating on the street.

STREET FOOD

Street food tends to be absurdly cheap and is often delicious, especially the grilled fish.

On street corners and around bus stations, especially in the morning, you'll see small booths selling pieces of bread with fillings or toppings of butter, chocolate spread, yogurt, mayonnaise or sardines. In Francophone countries, the bread is cut from fresh French-style loaves or baguettes, but in Anglophone countries the bread is often a less-enticing soft, white loaf.

In the Sahel, usually around markets, women with large bowls covered with a wicker lid sell yogurt, often mixed with pounded millet and sugar. You can eat it on the spot or take it away in a plastic bag.

In the evenings you can buy brochettes (small pieces of beef, sheep or goat meat skewered and grilled over a fire) or lumps of roast meat sold by guys who walk around pushing a tin oven on wheels. Around markets and bus stations, women serve deep-fried chips of cassava or some other root crop.

In Francophone countries, grilled and roast meat, usually mixed with onions and spices, is sold in shacks. These are called *dibieteries* in some places, and you can eat on the spot or take away.

Another popular stand-by in the larger cities are Lebanese-style shwarmas, thin slices of lamb grilled on a spit, served with salad (optional) in Lebanese-style bread (pita) with a sauce made from chickpeas.

SIT-DOWN MEALS

West Africa abounds in restaurants, from fine and varied cuisine in capital cities to one-wooden-bench tin shacks in smaller towns. The smallest, simplest eating houses usually have just one or two meals available daily; if you spend most of your time eating in these places, your meals will be pretty straightforward (bowls of rice or another staple served with a simple sauce).

In slightly smarter places, your choice may also include fried chicken or fish served with *frites* (hot chips). Cooked vegetables, such as green beans, may also be available. Up a grade from here, mainly in cities, you'll find midrange restaurants catering to well-off locals and foreigners. Some serve only 'international' dishes (some also do local dishes though) and these meals are usually expensive, particularly if some of the ingredients have been imported from Europe. In just about every capital city in West Africa, you'll come across at least one French and one Chinese restaurant, and often a handful of other international restaurants.

Vegetarians & Vegans

As a vegetarian in West Africa – challenging, though possible – you'll end up eating the same things again and again. The concept of vegetarianism is

West Africa (Festivals & Food), by Ali Brownlie Bojang, is a simply told look at some of West Africa's most interesting festivals and the foods (with recipes) that are prepared to celebrate them.

'My Cooking' West-African Cookbook, by Dokpe L Ogunsanya, is an exuberantly presented cookbook that's ideal for researching before you go to get an idea of what to look for.

Betumi (www.betumi.com) is dedicated to traditional and contemporary cuisine; a useful feature is the online forum where people write in with ideas and places to track down ingredients; it's especially helpful for American readers.

rarely understood in West Africa, and vegetarian restaurants are rare. Your best bet is often Asian restaurants in capital cities, which always have some vegetarian dishes. The main challenge is likely to be keeping some variety and nutritional balance in your diet, and getting enough protein, especially if you don't eat eggs and dairy products.

If you do eat eggs and dairy products, pizzas and omelettes make a change from ubiquitous bean-and-vegetable dishes. The French may have bequeathed a love of coffee and good bread to its former colonies, but cheese never quite caught on, apart from the ultra-processed triangular varieties in supermarkets. Expensive imported cheese is usually available in capital cities.

Vegetarian street food possibilities include cassava, yam and plantain chips, bread with mayonnaise, egg or chocolate spread, and fried dough balls. Alternatively, head for the markets and do your own catering. There's always plenty of fresh fruit and vegetables, as well as bread and tins of margarine or tomato paste. Banana and groundnut (local-style peanut butter) sandwiches made with fresh bread are a nutritious option, while it's sometimes possible to find takeaway spaghetti and tomato sauce served in banana leaves.

Keep in mind that even the most simple vegetable sauce may sometimes have traces of meat or animal fat in it, and chicken or fish are usually not regarded as 'real' meat. The ubiquitous Maggi cubes also often contain chicken. If you're invited to someone's home for dinner, meat – a luxury for most local residents – is often reserved for special occasions or honoured guests. This means that the beast in the cooking pot bubbling away on the fire may well have been slaughtered in your honour, so give some thought to how you might deal with this situation in advance.

> Troth Wells' *New Internationalist Food Book* is more than just a recipe book - it tells vignettes from a whole host of countries and puts food at the heart of Africans' daily struggle for survival.

Food & Drink Glossary

afra	grilled meat, or grilled-meat stall
agouti	a rodent of the porcupine family, known as grasscutter or cane rat in Anglophone countries; it's popular in stews
aloco	fried bananas or plantains with onions and chilli
attiéké	grated cassava
benchi	black bench peas with palm oil and fish
bissap	purple drink made from water and hibiscus leaves
brochette	cubes of meat or fish grilled on a stick
buvette	small bar or drinks stall
caféman	man serving coffee (usually Nescafé), sometimes tea, and French bread with various fillings in Francophone countries
capitaine	Nile perch (fish)
carte	menu
cassava	a common starch staple eaten as an accompaniment; the leaves are eaten as a green vegetable; also called *gari* or manioc
chakalow	millet beer
chop	meal, usually local style
chop shop	a basic local-style eating house or restaurant (English-speaking countries)
cocoyam	starch-yielding food plant, also called taro
couscous	semolina or millet grains, served as an accompaniment to sauce
dibieterie	grilled-meat stall
domodah	groundnut-based stew with meat or vegetables
épinard	spinach
felafel	Lebanese-style deep-fried balls of ground chickpeas and herbs
feuille sauce	sauce made from greens (usually manioc leaves)
foutou	sticky yam or plantain paste similar to *fufu;* a staple in Côte d'Ivoire
frites	hot potato chips or French fries

fufu	a staple along the southern coast of West Africa made with fermented cassava, yam or plantain which is cooked and puréed; sometimes spelt *foufou*
gargotte	simple eating house or stall in Senegal, Guinea and The Gambia; also spelt *gargote* or *gargot*
gari	powdered cassava
gombo	okra or lady's fingers
groundnut	peanut; sometimes called *arachide*
haricot verte	green bean
jaxatu	bitter flavouring
jollof rice	common dish throughout the region consisting of rice and vegetables with meat or fish; called *riz yollof* in Francophone countries
kedjenou	Côte d'Ivoire's national dish but available elsewhere; slowly simmered chicken or fish with peppers and tomatoes
kinkiliba	leaf that is sometimes used to brew tea
kojo	millet beer
koutoukou	a clear, strong home brew in Côte d'Ivoire
mafé	groundnut-based stew; also spelt *mafay*
Maggi	brand name for a ubiquitous flavouring used in soups, stews etc
maquis	rustic open-air restaurant, primarily serving braised fish and grilled chicken with *attiéké*
menu du jour	meal of the day, usually at a special price
palaver sauce	usually made from spinach or other leaves plus meat/fish
palm wine	a milky-white, low-strength brew collected by tapping palm trees
patate	sweet potato
pâte	starch staple, often made from millet, corn, plantain, cassava or yam, eaten as an accompaniment to sauce; also called *akoumé*
pito	local brew in northern Ghana
plantain	a large green banana that has to be cooked before eating
plasas	pounded potato or cassava leaves cooked with palm oil and fish or beef
plat du jour	the dish of the day, usually offered at a special price
poisson	fish
pomme de terre	potato
poulet	chicken
poulet yassa	grilled chicken in onion-and-lemon sauce
pression	draught beer
riz sauce	very common basic meal (rice with sauce)
rôtisserie	food stall selling roast meat
salon de thé	literally 'tearoom'; cafe
shwarma	a popular Lebanese snack of grilled meat in bread, served with salad and sesame sauce
snack	in Francophone Africa this means a place where you can get light meals and sandwiches; 'bar snack' means you can get a beer or coffee too
sodabe	a spirit made in Togo
spot	simple bar
sucrerie	soft drink (literally 'sweet thing')
suya	Hausa word for brochette
tiéboudienne	Senegal's national dish, rice baked in thick sauce of fish and vegetables; also spelt *thieboudjenne*
tô	millet or sorghum-based *pâte*
viande	meat
wigila	Songhaï speciality from Gao (Mali) of sun-dried dumplings dipped in a meat sauce made with cinnamon and spices
yam	edible starchy root; sometimes called *igname*

Spices of Life: Piquant Recipes from Africa, Asia and Latin America for Western Kitchens, by Troth Wells, has recipes, social and cultural information and some fascinating ideas for your next dinner party.

The Music of West Africa

Music put West Africa on the map. Years ago, even if no one knew exactly where Senegal was, they knew that Youssou N'Dour lived there, and the great Baaba Maal. They could tell you that Salif Keita came from Mali, and Mory Kanté from Guinea. That Nigeria was home to Fela Kuti and *juju* music emperor, King Sunny Ade. Reggae star Alpha Blondy defined Côte d'Ivoire. Saxophonist Manu Dibango was Cameroon, just as Cesária Evora was Cape Verde and Angélique Kidjo, Benin. All of these West African stars fuelled the global Afropop boom. Once filed under 'A' for Africa, they lent the world music genre much needed individuality, commerciality and cred.

Conakry's Radio Kankan (www.radio-kankan.com) is a French-language station devoted to news and music from the region.

The international success of these West African elders has paved the way for an apparently bottomless pot of talent. Desert rebels Tinariwen; dreadlocked Senegalese mystic Cheikh Lo; and his hotly tipped compatriot, Daby Baldé. The fresh prince of Côte d'Ivoire, Tiken Jah Fakoly, and its fresh princess, Dobet Gnahoré. Golden-voiced Mauritanian Daby Touré, and afrobeating politicos such as Nigeria's Femi Kuti (in looks, sound and sentiment, very much his father's son). Lura from Cape Verde, with her contemporary *morna* style, and Malians including ethereal songbird Rokia Traore, *kora* maestro Toumani Diabaté and husband-and-wife team Amadou and Mariam – whose Manu Chao–produced album, *Dimanche à Bamako*, went to the top of the global charts and stayed there.

Martin Scorsese presents the Blues: Feels Like Going Home (Martin Scorsese; 2003) follows musician Corey Harris' travels through Mississippi and West Africa, exploring the roots of blues music. Includes performances by Salif Keita, Habib Kolté, Taj Mahal and Ali Farke Touré.

Mentioning these names is only scratching the surface. Music is everywhere in West Africa, coming at you in thunderous, drum-fuelled polyrhythms, through the swooping, soaring voices of *griots* (traditional musicians or minstrels; praise singers) and via socially-aware reggae, rap and hip-hop. From Afrobeat to pygmy fusion, highlife to *makossa, gumbe* to Nigerian gospel, genres are as entrenched as they are evolving, fusing and reforming. Little wonder that here – in this vast, diverse region, with its deserts, jungles, skyscrapers, and urban sprawl – myriad ethnic groups play out their lives to music. Here are traditional songs that celebrate weddings, offer solace at funerals, keep work rhythms steady in the fields. Here are songs and rhythms that travelled out on slave ships to Cuba and Brazil. Songs that retell history and, in doing so, foster inter-clan and inter-religious respect.

In West Africa, too, are the roots of Western music (along with guitars, keyboards, Latin influences and other legacies of colonialism). Not for nothing did Senegalese rap crew Daara J title their 2003 international debut *Boomerang*. 'Born in Africa, raised in America', says member Faada Freddy, 'rap has come full circle'. As has the blues. A host of American blues musicians – Ry Cooder, Corey Harris, Taj Mahal, Bonnie Raitt – have found inspiration and affirmation in West Africa, in Mali in particular. 'I never heard American blues music before I started playing,' said the famed Malian guitarist, Ali Farke Touré, 'but when I did, I recognised it as African music, the music from my region'.

The great bluesman Ali Farke Touré, who passed away in March 2006, was the mayor of his hometown, Niafunké, a village near his farm on the Niger River in Timbuktu (Tombouctou) province. 'Your job on earth is to share what gifts God has given you,' he says. Check out his posthumously released album, *Savane*.

Even Blur and Gorillaz frontman Damon Albarn embarked on a love affair with West Africa, recording his hi-tech *Mali Music* album after a visit in 2000. His Honest Jons record label has since released a series of intriguing West African albums, including *Lagos Chop Up* and drummer Tony 'Afrobeat' Allen's *Lagos Shaking*. 'The amazing thing about West Africa,' Albarn has said, 'is that you can hear all the components of Western music there'.

You could, if you like, seek out the thriving West African scene in London or Paris, where many of the aforementioned West African acts have forged their international careers. But, just as Salif Keita relocated to Bamako in 2005

MUST-HAVE WEST AFRICAN ALBUMS

- *Dimanche á Bamako* (Because) by Amadou and Mariam
- *M'Bemba* (Universal Jazz France) by Salif Keita
- *In the Heart of the Moon* (World Circuit) by Ali Farke Touré and Toumani Diabaté
- *Worotan* (World Circuit) by Oumou Sangare
- *The Best Best of Fela Kuti* (MCA) by Fela Kuti
- *Nothing's In Vain* (Nonesuch) by Youssou N'Dour
- *Firin in Fouta* (Mango) by Baaba Maal
- *Juju Music* (Island) by King Sunny Ade and his African Beats
- *Miss Perfumado* (Lusafrica) by Cesária Evora
- *Amassakoul* (Independent Records) by Tinariwen

---

after 20 years in Paris, it really is better to soak it up in situ. 'A trunk never turns into a crocodile, no matter how long it stays in the water,' says Keita.

Trust us. Your musical tastes, attitude and perceptions will – like your iPod – never be the same again.

> Sterns Music (www .sternsmusic.com) is the Amazon.com of the world music scene, allowing you to search and buy from a large range of West African and other CDs and DVDs.

A POTTED HISTORY OF WEST AFRICAN MUSIC

The musical history of West Africa is closely linked to its diverse and long-established empires, such as Ghana's (6th to 11th centuries), where court music was played for chiefs, music accompanied ceremonies and chores, and was played for pleasure at the end of the day. In the vast Mali Empire (13th to 15th centuries), music was the province of one social caste, the *jelis,* who still perform their folk styles today. Correspondingly in Senegal, *griots* – Wolof culture's *kora*-strumming, praise-singing caste – trace genealogies, recount epics and span generations. There are myriad musical styles in West Africa, courtesy of its hundreds of ethnic groups and various Islamic and European influences, but the *jeli/griot* tradition is arguably the best known.

Senegal, The Gambia, Guinea, Mali, Mauritania, Burkina Faso and Côte d'Ivoire all share the same *jeli* tradition, though each linguistic group calls it something different and each has its own subtly different sound. They are acknowledged as oral historians – nearly all children know the epic of Sundiata Keita, the warrior who founded the Mali Empire (see the boxed text, p28) – and often as soothsayers, but, although they top the bill at weddings and naming ceremonies, *griots* occupy a lowly rank in their hierarchical societies. Many big West African stars faced parental objections to their choice of career. Others, such as Salif Keita – a direct descendent of Sundiata and, as such, not a *jeli* – made their reputations in exile.

> *In Griot Time: An American Guitarist in Mali* (2002) is an acclaimed account of Malian musicians and culture, written by a fellow musician who spent seven months in Bamako playing guitar with Djelimady Tounkara, formerly of the legendary Super Rail Band.

Oral tradition is equally strong in Nigeria, where stories of ancient Yoruba, Ashanti, Hausa and other kingdoms flourish. Like many a West African style, Yoruba music has its roots in percussion. Indeed, if there is any element common to the huge, diverse region that is West Africa, it is drumming. From the Ewe ensembles of Ghana – similar in style to those of Benin and Togo – to Senegal's *sabar* drummers, beating their giant instruments with sticks, drumming kick-started West Africa's musical heart. Often accompanied by ululation, vocal repetition, call-and-response vocals and polyrhythms, drums beat out a sound that immediately says 'Africa'.

As West African music travelled out on the slave ships (and brought other influences back with it later), so the music of the colonisers travelled in. The

Portuguese presence in Cape Verde created *morna*, music of separation, and *saudade* and creole-style *gumbe* in Guinea-Bissau. Western-style dance orchestras had the colonial elite fox-trotting on the Gold Coast. Francophone Africa fell in love with Cuban dance music, a genre, in rhythm and structure, remarkably close to Mande music. Cuban music (and guitar-based Congolese rumba) introduced modern instruments to the region, creating a swathe of dance bands such as Guinea's legendary Bembeya Jazz (a signifier of modern music, 'jazz' was commonly tagged on a band's name), who played local styles with Latin arrangements.

Post-independence, the philosophy of 'negritude' – or cultural rediscovery – arose among some 1960s-era West African governments. Popular Latin sounds were discouraged in favour of folkloric material. Electric Afropop began to incorporate traditional rhythms and instruments, such as the *kora* (a harp-like musical instrument with over 20 strings), *balafon* (xylophone) and *ngoni* (a stringed instrument). State-sponsored dance bands won big audiences and spawned even bigger stars. The first president of Senegal (poet Leopold Senghor) fostered the young Orchestra Baobab band, whose phenomenal 21st-century comeback continues. Mali's Le Rail Band du Bamako (sponsored by the Malian Railway Company) became an African institution that launched the careers of two of Africa's greatest singers: Salif Keita and Mory Kanté.

When the young Salif Keita defected to their foreign-style rivals, Les Ambassedeurs du Motel, there was uproar. Fierce, Oasis-vs-Blur-style competition ensued throughout the 1970s, making Bamako the dance music capital of West Africa (see p490). Meanwhile, in Nigeria, the poppy highlife sound of the 1940s, '50s and '60s gave way to genres with a strong percussive element, such as *juju* and *fuji*. The West's popular music genres – rock, soul, jazz, funk, pop – made their mark, each spawning its own 'Afro' equivalent. Today the likes of 1960s Sierra-Leonean Afro-soul king Geraldo Pino and Ghanaian Afro-rock collective Osibisa are being rediscovered by a new generation of Western hipsters.

The recording studios of Lagos offered commercial opportunities for Nigerian performers, as did those of 1980s Abidjan in Cotê d'Ivoire – a musical Mecca for artists from across the continent. But by the mid-1980s all eyes were on Paris, the city where Mory Kanté recorded his seminal club floor track 'Yeke Yeke', and where innumerable West African musicians lived. Big names moved back and forth between Paris, London and West Africa, recording cassettes for the local market and albums for the international one, as remains the case today. With the 1990s world-music boom, many stars – Youssou N'Dour, Salif Keita, Cesária Evora, King Sunny Ade – established their own record companies and signed up local talent.

Some savvy Western record labels pre-empted mainstream interest in West African music. London-based World Circuit signed the likes of Ali Farke Touré, Cheikh Lo, Oumou Sangare and Orchestra Baobab, arguably doing for West Africa what it did for Cuba with the Buena Vista Social Club. West African artists are now staples of international festivals including Womad and Glastonbury. Club producers have remixed Cesária Evora, Femi Kuti and Rokia Traore. West African albums make it into mainstream charts, West African musicians sell out Western venues and Western musicians look to West Africa for inspiration.

In West Africa, big-name artists attract hordes of followers wherever they go. The politicians who try to hijack such popularity are usually shrugged off. Youssou N'Dour, Baaba Maal et al are international ambassadors in their own right, stars who use their position (and their lyrics) to campaign against

I'll Sing for You (Je Chanterai Pour Toi; 2001) is an award-winning, life-affirming documentary featuring legendary Mali bluesman Boubacar 'KarKar' Traoré returning to his homeland after decades of self-imposed exile in France.

African Music Encyclopedia (www.africanmusic .org) offers a country-by-country, artist-by-artist breakdown for lovers of music from Africa and the African diaspora.

Cassette piracy is a huge problem in West Africa and many high-profile names have devoted themselves to the task of its eradication.

poverty, disease and illiteracy. Oumou Sangare sings, however obliquely, about women's rights. The rap movement in Senegal promotes peace and love. But freedom of expression is still curtailed; Femi Kuti's pro-democracy narratives are censored in Nigeria, just as his father's were.

Latin music remains popular in Mali. Guitar-based highlife is still a staple of Ghana, where hip-life – the country's very own hip-hop – is also huge; for more information, see the boxed text p331. Nigerian music isn't as popular in the West as it was; Mali, Guinea, Senegal and The Gambia are currently ahead in the popularity stakes. Traditional acoustic albums from that region have been enjoying a renaissance, and Salif Keita, Youssou N'Dour, Baaba Maal and Mory Kanté have all recently unplugged. Everywhere, musicians are creating, collaborating, experimenting. New, exciting performers are constantly emerging.

West African music has never been healthier. Styles may change, but one thing, at least, is certain: the drums will beat forever.

WEST AFRICAN INSTRUMENTS

West Africa's traditional instruments tend to be found in its rural areas and are generally fashioned from local materials – everything from gourds, stalks and shells to goat skin, cow horns and horse hair. Discarded objects and nature also have multiple musical uses; in Sierra Leone, empty Milo tins filled with stones were the core instrument for the genre called Milo-jazz. Hausa children in Nigeria beat rhythms on the inflated belly of a live pufferfish. The Pygmies of Cameroon beat rhythms on river water.

There are bells made of bronze in the Islamic orchestras of northern Nigeria, and scrapers made of iron in the south. In Cape Verde women place a rolled-up cloth between their legs and beat it as part of their *batuco* music (the singer Lura does this live, with silver lamé). Everywhere, there is men's music and women's music, men's instruments and women's instruments: in Mauritania, men play the *tidinit*, a four-stringed lute, and women the *ardin*, a sort of back-to-front *kora*. Accordingly, there are men's dances and women's dances. And most of these, like most instrumental ensembles, are fuelled by drums.

West Africa has a phenomenal variety of drums. Kettle, slit and talking drums; water, frame and hourglass-shaped drums; log, goblet and double-headed barrel drums. Drums used for ritual purposes, like the *dundun* drums of the Yoruba, which communicate with the *orishas;* drums made from tree trunks and used for long-distance messages; drums that mark the major events of one's life – baptism, marriage, death – and drums for entertainment. 'Talking' drums, such as the Wolof *tama,* a small, high-pitched instrument clamped under the armpit and beaten fast with a hooked stick, or the *djembe,* the chalice-shaped drum ubiquitous from Ghana to Senegal, and in the West's endorphin-inducing African drum circles.

There's a diverse array of string instruments too, from the one-stringed viol of the Niger Tuareg and the 13-string *obo* zither of the Igbo in Nigeria, to the 21-string *kora* – the harp/lute of the *griots* and one of the most sophisticated instruments in sub-Saharan Africa. *Kora* players are usually virtuosos, having studied their craft from childhood. Mory Kanté's amplified rock-style *kora* helped establish its reputation as a formidable solo instrument, while *kora* master Toumani Diabaté, son of the virtuoso Sidiki Diabaté, displayed its crossover potential by collaborating with everyone from flamenco musicians to bluesmen Ali Farke Touré and Taj Mahal.

Regarded by some as the precursor to the banjo, the *ngoni* (*xalam* in Wolof, *hoddu* in Fula, *konting* in Mandinka) is also popular with *griots*. A feature in the 14th-century courts of Mali, it has between three and five strings that are plucked, and is tricky to play. Another well-known *griot* instrument is the

YOUSSOU N'DOUR

Dressed in white, arms spread wide, Youssou N'Dour stands on stage and unleashes his startling tenor. 'Africa…all…my…people', he sings, unaccompanied, his voice curling sensuously skywards, his eight-piece band, Le Super Étoile, ready for action. As the crowd roars its response, N'Dour launches into the funky, riotous sound he's famous for. Hits come in Wolof, French and English, including his 1994 smash duet with Neneh Cherry, 'Seven Seconds'. West Africa's greatest musical hero is, as ever, on message. His pride in his culture is obvious.

'Africa needs new, positive images,' says the 47-year-old afterwards. 'For too long it has been seen as a place where war, poverty and sad things happen. But it is also a place of beauty and poetry, colour and music,' he sighs. 'It is up to African artists,' he adds, 'to bring these images to the West'.

For a long time it seemed to be up to Youssou N'Dour. One of a long line of Tukulor *griots*, N'Dour grew up singing alongside his mother at religious ceremonies. His swooping, soaring voice won him live slots on national radio and a boy-wonder status he exploited by hustling for gigs outside nightclubs like the Thoissane, the Copacabana-style venue in Dakar that he now owns. By 16 he was in the line-up of Ibra Kasse's Star Band and, soon after, Étoile de Dakar. Aged 18 he formed Le Super Étoile de Dakar, throwing in Latin influences, adding guitars and keyboards, and reclaiming the big Senegalese *sabar* drum. The sound, *mbalax*, spawned a phenomenon.

N'Dour set about straddling the commercial and traditional worlds. He introduced funk and fusion into his sound, then achieved world renown in the 1980s when he supported Peter Gabriel in concert and starred alongside Gabriel, Sting and Bruce Springsteen on the celebrated 1988 Amnesty International Tour. A series of glossy crossover albums followed, but it was 2002's acoustic *Nothing's In Vain* and 2004's inspired, Grammy-winning *Egypt* (a paean to Islam composed on Senegalese instruments and recorded with an Egyptian orchestra) that had critics doing backflips. Having cancelled a US tour in March 2003 in protest at the invasion of Iraq, the *Egypt* album was the album that he always wanted to make.

Among other projects, N'Dour owns a record label, Jololi, a cassette factory, a radio station, a newspaper and Xippi, the country's best recording studio, from where he produces rap artists for the local market ('Wolof rap will never be popular outside Senegal,' he says). He enjoys his role at the top, from where he channels his wealth into community projects. When he's not touring, and he tours often (scandalously, he was the only African star to play at the 2005 Live8 concert in Hyde Park), N'Dour regularly gigs at the Thoissane where, though he's rarely onstage before 3am, he always gets a stomping, shouting hero's welcome.

'I have a message to deliver to the world,' says N'Dour, 'and that message is in the music'.

balafon, a wooden xylophone with between 18 and 21 keys, suspended over a row of gourds to amplify the sound. The *balafon* is often played in pairs, with each musician – one improvising, one not – striking the keys with wooden mallets. The Susu people of Guinea are renowned *balafon* experts.

There are other xylophones with different names in West Africa, xylophones fashioned from huge logs, or xylophones amplified by boxes and pits. There are wind instruments (Fula shepherds play melodies on reed flutes) and brass instruments (the Niger Tuareg favour the *alghaita shawm* trumpet) and voices used as instruments – such as the timeless vocals of the *griots*, the polyphonic singing of the Pygmies and the sung poetry of the Tuareg.

Across the region, percussion vies and blends with brass, wood and wind instruments. In urban areas, traditional instruments complement and ground modern instruments. West Africa is, indeed, a hive of musical activity, thrumming to its own collective orchestra.

Songs of West Africa (2000) contains over 80 traditional African folk songs and chants in six languages, along with extensive translations, music fundamentals, a pronunciation guide and introductions to West African society. Oh, and a sing-along CD.

WEST AFRICAN MUSICAL STYLES

While many of West Africa's mega-successful artists might be classified as 'Afro-pop', thanks to commercial sales at home and/or in the West, the

TINARIWEN

Tinariwen loosen their turbans when they play away from home. Sand is never a problem outside of the Sahara. Back home it gets into ears and mouths, making it hard to sing, and under the fretboards of their Fender Stratocasters, making them hard to play. Not that this most rugged of guitar bands, a collective of Tuareg nomads from Kidal, a dusty town way out past Timbuktu, are bothered. Even their name means 'desert'. The sound conjured by their chants, ululations and call-and-response vocals, hand claps, hand-drums and wall of guitars, is all space and spirit. Their attitude – reflective, angry, resilient – is pure desert blues.

And if anyone has the right to play the blues, it's the Tuareg. These nomadic pastoralists once roamed the Sahara with their cattle, camels and goats, but African independence left them exposed to old enmities in the 1960s, and their living was devastated by drought in the following decades. Conflict with the Malian authorities was ongoing – eventually leading to a bloody rebellion (see p525) – and in the 1980s many Tuareg ended up in Libyan President Gadafi's training camps, where they learned how to play guitar. Legend has it they went to battle with Kalashnikovs in one hand and guitars slung across their backs.

'Desert life is hard,' says bandleader Ibrahim Ag Alhabib, 45, through a cloud of cigarette smoke, 'our own music, our own poetry is vital'. Tinariwen's songs tell the lives of their dispossessed kinsmen; passed on by generations of cheap cassette recordings, they have become as anthemic in the Sahara as those of, say, the Rolling Stones or White Stripes – bands with whom they've been compared. 'I have had sadness from an early age,' says Ibrahim. 'I saw my father killed by Malian soldiers. I grew up in exile in Algeria, fending for myself.' Music offered an escape. In the camps he met other musically minded freedom fighters. They threw out the traditional lute and one-stringed fiddle, and set their traditional rhythms to the electric guitar. 'At first we improvised with tin cans, sticks and string. Then somehow we got hold of guitars and taught ourselves how to play.'

They became so popular that the Malian government outlawed possession of their cassettes. 'But we were singing about hardship, about the desert, about taking pride in your heritage,' Ibrahim insists. In 2000 a rejigged Tinariwen recorded their debut album, *The Radio Tisdas Sessions*, in Kidal's electricity-starved local radio station. In 2001 they hosted the first annual Festival in the Desert in Essakane (see p521), an interclan get together so unique and exotic that the likes of Damon Albarn and Robert Plant have suffered the three-day slog to get there.

'The Tuareg have always placed a great importance on gatherings,' offers Ibrahim. Which is why, perhaps, Tinariwen's seven-strong touring line-up – six tough men and one demure but feisty woman, all in pale, flowing robes – have become a staple of the international festival circuit. They won a BBC World Music Award (Africa) for their second album, 2004's *Amassakoul* and, with their mesmeric sounds and effortless left-field cred, have become *the* world music name to drop. Their stunning 2006 album *Aman Iman: Water is Life* brought Tinariwen to a whole new international audience.

'Life has improved for the Tuareg people,' says Ibrahim, 'and I know Tinariwen have helped. Our message is being heard further away'. He dusts some imaginary sand off his shoe. 'We just want to take people with us,' he says, 'and the place we are going is back home'.

region boasts a gamut of distinctive musical styles. The following are just a few of them.

Afrobeat

Co-created by the late, great Fela Anikulapo Kuti, Afrobeat is a hybrid of Nigerian highlife, Yoruba percussion, jazz, funk and soul. Fela, a singer, saxophonist and bandleader, and one of the most influential 20th-century African figures, used Afrobeat to give voice to the oppressed. His onstage rants, tree-trunk-sized spliff in hand, were legendary. A succession of governments tried to shut him up. When he died of AIDS in 1997, a million people joined his funeral procession through Lagos (see p620 for more). His son, Femi, has picked up the baton, releasing fine albums such as *Shoki Shoki* and reopening his father's Lagos night club, the Shrine. A host of Fela imitators –

Tony Allen, the masked Lagbaja, and Fela's youngest son, Seun – keep the flame alight. A recent surge in interest has seen Afrobeat crossover into dance mixes, hip-hop and reggae collaborations.

Cape Verdean Music

Cape Verdean music came late to the West. The undisputed star of the bluesy, melancholy songs (known as *morna*) is the 'barefoot diva' Cesária Evora, a ciggie-puffing grandmother erroneously thought to appear onstage without shoes in support of the disadvantaged women in her country ('No,' she says, 'I just don't like wearing shoes'.). European influences are obvious in *morna*, the equivalent to Portugal's *fado*, while Africa is at the fore in other genres such as the dance-oriented *coladeira*, accordion-led *funana* and percussive women's music, *batuco*. Look out for recordings by *morna* tenor Bana, the Lisbon-based Lura and Tcheka, a singer/songwriter and guitarist who plays beats that are normally played on percussion.

Gumbe

Closely associated with Guinea-Bissau, *gumbe* is an uptempo, polyrhythmic genre that fuses about 10 of the country's folk music traditions. Lyrics, sung in Portuguese creole, are topical and witty; instruments include guitars and the water drum, an upturned calabash floating in a bucket. Civil unrest rendered *gumbe* a latecomer to the West, until the Lisbon-based Manecas Costa brought out his acclaimed 2004 album *Paradiso di Gumbe*. In Sierra Leone, *gumbe* evolved from the breezy, calypso-style guitar music called palm-wine. The late SE Rogie and London-based Abdul Tee-Jay are probably the best-known exponents.

Highlife

Ghana's urban, upbeat highlife, which started off in the dancehalls of the colonial Gold Coast, has had a ripple effect throughout West Africa. Trumpeter and bandleader ET Mensah was the post-war, pan-African king of this sound, a blend of everything from Trinidadian calypso, brass band music and Cuban son, to swing, jazz and older African song forms. Osibisa were *the* 'Afro-rock' pop/highlife group of the 1970s. Today's hybrids include gospel, hip-hop (hip-life) and the ever-popular guitar highlife. The Western Diamonds, Amekye Dede and Jewel Ackah are popular artists. Highlife is also a staple of Sierra Leone, Liberia and (with a Congolese influence) Nigeria. Check out early recordings by Dr Victor Olaiya, Nigerian highlife's 'evil genius' and his band, Cool Cats.

Juju

Juju music evolved from a mix of traditional Yoruba talking drums and folklore, and popular palm-wine guitar music. *Juju's* best known ambassador, King Sunny Ade, has been deploying his relentless blend of ringing guitar lines, multilayered percussion, tight harmonies and booty shaking for four decades now. In Nigeria he's known as KSA, the Minister for Enjoyment. Competition with his main rival, Chief Commander Ebenezer Obey, continues, with the likes of Sir Shina Peters close behind. *Juju* is not to be confused with the Arabesque percussion frenzy that is *fuji*: main players here include elder statesman Sir Ayinde Barrister and innovators Pasuma Wonder and Adewale Ayuba, whose recent award-winning collaboration with Adé Bantu, *Fuji Satisfaction,* added Afrobeat, ragga, rap and hip-hop.

Makossa

A fusion of highlife and soul, influenced by Congolese rumba and characterised by electric guitars, Cameroon's distinctive pop-*makossa* music remains

Afropop (www.afropop.org) aims to be the premier destination for web denizens interested in the contemporary music of Africa and the African diaspora; highlights include streaming audio and a searchable database.

Fela Kuti: Music is the Weapon (1982) is a hard-hitting documentary filmed in Lagos, mixing interviews with Kuti with footage of life at his Kalakuta Republic, and performances at his Shrine nightclub. Comes with a double CD of Kuti's best-known songs.

one of West Africa's most vibrant dance genres. Its biggest star is still the jazz-minded sax player and singer Manu Dibango (track down his 1973 release, *Soul Makossa*), who has worked in related genres such as *mangambe, assiko* and *bikutsi,* and regularly sells out London venues such as Ronnie Scott's. The ever-adventurous Francis Bebey is another big name, while Sam Fan Thomas has popularised *makassi,* a sort of *makossa*-lite. Other names include Toto Guillaume, Ekambi Brilliant and the guitarist Vincent Nguini.

Mbalax

Africanhiphop.com (www.africanhiphop .com) has been mapping the development of African hip-hop culture since the '90s; it features links, new productions and contributions from the artists themselves.

Taken from the Wolof word for rhythm, *mbalax* is Senegal's primary musical genre, an intensely polyrhythmic sound that evolved in the 1970s from Afro-Cuban dance bands such as the Star Band and Orchestra Baobab, and then fiercely reclaimed its African roots. Youssou N'Dour was the first to introduce more traditional elements, including *tassou* (a form of rap), *bakou* (a kind of trilling) and instruments such as the *tama* and *sabar* drums. Popular *mbalax* artists include females Khar M'Baye Maddiagaga, Kine Lam and N'Dour's Britney-esque sister-in-law, Vivianne.

Reggae, Rap & Hip-Hop

Afro-reggae, rap and hip-hop are huge throughout West Africa. Elder Ivorian statesman Alpha Blondy has enjoyed a 20-year career, spawning hits like the classic 'Jerusalem', recorded in Jamaica with the Wailers. His younger, equally political, compatriots include Serge Kassy and Tiken Jah Fakoly. Ivorian hip-hop includes the gangsta-style rap *dogba,* which contrasts with the socially aware, anti-bling Wolof rap of Senegalese outfits such as Daara J and Positive Black Soul. There is a growing Mandinka rap scene in Mali (check out the album *Mandinka Rap From Mali* (Naxos World) by the rapping *griot* duo Les Escrocs). Majek Fashek is the best-known Nigerian reggae artist, and Nigerian hip-hop musicians include Eedris Abdulkareem – he of the much-hyped spat with 50 Cent – along with JJC and the 419 Squad. Rap Nigerien is a melange of different languages spoken in Niger – as deployed by groups such as Was Wong, Gogro G and Metaphor – and covers such topics as forced marriages, child labour and corruption. The Gambia's reggae scene is also one of the most exciting in West Africa; the best-known artists include Dancehall Masters, Rebellion the Recaller and Egalitarian.

Oumou Sangare is the owner of Bamako's Hotel Wasulu, a purpose-built 35-room hotel whose rooms are named after famous Malian musicians. There's an Ali Farke Touré room and, of course, an Oumou Sangare suite. Oh, and she is also the resident headliner.

Wassoulou

Wassoulou music is named after the region of the same name, south of Bamako in Mali, and the Fula people who inhabit it. Wassoulou is not *jeli* music – they have no castes – but is based on hunting songs. The women usually sing, and the men dance. The music is based on the *kamalengoni* or youth's harp – a sort of funky, jittery bass guitar invented in the 1950s – and is augmented by the thwack and slap of the *fle,* a calabash strung with cowrie shells and thrown and spun in the air. Having shot to fame with her 1989 release, *Moussoulou,* Oumou Sangare is still the biggest Wassoulou star, singing in her native Bambara about the injustices of life in West Africa: polygamy, arranged marriages, the price of a bride. 'There is still much work to be done,' she says.

Arts & Craftwork

West Africa's artistic heritage, which encompasses fascinating traditional sculptures, masks, striking textiles and jewellery, is tied very much to the land and its people. Most of the works you'll encounter were, in their original form, representations of the natural and spirit worlds and have changed little in centuries. The creation of these arts and crafts is often the preserve of distinct castes of blacksmiths and weavers who rely almost exclusively on locally found or produced materials. Thus it is that, although you'll find some pieces that have been developed for the tourist market, the overwhelming majority of art forms come to life precisely because they still carry powerful meaning for West Africa's diverse peoples.

Lovers of West African art should make a beeline for the Musée International du Golfe de Guinée (p776) in the Togolese capital Lomé.

MASKS

In West Africa masks were rarely produced for purely decorative purposes. Rather, they were highly active signifiers of the spirit world and traditionally played a central role in ceremonies that served to both accompany important rites of passage and to entertain. There is a staggering range of shapes and styles of mask, all of which are invariably rich in meaning; they range from the tiny 'passport' mask of the Dan (Côte d'Ivoire) to the Dogon *imina-tiou* mask (Mali), which can tower up to 10m in height.

Masks, which are usually created by professional artisans, can be made of wood, brass, tin, leather, cloth, glass beads, natural fibres and even (in the case of the Ashanti) gold. They come in numerous forms, including face masks, helmet masks (which cover the whole head), headdresses (which are secured to the top of the head), the massive *nimba* masks of the Baga people in Guinea (which are carried on the dancer's shoulders) and the famous ivory hip masks from the Kingdom of Benin (present-day Nigeria), which are worn around the waist.

West African masks are usually classified as anthropomorphic (resembling the human form) and zoomorphic (the representation of deities in the form of animals). Anthropomorphic masks are often carefully carved and very realistic. Many groups use masks representing beautiful maidens, whose features reflect the aesthetic ideal of the people. The zoomorphic masks mostly represent dangerous and powerful nature spirits, and can be an abstract and terrifying combination of gaping jaws, popping eyes and massive horns. Some masks combine human and animal features. These convey the links between humans and animals, in particular the ability to gain and control the powers of animals and the spirits they represent.

The mask is only part of a complex costume that often covers the dancer's entire body. Made of plant fibre or cloth, often with elaborate appliqué, the costume is usually completed with a mane of raffia surrounding the mask. Most masks are associated with dance, although some are used as prestige symbols and are worn as amulets.

TEXTILES

Few places in the world can match West Africa for the beauty, vitality, colour and range of its textiles. Contrary to what many travellers expect, men are the main producers of textiles (the *bogolan* cloth of Mali is an exception), weaving wool, cotton, nylon, rayon and silk on a variety of looms. Most of West Africa's textiles follow the strip-cloth technique, whereby cloth is woven in

Some art historians believe that one of Picasso's most famous paintings - *Les Demoiselles d'Avignion* - depicts women wearing ceremonial Dogon masks.

The Art of West Africa (www.artofwestafrica .com) sells high-quality West African masks and sculptures. Alongside images of signature art forms and collectors-only prices, brief but informative descriptions make it worth a visit.

African Elegance, by Ettagale Blauer, is a magnificently photographed chronicle of African art forms and their role in modern Africa. The sections on masks and jewellery are of particular interest.

THE MASK COMES ALIVE

Behind almost every West African mask lies a story, often known only to members of a particular ethnic group. When masks and costumes are worn for a dance, which is accompanied by percussive music and song, they come alive and convey their meaning to the audience. Masked dances are used in initiation and coming-of-age ceremonies; in burial rituals, when dancing and celebrations assist the spirit of the dead to forsake the earth and reside with ancestors; in fertility rituals, which are associated with agriculture and the appeasement of spirits to ensure a successful harvest; and in the rituals surrounding childbirth. Masks fulfil the function of entertainment, with community-based dances and theatrical plays being created for social education and enjoyment.

The role of the mask is, however, changing. Christianity, Islam and the 20th century have all had a major impact on the animist masked dances of West Africa. Many dances are no longer performed, others have transformed from sacred rituals to forms of entertainment. Since the arrival in Africa of tourists and collectors, artisans have begun to produce masks for widespread sale. Although a departure from the mask's role in traditional society, tourism can serve to keep artisans employed in their traditional art – evidence, perhaps, that masking traditions are never static and continue to transmute over time.

It's still possible to see masked dances in West Africa, although they may be specially arranged 'tourist performances'. Getting to see the real thing is often a matter of being in the right place at the right time. For information on Dogon masks and related ceremonies, see the boxed text, p509.

---

narrow strips that are then sewn together. As many West Africans now wear Western clothes and traditional textiles are largely reserved for ceremonial occasions, the skills required to produce the finer textiles are disappearing, a trend that sales to collectors and tourists only partly ameliorates. For more information on Ghanaian textiles, see p331.

Kente Cloth

Kente Cloth; Introduction to History, by Ernest Asamoah-Yaw, is a fascinating journey through the history of Ghana's most famous textile with good coverage of pattern and name origins.

Clothing is one of the most important marks of distinction in Ashanti society and their colourful kente cloth is the most famous expression of Ashanti exuberance. The basic traditional garment for men is a long rectangular piece of *ntoma* (cloth) passed over the left shoulder and brought around the body like a toga. The earliest kente cloth was cotton, but from the 18th century Ashanti weavers began incorporating designs using unravelled, imported Dutch silk. Silk has since gone on to be the fabric of prestige and the most-expensive kente cloths contain silk (or imported rayon).

The weaving is done exclusively by men (usually working outdoors) who weave narrow, brightly coloured strips with complex patterns and rich hues. Kente cloth is worn only in the southern half of Ghana and is reserved for prestigious events. Although you'll find kente cloth on sale across Ghana, your best bet is to head to the Ashanti heartland, especially at Kumasi's Kejetia Market (p369) or the surrounding craft villages (p375).

The Ewe also weave kente cloth, but their designs are somewhat different and include motifs of geometric figures. Every design has a meaning and some designs are reserved exclusively for royal families.

Adinkra Cloth

African Textiles, by John Gillow, is at once visually eye-catching and a reasonably comprehensive study, including sections on Côte d'Ivoire, Mali, Sierra Leone, Cape Verde and the Niger Delta.

Just as impressive as the better-known kente cloth, *adinkra* cloth (a colourful cotton material with black geometric designs or stylised figures stamped on it) is also from Ghana. The word *adinkra* means 'farewell', and Ghanaians consider this fabric most appropriate for funerals.

Originally the printing was done on cotton pieces laid on the ground. Today, the cotton fabric is cut into long pieces, spread on a raised padded board and held in place by nails. The symbolic designs are cut on calabash stamps, and the dye is made from the bark of a local tree called *badie*. The printer dips the calabash into the hot dye and presses it onto the fabric. The rich colours are about far more than aesthetics: each colour has a special significance: vermilion (red) symbolises the earth, blue signifies love, and yellow represents success and wealth.

The village of Ntonso (p375), close to Kumasi in central Ghana, is famous for its *adinkra* cloth.

Bogolan Cloth

From the Sahel region of Mali comes *bogolan* cloth (called *bokolanfini* in Bambara, and often simply referred to as 'mud cloth'). This textile can be found in markets throughout West Africa, but its true home is in Djenné (p501) and Ségou (p494), both in Mali.

The cloth is woven in plain cotton strips, sewn together and dyed yellow using a solution made from the leaves of a local tree. If you thought mud was mud, think again – after weaving, the cloth is covered in designs using various types of mud from different sources: mud from sandstone outcrops is used for reds and oranges; mud from riverbeds is used for blacks and greys. The cloth is left to dry in the sun, and the mud designs are then removed, leaving their imprint – the effect is very striking.

Designs are traditionally geometric and abstract, but *bogolan* cloth made specifically for tourists is more representational, showing animals, markets or village scenes. Some designs are very complex and involve many hours of work by the artists, who are all women. *Bogolan* cloth is usually used for wall hangings and bedcovers, and is also sometimes used for making waistcoats, caps and bags.

Indigo Cloth

Another classic West African fabric is the indigo-dyed cotton worn primarily by the Tuareg as robes and headdresses. The indigo colour comes from the indigofera plant and the indigo vine; the plant is crushed and fermented, then mixed with an alkaline solution to produce the dye. The dyed cloth is often beaten with a mallet to produce a sheen. Among the Tuareg, cheaper dyed cotton from Nigeria or even China has begun to replace true indigo cloth, which can be outrageously expensive. Other West African peoples noted for their use of indigo include the Hausa, Dogon, Baoulé, Yoruba and Soninké, while it is also characteristic of Guinea's Fouta Djalon region.

Bogolan: Shaping Culture Through Cloth in Contemporary Mali, by Victoria L Rovine, is splendidly photographed and is a fine study of Mali's most recognisable textile art.

The Yoruba produce an indigo-dyed cloth, *aderi,* which has designs that are applied using the tie-dye technique, or by painting motifs with a dye-resistant starch. The Dogon also produce an indigo cloth, which has geometric patterns.

Other Textiles

The Fula have a caste of weavers, called Maboub, who produce blankets known as *khasa*. These are usually made from camel hair, although the term is sometimes used to describe cotton blankets as well. The Maboub also make rare and expensive wedding blankets. These large and elaborately detailed textiles are traditionally displayed around the marriage bed.

The Fon and the Fanti are known for their appliqué banners and flags. Shapes of people and animals are cut from colourful material and are carefully sewn onto a cloth panel.

The Hausa are famous for their embroidery, which was once hand-stitched onto their robes and caps. Although now machine-stitched, the designs remain unchanged. In keeping with Islam, Hausa designs are non-figurative.

The use of crosses in Tuareg culture (in jewellery and the shape of pommels on their camel saddles) led early European explorers to speculate that they were once Christians.

Northern Côte d'Ivoire is famous for its Korhogo cloth, a coarse, cream-coloured cotton adorned with geometrical designs or fantastical animals.

JEWELLERY

Jewellery is a West African tradition of extraordinary variety and, like all West African art forms, jewellery traditionally serves a purpose beyond the purely decorative.

Africa Adorned, by Angela Fisher, is an extravagantly beautiful coffee-table book that could just be the finest of its kind, with some exceptional and detailed sections on African jewellery.

Few jewellery items carry a wealth of associations quite like the humble bead, which is elevated to high art in this part of the world. Beads are often used as objects representing spiritual values and can play a major role in community rituals such as birth, circumcision, marriage and death. The availability of European products, which arrived via trans-Saharan trade caravans long before Europeans themselves, accelerated during the colonial period, altering the bead-making tradition significantly. Beads are now more likely to be made of glass, after local jewellers started copying the highly decorative *millefiori* trading beads from Venice, which featured flowers, stripes and mosaic designs. Discarded bottles and medicine jars were pulverised into a fine powder to be remade into glass beads and the Krobo in Ghana still melt powdered glass in terracotta moulds. In a slight variation, the Nupe in central Nigeria wind molten glass on long iron rods to make beads and bracelets. Referred to as *bakim-mutum* by bead traders (most of whom sell glass beads by weight, hence their other name, 'pound beads'), beads are commonly worn by village chiefs and elders as a sign of power and wealth.

A variety of other materials are used in Africa for making beads, including coral, shell, copal, amazonite, silver, gold and brass. In Mali you'll see large amber beads and ornate gold earrings worn by Fula women. The Dogon also treasure amber, and use it in their necklaces, bracelets and pendants. They also use beads made of stone and terracotta incised with geometric patterns. If you're fascinated by the history of beads, there's a small bead museum in Sevaré in Mali (p507).

Rings in West Africa can be stunning. In Burkina Faso, look for Bobo bronze rings, which often have intricate designs, including a tick bird, a warrior on horseback or a chameleon. In Mali, older Dogon men wear large bronze rings as a sign of status. Cowrie shells are often used to decorate jewellery; for a long time these shells were used as money in many areas of Africa.

In most areas of the region, the preferred metal for jewellery is gold; the Ashanti are famous for their goldwork in jewellery, ornaments and staffs. In and near the Sahara, however, the Tuareg and Moors prefer silver. The Tuareg are renowned for their intricate filigree silverwork in jewellery and in the decoration on the handles of their daggers. Tuareg men and women often wear silver crosses as pendants around their necks; in Niger, Mali and neighbouring Algeria these crosses differ from place to place, the most famous being the *croix d'Agadez,* while most are characterised by protective symbolism. Some incorporate circle and phallus designs, or fertility symbols; those representing a camel's eye or jackal tracks are symbolic of power and cunning.

Iron is no longer smelted in the Dogon Country; many Dogon blacksmiths now use iron taken from abandoned motor vehicles, which withstands heating and shaping better than new iron.

TOTEMS & TALISMANS

An important feature of traditional religions is the totem, an object (usually representing an animal) that serves as an emblem for a particular ethnic group, and is usually connected with the original ancestor of that group. It is taboo for a member of the clan whose totem is, for example, a snake, to harm any snake, as this would be harming the ancestor. Other common totems include lions, crocodiles and birds, although many of the animals themselves have disappeared from the West African wild.

THE BLACKSMITH – MASTER OF THE BLACK ARTS

In many West African societies, an almost mystical aura surrounds the blacksmith who, perhaps more than any other artisan caste, occupies a special place in community life. Feared due to their strange communion with fire and iron, which is believed to render them immune to evil spirits and give them special powers, and respected for the pivotal role they play in ritual and daily life, blacksmiths provide an unbroken connection to West Africa's past. They are the makers of all manner of tools, weapons and household implements, but they also serve as intermediaries (between social groups and between the human and spirit worlds) and operate at the heart of many traditional ceremonies.

Despite their pivotal role in traditional life, blacksmiths often live on the margins of the community with whom they work. Among the Dogon people of Mali, for example, blacksmiths may not marry outside the blacksmith caste, but the blacksmith's anvil is considered the foundation of the village; if the anvil is moved, it is believed that the village may drift. Within Tuareg society, blacksmiths (known as *inaden*) are customarily viewed with suspicion by other Tuareg and the blacksmiths traditionally lived on the periphery of towns and villages, even though Tuareg life would be impossible without them. Blacksmiths produce weapons and jewellery, and they're also healers, herbalists, poets, singers, skilled sacrificers of animals, advisers in matters of tradition and the custodians of oral traditions. Noble Tuareg women even confide in the *inaden*, using them as go-betweens in marriage negotiations and as mediators in love affairs. So important are they that no Tuareg festival could be complete without *inaden* participation, and anyone who tries to prevent them from attending is shunned by the whole community.

Other communities in which blacksmiths play a special role include the Bambara, Senoufo and Wolof.

Talismans (sometimes called fetishes) are another important feature in animism. These are objects (or charms) that are believed to embody a spirit, and can take many forms. For example, bird skulls and other animal parts may be used as charms by a learned elder for helping people communicate with their ancestors. The elders (usually men) responsible for these sacred objects are sometimes called fetish priests or *féticheurs*.

The most common charms found throughout West Africa are the small leather or metal amulets, often containing a sacred object, which are worn by people around the neck, arm or waist. These are called *grigri* and are usually worn to ward off evil or bring good luck. Many West African Muslims (including the Tuareg) also wear *grigri*, which are called *t'awiz* in other Islamic countries; there is often a small verse from the Quran inside and they are only considered effective if made by a marabout.

FIGURATIVE SCULPTURE

African sculpture is now considered one of the most dynamic and influential art forms around. Once relegated to curio cabinets and dusty museum store-rooms, and labelled as crude, barbaric and primitive, African carving finally gained credibility in the early 20th century when Picasso, Matisse and others found inspiration in its radical approach to the human form.

Most West African sculpture is carved in wood, but superb bronze and iron figures are created in terracotta and mud. The strange and uncompromising forms found in West African sculpture are rarely the unique creations of an inspired artist – the sculptures have always been made to fulfil specific functions, using centuries-old designs redolent with meaning.

In West Africa, sculpture is mostly used in connection with ancestor or spirit worship. Many groups believe that the spirits of the dead can have a major impact, both positive and negative, on a person's life. Ancestral figures

Starbook, by Ben Okri, is a stirring fictional fable that takes place among a mystical group of artists and artisans in West Africa in the lead-up to the colonial era.

West Africa: African Art and the Colonial Encounter, by Sidney Littlefield Kasfir, can be a little academic, but the influence of colonialism on African art forms is a fascinating subject.

are carved and placed in shrines and altars where they receive libations and sacrificial blood. Some groups carve figures that are cared for by women to ensure fertility and in the hope that the resulting child will inherit the fine looks represented in the sculpture. The famous *akuaba* 'doll' of the Ashanti is the best-known example of this. Prestige objects are also carved, such as figurative staffs of office, commemorative statues and other regalia used by kings, chiefs, traditional healers and diviners as emblems of power.

West African sculpture is usually created by a professional artist, who is almost always male and who has learned his craft through an apprenticeship. Mostly a family- or caste-specific occupation, the forms and skills are passed down from generation to generation, resulting in highly refined styles.

Like any non-static cultural tradition, the process can change: occasionally a virtuoso carver will introduce new elements that may then be incorporated by other artists. In many cases a carver will be commissioned to create a work. After payment has been arranged, the carver selects the wood required, which can involve lengthy rituals. He then blocks out the form using an adze, completes the finer details with a knife and, traditionally, sands the carving with a species of rough leaf.

Across the many styles produced in West Africa, some common characteristics exist. The figure is usually symmetrical and faces forward, the features are impassive and the arms are held to the side with the legs slightly bent at the knees. Certain features may be exaggerated, and the head is almost always large in proportion to the body.

The surface of the carving will often have tribal marks carved or burnt into the blackened face and torso, and there may be crusty deposits of sacrificial material, even though such rituals are practised less often now. Sometimes the carving is highly polished, or painted with ochre or imported enamel paint.

BRONZE & BRASS CASTING

West Africa's best-known castings were created for the Kingdom of Benin in present-day Nigeria. Plaques, statues and masks were produced to decorate the palaces and compounds of the kings and chiefs, and their discovery (and plundering) by Western governments and collectors did at least serve to challenge the prevailing view that African cultures were primitive.

West African brass and bronze is often cast using the *cire perdue* (lost wax) technique. The casting process involves creating a sculpture out of wax, which is then dipped in a silt-and-mud solution. When the sculpture is dry, clay is built around the form to create a strong mould. The mould is then heated and the wax is melted out. Molten bronze is then poured into the empty mould and, when cool, the mould is broken away to reveal the bronze sculpture. Each cast is therefore unique. For more on how to make a Benin brass figure, see the boxed text, p637. This process is thought to have produced the 1000-year-old beautifully intricate statues of the Ibo-Ikwu, which can be seen today in the National Museum in Lagos (p625). Today, latex is often used instead of wax, which creates even finer detail.

The Yoruba cast ritual staffs called *edan*. These comprise male and female figures in bronze, surmounting an iron tip and joined together by a chain. Figurative weights for weighing gold were cast by the Ashanti, and often symbolised the colourful proverbs for which they are known.

Among the British Museum's fine collection of Benin statues are 16th-century plaques depicting the Portuguese in knee breeches and boots, feathered hats, matchlocks, cross-hilt daggers and accompanied by dogs.

Peoples of West Africa

Perhaps more than anything else, it's West Africa's people and the richness of their cultural traditions that lure travellers to the region. Beyond the French-speaking world, this is Africa's least-known corner and the diversity of distinct languages, histories and customs you'll encounter in West Africa is astounding.

Following are brief profiles of some of the larger or better-known groups (ordered alphabetically).

ASHANTI

Inhabiting the heart of the now-thinning forest of south-central Ghana, the Ashanti, an Akan-speaking people, are among West Africa's best-known peoples. Their fame derives in part from their artefacts and symbols (among them kente and adinkra cloth; see p65) which have become prized among collectors in the West. But it's the Ashanti affinity with gold, with its echoes of West Africa's great empires of antiquity, which gives them their greatest resonance.

In the 18th century, the Ashanti king, the Asantehene, united the fractured feudal states of what is now Ghana and, ruling from his capital at Kumasi, brought peace and prosperity to the country; Ashanti political administration was among the most sophisticated in West Africa prior to the colonial period. Everything about the Ashanti kingdom glittered with gold: the Asantehene controlled the region's most prolific gold mines, the goldsmiths of the royal court were among West Africa's most practised artisans and the kingdom's trading reach extended across the world. The Asantehene's sacred golden stool, which may only be shown in public four times each century, became the ongoing symbol of Ashanti extravagance.

Ashanti power waned with the arrival of British colonial forces and, later, was subsumed into the multi-ethnic modern state of Ghana. But Ashanti culture maintains a strong hold over Ghana, and modern Ghanaian leaders ignore the traditional Ashanti rulers at their peril. Kumasi (p369) is littered with monuments and museums dedicated to Ashanti traditions.

BAMBARA

The Bambara (also known as Bamana) are the largest ethnic group in Mali. Concentrated in the south and centre of the country, they comprise around one third of the population.

Although a predominantly Muslim people, Bambara belief systems are laced with traditional beliefs and customs. Bambara men, for example, must pass through six secret societies during a seven-year coming-of-age initiation rite, a process that culminates in a symbolic death and rebirth. Ceremonies such as these are held in secret, but the symbols that accompany them, such as masks and music, are where travellers will most likely intersect with Bambara tradition. Masks in particular play a spiritually charged role and remain important signifiers of how Bambara see themselves; one example is the *chiwara* mask, an antelope-headdress that represents the mythical creature that taught the Bambara how to farm.

Bambara tradition decrees a highly regulated occupational caste system, among whose ranks are farmers, leather-workers, poets and blacksmiths. Each occupational group or caste has its own initiation rituals, for which particular masks are required, and only blacksmiths inherit the capacity to tap into the spiritual power, or *nyama,* that enables them to transform

The 1995 silver jubilee of the then-Asantehene Otumfuo Opoku Ware II became one of the most lavish traditional ceremonies in West Africa in modern times, attended by 75,000 people and showcasing an incredible collection of golden royal regalia.

One of the most famous Ashanti war leaders against the British was Yaa Asantewaa, queen mother of Ejisu, who in 1900 shamed the Ashanti army into entering battle by leading them herself (see p376).

Genii of the River Niger, by Jean-Marie Gibbal, is a fascinating study of the river peoples of eastern Mali, in particular their struggles to hold fast to traditional mythology in the face of Islam's march.

wood and iron into masks and other religious objects. Because *nyama* is inherited, blacksmiths must marry within their own occupational group. The significance of blacksmiths extends beyond masks: they make a range of items, such as hoes, door locks and guns, all of which are furnished with spiritual power as well as utility. Door locks often have a water-lizard symbol to protect the house from thieves, or a long-eared creature similar to a bat that is said to hear every sound, thus protecting the household.

BAOULÉ

The Baoulé of eastern and central Côte d'Ivoire, like the Ashanti of Ghana, are an Akan-speaking farming people. Their origins lie in Ghana, which they fled in the 16th century as Ashanti power grew and from this exodus they derive their name. As they fled west, so the story goes, they came up against a river which they were unable to cross. With their pursuers close behind, they threw their most prized possessions into the river, among them the son of their ruler, Queen Pokou, whereupon hippopotami rose up to provide a bridge, thereby allowing them to cross the river. The queen's lament of *baouli* (which means 'the child is dead') became the sorrowful name of a people.

The Baoulé claim to have resisted French colonial power longer than any other West African group, although other groups make similar claims. The Baoulé are distinguished by their belief in the *blolo* (meaning 'elsewhere' or 'the beyond'), another world, parallel to our own. A man may even have a *blolo bla*, a wife from beyond, and a woman a *blolo bian*, or other husband. Both can influence a partner's wellbeing, marital stability and sex life, usually negatively. Soothsayers play an important role in Baoulé culture; they're often used to 'call in' or 'bring down' the *blolo* partner to prevent further havoc. This can be done either by moulding a cone of fine kaolin clay mixed with secret herbs, or by fashioning a clay or wooden statue of the *blolo* partner, thus controlling the parallel-world partner.

For information on Baoulé crafts, see, p260.

Baoulé society is considered to be one of West Africa's most egalitarian: everyone, from village elders to slaves, traditionally had a voice in the important decisions of Baoulé life.

BOBO

The ancestors of the 100,000 Bobo people arrived in West Africa almost 1200 years ago and occupy western Burkina Faso, around Bobo-Dioulasso, and southern Mali. The Bobo traditionally minded their own business, preoccupied with communal village life and with little apparent interest in conquest. It was a recipe for survival: they made few enemies and thereby managed to escape subjugation by the powerful Mossi who ruled from Ouagadougou.

The Bobo cosmology revolves around the creator god Wuro, who creates balance in the world by dividing everything into pairs. In the Bobo worldview, human disruption to this natural order can only be rectified by Wuro, but as Wuro may neither be addressed nor spoken of nor depicted in any form, the Bobo communicate with Wuro through a mediating deity, Do. That effort to commune with Do gives the Bobo their most recognisable cultural forms, the renowned Bobo mask tradition, especially the famous butterfly and helmet masks. The large horizontal butterfly masks are typically about 1.5m wide and painted red, black and white. They are worn during funeral rites, and when invoking Do in planting-time ceremonies asking for rain and a good harvest. Other animals represented in Bobo masks include owls, buffaloes, antelopes, crocodiles and scorpions. The masks are usually tall, and have bold-coloured patterns similar to those adorning the butterfly masks.

The form of a butterfly is used in Bobo masks because butterflies appear in great swarms immediately after the first rains and are thus associated with the planting season.

DAN

The animist Dan (also known as the Yacouba) inhabit the mountainous area around Man in Côte d'Ivoire, spilling over the border into Liberia. Although part of the wider Mande tradition, they are set apart by their Dan language, of which there are more than 320,000 speakers. Until recently, Dan society lacked any overarching social organisation with each village looking after its own affairs, although the emergence of the secret leopard society (known as *go*) has become an important unifying vehicle for peacemaking between Dan communities. In Dan tradition, lavish gift-giving is considered an essential means of advancing socially

Masks are an important element of Dan culture and the Dan mask tradition is one of Africa's most highly developed. Each village has several great masks that represent its collective memory and which are glorified during times of happiness and abundance. Masks are regarded both as divinities and repositories of knowledge. They dictate the community's values that give the clan cohesiveness and help preserve its customs. For example, harvest-time yields, or whether a woman will give birth to a son or a daughter, are believed to depend on masks, and no important action is undertaken without first addressing a mask to request its assistance.

DOGON

The Dogon, who live along Mali's Falaise de Bandiagara (Bandiagara Escarpment), are among the region's most intriguing people. For a detailed summary of the unusual Dogon belief systems, masks and ceremonies, see the boxed text, p508.

The Dogon are traditionally farmers. Work for both men and women is a central feature of Dogon society. Crops such as millet and onions are planted in the fields below and atop the escarpment and on terraces created on the lower slopes. Unsurprisingly, many Dogon now choose to farm down on the plains where water is more plentiful, where traditionally there had been conflict with the Fula and Mossi. Now Fula groups bring their cattle to graze on harvested Dogon fields, thus providing fertiliser for the following year's crop.

Dogon: People of the Cliffs, by Agnes Pateaux, combines beautiful photography with text that gets to the heart of Dogon society, from the aura of blacksmiths to the changes assailing Dogon ways.

EWE

The Ewe people live in Ghana and are the most important ethnic group in southern Togo. The Ewe, who inhabit the forests and fertile riverine soils of Ewe land, are accomplished agriculturalists and their cultivation of yams (a staple of the Ewe diet) has taken on a near-mythical status. The annual Ewe Yam Festival, called Hogbetsotso, is the highlight of the Ewe year and involves farmers presenting their crops to the ancestors and purifying ceremonial stools where, the Ewe believe, ancestral spirits reside. Funeral rites are another intricate Ewe ceremony.

The Ewe also hold fast to complicated norms of behaviour. Among these, Ewe chiefs, who are elected by consensus, must keep their heads covered in public and must never be seen to be drinking. More generally, the Ewe are known for their hard work, tidy villages, their love of education, their spirituality, and the power of their traditional shrines and priests.

The arts play an important role in Ewe life, with their subtly coloured kente cloth (which they learned from Ashanti weavers taken as prisoners by the Ewe) and for their *vu gbe* (talking drums) taking centre stage. The tonality of the Ewe spoken language and the rhythm of particular phrases and proverbs are combined in drumming to produce messages that range from the commonplace, which everyone understands, to a specialised repertoire known only to the master drummers. Drum language is used for communication, especially in times of crisis and is an integral part of religious song and dance. Ewe dances are widely appreciated for their fast and intricate movements.

The traditional Ewe institution of *Trokosi*, decrees that young girls be given as virtual slave-wives to priests in order to appease the spirits.

FULA

One of the most widespread of West African peoples, the Fula (also called Fulani, Peulh or Foulbé in French-speaking countries) are tall, lightly-built people who have been settling across the West African savannah and Sahel for centuries. They number more than 12 million, and are found from Senegal to Cameroon, and sometimes beyond. The Tukulor (Toucouleur) and the Wolof of Senegal, as well as the Fulbe Jeeri of Mauritania, are all of Fula origin.

Cattle occupy a central position in society and the Fula are traditionally nomadic cattle herders, following their herds in search of pasture and living in seasonal grass huts resembling large beehives; they're famous for putting the welfare of their animals above their own. Those Fula with no cattle of their own often work as herdsmen, looking after other peoples' cattle. Islam also plays a central role: Town-dwelling Fula (referred to as Fulani Gida in some areas) adopted Islam as early as the 12th century and were major catalysts in its spread. Fula resistance to colonial rule was fierce, usually coalescing around a messianic Islamic leader.

The Africa Guide website (www.africaguide.com) has a great People and Culture section, which includes information on festivals, ceremonies and the traditions of a wide range of ethnic groups.

The nomadic Fula, or Wodaabé, are known for their public initiation ceremony in which young boys are lashed with long rods to the accelerating rhythm of drums, as part of their passage into manhood. There are many onlookers, including potential brides, and the boys must show no fear, though their ordeal leaves them scarred. At the annual Gerewol festival (see the boxed text, p604), where the young Wodaabé meet prospective marriage partners, men pay great attention to their appearance, adorning themselves with shining jewellery, feathers, sunglasses and elaborate make-up – anything to create an impression, and to look their best for the women. For information of the annual crossing of the Niger River by vast Fula herds in central Mali, see the boxed text, p497.

HAUSA

The dominant cultural group in northern Nigeria (Hausaland), the Hausa (with 27 million in Nigeria and almost six million in Niger) have always played an important role in West African history. From their bases in Kano, Katsina, Sokoto and Zaria, the Hausa developed a reputation as a fiercely independent mercantile people, with Islam the dominant force. This mix of spiritual devotion and worldliness means that you'll likely see Quranic script alongside symbols of modern technology, such as bicycles and aeroplanes, in the mud-relief patterns on house walls in the old quarters of Nigerian towns such as Kano and Zaria.

Traditionally, Hausa women rarely step from behind the walls of their compounds – many trade from home, while children are sent to run errands between compounds.

The emirs of the Hausa states are known for the pomp with which they live and travel. Their bodyguards traditionally wear chain mail, carry spears and ride strikingly caparisoned horses, while attendants on foot wear red turbans, and brilliant red-and-green robes. Except on ceremonial occasions, especially during the Islamic festivals of Eid al-Kebir (Tabaski) and Eid al-Fitr (see p816 for more on these festivals), these days you'll more likely see an emir riding through town in a large American car, with the horn sounding – very Nigeria.

Although the city states, caliphates and trappings of power of Hausaland are what brought the group its renown, rural communities are the bedrock of Hausa society. Many rural Hausa farm grains, cotton and groundnuts; sacks of groundnuts stacked in pyramids are one of the distinctive sights of many Hausa markets. Hausaland is also one of the few places where cloth is still dyed with natural indigo, and you'll probably see the drying cloths, patterned in shades of blue on blue, in contrast with the surrounding mud-red urban landscape.

IGBO

The Igbo (also known as Ibo) occupy densely settled farming areas in southeastern Nigeria. They form Nigeria's third-largest ethnic group with around 25 million Igbos in Nigeria alone. Theirs is not a happy history: their proximity to the Gulf of Guinea saw them devastated by slavery, while more than one million Igbo died during the Biafran War (1967–70).

The Igbo have a reputation for hard work, ambition and a love of education. Traditional-minded Igbo will not eat the new season's yam until Ikeji, the annual new yam festival, when thanks are given to the gods for a productive year. The most important Ikeji festival takes place in September at Arochukwu. Judges select the best village presentation of dance, parade and music.

Although predominantly Christian, many Igbo still practise the traditional religion of Odinani. An Igbo receives his destiny or *chi* directly from Chukwu, the benign god or 'great spirit' of creation. At death, a person returns his *chi* and joins the world of ancestors and spirits. From this spirit world, the deceased watches over living descendants, perhaps returning one day with a different *chi*. A traditionalist's daily preoccupation is to please and appease the *alusa*, the lesser spirits who can blight a person's life if offended and bestow rewards if pleased.

Half of a Yellow Sun, by Nigerian novelist Chimanda Ngozi Adichie, is a stirring tale of the Biafra War with a nuanced look at the often fraught relations between Nigeria's main ethnic groups.

LOBI

Tucked away in southwestern Burkina Faso, northern Côte d'Ivoire and northern Ghana, far from the centres of regional power, the Lobi have held fast to their traditions and ancestor-based belief systems more than most groups in the region. The Lobi are also distinguished by their architecture (they live in distinctive mud-brick compounds resembling small fortresses which they once defended using poisoned arrows) and by the fact that they don't use masks. Their name means 'Children of the Forest'.

Most Lobi woodcarvings are of human figures, typically 35cm to 65cm high, which represent deities and ancestors. The woodcarvings are used for ancestral shrines, and traditionally occupied every home. The Lobi also carve staffs and three-legged stools with human or animal heads, as well as combs with human figures or geometric decorations. Lobi carvings are distinguished by their rigid appearance, with arms generally positioned straight down, along the sides of the body. They are also notable for their realistic and detailed renderings of certain body parts, particularly the navel, eyes and hair.

Many Lobi ceremonies take place on or near the banks of the Mouhoun (or Black Volta) River which divides Ghana and Burkina Faso and, in Lobi tradition, separates this world from the afterlife. Fish and animals in the river are believed to be sacred, while fetishes, the spirit world and village priests still play an important role in daily Lobi life. In the remote Lobi capital of Gaoua (p159) in Burkina Faso, there's a small museum where you can learn more about Lobi culture. See also the boxed text on p160 for more on Lobi traditions.

More than half of the almost 280 million West Africans are Nigerians. The numbers of Yoruba, Hausa or Igbo alone each exceed the national population of every other national country.

Lobi tradition, backed by the accounts of some Christian missionaries, holds that a Lobi man once converted to Christianity and threw his fetishes in a nearby lake, whereupon the fetishes leapt from the water to reclaim him.

MALINKÉ

The Malinké (in some areas synonymous with, or closely related to, the Mandinka or Mandingo) are part of the larger Mande group, which also includes the Bambara and Soninké and is believed to have originated as early as 4000 years ago when agricultural peoples of the southern Sahara merged with the indigenous hunter-gatherers of the Niger River basin. Today, the Malinké are known as prolific traders and live in southern Mali as well as northern Guinea, Côte d'Ivoire, Senegal and Gambia. Historically, they were famed hunters and warriors, and were prominent converts to Islam from the

11th century. In the mid-13th century the Malinké founded the powerful Empire of Mali (p27).

Originally the Malinké were divided into 12 clans, each with its own king and highly stratified castes. The heads of these 12 clans formed a royal council, which elected a single leader, known as a *mansa*. The traditional hunter societies of the Malinké, with their secret initiation rites, still thrive today.

Music also accompanies almost all of the important events in Malinké life and its tradition of *jelis* or *griots* (an occupational caste of musician-storytellers) dates back to the days of the Empire of Mali. Griots were traditionally the custodians of West Africa's oral traditions and many born into the griot caste now rank among Mali's most famous musicians.

MOSSI

African Ceremonies, by Carol Beckwith and Angela Fisher, is a masterpiece, a stunning two-volume coffee-table book of photos of different rites and festivals from across Africa.

When the empires of Mali and Songhaï reigned over West Africa from the 13th to 16th centuries, one group remained outside their orbit: the Mossi, now the largest ethnic group in Burkina Faso, with their capital at Ouagadougou. In the 14th century they established powerful kingdoms in this area after leaving their original homeland around the Niger River, and held off the larger empires of the time through a fierce army of feared warriors. The Mossi are known for their rigid social hierarchies and elaborate rituals, and many Mossi continue to follow traditional beliefs. They also exert considerable political influence in Burkina Faso today and the Mossi ruler, the 37th Moro-Naba, is regularly consulted on important issues by the government. The Moro-Naba ceremony is still held at the Moro-Naba Palace in Ouagadougou every Friday (see p139 for details).

Artistically, the Mossi are best known for their tall wooden antelope masks, often more than 2m high and painted red and white. Female masks feature a human female figure, while male masks consist of a nonhuman plank-like structure. The masks were worn primarily at funerals.

SENOUFO

The Senoufo, a farming people who live in Côte d'Ivoire, western Burkina Faso and southern Mali, are, like the Lobi, renowned for having maintained their traditions in the face of assaults by colonialism, Islam and Christianity. The northern Côte d'Ivoirean town of Korhogo is considered the Senoufo capital.

Among the Senoufo, in addition to blacksmiths, the elaborate funeral rites are the domain of the powerful and secret Poro society – to become a member requires 20 years' training.

Animals are held in high regard in Senoufo culture, and when someone dies it is believed that they are transformed into the clan's animal totem. As a result, many Senoufo dances are associated with animals. One of these is the dance of the leopard men, which is performed in Natiokabadara, near Korhogo, as well as in other Senoufo areas when young boys return from their Poro (part of the secret Lô society) initiation-training sessions. In this and other dances, spirit masks (often of animal heads) are instrumental in making contact with the gods and driving away bad spirits.

When someone dies in traditional Senoufo society, the corpse is carried through the village in a procession, while men in grotesque masks chase away the soul of the deceased to ensure it leaves the village in peace and leaves for the afterlife. It is the blacksmiths who dig the grave and place the corpse inside, after which they present a last meal to the deceased, and then feast and celebrate.

SONGHAÏ

The Songhaï, the heirs to the Empire of Songhaï (see p28), live predominantly in Niger (where they are the fourth-largest grouping) and in northern Mali, between Timbuktu and Gao. They trace their roots back to the

7th or 8th century, when Aliman Za (or Dia) arrived at the upper Niger River from Mandinka (Malinké) lands further west, forcing out the local fisherpeople. Other theories claim that the Tuareg founded the original Songhaï state, while yet another hypothesis states that the ancestors of the Songhaï were the original inhabitants of the Upper Niger. The truth is probably a mixture of all three theories. Some Songhaï make a distinction between the Songhaï of Gao (supposedly of pure blood) and those of Timbuktu (who have mixed with Tuareg and Moors).

Songhaï villages are divided into neighbourhoods, each of which elects a head. These heads then come together to elect a village chief, who typically is of noble descent. Most Songhaï consider themselves Muslim, although their religious practices are often mixed with strong traditional elements, including ancestor worship and witchcraft. Large communities often have both a mosque and a *troupe* that specialises in mediums for spirit intervention.

> The Songhaï traditionally have strong bonds with their Tuareg neighbours. There's even an affectionate term in the Songhaï language that refers to the Tuareg as 'our Tuareg'.

TUAREG

The Tuareg are a nomadic people, who traditionally roamed the Sahara from Mauritania to western Sudan; they now live in Niger, Mali, Libya and Algeria, with smaller communities in Burkina Faso and Nigeria. Tuareg origins lie with the Berbers of North Africa (their language, Tamashek, has Berber roots) who migrated to the desert after the Arab-Islamic invasions of the 7th and 11th centuries. Droughts and political conflict have ensured that few Tuareg remain purely nomadic and most have had to abandon their traditional way of life; many have moved southwards to settle near cities.

The Tuareg traditionally follow a rigid status system, with nobles, blacksmiths and slaves all occupying strictly delineated hierarchical positions. The veils, or *taguelmoust*, that are the symbols of a Tuareg's identity serve as protection against the desert sand and wind-borne spirits, and as a social requirement; it is considered improper for a Tuareg man to show his face to a man of higher status. Traditionally, Tuareg men rarely remove their shawl to expose the lower half of the face in company and, when drinking tea, pass the glass under their *taguelmoust* so as not to reveal the mouth.

Tuareg women – who are not veiled and who enjoy an unusual degree of independence – weave artificial strands into their plaits and attach cowrie shells. They also can be recognised by their large pieces of silver jewellery.

> *The Pastoral Tuareg: Ecology, Culture, and Society*, by Johannes and Ida Nicolaisen, is a comprehensive two-volume study of the Tuareg with good photographs. Subjects range from traditions to the challenges faced by the Tuareg today.

WOLOF

The Wolof heartland is in Senegal, where they comprise about 43% of the population. They also live in Gambia (16%) and Mauritania (7%).

Although Islam has been an influence in Wolof areas since the 11th century, and Sufi Muslim Brotherhoods form the backbone of Wolof society, traditional beliefs persist. For example, there is a belief in a snake monster so terrible that to look upon it causes death. In order to guard against witches and other forms of evil, many Wolof wear leather-bound amulets containing written verses of the Quran.

Wolof society is hierarchical, with hereditary castes determining traditional occupations such as blacksmiths and *griots* (praise singers) and status. The Wolof, who are of Fula origin, tend to be tall and striking in their traditional flowing robes of white, dark blue or black. The women wear a series of loose, layered gowns, each a little shorter than the one underneath. Men wear long gowns over loose white pantaloons that overhang the knee.

> Famous members of the Senegalese Wolof community include musician Youssou N'Dour, the late film-maker Ousmane Sembène, and the current president of Senegal, Abdoulaye Wade.

YORUBA

The Yoruba, almost 30-million strong, are perhaps the largest ethnic group in West Africa, with their homeland extending from southwestern Nigeria into neighbouring Benin. It was here that the powerful Yoruba Kingdom of Ife (12th to 16th centuries) and Oyo Empire (17th to early 20th centuries) held sway over one of the region's most populous corners.

Most Yoruba traditionally prefer to live in towns, migrating seasonally to their more distant farmlands; the Nigerian cities of Lagos and Ibadan are considered important centres of Yoruban life. The urban culture of the Yoruba has facilitated the development of trade and elaborate arts, including the famous Benin bronzes. The old quarters of Yoruba cities contain large household compounds of extended families. Every town has an *oba* (crowned chief). The traditional head of all Yorubas is the *alafin*, who lives at Oyo, in Nigeria, while the *oni* (chief priest) lives at Ife. Formality, ceremony and hierarchy govern Yoruba social relations, and ostentation in dress and jewellery is a social requirement for women at traditional functions.

The Yoruba have the highest ratio of twin births of any group in the world and twins occupy an important role in Yoruba mythology.

Many Yoruba are now Christian, although traditional practices persist, among them the belief that ancestor spirits, which reside in an afterworld known as Kutome, hold powers of protection over the living. During the annual Egungun Festival, these ancestors are summoned by members of the secret Egungun masking society to return, so as to restore the cosmic balance upset by human failings, and to advise their descendants. The month-long festival is held between June and November every year and involves the ostentatious use of masks, fine cloth and drumming.

Environment

West Africa's environment stands at a crossroads. At one level the region's environmental woes and the precarious subsistence conditions in which many West Africans live read like a litany of an impending apocalypse, especially in the Sahel. At the same time, stunning success stories – such as the greening of central Niger and the survival of Mali's desert elephants – suggest that all may not be lost. Nonetheless, in 2008 the UN Secretary-General's Special Adviser on Conflict, Jan Egeland, on a visit to the region, described the Sahel as the world's 'ground zero' for vulnerable communities struggling to adapt to climate change. 'Many of the people here live on the edge even in normal times,' he warned, 'so if there will be dramatic climate change as many predict, they will go over the cliff if there is no investment in adaptation'. It is as simple and as complicated as that: West Africa faces some of the most pressing environmental issues of our time.

For advice on travelling responsibly throughout the region, see p17.

The UNEP's *Africa: Atlas of Our Changing Environment* (2008) is the definitive study of Africa's environment, with a detailed continental overview, country-by-country statistics and before-and-after satellite photos. It's available from Earthprint (www.earthprint.com).

THE LAND

West Africa spans some of the great landscapes of the African continent. Its geography is the story of three horizontal lines: a northern band of desert, a southern band of woodland and forest, and a semidesert zone in between known as the Sahel. Through it all snakes the region's lifeblood, the Niger River (see the boxed text, p80).

Although West Africa largely consists of a gently undulating plateau, there are some important highland areas: the borderlands between Nigeria and Cameroon rise to Chappal Wadi (2418m); the Jos Plateau (1781m) and Shebsi Mountains (2418m) in Nigeria; Mt Bintumani (1945m) in Sierra Leone; the rocky Aïr Mountains in Niger, rising to Mt Bagzane (2022m); Mt Nimba (1752m) in the border area between Guinea, Côte d'Ivoire and Liberia; and the Fouta Djalon in western Guinea (1538m). The peaks of the volcanic Cape Verde islands are also notable with the highest being Mt Fogo (2829m). Mt Cameroon (4095m) is the highest point in West Africa.

West Africa's highlands create headwaters for several rivers, including the Niger. Other major rivers include the Senegal River, which forms the border with Mauritania; the Gambia River, again giving its name to the country it flows through; the Casamance River in southern Senegal; the Volta River in Ghana and Burkina Faso; and the Benue River (a major tributary of the Niger) in Nigeria and Cameroon.

If West Africa is overshadowed by the looming Sahara desert to the north, it is barricaded by the equally formidable Atlantic Ocean to the south. Many major cities (including 12 out of 17 West African capitals) are strung out along the coast like beads in a chain, in some areas forming an almost constant linear urban sprawl, cut only by national frontiers.

A citizen of urban Britain, Australia or the USA, for example, consumes more than 50 times more of the earth's resources than a rural inhabitant of Niger or Guinea-Bissau.

The Sahara

The Sahara desert is a notoriously unwieldy beast to quantify, but most estimates put its size at 9.065 million sq km, comparable in size to the continental United States. The Sahara occupies more than half of Mali, 75% of Mauritania and 80% of Niger.

The Sahara may be the world's largest desert, but it is also the youngest. Thousands of years ago the Sahara was a fertile land, alternating between savannah grasslands, forests and lakes watered by relatively frequent rainfall. It was home to abundant wildlife – elephants, giraffes, hippos, lions

THE NIGER RIVER

Africa's third-longest river (4100km), the Niger owes its name to the Tuareg phrase *gher-n-gheren*, which means 'river among rivers', and its curious course has fascinated travellers for centuries.

The Niger begins its journey just over 200km from the Atlantic, at a spring in the Fouta Djalon highlands, on the Guinea–Sierra Leone border. Gathering strength and volume from countless mountain streams, the Niger flows deep into West Africa's heart, through the vast Niger Inland Delta of central Mali. From there, the Niger narrows and comes within touching distance of Timbuktu before it comes up against the impenetrable barrier of the Sahara and performs a long, laborious curve (known as the Niger Bend or Boucle du Niger). Thereafter, it courses down into Niger and crosses a slice of Benin before emptying into the Atlantic via a maze of swamps and channels (in Nigeria, west of Port Harcourt) called the Niger Delta.

Geographers believe that an ancient river called the Djoliba (many Malians still call the river by this name) rose in the Fouta Djalon Highlands, flowed past Timbuktu, before emptying into a salt lake called Juf, close to the salt mines of Taoudenni in what is now deep in the Sahara of northern Mali. At the same time, a river called the Quorra began in the Ahaggar Mountains of southern Algeria and flowed south into the Gulf of Guinea. When the Sahara began to dry out and become a desert (a process that began around 5000 BC), the two rivers altered course until, over the centuries, they joined to become the Niger.

Apart from its initial descent from the western highlands, the Niger flows on an extremely low gradient and is fed by highly variable rainfall. As such, its high and low points can vary by an extraordinary 10.7m and the river is highly susceptible to drought: in 1972 and again in 1984, the river almost dried up completely. Even more serious than the vagaries of seasonal fluctuations are the threats posed by human activity: by one estimate, the Niger's volume has fallen by 55% since the 1980s due to climate change, drought, pollution and population growth. Fish stocks have fallen, water hyacinth is a recurring problem and the formation of sand bars has made navigation increasingly difficult. Given that an estimated 110 million people live in the Niger's basin, problems for the Niger could cause a catastrophic ripple well beyond the river's shoreline.

The alarming signs of the river in distress prompted nine West African countries in 2008 to agree a US$8 billion, 20-year rescue plan to save the river. The plan includes dams, hydroelectric plants and the restocking of fish supplies. But with most of the funding yet to be found and the World Bank warning that the river could dry up entirely, the Niger's situation remains critical.

It may be almost 20 years old, but *The Strong Brown God*, by Sanche de Gramont, remains the most comprehensive geographical and human history of the Niger.

Sahara Conservation Fund (www.saharaconservation.org) is one of few sources of information on the wildlife of the Sahara, and the efforts being undertaken to protect it.

Sahara: A Natural History, by Marq de Villiers and Sheila Hirtle, covers the natural and human history of the Sahara like no other recent book, and the lively text makes it a pleasure to read.

and other African mega-fauna – as depicted in the rock art found across the Sahara, especially in Niger's Aïr Mountains (p603) and Mali's Adrar des Ifôghas (p528). The change began around 7000 years ago, when rains became less frequent and the land more arid. It was a gradual process that took 4000 years. As the Sahara became a desert, its people and wildlife retreated south. By 400 BC, the Sahara was the desert we know today, albeit on a smaller scale.

The definition of what constitutes a desert varies, but most geographers agree that it encompasses those lands that receive no more than 250mm (10 inches) of rain a year, or those zones where evaporation exceeds rainfall. An older way of measuring the desert's southern boundary is the point at which a prickly sub-Saharan weed called *cram cram* or *initi* ceases to grow and where *hadd*, a scrubby thorn bush, takes over.

Contrary to popular misconceptions, sand covers just 20% of the Sahara's surface and just one-ninth of the Sahara rises as sand dunes. More typical of the Sahara are the vast gravel plains and plateaus such as the Tanezrouft of northwestern Mali. The Sahara's other signature landform is the desert massif, barren mountain ranges of sandstone, basalt and granite such as the Aïr Mountains (Niger) and Adrar des Ifôrhas (Mali).

By one estimate, the Sahara is home to 1400 plant species, 50 species of mammals and 18 species of birds.

The Sahel

The Sahel – a horizontal band stretching from the Atlantic coast to the Nile – is the transition zone between the forested lands of the south and the Sahara to the north but, for its detractors, it possesses the redeeming features of neither. At face value the Sahel is indeed one of the direst stretches of inhabited geography on earth, beset by drought, erosion, creeping desertification, periodic locust invasions and increasingly infertile land.

That said, within its boundaries are many different subregions. Among these are zones that are variously described as semidesert savannah, Guinea savannah, Sudanese savannah, dry savannah or dry woodland savannah. In the north, near the true desert, the Sahel is dry, dusty, sparsely vegetated and barely distinguishable from the Sahara, but in the south, nearer the forests, it is greener and contains areas of light woodland fed by more plentiful rains.

Although the Sahel's boundaries are not fixed, the countries covered in this book that are considered to be all or partly in the Sahel are Senegal, The Gambia, Guinea, Mali, Burkina Faso, Niger and Nigeria. The northern parts of the coastal countries of Côte d'Ivoire, Ghana, Togo, Benin and Cameroon are relatively dry and sometimes described as having a Sahelian climate or vegetation.

WILDLIFE

Human beings rule in West Africa, and it's possible that, no matter how long you spend in West Africa, you may never see more than the occasional reptile or hear more than a troop of monkeys caterwauling through the trees but out of view. The once-plentiful wildlife of the region has been reduced by deforestation, encroaching deserts, ever-expanding human populations and drought to small, isolated pockets. As a result, West African animals are wild, wary and unaccustomed to large-scale safari tourism.

But, for all the doom and gloom, West Africa is the continent's most underrated wildlife-watching region. West Africa's excellent national parks (see p85) are home to many of Africa's classic mammal species, including elephants, giraffes, lions, leopards and a range of primates. Yes, you have to travel further to see the animals than elsewhere on the continent, and these animals may retreat into the canopy at the first sign of human beings. For wildlife-watching purists, however, this is how wildlife safaris used to be: a place where the sense of a real quest survives without carloads of camera-toting tourists outnumbering the animals.

West Africa is also a world-class birding destination; see p82. For a tailored itinerary through some of the best wildlife destinations in West Africa, see p24.

Animals

MAMMALS

First, some good news. Two of West Africa's most emblematic and endangered herds – the giraffes at Kouré in Niger (see the boxed text, p590) and Mali's desert elephants (p530) – are somehow holding on and, in the case of the giraffes, actually increasing in number. For other large mammals and where to see them, see the table, p86.

In most cases, West Africa's elephants exist in small, isolated herds and are considered endangered. In Côte d'Ivoire, for example, the vast herds that gave the country its name have been reduced to around 300 (see p263). Apart from Mali (see above), the best places to see elephants include Ghana's

Forty million metric tonnes of Saharan sand reaches the Amazon annually, replenishing mineral nutrients depleted by tropical rains. Half of this dust comes from the Bodele Depression on the Niger–Chad border, although the depression covers just 0.2% of the Sahara.

SOS Sahel International (www.sossahel.org in French; www.sahel.org.uk) is an NGO dedicated to the Sahel environment. It can be a good source of information on grassroots projects in the region.

African Silences, by Peter Matthiessen, is a classic on African wildlife; the passages on Senegal, The Gambia and Côte d'Ivoire are so beautifully written that you'll return to them again and again.

WILD WILDLIFE

If you set out in search of wildlife, remember that West Africa's wildlife is just that – wild. *Always* keep a healthy distance between you and any elephant, lion, rhino or other wild animal that you may be lucky enough to encounter. *Never* get between a mother and her calves or cubs, and invest in a telephoto lens instead of approaching an animal at close range. On safaris, heed the advice of your guide and respect park regulations, especially those that require you to stay in a vehicle. Exercise care when boating or swimming, and be particularly aware of the dangers posed by crocodiles and hippos.

Mole National Park (p380), Burkina Faso's Ranch de Nazinga (p161) and Cameroon's Parc National de Waza (p212).

Possibly the best-known and most easily observed mammals of West Africa are monkeys. These include several types of colobus and green or vervet monkeys. Other primates include mangabeys, baboons, galagos (bush-babies), as well as chimpanzees and the rare and endangered drill. Cameroon also hosts an endangered population of western lowland gorillas.

Mammals more readily seen include several beautiful antelope species, such as bushbucks, reedbucks, waterbucks, kobs, roans, elands, oribis and various gazelles and duikers; the sitatunga is more shy. The Sahel-dwelling dama gazelle is the largest gazelle species in Africa, but it is now close to extinction as its grazing lands have been taken over by cattle and reduced by desertification. The red-fronted gazelle may still survive in Mali's remote far east. Wild pig species include giant hogs and bush pigs (the West African species is often called the red river hog), which inhabit forest areas, and warthogs, frequently seen in drier savannah areas. Buffaloes in West Africa inhabit forest regions; they are smaller and redder than the East African version.

In the rivers, including the upper reaches of the Niger and Gambia Rivers, hippos can sometimes be seen, but numbers are low. Some hippos have adapted to live in salt water and exist in coastal areas such as the Orango Islands National Park (p446) in the Arquipélago dos Bijagós in Guinea-Bissau. A few forest areas, including Liberia's Sapo National Park (see the boxed text, p468) and Sierra Leone's Tiwai Island Wildlife Sanctuary (p757), are home to very small populations of elusive pygmy hippos, which are less aquatic than their larger cousins. Other marine mammals found in the region include dolphins, especially where the region's rivers meet the ocean, and humpback whales, which can be seen off Freetown Peninsula in Sierra Leone (see p753), especially in September and January.

Back on land, other highly endangered species that have somehow survived the human and climatic onslaught include: manatees (sea cows, a giant seal-like relative of the elephant) in Mali's Réserve d'Ansongo-Ménaka (p528), in Senegal's Parc National du Niokolo-Koba (p716), or in mangrove and delta areas along the coast, including the Parque Nacional do Catanhez (p450) in Guinea-Bissau; one of the world's last colonies of monk seals along Mauritania's remote Atlantic coast; olive baboons and the Sahara's only amphibian, the spurred tortoise, in the remote Aïr Mountains of northern Niger (p603); and the Saharan cheetah may still survive in northern Mali and Niger. See any one of these and you're a privileged traveller indeed.

African Bird Club (www .africanbirdclub.org) is ideal for those who love their birds, with plenty of interesting reading and West African bird-watching links.

BIRDS

West Africa lies along one of the busiest bird migratory routes between Europe and Africa, and more than 1000 species have been recorded. In short, West Africa is a birder's paradise. Many of the species are endemic, others are passing migrants, flying down the Atlantic coast to and from their wintering grounds, while some are African nomads moving within the continent in pursuit of seasons of plenty. Among those you're likely to see are flamingos, storks and pelicans (around waterways), beautiful gannets and fish-eating cormorants (in coastal areas), turacos – including the striking violet turaco – and African grey and red-billed hornbills.

One of West Africa's best bird-watching destinations is tiny Gambia, with more than 560 species recorded and several easily accessed bird-watching sites, among them Abuko Nature Reserve (p311), Tanji River Bird Reserve (p308) and Kiang West National Park and Baobalong Wetland Reserve (p315).

Senegal also offers excellent birding, particularly in Parc National de la Langue de Barbarie (p712) and Parc National des Oiseaux du Djoudj (p712). Both are famous for vast pelican and flamingo flocks. Parc National du Niokolo-Koba (p716) and the Siné-Saloum Delta region (see p703) are some other terrific sites, and there are several other good sites in northern Casamance near Kafountine (p729).

Three little-visited, but first-rate birding destinations are Mali, Guinea and Sierra Leone. Mali has more than 655 recorded species. In the Niger Inland Delta, Egyptian plovers, hammerkops (which make an enormous nest), jaçanas (lily trotters), pied kingfishers, cattle egrets and majestic crowned cranes can be seen year round, but February is the best time to visit, when over-wintering species such as greenshanks, black-winged stilts, marbled teals and ferruginous ducks are resident. In Guinea (p400), the Îles Tristao (p412), Koumounkan (p412) and the Parc National du Haut Niger (p420) are three terrific birding spots among many.

Sierra Leone's Tiwai Island Wildlife Sanctuary (p757) hosts hornbills, kingfishers and the rare white-breasted guinea fowl. Around Mt Bintumani (p763), the endangered rufous fishing-owl has been sighted, while Outamba-Kilimi National Park (p762) supports kingfishers, waders, raptors and the spectacular great blue turaco. The rainforest-rich Gola Forest Reserve (p760) is another fine birding destination, home, at last count, to 333 bird species, including the Gola malimbe, while the Kambui Hills Forest Reserve (p759) is home to the white-necked rockfowl. Liberia's Sapo National Park (see the boxed text, p468) and Côte d'Ivoire's Comoé National Park (p264), each host in excess of 500 species.

Further afield, other destinations that draw birders include: Ghana's Mole National Park (p380); Nigeria's Yankari National Park (p648); Cameroon's Korup National Park (p194); and Mauritania's Parc National du Banc d'Arguin (p556).

REPTILES & AMPHIBIANS

West Africa's most notable reptile is the Nile crocodile, which was once abundant all over the region; few remain due to hunting and habitat destruction. Your best chance to see them is along the larger rivers such as The Gambia, Senegal and Niger, although an unlikely population also survives in Mauritania's Saharan oasis of Matmata (p564). Two lesser-known species, the dwarf crocodile and slender-nosed crocodile, also occur.

Turtles survive along the coast of West Africa and on some of the offshore islands. The females come to the beaches to lay eggs in the sand, sometimes several hundred at a time. The threats faced by turtles are considerable, and include damage by humans to nesting areas, hunting, and the effects of water pollution – turtles often mistake floating plastic bags for food. The best places to see sea turtles are at the conservation project at Ebodje (p219) in Cameroon, on the Cape Verdean island of Boa Vista (p247) in July-August, the João Vieira-Poilão National Marine Park (p446) in Guinea-Bissau, or in Ghana at Akwidaa Beach (p362) and Beyin (p364).

Birds of West Africa, by W Serle, is a must for birders who want to know what species are present and where you're most likely to see them.

It is estimated that 5000 million birds from Europe and Asia migrate to tropical Africa every year, a journey of up to 11,000km - less than half make it home, either dying en route or preferring to remain in Africa.

According to the UNEP, Mt Nlonako in southwestern Cameroon is the richest single locality in the world for snake species – a mere 63 different species.

West Africa has a full complement of both venomous and harmless snakes, but most fear humans and you'd be 'lucky' to even see one. The largest snake is the non-venomous python, which grows to more than 5m in length. It kills by coiling around and suffocating its prey – not the nicest way to go, but fortunately it doesn't usually fancy humans. The venomous puff adder, which reaches about 1m in length and enjoys sunning itself, isn't aggressive but, being very slow, it's sometimes stepped on by unwary people before it has had time to wake up. When stepped on, it bites. Take special care when hiking in bush areas, especially in the early morning when this snake is at its most lethargic. The Sahara is home to the venomous horned viper.

Lizards are ubiquitous in West Africa, from the desert to the rainforest and from the bathroom ceiling to the kitchen sink. The largest of these is the monitor (up to 2m in length), which spends a lot of time lying around rivers and water holes, perhaps dreaming of being a crocodile. You're more likely to see agama – lizards about 20cm long with purple bodies and orange heads, energetically doing press-ups on walls and boulders. And in any house or small hotel you'll inevitably see geckos running around on the walls or hiding behind pictures, with their sucker-like feet and near-transparent skin. They can appear alarming, but they're your friends – they love to eat mosquitoes.

The West African countries with the most expansive forest cover are Guinea-Bissau (73.7%), Cameroon (45.6%), Senegal (45%), The Gambia (41.7%) and Sierra Leone (38.5%). Mauritania (0.3%) and Niger (1%) have almost no forests left.

Plants

FOREST & WOODLAND

Much of West Africa's coastal area is between five and 10 degrees north of the equator, where rainfall is heavy. Dense rain-fed lowland forest (or just 'rainforest') contains trees that can reach heights of 45m. The upper branches form a continuous canopy, blocking light from the forest floor.

Forests or dense woodland can only be found in parts of Liberia, Sierra Leone, southwestern Côte d'Ivoire and southern and eastern Cameroon. Smaller areas of woodland exist in Benin, Ghana, Guinea, Nigeria and Togo.

An especially rich bounty of rainforests, set amid volcanic mountains, straddles the border between Nigeria and Cameroon – for more information see p177. In the east, Cameroon's rainforests connect West Africa to the vast Congo Basin in Central Africa.

THE BAOBAB: KING OF THE AFRICAN BUSH

There's nothing quite like the baobab (*Adansonia digitata*), whose thick, sturdy trunk and stunted root-like branches are an instantly recognisable symbol of Africa. Thanks to its unusual form, many traditional cultures believe that the tree displeased a deity who promptly plucked it in anger and thrust it back into the ground upside down. Or as that great writer on Africa, Ryszard Kapuściński, wrote: 'Like elephants among other animals, so are baobabs among trees: they have no equals'.

Despite the apparent misdemeanours of its ancestor, today's baobab is revered by local people. Its wizened appearance, combined with an ability to survive great droughts and live for many hundreds of years, ensures that the baobab is believed to possess magical powers. Old trees often develop cavities, which are sometimes used to inter a revered *griot* (traditional musician).

The baobab is found in most parts of West Africa and serves a variety of practical, often essential, purposes. The hollow trunk sometimes holds rainwater, making it a useful reservoir in times of drought. The tree's large pods (which resemble pendulous Christmas decorations and are sometimes called 'monkey bread') contain seeds encased in a sherbet-like substance that can be eaten or made into a juice-like drink. The pods themselves are used to make cups or bowls (often for drinking palm wine) and as fuel; they burn slowly and are especially good for smoking fish. The leaves of the baobab can be eaten when chopped, boiled and made into a sauce; they can also be dried and ground into a paste to use as a poultice for skin infections and joint complaints. Even the flowers are used as decoration at ceremonies.

PURIFY YOUR WATER & SAVE THE ENVIRONMENT

When confronted by West Africa's often overwhelming environmental issues, it's easy to feel helpless. But there is one small, but very significant thing you can do to minimise your impact on the environment: don't buy bottled water. Instead, purify tap water for your drinking needs. Plastic water bottles and plastic bags are one of the most visible scourges across the West African landscape; you'll find plastic water bottles (and half-litre bags of mineral water) everywhere for sale when they're full, and then again littering the streets, fields and roadsides once empty. Water purification has come a long way since the days of unappealing iodine treatments and one purification system we've trialled on the road in West Africa are Micropur tablets, although there are plenty of other brands on offer. The impact of travelling this way is easily calculated: if you drink 150 litres of purified water, you'll keep around 100 plastic water bottles off the streets, not to mention save a considerable amount of money (in the UK Micropur costs UK£6 per 100 tablets, enough to purify 100 litres).

SAVANNAH & SEMIDESERT

In the northern parts of the coastal countries the climate is drier, and forest and woodland yield to savannah and semidesert. Here, the landscape consists primarily of well-dispersed trees, especially acacia, and low scrub bush, although ribbons of dense gallery forest occur along river courses. Gallery forest is similar to rainforest but is fed by ground water rather than rain, so the vines characteristic of rainforest are absent.

DESERT

In true desert, rainfall and vegetation growth are minimal. Apart from desert grasses and small flowers, which can carpet the desert in colour after rains (even after lying dormant for years), the most striking plant is the *Calotropis procera*, otherwise known as the Apple of Sodom. Its prolific (but poisonous) green leaves should be no invitation to taste. Wild colocynth melons (think watermelons in the sand) produce brittle, gourd-like fruits that burst open in the sun and scatter their seeds on the wind, but should not be eaten.

> Nearly half of Togo's land is considered arable, making it one of only two countries in Africa with more than 40% of its land suitable for farming. Just 0.2% of Mauritania can support agriculture.

NATIONAL PARKS & WILDLIFE RESERVES

West Africa has some outstanding national parks and reserves that provide the last refuge for the region's wildlife, protected areas amid a growing sea of humanity. Others exist in name only.

Whatever their status, few West African parks are set up for tourism – national park offices are rare and trails are often poorly maintained. Visiting these parks usually requires arranging a visit through a private agency, preferably one from the park's hinterland and with a local guide to ensure that the proceeds of your visit benefit the local community.

Because national governments rarely devote funds to wildlife and biodiversity protection, the better parks are often those that receive some form of international assistance. Among these are the parks that have been inscribed on Unesco's World Heritage List: the Réserve de Biosphere du Dja (Cameroon); Parc National de Taï (Côte d'Ivoire); Parc National du Banc d'Arguin (Mauritania); Parc Regional du W (Benin, Niger and Burkina Faso); Parc National des Oiseaux du Djoudj and Parc National de Niokolo-Koba (Senegal). Other parks that have benefited from WWF or other international aid include Parc National de Campo-Ma'an and Limbe Wildlife Centre (Cameroon), and the Réserve de Douentza (Mali). Increasingly, local community groups are beginning to develop small-scale ecotourism projects, especially in Benin and Ghana.

> Benin has the highest ratio (23%) of protected areas to total territory, followed by Côte d'Ivoire (16.4%), Burkina Faso (15.4%) and Ghana (14.7%). Lagging behind are Cape Verde (0.56%), Mauritania (1.7%), Mali (2.1%) and Nigeria (2.1%).

MAJOR NATIONAL PARKS & WILDLIFE RESERVES

National park	Country	Wildlife	Best time to visit	Page
Parc National de la Pendjari	Benin	elephants, leopards, buffaloes, hippos and lions	Mar-May	p121
Parc Regional du W	Benin/Niger/ Burkina Faso	leopards, lions, cheetahs, elephants, baboons, Nile crocodiles, hyenas, over 300 bird species, 500 plant species	Mar-May; open mid-Dec–mid-Jun	p592 & p123
Ranch de Nazinga	Burkina Faso	elephants, monkeys, crocodiles	Jan-Mar	p161
Parc National de Waza	Cameroon	elephants, giraffes, lions, hippos	Mar-Apr	p212
Parc National de Campo-Ma'an	Cameroon	rainforest, buffaloes, elephants, mandrills	Dec-Apr	p220
Korup National Park	Cameroon	oldest rainforest in Africa, 50 large mammal species, over 300 bird species	Nov-May	p194
Limbe Wildlife Centre	Cameroon	rescued gorillas, champanzees and drills	year round	p188
Réserve de Biosphere du Dja	Cameroon	rainforest, buffaloes, grey-necked rockfowl	Dec-Apr	p215
Takamanda National Park	Cameroon	cross river gorillas	Dec-Apr	
Parc National de Taï	Côte d'Ivoire	rainforest, chimpanzees	Dec-Feb	p278
Kiang West National Park	The Gambia	baboons, colobus monkeys, hyenas, dolphins, crocodiles, over 300 bird species	Nov-May	p315
Tanji River Bird Reserve	The Gambia	over 300 bird species	Nov-May	p308
Ankasa Nature Reserve	Ghana	rainforest, forest elephants, leopards, bongos	Jan-Mar	p364
Kakum National Park	Ghana	rainforest, elephants, colobus monkeys, antelopes, 300 bird species, 600 butterfly species	Jan-Mar	p356
Mole National Park	Ghana	94 mammal species (incl elephants), over 300 bird species	Jan-Mar	p380
Wechiau Community Hippo Sanctuary	Ghana	hippos	Nov-Jun	p383
Parc National du Haut Niger	Guinea	dry rainforest, hippos and chimpanzees	Nov-Apr	p420
João Vieira – Poilão National Marine Park	Guinea-Bissau	sea turtles	Oct-Nov	p446

Increasing human encroachment and an ever-growing catalogue of environmental threats ensure that new national parks are rare. In 2008, Cameroon announced the establishment of the Takamanda National Park, along the border with Nigeria, to protect 115 cross river gorillas, the rarest gorilla species on earth with just 300 left in the wild. Guinea-Bissau's Parque Nacional do Catanhez (p450) is another landmark new park, while soon to join the ranks of national parks, is Sierra Leone's Gola Forest Reserve (p760).

From 1976 to 1996, there were almost 5000 oil spills (equivalent to three million barrels of oil) in Nigeria's Niger Delta, where there are 66 gas fields and 500 oil wells.

ENVIRONMENTAL ISSUES

The environmental issues confronting West Africa are many, all of them serious. Deforestation and desertification are perhaps the most widespread and urgent of the challenges, but soil erosion, air and water pollution, wildlife destruction, water scarcity, threats to coastal and marine ecosystems, over-

National park	Country	Wildlife	Best time to visit	Page
Orango Islands National Park	Guinea-Bissau	saltwater hippos, crocodiles	Nov-Apr	p446
Parque Natural dos Tarrafes do Rio Cacheu	Guinea-Bissau	hippos, manatees, panthers, gazelle, hyenas, over 200 bird species	Nov-Apr	p447
Parque Nacional do Catanhez	Guinea-Bissau	chimpanzees, elephants, colobus monkeys, baboons, manatees	Nov-Apr	p450
Sapo National Park	Liberia	forest elephants, pygmy hippos, chimpanzees, over 500 bird species	Nov-Apr	p468
Réserve de Douentza	Mali	elephants	Jan-Jun	p530
Parc National du Banc d'Arguin	Mauritania	migratory birds	Dec-Jan	p556
Afi Mountain Drill Ranch	Nigeria	rescued drills, chimpanzees	Oct-Feb	p643
Gashaka-Gumti National Park	Nigeria	chimpanzees, lions, elephants, hippos	Nov-May	p649
Yankari National Park	Nigeria	elephants, baboons, hyenas, lions, over 600 bird species	Nov-Mar	p648
Parc National de la Langue de Barbarie	Senegal	hundreds of bird species	Nov-Apr	p712
Parc National des Oiseaux du Djoudj	Senegal	pelicans, flamingos, over 350 bird species	Nov-Apr	p712
Parc National de Niokolo-Koba	Senegal	lions, 80 mammal species, 350 bird species	Dec-May	p716
Parc National du Delta du Saloum	Senegal	red colobus & patas monkeys, hyenas, sea turtles, dolphins	Nov-May	p704
Gola Forest Reserve	Sierra Leone	rainforest, 333 bird species, elephants, leopards, zebras, duikers	Nov-Apr	p760
Tiwai Island Wildlife Sanctuary	Sierra Leone	pygmy hippos, chimpanzees, 120 bird species	Nov-Apr	p757
Outamba-Kilimi National Park	Sierra Leone	elephants, primates, hippos, leopards, lions	Nov-Apr	p762
Parc National de Fazao-Malfakassa	Togo	elephants, monkeys, antelopes, over 200 bird species	Dec-May	p790

fishing, drought and the impact of cash crops such as cashews and rubber all pose significant threats to the West African environment.

To give you an idea of the scale of the problem, in the UN Environment Programme's (UNEP) landmark 2008 study *Africa: Atlas of Our Changing Environment*, deforestation was listed as one of the top three environmental problems in 14 out of 17 West African countries. This was followed by threats to biodiversity (nine countries) and desertification (six). While the international community may be leading the way in identifying the problem, it is generally local, community-based conservation programs that are providing the most durable and exciting solutions.

Up to 90% of natural gas from the Niger Delta oil fields is burned as waste, releasing massive amounts of carbon dioxide into the atmosphere and causing acid rain.

Deforestation

West Africa was once covered in forests, but only a tiny fraction of the original forest cover remains and even that is under threat. In 1990, for example,

BIODIVERSITY HOTSPOT: GUINEAN FORESTS OF WEST AFRICA

Of 34 internationally recognised 'biodiversity hotspots', eight are in Africa. In order to qualify as a biodiversity hotspot, a region must contain at least 1500 species of vascular plants (ie more than 0.5% of world's total) and have lost at least 70% of its original habitat. Although only one of these – the Guinean Forests of West Africa – is in West Africa, it is so vast that it passes through nine out of the 17 West African countries. This hotspot covers the heavily populated coastal belt and its hinterland, and includes Guinea, Sierra Leone, Liberia, Côte d'Ivoire, Ghana, Benin, Togo, Nigeria and southwestern Cameroon, as well as Equatorial Guinea and São Tomé & Príncipe. As such, it's a hugely significant indicator of the state of West Africa's environment.

The vital statistics of the territory falling within West Africa's biodiversity hotspot make for sobering reading. The original extent of West Africa's Guinean forests was 620,314 sq km, of which only 93,047 sq km remain. It is also home to 31 endemic threatened birds, 35 endemic threatened mammals and 45 endemic threatened amphibians. The most prominent of the threatened mammals are pygmy hippos, Liberian mongooses, 12 primate species (including chimpanzees and gorillas), the African golden cat and the elephant. It also has what is easily the highest population density of any of hotspot – 137 people per sq km.

Why all of this matters is simple: West Africa's Guinean forests are home to 320 mammal species (more than 25% of Africa's mammals and including more than 20 primate species), 785 bird species, 210 reptile species, 221 amphibian species and over 9000 plant species, of which 1800 are endemic. Despite being such an important storehouse for Africa's biodiversity, less than 20% of the territory is adequately protected. The hotspot's landmark conservation parks – Sapo National Park (Liberia), Kakum National Park (Ghana), Korup National Park (Cameroon) and the new Takamanda National Park (Cameroon) – provide an example of what can be done, but many more such protected areas are needed, as well as the development of conservation corridors, agro-forestry projects and a greater emphasis on ecotourism. Major threats include unregulated logging, mining, hunting (especially the trade in bushmeat) and human encroachment.

To learn more about West Africa's only biodiversity hotspot, visit the website www.biodiversity hotspots.org/xp/hotspots/west_africa/Pages/default.aspx).

According to the UNEP, deforestation in Mali caused economic damage amounting to an estimated 5.35% of GDP. An estimated 98% of Mali is at risk from desertification.

forests covered 42.1% of Liberian territory; 15 years later, the figure had dropped to just 32.7%. Other alarming falls were recorded during the same period in Benin (30% to 21.3%) and Togo (12.6% to 7.1%). Deforestation is similarly acute in Côte d'Ivoire; see p264 for more details.

The extent of the problem is evident from the causes – increased population growth, commercial logging, the clearing of trees for farming and slash-and-burn farming techniques – the effects of most of which are either irreversible or require massive investment from often-impoverished governments. Even assuming the best political will in the world, meagre government resources and aid funds are, understandably, directed to more pressing human needs, with long-term environmental protection seen as a luxury few can afford, even though such policies of short-term necessity merely serve to make the region more vulnerable to drought and famine. Potential earnings in global timber markets, for example, are infinitely more attractive (and lucrative) than preserving wildlife for the trickle of tourists who come to see it.

Sahara Fragile (www .saharafragile.org/PRO JET/project_sahara.htm) is dedicated to sustainable Saharan tourism with tips for minimising your impact on Saharan environments.

Conflict and refugee flows can also have important flow-on effects for local forest coverage. During the conflicts in Sierra Leone and Liberia, neighbouring Guinea played host to one of the world's largest refugee populations, especially in the Parrot's Beak region, wedged between its two neighbours. Satellite images from 1974 show that forests completely covered the Parrot's Beak wedge of Guinean territory; by 2002, satellite images showed that none of it had survived the massive human influx.

The results of deforestation can be devastating – bird and animal species lose vital habitats, local human populations lose their lifeblood, soil erosion sets in, fewer areas are cultivable, water catchments are reduced, and the availability of traditional building materials, foodstuffs and medicines is decreased.

Fortunately, it's not all bad news. In Cameroon and Liberia (home to about 40% of the last remaining 'Upper Guinean' rainforest that once stretched from Sierra Leone to Ghana), several international environmental organisations have pledged resources to help improve forestry and environmental management. That said, of all 17 West African countries, only in Cape Verde (where forest cover rose from 14.3% in 1990 to 20.7% in 2005) was the trend of deforestation significantly reversed.

Desertification

As forest cover diminishes, all too often the desert moves in. Desertification is one of the most serious forms of land degradation, and it's one to which the countries of the Sahel are particularly vulnerable. Some areas of the Sahel are losing over 50 metric tonnes of soil per hectare per year, and the desertification that results has reached critical levels in Niger, Mali and Mauritania, each of which could be entirely consumed by the Sahara within a generation. But desertification is also a problem for countries beyond the Sahelian danger-zone: a high-to-moderate risk of desertification exists in Sierra Leone, Liberia, Guinea, Ghana, Nigeria and Senegal, which all suffer from serious erosion.

The major causes are desertification are easy to identify – drought, deforestation and the over-exploitation of fragile soils on the desert margin – and are the result of both human activity and climatic variation. But one of the

Seeds of Famine, by Richard Franke and Barbara Chasin, is as dry as the Sahel dust, but essential reading for anyone keen to learn more about the connection between colonial policies and the droughts that still face the region.

GREENING NIGER: A SUCCESS STORY

When droughts struck Niger (and the rest of the Sahel) in 1968–74 and 1980–84, the country seemed destined for environmental oblivion. The desperate search for firewood and animal fodder denuded the landscape, accelerating the southward march of the Sahara, which left sandy wastelands where it went. Fast forward to 2009 and something remarkable has happened. Satellite images show that three of Niger's southern provinces (especially around Tahoua) now have between 10 and 20 times more trees than they did in the 1970s. According to the UNEP, this is 'a human and environmental success story at a scale not seen before in the Sahel'.

The secret to the success has been giving farmers the primary role in regenerating the land. Faced with arid soil where agriculture was almost impossible, farmers constructed terraces and rock bunds to stem soil erosion, trap rainfall and enable the planting of trees. Trees planted by the farmers now serve as windbreaks against the desert and, for the first time in a generation, agriculture (millet, sorghum and vegetables) is almost possible year round, even in the dry season, thanks to improved water catchment and soil quality. Farmers no longer uproot trees to plant crops, ploughing around them instead, with the result that crop yields have increased.

In what has become known as 'farmer-managed natural regeneration', the flow-on effects have been extraordinary: not only has agriculture become possible, subsistence levels have risen and the local economy is improving, and the region's groundwater table has also risen, in some places from a depth of 20m to 3m. In some areas, pockets of desert now resemble agricultural parklands with more than 200 trees per hectare. Even in years of drought when crops fail, the trees, a small proportion of which can be sold for cash, serve as a last bastion against starvation; in the 2005 food crisis, death rates from hunger in the three southern provinces were much lower than elsewhere in the country.

Similarly, the community-based Guesselbodi National Forest Project was launched not far from Niamey in 1980, in an attempt to enable reafforestation by encouraging villagers to build windbreaks and establish nurseries to reduce soil depletion.

Success stories such as these have prompted a change in the Niger government's environment policy, with priority now given to a decentralised approach that empowers local farmers to manage their own resources.

DISAPPEARING LAKES

One of the most worrying environmental trends in the Sahel in recent years has been the drying up of some of its largest lakes. Although this has been attributed to fluctuating rainfall levels across the region, there may be deeper, more global causes at work. A 2003 study by Columbia University found that changes in sea surface temperatures in the Atlantic were a major factor in causing droughts in the Sahel. Other, more recent, studies increasingly show a connection between sea surface temperatures and rising carbon dioxide emissions – in other words, human-driven global warming.

The best-known case is that of Lake Chad, which once straddled the borders of Chad, Niger, Nigeria and Cameroon, and whose waters are essential to the lives of 20 million people around its shores and in its hinterland. This was once the sixth-largest lake in the world and Africa's second-largest wetland, supporting a rich variety of wildlife. But falling rainfall, a growing population (and hence increased water consumption) and a notoriously shallow average depth of 4.11m have taken their toll: Lake Chad has shrunk by 95% over the past 35 years. Although a few recent years of greater rainfall have sparked a minor recovery, Lake Chad has retreated from Niger and Nigeria, and its extent in Chad and Cameroon is just one-tenth of the lake's original size.

Lake Chad is not the only lake to have fared badly. Mali's Lake Faguibine, west of Timbuktu, was once one of West Africa's largest lakes and provided an important water source for people in the region. Lake Faguibine depends almost entirely for its water on the flooding of the Niger River into nearby basins and lake levels have, accordingly, varied significantly throughout the 20th century. However, Lake Faguibine may have entered a period of terminal decline. Lower rainfall from the late 1980s and a fall in the Niger's flow (see the boxed text, p80) saw Lake Faguibine dry up completely in the 1990s; dramatic satellite images taken in October 2006 show that the lake remains completely dry. The consequences for the villages on the lake shore and the nearby town of Goundam could be devastating.

most significant causes in West Africa is the use of deliberately started fires. Such fires are sometimes necessary for maintaining soil quality, regenerating savannah grasslands and ecosystems, enabling livestock production and as a form of pest control. But all too often the interval between fires is insufficient to allow the land to recover, thereby exposing the soil to wind and heavy rains, and degrading the soil beyond the point of recovery.

West Africans are often blamed for the destruction of their own environment, but the reality is far more complex and there are other causes that date back even further. Many of the problems began in colonial times, when farmers were encouraged to plant thirsty cash crops (such as the peanut) that require intensive farming – traditional methods involved fallow periods, which allowed the soil to regenerate. Thus deprived of essential nutrients, the soil required fertilisers to recover, but these were often too expensive for poor farmers to afford. The soil began to unravel.

This process was exacerbated by well intentioned animal husbandry and well-building schemes funded by the EU in the 1960s and '70s. Herd sizes increased without any accompanying growth in pasturelands. In the absence of fodder, the additional cattle and goats ate the grasses and thorns that bound the soil together. Patches of desert began to appear around villages that once lay many kilometres south of the desert's southern boundary. As populations increased and enticements by Western seed companies prompted ever-more farmers to increase the land under cultivation, the few remaining trees and forests were cut down, thereby accelerating a process that began centuries ago.

Community-Based Conservation

Sustainable environmental protection usually works only by involving local communities and providing them with the material benefits (tourism, sustainability of resources for future generations) that derive from preserving pristine environments. For those who live hand-to-mouth, as many do in West Africa, long-term planning is often impossible and the pretty forests that Westerners are desperate to protect are actually a necessary and time-honoured resource for locals. Not surprisingly, therefore, the most encouraging environmental projects are those driven by local communities.

The Gambia is the star performer among West African countries when it comes to ecotourism, with a host of community projects, eco-lodges and wildlife parks. In addition to these, several forestry projects in The Gambia (such as the Ballabu Conservation Project – p311) recognise this delicate balance, fusing environmental protection with traditional sources of livelihood. Natural woodland areas are not simply fenced off, but rather used in a sustainable way for the benefit of local communities, with the emphasis on sustainable resource management. In The Gambia's Kiang West National Park, limited cattle grazing and (more controversially) rice cultivation is permitted. Dead wood can be used for timber, fruits and edible leaves can be collected, and grasses can be harvested for thatch. These products can be used or sold, but all activities take place without destroying the growing trees. In this way, local people view the forest as a source of produce, income or employment, and have a real incentive to protect it in the long term. Local inhabitants also take a leading role in environmental planning – at Niumi National Park, also in The Gambia, community groups have been established to give local people a formal voice in the park's management structure.

In Burkina Faso, small-scale NGO projects encourage farmers to return to traditional methods of cultivation, in particular the laying of *diguettes* or stone lines along field contours, which slow water run-off, maximise water penetration and reduce erosion. And in Niger, putting land conservation in the hands of local farmers has proved to be a stunning success; for more on Niger's green revolution see the boxed text, p89.

Wildlife conservation is another area where involving local communities is beginning to reap rewards. Apart from several locally run sanctuaries in Ghana – such as the Boabeng-Fiema Monkey Sanctuary (p377) and Wechiau Community Hippo Sanctuary (p383) – some of the best results are to be seen in protecting Mali's desert elephants (see p530). Another excellent example is the Tabala Conservation Zone (see the boxed text, p420) spanning the Guinea–Sierra Leone border.

Ecotourism is another important element in community-driven environmental protection, not least because it enables local communities to profit from the environment without destroying it. The concept is still in its infancy in West Africa, but things are moving fast.

Local community projects around Toubab Dialao and the Réserve de Popenguine (see the boxed text, p698) in Senegal are a fine example of community-driven conservation. In Côte d'Ivoire, a village tourism project reduced forest clearing and poaching in one of West Africa's largest stands of rainforest in Parc National de Taï prior to the conflict; many such projects are yet to restart now that peace has returned to the country, however.

For information on ecotourism projects in Ghana and Benin, see the boxed texts on p383 and p97, respectively.

For a list of places and businesses that meet our exacting standards of environmental sustainability, including ecotourism projects, see p910.

Until the intrepid Mungo Park reached the Niger River close to Ségou on 21 July 1796, European map-makers were convinced that the river flowed east–west and originated in the Nile or Lake Chad.

Benin

It's surprising that Benin barely registers in people's awareness when its role in history is so significant. The birthplace of voodoo and a pivotal platform of the slave trade for nearly three centuries, Benin is steeped in a rich and complex history still very much in evidence across the country.

A visit to this small, club-shaped nation could therefore not be complete without exploring the Afro-Brazilian heritage of Ouidah and Porto Novo, shivering at the litany of massacres of the Dahomeyan Kings or learning about spirits and fetishes in Ouidah and Lac Ahémé.

But Benin will also wow visitors with its natural beauty, from the palm-fringed beach idyll of the Atlantic coast to the rugged scenery of the north. The Parc National de la Pendjari and the Parc Regional du W are two of the best wildlife parks in West Africa. Lions, cheetahs, leopards, elephants and hundreds of other species thrive here, and the infrastructure to see them is remarkably good.

In fact, Benin is wonderfully tourist-friendly compared to most of its neighbours. There are good roads, reliable intercity bus services, professional guides to tour the country with and ecotourism initiatives that offer travellers the chance to delve deeper into local Beninese life: how does learning traditional fishing techniques or sleeping in a *tata somba* (round tiered hut) house sound?

Finally, Benin's ill-loved economic capital Cotonou may not be a love-at-first-sight sort of place, but spend a Sunday afternoon chilling out in Fidjrossé, hanging around the daring Fondation Zinsou or bargaining hard at the Dantokpa market and you'll soon find the big smoke has its perks too.

FAST FACTS

- **Area** 112,622 sq km
- **Capital** Porto Novo
- **Country code** ☎ 229
- **Famous for** Voodoo; slavery; the Kings of Dahomey; adopting Marxism; Angélique Kidjo
- **Languages** French, Fon, Yoruba, Dendi, Aja, Bariba, more than 50 in total
- **Money** West African CFA franc; US$1 = CFA493; €1 = CFA656
- **Population** 6.7 million
- **Visa** CFA10,000 at border, 30-day extension CFA12,000

HIGHLIGHTS

- **The Atakora Region** (p120) Rugged landscapes of northern Benin and rich Somba cultural heritage.
- **Lake Ahémé** (p111) Learn traditional fishing techniques and get up close and personal with voodoo traditions on the shores of Lake Ahémé.
- **Route des Pêches** (p104) From Cotonou's most happening beach to isolated fishing villages, this is Benin's deserted Atlantic coast.
- **Porto Novo** (p105) Benin's mellow capital city, with its vibrant Afro-Brazilian heritage and visionary sustainable farming centre.
- **National Parks** (p121 & p123) With three species of big cat, elephant, hippo, croc, monkey and much more, the W and Pendjari are two of West Africa's best wildlife parks.

ITINERARIES

- **One Week** Start off in busy Cotonou (p97) where good food, cold beers, great markets and insane traffic give you a taste of things to come. Porto Novo (p105), the tranquil capital, and Ganvié (p104) the lacustrine stilt village, are both within two hours taxi journey of Cotonou. A little further along the country's main roads are two historical highlights: Abomey (p111), home to the ruined palaces of the Kings of Dahomey, and Ouidah (p107) once a capital of the slave trade and now the centre of voodoo worship.
- **Two Weeks** After a few days spent exploring the city of Cotonou, take the slow Route des Pêches to Ouidah. Put your bags down at lovely Grand Popo (p110) for a couple of idle days and head north via the stunning shores of Lake Ahémé (p111). Head to Abomey via Lokossa, and then on to Natitingou (p118), gateway to the intriguing Somba country or the Parc National de la Pendjari for a safari.
- **One Month** With this much time on your hands, you should be able to delve into every corner of this small country. In addition to the above, head northeast to the Parc Regional du W (p123) via Dassa-Zoumé (p115) and its striking rocky outcrops.

CLIMATE & WHEN TO GO

In southern Benin, there are two rainy seasons: April to mid-July, and mid-September to late October. The rains in the north fall from June to early October. In the north, temperatures can reach 46°C, while the coastal south is cooler, with temperatures ranging from 18°C to 35°C. Harmattan winds billow out of the Sahara between December and March, and the hottest time of the year is from February to April. The coolest, driest time to visit is between November and February. See Climate Charts, p810.

Parts of the northern Atakora region occasionally receive heavy rainfall, and smaller roads throughout Benin may be impassable during the rainy seasons; especially those in the wildlife parks.

HISTORY

More than 350 years ago, the area now known as Benin was split into numerous principalities. One of the chiefs quarrelled with his brother for the right to succession and, around 1625, settled in Abomey. He then conquered the neighbouring kingdom of the Dan, which became known as Dan-Homey, meaning 'in Dan's belly' (see p114). The name was later shortened by the French colonisers.

Each king pledged to leave his successor more land than he inherited, a pledge kept by waging war with the neighbours, particularly the Yoruba of Nigeria. Meanwhile, the Portuguese, and later other Europeans, established trading posts along the coast, most notably at Porto Novo and Ouidah. The Portuguese, French, Dutch and English, whose forts can still be seen in Ouidah, spelled the town's name four different ways but pronounced it the same.

The Dahomeyan Kings grew rich by selling slaves to traders, who then gave them the guns that let them pillage their neighbours for slaves and land. For more than a century, around 10,000 slaves per year were shipped to the Americas (primarily Brazil and the Caribbean, in particular Haiti), taking voodoo with them. As a result Dahomey was dubbed the Slave Coast.

Early in the 19th century, the French colonised the kingdom of Dahomey, making it part of French West Africa (p105). During the 70-year colonial period, progress was made in education, and many Dahomeyans were employed as government advisers in French West Africa. The country's intellectual nature led

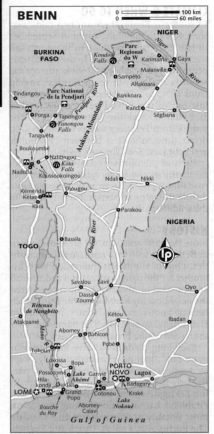

the French to nickname it 'the West African Latin Quarter'.

Independence & Le Folklore

When Dahomey became independent in 1960, Hubert Maga was elected the country's first president. Almost immediately, other former French colonies started deporting their Dahomeyan populations. Back home without work, they became the root of a highly unstable political situation. Three years after independence, having seen how easily some disgruntled soldiers in neighbouring Togo had staged a coup, the military did the same in Dahomey.

During the next decade, Dahomey saw four more military coups, nine more changes of government and five changes of constitution: what the Dahomeyans called in jest *le folklore*.

Revolution

In 1972 a group of officers led by Lieutenant Colonel Mathieu Kérékou seized power in a coup that initiated almost two decades of military dictatorship. The country then took a sharp turn to the left as he embraced Marxist-Leninist ideology and aligned the country with superpowers like China, the Soviet Union and North Korea. To emphasise the break from the past, Kérékou changed the country's flag and renamed it Benin, after the once-flourishing Nigerian Kingdom of Benin. He informed his people by radio on 13 November 1975, a date still etched into the memories of most Beninese.

The government established the schools it required to teach Marxism, along with collective farms, state enterprises, a central trade union, and a more militant spirit in the army. However, the revolution was always more rhetorical than real. The economy fell into a shambles: inflation and unemployment rose, salaries remained unpaid for months. People soon tired of living in West Africa's answer to Eastern Europe, and there were ethnic tensions between the president, a Natitingou-born northerner, and the Yoruba population in the south. There were six attempted coups in one year alone. Then in the late 1980s, workers and students went on strike.

In December 1989, as a condition of French financial support, Kérékou ditched Marxism and held a conference to draft a new constitution. Dissidents used the occasion to blame the government for bankrupting the country, and for corruption and human rights abuses. The 488 delegates then engineered a coup, relegating Kérékou to head of the army, and formed a new cabinet under former dissident Nicéphore Soglo.

The 1990s: Multiparty Elections

The first free multiparty elections were held in March 1991 and Soglo swept to power. However, his austere economic measures – following the 1994 devaluation of the CFA – came under fire, as did his autocracy and nepotism. Top jobs went to Soglo family members such as his son Liadi. Kérékou was voted back into power in March 1996, although he stuck

---

HOW MUCH?

▪ **Eco guided walk** CFA3000

▪ **Mashed yam** CFA200

▪ **Appliqué hat** CFA1500

▪ **Zemi-john** CFA200

▪ **National park entry** CFA10,000

LONELY PLANET INDEX

▪ **1L of petrol** CFA300-600

▪ **1L of bottled water** CFA500

▪ **Bottle of La Béninoise** CFA250

▪ **Souvenir T-shirt** CFA2000

▪ **Aloko (fried plantain)** CFA100

---

to the desperately needed economic measures implemented by his rival.

Five years later, in the March 2001 presidential elections, Kérékou and Soglo faced each other again. Soglo and fellow opposition candidate Adrien Houngbédji withdrew from the race, alleging electoral fraud, leading to a landslide victory for the incumbent president.

Benin Today

Kérékou's second and final five-year term in office finished with the presidential elections in March 2006, bringing an end to his 33 years at the top. The current president, Yayi Boni, former head of the West African Development Bank, beat Adrien Houngbédji in a run-off. In his campaign, based on the slogan of 'change', he pledged to fight corruption and revive the economy.

It hasn't been plain sailing however; despite winning a majority of seats in the parliamentary elections of 2007 and a number of local seats in the 2008 municipal elections, reforms have come about more slowly than hoped. With the next presidential election in March 2011, the pressure will be on President Boni to demonstrate he can be entrusted with a second mandate.

THE CULTURE
The National Psyche

Nicknamed 'the West African Latin Quarter' by the French for its intellectualism, Benin has a strong culture of discussion and debate.

Catholicism and Islam are highly important to their many followers, but the home-grown religion of voodoo is the most influential force.

Politically, the Beninese feel they have borne a lot to achieve their stable democracy and are wary of their troubled neighbours, Togo and Nigeria.

Beninese women may be a formidable presence on the streets but this is a firmly patriarchal society and they tolerate some inequality. However, they do have vital roles in society and the workforce – even in the Muslim north of the country (see below).

Daily Life

Benin's economy is primarily dependant on subsistence farming, which accounts for 38% of GDP. Yams, maize, cassava and corn are the principal food crops. The country's main exports are cotton, palm oil, cashew and cocoa beans, with cotton accounting for more than 75% of export earnings.

Benin's economic growth, achieved through political stability and economic management, is predicted to keep going at its slow but steady pace. Higher fuel and food costs have been partly offset by the increase in commodity prices (cotton, cocoa) and the expansion of Cotonou's port.

Most of Benin's ethnic groups are patrilineal and some still observe polygamy, although the practice is becoming increasingly rare among urban and educated Beninese. Marriages are still arranged by families and divorce is rare.

Most families support themselves through agriculture. Women control the local food distribution system, including the transport of produce to market and the subsequent barter and sale.

Average life expectancy is 56, with an AIDS rate of about 2.1%. Literacy is still low, with just 40% of the population aged over 15 able to read and write, but improving thanks to its young population: 45% are aged 14 or under.

Population

There is an array of different ethnic groups within Benin's narrow borders, although three of them account for nearly 60% of the population: Fon, Adja and Yoruba.

The Fon and Yoruba both migrated from Nigeria and occupy the southern and mideastern zones of Benin.

BENIN

ANGÉLIQUE KIDJO

Born in Ouidah in 1960 to a choreographer and a musician with Portuguese and English ancestry, Kidjo is a world musician in the true, boundary-busting sense of the phrase. Her music is inspired by the links between Africa and Latin America and the fusion of cultures.

In her 2004 album *Oyaya!*, Kidjo sings in four languages on tracks that dabble in Caribbean rhythms such as salsa, calypso and mambo. Her latest album, *Djin Djin*, released in 2007, was nominated for four Grammy awards and showcases appearances by Alicia Keys, Carlos Santana, Joss Stone, Peter Gabriel and Malian rock duo Amadou and Mariam, proof of how influential and international an artist she has become.

Kidjo now lives in New York and has been a Goodwill Ambassador for Unicef since 2002. She has also set up a foundation to promote the education of girls in Africa and has lobbied for fair trade and peace in Africa, a commitment that saw her sing at the Peace Ball for Barack Obama's inauguration in January 2009. Check out www.kidjo.com.

The Bariba and Betamaribé, who make up 9% of the population respectively, live in the northern half of the country and have traditionally been very protective of their cultures and distant towards southern people.

The nomadic Fula (also called Fulani or Peul), found widely across West Africa, live primarily in the north and comprise 6% of the population.

Despite the underlying tensions between the southern and northern regions, the various groups live in relative harmony and have intermarried.

RELIGION

Some 40% of the population is Christian, 25% is Muslim but most people practice voodoo, whatever their religion. The practice mixed with Catholicism in the Americas, where the Dahomeyan slaves took it and their Afro-Brazilian descendants brought it back. Christian missionaries also won over Dahomeyans by fusing their creed with voodoo.

The northern peoples practice voodoo under the name of fetishism, as evidenced by the fetish shrines outside the *tata somba* houses around Natitingou.

ARTS
Art & Craftwork

Benin has a rich cultural heritage, and its traditional art has brought international attention to the legendary kingdom of Dahomey. Traditionally, art served a spiritual purpose, but under the Fon kings, artisans and sculptors were called upon to create works that evoked heroism and enhanced the image of the rulers. They became the historians of the era, creating richly coloured appliqué banners that depicted past and present glories.

Other special examples are the clay polychrome bas-reliefs on the walls of the Musée Historique d'Abomey, now listed a Unesco World Heritage Site. They once used to decorate the palaces, temples and houses of Dahomeian chiefs.

Cinema & TV

The Quintessence film festival (www.festival-ouidah.org) takes place in Ouidah at the same time as the Voodoo Festival. The annual festival, which also tours the country, aims to promote films made in sub-Saharan Africa.

Expect Ivorian soaps on the commercial TV channels such as LC2 and Golfe TV. TV Nationale is the state-run channel.

Music

Angélique Kidjo, a major international star, is Benin's most famous recording artist (see above). Other well known Beninese artists include Gnonnes Pedro, Nel Olivier and Yelouassi Adolphe, and the bands Orchestre Poly-Rythmo and Disc Afrique.

Architecture

Benin has a substantial Afro-Brazilian architectural heritage, best preserved and most obvious in Porto Novo. Official institutions such as the Assemblée Nationale (parliament) or the Haute Court de Justice (high court) occupy the finest buildings but there are plenty of hidden gems to seek out in the capital's streets. Ouidah also has some good examples.

The Lake Nokoué stilt villages and the *tata somba* houses around Natitingou are remarkable examples of traditional architecture.

Sculpture

The *cire perdue* (lost wax) method used to make the famous Benin bronzes (made of brass) comes from Benin City in present-day Nigeria. However, the method spread west and *cire perdue* figures can be bought in Benin, particularly Abomey and Cotonou.

Figures called *bochio* are carved from the trunk of a tree and placed at the entrance of a village to discourage malevolent spirits. Some voodoo wood figures are combined with a variety of materials, such as bottles, padlocks and bones, to imbue them with power. Moulded figures of unfired clay represent Legba (a Fon god) and receive daily libations for the protection of the home.

ENVIRONMENT

Sandwiched between Nigeria and Togo, Benin is 700km long and 120km across in the south, widening to about 300km in the north. Most of the coastal plain is a sand bar that blocks the seaward flow of several rivers. As a result, there are lagoons a few kilometres inland all along the coast, which is being eroded by the strong ocean currents. Inland is a densely forested plateau and, in the far northwest, the Atakora mountains.

Wildlife thrives in Parc National de la Pendjari (p121) and Parc Regional du W (p123), with herds of elephants and several species of cat and antelope.

Deforestation and desertification are major issues because of the presence of valuable wood such as teak. In the north, droughts continue to affect marginal agriculture.

FOOD & DRINK

Beninese grub is unquestionably among the best in West Africa and very similar to Togolese food (p774), the main differences being in the names: *fufu* is generally called *igname pilé* and *djenkoumé* is called *pâte rouge* for instance. But whatever the name, you're bound to eat well in Benin.

The local beer, La Béninoise, is a passable drop. The adventurous could try the millet-based brew *tchoukoutou* or *sodabe* (moonshine).

COTONOU

pop 761,900

Cotonou is Benin's capital in everything but name: a vibrant, bustling, full-on city, and very much the economic engine of Benin. As a first port of call, it can be a little overwhelming, but life can be sweet in Cotonou, with good nightlife, great restaurants and excellent shopping (ideal for end-of-trip souvenirs).

Cotonou means 'mouth of the river of death' in Fon – a reference to the Dahomeyan kingdom's role in the slave trade. In 1868 the city was ceded to the French, but this was challenged in 1892 by the Dahomeyan king Béhanzin, leading to the Franco-Dahomeyan campaigns and the formation of the French protectorate of Dahomey.

BENIN'S BURGEONING ECOTOURISM

Eco-Bénin (www.ecobenin.org) is a small Beninese NGO promoting sustainable tourism. It runs activities in four sites across the country: Possotomé and Lac Ahémé (p111), Koussoukoingou (p120) in the Somba country, Alfakoara (p122) on the edge of the Parc Regional du W and Tanongou (p121) next to the Parc National de la Pendjari.

The basis of their activities is guided tours exploring the culture and heritage of the area. Circuits and prices are agreed with villagers and guides are always local. They receive comprehensive training and the fee visitors pay breaks down as follows: 45% for the guide, 25% for the community, 20% for track and equipment (pirogue, bikes etc) maintenance, 10% administration. Other services are being developed such as spending the night and eating with a local family.

Community funds are managed by a village committee and can be used to pay the school fees of disadvantaged children or to build village infrastructure such as pumps or market shelters.

As Benin suffers from a dearth of qualified and honest guides, this is a great initiative and the chance for travellers to get to know local Beninese.

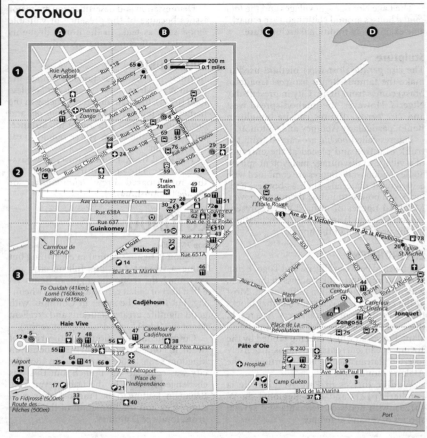

COTONOU

Place de l'Étoile Rouge is an imposing reminder of former President Mathieu Kérékou's dalliance with socialism.

ORIENTATION

The heart of town is around the intersection of Ave Clozel and Blvd Steinmetz. The area was undergoing significant works at the time of writing with the construction of a flyover. Heading north, Blvd Steinmetz runs perpendicular into Blvd St Michel, which becomes Ave du Nouveau Pont as you head east, just as Ave Clozel carries on the Ancien Pont. Both bridges head in the direction of Porto-Novo and Lagos. At the western end of town, following Ave Jean Paul II, is the popular Haie Vive area, as well as the airport.

Only major roads have names – small, unsealed alleyways are called *von* and directions are given with reference to another main street or a landmark.

Maps

The 1:15,000 IGN *Cotonou* map, which lists the city's hotels, cinemas, banks and markets, is available at bookshops.

INFORMATION
Bookshops

Librairie Notre-Dame (☎ 21 31 40 94; Ave Clozel; ⊙ 9am-12.30pm & 4-7pm Tue-Sat, 4-7pm Mon) Next to the cathedral, with an excellent selection of books on Benin (in French) and maps of Cotonou and Benin.

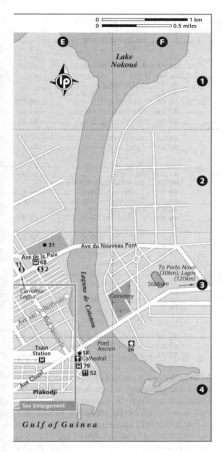

Sonaec (☎ 21 31 22 42; Ave Clozel; ✆ 8.30am-12.30pm & 3.30-7pm Mon-Fri, 9.30am-12.30pm & 4-6.30pm Sat) Smart bookshop with the latest periodicals, maps and some photography books on West Africa.

Cultural Centres
Centre Culturel Chinois (☎ 21 31 31 74; http://bj.china-embassy.org; Ave Jean Paul II; ✆ 9am-12pm & 3.30-6.30pm Tue-Sat) Shows films (see p103).
Centre Culturel Français (☎ 21 30 08 56; www.ccfcotonou.net; Ave Jean Paul II; ✆ 9.30am-12pm & 3-7pm Tue-Sat, closed Thu morning) This busy centre has a gallery, outdoor theatre, library and cinema.

Internet Access
Ave Clozel, Blvd Steinmetz and the Jonquet strip have the most internet cafes.

Cyber Café Le Teranga (☎ 21 30 29 29; Haie Vive; per hr CFA1000; ✆ 9am-midnight)
Cyber du Jonquet (☎ 21 31 71 54; Rue des Cheminots; per hr CFA500; ✆ 8am-1am Mon-Fri, 8am-midnight Sat, from 1pm Sun)
Cyber Océane (☎ 21 30 69 41; Haie Vive; per hr CFA400; ✆ 9am-11pm)
Star Navigation (☎ 21 31 81 28; off Blvd Steinmetz; per hr CFA500; ✆ 8am-10pm)

Medical Services
Pharmacie Camp Ghezo (☎ 21 31 55 52; Rue 240)
Pharmacie Jonquet (☎ 21 31 20 80; Rue des Cheminots) Open 24/7.
Polyclinique les Cocotiers (☎ 21 30 14 20; Rue 373) A private and efficient clinic at the Carrefour de Cadjéhoun; also has a dentist.

Money
All banks change cash but only Ecobank and SGBB change travellers cheques. There are plenty of ATMs in Cotonou, most of which accept Visa.

There's a thriving black market for currencies including the Nigerian Niara around the Jonquet district and Gare du Dantokpa.
Ecobank (✆ 8am-5pm Mon-Fri, 9am-1pm Sat) Blvd St Michel (**Blvd St Michel**); Rue 657 (**Rue 657**) Close to Marché Ganhi.
Polyclinique les Cocotiers (☎ 21 30 14 20; Rue 373)
Société Générale de Banques au Benin (Ave Clozel; ✆ 8am-5.30pm Mon-Fri, 9am-1pm Sat) Has a Visa cash machine.
Banque Atlantique (Blvd St Michel; ✆ 8am-5pm Mon-Fri, 9am-12.30pm Sat) Has a MasterCard and Visa cash machine.

Post
Main post office (off Ave Clozel; ✆ 7am-7pm Mon-Fri, 8am-11.30pm Sat)

Telephone
Telecom (OPT) building (Ave Clozel; ✆ 7.30am-7pm Mon-Sat, 9am-1pm Sun) You can make overseas telephone calls and send faxes.

Tourist Information
Direction du Tourisme et de l'Hôtellerie (☎ 21 32 68 24; Place de l'Étoile Rouge; ✆ 8am-12.30pm & 3-6.30pm Mon-Fri) Inconveniently located out of the centre, behind Pharmacie de l'Étoile Rouge and of limited use.

Visa Extensions
Direction Emigration Immigration (☎ 21 31 42 13; Ave Jean Paul II; ✆ 8am-12.30pm & 3-6.30pm Mon-Fri) Issues 30-day visas.

DANGERS & ANNOYANCES

The biggest danger in Cotonou is the traffic, the 80,000 reckless *zemi-johns* (taxi-motos or *zems*) in particular. They're unavoidable however, so always make sure that the driver agrees to drive slowly (*aller doucement*) before hopping on.

The Jonquet, the beach and the port area all have their fair share of undesirables: don't walk alone at night. Take a taxi to go home rather than a *zem*, but if you can't find one, watch your bag at traffic lights.

Keep an eye on your belongings in crowded areas such as the Grand Marché du Dantokpa.

SIGHTS

The seemingly endless **Grand Marché du Dantokpa** is Cotonou's throbbing heart, bordered by the lagoon and Blvd St Michel. Everything under the sun can be purchased in its labyrinthine lanes, from fish to soap, plastic sandals to goats, pirated DVDs to spare car parts. More traditional fare, such as batiks and Dutch wax cloth can also be found in the market building. The **fetish** section is at the northern end of the market. To appreciate just how huge and thriving Dantokpa is, climb the footbridge that crosses Ave de la Paix: it's exhausting just to look at it.

For a different kind of culture shock, head to the amazing **Fondation Zinsou** (☎ 21 31 50 51; www.fondationzinsou.org; Rue du Gouverneur Bayol; admission free; ☺ 10am-7pm, closed bank holidays). This fantastic exhibition space seeks to promote contemporary African art among Beninese people and has featured big names such as Malian photographer Malick Sidibe and home-grown visual artist Romuald Hazoumé (famous for his jerrycan creations). Children from local schools are regularly invited in and the foundation runs kids' art classes on Wednesday and Saturday. The chic boutique sells beautiful art books and the café serves expensive teas and fresh fruit juices.

COURSES

For Fon-language classes, call **Vinawamon** (☎ 97 87 37 72), also contactable via the Centre Culturel Français (p99).

BENIN

SLEEPING
Budget
Maison de Passage des Allemands (☎ 21 30 45 76; Haie Vive; r with air-con CFA7000; 🔀) This discreet villa next to Bar Le Lambi's is an absolute bargain if you manage to get a room: it was set up to accommodate German aid workers, and since there are only seven rooms and lots of aid workers, it's often full. Book well in advance. Bathrooms and toilets are shared but it is clean; you also get the use of the kitchen and an atmospheric patio and balcony. The only problem is the noise from the next door bar and traffic.

Hôtel Babo (☎ 21 31 46 07; Rue Agbeto Amadoré; s with fan/air-con CFA6000/10,000; 🔀) There's a good chance you'll be sharing the night with friends of the creepy-crawly variety but it's a big place and rooms cater for all needs, from air-con on the 1st floor to no fan or bednet on the 5th floor (the great views might be small comfort).

Le Chant d'Oiseau (☎ 21 30 57 51; www.chant doiseau.net; Rue du Collège Père Aupiais; s/d/tr with fan CFA9000/13,500/17,500, with air-con CFA16,500/22,000/27,500; 🔀 🖳) A safe, excellent budget option run by a catholic community and within walking distance of the lively Haie Vive area. The building looks a little austere with its concrete facade but the rooms are quiet and spacious, and the restaurant serves great-value food. There is also an internet cafe (per hour CFA500). Find it next to the well-known Collège Père Aupiais.

Midrange
Hôtel Benin Vickinfel (☎ 21 31 38 14; www.beninvickin felhotel.com; off Blvd Steinmetz; r from CFA15,500; 🔀 🛜) Don't be fooled by the grim exterior. This 33-room hotel is good value considering it's right in the city centre. Rooms are a little pokey but comfortable and very quiet (ask for one with a shower rather than a bath).

our pick **Chez Clarisse** (☎ 21 30 60 14; Camp Guézo; s/d with breakfast CFA25,000/30,000; 🔀 🖳) The closest thing to a guest house you'll find in Cotonou, this is a charming place, with seven immaculate rooms in a villa at the back of the popular Chez Clarisse restaurant. The owner is delightful and guests get the use of the lounge and of the small but perfectly formed pool. It's at the back of the US embassy.

Hôtel du Port (☎ 21 31 44 44; www.hotelduport -cotonou.com; Blvd de la Marina; s/d from CFA38,600/44,200, bungalow s/d CFA46,600/54,200; 🅿 🔀 🖳 🖳) This well-run hotel is the best midrange option

in Cotonou. Rooms are comfortable and the bungalows very spacious. The surrounding towers of containers from the next-door port are slightly surreal and in sharp contrast with the oasis-like pretty pool (nonguest CFA2500), garden and *paillote* (straw awning) restaurant-bar (meals CFA3800 to CFA6500).

Hôtel du Lac (☎ 21 33 19 19; www.hoteldulac-benin .com; r CFA40,000-60,000; 🔀 🖳 🖳) A good midrange choice on a breezy spot at the edge of the lagoon. Rooms are sunny, spacious, exceptionally clean and most have water views. The restaurant (meals CFA2500 to CFA4800) has a great panoramic terrace and the pool is popular at the weekend (adult/child CFA2500/2000). The only downside is that it's a little out of the way, on the other side of the river close to the Ancien Pont.

Alex's Hotel (☎ 21 04 36 86; Rue 108; s/d from CFA41,500/53,500; 🔀) Cotonou's Hotel California, with mildly erotic art decorating the corridors, sweetly scented rooms and enormous leather sofas crowding the reception area. There are city views from the roof, a gym (you'll definitely be working up a sweat) and a popular karaoke bar and nightclub, Cristal Palace (p103).

Top End
Novotel Orisha (☎ 21 30 56 69; www.novotel.com; Blvd de la Marina; r CFA85,000; 🅿 🔀 🖳 🖳) This super swish Novotel comes complete with design furniture, funky bar, beautiful swimming pool and decked out terrace featuring 'day beds' and wooden loungers. Rooms follow the same cool design style: not very African, but definitely comfortable and excellent value.

Benin Marina Hotel (☎ 21 30 01 00; www.benin -marina-hotel.com; Blvd de la Marina; r with city/ocean view CFA121,000/134,000, bungalow CFA155,000; 🅿 🔀 🖳 🖳) Luxury accommodation in true West African style: in a concrete bunker. The inside has more charm, with African tapestries lining the corridors and tasteful decor in the rooms. There is also a circular pool (nonguest adult use costs CFA4500, child CFA3500), with a poolside restaurant and a busy nightclub.

EATING
All restaurants listed below are open for lunch and dinner.

African
Chez Léa (off Rue des Hindous; meal CFA1500) Fill up on *poulet moyo* at this crazily popular lunch joint

set up under an awning and corrugated iron roof. Plates are piled high with chicken, *aloko* (fried bananas), fries, rice, peas and salad. Perfect to fill up on the cheap and take in the vibe from Cotonou's working crowd.

Maquis Le Lagon (☎ 97 44 29 94; off Blvd Steinmetz; meals CFA2000) On a quiet *von* (alleyway), friendly Le Lagon serves African-sized portions of fish or chicken – or if you dare, beef tongue – with staples such as *attiéké* (grated cassava) and *aloko* on the side. The tables on the street are perfect for people-watching.

Chez Maman Bénin (☎ 21 32 33 38; Rue 201A; meals CFA500-3000) This long-standing no-frills canteen off Blvd St Michel has a large selection of West African dishes scooped from steaming pots. There's a couple of blaring TVs showing the latest football action. Low-key but good fun.

ourpick **Pili Pili** (☎ 21 31 29 32; Quartier Zongo; meals CFA2500-3800) This *maquis* (open-air restaurant) rates highly with Beninese and expats for its amazing West African food. Prices are reasonable and the jugs of freshly squeezed pineapple juice at lunch time are a refreshing godsend. It's on the second *von* to your right as you head down Ave Togbé from Carrefour Unafrica.

Asian

Hai King (☎ 21 30 60 08; Carrefour de Cadjéhoun; mains CFA4000; ⏰ 10am-2.30pm & 6-11.30pm) You'll easily spot this popular Chinese restaurant by the dozen red lanterns decorating its facade. Close to Haie Vive, it serves great Chinese food on an atmospheric covered roof terrace overlooking the bustling Carrefour Cadjéhoun.

Royal Garden (☎ 21 30 03 20; Haie Vive; meals CFA3500-5000) This Indian-run restaurant with garden seating, on the same street as Le Livingstone, does a delicious curry and is popular with the few Brits living in Cotonou.

European

La Verdure (☎ 21 31 31 75; off Ave Clozel; meals around CFA6000) Tucked away, just west of Blvd Steinmetz, is this great little French seafood restaurant in a leafy garden, which also has a nice bar with a pool table.

Chez Clarisse (☎ 21 30 60 14; Camp Guézo; mains CFA3500) This small French restaurant, in a pretty residential area next to the US embassy, is a perennial favourite that churns out excellent European and African specialities. Service can get overwhelmed on busy nights though.

Le Costa Rica (☎ 21 30 20 09; Centre de Promotion de l'Artisanat; mains CFA4000) This French-owned joint

serves excellent home-made pasta, wood-fired pizzas and Provençal fare. It's also one of the few places to serve draft beer in Cotonou.

Chez Mimi (☎ 21 31 49 07; Rue d'Abomey; mains from CFA5000) Run by the savvy Mireille, this 'maquis de luxe' is Afro-European fusion cuisine at its best: home-made fresh fruit punch, divine monkfish gratin and delicious desserts all served in a lovely alfresco setting. To find it, turn off Rue Capitaine Adjovi opposite Pharmacie Zongo.

Les Trois Mousquetaires (☎ 21 31 61 22; Ave Dodds; mains from CFA9000) Cotonou's gastronomic highlight, this fine establishment serves delicate French cuisine such as *cocote de la mer au cidre* (cider seafood stew, which doesn't sound anywhere near as elegant in English!) or roast veal rib. The wine list is extensive too and the old colonial dining room is the perfect setting for a sophisticated evening. Book ahead.

Lebanese

Fleur de Sel (☎ 97 59 19 59; off Rue 651A; mains CFA3500) Savour Lebanese specialities with a side of ocean breeze and great port views at this beach-side restaurant. As well as succulent kebabs and unctuous hummus, the house also serves fab seafood, with lobster, crayfish and whole fish big enough to feed a party of 10. Find it down the road from the Chambre de Commerce et d'Industrie du Bénin.

Cafés & Patisseries

Boulangerie-Pâtisserie (Route de l'Aéroport; ⏰ 7am-8pm) The bread, croissants, éclairs and cakes from this little bakery next to the Air France office can rival those of any French bakery.

La Gerbe d'Or (☎ 21 31 42 58; Ave Clozel; ⏰ 6am-10pm) It's overpriced and the cakes are not always as fresh as they ought to be, but the cafe upstairs sells good ice creams.

Quick Eats

There's an amazing number of food joints that spring up at meal times. It's mostly omelette stalls in the morning (can't beat an omelette sandwich and a cup of Milo for CFA400 to kick-start the day), sandwich bars at lunch time and smokin' *brochettes* (kebabs) in the evenings. All are incredibly cheap and often a good place to chat with locals.

Self-Catering

In the centre, around Marché Ganhi, are a number of good supermarkets, including

La Pointe (☎ 21 31 69 45; off Ave Clozel; ☺ 9am-8pm) and **La Championne** (☎ 21 30 69 43; Haie Vive; ☺ 9am-10pm).

DRINKING

Haie Vive, near the airport, is a good, safe area by night, with many of the city's best bars and restaurants.

Le Livingstone (☎ 21 30 27 58; livin@leland.bj; Haie Vive; meals CFA3500-4500; ☺ 11am-late) Hugely popular with expats (many of whom live just round the corner in the leafy district of Haie Vive) who come here to chill out to the tune of Western pop and sport channels. It also serves ace but expensive pizzas (CFA5000). Perfect if you're in need of home comforts.

The nameless **our pick** **buvette** at Carrefour Cadjéhoun is a brilliantly atmospheric spot for sundowners. Tables spill out of nowhere as soon as darkness falls (if you walked passed during day time you wouldn't even know there's a bar) and there is often live music.

The Jonquet strip is bristling with pumping music and wild and wicked bars, such as **Le Soweto** (☎ 97 44 17 49; Rue des Cheminots; ☺ 7am-4am).

ENTERTAINMENT
Cinemas

You can see films in French at the Centre Culturel Français, which issues monthly pamphlets with upcoming program details, and at the Centre Culturel Chinois on Saturday at 8pm.

Nightclubs

The decadent bars on Jonquet strip are generally open through the night, often without a cover.

New York, New York (Halle des Arts, Centre de Promotion de l'Artisanat; admission CFA4500; ☺ 10pm-dawn) A glitzy hall of mirrors, frequented by some of the friendliest young ladies you'll encounter this side of Lomé.

Cristal Palace (☎ 21 31 25 08; admission CFA3500; ☺ 11pm-dawn Tue-Sun), at Alex's Hotel, has a karaoke bar. Benin Marina Hotel's **Le Téké** (☎ 21 30 01 00; Blvd de la Marina; ☺ 9pm-late Tue-Sun) is also fun at weekends (salsa classes at 10pm on Friday for CFA5000) and organises regular 'beach parties' by the pool.

Live Music

Le Repaire de Bacchus (☎ 21 31 75 81; Ave Proche; ☺ 11am-midnight, to 2am Thu, to 4am Fri & Sat) With live jazz on Thursday from 10.30pm, and music such as rumba and Côte d'Ivoire sounds on Friday and Saturday, this place is positively groovy.

SHOPPING

Centre de Promotion de l'Artisanat (Blvd St Michel; ☺ 9am-7pm) There are more beckoning hands than quality work in this large centre, but it's worth a look to get your cultural bearings. The boutiques sell woodcarvings, bronzes, batiks, leather goods, jewellery and appliqué banners.

Marché Ganhi, which takes up a whole block between rue des Hindous, rue du Gouverneur and Ave Clozel, is good for fruit and veg, and bits and pieces such as CDs, baskets and roast peanuts.

For quality Dutch wax fabric, head to the elegant boutique **Woodin** (Rue des Hindous; ☺ 8.30am-1pm & 4-7pm Tue-Fri, 9am-1pm Sat, 3.30-7pm Mon) where *demi-pièces* (see the boxed text, p782, for our tips on buying fabric) start at CFA14,000.

GETTING THERE & AWAY
Air

The international airport is on the western fringe of town. It has a pharmacy, a small grocery shop, two bureaux de change that don't change travellers cheques and a Visa cash machine.

For information on airlines flying to Cotonou see p126.

Bush Taxi, Minibus & Bus

Cotonou has a rather confusing number of stations for minibuses, buses and bush taxis. It's easiest to ask a taxi or a *zemi-john* to take you to the right one.

Gare Jonquet (Rue des Cheminots), a couple of blocks west of Blvd Steinmetz, services western destinations such as Ouidah (CFA700, one hour), Grand Popo (CFA1500, two hours) and Lomé (CFA3500, three hours).

Bush taxis for Porto Novo (CFA500-700, 45 minutes) and Lagos (CFA3000; three hours) leave from **Gare du Dantokpa** (Ave de la République) at the new bridge; those to Abomey-Calavi (for Ganvié, CFA400, 25 minutes) and Abomey (CFA2200, two hours) leave just north of Rond-Point de l'Étoile Rouge.

For more distant destinations such as Parakou, Malanville or Natitingou, take the bus (p127) – cheaper, faster and altogether better.

BENIN

For information on international buses to/from Cotonou, see p127.

GETTING AROUND
To/From the Airport
A private taxi from the city centre to the airport costs around CFA2000, although drivers will demand double this amount *from* the airport. There are also plenty of *zemi-johns* who will be quite happy to load you and your luggage for much less.

Taxi, Zemi-John & Shared Taxi
A *zemi-john* will whiz you around town for CFA100 to CFA300 depending on the distance.

Fares in shared taxis run from CFA150 to CFA400. Otherwise, taxis can be hired for CFA2000 per hour; rates increase from early evening on. Gare du Dantokpa is a good place to pick up taxis.

AROUND COTONOU

GANVIÉ
The main attraction near Cotonou is Ganvié, where 30,000 Tofinu people live in bamboo huts on stilts several kilometres out on Lake Nokoué. The Tofinu fled to this swampy region in the 17th century to escape from the Dahomey slave-hunters, who were banned by a religious custom from venturing into the water.

They live almost exclusively from fishing, which they do by planting branches on the muddy lagoon bottom. When the leaves on the branches begin to decompose, the fish congregate there to feed. Stilts are made of ebony and have to be replaced every 20 years or so. Because of this maintenance issue, 'hard' structures have started appearing for bigger and/or communal buildings such as the school and the church.

The town has become a tourist magnet but is a victim of its own success: pollution of the lagoon is a chronic problem and guides seem more interested in making a quick buck than providing an informative commentary.

Sleeping & Eating
Hôtel Carrefour Ganvié Chez M (☎ 95 42 04 68; hotelcarrefourchezm@hotmail.fr; r from CFA5000) This quaint hotel in the middle of the village has 11 rooms with balconies, mosquito nets, and some with ensuite bathrooms. It's quite an unusual setting but the noise from the diesel water-pump across the stream is a bit of a nuisance. Guests get free transport back to Abomey-Calavi. Meals are available for CFA2500 to CFA3000.

Getting There & Away
From Place de l'Étoile Rouge, get a taxi to Abomey-Calavi (CFA400, 25 minutes), not to be confused with Abomey. The embarkation point is 800m downhill. At the **official counter** (☎ 95 05 27 01; ☺ 9am-6pm), return fares to Ganvié for one person in a regular/motorised pirogue are CFA6050/7050; CFA4050/5050 each for two to four people; CFA3050/4050 for five to nine; CFA2550/3050 for 10 or more. Prices include a circuit of the village with stop-offs. The whole trip takes about 2½ hours.

ROUTE DES PÊCHES
West of Cotonou, past the airport and all the way to Ouidah, is the sandy **Route des Pêches**, a land of seemingly endless beaches and fishing villages, a world away from the big-smoke mayhem.

Fidjrossé and its immense beach is the place to hang out and be seen on Sunday afternoon in Cotonou. Beninese families turn out en masse to exchange gossip, parade new hair-dos and chill out with a beer. Stop at the tiny **Festival des Nems** (portion CFA300) in its blue beach hut for the best spring rolls in West Africa and wash it down with a bottle of Castel or Flag from one of the beach vendors.

As you leave Cotonou behind, the suburb gives way to thatched huts and palm groves. Many expats rent little *paillotes* for the weekend around here. For those just passing by, there are many popular restaurants along the route. **Wado** (☎ 97 77 66 66; www.wado.net; mains CFA4000) is the hang out of choice for the surfing crowd. As well as cool vibes, it serves mostly European fare.

The hidden gem on this bit of coast however, is the idyllic **ourpick Bab's Dock** (☎ 97 97 01 96; domhaumont@yahoo.fr; mains CFA6000; ☺ 10am-7pm Sat, Sun & bank holidays). This secluded retreat on the edge of the lagoon was built by a Belgian couple who fell head over heels for this slice of paradise. Almost everything is made of local wood – the tables, the bar, the deck – and was built with the help of local villagers. You can swim in the shallow waters of the lagoon, canoe and even sail or just relax in a hammock, rocked by the lagoon breeze. Food is European in style but local in production. A guesthouse with four rooms was in construction at the time of writing. Bab's Dock is 11km from Cotonou; there is no public transport there. A secure car park is signposted from the route; from there, a boat takes you to the restaurant through thick mangrove and open-sky lagoon. There is an admission fee (CFA2500) for the day, which covers the car park and boat trip.

THE SOUTH

Benin's south is an enticing but intriguing mix of heavenly shores and momentous history. Ouidah and Porto Novo brim with what remains of the riches accrued by European slave traders, while time seems to stand still in palm-fringed Grand Popo and tranquil Lac Ahémé. It is also the birthplace of the much demonised voodoo religion and was once the stronghold of the mighty Dahomey Kingdom based in Abomey.

PORTO NOVO
pop 223,168
Nestling on the shores of Lake Nokoué, Porto Novo is Benin's unlikely capital. Just 30km east of Cotonou and 15km from the Nigerian border, the city has somehow escaped the manic nature of its neighbours and carries on instead at a mellow, unperturbed pace. Its leafy streets, wonderful colonial architecture and interesting museums make it a fabulous two-day escape from full-on Cotonou.

Porto Novo has been Benin's official capital since it was used as such by the French, whose colonisation followed the Wars of Resistance that began here in 1890. The Portuguese named the city after Porto when they established a slave-trading post here in the 16th century. Some of this colonial legacy can be seen in the Musée da Silva, which examines Afro-Brazilian culture, and the statue in Place Jean Bayal celebrating cooperation between the Yoruba and Creole peoples.

Basic information about the city can be found online at www.porto-novo.org. There are three banks and a post office in the city centre.

Sights & Activities
CENTRE SONGHAI
There is something amazing about the fact that **Centre Songhai** (☎ 20 24 68 81; www.songhai.org;

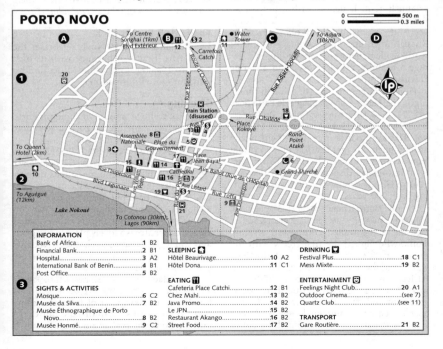

PORTO NOVO

Route de Pobè) is more than 20 years old. Everything it stands for – sustainable development, using local resources, blending traditional and modern techniques, recycling – was considered visionary when it was set up in 1985. The brainchild of a Dominican monk of Nigerian descent who wanted to boost the quality of life in rural areas, Songhai is now a major research, teaching and production centre in sustainable farming.

There are daily **guided tours** (1hr tour CFA500; ☉ 8.30am, 10.30am, noon, 3.30pm & 5pm Mon-Sat) to visit the plantations and workshops. You can also buy the centre's products in their shop, anything from fresh quail eggs to biscuits and preserves. Songhai is about 1km north of town. Every *zem* knows it so you won't have difficulties getting there.

MUSEUMS
Porto Novo has three rather original museums, which will fill you in on history, culture and tradition.

The privately owned **Musée Da Silva** (☎ 20 21 50 71; Ave Liotard; admission CFA2000; ☉ 9am-6pm) is a wonderfully eccentric and eclectic African establishment. It begins with a tour of an Afro-Brazilian house dating back to 1870, veers into rooms filled with old typewriters, Russian *kepis* and photocopied portraits of world leaders, before finally ending in a garage containing a Rolls Royce and a Harley Davidson hotrod.

Housed in another pretty colonial building is the **Musée Ethnographique de Porto Novo** (☎ 20 21 25 54; Ave 6; admission CFA1000; ☉ 8am-6pm Mon-Fri, from 9am Sat, Sun & holidays, closed 1 May & 1 Jan). The top floor is organised thematically around birth, life and death, with everything from costumes to carved drums. Downstairs is an impressive display of the Yorubas' inventive Gelede ceremonial masks, some dating back 200 years.

Finally, **Musée Honmé** (☎ 20 21 35 66; Rue Toffa; admission CFA1000; ☉ 9am-6pm, to 5pm Sat & Sun) is housed in the walled compound of King Toffa, who signed the first treaty with the French in 1863. The kingdom of Porto Novo was one of the longest lasting in sub-Saharan Africa, running from 1688 to the 25th king in 1976, when the five dynasties had a disagreement and let the kingdom die. The site hasn't been well maintained and you'll need some imagination to make something out of the bare chambers but the guide, François, puts on a good show.

PIROGUE TRIPS & WALKING TOURS
The 12km pirogue trip to the stilt village of Aguégué is a less touristy option than Ganvié. Among the guides offering to oblige are Hilaire and his company **Iroko Tours** (☎ 97 17 59 82, 93 80 60 59; iroko1992@yahoo.fr). Half-day trips cost CFA15,000 for two people, and CFA7000 per extra person. Hilaire also offers themed walking tours of Porto Novo, exploring either the voodoo culture or architectural highlights of the capital's Afro-Brazilian heritage, such as the multicoloured **mosque**, once a 19th-century church and now a flamboyant example of the fusion of cultures.

GRAND MARCHÉ D'ADJARA
The **market** in the small town of Adjara, 10km north of Porto Novo on a back road to Nigeria, is one of the most colourful in Benin. Held every fourth day, it's stocked with fetishes, grigri charms, unique blue and white tie-dyed cloth, some of the best pottery in Benin, *tam tams* and other musical instruments. Shared taxis to Adjara leave Porto Novo *gare routière* on market day – or take a *zemi-john*.

Festivals & Events
In mid-January Porto Novo celebrates the city's Afro-Brazilian heritage with its own version of **Carnival**. Contact the Musée da Silva (left) for more information.

Sleeping
There isn't a huge amount of choice in Porto Novo and standards are not particularly good. Below is the cream of the crop.

ourpick Centre Songhai (☎ 20 22 50 92; Route de Pobè; r with fan CFA4000, with air-con CFA12,500-15,500; P ✕ ⌑) Built to accommodate its numerous visitors, the 70 rooms at Centre Songhai (see p105) are basic but clean. Fan rooms have a shower cubicle but shared toilets. Air-con rooms have bathrooms and are still very good value. The centre is a lovely place to hang out and you'll get a chance to chat with students at the *maquis*-bar. There is also an internet cafe (per hour CFA250).

Queen's Hotel (☎ 20 24 79 83; quennhot2005@hotmail .com; off Route de Louho; r CFA9500-12,500; P ✕) This low-key hotel 2km west of town has some good-value rooms (comfortable but dark) and an excellent restaurant. Find it down the first road to your left after Carrefour Djassin Tokpa.

Hôtel Dona (☎ 20 22 30 52; www.hoteldona.com; Blvd Extérieur; s/d/tr CFA10,500/14,500/16,500; **P** ⊠) Rooms are quite plush at this pink establishment: those at the front benefit from balconies but are a little noisier because of the traffic on the boulevard. The rooftop panoramic restaurant is a nice spot to relax and Nicole, the friendly manager, is a good source of information.

Hôtel Beaurivage (☎ 20 21 23 99; Blvd Lagunaire; r CFA15,500-25,500; ⊠) Tired but spacious rooms (and new beds, finally!) with the town's best lagoon views and a wonderful terrace bar and restaurant. Even if you don't sleep here, you should definitely come for sundowners.

Eating

Chez Mahi (Ave 6; meals CFA500-1000; ⊠ lunch Mon-Sat) Locals swear by this restaurant, just south of Place Kokoyé; it's not an attractive place (unpainted concrete walls) but the mashed yam is excellent and the atmosphere jovial.

Java Promo (☎ 20 21 20 54; Place du Gouvernement; meals CFA1500-3000; ⊠ breakfast, lunch & dinner) Hidden behind the aquamarine shutters of a crumbling colonial building and shielded from the sun by a big *paillote*, this is a popular haunt for an omelette at brekkie or meat and pâte for lunch.

Le JPN (☎ 20 21 38 66; Jardin des Plantes et de la Nature, site 2; meals CFA2500; ⊠ 10am-6pm Tue-Thu, to 11pm Fri-Sun) Set in a leafy park southwest of the Assemblée Nationale, this place offers breakfast, lunch and the odd stream of ants.

Centre Songhai (☎ 20 22 50 92; Route de Pobè; menu du jour CFA5000; ⊠ breakfast, lunch & dinner) The posher of the centre's two restaurants offers mouth-watering cuisine and CFA500 carafes of wine. More informal, and very popular with students, is the *maquis*-bar which serves traditional African dishes (CFA1200) and cold beer. Both restaurants use the centre's products.

Restaurant Akango (☎ 20 21 56 12; Rue de l'Inspection; mains CFA3000; ⊠ lunch & dinner) Lavish dishes such as *coq au vin* or braised fish are the order of the day in this elegant restaurant on a quiet side street opposite a ministerial building.

QUICK EATS

Cafeteria Place Catchi (Carrefour Catchi) The usual cluster of Milo, condensed milk and coffee tins jostle for space with eggs and tin plates at this popular breakfast stall. Particularly handy since Cotonou-bound taxis tend to congregate on either side of the square.

There are plenty more food stalls around Carrefour Catchi and the parks around the cathedral.

Drinking

Java Promo, Le JPN and the *maquis*-bar at Centre Songhai are also popular watering holes.

Festival Plus (☎ 20 22 39 79; Rue Obalédé) Great Afro-Brazilian beats and cheap beer are in store at this bright-yellow, Flag-sponsored bar.

Messe Mixte (Blvd Lagunaire) This bar is popular with military personnel from the academy next door but the atmosphere is relaxed. There's also a little *maquis* at the front in the evening if you get peckish.

Entertainment

The town's most popular club is **Feelings Night Club** (Blvd Extérieur; admission CFA3000; ⊠ Fri & Sat), 1km north of Hôtel Beaurivage. There is also **Quartz Club** (Blvd Extérieur; admission CFA3500; ⊠ Fri, Sat & holidays) at Hôtel Dona. Both establishments open around 10pm but it doesn't really get going until midnight.

The **outdoor cinema** (CFA500) at Musée da Silva sporadically shows French films.

Getting There & Away

Plenty of minibuses and bush taxis leave for Cotonou (minibus/bush taxi CFA500/700, 45 minutes) from the *gare routière* and Carrefour Catchi. To Abomey from Porto Novo is CFA2700.

For Nigeria, you can get a taxi to the border-point in Kraké (CFA700, 30 minutes) but you'll have to change to go on to Lagos.

Getting Around

If Cotonou hasn't scared you off *zemi-johns*, they are the best way to see Porto Novo. Alternatively all the major sites and facilities are within half an hour's walk of each other.

OUIDAH

pop 87,200

Some 42km west of Cotonou is Ouidah, a relaxed, relatively prosperous town and a must-see for anyone interested in voodoo or Benin's history of slave-trading. Until a wharf was built at Cotonou in 1908, Ouidah had the only port in the country. From the 17th to the late 19th centuries (with trade peaking during the 19th century), captured country-men from across West Africa left Ouidah for the Americas.

A visit to the beach, from where the slaves once left, is well worthwhile. The 4km journey there from town takes you past a lagoon with fishermen and a small stilt village.

The annual **Voodoo Festival** (see opposite) is celebrated here in January. The **Quintessence Film festival** (www.festival-ouidah.org), where the top honour is the Python Royal (of the award rather than animal variety!), runs at the same time.

Information

There are several internet cafes on Rue Olivier de Montaguere, including **FIC** (per hr CFA350; 8.30am-11pm) and **Cyber PKCOM** (per hr CFA300; 9am-11pm).

Continental Bank Bénin (☎ 21 34 14 32; Place du Marché; 8.30am-noon & 3-6pm Mon-Fri) changes cash.

Sights & Activities
MUSÉE D'HISTOIRE DE OUIDAH
This **museum** (☎ 21 34 10 21; www.museeouidah.org; Rue van Vollenhoven; admission CFA1000; 8am-12.30pm & 3-6pm Mon-Fri, 9am-6pm Sat & Sun), two blocks east of the market, is housed in the beautiful Fortaleza São João Batista, a Portuguese fort built in 1721. It's one of the best museums of its kind, with exhibits focusing on the slave trade and the resulting links between Benin, Brazil and the Caribbean. You'll be shown voodoo arte-facts, skulls, photos showing the influence of Dahomeyan slaves on Brazilian culture, and traces of Brazilian architecture that the repatri-ated slaves brought back to Africa.

ROUTE DES ESCLAVES
The 4km Route des Esclaves, now the main road to the beach, starts near the Musée d'Histoire de Ouidah at **Place Chacha**, the old auction square. Once sold, slaves would make their way down to the coast to board the ships. Lining the sandy track now are fetishes and monuments such as the Monument of Repentance and the Tree of Forgetfulness. Slaves were forced to circle the tree that once stood here, to forget the land they were leaving.

There is a poignant memorial on the beach, the **Point of No Return**, with bas-relief depicting slaves in chains. It's such a beautiful spot that it's hard to fathom that 12 million people were deported from this very shore.

Guides from the Musée d'Histoire will offer to show you the Route des Esclaves

OUIDAH

0 _____ 500 m
0 _____ 0.3 miles

INFORMATION
Continental Bank Bénin.....................1 B5
Cyber PKCOM....................................2 A4
FIC..3 A4
Hospital...4 B5
Place Chacha....................................5 B5
Post Office...6 A5

SIGHTS & ACTIVITIES
Basilica..7 B5
Casa do Brazil...................................8 A5
Grand Marché...................................9 B5
Musée d'Histoire de Ouidah..........10 B5
Temple des Pythons.......................11 B5

SLEEPING
Oasis Hôtel......................................12 B5

EATING
Evivi...13 A5
Le Diplomate...................................14 B5
Maquis Benin...................................15 A3

DRINKING
La Carapace.....................................16 B5
Liberty's...17 A5
Maquia Cabana................................18 A4

TRANSPORT
Gare Routière...................................19 B5
Shared-Taxi Stop (to Grand Popo & Togo)..20 A3

by *zem* for an extra fee. It's probably a bet-ter bet than picking a random guide off the street: CFA4000 should cover it.

CASA DO BRAZIL
Sometimes called La Maison du Brésil, this **museum** (☎ 21 34 18 63; Ave de France, admission CFA1000; 9am-6pm) gives an overview of the African

---

CELEBRATING VOODOO

Voodoo, or *vodou,* got its current name in Haiti and Cuba, where the religion arrived with Fon and Ewe slaves from the Dahomey Kingdom and mixed with Catholicism. It was originally called *vodun* in Benin and Togo, a word that means 'the hidden' or 'the mystery'.

The practice conforms to the general pattern of West African religions, with a supreme god, Mawu, and a host of lesser spirits that are ethnically specific to their followers and to the part of the spiritual world inhabited by a person's ancestors. Traditional priests, or *juju* men, are consulted for their power to communicate with particular spirits and seek intercession with them. This communication is achieved through spirit possession and ritual that often involves a gift or 'sacrifice' of palm wine, chickens or goats. The grace of the spirits is essential for protection and prosperity, and some spirits can be harnessed for malicious and selfish ends.

A fetish is an object or potion imbued with the spirits' power. Fetish markets are like voodoo pharmacies. The buyer has a prescription of the items the priest needs to make the required concoction – such as a parrot's tail or a cobra's head. It's all a bit grisly to the Western eye but far from the skulduggery depicted in Hollywood.

Hollywood aside, Benin's own government hasn't always been supportive either. Kérékou's Marxist government outlawed voodoo as being inimical to a rational and socialist work ethic. But when a democratic government was installed here in 1989, traditional religious practice was permitted. And finally, voodoo was formally recognised as a religion by the government in February 1996.

Since then, 10 January, **Voodoo Day,** has been a bank holiday, with celebrations all over the country. Those in Ouidah, voodoo's historic centre, are amongst the best and most colourful, with endless singing, dancing, beating of drums and drinking. It's certainly eye-opening, but those expecting to see *The Night of the Living Dead* will be sadly disappointed.

Diaspora. The house itself is the former residence of the Brazilian governor and was later occupied by a Portuguese family until they were ousted in the early 1960s.

TEMPLE DES PYTHONS

The voodoo **python temple** (☎ 95 40 08 90; off Rue Colombani; admission CFA1000, photos CFA5000; ☽ 8am-7pm) is now more of a tourist trap than a sacred site. The guide explains some of the beliefs and ceremonies associated with the temple, ushers you into a room containing 40 sleepy pythons, drapes one round your neck, and asks for a *cadeau.*

SACRED FOREST

A generation ago, the peaceful **Fôret Sacrée** (☎ 97 68 89 22; admission incl guide CFA1000; ☽ 8am-6pm) was off-limits to the uninitiated. It contains the huge and rare 400-year-old iroko tree that King Kpassé, founder of Ouidah, is reputed to have turned himself into while fleeing enemies. The forest is now a tranquil place, dotted with sculptures that symbolise voodoo and animist deities and beliefs.

CASA DEL PAPA

Nonguests can use the facilities at this resort (see p110): swimming pool (adult/child CFA3500/2500), volleyball and tennis courts (per hour CFA3500).

Sleeping

Edelweiss Les Retrouvailles (☎ 21 10 10 86; Rue du Général Dodd; r with fan/air-con CFA6500/15,500; P ⊠) About 1km east of the Musée d'Histoire de Ouidah, past the French military cemetery, this excellent budget choice is set in leafy grounds with a *paillote* restaurant (meals CFA2000 to CFA3500) and a children's playground. Bungalows are clean and airy and the management really friendly. The name of the hotel will draw a blank with most *zems* so try asking for 'Les Paillotes'.

Oasis Hôtel (☎ 21 34 10 91; Rue van Vollenhoven; r CFA10,500-15,500 ⊠) The only central hotel but not the best: rooms are noisy and overpriced, as is the restaurant (meals CFA4500). It does have a nice rooftop bar however, with superb views, and the location is very handy.

Le Jardin Brésilien Auberge de la Diaspora (☎ 21 34 11 10; r CFA10,000-25,000; P ⊠ ⊠) On the beach near the Point of No Return, this tranquil place is a good midrange choice. Go for a category B room with air-con and fab views and avoid the fan rooms – overpriced and a furnace because of the lack of shade. The restaurant (meals CFA3000 to CFA9000) is

BENIN

pricey but in a beautiful setting and has a good selection of fish.

Casa Del Papa (☎ 95 95 39 04; ww.casadelpapa.com; Ouidah Plage; d incl breakfast CFA47,000-68,000; P ⊠ ♨) Squeezed between the ocean and the lagoon, Casa del Papa is the closest thing to an exclusive resort you'll find on the coast. It's packed with wealthy Cotonou residents at weekends but eerily quiet the rest of the week. There are numerous activities on offer as well as excursions across the lagoon and to the nearby Bouche du Roy (see right). The hotel is 7km beyond the Point of No Return on a road that is unsafe at night. There is no public transport to get there.

Eating

For a tasty meal, the hotels listed above are your best bet. For cheap bites or on-the-go food, try **Evivi** (Rue F Colombani; meals CFA1000, ☽ lunch & dinner), in a pleasant courtyard opposite the post office. **Le Diplomate** (Rue F Colombani; snacks CFA400, ☽ breakfast, lunch & dinner), with its sky-blue cladding and breakfast bar is perfect for a quick omelette. **Maquis Benin** (Route de Togo; meals CFA700, ☽ breakfast, lunch & dinner) is good for brochettes before boarding a taxi on the way to Togo or Cotonou.

Drinking

The town centre is peppered with small bars, notably **Liberty's** (Rue d'Orgre), or **Maquia Cabana** (Rue Olivier de Montaguere) with its Caribbean rhythms. Close to the basilica is **La Carapace** (Rue F Colombani), an attractive bar in the courtyard of a decaying colonial building.

Getting There & Away

Bush taxis to Cotonou (CFA700, one hour) sometimes leave from the taxi stop on Rue van Vollenhoven but it's easier and quicker to get a *zem* (CFA200) to Carrefour Bénin where you can also catch taxis to Grand Popo (CFA600, one hour) and the Hilakondji border (CFA1000, 1½ hours).

GRAND POPO

Some 82km from Cotonou and 20km from the Togo border at Hilakondji, Grand Popo is a wonderful spot to spend a few tranquil days. The village is rather sleepy but has plenty going on at the weekend when Cotonou residents come to escape the big smoke. It's a perfect base to explore the Mono River, go for a long walk on the beach, and learn more about voodoo culture.

Sights & Activities

VILLA KARO

On the main street through the village is this Finnish-African **cultural centre** (☎ 22 43 03 58; www .villa-karo.org) with a small **gallery** (☽ 8-11am & 4-6pm Mon-Fri, 8-11am Sat) that runs great exhibitions. There's also a library with books in French, Finnish and English, a free open-air cinema from 8pm on Friday evening, and a free concert on the first Saturday of the month.

PIROGUE TRIPS

Local guide **Gaston** (☎ 95 85 74 40) organises excursions on the **Mono River** or to the **Bouche du Roy**, where the river meets the ocean. Trips on the river last about two hours and cost CFA5000 per person but those to the Bouche du Roy cost CFA45,000 as you need a motorised boat. Boats fit up to eight people and the trip lasts about six hours. Gaston works with Cotonou-based NGO **Nature Tropicale** (www .naturetropicale.com) on the protection of marine turtles and sometimes gets visitors involved.

Sleeping & Eating

Lion Bar (☎ 95 42 05 17; kabla_gildas@yahoo.fr; r CFA5000) Signposted down a track from the main street, you'll easily find this reggae land by following Bob Marley's languorous beats. It's the hideout of choice for Cotonou's expat beatniks and oozes peace and love: drinks flow at all hours of the day and night, parties are a staple, rooms are super funky and the shared facilities surprisingly clean. Meals cost CFA1500. It's right on the beach and you're free to pitch your tent for CFA2500.

Awalé Plage (☎ 22 43 01 17; www.hotel-benin-awale plage.com; Route de Togo; d with fan/air-con CFA14,000/22,000, f with fan/air-con CFA20,000/28,000; P ⊠ ♨) This lively resort, on the main coastal highway west of the Grand Popo turn-off, is good fun. The accommodation bungalows are impeccable, there is an excellent beach bar, the restaurant (meals CFA2500 to CFA6000) is good, and you can hire boogie boards. Staff are dressed as pirates and they throw monthly full-moon parties, with poolside live music.

ourpick **Auberge de Grand Popo** (☎ 22 43 00 47; www.hotels-benin.com; camping per person CFA1500, d CFA17,000-25,000; P) Right by Grand-Popo's seemingly endless beach, where the road stops and palm trees take over, the auberge (see also p123 for booking info) is one of the most atmospheric spots in Benin. Rooms are split between three beautiful colonial buildings and have retained their colonial charm with shutters instead of windows, fans, mosquito nets, white-washed walls and simple wooden furniture. The attractive terrace restaurant (meals CFA3800 to CFA9000) has an impressive menu and wine selection, with jazz or classical music in the background.

Shopping

Aux Beaux Arts (Main St; 🕑 10am-6pm), on your left as you drive down towards the Auberge, is a tiny shop selling highly original and beautifully crafted calabash lamps. They come in all shapes, colours and sizes. Prices start at CFA12,000 for small models and CFA25,000 for bigger ones.

Getting There & Away

From Cotonou, take a bush taxi from Gare de Jonquet (CFA1500, two hours) and have it drop you off at the Grand Popo junction on the main coastal highway, 20km east of the Togo border crossing at Hilakondji. The beach and village are 3.5km off the main road and are easily accessible via *zemi-john* (CFA250).

POSSOTOMÉ & LAKE AHÉMÉ

The fertile shores of Lake Ahémé are voodoo strongholds and even non-believers will admit there is something very spiritual and peaceful about this area. It's a wonderful place to spend a few days, particularly around Possotomé, the area's biggest village.

Possotomé itself is famous for its thermal springs, the country's primary source of mineral water. The springs themselves are an anticlimactic trickle but you can fill up your bottle for free (although note that the water comes out warm).

Lake Ahémé features Eco-Bénin's (see p97) flagship **trips and excursions** (www.lacaheme .com). Learn traditional fishing techniques with Lucien (so graceful when they do it, so comical when we try!) or go on a fascinating two-hour botanic journey with Justin to hear about local plants and their medicinal properties. There is half a dozen thematic circuits to choose from (from two hours to day trips, CFA3500 to CFA12,000), all run by delightful local guides. As with all Eco-Bénin backed initiatives, 25% of the fee you pay goes back to the community.

Sleeping & Eating

ourpick Camping de Possotomé (☎ 90 11 53 35; camping CFA2500) How does watching the sun rise over Lake Ahémé sound? This campsite, on an idyllic spot on the sandy lakeshores right in the centre of the village, is run by Eco-Bénin guides. It's basic (bucket showers and toilets) but very atmospheric. Justin, the cook, will whisk up African wonders for sustenance (omelette breakfast CFA1000, meals CFA2500) and you can hire a tent and mattress if you don't have your own.

Auberge Palais des Jeunes (☎ 95 96 12 87; d/tw CFA5000/7500) Simple but spotless rooms in the centre of the village. The *paillote* bar-restaurant (mains CFA1500) serves French and American cuisine and turns into a nightclub on Saturday night.

Hôtel Chez Théo (☎ 22 43 08 06; www.chez-theo .com; r CFA5000-20,000; P 🔀) In a stunning lakeside location, Chez Théo is divine. Rooms are impeccable, with African batiks decorating the walls. A path through a well-maintained garden leads to a great bar-restaurant (mains CFA3000) on a stilt platform with wondrous views. There is also a lounge area, with hammocks and comfy armchairs, perfect to read a book or fall asleep to the sound of splashing waves. Find Chez Théo about 600m north of the village on the lake's shore.

Village Club Ahémé (☎ 22 43 00 29; village aheme@yahoo.fr; r CFA15,000-25,000; P 🔀) This 20-room hotel on the water's edge is popular for seminars and conferences so it's often full. Facilities are good, if a little corporate-looking, and the beach is beautiful. Staff are friendly and can help you organise excursions around southern Benin. Meals are CFA5000 to CFA6500.

Getting There & Away

From the main coastal highway take the turn-off north to Lokossa (20km) and Comé (700m), from where a road heads east to Possotomé (18km). Taxis that plough the Hilakondji–Cotonou route will generally drop you off at the Comé turn-off, from where the only option to Possotomé is a *zem* (CFA1000).

ABOMEY
pop 114,600

The name is mythical, and not without reason: Abomey, 144km northwest of Cotonou in Fon country, was the capital of the fierce Dahomey Kingdom and a force colonial powers had to reckon with for centuries. Nowadays Abomey is a rather quiet place, although the numerous

BENIN

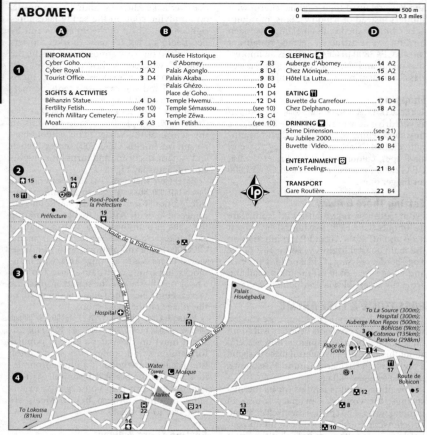

ABOMEY

0 ——————— 500 m
0 ——————— 0.3 miles

INFORMATION	
Cyber Goho............................1 D4	
Cyber Royal.........................2 A2	
Tourist Office......................3 D4	

SIGHTS & ACTIVITIES	
Béhanzin Statue....................4 D4	
Fertility Fetish...................(see 10)	
French Military Cemetery........5 D4	
Moat...................................6 A3	

Musée Historique	
d'Abomey.........................7 B3	
Palais Agonglo....................8 D4	
Palais Akaba.......................9 B3	
Palais Ghézo......................10 D4	
Place de Goho.....................11 D4	
Temple Hwemu...................12 D4	
Temple Sémassou...............(see 10)	
Temple Zéwa......................13 C4	
Twin Fetish.......................(see 10)	

SLEEPING	
Auberge d'Abomey.............14 A2	
Chez Monique....................15 A2	
Hôtel La Lutta....................16 B4	

EATING	
Buvette du Carrefour............17 D4	
Chez Delphano...................18 A2	

DRINKING	
5ème Dimension...............(see 21)	
Au Jubilee 2000.................19 A2	
Buvette Video....................20 B4	

ENTERTAINMENT	
Lem's Feelings....................21 B4	

TRANSPORT	
Gare Routière.....................22 B4	

Rond-Point de
la Préfecture

Préfecture

Route de la Préfecture

Palais
Houégbadja

Route du Palais Royal

Route de l'Hôpital

Hospital

Water
Tower   Mosque

Market

To Lokossa
(81km)

To La Source (300m);
Hospital (300m);
Auberge Mon Repos (500m);
Bohicon (9km);
Cotonou (135km);
Parakou (298km)

Place de
Goho

Route de
Bohicon

ruins and artefacts left behind by the kings of Dahomey make it clear it wasn't always so. In fact, the French were so fearful of Abomey's power that they deliberately designed the railway line between Cotonou and Parakou so that it would run 9km east of Abomey, in what is now Bohicon.

The legacy is that Bohicon has overshadowed Abomey commercially. Most buses and taxis stop in Bohicon, from where you have to connect for Abomey, and the area's main market is in Bohicon.

Information

You can get internet access at **Cyber Goho** (☎ 22 50 11 46; Place de Goho; per hr CFA500r; ☼ 7am-10pm Mon-Sat, from 10am Sun) and **Cyber Royal**

(☎ 22 50 16 85; Rond-Point de la Préfecture; per hr CFA500; ☼ 8am-10pm).

The newly opened **tourist office** (Office du Tourisme d'Abomey; ☎ 22 50 15 77; Place de Goho; ☼ 9am-1pm & 3-6pm Mon-Fri, 9am-4pm Sat) can provide information about Abomey's main sights and keeps a list of accredited guides (some of whom speak English or German).

All banks are in Bohicon and none of them change travellers cheques.

Sights

The kings of Dahomey were certainly a bloody lot, and their litany of slave-trading, human sacrifice and war is illustrated by the bold appliqué banners hanging in the **Musée Historique d'Abomey** (☎ 21 50 03 14;

GÉNÉRATION GOGOHOUN

They're aged 11 to 17; they live in two rural villages in southern Benin, Hlodo and Sagon, and they dream of being school teachers, doctors, custom officials, diplomats or artists. They could be your average Benin schoolchildren, but **Génération Gogohoun** (www.gogohoun.com) are instead embracing an all singing and dancing future, literally.

Gogohoun is a group of 30 school children who sing and dance about issues they encounter in everyday life such as emigration, AIDS, child labour or unemployment. If it doesn't sound all that upbeat, wait till you hear them sing (we dare you not to wiggle, clap or tap!) or even speak: 'You can do anything with culture,' they'll tell you. 'It's always difficult with work, but you must never give up.'

Their songs are all based on Adja rhythms, ancestral, rhythmic beats used in traditional ceremonies in the Zou and Mono areas. Originally called Agbahoun and characterised by its jerky buttock moves, it was adapted as a slightly less raunchy dance and renamed Gogohoun – although women in the villages will be keen to show you how it's *really* done!

Génération Gogohoun is the product of not-for-profit Franco-Beninese artists' group Cacy-Albatros-Tingo Gars, whose aim is to promote a better and fairer society through art. The message is definitely getting through and the Gogohoun write and choreograph all their songs themselves. Professional choreographers and stage directors funded by the NGO and occasional grants from international donors help them with the professional finish during school holidays.

In 2008, Génération Gogohoun did their first tour of Benin and played their show, Fiers d'Être Villageois (Proud to Be a Villager), in Boukoumbé, Parakou, Lokossa and the CCF in Cotonou. More tours and shows are planned in 2009 and 2010, grants allowing. Check the website for updates.

www.epa-premanet/abomey; Rue du Palais Royal; admission CFA1500; 9am-6pm). One of the tapestries shows Glélé using a dismembered leg to pound his enemy's head, another shows a head being crushed in a vice.

The same is true of the many exhibits on display in the museum, such as Ghézo's throne, which is mounted on the skulls of four enemies. The museum is housed in two palaces – all that remains of what was once one of the most impressive structures in West Africa, with a 4km perimeter and a 10m-high wall enclosing 44 hectares and a court of 10,000 people. There were originally 12 palaces, as every king built a new one.

The final king of Dahomey, Béhanzin, torched the place while fleeing the French in the late 19th century. His forces had been fighting the invaders using their own guns – bought from the Germans in Togo – but the French got the last laugh when they turned the palace into their administrative centre.

The bas-reliefs on the exterior, which illustrate the gory history of Dahomey, were a major factor in Unesco's decision to classify the structure as a World Heritage Site.

The admission fee includes a guide (only French is spoken), who will take about an hour to show you round the courtyards, ceremonial rooms and burial chambers. The tour finishes at the Centre des Artisans, where you can buy appliqué banners and bronze figurines made using the *cire perdue* method.

Tourist office–run **tours** (2hr tour for 1/2 people CFA3000/4000; day trip of the wider area CFA9500/15,000) will take you round the many other palaces, ruins and important sites of the Dahomeyan empire (see p114).

Sleeping

Accommodation in Abomey is skewed towards the bottom of the scale but there are some good, mellow choices.

Hôtel La Lutta (95 34 42 71; r CFA4000-4500) This rundown hotel is lost among a maze of sandy streets 300m southwest of the market – take a *zemi-john*. Run by local legend Da (Adjolohoun Jean-Constant), it's an eccentric establishment, with overgrown trellises in the garden and extraordinary plumbing in the rooms. Da prides himself in his *sauce arachide*; meals are CFA1600-2500. He's also a wonderful storyteller and can take you on a tour of Abomey (CFA4000).

Auberge Mon Repos (97 31 00 01; off Route de Bohicon; r CFA5500) Staff bend over backwards to welcome visitors to this respectable budget hotel, signposted on the right as you head towards Bohicon. Rooms are pocket-sized but clean and there is a decent restaurant (mains from CFA1200).

BENIN

THE ROUTE OF KINGS

Exploring Abomey's **Dahomey Trail** could provide the best insight you'll get into Benin's gothic history.

Tours generally start at the remains of the **moat** built in 1645 by the first king, Houégbadja. The moat, 42km around and 60m deep, gave Abomey its name – *abo* means 'moat' in Fon and *mey* means 'inside'.

Nearby is the **Palais Akaba**. Akaba goaded his enemy Dan by telling him he would build in his belly. In classic Dahomey style, Dan did indeed wind up with his belly cut open, buried beneath a tree outside the palace. The name of the kingdom thus mixes Dan's name with the words *ho* (belly) and *mey*.

At **Place de Goho**, the story leaps ahead to the late 19th century with the **Béhanzin statue**. He agreed to sign a treaty here with Colonel Dodds and the French forces – *goho* means 'meeting' – but his soldiers instead fired on them. The French casualties of the battle are in the **cemetery** nearby.

The ruins of the **Palais Ghézo** and **Temple Sémassou** show that life was just as tough for earlier rulers. When the baby Sémassou was born prematurely in the street, before he (the baby) died he prophesised that terrible events would befall the kingdom. After Glélé's henchmen disposed of the baby's body in a bush, Dahomey suffered 21 days of war, plague, and destruction. When Glélé discovered his henchmen's' disrespectful action, the oracle advised him to build a temple to encourage Sémassou's annunciation.

Among the many curiosities in this quarter are a **twin fetish** and a large white **fertility fetish**. Local women would straddle the latter's oversized erect penis to ensure fertility, until it was mysteriously snapped off.

The 18th-century **Palais Agonglo** is the best kept of Abomey's 12 palaces, with bas-reliefs inside listing the names and symbols of the great kings and chiefs. Agonglo also had an unusual son, the midget Hwemu. Saying he was returning to the voodoo world, Hwemu walked into the sea at Cotonou and turned into a fish. The oracle advised Agonglo to build **Temple Hwemu** for his son, whose name comes from the words *hwe* (fish) and *mu* (raw).

The palace of Ghézo, who had over 200 wives and established the army of female Amazon warriors, can still be seen, along with **Temple Zéwa**. The temple was built to appease the spirits of a traitorous group of Ghézo's wives, who he had executed by covering in red palm oil and leaving them for the ants to eat. Zéwa was the last to die.

---

ourpick Chez Monique (☎ 22 50 01 68; northwest of Rond-Point de la Préfecture; r CFA7500–12,000; **P**) This amazing pleasure garden, complete with antelopes, crocodiles, tortoises, monkeys, murals of Amazons, flower bushes and wood carvings, is a hive of activity. There is always something happening at Monique's and staff will treat you as if you were part of the family. The breezy rooms are impeccable too, with tiled floors and mosquito nets. Our only quibble is that the onsite restaurant is not that great; opt for a contemplative drink in the garden instead.

Auberge d'Abomey (☎ 97 89 87 25; www.hotels-benin.com; Rond-Point de la Préfecture; s/d with fan CFA11,500/12,500, with air-con CFA15,500/18,500; ❄) The latest addition to the reliable 'Auberge de…' chain (see also p123), with signature understated decor and a colonial feel. It's a small place with just a handful of rooms and a lovely garden: in winter, the half dozen mango trees lining the paths groan under the weight of ripe fruit.

Eating

There are plenty of food stalls around the market, otherwise try some of the *maquis* below.

ourpick Chez Delphano (☎ 93 64 02 40; meals CFA1600) If we had to choose a best *maquis* in Benin, this might be it. The owners, Pierre and Marguerite, are partial to a party and a bit of dancing, and if you're lucky, they might even show you some moves. Marguerite is a fine cook and prepares exquisite Beninese cuisine. She also learnt how to make *crêpes* from a Belgian guest, which she serves in the morning with fresh ground coffee and a mountain of fruit. Yum! Find Chez Delphano north of Rond-Point de la Préfecture, on the way to Chez Monique.

La Source (☎ 22 50 19 96; Route de Bohicon; meals CFA2500) As well as being one of the smarter bars in town, La Source serves hearty helpings of chicken and chips or couscous.

Buvette du Carrefour (Route de Bohicon) This is a popular and friendly place for a drink at all hours of the day. The *maquis* at the back gets busy at lunch time too and dishes out the usual pâte and sauce for a handful of francs.

Drinking

There are countless drinking holes in Abomey, the majority concentrated around the market and *gare routière*. Try **Buvette Video** with its multicoloured parasols and tiny courtyard or the lively **5ème Dimension** (Route de l'Hôpital). North of town, on Route de la Préfecture, **Au Jubilee 2000** is easy-going.

Entertainment

Lem's Feelings (Route de l'Hôpital; admission CFA2500; ☾ 10pm-dawn Fri & Sat) An animated crowd is found at this air-conditioned club, not far east of the market. Entry includes a drink.

Getting There & Away

Plenty of bush taxis depart from Cotonou (CFA2400, three hours), sometimes with a connection at Bohicon (9km east of Abomey).

Bush taxis (CFA300) and *zemi-johns* (CFA500) frequently run between Abomey and Bohicon. Vehicles going to Parakou leave frequently from the *gare routière* in Bohicon.

Inter City Lines (☎ 21 00 85 54) and **Confort Lines** (☎ 21 32 58 15) buses (from Cotonou to Parakou, Malanville and Natitingou) leave Cotonou at 7am daily. They stop in Bohicon (CFA2500, three hours) on the way so you can travel northwards in the morning or catch the Cotonou-bound services from Parakou, Malanville or Natitingou in the afternoon (ring to double check the time).

DASSA ZOUMÉ
pop 21,900

Dassa Zoumé, the 'city of 41 hills', is a wonderfully scenic part of the country. Awesome rock formations pepper the lush green landscape and the town's sleepy streets seem to mould themselves round these stony giants. Every August, Catholic pilgrims pay a visit to **La Grotte** (cave), where the Virgin Mary is said to have appeared. Behind the cave, and the imposing basilica, a short walk leads to the 13 shrines hidden among the rocks.

Slow internet is available at **La Maison des Tics** (per hr CFA600; ☾ 8am-11pm) on the main roundabout. There is a **Bank of Africa** (☾ 8-11.30am & 3-5.30pm Mon-Fri) in town, and plenty of cheap food stalls lining the main road.

Auberge La Cachette (☎ 22 53 02 11; r CFA5000), situated near the hospital, is a small, rustic hotel with no-frills rooms but a great little *maquis*-restaurant (meals CFA2000). The owners are charming too.

Auberge de Dassa Zoumé (☎ 22 53 00 98; www .hotels-benin.com; s/d with fan CFA11,500/12,500, with air-con CFA15,500/18,000; ☒) is the best hotel in town, and part of the Auberge chain (see also p123). It is opposite the *rond-point* (roundabout) on the main highway. The excellent restaurant (mains CFA3500) overlooks an ostrich farm and is a prime spot for spectacular sunsets.

Getting There & Away

The transport hub in Dassa is the main roundabout where you can catch bush taxis or buses north and south. You'll find bush taxis to/from Dassa Zoumé to Cotonou (CFA3000, four hours), Bohicon (CFA1500, 1½ hours) and Parakou (CFA3500, three hours).

Otherwise Inter City Lines and Confort Lines buses also stop there. Dassa is where the main north-south road splits, with one road continuing towards Natitingou and Burkina, the other towards Parakou and Niger.

THE NORTH

Northern Benin's arid, mountainous landscape is a world away from the south's beaches and lagoons but all the more attractive for it. It's all about the natural heritage around here – what with two fantastic wildlife parks and a mountain range – something that is obvious in the northerners' affection and pride for their land. It is ethnically more diverse than the south, and Islam is the main religion, but voodoo is still present.

PARAKOU
pop 198,000

Once a major slave-market town, Parakou now has a prosperous, busy atmosphere, with the most facilities you'll find in northern Benin.

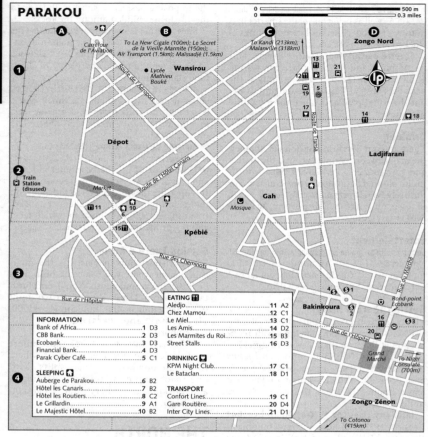

PARAKOU

INFORMATION	
Bank of Africa	1 D3
CBB Bank	2 D3
Ecobank	3 D3
Financial Bank	4 D3
Parak Cyber Café	5 C1

SLEEPING 🏠	
Auberge de Parakou	6 B2
Hôtel les Canaris	7 B2
Hôtel les Routiers	8 C2
Le Grillardin	9 A1
Le Majestic Hôtel	10 B2

EATING 🍴	
Aledjo	11 A2
Chez Mamou	12 C1
Le Miel	13 C1
Les Amis	14 D2
Les Marmites du Roi	15 B3
Street Stalls	16 D3

DRINKING 🍸	
KPM Night Club	17 C1
Le Bataclan	18 D1

TRANSPORT	
Confort Lines	19 C1
Gare Routière	20 D4
Inter City Lines	21 D1

There isn't much to keep you here, but with *buvettes* (small bars) and excellent *maquis* lining the town's dusty streets, Parakou makes a relaxing stop-over en route to the regional wildlife park of the W (see p123).

The town is quite spread out, with no obvious centre for restaurants or bars. Bus stops congregate north of town and there is a small cluster of hotels and *maquis* close to the now-disused train station, west of town. The *gare routière* and banks are in the southeast corner.

The **Bank of Africa** (Route de Transa) has a 24-hour ATM and there is internet at **Parak Cyber Café** (per hr CFA400; 🕙 9am-midnight).

Travellers continuing their journey north to Niger can get their visa at the consulate (see p124) if they don't already have one: the border at Malanville no longer issues them.

Sleeping

Hôtel les Canaris (☎ 23 61 11 69; off Route de l'Hôtel Canaris; r with fan/air-con CFA6500/9500; 🐟) Rooms at this long-standing budget establishment are nothing to write home about, but the management is friendly, it's clean and there are some great restaurants nearby.

ourpick Auberge de Parakou (☎ 23 61 03 05; www.hotels-benin.com; Route de l'Hôtel Canaris; s/d with fan CFA10,000/12,000, with air-con CFA14,000/16,000; P 🐟) This delightful auberge (see also p123) is great value for money with large, spotless rooms with tiled floors and mosquito nets. The lounge area with its pool table, library and patio is perfect to chill out in the evening and the excellent French restaurant serves a bargain three-course meal plus draught beer for just CFA4500.

Le Majestic Hôtel (☎ 23 61 34 85; www.lema jestichotel.com; Route de l'Hôtel Canaris; s/d with fan CFA12,500/14,500; with air-con from CFA22,500/24,500; ⚡) The closest thing you'll find to a boutique hotel in Benin, Le Majestic is a delightful three-storey villa with balconies and a pretty garden. The interior is similarly stylish with wrought-iron furniture and pretty fabrics. Top pick is room 208. Mains at the excellent restaurant cost CFA3500.

Le Grillardin (☎ 23 61 27 81; Carrefour de l'Aviation; r CFA21,500-29,500; ⚡ ⚡) You'll find this pretty establishment, with its L-shaped pool and carefully tended garden, north of town. Rooms are a little pricey but well appointed and quiet despite being near the main road.

Hôtel Les Routiers (☎ 23 61 04 01; Route de Transa; s/d from CFA26,000/28,000; Ⓟ ⚡ ⚡) This establishment, 500m north of the heart of town, has long been the most popular top-end hotel in Parakou. You can't help but relax by the green pool or in the exotic garden buzzing with parakeets. There's also a good, but expensive, French restaurant (*menu du jour* CFA8000, meals from CFA5000).

Eating

Aledjo (off Route de l'Hôtel Canaris; meals CFA500; ⏱ 7am-11pm) A typical 'point-and-choose' African canteen with a busy kitchen doling out huge servings of rice or *pâte* and sauces.

ourpick Le Secret de la Vieille Marmite (☎ 90 94 24 37; off Carrefour de l'Aviation; meals CFA1000) You can't miss 'the secret of the old cauldron' with its lively ambiance and bright-blue cladding. It does some of the best Beninese grub around; definitely one of our favourites.

Les Marmites du Roi (☎ 23 61 25 07; off Route de l'Hôtel Canaris; meals CFA3500-4000) This relatively upmarket *maquis* serves excellent African cuisine. You dine outdoors under a big patio; it's a shame it's all concrete and neon lights but focus on the food and you'll have a fine evening.

La New Cigale (☎ 97 89 11 98; off Carrefour de l'Aviation; meals CFA2500-4500) Pleasant restaurant serving pizza and French food.

Les Amis (☎ 23 10 05 37; off Route de Transa; meals CFA1500-3500; ⏱ closed Mon) This hip-hop-playing pizzeria attracts a young crowd to its covered garden and pool table. Great atmosphere and lovely staff.

QUICK EATS

Le Miel (☎ 23 61 00 67; Route de Transa; meals CFA1000-2500) This small grocery-shop-cum-bakery has a fab selection of cakes and vegetarian savouries such as cheese pasties, as well as yoghurts, biscuits and other basic essentials.

Chez Mamou (Route de Transa; meals CFA250; ⏱ from 7pm) Friendly *buvette* serving good, cheap food such as *wagassi* (cow's milk cheese) and macaroni.

There are plenty of street vendors around the *gare routière*.

Drinking

KPM Night Club (off Route de Transa) zooks the night away under tall teak trees. There is a BBQ stand loaded with fish and guinea fowl at the front if you're in need of sustenance.

Le Bataclan (off Route de Transa; admission Thu/Fri/Sat CFA1500/2500/4000; ⏱ Thu-Sat) is a Parakou favourite. The place fills up after midnight, especially on Saturday.

Le Secret de la Vieille Marmite is another good spot for a drink. Otherwise try the countless *buvettes* that line the roads.

Getting There & Away

BUSH TAXI, MINIBUS & BUS

From the *gare routière*, north of the Grand Marché, bush taxis and minibuses go regularly to Cotonou (CFA7100, eight hours), Kandi (CFA3300, 3½ hours), Malanville (CFA4500, five hours) and Djougou (CFA2500, two hours).

Inter City Lines (☎ 23 10 04 75; www.intercity lines.com; off Route de Transa) has two daily services to/from Cotonou (CFA7500, 7½ hours). Buses leave Cotonou at 7am and Parakou at 6.30am and 2pm (for the bus coming down from Malanville). **Confort Lines** (☎ 95 86 67 20; Route de Transa) also runs a daily service.

Aïr Transport (☎ 93 96 00 63) and **Maïssadjé** (☎ 90 03 38 04) run buses between Niamey and Parakou (see p127). The depots are about 1.5km north of town on the road to Niger. Ask a *zem*.

DJOUGOU

Djougou is a lively crossroads town 134km northwest of Parakou, bustling with people passing through on the way to Natitingou and Togo. It's well-known for its skilled craftsmen (weavers, blacksmiths, etc) but there's not much to keep you there.

The Tanéka villages around Badjoudè, near the Togo border, are very picturesque and home to thriving voodoo communities. **Bénin Aventure** (opposite) can organise tours of the area.

There is a Bank of Africa and an Ecobank, but surprisingly, no internet connection.

Auberge de l'Espace Tissage (☎ 97 58 91 93; Quartier Yaloua; r CFA5000) is a basic but spotless little auberge run by the local women's weaving cooperative. The six rooms share two impeccable bathrooms and toilets, and there is a nice communal area where you can chat to some of the women. You can also watch them at work: it takes one to two weeks to produce the beautiful fabrics which are then turned into outfits, bed or table linen (for sale in the adjoining shop). It's about 1.5km east of the centre. Ask a *zem*.

Motel du Lac (☎ 23 80 15 48; molacdjo@yahoo.fr; Route de Savalou; s/d with fan CFA12,000/15,000, with air-con CFA15,000/18,000; **P** 🞂) is on a peaceful spot near a lake, 3km out of town on the road to Cotonou, and is an unexpected retreat. Rooms are a tad over-priced but the views, breeze, lovely garden and atmospheric bar-restaurant (serving tasty French cuisine, with mains around CFA3500) make it worthwhile.

For eating, try **Le Quasar** (☎ 23 80 13 30; meals from CFA2500), an upmarket *maquis* with a slightly grandiose dining room but slow service, or **Buvette Le Passage** (meal CFA700), an open-air outfit under a huge mango tree, 50m down from Le Quasar.

Good nightspots include the rooftop bar **Le Baron** (🌣 from 6pm), west of town, which also has a nightclub on Saturday night.

If travelling to Kara, there are connections to the border (CFA1200, one hour). Bush taxis travelling between Parakou (CFA2500, two hours), and Natitingou (CFA1500, one hour) generally stop in Djougou. **Inter City Lines** or **Confort Lines** buses between Cotonou and Natitingou (see p120) also stop in Djougou, opposite Ciné Sabari.

NATITINGOU
pop 75,600

Affectionately known as Nati, Natitingou is the most vibrant town in northern Benin. About 200km northwest of Parakou and pleasantly located at an altitude of 440m in the Atakora mountains, it thrived under the influence of President Kérékou, who was born here.

Nowadays, it is a favourite among travellers with its easygoing attitude and per-fect location for exploring the Pendjari and the Atakora.

Orientation

Natitingou is split in half by the *goudron*, the main sealed road that heads north to Burkina Faso and south to Cotonou, also referred to as Route Inter-État. A maze of unpaved *vons* radi-

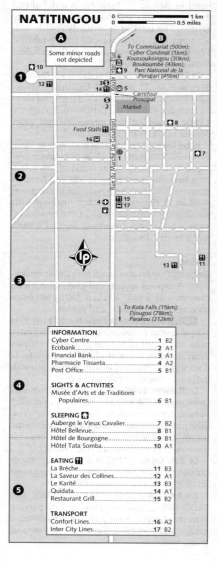

NATITINGOU

Some minor roads not depicted

To Commisariat (500m);
Cyber Condinat (1km);
Koussoukoingou (30km);
Boukoumbé (43km);
Parc National de la
Pendjari (45km)

Carrefour
Principal
Market

Food Stalls

To Kota Falls (15km);
Djougou (78km);
Parakou (212km)

ate from it; most have no name which makes getting around difficult. *Zems* are generally the way forward.

Information

You'll find basic information about the town on www.natitingou.org. For information about tours and excursions in the wider area, including the Atakora and the Parc National de la Pendjari (see p121), contact the Natitingou-based **ourpick** Bénin Aventure (☎ 23 02 00 17; www .beninaventure.com), a highly-recommended company run by three excellent local guides and a young French entrepreneur. The Pendjari authorities were also planning to open an information kiosk at Hôtel Bourgogne (right) at the time of writing.

Internet connection is available at **Cyber Condinat** (☎ 97 39 75 04; Route Inter-État; per hr CFA400; ⏲ 8am-11pm Mon-Sat, 10am-10pm Sun) north of town and **Cyber Centre** (☎ 98 77 29 37; Rue du Marché; per hr CFA400; ⏲ 8.30am-11pm Mon-Sat, from 10am Sun) in the centre.

There are a couple of banks in Nati: **Ecobank** (Rue du Marché; ⏲ 8am-6pm Mon-Fri, 9am-3pm Sat) at the main junction, and **Financial Bank** (Route Inter-État; ⏲ 8am-noon & 3-5pm Mon-Fri), a block north of the junction. Both change cash and travellers cheques but neither accepts credit cards.

The **Pharmacie Tissanta** (Rue du Marché; ☎ 23 82 10 13), at the southern end of town, is open 24/7. For more serious medical emergencies, **Hôpital St Jean de Dieu** in Tanguiéta is Italian-run and has a good reputation.

Sights & Activities

The **Musée d'Arts et de Traditions Populaires** (☎ 23 02 00 53; Route Inter-État; admission CFA1000; ⏲ 8am-12.30pm & 3.30-6.30pm Mon-Fri, 9am-noon & 4-6.30pm Sat & Sun), housed in a colonial building built by slaves at the beginning of the 20th century, gives an overview of life in Somba communities. The exhibition includes various musical instruments, jewellery, crowns and artefacts. Most interesting is the habitat room, which has models of the different types of *tata somba* (Somba houses; see p120).

You could also visit the **Kota Falls** (admission CFA400), 15km southeast of Natitingou, off the main highway. The walk down takes you through scenic woods and across a maze of streams. You can swim in the pool at the bottom of the falls or just sit down and read in the cool shade of the undergrowth. A great spot for a picnic.

Sleeping

Auberge Le Vieux Cavalier (☎ 23 82 13 24; fan/air-con r CFA6500/9000; ⊠) Water sometimes struggles to make it all the way to your bathroom at the top of the hill, but this is the only quibble about this otherwise great budget option in Nati. Rooms are small but clean with mozzie nets on the beds, and there is a funky courtyard decorated with murals and sculptures where the young and friendly staff often hang out.

Hôtel Bellevue (☎ 23 82 13 36; www.hotel-bellevue-benin.com; s/d with fan CFA8000/9000, with air-con CFA12,000/14,000; P ⊠ 💻) Perched at the top of a hill in a rambling garden, the Bellevue is a charming collection of sweet bungalows and *paillotes*. Myriam, the formidable owner, runs a tight ship and rooms are spotless, as is the food in the restaurant (much of which comes from her veggie garden). Myriam also makes jewellery, for sale at the reception, and there is a reliable, if expensive, internet connection (per hr CFA1000).

Hôtel de Bourgogne (☎ /fax 23 82 22 40; www .natitingou.org/bourgogne; Route Inter-État; s/d with fan CFA10,000/13,000, with air-con from CFA15,000/18,000; P ⊠) This delightful hotel will feel like a home away from home. Thérèse Oudot, the owner, is French honorary vice-consul and has been in Benin since the early '90s. She is a mine of information and wonderfully welcoming. Rooms were being repainted in warm colours at the time of writing and the restaurant is hands-down the best in town. For a refreshing afternoon treat in the atmospheric lounge, try the home-made fruit juices.

Hôtel Tata Somba (☎ 23 82 11 24; www.hoteltata somba.com; off Route Inter-État; r CFA30,000; P ⊠ 🖫) A regional institution, the hotel is a large, pink version of a *tata somba* house. The pretty swimming pool (nonguests CFA3000) takes centre-stage in the courtyard, with restaurant tables laid out in the shade (*menu du jour* is CFA6500). Rooms are everything you would expect from a high-end hotel, except for the bathrooms, painted in a scary shade of blue and rather dark as a result. The hotel can set up trips to the Pendjari.

Eating & Drinking

Natitingou has a fine array of places to grab a beer and a bite. Among the great *maquis* is **Le Karité** (mains from CFA500; ⏲ lunch only), world champion of *igname pilé* (pounded yam) and lost in a maze of alleyways on the eastern side of town (ask a *zem* to take you there). Also

THE SOMBA

Commonly referred to as the Somba, the Betamaribé people are concentrated to the southwest of Natitingou in the plains of Boukoumbé on the Togo border. They live in the middle of their cultivated fields, rather than together in villages, so their compounds are scattered over the countryside. This custom is a reflection of their fierce individuality, which has seen them resist both Dahomey slave hunters and the advance of Christianity and Islam.

The Dutamari-speaking Betamaribé's principle religion is animism – as seen in the rags and bottles they hang from the trees. Once famous for their nudity, they began wearing clothes in the 1970s.

What's most fascinating about the Betamaribé is their *tata somba* houses – round, tiered huts that look like miniature forts with clay turrets and thatched spires. There are some 10 types of them, including the *otchaou*, which are the same as the houses built by the Betamaribé's Tamberma relations nearby in Togo (see the boxed text, p797). The ground floor of a house is mostly reserved for livestock and defence mechanisms. A stepladder leads from the kitchen to the roof terrace, where there are sleeping quarters and grain stores.

good is **La Saveur des Collines** (☎ 90 66 55 18; mains CFA500-1500; ⓨ Mon-Sat), a no-frills canteen with an outdoor kitchen popular with the locals.

The nameless **restaurant grill** (☎ 95 28 37 58; mains CFA2000-4500) opposite the Pharmacie Tissanta is well-known in town for its penchant for blues and soul music. But as well as good tunes, there is excellent food such as grilled *capitaine* (Nile Perch) with yam fries or tasty pizzas.

A strong contender for most culturally enlightening bar-restaurant in the world, and popular with local aid workers, is **La Brèche** (☎ 90 92 43 20; menu du jour CFA4000), a *tata somba* house with views of the Atakora mountains. Book ahead for the house speciality: the *pierrade* (a hot stone surface on which you cook thin strips of meat).

Food stalls line Rue du Marché and there is a supermarket, **Quidata** (ⓨ 8.30am-1pm & 3.30-8pm Mon-Sat, 9am-2pm Sun), opposite Financial Bank.

Getting There & Away

From the *gare routière* on the main road, bush taxis and minibuses go to Parakou (CFA3500, five hours) via Djougou (CFA1500; 1½ hours), Boukoumbé (CFA2000, two hours) via Koussoukoingou (CFA1500, 1½ hours), and Porga on the Burkina border (CFA3000, 2½ hours) via Tanguiéta (CFA1500, one hour).

Bus services linking Nati and Cotonou (CFA8500, eight hours) include **Inter City Lines** (☎ 23 03 01 06; www.intercity-lines.com; Rue du Marché), opposite Pharmacie Tissanta, and **Confort Lines** (☎ 95 86 67 02; off Rue du Marché). Note that all buses arriving from Cotonou drop passengers off outside the post office. Cotonou-bound services however, pick passengers up at their respective offices. Services leave at 7am; book ahead or arrive early on the day.

THE ATAKORA REGION

On the Togo border, 43km southwest of Natitingou, **Boukoumbé** is the capital of Somba country, at the heart of the Atakora mountains. The drive there is stunning, bumping along a red *piste* (rough track) past corn fields and huge baobab trees. Boukoumbé itself is rather sleepy and uneventful, save for its lively market every four days, when *tchoukoutou* (sorghum beer, an acquired taste) gingerly flows. If you're crossing the border here, make sure you get your passport stamped at the commissariat (police station) as there is no border check point.

About 15km before Boukoumbé, you'll pass the mountain village of **Koussoukoingou** (also known as Koussou-Kovangou), famous for its stunning location and breathtaking views of the Atakora range.

Eco-tourism association **Perle de l'Atakora** (Pearl of the Atakora; ☎ 97 44 28 61; www.ecobenin.org /koussoukoingou), set up by Eco-Bénin (see the boxed text, p97) offers guided walks in the area (2½ to 3½ hours cost from CFA2000 to CFA4000) taking in local sights such as the famous *tata* houses (see above). You can also arrange to spend the night at a *tata* (CFA4500 per person including an evening meal). As with all Eco-Bénin projects, about 20% of what you pay goes back to the community.

Getting to the Atakora is best with your own transport, but bush taxis do ply the dusty *piste* between Nati and Boukoumbé (CFA2000, two hours). They're most frequent on Boukoumbé market day. Otherwise, *zemi-johns* (CFA5000, three hours) will take you: it's an exhilarating ride amid such a stunning landscape, although very dusty and tiring.

PARC NATIONAL DE LA PENDJARI

Amid the majestic landscape of the Atakora's rugged cliffs and wooded savannah live lions, cheetahs, leopards, elephants, baboons, hippos, a myriad of birds and countless antelopes. The 275,000-hectare **Pendjari National Park** (www.pendjari.net; admission per person CFA10,000, per vehicle CFA3000), 100km north of Natitingou, is the wildlife park *par excellence* in this part of West Africa.

The best viewing time is near the end of the dry season when animals start to hover around water holes, but the park is open year-round.

It adjoins the Parc National d'Arli in Burkina Faso and the Parc Regional du W, which, together, form the WAP (W, Arli, Pendjari) wildlife complex.

The park authorities have done tremendous work to promote responsible and quality tourism at Pendjari. Guides are now assessed every two years and given an A or B grade reflecting their level of expertise. The list of accredited guides can be found on the park's website, at park entrances and in Nati's better hotels. You stand a much better chance of seeing animals and learning about wildlife by sticking with these professional guides.

For more information, you can also drop in at the park's friendly **office** (☎ 23 83 00 85; www.pendjari.net) in Tanguiéta or buy the excellent

PARC NATIONAL DE LA PENDJARI & PARC NATIONAL D'ARLI

0 ─── 50 km
0 ─── 30 miles

To Kantchari (70km)
Diapaga
NIGER
BURKINA FASO
Parc Regional du W
Namounou
Tansarga
Koudou Falls
Campement des Chutes de Koudou
To Fada N'Gourma (60km)
Logobou
Kondio
Sampeto Park Entrance
Bigou
Parc National d'Arli
Arli
Koaba
Kérémou
BURKINA FASO
Tambarga
Pont d'Arli
Hôtel de la Pendjari
Zone Cynégétique (Buffer Zone)
Banikoara
Mare Yangouali
To Parc Régional du W Office; Kandi (69km)
Pama
Tindangou
Parc National de la Pendjari
Piste des Éléphants
Porga; Park Entrance
Zone Cynégétique (Buffer Zone)
Park Entrance
Batia
Relais de Tanongou
River
Mékrou
BENIN
Dassari
Tanongou Falls
Hôtel Baobab
Pendjari
Tanguiéta; Hôpital St Jean de Dieu; Parc National de la Pendjari Office
TOGO
To Natitingou (10km)

Guide Pratique de la Pendjari (CFA2000), from bookshops in Cotonou (see p98) or at park entrances.

Sleeping & Eating

Many visitors stay in Natitingou and make excursions from there, but you'll have a better chance of seeing animals if you stay at the park itself. For the rough and ready, **camping** is allowed at Mare Yangouali and Pont d'Arli. Guides will show you where.

More comfortable is **Hôtel de la Pendjari** (☎ 23 82 11 24; www.hoteltatasomba.com; r with fan/air con CFA21,000/29,000; ⊙ 15 Dec-31 Jul; ✗ ☒) at the heart of the park. Rooms are simple but adequate; there is an atmospheric bar-restaurant under a huge central *paillote* (meals CFA6000) and amazingly, a swimming pool.

On the park's periphery, **Relais de Tanongou** (☎ 23 82 11 24; www.hoteltatasomba.com; r CFA7000-10,000; ⊙ 1 Dec-31 May), next to the **Tanongou Falls**, is well located for an early-morning walk and swim. The spacious bungalows have a bathroom behind a dividing wall. Meals are CFA4000.

Spend a night with local villagers in Tanongou through **Eco-Bénin** (p97; s incl evening meal CFA4000-4500) who also offer a programme of **walks** (2-4hr CFA1000-4000) in the area.

In Tanguiéta, **Hôtel Baobab** (☎ 23 83 02 25; camping per person CFA1500, r with fan/air-con CFA6500/13,500; ℗ ✗) is popular with travellers but theft is an issue because of its out-of-town location. Meals are CFA5000.

Both the Pendjari and the Relais must be booked in advance because of their remoteness. You may be able to negotiate special rates at the very beginning and end of the season.

Getting There & Away

The main entrances to Pendjari are roughly 100km north of Natitingou. To get to the park from Natitingou, take the *goudron* (bitumen road) 50km north to Tanguiéta. From there, you can either head further north to Porga, 47km north on a good sealed road, or turn east and take the good *piste* to Batia, via Tanongou, 41km from Tanguiéta.

As hiking is not permitted in the park, travellers without vehicles could try to team up with other parties at hotels in Natitingou. Otherwise, many of the park's guides have their own vehicle, which you can rent. **Bénin Aventure** (☎ 23 02 00 17; www.beninaventure.com) rents 4WD vehicles for CFA75,000 a day (for up to four people) including a chauffeur-guide (A-rated by the park) and fuel.

Travel agencies such as Point Afrique, the 'Auberge de' chain (see opposite) and a handful of Western travel operators also offer tours of the park.

KANDI & AROUND

Kandi, 213km north of Parakou on the way to Niger, is the nearest town to Parc Régional du W (see opposite). The town itself doesn't have much in the way of sights, but it's a good base to visit the area.

The village of **Alfakoara**, 40km north of Kandi and on the edge of the park, is a good alternative for those who don't have the time or resources (financial and logistical) for an extensive tour of the W. Elephants have used the pond at Alfakoara since time immemorial and the village has an unusual track record of peaceful cohabitation with the tusked giants. You can easily access the **viewing platform** (admission CFA2500) from the main road and there is a good chance you'll see elephants in the dry season. Eco-Bénin has also set up **walking tours** (www.tour-communautaire-parcw.net; 1½-2½hr CFA2800-3300) from Alfakoara to learn more about Mokollé and Peul (Fula) traditions.

Sleeping & Eating

Auberge La Rencontre (☎ 23 63 01 76; r incl breakfast with fan/air-con CFA7500/14,500; ✗) The rooms are stuffy and the welcome lacklustre, but the rooftop restaurant (*menu du jour* CFA4500) is a nice spot to chill out.

Auberge de Kandi (☎ 23 63 02 43; camping per person CFA2500, d with fan/air-con CFA11,000/17,000; ✗) This auberge (see opposite for booking info) 2km north of Kandi has spacious but relatively bare rooms, and a delightful garden with frogs hopping about and birds singing their heart out. The French restaurant (meals CFA3800 to CFA4000) is the best in town.

For cheap *maquis* grub, try **Maquis C'est Ça Même** (Route de Ndali; meals CFA1000), a little turquoise number south of town, with a good vibe. **Maquis AEFI** (meals CFA800) on the southern roundabout, is a favourite nightspot among the locals with dancing under the stars and a kitchen that serves decent *pâte noire* and *wagassi* cheese as well as cold beers.

Getting There & Away

From Parakou, bush taxis head north to Kandi (CFA3300, 3½ hours). Inter City Lines buses between Malanville and Cotonou also stop in Kandi so you can head south early in the morning or to Malanville in the early evening.

For Alfakoara, catch a ride with a bush taxi heading north (CFA1000, one hour).

PARC REGIONAL DU W

Named after the W-shaped bend of the Niger River at the heart of the park, **Parc Regional du W** (www.parc-w.net; admission CFA10,000 plus per vehicle CFA3000; ☺ 15 Dec-15 Jun) covers 10,242 sq km in Burkina Faso, Niger and Benin, where the largest section of the park is. It was one of the first Unesco-recognised biospheres worldwide. You may see several species of cats and antelopes, buffalos, hippos, crocodiles and elephants.

Although W is twice as large as Pendjari, it has traditionally been the less popular park, partly because the latter has better access and infrastructure. Most of the tracks inside the park are still only passable during the dry season and remain rough. Access however, is improving: the road to Banikoara, 69km northwest of Kandi, is now sealed, leaving just 45km of good *piste* (track) to the park's entrance in Sampéto. The *piste* from Alfakoara has also been upgraded to a smooth strip of dirt rather than an overgrown, rock-ridden track following the construction of a new bridge over the River Alibori, which means a shorter drive to access the park from Kandi.

Visitors need their own 4WD and a guide (CFA3000-5000 per day). For the latter as well as more information about the park (including maps, camping possibilities and info on the park's fauna), contact the resourceful Kandi-based **Parc Regional du W office** (☎ 23 63 00 80; www.parc-w.net; ☺ 8am-12.30pm & 3pm-late Mon-Sat), about 1km south of town off the main road.

The best facility to stay at the park is the beautiful ourpick **Campement des Chutes de Koudou** (☎ 23 63 02 43; d CFA20,000). A night here should fulfil every *Out of Africa* fantasy: accommodation consists of luxury, semi-permanent tents, with a proper bed and a basic but elegant alfresco bathroom at the back. The Koudou falls are a prime drinking spot for local wildlife, so the *campement* (guest house) is one of the best places to watch animals in the park. And just in case you'd forgotten yours, the bar-restaurant has a pair of binoculars on standby. You can also pitch your own tent for CFA3000. Meals are CFA6000.

The park has three entrances in Benin: at Sampéto, near Banikoara, Alfakoara, and Kofonou, near Karimama on the Niger border.

MALANVILLE

This dusty town is in the far north on the Niger border, considerably closer to Niamey than it is to Cotonou, 733km away. Market day, held on Friday and Saturday, is a who's who of West African peoples, attracting traders from Togo, Nigeria, Burkina Faso and Niger. The town is busy every day of the week though, and you'll regularly see Fula people leading herds of hundreds of sheep across town.

Rose des Sables (☎ 23 67 01 25; r with fan & shared facilities CFA7000, with air-con & ensuite from CFA10,000; ❄), one kilometre south of town, is a cheap but not cheerful hotel. Bedbugs colonise the beds and the staff are a bit clueless but it's the only option if you're on a budget. Meals are CFA2500.

La Sota (☎ 97 64 97 48; s/d with fan CFA18,000/19,500, with air-con CFA22,000/25,000; P ❄ ☎) is run by the same management as Le Majestic in Parakou, and is an unexpected and great-value place. Rooms are a little underwhelming for the price but the facilities are tops, with a TV lounge, a good restaurant (meals CFA5000), a garden *maquis* outside and a great pool. The hotel is located 2km south of town on the banks of the River Sota.

Near the market, **Sous les Neems** (meals CFA500) serves *wagassi* (cow's milk cheese), pâté and cold beers. *Buvettes* and food stalls, selling everything from mashed yam to omelettes, line the main road through town.

Malanville is well connected with Parakou by bush taxi (CFA4500, five hours). Inter City Lines runs a daily service between Malanville and Cotonou (CFA11,000, 12 hours). Niger buses Rimbo and SNTV travel between Cotonou and Niamey via Malanville, but they are often full up (see p127). A *zemi-john* to Gaya in Niger, where you can get taxis to Niamey, is about CFA1200.

BENIN DIRECTORY

ACCOMMODATION

Accommodation in Benin is good value. Basic rooms with fan cost as little as CFA5000, while comfortable air-conditioned midrange rooms

BENIN

hover around CFA20,000. Top-end prices range from CFA35,000 outside Cotonou to over CFA100,000 in the economic capital.

The 'Auberge de' chain has consistently good hotels in Abomey, Dassa Zoumé, Grand Popo, Kandi, Koudou, Parakou and Savalou. Central reservations can be made on ☎ 21 31 38 62 or www.hotels-benin.com.

ACTIVITIES

The beaches along the coast are not safe for swimming because of strong currents. Stick to hotel swimming pools or the lagoon where you can also canoe (see p104 and p109).

Eco-Bénin (p97) runs guided themed walks in four locations across the country as well as pirogue and cycling excursions around Lake Ahémé (p111).

BOOKS

The Viceroy of Ouidah, by Bruce Chatwin, is a biographical sketch of the notorious Brazilian slave trader Francisco da Silva and how he and the kings of Dahomey built the trade. The vivid novella begins with a 20th-century reunion of the da Silva clan and moves back to the original Afro-Brazilian himself via his descendents, their dreams and disappointments.

Instruments of Darkness, by Robert Wilson, is the debut of this award-winning thriller writer, following an English 'fixer' through the Cotonou underworld as he searches for a fellow expat who has mysteriously disappeared.

Show Me the Magic, by Annie Caulfield, is a slightly glib but entertaining account by this English comic writer (who collaborated with the comedian Lenny Henry) about travelling around Benin in a taxi. She and her driver repeated the journey with Spice Girl Mel B for the documentary *Mel B Vodou Princess.*

BUSINESS HOURS

Businesses are open from 8am to 12.30pm and 3pm to 6.30pm Monday to Friday. Some banks are now open through lunch time and most open from 9am to 3pm on Saturday. Shops are open from 8am to noon and 3pm to 7pm Monday to Saturday and sometimes also on Sunday morning.

Midrange and upmarket restaurants are generally open for lunch and dinner (unless otherwise noted). Cafes and *maquis* tend to

---

PRACTICALITIES

- Cotonou's daily papers include *La Nation* and *Le Matinal*.
- Foreign newspapers and magazines can occasionally be found at newspaper stands.
- The state-owned ORTB broadcasts on the radio in French and local languages.
- Cotonou has some 15 commercial stations, including Radio Afrique (101.7MHZ).
- LC2 and Golfé Télévision are the most popular commercial channels, while ORTB runs one channel. None are particularly good.
- The electricity supply is temperamental and network cuts are also frequent.
- Benin uses the metric system.

---

be more informal and generally serve food throughout the day.

COURSES

Learn Fon in Cotonou (p100).

DANGERS & ANNOYANCES

Cotonou has its fair share of traffic accidents and muggings (see p100) so be careful, particularly at night (take a taxi). In Ouidah, avoid the roads to and along the coast.

There is little street lighting so bring a torch if you don't want to trip on the country's numerous dirt tracks.

If you are white, children – but also adults – will shout 'Yovo! Yovo!' (meaning white person) ad nauseam. It's normally harmless but tiresome, although travellers have reported being intimidated by the sheer scale of the phenomenon. Abomey is particularly bad.

EMBASSIES & CONSULATES
Embassies & Consulates in Benin

France Embassy (☎ 21 30 02 25; Route de l'Aéroport, Cotonou); Consulate (☎ 21 31 26 38; Rue 651A, Cotonou)
Germany (☎ 21 31 56 93; Ave Jean Paul II, Cotonou; ☻ 9am-noon)
Ghana (☎ 21 30 07 46; off Route de l'Aéroport, Cotonou; ☻ 8am-2pm)
Niger Embassy (☎ 21 31 56 65; Rue 651A, Cotonou; ☻ 8am-4pm Mon-Thu, to 1pm Fri); Consulate (☎ 23 61 28 27; Route de l'Hôpital, Parakou; ☻ 8am-1pm & 3.30-6.30pm Mon-Fri)

Nigeria (☎ 21 30 11 42; Blvd de la Marina, Cotonou; ⏰ 10-11.30am)
UK (☎ 21 30 12 74; Haie Vive) Officially, British Nationals must deal with the British Deputy High Commission in Lagos (p661). However, the Community Liaison Officer for the British community in Benin, Pauline Collins, based at the English International School, can be of some help.
USA (☎ 21 30 06 50; cotonou.usembassy.gov; Rue Caporal Bernard Anani, Cotonou)

FESTIVALS & EVENTS
Apart from the colourful annual Muslim celebrations in the northern towns – Djougou and Natitingou are especially good places to see them – the main event is the Voodoo Festival, held in Ouidah on 10 January (see p109).

Every four years or so, in late October or early November, there is the coming-of-age 'whipping ceremony' in Boukoumbé, which seems to go on until the young men are satisfied that they have literally beaten each other black and blue.

There are frequent voodoo celebrations in Ouidah, Abomey and on the shores of Lake Ahémé.

HOLIDAYS
Public holidays include the following:
New Year's Day 1 January
Vodoun 10 January
Easter Monday March/April
Labour Day 1 May
Ascension Thursday May
Pentecost Monday May
Independence Day 1 August
Assumption 15 August
Armed Forces Day 26 October
All Saints 1 November
Christmas 25 December

Benin also celebrates Muslim holidays. See p815 for more details.

INTERNET ACCESS
Internet is widely available across Benin, and at reasonable prices (per hour CFA200-500). The only town of any size that doesn't have any internet access is Djougou. Speed and reliability are another matter: network and electricity cuts are frequent and connections are slow.

INTERNET RESOURCES
Benin Tourisme (http://benintourisme.com) The best website, with highlights and lots of practical information (in English, French, Spanish and German).

République du Bénin (www.gouv.bj) The country's official portal (in French only).
Ville de Cotonou (www.cotonou-benin.com) Cotonou's main online resource, with news and travel info.

MAPS
The best map by far is IGN's 1:600,000 *République du Bénin Carte Touristique*. With good country detail and insert city maps of Porto Novo and Cotonou, it costs about CFA7500 in Cotonou bookshops.

MONEY
The unit of currency in Benin is the West Africa CFA (Communauté Financière Africaine) franc. All banks in the country change cash although outside of Cotonou, banks will only change euros. Cash advances against credit cards are possible at major banks in the capital. Banque Atlantique now accepts MasterCard.

Benin's neighbours all use CFAs apart from Nigeria, where the currency is the Naira. There is no official way to get hold of Naira in Benin but Cotonou has a healthy black market around the Jonquet district and Gare du Dantokpa.

Travellers cheques can be changed in Cotonou and Natitingou.

PHOTOGRAPHY & VIDEO
A photo permit is not required, but be careful when taking shots of cultural and religious buildings and ceremonies. Rules are not clear-cut, so it's best to ask first. A *cadeau* (gift) may be requested. For general information see p821.

TELEPHONE
International calls can be made at telecom offices and private telephone agencies throughout Benin. The cost per minute varies hugely but allow CFA400 per minute to Europe and North America, CFA600 to Asia.

Mobile phones are now a staple and the network coverage is surprisingly good. MTN is the main operator. A SIM card costs CFA2000, local SMS CFA50, international SMS CFA75 and international calls CFA125 per minute. Top-up vouchers worth anything from CFA500 to CFA25,000 are readily available.

TOURIST INFORMATION
There is a lacklustre tourist office in Cotonou (p98). The offices of both wildlife parks

(p121 and p123) can also help, as can Eco-Bénin (p97) and Bénin Aventure (p119).

VISAS

Visas are required for all travellers except nationals of the Ecowas (Economic Commission of West African States). If flying into Cotonou you will require a visa before arrival. A 30-day, single-entry visa costs UK£55 from the Beninese consulate in the UK; the embassy in the USA charges $100.

If crossing overland, it's far easier to get a visa at the border, where the 24-hour posts issue 48-hour, single-entry transit visas (CFA10,000).

You can then obtain a 30-day, single- or multiple-entry visa (CFA12,000) in Cotonou. The **Direction Emigration Immigration** (☎ 21 31 42 13; Ave Jan Paul II, Cotonou; ☺ 8am-12.30pm & 3-6.30pm) accepts applications between 8am and 11am and 3pm to 5pm Monday to Friday. These can be collected between 11am and 12.30pm or between 5pm and 6.30pm two days later. You will need one passport photo.

Visas For Onward Travel

For onward travel to Burkina Faso and Côte d'Ivoire, the French consulate issues three-month visas (CFA20,000) and transit visas (CFA6000) in 24 to 48 hours, with two photos required.

GHANA

The embassy no longer issues visas (although the Ghana embassy in Togo does – see p798) and requests travellers obtain visas in their home country before travelling.

NIGER

You must obtain a visa before travelling to Niger as border officials at the Malanville/Gaya crossing no longer issue visas. The embassy in Cotonou or the consulate in Parakou (p124) issue 30-day visas. They cost CFA22,500 and you'll need two photos. Officials say you should allow three to four working days but travellers have reported speedier processing.

NIGERIA

The Nigerian embassy issues only two-day transit visas to travellers with a Nigerian embassy in their home country. You need two photos, along with photocopies of your passport and, if you have one, your ticket

for onward travel from Nigeria. Fees vary according to nationality (CFA30,000 for UK, CFA68,000 for US, CFA20,000 for Australia) and are issued on the same day. You cannot get visas at the border.

TOGO

Seven-day visas for Togo (CFA10,000) are issued at the border (see p801).

WOMEN TRAVELLERS

Beninese men can be sleazy and women travellers will get a lot of unwanted attention. Particularly unnerving is militaries and other officials using their power to get more of your company than is strictly necessary, such as not letting go of a handshake, keeping hold of your passport or demanding your phone number. Always stay polite but firm and make sure you have a good 'husband story'. For more advice, see p826.

TRANSPORT IN BENIN

GETTING THERE & AWAY
Entering Benin

Benin's immigration regulations and officials are awkward. If flying into the country, you cannot obtain a visa on arrival. However, you can if entering by land, but the visa is only valid for 48 hours, and can only be extended in Cotonou. You'll also need a yellow fever certificate.

Air

The main airport is on the western fringe of Cotonou, in Cocotiers.

Air France has the most reliable and frequent services between Benin and Europe. For flight information, ticket sales and reconfirmations, the following airlines have offices in Cotonou:

Afriqiyah Airways (8U; ☎ 21 31 76 51; Blvd Steinmetz) Hub: Tripoli.

Air France (AF; ☎ 21 30 18 15; www.airfrance.com/bj; Route de l'Aéroport) Hub: Paris.

Air Ivoire (VU; ☎ 21 31 86 14; www.airivoire.com; Blvd Steinmetz) Hub: Abidjan.

Point-Afrique (6V/DR; ☎ 21 30 98 62; www.point-afrique.com; Route de l'Aéroport) Hub: Paris. Flights only in summer, organised tours the rest of the year.

Royal Air Maroc (AT; ☎ 21 30 86 04; www.royalairmaroc.com; Route de l'Aéroport) Hub: Casablanca

Land
BURKINA FASO
There's at least one bush taxi a day along the 97km of tarred road from Natitingou to Porga (CFA1900, two hours), where you can cross to Tindangou in Burkina Faso. Monday, Porga market day, is a good day to find a ride.

SKV (☎ 98 59 88 00) runs buses between Cotonou and Bamako (CFA35,000, 48 hours) via Ouagadougou (CFA17,000, 18 hours) on Wednesday and Friday (departure is at 8pm).

GHANA & CÔTE D'IVOIRE
Inter City Lines (☎ 21 32 66 69; www.intercity-lines .com) plies the interstate coastal route between Cotonou and Abidjan (CFA34,000, 28 hours) four times a week (Monday, Tuesday, Thursday, Friday). Cotonou–Accra costs CFA15,000.

STIF (☎ 97 98 11 80) has a service to Lomé (CFA4000, four hours), Accra (CFA8000, seven hours) and Abidjan (CFA27,000, 20 hours) every two days (departure at 1pm).

NIGER
From Malanville, 733km from Cotonou on tarred road, a *zemi-john* or shared taxi can take you across the River Niger to Gaya in Niger (*zemi-john*/shared taxi CFA1200/700). You cannot get a visa for Niger at the border – get one in Cotonou or Parakou (see opposite).

From Gaya, it's easier to find a Peugeot bush taxi to Niamey (CFA4250, five hours) or a minibus (CFA4600, 5½ hours) than it is to squeeze onto one of the Cotonou–Niamey coaches, which are usually full. From Cotonou, try **Rimbo** (☎ 95 23 24 82) with daily services to Niamey (CFA19,700, 19 hours), or **SNTV** (☎ 93 91 40 42; www.sntv.biz) also with daily trips (CFA17,500, 15 hours).

Crossing from Niger to Benin, you're unlikely to find bush taxis from Niamey to Benin so get to Gaya and cross the border on foot or with a *zem*.

NIGERIA
In Cotonou, bush taxis and minibuses leave for Lagos throughout the day from Gare de Dantokpa (CFA4000, three hours, excluding border crossing mayhem). There are no direct taxis to Lagos from Porto Novo so you'll have to change at the Kraké/Seme border (CFA700, 30 minutes). Make sure you have some Naira to continue your journey on the

other side. Another option is the Lagos–Accra bus service run by **ABC Transport** (☎ 21 33 33 77; www.abctransport.com), which stops in Cotonou (CFA4000, four hours).

There are countless checkpoints between Seme and Lagos, so travellers with their own vehicle will be better off crossing further north at Kétou, which then goes on to Ibadan.

You may have to grease a few palms at Kraké, although asking for a receipt is a good way to discourage corrupt officials. If hiring a taxi across the border, check whether the price includes bribes.

TOGO
Cotonou and Lomé are connected by frequent bush taxis (CFA3500, three hours), which regularly leave the Gare de Jonquet in Cotonou for Lomé. Alternatively, pick up a taxi to the border point at Hilakondji and grab another taxi on the Togolese side of the frontier. STIF buses also ply the route every other day (CFA4000, four hours).

Other crossings are at Kétao/Ouaké, on the Kara–Djougou road, and between Nadoba in Togo and Boukoumbé in Benin along a good *piste*. The latter crossing takes you through spectacular countryside but has little public transport except on Wednesdays, Nadoba market day.

GETTING AROUND
Bush Taxi & Bus
Minibuses and bush taxis are the principal means of transport between towns, and are faster than in many West African countries. There is sometimes a surcharge for luggage.

Benin now also has a range of excellent bus services. The best is **Inter City Lines** (☎ 21 00 85 54; www.intercity-lines.com) with comfortable seats, air-con and dreadful Ivorian soap videos which get the entire bus roaring with laughter. It runs daily services between Cotonou and Parakou (CFA7500, 7½ hours), Malanville (CFA11,000, 12 hours) and Natitingou (CFA8500, eight hours) stopping in all major towns en route. **Confort Lines** (☎ 21 32 58 15) also runs daily services between Cotonou and Natitingou (CFA8500, eight hours) and Parakou (CFA7000, 7½ hours).

These services have proved very popular with travellers and Beninese alike for their reliability, affordability and what feels like luxurious comfort compared to bush taxis, so book ahead.

Car & Motorcycle

Petrol costs between CFA300 and CFA600 per litre. Petrol is cheaper in Nigeria, so much of it is carried illegally across the border and sold on the black market at prices slightly below the official rate. Just look for the guys along the roads with 1L to 5L bottles.

If you're driving, you need an International Driving Permit. Roads are in relatively good condition throughout Benin with a couple of exceptions: the Cotonou–Bohicon road is appalling, as is a stretch of the Parakou to Kandi road. Both are scheduled to be resurfaced though, so smooth travels await.

Local Transport

TAXI

The omnipresence of *zems* has translated into the near disappearance of taxis for short journeys. Shared taxis still ply the main thoroughfares in big cities however, such as the Bohicon–Abomey stretch or the main axes between Cotonou's suburbs and the centre. Expect to pay CFA200 to CFA500 depending on the distance.

ZEMI-JOHNS

In nearly all towns, you'll find *zemi-johns* (scooter taxis). While they are by far the fastest and most convenient way of getting around, they are dangerous: most drivers behave like lunatics and helmets are not available.

Zem drivers wear numbered yellow and green shirts in Cotonou (various colours in other towns). Hail them just as you would a taxi, and be sure to agree on a price before the journey. The typical fare is CFA150 to CFA250. They are also an easy way to get to remote destinations.

Tours

The excellent **Bénin Aventure** (see p119) organises guided, tailor-made trips around Benin in a chauffeur-driven 4WD. Allow CFA75,000 a day (for up to four people) for car rental, fuel and guiding fees, CFA15,000-40,000 per night for a double room, and about CFA50,000 in excursion fees (park entrance etc). A great option for those not scrimping and saving and wanting more out of their trip.

More adventurous, and very much in the spirit of the Paris Dakar, is the **Brussels to Grand Popo by 2CV** rally organised by **Touareg Trail** (www.touareg-trail.be). Mechanic novices fear not however: if you don't have the resources or inclinations to take part in the full two-month adventure, Touareg Trail organises **Meet & Greet** (per person, full board, incl flights €2250), a 10-day trip that allows you to join the last leg of the race with a fully-prepared 2CV. The itinerary changes every year and may take in a neighbouring country. Fun on an epic scale.

Burkina Faso

Forget about big-ticket attractions in Burkina Faso. Bar a scattering of dunes and colourful markets in the Sahel, a range of eerie rock formations around Banfora in the southwest, and a couple of national parks (but none that can rival those in east or southern Africa), the country has few iconic calling cards. So why does it invariably win the hearts of travellers? The answer: the people. The Burkinabé (as people from Burkina Faso are called) are the country's greatest asset. They're disarmingly charming and easy-going. Wherever you go, you'll be greeted with a memorable *bonne arrivée* (welcome). It's this genuine welcome that makes travel in Burkina Faso such a delight.

The country's other big draws? Arts, craftwork and culture. There's a fantastic arts scene in Ouagadougou, the enjoyable and gloriously named capital, along with a famous musical tradition and beautiful handicrafts. Throw in Fespaco, Africa's premier film festival, and there's enough to engage your mind and senses for a couple of weeks or so. Burkina Faso is also alive with a vibrant cultural mix of peoples, from the proud Fulani people of the Sahel to the animist societies of the Senoufo or the Lobi. If you want to immerse yourself in local culture, opportunities abound, from drumming and dance lessons to cooking classes and theatre performances.

Tourism infrastructure is fairly limited, but there is a handful of gems, especially in Bobo-Dioulasso and Ouagadougou, in the form of adorable B&Bs and good restaurants, as well as family-run, eco-friendly *campements* in more remote areas.

Be warned: staying longer than you planned is a common issue.

BURKINA FASO

FAST FACTS

- **Area** 274,122 sq km
- **Capital** Ouagadougou
- **Country code** ☎ 226
- **Famous for** The coolest name for a capital city in the world; Thomas Sankara, Africa's Che Guevara
- **Languages** French, Moré, Fulfulde and Lobi
- **Money** West African CFA franc; US$1 = CFA493; €1 = CFA656
- **Population** 14.9 million
- **Visa** Available at borders (CFA10,000) or Burkina Faso embassies (up to CFA30,000)

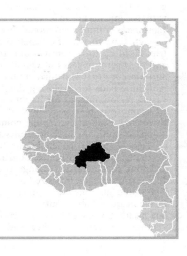

BURKINA FASO

HIGHLIGHTS

- **The Sahel** (p162) Colourful markets and camping out with camels under starry desert skies.
- **Ouagadougou** (p136) Famed arts scene, craft bargains, and dancing into the wee hours in a *maquis-dancing*.
- **Bobo-Dioulasso** (p149) Stunning Grande Mosquée and languid atmosphere.
- **Sindou Peaks** (p158) Martian landscape reminiscent of *Planet of the Apes*.
- **Tiébélé** (p161) Intricately decorated traditional houses in the heart of the Gourounsi country.
- **Ranch de Nazinga** (p161) Elephants stroll past your bungalow in this wildlife sanctuary.

ITINERARIES

- **One week** With only a week, plan on spending a couple of days in the capital, Ouagadougou (p136), which has few 'sights' but boasts a steamy nightlife, a thriving arts scene and fine restaurants. Then bus it to Bobo-Dioulasso (p149) and soak up the mellow vibes of this utterly charming city.
- **Two weeks** Consider further exploration of the southwest. Rent a mobylette or a bike in Banfora (p155) and make a foray into Senoufo country – make a beeline for the eerie Sindou Peaks (p158) and the mystifying Dômes de Fabedougou (p158). Push on to Niansogoni (p158), a fascinating village blessed with a scenic backdrop.
- **Three weeks** A third week would give you enough time to add the Sahel to your trip. Head up to Gorom-Gorom (p163) and the nearby villages of Oursi (p164) and Markoye (p164), which are the best launching pads for exploring this fascinating region, famous for its dunes and its clamorous markets; allow at least three days. Back in the capital, point the compass south to the colourful village of Tiébélé (p161), which boasts finely decorated traditional houses, and make a detour to Ranch de Nazinga (p161), where you can spot bus-sized elephants. You could also include Gaoua (p159), in the heart of Lobi country.
- **One month** Lovers of wildlife who are visiting between December and May

HOW MUCH?

- **Ouagadougou–Bobo-Dioulasso bus ride** CFA6000
- **Museum admission** CFA1000
- **Guide per day** CFA10,000 to CFA17,000
- **Internet connection per hour** CFA500
- **4WD rental per day** CFA55,000 plus petrol

LONELY PLANET INDEX

- **1L of petrol** CFA650
- **1L of bottled water** CFA500
- **Bottle of beer** CFA800
- **Souvenir T-shirt** CFA5000
- **Serve of riz sauce** CFA500

should make a three-day trip to Parc National d'Arli (p160).

CLIMATE & WHEN TO GO

The best time to visit is from mid-October to December. It can be downright wet between June and September, when the south can be uncomfortably humid and many roads throughout the country are impassable. By October you're less likely to find your travel plans disrupted by constant rains. From December to February the weather is marginally cooler (although if you've come from colder European climes you're unlikely to think so), with daily maximums only occasionally exceeding 35°C. During this period, the dry heat is more bearable, although dusty harmattan winds can produce hazy skies and sore throats in January and February. The hot season is from March to early June, when the mercury can rise well above 40°C in the capital. See also Climate Charts, p810.

Film enthusiasts won't want to miss Fespaco, Africa's premier film festival, which will run in late February in 2011. For more information, see the boxed text Fespaco, p135. For other festivals which you may want to attend, see p141.

HISTORY

The earliest known inhabitants were the Bobo, the Lobi and the Gourounsi, who were in the area by the 13th century. A century later, the

BURKINA FASO

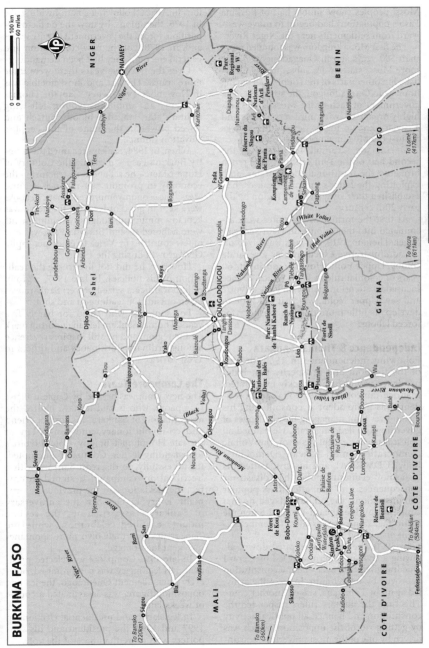

BURKINA FASO

Mossi peoples (now almost half of Burkina Faso's population) had begun to move westward from settlements near the Niger River.

The first Mossi kingdom was founded more than 500 years ago in Ouagadougou. Three more Mossi states were subsequently established in other parts of the country, all paying homage to Ouagadougou, the strongest. The government of each of the Mossi states was highly organised, with ministers, courts and a cavalry known for its devastating attacks against the Muslim empires in Mali.

During the scramble for Africa in the second half of the 19th century, the French broke up the traditional Mossi states, and, exploiting the latter's internal rivalries, had established their sway over the region by the early 20th century.

At first the former Mossi states were assimilated into the Colonie du Haut Sénégal-Niger. Then, in 1919, the area was hived off for administrative expedience as a separate colony, Upper Volta. However, during its 60 years of colonial rule in West Africa, France focused its attention mainly on Côte d'Ivoire and saw Upper Volta, which it did little to develop, as little more than a repository for forced labour.

Independence & Thomas Sankara

Following independence in 1960, dreams of the freedom and prosperity that independence would bring quickly evaporated. Maurice Yaméogo, Upper Volta's first president, was more adept at consolidating his own power than managing the challenges of governing the fledgling state. He banned all political parties except his own, the Voltaic Democratic Union-African Democratic Rally (UDV-RDA), and his crude attempts to fashion economic policy had disastrous consequences. In 1966, after mass popular demonstrations, the military staged its first coup, led by Lieutenant-Colonel Sangoulé Lamizana. Yaméogo was jailed for embezzlement on a grand scale.

In 1970, the military stepped down, allowing a civilian government led by Gérard Ouédraogo to take over under a constitution approved by referendum. In 1974 the army, led again by Lamizana, staged another coup. This time the military rulers suspended the constitution and banned all political activity by getting rid of the opposition, which was driven by one of the most powerful trade unions in Africa. Following a nationwide strike in 1975, the unions, by now the de facto opposition, forced the government to raise wages and, in 1978, got the new constitution and general elections they had been demanding.

Over the next five years there were three more coups. The last and most notable was in November 1982, when Captain Thomas Sankara, an ambitious young left-wing military star, staged a bloody putsch and seized power in the name of the People's Salvation Council.

When, in 1984, Sankara renamed the country Burkina Faso – meaning the Country of Honest Men – he set about restructuring the economy to promote self-reliance in rural areas. The economy improved, financial books were kept in good order, debt financing was kept to a minimum, budgetary commitments were adhered to and Burkina Faso was one of few countries in Africa to enjoy per capita GNP growth during the 1980s.

However, he did not live to see the realisation of his policies. In late 1987, a group of junior officers seized power; Sankara was taken outside Ouagadougou and shot.

For someone who ruled for barely five years, Thomas Sankara left an enduring mark on the region, and he still inspires reverence among ordinary Burkinabés and others in West Africa.

The Compaoré Years

The new junta was headed by Captain Blaise Compaoré, who is said to have plotted the assassination of Sankara, his former friend and co-revolutionary, and son-in-law of the late Houphouët-Boigny, Côte d'Ivoire's longstanding leader. Compaoré attempted, unsuccessfully, to discredit Sankara with a 'rectification' campaign designed to correct the 'deviations' of the previous government. Every 15 October, the anniversary of Sankara's assassination, the regime mounts a stilted celebration, while the 'Sankaristes' pay their own more spontaneous, genuine homage.

In late 1991 Compaoré was elected president. His legitimacy was compromised, however, when Clément Ouédraogo, the leading opposition figure, was assassinated a couple of weeks later.

In legislative and presidential elections in 1997 and 1998, the president and his supporters won more than 85% of the vote.

Burkina Faso Today

The country remains one of the more stable in the region, although rumblings of discontent continue. Street demonstrations in April 2000 forced the government to draft a constitutional amendment that limits presidents to two terms in office. Arguing that this two-term limit did not apply to terms served before the amendment was passed, and with the opposition divided, President Compaoré won re-election for a third term on 13 November 2005 with 80% of the vote. To no-one's surprise, in May 2007 the ruling CDP won 73 out of the 111 National Assembly seats in the election. President Compaoré intends to run for another term in 2010.

A still sensitive topic is the case of Norbert Zongo, a famous investigative journalist for *L'Indépendant*, who was killed in 1998. The case is still unsolved, despite regular marches, legal action and commemorations. In 2006, a judge dismissed charges against the only suspect in the case.

THE CULTURE
The National Psyche

Burkinabés are a laid-back lot, or, as they would say themselves, tranquil. Would-be guides can be persistent, but most are polite and friendly rather than annoying. If you breach local etiquette, most locals will be too polite to say anything.

Burkinabés have a genuine pride in their country, which manifests itself in a desire to embrace the modern world but at the same time remain unchanged by it. This is wedded to a belief that traditional ways of doing things remain important. If you're with a Burkinabé who encounters a chief from their ethnic group, the displays of deference can be quite moving. Although ethnic origin (along with religion) is the bedrock of identity, you'll see little if any antagonism between members of different ethnic groups.

People are also proud that in a troublesome region riven with conflict, they have become known as a beacon of stability. That doesn't mean that they love their president, but they acknowledge that, for all his faults, he has brought a measure of stability to the country – a quality that, in the absence of economic advancement, is extremely important to the Burkinabé. Many also express quiet anger that so many of their countrymen and women have been made scape-

goats in the conflict across the border in Côte d'Ivoire.

Daily Life

For all of their friendliness and relaxed nature, life for the Burkinabé is as tough as it gets. In 2008 the UN ranked Burkina Faso 173rd out of 179 countries across a number of quality-of-life indicators, ranging from income and infant mortality to literacy and life expectancy. Almost 50% of the population survives, barely, on less than US$1 a day.

As such, lifestyle is dictated by the daily need to survive. Families are large (the idea being that the more children you have, the more workers you will have to provide for the family) and usually live together in small houses (in urban areas) or family compounds (in rural places). As crops fail (as they did spectacularly in the aftermath of the 2004 drought and locust invasion), and with the influx of Burkinabé from Côte d'Ivoire, cities in Burkina Faso are growing at an alarming rate.

In rural Burkina Faso, traditional life remains largely unchanged by the passing years, with traditional religions, subsistence agriculture and village hierarchies still at the centre of rural existence.

Population

Occupying an area about half the size of France, the country is extremely diverse, with its almost 15 million people scattered among some 60 ethnic groups. The largest of these is the Mossi (48%), who are primarily concentrated in the central plateau area, which includes Ouagadougou. The Bobo (7%) live in the west around Bobo-Dioulasso, while the Senoufo (5%) live further south, around Sindu (some also live across the border in Mali and Côte d'Ivoire). The southwest around Gaoua is home to the Lobi (7%). East of the Lobi, and straddling the border with Ghana, are the Gourounsi (5%). In the Sahel areas of the north are the Hausa, the Fulani (also known as Peul-Fulani or Fula; 8%), the Bella and the Tuareg peoples, many of which are still semi-nomadic. The Gourmantché predominate in the east around Fada N'Gourma. Around 80% of Burkinabés live in rural areas.

RELIGION

Most of Burkina Faso's population observe either Islam (about 50%) or traditional animist beliefs based mainly on the worship of ancestors and spirits (40%) – although there is often considerable overlap. Muslims are concentrated particularly in Ouagadougou and the north, while the 10% of Burkinabés who are Christian live predominantly in the south.

ARTS
Arts & Craftwork

Burkina Faso has a vibrant contemporary plastic arts scene (painting, sculpture, wood carving, bronze and brass work, and textiles). Influential painters include Fernand Nonkouni, Samba Boly, Christophe Sawadogo, Bab'sSama and Sylvestre Zoungrana. Their work is exhibited in Ouagadougou galleries, cultural centres, collective workshops, hotels and restaurants, and at their studios. Leading sculptors are Siriki Ky (who founded Laongo, where international sculptors meet and carve the rock; see p147), Alassane Drabo, Xavier Sayago, Vincent Zoungrana and Hamado Kouragou. They specialise in bronze work. Most of them have exhibited across Europe and the USA. Some artists, such as Kely, turn scrap and lost objects into startling works of art.

Craftwork is also well developed, and there's no shortage of artisans' stalls and craft shops in Ouaga and Bobo-Dioulasso. While each ethnic group in Burkina Faso has its own artistic style, the work of the Mossi, the Bobo and the Lobi is the most famous. The tall antelope masks of the Mossi and the butterfly masks of the Bobo are perhaps the most recognisable, but the Lobi are also well known for their figurative sculptures. In the Sahel, artisans specialise in leatherwork. See also p65.

Cinema

Burkina Faso has a thriving film industry that receives considerable biennial stimulation from the Fespaco film festival held in Ouagadougou (see the boxed text, opposite).

Two Burkinabé film-makers who have won prizes here and developed international reputations are Idrissa Ouédraogo, who won the 1990 Grand Prix at Cannes for *Tilä*, and Gaston Kaboré, whose film *Buud Yam* was the 1997 winner of the Étalon d'Or. In addition to these well-known names, there are plenty of up-and-coming Burkinabé directors to watch.

Music

Burkina Faso's modern musicians draw on influences from across the continent (especially Mali, Congo and Côte d'Ivoire), Jamaican reggae and Europe.

In Ouagadougou and Bobo-Dioulasso, outdoor venues (usually cafes or bars) offer live music with both traditional troupes and modern ensembles on show. Music is also the mainstay of many traditional festivals and ceremonies across the country. In addition to hearing traditional music, you can also find out more about the instruments

---

LIFE AS A PAINTER

Burkina Faso is famous for its film-makers and dance performers, but less so for its painters, despite the fact that there's a prolific painting scene in Ouaga. We met Fernand Nonkouni, one of the best-known Burkinabé painters. 'My canvases are influenced by my previous job – I was a publicist. I include logos, geometric patterns and calligraphy in my paintings.' Is there a style specific to Burkina Faso? 'I'd say there's a style specific to French-speaking West African countries. Most visitors are struck by our palette – here we use lots of ochres, reds and browns, which are the colours of the soil. In Ghana, it's different. Because of the abundance of forests, Ghanaian painters use more greens and vivid colours, and their repertoire is more figurative; ours is more symbolic. Ghanaian painters are also lucky, because there are two schools of fine arts, which act as catalysts for emerging artists.'

Lucien Humbert, who runs Yiri Suma (p142) and sponsors many local artists, recognises that Burkinabé painters lack official support in Burkina Faso. 'Though there's no school of fine arts in Burkina, this country has lots of talented painters and plastic artists. Given that they don't get the support of public authorities, which prefer to sponsor sculpture, dance, theatre and the film industry, they tend to work in collectives. If they're lucky, they are discovered by gallery owners, who help promote them.'

FESPACO

Burkina Faso may, as one of the world's poorest countries, be an unlikely venue for a world-renowned festival of film, but the biennial nine-day pan-African **Fespaco** (Map p138; Festival Pan-Africain du Cinema; ☎ 50 39 87 01; www.fespaco.bf; Ave Kadiogo/Rte de Bobo, Ouagadougou), goes from strength to strength.

Fespaco began in 1969, when it was little more than a few African film-makers getting together to show their short films to interested audiences. Hundreds of films from Africa and the diaspora in the Americas and the Caribbean are now viewed every year, with 20 selected to compete for the prestigious Étalon D'Or de Yennenga – Fespaco's equivalent of the Oscar – as well as prizes in other categories (including TV). In 2009 the coveted prize for best film at Fespaco was won by the Ethiopian director Haile Gerima for his film *Teza*.

Fespaco has become an essential pillar of Burkina Faso's cultural life. Since its early days, it has helped stimulate film production throughout Africa and built on the passion for films among Burkina Faso's film-literate population. It has also become such a major African cultural event that it attracts celebrities from around the world.

Ouagadougou is invariably spruced up for the occasion and everyone seems to get in a festive mood. All the city's cinemas are used. Although you can buy individual tickets to screenings, they sell out fast and you're advised to purchase either a 'festival-goer's badge' (CFA25,000), which gives access to all screenings and official Fespaco ceremonies, or the 'Étalon Pass' (CFA10,000), which grants access to screenings. Hotel rooms are hard to find, so advance booking is essential.

Fespaco is held in Ouagadougou every odd year, in the second half of February or early March (in even years it is held in Tunis). The next Burkina Fespaco will be held in 2011. For more information about Fespaco, check out the excellent website.

and forms by visiting the excellent Musée de la Musique in Bobo-Dioulasso (p151).

Established local stars include the reggae performers Black So Man, Nick Domby, Traoré Amadou Ballaké, the Cuban-inspired Thomas Tiendrebeogo and Tidiane Coulibaly, and the soul and funk man Georges Ouédraogo. In Ouagadougou, listen out for Sonia Carré d'As, who's something of a local favourite. More contemporary singers and pop groups to look out for include Idak Bassavé, Sami Rama, Sissao, Alif Naba, Ahmed Smani, the jazz man Bill Akakora, Djata, Smockey, Zêdess and the hip-hop performers Yeleen. The most famous group internationally is Farafina, originally from Bobo and Victor Démé, also from Bobo-Dioulasso.

For more information, see also p57.

ENVIRONMENT
The Land
Landlocked Burkina Faso's terrain ranges from the harsh desert and semidesert of the north to the woodland and savannah of the green southwest. Around Banfora rainfall is heavier, and forests thrive alongside irrigated sugarcane and rice fields; it's here that most of Burkina Faso's meagre 13% of arable land is found. The country's dominant feature, how-ever, is the vast central laterite plateau of the Sahel, where hardy trees and bushes thrive.

The French named the country Upper Volta after its three major rivers – the Black, White and Red Voltas, known today as the Mouhoun, Nakambé and Nazinon Rivers. All flow south into the world's largest artificial lake, Lake Volta, in Ghana.

Wildlife
Parc National d'Arli, close to the border with Benin, is home to Burkina Faso's few remaining species of large animals, among them elephants, hippos, warthogs, baboons, monkeys, lions, crocodiles and various kinds of antelope.

National Parks
Burkina Faso's two main protected areas – Parc National d'Arli (p160), which allows access to the contiguous national parks of Benin just across the border, and Ranch de Nazinga (p161) – are in the far southeast of the country. Parc National des Deux Balés (p147), south of Boromo, is less set up for tourists but does host elephants. Parc Regional du W (p160) straddles Burkina Faso, Niger and Benin, but the best sections are across the border.

Unfortunately, hunting (including by tourists) is still a problem around the parks' perimeters.

Environmental Issues

Burkina Faso suffers acutely from two related forms of environmental damage: deforestation and soil erosion.

Nowadays, Ouagadougou is surrounded by a 70km stretch of land virtually devoid of trees. Firewood accounts for more than 90% of the country's energy consumption, and then there is commercial logging, slash-and-burn agriculture and animal grazing. When these ravages are added to the perennial threat of drought and the locust invasion of 2004, Burkina Faso's ecological future looks decidedly fragile.

But it's not all gloom. Some small-scale projects supported by nongovernmental organisations (NGOs) have been successful at the micro level at addressing these issues. For example, farmers have been encouraged to rely on groundwater rather than unpredictable rains, and to return to traditional methods of cultivation, in particular the building of *diguettes,* or stone lines, laid along field contours, which slow water run-off, maximise water penetration and reduce erosion.

FOOD & DRINK

Burkinabé food is influenced by Senegalese and Ivorian cuisines. Sauces, especially *arachide* (groundnut or peanut) or *graine* (a hot sauce made with palm oil nuts), are the mainstay and are always served with a starch – usually rice (it's called *riz sauce* or *riz gras*) – or the Burkinabé staple, *tô,* a millet- or sorghum-based *pâte* (a pounded dough-like substance). The Senegalese *yassa* preparation, consisting of grilled meat or fish marinated in a thick onion and lemon sauce, is also commonly found. Other not-to-be-missed dishes include the Ivorian *attiéké* (grated cassava), *alloco* (ripe bananas fried with chilli in palm oil) and *kedjenou* (simmered chicken or fish with vegetables).

One of the culinary highlights is *capitaine* (Nile perch). Grilled dishes of chicken, mutton, beef, guinea-fowl and fish also feature on the menu. If you're after more exotic offerings, make a beeline for stewed *agouti* (or grasscutter, a large rodent which is a whole lot easier to stomach if you don't see its rat-like resemblance) or *biche* (antelope).

In the Sahel, couscous (semolina grains) is widely available. In the southwest, try *fonio*

(a variety of couscous made with millet). Yam or sweet-potato chips are a great snack. For desserts, you'll certainly plump for *yaourt* (yoghurt), sometimes served with lashings of local honey (killer!), or *dégué* (yoghurt mixed with millet grains).

In Ouagadougou, you'll find a good array of eateries serving all types of cuisine. If you're on a budget, head for the ubiquitous *maquis* (small, local eateries), which generally offer simple dishes such as *riz gras, riz sauce* or grilled chicken. They usually double as bars.

Castel, Flag, Brakina, Beaufort and So.b.bra (pronounced *so-bay-bra*) are popular and palatable lager-type beers. If you're not catching an early bus out of town the next morning, try the local *dolo* (millet beer) in a *buvette* (small bar). Soft drinks and bottled water (Lafi or Jirma) are available everywhere. Locally produced juices include the hibiscus drink *bissap*, *gingembre* (ginger) and mango. Sad news for espresso addicts: prepare yourself for instant Nescafé.

OUAGADOUGOU

pop 1,455,000

If only all African capitals were as agreeable as Ouagadougou! Sure, Ouaga, as it's affectionately dubbed, lacks standout sights, and its architecture doesn't have much to turn your head, but stick around this bustling city long enough and you might fall prey to its unexpected charms.

The capital thrives as an eclectic arts hub, with dance and concert venues, live bands, theatre companies, beautiful handicrafts and, best of all, some genuinely talented painters whose works can be seen (and bought) in various galleries and workshops. It's rare to have a month go by without a special event. If your visit is in late February, try to make it coincide with Fespaco (see the boxed text, p135), Africa's major film festival, which attracts film buffs from all over the world.

If every town had a symbol, Ouagadougou's would surely be the *mobylette* (moped) – masses of them swarm down the boulevards like frantic bumblebees. At night, you'll see hundreds of them parked in front of the innumerable *maquis* that are dotted around the city, where the beat is alive and pumping.

If you need to pamper yourself, Ouaga has modern amenities and cosy guesthouses – bliss after so many saggy mattresses in the rural areas.

HISTORY

Ouagadougou became the capital of the Mossi empire in 1441 and, 250 years later, was chosen as the permanent residence of the Moro-Naba, the Mossi king. The town grew up around the imperial palace, and was extended during colonisation. The Mossi traditional chief remains Burkina Faso's most powerful, and the Mossi dynasty's 500-year presence in Ouagadougou marks the city out as unusual in a region where capitals were more often creations of colonial convenience than seats of ancient power. The completion of the railway from Abidjan (Côte d'Ivoire) in 1954 resulted in the city's rapid expansion.

ORIENTATION

It's easy to get disoriented in Ouagadougou as there are no landmarks. A compounding factor is that most accommodation options, restaurants, shops, bus stations and other services are scattered around the city. Adding to the confusion are the street names; main streets are signed, but their names have changed several times over the last few years, and old names continue to be used. Large buildings and roundabouts serve as de facto points of reference.

Take your bearings from the unmistakable globe at the centre of the busy Place des Nations Unies, from where the city's five main boulevards lead off. The 'centre' of town – where the streets are relatively ordered – lies west and southwest of this crossroads. At the heart of the city, the Grand Marché, which burnt down in 2003, should reopen by the time you read this. Gounghin, an arty neighbourhood, is west of the centre.

Some 5km south of the centre, the 'Ouaga 2000' development is part of an ambitious project of town planning, and it's rapidly becoming a separate little world, home to ordered streets, luxury villas and a presidential palace larger than the White House.

INFORMATION
Cultural Centres
Centre Culturel Français Georges Mélies (Map p140; ☎ 50 30 60 97; www.ccfouaga.com; Ave de la Nation; ☻ 9am-noon & 3-6.15pm Tue-Sat) Has a full

program of concerts, exhibitions and movies – pick up the monthly program for details.

Emergency
Commissariat Central (Map p140; ☎ 50 30 62 71; Ave Loudun) The first port of call for police-related matters.
Emergency (☎ 17 or 18)

Internet Access
Cybercentres (internet cafes) are easy to find. Most upscale hotels and guesthouses provide wi-fi access.
Cyberposte (Map p140; Ave Dimdolobsom; per hr CFA500; ☻ 7am-11pm Mon-Sat, 8am-noon Sun) Offers the most reliable connections and keeps longer hours.

Medical Services
There are numerous well-stocked pharmacies in the centre. For medical treatment or a consultation, expats recommend **Clinique Philadelphie** (Map p138; ☎ 50 33 28 71; Rue Maurice Yaméogo; ☻ 24hr).

Money
There are bureaux de change on Ave Kwame N'Krumah and at the airport (in the departure hall). Banks such as Biciab and Ecobank are also an option, but they keep shorter hours than bureaux de change and have longer queues. A quicker alternative is to change your euros at Marina Market (see p144) – this supermarket offers the best rates and stays open late (head to the manager's office).

You'll have no trouble finding banks with ATMs (Visa only) in the centre.

Post
Post office (Map p140; off Ave de la Nation; ☻ 7.30am-12.30pm & 3.30-5.30pm Mon-Fri) The main branch.

Telephone & Fax
For international and local calls, head to any *télécentre* booth – they are ubiquitous in Ouagadougou and stay open late.

Tourist Information
For reliable travel information, you could approach one of the privately run travel agencies in Ouagadougou (see below). Guesthouse owners are another excellent source of information.

Travel Agencies
For tours around Burkina Faso and further afield, the following companies are

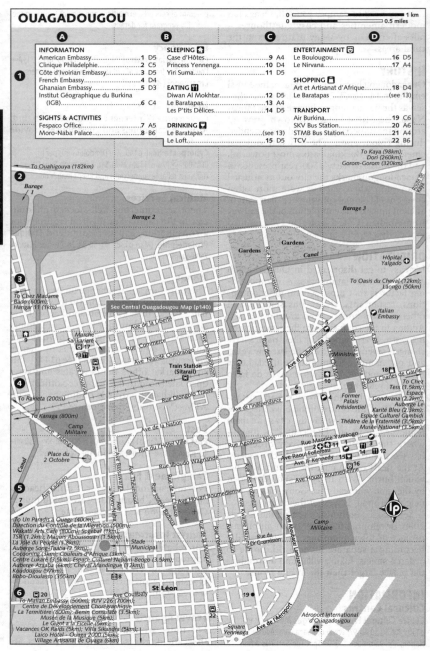

OUAGADOUGOU

BURKINA FASO

| 0 | | 1 km |
| 0 | | 0.5 miles |

INFORMATION
American Embassy.....................................1 D5
Clinique Philadelphie.............................2 C5
Côte d'Ivoirian Embassy.......................3 D5
French Embassy......................................4 D4
Ghanaian Embassy.................................5 D3
Institut Géographique du Burkina
  (IGB)...6 C4

SIGHTS & ACTIVITIES
Fespaco Office.......................................7 A5
Moro-Naba Palace................................8 B6

SLEEPING 🛏
Case d'Hôtes..9 A4
Princess Yennenga................................10 D4
Yiri Suma..11 D5

EATING 🍴
Diwan Al Mokhtar.................................12 D5
Le Baratapas..13 A4
Les P'tits Délices...................................14 D5

DRINKING 🍷
Le Baratapas ....(see 13)
Le Loft...15 D5

ENTERTAINMENT 🎭
Le Boulougou.......................................16 D5
Le Nirvana...17 A4

SHOPPING 🛍
Art et Artisanat d'Afrique....................18 D4
Le Baratapas ....(see 13)

TRANSPORT
Air Burkina..19 C6
SKV Bus Station....................................20 A6
STMB Bus Station.................................21 A4
TCV..22 B6

To Kaya (98km);
Dori (260km);
Gorom-Gorom (320km)

To Ouahigouya (182km)

Barage 1

Barage 2

Barage 3

Gardens

Gardens

Canal

Hôpital
Yalgado

To Chez Madame
Bado (600m);
Hangar 11 (1km)

To Oasis du Cheval (12km);
Laongo (50km)

See Central Ouagadougou Map (p140)

Italian
Embassy

Ave de la Liberté

Marché
Sankariaré

Rue Commerce

Ave d'Oubritenga

Ave Niande Ouedraogo

Train Station
(Sitarail)

Ministries

Blvd Charles de Gaulle

To Chez
Tess (1.5km);
Espace
Gondwana (2.2km);
Auberge Le
Karité Bleu (2.3km);
Espace Culturel Gambidi
- Théâtre de la Fraternité (3.5km);
Musée National (3.5km);

To Rakieta (200m)

Rue Diongolo Traore

To Kanaga (800m)

Former
Palais
Présidentiel

Ave de l'Independance

Camp
Militaire

Ave de la Nation

Place du
2 Octobre

Rue du l'Hôtel Ville

Rue Agostino Neto

Rue Maurice Yaméogo

Rue Ilboudo Wagnande

Ave Raoul Follereau

Ave JF Kennedy

To Un Paradis à Ouaga (400m);
Direction du Contrôle de la Migration (500m);
Wakatti Arts Cafe (800m); Sogebaf (1km);
TSR (1.2km); Maquis Aboussouan (1.5km);
La Jolie du Peuple (1.8km);
Auberge Song-Taaba (2.5km);
Cocooning (3km); Couleurs d'Afrique (3km);
Centre Lukaré (3.5km); Espace Culturel Napam-Beogo (3.5km);
Auberge Azaba (6km); Cheval Mandingue (12km);
Koudougou (97km);
Bobo-Dioulasso (355km)

Ave Houari Boumedienne

Camp
Militaire

To Malian Embassy (500m); RJV 226 (700m);
Centre de Développement Chorégraphique
- La Termitière (800m); Benin Consulate (3.5km);
Musée de la Musique (5km);
Le Gigot a la Ficelle (5km);
Vacances OK Raids (5km); Villa Sikandra (5km);
Laico Hotel - Ouaga 2000 (5km);
Village Artisanal de Ouaga (6km)

Ave Coulibaly

St Léon

Square
Yennenga

Ave de l'Aéroport

Aéroport International
d'Ouagadougou

recommended and can arrange English-speaking guides.

Couleurs d'Afrique (off Map p138; ☎ 50 34 19 56, 78 81 11 48; www.couleurs-afrique.com; Ave de l'Olympisme, Gounghin) Reputable operator southwest of the city. Can organise all kinds of tours, including guided off-road motorbike tours and treks, as well as 4WD rental.

L'Agence Tourisme (Map p140; ☎ 50 31 84 43; www.agence-tourisme.com; Hôtel les Palmiers, Rue Joseph Badoua) A well-established operator.

Vacances OK Raids (off Map p138; ☎ 50 38 88 63; www.okraid.com; Rue Bitto) South of town. Longstanding and reliable.

For purchasing domestic or international air tickets, head to **Satguru Travels** (Map p140; ☎ 50 30 16 52; Ave Kwame N'Krumah).

Visa Extensions

Direction du Contrôle de la Migration (off Map p138; Ave Kadiogo; ⏰ 7am-12.30pm & 3-5.30pm Mon-Fri) Southwest of town, this is also the place where you can get the Visa des Pays de l'Entente (CFA25,000), valid for two months in Burkina Faso, Niger, Togo, Benin and Côte d'Ivoire. For information on this visa, see p826.

DANGERS & ANNOYANCES

Ouagadougou is one of the safer cities in the region, but avoid walking around alone at night. Take particular care along Ave Yennenga, the southern reaches of Rue Joseph Badoua, and the Ave Kwame N'Krumah nightclub strip (see p145). Bag-snatching is also a slight problem. Never carry valuables with you.

SIGHTS

MUSÉE NATIONAL

The **national museum** (off Map p138; ☎ 50 39 19 34; Blvd Charles de Gaulle; admission CFA1000; ⏰ 9am-12.30pm & 3-5.30pm Tue-Sat) has an odd location, almost 4km east of the town centre. The displays of the various masks, ancestral statues and traditional costumes of Burkina Faso's major ethnic groups are the highlights. To get there, a taxi should cost no more than CFA2000.

MUSÉE DE LA MUSIQUE

It's worth popping your head into this **museum** (off Map p138; ☎ 50 32 40 60; admission CFA1000; ⏰ 9am-noon & 3-6pm Tue-Sat) if you have an interest in traditional music. The uncluttered displays include *tambours* (drums), flutes, xylophones and *luth* (harps) from around the country. Labels are in French. The museum is on Blvd Tengsoba (known as Blvd Circulaire) but

should be relocated to its original premises on Ave d'Oubritenga (Map p140) in 2010.

MORO-NABA PALACE & CEREMONY

Such is the influence of the Moro-Naba of Ouagadougou, the emperor of the Mossi and the most powerful traditional chief in Burkina Faso, that the government will still make a show of consulting him before making any major decision.

The Moro-Naba ceremony *(la cérémonie du Nabayius Gou)* takes place around 7am every Friday at the **Moro-Naba Palace** (Map p138). It's a very formal ritual that lasts only about 15 minutes. Prominent Mossis arrive by taxi, car and moped, greet each other and sit on the ground according to rank. The Moro-Naba appears, dressed in red, accompanied by his saddled and elaborately decorated horse. A cannon is fired, his most senior subjects approach to give obeisance and His Majesty retires.

The Moro-Naba reappears, dressed all in white and his servants invite his subjects to the palace for a drink.

It's a traditional ceremony, not something put on for tourists. Photos during the ceremony are not permitted.

ACTIVITIES

Very few visitors know that **horse riding** is available in Ouagadougou. There are two well-established equestrian centres, both run by French-Burkinabé couples. Both offer scenic horse rides around Ouaga for around CFA5000 per hour or CFA10,000 for three hours. Multiday treks in the Sahel or in Mali, including the Dogon Country, are also available.

Cheval Mandingue (off Map p138; ☎ 50 43 60 76, 76 61 43 56; www.chevalmandingue.com; ⏰ Tue-Sun) About 12km west of the centre, off the road to Bobo.

Oasis du Cheval (off Map p138; ☎ 50 39 33 71, 70 20 63 67; www.oasisducheval.com; ⏰ daily) About 12km east of the centre, off the road to Fada N'Gourma.

TOURS

To see more than just the usual tourist sights, of if you need a taxi for the day, you can contact the following guides. Both speak good English and can take you anywhere in Ouaga.

Eugene Compaoré (☎ 76 62 58 98; eugene_compaore@yahoo.fr) A full day costs around CFA20,000. Car rental is extra (about CFA30,000). Prices are negotiable.

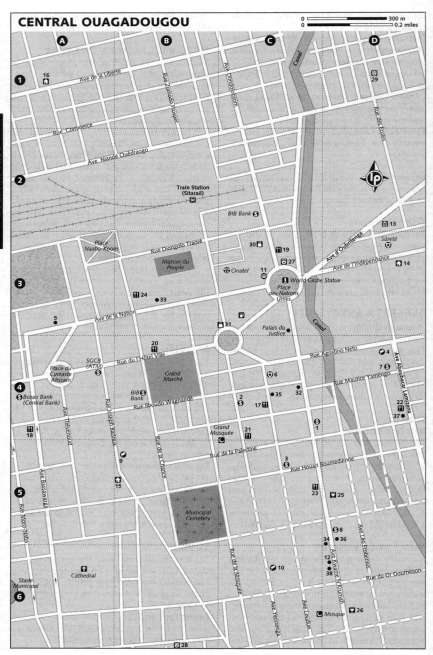

BURKINA FASO

CENTRAL OUAGADOUGOU

0 ——— 300 m
0 ——— 0.2 miles

A **B** **C** **D**

Ave de la Liberté
Rue Zinodo Prosper
Ave Dimdolobson
Canal
16
29
Rue Commerce
Rue des Écoles
Ave Niandé Ouédraogo

Train Station
(Sitarail)
BIB Bank
Ave d'Oubritenga
13
Place
Naaba-Koom
Rue Diongolo Traoré
30
19
Sûreté
Maison du
Peuple
Onatel
11
27
Ave de l'Indépendance
14
World Globe Statue
24
33
Place
des Nations
Unies
5
Ave de la Nation
31
Palais de
Justice
Canal
Rue Agostino Neto
4
Rue de l'Hôtel Ville
20
7
SGCB
(ATM)
6
Rue Maurice Yaméogo
Place du
Cinéaste
Africain
Grand
Marché
2
35
32
22
Bceao Bank
(Central Bank)
BIB
Bank
17
37
Rue Ilboudo Wagnandé
1
18
21
Grand
Mosquée
9
Rue de la Palestine
3
Ave Houari Boumédienne
15
23
25
Municipal
Cemetery
8
34
36
12
38
Cathedral
10
Rue du Dr Gournisson
Stade
Municipal
Mosque
26
28

INFORMATION		SLEEPING 🏠			ENTERTAINMENT 🎭		
Biciab	1 C4	Hotel Azalai	14 D3		Centre Culturel Français		
Biciab ATM	2 C4	Hôtel les Palmiers	15 B5		Georges Mélies	(see 5)	
Biciab ATM	3 C5	Le Pavillon Vert	16 A1		Jardin de l'Amitié	27 C3	
Canadian Embassy	4 D4				Le Kingstone	28 B6	
Centre Culturel Français		EATING 🍴			Le Music Hall	29 D1	
Georges Mélies	5 A3	Chez Tanti Propre	17 C4				
Commissariat		La Forêt	18 A4		SHOPPING 🛍		
Central	6 C4	Le Verdoyant	19 C3		Centre National d'Artisanat et		
Cyberposte	(see 11)	L'Eau Vive	20 B4		d'Art	30 C3	
Ecobank	7 D4	Marina Market	21 C4		Galerie Nuance	31 C3	
Ecobank	8 D5	Pâtisserie Koulouba	22 D4				
German Embassy	9 B5	Restaurant Akwaba	23 C5		TRANSPORT		
L'Agence Tourisme	(see 15)	Zama Chapelle	24 B3		Afriqiyah	(see 12)	
Nigerian Consulate	10 C6				Air Algérie	32 C4	
Post Office	11 C3	DRINKING 🍷			Air France	33 B3	
Satguru Travels	12 D6	De Niro	25 D5		Air Ivoire	34 D5	
		Le Moulin Rouge	26 D6		Air Sénégal International	35 C4	
SIGHTS & ACTIVITIES					Ethiopian Airlines	36 D5	
Musée de la Musique					Point Afrique	37 D4	
Future Site)	13 D2				Royal Air Maroc	38 D6	

BURKINA FASO

Salifou Kindo (☎ 70 40 33 70, 78 43 08 69; sakindo dekeke@yahoo.fr) A reputable guide and driver who has lived in London and Ghana. A full day costs around CFA20,000.

FESTIVALS & EVENTS

Apart from its lively nightlife, Ouagadougou is the undisputed capital of African film, hosting the biennial **Fespaco**, Africa's premier film festival (see the boxed text, p135).

In even-numbered years in late October or early November, Ouagadougou hosts the **Salon International de l'Artisanat de Ouagadougou** (www .siao.bf), which attracts artisans and vendors from all over the continent.

Other big-name festivals include **Jazz à Ouaga** (http://jazz.zcp.bf) in late April, **Ouaga Hip Hop** (www.wagahiphop.com) in October and **Festival International de Théâtre** (http://desik.free .fr), which is held in even-numbered years in late February.

SLEEPING
Budget

Espace Culturel Napam-Beogo (off Map p138; ☎ 50 35 35 14; www.napam-beogo.org; Gounghin; dm CFA4000, s/d with shared bathroom CFA6000/8500, d with private bathroom CFA10,000; 🖳) You've probably never stayed anywhere like this before, a 16-room guest house also operating as an artist residency (for musicians, dancers and theatre companies) and a crafts centre (based on fair trade). The rooms are utterly without frills but cut the mustard if funds are short, and the vibe is fun and casual, with your rent helping support educational and residency programs.

Cocooning (off Map p138; ☎ 50 34 28 14, 76 17 02 38; cocooning.faso@yahoo.fr; Gounghin; s/d CFA6500/8000)

Solo women travellers will feel at ease at this guest house, run with grace by Dalila, your French-Algerian host. She will go the extra mile to help you organise your sojourn in the city. The five fan-cooled rooms are clean and utilitarian, and the property, though lacking in greenery, is welcoming. Dalila's also active in supporting various orphan and disabled assistance programs, so there's a strong ethic here. Gourmet palates, you're in luck: she will treat you to French, African or North African specialities (meals from CFA4000).

our pick **Le Pavillon Vert** (Map p140; ☎ 50 31 06 11; hotelpavillonvert@yahoo.fr; Ave de la Liberté; s/d with fan & shared bathroom CFA7000/7500, with private bathroom CFA12,000/12,500, with air-con CFA16,500/17,000; 🖭) Under new management since 2009, the stalwart 'PV' is the best backpacker spot in Ouaga. Travellers of all backgrounds and nationalities will know the deal here: competitive prices, a lively bar and restaurant (excellent sausage tapas), a funky and relaxed atmosphere, and an assortment of well-kept rooms for all budgets. Top marks go to the plant-filled garden, which feels like an oasis in the evening. Bang for your buck. Reserve well in advance.

Auberge Song-Taaba (off Map p138; ☎ 50 34 65 70; Rue Toagba, Gounghin; s with fan CFA7200-8200, d with fan CFA9300-10,500, d with air-con CFA15,000; 🖭) This intimate inn offers bare yet secure rooms that open onto a verdant garden. Simple meals can be prepared, and bikes and *mobylettes* are available for rent. The owners support various community-based development projects, so you're sure that your money is well utilised. A good plan B.

ourpick Auberge Azaaba (off Map p138; ☎ 50 43 55 66, 70 75 36 32; www.maison-azaaba.com; Pissy; d with fan & shared bathroom CFA8500, with private bathroom CFA9500, with air-con CFA14,000; ❄ 🖳) What makes this guesthouse worth seeking out is how well it's maintained – Christophe, the French owner, and his Burkinabé associate Nico do care, and it is reflected in the four spotless rooms, the vast living room decorated with batiks and the appealing terrace. They're well clued up, speak acceptable English and can organise 4WD tours around the country. Meals (CFA3000) can be arranged with advance notice. There's a taxi rank 400m away.

Midrange

ourpick Case d'Hôtes (Map p138; ☎ 50 31 03 61, 78 00 86 16; www.case-hotes.com; s/d with fan & breakfast CFA11,500/16,000, with air-con & breakfast CFA16,000/22,000; ❄ 🖳 ⊚) This well-organised guesthouse, a block north of Ave de la Liberté is the perfect soft landing into Ouaga. Expect firm beds (bliss!) in the five rooms, crisp linen, a few artistic touches and spic-and-span bathrooms. Alain, the French owner, has a great deal of knowledge to impart about the capital. Good meals too (there's a cook), from CFA4000. The shady courtyard is the perfect spot for a reflective bottle of Brakina.

ourpick Yiri Suma (Map p138; ☎ 50 30 54 82; www.yirisuma.com; 428 Rue Maurice Yaméogo; incl breakfast s CFA15,000-20,000, d CFA18,000-23,000; ❄ ⊚) This sweetheart of a B&B conveniently positioned in a quiet avenue near the US embassy oozes panache. The five rooms are generously sized and expertly decorated with arts and crafts (the fact that the place doubles as an art gallery helps); beds are so plump you could pop them; and the bathrooms are so clean you could eat off the floor. Other perks include a soothing plant-filled garden, and a vast open-air terrace where breakfast and dinner (from CFA4000) are served. As well as the location, attentive service and comfort, it's the owner's passion for African arts and culture that makes this a magical spot.

Chez Tess (off Map p138; ☎ 76 03 06 06; http://tess.eklablog.com; Zogona; s/d with breakfast & shared bathroom CFA17,000/19,000, with breakfast & private bathroom CFA20,000/23,000; ❄ 🖳 ⊚) Can't speak a single word of French? Here you'll be glad to be welcomed in flawless English by Tess, a Swedish lady married to a Nigerien Tuareg. She runs a cosy B&B in a tranquil area, with four snug rooms decorated with a few artistic touches (the cheaper rooms share bathrooms), and will give you the low-down on all that's worth seeing and doing in Burkina Faso. A safe base for solo women travellers, too.

Un Paradis à Ouaga (off Map p138; ☎ 50 34 02 57; http://unparadisaouaga.free.fr; Gounghin, off Ave Kadiogo; s/d with breakfast CFA19,000/21,500, huts CFA21,500-23,500; ❄ 🐾) 'Paradise' might be pushing it a bit, but an atmosphere of dreamlike tranquillity wafts over this well-run B&B tucked away in a side street in a quiet neighbourhood. The neatly tended garden has places to lounge, the three rooms (including one occupying a stand-alone hut) are not luxurious but fresh and spruce, and there's a pool just ready for a refreshing dip. It's run by a French couple who travelled for three years around West Africa by 4WD, so you'll get plenty of advice if you've got your own wheels. Meals can be arranged.

ourpick Auberge Le Karité Bleu (off Map p138; ☎ 50 36 90 46; karite.bleu@yahoo.fr; Zone du Bois, 214 Blvd de L'Onatel; s incl breakfast CFA25,000-35,000, d 28,000-38,000; ❄ ⊚) Hidden behind ochre walls in a residential neighbourhood, this adorable B&B is one of those whispered secrets that are passed around by word of mouth. The owner's creative vision has inspired an inn of spiffy rooms and personalised service, and the ambience of the well-manicured garden is wonderful to unwind. The five rooms and two quirky huts, all adorned with masks and paintings, make you look forward to spending the night here. Feeling peckish? Espace Gondwana is a few doors away. It's about 2km west of the centre.

Hôtel les Palmiers (Map p140; ☎ 50 33 33 30, 78 81 30 96; www.hotellespalmiers.net; Rue Joseph Badoua; d CFA32,000-41,000; ❄ 🖳 🐾) This hotel is something special, an oasis blending African touches with European levels of comfort. All the rooms, which are arranged around a leafy compound, are embellished with local prints and traditional wooden masks. The garden is compact but easily one of the nicest in Ouaga, with a small pool, a bar and restaurant and birds humming in the trees. The location – on a quiet street but just a short walk from the centre – is another bonus. Book ahead.

Top End

Princess Yennenga (Map p138; ☎ 78 85 10 48; patriceb2@gmail.com; d CFA55,000; 🅿 ❄ 🖳 🐾) Easily the most luxurious venture in central Ouaga, Princess Yennenga is a good place to post up for a few days if you want a sophisticated level of comfort in peaceful surrounds. The property consists of 14 boutique-style villas cocooned in exotic gardens and kitted out with elegant African furnishings. Other highlights include a swimming pool, a craft shop and a restaurant. Payment is by cash only.

Hotel Azalai (Map p140; ☎ 50 30 60 60; www.aza laihotels.com; Ave de l'Independance; d from CFA60,000; P ⬛ ⬛ ⬛ ⬛) One of Ouaga's swankiest hotels, the Azalai makes for a splendid stay right in the centre, with 176 rooms outfitted with all the trimmings. With shops, restaurants, bars and a gym, it's always alive with action. There's also an enormous swimming pool complete with sunloungers, which casts a resort-like ambience on the whole property.

Laico Hotel – Ouaga 2000 (off Map p138; ☎ 50 37 49 02; www.laicohotels.com; Ouaga 2000; d CFA110,000; P ⬛ ⬛ ⬛ ⬛) Lying about 5km from the town centre in Ouaga 2000, this muscular building won't appeal to fans of minimalism, but the list of facilities is prolific, with two restaurants, a gym, a business centre, conference rooms, bars, a nightclub and a sparkling swimming pool. There are 231 rooms on offer here, with thick carpets and mahogany-like furniture.

EATING
Restaurants

Wakatti Arts Café (off Map p138; ☎ 50 34 58 00; Zone Industrielle de Gounghin; mains CFA1000-6000; ☽ lunch & dinner Tue-Sun) After a brilliant career in France, charismatic choreographer Irene Tassembedo settled back in Ouaga in 2008 and took over this atmospheric *maquis*. A chilled-out universe is created here by a large open-air dining area overflowing with tropical plants and a swimming pool. It's very quiet during the day, but there's live music at weekends from 9pm. The menu focuses on African staples.

Le Baratapas (Map p138; ☎ 78 85 24 80; Rue Commerce, Dapoya; dishes CFA1200-4500; ☽ 9am-11pm Tue-Sun) Ah, the Baratapas. Just around the corner from the STMB bus station, this snazzy spot has an arty vibe (see p144), the food is varied and creative (the Bobo Peul pancake, with smoked catfish, potatoes and cheese, is stunning), and Alain, the owner, is a delight. Highly recommended.

Restaurant Akwaba (Map p140; Ave Kwame N'Krumah; mains CFA2000-4000; ☽ lunch & dinner Mon-Sat) Don't be put off by the boring building – this discreet number is a reliable place to get an initiation to

lip-smacking African staples, such as *kedjenou poulet* (slowly simmered chicken with peppers and tomatoes), *alloco* (fried plantain bananas with red sauce) and *biche* (antelope).

Le Gigot a la Ficelle (off Map p138; ☎ 70 24 57 41; Blvd Tengsoba, known as Blvd Circulaire; ☽ dinner) You're going to like this slightly eccentric eatery: waiters shuffle between tables on roller skates! Food-wise, it's renowned for its *gigot* (grilled lamb), but the menu covers enough territory to suit all palates, including game and fish. There's also live music from 8pm and, at times, performances by jugglers and acrobats.

Diwan Al Mokhtar (Map p138:; ☎ 50 33 57 75; Ave JF Kennedy; mains CFA2000-7000; ☽ lunch & dinner Tue-Sun) The best Lebanese restaurant in town, Diwan serves up all of your favourite dishes from the motherland, including a superb assortment of mezes. A host of shwarmas and kebabs awaits if you're still hungry.

L'Eau Vive (Map p140; Rue de l'Hôtel Ville; mains CFA2000-7000; ☽ lunch & dinner Mon-Sat) This peaceful oasis is run by an order of nuns and promises an air-conditioned haven from the clamour outside; there's also a garden dining area out the back. The menu is mainly French but has the occasional nod to African flavours. Profits go to the order's charitable works and, for the truly surreal bit, don't be surprised if you're there at 9.30pm and the nuns sing 'Ave Maria' (you can join the choir).

La Forêt (Map p140; Ave Bassawarga; mains CFA2500-4000; ☽ lunch & dinner) La Forêt has earned a reputation as an atmospheric place for flavoursome African food, especially *poulet yassa* (chicken marinated in lime juice and onion sauce), *queue de boeuf* (ox tail) and *capitaine grillé* (grilled Nile perch). Dine alfresco around a pool in a leafy garden.

our pick Maquis Aboussouan (off Map p138; ☎ 50 34 27 20; Rue Simon Compaoré; mains CFA2500-4500; ☽ lunch & dinner Tue-Sun) A favourite of the Ouagalese and in-the-know tourists, this reassuring *maquis* is the place that you should reserve to sample your first *kedjenou poulet* or *kedjenou pintade* (slowly simmered chicken or guinea fowl with peppers and tomatoes), *attiéké* (grated cassava) and, for more adventurous tastebuds, *agouti* (a rodent – yes!). Fear not, fish also features on the menu.

Le Verdoyant (Map p140; ☎ 50 31 54 07; Ave Dimdolobsom; mains CFA3000-6000; ☽ lunch & dinner Thu-Tue) A favourite haunt of expats, the ultra-central Le Verdoyant is famous for its pasta and wood-fired pizzas (our expat friends swear they are 'the best in town', and we won't argue). If pizza and pasta aren't doing it for you, delve into salads, fish and meat dishes. The outdoor tables are pleasant and the service good.

ourpick Espace Gondwana (☎ 50 36 11 24; Rue 13.14, Zone du Bois; mains CFA4000-9000; ☻ lunch Mon-Sat, dinner daily) Espace Gondwana isn't just a restaurant, it's an experience, thanks to its sensational decor – we're talking a courtyard and four dining rooms richly adorned with masks, bronze carvings and traditional furniture. Each room is themed in a different style – Gourounsi, Mauritanian, Tuareg tent and Fula hut. The food impresses, too, with an imaginative menu that runs the gamut from frogs' legs and fish dishes to grilled meats and salads. Leave room for dessert (hmm, the explosively fruity Ivorian fondue!).

ourpick Villa Sikandra (☎ 50 43 30 99; Cissin; mains CFA5000-9000; ☻ dinner Wed-Mon) Style meets substance at this elegant eatery. Glide into one of Ouaga's most atmospheric villas – the place doubles as an art gallery – with a soothing soundtrack and order from a menu replete with beef, pork, chicken and veal dishes, as well as homemade pasta, fresh fish brought down from Ghana or Cote d'Ivoire and venison. Save room for the ambitious desserts (mango compote with almonds? More, please). Well worth the price tag.

Quick Eats

Pâtisserie Koulouba (Map p138; Ave Aboubacar Lamizana; snacks & pastries from CFA200; ☻ 6am-12.30pm & 4-7.30pm Mon-Sat, 6am-noon Sun) This pastry shop is famous for its dangerously addictive croissants and other carb-rich *viennoiseries* (pastries). It also serves snacks, ice creams and sandwiches (CFA1500).

Les P'tits Délices (Map p138; Ave JF Kennedy; snacks & pastries from CFA500; ☻ 7am-7pm) This snazzy tearoom near the American embassy is the sort of place to consider when you've been on the African road for a while and you're looking to sate a sweet tooth in stylish surrounds. Tea, (real) coffee, natural juices, appetising pies and fluffy cakes…stop! We're nearly licking the page!

Chez Madame Bado (off Map p138; off Rue 11.50, Kologh-Naba; grilled pork from CFA500; ☻ lunch Tue-Sun) After a typically Ouagalese experience? Seek out this unassuming hole-in-the-wall (in fact, a private compound), which specialises in *porc au four* (pork grilled in a traditional

oven) – a Gourounsi speciality. Tucked away in a side street (no sign; ask for directions), Chez Madame Bado is the sort of place you only find if you go looking for it. Come early – by 2pm the best morsels have sold out.

ourpick Chez Tanti Propre (Map p140; Ave Loudun; mains CFA500-1000; ☻ lunch & dinner Mon-Sat) You'll find no cheaper place for a sit-down meal in the centre. Order a *riz gras*, a *tô* or an *alloco* prepared grandma-style and plonk yourself on a wobbly bench on the terrace or in the neon-lit room. A fresh yoghurt will finish you off sweetly. Perfect for a quick bite at lunchtime.

Zama Chapelle (Map p140; Ave de la Nation; mains CFA600-1500; ☻ lunch & dinner) Zama Chapelle is not visible from the main drag – enter the Maison du Peuple compound and look for this refreshingly simple *maquis* on your left. Typical items include *langue de boeuf* (tongue) and, er, kidney. A good surprise.

Self-Catering

Marina Market (Map p140; Ave Yennenga; ☻ 8am-9pm Mon-Sat, 9am-8pm Sun) Opposite the Grande Mosquée, Marina Market has a wide selection (from Magnum ice creams to Special K breakfast cereal) and long opening hours.

DRINKING

For late-night drinking, one of the best areas is north of the centre, around Ave de la Liberté. Other G-spots of the city's bar scene include Gounghin and Ave Kwame N'Krumah, with plenty of atmospheric *maquis*.

De Niro (Map p140; ☻ 11am-late Mon-Sat) Patronised by crusty expats, De Niro – near Ave Houari Boumedienne – is an interesting place to sip a cold beer and enjoy a game of pool. It also serves simple meals.

ourpick Le Baratapas (Map p138; ☎ 78 85 24 80; Rue Commerce, Dapoya; ☻ 9am-11pm Tue-Sun) This could easily become your favourite spot in town – it's a hip bar with a cool ambience, a variety of rums and a mixed crowd, and you might hear some quality live music on Friday night. And this says nothing of the food (see p143).

Le Moulin Rouge (Map p140; Ave Kwame N'Krumah; ☻ lunch-late) With its large open-air terrace, Le Moulin Rouge is a good place to heart-start the night with a few bottles of Brakina.

Le Loft (Map p138; Ave JF Kennedy; ☻ 7pm-late Mon-Sat) This is a good choice if you want to just kick back with a perfectly crafted cocktail (from CFA2000) and soak up the loungey vibe. The Caresse du Soir (Evening Stroke), which mixes Champagne, cognac and sugar, will certainly put you in a good mood.

La Cave du Petit Paris (Map p138; off Ave Kadiogo; ☯ 9am-1pm & 4-7.30pm Tue-Sat, 4-7.30pm Mon) What about a glass or three of Bordeaux in this sophisticated wine bar? It serves good meals if your tummy's rumbling.

ENTERTAINMENT
Concerts, Dance & Theatre

The well-organised **Centre Culturel Français Georges Méliès** (Map p140; www.ccfouaga.com; Ave de la Nation) is a likely spot in the city for any major cultural happenings (such as concerts, exhibitions and theatre performances).

Other important venues:

Centre de Développement Chorégraphique – La Termitière (off Map p138; ☎ 50 30 23 44; http://cdc -latermitiere.net, in French; Samandin) This renowned complex specialises in contemporary African dance.

Espace Culturel Gambidi – Théâtre de la Fraternité (off Map p138; ☎ 50 36 59 42, 76 64 99 07; www .gambidi.org, in French; Blvd Charles de Gaulle) Near the Musée National, this eclectic cultural centre has a regular program of dance, theatre and traditional music.

Espace Culturel Napam-Beogo (☎ 50 35 53 14; www.napam-beogo.org; Gounghin) A nonprofit organisation, Espace Culturel Napam-Beogo is an artists' residency and promotes cultural understanding through dance, theatre and music.

Live Music & Maquis Dancing

If you think the time has come to showcase your dance-floor repertoire (but be prepared for stiff competition), you'll have plenty of opportunities to do so in the innumerable *maquis dancing* (simple open-air eatery-bars that feature live dance bands or sound-system jams – mostly Côte d'Ivoire beats – in the evenings). They are scattered all around Ouaga, but the most happening neighbourhood is Gounghin, west of the centre. Most venues really get rocking on Friday and Saturday nights. If you get the munchies, chow down on hot-off-the-grill chicken – this is the life!

RJV 226 (off Map p138; Ave Bassawarga) The biggest *maquis dancing* in Burkina Faso, RJV 226 has a *really* loud sound system and several dance floors under *paillottes* (straw awnings). Ivorian Coupé Décalé reigns supreme here.

Le Music Hall (Map p140; Rue des Ecoles) A large and always popular open-air club, leaning heavily on – you guessed it – Coupé Décalé.

La Joie du Peuple (off Map p138; Gounghin, near Ave Kadiogo) Everybody seems to have a good time at La Joie du Peuple, one of the most popular *maquis dancing* at the time of writing. The atmosphere is festive and the music always danceable.

Le Kingstone (Map p140) Near Rue Joseph Badoua, this place has cheap drinks and good reggae bands. However, it's in a rather intimidating neighbourhood.

Jardin de l'Amitié (Map p140; Ave Dimdolobsom) A lively *maquis* with live bands every evening around 8pm.

Wakatti Arts Café (Zone Industrielle de Gounghin; ☯ Tue-Sun) This *maquis* is a good place to catch live bands on Friday evenings and meet locals and expats.

Le Boulougou (Map p138; Koulouba, near Ave Houari Boumedienne) This Ouaga institution has been around for yonks and isn't showing signs of slowing down. A bar-eatery by day, it turns into a *maquis dancing* at weekends. Expect an older crowd. If you want to rub shoulders with hip-gyrating ladies dancing to African beats, this is the place!

Nightclubs

Ave Kwame N'Krumah has a few well-established discos, but the grooviest spot at the time of writing was **Le Nirvana** (Map p138; Ave Kouanda; cover charge CFA3500; ☯ Thu-Sun). Local DJs play a wide mix of sounds ranging from hip-hop to African beats.

SHOPPING

Ouagadougou is an excellent place to look for masks, woodcarvings, bronze work and paintings.

Galerie Nuance (Map p140; ☎ 50 31 72 74; nuancebf@ yahoo.fr; Ave Yennenga; ☯ 8.30am-12.30pm & 3.30-7pm Mon-Sat, 9am-1pm Sun) It's hard to beat this boutique for its combination of eclectic African art, textiles, clothing, carvings and jewellery, all at reasonable (and fixed) prices. It also supports local artists with occasional exhibitions.

Centre National d'Artisanat et d'Art (Map p140; ☎ 50 30 68 35; Ave Dimdolobsom; ☯ 8am-6pm) Profits here go directly to the artisan. Take some time to look over the bronze statues, wooden sculptures and colourful batiks, for there are some gems not found among the standard items elsewhere.

Village Artisanal de Ouaga (off Map p138; ☎ 50 37 14 83; Blvd Tengsoba, known as Blvd Circulaire; ☯ 7am-7pm) This government-run cooperative has, arguably, the widest range of products – clothing,

BURKINA FASO

BURKINA FASO

GO SHOP!

Even if you're not a visual-arts specialist, you'll love the range of original and fairly affordable artwork, especially paintings, bronzework and metal sculpture, on sale in Ouagadougou. You can't go wrong if you visit the following places.

Centre Lukaré (off Map p138; ☎ 50 46 48 59; centre_lukare@yahoo.fr; Gounghin; ✆ 8am-6pm) This collective is as atmospheric as it's genuine. Here you're guaranteed to see emerging artists at work, mostly painters, woodcarvers and metal sculptors.

Hangar 11 (off Map p138; ☎ 78 80 45 06; Kologh-Naba; ✆ by appointment) Set in an agreeable courtyard, this is another leading artists' collective, focusing on contemporary works, mostly paintings and bronze statues.

Le Baratapas (Map p138; ☎ 78 85 24 80; Rue Commerce, Dapoya; ✆ 9am-11pm Tue-Sun) The courtyard of this atmospheric den is filled with the innovative work of local artists and has occasional exhibitions.

Villa Sikandra (off Map p138; ☎ 50 43 30 99, 76 50 91 68; Cissin; ✆ 10am-8pm Wed-Mon) This upscale restaurant (p144) has a dedicated art gallery where you can admire (and buy) the works of Burkinabé and other West African artists. It's also a treasure trove of well-chosen handicrafts.

Two upscale B&Bs, Yiri Suma (p142) and Auberge Le Karité Bleu (p142), also sponsor local art and sell many leading and local artists' vibrant works. Espace Gondwana (p144), Laico Hotel – Ouga 2000 (p143), Espace Culturel Napam-Beogo (p141) and Centre Culturel Français Georges Mélies (p137) regularly feature art exhibitions. One good thing is that you can easily meet the artists – a number of them, such as Fernand Nonkouni (see the boxed text, p134), have their own studios and welcome visitors. Any art gallery will be able to provide you with their contact numbers.

---

textiles, leatherwork, painting, wood and metal carving, jewellery – and is ideal for getting a fix on prices and quality without the hard sell.

Art et Artisanat d'Afrique (Map p138; ☎ 50 33 43 40; www.africartisanat.com; off Blvd Charles de Gaulle; ✆ 9.30am-6.30pm Mon-Sat) This upmarket shop is literally packed to the rafters with all kinds of handicrafts from most West African countries.

Other places to check out:

Espace Culturel Napam-Beogo (☎ 50 35 35 14; www.napam-beogo.org; Gounghin) This craft makers' cooperative promotes local crafts and provides fair wages for its members. It has metalwork and woodcarvings. The manager, Lassane, has his own workshop and makes musical instruments and batiks.

Kanaga (off Map p138; ☎ 50 30 54 82; Larlé, near Ecole Nationale de la Police; ✆ 9am-6pm) Recommended for woodcarvings.

GETTING THERE & AWAY
Air

For details of international flights to/from Ouagadougou (some of which go via Bobo-Dioulasso), see p168.

Bus

Although there are loads of private companies, there are only five that you're likely to need for destinations within the country. Buses leave from the bus companies' depots rather than from the *gare routière* (bus station).

Undoubtedly the most comfortable buses are those of **TCV** (Map p138; Rue de la Mosquée) and **SKV** (Map p138; Ave Coulibaly), which both run services between Ouaga and Bobo-Dioulasso (CFA6000, five daily). Other reliable companies include **Rakieta** (off Map p138; Ave Yatenga), with services to Bobo-Dioulasso, Pô and Boromo, and **TSR** (off Map p138; Ave Kadiogo), which has services to Gaoua (CFA6000, three daily), Dori (CFA4000, two daily) and Bobo-Dioulasso (CFA6000, six daily).

STMB (Map p138; off Rue Commerce) has the most extensive network of routes throughout Burkina Faso (including those shown in the boxed text, below).

For Gorom-Gorom (CFA6000, six to seven hours), try STMB or the old clunkers of

---

BUS SERVICES FROM OUAGADOUGOU

Destination	Fare (CFA)	Duration (hr)	Frequency
Bobo-Dioulasso	6000	5	5 daily
Dori	5000	4-6	2 daily
Fada N'Gourma	4000	3-4	5 daily
Ouahigouya	2000	3	4 daily
Pô	3000	3	2 daily

Sogebaf (Ave Kadiogo), although it's easier to travel to Dori and arrange transport from there.

For details of services to Benin, Côte d'Ivoire, Ghana, Mali, Niger and Togo, see p169.

GETTING AROUND
To/From the Airport
The 2km taxi journey from l'Aéroport International de Ouagadougou to the city centre costs about CFA3000. Most gues houses can arrange transfer at the airport for about CFA3500 – a very convenient service, especially if you arrive (or leave) in the dead of the night with Royal Air Maroc or Afriqiyah.

Bicycle & Moped
The going rate to hire bicycles is CFA2000 a day, and for mopeds it could be anywhere from CFA3000 to CFA5000, depending on your negotiating skills; ask at your hotel. You can leave both bikes and mopeds safely for about CFA100 at one of the myriad two-wheeler parks around town.

Taxi
Shared taxis, mostly beaten-up old green Renaults, cost CFA300 for a short ride within town. The basic rate for a private taxi, which you commission just for yourself, is CFA500 – more for longer journeys. Rates double after 10pm.

If you're chartering a taxi for an hour or another set time period, agree on a price in advance.

AROUND OUAGADOUGOU

At **Laongo** (admission CFA2500; ⏱ 8am-5pm) there's a rich outcrop of granite, varying from grey to pink. Here, the Ministry of Culture had the inspired idea of inviting Burkinabé and international sculptors to meet, relate and carve the rock. The results of this and subsequent workshops are chiselled in the pell-mell of rocks and boulders.

To get here, take the Fada N'Gourma road to the village of Boudtenga (32km), then head northeast on a dirt road to the village of Laongo.

THE ROAD TO BOBO-DIOULASSO

BOROMO & PARC NATIONAL DES DEUX BALÉS
Halfway between Ouagadougou and Bobo, **Boromo** is a fine place to break your journey, with a good range of accommodation options. It also serves as the gateway to the **Parc National des Deux Balés** (park fees per person CFA3000; ⏱ Oct-Jun). Although the main section of the park is some distance from the town, there are several areas that are close to Boromo, and which are great spots to see elephants. The best time to visit is during March and April, when elephants head to the banks of the Mouhoun River for a cool drink and a romp in the water. Sightings can't be guaranteed, though.

Sleeping & Eating
Campement Le Kaicedra (☎ 76 62 65 40; http://kai cedra.waika9.com/camp.htm, in French; camping per person CFA3000, 2-/4-bed bungalow CFA18,000/22,000; ⏱ Oct-Jun) On the road to the national park, 7km from Boromo, is the newly refurbished and well-run Le Kaicedra. Digs are in nice bungalows in a peaceful setting right by the river, where elephants often come to drink. The staff can arrange guides (CFA2000), three-hour 4WD elephant safaris (CFA25,000 per 4WD) or pirogue trips (CFA2000). Transfers from the bus station in Boromo can be arranged (CFA10,000 per car). Meals are CFA5500.

Sama Camp (☎ 78 89 37 94, 76 08 25 96; www.sama -camp.com, in French; Boromo; s/d with shared bathroom & breakfast CFA4000/5000) At this friendly place, which you'll be hard-pressed to find, you'll get the best of both worlds: owner Philippe is French and his wife, Kadi, is Burkinabé. The atmosphere is delightfully chilled out, the neighbourhood is quiet, the ablution block is well scrubbed and the four rooms occupy a local-style house made of adobe bricks. Philippe has loads of advice on surrounding areas, while Kadi is a real cordon bleu cook (meals from CFA2000). Overall, it's simple, but there's plenty of heart. Pick-ups can be organised from the bus station, about 1km away.

KOUDOUGOU
pop 88,000
Burkina Faso's third-largest settlement, Koudougou, 97km west of Ouagadougou, is

BURKINA FASO

well worth the small detour from the main Ouagadougou–Bobo-Dioulasso road. Its distinctively Sahel-style **Grande Mosquée** in the centre of town is eye-catching, and its market is bigger, calmer and more interesting than anything Ouagadougou has to offer. Koudougou is also a convenient base for exploring Sabou and its crocodile lake, about 25km away.

You can purchase high-quality handicrafts and see craftspeople at work at the **Cité des Arts de Koudougou** (see right).

Stock up on delicious honey at **Wend Puire** (☎ 50 44 20 19; off Rte de Ouagadougou; ☯ 8am-6pm), which sells honey from local beekeepers. A 1kg pot costs CFA2000. Yes, it's organic!

If you want to meet a master bronze caster, seek out **Atelier Gandema, Mamadou et Fils** (☎ 50 44 00 48; off Rte de Sabou; ☯ 7am-6pm). You can buy small statues from CFA8000.

If you plan a visit in late November, try to make it coincide with the authentic **Nuits Atypiques de Koudougou** (www.nak.bf), which lasts about five days. It revolves around a series of dance, music and cultural performances.

You'll find banks with ATMs, *télécentres* and a Cyberposte in the centre.

Sleeping & Eating

Cité des Arts de Koudougou (☎ 50 44 33 35; www .citearts-koudougou.xdir.org, in French; Rte de Tresor s/d CFA5000/6000) We can't think of a better place for immersion in local culture. This small complex shelters various workshops employing resident craftspeople. Batiks, bogolan cloth, paintings, woodcarvings and traditional musical instruments – they're all made and sold here. Owners Apollinaire Nabaloum and Maurice Yamaeogo also organise dance and cooking classes as well as lessons in African percussion instruments. Accommodation-wise, it features three rooms that are clean, functional and well priced. The on-site restaurant is also recommended.

Hôtel Le Toulourou Plus (☎ 50 44 01 70; off Rte de Ouagadougou; d with shared bathroom CFA12,500, with private bathroom CFA18,000-25,000; ☒) Although it's starting to fray around the edges, Le Toulourou Plus offers tidy rooms with firm mattresses (luxury!), and its central yet quiet location is hard to beat. There's a decent on-site restaurant. Guests can also hire a hotel car (about CFA25,000) to visit Sabou.

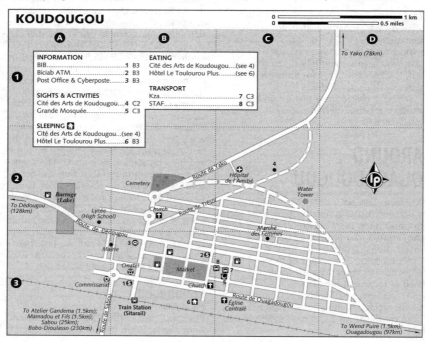

KOUDOUGOU

INFORMATION	
BIB...1	B3
Biciab ATM...............................2	B3
Post Office & Cyberposte.........3	B3

SIGHTS & ACTIVITIES	
Cité des Arts de Koudougou....4	C2
Grande Mosquée.....................5	C3

SLEEPING	
Cité des Arts de Koudougou...(see 4)	
Hôtel Le Toulourou Plus..........6	B3

EATING	
Cité des Arts de Koudougou....(see 4)	
Hôtel Le Toulourou Plus.........(see 6)	

TRANSPORT	
Kza...7	C3
STAF...8	C3

To Yako (78km)

Route de Yako

Cemetery

Barrage (Lake)

To Dédougou (128km)

Route de Dédougou

Lycée (High School)

Church

Route de Tresor

Hôpital de l'Amitié

Water Tower

Marché des Femmes

Marie

Onatel

Market

Commissariat

Route de Sabou

Train Station (Sitarail)

Church

Route de Ouagadougou

Église Centralé

To Atelier Gandema (1.5km); Mamadou et Fils (1.5km); Sabou (25km); Bobo-Dioulasso (230km)

To Wend Puire (1.5km); Ouagadougou (97km)

0 — 1 km
0 — 0.5 miles

BURKINA FASO

CROCODILE LAKES

If crocodiles give you a frisson, there are a couple of sacred lakes not far from Ouagadougou. The ritual's the same at both: you arrive; you're assailed by kids, from whom you buy a live chicken at a sacrificial price (about CFA1500, plus 'guiding fees'); the chicken's fed to a croc, which lumbers out of the water; then photos are taken of you, the kids and, grinning the widest, the croc.

Bazoulé is accessible from the village of Tanghin Dassouri, on the Bobo-Dioulasso road (about 30km west of Ouagadougou). Then head north for 6km on a dirt road.

Much more accessible is **Sabou**, which is around 90km west of Ouagadougou on the Bobo-Dioulasso road (27km from Koudougou). Sabou is well connected by bus to Ouagadougou (CFA2500) and Bobo-Dioulasso (CFA6000).

Getting There & Away

Kza and STAF, both near the mosque in the centre, have at least four buses a day to and from Ouagadougou (CFA1500, two hours).

For travel to Bobo-Dioulasso (CFA5000, five hours), Kza has one departure at 8am daily.

THE SOUTHWEST

Southwestern Burkina Faso ticks all the right boxes, with a heady mix of natural and cultural sights vying for your attention. And there's Burkina Faso's *pièce de résistance*: the much-loved city of Bobo-Dioulasso.

BOBO-DIOULASSO
pop 459,261

Bobo-Dioulasso (which means the 'Home of the Bobo Dioulas') is adorable. Bobo, as it's widely known, may be Burkina Faso's second-largest city, but it has a small-town charm and its quiet tree-lined streets exude a languid, semitropical atmosphere that makes it a favourite rest stop for travellers – one of West Africa's most enjoyable.

What's not to love in Bobo? It has a thriving market, a couple of interesting museums, a smattering of welcoming B&Bs and hotels, good restaurants, and numerous craft workshops. The spectacular mosque adds yet another dollop of atmosphere and character to the city. There's a lively music scene and, after dark, the district of Bolomakoté throbs. Drumming groups gather at local bars to get their African groove on – they play for themselves, but anybody is welcome to gather around and soak up the good vibes. Go on, delve in!

Orientation

The heart of town is the market, the Grand Marché. From the train station, Ave de la Nation leads southeast to Place de la Nation, while Ave de la Liberté heads northeast to Place du Paysan. The town's commercial core is the triangular area defined by these two roundabouts and the train station.

Information

There are plenty of freelance guides in Bobo. They can organise tours of the market, the mosque and craft workshops, as well as arrange trips to sights around Bobo.

Biciab, Ecobank and BIB are the most useful for travellers, as long as you're exchanging euros cash (and US dollars, if you're lucky). All have offices in the centre and are equipped with Visa-friendly ATMs. You'll also find several bureaux de change, but a quicker alternative is to change your euros at Marina Market (see p153) – this Lebanese-run supermarket offers the best rates and stays open late (walk to the manager's office, on the left as your enter).

Aspac (Association pour la Sauvegarde du Patrimoine Artistique et Culturel; ☎ 76 61 51 17, 20 98 15 02; www .aspac-burkina.com, in French; Blvd de la Révolution) Run by the friendly and knowledgeable Urbain Kam, Aspac offers high-quality eco-tours around the southwest and beyond. It has a strong ethic and operates on the principle of fair trade. Recommended.

Centre Culturel Français Henri Matisse (☎ 20 97 39 79; www.ccfhenrimatisse.com; cnr Ave du Général de Gaulle & Ave de la Concorde; ☺ 8am-12.30pm & 3-6.30pm Mon-Fri) Has a booklet outlining a monthly program of concerts and exhibitions.

Cyberposte (Ave de la République; per hr CFA500; ☺ 9am-9pm Mon-Sat, to 3pm Sun) At the post office; has the fastest connection among the several internet cafes in town.

BURKINA FASO

BOBO-DIOULASSO

0 |————————| 400 m
0 |————————| 0.2 miles

INFORMATION
BIB Bank (ATM)........................1 B3
Biciab (ATM)............................2 A3
Centre Culturel Français Henri
Matisse..................................3 D6
Ecobank (ATM)........................4 B3

SIGHTS & ACTIVITIES
Grand Marché..........................5 C4
Grande Mosquée.......................6 D4
Musée Provincial du Houët.........7 C6

SLEEPING 🛏
Campement Le Pacha.................8 A5
Casafrica.................................9 A6
Hôtel Restaurant Les 2 Palmiers...10 B4
L'Entente................................11 B3
Villa Rose...............................12 B5

EATING 🍽
Boulangerie Pâtisserie la Bonne
Miche....................................13 B3
Chama...................................14 B3
Dankan..................................15 B3
Don Gregori's..........................16 D5
Glacier Bon Yaourt Pâtisserie....17 C3
Hôtel Restaurant Les 2 Palmiers..(see 10)
Le Bois d'Ebene ....(see 21)
L'Eau Vive..............................18 B3
Les Bambous ....(see 24)
Mandé...................................19 B4
Marina Market........................20 A3

ENTERTAINMENT 🎭
Centre Culturel Français Henri
Matisse................................(see 3)
Le Bois d'Ebene......................21 B6
Le Macoumba Plus...................22 B3
Le Moonlight...........................23 A6
Les Bambous...........................24 C5

SHOPPING 🛍
Bobo Art................................25 B4
Grand Marché........................(see 5)
Handicraft Shops.....................26 A3
Handicraft Shops.....................27 A3

TRANSPORT
Air Burkina.............................28 A3
Rakieta Bus Station..................29 C4
SKV Bus Station.......................30 D3
STMB Bus Station.....................31 D3
TCV Bus Station.......................32 C4

To Mopti
(Mali; 535km)

0 |————| 100 m
0 |————| 0.1 miles

Gérédougou

To Musée de la Musique
and Aspac (2km);
ONTB (2km)

Hamdalaye

Sikasso-Sira

Kibidwé

Koko

To La Carine
d'Or (300m)

Train Station
(Sitarail)

Place
Amoro

Cathedral

Place du
Paysan

Stade
Wobi

Place de la
Révolution

See Enlargement

Municipal
Cemetery

Hospital

Place
de la
Nation

Gendarmerie

Haut
Commisariat

To Villa Bobo (1.5km);
Koro (13km);
Ouagadougou (355km)

To Hôtel Algouta (1km);
Le Zion (2.5km);
Dafra & Mare aux
Poissons Sacrés (6km)

To Airport (800m);
Koumi (14km);
Bathing Area (16km);
Forêt de Kou (18km);
Banfora (85km);
Gaoua (285km)

Brakina
Brewery

Bolomakoté

Route de Banfora

Ave de l'Indépendance

Ave du Général de Gaulle

ONTB (Office National du Tourisme Burkinabé; ☎ 20 97 19 86; Blvd de la Révolution; ☾ 7am-12.30pm & 3-5.30pm Mon-Fri) At the back of the SNC compound. Has a list of official guides and can recommend English-speaking guides. Expect to pay around CFA5000 per day within Bobo, or CFA10,000 per day if you're travelling beyond.

Dangers & Annoyances
Bobo-Dioulasso is generally a safe city. Avoid, however, the small river – more a trickle – where travellers report there's a risk of being mugged at night. You'll need resilience to outlast the particularly persistent hangers-on who lounge around the Grande Mosquée.

Sights
MUSEUMS
The modest **Musée Provincial du Houët** (Place de la Nation; admission CFA1000; ☾ 9am-12.30pm & 3-5.30pm Tue-Sat) showcases masks, statues and ceremonial dress from all over Burkina Faso. In the grounds are three traditional houses, each furnished in the style of its inhabitants: a Bobo house in red *banco* (mud brick), a Fulani hut of branches and woven straw, and a small Senoufo compound.

Musée de la Musique (☎ 20 98 15 02; Blvd de la Révolution; admission CFA1000; ☾ 8.30am-6pm Tue-Sun), operated by Urbain Kam (see p149), is a small museum recommended for those with an emerging passion for African music, as well as those keen to learn the difference between a *balafon* and a djembe.

GRAND MARCHÉ
Bobo-Dioulasso's centrepiece, the expansive Grand Marché is hugely enjoyable and atmospheric, and a wonderful (and largely hassle-free) place to experience a typical African city market. Occupying the inner circle are the fruit and vegetable stalls, watched over by colourfully clad women and surrounded by the overwhelming odours of the fish and meat sections. From here to the market's outer rim, impossibly narrow and labyrinthine lanes and makeshift stalls stock household wares and an excellent selection of African cotton prints. The market spills over onto the surrounding streets in a chaos of mopeds, wandering tradesmen and general clamour, which together provide a lively counterpoint to Bobo's otherwise tranquil streets.

GRANDE MOSQUÉE
The **Grande Mosquée** (admission to grounds CFA1000), built in 1893, is an outstanding example of Sahel-style mud architecture, with conical towers and wooden struts (which both support the structure and act as scaffolding during replastering). The exterior is captivating, especially at sunset when the facade turns golden and the faithful pass by on their way home or to the neighbouring mosque, often pausing for prayer in the mosque en route. The quiet and shady grounds in the immediate vicinity are interspersed with shelters and prayer mats for worshippers, and add to the charm of one of Burkina Faso's most memorable sites.

If you take one of the guides who hang around the vicinity, expect to pay around CFA3000 for explanations about the mosque and a short tour of the Kibidwe district; permission to take photos in the latter should be included in the price.

KIBIDWE
Just across the street to the east of the mosque is Kibidwe, the oldest part of town. You won't get around alone, so give in gracefully, make a contribution 'for the elders', and let yourself be guided. The best of the guides know their neighbourhood well, though their English is minimal. You'll see blacksmiths, potters, weavers, and **Sya** – the house of the ancestors, traditionally the oldest building in Bobo.

Festivals & Events
The best time to be here is during Bobo's **Semaine Nationale de la Culture** (www.snc.gov.bf, in French), a week of music, dance and theatre. It's held every even year in March or April. Held late December, the **Festival International Yeleen** (www.maisondelaparole.org, in French) features fairytale telling and concerts.

Sleeping
Staying in the city centre is convenient, but there are some imaginative choices in the quieter surrounding suburbs, easily accessed by taxi (about CFA300).

BUDGET
Casafrica (☎ 20 98 01 57; Rue 9.46, off Rte de Banfora; camping per person CFA1500, d with fan & shared bathroom CFA4000, with fan, shower & shared toilet CFA6000; ℗) This unabashed cheapie is what you'd expect: the beds are flimsy, the decor is plain, the facilities are a little outdated and the shared bathrooms have seen their fair share of bodies (and odours). But it's secure, the courtyard is attractive, there's a decent cheap bar and

BURKINA FASO

BURKINA FASO

FÊTES DES MASQUES

In the Bobo-Dioulasso region, whenever there's a major funeral, it's accompanied by a late-night *fête des masques* (festival of masks), which features Bobo helmet masks, as well as other types.

Masked men dance to an orchestra of flute-like instruments and narrow drums beaten with curved canes. Sometimes they're dressed in bulky black-and-brown raffia outfits, resembling scarecrows. Often the dancers carry long, pointed sticks with which they make enormous jumps. Each dancer, representing a different spirit, performs in turn, leaping, waving his stick and looking for evil spirits that might prevent the deceased from going to paradise. The onlookers, especially the children, are terrified and flee as the dancer becomes increasingly wild, performing strange acrobatic feats and waving his head backwards and forwards until he catches someone and strikes them. The victim, however, mustn't complain. That chase over, another begins, and the whole wild ceremony can last for hours.

restaurant, and the place is watched over by the friendly Ardiouma. The surrounding streets are quiet and very African with their laterite roads and overhanging trees.

Le Zion (☎ 78 86 27 25, 78 83 75 30; http://le.zion.free .fr; Kuinima; rooftop mattresses CFA1500, d with fan & shared bathroom CFA4500, with fan, shower & shared toilet CFA7000) On the outskirts of town and very much a part of the local community, Le Zion is run by a French-Burkinabé couple, Camille and Wassa. They offer unflashy yet clean rooms, built using traditional materials. You can also drag a mattress out on the rooftop and sleep beneath the star-studded skies. Never mind the cramped quarters, it's the whole package that stands out – live music most weekends, home-cooked meals (Camille is an adept chef), *mobylette* rental, loads of advice on the surrounding area, and a wonderfully chilled ambience. A perfect base for unfussy backpackers (less so if you're after hush and creature comforts). Give them a call and they'll come and pick you up from the town centre.

Campement Le Pacha (☎ 20 98 09 54, 76 61 16 01; lepachabo@yahoo.fr; Rue Malherbe; camping per person/car CFA2000/2500, d with fan & shared bathroom CFA9500-10,500, with air-con CFA17,500-18,500; P ⊠) An excellent first impression is made by the courtyard, one of Bobo's nicest, with a veritable forest of palms and potted plants, but there's no disguising the fact that the unadorned rooms are a tad disappointing for the price. However, visitors appreciate the convenient location and the great garden restaurant (mains from CFA3000). Bikers get a warm welcome from the owner, who's a biker himself.

MIDRANGE

our pick Villa Bobo (☎ 20 98 20 03, 70 53 78 17; http://myspace.com/villabobo; Koko; s/d with fan CFA8000/12,000, with air-con CFA12,000/17,000; P ⊠ 🖳 🖳 🛜) Seeking a relaxing cocoon in Bobo with homely qualities and a big dollop of atmosphere without the exorbitant price tag? This champ of a B&B run by Xavier, a French guy who fell in love with Bobo, has all the key ingredients, with three zealously looked-after rooms (two of which share bathrooms), prim bathrooms, plump bedding and a colourful garden. After a long day's sightseeing, nothing beats a dip in the small pool. Xavier speaks English and can arrange excursions in the area. He's also knowledgeable about Bobo nightlife and local music. Breakfast costs CFA1500, and there's a communal kitchen. Other perks include bike and moped rental.

our pick Hôtel Algouta (☎ 20 98 07 92, 78 85 84 42; www.hotel-algouta.com; Bolomakoté; d with fan CFA8000, with air-con CFA16,000; P ⊠ 🖳) Simplicity is the rule at the well-kept Algouta, and it works a treat. It offers a range of tidy, light and well-equipped rooms at remarkably reasonable prices, and the public spaces are enlivened with African handicrafts. Best of all, it's in a very quiet street and the onsite restaurant serves up excellent African food, including game dishes in the season. Free internet access.

Villa Rose (☎ 70 16 33 00, 20 98 54 16; www.villarose bobodioulasso.com; off Rue Malherbe; d with fan CFA9000, with air-con CFA14,000-16,000; P ⊠ 🖳 🛜) Not far from the railway line, this welcoming guesthouse run by a Dutch-Burkinabé couple, Franca and Moctar, hosts seven comfy (but not flash) rooms arrayed around a soothing garden. Breakfasts (from CFA1500) and dinners (from CFA2000) can be arranged on request. Franca, who speaks good English, is involved in various women's development projects in Bobo and will be happy to take you with her if you want to make contact with local charities.

L'Entente (☎ 20 97 72 05; Rue du Commerce; s/d with fan CFA9500/13,000, with air-con CFA18,500/21,000; **P** **⊠** **✿**) If you're seeking a billet in Bobo with tidy rooms, clean-smelling bathrooms and a central location, this fine pile is your answer. Pluses include a restaurant and a lovely garden.

Hôtel Restaurant Les 2 Palmiers (☎ 20 97 27 59; hotelles2palmiers@fasonet.bf; off Rue Malherbe; d CFA35,000-40,000; **P** **⊠** **✿**) This excellent option gets an A+ for its spacious, spotless rooms embellished with African knickknacks and, joy of joys, its spring mattresses (yes, *spring* mattresses!). There are only 10 rooms, which ensures intimacy and guarantees sweet dreams. Another bonus is the onsite restaurant, hailed as one of the best in Bobo. The location is better than it looks on the map – an easy walk into town but in a nice quiet street.

Eating

For self-caterers, **Marina Market** (Ave de la République; ✿ 8am-1pm & 4-8pm Mon-Sat, 9am-1pm Sun) has a good range of grocery items.

RESTAURANTS & MAQUIS

Les Bambous (p154), Le Zion (opposite) and Le Bois d'Ebene (p154) are congenial spots where you can enjoy well-prepared meals in pleasant surrounds, with live music most evenings.

Don Gregori's (Ave de la Révolution; mains CFA500-1000; ✿ lunch & dinner) This economical haunt with a small terrace and a vast neon-lit interior won't win any design awards, but it's the atmosphere you come here to ingest. Food-wise it focuses on African staples, such as *riz sauce* and *tô*.

our pick **Hôtel Restaurant Les 2 Palmiers** (☎ 20 97 27 59; off Rue Malherbe; mains CFA1000-4000; ✿ lunch & dinner) Everyone needs a slap-up meal once in a while and there's no better place than this upscale venture. The sinful menu roams from melt-in-your-mouth *filet mignon de porc* (a choice piece of pork) to *darne de thon rouge* (red tuna steak). Squeeze in a delicious homemade *crêpe* and you'll be in seventh heaven.

Dankan (Rue Malherbe; mains CFA1000-4000; ✿ lunch & dinner) With agreeable outdoor (but covered) tables, very reasonable prices and a wide-ranging menu specialising in African dishes, Dankan is an excellent deal. It's kept spotlessly clean and service is attentive. If you just eat *riz sauce* or couscous and drink tamarind juice, you'll be well fed for around CFA1500.

our pick **Mandé** (Ave de la Révolution; mains CFA1000-4000; ✿ lunch & dinner) Same menu (and same owner) as Dankan, so you can expect tasty African specialities at paupers' prices. However, the setting is much more romantic here, especially in the evening when the open-air terrace is moodily lit and waitresses are dressed like flight attendants. Very friendly and relaxed.

Chama (Ave Alwatra Diawara; mains CFA1000-4000; ✿ lunch & dinner) This clever little *maquis* is low on frills and high on conviviality, especially in the evening when the open-air terrace fills up with happy punters wrapping their lips around grilled chicken or delving into Nile perch. When you've eaten, grab a beer and challenge the locals to a game of pool inside.

our pick **La Canne d'Or** (☎ 20 97 15 96; Koko; mains CFA2000-5000; ✿ lunch & dinner) New owners have breathed fresh life into this villa-style eatery in a serene neighbourhood. It serves French fare with an African twist in a welcoming, light-toned interior, or on an inviting terrace. House faves include marbled frogs' legs, homemade spring rolls, antelope steak and Nile perch with almonds. If you've been on the road for a while, it'll all taste like manna from heaven.

L'Eau Vive (Rue Delafosse; mains CFA2500-5000; ✿ lunch & dinner Mon-Sat) The sister venue to the restaurant of the same name in Ouagadougou, and also run by nuns, L'Eau Vive offers imaginative French cooking and a varied menu. Main dishes all come with potatoes or vegetables and the dining area offers a star-filled canopy of the night sky.

QUICK EATS

Glacier Bon Yaourt Pâtisserie (Ave de la Révolution; yogurt from CFA300; ✿ 8am-late) Come to this stamp-sized outlet for the divinely sweet yoghurt – one mouthful, and you'll be hooked.

Boulangerie Pâtisserie la Bonne Miche (Ave Ouédraogo; ✿ 6am-midnight) Sugarholics flock to this buzzing pastry shop to re-energise on a bountiful selection of cakes and other goodies. The croissants are peerless: fresh, crusty and dense. Excellent baguettes too.

Drinking

Bobo-Dioulasso only really comes to life at the weekend. One exception is the popular quarter of Bolomakoté, which is rich in traditional music. Here you'll enjoy great music in small, unpretentious *buvettes* (small cafes that double as drinking places serving cheap meals), where

BURKINA FASO

you can drink *chopolo*, the local millet-based beer. Elsewhere – unless you're there very late on Friday or Saturday night – the bars are all pretty similar, with outdoor tables under straw *paillottes*. It's difficult to recommend anywhere in particular – there are so many, so just follow your nose to find one you like.

Entertainment
NIGHTCLUBS
Although most of Bobo's garden bars turn into dance venues late on Friday and Saturday night, **Le Macoumba Plus** (Ave de la République; ☼ Thu-Sat), near the market, is a dedicated nightclub. Another major player is **Le Moonlight** (Rte de Banfora; ☼ Tue-Sun). Both offer a mix of Western tunes and African beats. Cover charges (CFA3000) apply Friday and Saturday night only.

LIVE MUSIC
The Centre Culturel Français Henri Matisse (p149) and Aspac (p149) host concerts at least once a month.

Les Bambous (Ave du Gouverneur Binger; admission CFA500; ☼ 6am-2.30pm & 6pm-midnight Mon-Sat, 6pm-midnight Sun) This popular outdoor venue features a lovely garden area and traditional live music (especially djembe music) from around 9pm.

Le Zion (Kuinima; ☼ Fri & Sat) Another lively, but more intimate, place for live music (both modern and traditional), with plenty of local artists on Friday and Saturday night. It's very much a local bar, but is also popular with expats.

ourpick **Le Bois d'Ebene** (Ave de l'Unité; admission CFA500; ☼ noon-late) Watch your back, Les Bambous: music fans have started calling Le Bois d'Ebene the best venue in town for live music. It's less institutionalised than Les Bambous, it's big on atmosphere, and the garden is so coool.

Shopping
Bobo-Dioulasso is a good place to pick up wooden masks and other carvings – especially

---

A THUMPING GOOD TIME IN BURKINA FASO

After a unique cultural experience? Keen to learn West African music and dance? Consider taking drumming or dance classes. Ouaga, Bobo and the Banfora area have strong music traditions and are good places to look for drum (djembe, *balafon*) or dance teachers who give individual or group lessons. This is an effective way of learning about local traditions and having a good time. Sure, there's the language barrier, but for such activities it's not too much of a problem. A few contacts:

Aspac (p149) In Bobo-Dioulasso, this well-organised association offers week-long courses in African percussion as well as traditional dance courses. It has its own accommodation.

Association Soutrala Tyera (p158) This association, based in Sindou, is active in promoting responsible travel in the Senoufo country through cultural exchanges, including tailor-made courses in African percussion. You'll stay with local families in villages.

Bassirou Sanou (☎ 20 98 61 08, 76 60 69 59; Bobo-Dioulasso) We met Bassirou in person, and we were seriously impressed – he's one of the best players of the Malinké flute. Search for 'Bassirou Sanou' on YouTube and just listen – mystical. He gives classes.

Campement Farafina (p157) In Tengréla. Owner Solo is a skilled percussionist and teaches djembe, *kora* and *balafon*.

Centre Culturel Français Georges Mélies (p137) Organises dance and drumming classes, and can direct you to musicians and choreographers.

Centre Culturel Français Henri Matisse (p149) Can put you in touch with musicians in Bobo-Dioulasso.

Centre de Développement Chorégraphique – La Termitière (p145) In Ouagadougou. Features a range of dance classes and workshops.

Cité des Arts de Koudougou (p148) In Koudougou, this cultural beehive offers dance and drumming classes.

Espace Culturel Gambidi – Théâtre de la Fraternité (p145) In Ouagadougou. Organises dance and traditional music courses.

Irène Tassembedo (☎ 50 31 16 51, 76 58 72 72; www.irenetassembedo.com; Ouagadougou) Famous choreographer Irene Tessembedo had plans to open an international dance school in Ouagadougou when we met her – contact her for details.

Nabissa (p157) Owner Philippe knows all (good) musicians in Banfora and can refer you to competent teachers.

Lobi and Bobo items – and there are some good handicraft shops dotted around the town centre and in the southwestern quarter of the market.

One small shop that stands out for its variety of masks, statues and light sales pitch is **Bobo Art** (Rue Malherbe; ☿ 8am-7pm Mon-Sat).

For clothing, the Grand Marché is your best bet; for a tailor-made shirt expect to pay CFA1500 for cloth, plus CFA1500 for labour.

Getting There & Away
AIR
Air Burkina (☎ 20 97 13 48; Ave du Gouverneur Clozel) Has two flights per week to/from Ouagadougou (CFA50,000). For details of international flights from Bobo, see p168.

BUS
STMB (Blvd de la Revolution), **TCV** (Rue Crozat) and **SKV** (Blvd de la Revolution) have the best buses to Ouagadougou (CFA6000, five hours), with five daily departures each.

For getting around the southwest, **Rakieta** (Ave Père Nadal) is a reliable company that has regular departures for Banfora (CFA1500, 1½ hours, six daily). Another option is TCV, with six daily services to Banfora (same price).

For details on transport to Côte d'Ivoire, Ghana and Mali, see p169.

Getting Around
TO/FROM THE AIRPORT
Expect to pay CFA300/1500 for a shared/private taxi between the airport and the city centre.

BICYCLE & MOPED
To hire a bicycle for the day, ask at your hotel or guesthouse. A reasonable price is CFA2000 per day.

For a moped, expect to pay at least CFA4000 a day, and up to CFA7000 for a motorbike.

TAXI
Shared taxis are plentiful and most trips within town cost from CFA300. Prices increase after 10pm and luggage costs extra.

AROUND BOBO-DIOULASSO
The traditional houses in the villages around Bobo-Dioulasso are characterised by their tall conical roofs and narrow storehouses linked by earth walls, which give the compounds the look of squat medieval castles.

Forêt de Kou
About 18km west from Bobo-Dioulasso, the 115-hectare **Forêt de Kou** (admission CFA1000) is a lush forest that shelters lots of bird species. It's crisscrossed by a network of walking paths.

Fancy a dip? About 16km west of Bobo-Dioulasso, just off the road to Bama (it's signposted) and past the Ecole des Eaux et Forêts, you'll find a small **bathing area** (admission CFA500) in the Kou River. Although it's popular at weekends, you'll probably have the place to yourself during the week.

Koumi
On the road to Sikasso, about 14km southwest of Bobo-Dioulasso, the village of Koumi has some fine ochre two-storey adobe houses, typical of the area. Admission costs CFA1000, plus guiding fees.

Koro
The village of **Koro** (admission CFA1000) is 13km east of Bobo, just off the main Ouagadougou road. Perched on the hillside, its houses – built amid rock formations – are unique in the area, and there are fine panoramic views over the countryside from the top of the village.

Mare aux Poissons Sacrés
This sacred fish pond is around 6km southeast of Bobo, in the village of **Dafra**. The surrounding hills and pond, at the base of a cliff and a 20- to 30-minute walk from the nearest parking spot, are memorable; the fish are less so. Chickens, which you can buy on the spot (CFA1500), are sacrificed and thrown to the overgorged *poissons sacrés* (sacred fish). It's all rather gruesome, with chicken feathers everywhere. Don't wear gold jewellery or anything red; both are prohibited at this sacred spot.

A taxi there and back from Bobo-Dioulasso will cost at least CFA6000.

BANFORA
pop 76,000

A sleepy little town, Banfora lies in one of the more beautiful areas of Burkina Faso. As such, it serves as a good base for exploring the lush, green surrounding countryside, not to mention seeing the hippos of Tengréla Lake, the cascading waters of the Karfiguéla Waterfalls and the otherworldly Sindou Peaks.

It's also a necessary gateway to the Lobi country further east.

Banfora has several banks with ATMs, a Cyberposte and innumerable *télécentres*.

In Banfora itself, the perimeter of the market, with its women selling fruit and vegetables, is more interesting than the actual market – especially on the northern side. There are also some good hotels and places to eat.

As you wander around town, you're likely to be accompanied by guides keen to show you the neighbouring sights. Your best bet is to ask at your hotel for a recommendation. We found one English-speaking guide, **Lateef Dada** (☎ 78 82 31 97; jlateefdada@yahoo.fr), who has a good reputation. He charges CFA11,000 per day for up to three people (transport is extra).

Sleeping

Camping Siakadougou (☎ 76 43 30 89; camping per person CFA2000, d CFA3000-4000) A sensible choice for budget travellers. Siaka will welcome you warmly in his plain but well-run *campement*, with five traditional huts arranged around a courtyard. Simple meals are available on request. It's a 10- to 15-minute walk to the centre, in a quiet neighbourhood off the road to Karfiguelá. Give Siaka a call on arrival and he'll pick you up at the bus station.

Le Calypso (☎ 20 91 02 29, 70 74 14 83; famille _houitte@yahoo.fr; Rte de Bobo-Dioulasso; dm CFA2500, d with fan & shared toilet CFA6500, with fan CFA8500-10,000, with air-con CFA15,000; 🕮 🖳) This newish property caters to all budgets. On a shoestring? Opt for a bed in the neat dorm. In search of more privacy?

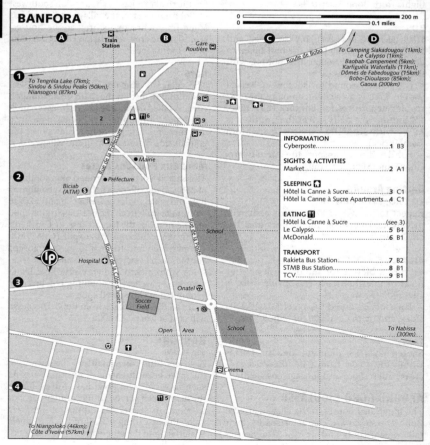

BANFORA

0 ____ 200 m
0 ____ 0.1 miles

To Tengréla Lake (7km); Sindou & Sindou Peaks (50km); Niansogoni (87km)

Train Station

Gare Routière

Route de Bobo

To Camping Siakadougou (1km); Le Calypso (1km); Baobab Campement (5km); Karfiguéla Waterfalls (11km); Dômes de Fabedougou (15km); Bobo-Dioulasso (85km); Gaoua (200km)

Rue de la Préfecture

Mairie

Préfecture

Biciab (ATM)

Rue de la Poste

School

Hospital

School

To Nabissa (300m)

Onatel

Soccer Field

Open Area

School

Cinema

To Niangoloko (46km); Côte d'Ivoire (57km)

INFORMATION
Cyberposte..................................1 B3

SIGHTS & ACTIVITIES
Market..2 A1

SLEEPING
Hôtel la Canne à Sucre..................3 C1
Hôtel la Canne à Sucre Apartments...4 C1

EATING
Hôtel la Canne à Sucre..............(see 3)
Le Calypso..................................5 B4
McDonald....................................6 B1

TRANSPORT
Rakieta Bus Station......................7 B2
STMB Bus Station.........................8 B1
TCV...9 B1

Upgrade to a fan-cooled unit. Want a few more creature comforts? The rooms with air-con are your answer. All units are sparkling clean, and there's an airy compound. Look no further if you need to recharge the batteries. Sensational value.

Hôtel la Canne à Sucre (☎ 20 91 01 07; www.banfora.com; off Rue de la Poste; d with fan CFA8000, with air-con CFA20,000-30,000, 4-bed apt CFA49,000; ✖ 🖳) Sweeeet! The immaculate rooms are kitted out with African woodcarvings and cloth, there's not a speck of dust in the huge bathrooms, the apartments across the road are comfy and the leafy garden feels like heaven after a tiring day…without a doubt Canne à Sucre is Banfora's most complete atmospheric hotel. If you're watching your money, opt for the fan-cooled rooms (needless to say, they're less eye-catching).

Eating
Nabissa (☎ 76 25 33 36, 75 27 68 86; mains CFA800-3000; ✖ 8am-late) Run by Philippe, a former postman in France and a keen musician, this bar-restaurant is a cool spot to sink your teeth into a chicken in *soumbala* sauce or a *porc au four* (oven-baked pork). The homemade French fries (potato, yam or sweet potato) are superlative too.

McDonald (off Rue de la Préfecture; mains CFA1000-3000; ✖ lunch & dinner Thu-Tue) Why can't all McDonalds have so much zest? This cool den off the main drag boasts an inviting covered terrace that doubles as a little art gallery. It churns out a good range of satisfying dishes, including a *hamburger frites* (burger with fries), salads and chicken, as well as pancakes and fruity concoctions, including a wickedly strong ginger juice.

Le Calypso (☎ 20 91 10 28; off Rue de la Poste; mains CFA1000-3500; ✖ breakfast, lunch & dinner) Under the same ownership as the eponymous hotel but in a different location, Le Calypso is distinctive for its mellow atmosphere – picture a verdant courtyard dotted with straw *paillottes* beneath a mango tree – and well-produced local dishes. Everything here is tasty, but two personal recommendations are the *capitaine à la crème* (Nile perch in a cream sauce) and *brochettes de capitaine* (skewered Nile perch).

Hôtel la Canne à Sucre (off Rue de la Poste; mains CFA2000-5000; ✖ lunch & dinner) The restaurant here is the best place to eat in the area, with delightful open-air dining, a well-chosen wine list, good service and a varied menu that spans European and African flavours. Will it be frogs' legs, or minced beef with ginger? Splash out – you deserve it.

Drinking & Entertainment
You'll find a gaggle of *buvettes* in Banfora, which are all good for a sundowner, but the most atmospheric venue at the time of writing was, by far, **Nabissa** (☎ 76 25 33 36, 75 27 68 86; ✖ 8am-late). There's traditional live music at 9pm, with *balafon*, djembe and local songs, and more modern tunes at weekends. Don't miss it.

Getting There & Away
Rakieta (Rue de la Poste) has regular departures for Bobo-Dioulasso (CFA1300, 1½ hours, six daily) and Gaoua (CFA5000, 3½ hours, one daily). **STMB** (Rue de la Poste) also leaves three times a day for Bobo-Dioulasso, while **TCV** (Rue de la Poste) has six daily services.

AROUND BANFORA
You'll need wheels to visit the wonderful attractions surrounding Banfora. If you take a guide, they can help you make the arrangements – for information on guides see p155; alternatively, ask at your hotel. Nabissa (left) in Banfora rents mopeds (CFA4000) and motorcycles (CFA6000) that are properly maintained and provides roadside assistance in case of breakdown – a winning formula. A motorcycle is advisable if you're making the longer journey to the Sindou Peaks and beyond.

Tengréla Lake
This 100-hectare **lake** (Lac de Tengréla; admission CFA2000), around 7km west of Banfora on a good dirt road, makes a pleasant ride and is easy to find. You'll see fisherfolk, a variety of bird life and, if you're lucky, hippos (your best chance of seeing them is in the drier months, especially from January to April). The admission price includes a pirogue trip.

Wanna laze a few days away in the area? Park your backpack at **Campement Kenignigohi – Chez Seydou** (☎ 70 24 68 93, 70 29 34 61; Tengréla; d/tw with shared bathroom CFA3000/6000), a five-minute walk from the lake, or at the Rasta-run **Campement Farafina** (☎ 70 24 46 21, 71 38 94 40; so loisa6@hotmail.com; Tengréla; d/tw with shared bathroom CFA3000/6000), about 500m further down, which sports cheery reggae paintings on the outside walls. Both places are simple but clean and high on character. They can arrange pick-ups from the bus station in Banfora (CFA3000) and organise bike and moped rental as well as village visits and cultural tours. They also prepare meals on request. The musically inclined will opt for Campement Farafina – the owner, Solo, is an adept percussionist and gives drumming lessons. He also has a craft shop packed with djembe and *balafon*.

To get to the lake, take the dirt road that forks right at the Total petrol station in Banfora, then, after about 6km, turn left for the village of Tengréla. The lake is a further 1km beyond the village.

Karfiguéla Waterfalls

Some 11km northwest of Banfora, these **waterfalls** (Cascades de Karfiguéla; admission CFA1000) are at their best during and just after the rainy season, when, unfortunately, the dirt tracks leading to the falls can be impassable. But, whatever the season, it's worth the journey. From below, you approach the falls through a magnificent avenue of mango trees, and the chaotic jumble of rocks over which the water sprays are a sight in themselves. Our tip: bring a picnic.

If you need to cool off, you can take a dip in the lovely natural pools on the upper part of the waterfalls (take the steps to the right of the falls). Pure bliss!

Baobab Campement (☎ 76 01 28 18; camping per person CFA1500, d with shared bathroom CFA5000), about 5km from Banfora on the road to the waterfalls (a further 1.5km), is a laid-back budget place that gets good reviews from travellers. The mud-brick huts are simple but satisfying and blend effortlessly into the environment. Paul and his family do a good job of preparing tasty meals, including wood-fired pizzas. Bikes and mopeds are available for hire. A taxi from Banfora's bus station costs about CFA3000.

Dômes de Fabedougou

Arriving at this site, you'll pinch yourself to see if it's real. The scenery is unique: the **Dômes de Fabedougou** (admission CFA1000) consist of huge limestone formations that have been sculpted over millennia into quirky, dome-like (some would go for 'phallic') shapes by water and erosion.

To get to the Dômes from Bobo, take the road to Sindou and then turn right at a sign near the Karfiguéla falls turn-off. Then ask for directions (the dirt track skirts cane fields and

is not easy to find). You can also walk the 3km from Karfiguéla waterfalls, but you'll need a guide to lead you to the Dômes because the path isn't waymarked.

Sindou

Sindou = fantastic rock formations. One of Burkina Faso's most spectacular landscapes, the **Sindou Peaks** (Pics de Sindou; admission CFA1000) are a geological wonderland. This narrow, craggy chain features a fantastic array of tortuous cones that were sculpted and blasted by the elements; they were left behind when the surrounding softer rocks eroded away. This outlandish landscape could be the perfect backdrop for another version of *Planet of the Apes*, especially given that macaws can regularly be seen hopping amid the rock formations.

The best moment to visit the area is at dawn or in the evening, when the sun sets behind the cones – don't forget your camera!

This fantasyland is ideal for a one-hour stroll amid the cones, a day hike, or even a couple of days' **trekking**. Coming from Banfora, the main gateway is about 1km before the entrance to Sindou town. There's a little booth staffed by guides. They belong to the **Association Soutrala Tyera** (☎ 76 08 46 60; mokopic@yahoo.fr), which was formed to promote community tourism and cultural exchanges. It's run by Moko, a dynamic Senoufo guide who knows the region intimately and can organise village stays, cultural tours (such as music or cooking courses; CFA15,000 per person per day) and various circuits in the Senoufo country, including moped trips (CFA27,000 per person per day) and bike tours (CFA21,000 per person per day). You'll find him (or his brother) at the booth.

In Sindou, you can stay at the humble **Campement Djatiguiya** (☎ 76 24 71 61, 70 71 57 28; r CFA4000). A more atmospheric option is **Campement Soutrala** (☎ 76 08 46 60; r per person CFA2500), operated by Association Soutrala Tyera. It offers a cluster of mud huts in a peaceful setting, near the guides' booth, and has views of the rock formations.

Coming from the village of Loumana, about 23km further west, a few minibuses stop in Sindou on their way to Banfora's *gare routière* (CFA1250). The last one leaves Sindou at around 11am.

Niansogoni

You've reached *le bout du monde* (the end of the world) in Niansogoni, still the country's undug tourism gem. Well off the beaten path thanks to its splendid isolation – it's 37km southwest of Sindou, near the border with Mali – this tiny settlement is a terrific place to kick back for a few days and a fantastic opportunity to experience local life. The scenery is gorgeous, with a series of limestone hills, cliffs and escarpment-like formations that loom on the horizon – all told, it looks like the Dogon Country in miniature. From Niansogoni, you can walk to an old village nestled in an alcove of the escarpment, where you can see old granaries and dwellings.

From Sindou, it's a long way along a dirt track to Niansogoni (no public transport). But the reward is sweet. The **Campement de Niansogoni** (☎ 76 48 06 59; Niansogoni; s/d with shared bathroom CFA3000/6000) offers simple yet well-maintained huts with thatched roofs. The setting? There's a limestone cliff as a backdrop. Meals are available and there's a small shop where you can buy crafts, cashew nuts and dried mangoes (killer!). And yes, beer is available (though a bit too lukewarm the day we dropped by). The owner, Richard Traoré, is passionate about his region and he'll be happy to arrange all kinds of excursions, including village visits, hikes and multiday treks.

GAOUA

Gaoua is a good base for exploring Lobi country, an area that's culturally distinct. There's a vibrant Sunday market and, if you like your music traditional and untainted, Gaoua has plenty of great *boîtes* (informal nightclubs) with live music. There is one bank with an ATM and a Cyberposte. Be sure to visit the well-organised **Musée de Poni** (☎ 20 90 01 69; admission CFA2000; ☼ 7am-6pm), which is the perfect introduction to Lobi culture and traditions.

The weak point in Gaoua is the lack of good accommodation options, though this should have changed by the time you read this (there are plans to build a new hotel). The old-fashioned **Hôtel Hala** (☎ 20 90 01 21; s/d with fan CFA12,500/15,000, with air-con CFA23,000/27,500; 🅿) features bog-standard rooms that are ludicrously overpriced, and the restaurant serves bland fare. Shoestringers can opt for **Campement Tranquille – Chez Kader** (☎ 70 01 32 26, 20 90 07 87; r per person incl full board CFA7500). Digs are in spartan but adequate mud huts. Kader is a congenial guide (and an accomplished sculptor) who can take you to nearby Lobi

villages. Give him a call and he'll pick you up at the bus station.

Gaoua's only true restaurant, **Les 4 Saisons** (☎ 20 90 04 57; mains CFA800-2500; ☼ breakfast, lunch & dinner) has a relaxed atmosphere and a varied menu, with salads, African staples and a criminally sweet vanilla yoghurt. It's right in the centre.

If you're after sustainably produced local handicrafts, the women-run **Association Pour la Promotion Feminine de Gaoua** (APFG; ☎ 20 90 00 78; ☼ 8am-12.30pm & 3-6.30pm Mon-Sat) sells shea-butter soap and creams, pottery, and textiles.

Getting There & Away

The *gare routière* is on the outskirts of town. You'll find bus services to Bobo-Dioulasso (CFA5000, five hours, two to three daily) and Ouagadougou (CFA6000, three to four daily, seven hours). Direct services to Banfora are scarce; it's best to go to Bobo and find onward connections.

THE SOUTH & SOUTHEAST

A journey into southern and southeastern Burkina Faso is much about viewing wildlife, but don't miss Tiébélé in the Gourounsi country, which is famous for its distinctive architecture.

FADA N'GOURMA
pop 42,000

If you're heading for Niger or the parks of southeastern Burkina Faso and Benin, you'll most likely pass through Fada N'Gourma (or Fada, as it's known), some 219km east of Ouagadougou. It's a sprawling town, with a mildly interesting market, but not enough to detain you any longer than the time it takes to change bush taxis and buy a pot of *miel du Gourma*, the locally produced honey, which is readily available at many roadside stalls.

You'll find banks with ATMs and a Cyberposte for internet access.

Sleeping & Eating

There are lots of *maquis* dishing up inexpensive fare along the main drag.

Panache Hotel (☎ 40 77 03 73; www.panache hotel.com; d with fan CFA10,000-15,000, with air-con CFA15,000-25,000; 🅿 🌆 🅟 🛜) What a good surprise. The Syrian-run Panache must be

---

LOBI TRADITIONS

Lobi traditions are some of the best preserved in West Africa. Perhaps because of this, Lobi art (in particular the wooden carvings) is highly regarded by collectors.

For travellers, the most obvious manifestation of those enduring traditions is the architecture of rural Lobi homes. The compounds are rectangular and – rare for mud constructions – sometimes multistorey. Each structure, with high mud-brick walls and small slits for windows, is like a miniature fortress. Unlike most Africans, who live in villages, the Lobi (like the Somba and the Tamberma in northern Benin and Togo), live in their fields; a family compound may be several hundred metres from its nearest neighbours.

The Lobi are also known for holding fast to their cultural rituals. For example, the *dyoro* initiation rites, which take place every seven years, are still widely observed. As part of this important rite of passage, young men undergo three to six months of severe physical tests of their manhood, and learn the clan's oral history and the dos and don'ts of their culture.

In rural areas the Lobi often don't warm easily to foreigners. Your best bet is to hire a guide in Gaoua (ask at Hôtel Hala – see p159), who will take you to interesting settlements, such as Holi, Tambili and Doudou. There are lots of female gold miners working around Doudou, and Doudou's market (one every five days) is famous for its gold trade. Don't take photos without permission. In towns such as Gaoua, however, the Lobi can be very friendly, and if you're invited to have some *chopolo*, the local millet beer, by all means accept. For more on the Lobi, see p75.

---

one of the most comfortable hotels outside Ouagadougou, with a lovely pool, squeaky-clean rooms, immaculate bathrooms, a neat garden, an onsite restaurant and well-sprung mattresses. Priceless!

Getting There & Away

STMB has five daily buses between Fada N'Gourma and Ouagadougou (CFA4000, three to four hours), while Rakieta has four daily services (CFA4000).

STMB has a daily service to Niamey (Niger; CFA9500) and two weekly services to Lomé (Togo; CFA16,500). You'll also find bush taxis and minibuses to the border with Benin (CFA4000), but they only leave when they're full.

Transport for the national parks of the southeast is scarce.

KOMPIENGA LAKE

About 100km south of Fada N'Gourma, you'll reach **Pama**, the main gateway to **Kompienga Lake**. Expats and visitors in the know come here to maroon themselves for a languid holiday at **Campement de Thialy** (☎ 70 30 13 94; thialyburkina@yahoo .fr; Kompienga; d per person incl full board CFA30,000; ✦ ✦), which must be the most atmospheric *campement* in the country. How many *campements* do you know that occupy a secluded peninsula on a lake? Once you get over the setting, the facilities are pretty astounding too, especially give the isolation: the eight rooms are well de-

signed and comfortable, and there's a pool and a restaurant. Various excursions and activities are offered, from pirogue trips on the lake to visits to nearby parks and reserves. Paradise found? You be the judge. To get there you'll need your own wheels or to arrange transfers with the owners.

PARC NATIONAL D'ARLI

In the southeast, on the border with Benin, **Parc National d'Arli** (admission CFA5000, plus obligatory guide CFA4000; ✦ 15 Dec–15 May) is Burkina Faso's major national park, but don't get too excited – it's not very well maintained and access is tricky if you don't have your own vehicle. It adjoins (and belongs to the same ecosystem as) Benin's Parc National de la Pendjari (p121), which is deservedly more popular. It's a long journey to get here from anywhere, but if you combine it with the Parc National de la Pendjari – at the frontier, you can buy a 48-hour visa for CFA10,000 – it could be worth it nonetheless.

Animal species common to the parks on both sides of the border include hippos, elephants, warthogs, baboons, monkeys, leopards, crocodiles and various kinds of antelope. Bird species are also varied.

With your own vehicle, you can also see the Burkina Faso side of **Parc Regional du W** (✦ usually 15 Dec–15 May), to the east of Arli on the Nigerien border; the entrance is via Diapaga. This park straddles Burkina Faso, Niger and Benin; see p592 for more details.

Getting There & Away

The only realistic option for visiting the park is to hire a 4WD with driver (at least CFA55,000 per day plus petrol), or you can take an organised tour (see p137 for more details) – any reputable travel agency in Ouagadougou can organise a tailor-made trip (three days is a minimum).

RANCH DE NAZINGA

The 97,000-hectare **Ranch de Nazinga** (Réserve de Nazinga; ☎ 50 41 36 17; per vehicle CFA1000, per person CFA8500, guide CFA2500, camera permit CFA1000; dm CFA5000, 2-bed apt CFA10,000, bungalows CFA12,500; ☽ 6am-6pm), near Pô and the Ghanaian border, has become a highlight on many a wildlife lover's itinerary over the last few years. The park has antelopes, monkeys, warthogs, crocodiles and plenty of birds, but elephants are the stars of the show, especially during the drier months (January through March), when they can regularly be seen roaming the Ranch. Sightings are not guaranteed, though. Accommodation-wise, don't expect a stylish lodge; guests stay in basic dorm-style rooms or in lacklustre bungalows, but they're only metres away from the Ranch's main watering hole, which attracts all kinds of game. Guided nature walks can be organised. Overall, Ranch de Nazinga is low-key.

If the Ranch is full, or if you want to do Nazinga in style, opt for **Campement de l'Elephant – Nahouri Safari** (☎ 70 29 78 78, 70 11 31 31; www.nahourisafari.com, in French; d from CFA22,000; ☒ 🖳), which sports impeccable rooms with all mod-cons and a restaurant that offers gourmet dishes. It's popular with hunters, but tourists are welcome. It's just before the gateway to the Ranch, about 19km from Pô (it's signposted). It's also a lovely plan B if you can't reach the park by sunset.

Driving time from Ouagadougou to Ranch de Nazinga is three hours; a 4WD is essential. Take the surfaced road south to Pô (176km), then a dirt road west towards Léo. After 15km you'll come to a sign pointing south to Nazinga, some 40km further.

TIÉBÉLÉ

Tiébélé, 40km east of Pô on a dirt track, is a wonderful detour if you're travelling up from Ghana, but it's also well worth visiting from Ouagadougou. Set in the heart of the green and low-lying Gourounsi country, Tiébélé is famous for its *sukhala* (colourful and fortress-like windowless traditional houses). Decorated by women, who work with guinea-fowl feathers, in geometrical patterns of red, black and white, the houses offer an antidote to the monochrome mud-brick villages found elsewhere in Burkina Faso. Once a Gourounsi capital, Tiébélé has an exceptional **chief's compound** (admission CFA2000). You can also go another 11km to **Tangassogo**, which also boasts a superb chief's compound.

Sleeping & Eating

Auberge Kunkolo (☎ 50 36 97 38, 76 53 44 55; d with fan & shared bathroom CFA5000) This is a wonderfully laid-back Tiébélé haven, with meals, a plant-filled courtyard and nice rooms that borrow from local traditional designs. You can also sleep on the rooftop (CFA2500). Bikes are available for hire (CFA1000 per day). It's about 600m past the chief's compound.

Other options:

Auberge de la Tranquillité (☎ 76 59 00 13; d with shared bathroom CFA5000) Has brightly painted huts.

Village d'Accueil Jean Viars (☎ 76 40 37 01; d with shared bathroom CFA5000) Almost across from the chief's compound.

Ignore the so-called guides waiting for tourists in Pô or at the entrance to Tiébélé –

GETTING UP CLOSE & PERSONAL WITH ELEPHANTS *Jean-Bernard Carillet*

I had already approached herds of elephants in southern Africa, but what happened to me in Ranch de Nazinga was beyond belief. I knew I had a good chance of seeing them (I was there in February), and I expected to spot them at dawn or sunset, when they congregate near the watering hole. After arriving in the camp and checking in, I went to my room for a little nap. I sat on my bed and…looking through the window, I saw a voluminous proboscis grazing foliage about 3m away from the room! I couldn't believe my eyes – a herd of truck-sized elephants (I'd say at least six individuals) was roaming shamelessly among the camp, *very* close to the sleeping quarters, totally undisturbed by the presence of tourists. Call it luck – I met frustrated tourists who visited Nazinga the previous day and they could only spy elephants in the distance.

they'll try to take you to Auberge des Manguiers in Tiébélé, about which we had negative reports.

In case you need to stop overnight in Pô, you can stay at **Hôtel Tiandera** (☎ 50 40 34 39; d with fan CFA7000, with air-con CFA12,500; ✱), on the road to Ouagadougou.

Getting There & Away

From Ouagadougou, STMB has two daily buses to Pô (CFA3000, three hours) and Rakieta has four daily services (same price). Buses travelling between Kumasi (Ghana) and Ouagadougou also pass through Pô.

From Pô, there are semi-regular bush taxis to Tiébélé (CFA1500) on market day (Saturday). Otherwise you'll have to charter a taxi (from CFA20,000).

THE SAHEL

Northern Burkina Faso is dominated by the desolate confines of the Sahel. It's certainly inhospitable most times of the year, but there's a lot to love about this area: stupendously colourful markets (it's worth timing your trip around them), fascinating local cultures and traditions, and landscapes that are much less monotonous than you'd think. It's still a secretive world with a peculiar appeal, and it begs exploration. Independent travel is a bit tricky to organise, but with a bit of time and gumption you should do it all right.

OUAHIGOUYA

pop 73,000

If you're reading this section, chances are great that you're heading to the Dogon Country in Mali (p507). Ouahigouya (pronounced waeegee-ya), 182km northwest of Ouagadougou by sealed road, is a bustling yet intimate town but doesn't have much to captivate you, and most people stay here only long enough to find onward transport to Mali. With a few hours to kill, you can wander around the lively market, then head northeast to the expansive but modest **Maison du Naba Kango**, which dates back to the days of the Yatengo kingdom, a precolonial rival of the principal Mossi kingdom, centred in Ouagadougou.

Ouahigouya has banks with ATMs (Visa only) and télécentres. For internet access, **Cyberposte** (off Ave de Mopti; per hr CFA500; ✆ 7.30am-

10pm Mon-Sat, 8am-noon Sun), at the post office, has the best connections.

You can bunk down at the Syrian-run **Hôtel Dunia** (☎ 40 55 05 95; mbachourf@yahoo.fr; Rue de Paris; s/d with fan CFA8000/10,000, d with air-con CFA20,000; ✱), which provides a homely atmosphere. Rates are somewhat inflated, though. Avoid the fan-cooled rooms downstairs as they are a tad sombre. There's a sitting room with satellite TV and a shaded area in front. Madame can cook Middle Eastern dishes (meals from CFA3000).

If funds are short, consider staying at **CIFER/BLO** (☎ 40 55 00 38; dm CFA2000, s/d with fan CFA6600/8500, with air-con CFA11,300/13,200; ✱), at the entrance of the town when coming from Ouagadougou (ask for 'seezess'). The rooms are tired and not everything works, but it's secure and OK for a night's snooze.

Avoid Hôtel de l'Amitié, which is ridiculously overpriced.

You'll find plenty of *maquis*-style restaurants in the centre.

Getting There & Away

STMB has four daily services between Ouagadougou and Ouahigouya (CFA2000, three hours). Ouahigouya's *gare routière* is just off the main drag.

For details on getting to Mali, see p169.

DORI

pop 21,000

Not so long ago, Dori, 261km northeast of Ouagadougou, was an excellent base in which to organise camel or 4WD forays into the fascinating Sahel. Nowadays, travellers use Dori as a mere overnight stop before heading further north to the 'real Sahel', including Gorom-Gorom (two hours further north), Oursi, Markoye, Gandefabou or even remote Tin-Akof, which all boast atmospheric *campements*.

That said, Dori's **Friday market** is worth a gander if you have a few hours to spare. See the blacksmiths and other craftsmen working leather items. If you want a guide to show you around, ask at Sahel Hébergement (be sure to agree on a price before setting off).

A word of warning: you'll have to cope with a fair share of 'guides' touting at the bus station, all eager to sell you camel trips and tours to nearby villages.

Dori has a bank with ATM (Visa only), a **Cyberposte** (per hr CFA500; ✆ 8am-9pm Mon-Sat, to noon Sun) and a wealth of *télécentres*.

Sleeping & Eating

Sahel Hébergement (☎ 40 46 07 04; d with fan & shared toilet CFA4500, with fan & private bathroom CFA5000, with air-con CFA10,000; ❄) This honest-to-goodness joint provides simple rooms that have benefited from a lick of paint and sees a steady stream of travellers passing through. It's a fair old walk east from the centre, but the outskirts-of-town location does mean a multitude of stars in the night sky and quiet, quiet nights.

Annexe Sahel Hébergement (☎ 40 46 00 36; d with fan CFA5000, with air-con CFA10,000; ❄) A hop, skip and jump from Sahel Hébergement (same owners), this place sports unadorned but cleanish rooms with bathrooms that won't make you squirm.

Hungry? You can eat simply at **Maquis Le Regal** (riz gras CFA500), across the street from Annexe Sahel Hébergement, or at **Le Relais** (mains CFA750-3000), a few doors from Sahel Hébergement. Nearby, the outdoor **Le Venus** (meals CFA400-700) serves filling meals at unbeatable prices.

Getting There & Away

A few companies operate daily services between Dori and Ouagadougou (CFA4000, four to six hours). STMB and TSR are the best.

For Gorom-Gorom it's a dirt track all the way. Bush taxis (CFA2000, two hours) are plentiful on market day; otherwise, they leave when they're full, so nothing's guaranteed.

There are also intermittent services to Markoye (CFA3000).

AROUND DORI
Bani

Bani, about 35km south of Dori on the road to Ouagadougou, is home to seven exceptional mud-brick mosques. You'll know you've arrived at this small, predominantly Muslim village when you see the minarets, the only structures over one storey tall, stabbing like fingers at the sky. Begin at the large mosque in the centre of the village and continue up the hill to the outlying structures. Their facades extravagantly decorated with relief carvings, these unique structures are among the finest in Burkina Faso.

Local guide Cissé Souabou provides an informative commentary (in French only) on the town's mosques. He charges a negotiable CFA5000 for his services and can be found at Auberge de Fofo.

The rustic **Auberge de Fofo** (☎ 76 44 63 84; camping CFA1500, d with shared bathroom CFA2500) has ultra-basic rooms with bucket showers, and simple meals are available. You can also sleep on a mattress on the rooftop.

All transport between Ouagadougou (CFA5000) and Dori (CFA1000) stops here.

GOROM-GOROM

You're now venturing into the heart of the Sahel region. Gorom-Gorom's Thursday **market** ranks as one of the most colourful in the country. Its charm lies in the fact that it's an authentic local market, drawing traders from all around the surrounding countryside. As such, its focus is entirely local, and tourists are simply part of the menagerie. The merchandise is also not aimed at tourists, so it's a chance to soak up the atmosphere of an important regional African market – the like of which is disappearing elsewhere – rather than a place to come in the expectation of doing some souvenir shopping. The animal market, where camels, goats, sheep, donkeys and cattle are all traded, is just beyond the nearby town pond. The market gets into full swing about 11am.

Gorom-Gorom is also a good base for organising **camel trips** to nearby villages and dunes. You'll probably be approached by self-proclaimed 'official guides', but it's best to arrange such trips through your hotel or *campement*. A small jaunt around Gorom costs about CFA6000. A two-day, one-night excursion to a nearby oasis should set you back around CFA15,000 (mineral water is extra; also add CFA10,000 for the guide), and a three-day expedition taking in Oursi costs around CFA17,500 per person per day (plus guiding fees). We met one guide who can get by in English; ask for Maiga Lasso.

Upon entering the town, you have to register at the commissariat and pay a 'tourist tax' of CFA1000.

There's no bank in Gorom-Gorom, so bring plenty of cash.

Sleeping & Eating

Relais du Campement Edjef – Chez Rissa (☎ 40 46 93 96; r with shared bathroom per person CFA4500) What this fine *campement* lacks in luxury it more than makes up for with ambience. Beds are in mud huts or under the stars, and the family who owns it serves as cook, guide and general organiser of most things you can do in and around Gorom-Gorom. The food is good and hearty. They also own Campement Edjef in Gandefabou (opposite), which is now their main base.

Hôtel de l'Amitié (r CFA5000) Things not to expect here: orthopaedic mattresses (our backs still ache), atmosphere and diligent service. But bathrooms are in good working order, sheets are clean and it's secure. The onsite restaurant (mains CFA1000 to CFA3000) is so unashamedly bare – greyish concrete floors and walls, neon lighting – that you might end up finding it atmospheric! At least the food is good, with copious plates of spag, couscous or grilled chicken. Thumbs up for the devilish yoghurt (CFA700), too.

Tasofaste (meals CFA400-1000) Delectable potato stews are on offer at this homely place.

Restaurant Kawar (meals CFA400-1500) This friendly place, noticeable for its roofs of corrugated iron, is one of a few modest eateries dotted around town.

Mouton Au Four (oven-baked mutton from CFA600), After something really special? Head to the Mouton Au Four, beside the soccer field. It's unsigned; look for a shack, behind which lies a mud-brick oven. Friendly Abdullaye cuts morsels of Sahelian mutton, puts them in the oven, and then serves them on a small plate, accompanied with spices. Delicious!

Drinking & Entertainment

Dancing Banguia (salads from CFA800) Take your Mouton Au Four plunder to this nearby place, an unpretentious *maquis* with a lovely shady area, and wash it down with a cold Brakina. As the epicentre of Gorom-Gorom's 'nightlife', Dancing Banguia is also a good, earthy place to spend an evening.

Getting There & Away

The road between Dori and Gorom-Gorom was in good condition at the time of writing, although it can get washed away in the wet season.

Sogebaf has two weekly direct services between Ouagadougou and Gorom-Gorom, usually on Wednesday and Sunday (CFA6000, six to seven hours), but it's easier to catch a bus to Dori and then arrange onward transport. Bush taxis ply the route from Gorom-Gorom to Dori (CFA1500, two hours) a few times daily.

AROUND GOROM-GOROM

Now we're talking. For the true Sahelian experience, we suggest that you spend a couple of days

in the small settlements around Gorom-Gorom. Given that public transport is infrequent and unreliable, your best bet is to hire a 4WD with driver (at least CFA40,000 per day, plus petrol) in Gorom-Gorom (or in Ouagadougou), or to arrange transfers with the *campements*.

In **Oursi**, some 35km northeast of Gorom-Gorom, you'll enjoy some spectacular sand dunes; if you can tear yourself from your bed, set off at 4am to catch the sunrise gilding their crests. Oursi's colourful Sunday **market** is not to be missed. The village boasts a small **museum** (admission CFA2000; ☺ 8am-noon & 3-5pm), perched on a dune about 1km away from the village. It does a good job of explaining the area's history and culture, with panels (in French) and pictures.

Another worthwhile excursion is to the pretty town of **Markoye**, 45km northeast of Gorom-Gorom, reached via a dirt track. In the heart of Fulani country, Markoye has a vibrant camel and cattle **market** every Monday. If you don't have a 4WD, a battered bush taxi leaves Gorom-Gorom early on Monday morning and returns at 6pm (about CFA2000).

Some 15km southeast of Gorom-Gorom, **Koirizena** is your typical Sahelian town and is noteworthy for its handicrafts. **Market** day is Saturday.

Gandefabou, 30km northwest of Gorom-Gorom, reached via a sandy track, is also well worth the trip, if only for its well-organised *campement* (see opposite).

It's a gruelling ride to get to **Tin-Akof**, 75km north of Gorom-Gorom, at the Nigerien border, but it's hard not to be touched by the end-of-the-world feeling that emanates from this tiny settlement by the Beli River.

From Oursi, Markoye, Koirizena, Gandefabou and Tin-Akof, it's easy to organise **camel trips** into the surrounding desert, which should cost around CFA25,000 per person per day for a well-provisioned trip, including food. Make sure you know exactly what you're getting for the price, which should include sleeping bags (you'll be sleeping in the open air) and ample food.

Sleeping & Eating

If you're looking for eco-friendly accommodation options and cultural immersion, the Sahelian *campements* will fulfil your expectations. All places concoct simple meals (about CFA1500 for breakfast and CFA3500 for lunch or dinner), have shared shower (with bucket)

THE PEOPLE OF GOROM-GOROM MARKET

You'll see a variety of Sahel and Sahara ethnic groups at the market. The Tuareg are easily identified by their long, flowing robes (boubous), indigo turbans and elaborate silver swords, and can often be seen riding proudly on their camels or haggling in the animal market over the price of camels and goats. The Tuareg's former slaves, the Bella, have taken over many of their erstwhile masters' skills in leatherwork, and both the men and the women favour black or grey gowns with wide belts of richly decorated leather.

You'll also see Songhaï farmers and Fulani herders (who wear the distinctive, conical straw hats). But it is the Fulani women who most catch the eye. You'll recognise them by their vivid, multicoloured dresses and complex hairstyles – usually braided and decorated with silver threads, tiny chains and colourful beads. These women carry their wealth with them in the form of beads, bracelets, heavy earrings or necklaces.

---

and toilet (some of the squat variety), and can organise camel or 4WD trips as well as cultural tours, which allow plenty of interaction with the locals. These *campements* are rustic (no electricity, no running water) but in keeping with local architecture.

Gîte de Markoye (☎ 70 31 76 93; Markoye; r per person CFA3000) The cheapest of the Sahelian *campements*, Gîte de Markoye is also the most compact, with five mud houses right in the centre of the village. It's well run and congenial.

Campement Assaline de Tin-Akof (☎ 50 46 33 60, 70 67 27 29; http://site.voila.fr/campement-assalim, in French; Tin-Akof; r per person CFA4000) Ouaga-based expats in search of an escape hatch recommend this place by the Beli River, at the Nigerien border. The sense of being somewhere *really* remote is a highlight of coming here. Sleep in a mud house or drag a mattress out and enjoy a starry night. Pirogue trips can be organised. Bring bottled water.

Campement Edjef (☎ 40 46 68 54, 70 61 21 30; www .gandefabou.org; Gandefabou; r per person CFA4500) One of the Sahel's best organised *campements*, the Tuareg-run Edjef is positioned in an idyllic spot on a sand dune, with sweeping views over a valley – sunset is the time you'll most appreciate staying here. Transfers by motorbike from Gorom-Gorom or Dori can be arranged for about CFA15,000.

Gîte Aounaf (☎ 40 46 70 12, 70 25 62 15; Oursi; r per person CFA5000) Another good camp in a scenic location, with soft sand and a clutch of attractive mud huts and traditional thatch-and-straw Fula tents, on the outskirts of Oursi.

Village d'Accueil de Koirizena (☎ 70 44 58 21, 75 21 24 29; Koirizena; full board per person CFA15,000; ⊙ Oct–May) This well-kept *campement* has bags of character. The mud huts are scattered around a neat compound and the toilet block is kept

functional. It's one of the best places to get acquainted with village life. Prices include encounters with craftspeople and traditional dance performances. Transfers by motorbike (CFA7500) can be arranged from Dori.

BURKINA FASO DIRECTORY

ACCOMMODATION

Ouagadougou and, to a lesser extent, Bobo-Dioulasso and Banfora have a good range of accommodation to suit most budgets, with some imaginative and comfortable choices in each town. The last couple of years have seen the development of appealing B&Bs, which are very popular among travellers. Elsewhere, you may need to take what you can find, as choice is limited.

Throughout this chapter, we've considered budget accommodation as costing up to CFA12,000/16,000 for a single/double with air-con, midrange CFA12,000/16,000 to CFA32,000/41,000, and top end from CFA32,000/41,000 and up.

While staying in Ouagadougou and Bobo-Dioulasso you have to pay a *taxe de séjour* at each place you stay, also known as a *taxe communale*. It's a once-off payment, irrespective of the number of nights you stay at a hotel, and is calculated at CFA500 per person.

ACTIVITIES

Burkina Faso is more for seeing than for doing, although there are opportunities for hiking and cycling around Banfora (p155), as well as horse riding around Ouagadougou

---

PRACTICALITIES

- Electricity supply is 220V and plugs are of the European two-round-pin variety.

- International versions of French- and (a few) English-language publications are available in Ouagadougou and Bobo-Dioulasso.

- BBC World Service (www.bbc.co.uk /worldservice) is on 99.2 FM in Ouagadougou. For French-language FM services, tune in to Horizon FM (104.4) and RFI (94).

- Burkina Faso uses the metric system.

(p139). You can also do camel expeditions around Gorom-Gorom in the north (p164).

BOOKS

Tracking down books on Burkina Faso can be a frustrating task, although many books that are unavailable elsewhere can be found at **Abebooks** (www.abebooks.com).

African Cinema and Europe: Close-Up on Burkina Faso by Teresa Hoefert de Turegano is a wonderful primer for Fespaco and one of the few studies devoted to the country's most unlikely industry.

Thomas Sankara Speaks: The Burkina Faso Revolution, 1983–87 by Thomas Sankara (edited by Samantha Anderson) charts the rise and fall of the man known as Africa's Che Guevara through his charismatic speeches.

The Parachute Drop by Norbert Zongo is an eerily prescient novel by the journalist who was killed in 1998, sparking demonstrations in Ouagadougou.

BUSINESS HOURS

Banks are typically open between 7am and 11am, and 3.30pm to 5pm Monday to Friday. Bars normally serve from noon until late, and nightclubs generally go from 9pm into the wee hours. Restaurants usually serve food between 11.30am and 3pm, then open again from 6.30pm to 10.30pm. As a rule, shops and businesses operate from 7.30am to noon and 3pm to 5.30pm Monday to Friday, and 9am to 1pm Saturday.

COURSES

For information on music and dance courses available throughout the country, see the boxed text, p154.

DANGERS & ANNOYANCES

Burkina Faso is one of the safest countries in West Africa. Crime isn't unknown, particularly around big markets, cinemas and *gares routières* (bus stations), but it's usually confined to petty theft and pickpocketing.

EMBASSIES & CONSULATES

Embassies and consulates listed below are in Ouagadougou.

Benin (off Map p138; ☎ 50 38 49 96; 401 Rue Bagen Nini)
Canada (Map p140; ☎ 50 31 18 94; ouaga@dfait-maeci.gc.ca; 586 Rue Agostino Neto) Represents Australia in consular matters.
Côte d'Ivoire (Map p138; ☎ 50 31 82 28; cnr Ave Raoul Follereau & Blvd du Burkina Faso)
France (Map p138; ☎ 50 49 66 66; www.ambafrance-bf.org; Ave de l'Indépendance)
Germany (Map p140; ☎ 50 30 67 31; amb.alle magne@fasonet.bf; Rue Joseph Badoua)
Ghana (Map p138; ☎ 50 30 76 35; Ave d'Oubritenga)
Mali (off Map p138; ☎ 50 38 19 22; 2569 Ave Bassawarga) Just south of Ave de la Résistance.
Niger (Map p140; ☎ 50 30 53 59; Ave Yennenga)
UK (Map p140; ☎ 50 30 88 60; consulat-uk@fasonet.bf; Impasse Thevenoud, Secteur 1) British honorary consul at ICI (Initiatives Conseil International), near the cathedral.
USA (Map p138; ☎ 50 30 67 23; http://ouagadougou.usembassy.gov; 622 Ave Raoul Follereau)

FESTIVALS & EVENTS

Fespaco, the biennial festival of African cinema, takes place in Ouagadougou in odd-numbered years during February or March. For further information on the festival, see the boxed text, p135. In even-numbered years, Ouagadougou hosts the Salon International de l'Artisanat de Ouagadougou (p141) during October or November, and Bobo-Dioulasso stages the Semaine Nationale de la Culture (p151) in March or April.

For more information on the traditional festivities (or *fêtes*) in the Bobo-Dioulasso area, see the boxed text, p152.

HOLIDAYS

New Year's Day 1 January
Women's Day 8 March
Good Friday & Easter Monday March/April
Labour Day 1 May
Ascension Day 4-5 August
Anniversary of Sankara's Overthrow 15 October
All Saints Day 1 November
Christmas Day 25 December

Burkina Faso also celebrates Islamic holidays, which change each year. See p816 for details of Islamic holidays.

INTERNET ACCESS

Broadband is finally being rolled out in Burkina Faso. You'll find internet cafes in larger cities, but your best bet is to head to Cyberposte outlets, which are within (or next door to) the post office, keep longer hours and have the best connections (rates are CFA500 per hour).

Wi-fi access is increasingly available in hotels and guest houses in Ouagadougou and Bobo-Dioulasso.

INTERNET RESOURCES

Artists in Burkina Faso (www.artistebf.org) A good site (with an English version) covering music, dance and cinema in Burkina Faso.

Fespaco (www.fespaco.bf) Website of Africa's favourite film festival.

Ministry of Culture, Arts & Tourism (www.culture .gov.bf) It's a bit clunky, but this government site has good (French-only) information on dance, cinema, music and literature in Burkina Faso.

LANGUAGE

The country's official language is French. Of some 60 local languages, the most significant is Moré, the language of the Mossi and others living on the central plateau, which is spoken by more than half the population. Dioula is the language of the market, even though in Burkina Faso it's nobody's mother tongue (it's closely related to Bambara, the language of neighbouring Mali). Other significant local languages include Fula, Gourmantché and Gourounsi.

See p860 for a list of useful phrases in French, Moré, Dioula and Fula.

MAPS

Burkina Faso (1:1,000,000), a map published by the French-based Institut Géographique National (IGN), is the most widely available. You can buy it at the **Institut Gèographique du Burkina** (Map p138; IGB; ☎ 50 32 48 23; Ave de l'Indépendance) in Ouagadougou, or in many European bookshops. IGB in Ouagadougou sells detailed city maps (CFA2500 each) for Ouagadougou and Bobo-Dioulasso.

For more information on maps, see p817.

MONEY

The unit of currency in Burkina Faso is the West African CFA franc. The best foreign currency to carry is euros. Travellers cheques are not useful; euros in cash and an ATM card (Visa only) are the way to go.

Banks that will change money with a minimum of fuss include Banque Internationale du Burkina (BIB), Ecobank and Banque Internationale pour le Commerce, l'Industrie et l'Agriculture du Burkina (Biciab). Quicker alternatives are the exchange bureaus and the Lebanese supermarkets in Ouagadougou and Bobo-Dioulasso, which keep longer hours, have no queues and offer the best rates (the best rates are offered for notes in denominations of 50 and 100 euros).

ATMs are astonishingly functional and available in larger cities, including Ouagadougou, Bobo-Dioulasso, Fada N'Gourma, Banfora and Ouahigouya, but keep in mind that they only issue cash advances against Visa (not MasterCard) and transaction fees are prohibitive (about €10 per withdrawal); take out as much as the machine lets you each time.

TELEPHONE & FAX

You can make international phone calls at any *télécentre* (phone booths equipped with metered telephones). *Télécentres* are ubiquitous in Burkina Faso. International calls cost from CFA500 per minute to Europe and the US, and from CFA1500 per minute to Australia.

Mobile phone (cell) coverage is excellent across all of Burkina Faso. Local mobile companies include Telmob, Zain and Telecel. Mobile phone numbers start with 70, 73, 76 or 78. If you have a GSM phone and it has been 'unlocked', it's possible to buy a SIM card (from CFA2000) with either of the three local network operators. Then you can buy top-ups, starting from CFA200 (and up to CFA5000) – they're on sale everywhere. Zain is the most expensive but has the best coverage.

There are no telephone area codes in Burkina Faso.

VISAS

Everyone except Ecowas (Economic Community of West African States) nationals needs a visa. You can buy a tourist visa at Ouagadougou airport for CFA10,000 (paid in local currency; head to any bank or bureau de change in the centre and come back with the requisite amount). The visa is issued in 48 hours – the police will give you an authorisation until your passport is returned. Travellers also report that visas are issued at Burkina Faso's land borders for the same price, although they're invariably issued on the spot.

Burkina Faso embassies require two photos and may ask for proof of yellow fever vaccination. Visas cost US$100 in the USA, while single-/multiple-entry three-month visas cost €20/30 in Europe. In countries where there is no Burkina Faso embassy, French embassies sometimes issue 10-day visas on the country's behalf.

Note that you can obtain the Visa des Pays de l'Entente in Ouagadougou (see p139). The Visa des Pays de l'Entente is a multi-country visa that covers travel in Benin, Burkina Faso, Côte d'Ivoire, Niger and Togo (see p826).

Visas for Onward Travel

Burkina Faso is a good place to stock up on visas.

BENIN

Visas are issued the same day (CFA15,000) and are valid for three months. You need two photos and photocopies of your passport. If you just want to slip over the border to Benin to explore Parc National de la Pendjari, you can get a 48-hour visa at the border post.

CÔTE D'IVOIRE

A one-month single-entry visa costs CFA20,000 (CFA10,000 for French citizens) with one photo.

The northern land borders were open and secure at the time of writing, but check the situation while in Burkina Faso.

GHANA

The Ghanaian embassy issues two-month visas within 24 hours for CFA15,000; you'll need four photos (make sure they're identical).

MALI

One-month visas cost CFA20,000 and are issued the same day. You need to supply two photos.

NIGER

A one-month single-entry visa costs CFA20,000, requires one photo and is issued in 72 hours.

TRANSPORT IN BURKINA FASO

GETTING THERE & AWAY
Entering Burkina Faso

If you've travelled in Africa for a while, entering Burkina Faso is a pleasure. You'll almost never encounter anything other than quick efficiency at Burkina Faso's borders, with not a single suggestion that a bribe may be necessary to speed up the process or smooth over 'misunderstandings'.

Proof of yellow fever vaccination is, however, mandatory and is often checked.

Air

Burkina Faso's two international airports are Aéroport International de Ouagadougou and Aéroport International Borgo (Bobo-Dioulasso).

The following airlines have offices in Ouagadougou.

Afriqiyah (airline code 8U; Map p140; ☎ 50 30 16 52; www.afriqiyah.aero) Hub: Tripoli. Represented by Satguru Travels.

Air Algérie (airline code AH; Map p140; ☎ 50 31 23 01; www.airalgerie.dz) Hub: Algiers.

Air Burkina (airline code 2J; Map p138; ☎ 50 49 23 43; www.air-burkina.com) Hub: Ouagadougou.

Air France (airline code AF; Map p140; ☎ 50 30 63 65; www.airfrance.com) Hub: Paris.

Air Ivoire (airline code VU; Map p140; ☎ 50 30 04 50; www.airivoire.com) Hub: Abidjan.

Air Sénégal International (airline code V7; Map p140; ☎ 50 31 39 05; www.air-senegal-international.com) Hub: Dakar.

Ethiopian Airlines (airline code ET; Map p140; ☎ 50 30 10 24; www.ethiopianairlines.com) Hub: Addis Ababa.

Point Afrique (airline code BIE; Map p140; ☎ 50 33 16 20; www.point-afrique.com) Hub: Paris.

Royal Air Maroc (airline code AT; Map p140; ☎ 50 30 50 81; www.royalairmaroc.com) Hub: Casablanca.

WEST AFRICA

Air Burkina (CFA151,000) and Air Ivoire (CFA134,000) fly from Ouagadougou to Abidjan several times a week each. Air Burkina also flies from Bobo-Dioulasso to Abidjan twice weekly (CFA150,000).

There are three weekly flights from Ouagadougou to Bamako (Mali) with Air

Burkina (CFA138,000) and Air Sénégal International (CFA172,000). Air Burkina also flies to Niamey (Niger) at least twice a week (CFA202,000).

For Dakar (Senegal), Air Burkina (CFA251,000) and Air Sénégal International (CFA275,000) each fly from Ouagadougou at least three times a week.

Other destinations served by Air Burkina include Lomé (Togo; CFA184,000, twice weekly), Cotonou (Benin; CFA190,000, four times weekly) and Accra (Ghana; CFA186,000; three times weekly).

Land

The main border crossings are at Niangoloko for Côte d'Ivoire; Tanguiéta for Benin; 15km south of Pô or Hamale for Ghana; Sinkasse for Togo; east of Kantchari for Niger; and Koloko or west of Tiou for Mali. Borders tend to be closed by 5.30pm or 6.30pm at the latest. Remember that there is a time change of one hour going from Burkina Faso into Benin or Niger (both ahead of Burkina Faso).

BENIN

SKV and TSR have a twice-weekly bus service from Ouagadougou to Cotonou (CFA20,000, 20 hours), while TCV has a weekly departure (on Sunday).

The alternative is to take a bus (eg STMB) to Fada N'Gourma (CFA4000, five hours, 225km), from where bush taxis and minibuses lie in wait (sometimes all day because transport to the border – CFA4000 – is scarce and fills up slowly).

CÔTE D'IVOIRE

Passenger-train services between Burkina Faso and Côte d'Ivoire (three weekly) have resumed, but it's a long, tiring journey to Abidjan (at least 36 hours!). We haven't heard bad reports about this ride, but it's wise to get an update while in Bobo before setting off.

TCV has a daily bus service to Bouaké from Bobo-Dioulasso (CFA12,000, 22 hours). You could also take one of Rakieta's two daily buses from Banfora (CFA800, one hour) to Niangoloko, from where onward transport may be possible.

GHANA

SKV and STMB have two buses per week from Ouagadougou to Kumasi (CFA10,000,

720km), while TCV has a weekly service (on Sunday) to Kumasi.

STMB has two buses per day from Ouagadougou to Pô (CFA3000, three hours), 15km from the border, from where there's infrequent transport to the border (CFA1500) and on to Bolgatanga in Ghana (CFA1250). If you're coming the other way, Burkinabé bush taxis wait on their side of the border to take you to Pô.

The other frequently used border crossing is at Hamale in the southwest of Burkina Faso. Coming from Ghana, you may have to stay at Hamale's cheap hotel and catch a bus to Bobo-Dioulasso the next morning. From Bobo-Dioulasso, Rakieta has two buses per day (at 8am and 2.30pm) to Hamale (CFA4500) that pass through Banfora en route.

MALI

Almost every bus company in Bobo-Dioulasso offers a daily service to Bamako (CFA11,000, 14 hours). The best buses are TCV's, which leave Bobo-Dioulasso at 6.30am or Ouagadougou (CFA18,000) at 11pm. SKV also has excellent buses, but they only ply the route twice weekly (CFA10,000 from Bobo-Dioulasso, CFA15,000 from Ouagadougou).

If you're heading from Bobo-Dioulasso to Mopti, your best bet is to change in Bla (Mali; CFA9000), where you'll easily find onward transport.

If you're going to the Dogon Country, the road from Ouahigouya to the border is in good condition but deteriorates on the Malian side. Bush taxis leave Ouahigouya from Koro (CFA3000, three to four hours) in the morning from a side street not far from the STMB bus station. From Koro you'll need to connect by bush taxi to Bankass and then Mopti; you stand a better chance of finding onward transport on Saturday, market day in Koro.

NIGER

SKV and STMB each have a daily service between Ouagadougou and Niamey via Fada N'Gourma (CFA10,000, eight to 10 hours).

TOGO

SKV and TSR have twice-weekly services to Lomé (CFA15,000 to CFA17,500, 21 hours) while STMB and TCV have weekly departures.

If you want to break up your journey, you can take an STMB bus to Sinkasse (CFA5000, twice daily), which straddles the border, and find onward transport to Dapaong in Togo. The border is open from 6am to 6pm.

GETTING AROUND
Air
Air Burkina has two flights a week between Ouagadougou and Bobo-Dioulasso (CFA46,000).

Bus
Buses are the most reliable and comfortable way to get around. There are a multitude of companies from which to choose, although STMB, TCV, TSR, SKV and Rakieta buses are better maintained and more reliable than other companies'. STMB has the most extensive network in Burkina Faso. Buses invariably leave from their own stations, rather than the *gares routières*.

Buses almost always operate with guaranteed seating and fixed departure times.

Bush Taxi & Minibus
Minibuses and bush taxis, mostly ageing Peugeot 504s, cover outlying communities that large buses don't serve. Most leave from the *gares routières*, and morning is the best time to find them. Minibuses are usually a third cheaper than Peugeot taxis but can take an age to fill up.

Car & Motorcycle
Burkina Faso's road network is excellent, with the sealed roads connecting major cities driveable year-round. During the rainy season, you may find your progress impeded by rain barriers, which are lifted once temporary flooding further down the road has abated.

Travel agencies in Ouagadougou (p137) can organise 4WD rental for about CFA55,000 per day (with driver). Petrol is extra.

Local Transport
All reasonable-sized towns have taxis that can be shared (usually for CFA300) or chartered (rates start at CFA500 for short trips).

Tours
Consider taking a tour or hiring a 4WD (CFA55,000 per day, plus petrol) to visit the wildlife parks and reserves in the country's southeast, where public transport ranges from infrequent and inconvenient to nonexistent. For details, see p137. Tours are also necessary for exploring the desert regions north of Gorom-Gorom.

Train
There are three weekly services from Ouagadougou to Bobo-Dioulasso (and on to Abidjan), but buses are much faster and more convenient.

Cameroon

For many, the word 'Africa' conjures a certain image: dense jungle of deep green, women balancing baskets on their brightly wrapped heads, men strolling down rust red roads made of earth that looks like Mars, whip-thin herders driving cows and goats across dry yellow grasslands, Pygmies whispering through the forest and masked dancers jumping in rhythm in front of mud-and-thatch huts, their carved faces fascinating.

This, then, is Cameroon, a country that markets itself, with some justification, as all of Africa in one. The description is apt, even eerie: physically, from the southern rainforests to the lazy beaches, from the Mountain of Thunder, an active volcano, to the brown hills of the Sahel and across to the wild eastern frontier that tempts the adventurous; culturally, in its blend of religions and ancient tribal traditions; linguistically, as one of the few Anglophone and Francophone nations in the continent. Even politically – Cameroon is both blessed by the stability many African nations vie for and hamstrung by accusations of corruption.

This, too, is Cameroon. But that's the reward of travelling here: seeing Africa at her most quintessentially African, warts and all. None of it stops us from loving this country and the continent she encompasses, an affection that's easy to feel as your first Cameroonian evening slips over you, and *makossa* music or a guitar made of gourds sets the rhythm, the street smells like roasting bananas and all that stands between you and African bliss is grilled fish and a sweaty beer.

CAMEROON

FAST FACTS

- **Area** 475,440 sq km
- **Capital** Yaoundé
- **Country code** 237
- **Famous for** International football success
- **Languages** French, English, Bamiléké, Fulfude, Fulani and Ewondo
- **Money** Central African CFA franc; US$1 = CFA493; €1 = CFA656
- **Population** 18.4 million
- **Visa** Arrange in advance, US$60

CAMEROON

HOW MUCH?

- **Ingredients for juju fetish** CFA500
- **100km bus ride** CFA1000
- **Moto-taxi ride across town** CFA150
- **Bottle of palm wine** CFA1000
- **Carved mask** CFA15,000-30,000

LONELY PLANET INDEX

- **1L of petrol** CFA375
- **1.5L of bottled water** CFA450
- **Bottle of '33' beer** CFA600
- **Souvenir football shirt** CFA3500
- **Stick of brochettes** CFA100

HIGHLIGHTS

- **Mt Cameroon** (p191) Don your hiking boots to climb the mist-shrouded slopes of West Africa's highest peak.
- **Maroua** (p208) The surreal streets of the crossroads of the Sahel.
- **Ebodjé** (p219) Sea turtle lays her eggs along a pristine beach, before you settle to sleep in a hut in remote, rural Africa.
- **The Grassfields** (p197) Green plateaus along the edge of dozens of traditional chiefdoms.
- **Mandara Mountains** (p210) The red dust and sharp mountains of Cameroon's wild north.

ITINERARIES

Travel in Cameroon can be slow, especially off main routes, including in the Ring Road area and in the far north around Maroua. Allow plenty of time and keep your schedule flexible.

- **One Week** With just a week of travel, starting from either Douala (p183) or Yaoundé (p178), head to Limbe (p187) for a night or two to get your bearings. Then – if you have a bit of an adventurous bent – head either to Mt Cameroon (p191) or to Korup National Park (p194) for a few days exploring (in the dry season only), finishing again in Douala. Alternatively, if you're more interested in culture and history, go from Douala to Foumban (p203) via Bafoussam (p201). After a night there, head to the Ring Road area (p197), ideally fitting in a day in Bafut (p200) and another on the stretch between Sabga (p197) and Kumbo (p198). Finish back in Douala or Yaoundé.
- **Two or Three Weeks** With two weeks, spend the first week exploring the Ring Road area (p197) and visiting Foumban (p203). Then you could head to Yaoundé (p178) from where you can head north to Maroua (p208) and venture into the Mandara Mountains (p210) for a few days trekking – this last leg is easier to accomplish with three weeks.
- **One Month** With a month or more you'll have time to expand this itinerary, perhaps starting with a night or two in Limbe (p187) followed by climbing Mt Cameroon (p191) or visiting Korup (p194), before making your way up to Bamenda (p195) and the Ring Road area (p197). During the dry season, you could then go from Kumbo (p198) on the Ring Road direct to Foumban (p203); otherwise head to Foumban via Bafoussam (p201). From here, make your way to Yaoundé (p178) to rest for a day or two, before heading north by train to N'Gaoundéré (p205) and beyond. Spend the remainder of the time exploring northern Cameroon (p205). If you have time, detour south to Kribi (p216) and Ebodjé (p220) to see sea turtles and rainforest – all at once.

CLIMATE & WHEN TO GO

The north has a single wet season from April/May to September/October. The hottest months here are March to May, when temperatures can soar to 40°C, although it's a dry (and therefore somewhat bearable) heat. The south has a humid, equatorial climate, with rain scattered throughout the year and almost continual high humidity. The main wet season here is June to October, when secondary roads often become impassable. From March to June are the light rains.

Throughout Cameroon, November to February are the driest months, though dust from harmattan winds greatly restricts visibility. These are the best months to visit, although you'll have harmattan haze during much of this time (which is not good for photography). The worst months are between July and October, when it rains almost everywhere and many roads are impassable. See also Climate Charts, p810.

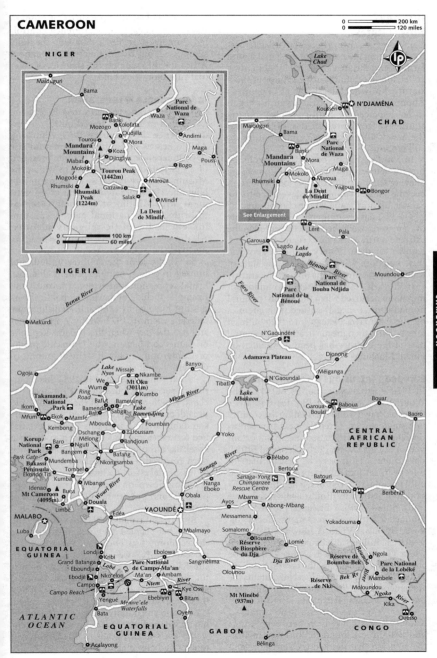

CAMEROON

HISTORY
Early Cultures

Cameroon has always been an African cross-roads, linking the nomads of the Sahel, Bantu farmers and the area's original inhabitants, a collection of ethnolinguistic groups of short stature known collectively as 'Pygmies'. About 2000 years ago, the Pygmies began to be displaced by Bantu peoples moving southeast from present-day Nigeria and the Sahel, although large communities do still remain.

In 500 BC, Hanno of Carthage wrote the first foreign account of seeing Mt Cameroon. Starting from around this period Cameroon became a major supplier of slaves, first to the Sahara, up north, and later to Europeans.

The first nation group most historians note in Cameroon were the Sao, who settled in the extreme north near Kousséri and Lake Chad. Known for their pottery and bronze-work, their kingdom was absorbed by the state of Kanem-Borno around the 8th or 9th century.

In the early 15th century another important migration occurred when the Fulani (pastoral nomads from Senegal) pushed their enemies off the Adamawa Plateau into the southern forests. Since then the north and north-central part of the country has been dominated by Fulani Muslims.

European Intrusions & Colonisation

In 1472 Portuguese explorers sailed up the Wouri River, naming it Rio dos Camarões (River of Prawns) and christening the country in a single stroke. Over the next two centuries, coastal Cameroon became an important port of call for Dutch, Portuguese and British slave traders. However, the first permanent European settlements were not established until the mid-19th century, when British missionaries arrived in protest against the slave trade. In 1845 British missionary Alfred Saker founded a settlement in Douala, shortly followed by one at Victoria (now Limbe).

British influence was curtailed in 1884, when Germany signed a treaty with the chiefdoms of Douala and the central Bamiléké Plateau – although for the local inhabitants the agreement meant little more than a shift from one form of colonial exploitation to another.

After WWI the German protectorate of Kamerun was carved up between France and Britain – a linguistic and administrative division that marked the start of a fault line still evident in the politics of modern Cameroon. Local revolts in French-controlled Cameroon in the 1950s were brutally suppressed, but the momentum throughout Africa for throwing off the shackles of colonial rule soon took hold.

Independence & Federalism

Self-government was granted in French Cameroon in 1958, followed quickly by independence on 1 January 1960. Ahmadou Ahidjo, leader of the Union Camerounaise (UC) independence party, became president of a newly independent state in which the Muslim-majority north was seeking to join Nigeria. The federated system of government with Ahidjo at the helm seemed to bridge these national gaps because of his ethnic-linguistic-religious identity: Ahidjo was a Muslim, French-speaking northern Fulani.

So Ahidjo kept the country united, and himself in power, using expedient alliances, brutal repression and regional favouritism. Examples include outlawing all political parties but his own in 1966 and abolishing the federal system in 1972. Many Anglophones still rue the day when the Federal Republic of Cameroon became the United Republic of Cameroon (today it's the Republic of Cameroon, full stop).

When Ahidjo resigned in 1982, his hand-picked successor, bureaucrat Paul Biya, declared Ahidjo an enemy of the state. The old president (genuinely shocked and understandably angry about this turn of events) fled to France and was sentenced to death in absentia, although his reputation has since been restored. In reality, Biya owed much to his predecessor, including a capacity for cracking down on real and imagined opponents, and preserving a fragile balance of vested interests.

Biya was initially able to weather the storms that plagued his government because the economy was booming. Prior to 1985, per capita GNP was one of the highest in sub-Saharan Africa, due largely to plentiful natural resources (oil, cocoa and coffee) and favourable commodity prices. When these markets collapsed and prices plunged, Cameroon's economy went into freefall. It has never really recovered and the shockwaves are still being felt by the country in today's globalised economy.

Elections & Emergencies

The clamour for freedom couldn't go ignored indefinitely. In 1991 Biya was forced to legalise opposition parties and multiparty elections were grudgingly held the following year – the first for 25 years. The Cameroonian Democratic People's Movement, led by Biya, hung on to power, despite widespread allegations of vote-rigging and intimidation. The main opposition party, the Social Democratic Front (SDF), boycotted subsequent parliamentary elections amid claims its presidential candidate had been denied a legitimate victory – claims backed up by many international observers including the National Democratic Institute (NDI).

In the 1990s, Biya's uneasy rule was often at an arm's length, as the president spent increasing amounts of time in France. At home, Cameroon lurched on in its customary state of uneasy stability and political stagnation. A small war with Nigeria over ownership of the oil-rich Bakassi Peninsula flared up in 1994 and again in 1996, deflecting attention from domestic problems (the peninsula has since been declared Cameroonian). In December 1999 further domestic clampdowns followed the shock (if short-lived) declaration of independence for Anglophone Cameroon by the Southern Cameroons National Council (SCNC) on Buea radio, again exposing the country's deep political problems.

Cameroon Today

In October 2004, with the opposition movement fractured, presidential elections returned Biya to power, for his 'second' seven-year term – the constitutional limit. International observers again complained that the process lacked credibility, in part due to the number of dead people who apparently turned up to vote for the status quo.

The economy continues to face severe difficulties. In 2004, Transparency International rated Cameroon 129th out of 146 countries on its corruption index, and corruption still gnaws away at the foundations of the country. Cameroon's failure to qualify for the World Bank's debt relief program in the same year was blamed primarily on institutionalised corruption.

The arrival of Chinese immigrants in great numbers – especially visible in Yaoundé and Douala – is also changing the face of the country. Cheap Chinese motorbikes have made private transport a possibility for many Cameroonians and 'Medecine Chinois' shops can be found offering acupuncture in small villages. But corruption remains Cameroon's great bogeyman. A significant proportion of Cameroonians have complained that they have had to pay bribes to get government services, and the paperwork for opening a business takes a very long time to process compared to the rest of Africa, a view reflected by various international observers. Until this malaise is seriously addressed and genuine political openness is permitted, Cameroon will continue to limp along for the foreseeable future.

THE CULTURE
The National Psyche

It's hard to pigeonhole 280 distinct ethnolinguistic groups divided by colonial languages, the urban-rural split and Christianity and Islam, among other factors, into one cutout identity. The Cameroonian psyche is, ultimately, any and everything African – like everything else in this country, diversity is the key.

A few characteristics do seem shared across Cameroon's divides. One is appreciation of fun – anything worth doing isn't worth much if done dour. Belief in traditional powers like witchcraft is often offset by an inferiority complex that comes from being told, by government and religious officials, such beliefs are holding Africa back. Finally, many Cameroonian possess a half-laconic, half-angry sense of frustration with the way things are. Most seem aware that while their country does OK compared to its neighbours, they could be immeasurably better off if corruption didn't curtail so much potential. Mixed in with this frustration is a sort of resignation – 'such is life' – an acceptance that comes off as serenity in good times, simmering rage in bad times.

There's a distinct gap between Francophone and Anglophone Cameroonians, albeit felt more predominantly by the Anglophone minority. The country is far from being truly bilingual, and Anglophones complain of discrimination in education (most universities lecture in French only) and in the workplace. The siting of the Chad oil pipeline was a particular bone of contention – rather than having it terminate in Anglophone Limbe, which has an oil refinery, it was directed to Kribi, in President Biya's home province, in what some activists claim was a deliberate act of marginalisation.

SPORT

Cameroon exploded onto the world's sporting consciousness at the 1990 World Cup, when the national football team, the Indomitable Lions, became the first African side to reach the quarterfinals, led by the legendary Roger Milla, the oldest player to score in the World Cup.

Football is truly the national obsession, and the one thing that unites the country. Every other Cameroonian male seems to own a copy of the team's strip, and in any bar and there'll be a match playing on TV. When Cameroon narrowly failed to qualify for the 2006 World Cup, the country's grief was almost tangible. Nevertheless, the Lions hold a proud record in the continent-wide Cup of Nations, winning the trophy four times – most recently in 2002. Cameroon's (and Africa's) current top player is the revered Barcelona striker Samuel Eto'o.

RELIGION

Christianity is the most followed religion in Cameroon, with adherents making up around 40% of the population. About a quarter of Cameroonians are Muslim, which is the predominant faith in the north. The remainder follow indigenous religions, including the Kirdi – fiercely non-Muslim animists in the north – and the spirit faith of the Baka. But these numbers are deceptive, as Cameroon's religions blend more than many adherents will admit; even where Christianity and Islam dominate, they're influenced by traditional practices.

This is a complicated matter, as Christians and Muslims are constantly told that their faiths are above the spirit world, yet in that placement, something of a part of it too. For some, but certainly not all Cameroonians, God and Allah are conceptualised as traditional spirits who have more power than local 'witchcraft'. There's any number of movies where a wandering preacher takes down idol-worshipping baddies in the jungle by a) saying God is greater than spells and curses, and then b) calling God down in the form of magic lightning against said idols.

ARTS
Literature

In addition to Mongo Beti (see p49), well-known literary figures include Kenjo Jumban, whose novel *The White Man of God* deals with the country's colonial experience, and Ferdinand Oyono, whose *Houseboy and The Old Man and the Medal* also deal with colonial themes. *The Crown of Thorns* by the prolific Linus Asong is well worth reading for insights into tribal society in northwestern Cameroon.

Music

Sit anywhere in this country and music will eventually start playing, and when it does, someone's booty will shake. Manu Dibango is the king of *makossa*, a fusion of highlife and soul that sprang from the clubs of Douala. He brought international fame to Cameroon in the 1980s with his hit 'Soul Makossa'. Moni Bilé is another great exponent of the style. In competition is the more danceable *bikutsi* style, originally from Yaoundé. With its martial rhythms and often sexually charged lyrics, it's guaranteed to get the hips moving – listen out for 'Les Têtees Brulées'.

Craftwork

The northwestern highlands area is known for carved masks, which have become the face of the African aesthetic in many curio shops and museums around the world. Masks are essentially transition pieces, conduits between the spirit world and ours; when donned during the proper ceremonies, the wearer is believed to be straddling the two realities of natural and supernatural.

Cameroon also produces some highly detailed bronze- and brass-work (including figurative art and pipes), particularly in Tikar areas north and east of Foumban. Carved wooden stools are generally round, except around Douala, where you'll see rectangular stools similar to those found elsewhere along the West African coast.

The areas around Bali and Bamessing (both near Bamenda) and Foumban are rich in high-quality clay, and some of Cameroon's finest ceramic work originates here.

ENVIRONMENT
The Land

Cameroon is as diverse geographically as it is culturally. The south is a low-lying coastal plain covered by swathes of equatorial rainforest extending east towards the Congo Basin. Heading north, the sparsely populated Adamawa Plateau divides the country in two. To the plateau's north, the country begins to dry out into a rolling landscape dotted with rocky escarpments fringed to the west by the barren, beautiful Mandara Mountains. That range forms the northern extent of a volcanic chain that forms a natural border with Nigeria down to the Atlantic coast, often punctuated with stunning crater lakes. Most are now extinct, but one active volcano remains in Mt Cameroon – at 4095m the highest peak in West Africa.

Wildlife

Cameroon's rainforests, especially those in the rich volcanic mountains bordering Nigeria, enjoy exceptional biodiversity. In 2005, British scientists surveyed over 2400 plant species in the Kupe-Bakossi region, with a tenth of them completely new to science – making this Africa's top location for plant biodiversity. The range of animal species is no less spectacular. Cameroon's forests host populations of lowland gorillas and chimpanzees and are home to the fierce-looking drill – the most endangered primate species in Africa – which is restricted to Cameroon and Nigeria.

Larger mammal species include elephant, buffalo and lion, which are best observed at Parc National de Waza in the dry season. Elephants and buffaloes also exist in reasonably healthy numbers in the rainforests, but are rarely seen due to the dense vegetation. Bénoué and Bouba Ndjida parks, near Garoua, also host populations of large animals – including a small number of black rhinos – but wildlife concentrations are not as high as in Waza.

Waza is the main wildlife-viewing park and the only one readily accessible to visitors. Korup National Park has the best visitor facilities of Cameroon's protected rainforest areas, but rainy-season access is problematic. Eastern rainforest holds no less diversity – Dja is a World Heritage Site – but infrastructure is terrible, and a visit only for the most adventurous.

Environmental Issues

Cameroon's government has had only limited success in balancing the interests of commercial logging and environmental protection. Timber is big business; the most common banknote – the CFA1000 – shows heavy machinery cutting down the forests. New logging roads are driven into local communities, followed by the bushmeat trade, once a subsistence activity. Urban demand for bushmeat is massive, and it's thought that Yaoundé and Douala have the largest bushmeat consumption in West Africa. Although the government has shut down the main bushmeat markets in both cities, you can still find 'mundane' bushmeat – usually porcupine – on menus at the poshest hotels, which speaks to the trade's popularity at all levels of society.

The gazetting of eastern rainforests into national parks and the creation of new primate reserves in the south are pluses, and the ecotourism flame in general seems to be catching across the country. A great example is Limbe, where a once-nightmarish zoo now rehabilitates captured primates, educates locals about environmental issues, and has become the most popular site in the city by far.

FOOD & DRINK

Cameroonian food is pretty functional: starch and meat and not much flavour. The usual meal is rice *(riz)* or *fufu*, a generic term for mashed yam, corn, plantain or couscous, served with overcooked chicken, beef or goat, usually in soup-ish form. *Fufu* is especially heavy; you fill up on half a ball but it is fun to eat with. You rip off bits with your fingers, roll them into a ball and scoop out your meat, which hopefully isn't cooked *okoroko* style – a kind of semiviscous soup that only gets…well, gooier when mixed with *fufu*. Interestingly, pasta is becoming a more popular base for meals as it is cheaper than rice.

On the tastier side of the culinary spectrum are outdoor grills where you can get amazing fish slathered in spicy peanut sauce and fatty bits of smoky *suya* (grilled beef). The former is always cooked by women; the latter by men. Side dishes vary throughout the country, but you can generally rely on delicious fried plantains or blander *batons* (sticks) of steamed manioc, also called *feuilles*. A popular sauce is *ndole*, made with bitter leaves similar to spinach and flavoured with smoked fish – it's good stuff.

Chop houses (often a table and bench) serve food throughout the day, but there are usually only one or two dishes on offer.

BEER MONEY

If there's one thing Cameroonians love as much as football, it's drinking beer: the country has one of the highest rates of alcohol consumption in Africa. Competition between breweries is fierce, and this recently spilled over into a series of promotional offers, luring punters with free prizes hidden under the tops of beer bottles. Cars, phones or free booze were all on offer; for a short time the tops became an unofficial form of currency.

Major towns will have at least one restaurant where you can get Western-style cuisine, with Chinese and Lebanese dishes commonly available.

Cameroon has some of the best patisseries in Africa: cakes, baguettes and beignets – sweet fried dough – are never too far away, and beignets make for good breakfasts.

Beer is available everywhere, including the Muslim north. Castel and 33 are the most popular brands – billboards for the latter make handy road signs on bus trips – announcing when you're '33'km from your destination. Guinness is also consumed in huge quantities. Palm wine is popular in the south and west – don't be fooled by its innocuous milky demeanour: it's lethal. Mineral water is sold in all major towns.

YAOUNDÉ

pop 1.1 million

Let's be brutally honest: West Africa is famous for many things, but pleasant cities – especially capitals – are not one of them. Then Yaoundé comes along. Green, spaced over seven hills, green again; she's not exactly a garden city, but the capital feels planned, thoughtfully laid-out and self-contained. Plus, her hilly geography wards off the worst of the humidity of the plains, making this a fine spot for a stop before getting a visa and/ or heading off into the rest of Cameroon.

ORIENTATION

Central Yaoundé is easy to navigate. The anchor is Place Ahmadou Ahidjo. From here, Ave Ahidjo runs northwest past the Marché Central and good hotels and restaurants (especially near Ave Kennedy Blvd); par-

allel, Blvd du 20 Mai leads past the landmark Hilton to the administrative district (Quartier du Lac). Here, the road winds uphill to Carrefour (Rond-point) Nlongkak, a major roundabout. About 1.5km further up is Carrefour Bastos and the upscale Bastos residential quarter, where many embassies and restaurants are located. Overlooking town to the northwest, about 5km from the centre, is Mt Fébé.

INFORMATION

Cultural Centres

British Council (Map p179; ☎ 220 3172; Ave Charles de Gaulle)

Centre Culturel Français (Map p181; ☎ 222 0944; Ave Ahidjo) Stages lots of free film screenings and theatre productions.

Internet Access

Expect to pay CFA500 per hour for internet access.

Cometé Internet (Map p181; Rue de Narvik) One of several near the US embassy.

Espresso House (Map p179; Carrefour Bastos; per 30min CFA1000) Has broadband.

Medical Services

Pharmacie Bastos (Map p179; ☎ 220 6555; Carrefour Bastos) A well-stocked pharmacy.

Polyclinique André Fouda (Map p179; ☎ 222 6612) For medical emergencies; in Elig-Essono southeast of Carrefour Nlongkak.

Money

Bicec (Map p181; Ave Ahidjo) Near Place Ahmadou Ahidjo. Has an ATM.

Crédit Lyonnais (Map p181; Ave Monsigneur Vogt) Near Place Ahmadou Ahidjo.

Express Exchange (Map p181; Ave Kennedy) Changes travellers cheques and US dollars.

SGBC Ave Monseigneur Vogt (Map p181; Ave Monseigneur Vogt); Ave de Gaulle (Map p179; Ave Charles de Gaulle) Both have ATMs.

Post

Central post office (Map p181; Place Ahmadou Ahidjo; 🕑 7.30am-3.30pm Mon-Fri, to noon Sat)

Post Office (Map p181; Ave Foch; 🕑 7.30am-3.30pm Mon-Fri, to noon Sat)

Visa Extensions

Ministry of Immigration (Map p181; ☎ 222 2413; Ave Mdug-Fouda Ada) Issues visa extensions. Bring one photo plus CFA15,000.

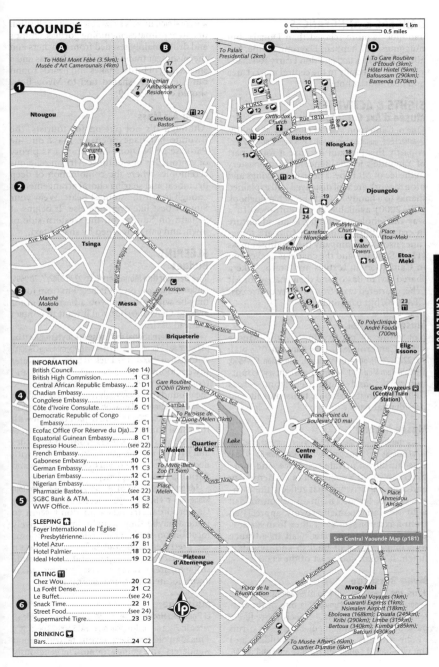

YAOUNDÉ

0 ———— 1 km
0 ———— 0.5 miles

CAMEROON

INFORMATION
British Council..........................(see 14)
British High Commission...............**1** C3
Central African Republic Embassy....**2** D1
Chadian Embassy.......................**3** C2
Congolese Embassy......................**4** D1
Côte d'Ivoire Consulate................**5** C1
Democratic Republic of Congo
  Embassy..............................**6** C1
Ecofac Office (For Réserve du Dja)...**7** B1
Equatorial Guinean Embassy...........**8** C1
Espresso House........................(see 22)
French Embassy........................**9** C6
Gabonese Embassy.....................**10** C1
German Embassy.......................**11** C3
Liberian Embassy.....................**12** C1
Nigerian Embassy.....................**13** C2
Pharmacie Bastos.....................(see 22)
SGBC Bank & ATM.....................**14** C3
WWF Office...........................**15** B2

SLEEPING
Foyer International de l'Église
  Presbytérienne.....................**16** D3
Hotel Azur...........................**17** B1
Hotel Palmier........................**18** D2
Ideal Hotel..........................**19** D2

EATING
Chez Wou.............................**20** C2
La Forêt Dense.......................**21** C2
Le Buffet............................(see 24)
Snack Time...........................**22** B1
Street Food..........................(see 24)
Supermarché Tigre....................**23** D3

DRINKING
Bars.................................**24** C2

To Palais
Presidential (2km)

To Hôtel Mont Fébé (3.5km);
Musée d'Art Camerounais (4km)

To Gare Routière
d'Étoudi (3km);
Hôtel Hintel (5km);
Bafoussam (290km);
Bamenda (370km)

Ntougou

Nigerian
Ambassador's
Residence

Carrefour
Bastos

Palais de
Congrès

Orthodox
Church

Bastos

Nlongkak

Rue Fouda Ngono

Djoungolo

Ave Ngu Fondha

Tsinga

Carrefour
Nlongkak

Presbyterian
Church

Place
Etoa-Meki

Préfecture

Water
Towers

Etoa-
Meki

Marché
Mokolo

Mosque

Messa

Rue Briqueterie

Briqueterie

To Polyclinique
André Fouda
(700km)

Elig-
Essono

Gare Routière
d'Obili (2km)

Blvd Manga Bell

Samba

To Paroisse de
N'Djong-Melen (1km)

Melen

Quartier
du Lac

Lake

Gare Voyageurs
(Central Train
Station)

Rond-Point du
Boulevard 20 mai

Centre
Ville

To Mvog-Betsi
Zoo (1.5km)

Place
Melen

Place
Ahméidou
Ahidjo

Plateau
d'Atemengue

See Central Yaoundé Map (p181)

Place de la
Réunification

Mvog-Mbi

To Central Voyages (1km);
Guaranti Express (1km);
Nsimalen Airport (18km);
Ebolowa (168km); Douala (245km);
Kribi (290km); Limbe (315km);
Bertoua (340km); Kumba (385km);
Batouri (430km)

To Musée Afhemi (6km);
Quartier Damase (6km)

DANGERS & ANNOYANCES

Yaoundé is more relaxed than Douala, but muggings still happen. Daytime is fine, but after dusk take a taxi and don't carry too many valuables, especially in the central market area and near tourist hotels.

SIGHTS & ACTIVITIES

Musée d'Art Camerounais

One of Cameroon's better **museums** (off Map p179; Quartier Fébé; donation requested; 🕑 3-6pm Thu, Sat & Sun) is partly this pleasant because it forms part of Yaoundé's idyllic Benedictine monastery in the lee of Mt Fébé. The usual carvings and bronze-work are well displayed and explained thanks to a handy English-French guidebook (CFA2000) available at the entrance. In a way the whole monastery is an adventure in cross-cultural education; *kora* are sometimes used to accompany the singing at mass (11am Sunday), and the chapel is decked out in Cameroonian textiles and crafts. Take a shared taxi to Bastos and then change for Mt Fébé; chartered taxis from the city centre cost CFA2000, but bargain hard.

Musée National

Not quite as captivating as the Musée d'Art Camerounais, this **museum** (Map p181; ☎ 2222 2311; off Ave Marchand; admission CFA1000; 🕑 9am-4pm Mon-Sat) is small and dusty, counting masks and sculptures from across Cameroon in its exhibits, housed in the old presidential palace.

Musée Afhemi

This **museum** (off Map p179; Quartier Nsimeyong; admission CFA3000; 🕑 9am-8pm Tue-Fri, 10am-8pm Sat & Sun) is technically a private residence, and more gallery in spirit: a collection of Cameroonian and regional artwork that reflects the owner's eclectic tastes. The main reason to visit is to see Cameroonian artwork appreciated from a connoisseur's – rather than an academic's – point of view. Call in advance to arrange a tour in English and, possibly, lunch. It's 6km southeast of the centre.

Mvog-Betsi Zoo

This **zoo** (Mvog-Betsi; off Map p179; admission CFA2000, camera fee CFA5000; 🕑 9am-6pm) is one of the better ones in West Africa – it feels more like a park than an arrangement of cages. Co-run by the Ministry of Forestry & Wildlife and the UK-based **Cameroon Wildlife Aid Fund** (CWAF,

www.cwaf.org), there's a sizeable onsite collection of native primates, including gorillas, chimps and drills, mainly rescued from poachers and the bushmeat trade. A few lions, hyenas and a smattering of birds, snakes and lizards round out the mix. A shared taxi to Mvog-Betsi should cost CFA200.

Open-Air Mass

Although it's not put on for tourists, the Ewondo-language open-air mass outside Paroisse de N'Djong Melen attracts plenty of visitors. It's one of those African religious ceremonies where the combination of deep drumbeat and soaring choral arrangement is enough to stir the stoniest heart. Wear your Sunday best like everyone else. It begins at 9.30am on Sunday on the western side of town, and can be reached by shared taxi.

SLEEPING

Budget

The **Benedictine Monastery** (☎ 2220 0947, 7770 9695; mission@icccnet.com) on Mt Fébé, 5km from town, may be willing to rent you a basic room for around CFA8500, but you'll want to contact it ahead of time.

Foyer International de l'Église Presbytérienne (Map p179; ☎ 985 236; off Rue Joseph Essono Balla; camping CFA2000, dm CFA3000, d CFA4000; 🅿) Tucked behind the water towers looming over Nlongkak, rooms and (communal) facilities are simple and clean, and the grounds have enough trees to laze under.

Hotel Palmier (Map p179; ☎ 2220 4593; Nlongkak; r CFA6800-10,000; 🌀) In a busy part of town with the usual controlled chaos of a market street outside, this hotel suffers from missing tiles and broken air-con but makes an effort with decent, large-as-life rooms, carved statues and Africana artwork aplenty.

Ideal Hotel (Map p179; ☎ 2220 9852; Carrefour Nlongkak; r CFA8000; 🅿) Recommended by Cameroonian friends who don't seem to mind (maybe they actually love) the lively location on Rond-point Nlongkak. Rooms are pretty enough, and balconies make up for the lack of light (plus you get Yaoundé smog for free). If you're visa hunting, this is a well-located-for-embassies option.

Midrange

El Panaden Hotel (Map p181; ☎ 2222 2765; elpanaden@ yahoo.fr; Place de l'Indépendance; r CFA15,500-28,000; 🌀) This is an old travellers' favourite, with a good wanderers' vibe going around. The generously

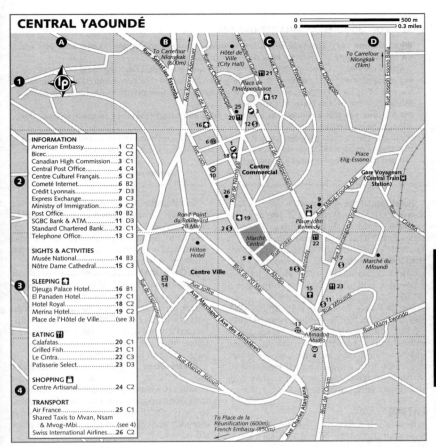

CENTRAL YAOUNDÉ

INFORMATION
American Embassy....................1 C2
Bicec.......................................2 C2
Canadian High Commission....3 C1
Central Post Office..................4 C4
Centre Culturel Français..........5 C3
Comété Internet......................6 B2
Crédit Lyonnais.......................7 D3
Express Exchange....................8 C3
Ministry of Immigration..........9 C2
Post Office............................10 B2
SGBC Bank & ATM.................11 D3
Standard Chartered Bank........12 C1
Telephone Office....................13 C3

SIGHTS & ACTIVITIES
Musée National.......................14 B3
Nôtre Dame Cathedral............15 C3

SLEEPING
Djeuga Palace Hotel................16 B1
El Panaden Hotel....................17 C1
Hotel Royal............................18 C2
Merina Hotel..........................19 C2
Place de l'Hôtel de Ville.........(see 3)

EATING
Calafatas...............................20 C1
Grilled Fish............................21 C1
Le Cintra...............................22 C3
Patisserie Select.....................23 D3

SHOPPING
Centre Artisanal.....................24 C2

TRANSPORT
Air France..............................25 C1
Shared Taxis to Mvan, Nsam
  & Mvog-Mbi.....................(see 4)
Swiss International Airlines.....26 C2

CAMEROON

sized and (importantly) spotless rooms often come with balconies. Next door, La Terrasse bar is a handy late-night stagger away.

Hotel Royal (Map p181; ☎ 2223 1953; Centre Commercial; r CFA15,000-32,000) On the outside it looks like a Brutalist bomb shelter, but on the inside the Royal is a decent midrange deal, with clean rooms and a central location that's about equidistant between the central market and the Place de l'Indépendance.

Hôtel Hintel (off Map p179; ☎ 2220 0466, 2220 0467; www.hintelhotel.com Ngouosso; next to hospital; r CFA25,000-35,000;) The Hintel is a bit outside of town (unless you're visiting the General Hospital, in which case it's very convenient). It's part of the appeal; quality midrange and all the more serene for being secluded from centre ville.

Hotel Azur (Map p179; ☎ 2221 1640/1; Bastos; r CFA35,000-45,000;) A modern hotel in a quiet and secluded location. The cheaper rooms feel a bit pinched for the price, but the more expensive ones are big enough to get lost in. Most have balconies, and those at the back have gorgeous views over the hills.

Top End
Merina Hotel (Map p181; ☎ 2222 2131; www.cameroon-plus.com; Ave Ahidjo; r CFA32,000-41,500;) The Merina is strictly business-class, catering to foreign suits and Cameroonian politicos. While it's a bit overpriced for what you get, rooms are comfy, the location is as central as the equator and there's vaguely reliable wi-fi.

ADAMOU MBOUMBOU, FINANCE OFFICER

When Obama says 'To those who cling to power through corruption...know that you are on the wrong side of history,' how does that make you feel?

It makes me hope that our politicians will listen to him. We cannot have the same president ruling us for so many years without them going corrupt, and in that corruption, they are hurting the rest of us for their gain. But things are changing...in some places. In Ghana, for example. Maybe this change can come to Cameroon.

Do Africans see this president as someone who will bring resources to their village, the 'village' being Africa?

We understand a black president cannot save Africa. But it does make us feel anything is possible, that there can be a change, and you must understand this is a feeling that is very important for Africans in countries like ours to hold onto.

Names were changed in this interview.

Hôtel Mont Fébé (off Map p179; ☎ 2221 4002; Mont Fébé; r CFA60,000; P ⚡ ☎) If you're going to sleep on Mont Fébé's slopes, do so in style, right? This is our favourite option in Yaoundé's outskirts, a cool mountain retreat with lovers' lane lookouts, good rooms, a golf course and a restaurant with – ah, yes Jeeves – a poolside buffet. The hotel also operates a shuttle bus to the airport for guests.

Djeuga Palace Hotel (Map p181; ☎ 2222 6469; www.djeuga-palace.com; Rue de Narvik; r from CFA72,000; ⚡ ☎) The four-star Djeuga Palace steals some thunder from the international chains in town. Rooms are as plush as a jewel box and come with good views, all embellished by the expected complement of swanky bars and restaurants and a small pool.

EATING

Patisserie Select (Map p181; Ave Monseigneur Vogt; baked goods CFA200-1000; ☺ breakfast, lunch & dinner) This excellent bakery sells delicious lines of croissants, beignets, pizzas and sandwiches – there's even a hamburger or two kicking around behind the glass cases. Popular with expats and well-heeled Cameroonians.

Le Buffet (Map p179; Carrefour Nlongkak; mains from CFA500; ☺ 11am-9pm) The name gives this place away – there's a long, heated servery where you can help yourself to various stews, chicken, fish and as much rice and plantain as you like.

Snack Time (Map p179; Carrefour Bastos; mains from CFA2700; ☺ 10am-11pm) This bright place serves up a menu straight from an American diner, with a few Lebanese and Italian dishes thrown in for good measure. The bean burritos (CFA3000) are decent, and the vegetarian pasta a treat for those suffering from a surfeit of meaty Cameroonian stews.

Chez Wou (Map p179; Rue Joseph Mballa Eloumden; mains from CFA4000; ☺ lunch & dinner) One of Yaoundé's older Chinese restaurants, this has nice tables set under a wide porch, a comprehensive menu and a complement of Chinese expat clientele – always a good sign.

Le Cintra (Map p181; Ave Kennedy; dishes from CFA4000; ☺ lunch & dinner) This is as close as we got to finding the sort of Cameroonian French restaurant where we'd film a movie about the colonial period with an Edith Piaf soundtrack. It's unfortunately not quite that atmospheric, but it makes an effort, and the French mains (*steak au poivre*, etc) make up the extra mile.

La Forêt Dense (Map p179; Rue Joseph Mballa Eloumden; meals from CFA5500) Every African capital has the restaurant where you get the local traditional stuff done up sexy and overpriced; welcome to La Forêt. If you've ever wondered what *crocodile mbongo* tastes like, this is the place to find out.

Quick Eats

Calafatas (Map p181; Rue de Nachtigal; pastries from CFA200; ☺ 8am-6pm) People cross the city to get their pastries from Calafatas, and you should too. Although it's open all day, all the best choices are gone by late morning, leaving little but baguettes.

Around Carrefours Bastos and Nlongkak you can find grills serving *suya* (brochettes) throughout the day. On Place de l'Indépendance, near El Panaden Hotel, you'll find the usual fish ladies plying their tasty stock in grilled trade.

DRINKING

The best bars are in Carrefours Bastos and Nlongkak, most with open-air seating facing the street – great for people-watching. Solo female travellers might find the atmosphere in some uneasy once the sun dips. It's difficult to recommend anywhere in particular – there are plenty, so follow your nose to find one you like. The bars in pricier hotels seem to become sex-worker (and client) central in the late hours.

SHOPPING

Centre Artisanal (Place John Kennedy) This large government-run establishment is a good place to get an idea of what handicrafts are available in Cameroon, although prices are high. Woodcarving dominates what's on offer.

GETTING THERE & AWAY
Air

For international flight connections to Yaoundé, see p223. For internal flights, the current option is **Elysian Airlines** (☎ 9909 8748; www.elysianairlines.com), offering a spotty schedule that flies to Douala (CFA28,500, 45 minutes), Garoua (CFA96,400, three hours), N'Gaoundéré (CFA86,500, 2½ hours) and Maroua (CFA125,000, four hours).

Bus

Central Voyages and Guaranti Express have services to Douala, (CFA3800, three hours) leaving regularly during the day. Central Voyages also has a 'prestige' service costing CFA7500. Its office is south of the centre in Mvog-Mbi; unlike most companies, you can book 1st-class tickets a day before and they leave on time. Guaranti Express is recommended for Limbe (CFA5000, five hours), Bamenda (CFA5000, six hours), Bafoussam (CFA2500, three hours) and Kumba (CFA4000, four hours). Its office is in Quartier Nsam, 3km south of the centre.

Otherwise, all other transport for Kribi, Bertoua, Batouri and other destinations in southern, central and eastern Cameroon, departs from Blvd de l'Ocam, 3km south of Place Ahmadou Ahidjo. For Kribi (CFA3500, 3½ hours) look for La Kribienne or Jako Voyages, running throughout the day. For Bertoua and points east, use Alliance Voyages, departing early each morning to Batouri (CFA6000, at least eight hours). There is also plenty of transport from here to Ebolowa, Limbe, Buea and Kumba.

Transport to Bafoussam (CFA3500 to CFA4000, five hours) and points north, departs from Gare Routière d'Etoudi, 5km north of Centre Ville, and is where most agencies

have their offices; the best one is Binam. You can find vehicles to Bamenda here – though it may be quicker to get something to Bafoussam and transfer. Transport to Bamenda also departs from Gare Routière d'Obili on the western edge of town.

Train

There is a daily Camrail train to N'Gaoundéré, departing at around 6pm from the **train station** (Gare Voyageurs; ☎ 2223 4003, 2222 1305). For more information on train travel, see p226.

GETTING AROUND
To/From the Airport

A taxi to Nsimalen Airport from central Yaoundé (40 minutes) should cost CFA4000 to CFA6000. There is no public transport.

Taxi

Shared taxis are the only public-transport option. There are no minibuses and surprisingly, Yaoundé doesn't permit *moto-taxis* (motorcycle taxis). Fares are CFA200 for short to medium length rides – flag a taxi down on the street and shout out the name of the quartier, *rond-point* or landmark near where you wish to go; the driver will sound his horn if he's going your way. Charter taxis start from CFA1000.

DOUALA & THE SOUTHWEST

Imagine Africa: a wormy red track and a pressing in of vegetation so intensely green you can almost taste the colour. Kids in cast-off T-shirts balance trays of nuts, fruits and cigarettes on their heads, and music is as imminent as heat. This image comes alive in the Southwest and Littoral Provinces of Cameroon. The country's economic heart intermittently beats in Douala, and from here it's a short hop to the haze and laze of beach towns like Limbe and the savannah-carpeted slopes of the Mountain of Thunder – Mt Cameroon.

DOUALA
pop 1.7 million

Sticky, icky and as frenetic as Cameroon gets, Douala isn't as bad as some say, but likely not your first choice for a honeymoon, either.

By any measurement but political power this is Cameroon's main city: primary air hub, port, business centre, and bit of a chaotic mess. There are few charms, but as veins go this is the main one: set your finger here to gauge Cameroon's pulse.

Orientation

Douala's 'centre' is the expensive Akwa district, bisected by Blvd de la Liberté, where you'll find many hotels, internet cafes, banks and restaurants. South of here, along and near Rue Joss in Bonanjo, is the administrative quarter, with airline offices, government buildings and the central post office. The rest of Douala is a series of built-up districts that have grown into satellite cities strung together by shared taxis, a whim and a prayer.

Information

INTERNET ACCESS

Places open and close with the drop of a hat. The following are reliable:

Cyberaljo (per 3hr CFA1000) Near Cinema Wouri.

Cyberbao (Blvd de la Liberté; per hr CFA400)

MEDICAL SERVICES

Pharmacie du Centre (Rue Joffre)

Pharmacie de Douala (Blvd Ahidjo)

MONEY

Hôtel Akwa Palace has plenty of touts outside for changing cash out of hours. Be on your guard.

Bicec (Blvd de la Liberté, Akwa) Recommended for changing money; the Akwa branch has an ATM.

Crédit Lyonnais Akwa (Rue Sylvani); Bonanjo (Rue Joss) Recommended for changing money.

Ecobank (Blvd de la Liberté) With ATM.

Express Exchange (Blvd de la Liberté) Conveniently changes travellers cheques and US dollars.

SGBC (Rue Joss) With ATM.

Standard Chartered Bank (Blvd de la Liberté) Recommended for changing money.

POST

Central post office (Rue Joss)

TRAVEL AGENCIES

Saga Voyages (☎ 3342 1203; Rue Tobie Kuoh) A well-organised, professional agency.

Dangers & Annoyances

Muggings happen: if you'd rather be safe than sorry it's recommended to take a taxi after dark. Leave valuables in a safe place, and be extra careful around nightspots.

Sights & Activities

This is a commercial city, so get a feel for the commercial areas: the docks (visible from the verandah of Foyer du Marin) piles up with offloaded containers; **Marché de Lagos** (cnr Rue de New Bell & Rue Congo Pariso) bumps along like an African market day on steroids; and the **Marché Chinois** (New Bell), hums with the mercantile activity of Cameroon's latest round of immigrants. These are the Chinese shopkeepers selling, as one local puts it, 'Things that are very cheap. But breakfast.'

Or relax in one of Douala's pools. The best is at **Hôtel Akwa Palace** (Blvd de le Liberté; nonguests CFA4000); alternatively try the **Hotel Beausejour Mirabel** (Rue Joffre; nonguests CFA1500), both in Akwa.

Sleeping

BUDGET

Église Évangelique de Cameroon (☎ 342 3611; eec@wagne.net; Rue Alfred Saker; s/d/tr CFA6500/8000/11,000) This is adequate as church missions go, but it's a bit tired and in need of love. The rooms are very basic, and facilities are shared.

Centre d'Accueil Missionaire (☎ 342 2797; progemis.douala@camnet.cm; Rue Franceville; r with/without shower CFA8000/7000; P ⊠ ⓢ) Praise be to this Catholic mission, with its clean twin rooms, pleasant verandah and pool. Next to the pink Axa building.

Hotel Hila (☎ 342 1586; Blvd de l'Unité; s CFA10,000-12,000; d 15,000; ⊠) The Hila's plus is its location: good for getting to Yaoundé. Its minus is the busy road outside, with cheers and jeers bridged by a middle ground of rooms that are seriously spartan. A CFA20,000 deposit is required on checking in.

MIDRANGE

Hotel Ste Juliette (☎ 3342 3885; info@beausejour-mirabel.com; Rue Joffre; r CFA15,000; ⊠ ⓢ) Ste Juliette defines 'midrange' – for air-conditioned comfort it's cheap and cheerful, even if rooms are boxy. There's an onsite, very small mosque, as this place is Muslim-run (but open and friendly to all comers).

Foyer du Marin (☎ 3342 2794; douala@seemannsmission.org; Rue Gallieni; s/d CFA15,000/28,000; P ⊠ ⌑ ⓢ) Every Third World city of a certain size gets one surreal hotel, and this is Douala's: a dark wood veranda shading British overlanders, tattooed NGOers, dressed to impress locals and the odd journalist, plus a crystal pool and…German merchant marine regulations. This is the German Seaman's Mission, and tidy rooms are kept as such for tourists and sailors on shore leave. Fills fast – book early.

Hotel le Nde (☎ 3342 7034; Blvd de le Liberté; s/d CFA18,000/21,000; ⊠) You can feel this place struggling not to slip the moorings of time and become a hotel of British West Africa (note the Union Jack crest) colonial days. The moulded furniture ambience is actually charming and more than makes up for average (if pleasant) digs.

Hotel Beausejour Mirabel (☎ 3342 3885; info@ beausejour-mirabel.com; Rue Joffre; r CFA25,000-27,000; ⊠ ⊠) The Mirabel's lobby isn't as impressive as the Akwa Palace, but rooms are just as lovely and the price a little cheaper. Nonguests can use the pool for CFA1500 per day.

Parfait Garden (☎ 3342 6357; hotel.parfait -garden@globalnet2.net; Blvd de le Liberté; r from CFA35,000; ⊠ ▭ ☎) These spacious rooms could do with carpeting (as opposed to linoleum), but they're gorgeously maintained, by fully decked-out bellhops to boot. Service is lovely; the wi-fi connection not so much, at least when we stayed.

Hôtel Akwa Palace (☎ 342 2601; akwa.palace@ camnet.cm; Blvd de le Liberté; s/d CFA38,000/45,000; ℗ ⊠ ▭ ⊠) Very much the best hotel in town, the Akwa Palace is the sort of place where movies about the indolence of expat existence are filmed. Rooms are plush, staff obsequious and decor tasteful.

Hotel Frais Palace (☎ 342 3885; Rue Joffre; r CFA45,000; ⊠ ⊠) Decidedly cool and comfortable, this is one of Douala's largest hotels. Some of the rooms have pseudo gold lamé sheets, which is either tacky or awesome depending on your taste, but they're all comfy. Plus: internet connections are reliable – exceedingly rare in Cameroonian hotels.

Eating & Drinking

There are plenty of good restaurants along Blvd de le Liberté, selling a spectrum of international cuisine.

Méditerranée Restaurant (Blvd de la Liberté; mains from CFA2500; ⊗ 8am-midnight) With an open terrace – but still cleverly sheltered from the busy road – the Méditerranée is perennially popular. As the name suggests, the menu mixes Greek, Italian and Lebanese dishes, and sadly, a big population of sex workers prowling at night.

Foyer du Marin (Rue Gallieni; kebabs from CFA1000; ⊗ 7-10pm) The nightly grill at this hotel is worth making a diversion for; great kebabs, chicken and juicy German sausage. A Douala expat institution.

Saga African Restaurant (Blvd de la Liberté; mains from CFA1200; ⊗ noon-10pm) Opposite Parfait Garden, the Saga serves an interesting mix of continental and local classics like *ndole* done up for tourists.

Delice (Blvd de la Liberté; snacks from CFA500; ⊗ 7am-9.30pm) A great early-morning stop for pastries and coffee; good toasted sandwiches, cool aircon and comfy seating.

STREET EATS

Grilled fish & beer (Rue de la Joie; fish from CFA1000; ⊗ 10am-late) Are there four better words? Also try Blvd del la Réunification, or really just about anywhere. Order the catch of the day, retire to a drinking hole to sink a cold one while your meal is on the barbecue. It's served to your table with plantains or *baton* – delicious!

Street food stalls (Rue Joffre; meals from CFA800; ⊗ 10am-9pm) This market street has plenty of options for filling Cameroonian food – mostly simple stalls with little more than a bench and table.

Entertainment

Douala is known for its nightlife, which is far more charged than Yaoundé. Asking locals is the best way to find the current hot spots; when we visited the area near the airport was happening, with bars and nightclubs dancing until dawn on weekends.

Shopping

Centre Artisanal de Douala (Marché des Fleurs, Ave Charles de Gaulle) Stock up on Cameroonian handicrafts, including carvings, metal- and leather-work and fabrics. Bargain hard.

Getting There & Away

AIR

Douala is the main entry point for international flights into Cameroon. The airport can be pretty chaotic, with plenty of hustlers; brace yourself. For internal flights, there's only **Elysian Airlines** (☎ 9909 8748; www.elysianair lines.com) which flies to Yaoundé (CFA28,500, 45 minutes), Garoua (CFA96,400, three hours), N'Gaoundéré (CFA86,500, 2½ hours) and Maroua (CFA125,000, four hours).

DOUALA

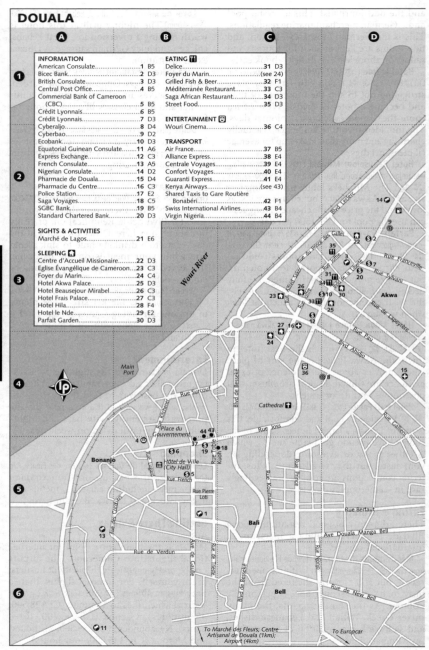

INFORMATION
American Consulate......................**1** B5
Bicec Bank.................................**2** D3
British Consulate..........................**3** D3
Central Post Office.......................**4** B5
Commercial Bank of Cameroon
  (CBC)....................................**5** B5
Crédit Lyonnais............................**6** B5
Crédit Lyonnais............................**7** D3
Cyberaljo...................................**8** D4
Cyberbao...................................**9** D2
Ecobank..................................**10** D3
Equatorial Guinean Consulate......**11** A6
Express Exchange.......................**12** C3
French Consulate........................**13** A5
Nigerian Consulate......................**14** D2
Pharmacie de Douala...................**15** D4
Pharmacie du Centre....................**16** C3
Police Station.............................**17** E2
Saga Voyages............................**18** C5
SGBC Bank................................**19** B5
Standard Chartered Bank..............**20** D3

SIGHTS & ACTIVITIES
Marché de Lagos.........................**21** E6

SLEEPING 🏠
Centre d'Accueil Missionaire...........**22** D3
Eglise Évangélique de Cameroon.....**23** C3
Foyer du Marin...........................**24** C4
Hotel Akwa Palace......................**25** D3
Hotel Beausejour Mirabel..............**26** C3
Hotel Frais Palace.......................**27** C3
Hotel Hila.................................**28** F4
Hotel le Nde..............................**29** E2
Parfait Garden...........................**30** D3

EATING 🍴
Delice......................................**31** D3
Foyer du Marin......................(see **24**)
Grilled Fish & Beer......................**32** F1
Méditerranée Restaurant...............**33** C3
Saga African Restaurant................**34** D3
Street Food...............................**35** D3

ENTERTAINMENT 🎭
Wouri Cinema............................**36** C4

TRANSPORT
Air France.................................**37** B5
Alliance Express..........................**38** E4
Centrale Voyages........................**39** E4
Confort Voyages.........................**40** E4
Guaranti Express.........................**41** E4
Kenya Airways.......................(see **43**)
Shared Taxis to Gare Routière
  Bonabéri...............................**42** F1
Swiss International Airlines.............**43** B4
Virgin Nigeria............................**44** B4

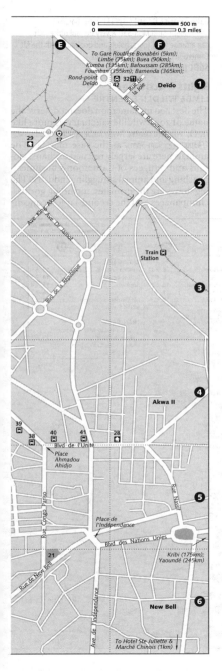

BUS

There are two main transport hubs. In central Douala, bus agencies including Centrale Voyages, Confort Voyages, Alliance Express and Guaranti Express all have depots along Blvd de l'Unité, and run services primarily to Yaoundé (CFA3800, three hours) and Limbe (CFA2000, three hours) throughout the day. Centrale Voyages also has a 'prestige service' to Yaoundé with comfier seats and drinks and snacks provided (CFA7500).

For other destinations, agency and non-agency transport uses the sprawling Bonabéri *gare routière*, 6km north of the city centre across the Wouri River bridge. Typical minibus fares include Limbe (CFA1000, 90 minutes) Bamenda (CFA5000, seven hours), Bafoussam (CFA3500, five hours) and Foumban (CFA5000, six hours).

If you arrive via Bonabéri, there will be charter taxis waiting to take you to town. Otherwise, walk to the main road and get a share taxi to Rond-point Deïdo (CFA200), where you'll need to get another shared taxi to wherever you're going. Charter taxis from the centre to Bonabéri generally charge CFA3000. At Rond-point Deïdo you can sometimes find shared taxis going all the way to Limbe (CFA2000, 70 minutes).

TRAIN

There's a twice-daily train (☎ 3340 6045) to Yaoundé but, as it takes around two hours longer than the bus, it's little used by travellers. Tickets cost CFA3000 to CFA6700 depending on the class. A daily service runs to Kumba, but is poorly maintained and painfully slow.

Getting Around
TO/FROM THE AIRPORT

Chartered taxis from Akwa or Bonanjo to the airport cost CFA3000 (CFA4000 at night).

TAXI

Shared taxis anywhere in town cost CFA200; charters cost from CFA1000. A short ride on a *moto-taxi* (locally called 'bendskins') costs from CFA100 to CFA150.

LIMBE
pop 50,000

Pop an 'O' in place of the 'E' at the end of Limbe, add 'tropical' to the front and you've got a fair idea of what this town is all about – chilling out by the ocean with a beer and some fish. Popular with both foreign and Cameroonian tourists, the main hub of the Anglophone Southwest is a sultry place, sweating and partying in the shade of Mt Cameroon and with hills overgrown with banana plantations. On clear days you can look out across the bay to not-so-distant Equatorial Guinea.

Information

The banks change money, but don't rely on travellers cheques.

Bicec (Ahidjo Rd) Has an ATM.

Bifunde Computer Centre (Bota Rd; per hr CFA800) Very fast internet access.

Computer World (Banley St; per hr CFA400; 🕑 closed Sun)

Fako Tourist Board (☎ 333 2861; Banley St; 🕑 7.30am-5pm Mon-Sat) A very helpful office that can arrange local tours, hotels and bookings with the Mt Cameroon Ecotourism Organisation.

SGBC (Beach Rd) Has an ATM.

Sights & Activities
LIMBE WILDLIFE CENTRE

The best zoo in Cameroon doesn't deserve the name of zoo; 'wildlife sanctuary' is more like it. Or **wildlife centre** (www.limbewildlife.org; admission CFA3000; 🕑 9am-5pm), as the case may be. The animals here are largely rescued orphans, victims and refugees of Cameroon's bushmeat, poaching and animal smuggling industry. The big draws are the primates, including gorillas, chimpanzees and the second-largest concen-

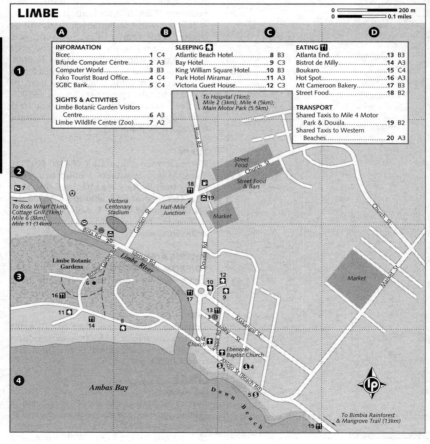

LIMBE

0 —————— 200 m
0 —————— 0.1 miles

INFORMATION
Bicec...1 C4
Bifunde Computer Centre..............2 A3
Computer World...............................3 B3
Fako Tourist Board Office...............4 C4
SGBC Bank...5 C4

SIGHTS & ACTIVITIES
Limbe Botanic Garden Visitors
Centre..6 A3
Limbe Wildlife Centre (Zoo)..........7 A2

SLEEPING 🛏
Atlantic Beach Hotel........................8 B3
Bay Hotel...9 C3
King William Square Hotel............10 B3
Park Hotel Miramar.......................11 A3
Victoria Guest House.....................12 C3

EATING 🍴
Atlanta End.....................................13 B3
Bistrot de Milly..............................14 A3
Boukaro...15 C4
Hot Spot..16 A3
Mt Cameroon Bakery....................17 B3
Street Food......................................18 B2

TRANSPORT
Shared Taxis to Mile 4 Motor
Park & Douala...............................19 B2
Shared Taxis to Western
Beaches..20 A3

To Hospital (1km);
Mile 2 (3km); Mile 4 (5km);
Main Motor Park (5.5km)

Street
Food
Church St.
Street Food
& Bars

Buea Rd

Catden St

Victoria
Centenary
Stadium
Half-Mile
Junction
Market

To Bota Wharf (1km);
Cottage Grill (1km);
Mile 6 (8km);
Mile 11 (14km)
Bota Rd
Idenao Rd
Limbe River

Botanic Garden Rd

**Limbe Botanic
Gardens**

Dimad Rd

Makangal St

Market

Church St

Market St

Banley St
Old
Church
Ebenezer
Baptist Church
Ahidjo St (Beach Rd)

Ambas Bay

Down Beach

To Bimbia Rainforest
& Mangrove Trail (13km)

THE GROUNDING OF CAMEROON AIR

After years of losing money, shoddy safety specs and failed attempts to rise from the ashes, Cameroon Airlines shut down in March 2008. The only domestic carrier in service as of research was Elysian Airlines, which has an untested safety record. Your other option for flights between Cameroonian cities – until Camair Co revives or another carrier is granted the right to start internal flights – is to fly outside of Cameroon, then back into your domestic destination. Welcome to Africa.

---

tration of captive drills on Earth. The centre works to educate Cameroonians on conservation issues and works with local villages on antipoaching initiatives. Interested visitors may even 'adopt' a primate, to help pay for their care, from CFA20,000 per year.

LIMBE BOTANIC GARDENS
The second -oldest and biggest botanical **gardens** (www.mcbcclimbe.org; admission CFA1000, camera fee CFA2000; 🕒 8am-6pm) in Africa are the home of, among others, cinnamon, nutmeg, mango, ancient cycads and an unnamed tree locals describe as 'African Viagra'. There's a small **visitors centre** (guides CFA1000) and an area with Commonwealth war graves. Guides aren't required but are highly recommended.

BIMBIA RAINFOREST AND MANGROVE TRAIL
About an hour south of Limbe is a **mangrove forest** – the only coastal lowland rainforest remaining between Douala and Limbe – where experienced guides can take you on day tours through some rather lovely submerged woods and old slave-trading sites. Bird-watching opportunities abound, and it's a lovely natural escape. Prices are: CFA5000 for the local development fee, which goes towards the village of Bimbia and mangrove preservation; CFA3000 per guide; and CFA15,000 for a bush taxi from Limbe (currently the only way here, although there was talk of arranging cheaper local transport), making this a trip best done in a group. To arrange tours talk to the guys who hang around the botanic gardens, arrange a trip through the Fako Tourist Board (opposite) or contact **Bimbia Rainforest & Mangrove Trail** (☎ 3333 3325; www.bbcforest.org/eco; bbcnaturetrail@yahoo.com).

Sleeping
Park Hotel Miramar (☎ 332 2332; Botanic Garden Rd; campsites CFA5000, s/d CFA13,650/18,400; P 🐾 🖵) These cute, stucco and blue cottages lip onto a wave-kissed cliff backed by screaming jungle – very romantic. It's Limbe's most popular hotel, but there's no sense of crowds, just quiet and escape. All prices include breakfast.

Bay Hotel (☎ 773 3609; off Makangal Street; r CFA7000-9000, ste CFA10,000) The Bay is the best of a triple-cluster of hotels in this corner of Limbe, with big rooms that, in some cases, come with wide verandahs – all good for catching the sea breeze. Unfortunately they also tend to pick up the noise of the party people in the nearby bars.

Victoria Guest House (☎ 333 2446; off Makangal Street; r with fan CFA6000-9000, with air-con CFA12,000-16,000; 🐾) Fine in a pinch, this budget option offers decent digs. You'll feel more content in cheaper rooms than paying the midrange price tag – especially compared with what else is on offer in town.

King William Square Hotel (☎ 333 2529; Makangal Street; s/d from CFA10,000/11,500; 🐾) The third of the cluster of hotels in this area, the King William is a workhorse: solid and boring. Look at more than one room – Limbe's damp atmosphere seems to have taken hold in a few.

Atlantic Beach Hotel (☎ 332 2689; r CFA16,500-23,500; P 🐾 🖵) There's a slightly romantic state of dishevelment to this hotel, although we want to say: it is kinda dishevelled. The sea-view rooms do indeed have nice vantages over the water, but garden- (more like 'parking lot') view rooms give more space for your franc. Bizarrely, the more expensive rooms come with two breakfasts, even if you're travelling solo.

Eating
You can find tasty street food around Half-Mile Junction, along with a good selection of grocery shops and bakeries.

Boukaro (Down Beach; dishes from CFA800-2500) You'll find this cluster of open-air grills with attached seating where the fishing boats haul up on the beach. Soak up your beer with something from the sea that was probably happily unaware it would be your dinner a few minutes before you ordered it.

Hot Spot (off Botanic Garden Rd; mains from CFA2000) On a low hill, there are moonlight-on-the-bay views here that are romantic as hell, plus good meals to boot. Take a torch for the walk home at night.

CAMEROON

Bistrot de Milly (Botanic Garden Rd; mains from CFA2000) Peer hard onto Ambas Bay and you may be able to spot Equatorial Guinea as you polish off some excellent seafood and the cold drink of your choice.

Mt Cameroon Bakery (Idenao Rd; mains from CFA2500) Although this spot does do nice beignets in the morning, in the evening it becomes a hopping resto/bar, serving French-ish standards and lots of loud music. The pork in mustard sauce is lovely, assuming it's on the somewhat changeable menu.

Cottage Grill (mains around CFA5000) This cosy place really does feel like your own white picket fence cottage and offers personalised dinners in a rich and heavy style, usually featuring beef, chicken or fish as your main. It's tucked away down a back street; follow the signs from the Limbe Wildlife Centre.

Atlanta End (Banley St) This nightclub/bar seems to always be partying until the wee hours; it can get pretty wild, which can be lots of fun or a little intimidating depending on your threshold for African nightlife.

Getting There & Away
BOAT

Ferries run every Monday and Thursday from Limbe to Calabar (p639) in Nigeria (CFA37,000, 10 hours), departing around 11pm and returning on Tuesday and Friday at 6pm. Operator **Destiny** (Bota Wharf) sell tickets on the day of departure at Bota Wharf, 1km west of town, from where the ferry also departs. You give up your passport on boarding, which is returned when you reach Nigerian immigration. There's no food or drink for sale on the ferry and seats are in short supply, so board early if possible. It's possible to change CFA for Nigerian naira at Bota Wharf.

Ferries no longer operate to Malabo in Equatorial Guinea, although you can arrange a speedboat (popularly called 'stick-boats' – we like 'death trap') from Bota for around CFA65,000. The trip takes four hours, but the boats have poor safety records and cannot be recommended. If you must take one, invest in a life jacket.

BUS & TAXI

The main motor park is Mile 4, about 5km from town on the Buea road. When arriving you may be dropped here, in which case it's a CFA100 share taxi to Half-Mile Junction in central Limbe.

Minibuses depart throughout the day from Mile 4 to Buea (CFA700, 25 minutes), Douala (CFA1300, 90 minutes) and Kumba (CFA1700, 2½ hours). Share taxis also depart to Douala (CFA2000, 70 minutes) and Buea (CFA750, 20 minutes) from Half-Mile Junction. Chartering a taxi to Douala costs around CFA10,000.

Mile 6 (CFA150, 10 minutes) and Mile 11 (CFA200, 15 minutes) depart from Idenao Rd near the stadium. To Mile 11 they can take a while to fill – expect to pay at least CFA2500 for a charter.

AROUND LIMBE
Beaches

Black – well, ashy brown – sand volcanic beaches curl north of Limbe, each one bearing an unromantic numerical name; ie Mile 5 beach, Mile 6 etc. The best are at Mile 8 (especially at Batoke village) and Mile 11. There's also a not-quite-as-nice beach at Mile 6, and those cute monkeys can – hey, come back with my wallet! – be a problem. Take local advice before swimming; currents are strong and riptides can be dangerous. On the road just before Mile 11 you can see the lava flow from Mt Cameroon's 1999 eruption. If you're heading this way, have a car or take shared transport heading towards Mile 11.

A good place to stay is **Hotel Seme Beach** (☎ 7774 9446, 9638 4838; www.sembebeach.com; Mile 6 Rd; r from CFA18,000, ste CFA41,000; P ⊠ ⬚) at Mile 11, which fronts the beach and is as traditionally 'resort-y' a spot as you're likely to find around here.

BUEA

Basically built into the side of Mt Cameroon, Buea (pronounced boy-ah) has a hill station's coolness, especially compared to sticky Limbe. If you're going up the mountain you're inevitably coming here. From 1901 this was briefly the German colonial capital, and has long been a popular tea-growing centre; Tole Tea Plantation, south of town, is a major local employer.

Information
Bicec (Upper Farm Rd)
Express Exchange (Molyko Rd) Actually changes euros, dollars and travellers cheques.
Mt Cameroon Ecotourism Organisation (☎ 3332 2038; mountceo@yahooo.uk; Buea Market; ⊗ 8am-5pm

Mon-Fri, 7am-noon weekends) Can arrange tours of the Tole Tea Plantation.

Nigerian Consulate (☎ 3332 2528, 3332 2537; Nigeria Consulate Rd; ⏲ 8am-4pm Mon-Fri) Convenient for visas for onward travel.

Sleeping & Eating

Paramount Hotel (☎ 3332 2074; Molyko Rd; s/d with cold water CFA6000/10,000, with hot water CFA14,000/17,000; P 🖥) The Paramount lives up to its name, a good-value sleep that brings a bit of flashness to otherwise-middling Buea lodging. The pretty rooms come with TVs and are a nice respite from the mountain.

Parliamentarian Flats (☎ 3332 2459; Nigeria Consulate Rd; s/d CFA5000/10,000; P) There's a stripped-down feeling and no showers here, but if you've slogged up Mount Cameroon you'll appreciate the deep baths – and the water heater to help fill them.

Presbyterian Church Synod Office (☎ 332 2336; Market Rd; camping CFA1000, s/d with bathroom CFA3000/5000, without bathroom CFA2500/4000; P) As with most church guesthouses, this is a friendly locale that's kept thoughtfully (and spotlessly) clean. The rooms are fine for the price, and a communal kitchen keeps self-caterers happy.

There are several cheap eating places on Molyko Rd around the Paramount Hotel.

Getting There & Away

The motor park for onward transport is at Mile 17, about 6km from town along the Limbe Rd. Minibuses run throughout the day to Limbe (CFA700, 25 minutes), and less frequently to Douala (CFA1500, two hours) and Kumba (CFA1800, two hours). A shared taxi from Mile 17 to Buea Market is CFA150.

MT CAMEROON

Raised like a dark fist over Southwest Province is West Africa's largest mountain: Mongomo-Ndemi in Bakweri, ie the Mountain of Thunder. Topping out at 4095m, Mt Cameroon is actually an active volcano that last erupted in…2000. Ooh, that's a little recent, isn't it? Well, the Mountain of Thunder seems pretty unstormy now. Scientifically, it's cluttered with endemic plants and birds thanks to unique climatic conditions that make it a biodiversity hotspot.

November to April is the main climbing season. Although it's possible to climb the mountain year-round, you won't get much in the way of views during the rains. Late spring

offers the best vantages – if not to the valley below, then at least for the stars at night.

Routes

There are several routes to the top and numerous trails on the lower slopes. None require technical equipment, but warm clothes are essential near the summit and waterproof gear a must. The quickest is the **Guinness Route**, a straight up-and-down climb that can be done in 1½ days, though it's quite steep in parts. Along this route are three poorly maintained **huts** (at 1875m, 2860m and 3740m), with plank beds and silk sheets doused in Chanel No 5…kidding. Just planks.

It's better to take two nights on the mountain to experience its ecosystems and explore less-travelled routes; there are also five-day hikes and more. One popular two-night, three-day combination ascends via the Mann Spring route and descends via the Guinness Route. With more time, it's possible to descend via **Musingile** on the mountain's northern side and from there go through the forest to Koto (northeast of Idenao). Alternatively, the steep **Radio Station route** ascends from **Bonakanda** village through scrub and grassland to a hunter's camp at Nitele and on to the summit.

If you're not feeling up to tackling the entire beast, you can make the grasslands of the middle slopes in a day, where you can see the upcountry landscape that feels worlds away from Southwest Province's normal jungle.

If you're spending the night you'll need camping equipment. For all routes you should be self-sufficient with food and water. The only water points on the mountain are at Hut 1 on the Guinness Route and at Mann Spring.

Guides & Permits

Treks are arranged in Buea through the professional **Mount Cameroon Ecotourism Organisation** (☎ 3332 2038; mountceo@yahooo.uk; Buea Market; ⏲ 8am-5pm Mon-Fri, 7am-noon Sat & Sun). The organisation works closely with 12 villages around the mountain, employing locals as guides and porters. All trekkers pay a 'stakeholder fee' of CFA3000, which goes into village-development funds and is used for community projects; the office also sells locally produced handicrafts.

Guides, well trained in local flora and fauna, cost CFA6000 per day (maximum five trekkers per guide); porters cost CFA5000. Establish a

CAMEROON

comfortable pace for yourself; some guides have a tendency – conscious or not – of rushing up the mountain. Equipment can be hired on a daily basis, and expect to spend around CFA2000 per day on food for the trek – Buea market has a decent selection of basics.

It's usually possible to arrive in Buea in the morning and arrange everything to start trekking in the afternoon, but it's better to make advance bookings. Treks can be booked through the Fako Tourist Board in Limbe (p188), while guides prowl Limbe looking for trekkers – they'll find you, don't worry. You might get gouged on transport fees to Buea – this isn't necessarily intentional, but hire cars really are expensive. If in doubt, use local transport.

Mt Etinde

Small but steep Mt Etinde (also known as Petit Mt Cameroon), a 1713m subpeak on Mt Cameroon's southern slopes, is an extinct volcano geologically older than its larger neighbour. Climbs can be arranged through the Mt Cameroon Ecotourism Organisation in Buea (p190) or the Fako Tourist Board in Limbe (p188). It costs CFA6000 per guide plus a CFA3000 per person 'stakeholder' fee, and CFA1000 to CFA2000 for the local chief, whose permission you need to climb. You'll also need to bring a bottle of whisky for the ancestral spirits.

It's possible to walk from Limbe to the mountain, in which case you should allow one (long) day for the entire trip. Otherwise

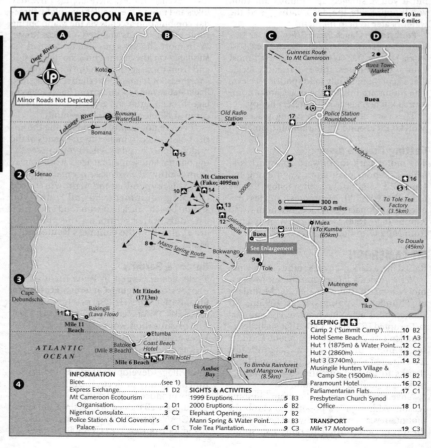

MT CAMEROON AREA

Minor Roads Not Depicted

Mt Cameroon (Fako; 4095m)
Mt Etinde (1713m)

Guinness Route to Mt Cameroon

Buea Town Market
Buea
Police Station Roundabout

To Tole Tea Factory (3.5km)

Muea
To Kumba (65km)
To Douala (45km)

Mann Spring Route

Bokwango
Tole
Mutengene
Tiko

Cape Debundscha
Bakingili (Lava Flow)
Mile 11 Beach
Etumba
Batoke (Mile 8 Beach)
Coast Beach Hotel
Fini Hotel
Mile 6 Beach
Ekonjo
Limbe
Ambas Bay
To Bimbia Rainforest and Mangrove Trail (8.5km)

Idenao
Koto
Bomana Waterfalls
Bomana
Old Radio Station
Onge River
Lokange River

ATLANTIC OCEAN

INFORMATION	
Bicec	(see 1)
Express Exchange	1 D2
Mt Cameroon Ecotourism Organisation	2 D1
Nigerian Consulate	3 C2
Police Station & Old Governor's Palace	4 C1

SIGHTS & ACTIVITIES	
1999 Eruptions	5 B3
2000 Eruptions	6 B2
Elephant Opening	7 B2
Mann Spring & Water Point	8 B3
Tole Tea Plantation	9 C3

SLEEPING	
Camp 2 ('Summit Camp')	10 B2
Hotel Seme Beach	11 A3
Hut 1 (1875m) & Water Point	12 C2
Hut 2 (2860m)	13 C2
Hut 3 (3740m)	14 B2
Musingile Hunters Village & Camp Site (1500m)	15 B2
Paramount Hotel	16 D2
Parliamentarian Flats	17 C1
Presbyterian Church Synod Office	18 D1

TRANSPORT	
Mile 17 Motorpark	19 C3

CAMEROON

RACE OF HOPE

The Mt Cameroon Race, or 'Race of Hope', has been held annually around the last weekend of January since 1973, attracting an international group of competitors and many spectators. During a gruelling mountain marathon of 40km, competitors use the Guinness Route to reach the summit. Considerably faster than the leisurely trek most people opt for, winners usually finish in a staggering 4½ hours for men, and 5½ hours for women. For more information contact the Fako Tourist Board in Limbe.

---

take a shared taxi to Batoke, from where you can charter a taxi to either Ekonjo or Etumba (Etome), two villages at the mountain's base. From either the ascent should take half a day. The idea with the whisky is half is poured out at the summit as a libation for the spirits, while the other half is consumed – fun walk down!

KUMBA

Kumba is a frenetic Anglophone town with friendliness to spare. It's a major cocoa-producing area, site of one of the country's largest markets and worth a day of exploring, especially considering the proximity of magical (literally) Barombi Mbo lake. On weekends check the rusty little **amusement park** (admission CFA500), a good spot for a family fun day out. The hill behind the park is sacred; locals say construction crews that try to build on it will automatically lose two members.

Barombi Mbo Lake

'If you swim here, the witchcraft will drown you!' we were warned. But along with the dark powers the lake possesses, you'd need to add scenic beauty. It's a volcanic, dark dollop in the midst of a landscape of jungly hills and dusty tracks. Men pole around in dugout canoes catching zebra-striped fish for European pet shops. Bargain hard and they'll take you on the water for CFA7000. There's a CFA2000 entrance fee (not always collected) and small **restaurant** (dry season) nearby.

Take a shared taxi (CFA300) from Kumba towards 'Upstation' and ask the driver to drop you at the junction, about 3km from town. From here, it's about 2km further and a pleasant, hilly walk to the lake. A *moto-taxi* the whole way costs around CFA2000.

Sleeping & Eating

Kanton Hotel (3335 4382; Buea Rd; r CFA6000-8000; P) It may look like a bomb shelter, but rooms are surprisingly big and clean, especially ones with balconies. Be warned – it gets loud come evening.

Shamrock Hotel (7744 8324; Preventive Rd; r CFA10,000-15000;) There's big thick blankets, fake flowers and teal-ish walls about, but the real draw is the staffmembers, who are just friendly as hell.

Vienello Hotel (3335 4603; Buea Rd; s/d CFA18,000/35,000; P) Kumba's most up-scale spot is more gaudy than classy, but there's internet downstairs, a nice restaurant that churns out Cameroonian standards and decent if overpriced rooms. The owner gives good tours of the surrounding area.

Street eats are available everywhere after nightfall, and all of the above hotels have attached restaurants. Shamrock and Vienello serve the best of the bunch.

Getting There & Away

BUS

Tonton Express and Mondial Express have depots on Commonwealth Ave near the market, and run regular daily services to Yaoundé (CFA4500, six hours), Douala (CFA2000, two hours), Bamenda (CFA4000, around six hours), Bafoussam (CFA2000, three hours), Limbe (CFA1500, 2½ hours) and Buea (CFA1500, two hours). Tonton Express has the most departures, but get there early.

Transport to Ekondo Titi (where you can find vehicles to Mundemba and Korup National Park) goes from Mundemba Rd motor park, and costs CFA2500 in the dry season. Fares double during rains, and the 2½-hour journey can triple in duration.

TRAIN

There's four trains daily between Douala and Kumba, but as it's faster to take the bus, no one seems to use them. If you're a railhead, consider taking the bus from Douala to Mbanga, and the train from there to Kumba (CFA500, one to 1½ hours). Trains pass Mbanga every few hours from about 9am to 4pm.

MANENGOUBA LAKES

Lakes and mountains make for scenic goodness; how much more so when you throw in fuzzy African grassland and an extinct volcanic caldera. These are the variables in an

CAMEROON

equation that produces 'Man' and 'Woman' crater lakes, set in a grassy caldera southeast of Bangem. Witchcraft abounds here, which is partly why camping and swimming is permitted at Woman Lake, but not Man Lake. A visit costs CFA1000, which you're supposed to pay at the police station in Bangem (get a receipt), though it's often easier to pay the guy near the lakes who approaches you to collect it.

The lakes are about three hours uphill on foot from Bangem; locals will point the way. Once you reach the rim you'll need to hike through the caldera, past grazing cattle and Fulani herdsmen, to reach the lakes on the far side.

The most direct way from Kumba to Bangem is via **Tombel**, but the road becomes atrocious at a hint of rain, so it's faster to go first to **Mélong** (about halfway between Kumba and Bafoussam), from where it's just CFA1500 and 45 minutes in a shared taxi to Bangem. It takes at least half a day to reach Bangem from Kumba.

KORUP NATIONAL PARK

Korup is the most accessible of Cameroon's rainforest preserves. The biodiversity is mind-boggling; within 1259 sq km are over 300 species of birds, 50 species of large mammals, 620 species of trees and over 100 medicinal plants. All of the above can be explored via some 100km of marked walking trails, led by guides who often work with field researchers. Two days is an ideal visiting time.

The starting point is Mundemba village, about 8km before the park gate. There's an **information centre** (☎ 7778 7883; www.panda.org /Africa/korup; entry per day CFA5000; ⓨ 7.30am-5.30pm daily Nov-May, to 3.30pm Mon-Fri, to 8.30am & 4.30-5.30pm Sat & Sun Jun-Sep). Phoning ahead of your visit is strongly advised to discuss your requirements with the tourist officer; you must hire a guide (CFA4000 per day, plus CFA1000 per night). Porters can also be arranged (CFA2000 per day plus CFA1000 per night, maximum load 25kg), as can rental of sleeping bags, foam mats and cookware. Pay all fees direct to the tourist officer, and ignore requests from anyone else for extra 'stakeholder' fees. Bring insect repellent.

Sleeping & Eating

There are three **camp sites** (per person CFA3000) in the park's southern section: Isriba Inene, about 2km from the entrance; Rengo (9km); and Chimpanzee (10km). Each has simple

huts with wooden beds and mosquito screens, water and a cooking area. You'll need to bring your own food and sleeping mat. You're not expected to supply food for guides and porters, but clarify this before setting off. Basic supplies are available in Mundemba.

Sure to Sure Guesthouse (☎ 754 5009; r CFA5000-6000) At the southern end of Mundemba, this place has simple rooms with fans. Other local hotels have rooms have rooms costing between CFA4000 and CFA7000.

Getting There & Away

There's usually at least one taxi brousse (bush taxi) daily in the dry season between Mundemba and Ekondo Titi (CFA2000, two hours), from where you arrange transport to Kumba. Rainy season transport is more ad hoc, takes longer and costs more.

From Mundemba to the Korup National Park gate at Mana Footbridge, you can either walk or go via a park vehicle (CFA8000 return per vehicle, 10 people maximum including guide and porters). An amazing suspension bridge crosses the Mana River here, almost worth the park-entrance fee alone.

If you have the money, a great way to depart or arrive in Korup is by boat (carrying six people) along the Mana River. Staff can arrange pick-ups or drop-offs as far south as Idenao, through the Bakassi Peninsula (around CFA280,000 one way). The boat can also be rented for shorter excursions along the river to explore the **mangrove swamps** (per 3hr CFA100,000) or visit nearby **Pelican Island** (CFA160,000). All boat trips need to be arranged in advance through the Korup Information Centre.

There's another entrance to Korup at Baro, west of Nguti, which can be reached by taxi brousse from Mamfe in dry season.

MAMFE

Mamfe is the last town of note before southern Cameroon's main crossing station into Nigeria at Ekok, 60km further west. It's also, along with nearby **Kembong**, a very powerful city for witchcraft (you're usually told this matter-of-factly a few minutes after bringing Mamfe up in any context). You may have more to worry about from Nigerian border guards. Situated on the banks of the Cross River, Mamfe isn't particularly attractive, but there are a few well-preserved colonial homes in town.

There's no bank at the border, so you'll need to ask at shops or the market if you're looking for Nigerian naira. Bicec bank in Mamfe is occasionally willing to change cash euros (no travellers cheques), but shouldn't be relied upon.

The Nigerian Office for Immigration & Emigration is worth a visit if you're border crossing, although this isn't required (immigration formalities occur at the border). The office is in the centre between the main roundabout and Bayang Garage; locals can point the way.

Sleeping

Eta Plaza (☎ 3334 1393; r CFA3000) It's basic, but good enough if you're pinching pennies.

Data Club Guest House (☎ 3334 1399; r from CFA10,000; 🔀) Easily the best lodging in Mamfe, on the northeastern edge of town.

Getting There & Away

Transport connections in all directions are good. Roads, on the other hand, suck. Travelling during the rains will be your own personal hell. The main motor park is 500m southwest of Mamfe's central intersection.

Transport goes throughout the day to the border at Ekok, 60km away. The main lines are Ali Baba and Tonton Express, and the price roughly CFA1800 in the dry season, though this can reach CFA4000 during the rains (when you'll frequently have to get out and push). A faster (and pretty much as safe) option is taking a pirogue down Cross River to Ekok.

The mountainous road from Mamfe to Bamenda (around CFA9000) is gorgeous, but there's perilous drop-offs aplenty and it's only an option in the dry season. It's better to take the longer southern route via Kumba (CFA5000, six hours), travelling on from there.

There's usually at least one vehicle daily between Mamfe and Nguti (for Korup National Park), although there's almost no traffic from Nguti into the park

NORTHWEST PROVINCE

This is a most rewarding province for travellers, the green hills contrasting with the humid coast. And you know those fantastic wooden masks you've spotted in a book or museum. If you looked at the label or caption it likely read 'Grassfields, Cameroon'. Well, here you are. Cameroon's Anglophone Northwest, with its secret societies, traditional chiefdoms and yes, masks and masked dancers, of great significance to African culture.

BAMENDA
pop 235,000

Dust. Red dust. Clouds of it get kicked up by cars and cows and hover above the bustling capital of Northwest Province. Through said dust sprawls the largest Anglophone city in Cameroon, tumbling down some of those green hills at over 1000m altitude. It's also the entrepreneurial heart of political opposition to President Paul Biya plus a good base for exploring the province it administers, in particular the Ring Road circuit.

Orientation

Most transport drops you at Upstation, overlooking Bamenda town proper. From here the road winds down to Nkwen District, which has a good market, follows Cow St and Sonac St and eventually reaches City Chemists' Roundabout and the main drag – Commercial Ave.

Information

Express Exchange (near City Chemists' Roundabout) Changes travellers cheques as well as US dollars cash and euros.

Horizon Internet (Commercial Ave; per hr CFA3000) Internet access.

Maryland Cybercafé (Commercial Ave; per hr CFA300) Also has internet phone.

Polyclinic (Bali Rd)

SGBC Bank (Commercial Ave) Has an ATM.

Tourist office (☎ 336 1395) Can provide basic maps and dates of local festivals.

Sleeping

Baptist Mission Resthouse (☎ 3336 1285; Finance Junction; dm CFA2500; 🅿) Drawbacks first: it's a shared cab to the town centre and service can be absent-minded. Now the good news: it's cheap, it's secure and it's clean as all get out, three concepts that are a holy trinity indeed for tired travellers.

Ex-Serviceman's Rest House (☎ 7624 6185; Hotel Rd; r CFA5000) This low-slung compound is, indeed, intended for ex-soldiers, but if any of the 10 rooms are available they'll be happily rented out. It's a great deal, but with that said, solo female travellers may feel out of place. There's a loud bar next door, which is a boon or a burden depending on your disposition.

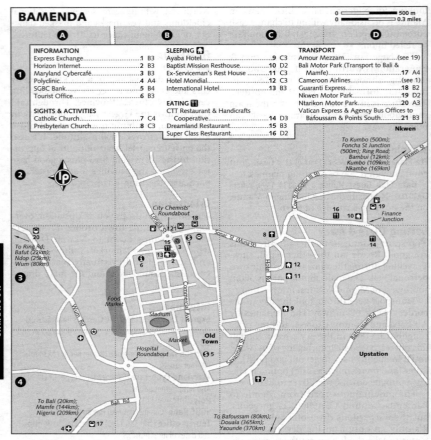

BAMENDA

0 ——— 500 m
0 ——— 0.3 miles

INFORMATION	
Express Exchange	1 B3
Horizon Internet	2 B3
Maryland Cybercafé	3 B3
Polyclinic	4 A4
SGBC Bank	5 B4
Tourist Office	6 B3

SIGHTS & ACTIVITIES	
Catholic Church	7 C4
Presbyterian Church	8 C3

SLEEPING	
Ayaba Hotel	9 C3
Baptist Mission Resthouse	10 D2
Ex-Serviceman's Rest House	11 C3
Hotel Mondial	12 C3
International Hotel	13 B3

EATING	
CTT Restaurant & Handicrafts Cooperative	14 D3
Dreamland Restaurant	15 B3
Super Class Restaurant	16 D2

TRANSPORT	
Amour Mezzam	(see 19)
Bali Motor Park (Transport to Bali & Mamfe)	17 A4
Cameroon Airlines	(see 1)
Guaranti Express	18 B2
Nkwen Motor Park	19 D2
Ntarikon Motor Park	20 A3
Vatican Express & Agency Bus Offices to Bafoussam & Points South	21 B3

Nkwen

To Kumbo (500m);
Foncha St Junction
(500m); Ring Road;
Bambui (12km);
Kumbo (109km);
Nkambe (169km)

Finance Junction

City Chemists' Roundabout

Sonac St (Muna St)

To Ring Rd;
Bafut (22km);
Ndop (25km);
Wum (80km)

Food Market

Stadium

Old Town

Market

Hospital Roundabout

Upstation

To Bali (20km);
Mamfe (144km);
Nigeria (209km)

Bali Rd

To Bafoussam (80km);
Douala (365km);
Yaounde (370km)

International Hotel (☎ 3336 2527; off Commercial Ave; r CFA15,000-18,000) Very convenient for buses, and service is friendly enough. The interior is a bit drab and mildewed at the walls, but rooms are big and most come with balconies offering sweeping views over, er, 'scenic' Bamenda.

Hotel Mondial (☎ 3336 1832, 7793 8378; off Hotel Rd; s/d CFA14,000/16,000; **P**) The Mondial feels a little more modern than its equivalents elsewhere in Bamenda – positively plush, even. It's not the Hyatt, but it's a good upper-midrange effort for the area.

Ayaba Hotel (☎ 3336 1356; ayabahotel@refinedct.net; Hotel Rd, Upstation; r CFA24,000-60,000; **P** ⊠ ☎) This is Bamenda's most luxurious option, but it's overpriced., unless you love the idea of sleep-

ing in a hotel with architecture and furniture straight out of the '70s (complete with ageing around the edges). In that case, buddy, have you found the right hotel.

Eating

If you can find it, try the Northwest's regional speciality: *amajama*, or chopped huckle-berry leaf, generally served with some kind of meat sauce.

CTT Restaurant & Handicrafts Cooperative (nr Finance Junction, Upstation; mains from CFA1000; ⏰ 8am-9pm) The food here is decent – OK Cameroonian and slightly better Western fare, but the real draw is the surrounds, specifically a workshop of regional handicrafts and great views sweeping to Bamenda below.

Dreamland Restaurant (Commercial Ave; mains from CFA1300; 7am-11pm) This is a bustling buffet, where you can catch some football at night, get flirty with friendly waitresses and enjoy a very good execution of steak and chips and – holy hell, really? In Cameroon? – a salad bar for those needing a graze.

Super Class Restaurant (☎ 3307 1792; nr Finance Junction; meals CFA3000-7000; lunch & dinner) A Cameroonian friend sagely informs us, 'Many whites meet here.' 'Many' is a relative term, but there were a few missionary types around when we visited, enjoying both African standards and decent (if expensive) pizzas.

Getting There & Away

Most agency offices for destinations to the south are on Sonac St. To Yaoundé (CFA5000, six hours), Vatican Express and Guaranti Express are the best. The same agencies operate daily services to Douala (CFA5000, seven hours). Sonac St is also the departure point for Bafoussam (CFA1500, 90 minutes), from where you'll find more transport heading south.

Nkwen Motor Park has transport to the east stretch of the Ring Road including Ndop (CFA1200, 90 minutes) and Kumbo (CFA3000, five hours). Amour Mezzam Express has the most departures. The west stretch of the Ring Road is served by Ntarikon Motor Park, with minibuses to Wum (CFA2000, two hours).

AROUND BAMENDA
Bali

Bali is a friendly small town about 20km southwest of Bamenda and makes a good day excursion for those looking to meet an African fon (chief). In point of fact there were almost two fons here: back in 2007, a part of the current fondom attempted to break away, sparking a war that was only settled through government intervention.

The fon's **palace** is fronted by a mural of a tiger, the chief's sacred animal (tigers aren't native to Africa). The mural runs across what looks like a public traffic shelter, but don't step on the platform: this space is reserved for fons only. You'll likely get a tour from a palace retainer and be asked to donate some money – around CFA1000 – to the palace. Inside the musty compound more tiger iconography abounds; the inner sanctum is protected by a magic tree that they say strangles unwelcome intruders.

The *lele* (end-of-year festival) takes place here in late December, with traditional dancing and suchlike. Shared taxis run frequently between Bamenda and Bali (CFA250, 15 minutes).

RING ROAD

The Northwest highlands bear the pretty name 'Grassfields,' an appellation too pleasant to really capture the look of the landscape. These aren't gentle fields; they're bright green and yellow valleys and short, sharp mountains, clad in a wiry constriction of palm fronds, creeper vines, tall grass and red earth. Here and there white waterfalls lip over dark cliffs, clouds of mist rising with wood smoke and dung smoke that marks the location of villages speckled on this deceptively inviting – but hard and rugged – terrain.

A 367km Ring Road runs a circle around the Grassfields, and if it were in better shape, it'd be one of Cameroon's great scenic drives. In fairness, it still can't be missed – but get your butt ready for some bumpy, red-earth roads. The payoff? Mountains dolloped with lakes, cattle loping into the hills and one of the greatest concentrations of fondoms in Cameroon.

Tourism is DIY here. At the time of research vehicles weren't going past Wum, and the trip from there to Bamenda was a painful three hours. Trekking, cycling and camping are all options, but always ask the permission of the local chief, and bring some gifts (whisky always works). For those heading east (anticlockwise) by vehicle, the road is decent from Bamenda to Kumbo. From Wum, a rough dirt road leads south to Bafut, from where it's a short skip back to Bamenda. Transport links along the Ring Road are reasonable, but not particularly frequent.

There's nowhere to change money, so stock up on CFA before leaving Bamenda.

Sabga, Bamessing & Ndop

The road east of Bamenda to Kumbo runs through thickets of tall grass, past hills that are sandy and rock-studded in the dry season and green as a springtime lawn after the rains.

The most dramatic of the hills dusting this road is Sabga Hill, on the eastern side of the village of the same name. Ask to be dropped off about 500m after the village by the 10%

CAMEROON

CAMEROON

gradient sign. It's a 120m scramble to the top and a blue view of the valleys, waterfalls and low ranges of the Mbam Massif in the distance, which are particularly alluring under the fire of a local sunset. Bring a torch for the walk down; there's a path of sorts, but it can get slippery.

From Sabga, the route continues to Bamessing. The arts and crafts of the Grassfields, particularly masks and wood-carvings, are famous throughout Cameroon and this is a good place to buy them. There are several cooperatives along the road that sell carved wood. The **Prescraft Centre** (Bamessing; ✪ 9am-5pm Mon-Sat) has fascinating tours of the pottery centre, where you can watch the whole process, from digging the clay from local riverbeds to firing the finished articles. The centre is badly signed 1km off the main road, so ask for directions.

The tar road from Bamenda finishes at **Ndop**, after which it's rough dirt roads to Nkambe. Ndop is large enough to have a petrol station, post office and the only sleeping options on this stretch of Ring Road.

Ndop Guest Home Hotel (r CFA3000-7000) is run by a friendly manager who always seems willing to cut a deal, which is just as well as rooms aren't always up to scratch – look at a few before settling.

Further from the main road is **Green Valley Resort** (☎ 3336 3400; r CFA5000) which has better beds and an onsite, if kinda meagre, restaurant. Amour Mezzam, on the north side of Ndop, has daily minibuses to Bamenda (CFA1200, 90 minutes).

A two-hour drive north of Ndop is **Jakiri**, which serves as a junction for the rough but stunning road southwest to Foumban (and apparently, as receptacle for all the dust in Africa). The **Trans-Afrique Hotel** (Jakiri; r CFA4000) will do if you get stuck here waiting for transport.

Kumbo

In another life, Kumbo should have been a hill station and colonial getaway. It's got the atmosphere of escape such retreats often possess: the largest town in the Grassfields perches at a cool 2000m above sea level, a little warren of roads worming across a

---

HIS MAJESTY DR GANYONGA III, FON OF BALI, NORTHWEST PROVINCE, CAMEROON

What do you consider your responsibilities are as the fon of Bali?
As the Paramount Fon of Bali, I ensure peace, solidarity and development in Bali fondom. As an auxiliary of that I see that foreigners in Bali live in peace and comfort. There is a traditional council held in the palace once every month that settles disputes; its members are made of notables of all the quarters and villages within Bali. I also suggest developmental projects to the Government for my fondom. One of my greatest responsibilities is maintaining the colonial boundaries of Bali.

Do you want tourists and travellers to come to Bali?
Yes. Bali's people are very hospitable, welcoming, and need travellers to come to their land so they can exchange ideas. Bali is Cameroon in miniature. We need more visitors, especially in the third week of December during the celebration of our annual Lele festival, which portrays the traditional dignity of a Bali man and our traditional artefacts.

What is your favourite place in your kingdom?
My favourite place in my kingdom is the palace. Not because I live there, but because it is the favourite place for all Balians and some Cameroonians and foreigners. People come from far and near to Bali and if they are not here for serious administrative assignment, the first place to visit is the palace.

What do Westerners have to learn from Bali?
Westerners should know Bali is the cultural heart of the Northwest. We have one of the best cultures in the Grassfields, one that has been maintained with adjustments that other villages in the area have copied up till the present date. We've modified the Lele festival, death celebrations, traditional marriages, widowhood mourning periods (reduced to three days), succession after the death of a family head, notables putting red feathers in their traditional caps and so on. These practices are now copied by neighbouring villages in the region and Cameroon at large.

As told to Adam Karlin

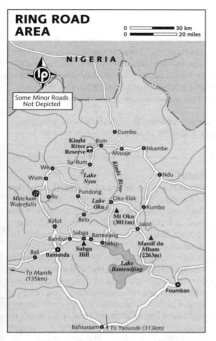

RING ROAD AREA

NIGERIA

Some Minor Roads Not Depicted

brown hill that claws at a clean, dry sky. The Panso, one of the major traditional kingdoms in the northwest, call Kumbo home, and in mid-November, the town hosts a huge horse-racing festival.

Kumbo is an important junction town with a relaxed air – a good base for exploring the Ring Road in more depth. There are plenty of bars and cheap eats, along with a post office and an internet cafe opposite the cathedral. Lolika Handicrafts Training Centre, near the market, is good for souvenir shopping.

SLEEPING & EATING
Ring Road Travellers Inn (☎ 348 1480, 348 1655; r with/without bathroom CFA5500/35000) Right on the town square, this place could hardly be better located, but rooms are pretty basic. If you want a little more comfort, opt for the following options.

Merryland Hotel (☎ 348 1077; s/d CFA5000/10,000; P) Management here was extremely accommodating during our visit, making us feel more at home than in a hotel. The hot showers are just what's needed after the dust

of the road, and rooms, despite their vaguely floral print–meets–West African pit stop motif, were well appointed for the price.

Fomo 92 (☎ 348 1616, 7777 8084; s/d CFA7500/15,000) Just north of the cathedral, there are lots of stairs and corridors in this hotel, which seems to tumble down the hill; but all paths lead to comfy carpeted rooms. There's a decent restaurant at the bottom to boot.

BB91 (mains from CFA1500; ☽ 10am-11pm) Next to the cathedral, this restaurant is a decent spot to sink a beer, but for food you may want to try the stalls across the street.

GETTING THERE & AWAY
Amour Mezzam Express, south of the market, runs daily to Bamenda (CFA3000, five hours), stopping at all points along the way. It occasionally goes to Yaoundé (CFA8000, 24 hours) via Foumban. Minibuses also run north to Nkambe (CFA2000, two hours) from just north of the square; and to Oku (CFA1200, one hour) leaving from Oku Rd, past the petrol station.

Nkambe & Missaje
Nkambe is the only town of any size between Kumbo and Wum. It's a cool city (temperature wise) plunked down at high altitude, swathed in long gasps of grassland and tea plantations centred on the village of Ndu. Heading north, the earth road steadily deteriorates in quality, and even the road here from Kumbo is sometimes closed.

Millennium Hotel (s/d CFA5000/10,000) is at the end of a very long (1.5km) road at the southern end of town. Doubles are big and decent, but make the singles look disappointing in comparison. A taxi here from town will set you back a steep CFA1000. There's a restaurant and 'occasional' nightclub.

Otherwise try the **Holy War Complex** (r with/without bathroom CFA5000/3000), a rock-bottom option with an irresistible name – the Holy War chain seems to own half the shops on this stretch of the Ring Road. Rooms aren't great, but at least they're cheap. Minibuses run from Nkambe to Bamenda, but not every day – check ahead (CFA5000, 10 hours).

At **Missaje**, about 20km west of Nkambe, the driveable road ends, and you'll need to continue on foot or mountain bike if you want to complete the circuit (it's all downhill from Nkambe to Wum). Allow a full, very scenic day on foot between Missaje and We (13km

CAMEROON

THE DEATH LAKE OF WEST AFRICA

North of We, the Ring Road gets even toothier and reliable transport is a contradiction. Northeast of here is **Lake Nyos**, just off the Ring Road and south of the village of the same name. This volcanic crater lake was the site of a vast gas leakage in 1986, which resulted in the asphyxiation of 1700 people. Villagers were at work in their fields and died where they stood. A build up of carbon dioxide gas from a subterranean magna pocket? That's science for you, but local conspiracy theories still blame the disaster on Western misadventure, and some police told us the real culprit was Al Qaeda.

The seldom-visited **Kimbi River Reserve** is just north of Nyos, though you'll need your own vehicle to explore, a tent if you plan to overnight and a lot of willpower – this isn't an easy area to reach.

northeast of Wum). That's assuming you don't get lost, so bring two days' worth of provisions and strongly consider hiring a Fulani herdsman as a guide, although be aware many only speak Fulfulde. If you get stuck in Missaje, the only place to stay is in one of the unappealing rooms behind the local bar.

Wum

Wum isn't much of a town, but it's the largest settlement on the western side of the Ring Road and the end of public transport if you're travelling in a clockwise direction. The way here is jaw-dropping – up and over a rocky, rough road with the flat fields that this land is named for moving slowly ahead of you, towards small clumps of dark mountains.

About 20km south of Wum are the **Metchum Falls**, a white cascade that streams down a dry jungle valley. The falls aren't visible from the road, so you'll need to ask someone to point out the spot for viewing them. Don't lean on the makeshift rail, as several visitors plunged to their deaths here some years ago.

There are several undistinguished guesthouses in Wum, the best of which is probably **Morning Star Hotel** (r about CFA4000), with simple but tidy rooms tucked into a largeish two-storey compound that wraps around the base of a hill. It's at the southern end of town, off the main road.

Symbol of Unity has daily buses between Wum and Bamenda (CFA3000, three hours). It's possible to go in a loop from Wum to We (13km north) and from there turn south back to Bamenda via Fundong and Belo. In Fundong, there's inexpensive accommodation at Tourist Home Hotel. Guaranti Express usually has a minibus daily between Fundong and Bamenda. Continuing north of here by vehicle can be difficult.

Bafut

Blessed by good rains and rich earth, the Tikar of Bafut have traditionally held claim to one of the most powerful fondoms in the area. Their land is fertile and fat; here the bloodred dirt sprouts thick fields of maize and cassava instead of being blown into the dry jet stream. In late December, Bafut holds a huge four-day celebration to mark the end of the year's ancestor worship, with masked dancing and drumming; this is a must-not-miss if you're in the area. The town also holds a large market every eight days (every 'country Sunday'). There's no accommodation at Bafut, but there are a couple of very basic eateries by the town square.

The **Makon palace compound** (admission CFA1000, camera fee CFA1500, museum CFA2000) is a low red structure often surrounded by kids playing soccer – more than a few of whom are the offspring of the fon and his 150-or-so wives (not all of whom are presently in residence). The compound is anchored by the sacred Achum building, centre of secret-society activity and off-limits to everyone except the fon and his close advisors. Behind the Achum is the royal reserve, a hunting ground strictly reserved for the fon alone when he takes on the form of a leopard, one of his many powers. You may get invited into a tattered receiving room; otherwise, the main thing to see here is an impressive museum partly supported by the Italian government.

The local artefacts are fascinating, including a beaded lizard crown worn during inauguration ceremonies, a jacket of feathers collected from birds in tributary states, intricately carved thrones (only the fon can sit in chairs carved with human figures) and a suit of German armour, a gift from German explorers who slaughtered a historical fon's army with machine guns (our guide told us if the fon had known the Germans were coming, he would have turned them to stone). As in many fondoms, the heir to the throne is kept unaware of his identity until his father dies; the bearers of this knowledge are restricted to secret-society members. The current fon made the progressive move of abolishing the law that required the widows of a dead fon to go about naked following their husband's death.

About 5km from the palace along the Bamenda road is **Savanna Botanic Gardens** (Saboga; ☎ 3302 8055; admission CFA1000, camera CFA1000) designed by a local professor. There's no politically correct way of putting this: Westerners tend to find the gardens tacky to the point of smirking; locals consider them dignified grounds for reflection. Come to your own conclusions, as you wander amid replicas of the birth of Jesus (our guide accidentally kicked the manky doll standing in for baby Jesus) and the 'Equality Exhibition' (two mannequins: a white man, 'The West,' draped in mobile phones and firearms, standing amid computers; holding a chained screaming black woman, 'Africa', wearing words like, Debt, HIV and Witchcraft). You can stay in the Garden's **guesthouse** (r CFA7000); do us a favour and free the poor caged monkey.

A shared taxi to Bamenda is CFA300 (20 minutes). A daily minibus north to Wum passes through Bafut, but transport is easier to arrange in Bamenda.

WEST PROVINCE

West Province straddles Cameroon's fault lines – between the high dust of the Adamawa Plateau and green clouds of the southern forests; the linguistic border between Anglophones and Francophones (despite this technically being a Francophone province); and the religious gulf between evangelical Christianity, ancestor worship and Islam. Bafoussam is the busy commercial centre of the agriculturally rich highlands, while mainly Muslim Foumban is home to the magnificent sultan's palace – itself a blend of traditional West African animism and Islam – and some of the best handicrafts markets in Cameroon.

BAFOUSSAM

There's little to initially love about Bafoussam. The Bamiléké stronghold dominates the nation's coffee and cocoa production and seems haphazardly built on agriculture money and a

refined sense of chaos. But it's friendly as hell and has an electric feel that's worth a day of exploration. Plus it's close to one of the best traditional palaces in the country.

Sights
Thanks to old tribal politics and modern business connections (including, it is rumoured, ownership of defunct Cameroon Airlines), the local fondom in **Bandjoun** (about 15km south of Bafoussam) and its **chefferie** (Dja; admission CFA2000; www.museumcam.org; ☺ 10am-5pm) has traditionally been one of the richest in Cameroon. The proof is in the infrastructure; roads here are nicely paved and electricity surprisingly reliable.

The *chefferie's* main building is an excellent example of traditional Bamiléké architecture, with its square base and totem pole-ish pillars supporting a thatched roof that looks like it could shelter half of Africa. The attached museum is particularly well maintained and modern, with excellent displays of Bamiléké art and secret society costumes. The entire edifice is located in Dja, near the Yaoundé intersection, about 15 minutes walk from the main road.

Another, smaller **chefferie** (Bafoussam; admission CFA4000) is just off the main road at the southern end of town; half the admission should be enough. This palace isn't as well maintained and the 'museum' feels like the fon's spare attic, but it's worth a visit for the local two 'tortoises of justice' whose movements determine the innocence or guilt of criminals.

Information
For changing cash try **Bicec** (Ave Wanko) at the southern end of the street, or **SCB-Crédit Lyonnais** (nr Carrefour Total) along the Foumban road – a good landmark; as always, travellers cheques are a hassle.

For web access, call into **L'Excellence Internet** (Route de Foumban; per hr CFA400).

Sleeping
Hôtel Fédéral (☎ 3344 1309; Route de Foumban; s/d CFA8000/9000) This place offers good value and with a decent bar to boot; rooms are neat, tidy and quite spacious considering the price. The nearby **Prestige** (☎ 7751 4503; Route de Foumban; s/d CFA8000/10,000) offers almost exactly the same.

Hotel le Confident (off Carrefour Total; s/d CFA6000/10,000) The rooms here aren't quite as unsoiled as those at the Federal and Prestige,

CAMEROON

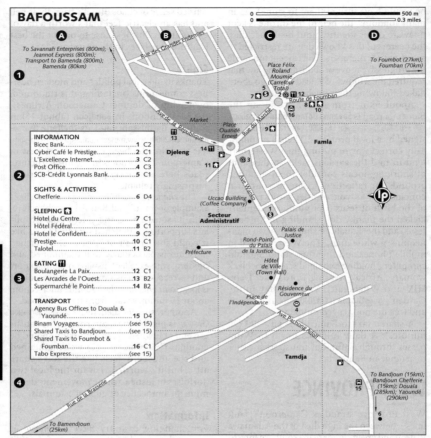

BAFOUSSAM

0 ——— 500 m
0 ——— 0.3 miles

To Savannah Enterprises (800m);
Jeannot Express (800m);
Transport to Bamenda (800m);
Bamenda (80km)

Rue des Grandes Endemies

To Foumbot (27km);
Fouman (70km)

Place Félix
Roland
Moumie
(Carrefour
Total)

Route de Foumban

Ave de la République

Market

Place
Ouandé
Ernest

Rue du Marché

Famla

Djeleng

INFORMATION
Bicec Bank.......................................**1** C2
Cyber Café le Prestige......................**2** C1
L'Excellence Internet........................**3** C2
Post Office......................................**4** C3
SCB-Crédit Lyonnais Bank................**5** C1

SIGHTS & ACTIVITIES
Chefferie..**6** D4

SLEEPING
Hotel du Centre..............................**7** C1
Hôtel Fédéral..................................**8** C1
Hotel le Confident...........................**9** C2
Prestige..**10** C1
Talotel..**11** B2

EATING
Boulangerie La Paix.......................**12** C1
Les Arcades de l'Ouest...................**13** B2
Supermarché le Point.....................**14** B2

TRANSPORT
Agency Bus Offices to Douala &
    Yaoundé...................................**15** D4
Binam Voyages..........................(see 15)
Shared Taxis to Bandjoun.............(see 15)
Shared Taxis to Foumbot &
    Foumban.................................**16** C1
Tabo Express.............................(see 15)

Ave Wang

Uccao Building
(Coffee Company)

Secteur
Administratif

Palais de
Justice

Rond-Point
du Palais
de la Justice

Préfecture

Hôtel
de Ville
(Town Hall)

Résidence du
Gouverneur

Place de
l'Indépendance

Ave Pachong Adolf

Tamdja

To Bandjoun (15km);
Bandjoun Chefferie
(15km); Douala
(285km); Yaoundé
(290km)

Rue de la Brasserie

To Bamendjoun
(25km)

but they make up for it by being comfortably large enough to accommodate a small party. It's located on an unnamed street running south of Carrefour Total.

Hotel du Centre (☎ 3344 2079; Carrefour Total; r CFA12,000-20,000) Although its located in a blocky bomb shelter–chic building, rooms are nonetheless open and fresh, many come with balconies and the toilets – bless – have seats. It's well located (as the name suggests) and a useful landmark; some tidy negotiations can bring this hotel comfortably into the budget category.

Talotel (☎ 3344 4185; hoteltalotel@camnet.cm; Place Ouandé Ernest; s/d CFA30,000/70,000; P ⚄ ▢) The poshest hotel around offers perfectly fine if not spectacular rooms. There's a strong bush-chic theme going on – if you like corny African murals, you're in the right spot.

Eating

Rue de Marché and Route de Foumban are good for street food and cheap eats.

Les Arcades de l'Ouest (off Ave de la République; ⏱ 9am-late) Opposite the market, this is good for cheap Cameroonian food. Wash it down with copious amounts of beer deep into the night. There's occasional live music on weekends.

Boulangerie La Paix (Route de Foumban; pastries from CFA150; ⏱ 8am-10pm) This patisserie sells good bread and sticky sweet treats in the mornings, and acts as a handy general food shop during the rest of the day. **Supermarché le Point**

CAMEROON

(Ave de la Répubiqe), at the opposite end of Rue de Marché, fulfils the same function.

Getting There & Away

Binam Voyages, Tabo Express and other agency buses to Yaoundé (CFA2500 to CFA3000, three hours) and Douala (CFA4000, five hours) have their offices at the southern end of town along the main road. Shared taxis to Bandjoun (CFA300, 15 minutes) leave from here throughout the day.

Transport to Bamenda leaves from the Bamenda Rd, 2km north of the centre (CFA150 in a shared taxi). Agencies include Savannah Enterprises and Jeannot Express and take 90 minutes (CFA1500).

Minibuses to Foumban (CFA800 to CFA1000, one hour) depart from near the petrol station, downhill from Carrefour Total. Many nonagency vehicles only go as far as Foumbot (CFA500, 30 minutes), where you'll need to change to reach Foumban (CFA500, 45 minutes).

FOUMBAN

Foumban has a deep tradition of homegrown arts and traditional monarchy centred around a sultan who resides in a palace plopped architecturally-conceptually between Mali and the Maghreb. In other words, this town is schizophrenically (in a good way) torn between West and North Africa, as if the Sahel and its sharp music, bright robes and Islam – this is the most Muslim city in the south – was slowly creeping into the eastern corner of West Province. Try and be here for Tabaski (see p816), when horse races and parades mark the end of Ramadan.

The Grand Marché is a warren of narrow stalls and alleys which are great fun to explore; the paths eventually lead to where the Grande Mosquée faces the palace. There's a slow **internet café** (east of market). **CPAC bank** (south of market) may change euros if you're lucky, but it's best to do your changing in Bafoussam.

Sights & Activities
PALAIS ROYAL (ROYAL PALACE)

There are plenty of traditional kingdoms in Cameroon, but most layer a veneer of Christianity onto a base substrate of traditional culture. In Foumban's royal **palace** (admission incl museum CFA2000, camera fee CFA1500; ☽ 8.30am-6pm), traditional culture and Islam seem to blend in equal measure. The effect is both accidental and intentional; this king-

dom is known for rulers who are into mixing. Take the designer of the palace itself, Ibrahim Njoya, 16th sultan of Foumban, developer of his own alphabet, Shumon, and his own religion, a combination of Christian, Islamic and animist beliefs. Other rulers have mixed cultures less peacefully, like the 11th sultan, who told his subjects he would unite the surrounding countryside, '…by blood and dark iron. War! Is my business!'

The 20th-century palace is one of the great centres of the Bamoun people, whose symbol, the double-headed snake, is ubiquitous in Foumban (said snake was adopted as a symbol by the war-crazy 11th sultan, who once defeated two armies at once and adapted the animal onto the Bamoun coat of arms). The upstairs museum's artefact collection – including calabashes decorated with human jawbones, secret-society uniforms and Shumon primers – is fascinating, but labelling is in French, and English-speaking guides are in short supply.

VILLAGE DES ARTISANS

A long street packed with workshops about 1.5km south of the market, this 'village' (OK: shopping arcade) is a mix of every Africana curio emporium you've ever visited. As such, it's an ideal place to pick up everything from woodcarvings and leatherwork to life-size bronze statues of royal lions, and while a lot of the stuff is replicated, you do occasionally find some unique pieces. The village is one of the few places in the country where you can expect some tourist hustle, but it's not too intense. Initial asking prices tend to be waaaay above actual value.

At the end of the road, the small **Musée des Arts et des Traditions Bamoun** (admission CFA1000; ☽ 9am-5pm) houses the private collection of Mosé Yeyap, a wealthy Bamoun during Ibrahim Njoya's time, who collected art and historical artefacts. Tours are in French and included in the admission.

Sleeping

Mission Catholique (Rue de l'Hotel Beau Regarde; dm CFA2500) Head here if you're out of options – it's pretty spartan and you have to ask to be brought water. If you ask very nicely, they might let you pitch a tent.

Hôtel Beau Regarde (☎ 3348 2183; Rue de l'Hotel Beau Regarde; r 6500-10,000) 'Shabby but big' about sums it up. The rooms are, well, roomy, and

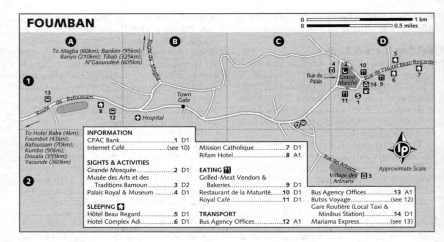

FOUMBAN

0 _____ 1 km
0 _____ 0.5 miles

INFORMATION	
CPAC Bank	1 D1
Internet Café	(see 10)

SIGHTS & ACTIVITIES	
Grande Mosquée	2 D1
Musée des Arts et des Traditions Bamoun	3 D2
Palais Royal & Museum	4 D1

SLEEPING	
Hôtel Beau Regard	5 D1
Hotel Complex Adi	6 D1

Mission Catholique	7 D1
Rifam Hotel	8 A1

EATING	
Grilled-Meat Vendors & Bakeries	9 D1
Restaurant de la Maturité	10 D1
Royal Café	11 D1

TRANSPORT	
Bus Agency Offices	12 A1

Bus Agency Offices	13 A1
Butsis Voyage	(see 12)
Gare Routière (Local Taxi & Minibus Station)	14 D1
Mariama Express	(see 13)

decently priced for what you get (a bed, floor space, and an OK if worn bathroom) but the entire place could use a decent scrub and a bit more brightness beyond the current Hannibal Lecter lighting scheme.

Hotel Complexe Adi (☎ 743 1181; Rue de l'Hotel Beau Regarde; r CFA8000-10,000) Look for the giant voodoo statue of a man studded by nails to find Adi's entrance – now that's better than a doorman. While the rooms here are clean, they're a bit smallish, and the bar downstairs gets pretty loud.

Hotel Baba (☎ 3348 2748; off Route de Bafoussam; s/d CFA10,000/15,000) This series of detached chalets is located a bit west of the city. The modern cottages are sizeable and sleepworthy in a 1970s family hotel–sorta way and decently upmarket for this corner of Africa, although nothing particularly special either.

Rifam Hotel (☎ 3348 2878; Route de Bafoussam; s/d CFA15,000/25,000; 🏊) Head a little way outside town near Hotel Baba to find Foumban's most luxurious lodgings. At the Rifam your CFA goes towards a room, satellite TV, sunken bathtub and a balcony you could fit a family on.

Eating

The area just east of the *gare routière* is good for grilled meat; go to the nearby bakeries to make up a quick sandwich. The streets along the Grand Marché are also good for quick eats on the hoof.

Royal Café (meals from CFA2000; 🕗 8am-10pm) On the southern side of the Grand Marché,

this has good meals and a patio with views. It's down a flight of steps and is easy to miss; look for the white building and red signboard.

Restaurant de la Maturité (meals from CFA2000; 🕗 8am-10pm) Opposite the *gare routière* at the eastern end of the market is this other option, with decent salads and omelettes.

Getting There & Away

All agencies running transport to Bafoussam (CFA800 to CFA1000, one hour) have their offices on Route de Bafoussam at the entrance to town, west of the town gate and about 3km from the market (CFA100 in a shared taxi). Moungo Voyages and Butsis Voyage have a few daily direct departures to Yaoundé (CFA3000, five hours) and Douala (CFA4500, six hours); otherwise you'll need to change vehicles in Bafoussam. Nonagency minibuses depart from the *gare routière* near the market.

Transport between Foumban and Kumbo (CFA3000, around six hours) runs all year, although travel times vary according to the rains. Although the road is very poor, it's easily one of the most beautiful in the country, skirting along the edge of the spectacular Mbam Massif. Ask for Mariama Express.

It's also possible during the dry season to find vehicles going northeast to Banyo, from where you can continue to N'Gaoundéré via Tibati; you should allow several days for this journey (see p207 for more).

NORTH & EXTREME NORTH PROVINCES

We'll admit: Cameroon milks the 'All of Africa in one country' slogan for all it's worth. You have all those thick forests and breezy green plains south of the Adamawa Plateau, which serves as Cameroon's localised equator. And now the north of the nation gives you the fringe of the world's greatest dry zone. This, friends, is the Sahel, a red and ochre and yellow and brown rolling sea of dust, dirt and strange, utterly beautiful hills and pinnacles of rock, crisscrossed by the dry wind, the thin strides of Fulani and the broad steps of their long-horned cattle.

N'GAOUNDÉRÉ

The gateway to the north has the allure of the edge and the energy of a transfer point. Here the railway line terminates and the great bus and truck routes to the far north and Chad begin. Vehicles scream and stream north from here, packed with passengers and Maersk cargo containers. The sense of adventure imparted upon reaching the Sahel is helped by the sight of government soldiers – there's a major training facility nearby – striding through the desert lanes with AK-47s strapped to their backs and extra banana claps taped to the stocks of their guns.

Some parts of N'Gaoundéré have bad reputations for safety at night, including the area around the stadium, and north of the cathedral. If in doubt, take a *moto-taxi*.

Information

The **Ministry of Tourism Office** (☎ 2225 2589; Ave Ahidjo) is a good bet for info on the surrounding area.

Bicec and Crédit Lyonnais, in the town centre, change cash and possibly travellers cheques and have Western Union offices.

The most reliable internet in town is found at **Complexe Lin Business Center** (Rue De la Grande Mosquée; per hr CFA300), although you might need to queue.

Palais du Lamido

To enter the **palace** (admission CFA2000, guide CFA1000, camera fee CFA1000; ⏱ 9am-5pm) of the *lamido*, or local Muslim ruler, you pass between three pillars stuffed with the remains of individuals who were buried alive to consecrate the site of the royal residence. One of Cameroon's more macabre foyers, yes, which leads into a complex of low-slung, heavily thatched roundhouses whose aesthetic feels more West African than Islam. Some rooms are underwhelming, but if you come on a Friday or (especially) Sunday, when nobles pay their respects and thin, gorgeous desert music settles over the nearby square dominated by the Grande Mosquée, there's a palpable sense of being…well, somewhere else.

Beware of black-painted areas within the compound – these sections are reserved for the *lamido*.

Sleeping

N'Gaoundéré's cool climate renders air-conditioning unnecessary in hotels.

Hôtel Transcam (☎ 2225 1252; r CFA25,000-60,000; 🅿 📺) Transcam offers much the same as many 'best hotels in town' in Cameroon: a somewhat out-of-the way location (1.5km southwest of the centre) and rooms that are, relative to local lodging, very nice: spotless digs, carpeted or linoleum floors, TVs and big, bouncy beds. There's also that same feeling you're a businessman in the late '60s–early '70s, but such is life, and a small price to pay for comparative luxury and a posh restaurant.

Auberge Pousada Style (☎ 2225 1703; r CFA5000-9000) A basic but friendly resthouse that's kept as clean as a barracks (has about the same atmosphere as well, but oh well). Take a *moto-taxi* late at night in this area.

Hotel de la Gare (☎ 2225 2217, 9905 0451; r CFA8500) This is probably N'Gaoundéré's best-located hotel, offering easy access to agencies and the train station. Rooms are tidy, if not much else.

Hôtel Le Relais Saveur (☎ 2225 1141; r with/without TV CFA18,000/15,000) Well located, near the intersection of Rue du Petit Marché and Rue de la Grande Mosquée, rooms here are scrubbed if a little musty. Try not to wrinkle your nose too much and enjoy a beer at the attached bar.

Nice Hotel (☎ 2225 1013; Rue de Garoua; r from CFA18,000) With spacious rooms, a peaceful, leafy setting (leafy, we might add, is pretty rare in N'Gaoundéré) long cool corridors and (French-language) TV in all rooms, the

CAMEROON

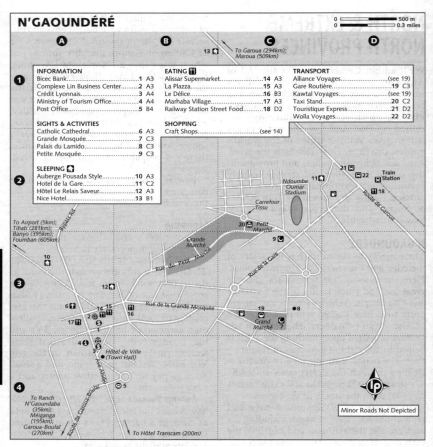

N'GAOUNDÉRÉ

0   500 m
0   0.3 miles

To Garoua (294km);
Maroua (509km)

INFORMATION
Bicec Bank.....................................**1** A3
Complexe Lin Business Center......**2** A3
Crédit Lyonnais.............................**3** A4
Ministry of Tourism Office............**4** A4
Post Office....................................**5** B4

SIGHTS & ACTIVITIES
Catholic Cathedral........................**6** A3
Grande Mosquée...........................**7** C3
Palais du Lamido..........................**8** C3
Petite Mosquée............................**9** C3

SLEEPING
Auberge Pousada Style.................**10** A3
Hotel de la Gare...........................**11** C2
Hôtel Le Relais Saveur..................**12** A3
Nice Hotel...................................**13** B1

EATING
Alissar Supermarket......................**14** A3
La Plazza.....................................**15** A3
Le Délice.....................................**16** B3
Marhaba Village...........................**17** A3
Railway Station Street Food..........**18** D2

SHOPPING
Craft Shops.............................(see 14)

TRANSPORT
Alliance Voyages.......................(see 19)
Gare Routière..............................**19** C3
Kawtal Voyages........................(see 19)
Taxi Stand...................................**20** C2
Touristique Express.......................**21** D2
Woïla Voyages.............................**22** D2

To Airport (5km);
Tibati (281km);
Banyo (395km);
Foumban (605km)

Bypass Rd

Ndoumbe
Oumar
Stadium

Train
Station

Route de Garoua

Carrefour
Tissu

Petit
Marché

Rue du Petit Marché

Grande
Marché

Rue de la Gare

Rue de la Grande Mosquée

Grand
Marché

Hôtel de Ville
(Town Hall)

Route de Garoua-Boulaï

To Ranch
N'Gaoundaba
(35km);
Méiganga
(155km);
Garoua-Boulaï
(270km)

To Hôtel Transcam (200m)

Minor Roads Not Depicted

CAMEROON

Nice is just that, and as good as midrange options get in town.

Ranch de N'Gaoundaba (☎ 225 2469, 9970 8115; Route de Meiganga; camping CFA2000, s/d CFA10,000/12,000, ste from CFA20,000) Kick back in your quality *boukarou* (Sahel hut), watch a crater lake move by in African time and wonder when your next horse trek to the dry hills is going to take place at this lovely former hunting lodge, 35km southeast of N'Gaoundéré. Once you've done all of the above, repair to the local bar and restaurant for a stiff drink (we hear the gin and tonic's divine) and a good meal. The ranch is only open from November to May; if you're using public transport it's about a 3km walk off the main road.

Eating

The best street food is easily found at the row of shops, stalls and bars opposite the train station, worth a detour even if you don't have a train to catch. We recommend wolfing the local *suya* (beef); this is cattle-herding country, and for about CFA1000 (plus a hundred or so more for plantains) you'll be enjoying a very fine grilled steak. Try some local honey (*miel* in French) while you're around; it's for sale in plenty of shops and is famous throughout Cameroon.

La Plazza (☎ 2225 2508; Rue de la Grande Mosquée; meals from CFA3000; ☺ 9am-midnight) Something of an N'Gaoundéré institution, this place has dining inside or outdoors, live music every evening and serves cold draught beer from the thatched bar. The Lebanese and pasta dishes are excellent, but don't miss the perennially popular Sunday buffet from noon (CFA5000).

Marhaba Village (mains from CFA1500; 9am-11pm) An open-air restaurant, with a snack bar and a more formal eating area. A central location makes it good for people-watching.

Le Délice (meals from CFA1500; 9am-11pm) A friendly place off the western end of Rue de la Grande Mosquée, this is one of several in the immediate area serving Western and Cameroonian dishes.

Alissar supermarket is well stocked for essentials and imported goods. The main market is the Petit Marché; the Grand Marché only sells vegetables.

Shopping
For reasonably priced, quality crafts, try the shops next to Alissar supermarket. For textiles, go to Carrefour Tissu.

Getting There & Away
AIR
Elysian Airlines (9909 8748) has flights to Douala and Yaounde, both for CFA86,500, and to Garoua for CFA28,500 – but call ahead to confirm. The airport is about 5km west of town (CFA1500 in a taxi).

BUS
For Garoua (CFA3500, five hours) and Maroua (CFA6000, eight hours), Touristique Express and Woïla Voyages are best, with several buses daily from about 6am. Both have depots near the train station. It's a long, tiring trip, but the road is decently maintained throughout.

The adventurous, with plenty of stamina and time, can consider going southeast to Garoua-Boulaï (CFA4000, 12 hours). Kawtal Voyages operates a service most days from the *gare routière* by the Grande Mosquée. The travel time is approximate, vehicles are battered, roads earthen and you should think twice (and ask ahead) before attempting this during the rains.

Only marginally less strenuous is the road southwest to Foumban. Kawtal Voyages also operates this route, as far as Banyo (CFA5000, around 10 hours). Otherwise, travel as far as Tibati with Alliance Voyages and change there. From Tibati to Banyo roads are semi-maintained, but otherwise they switch between broken tar and bumpy earth (and need-

less to say, buses don't come with recliners, in-coach DVD or air-con). There are a couple of basic auberges at Banyo, from where it's another six hours to Foumban.

TRAIN
The train is the best budget option if you're heading to Yaoundé or eastern Cameroon via Bélabo. Tickets are bought on the day of departure from the town's futurist concrete train station; the train leaves every evening at 6.30pm – see p226 for further details.

Getting Around
Moto-taxis (CFA100 to CFA150) are the main way of getting around. They're beefy Honda bikes instead of the weedy Chinese numbers found elsewhere in Cameroon, so hold on tight. Yellow taxis can be found at the Petit Marché and *gare routière*.

GAROUA
Garoua's a pleasant enough spot to spend the night or wait for a vehicle transfer, which is the extent of most people's time and plans here. You may need to make a stopover if you're overlanding into Chad; pay a visit to the **Chadian Consulate** (2227 3128) for visas (sometimes unavailable here, so check beforehand) or make friends with a member of Garoua's huge Chadian expat community.

Parc National de la Bénoué
On the road from N'Gaoundéré to Garoua you'll pass through **Parc National de la Bénoué**. Unfortunately, you'll pass through it, in a bus where locals happily toss food out of the window to attract baboons, elands, buffalo etc (there's even a chance you'll see lions off the side of the road). These activities and general human pressure is exerting a strain on the park's wildlife, which includes, beyond the above, hippopotami, crocodiles and some 300 bird species. To arrange a tour, contact guides like **Janick Pelleteret** (2227 2694, 3342 5338) or **Borge Ladefoged** (2227 2778) in Garoua; you'll have to arrange fees, but expect to spend at least €60 a day on transport costs alone.

Sleeping & Eating
There are no good sleeping options within walking distance of the bus stand; you'll need to hire a *moto-taxi* for the following hotels.

Auberge Hiala Village (2227 2407; r CFA5000-7000; P) This hotel, tucked away near a wharf over the Benoueu river, is good enough for its cute *boukarous*, shady gardens and clean rooms, but the pricing comes off as a genuine thrill. Did we mention some of the showers are open air? Hot.

Relais St-Hubert (☎ 2227 3033; Rue d'Yves Plumey; boukarous CFA18,000-23,000, r in the Grand Bâtiment CFA25,000; 🖳 🖳) Idi Amin at his most Africana obsessed could have designed parts of this hotel, which has a sort of futurist-tribal chic vibe going on. However you feel about the external architecture, the rooms are a refreshing break from the dusty Sahel.

Super Restaurant (Route de Maroua; mains from CFA1000; 🕙 9am-11pm) They've got lots of great snacks, but the super draw here is juice. Fresh, utterly refreshing, fortifying juice.

Getting There & Away

Elysian Airlines (☎ 9909 8748) flights connect Garoua with Douala and Yaoundé (CFA96,400 for both). There used to be flights to N'Djaména in Chad before Cameroon Airlines went under; check at the airport (☎ 2227 2346), 5km northwest of the centre, to see if they have resumed.

Woïla Voyages and Touristique Express have several buses daily to Maroua (CFA2500, 2½ hours) and N'Gaoundéré (CFA3500, five hours), departing from their depots near the market. Touristique Express can also book tickets for the N'Gaoundéré-Yaoundé train.

Moto-taxis are the main way around town (CFA100 to CFA150).

MAROUA
pop 214,000

If you've seen *Star Wars* and remember Mos Eisley, spaceport in the desert, you know exactly what Maroua looks like: low, red and brown streets running like dry riverbeds between squat and rounded beige buildings, all of it overtaken day and night by a colourful cast – Fulani, Chadians etc – in robes of sky blue, electric purple and blood red, as if their clothes contain all the colours that have been leeched out of the surrounding sun-swept semidesert.

This is Cameroon's northernmost major town and its best base for exploring the Extreme North Province, particularly the Mandara Mountains, as well as a good place to plan border crossings into Nigeria and Chad.

Information
INTERNET
Braouz (nr Relais de la Porte Mayo; per hr CFA750) The fastest, most reliable connections.
Marouanet (Rue Mobil; per hr CFA400)

MEDICAL SERVICES
Meskine Hospital (off Garoua Rd) Try this hospital, west of town, for emergencies.

MONEY
Bicec (Route de Maga) Has an ATM.
CCA Bureau de Change (Route de Djourgou) Worth trying if the main banks won't help you change money.
SGBC (Route de Djourgou) Has an ATM.

POST
Post office (Ave de Kakataré)

TOUR OPERATORS
Ministry of Tourism office (☎ 2229 2298; Quartier Domayo) May be able to hook you up with good tour groups. There are also numerous operators who can arrange trekking in the Mandara Mountains, visits to Parc National de Waza and can hire 4WDs with drivers. Better ones include the following:
Extrême Nord Safaris (☎ 2229 3356; deliteri@ hotmail.com)
Porte Mayo Voyages (☎ 2229 2692, 9984 1573; Pont Rouge) Based in Relais de la Porte Mayo.
Fagus Voyages (☎ 9986 1871; www.fagus voyages.com)

Sights
The **Marché Centrale** (🕙 daily) exhibits all the exotic beauty of the Sahel in buyable, market-driven form. It's as good for people-watching as it for buying a Cameroon gift; you can pick up some good local crafts here, or go to the **Centre Artisanal** at the end of the market.

The **Musée d'Art Local de Diamaré** (Marché Centrale; admission CFA500; 🕙 9am-6pm) is small and cluttered, but has a few good pieces describing local cultures and is worth a visit by any budding anthropologist (or anyone interested in local ethnicities).

Sleeping
BUDGET
Auberge le Voyageur (☎ 2229 2100; Rue Mobil; r CFA5525-8500; 🖳) Only if other options are full or you want to be near the Marché Centrale, as some rooms are dingy, and you need to pay extra to get air-con.

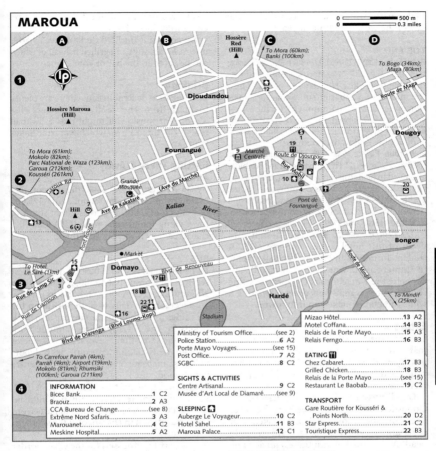

MAROUA

0 ___ 500 m
0 ___ 0.3 miles

INFORMATION	
Bicec Bank	1 C2
Braouz	2 A3
CCA Bureau de Change	(see 8)
Extrême Nord Safaris	3 A3
Marouanet	4 C2
Meskine Hospital	5 A2
Ministry of Tourism Office	(see 2)
Police Station	6 A2
Porte Mayo Voyages	(see 15)
Post Office	7 A2
SGBC	8 C2
SIGHTS & ACTIVITIES	
Centre Artisanal	9 C2
Musée d'Art Local de Diamaré	(see 9)
SLEEPING	
Auberge Le Voyageur	10 C2
Hotel Sahel	11 B3
Maroua Palace	12 C1
Mizao Hôtel	13 A2
Motel Coffana	14 B3
Relais de la Porte Mayo	15 A3
Relais Ferngo	16 B3
EATING	
Chez Cabaret	17 B3
Grilled Chicken	18 B3
Relais de la Porte Mayo	(see 15)
Restaurant Le Baobab	19 B3
TRANSPORT	
Gare Routière for Kousséri & Points North	20 D2
Star Express	21 C2
Touristique Express	22 B3

CAMEROON

Relais Ferngo (☎ 2229 2153, 7992 7364; off Blvd de Diarenga; r CFA6000; P ⊠) By far the best value in town: sleep in airy, whitewashed *boukarous* in the shade of willowy neem trees and…well, do whatever (how about take an open-air shower in the alfresco but walled-off bathrooms?). There are some good *suya* stalls just around the corner for those needing a beef fix.

Motel Coffana (☎ 9970 9643; off Blvd de Diarenga; r CFA6000-10,000; P ⊠) You'll find nicely turned out *boukarous* here, freshly painted and welcoming. Cheaper rooms in the main block have fan only, but are airy enough with their high ceilings. Plus: the service is some of the friendliest in Cameroon. Say hi to the resident chickens and enormous turkey in the morning.

MIDRANGE & TOP END

Relais de la Porte Mayo (☎ 2229 2692; Pont Rouge; s/d CFA13,900/16,900, apt CFA18,500; ⊠ ☐) French-run and popular with tourists, this is as good as Maroua lodging gets. It is skilled at giving a relaxed, modern-amenities-but-you're-still-in-the-Sahel kinda vibe, with roomy *boukarous*, a good (if touristy) restaurant-bar and fancy souvenir shop-cum-boutique.

Hotel le Saré (☎ 2229 1294, 9964 4044, 7758 6060; www.hotellesare.com; Quartier Pitoire; r from CFA15,000; P ⊠ ☐ ☎) Set amid seclusion, this is a classy place sprawled over large, shady grounds that hide sculptures by local artists, a pool and, rather bizarrely, two pet ostriches. Rooms are tidy and come in a variety of shapes and sizes –

as do tariffs, which change according to the day of the week and time of year.

TOP END

Hotel Sahel (☎ 2229 2960, 2229 3011; Blvd de Diarenga; r CFA15,000-25,000; ℗ ✖) Here's a high-end option that feels like a Holiday Inn plopped into the middle of a Saharan/sub-Saharan transition zone. That's a compliment, by the way – service is professional, rooms are cleaned with soldierly precision and an expansion wing should only add to the goodness.

Maroua Palace (☎ 2229 3164; Centre Ville; s/d CFA20,000/22,000; ℗ ✖) If you've got francs to blow and need to be in the centre of town, try this option. It's modern and has comfortable rooms and facilities – but struggles to find much of a personality beyond a slightly dour exterior.

Mizao Hôtel (☎ 2229 1300; Quartier Sonel; s/d CFA22,600/36,000; ℗ ✖ ⛽) The design and decor of this hotel comes with more 1970s student dormitory ambience (a popular theme in Cameroon, if you haven't noticed), but it's none the worse for it. It's a perfectly fine choice, but you may find yourself waiting a while for a taxi to take you into town.

Eating

The local speciality is a smooth avocado salad that – yes – tastes a lot like guacamole. It's usually made with sugar, so if you don't like your salad sweet, ask them to hold off (sans sucre) beforehand.

Grilled Chicken (dishes from CFA1000; ☺ 10am-midnight) Opposite the Champs Elysée Bar, this place does fantastic whole chickens, cooked over coals and served with bread and avocado salad. As it's Muslim-run there's no alcohol, but they'll happily bring your meal to you if you prefer to sit in the bar next door.

Restaurant le Baobab (nr Marché Centrale; dishes from CFA2000; ☺ 7am-11pm) This pleasant spot has outdoor seating under thatch, good atmosphere and better food. Check what's available – the lunchtime menu can be a bit limited.

Relais de la Porte Mayo (dishes from CFA4500; ☺ 7am-11pm) For upscale dining, this is Maroua's best option, evidenced by its popularity with the local French community. There's good French and Italian options, and a cheaper snack menu available from the bar.

Chez Cabaret (street food from CFA800) Variety acts, from stand-up comedians to girls who shake it with a hustle Beyoncé would approve of, take to a stage watched by dozens of drunk locals. It's sort of like local dinner theatre. Gone wild. In Africa.

Several stalls on Blvd de Renouveau offer up brochettes, suya and grilled fish, all of which can be eaten in the bar of your choice.

Drinking

Bars line Blvd de Renouveau – there are plenty to choose from. They're all of a muchness – listen out for music you might like, a football match on the TV, or whichever vibe takes your fancy.

Getting There & Away

AIR

Elysian Airlines (☎ 9909 8748) flights connect Maroua with Douala and Yaoundé (CFA125,000 to both cities). The airport is 20km south of town along the Garoua road (CFA3000 in a chartered taxi, if you can find one).

BUS

Touristique Express (Blvd de Diarenga) has the best services for Garoua (CFA2500, 2½ hours) and N'Gaoundéré (CFA6000; eight hours). There are several buses daily to both, mostly in the mornings from about 6am. You can also book tickets for the N'Gaoundéré–Yaoundé train here at the same time. Several other agencies operate the N'Gaoundéré route, with depots on the same road; Star Express in the centre is also good.

Plentiful transport to Mokolo (CFA1000, 90 minutes) and less frequently to Rhumsiki (CFA2000, around three hours) departs from Carrefour Parrah in Djarangol at the southern end of town.

Transport to Kousséri for the Chad border (CFA3500, five hours) departs from the gare routière on Maroua's eastern edge. Minibuses to Banki for the Nigerian border (CFA2000, two hours) also depart from here.

Getting Around

There are no taxis in Maroua; motorbikes cost CFA150, more for long-haul hops.

MANDARA MOUNTAINS

Basalt cliffs dot a volcanic plain while dust storms conceived on the Nigerian border sweep out of the sunset onto thorn trees, red rock cairns and herds of brindle cattle…and frankly, you wouldn't be half surprised to see a cowboy or a dragon or both pass across this awesome, evocative landscape.

The Mandara Mountains run west from Maroua to the Nigerian border and have become very popular – justifiably so – with Africa trekkers. With that said, 'very' popular is a relative term. Although the kids here do tend to ask for 'one pen' or 'cadeau' with worrying regularity, this definitely ain't Thailand.

The villages that dot these ranges are as captivating as the vistas they are built on, including **Rhumsiki**, with its striking mountain scenery; and **Djingliya** and **Koza**, set against steep terraced hillsides. Then there's **Tourou**, known for the calabash hats worn by local women; and **Maga**, with its unique domed houses made entirely of clay. Hiking between villages is one of the best ways to appreciate the scenery and culture alike.

There is accommodation in Rhumsiki (itself the gateway to the region), Mokolo, Mora, Waza, Maga and a few other villages, but infrastructure is awful otherwise. Local minibuses usually set off around 6am. *Mototaxis* are sometimes the only option for getting around, and the drivers know it.

In any case, and we can't stress this enough: change enough CFA to see you through before leaving Maroua.

One popular circuit goes from Maroua to Mora (with possible detours to Parc National de Waza and to Oudjilla), and then southwest via Koza, Djingliya and Mokolo to Rhumsiki, finishing back in Maroua. This can easily be broken down into two- or three-day treks (catching motorised transport between certain spots), giving a great taste of the region.

Mokolo

Mokolo, centre of the Mafa people, is about 80km west of Maroua along a bitumen road. There's not much here, but it's an important transport hub. If you find yourself having to wait for a ride, pop over to the local youth centre, just downhill from the bus stands. The centre was started by an American émigré who has hired friendly-as-hell staff and stocked a surreally out-of-place library full of the stuff pop literati love to read (David Sedaris etc). If you need to stay in Mokolo for the night, head for **Hotel Touristique le Flamboyant** (☎ 2229 5585; r CFA12,000-14,000; 🞬). Located near the Total petrol station, this is the most comfortable place in town, with clean boukarous, a nice restaurant and a good, touch of green on the Sahel atmosphere.

GETTING THERE & AWAY

Most transport departs from the market, in the town centre. Tsanaga Voyages go several times a day to Maroua (CFA800, one hour). Transport onward to Rhumsiki is much less frequent; your best bet is the bus from Maroua, which passes through midmorning. Otherwise, it's a bumpy, and likely very expensive (CFA3000) 55km ride by *moto-taxi*. There's a daily bus to Koza (CFA1500, two hours).

Rhumsiki

If you're missing the American or Australian Painted Deserts, you've found the right spot here. The mountains, particularly much-photographed **Rhumsiki Peak**, lean in aggressive dominance over desert soil and gashed valleys that become almost purple under the big sky sunset.

Sound nice? It is, although the drawback is an overtouristed vibe. Expect to be offered a lot of treks, hikes etc by local kids. Be warned: while most of these youngsters know their way around the hills, some may have no concept of how to properly pace a long walk. If you can find and contact a recommended guide before you arrive (Lonely Planet's Thorn Tree forum is a good resource), you may save yourself some headache. Hiking rates start at about CFA10,000 per day, including simple meals, accommodation in local homes, camping (with your own tent or on mats in the open) and a guide. If you're self-sufficient, it's perfectly feasible to strike out on your own.

Most routes are between half a day and four days, and some cross briefly into Nigeria, just 3km away; no visa is necessary as long as you don't continue further into the country. Horse trekking is also popular – in this case, expect to pay the trekking fee plus horse hire, generally around CFA8000 per day. Be warned: these horses don't seem to come with saddles, just blankets and really bony spines.

The local *feticheur* will divine your future by looking into his bucket of crabs; he and brass carvers and other trinket sellers usually factor into trek itineraries. It's a very soft sell, so don't be too put out by people trying to make a living.

SLEEPING & EATING

Except as noted, all places are along the main road, listed here in the order you

CAMEROON

reach them when arriving from Mokolo. All arrange trekking.

Kirdi Bar (camping per person CFA1000, r per person CFA2500-5000) There's some basic *boukarous* here and an exuberantly friendly manager who will vow to make you the meal of your life for about CFA2500. He whips up a decent pizza, but the best part of our meal was fresh local bread, somehow sweet and yes, almost sandy (or at least gritty), enjoyed by candlelight under a blanket of stars.

Auberge Le Kapsiki (☎ 2229 3356; s/d CFA5000/7500) Also called 'Le Casserole' (for the onsite restaurant), the *boukarous*-style accommodation here is spartan but adequate. Meals at the fine-dining (OK, 'good dining') restaurant cost around CFA2500.

La Maison de l'Amitié (☎ 2229 2113, 9952 7825; r CFA8500-12,000) The *boukarous* here feel a bit more modern, what with their wireless internet…kidding. They are nicely turned out, though, and there's an onsite restaurant. It's at the far end of town, about 150m off the main road.

Auberge Le Petit Paris (☎ 2229 5173; r CFA10,000-20,000) More *boukarous* are the order of the day here – green on the outside, plain on the inside. They're clean and tidy, there's a restaurant etc. Alternatively, dine at Le Casserole, opposite.

Campement de Rhumsiki (r CFA14,800-25,000) High-end *boukarous* or straight-up luxury (well, relative luxury) cottages are the order of the day here, along with large, shady grounds, overpriced restaurant and of course, attached souvenir shop – because there's no better way to finish a trek in the Extreme North highlands than with the purchase of some kitsch.

GETTING THERE & AWAY

Transport to and from Rhumsiki is best on Sunday, Monday and Wednesday – get up early for the 6am starts, but always check what's running the day before travel. There's a minibus most days to Maroua (CFA2000, around three hours), passing through Mokolo. Except on market day, transport dries up by around 2pm. A *moto-taxi* to Mokolo costs around CFA3000; rucksacks are better balanced between the handlebars than on your back.

Mora

Mora is in the heartland of the Wandala (Mandara) people and is the last settlement

---

MARKET DAY

Getting to and from villages in northern Cameroon (and elsewhere) via public transport is always easier on market day, as there are many more vehicles. Some local market days are as follows:

Town	Market day
Bogo	Thursday
Koza	Sunday
Maroua	Monday
Mogodé (north of Rhumsiki)	Friday
Mokolo	Wednesday
Mora	Sunday
Pouss (northeast of Maga)	Tuesday
Rhumsiki	Sunday
Tourou	Thursday

---

of any size before reaching the Nigerian border. Try to time your visit for the large Sunday market, one of the best tastes of local culture in the region. About 11km west is Oudjilla, a touristy Podoko village. Apart from the scenery, the main attraction is the **compound** (saré; donation CFA1000) of the village chief and his many wives, but you need to gain permission from someone to enter, and while said permission is usually granted, if the chief isn't in, you're stuck outside.

Auberge Mora Massif (r CFA4000-7000) is the best place to stay in Mora. The *boukarous* are as spacious as some hotel suites, and situated under strands of bougainvillea which shower the alfresco showers with little carpets of purple petals. It's 400m west of the main junction.

Campement Sanga de Podoko (r CFA4000) has acceptable *boukarous* rooms plus a bar, restaurant and desultory staff all thrown in as a bonus. It's east of the main road near the Total petrol station.

Minibuses go daily between Mora and Maroua (CFA800, one hour). The main way to reach Oudjilla is by *moto-taxi*.

PARC NATIONAL DE WAZA

Dry, dramatic and baking under the bone white Sahel sunlight, **Waza** (admission CFA5000, plus per vehicle CFA2000, camera fee CFA2000; ⏰ 6am-6pm 15 Nov–15 May) is the most accessible of Cameroon's national parks and the best for viewing wildlife. While it can't compare with East African parks, elephants, hippos, giraffes, antelopes, a whole mess of birds and yes, lions (you're lucky to see them) all wander amid two floral zones: an intermittently flooded plain and forests of spidery acacia. Late March to April is the best time for viewing, as the animals congregate at waterholes before the rains. The park is closed during the rainy season.

A guide (CFA3000 per day) is obligatory in each vehicle and walking isn't permitted.

Sleeping

Waza can easily be done as a day trip from Maroua if you start early (bring a packed lunch). Otherwise, there are two places to stay near the park entrance.

Campement de Waza (☎ in Maroua 2229 1646, 2229 1165, 7765 7717, in Waza 7765 7558; r CFA16,000; ❷) Plonked onto a hill amid smooth white and red boulders are these *boukarous*, with views that stretch out to the scrub plains and small mobs of lizards thrown in gratis. The huts are comfy, staff is obsequious and onsite restaurant good for sinking a beer post-lion-spotting.

Centre d'Accueil de Waza (☎ 2229 2207; camping per person CFA2500, r CFA7500) The Centre is much more efficient and spartan than the Campement, and cheaper too: you get bare *boukarous* with shared toilets and that's about it. Meals can be arranged (CFA2000) and there's a small kitchen onsite.

Restaurant Chez (☎ 7796 4764; r around CFA2500) There's some very simple rooms at the back of this restaurant-bar in nearby Waza village, just north of the park entrance. Other businesses in the village will also likely rent rooms to anyone looking hopeful enough.

Getting There & Away

The park entrance is signposted and lies about 400m off the main highway. Unless you have your own wheels, the best way to visit is to hire a vehicle in Maroua (about CFA40,000 per day plus petrol). See p208 for listings of tour operators. A 4WD is recommended.

To access the park by public transport, catch any bus between Maroua and Kousséri, which should be able to drop you at the park turnoff. After that you'll be reliant on hitching a lift into the park itself, which could involve a long wait.

During the dry season, it's possible to drive through the park and exit at Andirni, about 45km southeast of Waza village. The road from Andirni to Maroua via Bogo is only partially paved, and is sometimes impassable during the wet season.

EAST PROVINCE

The north of Cameroon may be windswept and wild, but the East claims the bad-boy title of frontier in spirit. Timber barons, Chinese resource-extraction teams, bushmeat hunters and the always pleasant (ha!) Central African Republic border make for a region that shouldn't be approached by tame travellers. It's hard going, although it's pretty going too: quintessential Central African green jungle and red laterite earth roads. The rainforest is the main attraction, by which we mean Cameroon's sweep of the Congo Basin, which takes in Parc National de la Lobéké, Boumba-Bek and Nki forest reserves, and the Réserve de Biosphère du Dja.

GAROUA-BOULAÏ

Garoua-Boulaï isn't some tribal dialect for 'fast money' but it could be. On the Central African Republic (CAR) border, the town was once known for bars, trucks, prostitutes and an alarmingly high HIV infection rate. It still has all of the above – plus money pouring in from natural resource exploitation.

There are several unappealing and unrecommended auberges with rooms for about CFA2000. Better is the **Mission Catholique** (dm for a donation, r about CFA5000) with dorm beds and a few rooms.

The road to N'Gaoundéré is in decent condition. Going towards Yaoundé the road to Bertoua is dirt, after which the remaining 247km are tolerably paved. from Garoua-Boulaï to N'Gaoundéré – it's dirt until you reach Bertoua, after which there's 247km of tolerable asphalt. During the dry season, there's one bus daily (CFA4000, 12 hours) and many police checkpoints. Ask around before travelling – sporadic banditry persists along the CAR border.

Vehicles go several times daily on a fair road to Bertoua. For details on getting to CAR, see p224; the border is on the edge of town next to the motor park.

BERTOUA

Bertoua is as nice as East Province gets – thanks, logging money! Said cash has brought bitumen, banks and a bit of variety when it comes to eating and sleeping. Otherwise, there's not a hell of a lot here to hold a traveller down.

Sleeping & Eating

Hôtel Mansa (☎ 2224 1650; Mokolo II; r CFA25,000-35,000; ☒) The Mansa is Bertoua's best place, complete with a restaurant (wow!), and is worth a splurge if you've been lost in the forest.

Hôtel Montagnia (☎ 2224 1186), near the *gare routière*, and Hôtel Mirage, near the main post office, both have basic rooms for around CFA7000.

Café Moderne (meals from CFA500) is found at the *gare routière*. Other similarly inexpensive places include Grille de la Ménagère (near the Orange phone mast) and Chez Odette, just off the road near La King textile store.

Getting There & Away

To Yaoundé, the main lines are Alliance Voyages and Djerem Express (CFA5000, about seven hours); most transport uses the southern route via Abong-Mbang and Ayos. The road is unpaved to Ayos (OK when dry; bad in rains), and bitumen from there to Yaoundé.

Minibuses go daily to Garoua-Boulaï, and on to N'Gaoundéré (CFA7500, one day); the road is unpaved to Garoua-Boulaï and paved the rest of the way to N'Gaoundéré. There's also daily transport to Batouri (CFA1500, three hours), along reasonable roads and to Bélabo (CFA1000, one hour), where you can catch the Yaoundé–N'Gaoundéré train.

BÉLABO

The halfway point on the Yaoundé–N'Gaoundéré train line, Bélabo is the rail entry point for the east. There's not much to the place except a pumping station and an edgy feel; unfortunately, taking the train means hanging around at the station at midnight, when the train arrives (from both directions), assuming it's on time. On arrival, hire a taxi or *moto-taxi* to take you to your hotel; walking alone isn't safe. If you're departing Bélabo with a 1st-class train ticket, you can wait in the VIP lounge rather than out on the street.

About 25km west of town, off the road to **Nanga Eboko**, is the privately run **Sanaga-Yong Chimpanzee Rescue Centre** (donations welcome), which offers sanctuary to about 20 chimpanzees and promotes local education efforts.

For accommodation, try **La Girafe** (r from CFA8000) on the edge of town. There are a couple of cheaper places, including the very basic **Hôtel de l'Est** (r from CFA2000). The best food is at Mama Etémé, behind the health clinic.

Transport goes several times daily along the paved road between Bertoua and Bélabo (CFA1000, one hour). To get to the chimpanzee centre, you'll need to charter a taxi or *moto-taxi* – expect to pay at least CFA1000.

BATOURI

Batouri is the last sizeable town before heading into either the CAR, or the forest reserves of the southeast – you'll likely want to break up your journey here if heading to either of them. It's located 90km east of Bertoua on a poor road.

Budget accommodation is available at **Hotel Le Coopérant** (☎ 2226 2300; r CFA5000) in the town centre. **Hôtel Mont Pandi** (☎ 2226 2577; r CFA11,000; ☒) is an even better bet if you're in need of a treat, like, say, an attached restaurant (treats are relative out here).

There are several buses daily to Bertoua, with the first leaving at about 8am, and usually at least one bus daily to Yaoundé. Local agencies include Atlantic Voyages and Narral Voyages. To Yokadouma, there's daily transport departing in the morning; allow half a day, more in the wet season. There is also transport at least once daily to Kenzou and the CAR border, departing Batouri at about 5am.

YOKADOUMA

Logging has brought Yokadouma a fast-paced Wild West feel, with its attendant bushmeat markets and displaced 'Pygmies'. The **WWF** (p179; ☎ 2221 7083; www.wwfcameroon.org, www.panda .org/who_we_are/wwf_offices/cameroon) can help with arranging visits to Parc National de la Lobéké, and Boumba-Bek and Nki forest reserves.

The best place to stay is **L'Elefant** (☎ 2224 2877; r from CFA8000; ☒). Otherwise, there are numerous cheaper and more basic choices, including **Alliance Auberge** (☎ 2224 2840) and **Caravane Bayoka** (☎ 2224 2815). Neither of these comes particularly well recommended.

All transport departs early. To Moloundou, apart from hitching a ride in a comfortable Land Cruiser, the best bet is Alliance Voyages, with one bus daily in the dry season (CFA5000, about eight hours). During the wet season, the journey can take several days.

MOLOUNDOU

You'll need to pass through this border town if you're heading for Réserve de Nki or Ouesso (Congo).

There are two basic places to stay, **La Forestière** (r from CFA3000) and **Beausejour** (r from CFA3000).

Alliance Voyages has one bus daily in the dry season to/from Yokadouma (CFA5000, about eight hours).

RÉSERVE DE BIOSPHÈRE DU DJA

The Réserve de Biosphère du Dja, as recognised by Unesco, protects about 526,000 hectares of primary rainforest. As with Lobéké and the other southeastern forest reserves, visiting here is a serious undertaking; you'll need to be completely self-sufficient. There are few people in the reserve area, but there are Baka communities around its borders, particularly along the old road rimming Dja's northern edge.

The reserve is managed by **Ecofac** (Map p179; ☎ 2220 9472; www.ecofac.org; Bastos) in Yaoundé, and you should visit its offices for information and to arrange a visit. There's a wide range of primates including chimpanzees, colobus monkey, mangabey, elephants and the honey badger.

The best starting point for a visit is **Somalomo village**, on the reserve's north edge. There's a training centre here with basic **rooms** (per night CFA10,000). Accommodation must be arranged in advance, along with meals (unless you plan to be self-sufficient). There's no food other than basic foodstuffs available in Somalomo. You'll also need a good water filter. Guides (CFA3000 per day) are obligatory and can be arranged at Somalomo, as can porters (CFA2000 per day).

The main route from Somalomo into the reserve is a 30km hike south to Bouamir, where you can **camp** at the site of an old research base and hike out again along the same path. Allow close to a week for a visit from Yaoundé, including a day each way to/from Somalomo, a day's hike in and out to Bouamir, and several days' camping. You'll need your own tent. At Bouamir, you're likely to see buffaloes and birds.

It's also possible to enter Dja from Lomié, to the east, although guides aren't as well organised there as in Somalomo. The best

time to visit Dja is during the drier season between December and February, although visits are possible into June.

LOBÉKÉ, BOUMBA-BEK & NKI

These three designated areas protect large sections of southeastern Cameroon's rainforests. They are also the focus of a joint initiative between the Cameroon government and the WWF to halt timber exploitation and poaching, and to protect the forests as well as local Baka communities (who depend on the forests for their livelihood). Lobéké, with more than 2000 sq km, was declared a national park in 2001; Boumba-Bek and Nki are forest reserves, though they're supposed to achieve national park status in the near future within a single 7500 sq km protected area.

Lobéké is the most accessible of the three areas, but all are difficult to reach, and you should only contemplate coming if you have lots of time, patience and endurance. December to March are the best times to visit – the dry weather means better accessibility and lighter vegetation, which can increase your chances of spotting wildlife.

Lobéké

Lobéké has large populations of forest elephants, chimpanzees and gorillas, although the dense vegetation means that sightings can be hard to come by. The best option is to use some of the miradors (viewing platforms) which have been constructed in more open areas and let the wildlife come to you.

A visit to Lobéké starts in Yokadouma. Park fees (CFA5000 per person per day) and guide fees (CFA3000 per guide per day) are payable at the **Ministry of Finance office** (Yokadouma); get a receipt to show at the park gate. You should also check in at the **WWF office** Campo (☎ 9711 0115; www.wwfcameroon .org); Yaoundé (Map p179; Bastos; ☎ 2221 6267) to get current information on accessibility and logistics. WWF can often help with transport (CFA4000) into the park through the **WWF suboffice** (Mambele), 160km south of Yokadouma. You'll need to be self-sufficient for food in the park.

If you get caught in Mambele for the night, there's accommodation at **Le Bon Samariten** (r from CFA2000). You can also find food and bottled water in town.

Boumba-Bek & Nki

Réserve de Nki – the most pristine of the three areas – is accessed via Moloundou, then by boat westwards along the Dja River, and finally on foot into the forest. WWF project staff can assist with boat arrangements; plan on about CFA170,000 per five-person boat.

Réserve de Boumba-Bek can be accessed via Ngola (north of Mambele on the Yokadouma road), from where you head west by vehicle and foot to reach the Boumba River and the reserve.

If you get to either of these forest reserves, you'll be as remote in deepest Cameroon as it's possible to get.

SOUTH PROVINCE

One of the seminal moments of Cameroonian history was the forced migration of peoples from the Adamawa Plateau into what most locals still call 'the forest' – the great jungle belt that lie across Africa's belly. In this country, South Province is the belt's buckle. You will see jungle here that redefines your concept of lush; you will not see, unless you're very lucky, some of the inhabitants of the deepest stretches of forest. Elephants, Pygmies and animals and plants yet unseen by outsiders' lurk in this jungle, which reaches towards the blue Atlantic, white waves and some of Cameroon's best beaches.

KRIBI

Cameroon isn't exactly world-renowned for her beaches, which frankly suits us fine – more Kribi for those in the know. Which happens to be lots of people – most of Cameroon, her expats and Francophone tourists from around the world – but very rarely does the vibe here feel anything like 'crowded beach resort', despite this being the country's exemplar of the genre. The sand is fine and golden, the water cool and inviting (but prone to hard rips; be careful) and all of the above is kept refreshingly clean. Plus, the seafood is fresh, and when it's paired with a cold beer, a grilled banana and a starry sky…well, there are times when Africa hugs you.

Book ahead on weekends and holidays; otherwise, Kribi can be pretty sleepy. There are also a few attractive beaches to the north and south, including at Londji, about 15km from town, but barely any accommodation options. Kribi has its dangers: gangs who wander the beach at night. Don't camp and avoid walking along the sand after dark.

Information

You may want to stock up on CFA before coming to Kribi. **Bicec bank** (Rue des Banques) will change cash euros. **Club Internet de Kribi** (Rue des Banques; per hr CFA500) has the most reliable internet connections. The **Ministry of Tourism Office** (☎ 3346 1080) is occasionally useful, and may help with trips to Campo-Ma'an National Park.

Sleeping

Kribi is as expensive as Cameroon gets outside of Yaoundé and Douala. If you're visiting during the rainy season or midweek, it's always worth bargaining at hotels.

BUDGET

Hotel Panoramique (☎ 3346 1773, 9694 2575; hotel panoramique@yahoo.fr; Rue du Marché; r CFA6000-14,000; 🐾) This semisprawling compound feels like a down-at-heels villa evolved into low-rent flophouse. Some rooms are good value – clean peach walls and crisp white sheets – but at the cheapest end of the spectrum you get swept into an ugly annexe with the dust and roaches. Located in town.

La Kienke (☎ 3346 2126; r from CFA15,000; P 🐾) Stucco walls and locker room–tiled floors make this hotel come off as an old-school beach resort, even though it's not on the beach. Nonetheless, La Kienke provides relatively cheap comfort in Kribi town.

Hotel Tara Plage (☎ 3346 2083; Route de Campo; r with/without air-con CFA16,000/CFA12,000; P 🐾) Tara Plage is a little away from town, so while the vibe is mellow, you're sort of stuck here amid onsite amenities…which, on the plus side, include a kick-butt restaurant. Advance booking is recommended.

MIDRANGE

Framotel (☎ 3346 1541, 3346 1640, 9994 8222; www.cam eroun-evasion.com; r from CFA20,000; 🐾 🖵) Framotel is a low-slung compound of guest villas and apartments that may put you in mind of the cheap and cheerful rentals your family used on holidays. It's apparently good enough for the UN, whose staff had the place booked out when we visited. Located 150m up a side road a little north of Kribi; the road entrance is op-

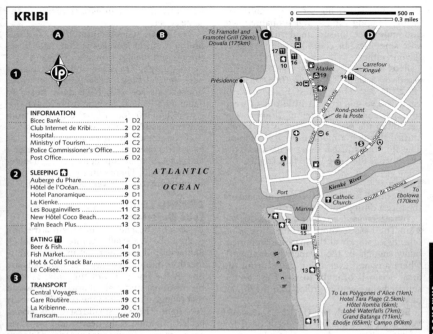

posite Framotel Grill (see p218). Two nearby hotels offer identical accommodation.

Hôtel de l'Océan (☎ 3346 1635; off Route de Campo; r CFA20,000-24,000; P) A fair few expats and foreign tourists were drying off the ocean in their Speedos when we walked into this cluster of lemon yellow beach blocks, which almost slip into the sea. Rooms are cool and breezy in a concrete corral kind of way, with good views of the sun slipping past the salt-wind horizon.

Les Polygones d'Alice (☎ 3346 1504, 7770 0439; Route de Campo; r CFA25,000; P) First: yes, 'Alice's Polygons' may be the best-named hotel in Cameroon. Second: the name isn't an exaggeration – this is a big white octagon covered in something like bathroom tiles, which we assume is supposed to impart a sort of seashell exterior, kind of like the Sydney Opera House. In hyperbole-land. Anyway, rooms are modern and comfy as hell.

New Hôtel Coco Beach (☎ 3346 1584; off Route de Campo; s CFA15,000-28,000, d CFA25,000-32,000, tr CFA46,000; P) If a little *metropole* brasserie dropped onto the buttery sand of Kribi appeals, may we direct you to Coco Beach?

There's an endearingly cluttered Gallic flair to this spot, accentuated by a great restaurant that serves foie gras by the sea – which pretty much laps up on your shoes.

Les Bougainvillers (☎ 9608 4745; off Route de Campo; r CFA25,000-35,000; P) 'The Bougainvillers' sounds like the name of an old-school funk band, and if there was such a band they'd likely crash this waterfront hotel, with its covered walkways, smooth orange tiles and frankly fantastic rooms – you get plush beds, sparkly clean everything and balconies that look out onto screaming jungle or, if you're lucky, palms blowing over whitecaps. Funk on, Bougainvillers.

Auberge du Phare (☎ 3346 1106; off Route de Campo; r CFA28,000-40,000; P) Blond wood accents, navy blue sheets and nautical embellishments give rooms some character, while the peeling courtyard, crystal pool and thatched tiki-tacky bar provides a sense of tropical indulgence. The major drawback is the tariff; du Phare is nice enough, but rates are frankly overpriced.

Palm Beach Plus (☎ 3346 1447; hotelpb@iccnet .cm; Route de Campo; r CFA25,000-75,000; P) Palm

CAMEROON

Beach Plus is the big scoop of vanilla on Kribi's lodging sundae: it'll probably make you smile. Nice, for sure: modern and stuffed with amenities (air-con, TV), but not a lot of flavour, either.

Hotel Ilomba (☎ 3346 1744, 9991 2923; illomna@ bluewin.ch; Route de Campo; s/d CFA25,000/30,000; P ☒ ☐ ☒) The poshest hotel in Kribi isn't; you've got to go a little out of town to experience the illustrious Ilomba. The best thing the place has going is *boukarous* stuffed through a modern luxury machine, The Ilomba is just a short walk along the beach from the Lobé Waterfalls (right).

Eating

All the beach hotels have restaurants, and are the nicest dining options in Kribi.

Fish market (meals from CFA1000; ☼ 10am-5pm Wed & Sat) The best seafood in Cameroon is on offer twice weekly at the marina (supported, oddly enough, by the Japanese government), where any and everything culled from the local ocean is brought to you fresh as the sunrise before getting grilled into the dinner of your dreams.

Beer & Fish (meals from CFA1000; ☼ 10am-late) When the fish market is closed, head for Carrefour Kingué, where you'll find plenty of ladies doing what Cameroon does best: grilling fish, smiling, flirting, calling their friends to bring you a cold beer and generally making the world right.

Hot & Cold Snack Bar (snacks & fast food CFA500-1500; ☼ 8am-10pm) Opposite Central Voyages bus office, this bar is like a German car: clean, efficient and reasonably priced. The menu includes omelettes, chicken and chips and suchlike.

Framotel Grill (mains from CFA2000) Located a little north of town, this is a good spot for feeling sand between your toes, stars above your head and fresh beer and fish on your lips.

Le Colisee (mains CFA3000-7000) If you put up a sign that screamed 'Air-con! Pizza!', you'd probably attract some attention in Kribi; Le Colisee figured they'd just have air-con and pizza and advertise via a building that looks like a dealer's Italian-style villa. Despite the look of the place there's no cocaine on the menu – just good Italian mains and some of the best (and only) pizza around.

Getting There & Away

Bus agencies have offices on Rue du Marché in the town centre. Nonagency transport leaves from the main *gare routière*, on the same street.

To Douala (CFA1800 to CFA2000, three hours), Central Voyages is best, with buses throughout the day from about 5.30am.

To Campo, Transcam and La Kribienne have several buses daily (CFA2000, three hours). All agencies have daily buses to Yaoundé (CFA3000, 3½ hours). Ebolowa transport (CFA3500, four hours) only runs from November to May due to the poor roads.

If you don't fancy the long walk along the beach to Lobé Waterfalls, you can charter a taxi (CFA2500) or hop on the back of a *moto-taxi* (CFA500). There's little public transport, so pay extra to the driver to wait for you.

AROUND KRIBI
Lobé Waterfalls

Besides the beaches, Kribi's main attraction is the Lobé Waterfalls (Chutes de la Lobé), 8km south of the town. Set in a very pretty location in a curved bay, the waterfalls are one of the few (but not the only, as local promotional materials claim) in the world that plunge directly into the sea – it's a really cool sight. There's a small restaurant serving grilled fish and drinks nearby and touts will approach you offering pirogue trips upstream to a 'Pygmy village'. Said village is depressing, but the boat trip itself is lovely. Expect to pay around CFA5000 for a 90-minute round-trip, or just opt for a 10-minute trip past the rapids to the larger falls behind.

EBOLOWA

Ebolowa, capital of Ntem district, has apparently come into some money – for a Cameroonian town of its size it's almost shockingly well developed. As a traveller destination its main use is as a possible stopping point en route between Yaoundé and Equatorial Guinea or Gabon; otherwise, the big attraction is an artificial Municipal Lake in the centre of town. Whoopee.

The best accommodation is at **Hôtel Porte Jaune** (☎ 2228 3929; Route de Yaoundé; r CFA10,000-12,000) in the town centre, with decent rooms and meals. Of a similar standard is **Hôtel le Ranch** (☎ 2228 3532; Centre Ville; r CFA7000-20,000) near the police station, and **Hôtel Nuit Ailleurs** (☎ 2228 3895; Place Ans 2000; r CFA17,000-25,000). There are several cheaper, undistinguished auberges near the main roundabout, including **Hôtel Âne Rouge** (Place Ans 2000; r CFA4000).

'PYGMIES'

The term 'Pygmies' is used by outsiders to refer to a diverse group of people – many of whom are short in stature – living in the forested areas of southeast Cameroon and Central Africa. Traditionally, these people have lived by hunting and gathering forest resources which they either use themselves or trade in exchange for cultivated foods. Although 'Pygmy' is used generically, the Pygmies do not view themselves as one culture, nor do they identify themselves as Pygmies. Rather, they belong to various distinct ethnolinguistic groups. In Cameroon, the most numerous are the Baka. Other groups include the Kola, the Medzan, the Aka and the Bofi.

Since early in the 1st millennium, these peoples and their traditional way of life have been under threat – first by Bantu groups, who forced them to withdraw as they migrated southeast through traditional Pygmy areas; later by colonial masters, who forced the Pygmies into more easily 'managed' (read: 'exploited') roadside settlements and, more recently, forces such as multinational logging companies, mining interests, and government policies that encourage Pygmies to adapt a more sedentary lifestyle. Now, while most Pygmies remain at least partially nomadic, many live in interdependent relationships with neighbouring Bantu farming peoples, although their exploitation continues.

Most Pygmies follow traditional religions, which typically centre around a powerful forest spirit, with the forest viewed as mother, father and guardian. Among the Baka, this forest god is known as Jengi – which is also the name given to celebrations marking the rite of passage of young Baka men into adulthood.

During the dry season, there's at least one vehicle daily along the rough road between Ebolowa and Kribi. There are also several vehicles daily to Yaoundé (CFA3000, three hours).

Several vehicles, including those of Arc-en-Ciel, depart in the morning for Ambam (CFA1000, one hour). From there you can find transport towards Ebebiyin (Equatorial Guinea) or Bitam (Gabon).

If you get stuck in Ambam, the (very) basic **Amam Sejour** (r CFA3000-5000) rounds out the budget end of the scale, **Hôtel La Couronne** (r CFA10,000-15,000) is fair quality while **Chateau Palace** (☎ 9960 2023; r CFA16,500-20,000), the top-end option, has TVs, air-con and (why not?) a piano bar.

CAMPO & EBODJÉ

Campo is the last town before the Equatorial Guinea border. Taking the road here is half the attraction – it's a hard but rewarding slog through immense rainforest and past Pygmy villages with views out to the ocean and fire-spouting petrol platforms shimmering in the west.

For travellers, Campo mainly serves as a jumping-off point for visiting Parc National de Campo Ma'an, as well as a community tourism project in nearby Ebodjé. There's scruffy accommodation, simple meals and very friendly faces at **Auberge Bon Course** (☎ 7451 1883; Campo; r CFA5000) at Bon Course Supermarché at the main junction.

Ebodjé, a small fishing village 25km north of Campo, is home to a sea turtle conservation project and ecotourism site run by **KUDU Cameroun** (☎ 3348 1648, 9622 0829; bebeaclotilde@yahoo .fr). Visitors are taken out at night to spot egg-laying turtles, although there's no guarantee you'll see any – some tour groups encounter none, some as many as six. Even if you don't see any turtles, the beach is gorgeous, pristine and better than anything you'll see in Kribi. Plus the sense of silence and starry-skyness as night falls in the village, which lacks electricity, is magical. If you do see a turtle you can help tag it and carry its eggs to a protected hatchery pen, from where you can release baby turtles back into the ocean.

The total cost of a **turtle walk** (per person around CFA10,500) includes accommodation in a local home, a village development fee, meal and tour. A proportion of all fees helps locals, many of whom have been trained as guides to the area, and for between CFA5000 and CFA10,000 you can arrange trips up local rivers or cultural nights with traditional dancing and singing. This is a great way to experience a tropical escape minus any resort-type commercialism; just remember to bring your own water or filter, mosquito net and sleeping sheet.

Getting There & Away

There are daily minibuses between Campo and Kribi (CFA1500) which also stop at

Ebodjé. *Moto-taxis* to Campo Beach (for Equatorial Guinea) cost CFA500. For information on crossing the border, see p225. Taxis to Ebodjé from Campo cost CFA500. *Moto-taxis* to Ebodjé cost around CFA2000.

PARC NATIONAL DE CAMPO-MA'AN

Campo is the starting point for visiting the Parc National de Campo-Ma'an (2608 sq km), which protects a dense rainforest thick with buffaloes, elephants and mandrills. The animals are rarely seen because of the heavy vegetation, but the park is being continually developed by WWF as an ecotourism destination. Before planning a trip, check with the **WWF office** (www.wwfcameroon.org) Campo (☎ 9711 0115); Yaoundé **(Map p179; Bastos; ☎ 2221 6267)** to see what progress is being made.

There's little infrastructure in place and you'll need your own 4WD to get here. The CFA5000 entry fee can be paid at the **tourist office** (Campo); get a receipt to show at the park entrance at the village of **Nko'elon**. Staff at the office can also help you arrange a guide (obligatory, CFA3000 per day).

CAMEROON DIRECTORY

ACCOMMODATION

Budget rooms are no-frills, with a narrow double bed and usually a cold-water shower. Sometimes they can be pretty grotty. In larger towns you can also find comfortable midrange options with reliable hot water and French satellite TV. Some church missions take travellers and can be excellent value, as they are usually clean, cheap and well run.

PRACTICALITIES

■ The *Cameroon Tribune* is the government-owned bilingual daily. The thrice-weekly *Le Messager* (French) is the main independent newspaper.

■ Most broadcast programming is government-run and in French, through Cameroon Radio-TV Corporation (CRTV). TVs at top-end hotels often have CNN or French news stations.

■ Electricity supply is 220V and plugs are of the European two-round-pin variety.

■ Cameroon uses the metric system.

Outside Yaoundé and Douala, international-standard top-end accommodation is hard to find. Throughout this chapter, we've considered budget accommodation as costing up to CFA15,000, midrange CFA15,000 to CFA40,000 and top end from CFA40,000 and up.

Camping is not generally recommended, except in the remote countryside. You should always ask permission from the village headman before pitching a tent.

ACTIVITIES

The two most popular areas are Mt Cameroon (p191) and the Mandara Mountains (p210). It's possible to organise treks with guides in both areas. On Mt Cameroon you'll either camp or stay in mountain huts; in the Mandaras you generally stay with villagers. The Ring Road near Bamenda also offers great hiking possibilities, but there's nothing organised so you'll need to be self-sufficient.

BOOKS

Cameroon with Egbert by Dervla Murphy is another outing with the trusted travel writer, here with a recalcitrant horse – the eponymous Egbert – and teenage daughter in tow. Great to get you in the mood for a trip

An Innocent Anthropologist by Nigel Barley speaks of the culture clash that can ensue between an anthropologist and 'his' subjects – here the Dowayo of northern Cameroon. It's very engagingly written.

Gerald Durrell's *A Zoo in My Luggage* and *The Bafut Beagles* are two gloriously told accounts of the naturalist's animal-collecting trips to Cameroon in the 1950s and '60s.

Culture and Customs of Cameroon, by John Mukum Mbaku, is an academic but still highly accessible ethnological guide to Cameroon – a must-read for those wanting to really get under the skin of the country.

BUSINESS HOURS

Government offices are officially open from 7.30am to 3.30pm Monday to Friday. Businesses open from 7.30am to 8.30am until 6pm or 6.30pm Monday to Friday, generally with a one- to two-hour break sometime between noon and 3pm. Most are also open from 8am to 1pm (sometimes later) on Saturday. Banks are open from 7.30am or 8am to 3.30pm Monday to Friday.

CUSTOMS

There are no limits on importing currency or on exporting CFA to other Central African CFA countries (Chad, CAR, Congo, Equatorial Guinea and Gabon). When departing the Central African CFA zone, you are permitted to export a maximum of CFA25,000.

DANGERS & ANNOYANCES

Yaoundé and Douala carry bad reputations for casual street crime. Be particularly wary around bus and train stations and outside banks and expensive hotels. By day you should be fine, but taxis at night are often recommended. The same caution should be applied late at night in N'Gaoundéré and Bafoussam. Avoid carrying valuables on the street.

Some parts of the north and east – most notably the area bordering the Central African Republic – are prone to banditry. Minibuses sometimes travel in convoys to avoid problems, although there's some who complain this is so people can earn an extra 'protection fee'.

Corruption is arguably Cameroon's worst problem. The form most often encountered by travellers is at interminable roadside police checkpoints. Although most attention is focused on locals, always keep your passport (or certified copy – see the boxed text, right) and vaccination certificate *(carte jaune)* handy. Police often seek out the most minor infraction. Travellers with their own vehicles may be asked to show their complete service history and ownership papers. Smile, be patient and polite, and most 'problems' will evaporate without having to put your hand in your pocket.

The most serious problem you are likely to encounter in Cameroon is dangerous driving. Minibus drivers in particular pay little heed to road safety or speed limits, which can make for nervous travelling – see the boxed text, p226 for more information.

EMBASSIES & CONSULATES
Cameroon Embassies & Consulates

In West Africa, Cameroon has embassies in Côte d'Ivoire, Nigeria and Senegal. Check the appropriate country chapter for details.

Embassies & Consulates in Cameroon

The following embassies and consulates are in Yaoundé, except as noted. Australians and New Zealanders should contact the Canadian

---

IDENTIFY YOURSELF

In Cameroon it is a legal requirement to always carry identification, and they're particularly prone to checking your paperwork up north. If you're not happy with always keeping your passport on you – understandable if going out at night in Yaoundé or Douala – it's possible to get an officially certified copy. Photocopy the title and visa pages (with your entry stamp) of your passport, and go to the main police office in any large town during office hours and ask to be 'legalised'. The process is quick and easy, leaving you with a passport copy with enough official stamps to satisfy the surliest checkpoint police. The certification costs CFA1000.

High Commission in an emergency. Opening hours noted are for visa applications.

Canada (Map p181; ☎ 2223 2311; Immeuble Stamatia-des, Place de l'Hôtel de Ville, Centre Ville)

Central African Republic (Map p179; ☎ 2220 5155; 41 Rue 1863, Bastos; ☾ 8am-3pm Mon-Fri)

Chad Garoua (☎ 2227 3128); Yaoundé (Map p179; ☎ 2221 0624; Rue Joseph Mballa Eloumden, Bastos; ☾ 7.30am-noon & 1-3.30pm Mon-Fri)

Congo (Map p179; ☎ 2223 2458; Rue 1815, Bastos; ☾ 8am-noon Mon-Fri)

Equatorial Guinea Douala (☎ 3342 2729; Rue Koloko; ☾ 9am-3pm Mon-Fri); Yaoundé (Map p179; ☎ 2221 0804; Rue 1805, Bastos; ☾ 9am-3pm Mon-Fri)

France Douala (☎ 3342 6250; Ave des Cocotiers, Bonanjo); Yaoundé (Map p179; ☎ 2222 7900; Rue Joseph Atemengué, nr Place de la Réunification)

Gabon (Map p179; ☎ 2220 2966; Rue 1816, Bastos; ☾ 9.30am-3pm Mon-Fri)

Germany (Map p179; ☎ 2221 0056; www.jaunde.diplo .de; Ave Charles de Gaulle, Centre Ville)

Japan (☎ 2220 6202; 1513 Rue 1828, Bastos)

Liberia (Map p179; ☎ 2223 0521, 2221 1296; Blvd de l'URSS, Bastos)

Nigeria Buea (☎ 3332 2528; Nigeria Consulate Rd; ☾ 8am-4pm Mon-Fri); Douala (☎ 3343 2168; Blvd de la Liberté); Yaoundé (Map p179; ☎ 2223 4551; Rue Joseph Mballa Eloumden, Bastos; ☾ 9.30am-3.30pm Mon-Fri). Visas not issued in Douala.

UK Douala (☎ 3342 8896; Immeuble Standard Chartered, Blvd de la Liberté); Yaoundé (Map p179; ☎ 2222 0545; ukincameroon.fco.gov.uk; Ave Churchill, Centre Ville)

USA Douala (☎ 3342 5331; Immeuble Flatters, off Ave de Gaulle, Bonanjo); Yaoundé (Map p181; ☎ 2220 1500; Ave Rosa Parks, Centre Ville)

CAMEROON

FESTIVALS & EVENTS

Tabaski (p816) is the biggest festival celebrated in Cameroon. If you're in the country at the time, head for Foumban, which holds the largest celebration, with a great procession led by the Bamoun sultan (p203). In late January/early February Cameroonian and international athletes gather for the Race of Hope to the summit of Mt Cameroon (p193), attracting crowds of spectators. Finally, it's always worth checking if the national football team is playing when you're in Cameroon – there'll be impromptu festivals in bars across the country if they score the winning goal.

HOLIDAYS

Public holidays include the following:
New Year's Day 1 January
Youth Day 11 February
Easter March/April
Labour Day 1 May
National Day 20 May
Assumption Day 15 August
Christmas Day 25 December

Islamic holidays are also observed throughout Cameroon (see p816).

INTERNET ACCESS

Internet access can be found in any town of a reasonable size. Connections aren't bad for Africa. Costs average CFA300 to CFA600 per hour. Bigger hotels sometimes offer wi-fi.

INTERNET RESOURCES

www.cameroononline.org A Cameroonian news portal website.
www.ecofac.org A Central African conservation organisation, heavily involved with projects in Cameroon.
www.fifa.com/associations/association=cmr/ All things to do with Cameroonian football.
www.panda.org/who_we_are/wwf_offices /cameroon/ World Wildlife Fund in Cameroon
www.postnewsline.com Online version of the *Post* newspaper

MONEY

The unit of currency is the Central African CFA franc, which is pegged to the West African CFA (p171), but not interchangeable. Bring euros, as other currencies can be hard to change, attract poor exchange rates and high commissions. The main banks for changing money are Bicec, SGBC, Crédit Lyonnais and Standard Chartered Bank.

Stock up on CFA when you can, as foreign exchange is difficult in small towns.

Cash is king in Cameroon. Although major banks advertise the fact that they change travellers cheques, in reality this isn't always the case. You'll need to bring the original purchase receipts and be prepared to take around a 5% hit on commission. Even then, there's no guarantee the bank will accept the cheques – most cashiers tend to look with extreme distaste at anything other than euros. A new chain of private money-changers, Express Exchange, is the traveller's saviour, with its readiness to change cheques and US dollars cash.

Most towns now have at least one ATM, always tied to the Visa network – a card is always a better option than travellers cheques. Banks won't generally offer cash advances on credit cards. Western Union have branches throughout Cameroon for international money transfers; the fee is only paid by the sender.

Men with bundles of CFA hang around major hotels willing to change cash quickly. This can be convenient out of business hours, but the usual caveats on changing money on the street apply. Large-denomination notes attract better rates.

POST

Yaoundé and Douala have reliable poste restante at their central post offices, with letters held for about two weeks (CFA200 per each letter collected). International post is reliable for letters, but international couriers should be preferred for packages – there are branches in all large towns.

TELEPHONE

Your best bet is internet phone calls, now generally offered by internet cafes – expect to pay between CFA50 and CFA250 per minute worldwide, although you often won't get much privacy. For calls within Cameroon, the quickest option is a street-side phone stand – usually a lady sitting at a table with a mobile phone. National calls are around CFA100 per minute.

Mobile phones are everywhere in Cameroon, which has two GSM networks – MTN and Orange. Local SIM cards cost from CFA5000, depending on the amount of credit purchased.

VISAS

All visitors to Cameroon require visas. Prices range from around US$60 for a one-month single-entry visa, to around US$110 for a three-month multiple-entry visa. Issuing time varies from 24 hours to a week. Applications made in West Africa are generally straightforward; applications at embassies in Europe and the USA often require a confirmed flight ticket, hotel reservation and proof of funds (copy of a recent bank statement).

Visa Extensions

You can obtain visa extensions at the **Ministry of Immigration** (Map p181; Ave Mdug-Fouda Ada) in Yaoundé, where one photo plus CFA15,000 is required.

Visas for Onward Travel

For contact details of embassies and consulates in Cameroon, see p221. Visas listed below are obtained in Yaoundé unless noted, and costs may vary according to nationality. Please note the following information is extremely subject to change.

CENTRAL AFRICAN REPUBLIC (CAR)

A one-month single-entry visa costs CFA35,000, requires two photos, and is processed within 24 hours.

CHAD

A one-month single-entry visa costs CFA30,000, requires two photos and a passport photocopy. It is issued on the same day (for morning applications). Visas are sometimes also issued at the consulate in Garoua (see p207).

CONGO

One-month single-entry visas for Congo cost CFA70,000, require two photos, and are issued in 24 hours.

DEMOCRATIC REPUBLIC OF CONGO

While they don't share a border, Cameroon is a popular place for overlanders to get DRC visas. A one-month single-entry visa costs CFA45,000, requires three photos and a passport photocopy, and is issued on the same day.

EQUATORIAL GUINEA

One-month single-entry visas cost CFA37,000 for most nationalities, and require two photos and a passport photocopy. Applications are processed in 24 hours, and may also be made at the consulate in Douala.

GABON

A one-month visa for Gabon costs CFA37,000, requires one photo and takes one day to issue.

NIGERIA

A one-month single-entry visa costs CFA52,500 and takes 24 hours to process at the Yaoundé embassy, with two photos, a passport photocopy, proof of funds and letter of invitation from a Nigerian resident or business required (see p663). The consulate in Buea (p190) is a better place to apply, waiving the proof of funds, and issuing the same visa for CFA39,000 in a couple of hours. The Douala consulate only accepts applications from Cameroon residents.

WOMEN TRAVELLERS

Women can expect few problems in the north. In the south you may encounter hissing or comments, but rarely anything threatening. For more information, see p826. Tampons are available in Douala, Yaoundé and occasionally in larger towns.

TRANSPORT IN CAMEROON

GETTING THERE & AWAY
Entering Cameroon

A valid yellow-fever certificate is required for all those entering Cameroon, even if arriving by air from a country where the disease is not endemic.

Air

Douala is Cameroon's air hub, with daily flights to Europe and connections to all neighbouring countries. Intercontinental carriers include Air France, KLM, Kenya Airways, Afriquiyah Air and Swiss International Airlines. There is also an international airport at Yaoundé (with connections several times weekly to Europe), but the following airline offices are all in Douala.

CAMEROON

Afriqiyah Air (8U; ☎ 3343 0363) Hub: Tripoli.
Air France (AF; ☎ 3350 1515; Place du Gouvernement) Hub: Paris.
Brussels Airlines (SN; ☎ 3342 0515; Ave du Galle) Hub: Brussels.
Kenya Airways (KQ; ☎ 3343 9499; off Rue Joss) Hub: Nairobi.
Swiss International Airlines (LX; ☎ 3342 2929; Rue Joss) Hub: Zurich.
Virgin Nigeria (VK; ☎ 3342 7627/8, 3342 7869; Rue Joss) Hub: Lagos.

AFRICA

Websites can be more reliable for booking than phone calls.
Bellview Air (VK; ☎ 3343 2131, 3343 1812; www .flybellviewair.com) Hub: Lagos.
Elysian Airlines (☎ 9909 8748; www.elysianairlines .com) Hub: Yaoundé.
Kenya Airways (KQ; ☎ 3343 9499; off Rue Joss, Douala) Hub: Nairobi.
Toumaï Air Tchad (LX; ☎ 3343 0122; www.toumaiair .com; Bonanjo) Hub: N'Djamena.
Virgin Nigeria (VK; ☎ 3342 7627/8, 3342 7869; www .virginnigeria.com; Rue Joss, Douala) Hub: Lagos.

EUROPE & NORTH AMERICA

Return fares between Cameroon and Europe are around €650 or more. Air France has daily flights between Paris and Douala, and flies several times weekly between Paris and Yaoundé. Afriquiyah Airlines flies several times a week between London and Douala and Yaoundé. Swiss Air has flights twice weekly between Zurich and Douala, and goes weekly to and from Yaoundé. Royal Air Maroc flights connect Douala with many European capitals via Casablanca. All connections to and from North America are via Europe.

Land

With the exception of Nigeria, all of Cameroon's neighbours use the Central African CFA, so when crossing most of these borders you won't need to switch currencies.

CENTRAL AFRICAN REPUBLIC

There are two main crossing points, each guaranteeing bumpy rides on poor roads – fun work in the rainy season. The standard route is via Garoua-Boulaï, which literally straddles the border (p213). It's the best route if you're travelling from north Cameroon. Semi-regular buses and trucks go from Garoua-Boulaï

> **DEPARTURE TAX**
>
> A departure tax of CFA10,000 is charged for all flights leaving Cameroon. Domestic flights incur a departure tax of CFA2500.

to Bangui, taking two days with an overnight in Bouar.

An alternate, and equally rough route is via Batouri further south (p214). Once in Batouri, there's usually one vehicle at dawn to Kenzou. At the border, you'll need to walk across and catch a vehicle on the other side to Berbérati.

CHAD

Minibuses run daily from Maroua to Kousséri, where *moto-taxis* will take you the 10-minute ride to the border at Nguelé, marked by a bridge. Travellers and locals alike can get hit hard here – Chadian immigration usually insist on an arrival or departure 'tax' of around CFA3000, while on the Cameroon side yellow-fever certificates are scrutinised for perceived infractions to attract a 'fine'. From Nguelé, it's a short hop by minibus to N'Djména (CFA300, 15 minutes).

A more obscure crossing is possible into southern Chad, via the towns of Bongor or Léré, and through a combination of taxis brousses and, in the case of Bongor, a pirogue (dugout canoe) across the Logone River – one for the adventurers.

CONGO

The overland route to Congo is strictly for the hardcore – it's a long, rough journey through dense rainforest on rutted dirt tracks, best tackled in the dry season. The nearest town to the border on the Cameroonian side is Yokadouma (p214). From here, take any transport going to Moloundou, and on to the border crossing at Sokambo (near Ouesso) on the Ngoko River. Pirogues carry you across the river into Congo; a ferry carries motorbikes and cars. Expect officials to have their hands out. There is onward transport to Pokola, where you must register with the Congolese police. From Pokola there is a barge (which can carry vehicles) to Brazzaville about three times a month, which takes around one week depending on the height of the river. A logging road from Pokola to Brazzaville has apparently been under construction for years now.

The Congo border has frequently been closed in recent years, so check in advance – it's a long trip back if no one lets you through.

EQUATORIAL GUINEA & GABON

The main border crossings into Equatorial Guinea and Gabon are a few kilometres from each other, and are accessible from the Cameroonian town of Ambam. In Ambam the road splits, the easterly route heading for Bitam and Libreville (Gabon) and the westerly route heading for Ebebiyin and Bata (Equatorial Guinea).

For Gabon, taxis brousses go from Ambam to Aban Minkoo (CFA500 to CFA700, 45 minutes), where a bridge across the Ntem River leads into Gabon. Immigration is at the town of Bitam, a further 30km away (CFA500, 30 minutes). From Bitam, there are regular buses to Libreville. Road quality is good, sealed all the way from Yaoundé to Libreville.

For Equatorial Guinea, taxis brousses go from Ambram to the border at Kye Ossi (CFA1000, one hour). Getting stamped out of Cameroon is no problem, but officials on the other side may hit you for 'un cadeau'. From Kye Ossi, it's a short taxi ride to Ebebiyin (CFA500, 10 minutes), where you can arrange onward transport to Bata (try to cross early to make the connection).

There is also a border crossing into Equatorial Guinea on the coast near Campo, but it's frequently closed. If it is open, *moto-taxis* make the short hop to Campo Beach, from where pirogues quickly cross the Ntem River into Equatorial Guinea. Once across the river and stamped in, there's generally at least one pick-up daily to Bata.

NIGERIA

There are two main border crossings into Nigeria, in the south and north. The busier is at Ekok, 60km west of Mamfe. There's frequent transport in the dry season between Mamfe and Ekok, and pirogues ply the river between the two (see p195). Immigration procedures are relaxed if your papers are in order. Once over the border, catch a shared taxi from the Nigerian border village of Mfum to Ikom (N60, 30 minutes), from where you can arrange transport to Calabar. On the Cameroonian side the road is in poor condition during the dry season and atrocious once the rains hit.

In the north, it's straightforward to travel from Maroua to Maiduguri. Minibuses run daily from Maroua to the border at Banki, with frequent police checkpoints on this road. Banki is a dusty village straddling the border; Cameroonian immigration is opposite the bus stand, and there are plenty of moneychangers. Border formalities are no nonsense. On the Nigerian side, a short N20 *moto-taxi* ride will take you to the bus stand and minibuses or bush taxis continue to Maiduguri (N370 or N500 respectively, 2½ hours).

Sea

EQUATORIAL GUINEA & GABON

There are no organised passenger services by boat to Equatorial Guinea or Gabon, although ad hoc transport can sometimes be arranged to Malabo from Limbe (p190). It might be worth checking at Douala port if there are any ships sailing to Libreville that will accept passengers.

NIGERIA

A twice-weekly ferry sails from Limbe to Calabar on Monday and Thursday, and in the opposite direction every Tuesday and Friday – see (p190). There is an occasional service from Douala, but no timetable – ask at the Douala port. 'Stick boats' – fast speed boats – also run this route, often piloted by smugglers. Although cheaper than ferries, they have poor safety records and what you save on the fare you'll shell out on bribes to Nigerian immigration and navy officials.

GETTING AROUND
Air

Cameroon Airlines shut down in March 2008, and plans to revive as Camair Co remain stalled. The only domestic carrier in service as of research was privately owned **Elysian Airlines** (☎ 9909 8748; www.elysianairlines .com), which flies between Douala, Yaounde, Maroua, Garou and N'Gaoundéré.

Bus

Agency (agences de voyages) buses run along all major and many minor routes in Cameroon. The major exception is across the Adamawa Plateau between Yaoundé and N'Gaoundéré; this crossing is best done by train. On the busier intercity routes vehicles are often large and reasonably comfortable; otherwise expect cramped minivans or

30-seater 'Coastal' buses. See destination sections for agency listings. Each agency has its own office in the towns it serves, and arrivals and departures are from here, rather than the town motor park or *gare routière*. Ask staff at your hotel which agency is best for your destination, and arrive at the office at least one hour before departure for decent seats.

On shorter routes, there are also taxis brousses, which use the main, and invariably chaotic, *gare routière* for departures/arrivals. In many towns, there will be several *gares routières*, so you'll need to find the one for the direction in which you're travelling – they're often named after their main destination. Whenever you get there you'll likely have a wait, although transport is usually best in the early morning.

If you know your way around, shared taxis are cheapest, but generally, and especially if your luggage is unwieldy, it's better to charter a taxi.

Major routes are sealed, including Douala–Yaoundé–Bafoussam–Bamenda, Douala–Limbe, Bafoussam–Foumban, and N'Gaoundéré–Kousséri. Otherwise, much of the country's road network is an unpaved endurance test.

Car & Motorcycle
Some people bring their own vehicle to Cameroon. If you're prepared for the rigours of African roads (see p845), then Cameroon shouldn't bring too many surprises. The main problem is police checkpoints; staff at many of them will be curious to look inside a foreign vehicle. Prepare to show lots of paperwork. There are also frequent toll points usually costing CFA500 – look for officials wearing orange uniforms. During the rainy season, some roads (notably the Ring Road and in the south and east) operate rain gates to prevent large vehicles – which can include many 4WDs – passing.

Taxi
Shared taxis are the main form of local transport within a town – even in a city like Yaoundé there are no local buses. Stand on the roadside in the direction you want to go and shout your destination when a shared taxi passes. If the driver is going your way, he'll toot the horn. The standard fare is a bargain CFA150, more for far-flung destinations or after 10pm.

> **ROAD HAZARDS**
>
> 'Drivers! Your vehicle is a means of freedom, not of death!' warns a sign at one bus station in Cameroon – and with good reason. Road accidents are probably the biggest safety risk you'll meet while travelling in the country. Speeds are high, drivers are often tired from long hours at the wheel, and overtaking on blind corners is a badge of honour.
>
> Avoid night travel and try not to get in vehicles which are loaded so high on top that their balance is off. Reconsider sitting in the front seat next to the driver – not only is this the 'death seat' in the event of a crash, but you'll avoid the frightening temptation to keep glancing at the speedometer to see what speed you're hurtling along at.

While the vast majority of shared-taxi rides are without incident, there have been robberies in Douala and Yaoundé, so it pays to keep your wits about you. If you're female, avoid getting in a vehicle with only men as passengers, especially at night.

To charter a taxi for yourself (taxi course or depo), the base rate for town rides is CFA1000. If there aren't already other passengers in the taxi, make it clear to the driver whether you want a depo, or not. At motor parks (gares routières), most taxis waiting for incoming buses are for hire only.

Motorcycle taxis (moto-taxis or motos) are popular, especially in the north. They charge between CFA100 and CFA150 in town, more at night or anything away from the central area. Hail the driver and tell him your destination. In some areas (eg around Maroua), motos are also used for longer journeys when there is no vehicle transport. This is fun for a few kilometres, but gets uncomfortable soon after. If you've got a rucksack, ask the driver to put it between his handlebars, rather than unbalancing yourself by keeping it on your back.

Train
Cameroon's rail system (Camrail) operates three main lines: Yaoundé to N'Gaoundéré, Yaoundé to Douala, and Douala to Kumba. In practice, only the first is of interest to travellers, as it's the main way to get between the southern and northern halves of the country. The other routes are quicker by road.

Trains go daily in each direction, departing Yaoundé at 6pm, and N'Gaoundéré at 7pm. Arrivals are about 11am the next morning if all goes according to schedule (ha). It's not unknown for the train to jump the rails, which can turn overnight trips into three days. At least you'll see the scenery en route.

For seating, there's a choice of comfortable 1st class couchettes (sleeping compartments) for CFA25,000/28,000 per person in a four-/two-bed cabin; 1st-class airline-style seats (CFA17,000); and crowded 2nd-class benches (CFA10,000). The couchettes are the only recommendable option, in part because you'll be in an enclosed cabin. Seats in 1st and 2nd class are in open wagons, with no way to secure your bag. Even in couchettes, be alert for thieves.

The train has a restaurant car where you can buy surprisingly good meals (dinner CFA2500, breakfast CFA1000). If you're in 1st class, someone will come and take your order and deliver it to your couchette. At every station stop, people offer street food at the windows.

Couchettes can be reserved 24 hours in advance, but are paid for on the day of travel; useful, since if the train is delayed, you'll have some flexibility to change your plans. You'll need to purchase the ticket no later than about 9am on the morning of departure, as thereafter all unpurchased seats are put back up for sale. If you're going north to south, Touristique Express in Maroua and Garoua also sells advance train tickets at its depots.

CAMEROON

Cape Verde

Set sail with the Saharan trade winds and for days on end your good ship will rock and roll across stormy Atlantic seas. Ahead of you the horizon will stretch blue and unbroken and your journey will feel as if it'll never end. But then, just before you're halfway to Brazil, an island rises into view. You have reached Cape Verde, an archipelago that is of Africa, but not a part of it. Instead it's a magical place where the land and its people look and feel like the stunning offspring of Mediterranean, African and Caribbean lovers.

Though they might be but a miniscule dot on the map, these islands pack a punch. On the westerly islands piercing green valleys of flowers are hidden by craggy peaks with pine trees for headdresses. While to the east, wispy white dunes merge with seas of indigo blue on beaches of soft sand that invite you to stay for just another day.

Thanks to its remote location it's perhaps not surprising to learn that Cape Verde is very different to the rest of Africa. It's the most Westernised country in the region and the people are richer, better educated and healthier than almost anywhere else on the continent. Indeed, life here can sometimes feel like life in an American hip-hop video. Everywhere you go muscle-bound men walk with swagger and girls with Caribbean eyes swing their hips to the constant beat of the music for which Cape Verde is famed.

All things considered, this is a place that is so utterly unique and so special that it cannot but leave you enchanted.

CAPE VERDE

FAST FACTS

- **Area** 4035 sq km
- **Capital** Praia
- **Country code** ☎ 238
- **Famous for** Singer Cesária Évora, windsurfing
- **Languages** Portuguese, Crioulo
- **Money** Cabo Verde escudo (CVE); US$1 = CVE85.75, €1 = CVE113
- **Population** 427,000
- **Visa** All non–Cape Verdean citizens require a visa; one-month tourist visas, issued on arrival at airports and ports, are €25 (payable in euros only).

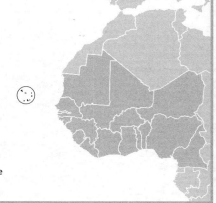

HOW MUCH?

- **Taxi ride in Praia** CVE150
- **São Vicente to Santo Antão ferry** CVE700
- **Espresso coffee** CVE50
- **Guide to climb Mt Fogo** CVE3000
- **Fresh grilled tuna with rice and chips** CVE650

LONELY PLANET INDEX

- **1L of diesel** CVE167
- **1L of bottled water** CVE80
- **Bottle of beer** CVE100
- **Souvenir T-shirt** CVE1000
- **Plate of cachupa (bean and corn stew)** CVE250

HIGHLIGHTS

- **Mardi Gras** (p239) Swinging hips, elaborate costumes and dirty dancing; Mindelo's Mardi Gras celebration is one of the sexiest and most colourful festivals in Africa.
- **Santo Antão** (see the boxed text, p242) Hiking the misty and pine-clad ridges, the sheer canyons and the verdant valleys of Cape Verde's most spectacular island.
- **Mt Fogo** (see the boxed text, p245) Views to admire from the summit of this stunning, cinder-clad mountain, the country's only active volcano and, at 2829m, its highest peak.
- **Windsurfing** (p245 and p247) Riding t giant waves of Sal and Boa Vista – two of the world's finest windsurfing destinations.
- **Traditional music** (p232) Smoky back-room bars, listening to musicians wave loved ones goodbye with a *morna* (mournful old-style song).

ITINERARIES

- **One week** Fly into Sal (p245) and unwind for a couple of days on the beaches at Santa Maria (p246), which is a windsurfer's mecca. Next, head to Mindelo (p239), located on São Vicente, the country's cultural centre and prettiest town, and spend a day hopping from bar to

bar. From Mindelo, an hour-long ferry ride lands you in mountainous Santo Antão (p241), where stunning hikes cap off your trip.

- **Two weeks** From Santo Antão, head over to Fogo (p243) and lace up your hiking boots for a scramble up the perfectly formed volcanic mass of Mt Fogo. Recover from this with a day dozing in the pretty squares of São Filipe (p244), the island's capital, and then another day or two exploring the wine and coffee country on the northern side of the island. Finally, wind down on the fine and largely deserted beaches of Boa Vista (p247)or Maio (p250).
- **Three weeks** With three weeks, you can do all of the above, and have time to take in the scene in Praia (p234), the capital of Cape Verde, after which you can explore the mountains and beaches of Santiago's hinterland (p234).

CLIMATE & WHEN TO GO

Cape Verde is pleasant year-round. Even during the so-called rainy season from mid-August to mid-October, weeks can go by without a downpour. Thanks to cooling ocean currents and offshore winds, Cape Verde has the lowest temperatures of any country in West Africa, and also some of the most moderate, ranging from a minimum night-time average of 19ºC in February to a maximum daytime average of 29°C from May to November.

From December to March you will need a sweater in the evenings and it's a good idea to pack an extra bed sheet, as hotels rarely provide enough bedding to keep you warm. Winter months are marked by strong winds, which blow in dust all the way from the Sahara.

See Climate Charts, p810, for more.

HISTORY
Slavery, Drought & Neglect

When Portuguese mariners discovered Cape Verde in 1456, the islands were uninhabited but fertile enough to attract the first group of settlers six years later. They founded Ribeira Grande (now Cidade Velha), the first European town in the tropics, on the island of Santiago. To work the land, settlers almost immediately began to import slaves from the West African coast. Plans by Genoese investors to create large sugar plantations never paid off, especially after the Caribbean proved so productive. However, the islands'

CAPE VERDE

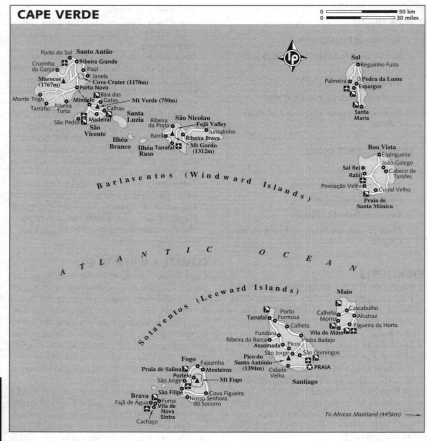

CAPE VERDE

remote yet strategic position made them a perfect clearinghouse and victualling station for the transatlantic slave trade.

Cape Verde's first recorded drought occurred in 1747; from that date they became ever more common and, in the century from 1773, three droughts killed some 100,000 people. This cycle lasted well into the 20th century. At the same time, the island's economic clout fell as Britain, France and the Netherlands challenged Portugal's control over the slave trade. As a result, Lisbon invested little in Cape Verde during the good times and offered almost no help during bad times. To escape hunger, many men left the islands, principally to work as hired hands on American whaling ships. Even today, Cape

Verdean communities along the New England coast rival the population of Cape Verde itself, and foreign remittances account for as much as 20% of GNP.

Cape Verde's fortunes revived with the advent of the ocean liner and they became an important stopover for coal, water and livestock. When the aeroplane replaced the ocean liner, Cape Verde responded in kind, opening an international airport on Sal in 1948 that was designed to service long, transatlantic flights.

Independence

Because much of Cape Verde's population was mixed race, they tended to fare better than fellow Africans in other Portuguese colonies. Beginning in the mid-19th century, a privileged few even received an education, many going on to help administer mainland colonies. By independence, 25% of the population could read (compared with 5% in Guinea-Bissau).

However, to the chagrin of the Portuguese, literate Cape Verdeans were gradually becoming aware of the nationalism simmering on the mainland. Soon, together with leaders of Guinea-Bissau, they had established a joint independence movement. In 1956 Cape Verdean intellectual Amilcar Cabral (born in Guinea-Bissau) founded the Marxist-inspired Partido Africano da Independência da Guinée Cabo Verde (PAIGC), later renamed the Partido Africano da Independência de Cabo Verde (PAICV).

As other European powers were relinquishing their colonies, Portugal's right-wing dictator, António de Salazar, propped up his regime with dreams of colonial greatness. From the early 1960s, one of Africa's longest wars of independence ensued. However, most of the fighting took place in Guinea-Bissau, and indeed many middle-class Cape Verdeans remained lukewarm about independence.

Eventually, Portugal's war became an international scandal and led to a nonviolent end to its dictatorship in 1974, with Cape Verde gaining full independence a year later. Cape Verde and Guinea-Bissau seriously considered uniting the two countries, but a 1980 coup in Guinea-Bissau ended talks.

Cape Verde Since Independence

On gaining power the PAICV created a one-party state but also instituted a remarkably successful health and education program. Unfortunately, independence did not solve the problem of drought, and in 1985 disaster struck again. However, this time the USA and Portugal contributed 85% of the food deficit; their aid continues in a country that produces only about 20% of its food supply.

By the late 1980s there were increasing calls for a multiparty democracy, and in 1990 the PAICV acquiesced, allowing lawyer Carlos Veiga to found the Movimento para a Democracia (MPD). With a centre-right policy of political and economic liberalisation, the MPD swept to power in the 1991 elections. Privatisation and foreign investment – especially in tourism – brought only slow results, however, and in 2001 the PAICV reclaimed power and Pedro Pires became president.

Cape Verde Today

The 2006 elections were again won by the PAICV and Pedro Pires remains the president. In general things are looking up for Cape Verde; it's the most prosperous West African nation, with the best-educated population. The country has Special Partnership status with the EU and there has even been talk of its applying for full EU membership.

Tourism is the fastest-growing industry and huge tourist-resort construction projects are underway on Sal and Boa Vista. Sal now even has a professional-standard golf course, which, while it's true may encourage richer tourists to visit and therefore boost the local economy, is also a massive drain on the already very scant water supplies. In fact with the average golf course using as much water as a town of 18,000, this one development uses more water than many islands! How tourism, and the country's tourist-generated income, is affected by the worldwide economic situation and tourism downturn is likely to be one of the big talking points in Cape Verde over the next couple of years.

THE CULTURE
The National Psyche

If you arrive from mainland Africa, the lack of hustle among Cape Verdeans will likely come as a welcome relief. While they are gregarious, you may catch a whiff of a certain distance, even clannishness – partly a result of the islands' isolation (from the mainland as well as from each other) and perhaps partly because of a history of Sicilian-style vendettas among Portuguese landlords. However, patience and a well-timed smile can smooth most paths.

The European legacy is more marked here than in most parts of Portuguese-speaking Africa, yet Cape Verdeans will tell you their Crioulo culture is, at its core, African, citing especially their food and music. More recently, the huge expatriate community in the USA has also had its effect on attitudes, including a growing evangelical community and a general infatuation with the US.

Daily Life

Except for a small class of business owners and professionals who live like their Western counterparts, life in Cape Verde is not easy.

CAPE VERDE

RESPONSIBLE TOURISM IN CAPE VERDE

Cape Verde isn't a destination overrun with ecofriendly tourist practises but a little thought can go a long way to getting the ball running. Follow our guide here and holiday guilt-free.

■ Save water as much as you can – shower together (and you'll have more fun doing it!) and when using the toilet remember the mantra 'if it's brown flush it down, if it's yellow let it mellow'.

■ Avoid Sal's new golf course complex – think how much water that needs to stay green.

■ Try to support local businesses rather than international chains.

■ Avoid eating too much fish – especially tuna, shark and the like. Cape Verde's seas might be full now but they won't be for long if we all munch on seafood.

■ Don't hike off path in Santo Antão – you might damage fragile plantlife.

Terraced farms require enormous effort and arid weather keeps yields small. While the infrastructure, from roads to water, is rapidly modernising, you regularly see women toting water from common wells. A high percentage of households consists of single mothers with children, a legacy of male-only emigration patterns that dates to the 18th century.

Cape Verde boasts by far the highest GDP per capita (US$4200) in West Africa. The country's literacy rate of 76% is also the highest in the region. Virtually all children of primary-school age attend school, though attendance at secondary schools is considerably lower.

Population

Based on the UN's quality-of-life index, Cape Verde comes out on top in West Africa. From 1975 to 2008, life expectancy leapt from 46 years to 71 years, far higher than the sub-Saharan African average. The country also has one of the lowest population-growth rates in the region. It's the only country in West Africa with a population of primarily mixed European and African descent. About 40% of the population lives on Santiago – mainly around the capital, Praia. The rest of the people live largely in small towns, most of which are clustered in the agriculturally productive valleys. As tourism grows, so do the once-tiny populations of arid Sal, Boa Vista and Maio, all of which have seen an influx of foreign residents.

RELIGION

The vast majority of Cape Verdeans are Roman Catholic. Evangelical Protestantism is making inroads, accounting for some 10% of the population. Traces of African animism remain in the beliefs of even devout Christians.

ARTS
Craftwork

Traditional crafts include weaving, ceramics, baskets, mat making and batik. Be aware that most craft shops sell objects from the African mainland rather than Cape Verde itself.

Literature

While Cape Verde has the smallest population of any country in West Africa, its literary tradition is one of the richest. However, little of that has been translated into anything but Portuguese. Prior to independence, a major theme in Cape Verdean writing was the longing for liberation. Poet, musician and national hero Eugénio Tavares (1867–1930) composed lyrical *mornas* in Crioulo rather than Portuguese. In 1936, a small clique of intellectuals founded a literary journal, *Claridade,* whose goal was to express a growing sense of Cape Verdean identity. Themes of contemporary literature, best expressed by poet Jorge Barbosa's *Arquipélago,* remain constant: *sodade* (longing and/or homesickness), mysteries of the sea and an attempt to come to terms with a history of oppression.

Music

Much of Cape Verdean music evolved as a form of protest against slavery and other types of oppression. Today, two kinds of song dominate traditional Cape Verdean music: *mornas* and *coladeiras,* both built on the sounds of stringed instruments like the fiddle and guitar.

As the name suggests, *mornas* are mournful expressions of *sodade* – an unquenchable

---

CESÁRIA ÉVORA

Undisputed queen of the *morna* and Cape Verde's most famous citizen, Cesária Évora continues to wow the world with a voice that is at once densely textured and disarmingly direct. She began to gain an international audience in the mid-1990s but vaulted to stardom in 1997 when, at the second annual all-African music awards, she ran away with three of the top gongs, including best female vocalist. Suddenly people around the world were swaying to the rhythms of Cape Verde's music, even if they couldn't point the country out on a map. Évora has left her native Mindelo in favour of Paris, but the 'barefoot diva' refuses to put on airs, and has been known to appear onstage accompanied by a bottle of booze and a pack of ciggies.

---

longing, often for home. With faster, more upbeat rhythms, *coladeiras,* in contrast, tend to be romantic love songs or else more active expressions of protest. Cesária Évora (see the boxed text, above) is hands-down the most famous practitioner of both these forms. The ensemble group Simentera is the self-appointed guardian of traditional music, though it works to make it appealing to contemporary ears.

A newer style of music called *funaná* is built on fast-paced, Latin-influenced rhythms and underpinned by the accordion. Current practitioners include Ildo Lobo, Exitos de Oro and Ferro Gaita.

ENVIRONMENT
The Land
Cape Verde consists of 10 major islands (nine of them inhabited) and five islets, all of volcanic origin. Though none is more than about 50km from its closest neighbour, they represent a wide array of climates and landscapes. All are arid or semiarid, but the mountainous islands of Brava, Santiago, Fogo, Santo Antão and São Nicolau – all with peaks over 1000m – catch enough moisture to support grasslands as well as fairly intensive agriculture, particularly in windward-facing valleys. Still, only 20% of the land is arable. Maio, Boa Vista and Sal are flatter and almost entirely arid, with long, sandy beaches and desertlike interiors.

Wildlife
Cape Verde has less fauna than just about anywhere in Africa. Birdlife is a little richer (around 75 species), and includes a good number of endemics (38 species). The frigate bird and the extremely rare razo lark are much sought after by twitchers. The grey-headed kingfisher with its strident call is more common, though.

Divers can see a good range of fish, including tropical species such as parrotfish and angelfish, groupers, barracudas, moray eels, and, with luck, manta rays, sharks (including the nurse, tiger and lemon) and marine turtles. Five species of turtle visit the islands on their way across the Atlantic. Nesting takes place throughout the year, but in particular from May to October.

Environmental Issues
The greatest threats to the environment remain cyclical drought and soil erosion, exacerbated by deforestation and overgrazing – mostly by goats. To combat these problems, the country has constructed more than 15,000 contour ditches and 2500km of dams, and since the 1970s has been implementing a major reforestation program. On some islands, notably Santo Antão, Maio, Santiago and parts of Fogo the tree cover has noticeably increased over the past couple of decades, but on islands like Sal a tree remains as rare as a rainy day.

FOOD & DRINK
While Cape Verdean cuisine may include Portuguese niceties such as imported olives and Alentejo wines, it's built on a firm African base, with *milho* (corn) and *feijão* (beans) the ubiquitous staples. To these the locals add relative luxuries such as *arroz* (rice), *batatas fritas* (fried potatoes) and *mandioca* (cassava). From the sea come excellent *atum* (tuna), *garoupa* (grouper), *serra* (sawfish) and, most famously, *lagosta* (lobster). Other protein sources include *ovos* (eggs), *frango* (chicken) and, with increasing rarity, *cabrito* (goat), *porco* (grilled pork) and *carne de vaca* (beef). Vegetables – often *cenoura* (carrots), *couve* (kale) and *abóbora* (squash) – come in *caldeirada* (meat or fish stews), or simply steamed.

CAPE VERDE

Meals tend to be very simple wherever you go: a piece of grilled or fried meat or fish, accompanied by rice or *xerém* (corn meal) and your choice of steamed vegetables or French fries. Practically nowhere will you pay less than CVE500, yet even the fanciest place will rarely charge more than CVE800 (except for beef and shellfish, which cost significantly more). The classic dish is the ubiquitous *cachupa,* which consists of beans and corn mixed with whatever scraps of fish or meat that might be around. In the evening, it's served as *cachupa fresca* (stew), while in the morning it's often sautéed and typically served with a fried egg and sausage as *cachupa guisada.* For those with a sweet tooth there are concoctions of *cóco* (coconut), *papaia* (papaya) and banana, as well as flanlike *pudim* of either *leite* (milk) or *queijo* (soft goat cheese).

Thanks to the large number of Italian tourists and expats, some reasonable pizza and pasta dishes are starting to appear on even the most out-of-the-way menus.

For drinks, there's *grogue,* the local sugarcane spirit; *ponch* (rum, lemonade and honey); some reasonable wines from Fogo (the white and rosé are the best), Strela, a decent bottled local beer; and, of course, Portuguese beers and wines. A decent caffeine fix is available everywhere (coffee even grows on the slopes of Mt Fogo), but tea is much harder to find.

SANTIAGO

Santiago, the largest member of the archipelago and the first to be settled, is a little bit of all the other islands. It has the sandy beaches, the desert plains, the verdant valleys and the mountainous interior as well as the capital, Praia. All this makes it an essential stop on your Cape Verdean rambles.

Getting There & Away

AIR
Praia's airport is, together with Sal's, the main air hub for the islands. There are daily flights to Boa Vista, two daily to Fogo, three weekly to Maio and up to 10 flights daily to Mindelo and Sal. For more information, see p252.

BOAT
STM (☎ 2612564; Av Unidade Guiné-Cabo Verde, Praia) heads to Fogo (Monday and Friday;

CVE2000), Boa Vista (Wednesday; CVE2500), and Mindelo via São Nicolau (Tuesday and Friday; CVE4500). **Agência Nacional de Viagens** (☎ 2603101; Rua Serpa Pinto, Praia) offers irregular boats to Boa Vista (normally Tuesday or Wednesday; CVE2200) and onward to Sal. As these are cargo ships rather than proper ferries the actual departure times depend more on loading and off-loading times. The companies also have occasional boats to Fogo, Maio and São Vicente. For more ferry information, see p253.

Getting Around

CAR
Inter Cidades (☎ 2612525; www.intercidadesrentacar.cv; Achada de Santo António, Praia), near the Portuguese embassy, has reasonable cars at good prices. **Delcar** (☎ 2623717; www.delcar.cv; Achada de Santo António, Praia) has a similar service. There are also various car-rental offices at the airport.

MINIBUS
Private *aluguer* (for hire) minibuses to most towns leave from Sucupira Market, on the northwestern side of Platô, Praia's town centre. See individual towns for more.

PRAIA
pop 78,000

Cape Verde's capital and largest city, Praia, has the sprawling suburbs of any developing city, but in the centre, standing on a large fortresslike plateau (hence the name Platô) and overlooking the ocean, is an attractive old quarter with enough to keep you happily occupied for a day or two.

History

Praia became the Portuguese military and administrative headquarters in the 18th century after Cidade Velha, the island's first settlement, proved vulnerable to pirates. The city has undergone considerable growth since independence, with an infrastructure that has not always kept pace.

Orientation

Around Platô, the town tumbles onto the land below: to the east are Achada Grande and the port, and to the southwest is the more affluent, residential area of Achada de Santo António, where the parliament building and some embassies are also found. Due

CAPE VERDE

south of Platô is the beachfront area known as Prainha.

Information

There are ATMs throughout the city, especially around Praça Alexandre Albuquérque; the main post office is situated three blocks east of this square. There's no official tourist office as such; you're best off talking to a private travel agency. Internet cafes are surprisingly scarce.

Bocas Café (Achada de Santo António; per hr CVE100; 9am-10pm Mon-Fri, to 9pm Sat & Sun) Excellent connection speeds, supercheap international phone calls and a cafe to boot – what more could you ask for?

Cabetur (☎ 2615551; Rua Serpa Pinto) Travel agency.

Hospital (☎ 2601010; Av Mártires de Pidjiguiti) Located in Platô, east of Praça 11 Maio.

Praiatur (☎ 2615746; Av Amilcar Cabral) Travel agency.

Sofia Café (Praça 11 Maio; per hr CVE100) The only real internet café in Platô and with only four computers at that. At least you can get a drink while you wait.

Sights & Activities

Praia may lack the visual punch of Mindelo, but the old Platô quarter contains enough life and colour to entertain for a few hours. During your ambles around these multihued streets, be sure to spend some time ferreting around the small food **market** before heading over the road to the **Palácio da Cultura Ildo Lobo** (☎ 2619375; Praça Alexandre Albuquérque; 9am-6pm) with its ever-changing collection of contemporary Cape Verdean art. Praia provides a home to a worthwhile museum, **Museu Etnográfico de Praia** (☎ 2618421; Av 5 de Julho; admission CVE100; 9.30am-12pm & 2.30-6pm), which has a small collection of traditional Cape Verdean artefacts and a few treasures hauled up from the many ships that have glugged to the bottom of the surrounding ocean.

Sleeping

Accommodation in Praia is expensive – expect to pay 30% more here than for similar digs in the rest of the country. Breakfast is included in all the following prices unless otherwise stated.

Residencial Sol Atlántico (☎ 2612872; Praça Alexandre Albuquérque; with/without bathroom s CVE2000/1500, d CVE3000/2500;) This longstanding hotel above a travel agency has nicely old-fashioned rooms with starched white sheets, equally white walls and contrasting black furniture. The bathrooms can be a bit pongy.

Aparthotel Holanda (☎ 2623973; www.hotelholanda.com; Rua Saúde; with/without bathroom s CVE2700/1700, d CVE3500/2500;) What's orange, hollow on the inside and a magnet for travellers? The answer, of course, is the Aparthotel Holanda. This excellent choice, consisting of supremely clean rooms built around an inner courtyard, has rooms with desks, fans and, in some cases, little balconies overlooking the streets of this lively, and slightly slummy, area. The numerous sculptures and knickknacks add a little something. All up, it offers the best value in its class. Breakfast is extra.

Residencial Paraiso (☎ 2613539; Rua Serpa Pinto; s/d CVE2300/3500) At the leafy northern end of Platô, this large, well-run guesthouse has blindingly white rooms (though some of the bedsheets have dubious stains), piping-hot water and a decent breakfast.

Residencial Santa Maria (☎ 2614337; res.praia maria@cvtelecom.cv; Rua Serpa Pinto; s/d from CVE4770/5936;) The positioning of this sky blue hotel, right in the heart of all the action, couldn't be topped. The rooms, while not memorably good, aren't memorably bad either and make for a decent Praia base.

Hotel Praia Mar (☎ 2614153; praiamar@cvtelecom .cv; Rua do Mar; s/d from €102/128; P) On a breezy bluff pointing out to sea is Praia's glossiest address. The large rooms are comfortable, though no different to a thousand other business-class hotels anywhere else in the world.

Eating

The food scene in Praia is surprisingly limited. For a cheap quickie, try the kiosks on Praça Alexandre Albuquérque, which sell toasted sandwiches and hamburgers for CVE150 to CVE250.

Pão Quente de Cabo Verde (Platô) For the best pastries in town, don't mess around anywhere else. This laughably busy, Portuguese-run place is in a league of its own. You can eat in or take your delicately wrapped treat away with you.

Snack Bar Daniza (off Rua da Assembleia Nacional; mains from CVE200) This cute little side-street cafe has a great *cachupa guisada,* the classic Cape Verdean dish of sautéed maize with eggs and sausage, for CVE200.

Snack Bar Tama (chicken & chips CVE360) A real neighbourhood hang-out, Tama has a limited menu (chicken and chips or chips and chicken

CAPE VERDE

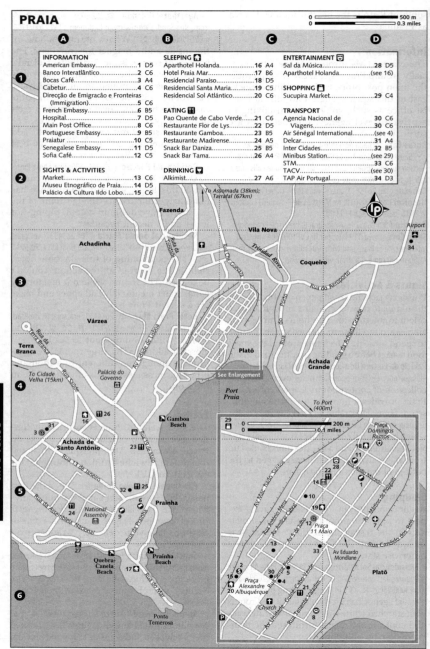

PRAIA

0   500 m
0   0.3 miles

INFORMATION
American Embassy.....................1 D5
Banco Interatlântico..................2 C6
Bocas Café................................3 A4
Cabetur.....................................4 C6
Direcção de Emigracão e Fronteiras
   (Immigration)......................5 C6
French Embassy........................6 B5
Hospital....................................7 D5
Main Post Office.......................8 C6
Portuguese Embassy..................9 B5
Praiatur...................................10 C5
Senegalese Embassy................11 D5
Sofia Café...............................12 C5

SIGHTS & ACTIVITIES
Market....................................13 C6
Museu Etnográfico de Praia....14 D5
Palácio da Cultura Ildo Lobo...15 C6

SLEEPING 🛏
Aparthotel Holanda.................16 A4
Hotel Praia Mar.......................17 B6
Residencial Paraiso..................18 D5
Residencial Santa Maria...........19 C5
Residencial Sol Atlántico..........20 C6

EATING 🍴
Pao Quente de Cabo Verde......21 C6
Restaurante Flor de Lys...........22 D5
Restaurante Gamboa...............23 B5
Restaurante Madirense.............24 A5
Snack Bar Daniza.....................25 B5
Snack Bar Tama.......................26 A4

DRINKING 🍷
Alkimist...................................27 A6

ENTERTAINMENT 🎭
5al da Música..........................28 D5
Aparthotel Holanda...............(see 16)

SHOPPING 🛍
Sucupira Market......................29 C4

TRANSPORT
Agencia Nacional de   **30** C6
  Viagens.................................30 C6
Air Sénégal International..........(see 4)
Delcar.....................................31 A4
Inter Cidades..........................32 B5
Minibus Station.....................(see 29)
STM..33 C6
TACV....................................(see 30)
TAP Air Portugal....................34 D3

To Assomada (38km);
Tarrafal (67km)

Fazenda

Vila Nova

Achadinha

Trinidad River

Coqueiro

Rua do Aeroporto

Airport

Várzea

Terra
Branca

To Cidade
Velha (15km)

Palácio do
Governo

Platô

See Enlargement

Achada
Grande

Port
Praia

To Port
(400m)

Gamboa
Beach

Achada de
Santo António

Prainha

National
Assembly

Praça
Domingos
Ramos

Rua Candido dos Reis

Quebra-
Canela
Beach

Prainha
Beach

Praça
11 Maio

Av Eduardo
Mondlane

Platô

Praça
Alexandre
Albuquérque

Church

Ponta
Temerosa

is about the limit), but it's all freshly made and bargain priced.

Restaurante Flor de Lys (Av 5 de Julho; mains from CVE600) The cheap and tasty dishes in this backroom restaurant include excellent grilled sardines. There's also a good range of pastries and a busy little bar. It's one of the few places in Platô for an evening meal.

Restaurante Gamboa (☎ 2612826; Rua 19 de Maio; mains from CVE800; ◷ noon-3pm & 7-11pm) Excellent service (a rarity in Praia) and the freshest, best ingredients make this the city's top choice.

Restaurante Madirense (☎ 2625005; Achada de Santo António; mains from CVE800) Run by the chatty Joaquim, this slightly formal place brings the tastes of one Atlantic rock to another.

Drinking

There are innumerable little bars with blaring TVs, upbeat music and lots of characters. Dive straight on in – the welcome is always warm and the beer cold.

Alkimist (Rua da Prainha) Just up from Quebra-Canela beach, Alkimist is a low-key but popular hang-out.

Entertainment

5al da Música (Quintal da Música; ☎ 2617282; Av Amílcar Cabral) For the best local music, head here most nights for live acts from around 8.30pm. There's also an overpriced restaurant.

Aparthotel Holanda (Rua Saúde; ◷ evenings Tue-Sun) The food at the restaurant attached to this hotel might not be up to scratch, but the fact that it attracts numerous up-and-coming local musicians for an evening jam makes it well worth stopping by.

Getting Around

TO/FROM THE AIRPORT

A taxi from the airport to Platô (5km) costs around CVE700 to CVE800. There's no regular bus service.

BUS

Small Transcor buses connect Platô with all sections of the city; short journeys cost from CVE70. Destinations are marked on the windshields.

TAXI

Taxis are plentiful and inexpensive – you can go from Platô to Achado de Santo António, for example, for about CVE200.

CIDADE VELHA

Dramatically situated on the sea, 15km from Praia, Cidade Velha (literally 'Old City') is on the tentative list for Unesco World Heritage status as the first European settlement in the tropics. Founded in 1462, the city became wealthy as a station for the transatlantic slave trade. Raids by pirates – including a particularly destructive visit from Sir Francis Drake in 1585 – eventually forced the Portuguese to move shop to Praia.

Remains from its heyday include the ruins of the **cathedral**, constructed in 1693, and the **pillory** on the old town square where enslaved captives were chained up and displayed. Perhaps more impressive is the town's position between the sea and the mouth of a canyon that, thanks to irrigation, remains green even in the driest months. For sweeping views, take the trail up to the dramatic, cliffside fort, **Fortaleza Real de São Filipe**.

Buses from Praia (CVE80, 20 minutes) leave from Sucupira Market. However, service is not regular, and the return trip can involve a long wait. Taxis charge about CVE3500 for a return trip, including an hour or two to visit the sites.

ASSOMADA

Heading inland from Praia, the desertlike plains gradually give way to the mountainous interior, home to fertile valleys and the sharp, volcanic peaks of the Serra do Pico de Santo António. The town of Assomada, though not particularly beautiful, occupies a narrow plain with fine views onto Pico de Santo António (1394m), making it a good base to hike through the surrounding mountains.

Picos, the town just south of Assomada, is home to the peaceful **Jardim Botanico Nacional** botanical gardens, situated about 2.3km off the main road.

Belying its initial dreary impression, **Asa Branca** (☎ 2652372; chinamsky@hotmail.com; r CVE2500) has clean, airy rooms and a downstairs restaurant that serves the usual fare (mains from CVE700). The **Hotel Avenida** (☎ 2653462; s/d CVE3000/3600) is a smart but sterile choice. Most of the rooms have balconies, some with mountain views.

In Praia, minibuses for Assomada (CVE250) leave from Sucupira Market starting at around 9.30am. For buses heading back to Praia, wave down a minibus on the main

CAPE VERDE

highway. Note that return service is most frequent before 8.30am.

TARRAFAL

With a small but fine white-sand beach and cooling breezes, Tarrafal is a favourite getaway from Praia, some 70km to the southeast. The town itself has a pleasant, hibiscus-lined main square, whose southern side serves as an open market. The beach is short but lovely and the surrounding area offers plenty of attractions. For watersports, including boat and snorkel rental, head to the French-run Pizzeria Alto Mira.

About 2km before the town centre is the former **prison**, where Portuguese authorities used to hold and interrogate political prisoners during the 1940s. It's now a **museum** (admission CVE100; ☼ 9am-6pm) and, although not well maintained, it remains a haunting reminder of colonial abuses.

Of much more interest is the newly formed **Parque Natural Serra Malagueta**, which covers the dramatic, tumbling ridges 15 minutes' drive back along the road to Praia. There are a number of spectacular and fairly well-signposted walking trails that weave up and down valleys and through little hamlets, and they might just provide a chance encounter with one of Santiago's elusive monkeys.

Sleeping & Eating

All the following rates include breakfast.

Hotel Sol Marina (☎ 2661219; s from CVE1800, d from CVE2300) Rooms are basic, but the beds are artfully made-up and the slat windows keep things cool. The downside is the cold showers, though as the water supply is fairly erratic that might not matter.

Baía Verde (☎ 2661128; r from CVE3800; 🖳) Simple but attractive bungalows, each with a hot-water bathroom and bunches of flowers (how romantic – oh, they're plastic!), are clustered under a grove of palms just back from the main beach. Best value in town.

Hotel Tarrafal (☎ 2661785; htltarrafal@cvtelecom.com; s/d CVE4000/4700; 🏊 🖳) Tarrafal's smartest option isn't actually all that smart. Rooms could do with a lick of paint and the pool isn't too inviting; otherwise, it's comfortable enough.

Pizzeria Alto Mira (mains from CVE500; ☼ 6.30-11pm) Among the town's limited dining options, Alto Mira serves up very tasty wood-fired pizzas as well as a few fish dishes. The Mediterranean courtyard setting is pleasant.

Hotel Baía Verde (mains from CVE800) This seems to be *the* place to go for lunch at the weekend. However, prices are high.

Getting There & Away

Minibuses from Praia (CVE500, around two hours) depart from Sucupira Market; service is most frequent from about 10am to noon – otherwise, waits can be long. From Tarrafal, minibuses leave from the western end of the central park.

SÃO VICENTE

Small, stark and undulating, São Vicente on its own would be fairly forgettable were it not for the beautiful Mediterranean town of Mindelo, Cape Verde's prettiest city and home to one of Africa's most raucous festivals. If you do need a break from the city, then Mt Verde (750m), the island's highest peak and only touch of green, is an easy day's hike. There are also some windy but fine beaches at Baia das Gatas and Calhau.

Getting There & Away

AIR

TACV (☎ 2321524; Mindelo) has six to 10 flights daily to and from Praia and two to three flights daily to Sal. Taxis to and from the airport cost CVE800.

BOAT

Ferries connect Mindelo with most islands, including daily boats to neighbouring Santo Antão. **STM** (Av 5 de Julho, Mindelo) also offers regular, twice-weekly boats to/from Praia via São Nicolau. For service to other islands, check at the ferry port, a short walk from downtown. See also p253.

Getting Around

The most convenient way around the island is by taxi from Mindelo, including trips to Monte Verde (CVE1500 return) and Calhau (CVE1200 each way). Alternatively, there are *aluguers* to Baia das Gatas that leave from the roundabout at the eastern end of Av 12 Septembro, Mindelo, and to Calhau that leave from near the Praça Estrela, Mindelo. Both cost around CVE250. Note that service is irregular and can involve long waits.

MINDELO
pop 50,000

Set around a moon-shaped port and ringed by barren mountains, Mindelo is Cape Verde's answer to the riviera, complete with cobblestone streets, candy-coloured colonial buildings and yachts bobbing in a peaceful harbour. Safely around a bend is the country's deepest industrial port, which in the late 19th century was a key coaling station for British ships and remains the source of the city's relative prosperity.

Mindelo has long been the country's cultural centre, producing more than its share of poets and musicians, and it's still a fine place to hear *morna* while downing something strong. Savvy locals, plus a steady flow of travellers, support a number of sophisticated bistros and watering holes.

Information

The phone and post offices are both very close to Praça Amilcar Cabral. There's a small tourist-information kiosk near the harbour, just off Av Marginal.

Banco Comercial do Atlântico (Rua da Libertad d'África) Has an ATM.

Caixa Económica (Av 5 de Julho) Has an ATM.

GlobalNet (Rua de Tejo; per hr CVE100; ☺ 8am-midnight)

Sights & Activities

Mindelo is a city to savour, taste and experience rather than a clinical list of 'sights' – an afternoon spent sitting in a sunny cafe is an afternoon well spent. The colonial heart of the city is centred on Rua da Libertad d'África, which runs from the harbour to the **Palácio de Presidente**, a pink colonial confection that now serves as the island's governing council.

Nearby is the recently restored **mercado municipal**, a great place to see the produce that Cape Verdeans manage to bring forth from seemingly barren lands. At the harbour is the **Centro Cultural do Mindelo** (☎ 2325840; admission free), which houses changing exhibitions of local arts and culture, a cafe, a craft shop, and a good book and music store. Jutting out into the harbour is the fortresslike **Torre de Belem** – a kitschy, Disney World version of the 15th-century tower that guards Lisbon's port. Just past the tower is the city's photogenic **fish market**. Heading about 1km north via the coastal road, you'll reach **Prainha Laginha**, the very pleasant town beach. It may be ringed by industrial-looking silos, but its waters are clean and crystal clear.

Festivals & Events

In February and March, Mindelo puts on the sexiest **Mardi Gras** (see below) this side of Río. Every August, the **Festival de Música** attracts musicians of all styles from around the islands and way beyond. Held at the Baía das Gatas, it's a three-day extravaganza of singing, dancing and partying. For more, see www.mindelo .info/gal_baia.php. At both these times finding accommodation or even an aeroplane seat is virtually impossible.

Sleeping

Residencial Atlântida (☎ 2313918; off Rua Santo António; s/d CVE1000/1400) You can't get any more basic (or cheaper) than these dosshouse rooms, but they are at least kept clean – which is more than you will be because there are no showers.

Pensão Chez Loutcha (☎ 2321636; Rua de Coco; s/d from CVE2400/3000; ☺) With a good restaurant and attractive, well-appointed rooms, this

CAPE VERDE

MINDELO'S MARDI GRAS

There's nothing like Mindelo's Mardi Gras (usually in February) anywhere else in Africa. Taking the best African beats and mixing it up with a healthy dose of Latin style and Brazilian sex appeal, the result is one sultry, raunchy party you'll never forget. Preparations begin several months in advance and on Sunday you can see the various groups practising for the procession. The saucy costumes, however, are worn only on Mardi Gras Tuesday. The weekend just prior to this sees a number of lesser processions and street parties, while on the Monday afternoon the whole city goes crazy as a huge street party takes place and people dress up in 'lesser costumes'. The Tuesday itself is a much more organised affair and after the procession has wound around the city a couple of times everyone seems to magically disappear. If you want to be a part of it, plan accordingly, as all flights and accommodation are booked up way in advance. If you can't make it to Mindelo then São Nicolau and Fogo put on a pretty good show as well.

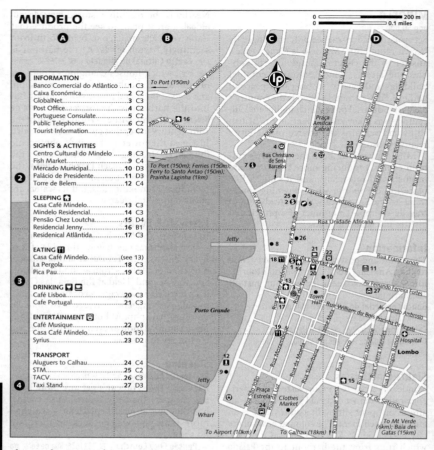

MINDELO

0 — 200 m
0 — 0.1 miles

INFORMATION
Banco Comercial do Atlântico 1 C3
Caixa Económica...........................2 C2
GlobalNet.....................................3 C3
Post Office...................................4 C2
Portuguese Consulate...................5 C2
Public Telephones........................6 C2
Tourist Information.......................7 C2

SIGHTS & ACTIVITIES
Centro Cultural do Mindelo 8 C3
Fish Market..................................9 C4
Mercado Municipal.....................10 D3
Palácio de Presidente.................11 D3
Torre de Belem...........................12 C4

SLEEPING
Casa Café Mindelo.....................13 C3
Mindelo Residencial...................14 C3
Pensão Chez Loutcha..................15 D4
Residencial Jenny.......................16 B1
Residencial Atlântida..................17 C3

EATING
Casa Café Mindelo...............(see 13)
La Pergola..................................18 C3
Pica Pau....................................19 C3

DRINKING
Café Lisboa................................20 C3
Cafe Portugal.............................21 C3

ENTERTAINMENT
Café Musique.............................22 D3
Casa Café Mindelo...............(see 13)
Syrius..23 D2

TRANSPORT
Aluguers to Calhau....................24 C4
STM...25 C2
TACV...26 C3
Taxi Stand.................................27 D3

CAPE VERDE

place makes a great base camp in Mindelo, but take a look at a couple of rooms as some are a bit cramped.

Residencial Jenny (☎ 2328969; Alto São Nicolau; s/d from CVE3600/4300; ✷ ☐) Set on a hill above the ferry dock, this modern hotel is comfortable, if characterless, but some rooms do offer fine views of the harbour.

ourpick Casa Café Mindelo (☎ 2318731; www.casa cafemindelo.com; Rua Governador Calheiros; s/d €40/60) One of the most exciting hotels in Cape Verde, the French-run Casa has just four rooms in a magnificently restored seafront building. The supercool rooms might be simple (common bathrooms), but they ooze big-city chic, with an arty African twist thrown in for good measure. Book ahead.

Mindelo Residencial (☎ 2300863; m.residencial@ gmail.com; off rua da Libertad d'Africa; s/d from CVE4770/6360; ✷ ☐) A flash new hotel in the centre with rooms piled around a sunny, glass-roofed courtyard. There are lots of African prints, but unfortunately the decor and imagination didn't extend to the rooms, which are a bit boring.

Eating

ourpick La Pergola (Alliance Française, Rua Santo António; mains from CVE450-600; ☺ 8am-7pm Mon-Fri, to 1pm Sat) At this excellent restaurant, set inside the sunny courtyard of the Alliance Française, meals are hearty and, typically for the French, very tasty. And it's all yours for laughably low prices.

MR GONCALVES

Carrying an oversized tool box with enough electrical testing and repair equipment to rewire the average palace, Mr Goncalves is a proud but worried man. Proud because this is his little baby, and worried because if it goes wrong months of hard work could go down the drain. Mr Goncalves is the architect behind one of the outlandish floats that Mindelo's Carnival is so renowned for and today is the big day. I asked him a little about the processes of building one of these floats.

'Our work begins almost as soon as the Carnival is over. We begin to think of ideas for next year and try out a few designs. Then we must raise sponsorship as most of these floats are sponsored by a local business and that takes time. This year was harder than normal because there is less money around. We don't start to actually construct the float until about six months before Carnival, but we only really do it at weekends as we must all work. We have to do it in secret as we don't want anyone else knowing what we are planning, because they give prizes for the best entries.'

Has he won this year?

'Ah, that we don't find out until much later today or tomorrow. Maybe!'

Casa Café Mindelo (Rua Santo António; mains from CVE700; ☯ 8am-midnight) Like father, like son: this superb waterfront restaurant and bar, below the equally good hotel, is Mindelo's favourite hang-out. It's the kind of understated, stylish place that wouldn't look out of place in Paris or London. The meals, which focus on the fruits of the sea, are excellent.

Pica Pau (Rua Santo António; mains from CVE800; ☯ 6-11pm) You know you must be doing something right when your customers start scrawling devoted messages of appreciation all over the walls. Specialising in seafood, this intimate little restaurant is the kind of place where all the punters start chatting away together.

Drinking & Entertainment

Evening breezes bring people out into the streets, and they inevitably head for Praça Amilcar Cabral (also called Praça Nova), where they sit, stroll, show off and flirt under the spreading acacia trees. Try either the tiny **Café Lisboa** (Rua da Libertad d'Africa) or **Café Portugal** (Rua da Libertad d'Africa) for an espresso or beer.

Syrius (cnr of Ruas Camoes & Senador Veracruz; admission from CVE300) Just around the corner from Praça Amilcar Cabral, Syrius is the city's perennially fashionable disco.

Casa Café Mindelo (Rua Santo António) In the evenings, this place has a chilled-out lounge feel, and sometimes live music on weekend nights.

Café Musique (Katem Musique; Rua da Libertad d'Africa) Come to this perennial favourite for its live music and bonhomie.

AROUND MINDELO

Few people venture beyond Mindelo's city streets to explore the rest of the island, but should you want to inhale some fresh air there are a couple of worthwhile sites. For panoramic views of Mindelo and all of São Vicente as well as Santo Antão and Santa Luzia, head to **Mt Verde** (750m). São Vicente's highest peak, it earns its name (literally 'green mountain') because of the cloud-fed lichen that cling to its rocky sides.

The island's best beaches are at **Calhau**, a weekend getaway 18km southeast of Mindelo. For information on getting to either of these, see p238.

SANTO ANTÃO

For many people the main reason for visiting Cape Verde is for spectacular Santo Antão, and it really is a good reason. This dizzyingly vertical island, ruptured with canyons, gorges and valleys, offers some of the most amazing hiking in West Africa. The second-largest island in the archipelago, it is the only one that puts the *verde* in Cape Verde. The northeast of the island, the most populated corner and the most popular with hikers, receives enough regular moisture to mean that forests of pine trees dominate the hill tops and tropical plants flourish in the steamier valleys.

To really get the most out of this island, set aside several days, prepare for some blisters and set out along the valleys and up the mountains on foot.

CAPE VERDE

HIKING SANTO ANTÃO

Dramatic canyons, cloud-soaked peaks and vertigo-inspiring drops all help to make Santo Antão a hiker's paradise. Walks here cover all ranges of abilities, from gentle hour-long valley walks to strenuous assents only for the fittest. If you're intending to do some serious hiking then get hold of the *Glodstadt Wanderkarte* hiking map. You may also consider hiring a guide; the going rate is around CVE2000. Hikes tend to begin or end on the transisland road. From here you can hitch a ride on a passing *aluguer*, or arrange for a taxi to wait for you ahead of time (around CVE2500 to CVE3000).

The classic hike is up the stunning **Valé do Paúl**. The route passes through verdant stands of bananas and fields of sugarcane until you reach Passagem, a pretty village where much of Cape Verde's *grogue* is distilled. Eventually you reach Cova crater (1170m), with its fascinating patchwork of farms. Nearby is the transisland road.

An easier, and absolutely spectacular, hike is along the coastal track from **Ponta do Sol** to **Fontainhas**. This hour-long walk takes you along a narrow path carved out of the cliff face that in places is so high and steep it's certain to send you into a cold sweat! Round a corner and there it is in front of you: Fontainhas, the most magnificently sited village in Cape Verde. It clings like a spider to a little ridge high above its fertile valley and a small, rocky cove.

There are numerous other possibilities, which any of the hotels listed here can advise on.

Getting There & Away

Due to dangerous cross winds, no flights currently operate to Santo Antão.

There are ferries daily between Mindelo and Santo Antão. While subject to change, the comfortable *Mar Novo* leaves Mindelo at 8am, returning at 10.30am. Then it leaves Mindelo again at 3pm, returning at 5pm. The trip costs CVE700 and lasts one hour. You must buy tickets 30 minutes before departure at the ferry-dock offices on both islands. Note that services may be more limited on Wednesday and Sunday. Crossings are short but can be rough during December and January.

Getting Around

If you want to see a lot of the island in a single day, your best bet is to hire your own *aluguer*, though expect to pay at least CVE6000 for a full day. You can usually arrange one when you arrive at Porto Novo. Alternatively, you can join locals on an *aluguer* headed toward Ribeira Grande (CVE400, one hour). There are also *aluguers* that leave Ribeira Grande at around 3pm to return to Porto Novo in time for the afternoon boat.

RIBEIRA GRANDE

Except for a small colonial heart, Ribeira Grande, the island's administrative centre, is not beautiful, though its position between steep cliffs and the roaring Atlantic is impressive. If you do get stuck here for the night,

Residencial Aliança (☎ 2212488; s/d CVE2400/1800) is basic but not at all bad for the price.

PORTO DO SOL

Porto do Sol feels like the end of the world, which in many ways it is. The sense of raw power here, with monstrous Atlantic waves exploding across the reefs and sheer cliffs reaching for, and often surpassing, the clouds leaves you feeling constantly in awe of nature. It's truly a wild place, but out of this wildness has grown a town with a pretty cobbled centre and a couple of enjoyable hotels and restaurants. It's an infinitely nicer baser than Ribeira Grande, just a few minutes' drive down the road.

Sleeping & Eating

Por de Sol Arte (☎ 2251121; porsolarte@yahoo.fr; s/d from CVE2200/2800) On the waterfront, this place is so multicoloured and playfully bright it looks like a playschool toy house. In fact, the playschool feel continues in the rooms, where the beds are made out of old tree trunks. More grown-up kids will find the hot-water showers and baths and the cool downstairs bar much to their liking. Very friendly.

Hotel Blue Bell (☎ 2251215; s/d CVE3700/4800) The closest thing the town has to a real hotel, the Blue Bell has rooms that are suitably 'real hotel' sterile, but comfort is guaranteed. No blue bells are visible from the room balconies, but the sea almost is.

Chez Teresa (mains from CVE600; ☒ 6-10pm) A cosy little Italian restaurant opposite the Hotel Blue

Bell, Chez Teresa has a lasagne that does wonders for your frizzled energy levels after a day spent hiking.

PAÚL

Located about 10km southeast of Ribeira Grande is idyllic Paúl, which consists of a pretty strip of pastel houses along the ocean and an equally pretty valley winding up into the heart of the island behind it. At the top of the valley is **Cova crater**, an extinct volcanic crater whose floor is a patchwork of farms and shocking greenery. It all makes for wonderful walking territory. Located on the water, **Residencial Vale do Paúl** (☎ 231319; r CVE1300) offers basic rooms with shared bathroom. Further inland, and perfect for groups or families staying a few days, is **Aldeia Manga** (☎ 2231880; www.aldeia-manga.com; r from €45), which is a large holiday house with bright and light rooms, soft pine furnishings and a garden that you'll struggle to tear yourself away from. Meals are available and the owners can advise on local walks.

PORTO NOVO

Arriving by ferry, the grubby port town of Porto Novo will be your first impression of Santo Antão. Don't worry; things rapidly improve! It's hard to think how this might happen, but if you did get stuck in Porto Novo you'll find a few reasonable places to stay, including the posh new **Santantao Art Resort** (☎ 2222675; www.santantao-art-resort.com; s/d from €47/66; 🖳 🏊), which offers good value a little to the south of town.

TARRAFAL

Lost in the burning desert beige of the west coast, the sleepy little oasis of Tarrafal, set along a beach of inky black sand, is a delight and the perfect place to rest, unwind and do nothing more strenuous than flip the pages of a book. Unlike at many of the beaches in Cape Verde, the high cliffs here shelter the beach from the worst of the winds. The **Pensão Mar Tranquilidade** (☎ 2276012; www.martranquilidade.com; cottages CVE3500) offers lovely stone-and-thatch cottages as well as good meals and all kinds of activities. Book ahead.

It's a good job Tarrafal is so nice, because after the long and bumpy journey in the back of an *aluguer* (CVE600 to/from Porto Novo) you'll want to stay a while. Transport is very limited, but something normally leaves Porto Novo heading this way every morning after the ferry disgorges its passengers.

FOGO

Whether you're being tossed and turned in the heavy seas during the boat ride from Praia or thrown about by unpredictable winds and turbulence in the tiny prop plane, the drama of Fogo begins long before you even set foot on its volcanic soils. The island of Fire (Fogo translates as fire) consists of a single, giant black volcano (which last erupted in 1995) that dominates every view and every waking moment on this dramatic island.

Life here isn't just about macho tectonic movements, though: **São Filipe** is easily one of the most attractive towns in the archipelago and can be used as a base for pretty drives around the eastern side of the island to the small town of **Mosteiros** – the drive takes you past terraced hillsides yielding mild Arabica coffee.

Getting There & Away

TACV (☎ 281228; São Filipe) has two daily flights to/from Praia. At writing time, Halcyon Air were due to begin direct Fogo–Sal flights. A taxi from the airport into São Filipe (2km) costs CVE300. Boats arrive at the tiny port 3km from town. If you can't stop gazing across the channel to tiny Brava, you might, with luck and very calm weather, find two boats a week rolling across the waves in that direction. A couple of different operators run this route, but it's all very disorganised and nothing can be taken for granted. For schedules, pop by **Agenamar** (☎ 2811012) or **Soluçoes Contablisticas** (☎ 2813267), which runs a much bigger, less weather dependent, but equally less regular, boat. Boats to Praia are also highly weather dependent (though less so than to Brava) and normally leave two to three times a week with Agenamar. The cost is CVE2000.

Getting Around

Minibuses around the island are relatively scarce. Most are based around the timings of the central market in São Filipe. That means they head to São Filipe in the early morning, and then back home later in the day; plan accordingly. Fares depend on distance but shouldn't

CAPE VERDE

cost more than CVE350. **Qualitur** (☎ 2811089; www.
qualitur.cv) offers self-drive cars from €60 per day
as well as excellent island-wide tours. See the
boxed text, opposite for more information on
getting to Chã das Caldeiras.

SÃO FILIPE

Set commandingly on the cliffs like the nest of
a seabird, São Filipe is a town of grace, charm,
immaculate Portuguese houses, and plazas full
of flowers and sleepy benches. Below, at the
base of the cliffs, lies a beach of jet black sand
and evil dumping waves; beyond, tantalising
on the horizon, squats the island of Brava. All
this makes São Filipe one of the most compelling and charming towns in Cape Verde.

Should the call of the ocean wave get to
you then note that strong currents (and some
recent muggings) make the town beach unsafe
for swimming, but you can join the locals at
the lovely **Praia da Salina**. Protected by strange
volcanic rock formations, the beach is located
17km to the north of town on the route to
Mosteiros. On 1 May, the town celebrates **Nhô
São Filipe**, its yearly citywide festival. Its Mardi
Gras celebration is also raucous.

Visitors interested in history and culture
should consider visiting **Dja'r Fogo** (☎ 2812879).
Run by a local artist, it serves as art gallery,
cafe, information point and launch pad for
informal trips around the island. It also offers rural accommodation in a house 8km
from São Filipe.

For internet access there's the **Micro Center**
(per hr CVE200; ◷ 10am-9pm).

Sleeping

Pensão Las Vegas (☎ 2812223; s/d CVE1700/2500) It
might not be as glam as its namesake, but
nevertheless it's a fun place to stay. The bright
rooms have terraces with sea views and hot
water bubbling forth from the showers.

Pousada Belavista (☎ 2811734; p_belavista@yahoo
.com; s/d CVE2300/3400; ✺) An elegant, understated,
impeccably run hotel built around an old colonial home. Rooms are well furnished, bathrooms are new (though some have cold water
only), and breakfasts are hearty. It's one of the
better-value guesthouses in Cape Verde.

Casa Renate (☎ 2812518; www.cabo-verde.ch; s/d
CVE3000/3500) In a beautiful colonial building
opposite the main church, this German-run

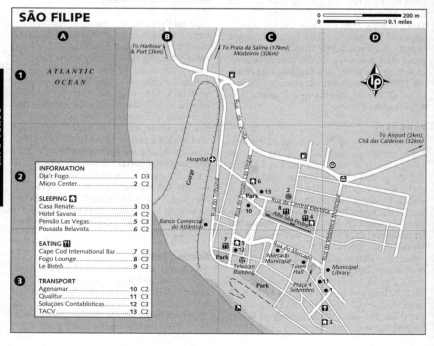

SÃO FILIPE

0 ——— 200 m
0 ——— 0.1 miles

INFORMATION	
Dja'r Fogo.....................1	D3
Micro Center...............2	C2

SLEEPING	
Casa Renate.................3	D3
Hotel Savana...............4	C2
Pensão Las Vegas........5	C3
Pousada Belavista.......6	C3

EATING	
Cape Cod International Bar.....7	C3
Fogo Lounge................8	C2
Le Bistrô.....................9	C2

TRANSPORT	
Agenamar...................10	C2
Qualitur.....................11	C3
Soluçoes Contablisticas....12	C3
TACV........................13	C2

ATLANTIC OCEAN

To Harbour & Port (3km)

To Praia da Salina (17km); Mosteiros (30km)

To Airport (2km); Chã das Caldeiras (32km)

Hospital

Gorge

Banco Comercial do Atlântico

Rua do Tribunal

Rua da Pensão Las Vegas

Park

Rua da Central Eléctrica

Alto São Pedro

Rua do Mercado

Rua da Biblioteca Municipal

Mercado Municipal

Telecom Building

Town Hall

Municipal Library

Park

Praça 4 Setembro

CAPE VERDE

CLIMBING MT FOGO

The conical 2829m-high Pico do Fogo volcano, shrouded in black cinder, rises dramatically out of the floor of an ancient crater known as Chã das Caldeiras ('Chã'). Bound by a half-circle of precipitous cliffs, Chã was born when, sometime in the last 100,000 years, some 300 cu km of the island collapsed and slid into the sea to the east. The main cone has been inactive for more than 200 years, though there've been regular eruptions in Chã. The latest, in 1995, threatened the village of Portela, whose famously friendly residents manage to grow grapes, coffee, beans and even apples in this forbidding landscape.

There's fascinating hiking along the crater floor, but most people come to climb the peak. While not technically difficult, it requires good physical condition, a hearty pair of boots, and a guide. There are plenty in Portela, and the going rate is around CVE3000. The taxing ascent – a climb of 1000m up a 30- to 40-degree slope – takes three to four hours, with some challenging scrambles near the top, but the views are magnificent. Afterwards, you can run down in 45 minutes!

Start climbing early to avoid the noon heat. Leave São Filipe by 5am by taxi (90 minutes, CVE5000 to CVE6000 with waiting time). The driver should be able to locate a guide. If you come by *aluguer* (CVE300; depart São Filipe around 11am), you will need to spend two nights in the Chã. Spend the afternoon after you arrive exploring the crater, and then make the ascent the next morning. Recover in the afternoon and then head back to São Filipe the next morning by *aluguer*, which leaves around 7am from Pedra Brabo.

In Portela you can stay at **Chez Patrick** (Pensão Pedra Brabo; ☎ 2821521; s/d CVE2226/3190), with basic rooms around a pretty, arcaded, plant-filled courtyard. The showers, being cold and communal, are a lot less comfortable than the rooms. There's also a cooperative that offers very basic rooms (no electricity or running water) in local homes for around CVE1200. Enquire with **Qualitur** (☎ 2811089; www.qualitur.cv) in São Filipe.

Finally, after you've struggled up the peak, what better way to reward yourself than with a drop of that locally produced wine? The vines are actually grown in the volcanic ash of the crater. For tastings and purchasing, visit the small cooperative in Portela (hours are very erratic).

house offers large, spotless apartments with a pleasing stonewashed look. Each apartment contains bedroom, living room, bathroom and terrace. It was up for sale at the time of research so might be very different in the future.

Hotel Savana (☎ 2811490; www.hotelsavanafogo.com; s/d CV3900/4500; 🏊) This startlingly yellow, renovated colonial building dressed up in showy pink bougainvillea is gorgeous. The rooms are surprisingly simple but have a certain elegance and the black volcanic rock decorations contrast nicely with the bright colours. There's also a perfect little pool.

Eating & Drinking

São Filipe is one of the best (and most reasonable) places in Cape Verde to try seafood.

Le Bistrô (mains from CVE500) German owner Renate serves up Italian and Cape Verdean dishes based on local seafood and produce. The rainbow-coloured table and chairs on the sunny terrace make this one of the nicer places to have a relaxing meal. Renate is also a great source of information about the islands.

Cape Cod International Bar (mains from CVE500) With staff and patrons getting on so well, and everybody wandering in and out of the kitchens willy-nilly, it can be quite hard to tell who actually works here. This friendly, family atmosphere will leave you feeling quite at home as you chow down on fresh seafood or chicken and chips. It's easily the most popular lunch spot with locals.

Fogo Lounge (mains from CVE600; 🕙 11am-midnight) As the drinks flow, afternoons quickly slip through to evenings at this cosmopolitan outdoor lounge cafe. Meals, which take a long time coming, are European based and rotate around pastas and kebabs.

SAL

Though flat, desolate and really rather dull, Sal boasts more tourists than any other island. They fall into three categories: hardcore windsurfers, the package-holiday crowd and those in transit to more interesting islands. The largest town is **Espargos**, located right next to the international airport, but most people stay near the fine beach in **Santa Maria**, 18km to the south.

Aside from the beach the only real attraction is the surreal, lunar **Pedra da Lume**, the crater of an ancient volcano where seawater is transformed into shimmering salt beds. It's located 2km west of Espargos; walk or take a taxi (CVE900 return).

Getting There & Away

AIR

TACV (☎ 2411338) has several flights daily to/from Praia and São Vicente, one a day to Boa Vista and three a week to São Nicolau (though these are often cancelled).

Halcyon Air (☎ 2418097) has daily flights to/from São Vicente and Santiago and three weekly flights to Boa Vista; a service to Fogo is due to begin shortly.

The airport has left-luggage facilities (CVE100 per bag per 24 hours), an ATM, a bureau de change (open 24 hours) and a tourist booth.

SEA

Interisland ferries call at Palmeira, the port about 4km northwest of Espargos. Schedules are irregular. Enquire at **Anaú Sal** (☎ 2411349), located near the taxi stand in Palmeira. For more details about interisland ferries, see p253.

Getting Around

Minibuses ply the road between Santa Maria and Espargos (CVE100, 25 minutes); all stop on the main road just in front of the airport. Taxis from the airport to Espargos (2.3km) charge around CVE200 during the day and CVE300 at night. Taxis to Santa Maria run to CVE700, CVE1000 at night.

SANTA MARIA

The good news is the beach. A sublime strip of gentle sand and ever-so-blue waters with world-class windsurfing and lots of fun-in-the-sun activities, but avert your eyes from this view and you're in for a shock. Santa Maria, the king of Cape Verdean resorts, is primarily a grim, wind-battered building site that in places resembles a war zone more than an international holiday resort. OK, maybe that's being a bit harsh – the central core has a certain charm, but if this is to be your only impression of Cape Verde then

you're going to be very disappointed indeed. Our advice? Get out as soon as you can.

There are several banks with ATMs and numerous internet cafes.

Activities

Surfzone (☎ 9978804; www.surfcabo.com), on the beach in front of Hotel Morbeza, rents the latest equipment for surfing, windsurfing and kitesurfing. Windsurf hire per day is €40 and kiteboard hire per day is €70; windsurf courses start at €35 and kitesurf courses at €60.

Fishing Center (☎ 2422050; www.caboverdefishing center.com; trips from €120) can arrange trawling (for wahoo, tuna and dorade) and deep-sea fishing. The travel agency **Barracuda** (☎ 2422033) offers sailing trips (half-day from €39 per person).

There are a number of scuba schools, including the **Orca Dive Club** (☎ 2421302; www.orca-diveclub -caboverde.com), which offers Padi Open Water courses for €340 and, for experienced divers, various boat and dive packages from €108. You can also rent snorkelling equipment for €3.

If you want to look for Nemo but don't want to get your water wings then salvation is available in the form of *Neptunus* – a bright yellow 'submarine' (it's actually a glass-bottomed boat disguised as a sub). One-hour trips, bookable through almost every hotel, cost €30 per person. Alas, the Beatles almost certainly won't be accompanying you.

Shopaholics will find plenty of opportunities to exceed their airline baggage allowance in the numerous **craft shops** throughout the town. Almost all of them are called some variation of No Stress, which actually isn't very true.

Sleeping

Most of the accommodation in Santa Maria consists of large package-tour hotels and privately rented apartments. For the independent traveller looking to hang out for just a night or two, options are decidedly limited and you're better off staying in Espargos and just coming here on day trips. If, however, you're planning on staying a while then the best option is to rent an apartment for the duration. **Aqui Sal** (☎ 2421325; www.aquisal.com) is one of the more established agencies where you can choose from a selection of apartments, houses or even just single rooms.

Otherwise the following places, all of which include breakfast in the price, are recommended.

Pensão Nhá Terra (☎ 2421109; nhaterra@hotmail.com; s/d from CVE4000/5000; 🖥 🐾) It's a little overpriced, but otherwise these smiley, happy rooms are spick and span, if a little dull. The best thing, though, is the roadside pool, complete with swimming palm trees! The restaurant is very good too.

Pensão Les Alizés (☎ 2421446; www.pensao-les-alizes.com; s/d €40/57; 🖥) The slightly old-fashioned rooms of the French-run Les Alizés, right in the thick of things, are a haven of calm. Rooms are given a bright, modern kick thanks to the copious amount of colourful art adorning the walls.

Hotel Morabeza (☎ 2421020; www.hotelmorabeza.com; s/d from CVE13,035/19,470; 🖥 🐾) Fronting a lively patch of beach, this well-run hotel has very comfortable rooms, the highlight of which are the eggshell-shaped sinks and enormous showers.

Eating & Drinking

Tam Tam (🕓 8am-midnight) This friendly, Irish-owned pub-restaurant serves big-boy fried breakfasts and, for the healthier, a fine *cachupa* (CVE300), as well as beer and cocktails. It's one of the most popular tourist drinking holes.

Restaurante Nhá Terra (mains CVE600-1100; 🕓 8am-10pm) Classic Cape Verdean dishes made with the freshest ingredients and served in the hotel's pleasant dining room.

Chill Out Cafe (mains CVE600-1000; 🛜) Behind the Nhá Terra, this is virtually a compulsory spot for a sunset drink. It also whips up light meals with a Western bent.

Entertainment

Pirata Pizzaria Disco Pub (🕓 until 4am Mon-Sat) Santa Maria's main disco is located just outside town on the road to the airport.

Getting There & Around

Taxis between Santa Maria and the airport cost CVE700 during the day and CVE1000 at night. Plenty of minibuses ply the road between Espargos and Santa Maria (CVE100), and all stop on the main road in front of the airport.

ESPARGOS

Located near both the airport and the ferry dock, Espargos – the island's capital – is a small, dusty, friendly town that feels more like the real Cape Verde than touristy Santa Maria.

Information

There are a number of banks with ATM around Praça 19 de Septembro.

DVD 6 (Praça 19 de Septembro; per hr CVE300) Has fast internet connections.

Sleeping & Eating

Both food and accommodation are cheaper here than in Santa Maria.

There are any number of poky little bars that'll do nicely for an evening beer and a morning pastry and caffeine kick. The Restaurante Sivvy on the main *praça* is one of our favourites.

Prices below include breakfast.

our pick **Pousada Paz e Bem** (☎ 2411782; Rua Abel Djassi; s/d/tr CVE2120/3180/3710) This superb buttercup yellow *pensão*, sitting just to the south of the main square, has spacious and astonishingly clean rooms that might be simple but are easily the best value on the island.

Residencial Santos (☎ hotel 2411900, shop 2413599; s/d CVE3000/4000) The well-scrubbed and polished rooms here are so large they virtually swallow Sal. Some even come with their own living room. It's a short way out of town to the east; if no one answers the hotel phone, try the shop number.

Restaurante Macaronesia (mains from CVE700; 🕓 12pm-11pm) The best – no, only – proper restaurant in Espargos has delectable tuna steaks and further fishy treats. The heavy R&B beats have the waitresses dancing their way over to your table. It's on the main street between the *praça* and the park.

Getting There & Away

Fares on the plentiful minibuses between Espargos and Santa Maria are CVE100.

BOA VISTA

pop 5000

With its feathery lines of dunes, stark plains and scanty oases you can't help but think of Boa Vista as nothing but a chunk of the Sahara that's somehow broken off the side of Africa and floated out here. Though the island offers some fantastic, but very wind-blown, beaches, incredible windsurfing, the pretty little town of Sal Rei, and an ever-increasing number of resorts and hotels, it's this desert

CAPE VERDE

interior that is the best reason for venturing out here.

INFORMATION

There are several banks with ATM on the *praça*. **Internet Café Boa Vista** (per hr CVE200; ☻ 9am-10pm) is three blocks east of the praça.

SIGHTS & ACTIVITIES

Of the beaches the town beach is attractive, but the longest and most beautiful, **Praia da Santa Monica**, is located about 25km away on the island's southern coast.

Homo sapiens aren't the only ones to have discovered the wonders of Boa Vista's beaches. Turtles come here in massive numbers in order to lay eggs. **Turtle-watching tours** are available in season (July to August) for €40 per person through both the **Migrante Guesthouse** (☎ 2511143; www.migrante-guesthouse .com) and **Morena** (☎ 2511445).

There's plenty to do for water enthusiasts: snorkelling, fishing, diving, whale- and turtle-watching and of course windsurfing and kitesurfing. **Migrante Guesthouse** (☎ 2511143; www.migrante-guesthouse.com) helps organise whale-watching tours. **Planet Surf Pool** (☎ 9929386; www.planetsurfpool.com) rents decent boards for around €60 per day. Windsurfing courses start at around €160 for a six-hour, one-on-one course; an eight-hour kitesurf will set you back €290. For diving, contact **Submarine Dive Center** (☎ 9924865), which provides both equipment and buddies for experienced divers, and Padi Open Water courses (€350) for those new to the world beneath the waves. Snorkelling equipment is also available for €10 per day.

If you're a landlubber, then a superb day can be spent touring the island in a rental 4WD. Your adventure will take you past peachy dunes and across searing plains with mirages dancing on the horizon. A good goal is the spooky village of **Curral Velho**, abandoned due to near-endless drought and now the home of ghosts and the odd passing fisherman. Another, equally spooky goal is the wreck of the **Santa Maria**, a rusting hulk of a ship laid out on a stormy stretch of beach to the north of Sal Rei. This would also make a decent half-day walk. You can hire a 4WD from **Morena** (☎ 2511445; boavistapoint@cvtelecom.cv) from €46 per day. If you don't fancy driving yourself, it can organise half- and full-day island tours.

SLEEPING

With an increasing number of tourists venturing to Boa Vista, accommodation can be tight. It's not a bad idea to book ahead.

Pensão Santa Isobel (☎ 2511252; s/d CVE2300/2700) This basic but friendly and well-looked-after *pensão*, right on the main square, feels as though it's been magically transported from small-town Portugal. Its rooms, though a bit poky, are easily the best budget pick in town.

Pensão A Paz (☎ 2511643; www.a-paz.it; s/d €30/45; ⌨) The chirpy, Italian-run A Paz, just off the southern end of the main square, has large, airy rooms decorated with boisterous African prints. The bathrooms have nice stone showers and there's a pleasing rooftop terrace.

our pick Migrante Guesthouse (☎ 2511143; www .migrante-guesthouse.com; s/d €50/70; ⌨) The gorgeous Migrante has five rooms set around a courtyard of mustard yellow and bougainvillea pink. Each room has dark wood floors, big, soft beds and black-and-white portraits hanging on the icy white walls, which help give it an artsy feel. The downstairs cafe is worth a bit of your time too.

EATING

Restaurante Santa Isabel (mains CVE500) Around the back of the *pensão* of the same name, this is a great place to tuck into cheap and tasty fish meals while locals down a beer and watch football or Brazilian soaps on the box in the corner.

Blue Marlin (mains CVE800-1000) A tiny restaurant with graffiti-covered walls on the main square, Blue Marlin serves easily the best seafood on Boa Vista (the owner's a big-game fisherman) and normally has an atmosphere to match the tastes. Book in advance as it's very popular.

GETTING THERE & AWAY

TACV (☎ 2511186) has daily flights to/from Praia (one hour) and Sal (25 minutes). New airline **Halcyon Air** (☎ 2511982) links Boa Vista to Sal, Santiago and São Vicente three times a week for slightly less cash than TACV. Ferries sail to Boa Vista from Praia on Wednesday (CVE2500); they then continue on to Sal (CVE2600) before returning the following day. *Aluguers* (from CVE100) ply the island's roads, but they're scarce. Taxis are readily available but costly – the short hop from the airport to town will set you back between CVE500 and CVE700.

CAPE VERDE

OTHER ISLANDS

BRAVA

pop 5000

Except for the occasional car that braves the cobblestone, cross-island roads, Brava seems to reside firmly in the 19th century. Its terraced hillsides are farmed with the aid of mules and life moves with a pace that would make a sloth sleepy. Its mountainous interior is undeniably breathtaking, though the flowers it used to be famed for have been in short supply recently, as drought has plagued the island for the past few years. Thanks to its distance from anywhere else and highly erratic travel connections, it's the island that receives the least amount of foreign tourism.

Vila de Nova Sintra ('Vila'), the tiny capital, sits on a little plateau regularly engulfed by clouds. From Vila there are some short but lovely hikes: eastward down to Vinagre via Santa Barbara and westward to Cova Joana and then on to Nosso Senhora do Monte or Lima Doce, both nearby. **Fajã d'Agua** is set dramatically between a rocky cove and impressive cliffs. Beyond Fajã lies Porteto, with its small but pleasant black-sand beach.

Aluguers ply the road between Fajã, Vila and the ferry port at Furna (CVE250 for the whole route, CVE100 from Vila to Furna). You can find a car and driver for a full-day tour of the island for as little as CVE2500 – ask around amongst the *aluguer* drivers. Plan ahead if you have a morning boat as transport can be scarce.

Sleeping & Eating

Pensão Restaurante Paul Sena (☎ 2851312; Vila de Nova Sintra; s/d per person CVE1500/2500) This *pensão* offers small, basic rooms that are clean, if musty smelling. The welcome you receive is a lot warmer than the water that spurts out of the showers. Paul will also prepare evening meals for around CVE500.

Pensão Sol na Baia (☎ 2852070; pensao_sol _na_baia@hotmail.com; Fajã; r from CVE3500) Run by a French–Cape Verdean couple, Sol na Baia offers a handful of tastefully appointed rooms, excellent French-inspired meals and a delightful garden full of birds and bees.

Getting There & Away

There are no flights to Brava so you'll have to brave the boat – and we really mean brave! Little more than a fishing trawler without even a nod towards passenger safety and comfort, this baby would make most of us nervous if we were just riding it around a calm boating lake; as it is you'll be heaving (literally – take some sick bags) your way across the treacherously rough channel between Fogo and Brava. Pack everything in watertight bags (including yourself) and hold onto the side rail of the boat very tightly. Still, you came here for adventure, right? Boats normally/sometimes/very occasionally make the crossing from Fogo twice a week, but at the merest hint of wind and swell and the boat is cancelled. Do not come here unless you have lots of time and patience – waiting a fortnight for a return boat is not at all unusual. For more information, see p243.

SÃO NICOLAU

pop 5000

São Nicolau hides its secrets well. First impressions are of a desolate and barren island, but hidden among those three ridges that dominate all views are lush and green valleys (at least, they are in years when the rains cooperate) and soaring peaks that rise up to **Mt Gordo** – at 1312m the island's highest peak.

Near the mouth of the fertile **Fajã Valley** lies **Ribeira Brava**, the island's capital. Long Cape Verde's religious centre, it was built inland to protect its treasures from pirates. Its narrow, hillside streets and tiled roofs are still reminiscent of 17th-century Portugal. Ribeira Brava's **Carnival** celebration is second only to Mindelo's.

You can go to Ribeira Brava by minibus (CVE400) or taxi (around CVE3000) from the unbeautiful town of Tarrafal, the island's port. A great option is to get off halfway at Cachaço and hike down through the Fajã Valley to Ribeira Brava. Any driver will be able to show you the way. The trail up to Mt Gordo also goes through Cachaço, passing through a protected pine forest before reaching the summit.

Sleeping & Eating

The following are in Ribeira Brava.

Pensão Jumbo (☎ 2351315; s/d from CVE1000/1400) Just across the riverbed from the Jardim, the Jumbo is good value, with clean, decent rooms.

Pensão Jardim (☎ 2351117; s/d CVE2000/3000) Located on a hill overlooking town and with breathtaking views, this spotless *pensão* has quaint, comfortable rooms and a very

CAPE VERDE

good rooftop restaurant (meals CVE800; order ahead).

Pensão Santo António (☎ 2352200; s/d CVE3000/3600; ✖) This sparkling place on the town's main square is sited in a beautifully renovated building and has comfortable, tastefully appointed rooms, some with views.

Getting There & Away

TACV (☎ 351161) has four flights a week to São Vicente and three a week to Sal. The airport is 5km southeast of Ribeira Brava (CVE500 by taxi). Flights are often cancelled.

Ferries stop off at Tarrafal at least twice a week while travelling between Praia and São Vicente. See p253 for more details.

MAIO
pop 5900

Glittering like a white crystal in a sea of turquoise, Maio is a place of squeaky-clean beaches and days that drift slowly by in a haze of sunshine and long conversations. The island is reputedly the friendliest in an archipelago full of friendly isles. Aside from the pretty main town of Vila do Maio and the beaches, the only other 'attraction' is the scrubby acacia-dotted interior that in barren Cape Verde constitutes a forest. But for the discerning traveller after something a little different, Maio is begging you to leave your footprints on its gorgeous beaches.

Hotel Bom Sossego (☎ 2551365; Vila do Maio; s/d from CVE2500/3500) is a bit overpriced and the cheaper rooms have cold-water showers only, but it's clean and well maintained. There's also a decent restaurant.

TACV (☎ 2551256) has three flights weekly to/from Praia (15 minutes). There's a very unreliable ferry service between Praia and Vila do Maio, which though supposedly weekly is more like fortnightly at best.

CAPE VERDE DIRECTORY

ACCOMMODATION

By West African standards, accommodation is expensive in Cape Verde, especially on Sal and in the city of Praia, where prices are some 25% more than in the rest of the country.

Most other places, you can expect to pay under CVE2000 for a basic but decent double with shared bathroom. For around CVE2500 to CVE4000, you can expect a modest but

---

PRACTICALITIES

- *A Semana, A Naçao* and *Expresso das Ilhas* are the weekly newspapers.
- Radio and TV is mostly limited to Portugal's, with Portuguese and Brazilian shows as well as Cape Verde news.
- Voltage is 220V with European-style twin-pronged plugs.
- Cape Verde uses the metric system.

---

quite comfortable midrange double with hot water and air-con. At the top end, there are mostly just resort hotels that cater to package tours, especially on Sal and Boa Vista. There are no camp sites, but camping on remote beaches is possible and generally safe.

ACTIVITIES

For active types, the main draws are windsurfing and kitesurfing, scuba diving and deep-sea fishing on Sal (p246) and Boa Vista (p247), plus trekking in the mountains of São Nicolau (p249), Brava (p249), Fogo (p245) and especially Santo Antão (p242). Surfing is growing in popularity on Sal (p245) and Santiago (p234), though in both cases the waves are quite inconsistent.

Diving in Cape Verde is well known for its diversity of species; dolphins, whales, sharks and rays are all occasionally seen. Because of currents, not all sites are suitable for beginners or inexperienced divers. Note that there is currently no decompression chamber in Cape Verde. The best months are from March to November; Sal (p246) and Boa Vista (p248) are the best-organised places in which to dive.

The windsurfing and kiteboarding conditions are amongst the best in the world on Sal, Boa Vista and lesser-known Maio (left). In fact, conditions are so good that Punta Preta in Sal hosts a leg of the Windsurf World Championship Tour every February. The 2007 event is still being talked about as having had some of the best ever conditions for a professional contest. Learning to windsurf or kitesurf here isn't cheap, though, with windsurfing courses starting at around €160, kitesurfing at €290. The best months are between mid-November and mid-May (and particularly January to March, when winds are strong and constant).

April to November (especially June to October) is good for fishing (rays, barracudas, marlins, wahoos, sharks); trekking and cycling are good year-round.

BOOKS

Publications in English about Cape Verde are scarce but include the *Historical Dictionary of the Republic of Cape Verde* by Richard Lobban, *Cape Verde: Politics, Economics and Society* by Colm Foy, *Antonio's Island: Cape Verde* by Marcelo Gomes Balla and *The Fortunate Isles* by Basil Davidson.

BUSINESS HOURS

Business hours are generally 8am to noon and 3pm to 6pm Monday to Friday, and 8am to noon or 1pm Saturday. Banking hours are from 8am to 3pm Monday to Friday. Note that for posted hours days are often numbered according to the Portuguese system from 1º to 7º (1º is Sunday, 7º is Saturday). Restaurants featured in this book are open from around noon to 3pm and 7pm to 10pm unless otherwise stated.

DANGERS & ANNOYANCES

While Praia is among the safest cities in West Africa, violent crime is not unknown here or in Mindelo, and pickpocketing and muggings are on the rise. Follow the same commonsense rules you would in any city. The rest of the country is very safe, though petty crime like pickpocketing is always a possibility.

EMBASSIES & CONSULATES

The following are in Praia, Santiago (Map p236), unless otherwise stated.

France (☎ 2615589; Rua da Prainha, Achada de Santo António)

Portugal (☎ 2626097; Rua da Assembleia Nacional, Achada de Santo António) Also Av 5 de Julho, Mindelo, São Vicente (call ☎ 2323130).

Senegal (☎ 2615621; Rua Abilio Macedo)

USA (☎ 2615616; 81 Rua Abilio Macedo)

FESTIVALS & EVENTS

Cape Verde's main festivals include Mardi Gras, which is held all over Cape Verde in February or March, the largest occurring in Mindelo (São Vicente); Nhô São Filipe (Fogo), held on 1 May; and the Festival de Música, held in Baia das Gatas (São Vicente) in August.

HOLIDAYS

Public holidays include the following.

New Year's Day 1 January
National Heroes' Day 20 January
Labour Day 1 May
Independence Day 5 July
Assumption Day 15 August
All Saints' Day 1 November
Immaculate Conception 8 December
Christmas Day 25 December

INTERNET ACCESS

The main towns of each island, and even other good-sized towns, have internet cafes with cheap and fast connections.

INTERNET RESOURCES

Cabo Verde (www.caboverde.com) Comprehensive tourism listings in English, Portuguese and Italian.
Cabo Verde 24 (www.caboverde24.com) General tourist information on the islands.
Cape Verde – History and Culture (www.umassd.edu/specialprograms/caboverde/cvhist.html) Historical and cultural information.
Cabo Verde Online (www.caboverdeonline.com) For news and current events.

LANGUAGE

Portuguese is the official language, but most Cape Verdeans speak Crioulo, an African-inflected version of medieval Portuguese, as their first language. For some useful words and phrases in Portuguese and Crioulo, see p860. French is widely understood; English is not.

MAPS

A good map of the islands is the German-produced AB Karten-Verlag *Cabo Verde* (1:200,000; 2001). An excellent hiking map for Santo Antão is the (also German) *Goldstadt Wanderkarte* (1:50,000; 2001) with around 40 suggested walks. The same company also produces maps to several other islands.

MONEY

The unit of currency is the Cape Verde escudo (CVE), divided into 100 centavos. It's not a hard currency, but it's stable; in January 2002 it was pegged to the euro. Most businesses also accept euros.

Banks are found in all the main towns and even some of the smaller ones, and most have

CAPE VERDE

ATMs that accept bankcards and Visa. Many also change travellers cheques and cash in all the main currencies (except the West African CFA franc).

Credit cards are increasingly accepted in even fairly modest establishments.

PHOTOGRAPHY & VIDEO
In general, Cape Verde is a wonderful place for photographers – Cape Verdeans love having their photo taken and many seem to be natural models. Even so, you should always ask permission first. Avoid photographing military installations.

POST
The postal service is cheap, reliable and reasonably quick. *Correios* (post offices) are open 8am to noon and 2.30pm to 5.30pm Monday to Friday, and Saturday mornings in some towns.

TELEPHONE
Every number for a fixed telephone line in Cape Verde has seven digits; all start with '2'. No area code is necessary. Public telephone booths are fairly plentiful, but you'll need a phonecard (available in CVE50/150 denominations at any post office and many small shops). Post offices often have call centres as well, which can be more convenient for expensive, international calls, which start at around CVE200 per minute. For better deals, keep an eye out for internet-based calling centres, which are starting to appear around the country and charge as little as CVE15 per minute to Europe.

Mobile phone reception is excellent. Mobile phone numbers are seven digits. If bringing a phone from home with roaming facilities it will connect automatically (though note that Cape Verde is not on the GPRS system so internet phones will not work here). Local SIM cards are available at all mobile phone offices and will work with unlocked phones.

VISAS
All visitors require a visa. Within West Africa, Dakar (Senegal) is one of the few

---

EMERGENCY
Fire (☎ 131)
Medical assistance (☎ 130)
Police (☎ 132)

---

places where you can get one. If there's no Cape Verdean embassy, enquire at the nearest Portuguese embassy.

That said, a one-month tourist visa can be obtained without any problems on arrival at the airports and at the ports of Praia and Sal. It costs €25 (payable in euros only – don't expect change to be available). Technically, there's a fine of CVE15,000 if you let your visa expire; in reality, if you're only a little over nobody is likely to care.

Visa Extensions
For an extension you need, in theory, to fill in a form, supply a photo and lodge the application at the **Direcção de Emigração e Fronteiras** (Map p236; Rua Serpa Pinto, Praia, Santiago); in reality, staff members here are likely to be highly confused if you turn up requesting an extension! Persevere – you'll probably succeed.

Visas for Onward Travel
Visas for Senegal can be obtained at that country's embassy in Praia. They cost around CVE500 and take up to 48 hours to process.

WOMEN TRAVELLERS
Cape Verde is one of the safest countries in West Africa for solo women travellers – no special precautions are required. For more general information and advice, see p826.

TRANSPORT IN CAPE VERDE

GETTING THERE & AWAY
Entering Cape Verde
Proof of yellow-fever vaccination is only required if you are coming from an infected area (see p856 for more details).

Air
Most international flights land on Sal, though Praia and Boa Vista are seeing an increasing amount of international activity and São Vicente is gearing up to receive its first international flights.

TACV has daily flights to Lisbon, and less frequent ones to Boston, Amsterdam, Fortaleza, Munich and Paris. There's also talk of flights to London and Rome. TAP Air Portugal has daily flights from Lisbon to Praia and Sal. Various charter flights fly to Sal and Boa Vista from the UK, Germany and Italy. These are generally the cheapest way of getting to the islands. See www.thomson.co.uk and www.tuifly.com for more.

From West Africa, TACV flies between Praia and Dakar (Senegal) three to four times weekly. Air Sénégal International has three flights weekly to/from Dakar, with connections to most major West African cities.

Scheduled airlines servicing Cape Verde include the following, all in Praia, Santiago (Map p236).

Air Sénégal International (airline code V7; ☎ 2617529; www.air-senegal-international.com; Rua Serpa Pinto) Hub Dakar.

TACV (airline code VR; ☎ 2608200; www.tacv.cv; Rua Serpa Pinto) Hub Praia.

TAP Air Portugal (airline code TP; ☎ 2615826; www.flytap.com; Praia International Airport) Hub Lisbon.

GETTING AROUND
Air
TACV serves all the inhabited islands except Brava and Santo Antão. Internal flights are slightly cheaper (note that we said cheaper, not cheap) if you buy tickets in Cape Verde. If you're taking two or more internal flights, you may want to purchase TACV's Cabo Verde AirPass (available from travel agencies abroad but not in Cape Verde). You have to arrive by TACV to qualify, but as its flights tend to be much more expensive than those of its competitors you'll rarely save any money by doing this.

Note that if flights are full it's well worth flying standby as no-shows are very common.

The cheapest TACV flights are at least CVE5000; the run between Praia and São Vicente, for example, is at least CVE10,000. Such prices quickly eat into even quite generous travel budgets.

Halcyon Air (☎ 2412360; www.halcyonair.com) is a new airline that at the time of research linked Santiago, Sal, Boa Vista and São Vicente and was shortly to add Fogo and Maio to its network. It charges about 25% less than TACV.

Boat
There are ferry connections to all nine inhabited islands, and prices are reasonable. However, be prepared for delays. Seas can be rough and most boats also carry cargo, so unloading time can be unpredictable. Sometimes departures are delayed by a day or more. There are cafes on board the bigger boats, but it's always a good idea to bring a reserve of water and snacks.

The most reliable – and comfortable – service is via SMT's *Tarrafal,* which connects Mindelo and Praia via São Nicolau. Twice a week, boats leave Mindelo in the early afternoon, arrive in São Nicolau in the evening, and then head to Praia overnight, arriving the following morning. In the other direction, the *Tarrafal* leaves in the evening from Praia, arriving the following morning at São Nicolau and in Mindelo around midday.

In addition, SMT boats run between Praia and Fogo on Monday and Friday, returning Wednesday and Saturday, and from Praia to Boa Vista on Wednesday, returning the following day.

The twice-daily service between São Vicente and Santo Antão is also very reliable. The trip lasts one hour and costs CVE700.

Agência Nacional de Viagens (☎ 2603101) offers irregular boats from Praia to Boa Vista (normally Tuesday or Wednesday; CVE2200) and onward to Sal, as well as irregular connections to Maio and Fogo.

Getting from Fogo to Brava is an exercise in patience, stamina and strong stomachs – see p249 for more.

Car
You can rent cars on many islands, but the only three that make the expense worth it are Santiago, Boa Vista and possibly Fogo. Consider a 4WD, as conditions are rough once you get off the few main roads. Cars cost from CVE5500 per day, including tax and insurance, with the first 100km free (CVE0.10 per kilometre thereafter). As tourism grows, international car-rental agencies are also setting up shop. Check at airports upon arrival.

Minibus & Taxi
Ranging from comfortable vans to pick-up trucks with narrow wooden benches, the *aluguers* provide regular connections between even relatively small towns on most islands. They pick up people at unmarked points around town, set off from their initial stop when they're more or less full, and drop passengers off anywhere on the way, on request.

Taxis are generally plentiful, with roundtown fares rarely topping CVE500. However, you could be stung fairly hard for an airport run or excursion.

Hitching is easy, though payment is sometimes expected. It's usually safe, but see p847 for a general warning on the possible risks.

CAPE VERDE

Côte d'Ivoire

Côte d'Ivoire: the name conjures images of starfish-studded beaches and pockets of deep-green jungle – the domain of forest elephants, tangled lianas, savannah palms and fat mahogany trees. It sounds poetic. It sounds like peace. It sounds like the name of one of the most developed nations in Africa.

Somehow, Côte d'Ivoire lost its footing. A 2002 rebellion tore the country in half and, from that moment on, travellers forgot about the beaches, hearing only the echoes of gunfire in their minds. It's time to stop remembering and start exploring, because Côte d'Ivoire is back. A reconciliation agreement has been signed, the rebels have been disarmed and the country is warmly embracing peace.

Head to Abidjan, where shimmering skyscrapers and cathedral spires pierce the heavens. When the daylight fades, sit back with a cocktail and watch the blue sky blush, making room for nightfall, warm laughter and the clever beats of *coupé-decalé*. Try *poisson braisé* and listen as musicians tease base notes from banjos. When you wake from slumber, make footprints on the eastern shores, embroidered with shells and sand dollars.

Though its beaches most certainly are, Côte d'Ivoire is not perfect. The skyscrapers of Abidjan stand tall but forests have fallen; elephants and chimps were among the casualties of war. Yet these early days of peace taste as good as the chocolate produced from this soil, and that's something worth sharing. It's time to forget the gunfire. These days, the only explosions you'll hear are fireworks.

FAST FACTS

- **Area** 322,465 sq km
- **Capital** Yamoussoukro
- **Country code** ☎ 225
- **Famous for** Cocoa, music, skyscrapers
- **Languages** French, Mande, Malinké, Dan, Senoufo, Baoulé, Agni, Dioula
- **Money** West African CFA franc; US$1 = CFA493; €1 = CFA656
- **Population** 20.1 million
- **Visa** Required by almost everyone (Americans are no longer exempt); arrange in advance

CÔTE D'IVOIRE

HOW MUCH?

- **Hand-spun Korhogo cloth** CFA10,000-30,000
- **Coupé-decalé album** CFA2000
- **Shared taxi across town** CFA200
- **Local celebrity magazine** CFA1700
- **Mobile phone top-up voucher** CFA1000

LONELY PLANET INDEX

- **1L of petrol** CFA425
- **1.5L of bottled water** CFA500
- **Bottle of Flag beer** CFA650
- **Souvenir football shirt** CFA3000
- **Plate of poisson braisé aloco** CFA800

HIGHLIGHTS

- **Abidjan** (p265) Eating haute Ivorian cuisine, dancing to *coupé-decalé* as night falls and never taking your eyes off the illuminated skyline.
- **Grand Bassam** (p275) Colonial streets galore and horse riding along white-sand beaches.
- **Man** (p280) Watching stilt dancers and trekking to the summit of Mt Tonkoui, with its view over three West African countries.
- **Assinie Mafia** (p276) Lazy pirogue rides, surfers sliding to the shore and *poisson braisé* under the stars.
- **Yamoussoukro** (p279) The quiet village that grew up to become a shining, modern capital.

ITINERARIES

- **One Week** Spend three days exploring Abidjan (p265) and its restaurants, live-music venues and sights. Head east to arty Grand Bassam (p275) and on to enchanting Assinie (p276).
- **Two Weeks** With an extra week you can throw in the charms of Sassandra (p277) and San Pédro (p278) and, if security permits, you can explore Parc National de Taï (p278) before crossing into Liberia. Alternatively, you could head north from Abidjan to Yamoussoukro (p279) and on to Man (p280).

CLIMATE & WHEN TO GO

Côte d'Ivoire has a humid, tropical climate with two rainy seasons: May to July and October to November. In the south of the country, annual rainfall is 1500mm to 2000mm. In the drier northern part of the country, the wet season extends from June to October with no intermediary dry spell. The south is very humid, with temperatures averaging 28°C. In the less-humid north, the average temperature is 26°C from December to February with midday maximums regularly above 35°C. Temperatures can drop to 10°C in the highlands. Come January, the dusty harmattan winds blow in from the Sahara, reducing visibility and prompting an epidemic of coughs and colds. See Climate Charts, p811.

HISTORY

The major ethnic groups in Côte d'Ivoire all migrated relatively recently from neighbouring areas. Around 400 years ago, the Krou (or Kru) people moved eastwards from Liberia while the Senoufo and Lobi moved southwards from Burkina Faso and Mali. It was not until the 18th and 19th centuries that the Akan people, including the Baoulé, migrated from Ghana into the eastern area and the Malinké (also called Mandingo) from Guinea moved into the northwest.

The Portuguese were the first Europeans to arrive. Compared with neighbouring Ghana, Côte d'Ivoire suffered little from the slave trade: European slave and merchant ships preferred other areas with better harbours. France took no interest until the 1840s when they enticed local leaders to grant French commercial traders a monopoly along the coast. Thereafter, the French built naval bases to keep out non-French traders and began a systematic conquest of the interior. To build

---

WARNING

Due to the risk of political insecurity in the north and west at the time of research, we were unable to travel to some areas outside of Abidjan. Instead, we relied on friends and journalists working in those places. At the time of writing, the British Foreign and Commonwealth Office was advising against travel to areas north of Bouaké and travel west of the line between the towns of Seguela and Guiglo.

CÔTE D'IVOIRE

CÔTE D'IVOIRE

the railway and work the cocoa plantations, the French conscripted workers from as far away as Upper Volta (present-day Burkina Faso). Cocoa was the country's major export; by the late 1930s, coffee ran a close second.

With a good third of the cocoa, coffee and banana plantations in the hands of French citizens, the despised forced-labour system became the backbone of the economy. Under this system, known as *la corvée*, young men were rounded up and compelled to work on private estates or public-sector projects, such as the railway.

Houphouët-Boigny

Born in 1905, the son of a wealthy Baoulé chief, Félix Houphouët-Boigny became Côte d'Ivoire's father of independence. In 1944 he turned to politics and formed the country's first agricultural trade union – not of labourers but of African planters. Opposing the colonial policy, which favoured French plantation owners, the planters united to recruit migrant workers for their own farms. Houphouët-Boigny soon rose to prominence and within a year converted the union into the Parti Démocratique de Côte d'Ivoire (PDCI). A year later, he allied the PDCI with the Rassemblement Démocratique Africain (RDA), becoming the RDA's first president. That year the French abolished forced labour.

Even before independence, Côte d'Ivoire was easily French West Africa's most prosperous area, contributing more than 40% of the region's total exports. Houphouët-Boigny feared that, with independence, Côte d'Ivoire and Senegal would find themselves subsidising the poorer ex-colonies if all were united in a single republic. His preference for independence for each of the colonies coincided with French interests.

Independence

In 1960, Houphouët-Boigny became the country's first president. While leaders throughout Africa offered varying strategies for development, Houphouët-Boigny favoured continued reliance on the former colonial power.

He was also one of the few leaders who promoted agriculture and gave industrial development a low priority – at least initially. Houphouët-Boigny's government gave farmers good prices and stimulated production. Coffee production increased significantly and, by 1979, Côte d'Ivoire had become the world's leading cocoa producer, as well as Africa's leading exporter of pineapples and palm oil. The Ivorian 'miracle' was foremost an agricultural one.

For 20 years, the economy maintained an annual growth rate of nearly 10%. The fruits of growth were widely enjoyed since the focus of development was on farming – the livelihood of 85% of the people. Another reason was the absence of huge estates; most of the cocoa and coffee production was in the hands of hundreds of thousands of small producers. Literacy rose from 28% to 60% – twice the African average. Electricity reached virtually every town, and the road system became the best in Africa, outside South Africa and Nigeria. Still, the many Mercedes and posh African residences in Abidjan's Cocody quarter were testimony to the growing inequality of incomes.

Houphouët-Boigny ruled with an iron fist and the press was far from free. Tolerating only one political party, he eliminated opposition by largesse – giving his opponents jobs instead of jail sentences.

The Big Slump

The world recession of the early 1980s sent shock waves through the Ivorian economy. The drought of 1983–84 was a second body blow. From 1981 to 1984 GNP stagnated or declined. The rest of Africa looked on gleefully as the glittering giant, Abidjan, was brought to

its knees for the first time with constant power blackouts. The miracle was over.

Houphouët-Boigny slashed government spending and bureaucracy, revamped some of the poorly managed state enterprises, sent home one-third of the expensive French advisers and teachers and, most difficult of all, finally slashed cocoa prices to farmers in 1989 by 50%.

The 1990 presidential elections were opened to other parties for the first time; however, Houphouët-Boigny still received 85% of the vote. As he became increasingly feeble, the guessing game of who he would appoint as his successor intensified. Finally, in late 1993, after 33 years in power as Côte d'Ivoire's only president, *le Vieux* (The Old Man) died aged 88.

A New Beginning, An Old Story

Houphouët-Boigny's hand-picked successor was Henri Konan-Bédié, a Baoulé and speaker of the national assembly. In 1995, Bédié achieved some legitimacy, receiving 95% of the vote in open presidential elections, but true democracy was stifled by the application of the new 'parenthood clause', which stipulated that both a candidate's parents must be Ivorian. After the elections, Bédié continued to discriminate against immigrants and their descendants, who for decades had fuelled the country's agricultural expansion. This persecution focused, in particular, on foreign Muslim workers in the north, but extended to all northern Muslims regardless of their origin.

In December 1999, Bédié's unpopular rule was brought to an end by a military coup led by General Robert Guéi; however, having deposed Bédié on the basis of his discriminatory policies, Guéi only pursued them further. The coup was quickly followed by military rebellion, violence and elections in 2000 in which Guéi was able to have his main opponent, Alasanne Ouattara, a former prime minister and IMF (International Monetary Fund) official, disqualified by the Supreme Court on the grounds that his mother was from Burkina Faso and that papers proving otherwise were forgeries. When Guéi tried to steal the subsequent result from winner Laurent Gbagbo, he was deposed by a popular uprising.

On 19 September 2002, a failed coup led to a full-scale rebellion and troops from the north gained control of much of the country.

Former president Guéi was killed early in the fighting: his death has never been investigated. In January 2003, President Gbagbo and leaders of the rebel factions met in Paris and signed the Linas-Marcoussis Peace Accord, creating a 'government of national unity' with representatives of the rebels taking places in a new cabinet. This was slowly but peacefully implemented, curfews were lifted and French troops cleaned up the lawless western border. On 4 July 2003 both sides officially declared the war over and vowed to work for demobilisation, disarmament and reintegration. The harmony was short-lived: the MPCI (Mouvement Patriotique de Côte d'Ivoire), now called the 'New Forces', pulled out of the government in September, citing President Gbagbo's failure to honour the peace agreement. Three months later, the north and south shook hands again.

No improvement in the country's situation was seen in 2004, and neither side drew any closer to its ultimate goal. In March, the PDCI accused President Gbagbo of 'destabilising the peace process' and quit the government. A few weeks later, after security forces in Abidjan opened fire on an opposition demonstration demanding Gbagbo implements the peace deal (killing 120 unarmed civilians), the New Forces followed suit. UN peacekeepers, under the UN Operation in Côte d'Ivoire (Unoci) banner, arrived soon after to help keep things rolling forward, or at least stop them from slipping back. New talks held in Accra in July resulted in yet another peace agreement and, once again, the government fell short of meeting its end of the bargain, so the New Forces rebels refused to disarm.

On 4 November 2004 President Gbagbo broke the ceasefire and began bombing rebel strongholds including Bouaké. Two days later, jets struck a French military base killing nine French peacekeepers. The French destroyed the Ivorian air force in retaliation, and then all hell broke loose in the streets of Abidjan. Thousands of foreigners were evacuated and dozens of Ivorians died in clashes with French soldiers. The government called off the mayhem after a few days but, for many, the anti-French sentiment behind it lingers even today.

The UN Security Council quickly imposed an arms embargo against the government and threatened to freeze the assets of individual leaders. Though his constitutional mandate expired on 31 October 2005, Gbagbo declared he would remain president until elections were held, while the rebels called for the appointment of an independent transitional government. Amid credible reports that President Gbagbo was rebuilding his air force, a UN resolution backed his bid to stay in office for another year. Elections were scheduled for the end of 2007.

In April 2007 French peacekeepers began a staged pullback from the military buffer zone, to be replaced gradually by mixed brigades of government and rebel troops. Gbagbo declared the end of the war and the two sides moved to dismantle the military buffer zone. But in June that year, a rocket attack on Prime Minister Soro's plane killed four of his aides, shaking the peace process further. The UN Security Council renewed arms sanctions for another year in order to push for early elections and, as 2007 drew to a close, rebels and government soldiers pulled back from the frontline.

Côte d'Ivoire Today

Violent protests about rising food costs shook the country in April 2008, causing Gbagbo to put the elections back to November. A month later, northern rebels began the long disarmament process. Just days before the planned elections, the government postponed them yet again, amid disorganised voter registration and uncertainty about the validity of identity cards – one of the issues that sparked the crisis in the first place. Voter registration has since got off the ground and elections have been tentatively planned for November 2009. Côte d'Ivoire is embracing a wary peace, but all eyes are on the ever-changing election date, which still has the potential to rattle the country.

THE CULTURE
The National Psyche

Ivorians have become used to living on an emotional rollercoaster. But it's both ironic and testament to their spirit that, though the north and south could not get along for so long, Ivorians have been able to reconcile living in a modern, relatively progressive society with the ravages of war. Côte d'Ivoire's conflict – or its crisis, as Ivorians say – did not devour the country, nor did it dampen the enthusiasm, joy for life or infectious spirit of its people.

In many ways, visiting Côte d'Ivoire doesn't produce the same kind of culture shock gener-

---

STILT DANCERS

Stilt dancing takes place as the sun is setting, when houses and compound walls are bathed in radiant ochre light. Most of the villagers participate in the cooperatively run performances. The stilt dancers' costumes are otherworldly; on their high stilts they don't resemble the human form in any way. Around their heads they wear cowrie shells and bells, and their bodies are hidden beneath ballooning straw overcoats. As their swirling dance progresses the acrobatic feats become more and more outrageous, until they are spinning at a terrific speed and hurtling themselves into the air, throwing their stilts over their heads then miraculously landing on them. The crowd goes wild. After each dangerous whirl the dancer approaches the chief and dignitaries, howling like a demented, wounded jungle bird until gifts of money are surrendered to their clutch.

Before they can dance publicly the dancers undertake three to five years of training. They tell no one, not even their wives, what they're doing. Once initiated, they become empowered to communicate with the spirits who, during the dancing, direct their elaborate stunts.

---

ated by visiting other West African countries. Creative pursuits, literature and world affairs are national passions. In the villages, the low literacy rate means the pursuit of art and craftwork has deepened. On an intellectual level, travellers to Côte d'Ivoire are welcomed as equals. You'll be greeted with open arms and enthusiasm, not simply because you're from another land, but because that's the Ivorian way. And should you find you need help in any way, you just couldn't be in better hands.

Daily Life

Life goes on. In Abidjan, babies are born to mothers with high-flying jobs. At the age of two or three, they practice walking with toys balanced on their heads – preparing for the life of a market woman they may choose to turn down in favour of a more glamorous occupation in Le Plateau. In some rural areas, particularly further north, daily life is a struggle. The crisis slashed jobs, ripped bank balances to shreds and tore bonds between friends. Though worries about the future and corruption are at the forefront of everyone's minds, humour infiltrates many aspects of daily life – and that goes for disarmed rebels, too.

And so Côte d'Ivoire finds itself in an unlikely position. The legacy of its past as an economic wonder lingers. It has kept certain aspects of it – love for the arts, some progress towards gender equality, an enriched perspective on life – but though the skyscrapers of Abidjan still stand tall, much has been lost.

Population

The 60-plus ethnic groups in Côte d'Ivoire can be divided, on the basis of cultural unity, into four principal groupings, each of which has affiliations with members of the same group living in bordering countries.

The Akan (primarily Baoulé and Agni) live in the eastern and central areas and constitute about 42% of the indigenous population. The Krou, 15% of the indigenous population, originated from present-day Liberia. The Bété are its most numerous subgroup and the second-largest ethnic group in the country.

The savannah peoples can be divided into the Voltaic (including Senoufo and Lobi) and Mande (Malinké and Dan) groups.

Life expectancy at birth is around 47.4 years; maternal morbidity and infant deaths are high, at 195 for every 100 births. Around 7% of the population lives with HIV.

SPORT

Throughout the conflict time, the only glue that bonded the country together was Les Elephants, the Ivorian national football team. With exports like Didier Zokora, Kolo and Yaya Touré and Arsene Oka, Côte d'Ivoire has a fantastic presence on widescreen TVs all over the world. Didier Drogba is perhaps the country's most famous footballer; he owns Le Queen bar on Rue Princesse in Abidjan (see p272).

RELIGION

Though the country has two of the most spectacular modern Catholic cathedrals in the world, only about 35% of the people are Christian, including some Protestants. Some 40%, mostly the Malinké and Dioula (plus most West African immigrants), are Muslims, living primarily in the north. Discrimination, both real and perceived, against the mostly Muslim north by the mostly Christian south

---

YAMOUSSOUKRO'S AMAZING BASILICA

For miles around, Yamoussoukro's spectacular Basilique de Notre Dame de la Paix broods on the humid skyline like a giant, pearl-grey boiled egg.

Its statistics are startling. Completed in 1989, it was built in three years by a labour force of 1500, working day and night in great secrecy. The price tag was about US$300 million and annual maintenance costs US$1.5 million. It bears a striking and deliberate resemblance to St Peter's in Rome. Although the cupola is slightly lower than St Peter's dome (by papal request), it's topped by a huge cross of gold, making it the tallest church in Christendom. Inside, each of its 7000 seats is individually air-conditioned, a system only used on the two occasions when it has been full: at its controversial consecration by a reluctant Pope John Paul II (the pope insisted on a hospital being built nearby as a condition of consecrating the basilica) and at the funeral of the man responsible for its creation, Pierre Fakhoury, an Ivorian of Lebanese descent.

The president was reluctant to discuss the details of its financing. He had done a 'deal with God' and to discuss God's business publicly would be more than indiscreet. Proponents of the basilica will rhetorically ask, were there no poor in France when Chartres Cathedral was lovingly built? And was England affluent when the spires of Canterbury Cathedral first stabbed the sky?

What is certain is that you'll catch your breath as you cross the threshold and see the 36 immense stained-glass windows, all 7400 sq metres of them, with their 5000 different shades of warm, vibrant colour. It's like standing at the heart of a kaleidoscope.

---

played a significant role in the conflict. Many Ivorians practice traditional beliefs and ancestor worship.

ARTS
Arts & Craftwork
Côte d'Ivoire's art is an expression of its path through history. Culturally diverse and steeped in artistic traditions, the country excels at pottery, sculpture, fabric and silverwork. Four ethnic groups stand out – the Baoulé, Akye, Dan and Senoufo.

The Baoulé are renowned for gold and brass casting, wooden sculptures, and mask and figure carving. In Baoulé culture ceremonial masks represent lesser deities and sometimes the souls of the deceased. It is deemed dangerous for anyone other than the owner of the mask to wear it; its energy is believed to have the power to transform the wearer. The Akye produce woodcarvings, weavings and pottery. Korhogo cloth is a coarse, cream-coloured cotton painted with either geometric designs or fantastical animals. Also prized are Dan masks of wood or copper from the Man region, and Senoufo wooden statues, masks and traditional musical instruments from the northeast.

There's a small modern art scene in Côte d'Ivoire. Christian Lattier, dubbed the 'bare-handed sculptor' is Côte d'Ivoire's most famous contemporary artist. He died in 1978. Nick Amon, who has a gallery in Grand Bassam (p276), is one of the most respected modern painters.

Music
Côte d'Ivoire used to be the musical crossroads of West Africa. Until the crisis, Abidjan was *the* place to come for a recording deal. Though now somewhat displaced by Dakar and Bamako, the economic heart of Côte d'Ivoire still has one hell of a pulse. Despite (or perhaps because of) the recent conflict, Ivorians have plenty to sing about. Music is a cornerstone of daily life and new genres are constantly evolving.

TRADITIONAL
Early Ivorian music, rooted in traditional culture, was characterised by polyphonic and polyrhythmic sounds, with input from percussion devices such as the talking drum and instruments like the balafon. Post-independence, the genres of *gbé gbé* and *dopé* emerged; both are rooted in traditional music.

Côte d'Ivoire is renowned for its stilt dances and there are numerous opportunities to watch them, particularly in the Man region.

CONTEMPORARY
Ernesto Djédjé, the pioneer of *ziglibithy* music, is considered the daddy of contemporary Ivorian music and the man who put Côte d'Ivoire on the music map. He led the San Pédro Orchestra in the early 1970s before forming the

group Les Ziglibithiens. *Ziglibithy* is a jerky, jazzy home-grown response to the imported styles that were leaking into the country around that time. It's worth lending an ear to Djédjé's 'Gnoantre-Ziboté' and 'Taxi Sognon', two of his most famous tracks. In 1982, he was honoured by then-president Houphouët-Boigny for his musical contribution to Ivorian society. A year later Djédjé died, at the age of 35.

When the late François Lougah emerged onto the scene in 1973, he made a similar impact. His music, which balances easy beats with powerful vocals, caused a storm all over the Francophone world; he toured until his death in 1993. His 1976 LP, *Au Zaire*, is pretty special.

In the late 1980s and early 1990s, reggae ruled Abidjan. The country's best-loved reggae export is the prolific Alpha Blondy, who

was named UN Ambassador of Peace for Côte d'Ivoire in 2005. Other reggae stars are Serge Kassy, Ismael Isaac and Tiken Jah Fahkoly. In the early 1990s came the *zoblazo* style of music, which mixed contemporary lyrics with traditional beats. *Zouglou*, a satirical genre popular with students, emerged soon after. Not entirely unrelated is *coupé-decalé*, which had a profound impact on the Ivorian psyche when it emerged in 2002 (see boxed text below).

To hear some of Côte d'Ivoire's musical talent in Abidjan, see p272. The Ki-Yi Mbock, on the outskirts of that city, is a hothouse for aspiring and established musicians. Led by the renowned Werewere Liking, the village has produced a number of highly acclaimed musical stars. Among them is Manou Gallo, who pins graceful, velvety lyrics to vibrant beats. Her contemporary, Dobet Gnahoré, is

---

COUPÉ-DECALÉ: CUT AND RUN

Picture the scene: it's 2002 and you're at the swish l'Atlantic nightclub in Paris. Around you, tight-shirted Ivorian guys are living it up – knocking back champagne, throwing euros into the air and grinding their hips on the dance floor.

Coupé-decalé is one of the most important music movements to hit Côte d'Ivoire. From the French verb *couper*, meaning to cheat, and *decaler*, to run away, the term loosely translates as 'cut and run'. It evolved as a comment on the shrewd but stylish Ivorian and Burkinabé guys – modern day Robin Hoods, if you like – who ran away to France at the height of the conflict in 2002, where they garnered big bucks and sent money home to their families.

Known as the 'jet set', they splashed the rest of their cash on the Paris club scene and it wasn't unusual for them to shower audiences with crisp notes. The late Douk Saga, one of the founders of the movement, was famous for wearing two designer suits to his shows. Halfway through, he'd strip provocatively and throw one into the crowd.

It wasn't long before this music genre took off in Côte d'Ivoire, becoming increasingly popular as the conflict raged on. With curfews in place and late-night venues closed, Ivorians started going dancing in the mornings. The more normal life was suppressed, the more they wanted to break free from the shackles of war. *Coupé-decalé,* the who-gives-a-damn dance, allowed them to do exactly that.

Early *coupé-decalé* was characterised by repetitive vocals set to fast, jerky beats. Lyrics were either superficial, facetious or flippant: 'We don't know where we're going, but we're going anyway,' sang DJ Jacab, and, for many Ivorians, listening to the music became a form of escapism. As the trend has matured, *coupé-decalé* lyrics have become smarter, more socially-aware and dripping with double and triple entendres. Listening out for the puns and wordplay may not be quite as challenging as the New York Times crossword, but it's not a million miles off either. The movement is now a source of national pride and, above all, a comment on Ivorian society. Despite years of conflict, misery and fear, Ivorians have never stopped dancing.

Today's *coupé-decalé* is cheeky, crazy and upbeat; to appreciate it fully you should get yourself to an Abidjan dance floor. Tracks to seek out include Bablée's 'Sous Les Cocotiers', Kaysha's 'Faut Couper Decaler', 'Magic Ambiance' by Magic System, DJ Jacab's 'On Sait Pas Ou On Va', 'Guantanamo' by DJ Zidane and Douk Saga's 'Sagacité' – a play on the title, which means 'shrewd'. The latter spawned the 'Drogbacité' dance craze, inspired by the footballer Didier Drogba. In 2006 DJ Lewis' hugely popular 'Grippe Aviaire' did for bird flu what early *coupé-decalé* did for the conflict – it replaced fear with joy.

another talented Ivorian songstress who tours worldwide. For more on Ki-Yi Mbock see the boxed text, p272.

Literature

Creativity and the pursuit of knowledge are highly valued in Côte d'Ivoire, so it follows that this country is blessed with one of the most lively literary scenes in West Africa. Though Ivorian literary circles have been thriving since the 1970s, drawing large audiences hasn't always been easy; the country's literacy rate is just 48.7%.

The Ivorian Bernard Dadié is one of Africa's finest writers. He's credited with writing Côte d'Ivoire's first play (*Assémiwen Déhylé* in 1936), first poetry anthology and first collection of short stories in French. He writes with warmth, even when expressing dissatisfactions. His must-read, published in 1970, is *Climbié*, an autobiographical account of his childhood. Other works translated into English include *The Black Cloth* (1987) and *The City Where No One Dies* (1986).

Ahmadou Kourouma's work is also outstanding. His 1981 masterpiece *The Suns of Independence* put him firmly on the African literary map. The story of a village chief deposed in the wake of independence, it was written as a comment on abuses of economic and social power. His second novel, *Monnew*, published in 1990, looks at African suffering, as does his third, *En Attendant le Vote des Bêtes Sauvages (Waiting for the Wild Animals to Vote)*. The writer Aké Loba is best known for *Kocoumbo* (1970), an autobiographical novel of an impecunious, uprooted African in Paris being drawn toward militant communism.

By the 1980s, many female writers were contributing to the rapidly increasing body of Ivorian literature. Among those who left their mark are Véronique Tadjo, Flore Hazoumé, Assamala Amoi and Goley Niantié Lou. Tanella Boni, a professor of philosophy at the University of Abidjan, is a highly regarded poet and novelist who received the Ahmadou Kourouma Prize for her novel *Matins de Couvre-Feu (Curfew Mornings)*. It was written in 2005 and evokes some of the distrust and discrimination that characterised the conflict. *Aya de Yopougon*, written by Marguerite Abouet in 2005, is a sweet and highly praised comic novel about three girls coming of age in 1970s Côte d'Ivoire.

Maurice Bandaman won the Grand Prix Litteraire d'Afrique Noire, Francophone Africa's most prestigious literary award, in 1993 for *Le Fils de la Femme-mâle*. His most recent novel, set in Abidjan, is *Meme au Paradis on Pleure Quelquefois (Even in Paradise, Sometimes We Cry)*. Also published in 2001 was Tiburce Koffi's *Terre de Misere (Land of Misery)*, a collection of short stories that explore the nature of humanity.

Cinema

Though it doesn't have the cinematic impact of countries like Burkina Faso and Senegal, Côte d'Ivoire's film industry bears fruit. Abidjan stages an annual festival of short films, le FICA; among its screening venues in 2008 was the city's main prison. In 2009, several Ivorian films made it into Fespaco, among them *Le Prix de l'Amour (The Price of Love)* by Léa Dubois Ziré and the strangely compelling *Il Nous Faut L'Amerique (We Need America)*, written by Koffi Kwahule and directed by Sidiki Bakaba, the current director of Abidjan's Palais de la Culture.

Côte d'Ivoire's most significant film director is probably the late Henri Duparc. His first picture was *Mouna ou le Reve d'un Artiste, (Mouna, or an Artist's Dream)* but his 1988 production *Bal Poussière (Dancing in the Dust)* is widely deemed his most powerful work. A comment on traditional polygamy, it's the story of a chief named Demi Dieu (after God he is, evidently, the owner of all things) on a quest for a sixth wife to fill every day of the week except Sunday.

Désiré Ecaré, who died in February 2009, was the director of the acclaimed *Faces of Women* (1985). He completed only three films in his lifetime and it was this one, though controversial and sexually explicit, that cemented his reputation as one of the greats. Bassori Timite's *Sur le Dune de la Solitude* and *La Femme au Couteau* are also well regarded, as is Roger Gnoan M'Bala's *Adanggaman* (2000).

ENVIRONMENT
The Land

Côte d'Ivoire's central area, where most of the coffee and cocoa grows, is generally flat. A pair of impoundments here have created lakes Buyo and Kossou, two of the largest lakes in West Africa. The north is characterised by a series of valleys, hills and plateaus, averaging around 300m. Man, with its rolling hill country, is punctuated by several peaks over 1000m. Mt Nimba (1752m), on the Guinean and Liberian borders, is the country's highest peak. In the extreme north you'll see savannah grassland interspersed with acacia and other bushes and trees.

Little remains of the dense rainforest that once covered most of the southern half of the country. The remainder is mostly confined to the southwest, inland from the coast and towards the border with Liberia; the largest tract is protected within the spectacular Parc National de Taï (p278).

Côte d'Ivoire's longest rivers are the Comoé (900km) and Bandama (950km).

Wildlife
ANIMALS
Once home to thousands of elephants, Côte d'Ivoire is now sadly a bit of a misnomer. The twin threats of poaching and habitat destruction have taken their toll and these days the only elephants you're likely to see are those immortalised in statue form in Abidjan, or Les Elephants, as the national football team is known. In the 1970s, there were believed to be as many as 5000 elephants in Côte d'Ivoire. Of course, the conflict hasn't helped matters and today there are believed to be less than 300 (largely to be found in Parc National de Taï). According to the 2008 IUCN Red List, African elephants are critically endangered in Côte d'Ivoire.

There are believed to be fewer than 1200 chimpanzees in the country, concentrated in the Taï and Marahoué national parks. They too are threatened; research carried out in 2009 has suggested that 90% may be wiped out within 20 years. To help prevent this, the French government has recently pledged CFA262 million to support protection programs. The country is also home to pygmy hippos, giant pangolins, aardvarks, rock hyraxes, hippos, sitatungas, buffaloes, duikers, waterbucks, kobs, roan antelopes, oribi, warthogs and minute populations of lions and leopards.

The bird-watching hotspot is Comoé national park in the northeast, which is believed to host around 500 species including storks, secretary birds and populations of Denham's bustards not found anywhere else in the country. If and when it becomes accessible again, Taï national park is a great place to view guineafowl, fishing owls, western wattled cuckoo-shrikes, nimba flycatchers, yellow-bearded greenbuls, black-headed rufous warblers and white-necked picathartes. Marahoué national park hosts a population of bee-eaters.

PLANTS
Côte d'Ivoire has a mix of dense rainforest, low-lying forested and non-forested savannah and grasslands. Deforestation has reduced the extent of large forested areas and it is unclear how many of the originally recorded 4700 plant species still remain. Bamboo, lianas and other climbing plants are common in forested areas, though cocoa bushes replace trees in many parts of the country.

NUT-CRACKING CHIMPS
The threatened chimps of Parc National de Taï have a special talent; they're one of the world's few documented groups of chimps to have mastered the knack of using fairly advanced tools. Animal behaviour researchers and some anthropologists believe their techniques mirror those of early humans. Here's how the chimps do it:

First the chimp selects a stone. The art of selection is believed to be passed down from generation to generation. Because no carving is involved, each stone must already look like a perfect nutcracker. Next, it heads to a tree bearing good nuts; it can't be any old tree, however, it must have a nook or tree stump nearby to serve as an anvil. With the golf ball–sized nut of choice in hand, it lifts the hammer and…wait! It takes at least seven years to master the art of nut cracking. The chimp's mother will have to give it a lesson first, and it'll have to grow a little. It takes around 1000kg of force to break open the nut without bashing it to pieces. Prime nut-cracking season runs from February to August. Each large nut contains around 30 calories so, on a good day, an expert nut cracker can break open around 100 of those, getting the necessary nutritional fill for the day. It's an exercise in precision, care and skill.

National Parks

Côte d'Ivoire's network of protected areas includes eight national parks, most of which were dedicated in the 1970s and 1980s. Parc National de Taï (p278) is a Unesco World Heritage Site protecting the largest remaining virgin rainforest in West Africa. It contains populations of chimpanzees noted for using tools, pygmy hippos and 11 species of monkey, including the endangered red colobus and Diana monkeys.

Parc National de la Comoé, in the savannah country of the northeast is a World Heritage Site in Danger. It was severely affected by the conflict and has also suffered from poaching and cattle overgrazing. It once hosted populations of lions, lesser white-nosed monkeys and hippos, though it is unclear how many of its species have been lost.

The country's other national parks include Parc National d'Assagny, a rainforest park east of Grand Lahou with good bird watching; Parc National des Îles Ehotilés, a marine park protecting six islands in the Abi Lagoon near Assinie; Parc National de la Marahoué, a savannah and woodland park northwest of Bouaflé; and Parc National du Banco on the outskirts of Abidjan.

At the time of writing, all but Comoé and Taï were accessible to tourists. It may be possible to arrange visits to Parc National de Taï in the near future; we advise you to check once you're on the ground.

Environmental Issues

Côte d'Ivoire has an appalling environmental record, with well-documented cases of illegal logging, poaching and poor park management. In the last 50 years, the country has lost almost a third of its forests. Between 1977 and 1987, when its hardwood exports exceeded Brazil's, a land over 20 times larger, 42% of Côte d'Ivoire's woodland was felled: the highest rate of destruction in the world. During the 1990s the rate of deforestation slowed to 3.1%, but this was still the fifth worst in Africa and nearly three times the continental average. According to 2008 figures, Côte d'Ivoire is still losing more than 3000 sq km of forested land a year.

Wood exported includes mahogany, samba, sipo, bété and iroko. Along with logging, the expansion of agricultural land has taken a devastating toll on the forests, and thus the diverse flora and fauna. The south was once covered in dense tropical rainforest but is now largely given over to coffee, cocoa and charcoal production, and massive groves of native palm, tapped for palm oil. Côte d'Ivoire is the world's largest cocoa producer, accounting for some 40% of the global market and a large proportion of the country's fallen forests. Cocoa forests are now a more common sight than jungle.

Even before the deforestation began, elephant poaching was a serious problem and, along with the loss of habitat, it dropped their numbers to an estimated few hundred. It is conceivable that the country's namesake will be completely wiped out in the future. For years the government, in flagrant violation of the UN Convention on International Trade in Endangered Species, did nothing to stop the sale of ivory.

In 1990, the country was considered the last chimpanzee stronghold in West Africa, harbouring an estimated population of 8000 to 12,000. Today there are only between 800 and 1200 chimps living in Côte d'Ivoire's national parks.

The country's large hydroelectric projects, such as those on the Sassandra River at Buyo and the Bandama River at Kossou, contribute to the country's electricity production, but have also caused ecological damage. There are also problems with water pollution from industrial and, in particular, agricultural effluent, notably in Lake Taabo. The country has been plagued with toxic waste scandals in recent years.

FOOD & DRINK

Almost a foodie's paradise, Côte d'Ivoire is blessed with a cuisine lighter and more flavoursome than that of its immediate coastal neighbours. *Poisson braisé*, sold everywhere from *maquis* to upmarket restaurants, is an absolute must. Try it at a *maquis*, where you'll be able to pick out the size and type of fish you want. It's then served grilled with lashings of onions and tomatoes mixed with ginger and other spices. You eat it by lightly pulling away the flesh with your hands. In Nouchi, the Ivorian street dialect, *braisé* means burned alive, yet this dish is delicately and lightly cooked – just one of the linguistic ironies and double entendres you'll come across in this country.

Poisson braisé is usually served with *attiéké*, grated cassava with a slightly bitter taste and the appearance of couscous. It's delicious. Another popular carb dish is *aloco* –

ripe plantain fried with chilli in palm oil. It can be a little greasy but it's great comfort food. *Fufu* is a doughy ball of boiled yam, cassava or plantain, pounded into a sticky paste similar to mashed potato and dipped into sauces or soups. Especially if you opt for the cassava version, be prepared to sweat it out later. *Sauce gombo*, sometimes called *gombo frais*, is a warming green okra soup; *sauce djoumgbré* has the same delicious ladies' fingers base.

Kedjenou – a whole chicken, or sometimes guinea-fowl, simmered with vegetables in a mild sauce and usually served in an attractive earthenware pot – is ubiquitous. Other meats widely available include brochettes (usually goat or beef) as greasy and fatty as they are spicy; *agouti* or grasscutter rat (tastes a bit like suckling pig; it's much bigger than a rat), *viande* (a generic term but it usually means beef), *herisson* (hedgehog) and other types of bushmeat, including monkeys and wild boar. Bushmeat is viewed as a delicacy throughout West Africa. If you're offered it, you might want to decline for environmental reasons, but if you're in a remote village your host may be offended.

The standard beer is Flag, though beer connoisseurs usually go for locally brewed Tuborg. *Bandji* is the local palm wine, which is very palatable when freshly tapped. Distilled, it makes a strong spirit called *koutoukou*.

ABIDJAN

pop 3.5 million
No, it's not a mirage. Rising curiously from the calm waters of a lagoon, Côte d'Ivoire's economic engine is, however, the stuff of fantasies. Take off your sunglasses, squint a little and admit it: the city's interlinked peninsulas and lagoons look more like Manhattan than the West African city you pictured. Restaurants dish up haute Ivorian cuisine, daring structures rub the clouds and hip boutiques welcome fashionistas. Abidjan, the capital in all but name, was an unimportant town until it became a major port in 1951 when the French finished the Vridi Canal connecting the Ébrié Lagoon with the ocean. Since then, its population has rocketed from 60,000 to 3.5 million. The old saying rings true: this, too, is Africa.

ORIENTATION
Abidjan spreads around the inlets and along the promontories of the large Ébrié Lagoon. Le Plateau, with its boulevards and skyscrapers, is the hub of the business and government districts. These days it's nearly a ghost town at night. Across a finger of the lagoon, east of Le Plateau, is the exclusive residential district of Cocody. North of Cocody lies the residential and restaurant district of Deux Plateaux. To the north of Le Plateau is Adjamé and the main bus station, the frantic Gare Routière d'Adjamé. South of Le Plateau, across two busy bridges is edgy Treichville. Zone 4, with its bars, nightclubs and arty shops, is fast becoming one of the hippest parts of Abidjan.The best way to get everywhere in Abj is by taxi, though buses are becoming more popular.

INFORMATION
Bookshops
Librairie de France (Map p268; ☎ 20-306363; Ave Chardy, Le Plateau; ☽ 8am-6pm Mon-Fri, 9am-5pm Sat) Though it's a little shabby, browsing here is like visiting a decent bookstore in Paris. Good selection of Ivorian fiction.

Cultural Centres
Goethe-Institut (Map p266; ☎ 22-400160; Rue 27, Cocody; ☽ 9am-noon & 2.30-6pm Tue-Fri) Shows European films and hosts local art exhibits.

Emergency
Ambulance (☎ 185)
Fire (☎ 180)
Police (☎ 110)

Internet Access
Cybercafes, most with speedy connections, are dotted all over the city. Rates average CFA600 per hour. Most of the midrange and top-end hotels listed in this chapter offer wi-fi.
Inkoo (Map p266; ☎ 21-247065; Cap Sud Centre Commercial & Gallerie Sococé, Deux Plateaux; ☽ 9am-8pm) Inkoo has speedy connections, a printing centre, phone booths, faxes and scanners.

Medical Services
Abidjan has a good range of medical facilities and it even has a couple of plastic surgeons. The US embassy publishes a long list of recommended practitioners on its website: http://abidjan.usembassy.gov.
Clinique de l'Indénié (☎ 20-215353; 4 Blvd de l'Indénié, Deux Plateaux)

ABIDJAN

0 ——— 1 km
0 ——— 0.5 miles

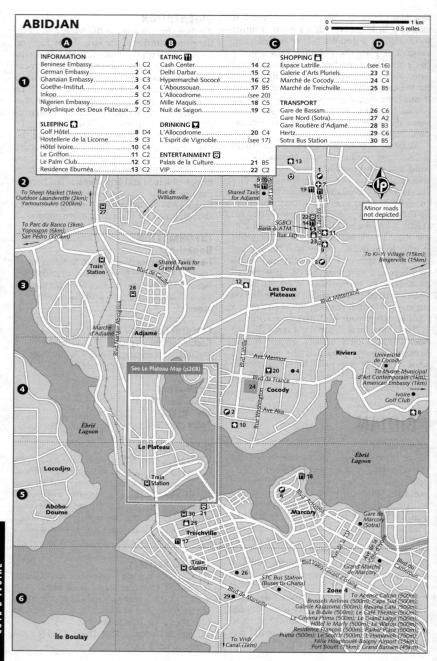

INFORMATION
Beninese Embassy..........................1 C2
German Embassy............................2 C4
Ghanaian Embassy.........................3 C3
Goethe-Institut..............................4 C4
Inkoo..5 C2
Nigerien Embassy..........................6 C2
Polyclinique des Deux Plateaux.....7 C2

SLEEPING 🛏
Golf Hôtel.....................................8 D4
Hostellerie de la Licorne................9 C3
Hôtel Ivoire.................................10 C4
Le Griffon....................................11 C2
Le Palm Club................................12 C3
Residence Eburnéa.......................13 C2

EATING 🍴
Cash Center..................................14 C2
Delhi Darbar.................................15 C2
Hypermarché Sococé....................16 C2
L'Aboussouan..............................17 B5
L'Allocodrome.......................(see 20)
Mille Maquis................................18 C5
Nuit de Saigon.............................19 C2

DRINKING 🍸
L'Allocodrome.............................20 C4
L'Esprit de Vignoble...............(see 17)

ENTERTAINMENT 🎭
Palais de la Culture......................21 B5
VIP..22 C2

SHOPPING 🛍
Espace Latrille.........................(see 16)
Galerie d'Arts Pluriels..................23 C3
Marché de Cocody.......................24 C4
Marché de Treichville...................25 B5

TRANSPORT
Gare de Bassam...........................26 C6
Gare Nord (Sotra).........................27 A2
Gare Routière d'Adjamé................28 B3
Hertz..29 C6
Sotra Bus Station 30 B5

To Sheep Market (1km);
Outdoor Launderette (2km);
Yamoussoukro (200km);

Rue de
Williamsville

Shared Taxis
for Adjamé

To Parc du Banco (3km);
Yopougon (6km);
San Pédro (320km);

SGBCI
Bank & ATM
Rue J40

Minor roads
not depicted

To Ki-Yi Village (15km);
Bingerville (15km)

Train
Station

Shared Taxis for
Grand Bassam
Blvd de Gaulle

Les Deux
Plateaux

Blvd Mitterand

Marché
d'Adjamé

Adjamé

Riviera

Université
de Cocody

See Le Plateau Map (p268)

Ave Mermoz

Blvd de France

Cocody

Ave Aka

To Musée Municipal
d'Art Contemporain (1km);
American Embassy (1km)

Ivoire
Golf Club

Ébrié
Lagoon

Le Plateau

Ébrié
Lagoon

Locodjro

Train
Station

Marcory

Gare de
Marcory
(Sotra)

Abobo-
Doumé

Blvd Achalme

Treichville

Grand Marché
de Marcory

Train
Station

STC Bus Station
(Buses to Ghana)

Blvd Valéry (Giscard d'Estaing)

Zone 4

Blvd de Marseille

To Agence Catran (500m);
Brussels Airlines (500m); Cape Sud (500m);
Galerie Kajazoma (500m); Havana Café (500m);
Le Bidule (500m); Le Café Theatre (500m);
Le Cinema Prima (500m); Le Grand Large (500m);
Hôtel le Marly (500m); Le Wafou (500m);
Residence François (500m); Parker Place (500m);
Prima (500m); Le Scotch (500m); L'Hamanieh (750m);
Félix Houphouët-Boigny Airport (15km);
Port Bouët (15km); Grand Bassam (45km)

To Vridi
Canal (3km)

Île Boulay

CÔTE D'IVOIRE

PISAM (Polyclinique Internationale St Anne-Marie; Map p268; ☎ 22-445132; off Blvd de la Corniche, Cocody) Recommended by UN staff. Intensive 24-hour care unit.

Polyclinique des Deux Plateaux (Pisam; Map p266; ☎ 22-413320; Deux Plateaux)

Money

Euros and dollars can be changed at main branches of banks in Le Plateau. Most branches of SGBCI and Cobaci have ATMs, though not all accept Visa and MasterCard.

Bicici Bank (Map p268; www.bicici.org; Ave Delafosse) Has an ATM.

SGBCI Bank (Map p268; www.sgbci.org; Ave Anoma) Good ATM option; accepts Visa, MasterCard and Maestro. The ATM has its own security guard.

Post

La Poste (Map p268; Pl de la République; ☉ 7.30am-noon & 2.30-4pm Mon-Fri) Western Union and poste restante.

Tourist Information

Côte d'Ivoire Tourisme (Map p268; ☎ 20-251600/10; Pl de la République, Le Plateau; ☉ 7.30am-noon & 2.30-4pm Mon-Fri) There's a good map on the wall and the helpful staff will be happy to shower you with brochures.

Travel Agencies

Agence Catran (off Map p266; ☎ 21-759163; Blvd de Marseille, Zone 4)

Amak Agence (☎ 20-211755; www.amak-international .com; Ground fl, Botreau Roussel Bldg, Le Plateau)

DANGERS & ANNOYANCES

Partly because of the conflict and partly because it's a sprawling, major city, you should keep your wits about you while visiting Abidjan. Though the city bears few war scars, the soldiers guarding checkpoints on the bridges tell a different story. You'll inevitably be stopped and asked for bribes; provided you have your papers with you, declining politely is acceptable. However, the minute you sense tension, you should comply with the request.

There is no longer such a severe distrust of the French, though those perceived to be from France may have slightly more hassle than others. Despite its reputation for crime, Treichville is relatively safe up to 15th Ave, though the bridges between Treichville and Le Plateau have long been notorious for theft, so don't walk over them, day or night. You might not even want to drive over Pont du Général de Gaulle during rush hour when many taxi

passengers get robbed. Travelling with a taxi driver you trust is recommended after dark. Your hotel should be able to recommend a reliable driver.

SIGHTS
Le Plateau

Abidjan's skyline is every bit as breathtaking as Chicago's, not least because it often takes travellers by surprise. **La Pyramide** (Map p268; cnr Ave Franchet d'Esperey & Rue Botreau-Roussel), designed by the Italian architect Rinaldo Olivieri, was the first daring structure.

Looming over the Cathédrale St-Paul are the towers of the **Cité Administrative** (Map p268; Blvd Angoulvant), featuring giant copper-coloured slabs with fretted windows. The shimmering **Ministry of Post & Telecommunications** (Map p268; cnr Ave Marchand & Rue Lecoeur), all rounded angles and curves soaring skyward, contrasts with its cuboid, right-angled neighbours. The **French Embassy** (Map p268; ☎ 20-200404; www.consulfrance-abidjan.org; 17 Rue Lecoeur) is also pretty impressive. Don't miss Blvd de la République.

Cathédrale St-Paul

Designed by the Italian Aldo Spiritom, this is a bold and innovative modern **cathedral** (Map p268; Blvd Angoulvant, Le Plateau; admission free; ☉ 8am-7pm). The tower is a huge stylised figure of St Paul, with the nave sweeping behind him like trailing robes. Inside, the stained-glass tableaux are as warm and rich as those of the basilica in Yamoussoukro. Make a point of seeing these three in particular: the one behind the altar depicting God blinding St Paul on the road to Damascus; the storm on Lake Galilee with Jesus pointing the way ahead as the disciples jettison the cargo; and, opposite, the tableau of the first missionaries stepping ashore to a scene of African plenty – elephants, gazelles, luxuriant palms and smiling villagers.

Musée National

The **museum** (Map p268; ☎ 20-222056; Blvd Nangui Abrogoua, Le Plateau; admission CFA2000; ☉ 9am-5pm Tue-Sat) houses a dusty but interesting collection of traditional art and craftwork, including wooden statues and masks, pottery, ivory and bronze. This is a good place to get a grounding in Ivorian traditions. There are also sculptures by Christian Lattier, one of Côte d'Ivoire's most celebrated artists.

CÔTE D'IVOIRE

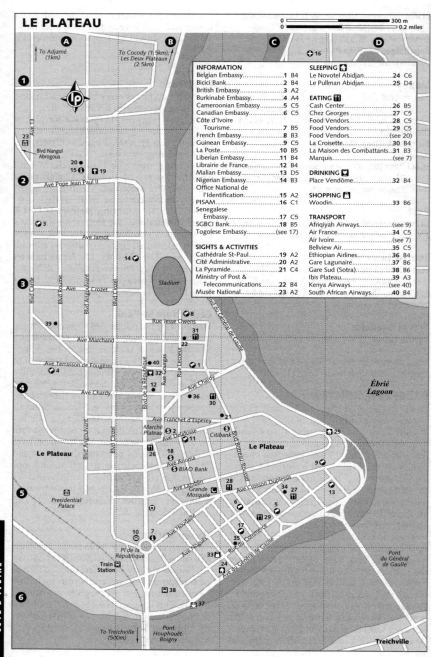

LE PLATEAU

To Adjamé
(1km)

To Cocody (1.5km);
Les Deux Plateaux
(2.5km)

Ave 13

Blvd Nangul
Abrogoua

Ave Pope Jean Paul II

Ave Jamot

Blvd Carde

Blvd Roume

Ave Angoulvant

Blvd Crozet

Blvd Clozel

Stadium

Rue Jesse Owens

Ave Marchand

Ave Terrasson de Fougères

Ave Chardy

Blvd de la République

Rue Gourgas

Rue Lecoeur

Ave Chardy

Ave Franchet d'Esperey

Blvd du Général de Gaulle

Blvd Botreau-Roussel

Marché
Plateau

Ave Delafosse

Citibank

Le Plateau

Ave Anoma

BIAO Bank

Ave Lamblin

Grande
Mosquée

Ave Crosson Duplessis

Ave Houdaille

Ave Noguès

Rue du Commerce

Pl de la
République

Train
Station

Ave du Général de Gaulle

Blvd Angoulvant

Blvd Clozel

Le Plateau

Presidential
Palace

Ébrié
Lagoon

Pont
du Général
de Gaulle

To Treichville
(500m)

Pont
Houphouët-
Boigny

Treichville

CÔTE D'IVOIRE

Musée Municipal d'Art Contemporain

This **art museum** (off Map p266; ☎ 22-471686; off Rte de M'Pouto, Riviera; admission CFA1000; ⊙ 9am-5pm Tue-Sat), situated beyond the Golf Hôtel has a thought-provoking collection of work by contemporary Ivorian and other African artists, and regularly mounts exciting, temporary exhibitions. You can have a guided tour for another CFA1000.

Parc du Banco

On the northwest edge of town is located the cool and shady **Parc du Banco** (off Map p266; Autoroute de Nord; admission CFA1000) rainforest reserve. It has pleasant walking trails, majestic trees and a lake, but you'll be lucky to see any wildlife. Though it's had some bad press in the past (escaped prisoners and ousted rebels hung out here during the crisis), if you pay CFA3000, the rangers will give you a safe guided tour. Near the park entrance is Africa's largest outdoor laundrette (see below).

The only reliable place to see animals in this city is the **Zoo d'Abidjan** (Autoroute Adjamé-Abobo; admission CFA300), situated on a hilly location. The zoo itself is popular with couples seeking a romantic picnic spot, though the caged lions look as dejected as you'd expect.

Sheep Market

Past the outdoor launderette, follow the road around until you reach the Muslim **sheep market** (off Map p266). Hundreds of thousands of goats and sheep of every possible colour and ilk are brought here every day, and it really is quite a sight. The market is frequented by farmers, butchers and *juju* practitioners, who use the horns in traditional African medicine. The rarest black goats go for as much as CFA250,000.

FESTIVALS & EVENTS

The **Marché des Arts et du Spectacle Africains** (MASA Festival; www.masa.francophonie.org) is a pan-African trade fair to promote dance, drama and music, but the highlight is the week of live performances. It used to take place in March and April of odd years, but recently dates have varied considerably. Abidjan's **short-film festival** (FICA; www.leblogdufica.com) is usually held every other even year in March or April.

SLEEPING
Budget

Abidjan suffers from a shortage of good budget accommodation. Treichville (particularly around Carrefour France-Amerique) has a few shoestring picks, though most of these are a little shady and not recommended.

Le Palm Club (Map p266; ☎ 22-444450; Blvd Latrille, Deux Plateaux; s CFA20,000; P ✗ ✆) Though it's certainly Abidjan's most well-equipped budget option (there's a pool and parking), it's a little drab. The basic but spacious rooms are popular with NGO workers.

L'Hamanieh (off Map p266; ☎ 21-756710/21-369155; Blvd Lorraine, s/d CFA20,000/25,000) Basic rooms are brightened with Ivorian art, but it's the location that's a winner: L'Hamanieh is within walking distance of the bars and shops on Blvd de Marseille.

Residence François (off Map p266; ☎ 21-244539; Rue Paul Langevin, Zone 4; s/d CFA20,000/30,000) Popular with long-term visitors, this is an OK budget option. Rooms, though basic, are clean and comfortable. There's TV but no internet.

Midrange

Hôtel le Marly (off Map p266; ☎ 21-258552; Blvd de Marseille, Zone 4; s/d CFA40,000/50,000, ste CFA60,000; P ✗ ✆) A low-key place, Le Marly offers simple plantation-style huts in a pretty garden setting. The staff are relaxed and friendly, and

---

THE OUTDOOR LAUNDRETTE

Every day some 375 *fanicos* (washermen), mostly Burkinabé and non-Ivorian, jam together in the middle of a small stream near the Parc du Banco, frantically rubbing clothes on huge stones held in place by old car tyres. Afterwards, they spread the clothes over rocks and grass for at least 500m (never getting them mixed up) and then iron them. Any washer not respecting the strict rules imposed by the washers' trade union, which allocates positions, is immediately excluded.

The black soap is sold by women who make it from palm oil in small wooden sheds on the hills surrounding the stream. The *fanicos* begin arriving with their loads around 6.30am, but it's best to come between 10.30am and noon when the action is at its peak. You'll get some superb photos, although payment is expected. In the afternoon all you'll see is drying clothes.

CÔTE D'IVOIRE

there's Ivorian art on the walls. It's at the end of a short track just off Blvd de Marseille.

Residence Eburnéa (Map p266; ☎ 22-527005; www .residence-eburnea.net, in French; 7eme tranche, Deux Plateaux; r CFA40,000-60,000; P ⊠ ⊜ ⊛) This friendly Ivorian-run guesthouse gets high ratings from travellers. Choose from several types of room, including charming duplexes and cute apartments with miniature kitchens and balconies. The whole place is clean, quiet and well-cared for. There's also a small pool.

our pick Hostellerie de la Licorne (Map p266; ☎ 22-410730; www.licogriff.com; Rue des Jardins, Deux Plateaux Vallons; r incl breakfast CFA40,000-70,000; P ⊠ ⊟ ⊛) Abidjan's most traveller-friendly option is also its most charming. Each room is clean, spacious and fun to look at; if you take the room at the end of the corridor, you'll share the enormous bed with plush, gold cushions and a furry leopard. Downstairs, there's a pool area, good restaurant, book swap, wine rack and jewellery for sale. Owned by a friendly, bilingual French couple, this is our favourite place to stay in Abidjan. Head to Rue des Jardins and follow the road as it winds behind the Total petrol station.

Le Griffon (Map p266; ☎ 22-416622; www.licogriff .com; Rue des Jardins, Deux Plateaux Vallons; r CFA40,000-70,000; ⊠ ⊜ ⊛) Owned by the daughter of the couple who run La Licorne, Le Griffon is every bit as special. This boutique hotel offers beautifully decorated themed rooms, dressed with Ivorian art and coffee-table books. With friendly staff, great food and a hot tub in the patio garden, it's a gem.

Le Wafou (off Map p266; ☎ 21-256201/2; Blvd de Marseille, Zone 4; r CFA48,000, ste CFA100,000; P ⊠ ⊜ ⊛) If the Flintstones won the lottery and moved to Mali, they'd live somewhere like this. Le Wafou's gorgeous bungalows take cues from traditional Dogon villages: rooms are beautifully and artistically decorated, with plush showers and great beds. At night you can enjoy great food and wine beside the stylish pool/bar area. The whole complex is set back from the road and has a great, unpretentious feel. It's good for kids, too.

Top End

Hôtel Ivoire (Map p266; ☎ 22-408000/72; www.hotel ivoire.com; Blvd de la Corniche; d CFA60,000, ste CFA300,000; P ⊠ ⊟ ⊛) In the 1970s the Hôtel Ivoire practically had diamonds on the soles of its shoes. There was a chandeliered piano bar,

ice rink, casino, cinema, pool and first-rate rooftop restaurant. It's being renovated but you can still stay here and marvel at the Côte d'Ivoire of yesteryear. Rooms are spacious and comfortable.

Golf Hôtel (Map p266; ☎ 22-431044; www.golfhotel -ci.com; Blvd de France, Riviera; r CFA90,000, ste CFA180,000; P ⊠ ⊟ ⊛) Flanked by the lagoon and the lush green Ivoire Golf Club, this top-end option is a winner. The 300-plus rooms are modern and very well equipped; some have balconies and stunning views. There's also an attractive pool, football pitch, tennis courts, lagoon beach and first-rate restaurant. Anyone can picnic in the relaxing grounds on Sundays (adult/child CFA5000/3000) Check the website for special offers.

Le Novotel Abidjan (Map p268; ☎ 20-318000; www .novotel.com; 10 Ave du Général de Gaulle, Le Plateau; r from €137; P ⊠ ⊟ ⊛) Abidjan's Novotel is up to the chain's usual high standards. Though many French travellers rate the cuisine at the Pullman more highly, there's a good restaurant, bar, pool, business centre, store and lagoon views. Free airport shuttle.

Le Pullman Abidjan (Map p268; ☎ 20-302020; www .sofitel.com; Rue Abdoulaye Fadiga, Le Plateau; r US$206, ste US$209; P ⊠ ⊜ ⊛) Among the best of Le Plateau's first-rate hotels, the Pullman has 209 gorgeous rooms with everything you could possibly want. There's an outdoor pool, business centre, airport bus and top-notch dining. It's part of the Sofitel chain.

EATING
Maquis

Mille Maquis should be your first stop. True to its name, this part of Marcory is teeming with *maquis* – it's a sprawling, overgrown food market. More than just a place to get a quick bite, Mille Maquis is as famous for the *coupé-decalé* music videos that have been filmed here as it is for its fare.

The un-named *maquis* behind Côte d'Ivoire Tourisme at Pl de la République, is a good place to fill up. The *aloco* won us over here.

If it weren't so friendly, Treichville's Maquis Rue 19 would look a bit like a witch's cavern. The huge cauldrons of sauces and soups empty nearby offices at lunchtime.

Food vendors near the port (opposite the Unilever building) and between Ave Noguès and Rue du Commerce are so popular that you'll have to wait in line. There's also a cluster of small, recommended lunchtime food vendors at the base of the towers of the Cité Administrative on Blvd Angoulvant.

Restaurants
IVORIAN
Le Nandjelet (opp cemetery, Blockosso; mains from CFA2000; ☾ dinner) Tucked away in Blockosso, this enchanting local spot offers good, basic fare. Make a beeline for one of the outdoor tables on the edge of the lagoon – they offer a breathtaking panorama of the Abidjan skyline. Who cares about the mozzies when the views are this good? It's not clearly signposted; ask passers-by if you're stuck.

Restaurant Mokla (Rue A49, Le Plateau; ☾ lunch) Easy to miss on Rue A49, the Mokla is a good plan for lunch au Plateau. Affordable but topnotch local food draws a suited and booted city crowd.

our pick **Galerie Kajazoma** (off Map p266; ☎ 21-246416; Rue G177/Marconi, Zone 4 ; mains from CFA7000; ☾ noon-late Mon-Sat) Part art gallery, part restaurant, this beautifully designed villa is one of our favourite places to eat in Abidjan. Grab a table in the garden or head inside, where everything is for sale, from painted plates to sofas, chairs, ironwork and carved Ivorian bowls the size of tables. Everything is designed and made on-site. The garden is sprinkled with fairy lights, artwork and little lamps. Try the *kedjenou* Kajazoma or the prawns with avocado and mango; there's also a great cocktail list.

L'Aboussouan (Map p266; ☎ 21-241309; Ave Valéry Giscard d'Estaing, Treichville; set menu CFA15,000) One of the top Ivorian restaurants in Abidjan (and therefore, probably, the world) L'Aboussouan ('family' in Akan) offers haute cuisine versions of popular Ivorian dishes, including first-class *kedjenou*. The owners also run L'Esprit de Vignoble, a highly regarded wine cellar-bar in the same building.

La Maison des Combattants (Map p268; Ave Marchand, Le Plateau; mains from C5000; ☾ lunch & dinner) Next to the war memorial, this renovated colonial building has a great range of dishes including *escargot*, *sauce feuille* (manioc-leaf sauce with beef tail, fish and crab) and other dishes not often found in sit-down restaurants.

FRENCH & EUROPEAN
La Croisette (Map p268; ☎ 21-759162; Ave Botreau-Roussel, Le Plateau; meals CFA8000-14,000; ☾ lunch & dinner) La Croisette is one of the city's best French picks

offering fine cuisine in stylish surroundings. The *sole meunière* is excellent.

Le Grand Large (off Map p266; ☎ 21-242113; 149 Blvd de Marseille; mains from CFA13,000; ☾ dinner) This Frenchrun dining room has a first-rate menu – everything from foie gras to crème brûlée, Irish coffee and chocolate and caramel tart. Upmarket, hip and welcoming.

Chez Georges (Map p268; ☎ 20-321084; www.restaurant chezgeorges.com; Rue du Commerce, Le Plateau; mains from C3000; ☾ lunch & dinner) We'd like to live in a restored colonial-era building like this. For now though, we'll have to make do with eating here. The menu is huge – everything from *salade roquefort* to stuffed crab, duck and *steak-frites* – though not to the detriment of the food. It serves good pizza too.

Hit Parade (Blvd Delafosse/Carrefour France-Amerique, Treichville; mains from C4000; ☾ lunch & dinner) Despite the dubious name this place is a fairly stylish affair with linen-covered chairs and a good ambiance. The bouillabaisse (CFA6500) is good.

ASIAN
Nuit de Saigon (Map p266; ☎ 22-414044; Rue des Jardins, Deux Plateaux; mains from CFA3500; ☾ lunch & dinner) Like a fine wine, La Nuit has got even better with age. Abidjan's best-known Vietnamese restaurant is still a local favourite. There's a great wine list, top service and a wide-ranging menu. The hot and sour soup (CFA3000) is excellent.

Delhi Darbar (Map p266; Rue des Jardins, Deux Plateaux; meals CFA4500-12,000; ☾ lunch & dinner Tue-Sun) A sound option for those in need of a curry fix. There's a good choice of Indian dishes, served in an attractive dining room.

Self-Catering
Abidjan has two established supermarket chains with stores in Le Plateau: Nour-al-Hayat and the cheaper, gaudier Cash Center (Map p268). The amazing **Hypermarché Sococé** (Map p266; Blvd Latrille) in Deux Plateaux is worth a visit for its own sake: there's everything from cheese and wine aisles to an entertainment section.

DRINKING
L'Allocodrome (Map p266; Rue Washington, Cocody) If you repeat its name fast, you get an idea of the kinds of rhythms that bring this place to life every night. L'Allocodrome is Abidjan's most famous *maquis* bar: individual food vendors compete for your business and on weekends

BEN MPECK

How many musicians perform in Ki-Yi Mbock? The group has 60 performers from three generations. It's a pan-African collaboration and we have members from all over Africa. Before the conflict, there were about 350 of us.

What effect did the conflict have on the group? It threatened to put a stop to everything. When Côte d'Ivoire erupted into war, it felt like a storm in the middle of the dry season. Everything was affected – our finances, our morale and our relationships with each other. We were unable to travel to international competitions, even though we'd been winning awards overseas up until then.

So what did you do? I worked on my music. You know, one good thing about the conflict – even the worst things in life aren't completely bad – is that Ivorians became more aware of their culture. All the expats packed up and left; Côte d'Ivoire was shut off from the rest of the world. During that time Ivorians learnt a lot about themselves.

How do you think the conflict has changed Abidjan? I fell for Abidjan the minute I moved here. It's such an open and welcoming city and that hasn't changed. What has changed is people's perceptions of it. I've started travelling abroad again and whenever I say I live in Abidjan, people look at me as if I've just said I live in Baghdad. In that respect, Abidjan is still getting hit by the crisis.

Ben Mpeck is a hip-hop artist who manages Côte d'Ivoire's national cultural group, Ki-Yi Mbock. Ben grew up in Cameroon but has been living in Abidjan for years.

there's dancing among the tables. It's huge, chaotic and really good fun: you'll learn more about Abidjan in one night here than you will anywhere else in this crazy city.

Havana Café (off Map p266; Rue Mercedes, Zone 4) Push back the wooden door and walk through the cute courtyard to find this ever-expanding bar, popular with travellers and expats. There's a tiled counter bar and the South American theme is reflected in the great mojitos and margheritas. We like it.

Le Bidule (off Map p266; cnr Blvd du 7 Decembre/Rue Paul Langevin, Zone 4) Though its walls – the colour of rust-red roads – are hung with African art, Le Bidule is an expat favourite. We know it's a bit of a gossip factory but it's also a place to have a damn good time. Things get going from Thursday onwards; earlier in the week it's a laid-back drinking lounge.

Le Café Theatre (off Map p266; Blvd du 7 Decembre, Zone 4) There are two faces to this classy-looking bar in Zone 4. Most of the time it's a posh champagne bar, but on Friday nights it becomes karaoke central.

Place Vendôme (Map p268; Blvd de la République, Le Plateau) Almost as fancy as its Parisian namesake, Vendôme attracts guys draped in bling and aspiring models. It's popular with Le Plateau's hot-shot business crowd.

Le Scotch (off Map p266; Rue Paul Langevin, Zone 4) Though it's not the hippest bar in town, Le Scotch still draws a good crowd. There's a great outside pool area (both kinds) and you can grab a bite to eat. It's good for early evening drinks.

ENTERTAINMENT
Live Music

Those who need convincing that Abidjan's music scene is as lively as ever should get themselves to Rue Princesse in the working-class district of Yopougon, 6km west of the centre. On Friday and Saturday nights the street becomes a cross between London's Notting Hill Carnival and Bangkok's Khao San Road. If you want to hear live or piped *coupé-decalé* and West African hip-hop, this is the place to be. President Laurent Gbagbo famously brought Jack Lang, France's former minister for culture, here in March 2008. Much to the amusement of the crowd, they went dancing at **Le Queen** (Rue Princesse, Yopougon) club – owned by the footballer Didier Drogba – to signify the end of the crisis.

Parker Place (off Map p266; www.parkerplaceabidjan.com; Rue Paul Langevin, Zone 4) The best drinking spot this side of Kingston. Parker Place's weekend reggae gigs have a cult following, not least because Alpha Blondy and Tiken Jah Fakoly played here before they were famous. The in-house band, The Wisemen, will have you jamming in no time. This is an Abidjan institution.

Ki-Yi Mbock (Map p266; ☎ 22-433866/01-573840; www.kiyi-village.org, in French; Riviéra II Bonoumin; shows from CFA7000) Dampened by the crisis, Côte d'Ivoire's spectacular national cultural group is back up and running. Under the tutelage of the phenomenal Werewere Liking, students from all over Africa perform highly regarded music, theatre and dance shows. The village also includes art, drama and recording studios, designed to nurture promising artistic talent. Dinner shows often take place on Wednesday nights, though not every week; call to confirm. A taxi is the best way to get here.

Palais de la Culture (Map p266; www.palaisdelaculture .ci; Ave 1, Treichville) Several venues are rolled into one at Abidjan's highly regarded cultural centre in Treichville. Though the concert halls have good acoustics, don't just come for the music. Dance, film and theatre get plenty of attention here too. Check the website for listings; there's no sense rocking up if you don't know what's on because the place is simply enormous.

Nightclubs

Le Ritz (Blvd Delafosse/Carrefour France-Amerique, Treichville) With a name like Le Ritz you'd expect either overdone glamour or a trashy, cheesy club. Thankfully, Le Ritz is neither. The place is dressed with plush white sofas, big pots of bamboo and vases of fake white dandelions. Not that you'll really care about the cool decor when the Ivorian beats are this much fun. DJs play *zouglou*, *coupé-decalé* and *boborama*. There's usually a CFA5000 cover.

Pinky's (☎ 09-586424; Blvd du 7 Decembre, Treichville) On the same strip as Ice, Pinky's is a small club that's big with expats. There's a circular dance floor and a well-stocked bar. It sometimes hosts themed parties.

Ice (Blvd Delafosse, Treichville) Lights, mirrors and the tight T-shirt brigade. At the time

of writing, upmarket Ice was getting props from Ivorian-born international footballers. Expect to hear hip-hop, RnB and sometimes *coupé-decalé*.

Le Mix (Rue Dr Blanchard) Le Mix draws big-name DJs, models, Ivorian celebs and suited, sunglass-clad businessmen. It's hip and pretty fancy.

VIP (Map p266; Rue des Jardins, Deux Plateaux) Another contender for the Abidjan club crown. Dress up and get down to American and Ivorian beats.

Cinema

Palais de la Culture (Map p266; www.palaisdelaculture .ci; Ave 1, Treichville) is your best bet for arthouse films. **Le Cinema Prima** (off Map p266; Centre Commercial Prima, Blvd Valéry Giscard d'Estaing) shows the latest from Hollywood.

SHOPPING

Marché de Cocody (Map p266; ☎ 20-310565; Rue du Commerce, Cocody) Until it was burnt down, this was Côte d'Ivoire's top arts and crafts market. Though the market has yet to be rebuilt, you can still shop for woodcarvings, nick-nacks, sculptures, handbags and jewellery in the area, though most of the stuff is now imported from Senegal. Until it's renovated, the road out of the city to Grand Bassam is a better bet for Ivorian crafts.

Marché de Treichville (Map p266; ☎ 20-310565; Treichville) If you're in the market for fabric or looking for a great (and inexpensive) tailor, the area around Treichville market is a good bet. You'll also find Maimouna Gomet's cocoa-fashion boutique, Felicite Mai, here (see the boxed text, below).

Galerie d'Arts Pluriels (Map p266; ☎ 22-411506 Rue des Jardins, Deux Plateaux) This fantastic art

---

ECO-FASHION: SWEET LIKE CHOCOLATE

Côte d'Ivoire is dripping with style and sartorial charm. Life in Le Plateau, Abidjan's business hub, is set to a soundtrack of clicking heels, and some of the city's streets look like extensions of the catwalk at the Palais de la Culture (see above). The latest trend to hit Abidjan is eco-fashion, or *waboua*, the philosophy that everything is useful. One of the pioneers of the eco-fashion movement is Maimouna Gomet, a young designer who has produced a line of clothing made entirely from disused cocoa sacks. Côte d'Ivoire, after all, produces more cocoa than anywhere else on the planet. Think skirts embroidered with dark thread, frayed shirts with cocoa beans for buttons, and a range of jewellery fashioned from torn strips of cloth and seashells. It's no surprise that other Ivorian designers are following in her footsteps. Gomet's Felicite Mai boutique is in the edgy Treichville district of Abidjan, where you'll find a handful of other eco-designers too.

CÔTE D'IVOIRE

gallery–shop is run by an Ivorian art historian. You can view and buy paintings, sculptures and jewellery from all over the continent. The prices, though high (a sculpture will cost you €800) reflect the quality of the stuff on show here.

Woodin (Map p268; ☎ 20-310565; Rue du Commerce, Le Plateau) This is part of a highly regarded West African group that sells quality Dutch wax-cloth clothing. It's a good bet if you're gift-hunting.

Abidjan has a handful of shiny shopping malls. **Cap Sud** (Map p266; Blvd Valéry Giscard d'Estaing) and **Prima** (Map p266; Blvd Valéry Giscard d'Estaing) include clothing shops, a couple of good bookstores and a music shop, while **Espace Latrille** (Map p266; Deux Plateaux) contains a range of stores including the revered Hypermarché Sococé.

GETTING THERE & AWAY
Air
The shiny Félix Houphouët-Boigny International Airport takes all of the international traffic. For details on international flights see p286 or p287 for domestic travel.

Bus & Bush Taxi
The main bus station is the disorganised Gare Routière d'Adjamé, some 4km north of Le Plateau. Most UTB and Sotra buses and bush taxis leave from here and there's frequent transport to all major towns. In theory, the earliest buses leave around 6am.

Bush taxis and minibuses for destinations east along the coast, such as Grand Bassam (45 minutes to one hour), Aboisso and Elubo (three hours) at the Ghanaian border, leave primarily from the **Gare de Bassam** (cnr Rue 38 and Blvd Valéry Giscard d'Estaing), south of Treichville. Transport for Grand Bassam also departs from Gare Routière d'Adjamé, but takes longer.

GETTING AROUND
To/From the Airport
A taxi ride from the airport to Le Plateau should cost between CFA4000 and CFA6000. The taxi stand is to the left of the main entrance. Most taxis are metered – you can either ask the driver to stick to the price his meter gives him, or you can bargain for a fixed price before getting in. Rates double after midnight. You'll probably be met by young guys

who insist on carrying your luggage to the taxi rank; though they can be pushy, they're generally harmless and are simply trying to make ends meet.

Boat
Abidjan has a commuter ferry service on the lagoon. It goes from Treichville to Abobo-Doumé (across the lagoon, west of Le Plateau), then to Le Plateau and back to Treichville again (in that sequence; it's a long ride from Treichville to Le Plateau). Taking a *bateau-bus* (boat-bus) is a great way to the see the city from a different perspective. The *gare lagunaire* (ferry terminal) in Le Plateau is 100m east of Pont Houphouët-Boigny. The fare from there across the lagoon to the Treichville ferry terminal, also east of Pont Houphouët-Boigny, is CFA200. There are several departures every hour from around 5am to 8pm.

The *bateaux-bus* also link Le Plateau with the *quartier* of Yopougon.

Bus
The city's Sotra buses tend to be crowded but they're as cheap as taking the commuter ferry (though the view doesn't compare). They display their route number, which also features on bus-stop signs, but only rarely their destination. The people waiting for a bus with you should know which ones go where.

The major Sotra bus station in Le Plateau is Gare Sud, south of Pl de la République. The other Sotra stations are Gare Nord in Adjamé, north of the train station, and another on Ave Christian in Treichville. Buses operate from about 6am to between 9pm and 10pm daily.

Car
International agencies – **Avis** (☎ 20-328007), **Budget** (☎ 21-751616) and **Hertz** (☎ 21-751105) – are represented at the airport and in Abidjan. Prices and terms vary but, in general, a small car is around CFA35,000 per day, including tax and compulsory insurance, plus CFA230 per kilometre. The price will rise if you want to leave the city. You are definitely better off arranging a car and driver with the many men who wait in front of the fancy hotels. You should be able to arrange one for the day for around CFA15,000 to CFA20,000. You could also try the car hire office attached to **Ibis Plateau** (Map p268; 7 Blvd Roume) or at any of the hotels in the top-end category. Alternatively, you can hire a taxi for the day (see opposite).

Taxi

Abidjan's orange taxis are reasonably priced, but drivers don't always switch on their meter without prompting. Make sure it's set to tariff No 1. The more expensive No 2 rate only applies between midnight and 6am. A trip from Le Plateau to Zone 4 cost around CFA2000 at the time of writing. If you want to hire a taxi driver for a day plan on paying between CFA18,000 and CFA30,000.

Woro-woro (shared taxis) cost between CFA250 and CFA700, depending on the length of the journey. They vary in colour according to their allocated area. Those between Plateau, Adjamé, Marcory and Treichville, for example, are red, while those in Les Deux Plateaux and Cocody are yellow; Yopougon's are blue.

THE EAST COAST

An easy weekend trip from Abidjan, the eastern beaches are reason enough to visit Côte d'Ivoire. A word of warning: arty Bassam and sleepy Assinie, blessed with cu-riously squeaky white sands, play havoc with even the best-laid plans.

GRAND BASSAM

Hugged by a long white sandy beach, laid-back Grand Bassam feels a world away from grid-locked Abidjan. Though it's now arty and shabby-chic, it wasn't so long ago (1893) that Bassam, as it's known, was declared capital of the French colony. Six years later a major yellow-fever epidemic broke out, prompting the French to move their capital to Bingerville. Shame on them, we think it's utterly charming.

Though the streets do have names in Bassam, nobody really uses them. The town is so compact that you'll be able to find everything you're looking for by use of nearby landmarks.

Sights

Much of the original colonial architecture is still in remarkably good shape; you can take it all in on an hour-long walk around town. The **Palais de Justice** (Blvd Treich-Laplene) should be your first stop. Built in 1910, it

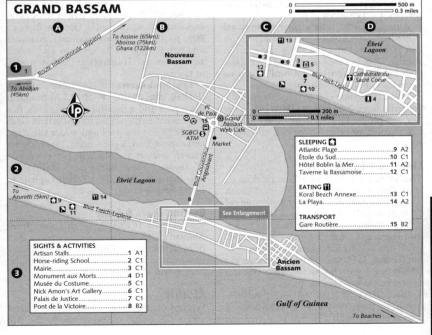

GRAND BASSAM

SLEEPING
Atlantic Plage...............................9 A2
Étoile du Sud.............................10 C1
Hôtel Boblin la Mer....................11 A2
Taverne la Bassamoise................12 C1

EATING
Koral Beach Annexe....................13 C1
La Playa....................................14 A2

TRANSPORT
Gare Routière............................15 B2

SIGHTS & ACTIVITIES
Artisan Stalls..............................1 A1
Horse-riding School.....................2 C1
Mairie..3 C1
Monument aux Morts...................4 D1
Musée du Costume......................5 C1
Nick Amon's Art Gallery...............6 C1
Palais de Justice..........................7 C1
Pont de la Victoire......................8 B2

was in this building that members of Côte d'Ivoire's PDCI-RDA political group – that of Houphouët-Boigny – were arrested by the French authorities in 1949, a struggle that preceded independence.

The **Musée du Costume** (☎ 21-301370; Blvd Treich-Laplene; admission by donation), once the governor's palace, now houses a collection of colonial clothing and artefacts. At the end of the boulevard is the **Monument aux Morts**, built in 1914 to honour, as the engraving states, 'France's fallen men'. The monument, dedicated to yellow-fever victims, shows a suffering white figure being watched over by a black woman. The **Pont de la Victoire**, which runs across the lagoon, is most famous as the site of a naked protest against the 1949 detainment of PDCI-RDA members.

Activities

The road from Abidjan to Bassam is one of the best spots on the coast to pick up art, craftwork and souvenirs but, for something special, head to Nick Amon's **art gallery** (Blvd Treich-Laplene). One of Côte d'Ivoire's most-respected contemporary artists, he'll greet you with paint-splattered clothing and a warm smile. His canvases start at around CFA50,000; profits go to an organisation that teaches street children to paint.

Augustin Édou runs a **horse-riding school** (1/2hr ride CFA13,000/20,000) on the same street. You can arrange riding trips along the coast at sunrise. Dugout canoe trips to see traditional crab fishers, mangroves and birdlife can be arranged with local boatmen.

If you time your visit to coincide with the colourful week-long **Fête de l'Abissa** (when the N'Zima people honour their dead) held in late October or early November, you won't be sorry.

Sleeping & Eating

The hotels listed here are all on, or close to, Blvd Treich-Laplene, Bassam's focal point. Though there are options on the other side of Le Pont de la Victoire, it makes much more sense to base yourself by the beach. The following places have their own restaurants but you'll find laid-back *maquis* dotted throughout Bassam. **La Playa** (Blvd Treich-Laplene; dishes from CFA4500) does a great line in upmarket versions of Senegalese and Ivorian dishes.

Atlantic Plage (☎ 05-504208/21-302971; Blvd Treich-Laplene; r with air-con CFA15,000; (P) (X) (D)) Atlantic is a good cheapie with a garden/pool area and

private beach. The handful of rooms have a nice Ivorian touch.

Hôtel Boblin la Mer (☎ 21-301418; Blvd Treich-Laplene; r with air-con CFA15,000-20,000; (P) (X)) Though the courtyard is a little shabby, Boblin is easily the best value in Bassam. Rooms are decorated with masks and woodcarvings, and the canopy beds come with the most attractive mozzie nets this side of Abidjan. The restaurant sits right on the beach and offers decent breakfasts.

Taverne la Bassamoise (☎ 21-301062; Blvd Treich-Laplene; r/bungalow incl breakfast CFA25,000/29,000; (P) (X) (D)) La Bassamoise is worth a visit for the courtyard alone. Just inside the gate, monkeys and parrots hang from every branch of a colossal tree. They're wooden, of course, just like the rest of the impressive statues that inhabit the grounds of this hotel. You'll meet policemen and forest rangers, pelicans and life-size leopards. Bungalows (a little shabby) are hidden underneath a canopy of bougainvillea; there's a restaurant, a 1950s-style beach area and two pools decorated with mosaics.

Étoile du Sud (☎ 21-302939; Blvd Treich-Laplene; r CFA45,000, ste CFA60,000; (P) (X) (📶) (D)) Though largely frequented by suits, Bassam's most upmarket option is a stunning place to stay. The hotel is dressed with stylish woodcarvings and sink-worthy sofas. Outside, there's a large pool with its own (excellent) restaurant and bar. Rooms are as spacious and stylish as you'd expect. It also offers the fastest wi-fi in town.

Koral Beach Annexe (☎ 21-30-2589; r with fan from CFA25,000; pizzas CFA8000; (P) (X) (D)) Although it has a pool and a handful of bungalows, this place is better known for its restaurant. Grab a table beside the pool and under the stars, and choose from a good menu that includes French starters and the best pizzas outside of Abidjan. From Étoile du Sud, take the lane that runs from Blvd Treich-Laplene to Blvd Lagunaire.

Getting There & Away

Shared taxis (CFA500, 40 minutes) from Abidjan's Gare de Bassam arrive faster than from Gare Routière d'Adjamé. In Bassam, the *gare routière* is beside the Pl de Paix roundabout, north of the lagoon.

ASSINIE

Perched on the tip of a long finger of sand where the Canal d'Assinie meets the Abi

Lagoon, quiet Assinie tugs at the heartstrings of overlanders, washed-up surfers and rich weekenders from Abidjan, who run their quad bikes up and down its peroxide-blonde beach. Somehow they all co-exist in relative harmony – partly because Assinie is split into several parts and partly because…well, it's just that kind of place.

Assinie is as quiet and low-key as it gets; at the time of research there was nowhere to get online and there are certainly no banks or ATMs. If you're here to surf, watch the undertows: they can be strong. Assinie is occasionally hit by power cuts, which, frankly, make it all the more romantic.

Sleeping & Eating

The following options are in Assouinde. Assinie Mafia has a small selection of resort-style hotels and the eccentric **Crocodile Dipi** reptile farm.

L'Hotel de l'Amitié (☎ 07-135300; s/d CFA20,000/30,000; mains from CFA2000) This great Burkinabé-run guest house tunes right into the Assinie vibe. The wooden dining area is so close to the sea that you can taste the sea spray. That doesn't detract from the enjoyment of the food, which includes perfectly cooked seafood and big French salads. This is the kind of place where you can share overlanding stories by candle-light over a good bottle of red.

Hôtel l'Océan (☎ 05-668189; r from CFA35,000) Our top Assouinde pick. Run by Ivorian/North African friends, whitewashed l'Océan effortlessly pulls off laid-back Assinie chic. Clean, attractive rooms look out over the ocean (as you might have guessed) and there's a great little restaurant and bar.

O Sole Mio (☎ 07-872771/05-964913; r CFA38,000, ste CFA48,000; 🖳) Antonio's (you'll be on first-name terms before long) beachfront set-up gets props for its luxurious rooms and wooden-roofed Italian restaurant serving gorgeous salads and pastas.

Getting There & Around

Coming from Grand Bassam, take a shared taxi to Samo (CFA2000, 45 minutes). From here you can pick up another car to Assouinde, 15 minutes away. Leaving Assouinde, you can take a pirogue (CFA100 plus luggage fee) across the calm lagoon that links Assouinde with Quartier France, followed by a shared taxi (CFA300) to reach Assinie Mafia.

THE WEST COAST

With sleepy deserted beaches fanned by soft sea breezes, patches of remaining rainforest and wild waves, exploring the west coast returns meaning to the word 'exploring'. So much of this region has yet to be documented by the rest of the world; so, leaving nothing but footprints, discover it your way.

SASSANDRA

Named after the river that feeds it, beautiful Sassandra has been overshadowed by San Pédro ever since the '60s. Though it's looking a little dog-eared these days, there's something quite endearing about that. It was originally established by the Portuguese in 1472, who named it São Andrea, then settled successively by the British and French, who developed it mainly as an outlet for timber from Mali. Though Sassandra's views are really its calling card, the colourful Fanti fishing harbour is a great spot mid-morning, when fishermen return with their catches.

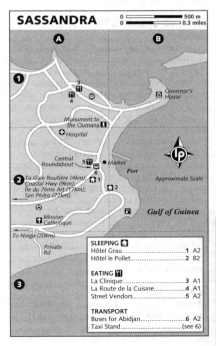

Sleeping & Eating

Hôtel Grau (☎ 34-720521; r with fan/air-con CFA5000/
CFA8000; ☒) This cheapie has clean rooms that
could use a good sea breeze. Nevertheless,
it's right in the centre of town, a short walk
from the market.

Hôtel le Pollet (☎ 34-720578; lepollet@hotmail.fr;
Rte du Palais de Justice; r with view CFA17,000, ste CFA38,000;
☒) Location, location, location. This white-
washed, three-storey place has the best one
in town, near the lighthouse overlooking
Sassandra. Rooms are splashed with Ivorian
art and feature sunken beds. The open-air Le
Phare Ouest restaurant whips up Ivorian and
European dishes.

There are plenty of street-food vendors
at the central roundabout plus some good
maquis like **La Clinique** (meals from CFA1000) and **La
Route de la Cuisine** (meals from CFA1000) near the post
office, grilling up the day's catch, which often
includes swordfish and barracuda.

Getting There & Around

UTB buses link Abidjan (CFA4000) with
Sassandra every morning; they leave from
Abidjan's Gare d'Adjamé.

AROUND SASSANDRA
Beaches

At the mercy of salty ocean sprays is wildly beautiful **Niega**, where the road ends. With its curling
breakers, it's enough to inspire poetic musings.
It's also a popular surfing venue hugged by a
pocket of forest. For a small sum, the village
boys will guide you along the narrow trails.

Best of Africa (☎ 34-720606; best@bestofafrica.org;
bungalows CFA40,000-60,000; ⓟ ☒ ⬜) sits 35km
east of Sassandra at Dagbego. This gorgeous
low-key resort offers wood-clad bungalows a
few metres from the calm waters of Dagbego
Beach. There's a good restaurant and the owners
can arrange hippo-watching trips (CFA40,000)
and canoe safaris up the Sassandra River.

Further upstream is **Île du 7ème Art**. Owned
by film director Yéo Kozoloa, it's a good
wildlife-watching spot. You might see hippos
and manatees on a boat tour (CFA8000) and
there are simple, inexpensive huts if you want
to stay the night.

SAN PÉDRO

Closer to Liberia than Abidjan, San Pédro has
a far-flung feel. Though its rapid growth in the
late '60s pushed San Pédro off the tourist map,
the country's second-biggest port is worth a

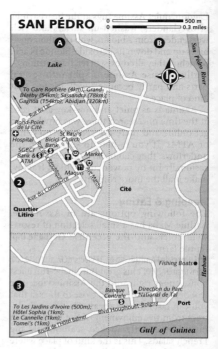

peek. There's not that much to keep you here,
but San Pédro is the jumping off point for
Parc National de Taï, as well as for Harper in
Liberia. Though the ocean has less of an un-
dercurrent than points further east, pollution
from freighters is the trade-off.

Les Jardins d'Ivoire (☎ 34-713186; Quartier Balmer; r
CFA25,000; ⓟ ☒ ⬤) has elegant rooms and phenomenal food. On the outskirts of town, **Hôtel
Sophia** (☎ 34-713434; Rue a la Plage; s/d CFA40,000/50,000;
ⓟ ☒ ⬤) is also pretty plush. There's a saltwater pool overlooking the bay, a laid-back
restaurant and fairly stylish rooms. Next door,
Le Cannelle (☎ 34-710539; r from CFA 25,000) has a decent restaurant. For pizza, head to **Tomei's**, a few
doors down from the Hôtel Sophia.

UTB buses link San Pédro with Abidjan
once daily (CFA5000). Shared taxis go west to
the balmy beaches of Grand-Béréby (CFA2500)
and east to Sassandra (CFA3000). For Harper,
just across the Liberian border, you can take a
shared taxi to Tabou (about CFA4000).

PARC NATIONAL DE TAÏ

Parc National de Taï (☎ 34-712353; www.parc-national
-de-tai.org), still technically the largest remain-

ing area of virgin rainforest in West Africa, is suffering. Long affected by illegal logging and poaching, the conflict didn't do it any favours, and its population of tool-using chimps (see p263) have hit their lowest numbers ever. Despite all that's been lost, the lianas, towering trees and swift streams create a cool, enchanting environment. Thanks to the WWF and other outside agencies, anti-poaching patrols continue. At the time of research, the park was still closed to visitors.

THE CENTRE

Though it's hardly the country's heartland, it does house the country's capital. The amazing Basilique de Notre Dame de la Paix is such a point of pride that it was spared during the November 2004 riots.

YAMOUSSOUKRO

Six-lane highways leading nowhere, streetlights brighter than the stars and impressive monuments too hard to get to, Yamoussoukro is one of Africa's peculiarities.

Félix Houphouët-Boigny's natal village was christened Ngokro (population 475). After stints as a French military station and a small agricultural town, Yamoussoukro (named after Queen Yamousso, who ran the village in the early 1900s) the capital burst forth in 1983. Unlike other defacto capitals, it has no embassies or ministries, but, even though its lights and roads might be better used elsewhere, many Ivorians speak proudly of it.

Some of the monuments are architecturally stunning; the Basilique de Notre Dame de la Paix with its many superlatives, Hôtel Président and the complex of structures that constitute the Institut National Polytechnique Houphouët-Boigny are worth a look. The best thing? You'll have it all to yourself. Plus, we hear rumours that Yakro, as it's affectionately dubbed, might be in line for a makeover.

Information
SGBCI Bank (Ave Houphouët-Boigny) Has a 24-hour Visa card–friendly ATM.
Tourist office (☎ 30-640814; Ave Houphouët-Boigny; ☽ 8am-noon & 3-6pm Mon-Fri) Arranges Baoulé dancing performances in nearby villages for around CFA50,000.

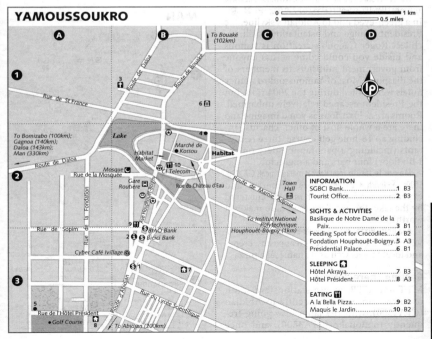

YAMOUSSOUKRO

INFORMATION
SGBCI Bank...........................1 B3
Tourist Office........................2 B3

SIGHTS & ACTIVITIES
Basilique de Notre Dame de la
  Paix...................................3 B1
Feeding Spot for Crocodiles....4 B2
Fondation Houphouët-Boigny.5 A3
Presidential Palace..................6 B1

SLEEPING
Hôtel Akraya.........................7 B3
Hôtel Président......................8 A3

EATING
A la Bella Pizza......................9 B2
Maquis le Jardin....................10 B2

CÔTE D'IVOIRE

Sights

BASILIQUE DE NOTRE DAME DE LA PAIX

Abidjan's spectacular **basilica** (Rte de Daloa; admission CFA2000; ☻ 8am-noon & 2-5.30pm Mon-Sat, 2-5pm Sun) will leave you wide-eyed. It remains in tip-top shape with English-speaking guides on duty. Don't forget to take your passport, which the guard holds until you leave. See the boxed test, p260, for more details.

HOUPHOUËT-BOIGNY'S LEGACY

Houphouët-Boigny's massive **palace**, where he is now buried, can be seen only from beyond its 5km perimeter wall. Sacred crocodiles live in the lake on its southern side and the keeper tosses them some meat around 5pm. The **Fondation Houphouët-Boigny** (Rue de l'Hôtel Président), on the south side of town, was built as the headquarters of the largesse-distributing association established by the former president.

Sleeping & Eating

Hôtel Akraya (☎ 30-641131; s/d CFA15,000/18,000) Yakro wasn't made for budget travellers and it's best budget buy is a bit out of the way. Rooms are bare but pleasant enough.

Hôtel Président (☎ 30-646464; www.hotelpresident .ci; Rue de l'Hôtel Président; r CFA55,000-250,000; P ⊠ ⊠) In a green-eyed nod to Abidjan's skyline, the Président is huge and ostentatious. Still, architect Roger Cacoub's creation is famous and inside you could come across anyone from government ministers to members of the diaspora. Most of Yamoussoukro's fancy hotels were looted during the 2004 riots, but the Président escaped relatively unharmed. Rooms are as luxurious as you'd imagine and there are a whole host of other 'charms', including an 18-hole golf course, three restaurants (including a panoramic eatery on the 14th floor) four bars and a nightclub.

Maquis le Jardin (opp Habitat market; meals CFA3000-5000; ☻ lunch & dinner) More upmarket and expensive than the other *maquis* clustered by the lake, the excellent food here makes it worthwhile.

A la Bella Pizza (Ave Houphouët-Boigny; meals CFA3500-5000; ☻ lunch & dinner) Serves great pastas, crêpes and local fare as well as its namesake pizzas.

Getting There & Away

MTT and UTB, whose stations are south of town, run buses frequently to Abidjan (CFA4500), with the latter also going frequently to Bouaké (CFA3800), and once

daily to Man (CFA5000) and San Pédro (CFA6000). You can also catch buses through to Bamako (Mali) and Bobo-Dioulasso and Ouagadougou (Burkina Faso) usually via Ferkessédougou.

THE NORTH

Northern Côte d'Ivoire, with its rust-red roads, craggy mountains and gradual descent into saffron-coloured savannah, feels like a no-man's land. Though it's aesthetically and culturally rich, this region has suffered like no other. Travel in this former rebel stronghold can still be risky, especially beyond Man and Bouaké.

MAN

Though it looks like paradise, during the war Man felt more like hell. It was taken by the New Forces in 2003 and war damage is still visible as you enter the town. Yet it's an absolute stunner; a succession of mountains rises out of the dusty earth like a many-humped camel carpeted in green and

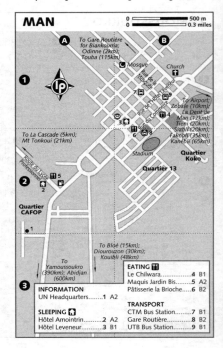

MAN

INFORMATION	
UN Headquarters	1 A2

SLEEPING ⌂	
Hôtel Amointrin	2 A2
Hôtel Leveneur	3 B1

EATING ⊞	
Le Chilwara	4 B1
Maquis Jardin Bis	5 A2
Pâtisserie la Brioche	6 B2

TRANSPORT	
CTM Bus Station	7 B1
Gare Routière	8 B1
UTB Bus Station	9 B1

grey. This is a great base for exploring surrounding villages and going hiking. At the time of research, UN staff and NGOs were still in town, so note that the region still has its issues. On the flip side, that's made Man a livelier place to visit, and there are some good sources of reliable information about the region in town.

There are no banks in Man but you can connect (slowly) at the web centre next to the Shell petrol station. You can head to Abidjan by shared taxi (CFA7000) or UTB bus (CFA7000). Taxis for N'zérékoré (Guinea) run via Sipilou. Check the security situation before attempting to travel this route.

Sleeping & Eating

Hôtel Leveneur (☎ 33-791776; Rue de l'Hôtel Leveneur; r CFA12,000; 🞩) Has the dishevelled backpacker thing down to a T, though we suspect it's not deliberate. Rooms are clean but a little bare…all part of the appeal.

Hôtel Amointrin (☎ 33-792670; Rte du Lycée Professionnel; standard/superior r CFA14,000/16,000; 🞩) This is the latest UN favourite and the place to be in Man. Good views, clean

rooms and a friendly crowd. The hot water works sometimes.

Le Chilwara (Rue du Marché; mains from CFA2000) is Man's best outdoor sit-down option. It offers some European dishes. Man has a whole host of decent *maquis*; **Le Boss** and **Maquis Jardin Bis** (Rte du Lycée Professionnel) both do great *attiéke* and brochettes. The **Pâtisserie la Brioche** (Rue du Commerce; croissants CFA240) is a great place for breakfast or morning coffee: the pastries are amazing.

AROUND MAN

It is currently considered safe to travel around the Man area. Check the security situation in the north before exploring further afield. If you're considering scaling Mt Tonkoui, give **La Dent de Man** (Man's Tooth) a shot first. North of town, this steep molar-shaped mountain hits a height of 881m. Allow at least four hours for the round trip, and bring snacks. The trek starts in the village of **Zobale**, 4km from Man. At 1223m, **Mt Tonkoui** is the second-highest peak in Côte d'Ivoire. The views from the summit are breathtaking and extend to Liberia and Guinea, even during the harmattan. The route begins about 18km from Man.

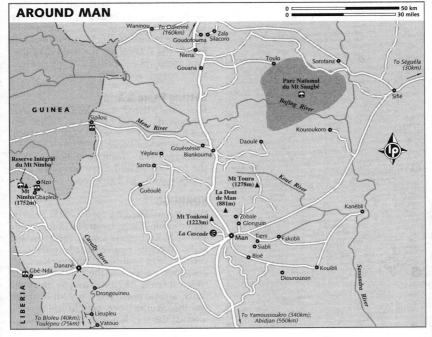

Man is also famous for **La Cascade** (CFA300), 5km from the town, a crashing waterfall that hydrates a bamboo forest. You walk a pretty paved path to reach it.

One of Man's most celebrated neighbours is **Silacoro**, about 110km north, which is famous for its stilt dancing (see p259).

BOUAKÉ

The beating heart of former rebel territory, gritty Bouaké isn't exactly a dream holiday destination. When the New Forces took Côte d'Ivoire's second-largest city in 2002, thousands fled. Before the war it had around half a million inhabitants; there's probably less than half that today. Most of the rebel fighters have been disarmed and at least 5000 weapons have

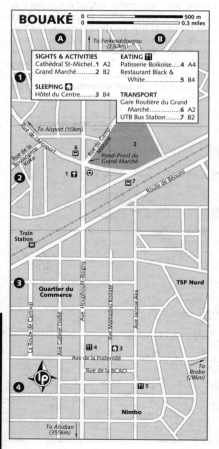

BOUAKÉ 0 ─── 500 m 0 ─── 0.3 miles

SIGHTS & ACTIVITIES
Cathédral St-Michel..1 A2
Grand Marché..........2 B2

SLEEPING
Hôtel du Centre........3 B4

EATING
Patisserie Boikoise.....4 A4
Restaurant Black &
White...................5 B4

TRANSPORT
Gare Routière du Grand
Marché.................6 A2
UTB Bus Station........7 B2

To Ferkessédougou (230km)
To Airport (10km)
Rue de l'Aéroport
Rue de la Boulangerie Koko
Rue du Camp Williams
Rond-Point du Grand Marché
Route de Béoumi
Train Station
Quartier du Commerce
TSF Nord
La Route de Carnaval
Ave Gabriel Dadié
Ave Houphouët-Boigny
Ave Mamadou Konaté
Ave Jacque Aka
Ave de la Fraternité
Rue de la BCAO
To Brobo (28km)
Nimbo
To Abidjan (355km)

been handed over to the UN. Even if peace persists in Bouaké, the transition period will be tough. Though there are some worthwhile sights around town, including the **park areas**, **cathedral** and **market**, we suggest you keep your ear to the ground and assess the situation before travelling.

Sleeping & Eating

Hôtel du Centre (☎ 31-633278/31-638457; Ave Mamadou Konaté; r CFA15,000; ☒) This trusty hotel is opposite a low-key *steak-frites* joint. The furniture doesn't look like it's changed since the '70s and, depending on your perspective, that'll either draw you in or send you running into former rebel territory. The latter would be a bit extreme – the staff here are friendly and there's a decent restaurant.

Hôtel Mon Afrik (☎ 06-349749/08-669182; nlciabid@ aviso.ci; Quartier Kennedy; s/d CFA20,000/30,000; ℗ ☒ ☒) Easily the best address in Bouaké. There's a pool, French restaurant and the interior of the terraced huts are as arty as any hip Abidjan hotel. The best part? It's run by the enthusiastic Madame Delon, who can advise you on all the dos and don'ts of Bouaké. It's just outside the city centre.

For food, head to **Restaurant Black & White** (Ave Jacque Aka; meals CFA4000-6000; ☺ lunch & dinner Tue-Sun) whose extensive menu is popular with (disarmed) former rebel leaders. **Patisserie Boikoise** (☎ 31-631033) on the main drag does good croissants and pastries, or you can head to the *maquis* around the market.

Getting There & Away

Buses and shared taxis depart from Gare Routière du Grand Marché. UTB has several buses a day to/from Abidjan (CFA7000) and one to San Pédro (GF8000) – both via Yamoussoukro – from its station south of the market. Shared taxis serve the same routes and charge a little less.

KORHOGO

Widely considered the capital of the Senoufo ethnic group, found largely in Cote d'Ivoire and Mali, Korhogo is famous for its art and crafts. With its rust-red roads, pockets of greenery and traditional homes, Korhogo does look a little like the painted cloth to which it lends its name. As you enter the dusty, artistic town, you'll spy Mt Korhogo and the main mosque, both of which reach towards the sky. Korhogo has had a rough ride in the last few years. Seized by rebels in 2002, it's since lost many in brutal gun battles. In 2004 the UN discovered mass graves in the town. If Korhogo is on your mind, be sure to consult reputable sources in Ferkessédougou or Bouaké before travelling here; at the time of research, the security situation was still a little dicey. The town is 225km north of Bouaké; shared taxis run between the two, via Ferkessédougou.

This is without a doubt the best place to shop for Korhogo cloth in Côte d'Ivoire and there are low-key galleries, antique stores and jewellery stands all over town. **Le Quartier des Sculpteurs** is fascinating. The **Hôtel Mont Korhogo** (☎ 36-860263/03-104707; opp Bicici Bank; r CFA12,500, ste CFA28,000; 🔊) is a safe place to lay your head. There's an attractive garden and pool; the rooms are comfortable and welcoming.

CÔTE D'IVOIRE DIRECTORY

ACCOMMODATION
Sleeping in Abidjan generally isn't good value. Reliable cheapies are hard to come by, largely because the city is frequented by business travellers more often than backpackers. For the purposes of the Abidjan section, budget accommodation is under CFA30,000, midrange averages around CFA45,000 and top end runs from CFA60,000 to CFA300,000. You'll find cheaper options in other parts of the country; there, hot water and internet access aren't usually included.

BOOKS
There is a wealth of books in French about the country's trials and tribulations. Especially recommended is Guy Labertit's *Adieu, Abidjan-Sur-Seine! Les Coulisses du Conflit Ivoirien*. Guillaume Soro's autobiography, *Pourquoi Je Suis Devenu Rebelle*, is a page turner. *Le Peuple N'Aime pas le peuple* by Kouakou-Gbahi Kouakou, describes the conflict as well in the title as it does in the content. In English, Susan Mullin Vogel's *Baoulé: African Art/Western Eyes* is a great look at Baoulé art.

BUSINESS HOURS
Shops open from 8am to 6pm, while government offices open from 7.30am to 5.30pm

---

PRACTICALITIES

- Among the nearly 20 daily newspapers, all in French, *Soirinfo, 24 Heures* and *L'Intelligent d'Abidjan* steer independent courses. *Gbich!* is a satirical paper.

- Radio Jam (99.3FM) and Radio Nostalgie (101.1FM) play hit music, while the BBC World Service broadcasts some programs in English on 94.3FM.

- Electricity voltage is 220V/50Hz; plugs have two round pins.

- Côte d'Ivoire uses the metric system.

Monday to Friday, with breaks for lunch. Banking hours are from 8am to 11.30am and 2.30pm until 4.30pm Monday to Friday.

DANGERS & ANNOYANCES
Any step in a peace process should be viewed with caution – the (hopefully) final one included. That said, there's no real reason why you shouldn't visit Abidjan, Yamoussoukro and the country's coastline. These areas were largely unaffected by the conflict and remain friendly and welcoming. But even in these places, we don't recommend that you travel after dark, even by shared taxi, and it's wise to take care at ATMs. In the same vein, it makes sense to avoid beaches and other non-lit areas once the sun has gone down.

At the time of research there were still security checkpoints in Abidjan and along the coast. Make sure your documents are in order and comply with requests if you feel tension. Travelling to Bouaké and further north was not recommended at the time of research. Though rebel groups have disbanded, disenchantment still runs high and the area is prone to sporadic outbreaks of violence. Again, this will change so check regularly for updates.

Finally, take care at the beach. The Atlantic has fierce currents and a ripping undertow; people drown every year, often strong, overly confident swimmers. Heed local advice.

EMBASSIES & CONSULATES
Most West African embassies take two to three days to process a visa application; you'll need to submit your application before noon. The following embassies and consulates are located

in Abidjan and are generally open between 8.30am and 3pm, with a break for lunch:

Belgium (Map p268; ☎ 20-219434/20-210088; 4th fl, Immeuble Alliance, Ave Terrasson des Fougères 01) Assists Dutch nationals.

Benin (Map p266; ☎ 22-414413; Rue des Jardins, Deux Plateaux)

Burkina Faso (Map p268; ☎ 20-211501; Ave Terrasson de Fougères) Also a consulate in Bouaké.

Cameroon (Map p268; ☎ 20-212086; 3rd fl, Immeuble le Général, Rue du Commerce)

Canada (Map p268; ☎ 20-300700; www.dfait-maeci .gc.ca/abidjan; Immeuble Trade Centre, 23 Ave Noguès) Assists Australian nationals.

France (Map p268; ☎ 20-200404; www.consulfrance -abidjan.org; 17 Rue Lecoeur)

Germany (Map p266; ☎ 22-442030; 39 Blvd Hassan II, Cocody)

Ghana (Map p266; ☎ 22-410288; Rue des Jardins; Deux Plateaux)

Guinea (Map p268; ☎ 20-222520; 3rd fl, Immeuble Crosson Duplessis, Ave Crosson Duplessis)

Liberia (Map p268; ☎ 20-324636; Immeuble Taleb, Ave Delafosse)

Mali (Map p268; ☎ 20-311570; Maison du Mali, Rue du Commerce) Also a consulate in Bouaké.

Niger (Map p266; ☎ 21-262814; Blvd Achalma, Marcory)

Nigeria (Map p268; ☎ 20-211982/223082; Blvd de la République)

Senegal (Map p268; ☎ 20-332876; Immeuble Nabil, off Rue du Commerce)

Togo (Map p268; ☎ 20-320974; Immeuble Nabil, off Rue du Commerce)

UK (Map p268; ☎ 20-300800; Immeuble les Harmonies, Blvd Carde)

USA (Map p266; ☎ 22-494000; http://french.cotedivoire .usembassy.gov; Riviera Golf)

FESTIVALS & EVENTS

Fêtes des Masques (February; villages around Man) Masks are an integral part of Dan society, serving as the community's collective memory and embodying a divine energy. The annual Fêtes des Masques brings together a great variety of masks and dances from the area.

Fête du Dipri (April; Gomon, 100km northwest of Abidjan) At midnight, naked women and children carry out nocturnal rites to rid the village of evil incantations. Before dawn the village chief appears to the sound of drums, and villagers are sent into a trance. An animated frenzy carries on throughout the following day.

Le Carnaval de Bouaké (March; Bouaké) This week-long celebration of friendship and life is one of West Africa's largest carnivals.

Fête de l'Abissa (October or November; Grand Bassam) A week-long, traditional carnival in which N'Zima people honour their dead and publicly exorcise evil spirits. Travellers can join in some parts of the celebration. Expect big street parties; you'll often see men dressed in drag.

HOLIDAYS

For more information on Islamic holidays, see p816. Public holidays in Côte d'Ivoire include the end of Ramadan as well as the following:

New Year's Day 1 January
Easter Monday March/April
Labour Day 1 May
Ascension Day 17 May
Independence Day 7 August
Assumption Day 15 August
All Saints' Day 1 November
Fête de la Paix 15 November
Christmas Day 25 December

INTERNET ACCESS

Ivorians love to be in touch with the diaspora and the rest of the world. You can get online in most parts of the country, with the exception of some rural areas. Abidjan has a wealth of internet facilities and relatively speedy connections. Many top-end hotels offer wi-fi.

LANGUAGE

French is the official language, spoken by almost everyone. In Abidjan you'll find some English speakers, though not enough to leave the French dictionary at home. The main regional languages include Mande and Malinké in the northwest; Dan/Yacouba in the area around Man; Senoufo in and around Korhogo; Baoulé and Agni in the centre and south; and Dioula, the market language, everywhere. See p860 for useful phrases in French, Dioula, Senoufo and Dan.

MAPS

The Michelin 1:800,000 map gives the best coverage of Côte d'Ivoire.

MONEY

Banks that offer a money-changing service include Bicici (Banque Internationale pour le Commerce et l'Industrie en Côte d'Ivoire), BIAO (Banque Internationale pour l'Afrique Occidentale), Cobaci (Compagnie Bancaire de l'Atlantique – Côte d'Ivoire), Citibank and SGBCI (Société Générale de Banques en Côte d'Ivoire). You can travel with US dollars or Euros – both are easy to change in Abidjan and large towns.

ATMs are widespread in Abidjan, Grand Bassam, Yamoussoukro and major towns. Most SGBCI branches have ATMs that accept Visa, MasterCard and sometimes Maestro. Though most ATMs are guarded, it makes sense to err on the side of caution and watch your bag when walking away. Credit cards are accepted at all international chains, as well as many top-end Ivorian hotels. Amex is usually OK. Commission charged on travellers cheques varies significantly from bank to bank. Large branches often have Western Union counters.

In Abidjan there's a black market for changing US dollars, concentrated in Treichville. Note that if you tell a taxi driver you want to change money, you'll probably be taken there first. The experience can be a little intimidating – groups of young men jump into the back of the cab, each offering a different rate. It makes sense to try the banks first.

TELEPHONE

If you have a GSM mobile phone, you can buy SIM cards from CFA2500. Street stalls also sell top-up vouchers, from CFA550. Calls generally cost between CFA25 and CFA150 per minute. Three of the most reliable phone networks are Orange, Moov and Kos. You can pick up phonecards (try Nasuba or Voneo) from many local stores, and you can make international calls from communications centres all over the country.

VISAS

Until 2009, US citizens visiting Côte d'Ivoire didn't need visas. That's now changed, and everyone except nationals of Ecowas states must apply for one. You'll need to arrange it in advance; visas aren't issued at Côte d'Ivoire's air and land portals. The cost varies depending on nationality and country of application. Visas are usually valid for three months and are good for visits of up to one month.

Note that you can obtain the Visa des Pays de l'Entente in Abidjan through either the Benin or Togolese embassies. The Visa des Pays de l'Entente is a multi-country visa that covers travel in Benin, Burkina Faso, Côte d'Ivoire, Niger and Togo (see p826).

Visa Extensions

Visa extensions, valid for up to three months, are issued by the **Office National de l'Identification** (Map p268; ☎ 20-254559; www.oni.ci, in French; opp Cathédrale St-Paul, Le Plateau; ✆ 8am-noon & 3-5pm Mon-Fri) in Abidjan. They are usually ready within two days. Bring four passport photos and a formal letter from youreslf or an employer.

Visas for Onward Travel

In Abidjan, you can get visas for onward travel to the following nearby countries:

BENIN

Visas cost CFA25,000 and you'll need four passport photos; they are usually ready the same or next day. The embassy also issues the Visa des Pays de Entente.

BURKINA FASO

Three-month single-/multiple-entry visas cost CFA30,000 and require two photos. There's also a consulate in Bouaké.

GHANA

Apply for visas (single/multiple entry CFA25,000/40,000) before 11.30am. You'll need four passport photos, though there's usually an on-site photographer.

GUINEA

One-month single-entry visas cost CFA32,000 for most nationalities. Everyone pays CFA96,000 for three-month multiple entry. You need three photos; visas might be ready the same day if you get there early.

LIBERIA

One-month single-entry visas, issued the same day, costs CFA30,000 for most nationalities. You need two photos.

MALI

For most nationalities, one-month single-entry visas cost CFA25,000; three-month multiple-entry visas cost CFA40,000. Bring four photos and a letter detailing your reason for visiting Mali and you can pick up your visa within 24 hours.

WOMEN TRAVELLERS

Other than the usual unwanted male attention, there are no real specific threats pertaining to women travelling in Côte d'Ivoire. Many female expats living in Abidjan take taxis alone late at night. Though there's no real reason why you shouldn't do the same, for the time being we recommend that you don't. If you're out late in the city, it's wiser to travel back with a friend or arrange a lift from a taxi driver you know. Though the chance of anything happening to you is minute, Côte d'Ivoire is still finding its feet after the crisis.

Ivorian men are generally warm and chatty, though flirtation is practically the national sport (in a recent poll by the French TV station Canal Plus, Ivorian men were ranked the third most unfaithful in the world). Note that unless you're on the beach or at the pool, showing your hips or lower belly is like giving the green flag. One way to generate respect among all generations of men is to talk about your (real or fictional) children. Though some Ivorian men don't value the ties of marriage, they do value motherhood (being married without children can be hard for Ivorian men to fathom).

You can buy tampons in major supermarkets and pharmacies in Abidjan and large towns. In Abidjan, a good bet is the amazing Hypermarché Sococé (p271), which feels like a French hypermarket.

TRANSPORT IN CÔTE D'IVOIRE

GETTING THERE & AWAY
Entering & Leaving Côte d'Ivoire
Whether you're travelling by air or by land, you'll need a yellow fever certificate to enter Côte d'Ivoire. If you don't have one you'll probably be ushered behind a curtain for an on-the-spot jab. There have been recent reports of travellers being asked for meningitis vaccination cards when crossing into Ghana at Noé.

Air
Félix Houphouët-Boigny is Côte d'Ivoire's swish international airport. Airlines serving Côte d'Ivoire include the following:

Afriqiyah Airways (Map p268; ☎ 20-338785; www .afriqiyah.be; Abidjan Universel Voyages, Ave Crosson Duplessis, Le Plateau)
Air France (Map p268; ☎ 20-202424; www.airfrance .com; Immeuble Kharrat, Rue Noguès, Le Plateau)
Air Ivoire (Map p268; ☎ 20-251400, 251561; www.air ivoire.com; Immeuble Le République, Pl de la République)
Bellview Air (Map p268; ☎ 20-320714; www.flybell viewair.com; Immeuble l'Amiral, Rue du Commerce)
Brussels Airlines (off Map p266; ☎ 27-232345; www .brusselsairlines.com; behind Supermarché Cap Sud, off Blvd Valéry Giscard d'Estaing) Offers short hops between Abidjan and Monrovia.

Ethiopian Airlines (Map p268; ☎ 20-215284; www .ethiopianairlines.com; Ave Chardy, Le Plateau)
Kenya Airways (Map p268; ☎ 20-320767; www .kenya-airways.com; Immeuble Jeceda, Blvd de la République, Le Plateau)
Slok Air (☎ 21-248867; www.slok-air.com; Immeuble les Dunes, Blvd Valéry Giscard d'Estaing)
South African Airways (Map p268; ☎ 20-218280; www.flysaa.com; Immeuble Jeceda, Blvd de la République, Le Plateau)

Land
At the time of research all major border crossings were open, though they may close around election times.

BURKINA FASO
The romantic (in a gritty way) Abidjan–Ouagadougou **Sitarail** (☎ 20-208000) sleeper takes two days. There are three trains weekly and you'll pay CFA25,000/35,000 in standard/first class

There are also daily bus services between Bouaké and Bobo-Dioulasso (CFA12,000, 22 hours).

GHANA
The crossing at Noé is pretty easy to navigate. It'll take you about three hours to reach it from Abidjan and, once you've passed Ivorian customs, it's a 10-minute walk (though there are waiting taxis, too) to the Ghanaian border post. Note that the border shuts at 6pm prompt, accompanied by a fancy flag ceremony.

The road between Abidjan and Noé is sealed and, for the most part, smooth. A taxi between the two will cost you at least CFA30,000. It's far cheaper to jump in a shared taxi at Gare de Bassam (CFA6000). STC buses also ply the route, charging CFA20,000 for a ticket to Accra. You'll pay a little extra for luggage. At the time of research there were three checkpoints on the route to Noé.

Negotiating the border crossings further north near Agnibilékrou and Bouna is less straightforward; plan for lengthy delays. Check the situation on the ground before heading up to Bouna in particular.

GUINEA
The most frequently travelled route to Guinea is between Man and N'zérékoré, either through Danané and Nzo or Biankouma and Sipilou. By bush taxi it is quicker to use the latter route, although the roads on both are bad. At the

time of research, you still needed to get clearance from the rebel authorities in Man.

LIBERIA
Intrepid overlanders seem to love the Tabou–Harper route, which sets you down in one of Liberia's prettiest towns. If you're planning on crossing at this border post, make sure you're not pressed for time. It can take a couple of days to reach Monrovia from Harper during the rainy season. The best jumping off point is San Pédro, from where you can take a shared taxi to Tabou. During the wet season you may then have to take a canoe to the Liberian side, followed by at least one motorbike.

The more sensible route is from Danané to Ganta via Sanniquellie. Minibuses and shared taxis make the quick hop from Danané to the border at Gbé-Nda. A bus takes this route from Abidjan to Monrovia (two days) several times a week.

MALI
Buses and shared taxis run from Abidjan, Yamoussoukro and Bouaké to Bamako, usually via Ferkessédougou and Sikasso in Mali. The road is good but, at the time of research, there were far more enjoyable things to do in Côte d'Ivoire than head to the extreme north. Keep an ear to the ground before travelling and stay away from this route during the Ivorian election.

GETTING AROUND
Air
Air Ivoire (see opposite) can't seem to commit to internal flights, but the situation may change as the country stabilises further. A (fairly) reliable alternative is **Sophia Airlines** (☎ 21-588043), which has five flights to San Pédro per week. Flying up north is tricky in the current political climate. Again, we expect that to change.

Bus
The country's large, relatively modern buses are around the same price and are significantly more comfortable than bush taxis or minibuses. Most have fixed departure times and don't charge extra for luggage. Journey times should ease once all the checkpoints have been removed.

Bush Taxi & Minibus
Shared taxis (ageing Peugeots or covered pick-ups, known as *bâchés*) and minibuses cover major towns and outlying communities not served by the large buses. They leave at all hours of the day but only when full, so long waits may be required. If you want to hasten your departure time, you can buy extra seats.

Car & Motorbike Taxis
Motorbike taxis aren't as common as the four-wheeled type, which are ubiquitous. For a private hire, you'll pay anywhere from CFA200 upwards, depending on the city, time and your bargaining skills. For information about Abidjan taxis, see p275.

Train
The romantically named *Bélier* and *Gazelle* trains link Abidjan with Ferkessédougou daily (CFA12,000, 1500km, 12 hours).

The Gambia

The tiny sliver of The Gambia is wedged into surrounding Senegal, and is either seen as a splinter in its side, or the tongue that makes it speak, depending on who you talk to. For most travellers, it's an easily negotiated country with a magnificent shoreline that invites visitors to laze and linger. But there's more to Africa's smallest country than sun and surf. Small fishing villages, nature reserves and historical slaving stations are all within easy reach of the clamorous resort zones on the Atlantic. Like a green belt around the coast, this area is dotted with inspired community projects, star-studded ecolodges and small wildlife parks that make this tiny nation a key player in responsible tourism.

Bird lovers might be tempted to book an annual holiday here (and many do). On a leisurely river cruise, you'll easily spot over 100 species, as your pirogue charts a leisurely course through mangrove-lined wetlands and lush gallery forests. Even if your ornithological skills don't go beyond identifying an inner-city pigeon, you'll be tempted to wield binoculars here, and can rely on an excellent network of trained guides to help you tell a pelican from a flamingo.

FAST FACTS

- **Area** 11,300 sq km
- **Capital** Banjul
- **Country code** ☎ 220
- **Famous for** Being the smallest African country; the *kora;* birds and beaches
- **Languages** Mandinka, Wolof, Fula, English
- **Money** Dalasi (D); US$1 = D26.48; €1 = D35.22
- **Population** 1.6 million
- **Visa** Not needed for nationals of Commonwealth countries, Germany, Italy, Luxembourg, the Netherlands, Ecowas (Economic Community of West African States) or Scandinavian countries. One-month visas of around US$45 for all others. To be purchased before travel.

HOW MUCH?

- **Soft drink** D20
- **Newspaper** D20
- **Sandwich** D70
- **French bread** D10
- **One hour's internet access** D30

LONELY PLANET INDEX

- **1L of petrol/gas** D30
- **1L of bottled water** D30
- **Bottle of Julbrew** D25
- **Souvenir T-shirt** D200 to D500
- **Shwarma** D60

HIGHLIGHTS

- **Atlantic coast resorts** (p298) Fabulous food to indulge in before partying the night away.
- **Janjangbureh** (Georgetown; p316) Upriver cruises past islands, small holiday camps and nature reserves.
- **Gambia River National Park** (p317) Chimps to chatter with and tropical islands.
- **Banjul** (p295) Bargain/negotiate in crammed Albert Market.
- **Kartong** (p310) The sun slides into the Atlantic in front of your exclusive ecolodge.
- **Makasutu Culture Forest** (p311) The whole country is squeezed into 10,000 hectares of abundant nature.

ITINERARIES

- **Three days** Over a long weekend, you can explore quite a large part of the Gambian coastal area. Spend a good amount of time in bars and on the beaches of the Atlantic coast (p298), tying in the occasional day trip to the surrounding areas. The busy market town of Serekunda (p298) is close by, and the pretty museum and bird reserve of Tanji (p308). Southwards of Tanji, the ecofriendly lodgings, empty beaches and community activities of Gunjur (p310) and Kartong (p310) invite you to linger.
- **One week** Start your trip as above, then head from Lamin to Makasutu Culture Forest (p311). Spend the night in Gambia's most exclusive hotel, then visit

Abuko Nature Reserve (p311), Gambia's smallest stretch of protected nature, and suck oysters at Lamin Lodge (p312), a creaking wooden restaurant nestled in the mangroves. The small and dusty capital, Banjul (p294), sits just 20 minutes from the coastal resorts, and tempts with a lively market and colonial architecture. Near the airport, you can taste fresh food at the community-supportive Gambia is Good Farm Yard (see the boxed text, p312). Get up early, catch the ferry to the north bank and visit Jufureh (p314) and beautiful Ginak Island (p313).

- **Two weeks** Ambitious travellers can visit almost the entire country in a couple of weeks. Having spent the first week in the proximity of the coastal resorts, treat yourself to a river trip up to Janjangbureh (p316). Or follow the southern shore by road, stopping at Bintang Bolong (p314), then carrying on to Janjangbureh, from where you can visit the chimp project at Gambia River National Park (p317) and check out the busy market of Basse Santa Su (p317).

CLIMATE & WHEN TO GO

Gambia's tourist season is almost entirely concentrated during the dry, cooler months from November to February, when daytime temperatures reach a maximum of around 24°C (75°F). This is also the best time to watch wildlife and birds. From mid-February to April, the average daytime maximums rise to 26°C (79°F).

The wet season starts around late June and lasts until late September. During this time, temperatures rise to around 30°C (86°F). The rains wash away some of the roads, rendering certain journeys upcountry impossible. Malaria is widespread and the stifling heat can become uncomfortable. On the other hand, everything is greener, and many places reduce their prices by up to 50% (unless they close completely).

HISTORY

Ancient stone circles, such as the famous Wassu group in eastern Gambia (a Unesco World Heritage Site), and burial mounds indicate that this part of West Africa has been inhabited for at least 1500 years.

By the 13th century, the area had been absorbed into the Empire of Mali, which

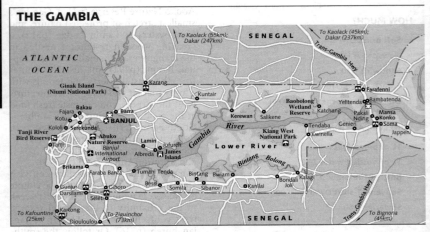

THE GAMBIA

stretched between present-day Senegal and Niger. A group of Malinké from Mali came to settle in the area of present-day Gambia and Guinea-Bissau, establishing a small outpost to the empire. They developed a distinctive culture, and today form the largest ethnic group of Gambia – the Mandinka.

The first Europeans to reach Gambia were Portuguese explorers in 1455. By 1650, they had been eclipsed by the British, who established Fort James on an island 25km upstream from the mouth of the Gambia River. The frequent skirmishes between French, British and other powers indicate the fierce fighting over land and influence that marked this era.

While the Europeans traded tobacco and gunpowder for ivory and gold, it was the purchase of slaves for shipment that most upset the traditional balance. Encouraged by European traders, local chiefs invaded neighbouring civilisations and took captives, selling them to the Europeans. In 1783, Britain gained all rights to trade on the Gambia River, and Fort James became a major slave shipment point.

The Colonial Period

When the British abolished slavery in 1807, Royal Navy ships began capturing slave ships of other nations, and Fort James was converted from a dungeon into a haven. As part of this crusade, in 1816, the British built a fort on Banjul island, and established a settlement that was named Bathurst.

The Gambia River protectorate was administered from Sierra Leone until 1888, when Gambia became a full colony. For the next 75 years, though, Gambia was almost forgotten, and administration was limited to a few British district commissioners and the local chiefs they appointed. Britain actually tried to trade Gambia for other colonial territories, but no one was interested.

In the 1950s, Gambia's groundnut plantations were improved as a way of increasing export earnings, and other agricultural schemes were implemented. But there was little else in the way of services; by the early 1960s, Gambia had fewer than 50 primary schools and only a handful of doctors.

Throwing off the British Yoke

In 1960, when other West African nations had already gained independence, David Jawara founded the People's Progressive Party (PPP). The political landscape was hardly developed, and, given the colony's small size, Britain doubted that an independent Gambia could be economically self-sustaining.

Still, Gambia became independent in 1965. Jawara was nominated prime minister, and Britain's Queen Elizabeth II remained titular head of state. Bathurst, now renamed Banjul, became the country's capital.

A viable future still seemed unlikely, but during the next 10 years, the world price for groundnuts increased and Gambia became a popular tourist destination, both factors which boosted the local economy.

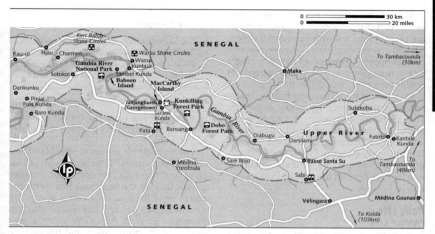

In 1970, Gambia turned into a fully independent republic, with Jawara as president. The first signs of discontent came in 1980, when disaffected soldiers staged a coup. In accordance with a mutual defence pact, the Senegalese army helped oust the rebels and, acknowledging his debt, Jawara announced that the armies of Gambia and Senegal would be integrated. But the swiftly formed Senegambia Confederation dissolved in 1989.

Jammeh Coup

In April 1992 President Jawara and the PPP were re-elected for a sixth term, yet overthrown only two years later (on 22 July 1994) in a bloodless coup. The coup leader, 29-year-old Lieutenant Yahya Jammeh, announced a new government, to be headed by the Armed Forces Provisional Ruling Council (AFPRC). Jammeh and the AFPRC ruled initially until 1996, when elections were held. Jammeh won the votes, turning neatly from coup leader to civilian president.

To consolidate this support, Jammeh announced a series of ambitious schemes to rebuild the country's infrastructure and economy. A new airport was constructed, a national TV station opened, and new clinics and schools were promised for the upcountry provinces. Despite a clamping down on free press, and human rights abuses that included the shooting of several protesting students in 2001, many people apparently came to regard Jammeh as a force for good, and in

October 2001, voted him in for a second five-year term.

Gambia Today

Today, Jammeh is still in power, and his leadership style seems more authoritarian than ever. Opposition voices have a hard time getting heard, journalists live in fear of oppression (as the media watchdog Reporters Without Borders reports regularly), and the nation's active secret service puts a dampener on open debate. Most worryingly, perhaps, are Jammeh's more bizarre endeavours, such as his claim to have found cures for HIV/AIDS and asthma, which he administers before rolling cameras in weekly TV shows. A 2003 announcement that oil had been discovered off Gambia's shores has so far not led to drilling (and is hotly debated), and Gambia's economy remains weak. Still, in conflict-plagued West Africa, Gambia remains a stable country.

THE CULTURE
The National Psyche

Holiday brochures like to describe Gambia as the 'Smiling Coast', a welcoming 'gateway to Africa', where local culture is easily accessible. Wiping the gloss off those descriptions, some of the smile still remains, though real hospitality is more easily found upcountry, away from the coastal resorts where mass tourism has somewhat distorted social relations and the respectful interaction otherwise typical of the country.

Years of authoritarian rule have also resulted in a certain climate of distrust. Conversations are often conducted with care, and few people will express their views on governmental politics openly – you never know who might be listening. Short-term travellers might not readily notice this, seeing that the government is keen to present a gleaming holiday image to the tourist community, whose dollars are vital to the local economy. Yet being aware of the troubles that the population faces will help you to understand silences in conversation or the avoidance of topics, and gradually grant you an insight into the real Gambia, the one that lies beyond the polished smiles and tourist hustling.

Daily Life

FAMILY LIFE

In Gambia, as anywhere else in Africa, the extended family plays an important role in a person's life. The network of relatives widens even more in polygamous families, which still account for a large amount of marriages in Gambia.

Unmarried children, particularly women, stay at their parents' home until they are married, which is when men found their own household, and women join that of their husband. After a divorce, women usually join the home of their parents. Single-woman or single-mother households are virtually unheard of.

EDUCATION

Despite some measures taken by the government, Gambia still suffers fairly low literacy rates: 40% of boys are estimated to be able to read and write, and for girls this drops by another 15% to 20%. In theory, primary education is available to all children, but girls especially often drop out early if the family can't afford continued education or needs their help at home. While numbers of girls and boys are still fairly equal at primary level, most girls don't even complete their primary exams, let alone attend secondary school or university.

Population

With around 115 people per sq km, The Gambia has one of the highest population densities in Africa. The strongest concentration of people is around the urbanised zones at the Atlantic coast, the area many people migrate to from the upcountry towns to try

---

THE GAMBIA

The Gambia's official name always includes 'The', but this is often omitted in everyday situations. In this book we have usually omitted 'The' for reasons of clarity and to ensure a smooth-flowing text.

---

to make a living from the tourist industry. About 45% of Gambia's population is under 14 years old.

The main ethnic groups are the Mandinka (comprising around 42%), the Wolof (about 16%) and the Fula (around 18%). Smaller groups include the Serer and Jola. With the exception of the Jola, these ethnic groups are structured in a hierarchical fashion that has its origins in West Africa's precolonial empires. The freeborn (rulers and traders) are traditionally at the top of society, followed by professional occupational groups, including *griots* (musicians) and blacksmiths, and formerly slaves. These structures still determine much of social life, though other aspects, such as economic success and education are also relevant.

RELIGION

Islam is the dominant religion – about 90% of Gambia's population is Muslim. The Wolof, Fula and Mandinka people are almost exclusively Muslim, while Christian faith is most widespread among the Jola and the Serer. Traditional religious forms (sometimes called animism) are most commonly practised in the predominantly Christian areas, and elements of traditional religious practice have found their way both into Islam and Christianity.

ARTS

Architecture

Banjul has several grand colonial structures (such as the government buildings around July 22 Sq), as well as unpretentious clapboard houses, some still occupied by the descendants of freed-slave families who moved to Banjul from Sierra Leone in the early 1800s. Not far from Banjul you can see the remains of British colonial fortifications Fort James (James Island) and Fort Bullen (Barra). For contemporary architecture, visit Arch 22 and Banjul Airport, both designed by Senegalese architect Pierre Goudiaby Atepa.

Literature

William Conton is Gambia's best-known novelist; the 1960s classic *The African,* set in the colonial era, is his most famous work. Authors such as Ebou Dibba (*Chaff on the Wind;* 1986) and Tijan Salleh (*Kora Land;* 1989) are leading writers of more recent times.

Music

Africa's possibly most famous musical instrument, the *kora,* was created in the region of Gambia and Guinea-Bissau. Still today, Gambia remains an important centre of *kora* playing, whose dry, rhythmic styles differ from those of Mali. While *kora* players such as Amadou Bansang Jobarteh, Jali Nyama Suso, Dembo Konte and Malamini Jobarteh came to fame on the world music scene of the '80s, the country's young, contemporary artists are less known outside their country. Brothers Tata Dindin and Pa Jobarteh are kora masters, and Gambia's most famous player is Jaliba Kuyateh. All mix *kora* with Senegalese *mbalax* rhythms and myriad other styles.

In the 1960s, Gambia was hugely influential in the development of modern West African music. Groups like the Afro-funky Super Eagles and singer Labah Sosse had a huge impact in Gambia, Senegal and beyond. Former Super Eagle Juldeh Camara has released brilliant records of Fula fiddle fusions. Today, the country is most famous for its booming reggae scene, including artists such as Dancehall Masters, Rebellion the Recaller, Egalitarian and dozens more.

Painting & Sculpture

Banjul's national museum has a few good examples of traditional statues and carved masks on display.

Leading contemporary artists Njogu Touray and Etu produce colourful works from mixed materials. Fabric printers such as Baboucar Fall and Toimbo Laurens push the art of batik in new creative directions.

ENVIRONMENT
The Land

Gambia's shape and position epitomise the absurdity of the colonial carve-up of Africa. About 300km long, but averaging only 35km wide, Gambia is entirely surrounded by Senegal, with the small exception of an 80km coastline. With only 11,295 sq km, it is the smallest country in mainland Africa, and its flat territory is dominated by the Gambia River.

Wildlife
ANIMALS

Gambia doesn't tempt tourists with huge mammals, though warthogs, various antelope species, baboons, patas and colobus monkeys, hippos, and crocodiles can all be spotted in the national parks. In Gambia River National Park you can see the cute chimps of the Chimpanzee Rehabilitation Trust (CRA).

For bird-watchers, Gambia is a veritable paradise. More than 560 species have been recorded, including many migrants that spend the European winters here. Of particular interest to ornithologists are Egyptian plovers, swallow-tailed and red-throated bee-eaters, Abyssinian rollers, painted snipes and Pel's fishing owls. Good sites for bird-watching include all the protected areas listed under national parks, but also much humbler areas, such as hotel gardens in Kololi, Gunjur and Kartong, and the wetlands in Banjul. Upcountry, Georgetown and Basse Santa Su are particularly rewarding.

PLANTS

From the coast to Farafenni, dense mangroves line the Gambia River. Further up, where the water isn't saline, its banks are covered in abundant gallery forest. Away from the river, Gambia's position in the southern Sahel means that large areas are dominated by dry grassland and open savannah woodland.

National Parks

The Gambia has six national parks and reserves, covering 3.7% of the national land area. They are all open to the public. Abuko Nature Reserve (p311) bundles gallery forest, open bushland and Guinea savannah into one tiny territory, while Kiang West National Park (p315) protects habitats including mangroves, mud flats and dry woodland. Baobolong Wetland Reserve (p315) with its mangroves is north of the Gambia River, and Niumi National Park (p313) and Tanji River Bird Reserve (p309) are coastal, with dunes, lagoons, dry woodland and coastal scrub.

Several forest parks have been established to provide renewable timber stocks. Bijilo Forest Park (p299) is the best known, primarily as a nature reserve and bird-watching spot. At writing, work had started on the ambitious new conservation project Ballabu (p311), a vast corridor gazetted for animal projects and village development.

Environmental Issues

The main environmental issues faced by Gambia are overfishing, deforestation and coastal erosion. An impressive project using Dutch technology to regenerate the nation's beaches, badly eroded due to natural causes and illegal sand mining (the sand going into the construction of houses and hotels), is showing significant results. Areas such as Kotu and Kololi, where beaches had almost disappeared, now have their sand strands back – until the sea, or illegal sand mining, claims them again.

Away from the coast, deforestation is the biggest problem. Woodlands are cleared to match a growing demand for farmland, but trees are also felled to make firewood and charcoal, much of which is used to smoke fish (caught through overfishing).

FOOD & DRINK
Staples & Specialities

National dishes include *domodah* (rice with a thick, meaty groundnut sauce) and *benechin* (rice cooked in tomato sauce and decorated with carefully arranged chunks of fried fish, carrots, cassava and other vegetables). Along the coast, fish and seafood are prepared in many tasty ways.

Gambia has a rich array of locally produced juices, making it hard to choose between the hibiscus drink *bissap*, ginger beer, and *bouyi* (a thick, sweet juice made from the fruits of the baobab). At breakfast, the sweet herbal tea *kinkiliba* is often served. For a real caffeine punch, try a glass of *ataaya* (strong, sweet green tea, brewed and enjoyed in small groups), served with the free offer of an afternoon's socialising. A local alcoholic drink is the thick, yeasty palm wine.

Where to Eat & Drink

Gambia's Atlantic coast is blessed with an excellent restaurant scene. You'll find anything here, from filling local meals to refined international cuisine. If you're on a budget, you'll probably search for tiny local eateries called chop shops. Most of those only have one dish available at any time, usually a variant of Gambian rice and sauce. They're mostly frequented during lunch hours and don't serve outside meal hours.

Vegetarians & Vegans

In the tourist centres, many restaurants have good vegetarian choices. Things get harder upcountry, and in the local chop shops you usually won't find any veggie options – with the very tasty exception of *niebbe*. These are spicy, cooked beans served with bread and oil that are mostly sold at street stalls. They're considered 'humble food', as most people here prefer to eat meat if they can afford it, but delicious all the same. On the whole, prepare for a rather limited variety of choices during your stay.

Habits & Customs

Meals are traditionally eaten squatting on the floor, grouped around a large platter of rice and sauce where everyone digs in with a spoon or the right (and only the right) hand. It's polite to take your shoes off, and to finish eating while there's still food in the bowl to show you have had enough. The shocked comments of 'you haven't eaten anything, dig in' are an acceptance that you've finished, rather than actual invitations to eat more.

BANJUL

pop 35,000

It's hard to imagine a more unlikely, more consistently ignored capital city than sleepy sea port Banjul. Yet despite the shadow of neglect that haunts its sand-blown streets, Banjul is truly worth a visit. Its colourful markets and hectic harbour show urban Africa at its busy best, while the old museum and fading colonial structures are imbued with a sense of history that Gambia's plush seaside resorts lack.

HISTORY

Banjul was founded in 1816 by Captain Alexander Grant, on a small, swampy island that the colonial pioneer found to be a suitable spot for establishing control over the river and enforcing the observance of the Abolition of the Slave Trade Act. Initially named Bathurst, after the secretary of the British Colonial Office, it soon developed into a busy settlement. Population numbers swelled in the 1830s, when freed slaves were resettled here from Sierra Leone.

When Gambia achieved independence in 1965, Bathurst was granted city status, became the capital of the young nation, and was soon after renamed Banjul (the Mandinka word for 'bamboo' and the island's original, local name).

ORIENTATION

July 22 Sq is the centre of town. From here, several main streets run south, including Russell St, which leads past the bustling Albert Market into Liberation St. West of the October 17 Roundabout is the old part of Banjul – a maze of narrow streets, crumbling structures and clapboard houses.

Independence Dr runs northwest from July 22 Sq, becoming the main road out of Banjul. On the edge of the city, it goes around the vast structure of Arch 22 and turns into a dual carriageway, which, after about 3km, crosses Oyster Creek on Denton Bridge to reach the mainland proper.

INFORMATION

Standard Chartered Bank (☎ 4222081; Ecowas Ave) and **PHB Bank** (☎ 4428144; 11 Liberation St) both have ATMs that accept Visa cards and change money. They open 8am to 4pm Monday to Thursday and 8am to 1.30pm Friday.
Banjul Pharmacy (☎ 4227470; ☼ 9am-8.30pm) Across the road from the hospital.
Gamtel Internet Café (Jul 22 Dr; per hr D30; ☼ 8am-midnight)
Main post office (Russell St; ☼ 8am-4pm Mon-Sat) Near Albert Market.
Quantumnet (Nelson Mandela St; per hr D30; ☼ 9am-10pm) Internet access.
Royal Victoria Teaching Hospital (☎ 4228223; Jul 22 Dr) Gambia's main hospital has an A&E department, but facilities aren't great.

DANGERS & ANNOYANCES

Violent crime is rare in Banjul, but there are pickpockets. Their favourite hunting ground is the Barra ferry; be vigilant around the terminal and Albert Market as well.

SIGHTS & ACTIVITIES

Banjul feels more like a very large village than a national capital, and this sleepy atmosphere has a quaint kind of charm. The city's attraction lies not in grand sights but in intimate details, and these are best taken in on a casual stroll around town.

Albert Market

Since its creation in the mid-19th century, **Albert Market** (Russell St), an area of frenzied buying, bartering and bargaining, has been Banjul's hub of activity. From shimmering fabrics and false plaits, fresh fruits and dried fish to souvenirs at the **craft market**, you can find almost anything here and then some.

Arch 22

Designed by Senegalese architect Pierre Goudiaby Atepa, the **arch** (Jul 22 Dr; admission D100; ☼ 9am-11pm) is a 35m-high gateway built to celebrate the military coup of 22 July 1994. Its publicly accessible balcony grants excellent views over the city and coast. There's also a cosy cafe, a souvenir shop and a small **museum** (☎ 4226244) that enlightens visitors about the coup d'état and houses good exhibitions.

St Joseph's Adult Education & Skills Centre

Tucked away in an ancient Portuguese building, this **centre** (☎ 4228836; stjskills@qanet .com; Ecowas Ave; ☼ 9am-2pm Mon-Thu, to noon Fri) has provided training to disadvantaged women for the last 20 years. Visitors can take a free tour of sewing and tie-dye classes, and purchase beautiful craftwork at reasonable prices in the onsite boutique.

Old Town

Heading west from the ferry port, towards the wide Ma Cumba Jallow St and beyond, you reach the 'old town' – an unruly assembly of decrepit colonial buildings and Krio-style clapboard houses. It's no coincidence that they resemble the inner-city architecture of Freetown in Sierra Leone, as many of them still belong to families who came to Banjul from there, some as early as the 1820s.

National Museum

The **museum** (☎ 4226244; www.ncac.gm; Jul 22 Dr; admission D50; ☼ 9am-4pm Mon-Thu, to 5pm Fri-Sun) has interesting, if slightly dusty, exhibits about history and culture in the region. You can arrange introductory talks and even arts classes and craft workshops. It's also a good source of information about other arts projects in the country.

July 22 Sq

This central **square** is a colonial creation, now mainly used for governmental pomp

lonelyplanet.com

THE GAMBIA

BANJUL

| 0 | 1 km |
| 0 | 0.5 miles |

ATLANTIC OCEAN

To Denton Bridge Resort
& Oyster Creek (3km);
Bakau (7km);
Serekunda (15km);
Banjul International
Airport (30km)

Muammar al Gadhafi Ave

This Area
Strictly
Out of
Bounds

State
House

Main Entrance
to Albert Market

July 22 Sq

Freedom
Lane

Nelson Mandela St

October 17
Roundabout

Davidson Carrol St

Serign Sillah St

Old
Town

Tanbi Wetland
Complex
18

Imam Lamin Bah St

To Barra
(5km)

Kankujeri Rd

Cherno Adama Bah St

INFORMATION
Banjul Pharmacy	1 C2
Gamtel Internet Café	2 B1
German Embassy	(see 24)
Guinean Embassy	3 C3
Immigration Office	4 C4
Main Post Office	5 D2
Malian Embassy	6 C5
PHB Bank	7 D3
Quantumnet	8 D3
Royal Victoria Teaching Hospital	9 C1
Sierra Leone High Commission	10 C4
Standard Chartered Bank	11 D3

SIGHTS & ACTIVITIES
Albert Market	12 D2
Arch 22	13 A1
Fountain	14 D2
Museum Arch 22	(see 13)
National Museum	15 C2

Playground	16 C2
St Joseph's Adult Education & Skills Centre	17 D3
Tanbi Wetland Complex	18 B4
War Memorial	19 D2

SLEEPING
Corinthia Atlantic Hotel	20 B1
Princess Diana Hotel	21 A1

EATING
Ali Baba Snack Bar	22 D3
King of Shawarma Café	23 D3
Michel's Seafood	24 A1

SHOPPING
Albert Market	(see 12)
Craft Market	25 D2
Kerewan Sound	26 D2

TRANSPORT
Air Sénégal International	27 D3
Ferry to Barra	28 D4
Minibuses to Bakau	29 C2
Minibuses to Serekunda	30 C2

and public celebrations. Look out for the **war memorial** and the (now dried up) **fountain** to commemorate the coronation of King George VI of Britain in 1937. The colourful and well-maintained **playground** will excite little visitors more than the 19th-century architecture.

Tanbi Wetland Complex

The 6300-hectare site of the **Tanbi Wetlands**, with its mangroves and creeks, is a great bird-watching spot, with Caspian terns, gulls, egrets and several species of waders.

SLEEPING

Not many tourists stay in Banjul, and the best good hotels are along the coast.

Princess Diana Hotel (☎ 4228715; 30 Independence Dr; r D550) Slightly better than most Banjul doss-houses, because it has doors that lock, this modest hotel has occasional live music in the bar, and even a kind of breakfast in the morning.

Denton Bridge Resort (☎ 7773777; s/d D800/1000; ☒) Near Oyster Creek, this resort is a water-sports centre, a pirogue landing and an excursion point as well as a breezy, decent hotel with large rooms.

Corinthia Atlantic Hotel (☎ 4228601; www .corinthiahotels.com; Muammar al Gadhafi Ave; s/d incl breakfast D1500/2500; ☒ ☒ ☒ ☒) The jewel in Banjul's crown is this plush palace at the city entrance. It's got all the makings of a classy hotel (good restaurants, massage centre, nightclub), though its most amazing feature is the bird-watcher's garden.

EATING & DRINKING

Banjul's restaurant scene is so calm that many eateries roll down the blinds before the evening has even started. Around Albert Market and the northern end of Liberation St are several cheap chop shops and street stalls, where plates of rice and sauce start at about D25. Denton Bridge Resort and Atlantic Hotel also have good restaurants.

Ali Baba Snack Bar (☎ 4224055; Nelson Mandela St; ☺ 9am-5pm) Banjul's main snack choice has a deserved reputation for its tasty shwarmas (sliced, grilled meat and salad in pita bread) and falafel sandwiches.

King of Shawarma Café (☎ 4229799; Nelson Mandela St; ☺ 9am-5pm Mon-Sat) Serving delicious mezze and pressed fruit juice, this friendly place is even happy to adapt its opening hours on request.

Michel's Seafood (☎ 4223108; 29 Jul 22 Dr; ☺ 8am-11pm) Banjul's classiest restaurant, Michel's is particularly renowned for its seafood menu. Outside the hotels, this is your only real dinner option.

SHOPPING

In Banjul, the best place to go shopping is Albert Market (p295). If you enter via the main entrance, you will pass stalls selling clothes, shoes, household and electrical wares and just about everything else you can imagine. Keep going and you'll reach the myriad colours and flavours of the fruit and vegetable market. Beyond here you'll find stalls catering mainly for tourists; this area is usually called the craft market.

Near the main entrance, you'll also find **Kerewan Sound** (Russell St), Gambia's best place to buy CDs and cassettes, and one of the very few boutiques that sell recordings by Gambian artists.

GETTING THERE & AWAY
Air

For details of international flights to/from Banjul, see p321. To confirm reservations on a flight you've already booked, it's easiest to deal directly with the airline offices.

Air Sénégal International (☎ 4202117; www.air -senegal-international.com; 10 Ecowas Ave)

Brussels Airlines (Map pp300-1; ☎ 4466880; www .brusselsairlines.com; Bertil Harding Hwy, Kololi)

Boat

Ferries (D10 per passenger, D150 to D200 per car) travel between Banjul's **ferry port** (☎ 4228205; Liberation St) and Barra, on the northern bank of the river. They are supposed to run every one to two hours from 7am until 9pm and take one hour, though delays are frequent and one ferry is often out of action.

The ferries take vehicles, but car space is limited, and you might have to wait for a couple of hours (if it's any consolation – trucks can sometimes be there for days). You buy your ticket before going through to the waiting area; keep it until getting off, as it'll be checked on the other side. If you're coming from the northern side by car, you'll need to purchase your ticket at the weighing station (just after the junction where the north-bank road east to Farafenni turns off), about 3km from Barra.

Gelli-Gelli and Taxi

Gelli-gellis (minibuses) and public taxis to Bakau (D8) and Serekunda (D10) leave from the car parks near the National Museum (they're named after their destinations). You might have to pay a bit more for luggage. Once in Bakau or Serekunda, you'll be able to jump on another taxi to take you to any other place along the coast or upcountry (see also p308).

A hire taxi from Banjul to Fajara or Bakau will cost around D150 to D200; Kololi, Kotu and Serekunda might be a bit more. If you don't find an empty taxi passing, try the Corinthia Atlantic Hotel – there are always taxis parked outside.

GETTING AROUND
To/From the Airport

Tourist taxis wait outside the airport, 30km northwest of the city. To Banjul, Serekunda and the Atlantic coast resorts (Bakau, Fajara, Kotu and Kololi) they'll cost around D300 to D400.

For a slightly cheaper option, walk out of the terminal until you come to the public car park, where you might find a yellow taxi to take you for D200.

Gelli-Gelli & Shared Taxi

A short ride across Banjul city centre (known as a 'town trip') in a private taxi will cost about D25 to D50.

ATLANTIC COAST RESORTS & SEREKUNDA

For many tourists, the short 10km stretch from Bakau to Kololi is The Gambia, for others not at all. The bustling area has all the makings of a thriving holiday zone: rows of hotels and guesthouses, a wide selection of restaurants, vibrant nightlife and packed beaches.

While it's perfectly possible to pass your days here, spread-eagled on white sand, you can also get a feel for African culture without having to venture too far from the strand. Fields, lagoons and palm groves sit between the hotel fronts, and most of the villages that have merged into this big holiday park have retained much of their original, rural character. Bakau's old town, a lively concentration of clapboard, corrugated iron and colourful market stalls, begins only a few steps away from the gleaming hotel fronts. And a short drive takes you to Serekunda, a hot and

heaving market town that's bursting at the seams with traffic, people and a strictly local vibe. Even the most polished parts, such as the 'Senegambia tourist mile' of Kololi, are speckled with exciting small enterprises, offering sustainable alternatives for those who want to dig a little deeper into what makes this country tick.

ORIENTATION

The main road from Gambia's upcountry towns goes past Banjul International Airport and reaches Serekunda, where it divides: straight ahead is the dual carriageway for about 14km to Banjul; and to the left is Kairaba Ave, which leads to Bakau, Fajara, Kotu and Kololi.

In Bakau and Fajara, the main drag is Atlantic Rd, which runs parallel to the coast, linking Kairaba Ave and Old Cape Rd. Just south of Atlantic Rd, and running parallel to it, is Garba Jahumpa Rd (formerly, and still better known as, New Town Rd). Badala Park Way branches off Kairaba Ave at the Fajara end and leads to the hotel/beach areas of Kotu and Kololi. It crosses Kairaba Ave at the country's famous set of traffic lights.

INFORMATION
Bookshops

Most supermarkets stock magazines and postcards.

Timbooktoo (☎ 4494345; timbooktoo@qanet.gm; Garba Jahumpa Rd, Fajara; ☺ 10am-7pm Mon-Thu, to 1pm & 3-7pm Fri, 10am-8pm Sat) An excellent shop with a good range of fiction and nonfiction, maps, and local and international papers. The Cultural Encounters offices upstairs provide information on sustainable tourism.

Cultural Centres

Alliance Franco-Gambienne (☎ 4375418; alliancefg@ hotmail.com; Kairaba Ave, Serekunda; ☺ 9.30am-5pm Mon-Fri) Has language courses (in French and Wolof) as well as regular concerts, films, shows and exhibitions. The garden restaurant at the back is a calm place for a solid, cheap lunch.

Internet Access

Many of the large hotels have internet cafes, and wi-fi connections (typically free for patrons) are getting popular with restaurants and hotels. Connections are usually slow. Most internet cafes charge D25 per hour.

Gamtel Kololi (Senegambia Strip); Serekunda (☎ 4229999; gen-info@gamtel.gm; Westfield Junction, Serekunda; ☺ 8am-11pm).

Net Bar (☎ 44982128; Atlantic Rd, Bakau; ☻ 9am-midnight) Here there are headsets, and you may be able to plug in a laptop. There's a small snack bar outside.

Quantumnet (☎ 4494514; Kairaba Ave, Fajara; ☻ 8.30am-10pm) Round the corner from Timbooktoo bookshop.

Medical Services
Medical Research Council (MRC; ☎ 4495446; Fajara) If you have a potentially serious illness, head for this British-run clinic off Atlantic Rd.

Stop Steps Pharmacy (☎ 4371344; Kairaba Ave, Fajara; ☻ 9am-10pm Mon-Sat) Has several branches.

Westfield Clinic (☎ 4398448; Westfield Junction, Serekunda)

Money
The main banks – Standard Chartered, Trust Bank and PHB – have branches in Bakau, Serekunda and Kololi. See p318 for opening hours. You can also change money at hotels, or ask your reception to put you in touch with an informal changer.

All of the banks listed below have ATMs, though you'll often find that they're out of order, and withdrawal limits can be tight. Remember to change or withdraw all the money you need at the coast, before any trip upcountry.

PHB Bank Bakau (☎ 4497139; Atlantic Rd)

Standard Chartered Bank Bakau (☎ 4495046; Atlantic Rd) Serekunda (☎ 4396102; Kairaba Ave)

Trust Bank Bakau (☎ 4495486; Atlantic Rd) Kololi (☎ 4465303; Wilmon Company Bldg, Badala Park Way)

Post
The main post office is off Kairaba Ave, about halfway between Fajara and Serekunda. The smaller **Gampost Bakau** (☎ 8900587; Atlantic Rd, Bakau; ☻ 8.30am-4pm Mon-Thu, to noon Fri & Sat) has a telecentre and an internet connection.

Telephone
Your best bet for finding public telecentres is around Serekunda and Kairaba Ave. Try **Gamtel** Kololi (Senegambia Strip) Serekunda (Westfield Junction, Serekunda; ☻ 8am-11pm).

Tourist Information
Cultural Encounters (☎ 4497675; www.asset-gambia .com; Fajara) The excellent information centre of the Association of Small Scale Enterprises

in Tourism (Asset), above Timbooktoo bookshop, is perfect for finding out about sustainable-tourism options.

Travel Agencies
Tour specialists are listed on p322. Most also do ticketing.

DANGERS & ANNOYANCES
Petty thefts and muggings occur occasionally, particularly on the path around Fajara golf course and the beaches. Single women should avoid being alone on beaches, particularly after dark.

One of the major annoyances in this area is the unwanted attention of 'bumsters' or 'beach boys', who loiter in the tourist areas, almost forcing their services as guides onto travellers. 'Bumsterism' is a form of sex tourism that is concentrated in areas of the Atlantic coast. In Gambia, the main sex tourists are middle-aged European women looking for young men. If you're not part of that scene, you'll find the constant advances a pain, to say the least. Be firm in your refusals.

SIGHTS
Kachikally Crocodile Pool
In the heart of Bakau village, the **pool** (☎ 7782479; www.kachikally.com; admission D50; ☻ 9am-6pm) has over 80 Nile crocodiles; large, lethargic 'Charley' can even be patted. For locals, it's a sacred site, and they traditionally come here to pray, as the crocodiles represent the power of fertility. At the entrance to the pool, there's also a nature trail and a small museum, containing musical instruments and other cultural artefacts.

Botanic Gardens
Bakau's **botanic gardens** (☎ 7774482; adult/child D50/free; ☻ 8am-4pm) were established in 1924, during colonial times, and are a peaceful place whose shade and calm offer good bird-spotting chances.

Bijilo Forest Park
This **park** (☎ 9996343; admission D20; ☻ 8am-6pm) is a small wildlife reserve on the coast, just a short walk from Kololi. It's a beautiful place to visit, either on your own, or on a guided walk (4.5km, one to two hours). A well-maintained series of trails leads through the lush vegeta-

THE GAMBIA

ATLANTIC COAST RESORTS & SEREKUNDA

A   **B**   **C**   **D**

INFORMATION
Alliance Franco-Gambienne	**1**	G5
American Embassy	**2**	F4
Belgian Consul	(see 47)	
British High Commission	**3**	E3
Cultural Encounters	(see 19)	
Danish Consul	**4**	G3
Discovery Tours	**5**	E3
Gambia Experience	(see 47)	
Gampost Bakau	**6**	G2
Gamtel Office	**7**	H5
Gamtel Office	**8**	A5
Guinea-Bissau Embassy	**9**	G2
Mauritanian Consulate	**10**	B5
Medical Research Council	**11**	F3
Net Bar	**12**	G2
Norwegian Consul	(see 4)	
PHB Bank	**13**	G2
Post Office	**14**	G4
Quantumnet	**15**	F3
Senegalese High Commission	**16**	F4
Standard Chartered Bank	**17**	H5
Standard Chartered Bank	(see 9)	
Stop Steps Pharmacy	(see 62)	
Swedish Consul	(see 4)	
Tilly's Tours	**18**	A6
Timbooktoo	**19**	F3
Trust Bank	**20**	G2
Trust Bank	**21**	B5
Westfield Clinic	**22**	H6

SIGHTS & ACTIVITIES
African Living Art Centre	**23**	F3
Bijilo Forest Park Headquarters	**24**	A6
Botanic Gardens	**25**	G2
Eco Yoga Holidays	(see 46)	
Fajara Golf Club	**26**	E3
Kachikally Crocodile Pool	**27**	G2
Sakura Arts Studio	**28**	F5

SLEEPING
African Heritage	**29**	H2
Balmoral Apartments	**30**	B5
Banana Ville	**31**	D5
Coco Ocean Resort	**32**	C6
Coconut Residence	**33**	A6
Fajara Guesthouse	**34**	E3
Fountain Hotel	**35**	E3
Holiday Beach Club Hotel	**36**	A5
Jabo Guesthouse	**37**	H2
Kairaba Hotel	**38**	A5
Kanifeng YMCA	**39**	G4
Leybato	**40**	E3
Luigi's	**41**	D4
Ngala Lodge	**42**	F2
Praia Hotel	**43**	G5
Roc Heights Lodge	**44**	H2
Romana Hotel	**45**	G2
Safari Garden	**46**	E3
Senegambia Beach Hotel	**47**	A5

EATING
Ali Baba's	**48**	A5
Asie Marie Cinema	**49**	F6
Bakau Market	**50**	G2
Bendula Garden	**51**	H2
Bucarabu	**52**	D4
Butcher's Shop	**53**	E3
Calypso	**54**	H2
Clay Oven	**55**	F3
Come Inn	**56**	F4
Flavours	(see 46)	
Francisco's	(see 35)	
Gaya Art Café	**57**	A5
Green Mamba	**58**	A5
GTS Restaurant	**59**	A6
Harry's Supermarket	**60**	F4
Jojo's	**61**	A5
Kairaba Supermarket	**62**	F4
Keur Bouba J & Cotton Club	(see 79)	
Kora	**63**	A6
La Pailotte	(see 1)	
La Parisienne	**64**	F4
Luigi's Pizza & Pasta House	(see 41)	
Maroun's	**65**	H5
Ngala Lodge	(see 42)	
Paradiso Pizza	**66**	B5
Ritz	**67**	E3
Safe Way Afra King	**68**	F5
Sambou's	**69**	G2
Solar Project	**70**	G5
Solomon's Beach Bar	**71**	C4
Soul Food	**72**	F3
Yok	(see 23)	
Youth Monument Bar & Restaurant	**73**	H5

DRINKING
Blue Bar	**74**	F3
Chapman's	**75**	G2
Come Inn	(see 56)	
Lana's Bar	**76**	F6
Paparazzi	**77**	B5
Sinatra's	**78**	G2
Weezo's	**79**	E3

ENTERTAINMENT
Aquarius	**80**	A6
Destiny	**81**	D4
Jokor	**82**	H6

SHOPPING
Tropical Tour & Souvenirs	(see 38)	
AB Rent-A-Car	(see 47)	
African Heritage	(see 29)	
Bakau Market	(see 50)	
Equigambia	**83**	D5
Salam Batik	**84**	F6

TRANSPORT
Brussels Airlines	**85**	B5
Hertz	(see 90)	
Minibuses to Banjul	**86**	H6
Shared Taxis to Bakau and Serekunda	**87**	F3
Shared Taxis to Fajara & Bakau	**88**	H5
Shared Taxis to Kololi	**89**	F4
Tippa Garage	**90**	F6

0   500 m
0   0.3 miles

Senegambia

See Senegambia Enlargement

Kotu Point

Kololi Point

Kololi

Senegambia Strip

Bijilo Forest Park

To Gambia Tours (1km);
Tanji (8km); Kartong (38km)

THE GAMBIA

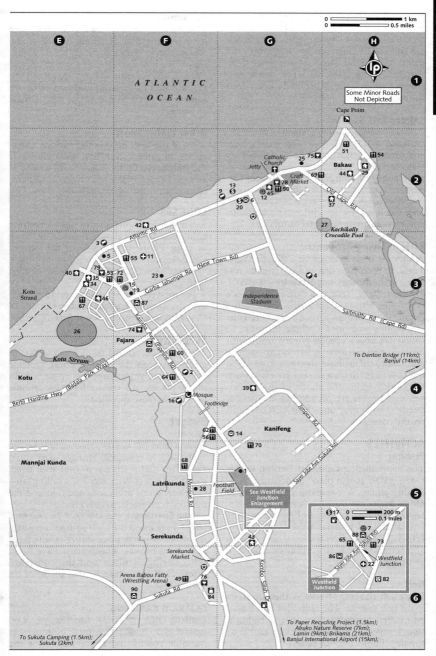

THE GAMBIA

tion, and you'll easily see patas and vervet monkeys as well as numerous birds (mainly on the coast side). The dunes near the beach are covered in grass and low bush, with tall palms just behind. Further back, away from the dunes, the trees are large, dense and covered in creepers. Absolutely don't feed the monkeys.

Sakura Arts Studio
Painter Njogu Touray's **studio** (☎ 7017351; Latrikunda) is full of colour and atmosphere and grants a private view of contemporary Gambian art. Using natural media, such as shells and sand, alongside colour, Touray carries the Gambian lands straight into his urban workshop. Ask him about his fascinating career, but also about his children's workshops and work in environmental campaigns.

African Living Art Centre
A fairytale cross between an antique gallery, a cafe, an orchid garden and an Oriental restaurant, the **African Living Art Centre** (☎ 4495131; Garba Jahumpa Rd, Fajara) is a hug of Gambia's arts scene. This is where Suelle Nachif hosts exhibitions, brings artists together, runs workshops and does a whole lot more to infuse Gambia's contemporary scene with new life. You can arrange to meet artists here and talk to them about their work, and find out how to participate in creative exchanges. Or simply enjoy the shade of the garden setting (flowers are yet another business of Suelle's) and enjoy one of the best cocktails on the coast.

ACTIVITIES
Fishing
The Sportsfishing Centre at Denton Bridge (Map p309) is the place to organise your fishing tours. A company based there is **African Angler** (☎ 7721228; www.african-angling.co.uk; Denton Bridge), specialising in light tackle, lure and anchored-bottom fishing in *bolongs* (creeks). It's very professional and able to accommodate experienced anglers as well as beginners.

Golf
Fajara Golf Club (☎ 4495456) is the country's main golf course. The club also has a pool and courts for tennis, squash and badminton. Temporary membership is available by the day. Enquire about rates.

Swimming
Most beaches in this area are relatively safe for swimming, though currents can be strong. Always check conditions locally before plunging in. The best sand strands are in Fajara and Kotu. If the Atlantic doesn't appeal, all the major hotels have swimming pools that are sometimes open to nonguests with a meal or drink.

Other Water Sports
Most of the large hotels offer various watersports to guests. Another good choice is the **Watersports Centre** (Map p309; ☎ 7773777) at Denton Bridge, where you can organise parasailing, windsurfing or catamaran trips.

COURSES
Safari Garden hotel always has something going on: African dance, drumming, batik or yoga. Phone to check what the current schedule is.

Salam Batik (see p307) runs recommended batik courses.

For total relaxation in beautiful surroundings, try Deepa's **Eco Yoga Holidays** (☎ in the UK 7779 240985; www.deepaspirit.com) at Safari Garden.

SLEEPING
You'll find everything from plush resorts to grotty dives on the Atlantic coast. Outside peak season, prices drop by up to 50% in many places. All rooms have bathrooms unless otherwise specified.

Budget
BAKAU
Romana Hotel (☎ 4495127; aframsromanahotel@yahoo .co.uk; Atlantic Rd; r from D350) You get what you'd expect for that price: a roof over your head, swept floors, a cold shower and a ceiling fan – the clean sheets are a nice addition and the outdoor hammock space is great.

Jabo Guesthouse (☎ 4494906; 9 Old Cape Rd; d D600) Never mind the high compound walls, this down-to-earth place surprises with large and clean rooms. The biggest have good self-catering facilities and the courtyard offers chill-out space in the shade of an orange tree.

FAJARA & KANIFENG
Kanifeng YMCA (☎ 4392647; www.ymca.gm; s/d incl breakfast D325/525; 🖳) This huge building has passable rooms and cheap meals for the

budget-bound. Rooms are very basic (only go for the top-floor ones that come with their own bathroom), but the knowledge that your stay here contributes to the impressive youth development projects run by the YMCA helps a sound sleep.

SEREKUNDA

Sukuta Camping (☎ 9917786; www.campingsukuta.com; camping per person D100, per car/van D20/28, s/d D240/460) This well-organised camping ground in Sukuta (southwest of Serekunda) also offers simple rooms for those that have temporarily tired of canvas. There are good washing (and laundry) facilities, great professional advice and an onsite mechanic to look after your car.

Praia Hotel (☎ 4394887; Mame Jout St; r D500; ☒) A few minutes' walk off Sayer Jobe Ave, right in the heart of fumes-filled and garbage-strewn Serekunda, this clean, spacious hostel with its large, wooden beds comes as such a surprise you may feel like hugging Mr Ceesay, the friendly manager.

KOTU & KOLOLI

Banana Ville (☎ 9906054; njieadama@hotmail.com; d D800; ☒) Very tiny and very simple, this is a great budget bet. Rooms are surprisingly spacious and have good self-catering facilities. And while the furniture looks a bit wonky, the beds are comfortable enough for a good night's sleep.

Midrange

BAKAU

African Heritage (☎ 4496778; www.africanheritagegambia.com; 16 Samba Breco Rd, Bakau; s/d incl breakfast D900/1000, apt 1500; ☒ ☒) Sometimes the best accommodation is found in unexpected places, such as this art gallery–cum-restaurant near the ferry jetty. Out the back, you have six clean, nicely furnished rooms and even an apartment for families and self-caterers. Room rates differ slightly depending on size and standard.

Roc Heights Lodge (☎ 4495428; www.rocheightslodge.com; Samba Breku Rd, Cape Point; s/d D1600/2350; ☒ ☒ ☒) This three-storey villa sits in a quiet garden that makes the bustle of Bakau suddenly seem very far away. Everything is arranged in an appealing decor of wood and tile simplicity. Even single rooms are large here. For even more space, you can book a self-catering apartment that comes with fully

equipped kitchens, bathtub, hair dryer, TV, telephone and plenty of space.

FAJARA

Fajara Guesthouse (☎ 4496122; fax 4494365; s/d D600/750; ☒ ☒) This cosy place exudes family vibes with its leafy courtyard and welcoming lounge. Some of the rooms are big enough to house couples with children. There's hot water, and self-caterers can use the kitchen for a small extra charge.

Leybato (☎ 4390275; www.leybato.abc.gm; d incl breakfast from D800) Hidden behind a small hill off Atlantic Rd, this cosy guesthouse overlooks the ocean from one of the best locations on the coast. Rooms vary in quality and price (go for the pricier ones; much better). Big selling point here is the beach location.

Fountain Hotel (Francisco's; ☎ /fax 4495332; francis coshotel@yahoo.co.uk; Atlantic Rd; s/d D800/1200; ☒ ☒) Recently renamed, this family hotel is still widely known as 'Francisco's'. Its intimate character has fortunately survived the baptism: the patio is still bathed in the shade of huge trees, the restaurant still does a fabulous roast on a Sunday (D175) and staffmembers are as friendly as ever.

Safari Garden (☎ 4495887; geri@gamspirit.com; s/d D1100/1500; ☒ ☒ ☒) The soul of this cute garden place with excellent service is managers Geri and Maurice, a couple so dedicated to Gambia and the possibilities for ecotourism and community action that travellers have been known to be drawn into their projects after even the briefest of stays. Ask them about Sandele Eco-Retreat (see p311).

KOLOLI

our pick **Luigi's** (☎ 4460280; www.luigis.gm; s/d incl breakfast D745/1100, apt from D2000; ☒ ☒ ☒) Once a pool restaurant with a couple of guest rooms, this has grown into a stunning complex with three restaurants and attractive lodgings set around the pool and Jacuzzi. Despite this tropical growth rate, the place manages to keep its family feel and you'll soon believe that you're a personal guest of Luigi's.

Balmoral Apartments (☎ 4461079; www.balmoralapartments.com; apt D1200; ☒ ☒) Perfect for families with children, this set of spacious, self-catering apartments does most things right in providing you with a relaxed home from home within walking distance of Kololi's busy stretch of restaurants and bars. You can even organise your own barbecues here.

Holiday Beach Club Hotel (☎ 4460418; www.holiday beachclubgambia.com; Senegambia; s/d 1500/2000; ⚡ ⚡) You're right near the Senegambia tourist mile at this resort hotel, but will feel miles removed once you've walked through the lush gardens to your private bungalow. The famous Bijilo monkeys leap right up to the private verandahs – great for wildlife feel, less exciting if they start nicking your jewellery.

Top End

In low season, many of those drop their (sometimes astronomical) prices.

FAJARA

our pick **Ngala Lodge** (☎ 4494045; www.ngalalodge .com; 64 Atlantic Blvd; ste per person D2000; ⚡ 💻 ⚡) Even the smallest room here is a large suite with its own Jacuzzi and handpicked paintings. Our favourite was the Rolling Stones room, kind of a stylish shrine to one of owner Peter's passions. It's not one for families – neither laid out nor intended for children – but it's ideal for couples. Perfect down to the frosted glasses, it also has one of Gambia's top-three restaurants.

KOLOLI

Senegambia Beach Hotel (☎ 4462717; www.senegam biahotel.com; Senegambia Strip; s/d incl breakfast D2800/3500; ⚡ ⚡ 💻 ⚡) With over 300 rooms, this is another giant on the scene. Its big winner is the stunning tropical garden surrounding the main building. It attracts plenty of birds, meaning you can tick the first tail feathers off the list while still lounging at the hotel pool.

Kairaba Hotel (☎ 4462940; www.kairabahotel .com; Senegambia Strip; s/d incl breakfast D4900/5700; ⚡ ⚡ 💻 ⚡ ♿) This president-owned place has more facilities than you can probably think of, including massage parlours, sports studios, a nightclub and a babysitting service. The right address for a holiday break wrapped in cotton wool.

Coco Ocean Resort (☎ 4466500; www.cocoocean.com; off Kombo Coastal Rd, Bijilo; ste D5000) With its pristine white walls, sculpted domes and wide, arched walkways, this aroma-wrapped wellness temple whispers relaxation. The minimum indulgence is the junior suite; honeymooners and big spenders can go for the royal treatment with private swimming pool.

Coconut Residence (☎ 4463377; www.coconutresi dence.com; Badala Park Way; ste incl breakfast from D6500; ⚡ 💻 ⚡) This is one of the few top hotels where luxury hasn't been traded for soul. All amenities and services come wrapped in sophisticated chic, from the landscaped gardens to the lavish suites. If you're in royal mood, go for a private villa with personal pool.

EATING

Mass tourism has made the Atlantic coast resorts one of the best areas to dine in West Africa; there's no shortage of places to eat and some real gems to tickle your tastebuds.

Self-caterers should head to Bakau market for fresh fruit and veg. There are plenty of supermarkets in this zone. Kairaba Ave has several choices. **Kairaba Supermarket** (Kairaba Ave) is large and well stocked, while **Harry's Supermarket** (⏰ 9am-10pm Mon-Sat) has the best hours. In Serekunda, **Maroun's** (Westfield Junction; ⏰ 9am-7.30pm Mon-Sat, 10am-1.30pm Sun) is a decent pick.

Bakau

Sambou's (☎ 4495237; Old Cape Rd; dishes from D100) This small, slapdash eatery has been around for years, which is more than some of the top food temples can say. They must be doing something right, then, at this very local, no-frills place, if it's only price or portion size.

Bendula Garden (☎ 4498223; www.bendulagarden .com; Kofi Annan St, Cape Point; dishes D250) This place is like an all-day happy hour. The drinks flow, the food fails to surprise, the music is live and the jokes are cheap. And though Mr Bass, the bubbly manager, insists that this spot is hassle-free, single women might disagree.

Calypso (Chez Anne & Fode; ☎ 4496292; ⏰ 9am-late; dishes D250) This cute, round beach bar serves delicious seafood, snacks and an African dish of the day between red-brick walls and attractive paintings. Sitting right on the beach, it also grants spectacular sunset romance at the right time of day. You can order a full English breakfast here all day (D225) or if you're the continental type, indulge in homemade cakes with thick cream.

Fajara

La Parisienne (☎ 4372565; Kairaba Ave; cakes around D30; ⏰ 6.30am-midnight; 🛜) French-style patisseries are very à la mode in Gambia, and excellent espresso and cappuccino, homemade ice cream, and warm croissants make this a particularly worthy teatime destination.

La Paillote (☎ 4375418; dishes from D50; ⏰ noon-4pm) The meal choice at the restaurant of the

Alliance Franco-Gambienne is between the African dish at a mere D50 and the European three-course meal at D100. Both are usually delicious – you'd have to try very hard to find better value anywhere.

Keur Bouba J & Cotton Club (☎ 4498249; Kairaba Ave, Fajara; lunch dishes D75; ◷ 9am-6am) With two venues wrapped in one, this restaurant and music club only closes for three hours every night. That means morning coffee between its warm, red walls, a huge plate of rice for lunch, and dinner à la carte before enjoying live jazz and salsa. One great day and not a traffic jam suffered.

Soul Food (☎ 4497858; Kairaba Ave; meals from D120) As the name promises, this is a place for generous portions of solid, sleep-enhancing meals. Think platters of rice dishes, mashed potato and rich sauces. The guesthouse upstairs has spacious but bare rooms.

Come Inn (☎ 4391464; meals around D200; ◷ 10am-2am) For a hearty meal, a good draught beer and a solid dose of local gossip, there's no better place than this German-style beer garden. It's popular with overlanders and pretty much anyone else who likes big portions at decent rates.

our pick Butcher's Shop (☎ 4495069; www.thebutchersshopgambia.com; Kairaba Ave, Fajara; dishes D169-285; ◷ 8am-11pm) Driss, the Moroccan celebrity chef, knows how to grill a pepper steak to perfection, subtly blend a sauce until the spices sing in harmony and present a freshly pressed juice cocktail like a precious gift. This place does a mean Sunday brunch (D200) from 10am to 4pm.

Flavours (☎ 4495887; dishes D200; ◷ 8am-midnight; V) If you've been wondering where all the great waiting staff are, quite a few have been hired by this fabulous little garden place, serving imaginative dishes for carnivores and vegetarians alike. Meals taste as great as they look and the atmosphere is as friendly as a hug.

Clay Oven (☎ 4496600; meals D250; ◷ 7-11pm; V) For Indian food, this place off Atlantic Rd is one of the best in the whole of West Africa. Just savour the Tandoori grill or any of the original desserts. With its scrubbed white walls, leafy garden and personalised service, the surroundings are right, too. And believe us, we tried, but Vimal wouldn't part with the slightest hint about his delicate spicings.

Ritz (☎ 9924205; meals D250; ◷ 8am-midnight) This tiny place with the aspirational name has for six years now given the impression of teetering on the verge of closing. And yet, it still serves generous portions of solid European fare in a Fajara side street.

Francisco's (☎ 4495332; cnr Atlantic Rd & Kairaba Ave; grills D250; ◷ lunch & dinner) There are few places where mixed seafood platters and grills taste better than in the shade of the giant palm trees in Francisco's tranquil garden.

Yok (☎ 4495131; African Living Art Centre, Garba Jahumpa Rd; meals D300; ◷ 12.30pm-midnight; V) No one should visit Fajara without eating at Yok, locally known as the Salon. You reach this Asian restaurant via the leafy, glass-roofed alleyway behind an impressively stacked antique and arts shop. It serves excellent Singaporean, Thai and Chinese fusion cuisine against a backdrop of gently flowing waterfalls and rustling palm trees.

Ngala Lodge (☎ 497672; Atlantic Rd; meals around D500; ◷ 11.30am-3pm & 7.30-11pm Mon-Sat; V) When we visited, Paul the manager was bent over the CVs of a range of star-spangled European chefs. Apparently the gig to heat the stove in one of Gambia's most renowned restaurants went to a Polish celebrity cook. This has always been the top address for sumptuous and lovingly presented meals; service and sea-view setting are impeccable.

Kololi
PALMA RIMA AREA
Solomon's Beach Bar (☎ 4460716; Palma Rima Rd; meals D100-200; ◷ 10am-midnight) At the northern end of Kololi beach, this cute roundhouse serves excellent grilled fish in a youthful atmosphere. As light and sunny as the reggae classics on loop.

Bucarabu (☎ 7797877; Palma Rima Rd; meals around D150) From breakfast parlour, grill party and tapas bar to cocktail lounge, there's hardly anything this place is not trying to be. The draught beer, darts and big-screen sports lead one to suspect that the place has a loyal British following. There's live music on Friday and karaoke night on Monday.

Luigi's Pizza & Pasta House (☎ 4460280; www.luigis.gm; Palma Rima Rd; dishes around D300; ◷ 6pm-midnight; ⬚ ♿ V) This is a praise song to Italy and its culinary achievements on two floors. The pasta is *al dente*, the pizzas are crisp and everything is cooked with the freshest ingredients. Kids get their very own menu and play area, so that parents on holiday can gaze across the sea from the terrace.

THE GAMBIA

SENEGAMBIA

GTS Restaurant (☎ 7777225; www.gambiatouristsupport
.com; Bijilo Park Rd; meals around D180; ☻ lunch & dinner)
This is the public face and fundraising initiative of a charity working to get Gambian
youngsters into school and enable them to
stay there. The relaxed restaurant has a real
youth vibe, with pool tables, table tennis and
occasional karaoke nights on offer.

Kora (☎ 4462727; Senegambia Strip; dishes D275-
350; ☻ 4pm-midnight; **V**) This dinner favourite
serves a range of very tasty meals, great cocktails and a vast selection of quality spirits in a
classy ambience. If you come with friends, try
the enormous mixed platter for four people
(D500 per person) that gives you a taste of the
best dishes on the varied menu. It also does
kids' dishes (D150), a rarity in Gambia.

Ali Baba's (☎ 9905978; Senegambia Strip; meals around
D300; ☻ 9.30am-2am) Everyone knows Ali Baba's,
so it's as much a useful meeting point as a
commendable restaurant. A fast-food joint
during the day, it serves dinner with a show
in its breezy garden. There are frequent live
concerts (mainly reggae), and important football matches on a big screen.

Paradiso Pizza (☎ 4462177; Senegambia Strip; pizzas
around D300) No one argued with the Paradiso's
claim that it serves the best pizza in town.
Amid the host of indistinguishable eateries
that line the Senegambia strip, this is a real
find. Sticking with the Italian theme, the espresso here is also real.

Gaya Art Café (☎ 4464022; gayaartcafe.com; Bertil
Harding Hwy; meals around D350; ☻ noon-midnight Mon-Sat;
V) Arty, veggie, healthy and organic, this is
an unlikely addition to Senegambia's loud and
boisterous food stations. Divine smoothies
and boosting salads are served in a relaxing
garden space.

Jojo's (☎ 7295711; Senegambia; dishes around D370;
V) Run by the former chef of the famous
Ngala Lodge, Jojo's, with its earthy, minimalist
ambience, sets out to rival established kitchens
of the country. The saltimbocca chicken with
olives and parmesan is divine, and for vegetarians, there's a great choice of salads. Breakfast
is pancakes and coffee.

our pick **Green Mamba** (☎ 6662622; www.green
mambagarden.com; dishes D450; ☻ 7pm-midnight; **V**)
A rare treat, this inspired restaurant is built
around the concept of an Oriental grill, meaning you get to pick the raw ingredients for
your personalised stir-fry and watch them
being cooked – unless you wish to relax over

an original local fruit cocktail while the attentive staff brings your plate over. Spread across
a large garden, tables grant a couple-enticing
amount of privacy. Also check for the party
and cinema nights.

Serekunda

Serekunda's small eateries are near the market
and taxi-station entrance, busy side streets
and near the taxi stands. Also popular is Asie
Marie Cinema, which isn't actually a cinema
at all but a darkened hall with football matches
on a big screen and cold beer in the yard.

Solar Project (☎ 7053822; solarprojectgambia@gmx
.ch; 18 Sainey Njie St, Faji Kunda; snacks D50-100; ☻ 7am-
midnight Mon-Sat) For ecofriendly eating options,
this small solar-powered café and workshop
is hard to beat. All of the omelettes, meatballs, cakes and dried fruit served here are
cooked on the parabolic solar-cookers you can
observe being made in the backyard.

Safe Way Afra King (dishes D50-150; ☻ 5pm-midnight)
This is a popular choice among Serekunda's
host of snacks, eateries and grilled meat
houses. Off the mosque road, it serves tasty
afra, sandwiches, *fufu* (mashed cassava), 'cow-
foot' and other African dishes.

Youth Monument Bar & Restaurant (Westfield
Junction; meals around D100; ☻ lunch & dinner) Right
on the junction, this is the local favourite for
cheap food and sports matches on screen. It's
a great place to meet the locals.

DRINKING

For entertainment, hotel bars compete for
attention with restaurants reinventing themselves as bars at night and with the glitzy
string of nightclubs along the coast. The line
between bar and club is often blurred, as punters turn precious table space (or table tops)
into improvised dance floors.

Chapman's (☎ 4495252; Atlantic Rd, Bakau; meals
around D150-250; ☻ 11am-10pm Thu-Tue) In Bakau,
this is labelled as 'the place where everyone seems to go'. It's usually packed with
a mixed crowd. Good, varied meals are
washed down with pints of draught beer and
good conversations.

Sinatra's (☎ 7781727; Atlantic Rd, Bakau) With
a different program every day (movies on
Monday, live music on Friday and Saturday,
grill party on Sunday afternoon) and the fixed
point of cheap draught beer to guide you
through it all, this is a place you're unlikely
to visit only once. The vibes here shift from

family day out to smoky jazz lounge or loose club night depending on day and time of day. The courtyard is particularly nice.

Weezo's (☎ 4496918; Kairaba Ave, Fajara) Fajara's favourite Mexican diner undergoes a fascinating transformation around sunset, when the lights get dimmed and tables are readied for spontaneous dancing, and sumptuous Mexican tortilla dishes are replaced with one of the best cocktail menus on the coast.

Come Inn (☎ 7049210; Kairaba Ave, Fajara; ✆ 10am-2am) Popular with anyone who knows how to handle a few pints, this beer garden is the place to compete for the biggest desert driving stories with drink-hardy Germans, Brits and Gambians.

Blue Bar (☎ 9991539; Kairaba Ave, Fajara; ✆ 11am-3am) Overlooking a calm stretch of the region's main artery, this cheerful, dimly lit bar has an excellent selection of drinks to be sipped in the relaxed vibes and good company on the outdoor terrace.

Paparazzi (☎ 4460600; Senegambia Strip, Kololi; ✆ 10pm-3am) This is a smart wine bar with dazzling decor and a tourist crowd. Don't stay away from your table too long or it may get pushed aside to make space for party steps to booming electronic beats.

Lana's Bar (☎ 7707684; Serekunda) This reggae-coloured drinking hole will happily soak you up after a tiring, lung-clogging walk along Serekunda's main artery. Sitting here with a cold beer, the Serekunda bustle washing over you, rather than you getting caught up in it, is not a bad way of wasting an hour. Unless you're a single woman, when it's torture by bad chat-up lines.

ENTERTAINMENT

Aquarius (☎ 4460247; Bijilo Forest Park Rd, Senegambia Strip, Kololi; ✆ 10am-3am) A smart cafe during the day, Aquarius turns into a glittering dance floor at night – a place where the beats are heavy and the crowds touristy. The drinks are expensive and the atmosphere is strictly party vibe – no place for a quiet drink.

Destiny (Kotu Beach, Kotu) A sparkling palace on three floors, this is where parties go on late, clothes are tight and tiny, and the beat is thumping. It's the nightlife version of a holiday beach club – great for glittering parties but the wrong address for local flavours.

Jokor (☎ 4375690; 13 Kombo Sillah Dr, Serekunda) This open-air club near Westfield Junction in Serekunda is a raucous local affair, and makes a convincing claim to be the most entertaining club of all. It's open, and packed, every night, and there's a live band (usually *mbalax* or reggae) on Friday and Saturday.

SHOPPING

Bakau Market sells fruit and vegetables, and has an adjacent handicrafts section stuffed to the rims with carvings, traditional cloth and other souvenirs. Serekunda is the place to hunt for good-quality batiks. There's no lack of small souvenir shops in this zone. The following indicates a few places that offer good choice and quality, or are totally original in their approach.

For music, your best choice is Kerewan Sound in Banjul (see p297).

African Heritage Centre (☎ 4496778; www.afri canheritagegambia.com; 16 Samba Breco Rd, Bakau) Near Bakau's Cape Point tip, you find this beautiful boutique with a range of original sculptures, batiks, paintings and souvenirs (as well as a good restaurant and a few rooms that you can stay in down the back).

Tropical Tour & Souvenirs (☎ 4460536; Senegambia Strip, Kololi) In the Kairaba Hotel, this hassle-free place has a good range of information, books, maps, arts and fashion. While there, ask about its Tropical Gardens project, an impressive little business of growing and preserving indigenous Gambian flora.

Equigambia (☎ 7798801, 7794374; www.equigambia .org; Kololi; ✆ 10am-6pm Mon-Sat) This is the place to purchase high-quality Gambian clothing, made by selected local tailors in an excellent employment-creation and training scheme. The brightly coloured children's, men's and women's collections are sold under fair-trade conditions.

Salam Batik (☎ 9820125; salam_batik_mp_art@ yahoo.co.uk; London Corner, Serekunda) Forget the mass-produced batik wares on display at various tourist markets. This inspiring little place sells original outfits, bags and other items at very reasonable rates. You'll become the proud owner of a unique and beautiful piece, while supporting local industry. Plans for batik workshops were in place when we visited. To get here, take an immediate left after Lana's Bar in Serekunda. It's on the left-hand side, after the big mango tree.

Paper Recycling Project (☎ 7707090, 7793358; gambianpaper@yahoo.co.uk; Fajikunda) A short drive out of Serekunda, this workshop, stunningly located on the edge of a *bolong* (creek) trains local residents in the art of paper making. The cards, boxes, bags and diaries on sale here are all made from recycled papers and colourful Gambian cloth. But that's almost a beautiful sideline; the real fun is in seeing this smooth project running and expanding – it's now planning to build a crafts village that will house other, small-scale craftsmen and women.

GETTING THERE & AWAY

Tippa Garage (Bakoteh Junction, Serekunda) is the main transport hub for *sept-places* (bush taxis) and *gelli-gellis* upcountry. Destinations include Soma (D70), though for travel upcountry you're better off going to Banjul (D15 in a shared taxi, D150 in a hire taxi), taking the ferry to Barra and getting onto taxis travelling the north-bank road from there.

For the south coast, you can get a *gelli-gelli* from Tippa Garage to Gunjur (D18). It passes Brufut, Sanyang and Tujering. A private taxi to Gunjur is around D150. Vehicles for Brikama (D12) leave from Westfield Junction. Bush taxis go from Serekunda to Kafountine and Ziguinchor in southern Senegal via the border at Séléti.

GETTING AROUND
To/From the Airport

A green tourist taxi from Banjul International Airport to Serekunda is around D400, and to any Atlantic coast resort it's D400. Yellow taxis cost about D200, depending upon your powers of negotiation.

There isn't any public transport to the airport, but minibuses between Brikama and Serekunda can drop you at the turn-off 3km from the airport.

Car & Motorcycle

There are also a few local one-man-and-his-car operations that advertise in hotels, shops and supermarkets. They can offer much better deals; just make sure the cars are in good condition, particularly if you're travelling upcountry.

AB Rent-a-Car (☎ 9320776; www.ab.gm; Senegambia Beach Hotel, Kololi)

Hertz (☎ 4390041; airport ☎ /fax 4473156; hertz@gamtel.gm; Tippa Garage)

Private Taxi

Green tourist taxis are usually parked outside big hotels, where they can be the only ones

allowed to enter. Their prices are relatively fixed and displayed on big boards – they are always more expensive than yellow taxis. The latter serve generally as shared taxis, but you can also hire them for individual rides; you just need to negotiate the rate. From Fajara to Banjul, for instance, you'll pay around D350 by tourist taxi, D150 in a yellow cab. A town trip around the coastal resorts by yellow taxi should cost around D50.

Hiring a taxi for a day to go around the Atlantic resorts and Banjul should cost around D1000 to D1500.

Shared Taxi

Shared taxis, called *six-six* (a short hop costs D6) operate on several routes at the coastal resorts. They connect Bakau to Westfield Junction and Serekunda, passing through Sabina Junction near the Timbooktoo bookshop at Fajara. You can also get *six-six* from the traffic lights junction to Senegambia Strip in Kololi and from there to Bakau. You simply flag a taxi down, pay your fare and get off where you want.

In Serekunda, minibuses (D6) to Banjul city leave from near Westfield Junction.

WESTERN GAMBIA

With its luxurious eco-lodges, community projects, nature reserves and historical sites, this region proudly indicates a whole new direction for tourism in The Gambia. From the riverbanks to the southern coast, you can catch intimate glimpses on life and nature here, and all within easy reach from the coast.

SOUTH COAST & INLAND
GETTING THERE & AWAY

From Tippa Garage in Serekunda, *gelli-gellis* go directly via Brufut and Tanji to Gunjur, but most go to Brikama first, where you have to change. For Kartong, it's another change in Gunjur.

Tanji & Around

Not long ago, the coast south of Kololi used to be lined with small, hard-to-access fishing villages. Now that a tarmac road connects the tourist centre in the north with Kartong, 50km further south on the Allahein River, the villages along its way are all transforming into

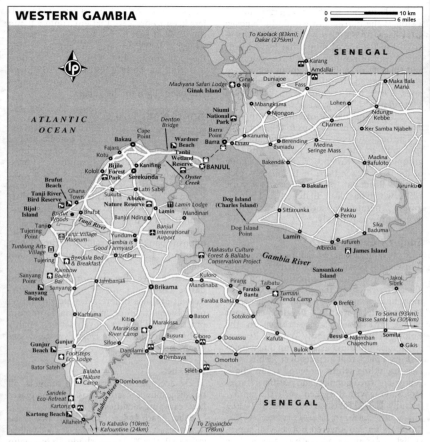

WESTERN GAMBIA

very viable tourist destinations. Impressively, many developments have been low-key, and with a real, green touch, making this zone a great area for exploring local life and environment without trampling all over it.

In Brufut, development has been most dramatic, transforming the sleepy village into an urban settlement with luxury housing. Small **Hibiscus House** (☎ 7982929; www.hibiscushousegambia .com; Brufut; r incl breakfast D2800; ⚒ ⚒) is, thankfully, tucked away at the end of a bougainvillea-lined dirt road and has attractive bungalows, an open-air Jacuzzi and a glass-fronted lounge. A short drive southwards takes you to Tanji, with its charming **Tanji Village Museum** (☎ 9926618; tanje@dds.nl; adult/child D100/25; ⚒ 9am-5pm) and the **Tanji River Bird**

Reserve (☎ 9919219; admission D35; ⚒ 8am-6pm), an area of dunes, lagoons and woodland that attracts a fantastic number of birds. Bijol Island, the off-coastal part of the reserve, is an important breeding ground for Caspian terns and grey-headed gulls. Only visit this fragile part in company of an official wildlife guide and outside breeding season; random visits endanger the project.

Tanji village, 3km south of the reserve office, has a couple of good lodgings. **Nyanya's Beach Lodge** (☎ 9808678, 4414021; s/d D400/600) has bright bungalows in a leafy garden on the bank of the Tanji River, a branch of the Gambia River, while **Paradise Inn Lodge** (☎ 9810112; r per person incl breakfast D660) sits in a bird-attractive garden (mangroves close by) in the village.

A little further south, in Tujering, put in a stop at the quirky and wonderful **Tunbung Arts Village** (☎ 9982102; etundow@yahoo.com) where artist Etu runs workshops that leave a colourful trail of random sculptures, paintings and splashes of paint throughout the garden and the skewed bungalows. Call or email for rates. A little further south again, **Bendula Bed & Breakfast** (☎ 7717481; www.bendula.com; s/d D490/740) is a simple and nature-oriented camp with drumming courses and trips to the herbalist.

The beautiful beaches of Sanyang, the next spot south on the coast, are popular with tour groups from the Kombos. Have a drink at one of its many beach bars, or if you stay, pick **Rainbow Beach Bar** (☎ 9726806; www.rainbow.gm; d D500), which has clean, thatched-roof bungalows, a generator, and a chef that knows how to grill prawns properly.

Gunjur & Gunjur Beach

One of Gambia's largest fishing centres, bustling Gunjur beach tempts with the impressive sight of pirogues rolling in, unloading their glistening catch on the shore. For Gunjur's more hidden sights, try a tour with the **Gunjur Environmental Protection & Development Group** (GEPADG; ☎ 8800986; gepadg@yahoo.com) to the Bolong Fenyo Community Wildlife Reserve it manages and the coastal lagoon that it helps restore, a place that attracts over 75 bird species, including white-crowned robin-chats, yellow-crowned gonolets and northern shovelers. Staying with the green spirit, the family-friendly **ourpick** **Footsteps Eco Lodge** (☎ 7411609; www.footstepsgambia.com; bungalows incl breakfast D2500; ▩ ▧) is an ecopowered house with super-stylish solar-powered rooms, composting toilets, freshly grown food and then some. **Gecko Lodge** (☎ 7778551; www.gecko-lodge.com; Gunjur; per person incl breakfast D1350) is equally superb in its design, all warm wood tones and earthen-coloured walls, best enjoyed during one of its yoga classes.

Five kilometres further south, **Balaba Nature Camp** (☎ 9919012; Medina Salaam; s/d D550/700) is a laid-back, environmentally friendly camp, sat amid dense savannah woodland. Manager Lamin offers drumming, dancing, bird-watching and other excursions.

Kartong

Picturesque Kartong is gradually turning into Gambia's prime location for ecotourism – its stunning setting between the Allahein River and the Atlantic coast attracted hoteliers keen to preserve that environment, and the work of **Kart** (Kartong Association for Responsible Tourism; ☎ 4495887) inspired ecothinking among the local community. A good time to come is during the **Kartong Festival** (☎ 9933193; www.kartongfestival.org), when regional dance troupes and bands light up the village.

SIGHTS & ACTIVITIES

Every visitor here gets taken to the **Reptile Farm** (admission D100) and the sacred **crocodile pool** of Mama Bambo Folonko. Ask Kart or your hotel for tours. The Kartong Community Forest is great for leisurely excursions and a great place to spot patas and red colobus monkeys. Put in a stop at the pretty **Lemon Fish Art Gallery** (☎ 9922884; www.lemonfish.gm), which has good exhibitions and a small shop, or arrange a pirogue tour along the river (note that the opposite bank is in Senegalese territory) with your hotel, KART, or the fishing centre, 3km out of town.

Most hotels offer drumming, batik and dance courses. Courses at Sandele Eco-Retreat are in a different league (including professional training in sustainable-tourism practice), and held in a lovely setting. Highly recommended here are Deepa's yoga classes on the beach.

SLEEPING

There are options here for all budgets, all boasting some eco-cred. Most Kartong places have camping facilities.

Boboi Beach Lodge (☎ 7776736; www.gambia-adventure.com; camping per person D300, d with/without bathroom D1200/800) Huge, shade-giving palm trees and waves lapping at your feet make this the prettiest camping spot in town. Rooms are a bit scruffy.

Equator Lodge (☎ 7851866; laminjamba@hotmail.com; www.equatorfoundation.com; incl breakfast camping D350, s/d D500/700) This recommended budget spot is run by a charity to finance the local healthcare centre.

Halahin Lodge (☎ 9933193; www.halahin.com; s/d incl breakfast D600/800) Just outside Kartong, Bouba Jaiteh's place is simple, friendly and solar-powered and promises local vegetables in the sauce.

Lemon Fish Art Gallery (☎ 9922884; www.lemonfish.gm; r D700) For a family feel, try Lemon Fish, where you stay in a lovely private house and can even use the kitchen.

Stala Adventures (☎ 9915604; www.stala-adventures .com; camping D245, full board per person D1500) This tranquil spot for fishing and birding is right on the Allahein River and perfect for pirogue tours. Solar panels and a water-recycling system boost its eco-credit.

our pick **Sandele Eco-Retreat** (☎ 4495887; www .sandele.com; half board per person r/lodges D1800/2500) Our favourite place, this stunning eco-castle has magnificent domes made from compressed bricks and dead wood. Its eco-pedigree is faultless, the setting and cuisine are divine, and the community commitment by managers Geri and Maurice is inspiring.

EATING

All of Kartong's hotels serve good food; you need to order in advance.

Umpacola Bar (☎ 4419111; silwia_barke@web.de; meals around D150; ☾ lunch & dinner) In the centre, this is Kartong's classic meeting place, great for cold beers, food and a chat.

Morgan's Grocery (snacks & meals D50-200; ☾ lunch & dinner) A 300m sand track west on the way to the crocodile pool, Morgan's is a great spot to pick up local information, book bird tours or simply chill with a drink.

GETTING THERE & AWAY

Kartong is temptingly close to beautiful Niafourang on the Senegalese side, but legal requirements complicate the short hop. You might be able to get your exit stamp at the Kartong immigration post at the exit from town, but there's no post on the Senegalese side. Phone Ousmane Sané at Tilibo Horizon in Niafourang (see p731) to check if he can help; otherwise stick to a pirogue tour.

Abuko Nature Reserve

For a park of only 105 hectares, the **Abuko Nature Reserve** (☎ 4375888; adult/child D35/15; ☾ 8am-6pm) has amazingly diverse vegetation and wildlife. Bird-watchers will love this place – more than 250 species have been sighted in the gallery forest, Guinea savannah and along Lamin Stream (keep an eye out for the Nile crocodiles in the waters). Species include African goshawks, oriole warblers, yellowbills, leafloves, green and violet turacos and many more, best observed on the trail through the birding extension. Several photo hides also reveal mammals, including bushbucks, duikers, porcupines and three monkey types: vervets, endangered western red colobuses and patas.

Abuko is an important hub of preservation work in The Gambia, largely thanks to the **Makasutu Wildlife Trust** (☎ 7782633, 4473349; m.wildlifetrust@yahoo.co.uk), which runs biodiversity research as well as ecotourism initiatives (see below).

If you are visiting for research purposes or to work as a volunteer you can stay at the reserve (D500 per person, less for longer stays).

A private taxi to Abuko from the Atlantic coast resorts costs about D300 to D400, including two hours of waiting time. Alternatively, you can take a minibus from Serekunda towards Brikama (D10). The reserve entrance is on the right (west) of the main road.

Makasutu Culture Forest & Ballabu Conservation Project

Makasutu means 'sacred forest' in Mandinka, or 'cultural theme park' in the language of tourist enterprise. **Makasutu Culture Forest** (☎ 9951547; www.makasutu.com; full/half day D750/550, night extravaganza D850) bundles a dazzling array of Gambian landscapes, traditions and wildlife into a territory of over 1000 hectares. A day in the forest includes pirogue tours through the mangroves, guided walks through savannah plains and gallery forest where you can watch palm wine being tapped, a visit to a crafts centre and much more.

Surrounding the forest, the **Ballabu Conservation Project** (Makasutu Wildlife Trust; ☎ 7782633; m.wildlifetrust@yahoo.co.uk; www.darwin gambia.gm) is one of Gambia's most ambitious projects of community-based conservation. The 85 sq km biodiversity belt not only protects animals but also aids the development of the 14 villages within the zone. Nature trails from Abuko and the Culture Forest were being sketched out when we visited; check with the Wildlife Trust as to how far they have progressed.

If you have the budget and feel like a treat, you can stay in the forest at the very exclusive **Mandina River Lodge** (☎ 9951547, 7777704; www .makasutu.com; s/d incl half board D3700/7400; ☒ ☒), a stunning ecoretreat with floating, solar-powered luxury lodges. Bookings are best made through the website. From October to April, the lodge works principally with Gambia Experience clients (p322); in low season it's open to all and the price drops by 50%.

From Brikama, take a *gelli-gelli* from Tippa Garage, Serekunda, to Brikama, then change

THE GAMBIA

for one to Kembujeh village (D7), from where it's a 3km walk. A hire taxi from Brikama is around D150, and if you phone the park beforehand you can be picked up from Brikama at 9am and dropped off with the park's 4.30pm bus (D100 one way).

Lamin Lodge

The quirky **Lamin Lodge** (☎ 4497603; www.gambia -river.com; meals around D300; ⏰ 9am-11pm) looks like a little boy's dream; it's a rugged, handmade log cabin on stilts, overlooking a mangrove creek. It's one of the most ingenious restaurant ideas around, and most tour groups stop here, either for meals (it does great fresh oysters and lush buffets), a relaxing break or a boat excursion with **Gambia River Excursions** (☎ 4494360; www.gambia -river.com). It organises plenty of imaginative boat trips on the Gambia River, including a fabulous Birds and Breakfast trip (D660).

A trip here is easily combined with time at Abuko Nature Reserve. Hiring a taxi from the coast, with a bit of waiting time, costs around D400.

Brikama

Three major junctions, crawling trucks, dust, heat and excitement – this is what Brikama is made of. Most people come here for the famous **crafts market** at the edge of town (on the right as you come in from Banjul or Serekunda). It's a hectic corner of covered stalls crammed with souvenir-style sculptures, improvised ateliers and hordes of eager salesmen. Music lovers should stay a little longer, visit some of the **kora player families** (see the boxed text, opposite) and perhaps book a class.

There's a hospital, a post office and a Trust Bank with an (unreliable) ATM. You can change money and check your mail at **Sonko Jileng Complex** (☎ 4483389).

SLEEPING & EATING

Brikama accommodation ranges from the barely inhabitable to the just about passable.

Nematulie Lodge (Chief's Compound; ☎ 9845959; nematulielodge@yahoo.com; off Banjul Hwy; s/d D200/400) In the centre, Nematulie is a decent option, with garden bungalows and a relaxing *bantaba* (terrace).

Alla la Daaroo Guesthouse (☎ 9912659; www.guest house.gm; Bakary Sambouya; s/d incl breakfast D350/530) Just 3km south of town, this reclusive guesthouse has five rooms and plenty of camping space in tranquil gardens. It welcomes families and can arrange tailor-made tours.

Nice to be Nice (☎ 7281909; ⏰ 7am-midnight; dishes around D150; Ⓥ) The best restaurant in town, this promisingly named place even claims to rustle up veggie food.

Kambeng Restaurant (Trans-Gambia Hwy) Another good address, this is the perfect place to line your stomach before a trip to the open-air nightclub Jokor's (Trans-Gambia Hwy; weekend admission around D100) – the best space to party in the whole country.

GETTING THERE & AWAY

Many minibuses (D10) pass through Brikama from Serekunda, about once every 10 minutes during the day.

If you're headed east, there is frequent transport to Soma (90), where you change for any other upcountry destinations. There

---

FRESH FOOD ON THE FARM

Near Yundum, the **Gambia is Good Farmyard** (Alhagie Darboe; ☎ 9891560, 4494473; Yundum; adult/child D100/50) is a place where you can watch your juice not only being pressed but also grown. Gambia is Good is a socially engaged marketing company that has since 2004 helped over 1000 poor (and mostly female) farmers to find buyers for the products of their small agricultural farms and provided the tourist enterprises on the coast with fresh, locally grown produce. On a visit to the farm, you can attend cookery classes (D500 per person, minimum of four people) and of course get to taste an organic Gambian stew in the restaurant (D250 including tour). Farmers introduce you to local horticultural techniques, improved nursery methods, new irrigation systems and plenty more. The project has won the Responsible Tourism Award for poverty reduction in 2008.

If you phone the yard before setting out they can pick you up and crank everything into gear before you arrive – and that includes preparing fresh juice and lunch. A return trip from the coastal resorts by taxi with a bit of waiting time costs around D400. If you book a cookery class, the transport is included in the fee.

KORA COURSES

For anybody interested in African music, Brikama should be an obligatory stop on the itinerary. The dusty town is home to one of the most renowned families of *kora* players in the country, a *griot* clan that reaches back several generations and has brought forth talents such as Dembo Konté, his son Bakari Konté, and Malamini Jobarteh and his sons Pa and Tata Dindin Jobarteh. This is a great place to learn traditional instruments – such as *kora*, *djembe* (a short, goat hide–covered drum) or *balafon* (xylophone) – from excellent players and teachers. You can also watch the instruments being made, and get an introduction to the *griots'* métier. Prices are entirely negotiable, and depend on duration and whether your stay and eat in your teacher's compound. For quotes and directions, call **Konté Kunda** (☎ Dembo 7776439, ☎ Jeli Bakari 9843706) or **Jobarteh Kunda** (☎ Moriba Kuyateh 9922045, 7738792; moriba143@yahoo.com). Both the Konté and Jobarteh compounds are located in Santhiaba, Brikama.

---

are also frequent bush taxis to Gunjur (D10), where you change for transport to Kartong.

Brikama is the best junction from which to reach the Casamance region in Senegal. A bush taxi to the Senegalese border in Séléti costs D50.

Sifoe, Darsilami & Marakissa

On a day trip from the coast, pass by **Sifoe** (between Gunjur and Darsilami) and visit the local **Beekeeping Association** (☎ 7781272; sifoe.beekeeping@yahoo.com; Sifoe-Kafo Farm). Manjiki Jabang, the president of the association, gives insightful tours of the farm and transformation workshops, explaining the various types of hives used, including a fabulous glass model that quite literally buzzes with bee activity. A small shop onsite sells honey, candles and batiks made with Sifoe wax.

The road from here to **Darsilami** is a stunning stretch of tropical landscape with imposing palm groves, wetlands and rice fields that provide plenty of bird-spotting opportunities. In the village, the friendly **Timberland** (☎ 9946981; www.senegam.net; full board per person D765) is kept in the spirit of village-style simplicity, including the experience of an outdoor shower. Rooms

are equipped with the basics for a comfortable night; toilets are shared.

It's only a short drive from here to **Marakissa**, a favourite spot for bird-watchers, who come to see white-breasted cuckoo shrikes, sunbirds, blue-breasted kingfishers, African darters and dozens of other species in the woodlands surrounding a calm river. **Marakissa River Camp** (☎ 7779487; marakissa@planet.nl; r per person incl breakfast D425; ☒) not only has welcoming accommodation in thatched huts near the river but also arranges trips (D150).

Marakissa and Darsilami are reached by bush taxi from Brikama (D10), for Sifoe hire a taxi in either Brikama or Gunjur (around D500).

NORTH COAST & NORTH BANK

Gambia's north coast stretches all of 10km from Barra at the mouth of the Gambia River to the border with Senegal. Since the colonial **Fort Bullen** closed its doors to the public there's little of interest here, but it's a major jumping-off point for trips to Farafenni, Jufureh and Ginak Island.

Ginak Island (Niumi National Park)

Niumi National Park spreads across a small corner of northwestern Gambia, including the long, narrow island of Ginak (also spelled Jinack), where the range of habitats (beach, mud flats, salt marshes, dunes, mangrove swamps, lagoons and woodland) makes for excellent bird-watching. Dolphins are occasionally spotted from the shore. In theory, the park protects small populations of manatees, crocodiles, bushbucks and duikers, plus various monkey species, but chances of spotting them are rather slim.

Despite being a conservation area, large parts of the park have been eroded. The best way to avoid these areas and head straight for the pretty bits is through guidance by Foday, the friendly manager of **Madiyana Safari Lodge** (☎ 9920201; www.paradiseisland-gambia.com; per person incl breakfast D800). This cute camp sits in a pretty spot on the western seafront and has accommodation in thatched huts, with kerosene-lamp lighting and open-air bucket showers – stargazing free of charge. The food here is excellent, and the cook loves indulging in preparing vegetarian meals on request.

The area is tricky to reach on public transport – contact Foday before setting out and arrange pick-up (D500). If you can't get him on the phone, ask at Calypso restaurant in

Bakau (see p304). Another good way to come is by arranging a boat tour with Hidden Gambia (p322).

Jufureh & Albreda

Jufureh became world famous in the 1970s following the publication of the book *Roots*, which describes the capture of Kunta Kinte – thought by author Alex Haley to be his ancestor – and transportation to America as a slave some 200 years ago.

His story has turned the tiny community into a popular tourist destination, though there's actually very little to see except the overblown village action that ensues as soon as the tourist boats arrive. Women pound millet at strategic points, babies are produced to be admired and filmed, and one of Haley's supposed descendants, the sister of the deceased Binde Kinte, makes a guest appearance at her compound. Note that there's a visitor's charge of D50 that's supposed to go to village-development projects.

Five hundred metres from Jufureh, Albreda is a little more peaceful. The main thing to see here is the ruined 'factory' (fortified slaving station) originally built by French traders in the late 17th century, and the **slavery museum** (☎ 4710276, 7710276; admission D50; ⏲ 10am-5pm Mon-Sat), which has a simple but striking exhibition tracing the history of slavery on the Gambia River.

The best place to stay is the **Kunta Kinte Roots Camp** (☎ 9905322; baboucarrlo@hotmail.com; s/d D500/1000) in Albreda – an ambitiously sized hotel with decent accommodation in colourfully decorated bungalows. If you phone before arriving, it can also organise excellent meals.

GETTING THERE & AWAY

The usual way to visit Jufureh and Albreda is by organised river tour (p322). All the tour operators along the Atlantic coast and several hotels have the 'Roots' Tour' in their catalogue.

Alternatively, take the ferry across to Barra, then find a shared taxi to Jufureh (around D25). There aren't many per day, so you need to set off early, or hire a taxi (around D1000 including a couple of hours' waiting time).

James Island

About 2km off the shore from Jufureh and Albreda, Unesco World Heritage–listed James Island is one of Gambia's most significant historical sights. It houses the remains of Fort James (1650s), an important colonial trading post since 1661, from where many slave boats left for the Americas.

Today the fort is largely in ruins, the only intact room being a food store. The biggest threat to its structures is natural erosion, which literally pulls away the grounds the ruins stand on. A financial injection from the Netherlands is supposed to go towards restoration, the opening of a visitors centre and a trail as well as an evaluation of the erosion.

Most people take in James Island as part of a Banjul–Jufureh Roots Tour, but you can also arrange a pirogue to take you over from Albreda (D500 per pirogue). Island admission including a visit to the museum of Jufureh costs D100.

CENTRAL & EASTERN GAMBIA

As Gambia is such a tiny sliver of land, nothing is really remote, but difficult transport connections on the north bank and an almost artistic chain of potholes along the southern route make the trip to the east an exciting, and occasionally frustrating, adventure. You can beat the roads and their many challenges by weaving boat journeys into your upcountry itinerary. Apart from being relaxing, it's also the way to see how the landscape subtly changes, from thick mangroves and creeks in the west to lush gallery forest with small islets further north. Bird calls and the barks of baboons accompany your journey, and, with a bit of luck, you'll get dolphins and hippos before your binoculars.

BINTANG BOLONG

Tucked away among the maze of shrubs lining the shores of the Bintang River is the spectacular **Bintang Bolong Lodge** (☎ 9929362; reception@ bintang-bolong.com; Foni Bintang Karanai; r per person D400), an intimate, ecofriendly camp made almost entirely from local mangrove woods and clay bricks. Stunning huts sit on stilts right on the river – you can leap from your balcony into a pirogue for a boat tour (per hour D800).

Gelli-gellis leave daily from Brikama (D30, one hour). If you can't face the wait for the bus to fill up, you can hire a private taxi (around

D2000). The driver needs to follow the main road east through the village of Somita, and at Killy turn left (north) along the dirt road to reach Bintang village and the lodge. Or just phone the place and arrange to be picked up (D750 to D2000, depending on where you come from).

TENDABA

Tendaba is a small village on the southern bank of the Gambia River, 165km upstream from Banjul. Thanks to the enduring **Tendaba Camp** (☎ 6401130, 9766588; tendaba@qanet.gm; bungalows per person D280, VIP r D1000), it's a fixed point on every tour itinerary upriver. Accommodation is slightly scruffy, though the restaurant is good (try the bush pig, a Tendaba staple)

The camp's attraction lies mainly in its position – opposite the Baobolong wetlands and in close proximity to Kiang West National Park – in short, it's a bird-watcher's dream destination. The camp arranges reasonably priced tours to both, as well as walks around the village and the nearby airfield.

Most hotels and tour operators arrange trips here at a cost – do some shopping around, as prices vary. To get here by boat, contact Hidden Gambia or Gambia River Excursions (see p322). Independent travellers on public transport can take a *sept-place* from Brikama or Serekunda to Soma. Get off at Kwinella; the camp (signposted) is 5km north along the dirt road. Camp manager Saja Touray can collect you from Kwinella. Otherwise it's a walk or trip by donkey cart.

BAOBOLONG WETLAND RESERVE & KIANG WEST NATIONAL PARK

Easily explored on a boat trip from Tendaba Camp, the **Baobolong Wetland Reserve** is a vast area of *bolongs* (creeks), lined by thick mangroves that seem to float on the waters. Fluttering egrets and herons (including white-backed night herons) accompany your leisurely river cruise, and you might spot rarer species, such as Pel's fishing owls and mouse-brown sunbirds. Clawless otters flit out of the undergrowth and glide into the waters, and the salt marshes and Guinea savannah behind the mangrove curtain are home to marshbucks.

Combine a trip here with a boat tour to Toubab Kollon point in **Kiang West National Park** (admission D35), where a hide often grants glimpses of bushbucks, warthogs and, if you're lucky, sitatunga antelopes. West from here,

an escarpment follows the river, making for a nice change from the otherwise flat lands. Intrepid bird-watchers come to Kiang West to see ground hornbills, ospreys, fish eagles, martial eagles and rare brown-necked parrots. Lacking infrastructure and facilities, it's not easily explored, though, as you'll notice if you attempt to visit the park on a 4WD tour from Tendaba.

SOMA

Junction town Soma has all the charm of a truck stop. This is where Dakar traffic passes through to get to Casamance, and Gambia's east–west vehicles put in a stop: a town to fill up the tank and the tummy and carry on with your journey.

To catch the ferry north to Farafenni, from where you can continue to Dakar or take the north-bank road westwards, you carry on northwards along the Trans-Gambia Hwy that passes through town, all the way to Yelitenda.

If you get stuck, the classic place to stay is the perfectly adequate **Moses Guesthouse** (☎ 4531462; r per person D125). Cleaner, and better company, is the welcoming Scout centre **Kaira Konko** (☎ 5531453; www.kairakonko.com; dm D150, r with/without bathroom D400/250), slightly out of town.

Getting There & Away

Sept-place taxis and *gelli-gellis* from the coast stop at the garage in the town centre, where you can change for a taxi to Janjangbureh or Basse. If you're heading north, take a local bush taxi to the Gambia River ferry at Yelitenda (D8), go across as a foot passenger (D10), and take one of the vehicles waiting on the northern bank at Bambatenda to Farafenni (D8), where you can find transport to Kaolack or Dakar.

FARAFENNI

Soma's north-bank sister feels a little more like an actual town than just a place to speed through, especially on Sunday, when the *lumo* (weekly market) doubles the dust and noise as traders drift in from as far as Dakar to sell their goods. There's no bank here; the nearest ATM is a longish drive to Senegal (make sure you have all the visas you might need to cross the border).

If you need to fill a day here, try a visit to **Kataba Fort**, 10km along the eastbound dirt road. Though reduced to its dusty foundations, this 1841 Wolof construction tells a half-forgotten story of old African kingdoms.

To spend the night, head for **Eddy's Hotel & Bar** (☎ 7621197; d from D400; [✖]), a welcoming place with a leafy courtyard that enjoys enduring popularity. It's also the best place to eat in town, though the lady on the Kuntaur side of the main crossroads rivals his kitchen with her excellent chicken sandwiches.

Getting There & Away

There are occasional direct *gelli-gellis* from here to Serekunda (D90) via the ferry, though you usually have to go to Soma and change. *Gelli-gellis* along the north-bank road to Kerewan (D60) are frequent, sometimes all the way to Barra. Most Dakar-bound transport goes from the Senegalese border. To get here, take a *gelli-gelli* from town (D6).

JANJANGBUREH (GEORGETOWN)

Founded by the British in 1823, Janjangbureh used to be a busy administrative centre and trading hub in the colonial era. Today, it moves to a sluggish rhythm and falls asleep as soon as nightfall drowns most of the town in darkness. Birdsong being the local music here, the town is one of Gambia's pilgrimage sites for ornithologists. Its brilliant midriver location makes Janjangbureh a great base for boat trips around the eastern region – feast your eyes on the abundant greenery that frames the river.

The traditional, and now officially reintroduced, name for the town and island is Janjangbureh, but most people still call it Georgetown. The island is 10km long and 2.5km wide, covered with fields of rice and groundnuts. It has ferry links to both riverbanks, but there is little in terms of infrastructure – no banks and no hospital, though internet access is available at **Gamspad** (☎ 5676159; per hr D25; [⏱] 9am-6pm).

Sights

On the waterfront, either side of the northern ferry landing, are the remains of two colonial warehouses, which local youth will try to 'sell' you as 'Slave Prison', also talking up a 'Freedom Tree' and 'Slave Market'. This is fictionalised history – though slaves were transported through Georgetown, these buildings were constructed much later. Nearby is the old **Commissioner's Quarters**, now inhabited by the district governor, and a **monument** outside the police station that recalls the 1823 building

of Fort George by the British. Further along the street, the **Methodist Church & School** (Owen St) tells of the 1824 introduction of Christianity to the region, and west of town you find the colonial **Armitage High School**. Janjangbureh's oldest building is its humblest; opposite the market, a small, weatherbeaten **wooden house** (Owen St) is one of the rare surviving examples of the typical housing built by freed slaves who settled here some 200 years ago.

Janjangbureh is a great base for exploring the east, including trips to **Gambia River National Park**, the historical stone circles of **Wassu** and **Kerr Batch**, and a visit to **Karantaba Tenda**, 20km from town, where an obelisk marks the spot where Scottish explorer Mungo Park started his journey to trace the course of the Niger River. Book an excursion with your *campement*.

Sleeping

Janjang Bureh Camp (☎ 9816944; www.gambia-river .com; s/d D300/500) Here colourful, quirky bungalows lie on a vast terrain between forest and water. It's slightly dusty, but fun, and a good base for river trips with Gambia River Excursions.

Baobolong Camp (☎ 5676133; fax 5676120; Owen St; s/ d D350/700) At the eastern end of town, across the river from Janjang Bureh Camp, Baobolong has a lovely riverine garden setting, though rooms aren't exactly spotless and plenty of young, male 'guides' haunt the place.

Bird Safari Camp (☎ 7336570, skype ☎ 01202884100; www.bsc.gm; per person ind breakfast D900; [▢] [▣]) Some 2.5km west, between forest and river, Bird is the remotest of the lot – not a problem if you come with a Hidden Gambia boat excursion, and fantastic if you're here for bird-watching.

Eating & Drinking

Few options exist outside the camps and lodges.

Talamanca Lodge (☎ 9921100; talamancalodge@ yahoo.com; Findlay St) Near the warehouses, Talamanca does great, local meals and even rents a couple of simple rooms.

Bendula Restaurant (Owen St) For reggae vibes and cold beers, the courtyard here is a good place to be.

Getting There & Away

Janjangbureh is only reached by ferry. Most bush taxis turn off the main road between

Soma and Basse Santa Su to drop off passengers at the southern ferry ramp – you should request this when entering the taxi. The ferry costs D5 for passengers and D75 for cars. For transport to Basse, you cross to the south, where you find bush taxis to Bansang, the place to change for Basse-bound cars.

GAMBIA RIVER NATIONAL PARK

South of Kuntaur, five islands in the Gambia River are protected as a national park. The heart of the park is the confusingly named Baboon Island, home to the **Chimpanzee Rehabilitation Trust** (CRA; www.chimprehab.com). Created by the late Stella Brewer OBE, it has successfully rehabilitated once-captured chimpanzees into the wild since 1976, when Stella first moved here with a truck full of chimps. The only (and most pleasant) way to get more than just a chance glimpse of the amazing creatures is by spending a night or more at the stunning **Badi Mayo Camp** (☎ 9947430; badimayo@ yahoo.com; per person D4000), where you get to stay in luxurious safari tents built on raised platforms. Red colobus and green vervet monkeys leap between the tall trees onsite, and you'll hear the chimps' calls from the islands across. The room rate includes all meals, pick-up and a tour around the islands with the chimp-feeding boat. Note that accommodation here is very limited – you can't just turn up.

In Sambel Kunda village, a relaxed horse-cart ride through bush grass and trees from Badi Mayo, you can visit the **Gambia Horse & Donkey Trust** (www.gambiahorseanddonkey.org.uk), where villagers are taught how to care better for their precious animals. On the way here, put in a stop at Chasin verandah, from where you get a fantastic view across the river, its islands and surrounding areas. Keep an eye out for the clawless otters, bush babies, hyenas, antelopes and of course the multitude of bird species that inhabit this area.

Getting There & Away

The best thing is to book a taxi from the coast (around D4000) when reserving your Badi Mayo tent. Otherwise you can make your way to Kuntaur, where Badi Mayo staff will pick you up by boat (free). If a stay at Badi Mayo explodes your budget, go to Kuntaur and contact **Faldeh** (☎ 9707770). He can take you on a tour around the park's navigable channel. And though that's not the same as staying at the camp with full chimp access, you might

still catch a chance glimpse of one, as well as see birds, hippos and the lovely scenery. Gambia's river-tour operators can all organise trips here. Hidden Gambia routes usually contain a stay here (see p322).

BASSE SANTA SU

Set on a beautiful waterfront, this easternmost town is the last major ferry-crossing point on the Gambia River and a transport hub for the surrounding area. It's a traditional trading centre, and as crammed and busy, rundown and forever deal-making as any West African junction town, and entirely defined by a market that claims every bit of ground.

Neither **Trust Bank** (☎ 5668907) nor **Standard Chartered Bank** (☎ 4668218) has an ATM, though they do change money. For phone calls, try the **Gamtel office** (☎ 4229999) opposite the post office. If you haven't found all the necessary immigration officials at the border, you can get your entry stamp from the immigration office in town.

Apart from a market stroll, a day here should include a stop at Traditions (see below), an imposing colonial warehouse on the riverside. It overlooks the ferry point (a lovely river spot) and is often visited by rare Egyptian plovers between June and February.

Sleeping

Traditions (☎ 5668760, 7335562; r D250) The best place to stay in town; here dedicated manager Sulayman Jallow has split some of the massive warehouse spaces into simple rooms with good mattresses and functional fans. Electricity is provided by a generator from 7pm to 7am. Phone before arrival, especially if you wish to arrange (invariably simple) meals.

Fulladu Camp (☎ 9906791; r per person D350) Across the river, Fulladu has bungalows on vast, leafy terrain.

Eating & Drinking

For food outside your lodging, try the chop shops around the taxi park, or the reggae-coloured **United Restaurant** (ferry terminal) that blasts *mbalax* from rickety speakers and serves Gambian food during lunch and dinner hours. Mike's Bar Peace & Love advertises 1L of gin for only D100, and the bizarre wall paintings inside somewhat betray the altered state of their creator.

Fija Jala Nightclub (☎ 9937121) The inviting sign outside proclaims this place 'the only

THE GAMBIA

and best nightclub in town' – that'll be where Basse's parties happen.

Getting There & Away

Gelli-gellis go to the ferry ramp for Georgetown (D60, one hour), Soma (D100, four hours) and Serekunda (D250, eight hours).

The ferry to the Gambia River's northern bank takes one car at a time, and the journey is quick (passenger/car D5/75). Small metal tubs can push you across for D50.

Very rusty *sept-place* taxis go to Vélingara (Senegal; D30, one hour), from where you'll be able to catch transport to Tambacounda (Senegal). The border crossing is usually smooth; just make sure you get all the correct stamps (sometimes – if the border guards are on their lunch break, for instance – this involves visiting the immigration post in Basse).

GAMBIA DIRECTORY

ACCOMMODATION

In the Atlantic coast resorts, there's plenty of choice in places to stay, from basic guesthouses and self-catering apartments to palatial hotels. Upcountry, your options are more limited, mainly to camps with accommodation in bungalows and roundhuts. Many places advertise themselves as ecolodges, but only some really are – we've indicated the best ones in the GreenDex (p910).

In this chapter budget accommodation is under US$30, top end is over US$75 and midrange is somewhere between the two.

ACTIVITIES

Tourists tend to come to Gambia either for the beaches – enjoying swimming in the sea or pools and watersports (no surfing, though) – or the bird-watching. Even in the tourist centres, there are many bird-watching opportunities close by. Pirogue and boat trips are another favourite and can be arranged in most places around the country (try an upriver tour; they're great). On boat or walking tours around some of the national parks, you'll get to see small wildlife as well as plenty of birds, and some places combine pirogue and fishing trips.

The increasing amount of sustainable tourism means there are many good village visits and community projects around.

> **PRACTICALITIES**
>
> ■ The electricity supply in The Gambia is 220V. Most plugs have three square pins, as used in Britain, though two round pins, as in continental Europe, are also in use.
>
> ■ *Africa Today* (Afro Media) has good political and economic news, plus business, sport and tourism. *Focus on Africa* (BBC) has excellent news stories, accessible reports and a concise rundown of recent political events. The local newspaper the *Point* (winner of the 2006 International Press Freedom Award) is famous for its critical view on Gambian politics and society.
>
> ■ The Gambia uses the metric system.

BOOKS

The most famous work relating to The Gambia is probably *Roots* (1976) by Alex Haley. A mix of historical fact and imaginative fiction, the hugely influential book describes the African-American author's search for his African origins.

For historical insights into the region, try Mungo Park's 19th-century classic *Travels in the Interior of Africa*, or the fictionalised version by TC Boyle (*Water Music*, 1882). Mark Hudson's *Our Grandmother's Drum* is an entertaining fiction with moving insights into Gambia's music scene.

BUSINESS HOURS

Government offices open 8am to 3pm or 4pm Monday to Thursday, and 8am to 12.30pm Friday.

Banks open 8am to 4pm Monday to Thursday, 8am to 1pm and 2.30pm to 4pm Friday, and 9am to 1pm Saturday.

Shops often close for lunch, opening 8.30am to 12.30pm or 1pm and 2.30pm to 5.30pm Monday to Thursday, and 8am to 12.30pm on Friday and Saturday.

Restaurants may be open all day but usually only serve lunch from 11am to 3pm and dinner from 6pm to 11pm. Most restaurants in the cities stay open until the last guest leaves, though in smaller towns and villages many close around 10pm, or whenever the food runs out.

Bars usually open around 8pm, tend to get going from 11pm onwards, and close around 3am or 4am.

CHILDREN

Children are generally welcome, though there's little in the way of child-centred activities. Most hotels offer the facility of adding an extra bed to a room. Children under two stay free of charge, and there's usually a 50% discount for those under 12.

Child-minding facilities are only available in a few hotels; top-end establishments and small, midrange guesthouses tend to be most accommodating. There's little in the way of professional babysitting agencies. Nappies and baby food are found in the big supermarkets, but upcountry you might encounter problems.

DANGERS & ANNOYANCES

Gambia is a fairly safe place to visit. Pickpocketing is a problem in busy areas (taxi points, markets and ferries), and muggings do occur occasionally.

Perhaps most annoying are the 'bumsters' near the coast, who try to make a living from hustling tourists, and are linked to sex tourism (see p299). Firm but polite refusal of their offers should keep them away.

Gambia's police checkpoints are notoriously irritating. Stay polite and friendly when faced with such behaviour – anger will only get you tied up in red tape. Women should be careful at beaches and on the road after dark – some readers have reported mild to serious hassles.

EMBASSIES & CONSULATES

Germany (p296; ☎ 4227783; 29 Independence Dr, Banjul; ✆ 8am-1pm, closed Tue)

Guinea (Map p296; ☎ 4226862, 909964; top fl, 78A Daniel Goddard St, Banjul; ✆ 9am-4pm Mon-Thu, to 1.30pm & 2.30-4pm Fri)

Guinea-Bissau (Map pp300-1; ☎ 4226862; Atlantic Rd, Bakau; ✆ 9am-2pm Mon-Fri, to 1pm Sat)

Mali (Map p296; VM Company Ltd, Cherno Adama Bah St, Banjul)

Mauritania (Map pp300-1; ☎ 4491153; Badala Park Way, Kololi; ✆ 8am-4pm Mon-Fri)

Senegal (Map pp300-1; ☎ 4373752; ✆ 8am-2pm & 2.30-5pm Mon-Thu, to 4pm Fri) Off Kairaba Ave.

Sierra Leone (Map p296; ☎ 4228206; 67 Daniel Goddard St, Banjul; ✆ 8.30am-4.30pm Mon-Thu, to 1.30pm Fri)

UK (Map pp300-1; ☎ 4495133/4; fax 4496134; http://uk ingambia.fco.gov.uk; 48 Atlantic Rd, Fajara; ✆ 8am-1pm Mon-Thu, to 12.30pm Fri)

USA (Map pp300-1; ☎ 4392856; http://banjul.usem bassy.gov; 92 Kairaba Ave, Fajara; ✆ 8.30am-12.30pm)

Several European countries have honorary consuls in Gambia, including Belgium (at the Kairaba Hotel, Kololi), Denmark, Sweden and Norway (above Tina's Grill, Saitmatty Rd, Bakau).

FESTIVALS & EVENTS

Two of Gambia's most interesting festivals:
International Roots Festival (☎ 4226244; www .rootsgambia.gm) Gambian and international music (and much more). Next on in 2010 and 2012.
Kartong Festival (☎ 9933193; www.kartongfestival .org) April or May. Village festival in southern Gambia; traditional dance troupes and contemporary music.

GAY & LESBIAN TRAVELLERS

Homosexuality is illegal in Gambia and can be punished with up to 14 years' prison. For many people, gay or lesbian relationships are also a cultural taboo. Needless to say, a scene exists, particularly at the coast, but you have to be very discreet.

HOLIDAYS

Apart from the state holidays below, Muslim holidays, such as Korité, Tabaski, Tamkharit and Moulid, are celebrated. Determined by the lunar calendar, they occur on different dates each year. See p816 for more information.

Holidays:
New Year's Day 1 January
Independence Day 18 February
Good Friday March/April
Easter Monday March/April
Workers' Day 1 May
Anniversary of the Second Republic 22 July
Christmas 25 December

INTERNET ACCESS

There are a few internet cafes in Banjul and around the Atlantic coast, and most upcountry towns have at least one sluggish cybercafe. Quantumnet is a main operator. Wi-fi is becoming more common, especially at the coast.

INTERNET RESOURCES

Access Gambia (www.accessgambia.com) Staggering amount of information on travel, hotels, restaurants and more.
Asset (www.asset-gambia.com) The home page of the Gambian Association of Small Scale Enterprises in Tourism lists plenty of interesting, one-man businesses.
One Gambia (www.onegambia.com) The portal for Gambian music.
Wow (www.wow.gm) Gambian news and entertainment portal with plenty of good stories and news items.

MONEY

The Gambia's unit of currency is the dalasi, which is divided into 100 bututs. Notes in circulation are D5, D10, D25, D50 and D100. There are great fluctuations in value. Check before setting out – exchange rates might have impacted on prices listed here.

ATMs

At the coast, the main banks (Trust, Standard Chartered, PHB) have ATMs. Upcountry, not only are ATMs rare but also you'll hardly find banks. ATMs can be unreliable (don't leave things too late), and withdrawal limits can be tight.

Black Market

If you travel in from Senegal, you'll be crowded by street changers as soon as you stop at the border. The police clamps down on black-market trading, though. To change out of office hours, you can ask your hotel reception. If you're staying in a budget to midrange place, the hotel can often call a street trader they know, rather than changing currency themselves at high commissions.

Cash

In Senegal and Gambia, major international currencies such as euros, US dollars and British pounds can be changed in banks and hotels in the capital cities, major towns and tourist areas. Upcountry, changing might be difficult and rates get worse.

Credit Cards

The use of credit cards is limited to mid-range and top-end hotels and restaurants, car rental, air tickets and some tours, but there's a real risk of fraud. Amex and Visa are the most widely accepted.

Moneychangers

All the major banks change money, as do exchange bureaus, which are found in the tourist zones. It's worth shopping around.

Tipping

Tipping is usually expected in upmarket places. At restaurants (discounting small eateries), you're expected to tip around 10%. You don't have to tip taxi drivers, but you do tip most people whom you've asked for a service.

Travellers Cheques

American Express travellers cheques can usually be changed at the banks near the coast, but not upcountry. Cheques in pounds sterling and euros are easier to change than cheques in dollars.

POST

The postal service is quite reliable, but it's slow. Letters from Banjul and the Atlantic resorts usually arrive in Europe within a couple of weeks; North America and Australasia take longer.

TELEPHONE & FAX

The easiest thing for calling is coming with an open mobile phone, and purchasing an Africell or Gamcel SIM. There are public telecentres (mainly Gamtel), but they're getting rarer, as mobile phone use increases.

There are no area codes. Calls are charged by the unit, and add up fast on a call abroad. National calls are cheap, but to call abroad, you'll pay around D50 per minute.

For directory assistance dial ☎ 151.

Mobile Phones

Gamcel or Africell SIM cards are D200 to D300. Local calls are a couple of dalasi, international calls over D20. Reductions apply after 9pm. Top-up cards are available everywhere from street vendors.

TIME

Gambia is at GMT/UTC. The country has no daylight savings. When it's noon in Gambia, it's 7am in New York, noon in London, 1pm in Paris and 10pm in Sydney.

TOURIST INFORMATION

The national **Gambia Tourism Authority** (☎ 4462491; www.visitthegambia.gm) has an informative website but no public-access offices.

For responsible choices:

Association of Small Scale Enterprises in Tourism (Asset; ☎ 4497675; www.asset-gambia.com; Fajara) At the Timbooktoo bookshop in Fajara, this great, informative office gives information on community enterprises.

Kartong Association for Responsible Tourism (Kart; ☎ 4495887; www.kartung.org; Kartong) Tries to boost ecotourism in Kartong.

VISAS

Visas are not needed by nationals of Commonwealth countries, Germany, Italy,

Luxembourg, the Netherlands, Ecowas and Scandinavian countries for stays of up to 90 days. For those needing one, visas are normally valid for one month and cost around US$45; you'll need to provide two photos.

Visa Extensions
Visa extensions are usually dealt with swiftly at the **immigration office** (Map p296; ☎ 4228611; OAU Blvd, Banjul; ⏱ 8am-4pm). They cost D250.

Visas for Onward Travel
For onward travel, get your visa from the relevant embassy. Most deal with requests within 48 hours. You cannot buy visas on the borders to Senegal.

WOMEN TRAVELLERS
While it's not exactly dangerous to travel on your own as a woman in The Gambia, unwarranted interest is a pretty steady travel companion. Guys won't hesitate to approach you and see how far they can go. It's up to you to set the boundaries. It's always better to refer to your boyfriend as your husband in order to see your relationship respected.

Beaches are prime hassle zones and are the areas where female readers report the most irritating advances.

Dress can help to a certain extent. Especially in rural areas, more modest, long clothing is recommended – you are travelling in a Muslim country. In the urban areas, tight jeans and tops are acceptable, and nightclubs get very sexy.

TRANSPORT IN THE GAMBIA

GETTING THERE & AWAY
Entering The Gambia
A full passport is essential for entering The Gambia. If you cross by land from Senegal, you might experience difficult officials, sometimes asking you for random stamps or papers. Stay polite, and make sure that your papers are in complete order – meaning: you've got a passport with a valid visa (if you need one) and your vaccination certificate.

Air
The Gambia's main airport is **Banjul International Airport** (BJL; ☎ 4473117; www.gambia .gm/gcaa) at Yundum, about 15km from the Atlantic coast resorts.

Most travellers arriving from Europe arrive on the competitively priced charter flights of **Gambia Experience** (☎ in UK 0845 330 2060; www.gambia.co.uk).

Air Sénégal International (airline code V7; ☎ in Banjul 4202117; www.air-senegal-international.com) Hub Airport International Léopold Sédar Senghor, Dakar, Senegal.

Brussels Airlines (airline code SN; ☎ in Kololi 4466880; www.brusselsairlines.com) Hub Brussels Airport, Brussels, Belgium.

Land
If you travel by land, you'll invariably enter from Senegal. There are frequent connections between Dakar and Banjul. Most pass through the border crossing at Karang. You need to change vehicles twice – first into a minibus to cross the 'no man's land' between the Senegalese and Gambian border posts, then into a taxi of the nation you're entering. To get to Banjul, you'll have to take the ferry in Barra. If you're coming from Dakar and think you might miss the last ferry across to Banjul (it leaves at 9pm), you're better off staying in Toubacouta and getting the ferry from Barra to Banjul the next morning – there's no good accommodation in Barra.

A second option takes you eastwards from Banjul to Soma, where you cross the Gambia River to Farafenni, then travel along the Trans-Gambia Hwy to Kaolack and Dakar. It's a brave journey along a terrible road – adventure stuff, with risks.

There are a few border crossings between Gambia and the Casamance in Senegal. To get to Ziguinchor, you take a taxi from Brikama or Serekunda to the Senegalese border post at Séléti, where a bush taxi to Ziguinchor is CFA2500.

If you're heading for Kafountine, you could get yourself to Diouloulou via Giboro, then change for Kafountine. If you travel via the tiny border post Darsilami, make sure you get your border stamp on the Senegalese side as soon as possible (ask your hotel); the border itself isn't manned.

For the pirogue crossing from Kartong to Niafourang (via the Allahein River), see p311)

From Basse Santa Su bush taxis make the 27km trip to Vélingara (D30, one hour).

GETTING AROUND
Boat
There's no regular transport upriver, though the following tour operators run excellent river excursions.

Gambia River Excursions (☎ 4494360; www.gambia -river.com; Fajara) Does trips from Denton Bridge or Banjul, and upriver from Janjang Bureh Camp in Janjangbureh. Most trips are done by motorised pirogues of various sizes. Tours range from simple bird-and-breakfast excursions to tailor-made trips of several days.

Hidden Gambia (☎ in the UK 01527 576239, in Gambia ☎ 6467381; www.hiddengambia.com) Has an excellent set of excursions, including trips from Bintang to (and around) the Baobolong wetlands, Janjangbureh and the Gambia River National Park. Tours are done on a combination of fibreglass boats and wooden, motorised pirogues and can be tailor made.

Bus
When we visited, the once-deceased national bus service had just been revived via several express buses that ply Gambia's major routes. The green vehicles (still shiny at the time of research) connect the major coastal centres of Serekunda, Bakau, Sukuta, Banjul and Brufut from 7am to 7pm daily (D5). A good place to get them is Brufut Turntable or Tippa Garage in Serekunda. You need a lot of time if you intend to use them, especially for longer journeys, such as to Kerewan, Janjangbureh and Basse from Barra.

Bush Taxi
Gambia has borrowed the French term *sept-place* taxis to refer to the seven-seater Peugeots that link all major towns in the country. *Gelli-gellis* are minibuses, a bit cheaper but endlessly more tedious than *sept-places*.

They ply the south-bank road, despite its dismal state (see right), going from Serekunda's Tippa Garage to Brikama and Soma, where you'll normally have to change.

For a north-bank trip, they leave from Barra going to Kerewan, Farafenni and Janjangbureh before heading south for the trip from Janjangbureh to Basse.

Taxi prices are fixed and you'll usually be quoted the correct price, plus a fee for your luggage (usually between D25 and D50). Taxis move only when they're full and fill up quickest early in the morning (around 7am).

On the Atlantic coast, yellow taxis and green tourist taxis ply the roads. The latter are more expensive. See p308 for more information.

Car & Motorcycle
It's possible to hire a car or motorbike in Gambia's resort areas, but it's often advisable to hire a taxi with a driver, as driving on Gambia's dilapidated roads shouldn't be taken lightly.

Despite the British heritage, traffic in Gambia drives on the right.

Tours
See left for agencies organising boat tours.

Discovery Tours (Map pp300-1; ☎ 4495551; farma@ discoverytours.gm; 10 Atlantic Rd, Fajara) Has a good selection of country tours and multilingual staff.

Gambia Experience (Map pp300-1; ☎ 4461104; www .gambia.co.uk; Senegambia Beach Hotel, Kololi) Gambia's biggest tour operator. Does everything from charter flights and all-inclusive holidays to in-country tours. Good Senegal-Gambia tours can be organised through its Senegal Experience branch.

Gambia Tours (☎ 4462601/2; info@gambiatours.gm; www.gambiatours.gm) Southwest of Kololi, this efficient, family-run enterprise also deals with car rental, airport transfers and so on. Multilingual staff.

Tilly's Tours (Map pp300-1; ☎ 9800215; www.tillys tours.com; off Senegambia Strip, Kololi) Small company with responsible tourism products, working especially with local, small-scale providers. Profits go partly to UK-based charities working in The Gambia. You can even spend your gap year with them.

Ghana

Hailed as West Africa's golden child, Ghana deserves its place in the sun. Its beaches are buttered with thick white sand and its savannahs are blessed with the footprints of elephants – no wonder travellers can't get enough.

Often labelled Africa's greatest success story, Ghana's green-gold-and-red has been flying high since 1957. The country has long stood proud, a beacon of hope on a rocky West African coastline. The wind of change that once swept through Ghana is now a soft, salty breeze; it cools the air and kisses a coastline still haunted by the legacy of the slave trade.

Accra, Ghana's dancefloor, is where the music comes alive. Laced with laughter, hip-life permeates cocktail bars, swish clubs and restaurants. Let the hot sun hug you and the beat get under your skin; follow it as it draws you into its relentless rhythm, linking the dry dusty north with the spectacular seascape of the south.

Let it take you to the crashing waterfalls of the east and the world-class waves of the west, past mud-and-stick mosques and crumbling colonial architecture. Don't miss Mole National Park, where sunburnt savannahs host populations of elephants, antelopes and monkeys. At the end of a long, hot day, slip into the night and take a peek at the inky sky: we bet you the stars will be out.

There's a good reason they call Ghana 'Africa for beginners': you'll never want your trip to end.

FAST FACTS

- **Area** 231,000 sq km
- **Capital** Accra
- **Country code** ☎ 233
- **Famous for** Castles and forts, beaches, democracy
- **Languages** English, Twi, Dagbani
- **Money** Cedi (C); US$1 = C1.50; €1 = C2.40
- **Population** 23 million
- **Visa** Arrange in advance, US$80

GHANA

HIGHLIGHTS

- **The Coast** (p348) Dance and drum lessons on the beaches of Kokrobite and Anomabu; surf and sea turtles at Busua, Akwidaa Beach and Axim.
- **Ghosts of the slave trade** The forts of Cape Coast (p352) and Elmina (p357) are filled with the history of slavery.
- **Mole National Park** (p380) The world's most inexpensive safari.
- **The East** (p365) Hiking, boat trips and waterfall climbs in former German Togoland.
- **Wa** (p364) Hippos and Islamic architecture in a seldom-visited corner of Ghana.

ITINERARIES

- **Two Weeks** Two weeks is just about long enough to lock eyes with an elephant at Mole and pay a visit to the Ashanti villages around Kumasi, ending your trip on the beaches close to Accra. Begin in Accra (p335; two days), then fly up north (you could travel by road but it will rob you of a night) to Tamale (p377; two nights), then on to Mole (p380; two nights) and Larabanga (p381; one night) before heading down south to Kumasi (p369; two nights) and back to Accra (p335; one night). Then head out to Anomabu (p351; two nights) or Kokrobite (p348), before returning to the capital to catch your flight home.
- If you can bear to miss Mole, an alternative is to head to Kumasi (p369; two nights) first, then Cape Coast (p352; three nights) to explore Kakum and the surrounding area. You could then move further west to Busua (p360; two nights) and Akwidaa Beach (p362; three nights) before returning to Accra.
- **One Month** With a month, you can do all of the above plus throw in visits to the east and, if bus routes are on your side, to Wa (p382). If possible fly from Accra (p335) to Tamale (p377; one night) – if not take your time bussing it to Kumasi (p369) and then further north – and on to Mole National Park (p380) and Larabanga (p381). Continue west to Wa (p382) and the hippo sanctuary at Wechiau (p383), if time permits, and return to Kumasi. From there you can head south to Accra

and go on to visit the east: Akosombo (p365), on to Ho (p366) and Hohoe (p367) and back to Accra. Alternatively, head directly to the coastal resorts of your choice from Kumasi.

CLIMATE & WHEN TO GO

Ghana has a tropical equatorial climate, which means that it's hot year-round with seasonal rains. In the humid southern coastal region, the rainy seasons are from April to June, and during September and October; the dry months, November to March or July and August, are easier for travelling.

Throughout the year, maximum temperatures are around 30°C, dropping three or four degrees during the brief respite between rainy seasons. The humidity is constantly high, at about 80%. In the central region, the rains are heavier and last longer. In the hotter and drier north, there is one rainy season, lasting from April to October. Midday temperatures rarely fall below 30°C, rising to 35°C and higher from December to March when the rasping harmattan wind blows in from the Sahara. At this time, dust particles hang heavily in the air, making it constantly hazy, and temperatures plummet at night. Many Ghanaians come down with colds and coughs at this time of year. See also Climate Charts, p810.

The tourist high season is from June to August, but Ghana draws travellers year-round.

HOW MUCH?

- **Purse made from recycled water sachets** C5
- **Elephant safari** C0.75
- **Short taxi ride through Accra** C2
- **Hip-life album** C6
- **Barbecued bat** C1

LONELY PLANET INDEX

- **1L of petrol** C0.75
- **1.5L of bottled water** C1.50
- **Bottle of Star beer** C2
- **Souvenir football shirt** C8
- **Plate of jollof rice** C2

HISTORY

Present-day Ghana has been inhabited since at least 4000 BC, although little evidence remains of its early societies. Successive waves of migration from the north and east resulted in Ghana's present ethnographic composition. By the 13th century, a number of kingdoms had arisen, influenced by the Sahelian trading empires north of the region, such as that of Ancient Ghana (which incorporated western Mali and present-day Senegal). Fuelled by gold (of which Ghana has substantial deposits), trading networks grew, stimulating the development of Akan kingdoms in the centre and south of present-day Ghana. The most powerful of these was that of the Ashanti, who by the 18th century had conquered most of the other kingdoms and taken control of trade routes to the coast. This brought them into contact, and often conflict, with the coastal Fanti, Ga and Ewe people – and with European traders.

The Portuguese arrived in the late 15th century, initially lured by the trade in gold and ivory. However, with the establishment of plantations in the Americas during the 16th century, slaves rapidly replaced gold as the principal export of the region. The fortunes to be earned in the slave trade attracted the Dutch, British and Danes in the late 16th century. The Akan kingdoms grew rich on the proceeds of delivering human cargoes to collection points in coastal forts built by the Europeans, among whom competition for trading concessions was fierce.

By the time slavery was outlawed in the early 19th century, the British had gained a dominant position on the coast. The Ashanti continued to try to expand their territory and protect their interests and the coastal Ga, Ewe and Fanti peoples came to rely on the British for protection. Conflict between the British and the Ashanti sparked a series of wars that culminated in 1874 with the sacking of Kumasi, the Ashanti capital. However, the Ashanti remained defiant and in 1896 the British launched another attack, and this time occupied Kumasi and exiled the Ashanti leader, Prempeh I, to the Seychelles. The British then established a protectorate over Ashantiland, which was expanded in 1901 to include the northern territories.

Under the British, cocoa became the backbone of the economy and in the 1920s the Gold Coast became the world's leading producer. By WWI, cocoa, gold and timber made the Gold Coast the most prosperous colony in Africa. By independence in 1957 the Gold Coast was also the world's leading producer of manganese. It had the best schools and the best civil service in West Africa, a cadre of enlightened lawyers and a thriving press.

Independence

In the late 1920s a number of political parties dedicated to regaining African independence sprang up. However, these parties were identified with the intelligentsia and failed to recognise the grievances and aspirations of most of the population. In response, Kwame Nkrumah, secretary-general of the country's leading political party, the United Gold Coast Convention, broke away in 1949 to form his own party, the Convention People's Party (CPP). With the slogan 'Self Government Now', it quickly became the voice of the masses.

A year later, exasperated by the slow progress towards self-government, Nkrumah called for a national strike. Seeking to contain the situation, the British responded by imprisoning him. While he was there, the CPP won the general election of 1951 and he was released to become leader of the government. Ghana finally gained its independence in March 1957; it was the first West African country to do so. At independence, Nkrumah cast aside the name Gold Coast in favour of that of the first great empire in West Africa, Ghana, famed for wealth and gold.

Much remained to be done to consolidate the new government's control over the country. Factional and regional interests surfaced and there was powerful opposition from some traditional chiefs. Repressive laws were passed in an attempt to contain this opposition, and the CPP became a party that dispensed patronage and encouraged corruption. Meanwhile, Nkrumah skilfully kept himself out of the fray and became one of the most powerful leaders to emerge from the African continent. He was handsome, charismatic and articulate, and his espousal of Pan-Africanism and his denunciations of imperialism and neocolonialism provided inspiration for other nationalist movements in the region.

Nkrumah borrowed heavily to finance grandiose schemes, the most ambitious of which was the Akosombo Dam. This project to dam the Volta River was to be financed by

GHANA

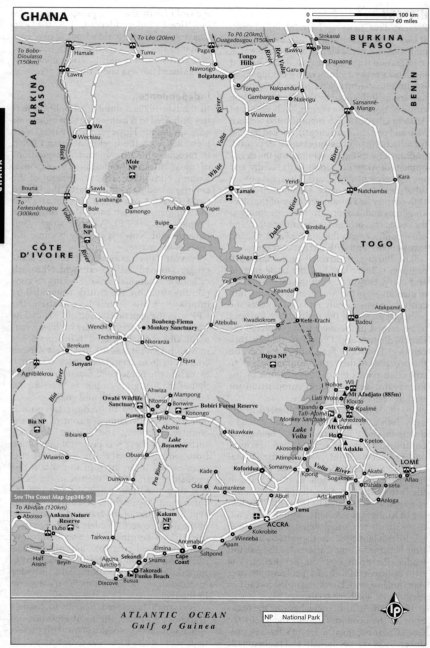

GHANA

GHANA

| 0 | | 100 km |
| 0 | | 60 miles |

To Bobo-
Dioulasso
(150km)

To Léo (20km)

To Pô (20km);
Ouagadougou (150km)

Sinkassé

**BURKINA
FASO**

Hamale

Tumu

Paga

Bawku

Bitou

Lawra

Navrongo

Tongo Hills

Garu

Dapaong

**BURKINA
FASO**

Bolgatanga

Red Volta River

Wa

Tongo

Nakpanduri

Wechiau

Gambarga

Nalerigu

Sansanné-
Mango

Walewale

Mole
NP

Black Volta River

To
Ferkessédougou
(300km)

Bouna

Sawla

Larabanga

White Volta River

Yendi

Kara

Bole

Damongo

Natchamba

Bui
NP

Fufulso

Yapei

Tamale

Oti River

Buipe

Doka River

Bimbilla

**CÔTE
D'IVOIRE**

River

Salaga

TOGO

Kintampo

Makongo

Nkwanta

Yeji

Kpandai

Atakpamé

Wenchi

Boabeng-Fiema
Monkey Sanctuary

Atebubu

Kwadiokrom

Kete-Krachi

Badou

Techiman

Nkoranza

Ferry

Jasikan

Berekum

Ejura

Digya NP

Bia
River

Sunyani

Hohoe

Wli

Agnibilékrou

Ahwiaa

Mampong

Mt Afadjato (885m)

Owabi Wildlife
Sanctuary

Ntonso

Bonwire

Bobiri Forest Reserve

Liati Wote

Klouto

Kpalimé

Bia NP

Kumasi

Ejisu

Konongo

Kpandu
Tafi-Atome
Monkey Sanctuary

Amedzofe

Bibiani

Abonu

Mt Gemi

Lake
Bosumtwe

Nkawkaw

Lake
Volta

Ho

Kpetoe

Wiawso

Obuasi

Akosombo

Mt Adaklu

Pra River

Kade

Atimpoku

Volta River

Akatsi

LOMÉ

Dunkwa

Asamankese

Koforidua

Somanya

Kpong

Sogakope

Denu

Aflao

Oda

Dabala

Keta

See The Coast Map (pp348-9)

Aburi

Ada Kassem

Anloga

To Abidjan (120km)

Aboisso

Ankasa Nature
Reserve

Kakum
NP

Tema

Ada

Elubo

ACCRA

Kokrobite

Tarkwa

Anomabu

Winneba

Apam

Half
Assini

Beyin

Agona
Junction

Sekondi

Shama

Élmina

Saltpond

Axim

Takoradi

Cape
Coast

Dixcove

Busua

Funko Beach

ATLANTIC OCEAN
Gulf of Guinea

NP   National Park

LP

the World Bank, other international banks and Valco, a US aluminium company. However, Nkrumah, abandoned by other backers, was obliged to short-change his country by accepting Valco's offer of the dam in return for all the electricity it needed, virtually at cost (see p365). With a steadily deteriorating economy, the expected private-sector demand never materialised, and the electrification and irrigation programmes were shelved for more than a decade.

In the end, unbridled corruption, reckless spending on ambitious schemes, his anti-Western stance and unpaid debts to Western creditors were Nkrumah's undoing. Worst of all, he alienated the army by setting up a private guard answerable only to him. In 1966, while the president was on a mission to Hanoi, the army ousted him in a coup. Exiled to Guinea, Nkrumah died of cancer six years later.

The Rawlings Era

Neither the military regime nor the civilian government, installed three years later and headed by Dr Kofi Busia, could overcome Ghana's corruption and debt problems. In 1972 there was another coup, headed by Colonel Acheampong, under whose inept leadership the economy worsened still further. As the cedi became increasingly worthless, food staples and other basic goods became scarce. In 1979, in the midst of serious food shortages and demonstrations against army affluence and military rule, a group of young revolutionaries seized power. Their leader was a charismatic, half-Scottish 32-year-old airforce flight lieutenant, Jerry Rawlings, who quickly became the darling of the masses.

As he had promised, the Armed Forces Revolutionary Council (AFRC) handed over to a civilian government several months later, after general elections. But first some major 'house cleaning' was done, resulting in the sentencing and execution of some senior officers, including Acheampong, and the conviction of hundreds of other officers and businessmen. The new president, Hilla Limann, unable to halt the country's downward spiral and uneasy with Rawlings' enormous grassroots support, accused him of attempting to subvert constitutional rule. This provoked a second takeover by the AFRC in January 1982, and this time Rawlings stayed for two decades.

Although Rawlings never delivered on his promised left-wing radical revolution, under his colourful leadership life became better for most Ghanaians. He yielded to World Bank and IMF pressure and carried out some tough free-market reforms, which included floating the cedi, removing price controls, raising payments to cocoa farmers and disposing of some unprofitable state enterprises. In return, the World Bank and the IMF rewarded Ghana amply with loans and funding. For a while, in the 1980s, Ghana was lauded as an economic success story, with an economic growth rate that was the highest in Africa.

In 1992, yielding to pressures from home and abroad, Rawlings announced a hastily organised referendum on a new constitution and lifted the 10-year ban on political parties. Opposition groups formed along traditional lines but divisions were deep. Without a united opposition front, Rawlings triumphed at the November 1992 presidential election, winning 60% of the vote. Humiliated, the main opposition parties withdrew from the following month's parliamentary elections, so Rawlings' National Democratic Congress (NDC) won and Rawlings was sworn in as president. Since 1992, Ghana has been a multiparty democracy with elections held every four years. Under the 1992 constitution, the government is headed by an elected president and a 200-member national assembly, which is also elected.

During the 1990s, Ghana made mixed progress. On the one hand, Rawlings seemed to have achieved a respectable democratic mandate, economic growth was maintained and Ghana continued to attract praise from the IMF. On the other hand, however, austerity measures, lack of improvement in social services, rising inflation, increasing corruption within the NDC and a hurried attempt by the government to launch an unpopular value-added tax in 1995 led to major civil unrest.

Rawlings' personal popularity was relatively unaffected and in December 1996 he was again elected as president. At much the same time, the appointment of Ghanaian Kofi Annan as UN secretary general boosted national morale. In 1998, in an effort to improve tax collection and spread the burden more equitably, VAT was successfully introduced. However, a drought in the late 1990s led to morale-sapping electricity and water rationing throughout the country, while a fall in the world price of cocoa and gold diminished Ghana's foreign-exchange earnings.

Ghana Today

Ghana is regarded by international analysts as West Africa's golden child; one of the continent's most stable and promising democracies. The cocoa-producing nation hit the jackpot in 2007 when oil reserves were discovered close to the west-coast surfing spot Cape Three Points. President John Kufuor, who ruled for eight years after the Rawlings era drew to a close, stepped down in 2009, paving the way for an NDC government headed by President John Atta Mills.

Ghana's 2008 election was widely regarded as a test of Ghana's ability to become a modern democracy. Despite an anxious two-round vote and marked tension between Atta Mills and his NPP competitor Nana Akufo-Addo, the election passed without serious violence. The NPP's Nana Akufo-Addo, darling of the West and a member of the Ashanti ethnic group, vowed to pour oil profits into free education, healthcare and the creation of jobs. John Atta Mills campaigned on a platform of change, scoring points with minority groups, the poor and the disheartened.

While Kufuor was viewed by the international set as a good man in West Africa, President Atta Mills' reputation has yet to be cemented. Under the Kufuor administration, primary school enrolment increased by 25% and many of Ghana's poor were granted access to free healthcare. When Kufuor was elected in 2000, he vowed to help elevate Ghana to a middle-class country within 15 years. Members of Accra's growing middle class say his biggest legacy is the creation of the Accra Mall, a shiny shopping mall on the outskirts of town, complete with the country's first multi-screen cinema.

When he came to power in 2009, President Atta Mills told Ghanaians that overspending by the previous government had left the country broke, with rising inflation and a tax deficit close to 15% of GDP. Nevertheless, inheriting power brought pressure to fairly distribute profits from the country's new-found oil wealth. The Cape Three Points area has proven reserves of more than 600 million barrels of oil. Along with natural gas, the International Monetary Fund predicts that the reserves could earn Ghana as much as $20 billion by the year 2030. At the request

of other African nations, the government has put in place a regulatory structure.

Some Ghanaians feel that as long as oil profits are poured into development, Ghana will progress at a fairly rapid speed. Many see oil as the key to a brighter future – a way of distancing themselves from the outdated concept of the third world, meeting UN development goals and joining the privileged in the first world. Others fear the profits from Ghana's new-found oil wealth may pass them by. Africa's resource-rich countries generally show lower growth rates than African nations with fewer resources; whether Ghana will be an exception remains to be seen.

Many of President Atta Mills' supporters come from underprivileged parts of the country, including the Jamestown district of Accra. If anyone is going to feel the effects of fairly distributed oil revenue and the meeting of Millenium Goals, it is them. On the other hand, should oil profits fail to speed development, they will be the ones to suffer. Either way, the new president's run in office is likely to prove pivotal for Ghana.

Among some Ghanaians, the king of the Ashanti is considered almost as influential as the president, in part because he rules with no term limits. Some Ghanaians living abroad send remittances to the king, some money comes from allowances paid by the government, and some of his wealth comes from taxes or tributes given by the people themselves. He has been instrumental in kick-starting education initiatives.

THE CULTURE
The National Psyche

When oil reserves were discovered off the coast in 2007, many Ghanaians felt like they'd won the lottery. Ghana has been on the cusp of change for some time and this, many felt, heralded a leap into the arms of the developed world. Others, jaded by the failings of long-gone leaders, didn't dare get their hopes up.

As you travel through Ghana, you'll see, hear, feel and smell every aspect of this country's struggle for place. Ghana can't be lumped in with the most underdeveloped parts of Africa. The broken roads of Guinea and Liberia are a world away from Ghana's smooth, sealed coastal highways. If you're a middle-class young professional living in the leafy 'burbs of Accra, life is good. Chances are you have running water, power, street lights and a fair wage. Your mobile phone never stops ringing, you go on dates to restaurants and the kids next door don't have to share a textbook in class. You don't know much about poverty, but your cousin on the other side of town does.

In Accra's poorest suburbs, places like Jamestown and Korle Gonno, streams of stagnant sewage mark the streets, babies are bathed in buckets and school-aged children sell water sachets in the street. Though education is supposed to be accessible to all, the reality is that uniforms are too expensive and textbooks, well…think again. Look around, if you decide to visit these areas, and you'll notice details that hint at greater problems. Few people, for example, wear glasses in these parts of town, and sadly it's not because everyone's sight is perfect. Despite the oil find, many poor Ghanaians aren't necessarily confident that their children's lives will look much different from their own.

For years Ghana has had a reputation as Africa's friendliest, most welcoming country. That's not strictly true; much of Africa welcomes travellers with open arms. What Ghana does possess is a huge joy for life. Celebrations are a big part of Ghanaian culture, and the good times don't stop when the last drink is served. Here, singing is a relied-upon means of expression; melodic tones drift down rust-red alleys and children practice dance moves in the street.

The extended family is the foundation of Ghanaian society. The Akan people are unusual in that they are matrilineal – you belong to your mother's clan. Clans are grouped under a chief, who in turn is answerable to a paramount chief, who is the political and spiritual head of his people.

You'll undoubtedly hear cat-calls of *obruni, obruni* or the ubiquitous West African hiss, used to attract attention. Neither call is really derogatory; the one time this author ignored the hiss, a kind passer-by was alerting her to the fact that she'd dropped something. Ghana, like most of Africa, operates on the principles of community life. No man is an island and everyone is part of a greater whole – that kind of thing. Newspapers, fruit and snacks are shared around on buses and it's polite to say hello to people you pass on quiet streets. Respect, too, is shared – show it and you'll get it back. Some Ghanaians who have lived

---

IN GOD'S NAME

From sleepy coastal villages to edgy, urban parts of Accra, you'll spot curiously-named shops, chop bars and businesses. Many of these take cues from religion, while others are influenced by family, friends and hopes for the future. Either way, they almost always rouse a smile in even the most travel-weary. Here are a few to look out for:

- Covered in the Blood of Jesus Hair Salon, Takoradi
- If God Say Yes Snack Shop, Accra
- Meek and Mild Preparatory School, Axim
- You May Cry For Me Chop Bar, Accra
- Jesus Loves Fashion, Accra
- If You Can Read This, Give Thanks to the Teacher Provision Store, Axim motor park

---

abroad argue that real change will only come about when professional Ghanaians feel confident they are at least the equal of any Westerner who sits across from them in the boardroom or at the negotiating table. You'll rarely hear anyone swear in Ghana.

Population

Ghana's population of 23 million makes it one of the most densely populated countries in West Africa. Of this, 44% are Akan, a grouping that includes the Ashanti (also called Asante), whose heartland is around Kumasi, and the Fanti, who fish the central coast and farm its near hinterland. The Nzema, linguistically close to the Akan, fish and farm in the southwest. Distant migrants from present-day Nigeria, the Ga are the indigenous people of Accra and Tema. The southern Volta region is home to the Ewe.

In the north, the Dagomba heartland is around Tamale and Yendi. Prominent neighbours are the Gonja in the centre, Konkomba and Mamprusi in the far northeast, and, around Navrongo, the Kasena. The Sisala and Lobi inhabit the far northwest.

For more details on the Ashanti people, see p71 and for the Ewe people, see p73.

SPORT

Ghana made back-page headlines worldwide when it hosted the 26th African Cup of Nations football tournament in 2008. With players like Michael Essien, Prince Tagoe, Sulley Muntari, Asamoah Gyan and Junior Agogo, the Black Stars almost made it to the finals before being knocked out of the competition by Cameroon.

Like much of West Africa, Ghanaians can't keep their feet off the ball and football is a real national obsession. Most football fans support one Ghanaian team and one international one. Manchester United and Arsenal are big favourites and you'll see strips, car air fresheners and even shops bearing their names all over Ghana. Head to any chop bar with a TV on a Saturday afternoon and you'll join a crowd of Ghanaians every bit as enthusiastic about the football as those attending the match. Ghana's most famous footballer is probably Michael Essien, nicknamed 'the bison', who also plays for Chelsea.

RELIGION

Ghana is a deeply-religious country and respect for religion permeates pretty much every aspect of life; you'll come across churches of every imaginable Christian denomination, sometimes even in the most far-flung villages. About 70% of Ghanaians are Christian. Pentecostal and charismatic denominations are particularly active, as are the main-line Protestant and Catholic churches. Branches of super-churches, like the Nigerian **Winner's Chapel** (www.winnersghana.com) are growing in popularity. Revivals are a big hit with families, and deliverance services, characterised by talking in tongues and the removal of bad karma through trance, fitting and the expulsion of bodily fluids, are, as you might imagine, a delight to watch. Christianity was introduced by European missionaries, who were also the first educators, and the link between religion and education persists.

About 15% of the population is Muslim; the majority are in the north, though there are also substantial Muslim minorities in southern cities such as Accra and Kumasi. Tamale, Wa and Larabanga have excellent examples of fine contemporary and traditional Islamic architecture.

Many Ghanaians also have traditional beliefs, notably in spirits and forms of gods who inhabit the natural world. Ancestor veneration is an important part of this tradition. Many people retain traditional beliefs alongside Christian or Muslim beliefs.

ARTS
Music

There's no doubt about it, Ghana's got rhythm. Whichever part of the country you visit, be it the gritty urban cities of Accra or Takoradi, the sun-drenched coast or soporific villages, Ghana's soundtrack will be a constant travel companion. From the age of three or four children are taught to dance, and we're not talking ballet. It's not unusual to see little kids copying the hip-grinding and ass-shaking that characterises the average Ghanaian party.

The best Ghanaian nights are those when the moon is high, the stars are out and tunes drift along bumpy red roads. Whether they're coming from a laptop, sound system or live band, you'll look around to see people jamming in the street.

TRADITIONAL

Court and ceremonial music is really only reserved for chiefs, rulers and royalty, though in Northern Ghana you can sometimes swing an invite to a public performance. The traditional music popular with ordinary Ghanaians has a strong percussion base, and includes instruments like the talking drum, *gonge* (one-stringed fiddle) and *seperewa,* a relative of the *kora* popular in francophone West Africa.

CONTEMPORARY

You can trace the roots of movements like high-life and hip-life back to palm-wine music, which has been intoxicating West Africa for centuries. Guitarists initially played at gatherings while revellers knocked back glasses of sweet palm wine, the fermented juice of the palm tree. As time went on the genre evolved to include elements of Caribbean harmonies, Congolese *soukous* and honey-glazed West African vocals. Though palm wine is still a popular drink, the genre is sadly winding down. The last of the greats include Daniel Amponsah (otherwise known as Koo Nimo) and the late SE Rogie.

High-life hit Ghana in the 1920s and popular recordings include those by ET Mensah, Nana Ampadu and The Sweet Talks. Accra trumpeter ET Mensah formed his first band in the 1930s and went on to be crowned the

HOMEGROWN BEATS

Until the early 1990s, Ghana's music scene was dominated by high-life, a mellow mix of big band jazz, Christian hymns, brass band and sailor sonnets. High-life began in the 1920s, when the trend for fancy European-style nights out leaked into Ghana (hence the name).

The first hip-life tracks aired in 1992, a hybrid of rhythmic African lyrics poured over imported American hip-hop beats. Ghana has been dancing to it ever since, and you won't be able to get through a few days here (let alone an entire trip) without letting the sweet sounds of hip-life into your world. It's more than just a music genre; it's an insight into Ghanaian society, steeped in its own traditions and languages but increasingly influenced by the diaspora in America and Britain.

Reggie Rockstone, Ghana's 'godfather of hip-life' is the man to listen to. His early work, such as the 1998 classic 'Keep Your Eyes on the Road' is a happy marriage of high-life notes and '90s lyrics. 'Eyes', a comment on Africa's relationship with the West, is another good bet. In 1999, Obrafuor exploded onto the hip-life scene with his track 'Kwame Nkrumah', a resounding tribute to the former leader and one that united the older generation with the experimental hip-life crowd. Obrafuor's *Pae Mu Ka* album is widely regarded as one of the most influential hip-life recordings ever made. Others to look out for include Obour, Castro, Tinny and Shoeshine Boy.

It follows that this genre, so strongly influenced by a sense of place in the world, has regional accents. Northern hip-life, produced predominately in the Muslim city of Tamale, is pretty different from the tracks produced down south. Up north, where the air is dusty and the land dry, hip-life takes cues from the haunting, melismatic style of music popular across the Sahel, with vocals sometimes in Dagbani. Arguably, nobody has had a greater impact on the northern hip-life scene than Big Adam. If you listen to only one album of his, make it *Asalamu-Alaakum*, acclaimed for its mesmerising Islamic praise vocals.

King of high-life, later performing with Louis Armstrong in Ghana. WWII brought an introduction to American swing to Ghana's shores, prompting the first complex fusion of Western and African music. Hip-life, which pretty much rules Ghana today, followed high-life in the early 1990s (see the boxed text, above).

Gospel music is also big in Ghana, as is reggae; gospel rap is another fusion of styles. Founded by Nana Danso Abiam, the Pan African Orchestra has recorded an album of neoclassical, Afrocentric symphonic music.

In the pecking order of the Ghanaian music scene, imported American hip-hop and Nigerian music closely compete for the number two spot after high-life. Tunes to look out for include P Square's 'No One Like You', anything by Akon, and Shakira's 'Hips Don't Lie'. There's only one rule to West African music and that's rhythm. If you can dance to it, you can bet your bottom cedi Ghana will be playing it.

Arts & Crafts

Ghana has a rich artistic heritage. Objects are created not only for their aesthetic value but as symbols of ethnic identity or to commemorate historical or legendary events, to convey cultural values or to signify membership of a group. The Akan people of the southern and central regions are famous for their cloth, goldwork, woodcarving, chiefs' insignia (such as swords, umbrella tops and linguist staffs), pottery and bead-making.

TEXTILES

The Ashanti in particular are famous for their kente cloth, with its distinctive basketwork pattern. It was originally worn only by royalty and is still some of the most expensive material in Africa. The colour and design of the cloth worn is yet another way of indicating status and clan allegiance. Different cloth is worn depending on the occasion. It is traditionally worn by high-ranking men at ceremonies to display their wealth and status. Kente is woven on treadle looms, by men only, in long thin strips that are sewn together. Its intricate geometric patterns are full of symbolic meaning while its orange-yellow hues indicate wealth.

In contrast, adinkra cloth is worn primarily on solemn occasions by both men and women. The symbolic designs are printed in black on cotton cloth that is usually dark grey, dark red or white.

The Ewe people of the southeast, who claim to have originally passed on the method of kente weaving to the Ashantis, produce both the Ashanti kente and their own Ewe kente, which is even more intricately woven.

ASHANTI STOOLS

Akan stools are among the finest in West Africa and incorporate designs that are rich in cultural symbolism. There's an Ashanti saying: 'There are no secrets between a man and his stool', and when a chief dies his people say 'The stool has fallen'. Ashanti stools are among the most elaborate in Africa. They are carved from a single piece of wood and the basic form is the same – a curved seat set on a central column with a flat base. Historically, certain designs, such as the seat supported upon the image of a leopard or elephant, were restricted to particular ranks within Ashanti society. The higher a person's status, the larger and more elaborate the stool.

Stools have a variety of functions and meanings. In official ceremonies, stools act as symbols of authority; on the death of their owner, consecrated stools are worshipped as homes to ancestral spirits. In most households, stools are articles of everyday use. A stool is the first gift of a father to his son, and the first gift bestowed by a man on his bride-to-be. Women's stools are different from men's. After death, the deceased is ritually washed upon a stool, which is then placed in the room for ancestral worship. Chiefs consider stools to be their supreme insignia. There are as many stool designs as there are chiefs, and the symbols are infinite.

OTHER OBJECTS

The *akuaba* doll is carved from wood and used as a household fetish to protect against infertility; these are easily identified by the extra-large round head. The Akan are skilled in the lost-wax method of metal casting, used to make exquisite brass objects, including weights used for measuring gold dust. Glass beads are made by grinding up glass of different colours and layering it in a mould to produce intricately coloured patterns. Around Bolgatanga in the north, fine basket weaving and leatherwork are traditional crafts. Drums and carved *owara* boards – the game of *owara* has various names throughout West Africa – are also specialities.

Architecture

With a mixture of 1960s-style block buildings and the remnants of colonial homes and forts, Ghana's architectural style is hard to define. The most striking architecture is arguably found in Northern Ghana, where the sun's hot rays illuminate the white clay facades of Sudanese-style mud-and-stick mosques. The best examples of these are probably in Wa and Larabanga.

As far as contemporary architecture goes, there's a nascent green architectural movement, with plans for eco-friendly constructions that utilise natural materials like bamboo. PozzoGhana, an alternative to expensive imported cement, is a mix of palm kernels, lime and local clays. It might well be used in the future to save building costs and curb over-reliance on imported materials.

Cinema

Ghanaians love the drama of the big screen, though Nigerian movies are far more popular than local productions. No traveller gets through a trip to Ghana without sitting through at least one of the Nigerian films shown on STC buses and in chop bars. They're usually characterised by excessive screaming matches, secret affairs and incidents which bring shame on entire families. Ghanaians love to watch these and usually turn them into participatory events. Even on bus journeys you'll often be given a running commentary alongside the film.

Ghana's film talent can't really compete with that of Senegal or Mali; an exception is Kwaw Ansah's 1989 classic *Heritage Africa,* which won first prize at the Fespaco film festival that year. In 2005, the Oprah Winfrey–produced documentary *Emmanuel's Gift* received a limited release outside the country. The film chronicles a young, handicapped Ghanaian man's bicycle ride across the country and his attempt to address the problems faced by the two million people (or almost 10% of the population) with disabilities in Ghana.

Literature

Ghana's literary scene, while still intimate, is beginning to resonate with the rest of the world. One of its key literary figures – and probably the most famous living Ghanaian writer – is Ayi Kwei Armah. Born in Takoradi, he studied at Harvard and Columbia universities before publishing his first novel in 1968,

The Beautyful Ones Are Not Yet Born. It's a finely-written story of the failure of an African ruling, told through the eyes of an anonymous railway office clerk, simply called 'the man', who struggles against both poverty and greed. By the same author, *Fragments* is also recommended. Both were written in the 1960s and '70s before Armah gave up the trappings of literary success and moved to an island off the coast of Senegal.

The Seasons of Beento Blackbird is a novel by Akosua Busia (daughter of Ghana's former prime minister and an actress in the film *The Color Purple*). She later co-wrote the screenplay adaptation of Toni Morrison's novel, *Beloved,* for the director Jonathan Demme. *The Seasons*, which follows the protagonist's fairly explicit love affairs with three men, was deemed pretty controversial when it first hit Ghana. *No Sweetness Here and Other Stories,* by Ama Ata Aidoo, also deals with how Africans come to terms with traditional culture in an increasingly cosmopolitan world.

The Two Hearts of Kwasi Boachi by Arthur Japin, based on a true story, is a novel about the tragic 19th-century exile of an Ashanti prince. *Ama: A Story of the Atlantic Slave Trade* by Manu Herbstein, winner of the 2002 Commonwealth Writers Prize for best first book, is a novelistic imagining of a young Ghanaian woman's tortured journey from slavery to freedom.

Kwesi Brew, who died in 2007, was one of Ghana's most eloquent poets. His only internationally published collection was *The Shadows of Laughter* (1968), but he also wrote a compassionate work on the downfall of Nkrumah. Atukwei Okai is a groundbreaking poet and the author of 'Oath of the Fontomfrom' and 'Logorligi Logarithms.' He was one of the first African poets to take the genre back to its rhythmic origins; he does readings worldwide. Other Ghanaian poets to look out for include Atukwei Okai, Kofi Anyidoho, Kobena Ayi Acquah and Kojo Laing.

ENVIRONMENT
The Land

Ghana is dominated by flat or gently undulating lowlands, with coastal plains punctuated by saline lagoons in the south, forested hill ranges in the centre and a low plateau in the northern two-thirds. All of the country lies below 1000m. Keta Lagoon east of Accra, near the Togolese border, is Ghana's largest lagoon. Dominating the eastern flank of the country is Lake Volta, formed when the Volta River was dammed in the mid-1960s. It's the world's largest artificial lake, about twice the size of Luxembourg. The highest hills are part of the Akwapim range in the east, which runs from just north of Accra, then east of Lake Volta and into Togo.

Wildlife
ANIMALS AND BIRDS

Ghana's national parks and reserves protect a variety of large mammals, including elephants, antelope species such as roans, kobs, hartebeests, water bucks, duikers and the endangered bongo, and primate species such as olive baboons, colobus and Mona monkeys and chimpanzees. The Black Volta River has a resident population of hippos; the best place to see them is at Wechiau Hippo Sanctuary (p383) near Wa. Nile crocodiles can be seen in various parts of the country but the crocodile ponds at Paga (p385) on the border with Burkina Faso are the best known. To see primates at close quarters, visit the sanctuaries at Boabeng-Fiema (p377) and Tafi-Atome (p367), where villagers have traditionally venerated and protected the resident populations of black-and-white colobus and Mona monkeys.

Forested areas contain numerous species of butterflies. Kakum National Park (p356), where some 400 species of butterflies have been recorded, and Bobiri Butterfly Sanctuary (p377) are some of the best places to see them.

The Volta estuary and coastal areas west of Accra (such as Kokrobite and around Winneba) are important turtle-nesting sites for green, leather-back and Olive Ridley turtles.

Ghana offers some of the best birdwatching in the world. In forested areas, birds such as hornbills, turacos, African grey and Senegal parrots and the rare white-fronted guinea fowl can be seen. The coastal wetlands around the Volta estuary and coastal lagoons are important resting and feeding grounds for some 70 species of indigenous and migratory water birds.

PLANTS

Ghana is rich in wildflower species and giant, sky-scraping trees. In the forests of the south there's a large number of Kapok trees and Khayas (African mahogany). The barks of certain trees are still used as medicinal aids, notably those of the Kaku tree (headaches), Dubini mahogany tree (blood tonic; as an enema for stomach pains), Otwere tree (used with honey to treat asthma) and the Pampuro tree (malarial fever). Kakum National Park (see p356) and Aburi Botanical Gardens (see p347) are Ghana's most significant accessible floral hotspots.

National Parks & Reserves

Ghana has five national parks and nine protected areas. Mole National Park (p380) in the northwest of the country protects savannah woodland and is the best place to see wildlife, including elephants, baboons and antelope species. Kakum National Park (p356), just inland from Cape Coast, is known for its canopy walkway and is a good place to see rainforest habitat and birdlife. The three remaining national parks, Bui, Bia and Digya, aren't really set up for visitors; if you want to go, make sure you have your own transport. Of the protected areas, Ankasa Nature Reserve (p364) near Elubo in the southwest is noted for its rainforest habitat and forest elephants. Owabi Wildlife Sanctuary (p376), near Kumasi, is one of several designated Ramsar wetlands conservation sites in Ghana. The **Ghana Wildlife Society** (www .ghanawildlifesociety.org) is an excellent resource.

Environmental Issues

The World Bank estimates that as much as 75% of Ghana's forest cover has been destroyed by logging, much of it illegal. Timber is one of the country's most important exports, and if it weren't for the designation of national parks, much of Ghana would have fallen to the ground. However, Ghana's environmental outlook is looking up, not least because of the sheer popularity of the country's community-based ecotourism projects (see the boxed text, p383).

Bizarrely, the future of logging might lie in Lake Volta, the world's largest artificial lake. In 2008 vast reserves of ebony, teak and mahogany were discovered underwater, buried in the lake bed. A venture to create timber from these lost forests could curb the illegal logging that sadly continues to threaten Ghana's greenery.

FOOD & DRINK

Fiery sauces and soups are the mainstay of Ghanaian cuisine and are usually served with a starchy staple like rice, *fufu* (cooked and mashed cassava, plantain or yam) or *banku* (fermented maize meal). Groundnut (peanut) stew is a warming, spicy dish cooked with liquefied groundnut paste (available at markets), ginger and either fish or meat. Palmnut soup (fashioned from tomatoes, ginger, garlic and chilli pepper as well as palmnut) is often served with oil floating on the top; it looks downright greasy but it tastes good.

Jollof rice, found throughout West Africa, is a spicier, greasier take on Spanish paella (though it has its own origins). You can buy this for a cedi or two from most chop bars, and it's a good filler-upper if you need a quick fix. Red-red is bean stew, sometimes served with fried plantains or yam chips. The meat used is usually chicken, goat or beef; guinea fowl replaces chicken in the north of the country. Grasscutter, a large rodent, is also popular. Fish, usually dried and smoked, is a common component of meals. *Omo tuo*, a special dish usually served only on Sunday, is mashed rice balls with a fish or meat soup. You'll also spot carts selling the cultish Fan Ice frozen yoghurts (C0.40).

ETHICAL FOOD

One of Ghana's most significant exports is cocoa and in 2009 the country signed a fair-trade deal to supply cocoa to British chocolate giant Cadbury. Forty thousand of Ghana's 700,000 farmers are benefiting from the collaboration, which might well encourage many of Ghana's city-dwellers to up sticks and move to the countryside.

Where to Eat

The cheapest food is sold at street stalls. Look out for people doling out rice, pasta and sauce from huge covered bowls set up on a wooden table. You can either eat it at the stall or take it away in a plastic bag or plantain-leaf parcel. Other food-stall staples include egg salad with rice, roast yam with spicy sauce, roast plantain with groundnuts, omelette in bread, and spicy kebabs. Inexpensive food is also available from chop bars, which serve a selection of dishes, usually with daily specials. Cheap places to eat are also referred to as 'catering services' and 'canteens'.

In Accra and other major centres you'll find a variety of cuisines, commonly Lebanese, Chinese and West African, but also Italian, French and Indian. Western fast food is hugely popular and there are plenty of outlets in Accra and other centres in the south. Most restaurants offer a choice of Western and Ghanaian dishes.

Regardless of where you eat, service is slow – sometimes frustratingly slow. If you can, it's almost always a good idea to order in advance and give an estimate of when you will return.

Drinks

Cold water is sold everywhere in plastic sachets or plastic bags for about C0.10. The stuff in sachets (called 'pure water') has been filtered, whereas the stuff tied up in plastic bags (called 'ice water') is just ordinary water. You just tear the corner with your teeth and suck.

A delicious home-made ginger ale is sold in some areas. As well as the usual brand-name soft drinks, bottled pure pineapple juice is available in some places. Generally, though, fresh fruit juice is difficult to find and expensive compared with the bottled drinks. Ghanaian tea is drunk from a huge mug with lots of evaporated milk and heaps of sugar.

Bars in Ghana are often referred to as a 'spot'. Decent, locally made beer is widely available. Popular brands include Star, Club, Gulder and Guinness.

Among home-brew alcoholic drinks, *pito* (millet beer) is the drink of choice in the north. Palm wine, which is more subtle, is the preferred tipple in the south. 'Tap before seven, drink before 11' is the local saying. As the day grows older the wine becomes less refreshing, more sour – and more seriously alcoholic. *Akpeteshie* is a fiery local spirit.

ACCRA

☎ 021, 024 / pop 2.9 million

Accra grows on you. When you first make eye contact – you peering through the steamed-up window of a 747, it looming large on the ground – you don't quite know what to make of each other. The capital's hot, sticky streets are perfumed with sweat, fumes and yesterday's cooking oil. Like balloons waiting to be burst, clouds of dirty humidity linger above stalls selling mangoes, *banku* and rice. Kids skip along rust-red alleys clutching school bags and each other's hands. From wooden chop bars comes the metallic clatter of pots and plates and the promise of spicy groundnut stew. The

city's tendrils reach out towards the beach, the centre and the west, each one a different Ghana experience. Like all capitals, Accra is what you make it. Ghana's beating heart probably won't inspire love letters but you might just grow to like it.

ORIENTATION

The centre of Accra is bounded by the semicircular Ring Rd West, Ring Rd Central and Ring Rd East. Its four major circles and interchanges are, from west to east, Lamptey, Nkrumah, Sankara and Danquah. Accra's jam-packed commercial heart is Makola Market. South of Makola, High St runs along the seafront. West of the city centre are the shantytown areas of Jamestown and Ussher Town, bordered by Korle Lagoon. East of the city centre is the beachside suburb of La. North of Makola, the commercial district extends along Nkrumah Ave and Kojo Thompson Rd, two parallel north–south highways that connect High St with the Nkrumah Circle area. The district of Adabraka, southwest of Nkrumah Circle, is where you'll find budget hotels and inexpensive bars and restaurants. East of Adabraka, the leafy residential areas of Asylum Down and North Ridge have some good accommodation options, and this area is another popular base for travellers. Easily Accra's most happening area is Osu, south of Danquah Circle, which has lots of fast-food joints, restaurants, internet centres and more expensive hotels. On the northern and eastern side of Ring Rd East are the upmarket residential areas of Cantonments, Labone and Airport, with embassies and upmarket hotels.

While most streets in Accra do have names, places are often identified by their proximity to landmarks – bear this in mind when taking taxis or asking for directions.

INFORMATION
Bookshops

A selection of imported novels, books on Ghana, magazines and newspapers are available at bookshops in and around Osu. The University of Ghana (p347) has an excellent bookshop, although Accra traffic can make it a hassle to get to.

Bookshelf.net (Map p340; 17th Lane, Osu) Stocks a reasonable selection of new and second-hand material. Opposite Frankie's.

GHANA

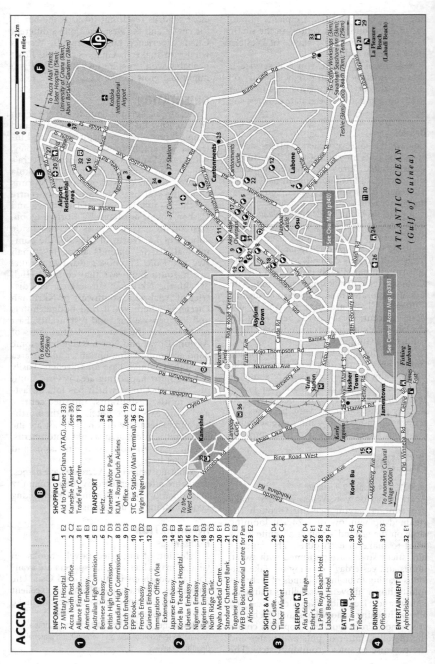

ACCRA

INFORMATION
37 Military Hospital.................................1	E2
Accra North Post Office.........................2	C2
Alliance Française...................................3	E1
American Embassy..................................4	E3
Australian High Commission..................5	E3
Beninese Embassy...................................6	E2
British High Commission........................7	D3
Canadian High Commission....................8	D3
Dutch Embassy.......................................9	D3
EPP Books...10	F3
French Embassy....................................11	D2
Guinean Embassy..................................12	E3
Immigration Office (Visa	
Extensions)..13	D3
Japanese Embassy.................................14	E3
Korle Bu Teaching Hospital..................15	B4
Liberian Embassy..................................16	E1
Nigerien Embassy..................................17	E3
Nigerien Embassy..................................18	D3
North Ridge Clinic.................................19	D3
Nyaho Medical Centre..........................20	E1
Standard Chartered Bank.......................21	D3
Togolese Embassy.................................22	E3
WEB Du Bois Memorial Centre for Pan	
African Culture.................................23	E2

SIGHTS & ACTIVITIES
Osu Castle...24	D4
Timber Market......................................25	C4

SLEEPING
Afia African Village..............................26	D4
Esther's..27	E1
La Palm Royal Beach Hotel...................28	F4
Labadi Beach Hotel...............................29	F4

EATING
La Tawala Spot.....................................30	E4
Tribes..(see 26)	

DRINKING
Office..31	D3

ENTERTAINMENT
Aphrodisiac...32	E1

SHOPPING
Aid to Artisans Ghana (ATAG)........(see 33)	
Kaneshie Market............................(see 35)	
Trade Fair Centre..................................33	F3

TRANSPORT
Hertz..34	E2
Kaneshie Motor Park.............................35	B2
KLM - Royal Dutch Airlines	
Office..(see 19)	
STC Bus Station (Main Terminal)..........36	C3
Virgin Nigeria.......................................37	E1

EPP Books (Map p336; Burma Camp Rd, Labadi) Has a fairly decent range of fiction, non-fiction and travel guides. Opposite the Trade Fair Centre.
Silverbird (Accra Mall, ☽ 10am-9pm Mon-Sun) This modern bookstore stocks an excellent selection of African and imported fiction and non-fiction.

Cultural Centres
Alliance Française (Map p336; ☎ 021 773 134; www .alliancefrancaiseghana.com; Liberation Link, Airport Residential Area). Cultural events and lectures.
British Council (Map p338; ☎ 021 610 090; www .britishcouncil.org/ghana; Liberia Rd) Air-con library with English newspapers and magazines. Organises cultural events and lectures.

Emergency
Ambulance (☎ 193/194)
Fire (☎ 192)
Police (☎ 191)

Internet Access
There are hundreds of internet cafes dotted all over Accra. Wi-fi is available at many top-end and midrange hotels.
Busy Internet (Map p338; ☎ 258 800; www.busy internet.com; 42 Ring Rd, Asylum Down; ☽ 24 hr) Ghana's sleekest web cafe by far. Fast browsing, printing services and a laptop lounge. There is a second (much smaller) branch in the Accra mall.
Mega Internet (Map p338; Ring Rd, Asylum Down; ☽ 8am-6pm) Flat-screen computers, all office-related services.
Osu Internet Café (Map p340; Mission St, Osu; ☽ 24 hr)
SharpNet (Map p340; Ring Rd East; ☽ 8am-9pm) As popular as Busy Internet but not quite as hi-tech.

Medical Services
Ask your embassy for a list of recommended doctors and specialists. The main public hospitals in Accra are included here. Pharmacies are everywhere, or try the supermarkets in Osu.
Korle Bu Teaching Hospital (Map p336; ☎ 021 665 401; Guggisberg Ave, Korle Bu) Accra's main hospital.
Lister Hospital (off Map p336; ☎ 021 812 325; www. listerhospital.com.gh; Airport Hills) Ultra-modern 25-bed hospital. Has lab, pharmacy and ER services. GP consultation C40.
37 Military Hospital (Map p336; ☎ 021 776 111; Liberation Ave) Near 37 Circle, recommended for traumatic injuries.
Nyaho Medical Centre (Map p336; ☎ 021 775 341; Airport Residential Area) Large, well-equipped facility.
Trust Hospital (Map p340; ☎ 021 776787; Cantonments Rd, Osu) Private hospital with general practitioner services.

Money
The main branches of Barclays and Standard Chartered banks are on High St; there are smaller branches around town, including one on Nkrumah Ave in Adabraka and Cantonments Rd in Osu. Almost all of their branches have working ATMs. Forexes are easy to find – try Kojo Thompson Rd in Adabraka and Cantonments Rd in Osu.

Post
Accra North post office (Map p336; Nsawam Rd) Just north of Nkrumah Circle.
Main post office (Map p338; Ussher Town; ☽ 8am-4.30pm Mon-Fri) Poste restante.
Osu Post Office (Labadi Beach Rd; ☽ 8am-4.30pm Mon-Fri) Poste restante.

Phone
Accra has plenty of card phones dialling but it's probably cheaper (if you're calling within the country) to visit one of the ubiquitous calling tables – literally a phone on a table. Inexpensive mobile phone SIM cards are available on almost every street corner; the MTN network is one of the most reliable.

Tourist Information
Tourist information counter A small counter in the international arrivals hall at the airport.
Tourist office (Map p338; ☎ 021 231 817, 021 2202 153; ☽ 8am-4pm Mon-Fri) Off Barnes Rd, 50m down Education Close. Some leaflets are free, others are for sale. Sadly it can't help with lots of practical information.

Travel Agencies
Travel agencies are dotted all over Accra, with plenty in Osu.
M&J Travel & Tours (Map p340; ☎ 021 773 498; 11th La, Osu)
Speedway Travel & Tours (Map p338; ☎ 021 227 744; Tackie Tawiah Ave)

Visa Extensions
Immigration office (Map p336; ☽ 8am-1pm; off Independence Ave) Near the Ako Adjei Overpass. You need two photos, a letter stating why you need an extension, and an onward ticket out of Ghana. Inconveniently, your passport is retained for two to three weeks while they process the application. Queue early.

DANGERS & ANNOYANCES
Accra is largely a safe city, though, like any capital, it has its share of bag-snatchers and theft. Take care around the Independence

GHANA

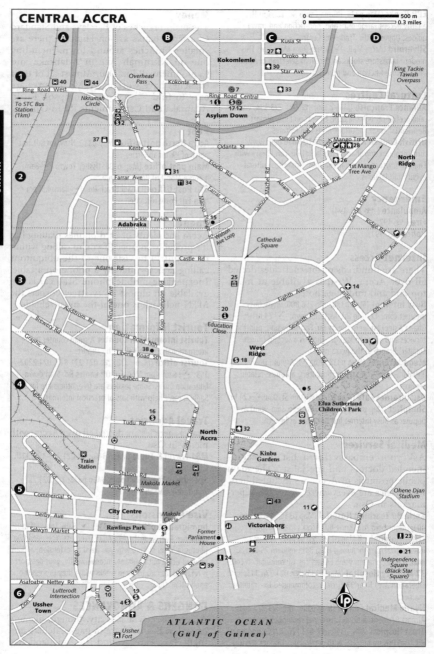

CENTRAL ACCRA

0 _____ 500 m
0 _____ 0.3 miles

Kokomlemle

Kusia St
27 Oroko St
30
Star Ave

Overhead Pass

Kokonte St

Ring Road Central

Asylum Down

Ring Road West

To STC Bus Station (1km)

Nkrumah Circle

40   44

42
2

37

Kente St

Paradise St

Odanta St

Eccfo Rd

King Tackie Tawiah Overpass

5th Cres

Samora Machel Rd

2nd Mango Tree Ave
6 29 28
26
1st Mango Tree Ave

North Ridge

Farrar Ave

31
34

Tackie Tawiah Ave

Adabraka

Adama Rd

Farrar Ave

Manyo Plange St

15

Watson Ave Loop

Cathedral Square

Castle Rd

9

Afram St   Mango Tree Ave

Samora Machel Rd

Kanda High Rd

Ridge Rd

Eighth Ave

8

North Ridge

Ridditrom Rd

Brewery Rd

Graphic Rd

Agbobloshi Rd

Nkrumah Ave

Kojo Thompson Rd

Liberia Road Nth

Liberia Road Sth

Adjaben Rd

25

20

Education Close

West Ridge

18

Eighth Ave

Seventh Ave

Independence Ave

Morocco Rd

Nasser Ave

14

13

5

Efua Sutherland Children's Park

Okai Kwei Rd

Marmladie Rd

Train Station

16

Tudu Rd

Tudu Crescent Rd

North Accra

32

Barnes Rd

35

Iberia Rd

Commercial St

Derby Ave

Selwyn Market St

Station Rd

Kimberly Ave

Makola Market

45   41

Makola Circle

City Centre

Rawlings Park

3

Kinbu Gardens

Kinbu Rd

43

11

Ohene Djan Stadium

Oval Rd

Zongo Ln

Zongo Rd

Pojan Rd

Thorpe Rd

High St

Former Parliament House

Dodoo St

Victoriaborg

28th February Rd

36

Asafoatse Nettey Rd

Lutterodt Intersection

10

Lutterodt St

19
4
22

Ussher Town

Zion St

Ussher Fort

24

39

23

21

Independence Square (Black Star Square)

ATLANTIC OCEAN
(Gulf of Guinea)

Square area, Jamestown and Nkrumah Circle. It's wise to stay away from unlit areas and avoid solitary strolls along beaches after dark. Probably the biggest hazard you'll face as a pedestrian is making sure you don't step off the curb into a ditch or a sewer. When crossing the street, look both ways several times and keep an eye out for taxis and tro-tros (minibuses) being driven like Scalectrix racing cars.

SIGHTS & ACTIVITIES
National Museum

Set in shady grounds, the **national museum** (Map p338; ☎ 021 221 633; Barnes Rd; admission C4.50; ☺ 9am-6pm Tue-Sun), features excellent displays on various aspects of Ghanaian culture and history. The displays on local crafts, ceremonial objects and the slave trade are excellent. There's some fine brass work, including weights used by Ashanti goldsmiths for measuring gold and the spoons they used for loading the scales with gold dust. Smaller displays feature masks, drums, wooden statues, gilded umbrellas and archaeology.

Makola Market

You can hear and smell Makola, Accra's most frenetic market, long before you reach it. It's a short walk from pavements overrun with vendors selling shoes and second-hand clothes to the market itself, an ever-expanding mass of stalls that suck you in like a vortex. Makola isn't the easiest place to shop, and you can forget about lingering over a purchase; before you know it the human undertow will deposit you deeper within the market. Makola's lanes hide everything from moisturiser to heels, jump leads, Chinese-made toys, wind-up radios and sacks of cocoa. The food vendors have some of the most fascinating displays – smoked fish, mountains of bread, pyramids of tomatoes and shallots, maize and millet, roast plantain and vast arrays of sweets, toffees and chewing gum. For new arrivals to Africa, it can be an intense experience, but it's a fun – though perhaps a little masochistic – Ghanaian initiation rite.

Independence Square & Osu Castle

This parade ground, also known as **Black Star Square** (Map p338), is a lavish nod to African independence. You can't always walk through **Independence Arch**, the square's centrepiece, but you can wander up to the **Eternal Flame of African Liberation**, lit by Kwame Nkrumah in 1961. The square was built to hold 30,000 – a number it has never attained.

From the square, looking east along the coast towards La, you can see **Osu Castle** (Map p336). Built by the Danes around 1659 and originally called Christiansborg Castle, it was the seat of government and was off limits to the public. The seat of government moved to Golden Jubilee House.

Kwame Nkrumah Memorial Park

It's all bronze statues and choreographed fountains at this peaceful park (Map p338; High St; adult/child C6/1; ☺ 10am-6pm) dedicated in the early 1990s to Kwame Nkrumah, Ghana's first president. Pointing the way forward with arm outstretched is an effigy of the man himself, who declared Ghana independent on this site in 1957. The park museum houses a curious collection of Nkrumah's personal belongings, including his presidential desk, bookcase, jacket and student sofa. A prolific writer and teacher, many of Nkrumah's book jackets are also on display. The park gardens are testament to his impact; trees have been planted by various heads of state and the entire park is on a monumental scale. He might not, however, have appreciated the fact that his index finger now points to billboards advertising fast-food restaurants and technology.

Jamestown

This historic division of Accra hides several interesting spots. Jamestown originated as a community that emerged around the 17th-century British James Fort, merging with Accra as the city grew. Alleys and grey paved streets wrap around courtyards and communities, colourful markets and colonial-era buildings. This is by no means a privileged part of Accra; slow-moving streams of sewage criss-cross the streets, school-age children play in gutters and unemployment is chronic. You should always ask for permission before photographing people. If you want to gain an insight into life in Jamestown, it's recommended that you go with a local guide (buying lunch and paying a fee is advisable), not least because you'll gain a better understanding of the issues that threaten this community. **Old Accra Community Guides** (☎ 0246 128 283, 0243 875 833) trains and employs young people from Jamestown, Ussher Town and Korle Gonno.

There are several boxing gyms – really nothing more than a makeshift ring on a concrete patio – that have nurtured a long line of neighbourhood kids who have become champions. For a great view of the city and the busy and colourful fishing harbour (haze and pollution permitting), climb to the top of the white-washed **lighthouse** (Map p336; nr James Fort). James Fort itself was used as a prison until 2008.

If you're walking back to the centre along Cleland Rd, which becomes High St, you could take a detour along Hansen Rd to see the **Timber Market** (Map p336); it's hard to find so you'll need to ask someone to show you where

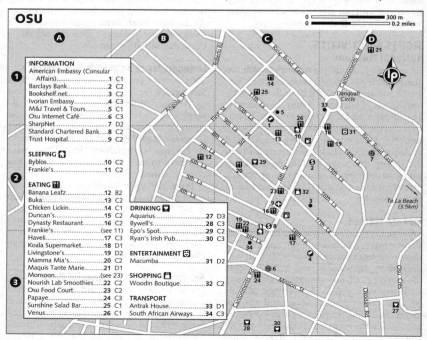

OSU

```
0          300 m
0          0.2 miles
```

INFORMATION
American Embassy (Consular Affairs)...............................1 C1
Barclays Bank..................................2 C2
Bookshelf.net...................................3 C2
Ivorian Embassy................................4 C3
M&J Travel & Tours........................5 C3
Osu Internet Café.............................6 C3
SharpNet...7 D2
Standard Chartered Bank............8 C2
Trust Hospital..................................9 C2

SLEEPING 🏠
Byblos...10 C2
Frankie's...11 C2

EATING 🍴
Banana Leafz.................................12 B2
Buka...13 C2
Chicken Lickin................................14 C1
Duncan's..15 C2
Dynasty Restaurant.......................16 C2
Frankie's.....................................(see 11)
Haveli..17 C3
Koala Supermarket........................18 D1
Livingstone's..................................19 D2
Mamma Mia's...............................20 C2
Maquis Tante Marie.......................21 D1
Monsoon.....................................(see 23)
Nourish Lab Smoothies..................22 C2
Osu Food Court.............................23 C2
Papaye...24 C2
Sunshine Salad Bar........................25 C1
Venus...26 C1

DRINKING 🍷
Aquarius...27 D3
Bywell's..28 C3
Epo's Spot......................................29 C2
Ryan's Irish Pub.............................30 C3

ENTERTAINMENT 🎭
Macumba..31 D2

SHOPPING 🛍️
Woodin Boutique............................32 C2

TRANSPORT
Antrak House.................................33 D1
South African Airways...................34 C3

Danquah Circle

To La Beach (3.5km)

To Mission St

Okodan Rd

THE LAST WORD IN STYLE

Being laid to rest inside a blushing-pink lobster may not be everyone's last request and there's certainly no guarantee you'll reach the afterlife faster in a coffin designed like a space shuttle. But for the last 50 or so years, a string of coffin designers in Ghana have been making death the last word in style. You can visit their workshops – fenced-in compounds that look more like fantasy farmyards than funeral parlours – in the Accra 'burbs of Teshie and La.

'We can make anything you want,' Daniel Oblie, who runs Hello Coffin Designs in Teshie, told us. Within reason, that is. Lions and tigers are usually reserved for village chiefs, and convention dictates that it's inappropriate to order, say, a coffin shaped like a jet plane when you're a modest taxi driver. Daniel's studio is teeming with every design imaginable, from crocodiles and roosters to bottles of palm oil, onions and cocoa beans. The last few years have seen Ghana embrace consumerism and orders for bottles of coke or bling-studded mobile phones are on the up.

But there's a serious edge to Ghana's lucrative coffin trade. Throughout West Africa, fancy funerals are viewed as the ultimate status symbol and families often spend more on them than weddings. Even some of the poorest families will pull together enough funds to spend on an elaborate funeral for relatives, even if it leaves them hungry for days. Fantasy coffins, the ultimate transport to the afterlife, cost between US$200 and $3000.

The caskets take around two weeks to make and some customers order in advance while others leave their last requests with relatives. Business, Daniel admits, can be hard to predict, but the coffin parlours get custom from tourists too, who sometimes take home miniature replicas to use for storage or souvenirs.

---

it is. The fetish section is fascinating, with its animal skulls, live and dead reptiles, strange powders, charms, bells, shakers, leopard skins, teeth, porcupine quills and *juju* figurines.

Head on to the **Holy Trinity Cathedral**, opposite Barclays on High St, which has a shady garden and, inside, a magnificent wooden barrel-vaulted roof.

WEB Du Bois Memorial Centre for Pan African Culture

Final resting place of the leading American/ naturalised Ghanaian who championed civil rights and pan-Africanism, the WEB Du Bois Memorial Centre (Map p336; 1st Circular Rd, Cantonments; entry C2; ☻ 8.30am-4.30pm Mon-Fri, 11am-4pm Sat) houses a research library for students of African unity and a collection of memorabilia. Towards the end of his life, Du Bois (pronounced as the American 'du boyse') was invited to Ghana to work on Nkrumah's Encyclopedia Africana; he died on this spot, in 1963, one day before Martin Luther King's 'I have a dream' speech.

Beaches

Accra's answer to Venice Beach or Bondi, **La Pleasure Beach** (Map p336; admission C2), also known as Labadi Beach, is about 8km east of central Accra, just before the Labadi Beach Hotel. Hot and hedonistic, at weekends the ocean is awash with the bold (undertows can be strong) and the beautiful. There's a lifeguard, as well as a few beachside eateries. Take a shared taxi or tro-tro from Tema station, Nkrumah Circle, any of the stops along Ring Rd Central or Labadi lorry station on High St. At the far quieter **Coco Beach**, about 7km further east towards Nungua, access to the beach is free or you can base yourself at the **New Coco Beach Hotel** which has a pool, bar and restaurant overlooking the shore. Take a taxi or tro-tro to Nungua and walk (about 20 minutes) or charter a taxi for the whole way.

SLEEPING

Accra has a good range of places to sleep, though prices are generally expensive. Osu is an excellent central base but the location usually commands hiked-up hotel bills. Cheaper options can be found around Ring Rd East, Adabraka and Asylum Down. Airport Residential, the pillow of politicians, is a leafy and luxurious part of town.

BUDGET

Accra's best budget options are outside of the city centre.

Savannah Seashore Inn (off Map p336; ☎ 024 3523 363; www.ghanaguesthouse.org; 35 Lagoon Rd, Teshie; d standard/king/superior C10/15/20) Owned by an American artist, this place makes simple seem sexy.

GHANA

GHANA

Basic mud huts with great ocean views, plenty of shade and a vegetarian snack bar. In the suburb of Teshie, about 25 minutes from the city depending on traffic.

Crystal (☎ 021 304 634; 27 Akorlu Close, Darkuman; camping US$15, dm/s/d US$10/15/20; 🖳 🛜) The hosts go out of their way to make travellers welcome at this lovely budget set-up in the quiet suburb of Darkuman. Rooms have private bathrooms, TV and fridges. There's a leafy communal lawn area, rooftop bar, wi-fi access and good Ghanaian food.

Kokomlemle Guesthouse (Map p338; ☎ 021 224 581; Oroko St, Kokolemle; r from C12) Basic, friendly and relaxed, the Kokomlemle has become something of a halfway house for long-term volunteers and travellers. Still, it's a good place for backpackers to crash too. Rooms are simple with shared bathrooms. Near the Technical Training College.

Anomomo Cultural Village (off Map p336; ☎ 024 4648 703; sharonswyer@hotmail.com; Korle Gonno; r C14) Everything is simple and ultra laid-back at this low-key beachfront set-up, run by a young, welcoming Ghanaian-British family. The handful of rooms (shared bathroom with buckets) attached to the family's outdoor courtyard, are basic and the decor is peeling. You'll sometimes hear reggae coming from the music room. Behind the Cambridge School in Korle Gonno.

New Haven (Map p338; ☎ 021 222 053; Ring Rd; s/d C15/28) For those who don't want to shell out to stay at the fancier Paloma eat-drink-sleep complex, this is an excellent compromise. Tucked behind that hotel on a back street, the New Haven is a nice place in its own right. Rooms are ensuite and spacious (some have enormous beds), there's a decent courtyard restaurant and you can pop into the Paloma for a beer. Book ahead.

Korkdam Hotel (Map p338; ☎ 021 226 797; 2nd Mango Tree Ave, Asylum Down; s/d C27/45; 🖳 🛜) The Korkdam's biggest draw is that it's one of the few budget options with (unreliable) wi-fi access. Rooms are large but shabby with running water, TVs, desks and paper-thin walls. Staff are friendly and there are usually charter taxis waiting nearby. A few steps from the Burkina Faso embassy.

Lemon Lodge (Map p338; ☎ 021 227 857; 2nd Mango Tree Ave, Asylum Down; r C20) Korkdam's next-door neighbour offers seven rooms arranged around a dingy reception area. Recent renovations have spruced the place up a little and

it's a reasonable budget option. Busy Internet is a 10-minute walk away.

Hansonic (☎ 021 300 849, 021 303 663; nr Kaneshie Market; s/d US$10/20, d with fan/air-con US$30/50; 🌐) This place gets top marks from budget travellers who don't mind being out in the sticks. Run by the man behind Cape Coast's kooky Hans Cottage Botel, rooms here are basic, clean and generally good value.

Ampax Hotel (Map p338; ☎ 021 234 157; Asylum Down; d with fan/air-con US$30/40; 🖳 🌐) A slightly more upmarket version of the Korkdam, this unfortunately-named hotel is in the same part of town. Rooms are bright, clean and good-value, though they're nothing to write poetry about. In theory, there's internet access.

MIDRANGE

Niagara Inn (Map p338; ☎ 021 230 118; niagara@ighmail .com; Adabraka; s/d US$40/60; 🌐 🖳) Down a quiet lane about 200m from Cantonments Rd, the Niagara has been hailed as the budget alternative to the (good) Niagara Plus down the road. Though this is not really a budget pick it is a reasonable one. Rooms are spacious and most have air-con.

Afia African Village (Map p336; ☎ 021 681 465; www.afiavillage.com; Liberia Rd; s/d C65/70, d with view C85; 🅿 🌐 🖳 🛜) One of the nicest places to stay in Accra. Though that might be because with a beachfront location, spectacular views and pretty garden, this doesn't feel like an Accra hotel at all. Rooms are beautifully furnished for this price bracket, and there's an art gallery, bar and the first-rate Tribes restaurant. Wi-fi is available for a fee.

Byblos (Map p340; ☎ 021 228 200; 11th Lane, Osu; r from US$65; 🌐 🖳 🛜) Smack bang in the middle of Osu, this is an excellent midrange option. There's a quiet courtyard set back from the main road and all 28 rooms are well-kept and air-conditioned, with hot water and wi-fi access. The adjacent Venus Cocktail Bar and Grill serves as the hotel's restaurant and offers good breakfasts.

Frankie's (Map p340; ☎ 021 773 567; www.frankies -ghana.com; Cantonments Rd, Osu; s/d US$59/98; 🌐 🖳 🛜) Frankie's is an Osu institution and an Accra landmark. Rooms here are stylish and clean and come with wi-fi access and hot running water. Downstairs, there's an ice-cream parlour, lounge bar and the famous fast-food joint of the same name. The front door opens out onto Oxford Street.

Paloma (Map p338; ☎ 021 228 700; Ring Rd Central; r from C70; [P] [icon] [icon] [icon]) Cool, comfortable rooms and bungalows with hot water, wi-fi and every comfort. The centrally-located complex includes several restaurants with good food (including breakfast pancakes), a sports bar, garden area and courtyard bar. There's car parking and a taxi service.

TOP-END

Esther's (Map p336; ☎ 021 772 368, 021 765 750; www .esthers-hotel.com; Volta St; Airport Residential Area; s/d/ste US$135/165/180; [icon] [icon] [icon] [icon]) This gorgeous boutique hotel will have you at hello. Set in a colonial-style building, the most expensive rooms are blessed with polished parquet floors, beautiful lamps, desks and sofas. Showers are hot and spacious, and there's wi-fi, satellite TV and a low-key restaurant that does fabulous breakfasts. Five minutes from Kotoka Airport by taxi.

Labadi Beach Hotel (Map p338; ☎ 021 772 501; www.legacyhotels.co.za; Labadi Beach; s/d US$270/310; [P] [icon] [icon] [icon]) Famous as much for its former guests – Tony Blair, Queen Elizabeth II – as for its comforts, the South African chain's offering is one of the most sumptuous in town. The stylish rooms, pool area and interior have a colonial twist and there's every style of room imaginable, including two specially-adapted rooms for disabled guests. Rates include a lavish breakfast.

La Palm Royal Beach Hotel (Map p336; ☎ 021 771 700; www.gbhghana.com; La Beach; r US$200-350; [P] [icon] [icon] [icon]) God forbid there should ever be a disaster in Accra, but if there were everyone would come here. It's a little city-state unto itself, complete with large conference centre, casino, several restaurants, a pool complex (the nicest in the city), a lounge with a big-screen TV, an ice-cream shop etc. Almost every expat in town on the weekend heads here at some point. There are rooms of varying size and quality.

Novotel Hotel (Map p338; ☎ 021 667 546; www .novotel.com; Barnes Rd, Accra North; r from US$170; [P] [icon] [icon] [icon]) Right in the crazy, chaotic heart of the city, the Novotel is a refuge of modernity and quiet. It's worth a stop at the pool or cafe if only to break up a day of sightseeing. All the rooms are modern and up to business-class quality; be sure to ask for one with a view. One of several international chains with a presence in Accra.

EATING

Accra has the best choice of restaurants in the country, and the food will seem like haute cuisine if you're returning to the city after time spent elsewhere in Ghana. Osu is China Town, Little Italy and your mall food court rolled into one long clogged road. Some of the upmarket restaurants where you'll spend at least C30 are found off the main road, down one of the residential streets.

Most of the midrange and all of the top-end hotels have restaurants and are especially recommended for breakfast splurges. If you're self-catering, the supermarkets in Osu are best, especially **Koala Supermarket** (Map p340; Cantonments Rd) just off Danquah Circle at the top of Cantonments Rd. **Max Mart** (Map p340; Liberation Rd) is another; note that it also accepts Visa cards. The **Accra Mall** (off Map p336; nr Tetteh Quarshie Interchange) is home to South African supermarkets Game and Shoprite; these are shinier, sleeker and cheaper than central Accra's equivalents.

African

La Tawala Spot (Map p336; South Labadi; plates around C3) Big, tasty plates of *jollof rice*, the sound of the ocean and a banter with the locals. Simple pleasures.

Buka (Map p340; 10th Lane; mains from C5) Dig into Ghanaian, Nigerian, Togolese and Senegalese specials at hip Buka. The stylish second-floor open-air dining room seals the deal.

Duncan's (Map p340; 10th Lane; mains from C5) Duncan's is another one of those low-key, outdoor chop bars that manages to get it right. Fresh, grilled fish and simple Ghanaian dishes draw a mixed, appreciative crowd.

Maquis Tante Marie (Map p336; ☎ 024 3225 181; www.maquistantemarie.com; Accra Mall; mains from C7) Hardly a *maquis*, this sumptuous dining room serves upscale versions of Ghanaian and other regional dishes, among them grilled *tilapia*, *fufu* and palmnut soup. There's another branch in North Labone (Map p340; ☎ 021 778914; 5th Norla Link, North Labone).

Tribes (Map p336; Afia African Village; mains from C7; [icon] 7am-10pm) While not quite haute cuisine, the excellent food and location make Tribes one of the best places to go for a relaxed supper. The decked outdoor dining area overlooks a lush garden. The vanilla ice cream with papaya and ginger sauce is recommended.

Livingstone's (Map p340; Osu; mains from C10) First-class West African and French food in an upmarket, atmospheric dining room. The French owner struck gold when he created this restaurant above a wine shop. If you're facing the entrance to Koala supermarket, it's the first right.

Rhapsody's (off Map p336; ☎ 024 3225 181; www.rhapsodys.co.za; Accra Mall; mains from C10) There's a light, stylish dining room and an outdoor patio at this South African–owned chain. The line-up includes dishes like avocado-brie fillet steak, African-inspired curries and chocolate fudge cake. There's a good wine list, too. It becomes a lively drinking spot on weekends.

Asian & Middle Eastern

Haveli (Map p340; 18th Lane; mains from C7; ✖) Bollywood, the Kama Sutra and the Taj Mahal; there are a thousand reasons to love the Indian subcontinent. Here's another. Push back the mosaic door to find a plain but atmospheric dining room and friendly servers. Excellent Indian and Pakistani dishes and not just chicken tikka masala either.

Banana Leafz (Map p340; 6th Lane, Osu; mains from C7; ✖) Indian-Indonesian fusion turned out to be an unhappy marriage. Separate menus it is then, at this not-so-atmospheric Osu eatery. Only really worth a visit if you're craving satay.

Venus (Map p340; 11th Lane, Osu; mains from C7; ✖ ⬁) It's not love, but it hits the spot. Excellent Lebanese dishes served in a friendly, laid-back indoor/outdoor setting. Grab one of the plush sofas at the back before the late-night drinks crowd arrives.

Dynasty (Map p340; Cantonments Rd; mains from C8; ✖) Though it does look somewhat regal, we're not sure what the name has to do with this fancy Chinese place. Joan Collins is nowhere in sight, and it's certainly not dy-nasty because the food here is excellent. White tablecloths and linen napkins. Sunday night is dim sum night.

Monsoon (Map p340; Oxford St; mains around C10; ✖) Who comes to Africa in search of the perfect California roll? You'd be surprised. West Africa has a number of great sushi bars and dressy Monsoon ranks somewhere in the middle. Overpriced sashimi served in a stylish dining room/open-air terrace.

European & American

The Orangery (Map p338; Farrar Ave, Adabraka; mains from C3) The Orangery is a pretty, if a little shabby, place decorated with potted plants and specialising in sweet and savoury pancakes, muffins,

waffles and crepes. Non-breakfast specialities include moussaka and seafood bouillabaisse.

Nourish Lab (Map p340; 3rd Lane; smoothies from C3; ⬁ 8am-10pm; ⬁) Escape the heat at this air-conditioned smoothie bar. The staff will whip up anything you fancy – though there's an extensive menu of good concoctions – while you sit back on the sofas, use the free wi-fi or watch MTV.

Sunshine Salad Bar (Map p340; ☎ 024 4383 064; Oxford St, Osu; mains C5-10; ⬁ 9am-5pm Mon-Sat) Like blue skies and lie-ins, everyone loves the Sunshine Bar. Plates brim high with wonderful big salads, wraps and brown-bread sarnies. There's a good range of fresh juices and vegetarian salads. There's also another branch on Embassy Rd which has a shady, fan-cooled outdoor courtyard.

Paloma Restaurant (Map p338; Ring Rd Central; mains from C5; ✖ ⬛) A safe bet, especially if you're feeling the need for comfort food. The line-up includes Ghanaian mains, mezze, burgers and sandwiches.

Mamma Mia's (Map p340; ☎ 021 264 151; 7th Lane; pizza from C7) Expats swear by the pizza here and the pretty outdoor garden dining area makes everything taste better. Spaghetti and kid-friendly chicken fingers are also served.

Frankie's (Map p340; Cantonments Rd; mains from C7; ⬁ 7am-midnight) You get stainless steel tables, big screen sports and a vast menu covering everything from hot dogs to mezze. Though it feels a bit like the kind of diner you might find at a bowling alley, Frankie's is a crowd-pleaser. Popular with tourists, volunteers, middle-aged professionals and Ghanaian teenagers on first dates. There's an ice-cream parlour in the same complex.

For a fast food fix, **Osu Food Court** (Map p340; Cantonments Rd; ✖ ⬛) is in a mini mall with a coffee shop and bakery, a pizza joint and a couple of fried-chicken places. **Papaye** (Map p340; Cantonments Rd) is the closest thing to the golden arches and **Chicken Lickin** (Map p340) is the winged-bird equivalent. The food court at the **Accra Mall** (off Map p336; nr Tetteh Quarshie Interchange) is also a good bet.

DRINKING

Accra's drinking spots start to fill up from about 7pm most evenings. Bars generally stay open late.

Aquarius (Map p340; Osu Crescent, Osu) This little place is tucked down one of Osu's winding residential streets, and has German beer on tap, German food on the menu and pub games like pool, pinball and darts.

Ryan's Irish Pub (Map p340; Osu; ⊠) This Osu gastro-pub is polished, homely and welcoming. If it's sweet stuff you're after, there's an excellent cocktail and dessert list (sticky toffee pudding, apple pie) but remaining true to its roots, there's beer on tap and footy on TV.

Epo's Spot (Map p340; Osu; ⊠) If the stars are out, you're in for a treat. Climb to the rooftop terrace of this low-slung building for cold drinks and good conversation. Epo's Spot is popular with Ghanaian couples who order simple dishes from the chop bar next door. If you can't see the stars, grab a bottled one instead.

The Office (Map p336; Osu; ⊠) Here's the deal; you're going to have to pay to go to work but in return, you can spend the day sipping cocktails and flirting with your hot colleagues. Deal? Furnished with desks and ring-binders, this theme bar feels like a drunken office party. Thankfully there's no photocopier but there is a cover charge on Friday and Saturday.

Bywell's (Map p340; Cantonments Rd, Osu) Live music Thursday and Saturday nights transforms this otherwise cool hangout at the southern end of Cantonments Rd into a fun party.

Champs (Map p338; Ring Rd Central; ⊠) Part of the Paloma Hotel complex, this expat hangout beams in sports from abroad. Thursday is quiz night, Friday is karaoke night, Saturday is live music night and Sunday movie night. One of the few places in Accra that serves Mexican food.

ENTERTAINMENT
Nightclubs
Accra is Ghana's biggest city and the birthplace of highlife, hip-life and other hybrid music genres so it's not surprising this city loves to dance. Thursday, Friday and Saturday are the big club nights and nowhere really gets going until 11pm or so. Osu is the biggest player on the drinking scene but there are club venues all over town. There's usually a cover charge (from around C5).

Tantra (Map p340; behind Barclays Bank, off Oxford St, Osu; cover C5-10; ⊠) Hip-hop and hands-in-the-air house at Accra's hottest superclub. Draws celebs and a mixed, fun crowd.

Aphrodisiac (Map p336; 48 Lumumba Rd, Airport Residential Area; cover C5-10; ⊠) Tantra's biggest competitor. Open Wednesday (francophone night) to Sunday, with ladies and old school nights in between.

Wakiki (Map p338; Nkrumah Ave) Famous for its Monday night sessions, you'll either get lost in the music or the building.

Macumba (Map p340; Ring Rd East) The music's still playing at Macumba, Accra's best-known club. These days it's more like a hot and sweaty hook-up joint.

Cinema
Arguably one of former president John Kufuor's biggest legacies was the creation of the Accra Mall (Map p336) which houses a plush five-screen **cinema complex** (nr Tetteh Quarshie Interchange; admission from C7; ⏰ 10.30am-midnight). Hollywood is served up alongside popcorn and bucket-sized cokes. Every Tuesday is film night at Alliance Française (p337).

For smaller-screen viewing, head to Busy Internet (p335), which shows DVD releases on weekend evenings. Champs (opposite) also shows films on Sunday night.

Theatre
National Theatre (Map p338; ☎ 021 666 986; Liberia Rd) This Chinese-built theatre looks like the base for an enormous eternal flame. There are performances by West African playwrights and by the excellent National Symphony Orchestra.

Sports
Accra's Ohene Djan Stadium was renovated ahead of the 2008 African Cup of Nations matches. It now has a capacity of 40,000, cafes, bars and private boxes and hosts matches between **Accra's Hearts of Oak** (www.accraheartsofoak .com) and other Ghanaian teams, as well as international fixtures.

Boxing is the second most popular sport, and fights are held Friday and Saturday night periodically from November to April at venues throughout Accra. Contact the **Accra Boxing Association** (☎ 021 760 892; Labone) for details of fights and amateur training.

SHOPPING
The **Arts Centre** (Map p338; 28th February Rd; ⏰ 9am-5pm), formerly known as the National Cultural Centre, is the place to shop for crafts in Accra. It has a reputation as a hard-sell outlet, but a smile and a bit of patience ease the pain of being constantly cornered. You can come away with good-quality handicrafts from all over Ghana, including batik, kente and other fabrics, beads, masks, woodcarvings, drums, brass and leatherwork.

GHANA

For altogether more sedate shopping the **Trade Fair Centre** (Map p336; off Burma Camp Rd, La) has several stores selling high-quality goods at fixed prices or try **Aid to Artisans Ghana** (Map p336; ATAG; www.ataggh.com; Trade Fair Centre, off Burma Camp Rd, La; 8am-5pm Mon-Fri, 10am-4pm Sat), an NGO that offers practical assistance to Ghanaian artisans of crafts and furniture. **Woodin Boutique** (Map p340; Cantonments Rd) in Osu is a chic fabric shop that sells some of the most attractive textiles in the city. The **Loom** (Map p338; 117 Nkrumah Ave), 200m south of Nkrumah Circle, sells moderately priced to expensive paintings as well as woodcarvings, fabrics and statues.

Look out for roadside stalls selling crafts, such as pottery and cane chairs on the northwest corner of Tetteh Quarshie interchange (opposite the Accra Mall), near 37 Circle, tie-dye clothes, paintings, prints, shoes, leather bags and woodcarvings around Danquah Circle and along Cantonments Rd in Osu, and woodcarvings near La Beach.

Makola Market and the area around is particularly rich in fabrics, including batik and tie-dye. Zongo Lane, not far from the post office, has rows of small shops offering colourful prints. Expensive Dutch wax cloth is everywhere, but you can also find almost identical cloth made by Akosombo Textile Co that is almost as good and much cheaper. The market is also good for glass beads, and you'll find second-hand clothing everywhere, sold for a few cedis.

Accra's second major market, **Kaneshie Market** (Map p336; Winneba Rd) on the western side of the city, is also a good place to look for beads and textiles as well as basic goods and foodstuffs. Music CDs, some original, some bad copies – ask before buying – of Ghanaian and other African pop stars are sold around both markets, as are mostly poor-quality pirated knock-offs of Nigerian and Hollywood films. Shoes are another staple of Accra markets – for that matter anywhere in the country – though most come with names like 'Babidas' and upside-down swooshes which look eerily similar to another well-known trademark; better quality, handmade leather shoes are also sold.

On the outskirts of town, the shiny **Accra Mall** (off Map p336; 021 823 040; nr Tetteh Quarshie Interchange) is shopping heaven. Stores like Body Basics sell perfume, nail colours and make-up, while ZigZag, Lorinda and Kiki have racks of African and imported clothes. Stepping into South African supermarkets Game and Shoprite is air-conditioned bliss. You'll also find sports and electrics stores (selling digital camera cards), a five-screen cinema and an excellent food court.

If you want to take home an unusual souvenir, **Trashy Bags** (www.trashybags.org) are fashioned from thrown-away water sachets and recycled flour sacks. You can find them in stores in Accra and Cape Coast.

GETTING THERE & AWAY
Air
Kotoka international airport (Map p336) is served by major airlines, including British Airways, KLM–Royal Dutch Airlines, Air Kenya, Air Afriqiyah, South African Airways and the flag-bearing Ghana International Airways.

For a list of airline offices situated in Accra see p391.

Bus & Tro-tro
The main **STC bus station** (Map p336; 021 221 414/221 912/221 942; Ring Rd) is just east of Lamptey Circle. Buses leave hourly from early morning to early evening for Kumasi (C10, four to six hours) and Takoradi (C7, four hours), and four times a day to Cape Coast (C3.50, three to four hours) and Tamale (C21, 12 to 13 hours). STC buses also serve Ho (C3.50, four hours), Hohoe (C5, 3½ hours), Kpando and Aflao on the Togo border. All timetables and prices can change without warning; your best bet is to head to the station a day before departure to check and ideally to purchase tickets in advance. Other destinations include Wa, Bolgatanga (C24) and Bawku with trips three days a week. There are fewer trips on all routes on Sunday.

Private buses and tro-tros leave from four main motor parks. Those for Cape Coast, Takoradi and other destinations to the west leave from Kaneshie motor park, 500m northwest of Lamptey Circle. Neoplan motor park, 250m west of Nkrumah Circle, has buses to north points such as Kumasi and Tamale. From Tema station east of Makola market, tro-tros leave for local destinations as well as Tema and Aburi. From the chaotic **Tudu bus station** (Map p338; Makola Market) at the northeast corner of the market, tro-tros leave for destinations such as Aflao, Ada, Keta, Hohoe and Akosombo. In addition, there's a small station tucked in behind Tema station from which tro-tros go to Ho and Hohoe. Kingdom Transport Services (KTS) runs comfortable minivans with leather seats and air-con to Ho from here.

Train
There are train services between Accra and some suburbs, and between Kumasi and Takoradi, but these take forever and timetables are unreliable. For more details, see p393.

GETTING AROUND
To/From the Airport
When you step outside Accra's modern Kotoka international airport, you'll be ushered to the taxi rank for the journey into central Accra. Drivers may claim a set fare but there isn't one; you'll pay at least C5 (and sometimes a lot more) depending on where you're heading. You can gain an idea from what is fair from airport staff and Ghanaians on your flight; taxi fares fluctuate according to the price of gas and the shape of Ghana's economy. Tro-tros and shared taxis also leave from the small, well-organised station within the airport compound, though you'll have to wait for them to fill up.

Shared Taxis & Tro-Tros
Shared taxis and tro-tros travel on fixed runs from major landmarks or between major circles, such as Danquah, 37 and Nkrumah (usually just called 'Circle'). Fares are usually very cheap. Major routes include Circle to Osu via Ring Rd; Circle to the central post office via Nkrumah Ave; Tudu station to Kokomlemle; 37 Circle to Osu; Makola Market to Osu; and Circle to the airport. Major shared taxi and local tro-tro parks include Tema station and the ones at Nkrumah Circle and 37 Circle. In addition, transport to La leaves from the taxi park at Nkrumah Circle or from Labadi lorry station on High St.

At the stations, tro-tros and shared taxis often have the destination written on a placard. Elsewhere, flag one down and shout your destination – if they're going your way, they'll stop and pick you up. For Nkrumah Circle, point the index finger of your right hand towards the ground and make a circular motion.

Private Taxi
Taking taxis in Accra is convenient but since there are no meters the unavoidable haggling can get tiring. You will probably first be quoted a ridiculous amount. If you reply with an even more ridiculous low-ball you should be able to find your way to something fair. Any ride within the city shouldn't cost more than C6; short hops should be around half that price. Though most streets do have names in Accra, landmarks are a much more popular way of identifying a destination. If you're heading to one of the lanes in Osu, telling the driver it's near Frankie's is a much better plan than specifying the number and the lane. There's no need to sit in the back of Ghanaian taxis unless you really want to; riding up-front is expected.

AROUND ACCRA

UNIVERSITY OF GHANA
The University of Ghana was founded in 1948 on the northern fringes of Accra, 14km from the city centre in Legon. Its **Balme Library** (8am-4.30pm Mon-Sat) has a rich collection dating from the colonial era. Its botanical gardens are run down, but they're a pleasant place for a stroll. The university bookshop is probably the best in the country. To get there, tro-tros leave from Tema station in Accra or from the Ako Adjei Overpass.

ABURI BOTANICAL GARDENS & AKWAPIM HILLS
Built as the classic British hill station, a cool mountain retreat from the oppressive heat of the lowlands, Aburi still retains a hint of its former therapeutic appeal, at least as far as temperatures and views go. On clear days you can see Accra in the plains below, only 34km away. The entrance to the **botanical gardens** (8am-6pm), about 200m up from the tro-tro station, are framed by two rows of towering palm trees. The gardens themselves make for a peaceful stroll though they're not of the finely manicured variety. Established in 1890 with seedlings from all over the British Empire, they are home to an impressive variety of tropical and subtropical plants and trees. The oldest tree, more than 150 years old, is a huge kapok tree facing the headquarters building. It's the only indigenous one the British didn't cut down.

GHANA

The botanical gardens are the obvious tourist focus, though it's really the surrounding beautiful Akwapim Hills that warrant anything more than a day trip out here. The area is one of the best places in the country to explore by pedal power thanks to the enthusiastic **Aburi Bike & Hike Tours** (☎ 024 267 390); the small office is on the second floor of a home at the southern entrance of the gardens. A mountain bike, helmet, backpack, maps and repair kit plus a shower on return costs around C5. Day-long bike sessions or overnight guided biking and hiking tours are also offered.

Sleeping & Eating

Aburi Botanical Gardens Resthouse (☎ 087 622 022; r around C20) Unfortunately the resthouse here probably hasn't changed much since the colonial days, and while the surroundings are leafy the rooms are rundown. Some of the upstairs rooms have good views and therefore may be a better option than the bungalows.

Little Acre Hotel (☎ 087 622 078; r from C20) This is a little over 2km before Aburi on the road from Accra.

Rose Plot Restaurant is attached to the resthouse and prepares basic fare while the Royal Botanical Gardens Restaurant just down the hill has a better selection and pretty views.

Getting There & Away

Tro-tros to Aburi (C1, 1½ hours) leave regularly from the far eastern end of Tema station, behind the Makola Market in Accra, though the wait can be a half-hour or longer. You may have to wait a while for transport back to Accra on a Sunday. Regular shared taxis run north from Aburi to towns such as Mampong, Adukrom and Somanya, from where you can get connections to Kpong (for Akosombo and Ho) and Koforidua.

THE COAST

Ghana's stunning coastal region, stretching 550km from Côte d'Ivoire to Togo, is a place to worship the sun and confront the past. It's shingled with the remains of colonial castles, their roots firmly planted in the gold and slave trade. Follow the coastline and you'll find perfect party beaches, secluded honeymoon spots, slices of rainforest and world-class waves.

KOKROBITE BEACH
☎ 027

Coming from Accra, Kokrobite is a breath of fresh air. Endowed with a stretch of long white sand, the village has become something of an institution among backpackers and volunteers. Kokrobite is only 32km from the big smoke, but it feels a million miles away. All you'll need here is a pair of flip flops, a beach towel and a book to read. Though small and sleepy, the town is charming in a laid-back, bohemian way.

Drumming lessons are the main draw here and are a big hit with tired volunteers who are feeling out of sync. The Academy of African Music and Arts (AAMAL), founded by top percussionist Mustafa Tettey Addy, runs courses (from two hours to three

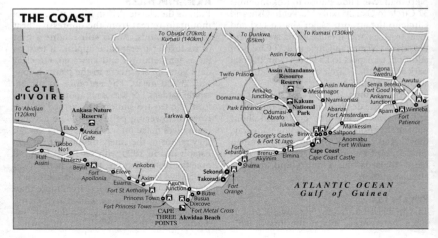
THE COAST

months) in African rhythms, tunes and dance. You can learn to play the balafon, a large wooden West African xylophone that resembles a rickety, wooden-planked bridge. Classes in *mbira*, the Zimbabwean equivalent, are also on offer. It's a 20-minute walk from Big Milly's along the beach. On Saturday and Sunday afternoon, let the rhythm grab a hold of you at one of AAMAL's live shows (usually about 3pm).

Between August and March beautiful leatherback turtles nest on the beach. You can also hire bodyboards and surfboards, though the swell is generally better further west. If you are going to swim or surf, always check conditions with the locals. There can be a powerful undertow on the beach.

Despite the good-times vibe, Kokrobite is a traditional coastal village and many people barely eke out a living. Theft can be a problem so it's wise to err on the side of caution, especially when out after dark.

Sleeping & Eating

Big Milly's Backyard (☎ sms 0287 288 889, 0242 206 971; www.bigmilly.com; camping with own/rented tent C3.50/6.50, dm/s C4.50/10, loft C3.50, d without/with bathroom C20/23, ste C65; P 🖭 🖳) Also known as Wendy's Place, Big Milly's is one of the most famous beachfront set-ups in Ghana. Here, hammocks sway from skinny palm trees, backpackers peruse the cocktail list and volunteers grab bar meals, served with a healthy dollop of laid-back hedonism. At weekends, the place erupts into a party, with live bands, ice-cold beers, bonfires

and barbecues. There's no need to shell out for the gorgeous suite; the regular rooms are clean, comfortable and artfully-decorated. Massages can also be arranged.

Kokrobite Gardens (☎ sms 0246 785 746; r C12; P) Even more relaxed than its neighbour, this Italian restaurant in a lush garden setting behind Big Milly's has a small selection of rooms and a large selection of great pastas and pizzas (from C4), made fresh.

Kokrobite Beach Resort (AAMAL; ☎ 024 380 854; s/d US$11/13; P) A beautiful 20-minute walk along the beach and up and over rocky outcroppings from Big Milly's – a road goes here as well – takes you to this rustic, seemingly abandoned resort famed for the attached AAMAL drumming school. The large rooms are old but the warped wooden floors charming and there's a simple restaurant and bar on the premises.

Bojo Beach Resort (☎ 0242 325 169; afamefuna14@ hotmail.com; P) Small boats shuttle guests across the freshwater lagoon to a beautiful stretch of sandy beach where you can order drinks and food and hire boogie or surfboards or just luxuriate in the quiet.

Getting There & Around

Tro-tros (C0.50, 45 minutes) to Kokrobite go from the western end of Kaneshie motor park in Accra. Depending on your ability to negotiate, a taxi from Accra will cost from C8 to C20.

FETE, SENYA BEREKU & BUDUMBURAM
☎ 027

Part beach-town with surf, part attractive fishing village, Fete (also known as Gomoa Fetteh) is set on a hill on the coast between Accra and Winneba. Senya Bereku, about 5km west, is the site of the impressive **Fort Good Hope** (admission C2), built by the Dutch in 1702. Originally intended for the gold trade, the fort was expanded in 1715 when it was converted into a slave prison. Well restored, it sits on the edge of a cliff above the beach and has good views. Shared taxis regularly ply between the villages or you could walk (with a guide).

About 4km from Fete is the settlement of Budumburam, which contrasts sharply with the beach life of Fete. It once housed 40,000 Liberian and Sierra Leonean war refugees. There's not much to see here, and at the time of writing you could not enter the settlement, but because of their interaction with West

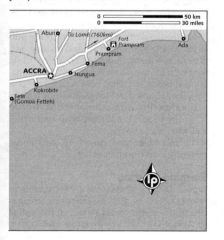

GHANA

GHANA

GOT NO COUNTRY

Thirty-five kilometres from Accra is a no-man's land of winding alleys, peeling concrete shacks and dirty yellow footpaths. This is Budumburam, which once housed 40,000 Liberian and Sierra Leonean refugees who had fled bloody conflicts in their homelands. As fighting raged on, months turned into years and flimsy tarpaulin tents turned into concrete homes. When the closure of Budumburam was announced in 2008/09, the stream of refugees trickled out of Ghana, returning to countries recovering from two of the worst conflicts West Africa has ever seen.

Some however, like Sunny Kolleh, a Liberian refugee, didn't want to go home, opting to resettle in Budumburam's neighbouring village. 'I'm staying in Ghana,' he told us. 'Why not? I have no other place to go.' Kolleh lost his house and family in the war. 'For now, I've decided to settle here in Ghana. I've made some Ghanaian friends. I don't have the right to vote in Ghana and I will never become a citizen, but I am happy to be able to stay. Life is better here – it's not perfect, but it's better for me. I think Ghana is very developed,' he said. At weekends, Kolleh goes down to the local football pitch, where he competes in Liberia v Ghana football matches. But even he admits he doesn't know which side to play for any more.

African refugees, the locals here have an interesting perspective on life; see the boxed text, above.

Sleeping & Eating

Till's No 1 (☎ 027 559 480, 0242 855 035; tillsbeachhotel.com; s/d US$50/60; P 🍴 🖳 🏊) Though not as fancy as the White Sands, Till's is still an attractive place to stay. This German-owned resort has comfortable rooms with balconies and sea views and a veritable Olympics worth of equipment for water and other games, including beach volleyball. There's a decent onsite restaurant. It's signposted as you enter Fete.

White Sands Beach Club (☎ 021 303 889; r from US$100; P 🍴 🖳 🏊) The spacious, individually designed Moroccan-themed villas at the White Sands are some of the nicest accommodation in Ghana. They're located on a spectacular beach with three superb restaurants. Bear left as you enter Fete and follow the main road down through the village until you reach the resort gates.

Fort Good Hope (r with fan US$7) Although it once held slaves in its dungeon, this fort has been developed into a guest house. You can sleep here in very basic rooms with shared bathrooms (bucket showers); it has a nice, breezy sitting area upstairs and a restaurant and bar on the premises.

Though not a perennial option, **Emily's Place** (behind Till's No 1) also sometimes has budget rooms.

Getting There & Away

From Kaneshie motor park in Accra, there are direct tro-tros to Senya Bereku (one

hour). Tro-tros also ply the scenic but bumpy cross-country route between Winneba and Senya Bereku (40 minutes). For Fete, take a Winneba-bound tro-tro from Accra and stop at Awutu junction on the main road, from where you can get a tro-tro direct to the village. Budumburam can be reached by shared or private taxi from Fete.

WINNEBA
☎ 0432

Traditionally known as Simpa, breezy Winneba gets props for its excellent University College of Education (UCEW), one of the best in West Africa and sometimes dubbed the Oxford of Ghana. It's good but it's not that good. The town itself is the largest between Accra and Cape Coast and on the first weekend in May, hosts the famous **Aboakyer** (Deer Hunt Festival).

On the outskirts of town, fishing boats pull in from early morning to around midday, and dozens of fishermen haul in their nets while singing a rousing tune. An impressive, palm-fringed beach stretches west from here for a couple of kilometres, though the slope is steep and swimming isn't recommended. Inland from the beach, the lagoon is an important wetland area for birds.

There's a Ghana Commercial Bank and a post office on Commercial St.

Sleeping & Eating

Lagoon Lodge (☎ 0432 22435; www.lagoon-lodge-winneba.com; r C8-35; P) This charming set-up is one of the nicest places to stay in the radius of Accra. It's rare in Ghana to find such a well-run, professional yet hospitable hotel and at budget prices no less. Run by Ghanaians with Aussie links, the Lagoon has 19 small, modern, perfectly kept rooms with enormous bathrooms and a pleasant courtyard restaurant (mains from C4) and bar that catches a great breeze in the evening. It's reached by heading down a winding track through the fields, signposted off the beach road.

Ghana Armed Forces Resthouse (☎ 043 22208; r C7) If you're contemplating staying anywhere other than the Lagoon Lodge, this place is worth a shot. Strictly utilitarian concrete, though it's in a peaceful enough setting on a hill overlooking the lagoon. Follow the road up past the UCEW South Campus and, where it forks, take the road on the right.

The restaurant at the Lagoon Lodge is the best place to eat and does great grilled seafood. There are several basic eateries serving cheap Ghanaian food on Commercial St and the road leading towards the UCEW South Campus.

Halo Halo is a typical spot for icy beers, though the food here gets mixed reviews and the music is loud. **Hut de Eric** (Hwy junction; mains C3) is the most comfortable restaurant you'll find in the area; it's a modern, large pavilion with outdoor seating serving Ghanaian staples and grilled meats.

Getting There & Away

Winneba is about 6km south of the main coastal road. There's a bus station in the town but tro-tros stop at the junction on the coastal road. Regular shared taxis (C0.40) run between the junction and Winneba town. Tro-tros to Winneba leave from Kaneshie motor park in Accra (C1.50, 1¼ hours) or from the Accra station in Cape Coast (1½ hours). From the junction, plenty of transport runs in both directions.

APAM

☎ 0432

For many travellers Apam is simply another of the pleasant villages that freckle Ghana's sunburned coastline. But colourful fishing boats and fantastic views from the ramparts of **Fort Patience** (admission C3) make Apam, 20km west of Winneba, worth a visit. The fort, built by the Dutch in 1697, is set on a hill overlooking the village and picturesque fishing harbour at one end of a wide sandy bay. Near the harbour is a great three-storey *posuban* (shrine), with mounted horsemen overlooked by a white-robed Jesus.

The fort also functions as a **guest house** (r C3). Very basic rooms with shared bathroom (bucket shower) are available. Simple meals can be prepared on request or there are food stalls along the main street. **Lynnbah Guesthouse** (☎ 0246 359 680; r C3), about 1km from the tro-tro station, is a more homely place to sleep.

Apam is about 9km south of Ankamu junction on the main coastal road, from where regular shared taxis and tro-tros run down to the village. Any tro-tro running between Cape Coast and Winneba or Accra will be able to drop you at the junction.

SALTPOND & ABANZE

There's nothing spectacular to draw you to **Saltpond**, though it's pleasant and friendly. In the town centre there is an interesting *posuban* reminiscent of those in Anomabu, complete with statues of weird and wonderful creatures. Two kilometres from Saltpond is the settlement of **Abanze**. The stirring remains of **Fort Amsterdam** (admission C3; 9am-5pm), also known as Fort Kormantin, are visible from the main coastal road, about 32km northeast of Cape Coast. The fort has a fantastic location high on a hill above Abanze village, and the views from the ramparts are wonderful. Established in 1598 by the Dutch, it was rebuilt by the English in 1645 as their first settlement along the coast of the Gulf of Guinea and named Fort York. When the Dutch recaptured it in 1665, they renamed it Fort Amsterdam as a stylish thumbing of the nose at the English who, the previous year and on the other side of the Atlantic, had taken possession of New Amsterdam and re-christened it New York. The fort is only partially restored, giving it a poignancy that many of the white-washed castles elsewhere along the coast lack.

Transport going west to Cape Coast can drop you at Abanze. From Cape Coast, take a tro-tro (20 minutes, C0.40) from Kotokuraba station as you head towards Mankessim and get off when you see the fort up on the hill to your right, just before Abanze. Returning to Cape Coast you may have to wait a while for an empty seat.

ANOMABU

☎ 042

Many travellers rate Anomabu's stunning beaches as second only to those further west, like Busua and Akwidaa. The sands and ribbons of low-key surf are certainly a big draw, but the village itself occupies an entirely different universe. There, life can be tough, contrasting sharply with a stay at one of the resorts. It's nice to see both sides of Anomabu; the village has its charms, among them seven **posubans**. The easiest to find is Company No 3's, which features a whale between two lions. It's about 50m from the main road, opposite the Ebeneezer Hotel. The most spectacular shrine is the one in the form of a large painted ship; it's in the area just west of **Fort William** (built by the British in 1753) which is now a prison.

The **Okyir Festival** is often held in the second week of October and is traditionally believed to cleanse the community from evil, hunger and disease.

Sleeping & Eating

Anomabu Beach Resort (☎ 024 291 562; anomabu@ hotmail.com; camping with own/rented tent US$6/15, hut without/with air-con US$27/38; P ⚡) Volunteers in need of downtime dream about this place. So, for that matter, do expats from all over West Africa, families included. Attractive bungalows set within a sandy and shady grove of coconut palms make it a favourite among backpackers too. You'll spend most of your time lounging on the beautiful white-sand beach or chowing down on seafood at the exquisite wood pavilion restaurant. Rates are higher on Friday and Saturday night.

Biriwa Beach Resort (☎ 0244 446 277; s/d with seaview US$50/60; P) This German-run resort has a shabby chic feel and fabulous views out over the ocean.

Getting There & Away

From Cape Coast, take a tro-tro (15 minutes) from Kotokuraba station heading for Mankessim and ask to be dropped at the Ebeneezer Rest Stop for Anomabu town; or at the turn-off for the beach resort, which is about 2km west of the Ebeneezer. From the turn-off, it's about 500m to the resort gates. The main tro-tro and shared taxi stop in Anomabu is just east of the Ebeneezer and plenty of vehicles run in both directions along the main coastal road.

CAPE COAST

☎ 042

Forever haunted by the ghosts of the past, Cape Coast is one of the most culturally-significant

spots in Africa. This former European colonial capital, originally named Cabo Corso by the Portuguese, was once the largest slave-trading centre in West Africa. At the height of the slave trade it received a workforce from locations as far as Niger and Burkina Faso. These men and women were kept locked up in the bowels of Cape Coast's imposing castle. From the shores of this seaside town, slaves were herded onto vessels like cattle, irrevocably altering the lives of generations to come.

Today, Cape Coast is an easy-going fishing town with an arty vibe, fanned by salty sea breezes and kissed by peeling waves. Crumbling colonial buildings still line the streets, while seabirds prowl the beaches and fishermen cast nets where slave ships once sailed. There's a host of good restaurants and bars, making Cape Coast a logical base for Kakum National Park and the sandy beaches further downstream.

Information

BOOKSHOPS

Black Star Bookshop (☎ 0244 928 737; Commercial St) Helpful owner stocks a good selection of page-turners.

INTERNET ACCESS

Cornell Internet (Commercial St; ☉ 9am-6pm)
Ocean View Internet (Commercial St; ☉ 24 hr) A few dozen computers. Printing, scanning, CD burning.

MONEY

There aren't many forexes in town. Coastal Forex on Jackson St is reliable.
Barclays Bank (Commercial St) Can change travellers cheques and cash; has an ATM.
Standard Chartered Bank (Chapel Sq) Near the tourist office. Can change travellers cheques and cash; has an ATM.

POST

Post office (Attebury Rd)

TOURIST INFORMATION

Tourist office (☎ 042 30265; off Jackson St; ☉ 8am-5pm Mon-Fri) On the 1st floor of Heritage House, a restored colonial-era building. Unless you're collecting brochures, the city itself is a better guide.

Sights

CAPE COAST CASTLE

Cape Coast's imposing, whitewashed **castle** (adult/student US$7/4, camera fee C0.50; ☉ 9am-5pm) commands the heart of town, overlooking the sea. First converted into a castle by the Dutch in 1637 and expanded by the Swedes in 1652, the castle changed hands five times over the 13 tumultuous years that followed until, in 1664, it was captured by the British. During the two centuries of British occupation, it was the headquarters for the colonial administration until Accra was declared the new capital in 1877.

Now extensively restored, Cape Coast castle deserves as much time as you can give it. Mountains of rusty cannonballs line the route walked by slaves and castle staff conduct excellent tours of the grounds every hour or so (less frequently on Sunday). You'll be shown into the dark, damp dungeons, where slaves sat waiting for two to 12 weeks, all the while contemplating rumours that only hinted at their fate. A visit to the condemned slave cell (not for the claustrophobic) contrasts sharply with the incredible Governor's bedroom, blessed with floor-to-ceiling windows and panoramic views of the ocean.

There's also an excellent museum on the first floor, detailing the history of Ghana, the slave trade and Akan culture. The castle

buildings, constructed around a trapezoidal courtyard facing the sea, and the dungeons below, provide a horrifying insight into the workings of a Gold Coast slaving fort. The guided tour, which lasts about an hour, ends with a passage through the Door of No Return.

FORT WILLIAM & FORT VICTORIA

It's worth the short but steep hikes up to Fort William, which dates from 1820 and now functions as a lighthouse, and Fort Victoria, originally built in 1702 and heavily restored in the 19th century, for the spectacular views. The castle and the two lonely look-outs originally formed a triangular lookout system between which signals could be passed. You can't go inside either of the forts.

Courses

Global Mamas (www.globalmamas.org) is connected to Women in Progress, a nonprofit group encouraging the growth of women-owned enterprises in Africa. It offers courses in fishing (C17), Ghanaian cookery (C25)

GHANA

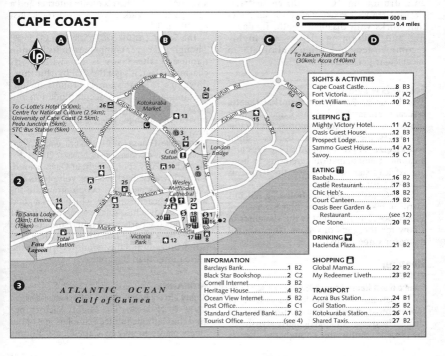

CAPE COAST

SIGHTS & ACTIVITIES	
Cape Coast Castle	8 B3
Fort Victoria	9 A2
Fort William	10 B2

SLEEPING	
Mighty Victory Hotel	11 A2
Oasis Guest House	12 B3
Prospect Lodge	13 B1
Sammo Guest House	14 A2
Savoy	15 C1

EATING	
Baobab	16 B2
Castle Restaurant	17 B3
Chic Heb's	18 B2
Court Canteen	19 B2
Oasis Beer Garden & Restaurant	(see 12)
One Stone	20 B2

DRINKING	
Hacienda Plaza	21 B2

INFORMATION	
Barclays Bank	1 B2
Black Star Bookshop	2 C2
Cornell Internet	3 B2
Heritage House	4 B2
Ocean View Internet	5 B2
Post Office	6 C1
Standard Chartered Bank	7 B2
Tourist Office	(see 4)

SHOPPING	
Global Mamas	22 B2
My Redeemer Liveth	23 B2

TRANSPORT	
Accra Bus Station	24 B1
Goil Station	25 B2
Kotokuraba Station	26 A1
Shared Taxis	27 B2

Map labels: To Kakum National Park (30km); Accra (140km); Residential Rd; Governor Rowe Rd; Sarbah Rd; Attebury Rd; Ashanti Rd; Slam Rd; Kotokuraba Market; Kotokuraba Rd; Commercial St; London Bridge; Crab Statue; Johnston Rd; Aboom Wells Rd; Aboom Rd; Coronation Rd; Wesley Methodist Cathedral; Beulah La; Royal St; Jackson St; Jukwa Rd; To C-Lotte's Hotel (500m); Centre for National Culture (2.5km); University of Cape Coast (2.5km); Pedu Junction (5km); STC Bus Station (5km); To Sanaa Lodge (2km); Elmina (15km); Market St; Total Station; Victoria Park; Victoria Rd; Intsin St; Fosu Lagoon; ATLANTIC OCEAN; Gulf of Guinea; To Kakum National Park

GHANA'S COASTAL FORTS

The chain of forts and castles (the terms are used interchangeably) along Ghana's coast is an extraordinary historical monument, unique in West Africa. Most of the forts were built during the 17th century by various European powers, including the British, Danes, Dutch, French, Germans, Portuguese and Swedes, who were vying for commercial dominance of the Gold Coast and the Gulf of Guinea. Competition was fierce and the forts changed hands like a game of musical chairs. By the end of the 18th century, there were 37 along the coastline. The forts were concentrated along this relatively short (around 500km) stretch of coast because access to the interior was relatively easy compared with the more swampy coastlines elsewhere along the West African coast, and because the rocky shore provided building materials. They were fortified not against the locals, with whom they traded equitably, but against attack from other European traders.

The forts were originally established as trading posts to store goods bought to the coast, such as gold, ivory and spices. Later, as the slave trade took over, they were expanded into prisons for storing slaves ready for shipping. Slaves were packed into dark, overcrowded and unsanitary dungeons for weeks or months at a time. If you tour some of the forts, you'll leave with a deep impression of just how brutally the captives were treated. When a ship arrived, they were shackled and led out of the forts to waiting boats through the Door of No Return.

If your time is limited, make sure you visit at least Cape Coast Castle (p352), which houses a superb museum, and St George's Castle (p357) at Elmina, both of which are deservedly Unesco World Heritage sites. With a bit more time, you could also visit Fort Metal Cross (p360) at Dixcove, Fort Amsterdam (p351) at Abanze and Fort Princes Town (p363) at Princes Town, all of which are atmospheric and have great settings. Fort Good Hope (p349) at Senya Bereku and Fort Patience (p351) at Apam are also worth a visit; both overlook busy fishing harbours.

and drumming (C15). **African Footprint** (☎ 042 31686; www.africanfootprint.dk) is an NGO that works with disabled youth. Its dancing and drumming classes are highly recommended and often culminate in spectacular performances.

Festivals & Events

The biennial **Pan-African Historical Theatre Festival** (Panafest), is held in Cape Coast. It showcases African contemporary and traditional arts, including music, dance, fashion and theatre. There are political lectures and a candlelit emancipation ceremony to honour African slaves. Of course, the festival is studded with parties too.

Cape Coast's **Fetu Afahye Festival**, a raucous carnival, takes place on the first Saturday of September. The highlight is the slaughter of a cow for the gods of Oguaa (the original name for Cape Coast).

Sleeping

BUDGET

Sammo Guest House (☎ 042 33242; Jukwa Rd; r C7.50-25; 💻) Sammo's corridors lead to a variety of rooms, most of which are comfortable and clean. The decor isn't particularly stylish but the place is comfortable enough and attracts

a young crowd. There's onsite internet and a little garden. Walk down a short track, just off Jukwa Rd.

The Savoy (☎ 042 32805; Sam Rd; r C13.50-69) Though it'll never compete with its London namesake, the Savoy is not without its charms. In fact, it's got the shabby-chic thing down to a T. There's a mix of rooms, including simple backpacker accommodation and larger chalets. Ancient Greek-style statues inhabit the lounge. There's an internet cafe next door.

Oasis Guest House (☎ 042 35958; ali_d@gmx.da; opp Victoria Rd; huts with shared/private bathroom C15/25; 🅿) Like a hip party spot, a night at Oasis is loud, hot and sweaty. Backpackers, volunteers and Cape Coast's beautiful people gravitate towards the beachfront bar, which does a good line in sandwiches, salads and cocktails. At weekends the party atmosphere lingers once you get back to your hut, where impotent fans turn fruitlessly and tiny windows bring in the noise rather than the breeze.

MIDRANGE

Mighty Victory Hotel (☎ 042 30135; r with fan/air-con C20/30; 🅿 ✖ 💻 🛜) The Mighty Victory, behind the Catholic Jubilee School, is one of the nicest places to stay in Cape Coast. Rooms are modern and cool, with crisp white sheets and hot running water. There's a good onsite restaurant, speedy wi-fi (for a fee) and the American-Ghanaian owners are friendly and welcoming. Mighty fine.

C-Lotte's Hotel (☎ 042 36393; www.c-lotteshotel.com; r with fan/air-con US$25/38; P ✹) The exterior of this three-storey hotel is tattooed with images of Ghanaian drummers and dancers. Step inside to find spacious, comfortable rooms with a touch of style.

Prospect Lodge (☎ 042 31506; www.prospectlodge .com; s/d US$25/40; P ✹ ▢ ⎵) Cape Coast's closest thing to a boutique hotel. Atop a steep hill, Prospect Lodge has fabulous views of the city, a terrace bar-restaurant and wi-fi. Rooms aren't particularly jazzy but they are bright and spacious, and the whole set-up has a great ambiance. The entrance is opposite the 'Man, Know Thyself' hardware store.

TOP END

Cape Coast Hotel (☎ 0233 4232 919; r US$45-55; P ✹) Popular with regional visitors, this smart, friendly hotel features huge, carpeted rooms with all mod cons. There's a decent onsite restaurant and pleasant grounds.

Sanaa Lodge (☎ 0233 4232 570; s/d US$65/80; P ✹ ⎙) On a hill overlooking the beach near the westernmost entrance to town, the Sanaa Lodge, Cape Coast's most upscale hotel, enjoys a tranquil location and rooms with all the modern amenities. The pool and poolside grill are worth the price alone.

Eating & Drinking

Restaurants in Cape Coast close fairly early; plan to eat before 9pm. Bars are open much later, especially on weekends.

Baobab (Commercial Rd; mains from C2; ☽ 9am-5pm) A hip organic food bar with a wholesome touch. Cecilia serves up great aubergine sarnies, soy lattes and glasses of *bissap* juice, a Senegalese staple made from hibiscus and ginger. Profits from the adjacent shop go to a local children's foundation.

One Stone (opp Oasis Guest House; mains from C2) This little place with a Rasta spin has backpacker breakfasts nailed. The menu includes fresh banana juice and chocolate pancakes (it's never too early for a chocolate fix). After dark, there are madingo cocktails to be had.

The Castle (mains from C3) Though not as impressive as its next-door neighbour (Cape Coast castle), this bar-restaurant is a charmer. Take a seat on the wooden decking, watch the waves roll in and soak up the relaxed but buzzy atmosphere. The fare (a mix of Ghanaian and international dishes) is good, though not sensational.

Court Canteen (mains from C3; ☽ 7am-8pm Mon-Sat) Enter the law courts to find this eatery, which serves hearty Ghanaian fare. The dolls dangling from the ceiling are a little off-putting but add to the overall quirkiness.

Hacienda Plaza (London Bridge; mains from C3) Fun, kitsch nightspot with a glitterball and 1980s vibe. On weekends, bring your dancing shoes; the rest of the time it's a bar with football or music videos on the TV. Simple meals are available. Head to London Bridge and look for the flashing palm tree.

Oasis (mains from C4) The pulse of Cape Coast's volunteer and backpacker scene, Oasis (attached to the guesthouse of the same name) always draws a fun crowd. The cocktail list is as good as the burgers and salads. At weekends Oasis turns into one big party, frequented by everyone from braided backpackers to local students.

Chic Hebs (mains from C5; ☽ 8am-6pm) The green, yellow and red flag flies high at this low-key spot. Does excellent veggie burgers and (bizarrely) even better onion bhaji burgers. There's a well-stocked bar and an arty shop attached.

There's a good **wine shop** (Commercial St) diagonally opposite Barclays Bank. It stocks a range of imported wines and the owner sometimes turns the patio into a seating area. Castle View Coffee Shop, run from a gazebo, sells filter coffee.

Shopping

Cape Coast is an arty, creative town and a fun place to shop.

Baobab (Commercial St) Does a great line in kente cloth and batiks. There are newspaper and magazine stands opposite the latter.

Global Mamas (☎ 042 36883; www.globalmamas.org) Racks of locally-made dresses, cute aprons and jewellery. Each piece is hand-finished and 'signed' by the seamstress; all profits go to the foundation.

My Redeemer Liveth (cnr Beulah La & Royal St) This is the place to pick up a trashy handbag (made from recycled water sachets and flour sacks).

Getting There & Away

STC buses pull into the **Goil petrol station** (Pedu junction), about 5km northwest of the town

GHANA

centre. There are buses twice a day to and from Accra (C5, three hours) and Takoradi (C3, one hour) and once a day to and from Kumasi (C5, four hours). Passenger taxis to Pedu junction leave from the **shared taxis station** (Commercial St), opposite the Cape Café.

There are two main motor parks in Cape Coast. The **Accra bus station** (cnr Sarbah & Residential Rds), serves long-distance routes, such as Accra and Kumasi. **Kotokuraba station** (Governor Rowe Rd), near the market, serves destinations around Cape Coast, such as Abanze, Anomabu, Kakum National Park and Takoradi. Shared taxis to Elmina (C0.75, 15 minutes) leave from the shared taxis station on Commercial St.

KAKUM NATIONAL PARK
☎ 042

Kakum is one of the world's most accessible rainforests. An easy day trip from Cape Coast, the **park** (entry C3) together with the neighbouring Assin Attandanso Resource, protects 357 sq km of jungle and semideciduous forest. It's home to over 300 species of bird, 600 species of butterfly and 40 mammal species, including forest elephants, antelopes, flying squirrels and colobus monkeys. With the exception of monkeys, you're extremely unlikely to spot any of the larger creatures, mainly because they stay away from the well-mapped trails.

Kakum's biggest draw is its 30m high canopy **walkway** (adult/student C9/5), which gives a monkey's eye view of the forest below. It consists of seven wooden viewing platforms linked by a string of bouncy suspension bridges. At best it's a fun, unusual way to see the rainforest and its inhabitants; on quiet days it's not unusual to come face to face with monkeys or colourful birdlife. Quiet days, sadly, are rare; Kakum is popular with large tour groups and excited schoolchildren whose laughter echoes through the rainforest. Though a little overhyped, it's an easily-earned adrenaline rush and shouldn't be missed. It takes a minimum of 20 minutes to complete, longer if you linger and savour the view. The canopy walk is a 20-minute hike (partly on paved trails) from the **park visitor centre** (main park entrance). In the visitor centre, there's a superb, ecologically sensitive display.

Although the hype can make it seem as if the canopy walkway *is* the park, there are other activities. **Guided hikes** (adult/student per hr C4/2) are a superb way to learn about the rainforest flora and its medicinal uses. You'll be talked through the uses of the Kaku tree, linked with headache treatments, and the Pampuro tree, traditionally used to treat asthma. Though this part of Kakum is well-developed, you'll want to wear hiking boots or sturdy shoes – the bite of a soldier ant is painful.

Off-the-beaten track enthusiasts can visit the **Mesomagor tree platform** (overnight C9) on the far eastern outskirts of the park. This section of Kakum is beautiful and wild; there's a chance of spotting antelopes and forest elephants, although the latter are generally shy. Mesomagor village is the home of the famous **Kukyekukyeku Bamboo Orchestra** and it may be possible to hear a performance. The main visitor centre has plenty of literature on Mesomagor and can help arrange a trip.

Sleeping & Eating

The visitor centre can arrange **camping** (with excursion C9) in the park and visits to the tree platform at Mesomagor with **homestays** (per person C9) in the adjacent village.

Most travellers use Cape Coast as a base for visiting the park, but a weird and wonderful alternative is **Hans Cottage Botel** (☎ 042 91456; www.hansbotel.com; camping US$5, r US$30, s/d with fan US$31/45, with air-con US$54/72; P ⊠ ⊛) on the road to Kakum. An old traveller favourite, this place is suspended over an artificial crocodile swamp (hence 'botel' rather than hotel). It's attractive in a shabby-chic way, and draws everyone from eccentric birdwatchers to hip groups of friends. It's the kind of place where you might spot retired twitchers pulling ripe passionfruits from trees, later finding yourself sharing a bottle of wine with them in the bar. Rooms are basic but comfortable and clean. There's an internet cafe, good restaurant and a pool. Though the enormous crocs are fed regularly, they technically roam free.

Kakum's **Rainforest Café** (main park entrance) serves basic food, snacks and homemade ginger juice.

Getting There & Away

From Cape Coast, tro-tros (C2, 45 minutes) that go past the entrance to the park leave from Kotokuraba station on Governor Rowe Rd. It's a five-minute walk from the main road to the park headquarters. Or, you could charter a taxi for about C30 round trip. To get to Mesomagor, take a tro-tro from Cape Coast to Nyamkomasi and a shared taxi from there to the village.

AROUND KAKUM

Three kilometres from Kakum, **Monkey Forest Resort** (☎ 0244 118 313; www.monkeyforestresort.com) is a new initiative devoted to abandoned primates and a wonderful place to spend a couple of hours. The caring Dutch owners have created an excellent habitat for the animals, which include civet cats. Mrs Doolittle's restaurant serves cold drinks and snacks to visitors. It's signposted from Kakum National Park Rd.

There's an interesting community-based ecotourism project at **Domama Rock Shrine** (⊗ 8am-5pm) 34km northwest of Kakum. The natural rock formation was once a sacred spiritual spot; sadly, its significance seems to have lessened but it's still quite a sight. Tours include canoe trips on a stretch of the Pra River. A charter taxi from Cape Coast should cost around C20.

ELMINA

☎ 042 / pop 20,000

Elmina, 15km from Cape Coast, has one of the most colourful fishing harbours in Ghana. On a narrow finger of land between the Atlantic Ocean and Benya Lagoon, it's also the site of St George's castle, one of the oldest European structures still standing in sub-Saharan Africa. Here, the air is salty, the people friendly and the architecture a charming mix of colonial remnants and elderly *posubans*. Elmina's charisma first attracted the Portugese in 1471, followed by the Dutch and later the British.

Sights

ST GEORGE'S CASTLE

Perhaps because it attracts fewer visitors than Cape Coast castle, wandering around this beautiful fort is a much more stirring experience. At the end of a rocky peninsula, **St George's Castle** (adult/student C7/4; ⊗ 9am-4.30pm), a Unesco heritage site, was built by the Portuguese in 1482, and captured by the Dutch in 1637. From then until they ceded it to the British in 1872, it served as the African headquarters of the Dutch West Indies Company. It was expanded when slaves replaced gold as the major object of commerce, and the storerooms were converted into dungeons. The informative tour (included in the entry fee) takes you to the grim dungeons, punishment cells, Door of No Return and the turret room where the British imprisoned the Ashanti king,

Prempeh I, for four years. Later, soldiers of the Royal West African Frontier Force trained at the castle. These days there are palm trees growing in the (dry) moat. The Portuguese church, converted into slave auctioning rooms by the Protestant Dutch, houses a museum with simple but super-informative displays on the history and culture of Elmina.

FORT ST JAGO

Facing the castle across the lagoon is the much smaller Fort St Jago, also a Unesco World Heritage site, built by the Dutch between 1652 and 1662 to protect the castle. The views of the town and St George's Castle from the ramparts of this partial ruin are superb.

FISH MARKET

The traditional name of Elmina is Anomansa, meaning inexhaustible supply of water. Watching the colourful pirogues pull in and out, breathing in the salty air and listening to the cacophony of shouts at the crowded Mpoben port is like having front-row theatre seats. The vast fish market on the lagoon side is also fascinating to wander around, particularly when the day's fishing catch is being unloaded in the afternoon.

OTHER SIGHTS

There are some fascinating **posubans** in town and a well-kept **Dutch cemetery**. To get to the cemetery from the castle take a left turn over the bridge and follow the road around which takes you past some of the *posubans*, decorated with brightly-coloured lions and other animals. On Lime St you'll see the interesting architecture of **Dolphin House**, which was built by the merchant trader Fred Dolphin in the late 19th century. The house is now a little rundown. At the top of the hill is an impressive **catholic church** built in the late 1800s. It is guarded by busts of significant Ghanaians, although sadly several busts are now missing.

Festivals & Events

Elmina's colourful **Bakatue Festival** takes place on the first Tuesday in July. It's a joyous harvest thanksgiving feast, and one of its highlights is watching the priest in the harbour waters casting a net to lift a ban on fishing in the lagoon.

GHANA

The first Thursday in January is **Edina Buronya** time, a sort of Christmas signifying Ghanaian-Dutch friendship with fishing, drinking and slaughtering – of a lamb.

Sleeping and Eating

Almond Tree Guesthouse (☎ 0244 281 098; www .almond3.com; r C32-63; P ✖) This boutiquey guest house is just past the Elmina beach resort. Rooms are named after famous Jamaicans and spruced with wicker furniture and yellow bed linen. The ones with wood floors and balconies are especially attractive. Breakfast is included.

Bridge House (☎ 042 91261; www.coconutgrove hotels.com.gh; s/d from US$50/60; ✖) The best place in Elmina to eat, drink and sleep, Bridge House (part of the Coconut Grove group) occupies a fabulous brick building right on the harbour. Rooms are clean and spacious; the outdoor courtyard is a charming place to eat, as long as you don't mind the (somewhat endearing) geckos occasionally nibbling at your toes. Plush bathrooms.

Coconut Grove Beach Resort (☎ 0242 91213; www .coconutgrovehotels.com.gh; s/d from US$95/105; P ✖) This luxurious resort, while not much to do with Elmina, has a fancy beachside location 4km west of Elmina and offers a variety of upmarket rooms as well as a pool, ball court and nine-hole golf course.

You can buy fresh seafood, including shrimp and crab, from buckets on the harbour. Halfway between Elmina and Cape Coast, **Mabel's Table** (Main coastal rd; ✖ lunch & dinner) serves excellent simple Ghanaian fare in a pretty outdoor setting. In the nearby village of Brenu-Akyinim, **Brenu Beach Resort** (r from US$10) sits on a gorgeous stretch of sand, dotted with palm trees and blessed with cool breezes. There are attractive, simple rooms and the nearby restaurant serves great lobster. From Elmina or Cape Coast, take a tro-tro west towards Takoradi and ask to be let off at the junction for Brenu-Akyinim. From here you should be able to get a passenger taxi to the village (5km).

Getting There & Away

The main taxi and tro-tro station is outside the Wesley Methodist Cathedral. From here you can get tro-tros to Takoradi (C10) or passenger taxis to Cape Coast. In Cape Coast, shared taxis (C0.75, 15 minutes) to Elmina leave from the station on Commercial St, a block north of Barclays Bank. A private taxi between Elmina and Cape Coast costs about C5.

SEKONDI-TAKORADI

☎ 031 / pop 300,000

Together, the conjoined sister cities of Sekondi and Tekoradi form the third largest urban centre in Ghana. Takoradi, the larger of the two, was just a fishing village until it was chosen as Ghana's first deep-water seaport; since then it has prospered. Now feeding on Ghana's oil boom, Takoradi (or Taadi as it's known) is growing larger by the day. Although you'll find modern (expensive) comforts and some good restaurants here, there's no real reason to stick around. About 100m from Sekondi Circle is the turn-off to **Monkey Hill**, a lightly forested escarpment that supports a small population of olive colobus monkeys.

Sekondi, the older of the two settlements, is roughly 10km northeast of Takoradi. The only reason you might venture into Sekondi is to take a quick look at **Fort Orange**, built by the Dutch in 1640 and now a lighthouse.

Information

There are internet cafes around Market Circle. Among the best is the sleek **e-base** (Liberation Rd; ✖ 24 hr). For ATM and money-changing services, there are branches of Barclays Bank and Ghana Commercial Bank on the southeastern side of the circle. The main post office is located on Axim Rd. Takoradi Hospital is the largest on the coast.

Sleeping and Eating

Hotel Arvo (☎ 031 21530; Collins Ave; r C20) This cheapie is a good fallback, especially if you're arriving late and are stuck for a place to crash. Staff are friendly and the location is central.

Hotel de Mexico (☎ 031 23923; r C30-40) Ok, so it's hardly Mexico but this is a good midrange option in Taadi's most attractive part of town. Rooms are comfortable, staff are friendly and you're right on Beach Rd roundabout.

You 84 Hotel & Restaurant (☎ 031 22945; Market Circle; r from US$20) Right in the heart of the action, this intriguingly named budget hotel is upstairs on the western side of Market Circle. The rooms, as you'd expect, aren't the quietest, and are a little on the small side. There's a restaurant and supermarket downstairs.

Planter's Lodge (☎ 031 22233; www.planters.com.gh; r/ste C150/220; P ✖ 🖥 ✖) Originally built to

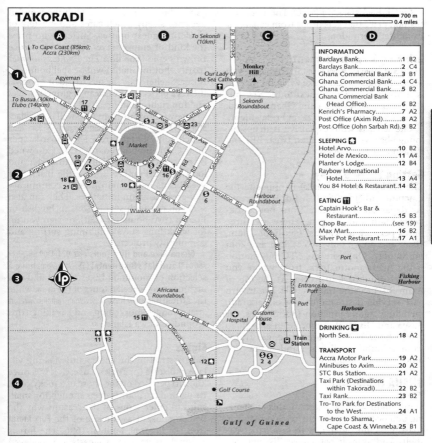

accommodate British Royal Air Force flying officers, Planter's is now a stylish hideaway popular with oil magnates and the Takoradi jet-set. There's six bungalows, each with colonial-style furniture; an excellent restaurant and outdoor pool.

Raybow International Hotel (☎ 031 22072; www .raybowhotel.com; r/ste US$92/139; P ⊠ ⬚ ☎) For those seeking modern comforts, the whitewashed Raybow compound is another good option. Each of the chalets has high-quality amenities, including wi-fi access, and the charming bamboo-and-wicker restaurant serves some of the best food in town. Breakfast included.

Takoradi attracts wealthy expats so eating and drinking here can be expensive. There are several budget eateries and lively drinking spots along Axim Rd, around Market Circle and on Liberation Rd.

Chop bar (Accra motor park; dishes from C1.50) This unnamed place right beside tro-tros departing to Accra, is unnamed but excellent. It offers simple, delicious dishes including a variety of spicy soups, *fufu* and jazzed-up spaghetti.

Bocadillos (☎ 31 20 356, Wiawso rd, Number 2 districts snacks from C2.50). Just south of the centre, this is an expat favourite. Its menu includes everything from great French pastries, including croissants, international and African dishes, cakes and ice cream.

Silver Pot Restaurant (Liberation Rd; mains from C5) This clean and calm oasis is good for a drink or meal of Ghanaian and continental cuisine.

Captain Hook's (Beach Rd; from C9) This is a fancy seafood place that gets props from expats for its lobster thermidor.

Drinking & Entertainment

North Sea (Axim Rd; mains from C5) This joint can get as chilly as its namesake when the air-con is cranked up. It's right next to the STC bus station and serves pizza and Ghanaian food. There's sometimes live jazz on Friday night.

Café de Paris, while expensive, is an upscale lounge bar with a bohemian twist. BBJ and Paragon are the hippest clubs.

Getting There & Away

The **STC bus station** (Axim Rd) is opposite the junction with John Sarbah Rd. It has regular departures for Accra (four hours) between 3am and 5.30pm. There are three buses per day to Kumasi (six hours, 4am, 10am and 4pm); only two at 8am and 2pm on Sunday. Opposite the STC bus station is the Accra motor park, from where you can get minibuses to Accra. At the top of Axim Rd, near the traffic circle, is a tro-tro park serving destinations west of Takoradi, including Agona junction (30 minutes, for Busua and Dixcove), Axim, Beyin and Elubo (three hours). There are passenger trains from Takoradi to Kumasi and Accra. For more details, see p393.

BUSUA & DIXCOVE

☎ 031

Some 30km west of Takoradi, this enchanting duo occupies a perfect stretch of Atlantic coastline, embroidered with sandbars, seashells and skinny palm trees. Busua, the largest of the two, reels in laid-back travellers and surfers chasing world-class waves. Dixcove, 2km away, is a lively fishing village. The area serves as the gateway to the dreamscape around Akwidaa, 11km further west.

Information

The nearest banking facilities are in Takoradi and the only reliable internet is at the Busua Beach Resort, which charges the extortionate rate of C1 for 10 minutes.

Activities

Busua is the kind of place that makes you want to kick off your shoes and never put them back on again. The mile-long sandy beach is lined with the peeling hulls of brightly-painted fishing boats, interspersed with the wooden decks of sleepy beach cafes and clusters of charming guest houses. Surfers who prize the kind of empty waves featured in Bruce Brown's epic 1966 film *The Endless Summer* (partly shot in Ghana) will be spellbound by Busua. Sheltered by the reef island of Abokwa, there's a perfect mix of clean beginners' waves and fun right-point breaks.

A few footprints from the swell is the **Black Star Surf Shop** (www.blackstarsurfshop.com; ☺ 9am-7pm) which rents longboards, shortboards (per hour C10) and bodyboards (C4). Co-owned by an eco-conscious Californian surfer and local legend Frankee Bordes, the Black Star spearheads local environment, community and green tourism initiatives. They can also sort you out with surf lessons in English or French (two hours for C30), or sign you up for week-long stays combining surfing and community projects.

Ghana Bike and Hire Tours (☎ 024 4209 587, 027 766 018) and **Nat's Bike Rental** (☺ 9am-7pm) have a selection of mountain bikes to rent and can organise two-wheeled tours of the area, while the **African Rainbow Resort** (www.africanrainbowresort .com) arranges snorkelling and kayaking trips around Abokwa Island.

Sights

Take a stroll to the cheery little fishing village of **Dixcove** (or Dick's Cove, as it was once known) perched on the shore of a rocky cove. Its natural harbour is deep enough for small ships to enter – one of the reasons why the British chose it as the site of the **Fort Metal Cross** (☺ 9am-5pm), built in 1696. The fort is as tough as its name suggests; it is believed to have endured more attacks than any other fort on the Ghanaian coast. It is now whitewashed and owned by a philanthropic and easy-going Englishman, Rob. From the ramparts, the recycled sails of fishing vessels (some are fashioned from old flour sacks) look like freshly-washed sheets billowing in the breeze. Local fishermen are sometimes willing to take visitors out on fishing excursions – if you choose to do this, slap on the sun cream.

Dixcove is a 30-minute walk over the headland to the west of Busua. Locals warn against walking the track alone; heed their advice and take one of Busua's many local guides with you. Alternatively, you could take a shared taxi inland to Agona junction and another from there to Dixcove. There's no main road directly linking Busua with Dixcove.

Sleeping

Most travellers opt to stay in Busua, which has a good selection of budget and upmarket lodgings, most within walking distance of the beach.

Sabina's Guesthouse (r without/with bathroom C7/12) Across the road from the Alaska, Sabina's is a good choice if you're on a tight budget. Basic rooms back onto the family courtyard, and if you don't mind the comedy curtains and slightly leaky tin roofs, you're onto a winner. Sabina's daughter sells popcorn in the shop next door – the perfect antidote to hot, sweaty weather. The family will happily whip up meals for guests, with vegetarian options.

Dadson's Lodge (☎ 024 4947 326; s/d C12/20; P) This two-storey rust-coloured lodge has been a budget favourite for years. Rooms aren't particularly inspiring but they're clean and decent enough. Staff are friendly and helpful and there's a ground-floor restaurant serving fairly inexpensive dishes.

Alaska Beach Club (huts without/with bathroom C15/20; P) Owned by an Alaskan with an eccentric sense of humour, this is the best value in Busua and popular with the overlanding crowd. Set in grassy grounds that back onto the beach, the simple red huts are well-maintained, with comfortable beds, desks and fans that actually work. Although the place is laid-back most of the time, when the bar hosts parties, they're almost always lively. You can also rent bodyboards.

Busua Inn (☎ 020 7373 579; www.busuainn.com; tw with fan US$23-49, with air-con US$45-57; P ✕) Staying at the Busua Inn feels like visiting the gastronomically gifted French relatives you never had. Owners Danielle and Olivier offer four clean, spacious and breezy rooms with sea views. There's a leafy terrace restaurant that backs onto the beach, serving excellent French and West African dishes against a fabulous wine list.

African Rainbow Resort (☎ 031 302 149; www .africanrainbowresort.com; s/d with fan US$45/50, s/d with air-con US$60/65; P ✕) Well-kept, stylish rooms with balconies overlooking a green front yard. With stacks of character, this is a great place to relax in style. The staff will help you arrange snorkelling and kayaking trips and there's a good onsite restaurant, artisan shop and rooftop bar, swathed in coloured lights come nightfall. The only downside is that it's not on the beach.

Busua Beach Resort (☎ 031 93307; www.gbh ghana.com; r from US$95/115; P ✕) Once the darling of former fighter-pilot-turned-president JJ Rawlings, this huge complex doesn't exactly fit the laid back Busua vibe. It's since been bought by a Ghanaian hotel chain and there's every amenity you dare imagine. Landscaped grounds spill onto the beach and contain several pools, a good kids' playground, tennis courts, jet ski hire and a fancy bar with (expensive) internet access. In theory, there's one budget room here (with fan US$20).

Eating & Drinking

There's no shortage of decent eateries in Busua and almost all lodgings have onsite restaurants. The French food at Busua Inn is pretty special, closely trailed by the pizzas at the African Rainbow Resort. There's certainly no shortage of locals who will catch seafood for you upon request; walking along the beach you can expect to be propositioned by an entrepreneurial chef or two. Among them is **Frank the Juice Man** (Busua Beach) who'll fill an empty water bottle with freshly blended mango and orange juice for a few cedis.

Service can be slow in Busua and many restaurants stop serving by 9pm – head out early or order in advance if you prefer.

Zweite Heimat (opp Dadson's Lodge; mains from C2) Also known as Nana's Place, this friendly backpacker joint is famous for its long communal table and wall scrawlings. Enthusiastic owner Nana Yaw will go out of his way to produce fresh Busua lobster (C10), cold beer or even Ghanaian dishes tailored to Western taste buds. A good find.

Sankofa Beach Bar (Busua Beach; drinks from C2) This laid-back and slightly ramshackle drinking spot is a great place for an early evening drink. A wooden terrace leads onto the beach, and you can place orders with the lobster men who roam the sands. The Sankofa also has a couple of inexpensive, basic rooms.

Okorye Tree (Busua Beach; mains from C3.50; ✕ 9am-9pm) Attached to the Black Star Surf Shop, the Okorye Tree does a roaring trade in chicken sandwiches and big burritos. Grab a table on the wooden deck, order a frozen margarita and watch the waves break. Because surfers often rise with the sun, they know how important a good breakfast is; the Okorye Tree serves it all day long. 'If this place can get it so right, why do others still get it wrong?' we overheard one visitor say.

Black Mamba Corner (Busua Beach; mains from C7) This German-run place is an adventure in itself. Located on a rocky tongue that licks the Atlantic; walk to the end of the beach and look for the sign across the water. Order at least a couple of hours in advance (preferably the day before) for good pizza and seafood. A word of warning: carry a torch (flashlight) and don't wear your best shoes.

Daniel the Pancake Man (Behind Sabina's Guesthouse; mains from C4) Fans of John Edward Everett's early 20th-century poetry – 'I'm the pancake man…I bake them brown and swallow them down and loudly call for more' – will love this place. Daniel the Pancake Man is probably more famous than the Kansan poet and he makes pretty good European-style pancakes to boot. Toppings range from standard lemon and sugar to lobster.

Getting There & Away

Busua and Dixcove are 2km apart, on separate roads leading to Agona Junction. From Takoradi, regular tro-tros leave for Agona junction from the station at the top of Axim Rd. From Agona junction there is frequent transport to both Busua and Dixcove, although there is no main road linking the two.

BUTRE

If you head east along the beach from Busua, after about 2km you'll reach the settlement of Butre, site of the ruined **Fort Batenstein**, built by the Swedish in 1652. Far sleepier than Dixcove, Butre is a great place to chill out.

Sleeping and Eating

Ghana Spirit (☎ 0277 686 224; www.ghanaspirit.com; dm/ huts C6/25; ⓦ) This lovely little slice of paradise opened in 2008. Owned by a young British-Ghanaian couple, the traditional round huts are cute with a bit of an edge. There's a great restaurant-bar, yoga is a possibility and amazingly, it offers wi-fi. A winner.

Ellis Hideout (☎ sms only 0207 369 258; www .ellishideout.com; dm C6, treehouses/bungalows C15/25) A few minutes' walk from Butre, separated by a short canoe ride or rickety wooden bridge, this beachfront place feels like a Robinson Crusoe–inspired adventure playground. It has a mix of bungalows and treehouse hideaways, all a little weather-beaten. The Swedish owner gives discounts to students and volunteers.

Fanta's Folly (☎ 0243 213 677; www.fantasfolly.com; d/tw US$36/47, family lodge US$60-72) This remote retreat offers simple, artistically-decorated bungalows between slices of beach and rainforest. The French-Nigerian owners are pretty talented in the kitchen, too. It's just before the village of Asemkow, 2km from Butre.

Getting There & Away

It's easier to walk to Butre than take transport. Walking east from Busua (about 2km), the footpath is fairly direct. The taxi route takes about 15 minutes and you'll probably have to charter a car (from C4 to C8).

AKWIDAA BEACH

The sleepy little village of Akwidaa sits on a beautiful sandbar, split by the calm waters of a lazy lagoon. Though the village itself is pleasant, it's the surrounding area that will take your breath away. In the shadow of bamboo groves and mangrove swamps, this is a stunning slice of Ghana, shingled with rocky outcroppings and buttered with lashings of white sand. The eco-lodges at Akwidaa Beach are doing more for the planet than they realise – many travellers who make it here wind up accidentally-on-purpose missing their flight home.

Sleeping and Eating

ᴏᴜʀ ᴘɪᴄᴋ Green Turtle Lodge (☎ sms only 024 4893 566; www.greenturtlelodge.com; camping with own tent C3, dm C5, d without/with bathroom C15/30) Volunteers and backpackers get a misty look in their eyes when they talk about the Green Turtle. Owned by a young English couple, this magical eco-resort is more than just a place to chill out. Built entirely from locally-sourced, natural materials, its cute bungalows are clean and airy with self-composting toilets. The beach bar plays laid-back tunes, the restaurant churns out chocolate-covered bananas and there's a stack of board games. Turtle spotting tours leave nightly and the owners can organise hiking trips and canoe safaris. Paradise.

Safari Beach Lodge (sms only ☎ 024 6651 329; www .safaribeachlodge.com; d without/with bathroom C30/40) Green Turtle's quiet, stylish neighbour has been turning heads on Akwidaa Beach. Brainchild of an ultra eco-conscious sommelier turned chef, Safari is big on attention to detail. Huts are furnished in the style of a Kenyan safari lodge, complete with four-poster beds, desks and artwork. Everything is designed from locally-sourced materials and the solar-heated showers are open to the sun and stars. It gets even better: the bar-restaurant makes phenomenal cocktails and the food…well, it deserves a Michelin star. This is rustic romance at its best.

Getting There & Away
Akwidaa Beach is about 11km west of Busua. From Agona Junction, any tro-tro heading to Akwidaa village can drop you at one of the two eco-lodges. If you're travelling by private transport or taxi, the entrance to Safari Beach Lodge is about 2km from the village, on the only (rough) road. Green Safari Lodge is the next large settlement. Neither lodge has public internet access and mobile phone signals can be unreliable.

CAPE THREE POINTS
About halfway between Akwidaa and Princes Town, Ghana's southernmost tip has the strange juxtaposition of being both a surf spot and the site of Ghana's recent off-shore oil find. This tiny finger of land boasts some of the best (and often empty) waves in West Africa, coupled with cool breezes that quite frankly, come as a spot of relief. If you're planning on surfing here, avoid the rocks and note that the breaks are best during the spring. The red and white **Cape Three Points lighthouse** was built in 1930 and from its base you can sometimes spot whales swimming close to shore between October and January. About 2km inland is the thriving **Cape Three Points Coastal Reserve**, which hosts an endangered population of Diana monkeys as well as at least 150 species of bird.

Cape Three Points is about 5km west of Akwidaa. Although share taxis don't regularly run between Akwidaa and Cape Three Points, you can charter one for a few cedi. Alternatively, the Green Turtle Lodge and Safari Beach at Akwidaa can arrange hiking trips. There are plans to establish an eco-heritage trail from Butre to Axim, taking in Akwidaa and Cape Three Points.

PRINCES TOWN
Some 15km west of Agona junction, Princes Town is suffering a bit of an identity crisis. Depending on who you ask, it's known as either Princes Town or Princess Town and the two seem to be interchangeable. Gender issues aside, its sandy beaches and attractive fort make for an interesting day trip, especially if you're keen to get off the beaten track. Perched atop a hill at the eastern edge of the village, **Fort Princes Town** (admission C5, camera fee C5/10; ☼ 9am-5pm) was founded by Prince Friedrich Wilhelm of Prussia in 1683. The partly restored fort is made from greyish local stone and this, together with the lush vegetation surrounding it, makes it one of the most attractive forts on the coast. There are superb views from the ramparts over the sandy bay and towards Cape Three Points, Ghana's southernmost point. At the start of the short trail up to the fort is a terrace bar and restaurant where you can get cold drinks and cheap seafood meals. The fort's helpful caretaker can arrange excursions in the area, such as canoe trips on the nearby lagoon, and trips up the River Kpani to visit a palm-wine distillery. It's also possible to stay in one of the fort's simple rooms.

The junction for Princes Town is about 15km west of Agona junction; any tro-tro heading west from Agona can drop you there. From here, it's about 18km to Princes Town along a scenic but rough dirt road.

AXIM
☎ 0342
Seventy kilometres from the border with Côte d'Ivoire Axim has as much in common with its francophone neighbour as with Ghana. Axim is pronounced French-style (usually Akzeem or Azeem). As you near it you'll notice the landscape changing; patches of dry land are replaced with thick, jungly forest. The town itself, the largest on the coast west of Takoradi, is fairly unremarkable but it's friendly enough and is flanked by spectacular rocky beaches. It's also the site of the huge **Fort San Antonio** (admission C7, camera fee C5). It was built by the Portuguese in 1515, making it the second-oldest fort on the Ghanaian coast. From the top of the fort, there are spectacular views of the stunning coastline in both directions. The live-in caretaker provides good, enthusiastically-acted tours of the fort and is also a good source of local knowledge.

Sleeping & Eating
Axim Beach Hotel (☎ 031 22260; www.aximbeach.com; r US$10, d with fan/air-con US$20/30, family villas with air-con US$100-200; ⚄ ⚂) Resorts as stunning as this are usually reserved for those with deep pockets, but this hotel caters to everyone. Bungalows and villas spill onto hilly slopes

overlooking the ocean. Inside, beds are made with crisp white sheets and bathrooms (with hot water) are finished with mosaics. Even the budget rooms are carefully-designed. The hotel has two onsite restaurants, wi-fi (for a fee) and surfboard hire. The hotel is a five-minute drive from Axim town, along a rough track – you can charter a taxi to take you there for C3.

ourpick **Lou Moon Lodge** (☎ 031 021 394; www.lou moon-lodge.com; d US$66-138, ste US$99-158) Overlooking an idyllic cove with safe waters, this stylish eco-wonderland is one West Africa's most enchanting resorts. Everything is beautifully-designed, from the light-filled bungalows with four-poster beds to the executive suites, which come with floor-to-ceiling windows and your own private island. The ultra design-conscious Belgian owners employ top Togolese chefs and the food, which includes lobster and homemade hibiscus sorbet, is phenomenal. You'll never want to leave. It's 6km from Axim, near the village of Ankobra.

Ankobra Beach Hotel (☎ 0342 22400; ankobra _beach@hotmail.com; bungalows US$40-100) The Ankobra is another highly recommended resort with an unbeatable location on a beautiful beach loaded with palm trees. The thatched bungalows may not have quite as much character as those at the Axim but they're comfortable and the restaurant is still pretty good. Activities such as canoe trips up the nearby Ankobra River can be arranged. Ankobra Beach is signposted off the main Elubo road, about 5km from the turn-off to Axim. From the main road, it's about 500m to the resort.

Frankfaus Hotel (☎ 0342 22291; s/d US$12/20) Axim town's only decent option is a two-storey building a few metres from the tro-tro station. Rooms are clean and nicely furnished and there's a good onsite restaurant.

Getting There & Away

Axim is 69km west of Takoradi, off the main Elubo road, which bypasses it. The tro-tro station is in the centre of town, across from the football pitch in front of the fort. There are regular tro-tros to Takoradi (30 minutes), which can drop you at Agona junction (for Busua and Dixcove) or the Princes Town junction. Heading west, for Elubo and Ankasa you may have to get a tro-tro to Esiama, a big transport hub on the main coastal road about 10km from Axim, and get onward transport from there. To Beyin, you'll have

to get a tro-tro to Eikwe and then transport on from there.

BEYIN & NZULEZU

About 65km west of Axim, is the village of **Beyin**. It's the site of Fort Apollonia, the last of the coastal forts west of Accra, and it's the departure point for visits to the stilt village of Nzulezu, suspended above the freshwater Amansuri Lagoon. **Nzulezu**, home to 500 people, is reached by canoe, which takes about an hour each way. At the Ghana Wildlife Society office on the outskirts of Beyin, you register and pay a fee of C5 per person, which includes the canoe trip and entry to the village (you can go any day except Thursday, which is deemed sacred). You pass through the **Amansuri Wetland**, Ghana's largest intact swamp. There's no shade on the lagoon so the earlier in the day you leave the better, and take plenty of water and a hat.

You can stay overnight in Nzulezu in a tranquil room over the water for C4 and simple meals can be arranged.

Beyin Beach Resort (☎ 027 5139 186; ninasarpong@ hotmail.com; bungalows $10-32) has four luxury bungalows, attractively furnished and in the style of Nzulezu dwellings. There's a good restaurant and book swap, and the English/Ghanaian owners can help you arrange trips to Nzulezu and Ankasa, as well as night hikes to look for turtles. There are discounts for volunteers.

Beyin is on a rough dirt road that leaves the main Elubo road about 20km west of Esiama. From there it's about 15km to Eikwe and then the road follows the coast to Beyin. From Takoradi, you may be able to get a direct tro-tro from the station at the top of Axim Rd but it's probably quicker to get a tro-tro to Esiama and then transport on from there. From Axim, there are a few tro-tros to Eikwe, from where you can get onward transport to Beyin. Alternatively, Axim Beach Resort and Ankobra Beach Hotel can charter a taxi to take you there and back. Heading to Elubo, you can get transport east from Beyin to Tikobo No 1 and onward transport from there.

ANKASA NATURE RESERVE

This rich slice of rainforest, 5km southeast of the border with Côte d'Ivoire, is relatively untouched by human hands. Although there's plenty of talk about Ankasa becoming Ghana's next wildlife-watching destination, it probably won't see a tourist invasion for quite some time, largely because its facilities are still very basic. But with a biodiversity far greater than that of Mole or Kakum (300 plant species have been recorded in a single hectare) those who make it here are richly rewarded. Together with the adjacent Nini-Suhien Reserve, Ankasa Nature Reserve comprises 500 sq km of wet evergreen jungle, teeming with bird and animal life. Thick pockets of foliage are cut by terracotta tracks and warm waterfalls. At Nkwanta, 8km into the park, is the **Bamboo Cathedral**, a naturally formed sanctuary on the edge of a small valley. Here, thick strands of bamboo have become intervowen over time, forming a colossal chamber that scrapes the sky. Smaller antechambers surround it.

Ankasa is home to populations of endangered black and white Diana monkeys as well as leopards, duikers, chimpanzees and bongos – the latter is being considered for the park symbol. Although there are forest elephants within the reserve, these animals are shy and you're much more likely to hear them than see them. The reserve is particularly rich in birdlife; more than 260 species have been recorded, including parrots, hornbills and the rare white-fronted guinea fowl. You'll almost certainly become acquainted with Ankasa's insect species. Watch out for the aggressive soldier ants – if your feet aren't fully covered as you walk through the jungle, they'll latch onto you with their strong, stubborn jaws.

The **park headquarters** (www.fcghana.com) is at the main **Ankasa Gate** (park entry C2.50) where you pay the entrance fee and can arrange hikes with helpful park rangers (by day or by night). There are **jungle camps** (per night C5) with running water at three locations – Ankasa Gate, Elubo Gate and Nkwanta. They are equipped with screenhouses, beds and hammocks – bring your own mosquito net, sleeping bag and plenty of food and water. As long as you cover up and bring bug spray, falling asleep to the sounds of Ankasa's nocturnal birds, big cats or monkeys can be a special experience.

Alternatively, you can stay at **Frenchman's Farm** (r C10), signposted about 500m before you reach Ankasa Gate. Owned by a friendly Ivoirian former film producer, it consists of a row of basic rooms on the edge of the forest. Frenchman, as he likes to be known, provides basic breakfasts and dinners to guests.

Ankasa Gate is about 6km north of the main road to Elubo and the Côte d'Ivoire border. You can jump on any tro-tro heading that way and ask to be dropped at the Ankasa junction, but be prepared for a 40-minute hike (at least) to the park entrance. Far better to charter a taxi from Elubo, Aiyanasi or even Axim.

THE EAST

Hugged by the Togoloese border, Eastern Ghana – also known as the Volta region – is prime hiking territory. Lush, fertile farmland is flanked by rocks and mountains offering beautiful vistas. The three waterfalls at Wli, Tagbo and Amedofe cleanse tired travelling souls, while Lake Volta offers peaceful river trips. With regular buses departing Accra, the East is an easy weekend getaway.

AKOSOMBO
☎ 0251

The scenic town of Akosombo was built in the early 1960s to house construction workers involved in the completion of the hydroelectric dam, which holds back the waters of Lake Volta, the word's largest artificial lake. It deserves a visit to take in the fabulous hilltop views, as well as this engineering marvel. It's also the terminus for a passenger-boat service north to Yeji.

Akosombo is about 7km north of the Accra to Ho road, 2km before the dam and 6km before the port. There's a Ghana Commercial Bank, post office and small visitor centre on the main road near the motor park in town. A wider selection of accommodation and eating options are available in Atimpoku, to the south of Akosombo, where the Ho road crosses the Volta at the impressive Adome Suspension Bridge.

Sights & Activities

The **visitors centre** (☎ 025 120 550) arranges **tours** (C2; ☉ 9am-3pm Mon-Sun) of the dam. An alternative is the *Dodi Princess*, more like a booze cruise than a love boat. It chugs out to nearby Dodi Island on Saturday, Sunday and holidays (adults C20), blaring hip-life music; the price includes lunch and a drink. Leaving at around 11am, the trip takes five hours, with two hours on the island, but you can stay on board if you want. Contact the Volta Hotel for reservations. It leaves from a well-signposted jetty beyond the dam, before the port. Any shared taxi heading for the port from the motor park can drop you at the jetty.

Sleeping & Eating

Benkum Motel (☎ 025 120 050; r from C10) Not the most attractive option in town, but once you're inside you don't have to look at it. Bargain rooms – comfortable, spacious and inexpensive, that is.

Adomi Hotel & Restaurant (☎ 025 120 095; r with fan/air-con C20/26; ⊠) Overlooking Atimpoku roundabout opposite the suspension bridge, the Adomi has basic but comfortable rooms with excellent views of the traffic.

Aylos Bay (☎ 025 120 901; r from US$30) Set in lush green grounds, the Aylos Bay has a warm, relaxed vibe. Hammocks are strung between trees and the stylish bungalows are good value. There's a garden bar and restaurant.

Volta Hotel (☎ 025 120 731; www.voltahotel.net; s/d US$98/108; ⊠ ⊠) Even without the panoramic views of the dam, the lake and the Akwamu highlands, the plush Volta Hotel makes an impression: top service, quality, modern rooms and a good restaurant. The bar has live music on most weekend nights. It's signposted from town.

Street food in Akosombo and Atimpoku includes specialities like takeaway fried shrimp and 'one man thousand' (minute-fried fish). In Akosombo town, try the **Kokoo-Ase Spot** (nr motor park) for a drink or bite to eat. Aylos Bay also has a pretty good restaurant.

Getting There & Around

The main transport hub is at Kpong, on the Accra to Ho road 10km south of Atimpoku. Regular tro-tros travel between Kpong, Atimpoku and Akosombo. From Accra, tro-tros for Kpong/Akosombo (C4) leave from Tudu station. Alternatively, get any transport to Ho from Accra or to Accra or Kpong from Ho and get off at the suspension bridge at Atimpoku.

For details about the boat between Akosombo and Yeji, see p392.

HO

☎ 091

Capital cities aren't always where the action is. While Ho, about 75km northeast of Akosombo, is a pleasant enough little town, it wears its status as the political and administrative seat of the Volta region like a baggy

sweater. Nevertheless, this friendly community is a peaceful place to base yourself while you explore the region.

Ho's streets are long and things are spread fairly far apart, although the STC bus station and main lorry park and the central market are next to one another, not too far from the Freedom Hotel. The town's backdrop is a range of hills with the distinctive Mt Adaklu to the south.

Information

There's a small **tourist office** (☎ 091 26560) on the 4th floor of an office complex next to the Goil petrol station on the Accra road. Barclays Bank is just down the road from here and has an ATM. For internet access, try Blessings or the business centre at the Freedom Hotel or Chances Hotel.

Sleeping

Hotel Tarso (☎ 091 26732; r with shared bath C7, r with fan/air-con C15/30; ⊠) The best of the budget options, the friendly Tarso has a mix of rooms, all of varying standards. The cheapest are still comfortable.

Fiave Lodge (☎ 091 26412; r from C10) On the Kpalimé road between the market and the Freedom Hotel, this is a small family-run guest house with a few rooms of varying quality, some with their own bathroom. Meals are available upon request.

Freedom Hotel (☎ 091 28151; www.freedom hotel-gh.com; r with fan/air-con C30/40, chalets C50; P ⊠ ⊠ ⊠) The best place in town to hang out is on the Freedom's rooftop lounge and bar with views over the road. It's also an excellent place to stay. The rooms and chalets are inviting – some have TVs, fridges and hot, pressurised showers.

Chances Hotel (☎ 091 28344; r/chalets from US$55/60; P ⊠ ⊠ ⊠) Chances is Ho's most upmarket hotel and worth the price. There's a beautiful pool, a good restaurant (mains from C5) and an internet centre.

Eating & Drinking

The **Freedom** (mains from C4) and **Chances** (mains from C5) hotels have the two best restaurants in Ho. **Phil's** (nr The Freedom) is a popular drinking spot and serves good local nosh, as does the not-so-central Pleasure Garden and the White House, a short way up the hill from the Hotel Tarso. Around the main lorry park and the STC bus station on the main street are plenty of stalls selling street food. Note that feline bushmeat may be among the dishes.

Getting There & Away

Ho's busy main lorry park is well organised. From here, regular tro-tros run between Ho and Hohoe (two hours) throughout the day. Other destinations include Accra, Amedzofe, Akatsi and Keta.

STC also runs one ridiculously early bus a day (C4, four hours) between Ho and Accra, leaving from the STC bus station on the main street in Ho around 4am. Possibly the most comfortable public transport available in Ghana are the KTS minivans connecting Ho and Accra (two hours). They leave when full from a little clearing on the left side of the Kpalimé road coming from the central market.

AROUND HO
Tafi-Atome Monkey Sanctuary

At Tafi-Atome, about 25km north of Ho, the villagers have created a **sanctuary** (admission & guided tour from C5) around the village to protect the sacred Mona monkeys that live in the surrounding forest. The monkeys are used to humans and roam around the village in the early morning and late afternoon, like teenagers just released from school. You can hire a bicycle to visit other sites in the area or stay for drumming, dancing and storytelling sessions in the evening. Basic accommodation and meals are available at the **guest house** (s/d C8/16) or at the homestays for a negotiated fee.

Biakpa Mountain Paradise

At Biakpa, sanctuary comes in the form of **our pick** Mountain Paradise (☎ 0244 166 226; www.mountainparadise-biakpa.com; camping C5, r C8-12) a former government resthouse converted into a fabulous mountain hideaway in the Avatime range. Though the architecture isn't much to write home about, you'll still want to sit on the terrace with a journal, pen and cold bottle of Star beer. There's a bookswap, good restaurant and staff can arrange hikes and canoe excursions along the Kulugu river. There are plans to extend the conservation programme already in operation in the area; the lodge marks its geographical centre. Shared transport between Ho and Hohoe stops at the village of Fume, 4km from Mountain Paradise – you might be able to persuade the driver to drop you at

the lodge for an extra fee. Alternatively, it's a short drive from Amedzofe.

Mt Adaklu

The views from the top of this majestic mountain, about 12km south of Ho, are worth the three-hour guided hike to get there. Surrounded by nine villages, the Adaklu area is part of a community-based tourism project. At the **visitor centre** (Helekpe) at the foot of the mountain, you pay a fee of C2 and are assigned a guide. Bring plenty of water and strong footwear.

Amedzofe

This mountain village is the main centre in the Avatime Hills, an area that offers breathtaking vistas, a waterfall, forests, cool climate and plenty of hiking opportunities. There's a community-run **visitor centre** (Amedzofe) where you pay a flat fee of C2 and can arrange hikes. Popular hikes include a 45-minute walk to **Amedzofe Falls** and a 30-minute walk to the summit of **Mt Gemi** (611m), one of the highest mountains in the area, where there is a 3.5m iron cross and stunning views.

Xofa Eco Village

What began as an admirable attempt to restore treelines on the eastern shore of Lake Volta became a **guest house** (☎ 021 514 989; www.xofa.org) in 2001. This set-up, which polarises travellers (some complain that the eco-initiatives have fallen by the wayside) offers accommodation in simple huts and activities including canoe trips and dance workshops. Make of it what you will, but be sure to contact them before turning up; at the time of research Xofa's future was unclear.

HOHOE
☎ 0935

In this soporific district capital you're likely to elicit nothing more than a friendly nod or smile, and it's this pleasant, laid-back vibe that make Hohoe the perfect jumping-off point for the nearby Wli Falls. It's also a staging point for travel across the border into Togo and north to Tamale via Yendi.

The action area of Hohoe (pronounced Hohoy) is the Accra road, which becomes the road to Jasikan and Bimbilla as it heads north out of town. Along here, south to north, you'll find the motor park, market and **tourism office** (Hohoe District Assembly Bldg), a Ghana Commercial

GHANA

Bank, and the post office. The road to Wli and the Togo border turns off the main road at the Bank of Ghana about 1km from the motor park.

Sleeping & Eating

Grand Hotel (☎ 0935 22053; r from C7) The Grand is the cheapest option in town and also the most central across from the Bank of Ghana. Basic rooms (shared bathrooms) are set around a concrete central courtyard and restaurant.

Taste Lodge (☎ 0935 22023; r from C18; P) The best budget option in town, partly because of the friendly and helpful owner. This comfortable set-up has five rooms, all with their own small balconies opening onto a shady courtyard. A good restaurant is attached and hot water is available upon request.

Evergreen Lodge (☎ 0935 22254; r from C20; P) Though the building doesn't have much character, rooms at the Evergreen are the most modern in Hohoe; the owners are big on attention to detail. A nice restaurant with cable TV is attached.

At night, Taste Lodge serves decent chow, as does The Grand. There's a lively chop spot known as **Kitcat** (Accra Rd).

Getting There & Away

STC buses leave Hohoe for Accra at the ungodly hour of 3am (C4, four hours) and leave Accra at 3.30pm daily. Tro-tros leave regularly throughout the day for Accra (four hours), Ho (one hour) and Akosombo (2½ hours). Tro-tros and shared taxis go to Wli Falls and the Togo border at Wli (30 minutes).

AROUND HOHOE
Wli (Agumatsa) Falls

After a scenic, undemanding 40-minute walk along a bubbling stream, it's hard not to gawk at Wli ('Vlee')'s 40m-high cascade. Those aren't birds but an estimated half a million bats swirling around near the top of the horseshoe-shaped cliff. If the icy water isn't an obstacle you can swim in the shallow pool at the bottom of the falls. The fee to enter the **Agumatsa Wildlife Sanctuary** (entry C7) which contains the falls is payable at the wildlife office. You can reach the lower falls by yourself but a hike to the upper falls (C2) is a demanding two-hour climb and a guide is necessary.

The German-owned **Waterfall Lodge** (☎ 0289 547 459; www.ghanacamping.com; r from C10) is a few

hundred metres from the wildlife office, and is a great place to sleep after a day at the falls. Some of the rooms are pretty wonderful. Tasty food is served indoors or in the palava hut on the lawn.

Regular tro-tros (40 minutes) and share taxis make the scenic run between Wli and Hohoe throughout the day. If you're heading for Togo, the Ghanaian border post at Aflao is on the eastern side of Wli (turn left at the junction as you enter the village). From there, it's a 10-minute walk to the Togolese side.

Liati Wote & Mt Afadjato

The pretty village of **Liati Wore**, 21km south of Hohoe, grounds Ghana's highest mountain, **Mt Afadjato** (885m) – nearby Aduadu peak is really the highest point in Ghana, but isn't considered a mountain because the height difference between the base and the peak is too small. Liati Wote is part of another community-based ecotourism initiative – check in at the visitor centre when you arrive to pay your fees and arrange a hike. It's a reasonably challenging two-hour climb to the summit of Mt Afadjato, which offers stupendous views of Lake Volta and the countryside below. There are also a couple of easier walks, including to Tagbo Falls, a 45-minute hike from the village through coffee and cocoa fields. The surrounding forest is filled with clouds of butterflies. There's a small guest house and eatery in town. Tro-tros leave for Liati Wote (one hour) from Fodome station in Hohoe.

KETA
☎ 0966

In this rarely-visited corner of Ghana, the **Keta Lagoon** is separated from the encroaching sea by a narrow strip of land and a sandy beach which in places is quite pretty. With all this wetland, it's a haven for birdwatchers. You can also check out the ruins of **Fort Prinzenstein**, built in 1784 by the Danes. Just along from the fort is the beach; other beaches are at Tegbi, Woe and Anloga on the road south of Keta.

Lorneh Lodge (☎ 0966 402 160; r from US$25;) has a row of concrete bungalows on a good swimming beach. Less expensive rooms are a few hundred metres away. There's a restaurant and internet access.

Tro-tros to Keta leave from Tudu station in Accra (three hours). From Ho, infrequent tro-tros head to Keta but it's quicker to go to Akatsi junction and on from there. East of

Keta towards Aflao and the Togo border, the sea has encroached on the road. Occasionally 4WDs make the trip when the water is especially low; otherwise there are frequent boats across and onward transport from there.

THE CENTRE

Like a magnet, the pull of Ghana's cultural heartland is hard to resist. Spilling over a series of hills, this region is the historic centre of the Ashanti and is endowed with lakes, thick patches of forest and settlements steeped in tradition. Kumasi, the country's second city, is the seat of the Ashanti King and marks the tip of a triangle that links the coast and Accra in a popular travel circuit.

KUMASI
☎ 051 / pop 1.5 million
Kumasi is worth as much time as you can give it. Once the capital of the rich and powerful Ashanti kingdom, Ghana's second city is still dripping with Ashanti traditions. Its heart, the huge Kejetia market, throbs like a traditional talking drum and its wares spill into the city so that no matter where you are in Kumasi, it sometimes feels like one enormous marketplace. Among the urban sprawl are green spaces, remains of colonial architecture and a number of great sightseeing spots – three reasons why many travellers speak fondly of the hilly city. The fourth, thanks to an elevation of 246m, is its climate. If you're coming from Accra or Tamale, you'll feel a slight drop in temperature, most noticeable between dusk and noon. Founded in 1695, the city was razed by the British in 1874 during the Fourth Ashanti War and now consists of a patchwork of lively neighbourhoods sewn together by a diverse mix of inhabitants.

Orientation
Kumasi sprawls over a vast hilly area. The heart of town is Kejetia Circle, a vast traffic-clogged roundabout. On the eastern side of the circle is Kejetia Market, which spills over onto the roads around it. West of the circle is the vast Kejetia motor park, the city's main transport park. South of the circle, the parallel Guggisberg and Fuller Rds lead past the train station. The district of Adum, just south of the circle, is the modern commercial district, where you'll find the major banks and shops. The STC bus station is on the southern edge of this district, a 10-minute walk from Prempeh II Roundabout.

Information

INTERNET ACCESS
Internet cafes are dotted all over town.
Bee Busy Internet (Asomfo Rd; per hr C0.80; ⏰ 24 hr) Has printing facilities and air-con.
Unic Internet (Bank Rd; per hr C0.60; ⏰ 7.30am-8.00pm) Next to the British Council.

MEDICAL SERVICES
Okomfo Anokye Teaching Hospital (Bantama Rd) A large complex near the National Culture Centre; Kumasi's main public hospital with 700-plus beds.

MONEY
All banks listed here change traveller's cheques and have ATMs. There are also several forexes for changing cash.
Barclays Bank (Prempeh II Roundabout) Other branches throughout the city.
Ecobank (Harper Rd)
Garden City Forex Bureau (Harper Rd) Has the best rates around.
Ghana Commercial Bank (Harper Rd)
Stanbic Bank (Harper Rd)
Standard Chartered Bank (Prempeh II Roundabout) Other branches throughout the city.

POST
Main post office (Stewart Ave; ⏰ 8am-5pm Mon-Fri) Opposite the Armed Forces Museum. Poste restante shuts at 4.30pm.

TOURIST INFORMATION
Tourist office (⏰ 7am-5pm Mon-Fri) In the National Cultural Centre complex. Staff can help arrange guided tours of the city and surrounding villages.

Sights

KEJETIA MARKET
The vast, infinitely disorienting Kejetia Market has a magical quality about it. From afar, West Africa's largest market looks like an alien mothership. Closer up, its rusting tin roofs give it the appearance of a circular shantytown. But once you take a deep breath and step through the gates into its interior, you'll quickly get swept up in the excitement of a market throbbing with life and commerce. Watch your step, often over railway sleepers, as you explore the narrow alleyways selling everything from groundnut paste, pungent

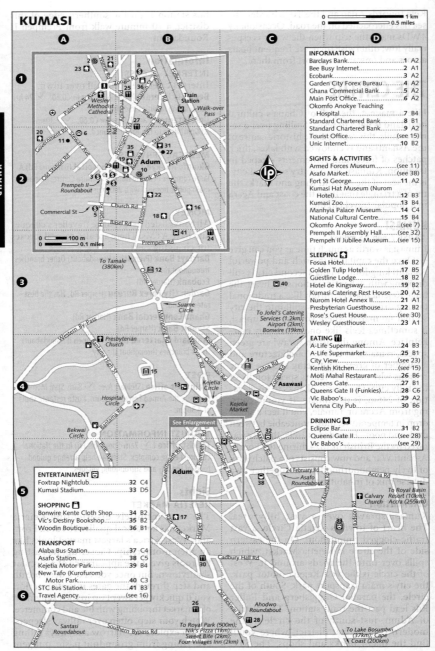

KUMASI

INFORMATION
Barclays Bank	**1** A2
Bee Busy Internet	**2** A1
Ecobank	**3** A2
Garden City Forex Bureau	**4** A2
Ghana Commercial Bank	**5** A2
Main Post Office	**6** A2
Okomfo Anokye Teaching Hospital	**7** B4
Standard Chartered Bank	**8** B1
Standard Chartered Bank	**9** A2
Tourist Office	(see 15)
Unic Internet	**10** B2

SIGHTS & ACTIVITIES
Armed Forces Museum	(see 11)
Asafo Market	(see 38)
Fort St George	**11** A2
Kumasi Hat Museum (Nurom Hotel)	**12** B3
Kumasi Zoo	**13** B4
Manhyia Palace Museum	**14** C4
National Cultural Centre	**15** B4
Okomfo Anokye Sword	(see 7)
Prempeh II Assembly Hall	(see 32)
Prempeh II Jubilee Museum	(see 15)

SLEEPING
Fosua Hotel	**16** B2
Golden Tulip Hotel	**17** B5
Guestline Lodge	**18** B2
Hotel de Kingsway	**19** B2
Kumasi Catering Rest House	**20** A2
Nurom Hotel Annex II	**21** A1
Presbyterian Guesthouse	**22** B2
Rose's Guest House	(see 30)
Wesley Guesthouse	**23** A1

EATING
A-Life Supermarket	**24** B3
A-Life Supermarket	**25** B1
City View	(see 23)
Kentish Kitchen	(see 15)
Moti Mahal Restaurant	**26** B6
Queens Gate	**27** B1
Queens Gate II (Funkies)	**28** C6
Vic Baboo's	**29** A2
Vienna City Pub	**30** B6

DRINKING
Eclipse Bar	**31** B2
Queens Gate II	(see 28)
Vic Baboo's	(see 29)

ENTERTAINMENT
Foxtrap Nightclub	**32** C4
Kumasi Stadium	**33** D5

SHOPPING
Bonwire Kente Cloth Shop	**34** B2
Vic's Destiny Bookshop	**35** B2
Woodin Boutique	**36** B1

TRANSPORT
Alaba Bus Station	**37** C4
Asafo Station	**38** C5
Kejetia Motor Park	**39** B4
New Tafo (Kurofurom) Motor Park	**40** C3
STC Bus Station	**41** B3
Travel Agency	(see 16)

GHANA

fruits and vegetables and imported Chinese toys to kente cloth, Ashanti sandals, batik and bracelets. Closer to the railway tracks you might see *juju* fetish items that look like they belong in a JK Rowling novel – vulture skulls, crocodile tails, parrot wings and dried chameleons. Locals navigate the labyrinthine market with expert knowledge; while the children of stall owners, some barely tall enough to see over the stands, seem to know exactly where to find their parents. The second an expression of lost panic crosses a traveller's face, one of the 10,000 stall owners will likely grab your hand and lead you through the chaos. The occasional freight train passes through the market, but if you're hoping to watch the spectacle, note that there's no timetable and the service can be subject to month-long delays.

Kente cloth, made locally, is a particularly good deal here. It's usually sold in standard lengths of 12m and price varies according to the composition of the material (cloth containing a mixture of cotton, silk and rayon is more expensive than all-cotton, for example) and weave (double weave is, naturally, more expensive than single). You can get cloth made up cheaply and expertly into whatever you want by the market's dressmakers, many of whom seem to work at the speed of light.

Make sure you finish your shopping well before dusk; when darkness cloaks the market it becomes doubly disorienting and the adjacent Kejetia taxi/tro-tro park fills up.

NATIONAL CULTURAL CENTRE
This **complex** (admission free; 🕙 8am-5pm) is set within peaceful, shady grounds and includes craft workshops where you can see brassworking, woodcarving, pottery making, batik cloth dyeing and kente cloth weaving; an art gallery and crafts shop; the regional library, tourism office and the small but informative Prempeh II Jubilee Museum. The craft workshops aren't always active, especially on Sunday, and it's all rather low-key, but the grounds are the perfect antidote to a morning at Kejetia market and a pleasant place to spend a few hours.

Prempeh II Jubilee Museum (adult/student/child C3/2/0.50; 🕙 9am-5pm Mon-Fri, 10am-4pm Sat & Sun) may be small but then most of the items on show are, too (there's no photography allowed). The museum is housed in a replica of a traditional Ashanti royal home, complete with internal courtyard and walls decorated with Ashanti murals. The tour included with the admission fee is a captivating introduction to Ashanti culture and history, from 1690 to the present day rule of King Otumfuo Osei Tutu. Among the museum's collection are two stools; one in silver, the other in fake gold. A Denkyira chief was purportedly sitting on the former at the time of an unforeseen attack by the Ashanti in 1699. The fake gold stool was used to deceive the British – who requested the famous Golden Stool, the rarest of Ashanti artefacts – in 1900. The original Golden Stool remains hidden away but you can see a photograph of it on display at the museum. You will also see artefacts relating to Ashanti King Prempeh II including the king's war attire, ceremonial clothing, jewellery, protective amulets, towels made from soft plantain fibre, royal symbols – including replicas of birds with their heads turned backwards, suggesting Ghana's constant acknowledgement of its Ashanti roots – and some fine brass weights for weighing gold.

MANHYIA PALACE MUSEUM
King Otumfuo Osei Tutu, the present Asantehene, or Ashanti King, has opened a section of Manhyia palace to tourists; you can also wander the grounds with the peacocks and pop into the adjacent **museum** (off Antoa Rd; admission C5; 🕙 9am-noon & 1-5pm), up the hill north from Kejetia Circle. The palace was built by the British in 1925 to receive Prempeh I when he returned from a quarter of a century of exile in the Seychelles to resume residence in Kumasi. On display is the original furniture, including Ashantiland's first TV, and various artefacts from the royals, with evocative photos of the time. More striking are the unnervingly lifelike, life-size wax models of the two kings and their mothers and of the most redoubtable queen mother, Yaa Asantewaa, who led the 1900 revolt against the British and who died in exile in the Seychelles.

Inquire here or at the tourist office if you'd like an appointment with King Otumfuo Osei Tutu, the 16th Asantehene. If you're lucky enough to get an audience, etiquette demands presentation of a bottle or two of good schnapps when meeting the royals. This curious custom is a legacy from the days when the Dutch traded with the Ashantis and would present the chiefs with schnapps as a token of goodwill. During the festivities of Adae the Asantehene receives visitors; travellers are more than welcome.

OKOMFO ANOKYE SWORD

The **Okomfo Anokye Teaching Hospital** is the unlikely setting for the small **museum** (Bantama Rd; admission C3; ☻ 9am-4.30pm) housing the Okomfo Anokye Sword, an important Ashanti monument. The sword has been in the ground for three centuries and has never been pulled out. According to Ashanti legend, it marks the spot where the Golden Stool descended from the sky to indicate where the Ashanti people should settle. The sword is a symbol of the unity and strength of the Ashanti people and if anyone ever pulls it out, their kingdom will collapse. It's housed in a small yellow building with red Ashanti symbols on the outside walls. When entering the hospital grounds from Bantama Rd, veer to the right so you avoid the smell of formaldehyde from the mortuary; it's behind Block C.

ARMED FORCES MUSEUM

Fort St George and its **museum** (Stewart Ave; adult/child C5/2; ☻ 8am-5pm Tue-Sat) deserve a visit for the extraordinary collection of booty amassed by the West Africa Frontier Force, forerunner of today's Ghanaian army, with items looted from the Germans in Togo during WWI and, in WWII, from the Italians in Eritrea and Ethiopia and from the Japanese in Burma. The fort, originally constructed by the Ashanti in 1820, was razed by the British in 1873 during the Fourth Ashanti War, and then rebuilt by them in 1896. The most interesting section relates to the British-Ashanti war of 1900, when the Ashanti, led by their queen mother, Yaa Asantewaa, temporarily besieged the fort, starving the British residents.

KUMASI HAT MUSEUM

The top floor of the Nurom Hotel on Ofinso Rd is a monument to one man's extraordinary hat fetish. The owner, the late Chief Nana Kofi Gyemfi II, spent his lifetime assembling an amazing personal collection of more than 2000 hats from all over the world. Beginning with his first headgear, back in 1928, there's a proud collection of fedoras, sombreros, boaters, bowlers and much more. To get to the hotel, take any tro-tro heading north from Kejetia Circle to Suame Circle or catch a taxi.

KUMASI ZOO

Though some of the members of the sad-looking collection of creatures in **Kumasi Zoo** (admission C1; ☻ 9am-5pm Mon-Sat), among them imprisoned squirrels and a skinny camel on its last, knobbly legs, might break your heart, the wardens are well-meaning enough and this zoo is hugely popular with families and curious schoolchildren. If you can bear it, it's worth a visit if only for its one unfenced exhibit – an immense colony of squabbling fruitbats. The bats live in the trees in and around the zoo; from its benches you can watch from a close vantage point. Even more spectacular is the sight of what looks like black stormclouds descending upon the city, as the bats depart for a night of hunting. As you leave the zoo, turn left and you'll see women selling spicy fried bats as snacks. Presumably the profit margins of such an operation (they simply climb into the trees and grab the bats) makes the risk of rabies and other infectious diseases worthwhile.

MAGAZINE AREA

Kumasi is made up of a number of districts, many of which used to perform a specific role for the Ashanti king. The Magazine area in Suame district was originally where artillery was made; now, however, it's a vast used-car workshop where rusty old wrecks are resuscitated. Piles and piles of rusting engine parts line the sides of the roads and the air is filled with the chinking sound of metal hitting metal. Worth a look as you pass through on your way north.

Festivals & Events

The 42-day cycle of the Ashanti religious calendar is marked by the **Adae festival**, a public ceremony involving the Asantehene. The tourist office has a list of exact dates. The **Odwira festival** is an important annual celebration.

Sleeping

BUDGET

Nurom Hotel Annex II (☎ 051 32324; Nsene Rd; r from C10) This hotel close to the Kejetia Market and lorry station can be noisy, but accommodation is roomy and clean, and the place is friendly enough.

Guestline Lodge (☎ 051 227 657; mahesh161us@yahoo.com; Prempreh II St; dm C8, s/d with fan C9/14, d with bath & air-con C39; ☻ 🖵) Vic Baboo's sleeping establishment soaks up plenty of backpacker traffic, largely because it's a block away from the STC bus station. There's a pleasant courtyard where you can order discounted meals from Vic Baboo's cafe but many of the rooms are looking decidedly grubby, running water is unreliable and the advertised internet cafe is but a fantasy. Nevertheless, the three-storey building is not without its charms.

Presbyterian Guesthouse (☎ 051 26966; Mission Rd; r C8; **P**) Set in attractive green grounds, this two-storey guesthouse is the most peaceful budget option in Kumasi. The basic rooms are very well maintained and as part of the deal you get use of a kitchen. There's also an onsite cafe, with meals from C2.50. Whatever your faith, this place is proof that cleanliness is indeed next (door) to Godliness.

Hotel de Kingsway (☎ 051 26228; Asomfo Rd; r with fan/air-con from C12/40; 🔀) The Kingsway is a bit like the hotel that time forgot. Old-fashioned furniture and old-fashioned manners are the order of the day. If you can bear the dark prison-style corridors and shabby rooms, this is a decent central option – the charming elderly night porter certainly thinks so.

Wesley Guesthouse (☎ 051 82984; r with air-con from C23; 🔀) Above the City View restaurant, this is a strong contender for the budget guest house crown. Though there are only nine rooms, they're modern, clean and air-conditioned. The building's entrance is at the side and you'll need to climb a few flights of stairs.

MIDRANGE

Kumasi Catering Rest House (☎ 051 26506; Government Rd; r with fan/air-con C30/50; **P** 🔀) This charming guest house set within shady grounds a short walk from the centre seems engaged in a single-handed attempt to bring 1970s-style furniture back into fashion. The rooms are huge and the bathrooms need their own area code. Also on site is a popular restaurant with a large menu (mains from C3.50).

Rose's Guest House (☎ 051 24072; Old Bekwai Rd; r C35; **P** 🔀) Within stumbling distance of the Vienna City Pub on the same grounds, Rose's offers several large and cool tiled-floor rooms. More expensive executive rooms have carpeting and cable TV.

Sanbra Hotel (☎ 051 31256; Bogyawi St; r C39-70; **P** 🔀) Attracts a mainly Ghanaian crowd, the lobby is reasonably decorated, rooms are fresh and spacious and some even have small balconies.

Fosua Hotel (☎ 051 37382; www.fosuahotel.net; r from C40; **P** 🔀 🖥) This smart hotel occupies the top floor of the Aseda office complex a block from the STC bus station. The 24 rooms here

are clean and comfortable, with hot water and room service, though each has a strange, small glassed-in space facing out in lieu of a balcony. Still, there are decent views out over the city and there's a forex bureau, travel agency, bar and restaurant in the same complex.

TOP END

Royal Basin Resort (☎ 051 60144, 0246 333 596; 10km east of city; s/d US$65/75; **P** 🔀 🏊) Opposite St Louis School, the Royal Basin is a perfectly ok option, although staying here does feel a little like being on a mediocre package holiday in Spain. If you need some down time, however, you can't go too wrong; there's an outdoor pool, jazz club and the rooms are clean and fairly comfortable.

Royal Park (☎ 051 39353; Old Bekwai Rd; d US$70-100; **P** 🔀 🛜 🏊) Rooms at this up-market Cantonese-run hotel are clean, design-conscious and modern, with granite-topped basins and decent beds. The decor is largely oriental and there's a good restaurant, casino and wi-fi access.

Four Villages Inn (☎ 051 22682; www.fourvillages.com; Old Bekwai Rd; s/d inc breakfast US$80/90; **P** 🔀) The Ghanaian-Canadian owners have pulled out all the stops at this totally charming guest house. Each of the four enormous air-conditioned rooms is decorated in a different style and there's a TV lounge, tropical garden and even an atrium. Wake to the smell of freshly-ground coffee and ask the owners, one of whom trained as a chef, about the tour services, golf club hire and DVD library.

Golden Tulip (☎ 051 83777; www.goldentulipkumasicity.com; Rain Tree St; r US$100-280; **P** 🔀 🖥 🛜 🏊) Everything you would expect from a swish international chain, including a pool and gym, hair salon, business centre and universal wi-fi access. Rooms are stylish and air-conditioned. You can book online.

Eating

For food stalls, head to the train station area, around Kejetia Circle and on the Hudson Rd side of the stadium. There are several small chop bars along Prempeh II Rd, a couple of which sell good, deli-style sandwiches.

Vic Baboo's (Prempeh II Rd; mains C3-10; 🕑 11am-9.30pm; 🔀) It's a hot, sticky afternoon in Kumasi and you're craving an ice-cold strawberry milkshake. Your British travelling companion is dreaming of chicken tikka masala. So you go to Vic Baboo's, an institution among

GHANA

travellers and expats. With the biggest menu in town, this place is whatever you want it to be – Indian takeaway, decent burger joint, Lebanese deli or cocktail bar. It also has ice cream, cashew nuts and popcorn. Last orders taken around 9pm.

King of Kings (Prempeh II Rd; mains C3-10; ☺ 6am-9.30pm; ☒) The King of Kings wins the crown for the best balcony restaurant in Kumasi (and there are a fair few contenders). There's a choice of 10 or so excellent speciality dishes, including good groundnut soup and *fufu*, and the Ashanti King theme isn't rubbed in your face (although you can hire red and black robes). There's also a great well-stocked bar offering juices, bar snacks and a good selection of African bitters and gins.

Sweet Bite (Ahodwo Main Rd; mains C3-9; ☒) It's worth a trip out to Sweet Bite, several kilometres south of Ahodwo Circle, for good Lebanese food like falafel, baba ganoush, hummus and kofta. Other options like burgers and seafood are on the menu.

Queens Gate (Prempeh II Rd; mains from C4) Serves everything from omelettes to soups, salads, burgers and good Ghanaian dishes on a 3rd-floor balcony restaurant. Sister restaurant of Queens Gate II, otherwise known as Funkies, at Apino Plaza.

City View (Asomfo Rd; mains from C4) Dining at City View, below the Wesley Guesthouse, is like being invited to a festive dinner party. Tables are laid with fancy napkins, stylish tablecloths and candles, but the place is wholesome, unpretentious and friendly. Ask for one of the two outdoor tables – you'll have your own private balcony and views of the city. Chinese food.

Vienna City Pub (Harper Rd; mains from C4; ☒) This place, formerly Ryan's Irish Pub, is a second home for some expats, who wash away their nostalgia beside the pool table, fußball and darts. The bar is a bit of a dive but you can get decent sandwiches and pizza in the adjacent restaurant. On the grounds of Rose's Guest House.

Kentish Kitchen (mains from C4; ☺ breakfast-6pm) Inside the grounds of the National Cultural Centre Complex, Kentish has Adirondack-style white wooden chairs, checked tablecloths and an outdoor picnic vibe. Local and international dishes, all fairly simple.

Queens Gate II (Apino Plaza; mains from C5) Locals still call this place 'Funkies', which quite frankly, feels much more apt. Good pizza and excellent kebabs in an outdoor garden

sprinkled with fairy lights. Manages to be both laid-back and lively; there's often a DJ playing loud hip-hop to what would otherwise be a quiet courtyard setting. There's a good wine shop in the plaza.

Moti Mahal Restaurant (Asokwa; mains from C5; ☒) One of the most expensive restaurants in Kumasi, with a large selection of Indian cuisine; because everything is a la carte the bill can add up. It's atop Martin's Complex, Asokwa.

Nik's Pizza (off Old Bekwai Rd; pizzas C8-10) New Image Kitchen, or Nik's as it's known, is a Kumasi gem. Friendly waiters serve excellent pizza (and only pizza, it's clearly what they do best) in a quiet, leafy garden setting. It's worth the 15-minute walk through Kumasi's fanciest neighbourhood. From Apino Plaza on the Old Bekwai Rd, turn left: Nik's is signposted from there.

SELF-CATERING
You can find basic provisions at the food shops along Prempeh II Rd. The best supermarket is the A-Life chain, which has a branch on Prempeh II Rd and another only two blocks from the STC station. Opoku Trading, opposite the post office, has a good selection of imported foods and toiletries. There's a good Lebanese grocery store next to Sweet Bite restaurant.

Drinking
Kumasi has lots of places to grab a drink; anywhere with 'spot' in the name is a giveaway. The best places are in Adum.

Eclipse (Adum Rd) A friendly beer joint with an outdoor patio on the street; inside it's all diamond-shaped mirrors and big-screen sports.

Vic Baboo's (Prempeh II Rd) Lacks the ambiance of most locally run places but Vic's long cocktail list tempts volunteers and backpackers.

Queens Gate II (Apino Plaza) The coutyard bar-restaurant is a good place to start the night.

Entertainment
Jofel's Catering Services (Zongo Rd) sometimes has live music on Saturday.

Club monkeys might like to point their dancing shoes towards hip-hop hall **Tsar** (by Kejetia Circle), the sightly divey **Foxtrap** (Maxwell Rd) or sleek and sexy **Kiravi** (Harper Rd), which draws Ghanaian celebs and DJs.

Kumasi Stadium (Hudson Rd) hosts football matches (about C3) most Sundays.

Shopping

Besides Kejetia Market (p369), if you're interested in high-quality locally produced textiles try the **Bonwire Kente Cloth Shop** (Bank Rd), a little hole-in-the wall near Prempeh II Roundabout or the Kumasi branch of the West African Woodin Boutique group – a block from the train tracks and Kejetia Market. **Vic's Destiny Bookshop** (☎ 051 24047; Bank St; 9.30am-6pm) sells pens, journals, art supplies and a small selection of novels. Among the thrillers is the occasional African literary gem. The **Malaria Prevention Shop** (9.30am-6pm) is an entire store dedicated to the downfall of Kumasi's flying needles. It sells coils, plug-ins and bug spray – not exactly the stuff of every shopaholic's wildest fantasies, but worth a visit if you're itching and scratching.

Getting There & Away

AIR

Kumasi airport is on the northeastern outskirts of town, about 5km from the centre. The most efficient airline is **Antrak** (www.antrakair.com) which flies twin-propeller jets between Kumasi and Accra twice a day (one-way around US$90). Antrak and American Airlines share an **office** (☎ 051 32261; Harper Rd) though opening hours can be unreliable.

BUS & TRO-TRO

The huge **Kejetia motor park** (next to Kejetia market) is the city's main transport hub, from where you can get tro-tros to most regional destinations as well as buses to Accra and other points south. In addition, transport for Accra, Sunyani, Cape Coast, Takoradi and local destinations such as Lake Bosumtwi leave from **Asafo station** (east of Asafo roundabout).

The **STC bus station** (www.intercitystc.com; Prempeh Rd) is a two-minute walk from Guestline Lodge. Buses to Accra (C7, four hours) leave regularly between 3.30am and 5pm. STC buses also stop at Cape Coast (C4, four hours) on their way to Takoradi (C7, five hours). There are two buses a day to Tamale (C12, eight hours). There are less frequent services to Alfao and Tema. STC services Ouagadougou (Burkina Faso; C20, Monday, Wednesday, Saturday and Sunday) from Kumasi; price includes an additional charge.

Non-STC buses to Tamale, Bolgatanga, Bawku and Ouagadougou leave from **New Tafo (Kurofurom) motor park** (Dichemso), about 2km north of Kejetia market. Smaller buses to Tamale and destinations in the Upper West region leave from **Alaba bus station** (off Zongo Rd), on the northwestern side of the market.

TRAIN

For details of the train service to Takoradi and Accra, see p393.

Getting Around

The best place to charter a taxi is in the carpark of the STC bus station on Prempreh Rd. A short hop around town should cost C1 to C3. Most shared taxi lines start at Kejetia motor park and across the street at the intersection of Prempeh II and Guggisberg Rds. From Ntomin Rd, shared taxis head south along Harper Rd, serving the areas of town beyond Ahodwo Roundabout. Taxis are often reluctant to cross Kejetia Circle (because the traffic is so bad) so consider breaking a long journey into shorter stages.

An alternative to hiring a taxi for the day, **Dodi Travel & Tours** (☎ 051 20421; www.dodighana.com; Hudson Rd) is a dependable place to hire a car; small to medium vehicles are US$70 per day. Guestline Lodge also has a **car rental service** (Mike; ☎ 0242 020 271) where standard vehicles (with air-con and driver) cost $60 per day and 4WD vehicles are $120 per day.

AROUND KUMASI
Craft Villages

Because of their proximity to Kumasi, the craft villages in the region offer a convenient if touristy way to see how some of Ghana's traditional workshops operate.

There are two villages just on the outskirts of Kumasi, on the Mampong road beyond Suame Roundabout. **Pankrono**, 8km away, is a major pottery centre. One kilometre further is **Ahwiaa**, known for its woodcarving and an aggressive sales approach. **Ntonso**, 15km further, is the centre of adinkra cloth printing. **Bonwire**, 18km northeast of Kumasi, is the most famous of several nearby villages that specialise in weaving kente cloth. At the visitor centre here weavers demonstrate their craft and sell their wares. Bonwire has become very touristy in the last few years; while that's a good thing for the village, you might choose to head to other less visited kente villages such as **Wonoo** or **Adanwomase**, or **Bepoase**, further north. Several villages northwest of Kumasi on the Barekese road specialise in beadmaking, including **Asuofia** and **Pasoro**. A scene from

Lesley Lokko's novel *Bitter Chocolate* takes place in the village of Bonwire.

The easiest way to visit the central region's craft villages is to hire a private taxi (about C30 for a full day). You can also arrange a tour through the Kumasi tourist office. Less convenient, especially if you want to make a number of stops in one day, is to get a tro-tro from Kejetia motor park for the villages on the Mampong road or from Antoa station for Bonwire.

Owabi Wildlife Sanctuary

For butterflies and birds, maybe a Mona monkey or two, visit this small **sanctuary** (admission C3; ☉ 9am-5pm) 16km northwest of Kumasi, just off the Sunyani road. It consists of 13 sq km of pristine forest cut by several footpaths around the Owabi reservoir. They've recorded 161 species of bird here. You have to be accompanied by a guide, which you can arrange at the entrance gate. You can take a tro-tro from Kejetia motor park to Akropong on the Sunyani road, from where it's a 3km walk. Alternatively, you could hire a taxi for the day and take in the village of Bonwire too.

Ejisu

The small junction town of Ejisu, about 20km east of Kumasi on the Accra road, is the birthplace of Nana Yaa Asantewaa and home to an eponymous **museum** (admission C2; ☉ 9am-5pm), built in the form of a traditional queen mother's palace. It houses a fascinating display of artefacts from the life of Yaa Asantewaa, the queen mother and chief of Ejisu. She's most remembered for resisting British rule and preventing the revered Golden Stool from falling into their hands. Also recommended is a visit to the **shrine** in nearby **Besaese**. This was where Yaa Asantewaa consulted before launching her attack against the British. Inside is an excellent display on traditional Ashanti shrines. There are a number of other harder-to-get-to shrines in the area that see few tourists.

Regular tro-tros to Ejisu (30 minutes) leave from Asafo motor park in Kumasi. The museum is about 1.5km from the motor park in Ejisu and Besease is about 2km further along the Accra road. You can either walk or flag down a taxi.

Lake Bosumtwe

With a depth of 86m, Lake Bosumtwe is a crater lake formed by the impact of a huge meteorite. The lake is hugged by lush green hills in which you can hike, visiting some of the small villages around its perimeter. Only 38km southeast of Kumasi, it's a popular weekend venue for Kumasi residents, who come here to relax, swim (the water is said to be bilharzia-free) and jet-ski. You can also cycle the lake's 30km circumference.

The lake takes its name from the Twi for 'good antelope'; legend has it that it was discovered by a hunter chasing one for his supper. Not only is Bosumtwe the country's largest and deepest natural lake, it's also sacred. The Ashanti believe that their souls come here after death to bid farewell to their god Twi. Historically, dugout canoes and boats were forbidden, but the tide has turned and at weekends Bosumtwe becomes a haven for watersport enthusiasts. The word on the street is that the lake has a magnetic forcefield; researches from Harvard University are currently looking into it.

SLEEPING & EATING

Rainbow Garden Village (sms ☎ 0243 230 288; www .rainbowgardenvillage.com; camping C6, dm C9, d C24-29) This laid-back German-Ghanaian owned place, 3.5km from Abono, is the Big Milly's (p349) of Lake Bosumtwe. The dorms and waterfront bungalows are popular with a backpacker and volunteer crowd; there are tours on offer and big, convivial campfires every weekend.

Lake Point Guesthouse (sms ☎ 0243 452 922; www .ghana-hotel.com; dm/d/tr C8/26/30) Not far from the secluded shore of the lake, this hotel's landscaped grounds and flowering gardens give it an air of a nature retreat. Rooms are bright and charming, there's a good bar-restaurant and a range of spa treatments available, including (aptly) mud massages. You can also rent pedalos.

Paradise Resort (☎ 051 20164 www.lakebosom twepardiseresort.com; US$55-65; ☒ ☎) A good option if you want to commune with nature but not completely immerse yourself in it. Twenty plush rooms – some with lake views; all with air and mod cons. There's also wi-fi access and helpful staff.

GETTING THERE & AWAY

Occasional tro-tros run direct to Abonu (C2) from Asafo motor park in Kumasi; alternatively, take a tro-tro to Kuntanase (45

minutes) and a passenger taxi from there
(C3, 15 minutes).

Bobiri Forest Reserve
This reserve protects a parcel of virgin, un-
logged forest about 35km east of Kumasi.
The main goal for visitors is **Bobiri Butterfly
Sanctuary** (admission C2), home to more than 300
species of butterfly and an arboretum. Even if
you're unlucky enough not to see any, this is
a serene and beautiful place to relax. Guided
walks of varying length are available or you
can hike unaccompanied on some of the trails.
The **guest house** (r C8) at the sanctuary is better
than many and each fan room with wood
floors has a painted wall mural. Simple meals
are available.

From Kumasi or Ejisu, take any vehicle
going to Konongo (including STC buses)
or further south, and ask to be dropped at
Kubease, from where you can charter a taxi
or attempt the 3km walk.

BOABENG-FIEMA MONKEY SANCTUARY
This **sanctuary** (admission C4) is an excellent example of community-based conservation. It
links the twin villages of Fiema and Boabeng,
165km north of Kumasi. The villagers have
traditionally venerated and protected the
glossy black-and-white colobus and Mona
monkeys that live in the surrounding forest,
and in 1975 successfully passed a law making
it illegal to harm them.

You can see the monkeys on guided walks
through the forest and there's a simple,
village-run six-room **guest house** (Fiema; d from
C5); camping is also possible here.

From Kumasi, take a tro-tro to Techiman
from Alaba station. From there, take a shared
taxi to Nkoranza, 25km east. There are regular passenger taxis from Nkoranza to Fiema,
about 20km away.

YEJI
There's no real reason to come to Yeji, a port
town on Lake Volta, unless you're disembark-
ing from the *Nana Besemuna*, a ferry that links
the town with Makongo. On the scenic Tamale
road, 216km northeast of Kumasi, Yeji's surroundings are far more attractive than the
town itself. The town is also the gateway to the
remote and rarely-visited **Digya National Park**,
comprising 3,500 sq km of wetland, jungle
and swampland. The park hosts populations
of forest elephants, leopards and endangered

manatees. However, you'll need a spirit of
adventure, lashings of patience and a 4WD
to enter the park. The **Ghana Wildlife Society**
(www.ghanawildlifesociety.org) should be your first
port of call.

Tro-tros run between Yeji and Antoa station in Kumasi (four hours). For Tamale, take
the twice-daily ferry (45 minutes) across to
Makongo on the east bank. Tro-tros run
between Makongo and Tamale (five hours).

For details of the ferry service to Akosombo,
see p392.

THE NORTH
The rust-red roads of northern Ghana wind
through flat grasslands, saffron-coloured savannah and patches of hot, arid scrubland.
Life happens more slowly here. Men in prayer
caps ride bicycles to mud-and-stick mosques;
elephants linger at the watering holes of Mole
National Park and goats wander around villages of baked clay huts. This dusty region,
shingled with fine examples of traditional
Islamic architecture, feels a million miles away
from the rest of Ghana.

TAMALE
☎ 071
The capital of northern Ghana, with its flat,
dusty avenues, was practically made for bicycles. You'll see clusters of them parked outside schools and markets; shiny blue metal
glistening in the hot Tamale sun. Ghana's
fourth-largest city underwent something
of a renovation in 2008 but the flat-roofed
buildings and shabby-looking shops remain.
One thing is certain; if the northern region is
Ghana's breadbasket, Tamale is its kitchen. If
you can take the heat, you'll discover a town
with plenty of good food, charm and a whole
lot of soul. (If you can't, don't panic: Mole
is cooler.)

Because Tamale (pronounced Ta-ma-le,
with syllables of equal length) is a major
transport hub for travellers on their way to
Mole or overland to Burkina Faso, it has a
nice selection of good-value hotels and restaurants. The heart of town is the sprawling **central market**, marked by the tall radio
antenna near the STC bus station. You can
buy pretty much anything here, including
parasols and trekking boots (only in men's
sizes) for Mole.

GHANA

Tamale's population is largely Muslim and there are several interesting **mosques** around town, notably on Bolgatanga Rd. The **National Cultural Centre** (off Salaga Rd), has an echoing auditorium where music and dance performances are occasionally put on; there are a bunch of craft shops around the back that rarely see shoppers. There's a **public library** with a nice collection of fiction and non-fiction books just south of Sparkles restaurant opposite the entrance to the football stadium.

Information

INTERNET ACCESS

Forsumel Internet Café (Salaga Rd)

Kalang ICT Centre (Gumbihini Rd; per hr C0.80; ⏲ 8am-10pm) On the same street as the Catholic Guesthouse and Swad Fast Food.

My.com Internet Café (per hr C0.80; ⏲ 7.30am-11.00pm) Directly opposite Relax Lodge.

MONEY

Man Forex Bureau is one of the only ones in town although the exchange rate at the Gariba Lodge is better.

Barclays Bank (Salaga Rd) Near the Giddipass Restaurant. Has an ATM.

Standard Chartered Bank (Salaga Rd) Opposite the market. Has an ATM.

TOURIST INFORMATION

Tourist office (☎ 2337 124 835; ⏲ 8.30am-5pm Mon-Fri) About 1.5km east of the centre, in the administration buildings. Brochures galore.

BIKE HIRE

All Stars (Bolgatanga Rd) and **Paniel Enterprises** (Bolgatanga Rd) rent inexpensive Tamale-style bicycles for kids and adults.

Festivals & Events

As if Tamale wasn't hot enough, it hosts an annual **Dagomba Fire Festival**, held in July. According to local legend a chief was overjoyed to find his missing son asleep under a tree. Angry that the tree had hidden his son, he punished it by having it burnt. On the night of the festival, pyromania takes hold and everyone rushes around with blazing torches. It's a little like an out-of-control sparkler party.

Sleeping

Tamale has a good mix of budget and top-end options. Touts meet the STC buses; if they tell

you the place you had in mind is full, it probably isn't. Most are working on commission for local (often perfectly OK) hotels.

BUDGET

TICCS Guesthouse (☎ 071 22914; www.ticcs.com; Gumbihini Link Rd; r C10; ℗ 🐱) Simple, airy rooms in leafy green surrounds at the Tamale Institute of Cross Cultural Studies, which also runs (long-term) courses in African Studies and Theology. Onsite there's the popular jungle bar, stalked by two resident cats.

Catholic Guesthouse (☎ 071 22265; Gumbihini Rd; r C14-25; ℗ 🐱) The most popular cheapie. Simple, air-conditioned rooms wrap around a pretty courtyard. There's a good restaurant and outdoor bar. Although the spacious green grounds give it a quiet and peaceful feel, this is a good place to meet other travellers.

King's Guesthouse (☎ 0208 380 950; Kalpophin Estates; r from C15; ℗ 🐱 🖳) Another courtyard set-up, King's has a range of rooms – some with satellite TV, fridges and air-con. Everything, from the rooms to the furniture, is miniature in a rather endearing way. Everything, that is, bar the constant smile on the face of helpful owner Kofi. There's also a (miniature) restaurant and a computer with internet access.

MIDRANGE & TOP END

Picorna (☎ 071 22672; Kaladan Park; r C23-58; ℗ 🐱) Like an ageing celebrity, the Picorna used to have it all. It was smart, pretty hot and had its own cinema and nightclub. It's booked in for a facelift, but in the meantime this is not the worst option in town. Staff are friendly enough and there's a quirky garden filled with statues of women and giraffes. Despite its issues, the Picorna still attracts a few birds, which come to drink at the pond at sunset.

Relax Lodge (☎ 071 24981; Gkc1955@yahoo.com; r from US$50; ℗ 🐱 🎧) Pretty in pink, this friendly Pakistani-run place has undergone renovation and is now a decent midrange option. There's a (good) Tandoori restaurant that breaks the rules a little by serving pizza.

Hotel Mariam (☎ 071 23548; Gumbihini Rd; r US$80-120; ℗ 🐱) A favourite with business travellers, the Mariam is the nicest place to stay in Tamale. The rooms are modern, clean and well kept, and there's a good restaurant with a large menu, though service isn't particularly quick. Find it a few kilometres from the centre, up the same street as the TICCS Guesthouse.

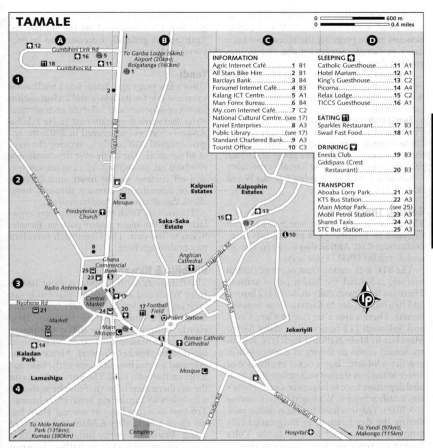

TAMALE

INFORMATION
Agric Internet Café..............1 B1
All Stars Bike Hire................2 B1
Barclays Bank.....................3 B4
Forsumel Internet Café.......4 B3
Kalang ICT Centre...............5 A1
Man Forex Bureau...............6 B4
My.com Internet Café.........7 C2
National Cultural Centre..(see 17)
Paniel Enterprises...............8 A3
Public Library..................(see 17)
Standard Chartered Bank....9 A3
Tourist Office....................10 C3

SLEEPING
Catholic Guesthouse.........11 A1
Hotel Mariam....................12 A1
King's Guesthouse.............13 C2
Picorna.............................14 A4
Relax Lodge......................15 C2
TICCS Guesthouse.............16 A1

EATING
Sparkles Restaurant...........17 B3
Swad Fast Food.................18 A1

DRINKING
Enesta Club......................19 B3
Giddipass (Crest Restaurant).................20 B3

TRANSPORT
Aboaba Lorry Park.............21 A3
KTS Bus Station................22 A3
Main Motor Park...........(see 25)
Mobil Petrol Station..........23 A3
Shared Taxis.....................24 A3
STC Bus Station................25 A3

GHANA

Gariba Lodge (☎ 071 23041; gariba@africaonline .com.gh; Bolgatanga Rd; d US$85-110; P ⊠ 🛜) Clean, stylish rooms (with hot water) in a tranquil garden setting. This place, though not the liveliest, is smart and upmarket without being pretentious. There's a good restaurant serving wine and guinea fowl. Staff are helpful and friendly. For a fee, you can use the fastest wi-fi connection in Tamale. About 7km north of the town centre on Bolgatanga Rd.

Eating & Drinking

There are plenty of food stalls around the market and along Salaga Rd where you can also sample *pito*, the local millet brew.

Sparkles (nr library; mains from C3; ⏲ 8am-8pm Mon-Sat) A mainstay on the Tamale restau-rant scene, Sparkles is popular with back-packers and volunteers, who cycle here from placements in nearby villages. It's a simple cafe serving good Ghanaian food alongside Western staples such as sandwiches.

Swad Fast Food (☎ 071 23588; Gumbihini Rd, nr Catholic Guesthouse; mains about C7; ⏲ 11am-10pm) Ah, Swad Fast Food. Ok, so the name may not do it for you but this is one of the best places to eat in Tamale. The speciality is Indian, but there's also French onion soup, red red, banku and (bizarrely) fish-finger sandwiches. You eat beneath thatched umbrellas in a pretty outdoor garden.

Jungle Bar (TICCS Guesthouse, Gumbihini Link Rd; meals C3-8) There should be more places like this in Ghana. The Jungle Bar, on the grounds of the TICCS Guesthouse, is on a leafy balcony with an all-wood bar, cable TV and comfy benches and is probably the nicest spot for a drink in Tamale. Serves kebabs, sloppy Joes and hot dogs.

Giddipass (Crest Restaurant; Salaga Rd) Sit back on the roof-top terrace and let an ice-cold beer and the sweet sounds of hip-life into your world.

Enesta Club (cnr Bolgatanga & Bank Rds; ⊙ Sat & Sun) Fun dancehall with a homespun reggae vibe. Crate diggers should visit the vinyl store of the same name, which sells a range of African records and CDs as well as Tamale's speciality – northern Ghanaian hip-life (see the boxed text, p331).

Getting There & Away

The airport is about 20km north of town, on the road to Bolgatanga; a private taxi there costs about C10. Antrak flies between Tamale and Accra for US$175 one way.

The STC bus station (just north of central market) is behind the Mobil petrol station. There are four buses daily to Accra (12 hours) and two buses a day to Kumasi (four to seven hours). There's also a service to Cape Coast and Takoradi (12 hours). The daily Metro Mass bus to Mole National Park (C4; four to six hours) leaves in theory at 2.30pm but in practice a lot later. Buy a ticket in advance or arrive at the bus station well before its scheduled departure time to be sure of a seat. There's also a daily service to Wa (eight hours), leaving at 5.30am. Tro-tros leave the main motor park during the day heading to Bolgatanga (2½ hours). For details of services to the Volta Region via Yendi and Bimbilla, see below.

Getting Around

During the daytime you won't have to wait more than a few minutes for a line taxi running along the Bolgatanga road to take you into town from one of the hotels. When night falls, finding transport on the street can be slightly harder. Most taxi drivers are happy to arrange a ride in advance.

TAMALE TO HOHOE

The route between Tamale and the Volta Region via Yendi and Bimbilla is rough, and there are few facilities for travellers, but it offers a fantastic off-the-beaten-track experience and some magnificent scenery. This route can be done in either direction and

takes a minimum of two days but if you've got time, it's worth breaking the journey up. Transport is generally infrequent so be prepared for long waits.

Yendi

Until a few years ago, Yendi was a traditional town notable for its palace and an interesting fusion of Moorish and Sahelian architectural styles. But when the paramount Ya-Na Yakubu Andani chief was murdered in 2002, the region erupted into conflict, claiming the lives of 40 townfolk. The battle over the chieftaincy rumbled on, prompting Accra to impose on-and-off curfews on the town until 2008. If you're considering passing through here, check the situation before travelling.

Tro-tros to Yendi (two hours) leave regularly from the main motor park in Tamale, 97km to the east. The Greenwich meridian passes through here.

Bimbilla & Nkwanta

This flat, dusty district capital is about 100km from Yendi and a convenient place to break your journey. It too has an interesting palace, home to the chief. Just off the main drag, clearly signposted, is the **Hilltop Guesthouse** (r C7), where basic rooms come with shared bathrooms (bucket shower). Meals can be prepared for you here or at one of the basic eateries on the main road. The lorry station is on the southern edge of town. From here, there's a daily bus to Tamale via Yendi (four hours). Tro-tros to Accra leave at around 11am but get there a little after 6.30am to be sure of a seat. **Nkwanta**, a pretty little village with a scenic mountain backdrop, halfway between Bimbilla and Hohoe, is another possibility for breaking your journey.

MOLE NATIONAL PARK
☎ 0717

At 4577 sq km, Mole (pronounced Mo-lay) is Ghana's largest national park and one of West Africa's best wildlife-watching spots. It consists of swathes of saffron-coloured savannah, criss-crossed by pockets of forest and shaded streams. There are at least 300 species of bird and 94 of mammal, including African elephant, kob, buffaloe, baboon and warthog (see boxed text p382).

There's one main escarpment, on which the motel and **park headquarters** (entry fee adult/student C4/2.50, camera fee C5) are situated, From here, you can embark on what must be the most inexpensive **safari** (adult per two hr C0.75) in Africa, entirely by foot and with unrivalled opportunities to get up close to beautiful, bus-sized elephants. Informative safari walks depart twice daily, leaving the park headquarters (diagonally opposite the motel) at 6.30am (sometimes half an hour later in the rainy season) and 3.30pm. Sturdy, covered footwear is a must for the two-hour walk through patches of jungle and scrub; if you come without, the rangers will insist on lending you a pair of ill-fitting wellington boots for a fee of C2. The walks are fantastic value and wind their way through woodland and arid savannah, finishing at the main waterhole. At the time of research, vehicle safaris were only possible for those with private vehicles and accompanied by a park ranger. Wheelchair users may be able to arrange adapted non-vehicle safaris (much of the park is flat).

The best time to see wildlife is during the ultra-dry harmattan season from January to March, when thirsty elephants congregate at the waterhole. However, Mole is worth a visit at any time of year. On one guided walk, it's usual to see as many as 20 elephants splashing around at the waterhole, though this is by no means guaranteed. It's possible (though rare) to come away having seen nothing at all.

The park entrance gate is about 4km north of the Larabanga turn-off. The park headquarters and the motel are a further 2km into the park. Metro Mass buses from Tamale pause in Larabanga before making a final stop right outside the Mole Motel.

You're not permitted to walk (or drive) in the park unless you're accompanied by an armed ranger. You are, however, allowed to walk unaccompanied along the road back to Larabanga – apparently the park isn't liable for people attacked outside its domain.

Sleeping & Eating

Mole Motel (☎ 0277 564 444, 0244 316 777; dm C8, r without/with air-con C35/45; ✱ ☲) Most of the world's motels have views of highways, car parks or non-descript suburban towns. Not Mole. Perched on a grassy ridge overlooking a waterhole, this low-key motel enjoys views of sweet grasslands, scrub and prancing antelopes. Monkeys hang (literally) beside the outdoor pool, warthogs sniff around the breakfast tables and from the sunloungers you can watch elephants thunder through the park. The motel itself is no stunner, but

frankly there are better things to look at. For a while there has been talk of renovations, but for now the enormous rooms are at least clean and bright, with running water and huge balconies. There's also a reasonable restaurant, serving a mix of Ghanaian and international fare (mains from C6). If you want to keep the mozzies away, try the excellent grilled fish in garlic, served with yam chips. The two viewing stations are a good place for a sunset beer. The motel is not technically wheelchair accessible, but those able to negotiate one or two small steps (mainly around the pool and bar area) will find it acceptable.

Mole Canteen (mains from C2.50; ✆ 8am-10pm) This little gem is tucked behind the park headquarters. Cheap, hearty northern fare is served largely to park rangers and their families. Good breakfast sandwiches.

Getting There & Away

Mole National Park is 135km west of Tamale, off the dirt road that connects Fufulso on the Kumasi to Tamale road with Sawla on the Kumasi to Wa road. The turn-off to the park is in Larabanga, 15km west of Damongo, a busy transport and market centre.

A daily Metro Mass bus runs from Tamale (C4, four to six hours), leaving some time after 2.30pm, once it's packed to the gunwales, and arriving at the park motel around 7pm if all goes well. You really need to get your ticket a day in advance or early the morning of the departure to be assured a seat. Depending on your perspective, and to some extent your luck, the journey is either a real African adventure or a hot, sweaty bus ride from hell. The same bus overnights at the park, returning to Tamale the next day, leaving the park at around 4.30am.

The alternative is to take any early-morning bus from Tamale heading to Bole or Wa and get off at Larabanga, then find onward transport by motorbike, private taxi or tro-tro.

LARABANGA

The tiny Muslim village of Larabanga is 4km from Mole and is most famous for its striking Sudanese-style mud-and-stick mosque, purported to be the oldest of its kind in Ghana. The town itself is hot, dusty and soporific; alleys wrap around traditional mud homes and bedraggled goats roam the streets. The village has some fine examples of the mud-walled domestic compounds decorated with geometric two-tone patterns that are a feature

GHANA

IN THE FOOTPRINTS OF ELEPHANTS

African elephants have inhabited Mole for centuries but the area was not declared a national park until 1971. In the 1920s and 1930s, villagers complained of an abundance of tsetse flies and subsequent outbreaks of sleeping sickness. Poachers quickly moved in, convincing villagers that eliminating the wild animals would curb the outbreaks. The open season only ended when the park became established some forty years later.

Today the park spans 4577 sq km and employs some 175 staff as rangers, caretakers and support workers. They live in Mole village, a short walk from the Park HQ, or in one of the other 35 communities in and around the park. With at least 300 species of bird, including blue-bellied rollers and raptors, Mole is a spectacular place to whip out the binoculars.

There's been 94 mammal species recorded; among them a steady population of 600 to 800 African elephants, more than 1000 buffaloes, olive baboons, several species of antelopes, warthogs and Nile crocodiles. There is a small population of lions, but sightings are rare, even among the park rangers, who spot one on average every five years. The first caracal sighting was in 2008; rangers believe Mole harbours a very small population of these nocturnal big cats.

of northern Ghana. It's also a good alternative base for exploring the park.

Villagers believe the **mosque** was built in 1421, when its founder, eager to find a site for a place of worship, came across a mystic stone on the outskirts of Larabanga. According to the story, he threw a spear from the site and constructed the mosque where it landed. Other, more controversial accounts, suggest the mosque was built several hundred years later. Make of its history what you will; whatever its age, the mosque is a fine specimen of Islamic-influenced African architecture. Everyone can visit the black-and-white exterior, but only Muslims (and even then special permission is required) may enter. The mosque is listed on the World Monuments Fund's List of 100 Most Endangered Sites; the Imam requests donations of C5 from all tourists.

Though the number of tour guides in Larabanga can be overwhelming at times, the village has come to rely on tourism for its bread and butter. Understandably everyone wants a slice of the pie, and some travellers have subsequently complained about scams. Nyekemeke Abudu Kony leads recommended, though expensive, **tours** (☎ 0243 454 931) of the village and surrounding area, including to the **mystic stone**. Several years ago, a road was planned which would have passed right through it; villagers successfully had its direction changed.

Most travellers stay with the well-known Salia brothers' **guesthouses** (☎ 0275 544 071; www. larabanga.netfirms.com; r C5) in the village. They have established a community-based project where you can hire bicycles, binoculars and bird-identification kits. Rooms are basic but comfortable, and have fans. You can even sleep on the roof, under a mosquito net and the stars. Good, basic meals are available on request. Because the Salia brothers have the monopoly on tourism, sometimes other villagers pose as the brothers to boost their income. There are several other good homestay options in Larabanga, but if you plan on staying with the Salia brothers, be sure of the identity of those meeting you at the bus. There are two general stores/basic restaurants in Larabanga and some villagers sell DVDs and sunglasses.

Transport from Larabanga is limited. To Tamale, there's the daily bus from Mole and a daily bus from Wa, both of which pass through town early in the day; heading east, there are two daily buses to Bole in the early afternoon, and a daily bus to Wa at around 9.30am. Tro-tros from the junction town of Sawla on the Kumasi to Wa road occasionally pass through on the way to Tamale.

To get to Mole, you can hire a bicycle or a private taxi/motorbike; walking is definitely not advisable in the heat of the day. There have been reports of robberies on this road, and so it's best to err on the side of caution when considering this route, especially alone or in the dark.

WA

☎ 0756

Few visitors make it to Wa, in the far northwestern corner of the country near the Burkina Faso border, but it's worth the slog getting here; not only as it's a departure point for visits to the Wechiau hippo sanctuary, but to check out the **palace of the Wa**

Na (as the chief is called). This palace, found behind the post office and Ghana Telecom complex, was built in the traditional Sahelian mud-and-pole style and you can take a quick tour of the crumbling remains inside.

Definitely worth a look is the beautiful **Great Mosque** and, behind it, an older mud-and-pole **mosque**. First pay your respects (and a small donation) to the Imam, who will expect you to sign his visitor's book.

About 5km past the Upland Hotel is the small village of **Nakori**, which has an impressive mud-and-pole mosque. There's no public transport; you'll have to take a private taxi from the motor park or it makes a pleasant walk (allow a good hour one way from the Upland Hotel).

Sleeping & Eating

The **Hotel du Pond** (☎ 0756 20018), **Kunateh Lodge** (☎ 0756 22102) and the **Catholic Guesthouse** (☎ 0756 22375) are all located within a few minutes walk of the motor park and offer wallet-friendly, comfortable rooms.

Though 3km west of the town centre, the smart **Upland Hotel** (☎ 0756 22180; r C40-60) has clean, spacious rooms and a great outdoor restaurant and bar.

There are plenty of food stalls and chop bars in and around the market area. The **Soldier's Bar** (dishes from C2) and **Prisoner's Canteen** (dishes from C2) near the football pitch serve good, cheap chow.

Getting There & Away

STC and City Express buses leave from the STC bus station by the main roundabout, travelling between Wa and Kumasi (three times a week), Accra (three times a week) and Tamale (daily). The Tamale bus makes a stop in Larabanga. There is a 10am City Express bus to Bolgatanga every day (C4.50). For tro-tros and OSA buses to surrounding villages and the Burkina border, head to the main motor park.

WECHIAU HIPPO SANCTUARY

About as far west as you can travel without changing languages, this remote hippo sanctuary along the Black Volta River is one of Ghana's most under-hyped ecotourism projects. Initiated by village chiefs in 1999, the 40km sanctuary is a safe haven for female hippos, who give birth in the flooded streams during the rainy season. Hippos are among West Africa's most threatened creatures; slash-and-burn farming has already destroyed some habitats. The sanctuary is sponsored by Canada's Calgary Zoo.

The C9 admission fee covers basic guest house accommodation (pit toilet and bucket shower) and canoe trips to see the hippos; November through June is the best time to see these prehistoric-looking beasts. Meals can be prepared but you'll need to bring your own provisions.

Wechiau village is reached by tro-tro (one hour, 46km) from the main lorry park in Wa. The Wechiau Hippo Sanctuary is about 20km from Wechiau. Transport uncertainties (roads sometimes become impassable in the rainy season from July to September) mean you really should plan to spend one night at the sanctuary itself rather than try to do it as a day trip from Wa.

WORKING TOGETHER: COMMUNITY-BASED TOURISM IN NORTHERN GHANA

Ten years ago the villagers of Mognori, 12km from Mole National Park, found themselves in a bit of a quandry. Their neighbours in Larabanga were beginning to reap the rewards of a burgeoning community-based tourism movement. But times were hard in Mognori; crops had been threatened by elephant destruction and fertile farmland was scarce. The answer lay in Mognori's lazy, slow-running river.

In 2006, funding (from both Ghanaian and international development sources) came through for an ecotourism project that would benefit the villages as well as visitors to Mole and Larabanga. The project launched soon after and visitors to the friendly, low-key **Mognori Eco-Village** (☎ 0274 301 583, 0275 543 056) can now take canoe safaris on the river (there are monkeys, birds and crocodiles) , watch drumming and dancing performances, and see shea butter being made and baskets weaved. You can also learn about traditional African medicine. Pigeons are sacred to the villagers and rumour has it that they will shun all water unless it has been blessed. Homestays can also be arranged.

BOLGATANGA

☎ 072

Bolgatanga – 'just call me Bolga' – was once the southernmost point of the ancient trans-Saharan trading route, running through Burkina Faso to Mali. As well as serving as a jumping-off point for travellers heading into the dust, it's an interesting base for exploring the surrounding villages.

Bolga's selling point is its renowned **craft market**, selling textiles, leatherwork, multi-coloured baskets and the famous Bolga straw hats. For baskets, you could also try the **basket shop** (Commercial Rd) near the intersection with Bazaar Rd.

Don't miss **Bolgatanga Library**, designed by the late J Max Bond Jr, one of New York City's most prominent architects. A small **museum** (off Navrongo Rd; admission C1; ⌚ 9am-5pm), behind the Catholic mission, has a display on the ethnology and culture of the northeast.

Information

There's a helpful **tourist office** (☎ 072 23416; Navrongo Rd; ⌚ 9am-5pm Mon-Fri) across from SSNIT House on Library Rd. There are sev-

eral banks and an ATM on Commercial Rd. SSNIT also houses an internet cafe.

Sleeping

Nsamini Guesthouse (☎ 072 23403; off Navrongo Rd; r from C7) A popular choice, this cute courtyard set-up is one of Bolga's best budget buys. Rooms are clean and staff are welcoming. It's up a lane leading off the Navrongo Rd.

Sand Gardens (☎ 072 23464; r with fan/air-con C30/35; 🏊) Rooms surround a large dirt compound, part bar, part restaurant, sometimes loud, but the concrete bungalows are clean and comfortable. To find it head east down Zuarungu Rd until you reach the fire station and turn left down the dirt road.

St Joseph Hotel (☎ 072 230 214; r from C10; 🏊) A mish-mash of rooms and an OK fallback option, St Joseph is located on a side road next to the National Investment Bank.

Tienyine Hotel (☎ 072 22355; Starlet 91 St; r from C30) Bolga's best upmarket option, this is part of the same complex as the recommended Comme Ci Comme Ça restaurant. Rooms are bright and welcoming.

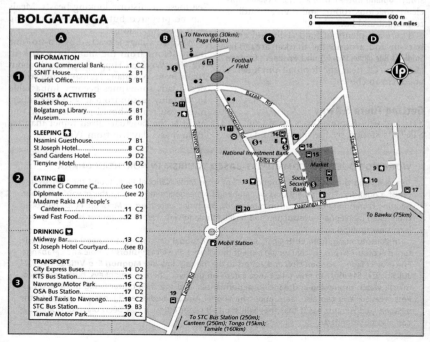

BOLGATANGA

0 — 600 m
0 — 0.4 miles

INFORMATION
Ghana Commercial Bank.............1 C2
SSNIT House.................................2 B1
Tourist Office.............................3 B1

SIGHTS & ACTIVITIES
Basket Shop................................4 C1
Bolgatanga Library....................5 B1
Museum......................................6 B1

SLEEPING 🛏
Nsamini Guesthouse...................7 B1
St Joseph Hotel..........................8 C2
Sand Gardens Hotel...................9 D2
Tienyine Hotel..........................10 D2

EATING 🍴
Comme Ci Comme Ça.............(see 10)
Diplomate................................(see 2)
Madame Rakia All People's
     Canteen..............................11 C2
Swad Fast Food.........................12 B1

DRINKING 🍷
Midway Bar...............................13 C2
St Joseph Hotel Courtyard........(see 8)

TRANSPORT
City Express Buses....................14 D2
KTS Bus Station........................15 C2
Navrongo Motor Park................16 C2
OSA Bus Station.......................17 D2
Shared Taxis to Navrongo.........18 C2
STC Bus Station........................19 B3
Tamale Motor Park....................20 C2

To Navrongo (30km);
Paga (46km)

Football
Field

Bazaar Rd

National Investment Bank

Abilba Rd

Market

Social
Security
Bank

Zuarungu Rd

To Bawku (75km)

Mobil Station

To STC Bus Station (250m);
Canteen (250m); Tongo (15km);
Tamale (160km)

GHANA

Eating & Drinking

There are plenty of food stalls on the stretch of Zuarungu Rd east of the intersection of Navrongo and Commercial Rds.

Madam Rakia All People's Canteen (Commercial Rd; dishes from C2) This wonderfully-named place has all kinds of northern Ghanaian food for all kinds of people.

Diplomate (cnr Bazaar & Navrongo Rds; mains from C2.50) At SSNIT House, this popular restaurant has something of the look of an English tearoom. It's comfortable and pleasant and serves good solid Ghanaian food.

Comme Ci Comme Ça (Starlet 91 St; mains from C3) This restaurant in the Tienyine Hotel compound is nothing more than a few plastic tables and chairs on a concrete patio but the food hits the spot.

Swad Fast Food (Navrango Rd; mains from C4) Lovers of the Tamale Swad won't be disappointed, as this eatery has the same eclectic menu of Indian, Chinese, Ghanaian and continental dishes.

For a beer, try **Midway** (Commercial Rd) and **Street View** (Commercial Rd) the courtyard at the St Joseph Hotel and **Meet Me There** (Bazaar Rd).

Getting There & Away

Tro-tros to Tamale (2½ hours) leave from the motor park on Zuarungu Rd east of the intersection with Navrongo and Tamale Rds. Tro-tros to Navrongo (30 minutes) and buses to Kumasi and Accra leave from the Navrongo motor park on Bazaar Rd. Passenger taxis to Navrongo leave from the taxi station diagonally opposite the National Investment Bank. The **STC bus station** (Tamale Rd) is about 800m south of the intersection with Navrongo and Zuarungu Rds. From here, buses leave daily for Accra (14 hours) and Kumasi (eight hours).

If you're headed for Ouagadougou in Burkina Faso, take a tro-tro to the border at Paga (40 minutes). To cross into Togo, take a tro-tro from the motor park behind the market to Bawku from where you can catch vehicles to the border (30km) and on to Dapaong (Togo), 15km further east.

AROUND BOLGATANGA

The **Tongo hills**, about 16km southeast of Bolga, are known for their balancing rock formations, panoramic views and the whistling sound the rocks make during the windy har-

mattan season. A popular goal is the village of **Tengzug**, about an hour's hike (a steep 4km) from **Tongo** village and 9km from Bolgatanga, above which are numerous sacred **shrines** (entry C5). Women, as well as men, must be topless and barefooted to enter. The most famous shrine, damaged by the British in the early 1900s, is the *ba'ar Tpmma'ab ua' nee* or Nana Tongo shrine. Tro-tros run regularly to Tongo from the main motor park behind the market in Bolgatanga. Travellers can arrange homestays or even sleep on the roof of a traditional mud home.

The **Red Volta River Valley**, between Bolgatanga and Bawku, is potentially a fascinating area to explore, with opportunities for learning about the distinctive local culture and architecture, hiking, canoeing and wildlife viewing (it's a migration corridor for elephants and other wildlife).

GAMBARGA ESCARPMENT

Southeast of Bolga, the Gambarga Escarpment extends towards the Togolese border. Along it is **Gambarga**, ancient capital of the Mamprusi kingdom; **Nalerigu**, the modern district capital; and **Nakpanduri**, the goal of most travellers to the area. A sleepy, unspoilt village of neatly thatched huts, perched on the edge of the escarpment, Nakpanduri has magnificent views and offers some fine hiking. You can stay at the **Government Rest House** (r C4), which has basic rooms in a pretty spectacular location. There are **camps for marginalised women** accused of witchcraft at several locations in the Gambarga Escarpment. It's not normally possible to visit but if you are invited, you'll gain insight into the traditional justice system that sadly persists throughout West Africa.

Nakpanduri and the other towns along the escarpment can be difficult to get to by public transport. Your best bet is to do the journey in stages: from Bolga, get any transport heading to Tamale and get off at Walewale, where the road to Gambarga turns off the Tamale road. From there, you should be able to get a tro-tro to Nalerigu, and from there to Nakpanduri, but it may take a while.

PAGA

Most people stopping in Paga are on their way to or from Burkina Faso but if you're in the general vicinity it's worth a visit even if you're not crossing borders. The town has become synonymous with its sacred **crocodile**

GHANA

ponds, now part of a formally organised community ecotourism project. Chief Pond is visible from the road, about 1km from the main motor park towards the Burkinabé border, while Zenga Pond is signposted off the main road, just after the motor park. At Chief Pond, you'll find official guides and a good informative booklet on the ponds. It costs around C3 per person to see the crocs, plus a little extra for the crocs' supper.

Just as (if not more) interesting, and highly recommended, is a tour of the chief's compound, the **Paga Pio's Palace**, a traditional homestead of the local Kasena people. There's no set fee for the tour but a donation is expected. You can arrange bicycle tours of villages in the surrounding area through Alhassan Village Tours, opposite Chief Pond. Alhassan offers the only accommodation in Paga; you can sleep on the roof of mud huts for a negotiated price and meals can be arranged.

You can also take a stirring tour of the remains of **Pikworo Slave camp** and cemetery 2km west of Paga. The detour is well worth it.

Regular shared taxis and tro-tros run between Paga and both Navrongo and Bolgatanga. From the motor park in Paga, you can either walk the 2km to the border post or you can pay the going rate for a private taxi.

GHANA DIRECTORY

ACCOMMODATION

If you're looking for a bargain, Ghana probably isn't it. Though there is some decent budget accommodation, Ghana will stretch your pockets more than you would like. Except for Accra, in this book budget refers to rooms under C30, midrange covers rooms to around C60 and top-end is over C60. In Accra, budget is under C50, midrange runs to C80, and top-end is over C80. You get much more for your money outside the big smoke.

Most room rates around the country already include 15% tax in their listed prices but some whack it on top of the rate – ask before taking a room, if you're unsure. Many midrange and top end hotels include breakfast though in the former category it usually consists of a basic coffee, rubber omelette and toast trio.

Off the tourist trail there are few hotels and guesthouses, but it's usually possible to arrange to sleep on a floor or roof somewhere. Most of the ecotourism projects offer overnight stays in simple guesthouses or homestays. Along the coast, there are some gorgeous beach resorts, some of which are within reach of a midrange budget. Camping is a possibility at some of these resorts and also at national parks and reserves. Many of the smaller coastal forts will be prepared to put you up for a few cedis. You'll likely be offered several homestays, too. If you meet someone who offers to put you up in their home, it's likely to be a genuine, generous offer. Still, it's wise to trust your gut instinct and employ as much caution as you would anywhere else in the world. If you do stay, giving a small gift or paying for lunch is an excellent idea.

ACTIVITIES

With such a beautiful long coastline, one of the best things to do in Ghana is head to the beach where you can surf or simply do nothing, which should be considered an activity. However, ask before swimming since currents and undertow make conditions unsafe. Good hiking can be found in the Volta Region around Ho (p367) and Hohoe (p368) in the east and in the Tongo Hills near Bolgatanga (p384) in the north.

BOOKS

Ekow Eshun's *Black Gold of the Sun: Searching for Home in England and Africa* is an excellent account of the author's journey to reconcile his Ghanaian and British roots. If you read it on the road, you'll follow him to Cape Coast, Mole, Bolgatanga and Kumasi. *In My Father's Land,* by Star Nyanbiba Hammond, is part-autobiography, part-novel inspired by the author's move from England to Ghana at the age of eight. Maya Angelou's *All God's Children Need Travelling Shoes* beautifully documents the author's emigration to Ghana. *Once upon a Time in Ghana: Traditional Ewe Stories Retold in English* by Anna Cottrell is an excellent introduction to Ghanaian folklore and fairytales.

Earth Architecture by the architect Ronald Rael, is a great collection of images that document the beauty of houses made from mud, sandstone and earth – in Ghana and elsewhere. *Ghana: A Portrait Revisited* is Peter Randall's classic too-big-for-your-rucksack coffee table book. Albert van Dantzig's *Forts and Castles of Ghana* remains the definitive work on the early European coastal presence.

Kwame Nkrumah, The Father of African Nationalism by David Birmingham is a comprehensive biography of the first African statesman; Nkrumah's own works give you an insight into the man and his beliefs. Paul Nugent's *Big Men, Small Boys and Politics in Ghana* is a good account of the Rawlings era. *Onions Are My Husband: Survival and Accumulation by West African Market Women* by Gracia Clark goes behind the market stalls, painting a portrait of life at Kumasi's markets.

BUSINESS HOURS

Banks generally open between 9am and 3pm Monday to Friday; some run until noon on Saturdays. In cities and major towns you can shop from 9am until 5pm or 6pm every day except Sunday, when it's only large stores that open. Administration buildings usually open early – from 8am until 1pm or so. Embassies tend to keep similar hours. In predominately Muslim areas, markets are quiet on Friday, the day of rest, and busier on Sunday.

Chop bars generally open around 6am for breakfast, restaurants a little later. Outside of big cities, dinner service stops early - it's wise to eat before 9pm.

CHILDREN

Ghana's a great place to take little ones and they'll receive a warm welcome from Ghanaians. While there aren't any theme parks or child-oriented activities, Mole National Park (p380), the canopy walk at Kakum (p356) and Cape Coast's castles (p352) make children wide-eyed. As far as beach resorts and restaurants go, most places welcome kids; the stylish Lou Moon (p363) is very child-friendly.

COURSES

Ghana is one of the more popular options for foreign students wishing to study in Africa, at least in part because courses are offered in English. Many universities in the US and Europe have collaborative programmes with the **University of Ghana** (www.ug.edu.gh) in Accra, the **University of Cape Coast** (www.ucc.edu.gh), and development studies programmes in Tamale.

The **University for Development Studies** (uds@ug.gn.apc.org), based in Tamale, studies rural poverty and the environment, combining academic work with practical training in rural communities. The **Tamale Institute of Cross-Cultural Studies** (TICCS; www.ticcs.com/index.htm) offers two Masters degree programmes – the MA in Cross-Cultural Development, and the MA in Cross-Cultural Ministry.

For drumming and dancing lessons, contact Big Milly's (p349) or the Academy of African Music & Arts (AAMAL; p348) in Kokrobite, the Global Mamas or African Footprint (p353) in Cape Coast, or almost any of the community-based tourism projects around the country.

DANGERS & ANNOYANCES

One of Ghana's competitive advantages, as far as tourism in West Africa goes, is that it's a stable and generally peaceful country. Having said that, ethnic violence continues to affect the very far northeast around Bawku; it generally has little effect on the rest of Ghana. Take care of your valuables on the beaches west of Accra and always try to be aware of your surroundings especially if you're walking alone at night. Otherwise, reckless tro-tro drivers, dehydration and open sewers are as bad as it gets.

PRACTICALITIES

- Accra's best daily papers include *The Daily Graphic, The Ghanaian Chronicle* and *The Mirror,* a Saturday newspaper in the style of a British red-top. You can find foreign press in Accra, Kumasi, Takoradi and in major hotels; current affairs magazines like Newsweek and The Economist are easier to find than international papers.

- The BBC World Service is widely listened to in Ghana; in Accra it's on 101.3FM.

- Popular Ghanaian radio stations include the excellent Joy FM (news and music; 99.7FM), Choice FM (102.3), Gold FM (90.5) and Atlantic FM (jazz).

- GTV and Metro TV are Ghana's biggest TV stations. Programmes and camera work don't always run smoothly. Satellite TV (referred to as DSTV across Africa) is available in some upmarket hotels.

- Electricity supply is 230V and three-pin British-style plugs are used.

- Ghana uses the metric system.

GHANA

DISABLED TRAVELLERS
Ghana is one of the easiest West African countries for disabled travellers to visit. Having said that, if you use a chair your budget will obviously have to stretch to cover the cost of hotels equipped with elevators and adapted rooms. Ghana's best hotel for wheelchair travellers sadly happens to be its most expensive – Labadi Beach (see p343) in Accra, which goes the full hog with two adapted paraplegic rooms. If you're adventurous and don't mind a bit of a challenge, there's nothing to stop wheelchair users from coming to Ghana. We met several throned travellers at Mole National Park (see p380).

EMBASSIES & CONSULATES
Ghanaian Embassies & Consulates
In West Africa, Ghana has embassies in Benin, Burkina Faso, Côte d'Ivoire, Guinea, Mali, Nigeria, Sierra Leone and Togo. For details, see the relevant country chapters.

Embassies & Consulates in Ghana
All of the embassies and consulates listed are in Accra. Most are open from 8.30am to 3.30pm Monday to Friday. Most West African embassies need visa applications in before noon.
Australia (Map p336; ☎ 021 777 080; www.ghana.embassy.gov.au; 2 Second Rangoon Close, Catonments)
Benin (Map p336; ☎ 021 774 860; Switchback Lane, Cantonments)
Burkina Faso (Map p338; ☎ 021 221 988; 2nd Mango Tree Ave, Asylum Down; ☒ 8am-2pm Mon-Fri)
Canada (Map p336; ☎ 021 228 555; 46 Independence Ave, Ako Adjei Overpass)
Côte d'Ivoire (Map p340; ☎ 021 774 611; 9 18th Lane, Osu; ☒ 9am-2.30pm Mon-Thu)
France (Map p336; ☎ 021 228 571; 12th Rd, Kanda)
Germany (Map p338; ☎ 021 2021 311; 6 Ridge Rd, North Ridge)
Guinea (Map p336; ☎ 021 7779 021; 4th Norla St, Labone)
Ireland (☎ 021 772 866; 5th Circular Extension)
Japan (Map p336; ☎ 021 775 616; fax 775 951; 8 Josef Broz Tito Ave, Cantonments)
Liberia (Map p336; ☎ 021 775 641; 10 West Cantonments Rd)
Mali (Map p338; ☎ 021 663 276; Liberia Rd, West Ridge)
Netherlands (Map p336; ☎ 021 231 991; nlgovacc@ncs.com.gh; 89 Liberation Ave, Sankara Circle)
Nigeria (Map p336; ☎ 021 224 962; E104/3 Independence Ave, Ringway Estate)
Niger (Map p336; ☎ 021 776 158; fax 774 395; 5 Josef Broz Tito Ave, Cantonments)
Togo (Map p336; ☎ 021 777 950; Togo House, Cantonments Circle, Cantonments)
UK (Map p336; ☎ 021 2021 665; fax 2021 745; 1 Osu Link, Ringway Estate) British high commission.
USA (Map p340; ☎ 021 776 601, 021 741 150 ghana.usembassy.gov; cnr 10th La & 3rd St, Osu)

FESTIVALS & EVENTS
Ghana observes the Muslim festivals of Eid al-Fitr, at the end of Ramadan, and Eid al-Adha, both of which are determined by the lunar calendar. See p816 for a table of Islamic holidays.

Ghana has many festivals, including Cape Coast's Fetu Afahye Festival (first Saturday of September; see p354), Elmina's Bakatue Festival (first Tuesday in July; see p357), the Fire Festival (p378) of the Dagomba people in Tamale and Yendi (dates vary according to the Muslim calendar) and various year-round Akan celebrations (p372) in Kumasi. Ghana's most famous festival, the Aboakyer or Deer Hunt Festival (p350) is celebrated in Winneba on the first weekend in May. Accra's tourist office sells a booklet on festivals. Panafest is celebrated annually in Cape Coast, Accra and Kumasi.

HOLIDAYS
Public holidays include the following:
New Year's Day 1 January
Independence Day 6 March
Easter March/April
Labour Day 1 May
Africa Day 25 May
Republic Day 1 July
Farmers' Day 1st Friday in December
Christmas Day 25 December
Boxing Day 26 December

INTERNET ACCESS
You can get online in all major towns and some smaller ones. Finding a speedy connection, however, is a bit hit and miss. Rates run from C0.60 to C3 per hour.

INTERNET RESOURCES
Daily Graphic (www.graphicghana.com) Ghana's most popular daily.
Ghana Expo (www.ghanaexpo.com) Breaking news, movies and music.
Ghana Review (www.ghanareview.com) News and politics site.
Ghanaweb (www.ghanaweb.com) Everything Ghana, from news to dating tips.
Joy Online (www.myjoyonline.com) Good source for fast news updates.

Museke (http://museke.com) West African tunes.
Nature Conservation Research Centre (NCRC; www
.ncrc-ghana.org) Haven for ecotourism info.

LANGUAGE

English is the official language. There are
at least 75 local languages and dialects. The
most widely spoken language is Twi, which
belongs to the Akan language group and is
spoken in different versions throughout most
of the central and southern parts of the country. The Ashanti version of Twi is not only
spoken throughout the Ashanti homeland
but also serves as a lingua franca for much
of the country and especially in Accra. Fanti
is spoken along much of the coast to the west
of Accra. Other prominent languages are Ga
in the Accra-Tema area, Ewe in the southeast
and Mole-Dagbani languages in the north.
See the Language chapter for useful phrases
in Ga (p860) and Twi (p860).

MONEY

In 2007, four zeros were lopped off the value
of the old Ghana cedi, making it the highest-
value currency in West Africa. For the most
part, Ghanaians have adjusted but you'll occasionally hear people asking for C10,000 when
they really want C1: don't be alarmed. The
new-and-improved cedi dropped the 'Ghana'
part of its name too, but that doesn't seem to
have really taken hold.

Cash

British pounds, US dollars and euros (in that
order) are the best to carry. Some hotels and
guesthouses accept payment in foreign currencies. Barclays and Standard Chartered
Banks exchange cash and well-recognised
brands of travellers cheques. Western Union
counters are widespread; try any major bank
or post office.

Forex bureaus are commonplace in most
major towns, though there are fewer in the
north. They usually offer a slightly better rate than the banks and stay open later.
Higher denomination bills receive higher
exchange rates. They don't generally change
travellers cheques.

ATMs

If you're arriving in Ghana from more
under-developed parts of West Africa,
you'll be in ATM heaven. Maestro, Visa and
MasterCard are accepted at most ATMs run
by Barclays and Standard Chartered Banks,
among others.

Credit Cards

Top-end hotels, and a few midrange ones,
will allow you to pay by Visa or MasterCard,
though there will sometimes be a surcharge.

Tipping

A service charge is rarely added to restaurant
bills. A tip of 5% to 10% is normal in high-end
restaurants. Use your discretion with long-
hire taxi drivers and guides; if you're hiring
someone for the day, paying for lunch is often
a good idea.

TELEPHONE

Mobile (cell) phones are ubiquitous in Ghana
and you'll hear their dulcet tones everywhere,
especially at around 5am when you're trying to sleep. SIM cards can be picked up in
shopping centres, communication centres
and, in fact, on most street corners. MTN
and Vodafone are likely to be reliable long-
term players. Most European and Australian
phones accept SIM cards; Americans are likely
to run into more problems and might want
to look into purchasing a phone (from C60)
on arrival.

Local, national and international calls (and
faxing) can easily be made from communication centres around town, though the connection may not be smooth and you might attract
a crowd of eavesdroppers. Little streetside
tables festooned with signs announcing which
cellphone providers they can call are everywhere, from Accra to small villages. These
generally cost from C0.40 to C2 per minute
and are the most convenient phoning option.
You can buy international calling cards all
over Ghana – try communication centres,
web cafes and supermarkets.

TIME

Ghana is on Greenwich mean time and does
not apply daylight-savings.

TOURIST INFORMATION

The website of the **Ghana Tourist Board** (www
.touringghana.com) is worth a look. Within Ghana,
the tourist board has a network of offices in
the major regional capitals, but staff aren't
always up to speed on the latest places to visit.
That said, the situation is improving and there
are some good centres.

GHANA

The **Nature Conservation Research Centre** (NCRC; www.ncrc-ghana.org), a major player behind the country's burgeoning community-run tourism efforts, has information on its projects.

VISAS

Visas are required by everyone except Ecowas (Economic Community of West African States) nationals. Though it's technically possible to pick up a visa upon arrival at Accra's Kotoka Airport, they only tend to be granted in rare cases. Flying into Ghana without a visa is not recommended. Land border officials might sometimes be a little more lenient, but procuring a visa in Côte d'Ivoire, Togo or Burkina Faso is highly advisable. In fact, if you're travelling overland, it's often cheaper to apply for a Ghanaian visa in these countries than in Europe or the US. Bear in mind that you'll have to give up your passport for a few days while it's processed.

Visas permit a stay of 60 days and can be single or multiple entry. They must be used within three months of the date of issue. Study and business visas sometimes run for longer periods of time, but each embassy seems to have its own rules.

Visa Extensions

You can get a visa extension at the **immigration office** (Map p336; ☎ 021 221 667) in Accra near the Ako Adjei overpass. Applications are accepted between 8.30am and noon Monday to Friday. You need two photos, a letter stating why you need an extension, and an onward ticket out of Ghana. Your passport is retained for the two to three weeks it takes to process the application.

Visas for Onward Travel

Most nationalities need a visa for onward travel throughout West Africa. Most embassies require you to submit applications before noon; they are usually finalised one, two or three days later.

BURKINA FASO

The embassy issues visas for three months on the same day if you get there early. You need three photos and rates fluctuate, but it costs about C50.

CÔTE D'IVOIRE

The embassy issues visas in 48 hours and you need two photos. Americans don't need a visa

to enter Côte d'Ivoire. Alternatively, you can get one at the Elubo border crossing.

TOGO

The embassy issues visas for one month on the same day. Alternatively, you can get a visa at the border at Aflao, but it's only valid for seven days and you'll need to extend it in Lomé.

WOMEN TRAVELLERS

Travelling solo as a woman through Ghana is generally a positive experience, though attracting unwanted attention from men is a given. However, it's not usually threatening or anything to worry about. Set the boundaries from the start and remember that you're in control of who you share your time with. Inventing a husband is a tried-and-tested idea that can help curtail unwanted attention. You could try wearing a 'wedding band' but it's not really necessary as not all married Ghanaians wear rings. Carrying a picture of your 'husband' or 'kids' works, though be prepared to explain why they're not with you. Having a boyfriend back home doesn't quite cut it as far as some men are concerned – you're not married, so they're still in with a chance.

If you're travelling as an unmarried couple, you might want to get in the habit of referring to your boyfriend as your husband in order to see your relationship respected. That said, if you don't have kids together, you might then be asked why your husband isn't up to fatherhood.

There's a reason Shakira's 'Hips don't lie' was adopted as one of West Africa's unofficial anthems. Breasts, and therefore low-cut tops, aren't taboo but butt-hugging jeans are another matter – the area from a woman's belly button to her hips is deemed highly sexual. Unless you're on the beach or by the pool, flashing yours will get you a scolding from other women; at worst, you might as well be walking topless through New York. Leave the low-slung jeans at home.

You can find tampons in major urban centres. In the capital, a safe bet is Koala Supermarket or the Accra mall. In Kumasi, head to A-Life and in Takoradi, Market Circle.

WORK & VOLUNTEERING

Ghana is one of Africa's top volunteering spots, and you'll find literally hundreds of organisations that arrange short and long-term placements. Take a look at any passing 4WD and odds are there's a decal on it with an acronym identifying it as an NGO or organisation that takes volunteers.

The US Peace Corps programme also has a significant presence. In Busua, the **Black Star Surf Shop** (www.blackstarsurfshop.com) arranges placements that combine community work with surfing. Other organisations include:

Bunac (www.bunac.org)

Cross Cultural Solutions (www.crossculturalsolutions .org) Volunteer programmes.

Global Vision International (www.gvi.co.uk)

Projects Abroad (www.projectsabroad.co.uk)

Travel Active (www.travelactive.nl) Dutch volunteer organisation.

Volunteer in Africa (www.volunteeringinafrica.org) Offers short- and long-term volunteer placements in health, education and eco-projects.

TRANSPORT IN GHANA

GETTING THERE & AWAY
Entering Ghana
You need a yellow fever vaccination certificate to enter Ghana. Though it's rarely checked at airports, border guards often ask to see it. Worst-case scenario: you'll be made to have a yellow fever jab on the spot – don't risk it. There have been reports of officials asking to see meningitis vaccination cards at the border with Côte d'Ivoire.

Air
Kotoka Airport in Accra is Ghana's international hub. In 2005, the dicey national carrier, Ghana Airways, was replaced by the much better **Ghana International Airlines** (www .fly-ghana.com), owned by the Ghanaian government and a US consortium. Its Boeing 747s fly between London and Accra (return from GBP400) every day, with frequent flights to Frankfurt. The cabin crew are Ghanaian and the pilots are leased from European airlines. Delta runs non-stop flights from New York. Other international airlines flying in and out of Kotoka include the following:

Afriqiyah Airways (www.afriqiyah.aero) Hub: Tripoli. Flights to Europe with stopover in Tripoli, Libya; office at Accra airport.

Air Ivoire (www.airivoire.com) Hub: Abidjan. Office at Accra airport.

British Airways (www.ba.com) Hub: London Heathrow.

Delta (www.delta.com) Hub: Atlanta, Georgia.

EgyptAir (www.egyptair.com; Ring Rd East, Osu, Accra) Hub: Cairo.

Emirates (www.emirates.com; Meridian House, Ring Rd Central, Accra) Hub: Dubai. Four flights a week connecting Accra and Dubai. Also offers short hops to Abidjan.

Ghana International Airways (www.fly-ghana.com; Silver Star Tower, Airport City, PMB 78, Kotoka International Airport) Hub: Accra.

Kenya Airways (www.kenya-airways.com) Hub: Nairobi. Serves destinations in West Africa as well as East Africa.

KLM-Royal Dutch Airlines (Map p336; www.klm.com; Ring Rd Central, Accra) Hub: Amsterdam.

Slok Air International (www.slok-air.com; No 3 Aviation Rd, Accra) Hub: Banjul.

South African Airways (Map p338; www.flysaa.com; Ring Rd Central, Asylum Down, Accra) Hub: Johannesburg.

Virgin Nigeria (Map p336; www.virginnigeria.com; La Palm Royal Beach Hotel, Accra) Hub: Lagos.

Land
Ghana has land borders with Côte d'Ivoire to the west, Burkina Faso to the north and west, and Togo on the east. The main border crossing into Côte d'Ivoire is at Elubo; there are less-travelled crossings between Sunyani and Agnibilékrou and between Bole and Ferkessédougou. Into Burkina the main crossing is at Paga, with other crossings at Tumu, Hamale and Lawra. Note that with the exception of the crossing into Togo at Aflao, all Ghana's borders close promptly – with a flag ceremony – at 6pm.

BURKINA FASO
Between Accra and Ouagadougou, the usual route is via Kumasi, Tamale, Bolgatanga, Paga and Pô. A direct STC bus runs to Ouagadougou from Accra three times a week (Monday, Wednesday, Friday). The bus leaves Accra at 9am, arriving in Ouagadougou the following afternoon. You can expect to sleep on the concrete at Bolgatanga STC station before crossing the border at Paga around 7am. The return journey is only slightly less tiring; buses leave Ouagadougou three times a week (8.30am Monday, Wednesday, Friday) and arrive in Kumasi the same day around midnight, and Accra at 6am the following day. Going the entire distance at once can be painful and most people do the trip in stages. From Bolgatanga, there are frequent tro-tros to the border at Paga (40 minutes), from where you

can get onward transport to Pô, 15km beyond the border, and Ouagadougou.

You can also enter Burkina Faso from the northwest corner of Ghana, crossing between Tumu and Léo or from Hamale or Lawra and onto Bobo-Dioulasso. From Hamale there are two daily buses to Bobo-Dioulasso. Léo is connected by bus to Ouagadougou. You can reach Tumu most easily from Bolgatanga, Hamale from Bolgatanga or Wa, and Lawra from Wa.

CÔTE D'IVOIRE

Crossing into Côte d'Ivoire at Elubo is relatively straightforward. You can make your way to the border post in stages, or take a tro-tro or air-conditioned van from Takoradi or an STC bus from Accra to Abidjan (around 13 hours). Once you reach Elubo, it's a 10-minute walk to the border itself and the same distance again to Noé on the Ivoirian side. Elubo is a typical border town of market stalls and cheap eateries. Noé is only slightly quieter; from there you can easily find transport to Abidjan, though be prepared to haggle for a fair rate.

Other much more adventurous crossings are from Kumasi via Sunyani and Berekum to Agnibilékrou (you'll have to do this in short stages as there are no direct buses) and between Bole and Bouna to Ferkessédougou.

TOGO

Tro-tros and share taxis run between Accra and Aflao (about C5, three hours). Efficient, air-conditioned STC buses ply the route from Abidjan to Lomé via Accra (C8 from Accra, four times a day). The border at Aflao, just 2km from Lomé, is open from 6am to 10pm daily but you should cross between 9am and 5pm if you need a Togolese visa (valid for seven days, extendable in Lomé) at the border. Tro-tros deposit you on the Ghanaian side of the border. Other crossings are at Wli near Hohoe and between Ho and Kpalimé. From northern Ghana, you can cross from Tamale via Yendi to Sansanné or Kara but road conditions – and therefore transport – can be hard to predict on this route.

GETTING AROUND
Air

Two domestic airlines, **Citylink** (☎ 021 785 725; www.citylink.com.gh) and **Antrak** (Map p340; ☎ 021 777 134; www.antrakair.com; Antrak House, Danquah Circle, Osu) operate in Ghana. Both have two to three flights daily between Accra and Kumasi (one

way US$60 to US$80, 45 minutes), three to four weekly flights to Tamale (around US$300 return) and regular flights to Takoradi and Sunyani.

Boat

A passenger boat, the *Yapei Queen*, runs along Lake Volta between Akosombo and Yeji, stopping at the town of Kete-Krachi and a few villages along the way. The journey takes in beautiful hills and is an experience in itself as well as an alternative to the travails of road travel. In theory it leaves the port at Akosombo at around 4pm on Monday and arrives in Yeji on Wednesday morning; in practice the departure and arrival times are much more fluid, with date changes common. The southbound service is scheduled, in the broadest sense of the term, to depart Yeji around 4pm on Wednesday, arriving in Akosombo on Friday morning. Tickets cost C10/5/4 in first/second/third class, and food and drinks are available on board. If you want one of the three first-class cabins, you have to reserve at least two weeks in advance – call ☎ 0251 20686 at Akosombo port to make a booking.

It's possible to jump on board freighter boats making the same trip; there is no fixed cost or schedule and you'll sleep on the deck. Akosombo port can point you in the right direction.

Bus

The best bus service in the country is provided by STC. Compared to other transport in the region it's fairly reliable and despite the loud Nigerian movies, you travel in air-conditioned comfort. It's wise to book in advance; tickets get snapped up fast on the more popular routes. STC charges a little extra for hold luggage – you'll have it weighed and be charged by the kilogram.

Sample fares and times from Accra include to Cape Coast (C3.50, 3-4 hours); Tamale (C21, 12-13 hours); Kumasi (C10, 4-6 hours). Bus fares and times from Kumasi include to Takoradi (C9, Monday to Saturday 6am and 12 noon, Sunday 7am and 2pm); Kumasi to Alfao (C14, Tuesday and Thursday 9pm); Accra (C10, eight buses daily, from 4am until 3.30pm); and to Cape Coast (C7.50, 3-4 hours).

From Tamale, sample fares are to Kumasi (C13, 6-8 hours); and to Bolgatanga (C25, 3 hours).

Other operators, which may have the only buses on some routes (such as between Tamale and Mole National Park), include Metro Mass, OSA, Kingdom Transport Services (KTS) and City Express. Fares are often much cheaper than those offered by STC but you can't predict what kind of bus you'll end up on or how packed it will be.

Car & Motorcycle

Driving is on the right in Ghana. Most main roads in Ghana are now in pretty good condition though almost all secondary roads are unsealed. Self-drive car rental is available in Accra but is not recommended unless you are used to all the quirks of driving in West Africa. An international driver's licence and many foreign countries' licences are recognised. It goes without saying that the driver should carry a licence at all times, but passengers travelling in a car driven by non-Ghanaians can also expect to have their ID checked by police angling for a bribe. Kola nuts, sold at tolls, keep Ghanaian drivers awake on long journeys.

FUEL

Petrol stations are easy to find throughout the country and range from simple roadside stands to fancy premises with air-conditioned shops. A litre of petrol cost around C0.75 at the time of research.

CARS

Hiring a car with a driver is a good option if you're short on time. Depending on the distance, car and driver's experience, factor in anything from US$40 to US$120 per day. Your hotel will be able to suggest local car-hire firms, or you can simply hail a taxi and ask to hire it for the day. Self-drive car rental is available at Kotoka International Airport and at the following locations:

Europcar (Map p338; ☎ 021 667 546; Heritage Tower, West Ridge)

Hertz (Map p336; ☎ 021 775 360)

U-Save (☎ 021 761 751; North Labone) Golden Tulip Hotel (Liberation Ave, Airport Residential Area) Affiliated with Avis.

ROAD HAZARDS

Ghana's main road hazards are other drivers. Accidents and injuries or even fatalities are all too common; one of the contributing factors is that so many vehicles stop suddenly to pick up or drop off passengers. Though many of Ghana's roads are impressive as far as West African standards go (the main coastal road in particular), poor roads are of course an issue, and unpaved and potholed roads threaten the condition of your vehicle.

Taxis

Throughout West Africa, you'll notice people standing by the side of the road making strange hand signals. While it can feel like they're in on a secret cult you don't understand, what they're really doing is waiting for shared taxis. Within towns and on some shorter routes between towns, shared taxis are the usual form of transport. They are cheap and run on fixed routes, along which they stop to pick up and drop off passengers. Passenger hand signals refer to the destination they wish to reach; pointing up, for example, often means the town centre, while circular hand movements sometimes denote a ring road. It's best to ask before trying these out – they vary from town to town. If you're waiting for a shared taxi to fill up and time is short it's always possible to pay for two or three seats rather than wait for the full load.

Private taxis don't have meters and rates are negotiable. It's best to ask a local in advance for the average cost between two points. You'll soon have a handle on what is fair. Taxis can be chartered for an agreed period of time from one hour to a day for a negotiable fee. Drivers will often try to renegotiate after a deal has been struck and you've started moving, saying things like 'it's really not enough' or 'you just give xxx more.' Stick to your guns, within reason. Most taxis don't have air-con, which isn't a problem unless the back windows don't open, which is actually not unusual.

Train

Ghana's train service should be viewed as a supplement, not alternative, to internal travel. Kumasi and Takoradi have had an on-off relationship with a night train for many years. When it runs, it takes around 13 hours. There is also a commuter service between Accra and Tema.

Tro-tros

Tro-tro is a catch-all category that embraces any form of transport that's not a bus or taxi. They cover all major and many minor routes and, without them, Ghana would come to a standstill. Except on real backcountry routes, tro-tros are minibuses of all shapes, sizes and degrees of roadworthiness. They don't work to a set timetable, but leave when full, having squeezed in as many passengers as they can. You can get a rough idea of when the tro-tro you're sitting in will leave by counting the number of passengers on board (though some may have done the same thing and subsequently escaped for lunch). The average tro-tro carries 11 to 14 passengers; if there are only five on board, you're usually in for a long wait ('the poor are rich in patience' wrote Ayi Kwei Armah in *The Beautyful Ones Are Not Yet Born*).

You can however, buy extra seats in order to hasten the departure time. The beauty of tro-tros is that you can pick them up any-

where along a route and they're extremely cheap. Most fares are under a dollar or two but frequently change by small amounts, and for that matter the fares on many routes are not given. For long journeys, though, buses are more comfortable and safer. Many tro-tro drivers demand a negotiable luggage fee though this seems to be applied fairly arbitrarily and is more commonly requested of foreigners than Ghanaians.

Most towns have an area where tro-tros and buses congregate, usually in or near the market. These are called lorry park or motor park (the terms are used interchangeably) or, quite often, station. You may hear the term tro-tro used, but taxis and minibuses are often just called 'cars'.

Guinea

Imagine you're travelling on smooth highway then get tempted by a tiny, dusty turn-off into rugged terrain, where spectacular surprises lurk behind every corner.

Guinea is that turn-off. This is a country blessed with amazing landscapes, from the craggy mountain plateau of Fouta Djalon to wide Sahelian lands and thick forests. Overland drivers are drawn here by rugged tracks, and the challenge of steering their vehicles over rocks, laterite and washed-out paths. Nature lovers can lose themselves on long hikes past the steep waterfalls, proud hills and tiny villages of the Fouta. And for music fans, the country is something of a pilgrimage site – this is where West Africa's 1960s sounds were created.

There's virtually no tourist infrastructure and creature comforts are scarce. Instead, you get to explore paths that few tourists travel.

For most Guineans, life has been tough since the country defiantly broke from France and ventured out on a difficult post-independence journey. Yet, despite the hard times, the country's diverse people have largely stood together through the decades, rather than turning on each other. In conversations and encounters you will catch glimpses of that strong stance, and hear about the nation's troubles as well as its hopes.

GUINEA

FAST FACTS

- **Area** 245,855 sq km
- **Capital** Conakry
- **Country code** ☎ 224
- **Famous for** Bauxite; Radical independence; Circus & Acrobatics School; Les Ballets Africains
- **Languages** French, Malinké, Pulaar (Fula) and Susu
- **Money** Guinean franc (GF); US$1 = GF4920; €1 = GF6654
- **Population** 9.5 million
- **Visa** Required in advance

HIGHLIGHTS

- **Îles de Los** (p410) Beautiful palm-fringed strands on which to sip fresh coconut juice.
- **Fouta Djalon** (p413) Trekking and swimming in the waterfalls of the majestic mountain plateaus.
- **Bossou** (p425) Chimpanzees to come face to face with.
- **Conakry** (p401) The capital's dubious dives for getting drunk on some of West Africa's best live music.
- **Forêt Classée de Ziama** (p423) Elephants in the virgin rainforest.

ITINERARIES

- **One week** Spend a couple of days in Conakry (p401), taking in the Îles de Los (p410) on a day trip. Then head to Fouta Djalon (p413), trekking to craggy mountains and steep waterfalls.
- **Two weeks** Add a leisurely trip through the towns, hills, palm groves and villages of Lower Guinea (p410) to the one-week itinerary, stopping at Bel Air and Sobané (p411) for another stretch of beach lazing. Take a detour to Faranah (p420) to explore the Parc National du Haut Niger (p420) and hike to the source of the River Niger. Alternatively, just stay in Fouta Djalon (p413) and strike out on an extended village-to-village trek (see p414).
- **One month** This is enough time to venture through all four of the country's regions, allowing you to reach remote villages, and maybe even the mighty Mt Nimba in Guinée Forestière (p425).

CLIMATE & WHEN TO GO

Guinea is one of the wettest countries in West Africa. Rainfall along the coast averages 4300mm a year, half of which falls in July and August, while the central mountainous region receives about 2000mm between May and October, although sometimes starting as early as March. Temperatures average 30°C along the coast, where it is always humid, and can fall to 6°C and below at night in the highland areas in December and January (see Climate Charts p810).

The best time to visit is November and December, when the rains have swollen rivers and waterfalls, and the landscape is green. Visits during the rainy season can be tough as

many roads become inaccessible (especially in the Forest Region), and the capital Conakry turns into a giant mud bath.

HISTORY
The Age of Empires & Colonisation

Most of the sociocultural make-up that defines Guinea to this day was established from the 13th century onwards, the age of West Africa's empires (p27). Following the fall of the Empire of Ghana, Susu and Malinké people migrated increasingly to the region, pushing some of the earlier, clan-based inhabitants, such as the Koniagui, Baga and Landuma, into new regions.

The legendary clashes of the Susu sorcerer king Soumaoro Kanté and Sunjata Keita, founder of the 13th-century Empire of Mali, took place on Guinean soil. The Empire's historical capital Niani is in Upper Guinea, though a visit here betrays little of its glorious past. The major migrations caused by the rise and fall of Mali established the 'cultural zones' of the Susu (Lower Guinea) and Malinké (Upper Guinea) lands that persist today. In between the two is the Fouta Djalon plateau, whose culture and history is defined by a very different course. Throughout the 17th century the area absorbed increasing Muslim Fula populations from Macina (in present-day Mali) and Fouta Toro (present-day Senegal), who increasingly took to converting the diverse ethnic groups resident in the area, and finally launched the first jihad

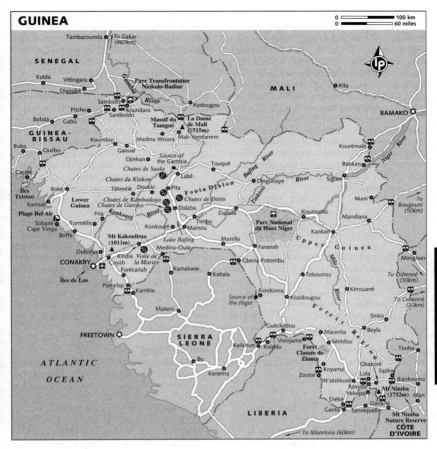

(holy war) in West Africa in 1725. This resulted in the creation of a sophisticated, Fula-led theocracy, and to this day the area remains an important centre of Islamic learning, and home to Guinea's Fula population.

The first Europeans to arrive on Guinean territory were the Portuguese in the late 15th and early 16th century, who landed on the coast near Boffa and Boké. In the mid- and late 18th century, the British held primary commercial interests in the area, establishing trading centres on the Îles de Los, and seeking control over the main rivers and Fouta Djalon. They finally lost influence to the French, who eventually colonised the entire territory, integrating it into their vast French West Africa. The divisions, and op-posed interests of the Fouta Djalon rulers and Malinké hero Samory Touré in Upper Guinea, facilitated the French advance, even though Touré put up an impressive effort of resistance (remnants of his fort are still found in Kerouané, Upper Guinea).

Guinea under Sékou Touré

In a bid to maintain control over the burgeoning independence movements of the 1950s, in 1958 General Charles de Gaulle offered the French West African colonies a choice between independence or integration in a Franco-African community. Sékou Touré, great rhetorician, trade unionist and the young voice of 1950s Guinea, was the only leader to say 'no' to de Gaulle, choosing complete autonomy following a referendum. He immediately became a legend, and president of the first French colony to gain independence. France's reaction, however, was severe. The administration, including teachers, withdrew instantly, isolating young Guinea and pushing huge obstacles into its path. Though the country received help and support from other nations (notably Eastern Bloc countries, who saw in this a chance to increase influence over their Cold War enemies) the country slipped gradually into crisis, only reinforced by the 1967 campaign of cultural revolution and socialist-style economic models. As many as one million Guineans fled into neighbouring countries.

Over the years, Touré's rule grew increasingly severe. Following an unsuccessful Portuguese-led invasion in 1970, he became paranoid, often speaking of a plot against his regime. Waves of arrests and executions followed; torture became commonplace. In 1976 Touré charged the entire Fula population with collusion in an attempt to overthrow the government. Thousands went into exile.

Towards the end of his presidency, Touré changed many of his policies in an attempt to lift the nation out of its deep crisis. He died of heart failure in 1984. A few days later, a group of army colonels staged a military coup, and military man Lansana Conté became the country's new president.

The Second Republic

A barely educated soldier and dedicated farmer, Conté certainly wasn't a favourite leader for Guinea's intellectuals. But tentative efforts to reform the economy in the mid-1980s, the introduction of a new currency (the Guinean franc) and the creation of a multiparty political system – ushered in via a new constitution in 1991 – showed some promise in the first couple of years of his rule. Yet this period of hope didn't last long. The recession years of the 1980s were an impossibly difficult time to boost a failing economy, and Conté proved an impenetrable leader, unwilling and unable to enter into dialogue with opposition leaders. Conté and his party, PUP, won three more elections, the fairness of which as fiercely disputed by opposition groups and international observers. Corruption became increasingly endemic and opposition leaders, notably Alpha Condé, one of the most powerful challengers, were frequently imprisoned.

Conflicts in neighbouring Liberia and Sierra Leone threatened to spill over into Guinea and, though they were successfully quashed by the military, over a thousand people lost their lives in Guinea's Forest Region and many were displaced.

Had Conté left power in time, people might have remembered him for keeping the country stable as neighbouring nations imploded. Yet he clung onto power, despite grave health problems that left him unable to walk, even speak, leave alone make clear decisions in the final years of his rule. In 2007, Guinean youth violently announced that they'd had enough. They took to the streets, setting towns alight across the country, demanding the creation of a new government. Conté gave in and nominated Lansana Kouyaté as prime minister. But the man proved a disappointment, and his dismissal in March 2008 was barely disputed.

Guinea slipped deeper into crisis as rising food and oil prices pushed the poorest families further into deprivation. In spring 2008, soldiers staged a mutiny over unpaid wages and rendered Guinea's streets insecure. In its wake, banditry and street crime (committed both by people in uniform and armed gangs) rose significantly.

Guinea Today

On 23 December 2008, two months after Guinea's 50th anniversary of independence, Lansana Conté died. Less than 24 hours later, the young, hitherto barely known army captain Moussa Dadis Camara declared that he had taken over power as head of the National Council for Democracy & Development (CNDD) in a bloodless coup d'état.

Claiming to have no other interest than stabilising the country and paving the way for free elections, Dadis Camara embarked on daring actions of 'cleaning the nation' and was enjoying widespread popularity at the time this book went to press.

While Guinean politics and public life had always been marked by closed doors and secrecy, he made a point of using the power of TV to impress his desire for transparency and the end of corruption. Every night, the entire country gathers around the TV to watch the news, nicknamed the 'Dadis Show' for being dominated by his virulent speeches and revelations of misrule and mismanagement by the former government. Within a couple of months, he had touched on some of Guinea's most explosive topics, such as the thriving drug trade (as bad here as in Guinea-Bissau, if less exposed) and the involvement of the Conté government in it, corruption among top military ranks, and the disastrous handling of Guinea's mining contracts (the nation sits on some of the world's largest bauxite, gold and iron reserves, yet little of this wealth flows into the country).

Some claim it's indeed little more than a 'Dadis Show', yet most Guineans seem grateful for this sudden openness and his courage, allowing him the benefit of the doubt to see what path Guinea will take. The stakes and risks are huge, particularly as international support for Dadis' regime is low, his enemies powerful, and economic reform extremely challenging in a climate of global recession.

THE CULTURE

The face of Guinean culture changes along with the natural zones you pass. Each of the country's main ethnic groups has its own, proud past, and yet there's an equally strong sense of national identity. Sékou Touré's 'no' to Charles de Gaulle may never have led the country to prosperity, but the act of having stood up against France is proudly remembered by many Guineans.

Today, Guinea is one of the world's poorest nations, despite sitting on some of the richest soils. That paradox puzzles people, and has recently pushed the nation's youth (over 50% of the total population) to claim its 'share' in violent demonstrations. It took Guinea decades to rise up against endemic corruption, economic mismanagement and poverty. The fact that the youth finally cried out instead of suffering in silence may indicate a huge cultural shift.

Population

Guinea's main ethnic groups are the Fula (about 40% of the population), Malinké (about 30%) and Susu (about 20%). Fifteen other groups, living mostly in the Forest Region, constitute the rest of the population. Susu predominantly inhabit the coastal region, Fula the Fouta Djalon and Malinké the north and centre. Non-Africans, mostly French and Lebanese, total about 10,000.

RELIGION

About 85% of the population are Muslims, 8% are Christians and the remainder follow traditional animist religions. Most Christians are in Conakry and the Forest Region; the animists are mostly in the Forest Region. While devoted followers of traditional beliefs continue to decline in number, the magic of the past is still respected by many Muslims and Christians: traditional medicines are common and sacred forests respected. There is little religious discord in the country and mixed families are common.

ARTS
Arts & Craftwork

Guinea is deeply associated with indigo – Fouta Djalon has a particularly strong tradition of weaving and dyeing the blue-white cloths. In the Forest Region, *bogolan* cloth (mud cloth) is also made.

Woodcarving, particularly the making of statues, is common in Upper Guinea. The statues made in Kankan are sold widely across West Africa. Fouta Djalon has a strong tradition of leatherwork – Labé's Maison des Artisans (see p417) is a good place to find out about local crafts. Little remains of the Baga mask traditions outside the performances of Guinea's ballet troupes.

In Conakry, you can check out some of the quirky recycled-metal sculptures (see p405), while in Dubréka, the arts exchange project by renowned painter Nabisco is a good place to find out about Guinea's visual arts (see p411).

Music & Dance

Guinea's musical heritage is astoundingly rich. Many of the country's ancient traditions have been reworked in the performances of Guinea's great ballets (including Les Ballets Africains) and *ensembles instrumentals* under Sékou Touré. Music was nurtured as part of the revolution and African-renaissance effort, and the use of traditional and modern elements by the nation's great bands (including Bembeya Jazz, Balla et ses Balladins, Keletigui et ses Tambourinis) ushered in the greatest era in popular West African music.

Today's stars, including Sekouba Bambino Diabaté and Ba Cissoko, can be seen performing in the clubs and bars of the nation's capital. For more about Guinea's music scene see the Music of West Africa chapter (p57).

Literature

Camara Laye's autobiographical first work, *The Dark Child* (1954), is one of the most famous novels from francophone West Africa. Most of Tierno Monenembo's brilliant works have unfortunately not been translated into English (with the exception of *The Oldest Orphan*).

Cinema

Guinea has a limited cinematic oeuvre, but what's produced is often great. Mohamed Camara's *Dakan* (1997) was the first film about homosexuality from sub-Saharan Africa, while Gahité Fofana's *Un matin de bonheur* (Early in the Morning, 2005) is a moving cinematic treatment of the tragic death of two Guinean emigrants. Cheikh Fantamady Camara's *Il va pleuvoir sur Conakry* (Clouds over Conakry) was one of the most widely acclaimed films from francophone West Africa in 2007.

ENVIRONMENT
The Land

Guinea has four distinct zones: a narrow coastal plain, the Fouta Djalon, northeastern dry lowlands and the Forest Region of the southeast. The Fouta Djalon plateau, rising to over 1500m, is the source of the Gambia and Senegal Rivers, and of much of the Niger (although the actual source of the Niger River lies to the south, near the Sierra Leone border). Southeastern Guinea is hilly and heavily vegetated, although little virgin rainforest remains.

Wildlife

Large animals are rarely sighted, though waterbucks, bongos, buffaloes and baboons wander the forests while crocodiles, manatees and hippos swim the rivers. The abundant birdlife includes brown-cheeked hornbills, long-tailed hawks, grey parrots and Nimba flycatchers. Two amphibians of note, both of which live on Mt Nimba, are goliath frogs and Nimba toads, which bear live young.

Guinea is one of West Africa's last (though dwindling) strongholds for chimpanzees, with significant populations in Fouta Djalon, Parc National de Haute Guinée and the Forest Region. The Jane Goodall Institute does amazing protection work here.

National Parks & Reserves

Guinea has many designated protected areas (*forêts classées*), although there is little enforcement of environmental regulations. The Mount Nimba Nature Reserve in the far southeast is a Unesco World Heritage Site, but this didn't stop the former government from opening an iron mine. Nearby is Forêt Classée de Ziama, where the rainforest remains pristine (for now, at least) and elephants are often seen.

The two main national parks are Parc Transfrontalier Niokolo-Badiar, of which the Guinean part is called Parc Regional du Badiar, near Koundara (p419), and Parc National du Haut Niger, northeast of Faranah (p420), though both suffer from neglect. The Jane Goodall Institute has started work on the establishment of a border-straddling park with Sierra Leone (see the boxed text, p420).

Environmental Issues

Guinea's environmental record is atrocious. Most large mammals are rapidly declining, while understaffing and underfunding mean that even the national parks don't provide much of a safe haven.

The primary concern is deforestation. Logging continues largely unchecked and has proceeded so rapidly in the south that the Forest Region really ought to adopt a new name. On the coast, much of the mangrove forest has been cleared for rice production, and overfishing is a growing problem. Large mining companies have pledged to improve their practices and there is some evidence this is happening.

FOOD & DRINK

Rice is the staple of Guinea, either served as *riz gras* (rice fried in oil and tomato paste and served with fried fish, meat or vegetables) or accompanied by a variety of delicious sauces. In Fouta Djalon, creamy sauces made from meat and potato leaves (*haako putte*) or manioc leaves (*haako bantara*) are common. The coast is great for grilled fish, while the best salads are prepared in Fouta Djalon.

Unfortunately, the tastiest meals are served in family homes – proper restaurants, sometimes even street rice bars, are rare outside Conakry, and chicken and chips might often be the only thing you'll find.

Guinea has plenty of basic (sometimes quite rugged) coffee bars where you can either enjoy a sweet, black *café noir* or rich *café au lait* made with Nescafé and powdered milk and usually served with French bread and butter. The most common beers are Skol, a light lager, and the darker Guiluxe and Flag.

CONAKRY

pop 2 million

Conakry doesn't try to please its guests, yet like women falling for the wrong guy, many fall in love with the city. There aren't a lot of sights in this sprawling mess of crumbling buildings; traffic jams and random police checks make getting around an exercise in extreme patience, and humidity and heat paste the city dust onto your skin. From the nauseating fish port of Boulbinet and street kitchens of Coronthie to the containers-turned-shops of Taouyah and Kaloum's office floors, this city goes about its business noisily and with ingenuity, proud and unruffled by the visitor's gaze.

HISTORY

The founding date of Conakry is usually given as 1887, the date the French commander Raffenel officially claimed ownership over the island of Tumbo (now the tip of the Kaloum peninsula). By then French presence was well established, and the British had just been shown that their influence was to be limited to the Îles de Los. People had, of course, inhabited Tumbo and the peninsula long before the French opened their first trading station – many of today's *quartiers* (neighbourhoods) were then tiny villages.

Via its busy port, Conakry grew rapidly throughout the late 19th and early 20th century, particularly once the railway linked the emerging city to Kankan (1913). After independence, it naturally became the capital of the young nation, and is today home to almost a quarter of Guinea's population.

ORIENTATION

Conakry's town centre sits on the southwestern tip of the peninsula. The area is called Kaloum, though most people just refer to it as *la ville* (the town). Kaloum's artery is the wide Ave de la République, where you find many offices, restaurants, internet cafes and the main bank. Three roads snake from Kaloum along the peninsula northeastwards out of town: Corniche Nord passes the main port and follows the northern shore; Corniche Sud runs past the fishing port, Boulbinet, and along the southern shore; and the Rte du Niger, from where the Autoroute (towards the airport) and Rte de Donka branch off at the landmark Pont du 8 Novembre. Rte de Donka connects several major communes, including Dixinn

with the stadium and a hospital, and vibrant Ratoma with its *quartiers* Taouyah, Kipé and Kaporo. The commune of Matam with its *gare routière* and *quartiers* Coléah and Madina (famous for its market) stretch out between Corniche Sud and the Autoroute.

Maps

Libraries, *papeteries* (newsagents) and Ave de la République street vendors sell Conakry maps for about GF30,000.

INFORMATION

The bimonthly, pocket-sized *Wonkhaï* magazine has cultural listings, news and features, while *Foty,* an intelligent glossy run by a couple of inspired young Guinean women, contains excellent tourist and arts info, as well as the latest star gossip.

Bookshops

La Maison du Livre (Map p402; ☎ 64248350; Carrefour Moussoudougou; ☻ 9am-1pm & 2-6pm Mon-Sat) Has a great range of books on the country, magazines, postcards and stationery.

Cultural Centres

American Center (Map p404; ☎ 65104000; Transversale 2, Ratoma; ☻ 9am-3pm Mon-Thu, to noon Fri) Has a good library with American books and magazines, an internet cafe and occasional events.
Centre Culturel Franco-Guinéen (Map p402; ☎ 63409625; www.ccfg-conakry.org, in French; Corniche Nord, Tumbo) A hub of cultural activity with regular concerts, films, exhibitions and more. Also runs a small cafe.

Internet Access

There are other, slow internet cafes, but those two are the best.
Cyber Rogbane (Map404; Rte de Donka; Ratoma; per hr GF6000; ☎ 8am-11pm) The main point in Ratoma; it has a generator.
MouNa (Map p406; Ave de la République, Kaloum; per hr GF6000, wi-fi per hr GF10,000; ☻ all day) Guinea's best internet cafe has wi-fi points, laptop booths and a cafe downstairs.

Medical Services

There are many good pharmacies along Ave de la République.
Clinique Pasteur (Map p406; ☎ 30430076; 5th Boulevard) Fairly good for malaria tests and minor injuries.
Hôpital Ambrose Paré (Map p402; ☎ 63351010; Camayenne) Considered the best in Guinea, though for anything serious it's best to get flown out to Dakar or Europe.

GUINEA

CONAKRY

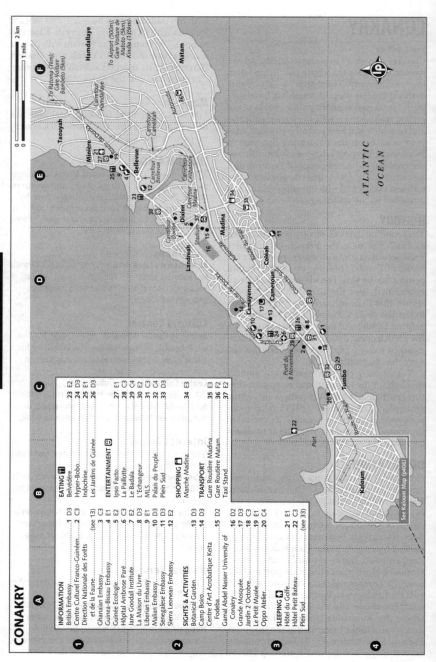

INFORMATION
British Embassy..................................**1** D3
Centre Culturel Franco-Guinéen........**2** C3
Direction Nationale des Forêts
et de la Faune..................................(see 13)
Ghanaian Embassy..............................**3** C3
Guinea-Bissau Embassy.......................**4** E1
Guinée Ecologie..................................**5** E2
Hôpital Ambroise Paré.........................**6** C3
Jane Goodall Institute..........................**7** E2
La Maison du Livre...............................**8** D3
Liberian Embassy.................................**9** E1
Malian Embassy.................................**10** D3
Senegalese Embassy..........................**11** D3
Sierra Leonean Embassy.....................**12** E2

SIGHTS & ACTIVITIES
Botanical Garden...............................**13** D3
Camp Boiro..**14** D3
Centre d'Art Acrobatique Keita
Fodeba...**15** D2
Gamal Abdel Nasser University of
Conakry..**16** D2
Grande Mosquée................................**17** D3
Jardin 2 Octobre.................................**18** C3
Le Petit Musée...................................**19** E1
Oppo Atelier......................................**20** C4

SLEEPING
Hôtel du Golfe...................................**21** E1
Hôtel Petit Bateau.............................**22** C3
Plein Sud...(see 33)

EATING
Belvédère...**23** E2
Hyper-Bobo.......................................**24** D3
Indochine..**25** E1
Les Jardins de Guinée.........................**26** D3

ENTERTAINMENT
Ipso Facto...**27** E1
La Paillotte..**28** C3
Le Badala..**29** C4
L'Echangeur......................................**30** C3
MLS...**31** C3
Palais du Peuple................................**32** C4
Plein Sud...**33** D3

SHOPPING
Marché Madina..................................**34** E3

TRANSPORT
Gare Routière Madina........................**35** E3
Gare Routière Matam.........................**36** F2
Taxi Stand...**37** E2

See Kaloum Map (p406)

To Ratoma (7km);
Gare Voiture
Bambéto (5km)

To Airport (500m);
Gare Voiture de
Matoto (5km);
Kindia (135km)

*ATLANTIC
OCEAN*

Money
Street changers line Ave de la République; a fairly reliable black-market spot is the so-called 'Wall Street', near Club Bembeya, though the usual precautions apply (see p818).
Bicigui (Map p406; ☎ 30414515; Ave de la République) The main branch claims to change travellers cheques, but doesn't always. The 24-hour ATM takes Visa.
SGBG (Map p406; ☎ 30456000; Cité Chemin de Fer) Changes cash; 24-hour ATM for Visa cards.

Post
DHL (Map p406; ☎ 30411221; 4th Blvd, Almamya)
Main post office (Map p406; 4th Blvd, Almamya; ☺ 8am-5pm Mon-Fri, to noon Sat)

Telephone & Fax
MouNa (Map p406; Ave de la République; ☺ 8am-10pm) Largest telecentre downtown.
Sotelgui (Map p406; ☎ 30452750; www.sotelgui.net, in French; Almamya; ☺ 8am-8pm Mon-Sat) Good for faxes, but won't handle phone calls.

Tourist Information
Direction Nationale des Forêts et de la Faune (Map p402; ☎ 30468123; Rte de Donka, Conakry) Information on Guinea's national parks.
Guinée Ecologie (Map p402; ☎ 60287994; madou salioupop@yahoo.com; Pharmaguinée Dixinn) A fantastic resource of environmental information, and rare place to find out about Guinea's birds; can arrange bird-watching tours and put you in touch with guides for visits to national parks and hard-to-reach chimp, birding and other sites.

Jane Goodall Institute (Map p402; ☎ 60216888; www.janegoodall.org; mcgauthier@janegoodall.org; Blvd Bellevue, Dixinn Centre 1) For information on chimpanzee protection and visiting chimp sites, email first to ask about being put in touch with guides. See also p412 and p420.

Travel Agencies
The following agencies, all on Ave de la République, are long established and very professional.
Ambassador Voyages (Map p406; ☎ 63270009; ambassadorvoyages@hotmail.com; 6 Ave de la République) Good ticketing service.
IPC Voyages (Map p406; ☎ 30455662; Imm Nafaya, Kaloum) Bookings and ticketing.
Mondial Tours (Map p406; ☎ 30433550; www.mondial tours.net, in French; Imm Nafaya, Kaloum) The best for tours around the country; also does ticketing and car hire.

DANGERS & ANNOYANCES
Following violent demonstrations and incidents of crime, Guinea had returned to its usual peacefulness when we visited. Still, the country was fragile and going through massive changes, and you need to check the latest political situation before you set out.

Madina Market and the Ave de la République have pretty bad reputations for bag snatching and pickpocketing, so keep an eye on your belongings. If there's any civil unrest, the youth areas of Kipé, Ratoma and Taouyah are often 'trouble spots'.

CAMP BOIRO
You can almost measure Guinea's attitude to the nation's first president, Sékou Touré, by the place accorded to his statue in the Musée National. Tucked away in a dusty corner after the end of the First Republic, it's gradually been shifted forwards, and has now already reached the main hall. The horrors of the worst years of the dictatorship have slowly drifted to the back of the collective memory, and no viable political models have been proposed since – and suddenly Sékou Touré can be talked about again.

In Guinea, the Association of the Victims of Camp Boiro has fought for years against the forgetting of the crimes committed under Touré's regime. They represent the families of more than 50,000 people that were tortured, kept in barbaric conditions and executed under his rule in the infamous Camp Boiro (Map p402) and similar prison camps across the country. The name of the camp has become synonymous with the most sinister aspects of Touré's regime – state oppression, paranoia and violence.

Under Lansana Conté, debate about the past was stifled. In early 2009, interim president Moussa Dadis Camara met with the victims' association and, although he focused on pleading for forgiveness rather than reparations, the conversation itself might indicate a new direction. At the time of writing, bulldozers were breaking down the walls of Camp Boiro to the relieved cheers of many. Little was known about the buildings supposed to be erected in its place, or whether a memorial to the victims was planned.

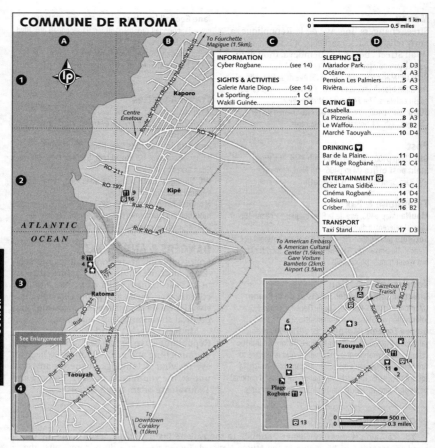

COMMUNE DE RATOMA

INFORMATION
Cyber Rogbane.................(see 14)

SIGHTS & ACTIVITIES
Galerie Marie Diop..........(see 14)
Le Sporting......................**1** C4
Wakili Guinée..................**2** D4

SLEEPING
Mariador Park....................**3** D3
Océane..............................**4** A3
Pension Les Palmiers.......**5** A3
Rivièra..............................**6** C3

EATING
Casabella..........................**7** C4
La Pizzeria........................**8** A3
Le Waffou..........................**9** B2
Marché Taouyah.............**10** D4

DRINKING
Bar de la Plaine...............**11** D4
La Plage Rogbané............**12** C4

ENTERTAINMENT
Chez Lama Sidibé...........**13** C4
Cinéma Rogbané.............**14** D4
Colisium..........................**15** D3
Crisber............................**16** B2

TRANSPORT
Taxi Stand......................**17** D3

Always carry your passport and vaccination certificates with you, especially if you're out in town after 11pm – *gendarmerie* checkpoints are set up at Pont du 8 Novembre (Map p402) and near the British Embassy (Résidence 2000; Map p402) and you will usually have to show your papers. If everything is in order you shouldn't have to pay any 'fines', though you might have to discuss a little with the often-intimidating soldiers.

SIGHTS

The **Musée National** (Map p406; ☎ 3051066; 7th Blvd, Sandervalia; admission GF5000; ⏰ 9am-5.30pm Tue-Sun), with its modest collection of masks, statues and musical instruments, is of vague interest, though the ancient, kapok tree–shaded **Cimetière**

de Boulbinet (Map p406; near Port de Boulbinet), abandoned in 1946, tells you a lot more about the lives and suffering of Conakry's former generations than the museum displays ever could.

Nearby, the grand **Palais des Nations** (Map p406; Boulbinet) served as the president's office until being destroyed in the February 1996 army rebellion. It's currently being renovated.

Seeing worshippers flock to Conakry's impressive **Grande Mosquée** (Map p402; Autoroute, Camayenne) on a Friday is amazing. Built in 1984, the mosque is a striking building that accommodates up to 10,000 people. Unless you're a practising Muslim, you'll have to content yourself with admiring it from the outside. Sékou Touré's grave is in a small gazebo on the grounds. The yellow-and-red **Cathédrale**

CONAKRY ACROBATICS

Just behind the large Dixinn Stadium, one of Conakry's most amazing spots announces itself with drumbeats, balafon sounds and shouts of excitement. This is where the **Centre d'Art Acrobatique Keita Fodeba** (Map p402; Dixinn Stadium) unites street kids and artists in focused daily practice. Launched by the success of the Guinean troupe Circus Baobab, this magical place takes stage performance to a whole new level. The centre not only trains some of Africa's greatest acrobats, it also provides youngsters with a whole range of skills. The discipline of practice for progress is one of them, and practical expertise in crafts, literacy and much more is also part of the rigorous training. The centre's success has made waves across the world – young performers have been sought out to participate in circus performances from East Asia to the US. Seeing them rehearse is inspiring, shining a light on possibility in a country where most people preach despair. And, if you've caught the bug, ask them to give you some classes – you might bring trapeze or juggling skills, along with a whole new insight into the lives of Guinea's youngsters, back from your travels.

Sainte-Marie (Map p406; Blvd du Commerce, Kaloum) isn't quite as impressive, though it's still a pretty structure.

If you drive into town on Corniche Nord, the funky scrap-metal sculptures of **Oppo Atelier** (Map p402; Corniche Nord, Tumbo) greet you on either side of the road. The welders can produce custom work and, if you come during the day, you can watch the statues being made.

The large **Botanical Garden** (Map p402; Rte de Donka, Camayenne) is a pleasantly cool place, great for relaxed walks under kapok trees. Near the Palais du Peuple, the **Jardin 2 Octobre** (Map p402; ☎ 66663685; Corniche Nord, Tumbo) had just been turned into a fabulous kids' playground when we passed, complete with merry-go-rounds and plenty of activities. It wasn't open at the time of research, so you'll need to enquire for rates and opening hours. Driving out of town, check out the large mosaics at the **Gamal Abdel Nasser University of Conakry** (Map p402; Route de Donka, Dixinn).

Tucked away in Minière, **Le Petit Musée** (Map p402; ☎ 64215498; Minière; 🕓 9am-7.30pm Mon-Sat), is a beautiful spot, built with imagination and decorated in the warm, earthen colours of Sahel architecture. It also features a small stage where you'll often get to see great theatre and music shows. In Taouyah, the tiny **Galerie Marie Diop** (Map p404; ☎ 63666660; mariediop@hotmail.com; Espace Rogbane, Taouyah) is a art gallery exhibiting Marie's original works. It sits in one of Conakry's bustling suburbs, and there's a good cafe next door.

ACTIVITIES

Le Sporting (Map p404; ☎ 62661251, 64287746; Taouyah; admission GF30,000; 🕓 8am-9pm), a sports centre with a sea view, has tennis, ping pong and squash facilities, as well as a pool and fitness club.

COURSES

Inquire for rates at the individual centres.

Centre Culturel Franco-Guinéen (Map p402; ☎ 63409625; www.ccfg-conakry.org, in French; Corniche Nord) Can arrange drum and dance lessons, and is a good place to meet artists.

Wakili Guinée (Map p404; ☎ 64204797; lamafoutah@yahoo.fr; Taouyah) Ba Cissoko's music centre arranges excellent *kora* classes, organises festivals, has a simple bar and possibly even accommodation by the time you visit.

Centre d'Art Acrobatique Keita Fodeba (Map p402; Dixinn Stadium) West Africa's most outstanding acrobatics school can arrange acrobatics and trapeze classes for serious students.

FESTIVALS & EVENTS

The **Festival Kora & Cordes**, run by Wakili Guinée (see above) regroups some of the leading acoustic groups from across West Africa. It's normally held in December. During the **Festagg** (www.festagg.com, in French) you get to enjoy live concerts by major bands from Guinea and beyond for a whole week. It's annual, and held around April/May.

SLEEPING

All places should back up electricity at night in case of shortages.

Budget

Inexpensive lodging is scarce and usually pretty seedy. For niceties like running water, electricity and reasonably clean sheets, you might have to invest a bit more. Good exceptions are noted below.

Plein Sud (Map p402; ☎ 60203535, 60542286; off Corniche Sud; r GF100,000-120,000; Ⓟ ❄) Conakry's most relaxed open-air restaurant has three clean, simple rooms right next to its large,

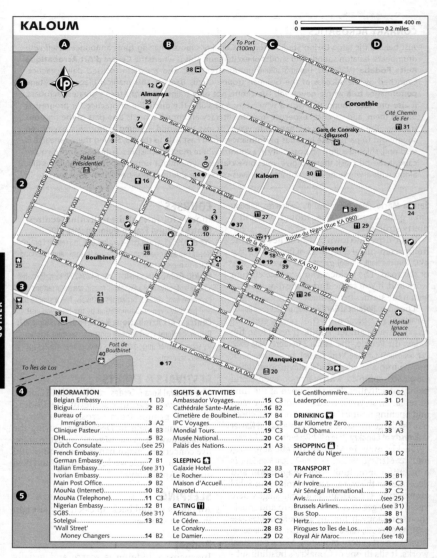

sea-view garden. The couple that run this place are lovely, too, making you feel like their personal guest.

Hôtel du Golfe (Map p402; ☎ 64259478; hoteldu golfedeguinee@yahoo.fr; Minière; s/d from GF160,000/170,000; ⓟ ⓧ) The building could hardly be any less attractive, but inside the gloomy, dark grey shell you find rooms that are surprisingly well

maintained, if slightly worn. The cheapest rooms are dark; invest GF20,000 more for a touch more comfort.

Maison d'Accueil (Map p406; ☎ 60420667; Rte du Niger, Kaloum; r with/without air-con GF200,000/75,000; ⓟ ⓧ ▣) Conakry's Catholic Mission has become so famous for its clean, simple accommodation that it's often fully booked. The setting is peaceful, the place is safe and there's an internet cafe downstairs.

Midrange

our pick **Pension Les Palmiers** (Map p404; ☎ 60593803, 62294484; ighussein@yahoo.fr; Rte de Donka, Ratoma; s/d incl breakfast GF200,000/250,000; ⊠ ⊠) Madame Ghussein has kept her cute guesthouse spotless while bigger places around her crumbled. The doily-adorned couches, cute living room and caring owner will remind you of your best visits to grandma's; the small garden, teeny pool and view over a lively stretch of beach are relaxing after a day out on town.

Hôtel Petit Bateau (Map p402; ☎ 63406106, www.hotelpetitbateau.net, in French; Port de Plaisance; s/d GF255,000/305,000; P ⊠ ⊠ ⊠) Past the rusty hulks and industrial zone, you reach this very pretty sea-view place with impeccable rooms, a large pool and a marina outside. It's a great address – if you've got your own wheels; taxis rarely pass here.

Océane (Map p404; ☎ 67909090; Rte de Donka, Ratoma; r incl breakfast GF265,000; P ⊠ ⊠) The pool is popular for weekenders, as well as being the best thing about this place. The rooms aren't particularly well maintained but have great views.

Mariador Park (Map p404; ☎ 60543053; Rue RO 128, Taouyah; r GF285,000; P ⊠) The cheapest place of the Mariador chain sits in tempting distance to Taouyah's nightlife zone. It's got a relaxing garden and the rooms are acceptable, though slightly rundown.

Galaxie Hotel (Map p406; ☎ 62089026; 5th Ave, Kaloum; s/d GF440,000/500,000; ⊠) The beds here are impressive enough to make a porn star blush. With clean, comfy rooms and small enough to feel like a pension, it's a decent inner-city choice.

Top End

Le Rocher (Map p406; ☎ 30477555, 60559877, essiar natoussi@yahoo.fr; Sandervalia; s/d incl breakfast 600,000/700,000; P ⊠ ⊠ ⊠ ⊠) The service is personalised, rooms impeccable and the food excellent at this small family hotel. The breakfast terrace alone, with a view across the waves, is worth the stay. Our favourite in this price range.

Rivièra (Map p404; ☎ 64223304; Taouyah; s/d GF600,000/700,000; P ⊠ ⊠ ⊠ ⊠) Rooms here are large and come with a breakfast bar, cooking facilities and comfy decor. A great choice outside the inner city.

Novotel (Map p406; ☎ 30415022; H0509@accor .com; Kaloum; r with/without seaview GF835,000/800,000; P ⊠ ⊠ ⊠) This is Conakry's typical choice for anyone from airline staff to foreign consultants, providing a good service, safety and noncommittal smiles to anyone who can afford it. A business hotel that does its job.

EATING
Kaloum

For good street food, try the Marché du Niger (Map p406) where bowls of rice cost less than GF6000.

Le Gentilhommière (Map p406; ☎ 60339023; Rue KA 040; meals GF25,000-40,000; ⊠ lunch & dinner) Gentilhommière doesn't look like much from the outside, but the bamboo, thatch and calabash interior invites you to stick around a while, as does the wide variety of African dishes.

Le Cédre (Map p406; 7th Ave; meals GF30,000-50,000; ⊠ lunch & dinner Mon-Sat) Excellent Lebanese and international cuisine, attentive staff and a relaxed atmosphere have made this one of Conakry's lunchtime favourites.

Le Damier (Map p406; ☎ 30411786; www.damier -conakry.com; Rte du Niger; meals GF30,000-70,000; ⊠ breakfast & lunch Mon-Sat; Ⓥ) It started 20 years ago as a simple patisserie and still sells the best bread and chocolates in town. The soul of this place is the cosy upstairs restaurant, however, where Guinea's young, upwardly-moving classes mingle over plates of varied and refined international cuisine. Don't miss out on the Sunday brunch.

Le Conakry (Map p406; ☎ 30412682; 4th Ave; meals GF35,000; ⊠ lunch & dinner Mon-Sat) Small and fairly French, this expat favourite has a great selection of simple dishes, rendered excellent through a few expert touches.

Africana (Map p406; ☎ 30413518; Manquépas; dishes GF25,000-40,000; ⊠ 9am-8pm Mon-Sat) The tables here heave with delicious Senegalese and Guinean meals and the place is always packed around lunchtime – come here before 2pm to make sure the best meals haven't gone yet. There's usually live *kora* music. It's located behind the Anglican church.

Dixinn & Coléah

Belvédère (Map p402; ☎ 60432526; Rte de Donka, Bellevue; meals GF25,000-60,000; ⊠ 2pm-2am) The large garden is a favourite for family parties, live concerts and filming music videos. The menu is made of fast-food staples, but the garden space is pleasant, there's a kids' playground and a gig every weekend.

Les Jardins de Guinée (Map p402; ☎ 64218938; Coléah; meals GF40,000-60,000; ☻ lunch & dinner) Once one of Conakry's great music venues, this spacious place is today one of the city's favourite restaurants, all thanks to the excellent French food and pizza served, to the tasteful decor of the garden space, and friendly staff. Come here for lunch, when it's less busy.

Indochine (Map p402; Minière; meals GF50,000-80,000; ☻ lunch Tue-Sun, dinner daily; ⓥ) It's been going for years and is still Conakry's first address for South East Asian cuisine. Meals are pricey, but the owners do invest a great deal in importing the perfect ingredients. One of the Conakry's classiest dining experiences.

Ratoma

Plenty of good street-food vendors and small eateries front Marché Taouyah (Map p404) and Carrefour Transit nearby.

Le Waffou (Map p404; off Rte de Donka, Kipé; meals GF15,000-30,000; ☻ lunch & dinner) You can buy Ivorian *attiéké* (grated cassava) at most Conakry street corners, but this thatch-roof eatery prepares it fresh and does it well. It sometimes features live bands on Friday nights.

La Pizzeria (Map p404; Rte de Donka, Ratoma; meals GF30,000-50,000; ☻ dinner Wed-Sun; ⓥ) It doesn't need to bother with a fancy name – the Ratoma grapevine has this humble house down as the nation's best pizza oven. Pizzas are large with thin dough and imaginative toppings; the vibe is family friendly.

Casabella (Map p404; ☎ 60217755; Taouyah; dishes GF55,000-80,000; ☻ noon-midnight Mon-Thu & 5pm-midnight Fri & Sat; ☒ ⌨ ⓥ) Between chubby baroque angels and faintly lit fountains, you get to enjoy spicy Mexican meals and good pizzas. The pool outside invites for sundowners.

Self-Catering

Well-stocked (but expensive) supermarkets include **Leaderprice** (Map p406; Cité Chemin de Fer) and **Hyper-Bobo** (Map p402; Camayenne).

DRINKING

Conakry has more conspicuous little drinking holes (*maquilles*) than your average Guinean street has potholes. Most can be fun if you're swaying a little yourself and thrive in the presence of male layabouts and pretty prostitutes. This is a handful of cute spots we like.

Bar de la Plaine (Map p404; Marché Taouyah) Squeezed between Taouyah's charcoal sellers, roadside barbers and rotating stands proffering second-hand bras, this humble terrace is where you soak up local atmosphere over a very cheap bottle of Guiluxe and indulge in chats with the musicians of the band Ba Cissoko (who own the place) and their keen fans.

Bar Kilometre Zero (Map p406; Boulbinet) Behind the Novotel, right at the point where Conakry's first-ever inches of tarmac were placed, you'll find this makeshift hut of hewn-together yellow planks. Step in and a cute bar with great views over the tip of Kaloum opens up.

Club Obama (Map p406; Boulbinet) The US President's name adorns dozens of bars across the country. This is a cute one, made from wooden planks, thatch sun-roofs and a curious assembly of huge fish skeletons. It's a humble place from which to observe the bustle of nearby Port de Boulbinet.

La Plage Rogbané (Map p404; Taouyah; ☻ lunch & dinner) In a brilliant communal effort, Taouyah's youngsters cleaned this stretch of beach to build a space for playing ball, flirting, running and watching sunsets to carry you far away from Conakry. The terrace bar is one of the city's most chilled-out spots, serving tasty seafood and cold beers amid engaging neighbourhood vibes.

ENTERTAINMENT

Conakry parties as though the weekend was invented right here. There are hundreds of clubs, ranging from grimy red-light huts to glitzy capital-worthy parlours, and many have live music.

Live Music

Some of Guinea's greatest stars play in some of Conakry's most dubious corners. Between those and the big, often international gigs at the stately **Palais du Peuple** (Map p402; Corniche Nord; Tumbo) and the **Centre Culturel Franco-Guinéen** (Map p402; www.ccfg-conakry.org, in French; Corniche Nord, Tumbo), you find a live show every day of the week, and most are free of charge.

La Fourchette Magique (Map p404; ☎ 60368650; Kaporo Port) Far out of town, this is where Guinea's intellectuals, bright young things and old-school revolutionaries debate the country's future over a few Skol and excellent live jazz.

L'Echangeur (Map p402; Dixinn II) Right on Dixinn junction, this humble bar looks completely unspectacular, yet it's where many of Guinea's biggest stars play on Saturdays in a bar overflowing with good vibes and cold beer. Bring a few Guinea francs to 'spray' the musicians in thanks for the praises they'll sing.

Le Badala (Map p402; ☎ 64709446; Corniche Sud; ☻ 3pm-midnight Tue-Sun) Its large roundhouse leans far out onto the shore; inside, there's a dusty glitterball suspended from a dented tin roof. Most weekends soft lights lend the place atmosphere and the popular band Les Espoirs de Coronthie spins out a few tunes.

Chez Lama Sidibé (Le Marsitaala; Map p404; ☎ 60542082) It's really just a bare house with a large fridge full of cold beers, but before nightfall, you get to enjoy the view from the raised shore across the bay. On weekend nights the crashing of shakers and call of Fula flutes rival the lapping of the waves, as famous singer Lama Sidibé hosts informal jam sessions.

La Paillotte (Map p402; Corniche Nord, Camayenne) If you're a fan of Guinea's 'Golden Age' of music this, the classic rehearsal space of many 1970s bands, is where the old stars still meet daily for drinks and nostalgic chats, and sometimes perform at the weekend.

Plein Sud (Map p402; ☎ 60203535; off Corniche Sud) One of the best places to hide from the dust of the city, this palm-shaded garden restaurant features live music by the classic Horoya Band every Friday and jazz on Saturdays, all enjoyed by one of Conakry's most relaxed crowds. The restaurant is brilliant, too.

Dancing
The harder life gets for Conakry's youth, the dizzier the club scene seems to become. The town is sprinkled with mirror-adorned, disco ball–dazzling nightspots (admission is usually around GF10,000–20,000).

Crisber (Map p404; Rte de Donka, Kipé; admission around GF20,000) Ratoma has the highest club density of all. The young and flash opens the ball. It's full of lipgloss-sporting girls in Barbie weaves and posing guys, and also has a good pool table.

MLS (Map p402; ☎ 65811811; Place 8 Nov; admission Fri-Sun GF50,000-100,000, Mon-Thu free; ☻ 5.50pm-5am) The very chic place is in a league of its own; subtly styled in polished wood, soft fabrics, spotlighting and handmade furniture, it's got to be one of West Africa's classiest clubs. Its support for imaginative youth projects means regular exciting events.

The city's top address at the time of research was the **Colisium** (Map p404; Carrefour Transit; admission around GF20,000) with its flash indoor dance floor and open-air chilling area. There's a handful of other clubs right there but, if you manage to move on, try the pretty **Ipso Facto** (Map p402; ☎ 64205609; Minière; admission around GF15,000) where you dance or play pool between Charlie Chaplin paintings and leather-clad chairs.

Cinemas
The beautifully renovated **Cinéma Rogbané** (Map p404; Rte de Donka, Taouyah) shows dated Hollywood blockbusters and the occasional African movie every weekend. Try also the Centre Culturel Franco-Guinéen (see p401).

SHOPPING
The hectic, noisy sprawl of **Marché Madina** (Map p402; Madina) is where you get everything from Chinese housewares to indigo cloth, and sometimes a lost copy of Plato between faded women's magazines with one of the many street booksellers. Marché du Niger (Map p406) isn't quite as crazy, and has fewer pickpockets too – it's a great place for buying fruit, veg and patchwork trousers.

GETTING THERE & AWAY
Air
Conakry has the only international airport. There were no scheduled domestic flights at research, though irregular charters by NGOs or private companies to N'zérékoré, Kamsar and Siguiri sometimes accept passengers.

Bush Taxi & Bus
There are three main *gares routières*: Bambeto, Madina and Matam (Map p402). Bambeto is the most popular departure point for taxis to Fouta Djalon, while Matam is the only one where you find the big, American school buses travelling to Kankan (GF100,000, 13 hours), Kissidougou (GF86,000, 12 hours) and N'zérékoré (GF150,0000, 20 hours), as well as taxis. From Madina, you usually find taxis to all destinations. As Matam is big and busy, taxis tend to fill up fairly quickly.

Leaving Guinea, there are several taxis daily from each *gare routière* for Freetown, (Sierra Leone; GF100,000, seven hours) and Diaoubé (Senegal; GF200,000, two days). For Bamako (Mali; GF200,000, 24 hours), cars use the Gare Routière Madina. The

GUINEA

three-day marathon to Monrovia (Liberia; GF150,000) begins at the Gare Routière de Matoto. See also p429.

GETTING AROUND
To/From the Airport
Chartering a taxi between downtown and the airport shouldn't cost more than about GF30,000.

Bus
A few buses run along the Rte de Donka and up the Autoroute past the airport. You can catch buses for both places downtown at the roundabout opposite the port but the ride is tedious. Tickets are around GF1000.

Car
Travel agencies (particularly Mondial Tours, see p403) can arrange car hire, and informal options are often advertised in hotels.

Avis (Map p406; ☎ 30454571; Novotel)

Hertz (Map p406; ☎ 64579935; Ave de la République)

Taxi
Shared taxis ply all major routes around Conakry (GF1000 per 3km zone). A car is full when there are four people in the back and two in front. The two main destinations from Ratoma are Kaloum (*ville*) and Madina. There's a very useful hand signalling method by which you indicate the direction you're taking to the driver: you'll have sussed it quickly by observing others using it, if not, just shout your destination as the taxi passes.

If you want to charter a taxi (called *déplacement*) you'll need to find an empty one and then negotiate your price. Downtown to Taouyah, for example, should cost around GF20,000. Dixinn–Taouyah is around GF10,000. Prices go up when the traffic jams are worse.

You usually find parked empty cabs at Carrefour Transit in Taouyah (see Map p404) and near the stadium in Dixinn (see Map p402).

AROUND CONAKRY

ÎLES DE LOS
When you step over the harsh tapestry of blue plastic bags and fish guts of Port de Boulbinet to catch your island-bound pirogue, you might find it hard to believe that a 20-minute boat ride will take you to tranquil stretches of palm-fringed sands. Once you arrive, there's little here to tell you that the Îles de Los were once under British control and used as prisons and slave-trading stations. Today they are popular for weekenders escaping Conakry's fumes.

Tiny **Île Room** has a great swimming beach, though the pretty, if overpriced hotel **Le Sogué** (☎ 64257059; r incl breakfast GF520,000; ⊙ Nov–mid-Jun; ⊠), which sits right on it, will charge you GF5000 for using it (parasols and mats cost extra). Further along, the rootsy **Konkoba** (☎ 64609286; r GF125,000) has tiny, not exactly spotless rooms, and offers percussion classes. In the village, the chilled-out guesthouse **Villa Elisa** (full board GF150,000) has decent rooms, energy by solar panels and lovely views over a rocky bit of shore. Near the pirogue landing, you'll find a couple of reggae-styled *campements* – the haunts of spliff-smoking, hammock-lounging djembe drummers.

Île de Kassa is closer to Conakry, and big (as well as beautiful) enough for short hikes. **Le Magellan** (☎ 64395420, 60367574; pascaldemattos@yahoo.fr; s/d from GF300,000/330,000; ⊙ Oct–mid-Jun; ⊠ ⊠) is the perfect place for a chilled weekend between smoothly washed rocks, sandy beach and pretty bungalows. Contact them to arrange a pick-up from Hôtel Petit Bateau (Map p402) – they run a regular boat every Saturday.

Île Tamara, used by the French and later by Sékou Touré as a penal colony, is not as popular as its beaches aren't particularly good, although it offers some interesting hikes. Fotoba, with its small Anglican church, is the main village.

Getting There & Away
Overcrowded pirogues (around GF10,000) leave regularly for Île de Kassa from Port de Boulbinet. For Room, you won't make it there and back in a day unless you hire a boat (return with waiting time around GF200,000 for Roume, less for Kassa).

LOWER GUINEA

Among the palm groves, sand beaches and rock-shore rivers of Lower Guinea, three different eras seem to coexist. In villages and on the remote Îles Tristao, Baga and Nalou populations continue traditional lifestyles, while Boké and Boffa bear the signs of the region's early colonial occupation. In Fria and Kamsar, you see the 'lungs' of modern Guinea at work – the massive bauxite mines and plants, around which modern towns have developed.

DUBRÉKA

A pretty town close to Conakry, Dubréka saw a fair bit of investment under Lansana Conté: it was his hometown. Art lovers should take a look at the Institut Supérieur des Arts, Guinea's national art school, though the more exciting arts project **Tafory** (Khorira) lies just out of town. Famous painter Nabisco and his wife Nicole have opened a space here for creative encounters, relaxation in beautiful surroundings and responsible travel ideas that support the local village. Accommodation is in local-style round huts. Ask in Dubréka, and follow the signposts to get there.

The **Cascades de la Soumba** (☎ 63352024; admission GF10,000), Dubréka's famous waterfalls, are close by. They're worth a visit from around June to December; in the remaining months they dry to a trickle. Near the falls, four **bungalows** (r GF280,000; P ☒) offer good quality accommodation and meals at the weekend. The signposted turn-off to the falls is 11km after the Dubréka junction on the Boké highway; the falls are 5km further down a dirt road. On your way, you pass the **Merveilles de la Soumba**, a lovely stretch of river, rendered a favourite weekend destination via several simple **bungalows** (☎ 64609620; r GF70,000), a good nightclub and sports grounds.

Ask someone at Dubréka junction to point out the **Le Chien Qui Fume** rock formation (supposed to resemble a smoking dog) on the side of **Mt Kakoulima** (1011m). There are some great hikes to be done here; you can bathe in a small pool at the foot of the mountain and sleep in the adjacent **campement** (r GF50,000). Taxis and minibuses leave regularly for Dubréka from Conakry (GF15,000).

FRIA
pop 100,000

Fria developed around Guinea's first bauxite mine, established already under colonial rule. The mining compound looms above the town, which winds up the green hills towards the plant, then down towards the Konkouré River. The town itself is pretty and there are a few interesting places nearby. About 15km from Fria, beyond Wawaya village, are the **Grottes de Bogoro**, a good place for a swim. The so-called **Plage de Konkouré** is reached via a 4km trek along a rough road, during which you get great glimpses of the river from above. People bathe here and fishermen can take you to the nearby caves. There are also interesting caves in **Tormélin**, between Fria and the Boké highway; they're about a 6km walk from the Tormélin mosque.

La Mariame (s/d GF60,000/85,000; ☒) is a clean, friendly guesthouse in the town centre. Staff at **Hôtel Yaskadi** (☎ 63856544, 65665415; signposted off Rte Unite; r with fan/air-con GF30,000/50,000; P ☒) is so good at arranging tours to Fria's surroundings that you almost forgive it for the bathroom tiles along the walls. The fanciest hotel (and nightclub too) is **Le Bowal** (☎ 64650510; airport road; r GF80,000-100,000; P ☒), which sits near a lake in the rainy season, merely a wide field in the dry months.

Among the town's restaurants, the **Rose de Casablanca** (near the hospital; meals around GF30,000) has simple meals and a well-stocked bar, as does Le Marakech on the entrance to town.

Conakry is easily reached by bush taxi (GF20,000, three hours). The 65km to Télimélé (GF35,000, four hours) takes you along one of Guinea's worst roads, though the grapevine talks about imminent repairs.

BOFFA
pop 20,000

Tiny Boffa, a former French-colonial trading point, only really comes to life once a year, in early May, when thousands of Christians march here from Conakry on their annual pilgrimage to Guinea's first **Catholic church** and mission. The original church, built in 1876 by the Holy Ghost Fathers, burnt down and was replaced by a pretty brick building in 1934. The building, as well as the lovely green terrain surrounding it, are well worth a glimpse.

If you get stuck, you can spend the night at the basic but acceptable **Niasa Bely** (r GF40,000).

BEL AIR & SOBANÉ

All along the Lower Guinea road, signposts try to lure you to Plage de Bel Air. The beach here really is beautiful in its golden sway, though the massive **Grand Hôtel de Bel Air** (☎ 63327010; r GF400,000, villa GF600,000; P ☒) put a damper on simple fun. Built by former president Lansana

GUINEA

Conté, the luxury place was showing the first signs of going the ashes-to-ashes way when we passed (we found it locked up and empty). Check the situation when you're there.

Three kilometres before Bel Air is the signposted turn-off for the **Village Touristique Sobané** (☎ 63937128; bungalows with/without air-con GF200,000/180,000; P ⚡), a relaxed site with a great beach (make sure you come at high tide), though the bungalows were suffering badly from neglect. For GF10,000 you get access to the beach without spending the night.

Without your own transport you'll need to charter a taxi in Boffa (GF150,000) or Boké (around GF300,000). A *moto-taxi* (motorcycle taxi) will be cheaper. Taking the long route along the 5km from the turnoff to Bel-Air, you pass some picturesque villages nestled among palm groves.

BOKÉ & KAMSAR
pop 120,000

The area of **Boké** was among the first to be claimed, and fought over, by colonial powers in the 19th century. The French explorer René Caillé set off on his tour along the Rio Nunez from here. A pillar erected in honour of the voyager reminds visitors of his journey while crumbling colonial warehouses along the river tell the story of colonial trade. The most impressive historical building is the 1878 French fort, **Fortin de Boké** (☎ 60682674; admission by donation; ⚘ 8am-6pm), which houses a dusty little museum with historical documents and a carelessly preserved collection of masks and artefacts.

Kamsar is very different in character – a recent town that has grown rapidly around a huge bauxite plant and its train tracks. There aren't any real sights here and, though the town is large and has reasonable infrastructures, it doesn't really have much character.

If you come with time and courage, undertake a pirogue trip to the **Îles Tristao**, a small set of mangrove-lined islands off the Kamsar coast. Rarely visited, those pretty isles are an important wetland and a fabulous bird-watching spot, as well as home to Nalou communities who have maintained very traditional lifestyles. Getting here is tough – a rough, five-hour pirogue trip. If you're up for it, contact the **Jane Goodall Institute** (☎ Mr Soumah 64081163, Bokar Sylla 65465076, Moussa Thiam 60201680; nr Boké Stadium) in Boké who can help you organise your trip. The institute works mainly on the protection of chimpanzees and can also indicate (and take you to) good chimp sites in the area.

Sleeping & Eating

Boké is the prettier town, but neither its **Hôtel Filao** (☎ 65247165; r with/without air-con GF80,000/55,000; P ⚡) nor **Hôtel Kakande** (☎ 60543486; r GF35,000-100,000), which sadly blocks its own great river views, are as good as the hotels you have in Kamsar.

There, the **Océane Plus** (☎ 30326604; s/d GF90,000/110,000; ⚡) near the port is a safe and friendly option for those on a low budget. **RBQ** (☎ 30326501; r from GF125,000; ⚡ ⚡) has good, slightly dark lodgings, and one bathroom per two rooms. The best thing about it is the large, clean pool.

Close by, **Hôtel le Kamsar** (☎ 63355262, 63351107; kikeyambe.kamsar@gmail.com; r GF270,000; P ⚡ ⚡ ⚡) is one of the best places in the country. Rooms are spacious and tastefully decorated with excellent bathrooms. The same owners run also the **Auberge de Kamsar** (☎ 63355262, 63351107; dishes around GF50,000; ⚘ 9am-3.30pm & 6.30-11pm Mon-Sat), one of very few upcountry restaurants that propose a varied menu of excellent dishes.

Behind the parking lot of the bauxite plant, you very unexpectedly find the airy **Club Nautique** (dishes around GF40,000), a restaurant that looks out onto the sea, has a relaxed atmosphere and good salads on the menu.

At the supermarket next to Auberge de Kamsar you can stock up on pricy European food and toiletries.

Getting There & Away

You get to Conakry (GF30,000, four hours) from either town or, via a very rough road through beautiful lands, to Télimélé (GF40,000, seven hours), where you can find transport to other towns in Fouta Djalon. Bush taxis run to Québo (Guinea-Bissau; GF50,000, six hours) on most days; the road is very bad. See also p429. Taxis between Kamsar and Boké are GF5000.

KINDIA
pop 100,000

Famous for its fruit, friendliness, football team and fierce army, Kindia is a spread-out town up the first mountain as you wind your way into Fouta Djalon. Conakry kids drift to Kindia for a night out in another town – it has a thriving club scene. You'll probably be more interested in the handful of natural sights close by. Kindia's postcard picture is the **Voile de la Mariée** (Bridal Veil Falls; admission GF5000) waterfall, 12km out of town, now a rather neglected site and not quite as impressive as the **Eaux de Kilissi** (☎ 62352251 Aboubacar Keita; Foulayah; admission GF5000). The site has two pretty falls and a natural amphitheatre that hosts occasional concerts; it's great for picnics. Aboubacar is a brilliant guide who can also indicate other sites to you. The falls are in Foulayah, the village preceding Kindia on the way from Conakry. Turn left at the market and follow the signs.

Looming in Kindia's background is the massive **Mt Gangan**, which you can hike up (around two hours) to enjoy the views. The turn-off in town is just before the military camp – any kid can show you the way.

Rarely visited is the small stretch of remaining virgin rainforest near Kindia, the **Forêt de Koumounkan**, an impressive site and brilliant bird-watching spot. Contact Guinée Ecologie (p403) to arrange a visit.

Information

The local Bicigui bank has an ATM, and there's a post office, telecentre and several poorly stocked pharmacies. Internet access is tricky.

Sleeping & Eating

Most of Kindia's hotels are tucked away behind the dusty roads of Khaliakhori, just off the Kindia–Conakry road. They're all signposted. **Le Sooli** (☎ 60490933, 65225704; Khaliakhori; s/d GF90,000/115,000; P ⊠ ☎), near the electric powerplant, is one of those. With Mathieu it's got the friendliest manager around – a guy who'll try to do the impossible to make you feel welcome. Rooms are clean with good beds and set in bungalows far enough away from the nightclub, bar and restaurant.

The spacious red huts of **Les Bungalows** (☎ 60298449; s/d incl breakfast GF130,000/160,000; P ⊠) are scattered around a large garden at the end of a Khaliakhori dust track. It's a great place to hide from the world. **Le Masabi** (☎ 64726569; s/d incl breakfast GF120,000/140,000; P ⊠) is on the side of the road as you come in from Conakry. The spacious rooms here are impeccable and even have a touch of flair. There's hot water and a strictly rationed breakfast. The only drawback: some of the staff can be astoundingly unaccommodating.

For food outside your hotel, try **La Gargotte** (next to Moroccan Bank; meals GF25,000), a backyard with vinyl-clad tables serving chicken and chips. **Le Mont Gangan** (meals GF25,000) offers the same menu but better people-watching, and there are a couple of eateries near the petrol station on the Conakry–Mamou road.

Getting There & Around

Daily taxi destinations include Télimélé (GF35,000, five hours), Mamou (GF22,000, three hours), Labé (GF35,000, six hours) and Conakry (GF13,000, three hours). There's also a daily Conakry-bound bus (GF10,000).

Public transport in town is mainly by *moto-taxi*. A short ride is GF1000. To the falls, you'll pay around GF6000 for a return with a bit of waiting time.

FOUTA DJALON

Not only the scenery changes from flat lands and palm groves as you wind your way up the serpentines of the Mamou route, the population changes too. You'll pass elegant old men in indigo *boubous* and striking ladies, white headwraps swept back as they walk to the mosque. The heartland of the Fula population, this impressive plateau is also an old centre of Islamic learning and former home to one of West Africa's most powerful Muslim theocracies (1725–1886).

Fouta Djalon is an amazing trekking terrain. Temperatures are cooler than in other parts of the country and the scenery, with its steep drops, tiered waterfalls and craggy mountainsides, is simply stunning.

MAMOU

Mamou, the gateway to Fouta Djalon, is a dusty junction town perched on a hill. Twenty-five kilometres west of town, at the village of **Konkouré**, is a beautiful waterfall, and 15km to the north is **Lake Bafing**, a Sunday getaway for picnics and swimming. The route to Dabola takes you past **Timbo**, former capital of the Fouta Djalon Empire, and an important religious centre for the Fula community. You can visit the mosque and a few ancient tombs, as well as speak to the village elders who'll be proud to relate the empire's story.

FOUTA TREKKING AVENTURE

Over 10 years of hiking and researching, the members of **Fouta Trekking Aventure** (Map p417; ☎ 60570279; www.foutatrekking.org) have identified the best hikes, cliffs, mountains and waterfalls in Fouta Djalon, one of the best trekking areas in West Africa. Better still, they work closely with the local villages in developing their circuits in order to minimise the negative impacts of tourism on fragile communities and channel economic benefits back to the villages. Tours can be tailored to individual wishes and last anything from a day to over a week. The rate is €25 per day, including the guide, food and accommodation, but excluding transport.

While they can take you to any place in the Fouta, their exclusive circuits are particularly recommended. They pass through the beautiful village of **Aïnguel**, where the huts of their *campement solidaire* (traditional-style lodging run for community benefit) are built in the unique, colourful style this community is known for. Twelve kilometres further, in **Leyfita** you get to cross an impressive vine bridge and see a few rarely visited waterfalls. The route to **Debeya** leads past further beautiful falls, to a quirky set of wooden 'ladders' made by the villagers. A similar, more famous set is the **Echelles de Lelouma** in Djinkan, wedged into the mountainside to connect the villages on the plateau to those in the valley.

All mentioned villages have a *campement*, almost exclusively handled by Fouta Trekking Aventure and the villages concerned. Further *campements solidaire* were under construction in Mali-Yemberem, and near the Kambadaga falls.

Nearby areas are also to be integrated in the Tabala conservation project (see p420).

Information

There's a bank with a 24-hour ATM, a post office and telecentre. The best place to get online is the École Forestière or the **cybercafe** (☒ 6-11pm) near the old cinema in town.

Sleeping & Eating

Most sleeping options in town are pretty grotty. Below are three better choices.

École Forestière (☎ 60572912, 60549643; Conakry Rd; r GF35,000; 🅿 🖳) Rooms at the forestry school are really meant for seminar attendees, but electricity, birdsong in the morning, an internet connection and clean rooms attract other travellers too.

Guesthouse Les Acacias (☎ 60329749; r incl breakfast GF120,000) On the road towards Labé, this cute, welcoming place is made up of four spacious rooms with clean bathrooms (there's hot water), comfy beds and a living room with satellite TV.

Hôtel Balys (☎ 60573070; Quartier Pétel, km4; s/d GF100,000/110,000, r with air-con GF155,000; 🅿 ☒ 🖳) Fake flowers, kitsch curtains and small seating corners with leather armchairs make the spacious bedrooms look like perfect replicas of Guinean middle-class lounges. This is a clean, bright and friendly option with a good

restaurant, on-and-off internet connection and car hire.

Outside hotels, you'll find food in the small eateries in town. Chez Willy near the Station Total and the nearby Restaurant Pergola were popular when we visited.

Getting There & Away

There's transport to all four corners of the country from Mamou. Bush taxis to Conakry (GF33,000), Kindia (GF22,000) and Faranah (GF30,000) leave from *gare routière* Conakry in town. Those for Labé (GF30,000, three hours). Dabola (GF30,000, two hours) and Kankan (GF70,000) go from the *gare routière conserverie*, while those for Dalaba (GF15,000, one hour) go from the *ancien gare routière*.

DALABA

Perched at a pleasant 1200m, Dalaba used to be an important therapeutic centre during colonial days. You can still visit buildings from this era, though the most amazing thing to do here is undertake hikes through the surrounding pine groves and villages, and to waterfalls.

The **tourist office** (☎ 67269348; Quartier des Chargeurs; ☒ 8.30am-6.30pm) is one of the few in the country that's really useful – thanks to the personal initiative of director Mamadou Diallo. Contact him to arrange village tours and even stays.

Sights

IN TOWN

The old French governor's residence, **Villa Sili** (1936) is fascinating in its decay. Next door, the **Case à Palabres**, decorated with beautiful Fula bas-relief designs, was used as a meeting hall by village elders. The caretaker will show you around both for a small tip.

The calm and curious **Williams-Bah Museum** (☎ 64368275; admission by donation; ☿ 9am-6pm; ☐) displays a few dusty masks and artefacts, as well as information on eminent African-Americans. There's also a small library. Mme Barry, who looks after this place, can also explain the finer details of the **Association des Couturières de Tangama** (☎ 64368275; ☿ 9am-4pm Mon-Sat), a great workshop to watch fabrics being made and dyed, and to buy the quality fairtrade products. On the main road, the **Cooperative des Cordonniers** (☎ 62529664) is Guinea's best place for purchasing leather goods, particularly sandals, wallets and pouches.

AROUND TOWN

One of Guinea's tallest waterfalls, the **Chutes de Ditinn**, takes a remarkable 80m drop straight down off the cliff. Bush taxis run from Dalaba to the namesake village (they're easiest to find on Thursday, market day), 32km away. The parking area is 5km further on; from here it's a 20-minute walk.

Just after the rainy season, the 10km hike to the **Chutes de Garaya** makes for a great day out (bring a picnic). They often attract baboon populations, and sometime even chimps. Monkeys are also often spotted on **Pont de Dieu**, a natural rock bridge. Closer to town, shady **Chevalier Gardens** was started in 1908 to determine which European plants could grow in Guinea. Next to it, the waters of **Lake Dounkimagna** nourish the products of the garden, including Dalaba's famous strawberries and other fruits and vegetables.

Sleeping & Eating

There's a hotel for every pocket here. To eat outside of these places, try the rice stalls in the village.

Auberge Seidy II (Chez Koffi; ☎ 60575370, r GF40,000) Koffi's veranda is a bright place, perfect for digging into the delicious chicken and chips he prepares for stranded travellers (he also

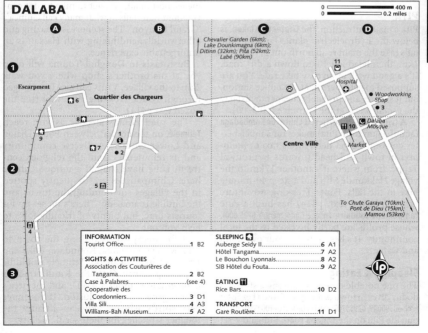

DALABA

INFORMATION		
Tourist Office	1	B2

SIGHTS & ACTIVITIES		
Association des Couturières de Tangama	2	B2
Case à Palabres	(see 4)	
Cooperative des Cordonniers	3	D1
Villa Sili	4	A3
Williams-Bah Museum	5	A2

SLEEPING ⌂		
Auberge Seidy II	6	A1
Hôtel Tangama	7	A2
Le Bouchon Lyonnais	8	A2
SIB Hôtel du Fouta	9	A2

EATING ⍗		
Rice Bars	10	D2

TRANSPORT		
Gare Routière	11	D1

does great West African dishes, but you need to order in advance). Rooms are reminiscent of the poetic quarters of a 19th-century lady, gazing out to inspire her memoirs.

Hôtel Tangama (☎ 60355607; s/d GF50,000/65,000; **P**) The whole set-up here is welcoming, right down to the fireplace in the lounge, but everything's a little dated, dusty and a tad rundown.

SIB Hôtel du Fouta (☎ 60276171; s/d GF100,000/ 125,000; **P**) Decline has also nibbled on Dalaba's largest hotel, though rooms are still good and the views from the terrace across the valley as spectacular as ever.

Le Bouchon Lyonnais (☎ 60346176, 64355105; r incl breakfast from GF150,000) The fresh, imaginative meals (GF40,000) served here make a fantastic difference from a week of fried chicken – there's even good wine. Three of the impeccable, darkish rooms (each with a large, specially made bed) share a clean bathroom.

Getting There & Away

Bush taxis go to Pita (GF12,000, one hour), Labé (GF22,000, two hours), Mamou (GF12,000, one hour) and Conakry (GF35,000, seven hours).

PITA

Pita's major attraction, the **Chutes du Kinkon**, is below the hydroelectric plant. To get to the falls take the main road north out of town for 1km, then head left 10km down a dirt road. It's a good walk or an easy bike ride. You are supposed to get a permit at the police station, but it's easier and probably cheaper to just pay the *gendarmerie* at the entrance (GF3000).

A trip to the three-tiered **Chutes de Kambadaga** (about 35km from Pita) makes for a much better day out. To get here, hire a taxi or *moto-taxi* in town and head towards Bourouwal Tappé, from where it's another 17km to the village Hakkunde Miti and a steep 40-minute hike to the falls. Fouta Trekking Adventure (see the boxed text, p414) has built a cute **campement solidaire** (village campement; r GF25,000), whose profits are partly invested in the local community. It's best to bring your own food and water.

Sleeping & Eating

The one notable exception among a string of dodgy dives in town is the spread-out **Chez Sister** (☎ 60590049, 62955707; r incl breakfast GF100,000), 4km outside Pita on the Dalaba road. Bungalow-set rooms are clean and pretty, there's hot water, and solar panels grant a few extra hours of electricity. Come at the right time of year and you might be able to pick bananas from the garden behind the terrace.

A few tiny eateries provide the usual steak, chips and chicken diet, though Chez Sall on the main road in Pita cooks up the best rice and sauce in town.

Getting There & Away

Bush taxis for Labé (GF12,000, one hour) and Dalaba (GF10,000, one hour) leave from the Rex Cinéma, and on a nearby side street for Doucki (GF15,000, 1½ hours).

DOUCKI & TÉLIMÉLÉ
pop 100,000

The road from Pita to Télimélé is a tough ride, but if you manage to take your eyes off the treacherous route, you'll take in some of the Fouta's most spectacular mountainsides. About 45km from Pita you pass the village of **Doucki** where the one-of-a-kind Hassan Bah (who speaks English, French and Spanish) runs a basic **campement** (GF25,000). You get to stay in a traditional Fula hut and eat local meals; best of all, you get to hike to slot canyons and waterfalls in what many call Guinea's 'Grand Canyon'. The scenery is amazing and otherworldly, and hiking with Hassan is an unforgettable experience.

Bush taxis to Donghol-Touma will drop you at his brother's shop where you walk 2km to the village. Visits can also be arranged through Fouta Trekking Aventure (see the boxed text p414).

The road climbs steeper as you reach **Télimélé**, on the border between Fouta Djalon and Lower Guinea. A diverse community and its remoteness from the religious centre in Labé have shaped a unique culture here. Chimpanzees are frequently spotted in the villages surrounding the towns and the birdlife is amazing. There's no set-up for tourists here, but plenty of friendly folks to help you out.

If the many roads linking the town to Pita, Kindia, Lelouma, Koundara, Boké and Fria were in good shape, Télimélé would be a thriving centre. Only the Kindia track is manageable without a 4WD, and the area's charm grows in its seclusion. If you have very sturdy wheels, you can attempt the tougher stretches for their scenic beauty.

GUINEA

LABÉ
pop 60,000

The four minarets of Labé's large mosque greet you from afar, welcoming you to the administrative centre of the largely Muslim Fouta Djalon. Most of town is dominated by the busy **Marché Central** – a dusty, nauseating affair, impressive for its activity.

Home to the impressive **Fouta Trekking Aventure** (☎ 60570279; www.foutatrekking.org; Quartier N'Djoulou), Labé is the perfect starting point for hikes around the region (see also the boxed text, p414).

Information

The Bicigui and SGBG banks have 24-hour ATMs and change cash, and you'll find a black-market changer on every corner in the market. The hospital isn't very well equipped. For internet access (per hour GF6000), try Aden de Labé or Cofobreak. The Radio Rurale is a good address for cultural information on the area and for getting in touch with some of Labé's fantastic Fula musicians *(nyamakala)*.

Sights

In town, a squeeze through the narrow alleyways of the **Marché Central** is an experience. The more exciting place to pick up craftwork, such as Fouta-typical indigo cloth or leather sandals, is the tall **Maison des Artisans** (☎ 60570830, 60364882; Quartier Kouroula; ⏲ 8.30am-5pm Mon-Sat). You can learn a lot about the role of crafts in the Fouta here and arrange visits to the workshops of weavers, dyers, blacksmiths, woodcarvers and other artisans.

At the entry of Labé, **Petit Musée du Fouta Djallon** (☎ 60571584, 30520010; admission by donation; ⏲ 8am-6pm), run by the renowned writer Koumanthio Diallo, is illuminating. It breathes life into artefacts and documents by presenting them in small scenes, has a reference library and also features occasional cultural events upstairs.

One of the closest hiking destinations is the stunning **Chutes de Saala**, about an hour's drive down a rugged road off the Rte de Koundara. You can picnic and swim here. Expect to pay about GF130,000 for a chartered taxi.

Sleeping

A very promising-looking ecolodge was under construction, a few houses south of the Fouta Trekking offices. Check if it's completed.

Hôtel de l'Indépendance (☎ 60570990; r GF35,000) Very rundown and with lax security, this is only

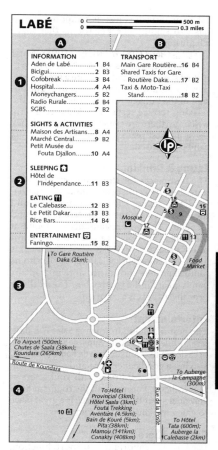

worth a look if you're really strapped for cash and desperate to stay near the town centre.

Auberge la Calebasse (☎ 60410851, 62235048; Quartier Ghadha Pounthioun; r GF50,000; P) Labé's best budget bet is very simple and tucked away in a residential *quartier* (you need to hire a *moto-taxi* to get here). Rooms are bare but clean, all the way to the sheets.

Hôtel Saala (☎ 60317422; r GF50,000, bungalow GF80,000; P) Only the bungalows are of good quality at the hotel of choice for Labé's wedding parties. The best nightspots are next door.

Auberge la Campagne (☎ 60571702, 60414300; Quartier Pounthioun; r incl breakfast GF100,000, camping GF30,000; P) The large rooms here are great value, but the option of camping on the

GUINEA

1st-floor terrace is just as tempting. It also has two slightly cheaper rooms that share a bathroom.

ourpick **Hôtel Tata** (☎ 60410851, 62235048; Quartier Pounthioun; r & bungalows GF100,000; **P** 🖳) The varnished slate floors and walls are a great idea – they keep things cool and attractive. The design of the bungalows here is as pretty as the relaxing terrace restaurant; kids are utterly welcome (there are even highchairs) and they serve the best pizza in town. Trekking tours can be organised.

Eating & Drinking

The best places for street food are the stalls near the *gare routière* and along the market. Rice and sauce, fried sweet potatoes and meat skewers are the going fare (all around GF5000). The best restaurants are found at the hotels. For small eateries, the backyard of **Le Calebasse** (meals GF20,000; 🕑 lunch & dinner) is good, and **Le Petit Dakar** (dishes GF15,000), with its football posters and corner store instead of a bar, is great for the youth vibes. The small bar near the airport is a calm spot.

Entertainment

The best nightclub in town is **Salaa Plus** (Hôtel Salaa), while the adjacent **Jardin de Saala** features occasional live music. **Bain de Kouré** (Mamou Rd) also has a good dance floor and open-air bar. **Faningo** (Labé Centre) brims with youngsters at the weekend. Forget about the rooms at **Hôtel Provincial** – but the airy terrace is a great place to enjoy live music and a cold drink.

Getting There & Away

Labé is an important transport junction. Bush taxis for Mali-Yemberem (GF35,000, four hours) and Koundara (GF65,000, eight hours) leave from Gare Routière Daka, 2km north of town. Shared taxis (GF800) for Gare Routière Daka leave from near the mosque in the town centre.

The best days to reach Senegal are Monday and Tuesday, when plenty of bush taxis head for the market in the Senegalese town of Diaoubé (GF120,000). Roads on the Guinean side are pretty bad, meaning that you usually have to spend a night at the border post even if leaving early. Works on the Labé–Koundara road was supposed to be imminent when we passed, though the political situation had enforced a temporary stop. See also p429.

Bush taxis for Pita (GF12,000, one hour), Dalaba (GF22,000, two hours), Mamou (GF25,000, three hours) and Conakry (GF55,000, eight hours) leave from the main *gare routière* in the centre.

MALI-YEMBEREM

Mali-Yemberem sits on the edge of the spectacular Massif du Tamgué, just before its precipitous drop towards Senegal and the plains below. At over 1400m Mali-Yemberem is the highest town in the Fouta; the climate is cool – sometimes downright cold – and the scenery superb. Its most famous icon is **Mt Loura** (1515m), known as **La Dame de Mali**, as the mountain curiously resembles a woman's profile. On a clear day, the 7km hike to the top is rewarded with breathtaking views across the Fouta, and all the way to Senegal and the Gambia River.

The gorgeous **Chute de Guelmeya**, 15km away, is the largest waterfall in the area and a good day trip, as are the pottery and weaving villages of **Toqué** and **Kolossi**.

Information

There's no electricity or running water in town, and only basic provisions. Sadio Souaré, who runs the small **Bureau de Tourisme** (☎ 60454712) can point you in the direction of local waterfalls, caves, mountains and artisan villages, as well as organise guides (GF30,000 per day). Sunday is market day here – look out for the **honey vendors**; they gather honey from the baskets you'll see in the trees lining the road to Labé. Opposite the market is the **Centre d'Appui à l'Auto-Promotion Féminine** (CAAF), a cloth-weaving cooperative with a small boutique that also sells pottery.

Sleeping & Eating

The construction of Mali's **campement solidaire** (☎ 60570279; r GF25,000) was almost complete when we passed. Accommodation will be in local-style huts. The other option in town is **L'Auberge Indigo** (☎ 60360165; r GF35,000; **P**), which has four simple rooms, two clean huts and grants access to the kitchen if you wish. Otherwise try one of the rice bars in town.

Getting There & Away

There are a few taxis between Mali-Yemberem and Labé (GF35,000, four hours), and an occasional direct connection to Conakry (GF70,000, 12 hours). Transport from Mali-

Yemberem to Koundara is only feasible on Saturday, market day in Madina Woura, where you change taxis. A clapped-out Land Rover leaves for Kedougou (Senegal; GF100,000) once a week or so during the dry season. Roads are so bad that the 120km can take more than 24 hours.

KOUNDARA

It's a tough trail along rough laterite paths to get to Koundara; everything in town (including arriving visitors) is covered in the red dust that the winds whirl up. Just north of Fouta Djalon, Koundara is home to a mixed population of Muslim Fula and the Bassari, Koniagui and Badiaranké people that inhabited the area long before the Fula arrived. The little **museum** (open whenever the caretaker is around) at the *préfecture* tells you a tiny bit about the town's past and culture. Most people come here to visit the **Parc Regional du Badiar**, the Guinean part of the Parc Transfrontalier Niokolo-Badiar, which also encompasses Senegal's Parc National du Niokolo-Koba. Together they encompass a 950,000-hectare protected area, of which about 50,000 hectares are in Guinea. Protection efforts are insufficient on the Senegalese side – in Guinea, things are even worse, and there's hardly any infrastructure to receive and guide visitors. Many of the park's large mammals have been hunted, though you might spot some bushbucks, wild boar and patas monkeys on a walk or motorbike ride through the open woodlands, gallery forest and savannah plains. Contact the Direction Nationale des Forêts et de la Faune or Guinée Écologie in Conakry for information on recent protection programs and details of arranging a visit (see p403 for the contact details).

Sleeping & Eating

Koundara isn't exactly blessed with hotels. Head for the antenna, where you'll find a couple of very basic and not very clean places. There are several roadside eateries serving omelettes and coffee or rice and sauce, and a lady who sells freshly tapped palm wine in huge calabashes near the market (ask around in town).

Getting There & Away

Bush taxis run frequently to Saréboïdo (GF8000, one hour) and daily to Labé (GF65,000, eight hours). For Boké go to Saréboïdo to find a car bound for Conakry (GF100,000, 15 hours) – only a sure thing on Friday, Saturday and Sunday. There are ferry crossings on both of these routes.

A bush taxi generally heads daily for Diaoubé (Senegal; GF65,000, six hours) along a pretty bad dirt road (hopefully to be sealed in the near future). For Gabú (Guinea-Bissau), also a rough journey, you'll need to take three taxis, changing at Saréboïdo and the border. See also p429.

UPPER GUINEA

In Upper Guinea (Haute Guinée), the hills and greenery of Fouta Djalon give way to the reds and browns of the country's grassy, low-lying savannah. Few travellers make it to this hot homeland of the Malinké people; those that do get to discover the Sahelian swing of its towns, perhaps listen to the great Mande *griots* and catch a glimpse of Guinea's biggest gold mines.

DABOLA

Dabola, the gateway to Upper Guinée, is a peaceful town, lined with mango trees and framed by hills. Put in a stop to visit the **Barrage du Tinkisso** (8km west of town, signposted on the Conakry road), which supplies electricity to the region. There's a popular picnic area at the bottom of the dam and, across the stream, there's a beach and a small waterfall.

Sixty-five kilometres north along a pretty bad road takes you to **Dinguiraye**, the place from where El Hadj Omar Tall set out to establish his huge Muslim empire and spread the spiritual teachings of the Tijanniya brotherhood in the 19th century. The huge, round mosque (1883) is one of the most famous in West Africa.

Sleeping & Eating

The two hotels in town are pretty decent and have electricity at night. **Hôtel Tinkisso** (☎ 60362210; Conakry Rd; s/d/ste GF60,000/90,000/140,000; P ☒) has clean rooms with curious wall-hangings. The two-room 'suites' are the best choice. A few steps further, rooms at **Mont Sincery** (☎ 60362248; s/d with air-con GF60,000/90,000, s/d without air-con GF50,000/75,000; P ☒) are shaded by giant mango trees; the terrace restaurant is inviting.

GUINEA

BUILDING THE TABALA CONSERVATION ZONE

The frontier zone between Guinea and Sierra Leone is a striking area of savannah, meandering rivers and woodlands. It also remains rich in wildlife: chimpanzees, elephants, panthers and aardvarks inhabit the zone, you'll find hippos and crocodiles in the waters, and the birdlife is simply amazing. Little has been done to protect this fragile realm, and the fact that it's located in border areas had rendered efforts even more difficult. Now the **Jane Goodall Institute** (Map p402; ☎ 60216888; mcgauthier@janegoodall.org; Dixinn Centre 1, Conakry) has started working on an ambitious conservation program, uniting seven communities from Madina Oula (Kindia), Soyah and Ourekaba (south of Mamou) southwards to Dembelia Sinkunia in Sierra Leone. Once fully developed, it's hoped that the zone will become a reserve to rival all others, built with community engagement and by enthusiastic staff. Already in the early stages, there's plenty to see. Contact the institute to arrange tours and find out about progress.

Outside your hotel, try any of the roadside eateries on the main junction downtown for omelettes, coffee, rice dishes and meat skewers *(brochettes)*.

Getting There & Away

Dabola is a junction town, but it's small, so it can take a long time for taxis to fill. There is usually one daily departure along the good laterite road to Faranah (GF27,000, two hours). Taxis to Mamou (GF30,000, three hours) and Conakry (GF80,000, nine hours) are more frequent. Transport is frequent to Kankan (GF50,000, four hours), though the road is a potholed disaster.

FARANAH

Perched on the Niger River and spread out near its waters and gentle hills, Faranah is one of the prettiest towns in Upper Guinea. President Sékou Touré came from Faranah and the city still bears his marks: there's an airstrip built to accommodate a Concorde, a crumbling presidential villa, his portrait painted on local shops and, on top of the hill, the **Cité de Niger**, built to host presidential guests. The Cité's handful of grand bungalows are all dilapidated but, since they're nice structures with fabulous vistas over the river, someone might just open a hotel here. Come for the view, a drink with the voluntary, gin-reinforced guardians, or to visit to the house of renowned Guinean djembe drummer **Fadoua Oularé**, who lives right behind and takes on serious students for a fee.

Faranah is the starting point for excursions to the **Parc National du Haut Niger** (admission GF5000); the entry is 50km from town in Sidakoro. Though it suffers neglect, a visit here can still be hugely rewarding. The park's 1200 sq km cover one of West Africa's last remaining tropical dry-forest ecosystems. With a good guide, patience and a bit of luck, you can see chimps, buffaloes, duikers and waterbucks, as well as hippos and crocodiles in the waters of the Niger. It's a brilliant area for birdwatching, and you can arrange pirogue rides along the Niger with the local fishermen. To organise a visit, contact either the Direction Nationale des Forêts et de la Faune or Guinée Ecologie (see p403 for their contact details).

Another good excursion is the trek to the **Source of the Niger River** (Koubikoro). It's a 160km drive to the village of Forokonia, from where a guided walk takes you there. Ask locally for cost and duration; we found Hotel del Niger particularly reliable in finding good guides.

Sleeping & Eating

The cheapest sleeper is **Hôtel Firya** (☎ 60581682; r GF60,000, villas GF80,000; P X), with just about passable rooms near the Niger River. Two kilometres from the centre on the way to Sidakoro, **Hôtel Bibisch** (Babylon; ☎ 64380077, 64375083; r with fan/air-con GF70,000/80,000; P X) has passable rooms and the best nightclub in town.

By far the best choice is the lovely **Hôtel del Niger** (☎ 64437946, 64078254, www.hoteldelniger.com, in French; bungalow GF100,000; P X X), where pretty, individual bungalows have wooden ceilings and comfy beds. The main house had been ravaged by a bushfire when we passed, but the bungalows were all in pristine condition. This is also Faranah's best address for organising excursions to the National Park and the source of the Niger.

Getting There & Away

The *gare routière* is on the main street next to the petrol station. Vehicles go daily to Kissidougou (GF30,000, three hours), Mamou (GF30,000, three hours), Dabola (GF27,000, two hours) and Conakry (GF70,000, nine hours). The road to Kabala (Sierra Leone; GF60,000, seven hours) is very bad, so there's little traffic, but taxis do go a couple of times a week. See also p429.

KOUROUSSA

About 65km from Kankan on the Dabola road, **Kouroussa** hasn't had electricity for such a long time that the local vendors got organised and equipped with solar panels. That means that the town has a busy, atmospheric market in the cool evening hours dotted with energy-saving bulbs.

Most people come here to pay homage to Guinean author Camara Laye (see p399), who was born here and whose family compound you can visit.

The basic **Motel Tando** (☎ 60272042; r from GF120,000; P) charges a great deal for lax security and unreliable water supply. The grand villa of **Hôtel Dominos** (r GF140,000;) in town has the better rooms, but only if the

generator is working, otherwise negotiate the price down.

Bush taxis go regularly from Kankan (GF15,000, one hour) and Dabola (GF35,000).

KANKAN

A rebellious university town and spiritual home of West Africa's Malinké population, the Sahelian city of Kankan has a unique character. The capital of the ancient Empire of Mali was at Niani, 130km northeast of Kankan, and though the region has hardly any historical monuments – with the notable exception of the remains of Samory Touré's 19th-century fort in **Kérouané** – the hot desert winds seem to blow in stories from the past along with the red dust that covers everything in town. Enigmatic Malinké hunters walk the roads, rifles slung over their backs. Just across the cute bridge over the tranquil Niger River, **Samory Kourou**, the hill from which Samory Touré's famed siege of Kankan and later standoff against the French colonialists took place, offers great views of the city. In town, squeezing through

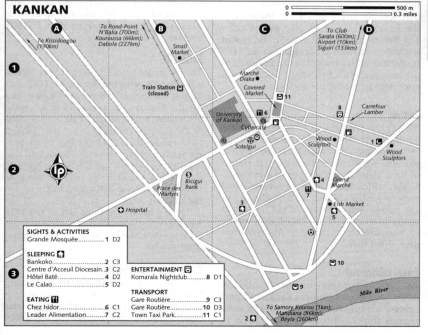

KANKAN

the narrow market streets is an experience – check out the grigri (talisman or charm) on sale – and the **Grande Mosquée** is a beautiful building that you might be allowed to visit, provided you're dressed appropriately.

Kankan's infrastructure is very poor, considering its size. Electricity is only available from private generators (take a torch!), and there are frequent water shortages. You can check your mail at a couple of internet cafe in town (powered only for a few hours every day), and charge your mobile at the restaurant Chez Isidor.

Sleeping

The clean, safe and reasonably priced rooms at the **Centre d'Accueil Diocesain** (☎ 60596757; r with/without private bathroom GF80,000/60,000; **P**), the Catholic mission guesthouse, are so popular that it's hard to find one available – phone in advance. Behind the fish market, the tiny **Le Calao** (☎ 63197836; r GF80,000; **P** 🗙) has surprisingly well-maintained rooms grouped around a calm yard. **Hôtel Baté** (☎ 60580222; s/d GF150,000/180,000; **P** 🗙) likes to think of itself as the first house in town, but is quite rundown. Check a few rooms to get a slightly better one (or one that actually locks), and avoid the ones in the annexe – they look like prison cells. The **Bakonko** (☎ 64712187, 62601672; r incl breakfast GF120,000-200,000) near the bridge over the Milo is much nicer; it's housed in the buildings of the historical Villa Syli where Sékou Touré once used to receive his guests.

Eating

Among the few eateries in town, **Chez Isidor** (Le Répère; ☎ 64359415; dishes around GF20,000; 🕑 7.30am-10pm) is the friendliest, and a great place to see Kankan life go by. It claims to be a 'culinary crossroads of five continents', which really means universal food such as grilled chicken and spaghetti, but also salads. Self-caterers can get fresh food at the markets and packaged stuff at the corner stores or at Leader Alimentation near Hôtel Baté.

Entertainment

The Malinké have a sophisticated music tradition and Upper Guinea, Kankan in particular, is home to many of Guinea's most famous singers. Still, live performances in

town can be hard to track down. Keep an eye open for wedding ceremonies – that's when the *griots* are at their best, and you'll usually be allowed to sneak a peek.

Kankan's nightclubs have certainly seen better days, but still get packed with students at the weekend. The slightly stuffy **Club Sarata** (admission GF7000; 🕑 Fri & Sat) is the enduring favourite – dress up for the party. Close by, the **Komarala Nightclub** (admission GF7000; 🕑 Fri & Sat) attracts a slightly younger crowd.

Getting There & Away

Bush taxis for places including Conakry (GF100,000, 13 hours), Kissidougou (GF50,000, five hours), Siguiri (GF30,000, two hours) and N'zérékoré (GF110,000, 12 hours) leave from the twin *gares routières* near the bridge. With the road sealed nearly the whole way, Bamako (Mali) can be reached in eight hours by bush taxi (GF100,000) while the big buses (GF70,000) take much longer. The best way to get to Côte d'Ivoire is via Bamako because the road to Odienné via Mandiana is so bad that taxi drivers don't use it. See also p429.

There's also a smaller bush-taxi stand near Rond-point N'Balia for Kouroussa (GF15,000, one hour) and Dabola (GF50,000, four hours).

SIGUIRI

The last major town en route to Mali, Siguiri is famous for being the birthplace of Guinea's biggest star, Sekouba Bambino Diabaté, and for the country's largest gold mine, some 25km from town on the Rte de la SAG. Next to the mine, temptingly called the 'Ashanti Gold Fields', there is a huge area where people wash the dug-up sands for second and third times to draw out the remaining gold dust. If you're lucky, you may get access to the area: not to search for gold, but to take in the amazing scene.

There's hardly anything left of the 1888 **French fort** atop a little hill just a few minutes from the *gare routière*, but the leafy site gives some shade.

Sleeping & Eating

The town's cheapo **Hôtel Tam Tam** (Siguiri Centre; r from GF60,000; **P** 🗙) has plenty of by-the-hour activity, though rooms are just about passable and the restaurant is reliable. The small **Hôtel**

Manden (☎ 64423550, 64263327; Rte de la SAG; r with/
without air-con GF140,000/80,000) is much better. It
has a calm terrace, ice-cold drinks and simple
rooms with wooden ceilings (the air-con ones
are much better). Djoma Hôtel (☎ 64861050; r from
GF140,000; P ⊠) at the airport is the best-main-
tained and most comfortable place in town.

Siguiri is one of the few places where rice
sellers in the street are hard to find – you're
best off eating in the hotels or self-catering.

Getting There & Away
Two roads lead to Mali from Siguiri.
Bush taxis go via Kourémalé to Bamako
(GF80,000, five hours). The second route
along the Niger River makes a great mo-
torbike trip during the dry season. See
also p429. Bush taxis also leave daily for
Kankan (GF30,000, two hours) and Conakry
(GF130,000, 15 hours).

FOREST REGION

Guinea's Forest Region (Guinée Forestière)
in the country's southeast is a beautiful area
of hills and streams, although deforestation
has taken a heavy toll and there are only
pockets of primary forest left. What little
remains, however, offers excellent wildlife-
watching, especially for chimpanzees
and elephants.

KISSIDOUGOU
Kissidougou, running seemingly forever
along the Conakry highway, is a good place
to break your journey south. The small
Musée Préfectoral (admission GF1000; ⊙ 9am-5pm Mon-
Sat) across from the police station has great
masks and objects deemed magical. The surrounding area, with gently rolling hills and
many villages, is great for bicycle tours. The
rarely visited village of Koladou, 30km down
a rough, nearly nonexistent road, has a vine
bridge above some rapids. If you go, take
some kola nuts for the village chief.

The town has many hotels, though most
aren't very good. Hôtel Mandela (☎ 60392542;
r GF30,000) is a decent budget option with
clean, basic rooms. A step up, the Hôtel
Mantise Palace (☎ 62645587; Quartier Yassafé; r with fan
GF60,000) is certainly not a palace, but a welcoming, good-value place. For both food and
lodging, Hôtel Savanah (☎ 60439754; Quartier Sobèla;
r with/without air-con GF80,000/60,000; P ⊠) is the

nicest option. The restaurant, surrounded by
flowers, is beautiful and the food varied and
tasty (around GF35,000).

Bush taxis go daily to Faranah (GF25,000,
two hours), Kankan (GF50,000, five
hours), Guéckédou (GF20,000, 2½ hours)
and Macenta (GF23,000, five hours). For
Conakry (GF86,000, 12 hours), many taxis
depart around 6pm.

MACENTA
The Forest Region begins in Kissidougou, but
the area's beauty really kicks in at Macenta, a
busy town ringed by hills and streams.

About 40km south of Macenta the
116,000-acre Forêt Classée de Ziama (admission GF100,000, mandatory guide GF25,000), one of
Guinea's few remaining virgin rainforests,
blankets the mountains. Elephants are sometimes spotted here, and you don't need a car
to enter the forest. Guides and information
are available at the headquarters in Sérédou,
though they request that you call the Centre
Forestier (☎ 33910389) in N'zérékoré first so
that staff can prepare for your visit.

Macenta's hotels have never been great
and certainly haven't gotten better over
the years. Hôtel Bamala (☎ 60585227, 66678789; r
GF30,000-40,000; P ⊠) sits 3km from the centre off the N'zérékoré road, while Hôtel Palm
(☎ 60526113; r GF15,000-40,000; P) is in the town
centre near the N'zérékoré gare routière.

Bush taxis head daily to Kissidougou
(GF40,000, five hours) and to N'zérékoré
(GF30,000, 2½ hours). Several taxis a day
take the rough road to Voinjama (Liberia;
GF30,000, two hours) via Daro; however, if
you're heading to Monrovia (Liberia) it's better to go from N'zérékoré. See also below.

N'ZÉRÉKORÉ
N'zérékoré, the major city in Guinea's Forest
Region, is a busy place and good base for
exploring the surrounding area. This is
Guinea's NGO central so you'll find many
foods and services unavailable in most other
cities. Market day is Wednesday.

The Musée Ethnographique (admission GF9000,
with photo permit GF15,000; ⊙ 8.30am-5pm Mon-Sat)
has a fascinating collection of masks and
fetishes, including two statues in the courtyard representing historical figures.

The pretty village artisanal sits at the
entry to town on the Macenta route. It's

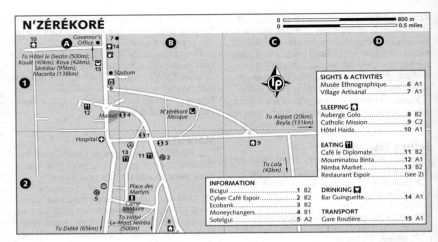

surrounded by a small forest of rubber trees, and you can watch craftspeople dye mudcloth and make raffia sacs (hand-crocheted one-piece raffia shoulder bag), and often witness traditional dancing.

Many local villages have vine bridges, particularly those along the Oulé River. Ask at the museum for advice and directions. There's a more accessible one near the hamlet of Koya, just north of Koulé, about 40km north on the Macenta road. Give the chief a small tip and he will get you a guide for the Pont de Liana (not to be confused with Pont Diana, a highway bridge nearby). Forty-five minutes and forty-five thousand butterflies later, you're there.

Information

Bicigui (ATM-enhanced) and Ecobank change cash, and you find moneychangers at the market and *gare routière*. You can get online at Cyber Café Espoir and Sotelgui.

Sleeping

All places (normally) have electricity from 7pm; food needs to be ordered in advance.

Catholic Mission (Quartier Dorota; r GF30,000; **P**) The Catholic Mission, on the east side of town, has simple but spotless rooms with shared toilets and mosquito nets. It's a nice, quite location, downhill behind the church.

Hôtel Haida (Gbama 1; r with fan/air-con GF35,000/40,000; **P** **X**) Rooms here are very basic but the restaurant is a secret favourite for many, with

excellent rice dishes, grilled fish and meat (around GF15,000).

Hôtel le Destin (☎ 60342105; Quartier N'ye; r with/without air-con GF70,000/60,000) This large place has six simple rooms. What makes the difference is the leafy courtyard, and it feels safer than other cheapos in town.

Auberge Golo (☎ 65538534, 60317065; Quartier Telepoulou; r GF100,000; **P** **X**) With a pretty flower garden, 15 good rooms and a friendly staff, this is a calm, welcoming place to spend a few nights. They can prepare pretty much anything you wish to eat.

Hôtel Le Mont Nimba (☎ 64384524; Quartier au Sud; r per person GF180,000-250,000; **P** **X** **R**) Set in a lush tropical garden, this large place has all the makings of a lush, quality hotel. The pool is a great addition and can be used by nonguests for a fee.

Eating & Drinking

For street food, try the *gare routière*.

Restaurant Espoir (meals GF5000-10,000; ☽ lunch & dinner) At lunch pause, you'll think the whole working community of N'zérékoré has converged at this simple restaurant. It's noisy and packed, but the rice is tasty.

Mouminatou Binta (meals GF7500-9000; ☽ lunch & dinner) This friendly woman whips up a mean *riz gras* and great plates of *fonio* (a form of millet) with meat.

Café le Diplomate (dishes around GF8000-20,000; ☽ breakfast, lunch & dinner) This is a great place for omelettes and *café au lait* in the morn-

---

HIKING UP MT NIMBA

Mt Nimba, Guinea's highest peak at 1752m, is part of the mountain range straddling Guinea, Côte d'Ivoire and Liberia. The area is protected as a Strict Nature Reserve and, following the licensing of an iron mine on the mountainside by the former Guinean government, as World Heritage in Danger. As it's a strict reserve, tourist activities are not normally accepted. You need to ask around to see whether you'll be allowed to climb up and either get a required permit at the *préfecture* in Lola, or hire a guide who can arrange this for you.

The summit, best reached from the village of Gbakoré, 18km southeast of Lola, offers phenomenal views of surrounding peaks in all three countries. It's a steep, winding four-hour trek to the top and a guide is mandatory. Come in the afternoon and you can climb the next day; come early enough in the morning and you might be able to summit the same day. The price is negotiable but count on around GF150,000. Food and lodging can be arranged in Gbakoré.

The Nimba mountains host a rich variety of plant and animal life. Nearly a dozen vertebrate species are endemic to the area, including some notable amphibians (see p81).

---

ing, or the corner to discuss politics with the regulars over *café noir*.

Bar Guinguette (☽ lunch & dinner) The gin comes by the bottle and most women have to be paid for at this raucous *buvette* (watering hole) at the entrance of town.

Nimba Market (☽ daily) This little supermarket has a fairly good range of imported goods.

Getting There & Away

Bush taxis depart daily from the well-organised *gare routière* for Lola (GF7000, 30 minutes), Macenta (GF30,000, 2½ hours), Beyla (GF33,000, four hours), Kankan (GF110,000, 12 hours) and Conakry (GF150,000, 20 hours).

Travel to Monrovia (Liberia) is a rough, all-day trip with many checkpoints – it's GF100,000 all the way there. Bush taxis go to the border at Diéké (GF19,000, three hours), where you get another car to complete the trip. For Côte d'Ivoire, you can get taxis to Man via Sipilou (GF40,000).

LOLA

Lola, near the borders of Liberia and Côte d'Ivoire, is the starting point for hiking up Mt Nimba, if it's permitted (see the boxed text, above). There are several mud-cloth cooperatives in town and if you ask around someone will lead you to one. Lola is also home to the endangered grey parrot. There are some places (called *dortoits*) around town where the birds sing daily at dawn and dusk. On Tuesday the market overwhelms the town.

Hôtel Heinoukoloa (☎ 65353556; r with/without fan GF35,000/25,000; P ✷), signposted 1km off the main road, has basic but acceptable rooms and a big hall that attracts plenty of beer drinkers. **Hôtel Nouketi** (☎ 65904945; r with/without fan GF25,000/15,000; P) is a bit calmer and has a flowery courtyard. Both say they'll switch on the power from 7pm to midnight, and neither do food – you'll either have to take a trip to the corner store for bread and sardines, or try the eateries in town.

Bush taxis head to N'zérékoré (GF7000, 30 minutes), Bossou (GF5000, 30 minutes) and Gbakoré (GF5000, 45 minutes). To Yekepa (Liberia; GF7000, 45 minutes) the road is pretty good. Heading towards Man in Côte d'Ivoire, it's a bad road whether you go via Danané or Sipilou. See also p429.

BOSSOU

The **Bossou Environmental Research Institute** (☎ 60584761; douakomakan@yahoo.fr) attracts researchers from around the world to study the famous chimpanzees in the surrounding hills (see p400). There's not much primary forest left, though the area remains scenic and, since the small groups of chimps are tracked, there's a good chance that you'll actually get to see them.

The **guesthouse** (s/d GF15,000/20,000) after the customs point has simple rooms with shared toilets. If there's space, you can also sleep at the research centre (ask for rates).

Instead of heading straight back to Lola, consider taking the seldom-travelled rocky track east to Gbakoré where you'll enjoy gorgeous views of Mt Nimba. About 4km before Gbakoré the road crosses a natural bridge cut through the rock by the Cavally

River. It's a magical little spot, ideal for a picnic and a swim.

GUINEA DIRECTORY

ACCOMMODATION

Guinea's handful of upmarket hotels tends to be very expensive, while good-quality rooms in the budget and midrange categories are rare. Many of the upcountry places have deteriorated over the years and few new ones have opened.

In this book, the budget category covers places under GF150,000 and top end encompasses hotels that cost over GF500,000.

Many of Guinea's towns are entirely dominated by their markets; the better hotels are more typically found on the outskirts of town to offer calm and easy access. Many have nightclubs attached.

Most hotels charge per room, rather than per person, though they may not readily accept two people of same sex sharing one room, or spontaneously ask for a slightly higher rate. Rooms with twin beds are almost unheard of outside the capital.

Though midrange and top-end hotels have generators, places outside Conakry normally only switch them on around 6pm or 7pm, leaving them to run until midnight when the regular supply often takes over until around 6am. Only in Conakry and the bauxite towns of Kamsar and Fria (where electricity is provided by the companies) can you expect 24-hour electricity.

A tourism tax of GF5000 per person applies to top-end and some midrange hotels.

ACTIVITIES

Guinea offers some of West Africa's best hiking opportunities – Fouta Djalon and Guinée Forestière are particularly good. Bird-watching here is fascinating, especially as it's less visited than places such as The Gambia and holds at least the same interest. Contact Guinée Ecologie (see p403) in Conakry: it can put you in touch with guides.

Guinea has many wild and scenic rivers to paddle; the biggest adventure is on the remote upper reaches of the Niger. The trip from Faranah to Kouroussa through Parc National du Haut Niger (p420) is highly recommended, but not for the inexperienced.

PRACTICALITIES

■ Guinea uses the metric system.

■ Electricity is 220V/50Hz; plugs have two round pins.

■ Guinea's best-selling newspaper is the satirical weekly *Le Lynx*.

■ The only TV station is the government-owned RTG, which shows a lot of sport and speeches.

■ The BBC World Service is broadcast in French on FM and English on short wave.

Music lovers flock to Guinea: it's got an amazingly rich live scene and there are plenty of opportunities to organise lessons. See p405 for options in Conakry and p420 for Faranah's main djembe teacher.

BOOKS

There's very little in English but, if you read French, you'll find plenty of detailed historical and cultural information in the works of the Harmattan and Karthala publishing houses.

BUSINESS HOURS

Government offices are open from 8am to 4.30pm Monday to Thursday and 8am to 1pm Friday. Most businesses are open from 8am to 6pm Monday to Saturday, except Friday when many close at 1pm. Businesses also close for an hour or so at lunch. Banking hours are from 8.30am to 12.30pm and 2.30pm to 4.30pm Monday to Thursday, and 8.30am to 12.30pm and 2.45pm to 4.30pm Friday.

CUSTOMS REGULATIONS

You're not allowed to export more than GF100,000 in local currency or US$5000 in foreign currency. You must have a licence to export precious stones; to export art objects you'll need a permit from the Musée National in Conakry (p404). The cost varies but averages 15% of the value for items worth less than GF50,000 and 25% of the value for more expensive pieces.

DANGERS & ANNOYANCES

At the time of writing, Guinea is calm and driven by hope, though the country's political situation remains fragile. Though violent riots have ceased, and the banditry and robbery that washed over the country following the politically motivated clashes have largely been brought under control, you will need to check the current situation before you set out. Most diplomatic services and NGOs still banned night travel at the time of research, considering the danger of roadblocks, extortion and car-jackings a risk. it's best to avoid journeys after nightfall.

Electricity and running water are all intermittent; even major towns such as Kankan don't have electricity, other than what's provided by private generators, and suffer water shortages.

EMBASSIES & CONSULATES

All of the following are in Conakry.

Belgium (Map p406; ☎ 30412182; Corniche Sud, Koulévondy; ⊗ 9am-12.30pm Mon-Fri)

Côte d'Ivoire (Map p406; ☎ 30451082; Blvd du Commerce; ⊗ 8.30am-2pm Mon-Fri)

France (Map p406; ☎ 30411655; Blvd du Commerce; ⊗ 7-11am Mon-Fri)

Germany (Map p406; ☎ 30411506; www.conakry.diplo.de; 2nd Blvd; ⊗ 8am-noon Mon-Fri)

Ghana (Map p402; ☎ 30409560; Corniche Nord, Camayenne; ⊗ 9am-3pm Mon-Fri)

Guinea-Bissau (Map p402; ☎ 60587336; Rte de Donka, Bellevue; ⊗ 8am-1pm Mon-Fri)

Italy (Map p406; ☎ 62663829; Cité Chemin de Fer; ⊗ 8.30am-noon Mon-Fri)

Liberia (Map p402; ☎ 30462059; Rte de Donka, Bellevue; ⊗ 9am-1pm Mon-Fri)

Mali (Map p402; ☎ 30461418; Corniche Nord, Camayenne; ⊗ 7.30am-1pm Mon-Fri)

Netherlands (Map p406; ☎ 30415021; Novotel, Rm 121) ⊗ 8-11am Mon-Fri)

Nigeria (Map p406; ☎ 30431131; Ave de la Gare; ⊗ 11am-1pm Mon, Wed & Fri)

Senegal (Map p402; ☎ 63409035; Corniche Sud, Coléah; ⊗ 8am-12.30pm Mon-Fri)

Sierra Leone (Map p402; ☎ 30464084; Carrefour Bellevue; ⊗ 9am-1pm Mon-Fri)

UK (Map p402; ☎ 63355329; britembconakry@hotmail.com; Corniche Sud, Residence 2000, Villa 1; ⊗ 8am-1pm Mon-Fri) Assists Australian and Canadian citizens also.

USA (Map p404; ☎ 65104000; http://conakry.usembassy.gov; Transversale 2, Ratoma; ⊗ 7.30am-noon Mon-Fri) The American Center is in the same building.

FESTIVALS & EVENTS

Major events in Conakry include the **Festagg** and **Festival Kora & Cordes** (see p405). In Kankan,

the **Fête des Mares** is held at the beginning of each rainy season and is a great opportunity to see top Mande music performed. During September's **Potato Festival**, the city of Mali-Yemberem (p418) throws a party for the farmers of the surrounding villages.

HOLIDAYS

Public holidays include the following:

New Year's Day 1 January
Easter March/April
Declaration of the Second Republic 3 April
Labour Day 1 May
Assumption Day 15 August
Market Women's Revolt 27 August
Referendum Day 28 September
Independence Day 2 October
Christmas Day 25 December

Islamic holidays are also observed, and Eid al-Fitr is one of Guinea's biggest celebrations; see p816.

INTERNET ACCESS

Internet services (usually GF6000 per hour) are easy to come by in Conakry; only a few towns have connections outside the capital.

INTERNET RESOURCES

Foutapedia (www.foutapedia.org, in French) Contains excellent cultural, historical and tourist information about Fouta Djalon.

Guinée News (www.guineenews.org, in French) The site where all Guineans get their news.

LANGUAGE

French is the official language and it is widely spoken throughout the country to varying degrees of proficiency. Major African languages are Malinké in the north, Pulaar (also called Fula) in Fouta Djalon and Susu along the coast. See p860 for a list of useful phrases in French, Malinké, Pulaar and Susu.

MAPS

Institut Géographique National's (IGN) 2002 map of Guinea is outdated but still useful. It's widely sold on the street and available from bookshops and stationery stores in Guinea (GF50,000).

MONEY

Banks outside Conakry exchange only cash, and even Conakry branches don't always take travellers cheques. The most easily changed currencies are euros, US dollars and CFA francs. Black-market dealers are widely used throughout Guinea. You usually find them (or they find you) near the markets of bigger towns. In Conakry, the best places are Ave de la République and nearby. Make sure you count every crumpled banknote of your thick pack of Guinea francs as not all are honest dealers.

The main banks of interest to foreigners are **Bicigui** (www.biciguinet.net) and **SGBG** (www.socgen .com) as they have ATMs that accept Visa cards and branches across the country. At the time of research the ATMs give you only up to GF200,000 (US$40) in one withdrawal – the machines can't handle any more banknotes at one time.

PHOTOGRAPHY & VIDEO

Photo permits are not required but you must be careful taking pictures. Guys in uniform don't like being snapped, and the streets teem with them. Don't take pictures of government buildings, airports, bridges, military camps and markets or you might get into trouble (and possibly have your camera broken). It's always best to ask people before taking their picture – a simple matter of respect. The same restrictions apply to video.

POST

Guinea's postal service is notoriously unreliable; packages especially often get 'lost'. Postcards should go through without problems; for anything more valuable use a private shipping service (p403).

TELEPHONE

For domestic and international calls there is a government-owned Sotelgui office in all large- and medium-sized towns, as well as a few private telecentres. There are five mobile-phone providers (maybe more by the time you travel) – the most popular ones are Areeba, Sotelgui, Intercel and Orange. Many of them offer excellent deals when purchasing a cheap mobile with a local SIM (from around US$22); top-up credit is available from street traders anywhere. If you have an open phone, or can get yours unlocked, you can just pick up a SIM and credit for a few dollars on the street. The massive competition has made calling cheap. On some networks, you can even call the US for less than US$0.10 per minute.

TOURIST INFORMATION

Depending on individual staff members, tourist information offices can be useful in some places, but they're not consistently helpful. It's worth trying a variety of sources, including travel agencies. See p403 for useful Conakry-based addresses and p413 for a good starting point in Fouta Djalon.

VISAS

All visitors, except nationals of Economic Community of West African States (Ecowas) countries, Morocco and Tunisia, need a visa. Visas, usually valid for three months, are not available at airports or land borders.

Visa Extensions

Visas can be extended for up to three months at the **Bureau of Immigration** (Map p406; ☎ 30441339; 8th Ave) in Conakry.

Visas for Onward Travel

Visa regulations, prices and the speed of processing change fast. It's best to contact the relevant embassy of your destination country early to find out how to proceed (see p427). You normally need a photocopy of the first three pages of your passport and provide two passport photographs, the relevant amount of money and a completed application form.

WOMEN TRAVELLERS

Solo women travellers will get a fair amount of attention – think kissing noises, random offers of marriage and unlikely declarations of undying love. Serious sexual harassment and rape are rarely reported by travellers.

Tampons are only available from the large supermarkets in Conakry and they're pricey – best to bring enough with you.

Many of the cheapish hotels upcountry attract a fair amount of by-the-hour business and can feel uncomfortable, sometimes even unsafe, for women. See also p826 for more general information.

TRANSPORT IN GUINEA

GETTING THERE & AWAY
Entering Guinea
A valid passport, visa and certificate of yellow-fever vaccination is required of all travellers.

Air

Guinea's only international airport is Conakry-Gbessia, 13km from the centre of Conakry. It can be quiet and easily negotiated in the mornings, and extremely exasperating at most other times. Make sure you keep your luggage tag: it'll be checked against the bag you're taking off the belt on arrival. Expect your bags to be checked by imposing customs ladies.

Direct flights from Europe are available with Air France and Brussels Airlines. Direct African destinations include Dakar (Senegal), Bamako (Mali) and Abidjan (Côte d'Ivoire). For most other inner-African flights, you connect either at Dakar or Abidjan.

The following airlines service Guinea and have offices in Conakry:

Air France (AF; Map p406; ☎ 64202203; www.airfrance .fr; 9th Ave, Conakry) Hub: Paris.

Air Ivoire (VU; Map p406; ☎ 64202096; www.airivoire .com; 5th Ave, Conakry) Hub: Abidjan.

Air Sénégal International (V7; Map p406; ☎ 30473700; www.air-senegal-international.com; Ave de la République, Conakry) Hub: Dakar.

Brussels Airlines (SN; Map p406; ☎ 63451061; www .brusselsairlines.com; Cité Chemin de Fer) Hub: Brussels.

Royal Air Maroc (RAM; Map p406; ☎ 63271111; Ave de la République, Conakry) Hub: Casablanca.

Land

CÔTE D'IVOIRE

The most frequently travelled route is between Lola and Man, either via Nzo and Danané or via Sipilou and Biankouma. By public transport, the latter is the fastest choice. From Kankan it is easiest to go via Bamako as the road to Odienné via Mandiana is very rough. There's also a seldom-travelled route between Beyla and Odienné (via Sinko). The roads here are also horrible, but taxis run from Kankan and N'zérékoré to Beyla where you can connect onwards.

GUINEA-BISSAU

Most people travelling by taxi get to Guinea-Bissau via Labé, Koundara and Gabú. You have to taxi hop between Koundara and Gabú; the road beyond the border is horrible (especially in the rainy season) but it can be done in a day if you start early in the morning.

Infrequent bush taxis go from Boké and Kamsar up the rough road to Québo. Going to Koundara (to get to Gabú) via Boké usually involves long waits for taxis to fill – your best bet is a weekend journey. With your own vehicle you can shave some distance, though not necessarily time, off this journey by going direct from Koumbia to Pitche.

LIBERIA

There is quite a lot of traffic to Liberia. The primary route is from N'zérékoré to Ganta via Diéké. Bush taxis go frequently from N'zérékoré to the border from where you can get a *moto-taxi* or walk the remaining 2km to Ganta for a Monrovia-bound taxi.

From Macenta, bush taxis go via Daro to the border and on to Voinjama, although the Voinjama road is terrible. The route south from Guéckédou to is similarly difficult. It's probably better to go from Macenta to Koyama, where you can find transport to Zorzor and on to Monrovia. Still, plan on a full day to reach the capital.

Another route goes from Lola via Bossou to Yekepa but traffic is sporadic beyond here. For all of these routes you buy a single ticket but change cars at the border.

MALI

Taxis and buses travel directly to Bamako from Kankan, Siguiri, Labé and Conakry. The road is sealed and in good, sometimes excellent, shape from Kankan to Bamako (except for a 50km-stretch in Mali), though you pass a terrible stretch of potholed tarmac between Dabola and Kouroussa. If you have your own, very sturdy, 4WD you can also go from Kankan via Mandiana to Bougouni, or Mali-Yemberem via Kita.

SENEGAL

Taxis to Senegal going via Koundara, the busiest route, stop at Diaoubé, a small town with a huge market, where you can connect to almost everywhere, including Dakar. Roads on the Guinean side aren't quite as bad as they used to be, but are still pretty awful. Sealing of the Koundara–Diaoubé route was supposed to be imminent at the time of writing but hadn't started yet. Plans to seal the rough road from Mali-Yemberem to Kedougou (Senegal) exist but are unlikely to be put in place soon.

SIERRA LEONE

The infamous Conakry–Freetown Hwy had once again been promised to be sealed soon when we visited; check the latest situation in the country.

GUINEA

From Kindia to Kamakwie there are regular taxis to the border at Medina-Oula, but little transport further south. The road on the Sierra Leone side is quite bad; during the rainy season the Little Scarcies River sometimes runs so high that the ferry shuts down. The road from Faranah to Kabala is also in bad shape and sparsely travelled, but taxis do go a couple of times a week.

If you cross from Guinea's parrot's beak, the point of land west of Guéckédou, go to Kailahun rather than Koindu because there is much more traffic there.

River

During the rainy season (July to November) barges run once a week or so from Siguiri to Bamako in Mali. It's a one-day journey downstream and at least two days coming back up.

Sea

The ferry service to Freetown is expected to begin again, so it's worth asking around at the port.

Tours

Fouta Trekking Aventure (Map p417; ☎ 60570279, www.foutatrekking.org; Quartier N'Djoulou) Excellent hiking tours and responsible tourism projects in Fouta Djalon.

Indigo (☎ 64407593; www.guinee-voyage.com) Has a range of trips through different parts of the country.

Mondial Tours (Map p406; ☎ 30433550; www.mondial tours.net, in French; Imm Nafaya, Kaloum) Excellent tour agency with interesting circuits around Fouta Djalon and Lower Guinea. It even offers tours to Senegal.

GETTING AROUND

While the main arteries connecting Conakry and the main towns in Fouta Djalon, Upper and Lower Guinea are fine, any small side trip or a journey to the Forest Region means tough driving on dirt paths. For round trips covering different parts of the country, you either need a very sturdy 4WD or you'll have very limited choices of routes. Overlanders can have a great travel adventure here, seeking out rarely travelled routes that lead through amazing scenery – you need to be an excellent driver and mechanic with a solid car though.

Air

At the time of research there were no internal flights other than those organised by the bauxite companies or NGOs (which you can sometimes get on).

Bicycle

Fouta Djalon is an excellent region for mountain biking. Villages are spaced closely enough that lodging and food are seldom a problem. You'll need to be fully equipped with spare parts, as you won't find fittings for Western-made cycles anywhere, though most towns have at least one shop that can mend flat tyres and take care of other basics. You're unlikely to find a decent bike for hire.

Bus

Big buses run between Conakry and Boké, Kindia, Mamou, Labé, Kankan and N'zérékoré. You can save a few hundred Guinean francs going by bus, though you'll probably spend more than that while you buy snacks and drinks as you wait for the driver to mend breakdowns and fix tyres.

Bush Taxi

In other West African countries, the big seven-seater Peugeots 505 are appropriately called *sept-place*. Not in Guinea, and for good reason – here they carry at least nine people. Whatever you do, don't take the front seat near the driver, as your legs will be straddling the gearbox, provoking close encounters between the gear-shifting hand and your private parts.

Expect at least one breakdown on even the smallest journey, meaning that travel times provided throughout this book are only rough indications. Guinean drivers are extreme risk-takers, placing their lives and those of their passengers completely in the hands of God, tempting Him with racing in rusty vehicles and overtaking manoeuvres in blind spots.

Taxis leave when they're full, and most people travel in the morning. You always have the quickest getaway around 7am to 8am.

For an even slower journey with bigger breakdown chances, take a minibus (*magbana*), which will cost a few Guinea francs less.

Rates given for taxi fares throughout the book should be regarded as rough indications – not because you'll have to negotiate (bush-taxi tariffs are usually fixed, and you can almost always rely on the driver to charge the correct rate), but because the Guinea franc fluctuates a lot, as do petrol prices, and with it taxi rates. In addition, rates may vary depending on the terrain. If it's uphill all the way, you may pay more, then have a slight saving on the way back.

All public transport goes to and from the *gare routière* in each town; you can ask to be dropped off anywhere along the way.

Another option is travelling with the post office van. It's a bit more expensive, and you'll stop in every town for the postman to do his job, but you get a seat to yourself and the buses are in fairly good shape. You need to book in advance (and in person) at the main post office.

Car & Motorcycle

If you're driving your own or a hired vehicle in Guinea, be sure that the insurance and registration papers are in order as they will be checked many times along the way. Hiring a car for travel upcountry is usually very expensive. See p410 for details of car hire in Conakry.

ROAD CONDITIONS

Good, sealed arteries lead from Conakry via Kindia, Mamou and Pita to Labé – from there to Mali-Yemberem it's rugged dirt track, as is the Koundara connection. Between Dabola and Kouroussa the tarmac is riddled with potholes; Kouroussa to Kankan and Siguiri is excellent. Towards the Forest Region, all routes are 4WD territory.

The coastal road from Conakry is sealed and in excellent condition as far as Boffa: that's when potholes trouble the tarmac all the way to Boké. Further north it's dirt track. The 'direct' connections between Labé via Télimélé towards Lower Guinea are beautiful but in extremely bad condition – only to be attempted with a sturdy 4WD.

GUINEA

Guinea-Bissau

History has not been kind to Guinea-Bissau. Decades of Portuguese colonisation, a long, painful liberation struggle and cycles of civil war have locked this pretty nation in grinding poverty. And when it seemed finally that peace would last, Guinea-Bissau gained an unwholesome reputation as West Africa's key entry port for hard drugs.

But the fact that you rarely hear good news from Guinea-Bissau doesn't mean that there is none – it simply doesn't make it to the news screens. The stories you will bring back from your trip are more likely to paint pictures of endless white beaches, thick rainforest and, most of all, the country's disarmingly friendly people.

Like a microcosm of Africa, this tiny nation contains a spectacular variety of landscapes, cultures and small-town scenes, all within easy reach from the capital, Bissau. The jewel in its crown is the labyrinth of tropical islands that makes up the Arquipélago dos Bijagós. With vast deserted sand strands and clear waters quivering with fish, these islands are a dream destination for sports fishers and sea-and-sun lovers. The fragile ecosystem is home to turtles, hundreds of bird species and rare saltwater hippos, and is protected as a Unesco Biosphere Reserve. Similar preservation efforts have so far saved the last vestiges of humid tropical rainforest and its thriving populations of monkeys, chimps and buffaloes, in the south of the country. All this natural beauty would have transformed a more stable country into a travelling hotspot. In Guinea-Bissau, you'll be one of very few visitors and get to enjoy stunning landscapes and culture far off the tourist trails.

FAST FACTS

- **Area** 36,120 sq km
- **Capital** Bissau
- **Country code** ☎ 245
- **Famous for** Cashews, island paradise, chimpanzees
- **Languages** Portuguese, Crioulo
- **Money** West African CFA franc; US$1 = CFA493; €1 = CFA656
- **Population** 1,416,000
- **Visa** All visitors except citizens of Ecowas nations require a visa; they need to be arranged before arrival

HOW MUCH?

- **Small souvenir mask** CFA2000
- **Taxi ride through Bissau** CFA500
- **Wi-fi in Bissau's better restaurants** free
- **Woven indigo cotton cloth (40cm x 80cm)** CFA6000
- **Main course in Western-style restaurant** CFA5000

LONELY PLANET INDEX

- **1L of petrol** CFA550
- **1L of bottled water** CFA1000
- **Bottle of Guinean Pampa beer** CFA1000
- **Souvenir T-shirt** CFA2500
- **Omelette sandwich from street vendor** CFA600

HIGHLIGHTS

- **João Vieira** (p446) Fresh coconut juice on the island's endless, palm-framed sand strands.
- **Orango** (p446) Rare saltwater hippos and the tombs of the kings and queens of Bijagós.
- **Bolama** (p443) Witness the crumbling colonial grandeur of the antique Portuguese capital.
- **Bissau** (p438) The narrow alleyways of Bissau Velho.
- **Parque Nacional do Cantanhez** (p450) Follow buffalo, chimp and elephant trails through dense rainforests.

ITINERARIES

- **One Week** Most travellers with only a week to spare spend a day or two in the capital Bissau (p437), which has few 'sights' but a pleasant, relaxing feel. This could be combined with a few days visiting the country's major attraction, the Arquipélago dos Bijagós (p442), southwest of Bissau. The island of Bubaque (p443) is the easiest to reach, with good beaches and a range of places to stay.
- **Two Weeks** If you have a second week to spare, consider further explorations of the Bijagós. Head to Orango (p446), with

its rare saltwater hippos, or the turtle colonies of João Vieira (p446). Relax on the white beaches of tiny islands, such as Kere (p446), before heading back to Bissau, taking in the ghost town on Bolama (p443) island on the way.
- **Three Weeks** A third week is best spent in the south, where you can travel the narrow creeks and lagoons of Parque Natural das Lagoas de Cufada (p450) and go chimp and elephant spotting in the Cantanhez rainforest (p450).

CLIMATE & WHEN TO GO

The rainy season is from June to October; it rains almost twice as much along the coast as inland. Conditions are especially humid in the months before the rains (April and May), when average maximum daytime temperatures rise to 34°C.

The best time to visit is from late November to February, when conditions are dry and relatively cool. February/early March is also Carnival time in Bissau, although smaller festivals take place in many towns to celebrate the end of the harvest in November and December.

See also Climate Charts p810.

HISTORY

A group of Manding people arrived in present-day Guinea-Bissau in around 1200, led by a general of Sunjata Keita, the legendary founder of the Empire of Mali. The region thus became an outpost of the empire, before transforming into the Kaabu kingdom, a state in its own right, in 1537. Gabú in eastern Guinea-Bissau was the capital of this small kingdom. See also p27.

WARNING

Only days before this book went to press, former president João 'Nino' Vieira and his chief of staff were assassinated by military – just a few months after elections had raised cautious hopes of lasting stability. The murders resurrected fear of a resurgence of civil war, and have brought into sharp focus the fragility of peace in this country plagued by corruption, military rivalries, poverty and drug smuggling. Always check the latest advice from governments, other travellers and local residents before venturing to Guinea-Bissau.

GUINEA-BISSAU

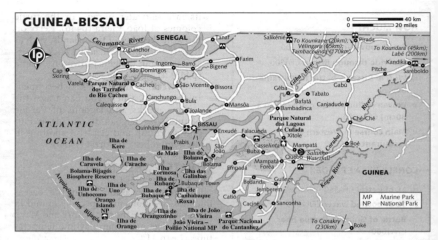

GUINEA-BISSAU

Colonial Period

Portuguese navigators began exploring the coast of West Africa in the 15th century, reaching what's now Guinea-Bissau around 1450. They found the region particularly attractive, with navigable rivers that facilitated trade with the peoples of the interior. Soon the Portuguese were shipping gold, salt and, above all, slaves from here. In the 17th century, Portugal lost control of much of the African coast but managed to hang onto its valuable Guinean ports.

With the decline of the slave trade in the 19th century, the Portuguese had to win control of Guinea-Bissau's interior if they wanted to continue to extract wealth from their possession. Portuguese Guinea-Bissau descended into one of the most repressive and exploitative colonial regimes in Africa, particularly accentuated when right-wing dictator António de Oliveira Salazar came to power in Portugal in 1926.

War of Liberation

By the early 1960s, African countries were rapidly gaining independence. While the transition from colonial to neo-colonial countries was fairly smooth in most French- and British-held territories, Salazar refused to relinquish hold on his African colonies. The result was one of the longest liberation struggles in modern African history.

The independence movement was led by writer and engineer Amilcar Cabral, who in 1956 helped found the Partido Africano da Independência da Guiné e Cabo Verde (PAIGC). In 1961, the PAIGC started arming and mobilising peasants. Though outnumbered by Portuguese forces, PAIGC troops won control of half the country within five years. Even Amilcar Cabral's assassination in 1973 did not stop the momentum for freedom. The PAIGC organised nationwide elections in the liberated areas and proclaimed independence, with Amilcar Cabral's half-brother, Luis, as president.

Independence

Unlike other colonial powers, Portugal had invested little in local development, and the new PAIGC government faced staggering problems. At the time of independence only one in 20 people could read, life expectancy was 35 years, and 45% of children died before the age of five.

Politically, the PAIGC wanted a unified Guinea-Bissau and Cape Verde. However, this idea died in 1980 when President Luis Cabral was overthrown in a coup while he was visiting Cape Verde to negotiate the union. João 'Nino' Vieira, an important military leader of the independence struggle, took over as president. Initially, Guinea-Bissau continued to follow a socialist path, and most businesses were state-controlled. But Vieira believed that Guinea-Bissau was making no progress under Marxism, and in 1986, following a coup attempt the previous year, the government completely reversed its policies, devalued the currency and began selling off state enterprises.

The 1990s

Vieira proved to be a shrewd politician, surviving three coup attempts while keeping the PAIGC in power against a background of growing discontent – most notably felt after the 1994 elections – that he won against contender Koumba Yala.

Despite some improvement, Guinea-Bissau's social and economic situation remained dangerously poor. Protests increased and came to a head on 7 June 1998 when General Ansumane Mane, former head of the army, staged a coup attempt, supported by large parts of the army and allegedly the separatist movement of Senegal. Senegal and Guinea became involved in the conflict, sending soldiers in support of Vieira and government troops loyal to the president. Fighting spread to villages, where many civilians were killed, and by late July, 300,000 people had been displaced.

Despite attempts by Portugal and several Ecowas states to negotiate peace, fighting continued. In May 1999, the military junta led by General Ansumane Mane conquered all of Bissau and personally escorted Vieira to the Portuguese embassy.

Unstable Peace

Transparent presidential and legislative elections were held in November, and a presidential run-off in January 2000 made Koumba Yala the president of the new civilian government. He quashed a coup attempt by General Ansumane Mane, who was later killed in a shoot-out at Quinhámel, 40km from the capital.

Yala's problems with the military had been temporarily solved, but it wasn't long before his relations with other sectors of the government, as well as with civic groups and the media, became strained. In 2001 and 2002 Yala seemed to court controversy, arresting journalists, defying court rulings, and sacking half the civil service.

In September 2003, a coup headed by General Veríssimo Correira Seabra removed the erratic Yala. Legislative elections were held in 2004, with Seabra as caretaker head of state. But, in October 2004, Seabra was killed by a faction of soldiers, and the country held its collective breath until presidential elections in 2005. Despite widespread fears of continued factional violence, the elections were held as planned and generally deemed free and fair. The winner was deposed president João Vieira, who had returned from exile in Portugal to run a successful campaign based on national reconciliation.

Guinea-Bissau Today

For the next three years, Vieira governed the country against a background of feuding army factions, political rivalry and another dangerous enemy – South American drug lords. From 2006 onwards, large-scale cocaine smugglers had increasingly shifted their operations from Cape Verde to Guinea-Bissau. Impoverished, with an army wracked by infighting (and not even enough fuel to put up a chase), and a coastline comprising tiny, uninhabited islands and hidden creeks, smugglers have reigned almost freely. Within three years, Guinea-Bissau has become West Africa's main portal for drug shipments from South America to Europe.

With the strong presence of drug cartels and ongoing army feuds, Guinea-Bissau did not find lasting peace. On 1 March 2009, the president's chief of staff, General Batista Tagme, was murdered, allegedly on President Vieira's command. The following day, Vieira himself was assassinated in what may have been an act of revenge by army officers. As this book went to press, cautious calm had returned to Guinea-Bissau, under the leadership of Interim President Raimundo Pereira, former head of the National People's Assembly, yet the future of this troubled nation remains extremely uncertain.

THE CULTURE
The National Psyche

Despite grinding poverty, a severely damaged infrastructure and wide religious and ethnic differences, Guineans are united by a neighbourly goodwill that is genuinely remarkable. Even in the capital city, where blackouts keep streets pitch black most nights, you can walk the streets with only a modicum of care. Outside the volatile political situation (see boxed text, p433), violence, and even aggressive sales techniques, are rare.

The mainland people share many cultural links with those of southern Senegal and western Guinea. However, the Bijagós people from the Arquipélago dos Bijagós have distinct, and fascinating, customs (see boxed text, p443).

Daily Life

Guinea-Bissau is one of the world's poorest countries, though regular rains and relatively

---

THE WORLD ACCORDING TO NGALA

If you travel from Bissau to Bafata, keep your eyes open for Guinea-Bissau's most unusual, and perhaps most striking exhibitions. Just after the Mansoa junction, Ngala, a toothless old Balante man has fenced in a patch of roadside and, as he says, created the world. That's probably only fair, after all, Ngala means 'God' in the Balante language. Ngala's creation is a small, thought-inspiring universe built from stone, brick and recycled materials. Just like that, to please those who pass, and make them think a little. The gleaming white fence surrounding his 3D social commentary spans dozens of eerie symbols. Christian crosses stand next to a toy-town mecca, peace doves fly over huge bazookas, and dozens of wooden sculptures of policemen, soldiers and two-headed women people the place. Ngala's world is certainly marked by the many struggles his home country has seen. He smiles when asked, quietly stating that 'all of this is part of the same world, war, peace, struggle, love', adding in a whisper that he remembers the liberation war, and models the things it makes him think of. And smiles again. This improvised museum will tell you more about Guinea-Bissau today than any of the papers sold on Bissau's streets.

You pass the place on the main road from Bissau to Bafatá. Pictures can be taken for a small donation, but the works can't be bought.

---

fertile land make outright hunger rare. In rural areas, most people scratch out a living from fishing and subsistence farming. Villages consist of mudbrick houses roofed with thatched grasses, and at night families gather around wood fires that are both the stove and, after dark, the only source of light.

For the vast majority, life is hardly easier in the urban areas. In a nation with virtually no industry, most people eke out a living as small-time merchants, hawking foodstuffs or cheap imports. But those who do escape poverty usually do so quite dramatically. You'll see fat 4WDs squeezing through dirt roads, in a country where fuel problems are frequent, and find Bissau's diners packed with a small, affluent elite.

Population

Current estimates put the population at about 1.4 million, divided among some 23 ethnic groups. The two largest are the Balante (30%) in the coastal and central regions and the Fula (20%) in the east and south. Other groups include the Manjak, Papel and Fulup (closely related to the Diola of Senegal) in the northwest, and the Mandinka in the interior. The offshore islands are mostly inhabited by the Bijagós people (see boxed text, p443).

In Bissau, there is also a significant minority with Cape Verdean and Portuguese ancestry that forms something of an urban elite. There are large numbers of Lebanese and Senegalese as well as a few French, especially in the commercial sectors.

For more information on Fula and Manding cultures, see p74 and p75 respectively.

RELIGION

About 45% of the people (mainly Fula and Manding) are Muslims; they live more in the northeast and south than along the coast. Christians make up less than 10% of the population. Most are Catholic, though evangelical Christians are increasing in number. Animist beliefs remain strong along the coast, in the south and in the Bijagós islands, and have a great influence even on the practices of those who espouse Christianity or Islam.

ARTS

The Bijagós people are famous for mask making and sculpture. Statues representing *irans* (great spirits) are used in connection with agricultural and initiation rituals. If you get the chance to celebrate Carnival on Bubaque island, you'll see many, including ferocious-looking bull-masks worn.

Eastern Guinea-Bissau is a centre of *kora* (a harplike instrument with over 20 strings) playing, being the ancient seat of the Kaabu kingdom, where the instrument was invented. The traditional Guinean beat is *gumbé*, though contemporary music is mainly influenced by zouk (a style of popular music created in the Caribbean and popular across Africa, with a lilting, sensual beat) from Cape Verde. Guinea-Bissau's classic band is Super Mama Djombo, recently reformed. Popular contemporary artists include Manecas Costa, Justino

Delgado, Dulce Nevas and Rui Sangara. You'll rarely see them perform though – the centre of Guinean pop is not Bissau, but Lisbon.

ENVIRONMENT
The Land
Guinea-Bissau has an area of just over 36,000 sq km (about the size of Switzerland), making it one of West Africa's smallest countries. The coastal areas are flat, with estuaries, mangrove swamps and patches of forest. Inlets indent the coast and high tides periodically submerge the lowest areas. Inland, the landscape remains flat, with the highest ground, near the Guinean border, just topping 300m above sea level. Off the coast is the Arquipélago dos Bijagós, consisting of 18 main islands and dozens of smaller ones.

Wildlife
ANIMALS
Hippos are common, including a rare saltwater species near Ilha de Orango (Orango Island). The Bijagós are also an important nesting ground for aquatic turtles. The Cantanhez rainforest in the southeast is the most westerly home of Africa's chimpanzee population. There is also a stunning variety of birds, especially within the coastal wetlands, including cranes and peregrine falcons. Dolphins, sharks and manatees inhabit the waters of Bijagós.

PLANTS
The natural vegetation of the inland areas is Guinea savannah, but on a drive through the country you'll hardly see anything but cashew plantations. Rice, groundnuts (peanuts) and maize are also cultivated and oil palms are common. The coastal zone is very low-lying and indented by many large creeks and estuaries that are lined with impressive mangroves.

National Parks
Guinea-Bissau has a number of protected areas, including the flagship Bolama-Bijagós Biosphere Reserve, which contains the Orango Islands National Park (p446) and the João Vieira-Poilão National Marine Park (p446). On the mainland, the Parque Natural dos Tarrafes do Rio Cacheu (p447), near the border with Senegal, protects a vast area of mangroves, while the southern Parque Natural das Lagoas de Cufada (p450) near Buba is characterised by its freshwater wetland. South of here Parque Nacional do Cantanhez (p450) has been gazetted to preserve the last vestiges of Guinea-Bissau's rainforests, as well as estuarine mangroves.

With some local guidance, parks can be visited quite easily. Cantanhez has a fantastic set-up of guides and information (you only need to get there), and in all other parks nearby hotels can help you out. You can also visit the **IBAP** (☎ 327106; www.ibap-gbissau.org, in Portuguese; Rua de São Tomé, Bissau) office, which oversees all parks.

Environmental Issues
A major environmental issue is the destruction of mangroves – some of the most important in Africa – on the coast, due to the expansion of rice production in seasonally flooded areas. Large areas of forest inland have been replaced with cashew plantations; there are now efforts to protect the remaining rainforests against human encroachment. A number of international bodies, such as UNEP, the WWF, and the impressive NGO Acção Para o Desenvolvimento (AD) are only some of the bodies working to preserve Guinea-Bissau's fragile ecosystems.

FOOD & DRINK
Seafood is the highlight of Guinean cuisine, from oysters and shrimp to the meaty *bica* (sea bream). Fish is generally either grilled or sautéed in an onion and lime sauce. Rice is the ubiquitous staple, sometimes supplemented with other starches like potatoes, yams, beans and *mandioca* (cassava). The national dish, *chabeu* (palm oil), takes some getting used to: it's deep-fried fish served in a thick, palm-oil sauce with rice. Vegetarian options are limited, but if you self-cater, you'll find plenty of fresh ingredients.

Local brews include palm wine. Go slow on the *caña* rum, and even slower on *cajeu*, a sickly sweet and dangerously strong cashew liquor.

BISSAU
pop 410,000
In the early evening, the fading sunlight lends the crumbling colonial facades of Bissau Velho (Old Bissau) a touch of old-age glamour. Dozens of generators set the town trembling, and ignite the lights of stylish bars and restaurants that form something

GUINEA-BISSAU

of a modern, indoor city in startling contrast with the worn exterior.

ORIENTATION

Bissau's main drag is the wide Av Amilcar Cabral, running between the port and Praça dos Heróis Nacionais. A block west on Av Domingos Ramos is the main market, the Mercado Central, and Praça Ché Guevara with the French cultural centre. On the north-western edge of the centre is the Mercado de Bandim. From here, Av de 14 Novembro leads northwest to the main *paragem* (bus and bush-taxi park), the airport and all inland destinations.

INFORMATION

Cultural Centres

Centre Culturel Franco-Bissao-Guinéen (☎ 3206816; Praça Ché Guevara; ☼ 9am-10pm Mon-Sat) This bright, modern centre has a library, art gallery, performance space and small cafe.

Emergency

Fire (☎ 118)
Police (☎ 117)

Internet Access

Restaurant Tamar (p441) and Oporto (p441) had free wi-fi connections when we visited, and the number of connected places is fast increasing.
Cybernet Café (Rua Vitorino Costa; per hr CFA1000; ☼ 9am-10pm) Slow but dependable connections.
Moby's Club (6685746; per hr CFA1500; to 10pm Mon-Sat, to 6pm Sun) Doubles as a cool cafe with live music.

Medical Services

Health services in Guinea-Bissau are very poor. If you need urgent medical attention, get flown out – if not to Europe or the US, then at least to Dakar.
Pharmacie Moçambique (☎ 3205513) Bissau's best-stocked pharmacy.
Policlinica (☎ 3207581; info@policlinica@bissau.com; Praça Ché Guevara) A better option than the main hospital.
Simão Mendes (☎ 3212861; Av Pansau Na Isna) Bissau's main hospital, in a desolate state.

Money

Bissau is the only place in Guinea-Bissau with ATMs, and even those only accept Guinean cards. Unless things have changed (and they might), you need to bring all the money you need in cash. To change money, either ask your hotel for an informal moneychanger, try **Supermercado Mavegro** (☎ 3201224; Rua Eduardo Mondlane; ☼ 3.30-6pm Mon, 9am-12.30pm & 3-6pm Tue-Fri, 9am-12.30pm Sat) or the following banks:
BAO (Banco da Africa Occidental; ☎ 3202418; Rua Gerra Mendes)
Ecobank (☎ 7253194; Av Amilcar Cabral) Changes dollars and euros.

Post

Main post office (Correio; Av Amilcar Cabral)

Telephone

For calls, it's easiest to bring an open mobile (cell) phone (or get yours unlocked on the market) and insert a local MTN or Orange SIM. If you travel widely in francophone West Africa, an Orange card is useful, as it will also work in Senegal, Mali, Guinea and Côte d'Ivoire. For fixed lines, try your hotel or the call centre at the main post office.

Travel Agencies

Weekend Loisirs Vacances (☎ 6830674; julienho@hotmail.com) Julien's colourful van can pick you up from the airport and take you around town, as well as arrange your ferry and boat tickets.

DANGERS & ANNOYANCES

See boxed text, p433, for dangers related to Guinea-Bissau's volatile political climate.

Unless the country has descended into war, you will probably find the discrepancy between violence on a political and military level hard to relate to the climate of peace that characterises Bissau city. You can walk around without being hassled and even the pitch-black Bissau nights usually don't feel unsafe. Beware of pickpockets near the port and in the markets, and carry a torch at night – both to avoid the odd mugging and the holes in the tarmac.

SIGHTS

A stroll through **Bissau Velho** (the old town) reveals a set of narrow alleyways, and derelict buildings, guarded by the **Fortaleza d'Amura**, which is unfortunately off limits to visitors. Along Av Amilcar Cabral, you see a series of majestic colonial houses, as well as ruins of the civil war. The most pertinent of these is the **former presidential palace** that dominates Praça dos Heróis Nacionais. With its bombed-out roof, and the shrapnel in its once graceful, neoclassical facade,

BISSAU

0 — 500 m
0 — 0.3 miles

INFORMATION	
BAO	**1** C5
British & Dutch Consul	(see 16)
Centre Culturel	
Franco-Bissao-Guinéen	**2** C5
Cybernet Café	**3** C5
Ecobank	**4** C5
Gambian Embassy	**5** B5
Guinean Embassy	**6** C5
IBAP Office	**7** B4
Main Post Office	**8** C5
Moby's Club	(see 40)
Pharmacie Moçambique	**9** B5
Policlinica	**10** C5
Portuguese Embassy	**11** C4
Senegalese Embassy	**12** C4
Serviço de Estrangeiros	**13** C4
Simão Mendes	**14** C5
Spanish Embassy	**15** C4
Supermercado Mavegro	**16** D5
Telephones	(see 8)
Weekend Loisirs Vacances	**17** C5

SIGHTS & ACTIVITIES	
Assembleia Ministério da Justiça	**18** B4
Former Presidential Palace	**19** C4
Fortaleza d'Amura	**20** D5

SLEEPING 🏠	
Aparthotel Jordani	**21** C5
Aparthotel Lobato	**22** C4
Hotel 24 Septembra	**23** C2
Hotel Kalliste	**24** C5
Pensão Centrale	**25** C5
Pensaõ Creola	**26** C5
Residencial Coimbra	**27** C5

EATING 🍴	
A Padeira Africana	**28** B5
Bistro	**29** D5
Casa dos Bifes	**30** B4
Dona Fernanda	**31** C3
Gelataria Baiana	(see 26)
Mana M'Butcha	**32** C5
Maria do Rio	**33** B5
Oporto	**34** C5
Papa Louca	**35** C4
Ponto de Encontro	(see 28)
Restaurant Coimbra	(see 27)
Restaurant Samaritana	**36** C4
Restaurant Tamar	**37** C5
Supermercado Bonjour	**38** C5
Supermercado Coimbra	(see 27)

DRINKING 🍷	
Chill Out	**39** C5
Moby's Club	**40** C5

ENTERTAINMENT 🎭	
Mansaflema	**41** B3
X Club	**42** C5

SHOPPING 🛍	
Artissal	(see 25)
Centro Artistico Juvenil	**43** A3

TRANSPORT	
Air Sénégal International	**44** C5
Canoas to Bolama	**45** D5
Expresso dos Bijagòs Office	**46** C5
TACV	**47** C5
TAP Air Portugal	**48** C4

Some Minor Roads not Depicted

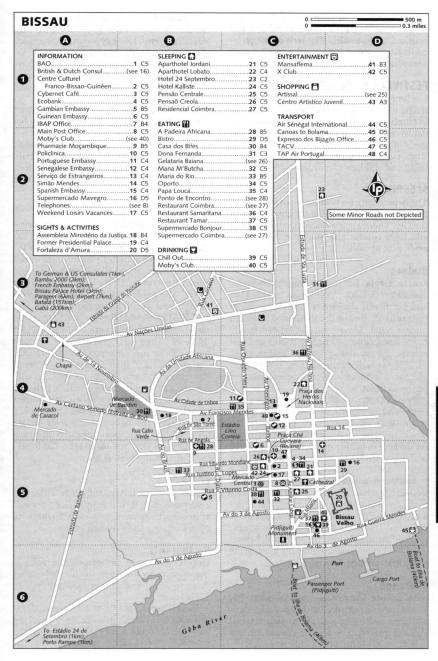

GUINEA-BISSAU

it's an ever-present reminder of the country's devastating civil war. The rebuilt and brushed-up **Assembleia Ministério da Justiça**, by contrast, is an architectural expression of democratic hopes.

FESTIVALS & EVENTS

For four days in February, Bissau is closed to traffic and opened to hundreds of **Carnival** folk in gumboots, raffia skirts, face paint and huge papier-mâché masks who race through the street blowing whistles. It's no sexy Caribbean street party, but great for good vibes, drumming and children's laughter.

SLEEPING

The dependence on generator power and imports for most items drive up hotel prices in the city. There are few decent budget options and for a comfortable stay, you have to set aside a bit of cash.

Budget

Pensão Creola (☎ 6633031; marcelkuehne@yahoo .com; s/d from CFA15,000/17,000) When bubbly Lina and her family decided to open their doors to travellers, Bissau finally owned a decent budget hotel. Their centrally located family home has simple, welcoming rooms and you can use the toy-strewn lounge (and its satellite TV) as well as the kitchen and terrace. Electricity is limited to five hours of generator power at night.

Pensão Centrale (☎ 3213270; Av Amilcar Cabral; r with shared bathroom CFA20,000) Dona Berta is a real Bissau icon, the eccentric grandma to the whole city. She has put up stranded travellers for decades in her historical, balcony-adorned building with dozens of basic rooms and great views from its wide terraces.

Aparthotel Jordani (☎ 3201719; Av Pansau Na Isna; s/d CFA25,000/30,000; ✂) With its dark blue walls, simple rooms and small courtyard, this is not a bad choice, even though there is cold water only and the generator is prone to breakdowns. The drawback is the nightclub behind – on weekends, you're better off joining the party than trying to sleep.

Midrange

Hotel Kalliste (☎ 6064215; r from CFA35,000; ✂) Rooms are thankfully better than the dark staircase and bored reception suggests, but still overpriced. The terrace restaurant and casino are great for a taste of Bissau life.

Aparthotel Lobato (☎ 3201719; Av Pansau Na Isna; s/d from CFA35,000/45,000; ✂ 💻) Tiny from the outside, this pretty, low-key lodging has a maze of rooms of varying standard in the back. Go for one of the slightly pricier ones, which have clean brick floors, comfy beds and hot water. Their internet cafe is across the road, and staff are incredibly helpful.

Hotel 24 Septembro (☎ 6822777; www.azalaihotels .com; r from CFA50,600; ✂ 💻 🍴) The stately, sober structure tells of this hotel's past as the nation's proudest state-run hotel. Now privately managed, it has been infused with a certain charm (the garden space is particularly nice), but still has a way to go to become a haven of comfort.

Top End

Bissau Palace Hotel (☎ 256260; www.bissaupalacehotel .com; Av de 14 Novembro; s/d CFA80,000/100,000; ✂ 💻 📶) This modern structure near the airport is aimed at high-flying business travellers – the ostentatious fake-leather chairs and plush carpets certainly try hard to convey that image. The garden space and pool are great though, and wi-fi is a nice touch.

OUR PICK **Residencial Coimbra** (☎ 6112122; www.res idencialcoimbra.com; Av Amilcar Cabral; s/d CFA85,500/101,000; ✂ 💻 📶) Even your grandmother couldn't bestow more care onto you than the charming, attentive and discreet hotelier who runs this family business. Rooms are spacious with tall ceilings, and decorated with a personal touch that makes them feel like little homes, complete with TV, DVD, stereo and minibar. There's wi-fi throughout and a leafy terrace for relaxation high above the dusty streets. If you need another reason to stay, the breakfast buffet is the best in town.

EATING

Bissau's varied restaurant scene comes as a surprise. You'll find simple rice bars and atmospheric eateries, and even a couple of places serving truly refined cuisine.

Restaurants

Unless otherwise indicated, the following restaurants are open for lunch (around noon to 3pm) and dinner (around 7pm to 10pm) daily.

Mana M'bucha (☎ 6701947; dishes around CFA2500; ✆ lunch & dinner) Don't mistake it for a parking lot – the concrete front yard may not be the most glamorous location, but you won't notice once you've tasted the grilled *bica* or prawns. A fine, local eatery in the heart of town.

Restaurant Samaritana (☎ 6131392; off Av Pansau Na Isna; mains CFA2500) Locally known as 'Chez Mamadou', this triangle of roadside greets you with a bar made from a cut-out container and buzzes with Guineans of all ranks and incomes eager to sample Mamadou's reliably delicious and solid Senegalese and Guinean meals.

Restaurant Tamar (☎ 6609349; mains CFA3500; 🖥 🛜) Try a palm-oil bathed *chabeu* or Cape Verdean *cachoupa* (rich stew, usually made from a corn and meat base) at this understated eatery in Bissau's old town while connecting to the net. That's what the locals do – until the live music kicks in and the tables get pushed out on a Friday night.

A Padeira Africana (☎ 6131393; Rua Marien N'Gouabi; mains CFA4000; 😎) This very air-conditioned Portuguese restaurant is a favourite dinner address for affluent Guineans and expats. It's great for meals and mingling, and the adjacent Ponto de Encontro is one of Bissau's best coffee and croissant places.

Maria do Rio (☎ 6786265; Rua Eduardo Mondlane; meals CFA4000) Bright and shiny, and a good place for pastries and morning coffee, or for an excellent range of international cuisine at lunch and dinner times. There's a good nightclub downstairs.

Dona Fernanda (☎ 6604942; mains CFA4500-6000; 🕒 7-11pm; **V**) Fernanda's leafy patio down a dirt road east of Estrada de Santa Luzia is a favourite address for huge salads and delicately spiced *bica* – often imitated but rarely matched.

Oporto (☎ 6622417; Rua Justino Lopes; 🕒 7am-11pm Tue-Sun; 🖥 🛜) What looks like a humble outdoor terrace from the mango-tree shaded street is in fact a tiny world of small-town glitz with movies on plasma screen, wi-fi and ice-cold beer.

Restaurant Coimbra (☎ 6112122; Av Amilcar Cabral; buffet CFA7500; **V**) Every night Bissau's most stylish restaurant offers a huge, varied buffet, renowned for its quality as well as for its excellent vegie choices (the owner is a vegetarian). The price doesn't seem so high once you know that red wine and water are included in the rate.

Bistro (☎ 3206000; 🕒 noon-3pm & 7-10.30pm) This cute corner stop serves some of Bissau's best cuisine, and without even bragging about it. It's run by a Frenchman, and clichés being what they are, this means very fine food indeed. Come here in the evenings, when the ambience is at its best.

Try also:

Gelataria Baiana (Praça Ché Guevara) Espresso and snacks overlooking Bissau's lively central *praça* (square).

Papa Louca (Av Francisco Mendes) Great for fast food, including shwarma (CFA1500) and pizza (CFA3000) and the table football outside.

Casa dos Bifes (mains CFA2500) With walls covered in yellow and ornamented tiles, the decor seems to promise a sauna session, rather than the juicy meat and rice Bissau's 'Don Beefsteak' serves up here.

Self-Catering

Get your juicy oranges and giant papayas at Mercado Central or Mercado Bandim. For the packaged stuff, the **Supermercado Coimbra** (Av Amilcar Cabral) is the best stocked, with rare imported treats the others don't have. **Supermercado Bonjour** (Rua Vitorino Costa) is another good choice.

DRINKING & ENTERTAINMENT

Moby's Club (☎ 6685746; 🕒 8am-8pm Mon-Wed, 8am-4am Thu-Sun; 🖥) Between painted palms and an improvised terrace heaving with computers, Bissau's party people sip on Pampa beer or push the wobbly rattan chairs to zouk away in rhythm with the live band.

Chill Out (Bissau Velho) The bright pop-art decor and shiny bar stools come as a shock to the eye when you step in from the crumbling old town. This is one for dressed-up party folks, though doesn't always get full enough to relax into a groove.

X Club (☎ 3213467; Rua Osvaldo Vieira) Join the odd assembly of hard-working UN staff, shady businessmen and sparkling party folk on their glitzy trip through the night. Like a potent aperitif, it prepares Bissau's night owls for dancing into the small hours of the morning.

Bambu 2000 (Av de 14 Novembro) The ambience at this bustling club out of town is relaxed and local. Less dressed-up than the X Club, it's the one with the more raucous party. There's food downstairs to refuel before heading home.

Mansaflema (near Av Nações Unidas) The rootsiest party of all happens at Mansaflema. This is where you'll learn that *gumbé* hip swing, or sway across the dance floor to sensual zouk beats under the glitter ball, Guinean-style.

SHOPPING

On the ground floor of Pensão Centrale, **Artissal** (☎ 6604078) has a fantastic choice of bedspreads, tablecloths, bags and other artisanal products made in the Papel weavery in Quinhámel (see also p446). On the sidewalk outside you can pick up wooden masks and bead bling.

A bit further out of town, the **Centro Artistico Juvenil** (Av de 14 Novembro) sells craftwork made from young trainees in a skills training and job creation project.

GETTING THERE & AWAY
Air
There are daily flights to Bissau with TACV, Air Sénégal International and TAP Air Portugal. See p453 for more information.

Boat
See right for the ferry service that links Bissau and Bubaque.

Sept Place & Transporte Misto
You can get *sept places* (Peugeot taxi seven-seaters) and *transporte misto* (literally 'mixed transport') buses to just about anywhere in the country, as well as to Senegal, at the outdoor *paragem* (bus and bush taxi park) about 5km outside town. It's always best to catch transport in the morning. For more information about travelling around the country, see p453.

To get to the *paragem,* take a *toca-toca* (small minibus) from the Mercado de Bandim (CFA100) or a taxi (about CFA1000) from anywhere in town.

GETTING AROUND
To/From the Airport
The airport is about 9km from the town centre. It only switches on its lights when a flight comes in, and that's when you will also find taxis outside. A taxi to town should be around CFA3000.

Taxi
Shared taxis – generally blue, well-worn Mercedes – are plentiful and ply all the main routes. In the town centre, trips cost CFA500. Longer routes vary and have to be negotiated.

Toca-Toca
These are small minibuses painted blue and yellow that run around the city. Rides cost CFA100. The most useful route for visitors goes from Mercado de Bandim along Av de 14 Novembro towards the *paragem* and airport.

ARQUIPÉLAGO DOS BIJAGÓS

It's from the skies that this magnificent set of islands, creeks and mangroves reveals its full beauty, with tiny islets, adorned with swishing palm trees and white, sandy bays, sitting on the turquoise waters. Eighty-seven islands make up the 10,000 sq km of the Arquipélago dos Bijagós. They differ in size, flora and fauna, but each is picture-perfect. Dolphins, hippos, manatees and sea turtles inhabit the waters, and the mangroves are important breeding grounds for migratory birds. The archipelago forms a complex and fragile ecosystem that is protected as a Unesco Biosphere Reserve.

More than 20 of the islands are inhabited, mainly by the elusive Bijagós people. Protected by unpredictable currents, swift tides and treacherous sandbanks, they have been able to maintain a fascinating, unique culture. Their rites and ceremonies remain largely hidden from the eyes of visitors, as their villages are usually far away from the beach in the heart of tropical forests.

Life on the Bijagós islands is defined by the rhythms of nature, and your visit will be too. Everything here depends on the tide – including timings of outings and availability of boats – and nothing happens fast. It's an idyllic place to unwind, not one for rushing.

Dangers & Annoyances
It's hard to imagine a more peaceful place – the greatest dangers are hence the natural kind: stingrays in the flat waters, sharks in the deep and unpredictable hippos near Ilha de Orango.

Getting There & Away
The Arquipélago dos Bijagós is temptingly close to Bissau, but hard to reach. The ferry **Expresso dos Bijagós** (☎ 6538739; Bissau Velho; CFA7500-12,500) normally leaves Bissau port for Ilha de Bubaque every Friday, returning on Sunday. Departure time from both places is around noon and can be as late as 3pm – exact timings depend on the tide – and the trip takes four to five hours. On any other day, your choice is between the rough and risky *canoas* (motor canoes; per

person CFA2500, six hours), where you'll be squeezed between dozens of people, pigs, chickens, bags of rice and dried fish, or the luxury option of hotel pick-up by speed-boat (per four-seater boat CFA150,000 to CFA200,000, 1½ hours).

An amazing way of visiting and getting around the islands is the mini-cruises offered by the charming 1950s boat **Africa Queen** (www .africa-queen.com). The one-week tour takes you around some of the far-flung islands and includes plenty of beach-lounging, walks and fishing excursions, as well as visits to Bijagós villages. Rates start from €950 for the week, including full-board, accommodation and all outings.

Getting Around

Travel between most islands is trying. Rubane and Canhabaque are still fairly easily (and cheaply) reached from Bubaque. For more far-flung places, you're best off arranging a boat trip with your hotel (CFA100,000 to CFA200,000 per four-seater boat depending on distance).

There are public *canoas* for local transport, but they're almost impossible to use. Timings are unpredictable and once you've been dropped off on the island of your choice, there's no telling when the next *canoa* will pass by to pick you up. Many islands don't have accommodation, leaving you without a place to spend the night(s) until the next boat arrives.

ILHA DE BOLAMA

Until 1941, Bolama was the Portuguese capital of the region. Since the transfer of the government to Bissau, it has largely been left to decay, and looks today like a place forgotten in time, strangely beautiful with its sagging colonnades and papaya trees sprouting from stately living rooms. You'll walk the town in a couple of hours, but if you're here with the public *canoa* (it leaves Bissau every Friday and Saturday; CFA2000, about three hours), you'll have to stay the night – the boat only returns the following day. And that's when you'll be grateful for the very decent rooms (CFA20,000) rented out by the NGO Prodepa that works here with artisanal fishermen.

ILHA DE BUBAQUE

At the centre of the Bijagós, Bubaque is home to the archipelago's largest town, as well as being its major transport hub. If you can't make it to remoter islands, Bubaque makes a fine place to unwind. To get to the most isolated spot, away from the small hotels, hire a bicycle or motorbike and track 17km through tropical land to the southern tip of the island. That's where the wide Praia Bruce tempts with soft sands – empty, apart from a couple of lazy cows. If you make the trip, make sure you're there for high tide, or you'll have to wade through mud before reaching the glistening waters.

The island only has electricity in the evenings (and then not always), but most hotels

---

QUEENS OF THE BIJAGÓS

Protected by the shallow channels and treacherous tides that wash their islands, the peoples of the Arquipélago dos Bijagós have, over the centuries, developed a largely matriarchal culture that is remarkably distinct from that of mainland Guinea-Bissau. The islanders are ruled by a king and queen (they're not married) who serve as co-regents – the king managing men's affairs and the queen managing women's affairs. Women often serve as chiefs of individual villages, and they're also the sole homeowners – only fair since they are entirely responsible for homebuilding, from brick-making to actual construction.

Marriage is also a matriarchal affair. On some islands, when a girl reaches puberty, the young men venture forth with as much rice and other goods as they can afford in the hope of buying their way into her favour. She chooses a suitor, but if she's not pregnant within a year, or if someone else makes a better offer, she can ditch her man and choose another. The man usually only stays around until she gives birth, then returns home and becomes eligible for other liaisons. Children take their mother's name and are often unable to identify their father.

The majority of the people remain almost untouched by modern civilisation, and their culture's survival depends entirely on its isolation. If you travel to the more remote islands, tread very, very lightly.

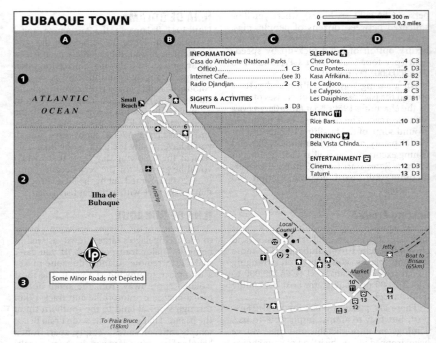

BUBAQUE TOWN

ATLANTIC OCEAN

Small Beach

Ilha de Bubaque

Airstrip

Local Council

Jetty

Boat to Bissau (65km)

Market

Some Minor Roads not Depicted

To Praia Bruce (18km)

INFORMATION	
Casa do Ambiente (National Parks Office)..............................1	C3
Internet Cafe..............................(see 3)	
Radio Djandjan.............................2	C3

SIGHTS & ACTIVITIES	
Museum.....................................3	D3

SLEEPING	
Chez Dora.................................4	C3
Cruz Pontes..............................5	D3
Kasa Afrikana............................6	B2
Le Cadjoco...............................7	C3
Le Calypso...............................8	C3
Les Dauphins............................9	B1

EATING	
Rice Bars...............................10	D3

DRINKING	
Bela Vista Chinda.....................11	D3

ENTERTAINMENT	
Cinema..................................12	D3
Tatumi..................................13	D3

have generators. Mobile phone coverage can be sporadic.

In February, you'll see plenty of traditional outfits at Bubaque's **Carnival** party.

Information

Casa do Ambiente (☎ 327106) Well-organised research centre and information office about the Biosphere Reserve of the Bijagós Archipelago. A small museum details the ecosystem of the islands and displays various artefacts.

Internet cafe (☎ 6549238; per hr CFA1000; ⏰ 9.30pm-midnight Mon-Fri, 8-11.30am & 7pm-midnight Sat & Sun) Surprisingly well equipped, will open at other times if someone's around.

Radio Djandjan This is the larger one of two community radio stations. It broadcasts local music and is the only means of communication to span the islands – hence the many announcements of private matters and events. Hugely interesting.

Sights & Activities

Bubaque's relaxed **market**, with its handful of vegetable, meat and fish stalls, rummaging pigs and playing kids is particularly good on a Sunday. There's no hassle, plenty of smiles

and unforgettable scenes of relaxed trading, gazing and teasing.

Northwest of town, near Les Dauphins bungalows, you can amble through the weather-beaten remains of what used to a massive, state-owned hotel, interspersed with tall oil palms.

On the southern side of Bubaque town, the small **museum** (☎ 6115107; admission CFA1000; ⏰ 10am-1pm & 4-7pm) of the Catholic mission has a nicely displayed selection of masks, statues and ritual items. If you're here for a whole day, try hiring a bicycle or motorbike for the 14km trip to secluded Praia Bruce.

Sleeping & Eating

There is a range of good accommodation in Bubaque, and all serve meals if you order ahead. For cheap eats, try the rice bars near the port.

BUDGET

Le Cadjoco (☎ 5949012, 6161638; r CFA10,000) If you're in a small group, you can book the four rooms and make this village-set place your private home. Otherwise you'll just be absorbed into the family of the lovely owners. There are fishing and boat excursions on offer and bikes available for hire (per day CFA5000). An excellent budget choice.

Chez Dora (☎ 6928836; sosybubaque@gmail.com; s/d CFA10,000/15,000) Barely through the front gate, you will already feel at home in this spacious, lovingly cared for mini-hotel. The bungalows are large, adorned with pretty splashes of colour and swept clean every morning. Best, though, is the garden restaurant, where you can dig into large platters of seafood and Dora's Portuguese specialities in the shade of a straw roof and mango trees.

Cruz Pontes (☎ 7252015, 7248430; s/d CFA10,000/ 15,000) The bungalows in the lovingly tended garden are slightly dark, but still good value. It doesn't quite match other budget options in vibrancy, but beats them when it comes to location – the shore and sea view are only steps away.

MIDRANGE & TOP END

Le Calypso (☎ 5949207; calypsohotel@neuf.fr; s/d CFA20,000/ 22,000; 🏊) Hard to decide where you relax better – in the lazy bar, the Mauritanian tent or by the sunny poolside. Rooms are cute, with colourful decor and a fan to provoke a breeze. Ask about day trips to Canhabaque, where you picnic on the beach and sleep in a bivouac.

Les Dauphins (☎ 6083146, 821156; direction@lesdauphins.com; r CFA30,000; 🖥 🏊 🛜) The leafy garden seems to hold more boats than bungalows. It's a fisherman's favourite with plenty of excursions on offer. Rooms are spacious and well maintained with white tiles and walls, though unspectacular apart from their coastal setting. Wi-fi is pricey at CFA5000 for 30 minutes.

Kasa Afrikana (☎ 7243305, 5949213; develayg@yahoo.fr; per person incl breakfast CFA30,000; 🖥 🖥 🏊 🛜) 'I've spent years searching for the perfect place to live, and I've found it on Bijagos', said the owner. He also built a pretty perfect lodging. Rooms are cushy, well equipped and welcoming – and that includes the large bathrooms. Wi-fi is CFA2000 a day, and you can check out paradise yourself on tailor-made excursions and fishing trips.

Drinking & Entertainment

The best entertainment in Bubaque remains a trip to the market, trying to learn Kreole while chatting to the women behind vegetable stalls, butcher boys and kids. Alcohol consumption being popular here, you don't need to look hard for a local-style bar selling *caña* or *cajeu* liqueur – stained curtains and sickly sweet smells are the giveaways.

Bela Vista Chinda (☎ 6060112) On the shore, the scruffy Bela Vista Chinda has a surprisingly nice terrace right on the water, perfect for an evening beer overlooking the activity of the local fishing centre next door.

Tatumi (admission CFA1000-2000) One class up, and the island's glitzy pride, this nightclub is where zouk beats carry local youngsters in close embrace over the dance floor.

A few steps along the road from Tatumi, a rootsy cinema plays French-language DVDs on a large-screen TV.

Getting There & Away

Bubaque is the arrival port of the Expresso dos Bijagós ferry; see p442 for contact and travel details.

To get to other islands, you're best off phoning the hotel you'll be staying with to arrange pick-up. Prices range from CFA4000 one way for the close-by islands to CFA200,000 per four-seater boat for Ilha de Orango or João Vieira. You can also try the Casa do Ambiente (opposite) to see if you can hitch a boat ride with the national park people, though it won't be much cheaper.

ILHA DE RUBANE

There's no cheap way of visiting the Bijagós islands, so you might as well blow the budget and head to Ilha de Rubane. Here the strikingly beautiful **Ponta Acachana** (☎ in Senegal 33-993 5161, in Guinea-Bissau 7250714; s/d CFA65,000/100,000; 🖥 🏊), a 10-minute boat ride from Bubaque, welcomes you with private, beautifully decorated bungalows and views across the sea (you regularly see dolphins from the rooms). For that really glamorous feel, shuck some oysters at the overflow pool, or dine on the wooden platform from where you can observe the coming and going of the boat fleet (it's a favourite with tourists as well as sports fishermen). This is a great place to unwind or even honeymoon.

The hotel has found the perfect way of combining a holiday in Guinea-Bissau with a Senegal stay. They can take you here from Cap Skiring in Senegal by light plane (per person CFA260,000) – not cheap, but an amazing way to travel, as you get a stunning bird's-eye views over the islands (see also p728).

GUINEA-BISSAU

They can also pick you up by boat from Bissau (CFA150,000) or Bubaque (CFA4000).

ORANGO ISLANDS NATIONAL PARK

Home to rare saltwater species of hippo and crocodile, Ilha de Orango and the surrounding islands together make up the Orango Islands National Park. The island is also the burial site of the Bijagós kings and queens (see boxed text, p443).

The only hotel, **Orango Parque Hotel** (☎ 521 9306, 675 5262; lreservas@cbd-habitat.com; s/d with full board CFA35,000/50,000), has attractive rooms with pretty, tiled bathrooms right on the beach. It's run in association with the local community, and reinvests in local development. Local village residents can take you on tours along the nearby creeks, as well as on hippo-spotting outings. Rely on your guide on the hippo tours – there are quite a few of these big creatures here, and they have volatile tempers and fast feet. You don't want to get on their wrong side!

Phone the hotel to arrange your transfer (around CFA320,000 for six people).

JOÃO VIEIRA – POILÃO NATIONAL MARINE PARK

At the far, southeast end of the archipelago, the João Vieira – Poilão National Marine Park consists of four islands and surrounding waters that together form one of the most important egg-laying areas for sea turtles on the Eastern Atlantic. The islands' wide, palm-sheltered beaches are paradisiacal, with sand that feels as soft as velvet and crunches like snow. The cute camp **Chez Claude** (☎ 6520374; www.bijagos-joaovieira.com, in French; full board CFA35,000) sits right on such a beach, though Claude, a rough soul and solitude-loving fisherman, will tell you that living here with a small family is not what Eden ought to be like. Every item has to be transported here on a two-hour boat trip, schooling is undertaken on a few plastic chairs behind the sands, and there are plenty of other worries linked to life in the wild. Yet, he still lives there after 13 years, and that might have something to do with the turquoise waters, swishing palm trees, and giant barracudas quivering in the sea.

The nearby island of **Mëio** is reputed to be among the finest of all. During the main egg-laying season of the green tortoises (October/November), the shores can teem with those rare creatures – an incredible sight. In the right season, you can watch dozens of sea turtles on the shore.

To get here, you can either take a boat trip with a Bubaque or Rubane hotel (around CFA150,000) or Claude has to pick you up (CFA200,000 from Bissau, CFA100,000 from Bubaque).

OTHER ISLANDS

Perhaps the most amazing island of all (and competition is intense) is the small, sandy **Kere**. It's perfect, in every way – including the rare absence of stingrays, which means undisturbed bathing in the clear waters kissing Kere's shores. There's a very fine little hotel, run by the managers of Orango Parque Hotel (see left). Contact them to arrange your transport here.

The island of **Canhabaque (Roxa)** is very different. It's large and inhabited, and close to Bubaque. Many of Bubaque's hotels organise excursions here, and on these you can catch a glimpse of village life in the Bijagós.

THE NORTHWEST

Northwest Guinea-Bissau offers two distinct experiences for the traveller. Varela, which sits just across the border from Senegal's Cap Skiring, shares its neighbour's gorgeous, wide beaches yet remains almost completely undeveloped. The region is also home to remarkably well-preserved mangrove swamps and the Cacheu River, with its hippos and crocodiles.

QUINHÁMEL

A wide, palm-shaded promenade lends this tiny town the grandeur it deserves, being the regional capital of the Biombo region. Thirty-five kilometres west of Bissau, this is the traditional home of the Papel people, and there's no better introduction to this ethnic group and their traditions than **Artissal** (☎ 6604078; artissal@gmail.com; ✆ 9am-5pm), a local collective devoted to the preservation and promotion of Papel weaving crafts. When we passed, they were just about to embark on a promising cultural tourism initiative, including visits to local craftsmen. See how far they've progressed.

Ask in town for the Portuguese lady who grills oysters (everyone knows her); they're divine. For a more substantial meal, try the palm-grove–set **Hotel Marazul** (☎ 6670637; r incl breakfast CFA40,000; ✗ ♨) on the river. It's nicely located, but as it is suffering the first signs of neglect, a meal may be a better choice than a stay.

Transporte misto go here from Bissau (CFA500). You can jump on at the airport roundabout. A return hire taxi from Bissau will cost around CFA15,000.

CACHEU & CANCHUNGO

Today a sleepy provincial town, **Cacheu** was the first capital of the region and an important trading centre under Portuguese colonial rule. The wide promenades, small port, and tiny, reconstructed fort grant a glimpse of the town's historical importance. The garrison's old cannons may be the ones that helped repulse the infamous English pirate Sir Francis Drake in 1567; nowadays they're joined by an odd assembly of out-of-fashion bronze statues, 'dumped' here for their retirement.

A visit here is best combined with a stop at **Canchungo**, where the large, relaxed market near the *rond-point* (roundabout) invites travellers to linger and spend a few francs on traditional pottery and woven baskets. Stop here on your way to Cacheu to order a plate of *caldeirada* (a thick stew, usually with a meat base) at **Casa Monteiro** (dishes CFA2500) near the *rond-point* – it will be ready on your return journey from Cacheu.

Keen birdwatchers should pay a visit to the **Parque Natural dos Tarrafes do Rio Cacheu**, near Cacheu town. Its over 200 bird species include flamingos, Senegal parrots and African giant kingfishers. Its gazelles, hyenas, manatees and other mammals are a lot harder to view. For more information, contact the **IBAP office** (☎ 327106; www.ibap-gbissau.org; Rua de São Tomé) in Bissau.

For a visit to both towns and the park, it's best to hire a car. There are also regular *transporte misto* from Bissau (CFA1000 to Canchungo, CFA3000 to Cacheu). To visit the park only, you can also hop on the daily *canoa* between Cacheu and São Domingos; the trip costs CFA2000 and takes around two hours. Schedules depend on tides.

SÃO DOMINGOS

On the border with Senegal, this busy junction town is where you carry out immigration formalities – usually a swift process.

There are small eateries, but for a bed, you'll have to make your way to Ingore on the way to Bissau.

All public transport from Bissau to Ziguinchor (CFA2500) and Varela (CFA3000) passes through here. The journey from Bissau to Ziguinchor takes about four to five hours – it should be much less once the bridge across the Cacheu River is completed.

VARELA

The beaches here are as wide and beautiful as those of Cap Skiring, but see far fewer visitors. Guineans love coming here for weekends out of town, but the terrible condition of the unpaved road from São Domingos discourages most that can't afford a 4WD. At least the bridge across the Cacheu was nearing completion when we passed. If that's followed by investment in the roads, you can expect a number of new guesthouses to join the Varela classic **Chez Fatima** (☎ 7270876; r CFA15,000), above the waves. Fatima is a lovely lady with a hotel to match her spirit. To visit her and her endless beach front yard, you can either brave the route on *transporte misto* (CFA3000, six to seven hours until the bridge is completed) or, if you come from Senegal, walk along the beach from Kabrousse, then take a pirogue. It's an easy 3km from Kabrousse – just make sure you get your exit stamp at Cap Skiring (see p727). Fatima can look after the Guinean formalities.

THE NORTHEAST

Travelling northeast from Bissau, the flat, wet coastal regions give way to drier and hillier land that serves as the transition into the Sahel. There is little to detain the traveller, although the forests and rivers are popular with hunters and fishermen, and the road between Gabú and the Guinean border winds through pretty hills as high as 300m – the highest point in the country.

BAFATÁ

Blow some tumbleweeds across the cracked tarmac of Bafatá's streets, and the ghost town atmosphere is perfect. The largest town in the northeast is the birthplace of Amilcar Cabral and looks as though not a lick of paint has

GUINEA-BISSAU

BAFATÁ

0 ⸺ 500 m
0 ⸺ 0.3 miles

SLEEPING 🛏
Aparthotel Triton........1 B1
Hotel Maimuna Capé..2 A2

EATING 🍽
Food Stalls......................3 B2
Ponto de Encontro..........4 A2

TRANSPORT
Minibus & Bush Taxi Park.5 B2

Old Airstrip

To Club Capé (15km)

Géba River

Old Market

Hospital

Pharmacy

Cabral Monument

To Gabú (50km)

Market Stalls

Some Minor Roads not Depicted

To Bissau (151km)

been added since he spent his childhood here. In its state of abandon, Bafatá's old town, with its withered Portuguese buildings, is eerily beautiful and the wide Gêba River that flows past adds to the complete tranquillity.

On the descent towards the river, the historical building of **Hotel Maimuna Capé** (☎ 6648383; s/d CFA10,000/15,000; 🛏) looks attractive from the outside, though the small rooms have lost much of their lustre. **Aparthotel Triton** (☎ 6938100; r CFA25,000; 🛏 🖳 🞈) on the former airstrip was brand new when we passed. Though trying hard to be luxurious, the homemade design with flimsy walls, plate-glass windows and ter-

races going nowhere resembled more a cheap Chinese construction kit.

A lovely walk along the laterite road opposite Maimuna Capé takes you through a village-type neighbourhood, past palm groves and across the river to the remote **Club Capé** (☎ 6648383; s/d CFA20,000/25,000). It's a striking, though often empty, place that opens only during hunting season (January to March).

Bafatá's classic eatery is the cosy **Ponto de Encontro** (Chez Celia; ☎ 6921690; dishes around CFA3500), which serves Portuguese food made from fresh local ingredients. You can follow it with an ice cream at Aparthotel Triton, otherwise it's the street food stalls near the market.

Transporte misto to Bissau (CFA3000), Gabú (CFA1500) and Buba (CFA3000) depart from the petrol station area.

GABÚ

In the 19th century, this northeastern town was the flourishing capital of the small, but important empire of Gabú (also called Ngabu or Kaabu). The short spell of glory has left no physical traces – only the epic songs of the *griots* (traditional caste of musicians or praise singers) keep its story alive (see boxed text, below). Today, Gabú is a lively up-country centre with a busy market illuminated at night by dozens of kerosene lamps. It's also a great base for excursions to **Boé** (40km from Gabú), from where you can hike up rocky hillocks that grant brilliant views across the plains.

TELLING TIME

Try as you might, a walk through the dusty, chattering market town of Gabú – entertaining as it might be – simply won't impress you with the centre's distinguished past. There are no grand monuments, no crumbling palaces, not even a sign to tell you that this was once the capital of the powerful kingdom of Kaabu (1537–1867). Yet even if its grand story is not immediately visible, it's certainly remembered. And Kaabu's living memory sits 40km further southwest, in a tiny village called Tabato. This extraordinary community is home to El Hadj Mountarou Diabaté and his extended family of *griots* (traditional caste of musicians or praise singers). For centuries, Diabaté's ancestors have played their music both for the region's kings and common people, remembered the greatest stories and told them to the public. When the village gets together, strumming *koras* and breaking into song you sense the grandeur of Kaabu's kings, elaborately painted in the *griots'* words.

Tabato is certainly not the only *griot* village around, but its family has chosen to open their world to others. Busking in the streets of Bissau, they raised enough funds to build a little museum, where you can look at the *griots'* instruments and hear about the stories of the region's past. It's also the place to arrange *kora,* drumming, *balafon* (xylophone) or singing courses, or simply drop by to enjoy the stories and songs (for a donation). Contact the Diabaté family on ☎ 6651847.

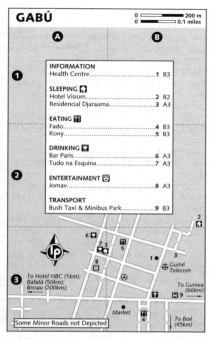

There's a small, scarcely equipped health centre, dozens of pharmacies, a telecentre, and internet access at Hotel HBC.

Where Gabú greets the banana gardens, the friendly **Hotel Visiom** (☎ 6866699; r with fan/aircon CFA8000/15,000; ✕) is a tranquil spot, with clean, simple accommodation in a cute garden. Rooms at the quirky **Residencial Djaraama** (☎ 6938442; r with shared bathroom CFA15,000) are a tad scruffier, but have infinitely more character. Each of the 1st-floor, balcony-adorned spaces is decorated in its unique tacky way – the spacious double with the huge last-supper wall carpet and wrought-iron furniture was our favourite. The classiest option is the large **Hotel HBC** (☎ 6444403; www.chasseen guinee.com; r CFA24,000; ✕ ☐ ⚐) at the entry of town, which has a good restaurant, tempting pool and sparkling bungalows.

For food outside your hotel, you need to pre-order. The busy **Kony** (☎ 7224485; mains CFA2000) does simple, tasty meals in clean surroundings. Near the market, burly Fula lady Fatime serves solid local meals at **Fado** (☎ 6630947; meals CFA2000), an unexpectedly large, round patio squeezed between huts and roofs.

Around the corner on the market, are several street stalls.

To dance off the rice-induced calories, head for **Jomav** (admission CFA500; ✕ Fri-Sun), an outdoor club that often has live music. Nearby, makeshift bars such as **Tudo na Esquina** (☎ 6768872) and Bar Paris attract drink-hardy locals for ice-cold beers.

Getting There & Away

Sept places and *transporte misto* go to Bissau regularly (CFA4000, six hours). See p453 for details on travelling from Gabú to Guinea or Senegal. You can easily change CFA into Guinean francs at the taxi rank.

THE SOUTH

With its wide river arms, gentle waterfalls and a stunning stretch of tropical rainforest, the south remains Guinea-Bissau's best-kept secret. The mermaid that's rumoured to comb her hair on the Saltinho rocks may be part of popular lore, but the shifting lands of Cufada, and Cantanhez's gigantic trees, buzzing bird islands and populations of manatees, chimpanzees, elephants and buffaloes are not. Bring a sturdy vehicle and plenty of patience.

Getting There & Away

Saltinho and Buba are easily reached by *transporte misto* from Bissau (CFA3000), a trip to Jemberem or any other far-flung destination necessitates a 4WD, and even then is only manageable in the dry season. See also p450.

SALTINHO

A pretty 1950s bridge crosses the Corubal River right where its waters wash over wide stones at Saltinho. Both bridge and waterfalls adorn most walls, logos and printed items at the relaxed **Pousada do Saltinho** (☎ 5900693; s/d CFA20,000/25,000; ✕). The hotel's bungalows are far too bright and pretty to leave them only to the sports hunters for which they're mainly intended, and the outdoor restaurant grants great vistas over the river.

BUBA

The planned construction of one of West Africa's biggest ports is bound to change the tranquil pace of this pretty town overlooking the mangroves. When we passed, this huge project was in its very early stages – Buba was still a provincial centre with wide, laterite alleys and dug-out canoes riding on the river, and the nearby **Parque Natural das Lagoas de Cufada** a peaceful stretch of wetlands and chattering birds. Contact the **IBAP office** (☎ 327106; www.ibap-gbissau.org; Rua de São Tomé) in Bissau or the Buba branch to find out about the latest developments and arrange your visits to the Cafatada Lagoon.

Possibly even more helpful is Gabi, the welcoming Portuguese manager of **Pousada Bela Vista** (☎ 6647011, 6072244; r CFA13,000; ☒). She can tell you about Buba behind-the-scenes and direct you to pirogues that travel the river, park and possibly even go to Bolama. Her place overlooks a beautiful bit of mangrove from a lovingly tended garden, and the bungalows are pretty, well maintained and bright.

Dedicated fishermen or hunters might also enjoy a stay at **Antonio Torre's** (☎ 6624632), who offers rooms in his family house from January to May. The place is set on a lovely stretch of river, though the gallery of hunting poses in the living rooms is nothing for delicate souls.

Transporte misto run regularly along the tarmac road from Bissau to Buba (CFA3000).

JEMBEREM & PARQUE NACIONAL DO CANTANHEZ

The road to Jemberem is as tough as it is pretty. It's a slim stretch of bouncy, washed-out red dust, lined on either side by gigantic tropical trees. Once you've made the last few kilometres, the forest suddenly opens onto a large, superbly organised Fula village. Thanks to the efforts of development agency Acção Para o Desenvolvimento (AD), this village is not only proud owner of a community TV station and radio, small hospital and school, but also to a fully-fledged ecotourism project designed to promote and support the adjacent **Parque Nacional do Cantanhez**, which surrounds Jemberem and was gazetted in 2008 to protect the last of Guinea-Bissau's rainforests. You cross it as you drive in, and large, tropical trees wave to you as you eat dinner at AD's eco-camp.

While the dense web of giant kapok trees, lianas and palm trees is already exciting for the jungle-thrill it provides on walks and bike tours, the best thing about this forest is the spectacular wildlife it preserves. Cantanhez is home to Africa's westernmost troupe of chimpanzees, as well as to buffaloes, elephants, baboons, colobus monkeys, antelopes and hundreds of birds. In the mangrove and island areas that also form part of the protected zone, plenty of fish, manatees, small hippos and a whole different assortment of birds thrive.

AD has designed a range of **trails** (CFA5000) that can be explored in the obligatory (and necessary) company of one of its trained community guards. On an early morning walk, you're almost guaranteed chimpanzee sightings (and you'll at least experience the aural pleasure of the jungle waking up). If you're here for a few days, you'll almost certainly get to see elephants, too.

This area is also of huge historical importance, having served as a refuge and fighting zone during the independence struggle. On the route from Guilege to Jemberem, you pass a site where old ammunition is still strewn across the ground. AD is currently developing it into a museum.

AD's **U'Anan Camp** (☎ 6060019, 6637263; d/q CFA15,000/25,000) can put you up in cute bungalows. It has running water and generator-produced electricity from 7pm to midnight. Contact AD before setting out, as it can put you in touch with a reliable 4WD driver to take you there. Expect to pay around CFA60,000 in car hire charges per day, excluding petrol. Don't attempt this trip in anything but a 4WD and only go during the dry season. Rains are heavy here, turning dirt tracks into rivers. To drive here, follow the road to Buba until Mampata Forea, where you leave the tarmac for 70km of track. Keep asking the locals to make sure you don't lose your way, or better, get a driver who knows where he's going.

GUINEA-BISSAU DIRECTORY

ACCOMMODATION

The lack of electricity and subsequent need for generator power pushes up prices for accommodation. There's hardly any budget bed that can be recommended. Even a midrange room of CFA35,000 may not be great, though it will have some security, a private bathroom and electricity. With few exceptions (that we've noted in this book), you'll have to pay upwards of CFA80,000 for something really nice. This situation repeats itself across the country (the Bijagós islands are expensive, too). If you want to travel with a certain amount of comfort, plan a generous accommodation budget, allowing a minimum of CFA35,000 on average per night.

ACTIVITIES

The Arquipélago dos Bijagós (p442) and especially Varela have great sandy beaches, and the waters around the Bijagós also offer some of the best deep-sea fishing in the world. Cycling is an excellent way to get around Guinea-Bissau, as roads are quiet and generally flat.

In the south, eg Parque Nacional do Cantanhez (opposite), you can set out on rewarding wildlife-spotting trips and nature hikes.

BOOKS

Patrick Chabal's *Amilcar Cabral: Revolutionary Leadership and People's War* is a fine antidote to cynicism about African politics, documenting the way the leader of Guinea-Bissau's revolution combined idealism, sharp analytical powers and political acumen.

Walter Hawthorne's *Planting Rice and Harvesting Slaves: Transformations along the Guinea-Bissau Coast, 1400–1900* examines the way European slavery radically changed the way of life of the stateless Balanta people of Guinea-Bissau.

Jonina Einarsdottir's *Tired of Weeping: Mother Love, Child Death, and Poverty in Guinea-Bissau* explores the unexpected ways women of Guinea-Bissau's matrilineal Papel cope with high rates of infant mortality.

BUSINESS HOURS

Opening hours for banks and government offices vary quite a bit, but are usually 8am to noon and 2pm to 5pm Monday to Friday, or 8am to 2pm Monday to Friday. The post offices are generally open Monday to Friday mornings only, but the main post office in Bissau is open 8am to 6pm Monday to Saturday. Larger shops are open 8am or 9am until 6pm Monday to Friday and 8am until 1pm or 2pm Saturday.

> **PRACTICALITIES**
>
> ■ The national radio and TV stations broadcast in Portuguese. Most interesting for travellers is Radio Mavegro FM (100.0MHz), which combines music with hourly news bulletins in English from the BBC.
>
> ■ Newspapers come and go quickly in Bissau. If you sit at one of the city's cafes or restaurants, a vendor will quickly be offering you the latest publication.
>
> ■ Electrical voltage is 220V with European plugs (2 round prongs).
>
> ■ Guinea-Bissau uses the metric system.

Some shops also close for an hour or two in the early afternoon. In most towns there are usually corner grocers that will stay open until 10pm or even later.

EMBASSIES & CONSULATES

All embassies and consulates are in Bissau, some in the centre, others along the road towards the airport.

France (☎ 3201312; cnr Av de 14 Novembro & Av do Brazil)

Gambia (☎ 3251099; Rua Vitorino Costa; ☷ 8.30am-3pm Sat-Thu, to 12.30pm Fri)

Germany (☎ 3255020; escritorio-bissau@web.de; SITEC Building; ☷ 9-11am Mon-Fri)

Guinea (☎ 3201231; Rua 12; ☷ 8.30am-3pm Sat-Thu, to 1pm Fri) East of the central stadium.

Portugal (☎ 3203379; Av Cidade de Lisboa; ☷ 8am-noon)

Senegal (☎ 3212944; off Praça dos Heróis Nacionais; ☷ 8am-noon)

Spain (Praça dos Heróis Nacionais; ☷ 8am-noon)

The consul for the UK and the Netherlands is **Jan van Maanen** (☎ 6622772; Supermercado Mavegro, Rua Eduardo Mondlane, Bissau). The US consular representative is a subpost to the **Dakar Embassy** (☎ Senegal 33 82 2100; consulardakar@state.gov; SITEC building).

FESTIVALS & EVENTS

Guinea-Bissau's main event is Carnival (see p440). The biggest party happens in Bissau, but Bubaque's has the more interesting masks and costumes.

HOLIDAYS

Public holidays include:

New Year's Day 1 January
Anniversary of the Death of Amilcar Cabral 20 January
Women's Day 8 March
Easter March/April
Labour Day 1 May
Pidjiguiti Day 3 August
Independence Day 24 September
Christmas Day 25 December

Islamic feasts such as Eid al-Fitr (at the end of Ramadan) and Tabaski are also celebrated. See p816 for a table of dates of Islamic holidays.

INTERNET ACCESS

There are several internet cafes in Bissau. They charge CFA1000 to CFA1500 per hour for slow, dial-up connections. Wi-fi is increasingly common, with many hotels and restaurants offering a free service. Outside of the capital, there is virtually no public internet access.

LANGUAGE

Portuguese is the official language, but no more than a third of the people speak it. Each group has its own language, but the common tongue is Crioulo – a mix of Portuguese and local words. As Guinea-Bissau is increasingly drawn into the Afro-Francophone world, you easily get by with French. See p860 for some useful phrases.

MONEY

At writing, there are no ATM machines accepting international cards in Guinea-Bissau, and credit cards are not accepted anywhere. You must plan to arrive with all the money you need in cash. Euros are the easiest to exchange. US dollars are more difficult, and sometimes impossible outside Bissau. You're strongly advised to change all the money you need in Bissau before heading up-country or to the islands, as there are virtually no banking facilities outside the capital.

The unit of currency is the West African CFA franc.

PHOTOGRAPHY & VIDEO

Photo permits are not required, but the usual restrictions apply. For more information, see p821.

POST

The postal service is slow – you're probably better off posting mail home from Senegal or Gambia.

TELEPHONE

For local calls, keep an eye out for signs reading *posto publico;* they are located at corner stalls. International calls can cost as much as CFA2200 to CFA5000, depending on where you call. There is also a call centre at the **main post office** (Av Amilcar Cabral) in Bissau.

The best thing to do is buy Orange or MTN SIM cards. If you don't have an unlocked phone, you can easily buy a cheap one. Top-up credit is available on every street corner.

Service can be unreliable in remote areas, including the Arquipélago dos Bijagós.

VISAS

All visitors, except nationals of Ecowas countries, need visas. These are normally valid for one month and are issued for around US$40 at embassies. They are not issued at land borders, but may be issued at the airport if you come from an African country where visas are not available. To avoid hassles, get one before you arrive.

Visa Extensions

Extensions are easy to obtain at **Serviço de Estrangeiros** (Praça dos Heróis Nacionais, Bissau). For virtually all nationalities, 45-day visa extensions cost around CFA4000 and are ready the same day if you apply early.

Visas for Onward Travel

Visas for the neighbouring countries of Guinea-Bissau can be obtained at their embassies in Bissau (see p451).

WOMEN TRAVELLERS

Compared to other West African countries, Guinea-Bissau is bliss for women travellers. There's none of the whistling and general sleazing about that can make places like Gambia, Senegal, Guinea or Nigeria tough terrain for lone female travellers.

It's best to bring all the tampons you need. You won't find any up-country, and if they have them in Bissau, they're expensive.

Dress codes resemble those of other West African countries. Long clothing is preferred in more conservative areas. Bissau is pretty relaxed about women's legs being exposed.

TRANSPORT IN GUINEA-BISSAU

GETTING THERE & AWAY
Entering Guinea-Bissau
A certificate with proof of a yellow fever vaccination is required of all travellers.

Air
Guinea-Bissau's only international airport is on the outskirts of Bissau. The main airlines flying to/from Guinea-Bissau are TAP Air Portugal (the only direct flight from Europe), TACV and Air Sénégal International (both via Dakar). Flights from Dakar to Bissau with both Air Sénégal and TACV are distressingly expensive, and you might consider taking a bush taxi to Ziguinchor and get on a cheaper, internal flight in Senegal from there. To fly between Bissau and anywhere else in Africa you have to pass through Dakar. The following airlines service Guinea-Bissau:

Air Sénégal International (V7; ☎ 3205211; www.air -senegal-international.com; Rua Osvaldo Vieira) Hub: Dakar.
TACV (VR; ☎ 3206087; www.tacv.com; Av Amilcar Cabral) Hub: Praia.
TAP Air Portugal (TP; ☎ 3201359; www.flytap.com; Praça dos Heróis Nacionais) Hub: Lisbon.

Land
The busiest crossing point to/from Senegal is at São Domingos, on the main route between Ingore and Ziguinchor. There are also crossing points between Tanaf and Farim, and near Pirada, north of Gabú on the route to/from Vélingara and Tambacounda.

To/from Guinea, most traffic goes via Kandika and Saréboïdo on the road between Gabú and Koundara. A less-travelled route, open only in the dry season, links southeastern Guinea-Bissau and western Guinea via Quebo and Boké (Guinea-Conakry).

GUINEA
Bush taxis go to the border daily from Gabú and Koundara (CFA5000). It can take all day to cover this 100km stretch, although the winding road through the Fouta Djalon foothills is beautiful. If you have to change transport at Saréboïdo, tying in with the weekly Sunday market will improve your options.

SENEGAL
Most overland travel between Senegal and Guinea-Bissau passes through Ziguinchor, Senegal and the Guinea-Bissau border town of São Domingos. When this book went to press, the toll bridge across the Cacheu River was nearing completion – it should be finished by the time you set out, which means you will be able to travel from Bissau to Ziguinchor in a couple of hours. As long as the ferry (passengers CFA100) is in operation, long waiting times make the length of a journey unpredictable. Bissau–Ziguinchor is CFA5000 by *sept place*.

GETTING AROUND
Boat
The main boat connection is the Expresso dos Bijagós that links Bissau to Bubaque island (see p442), a reliable, regular ferry service. Between individual islands, you also have regular *canoas*. The only stretch where the *canoa* trip is recommended is on the relatively short distance from Bissau to Bolama. All hotels in the Bijagós hire boats for fishing trips, excursions or pick-up from Bubaque, but that's always expensive.

Sept Place & Transporte Misto
Sept places are Peugeot 504 seven-seaters that link Guinea-Bissau's main towns. More common and far less comfortable are the large minibuses called *transporte misto* (literally 'mixed transport', though what exactly makes the mix special, we weren't able to find out).

In Bissau, short distances are covered by *toca-tocas*, which are smaller, blue-and-yellow minibuses.

The main roads between Bissau and the towns of Bafatá, Gabú, São Domingos and Buba are all tar and generally in a good state. The stretches from Buba to Jemberem and São Domingo to Varela are unpaved, and in seriously bad condition.

Mornings (before 8am) are always the best time to get transport. For an idea of fares across the country, from Bissau to Gabú (around 200km) is CFA3500 by *sept place*, CFA2000 by *transporte misto*.

GUINEA-BISSAU

Liberia

Peace and a modicum of stability have finally come to Liberia, a country that for decades has been a festering sore on West Africa's benighted coastline, known only for child soldiers and warlords. Having elected Africa's first female president and been subject to an unprecedented effort by the international community to get the shattered country back on its feet, Liberia is now safe and open for visitors once again.

This is a unique opportunity to travel through a country that is rebuilding itself after decades of violence, and one you should take if you get the chance – avoiding Liberia, while common enough for West African itineraries, will never help the country reintegrate into the region's mainstream.

Liberia itself is a lush, beautiful land criss-crossed by rivers and largely made up of impenetrable rainforest. It now again offers visitors a fascinating glimpse into one of West Africa's most hospitable and enigmatic societies. The country's artistic traditions – especially carved masks, dance and storytelling – rival those of anywhere in the region, and traditional culture remains strong. This was especially true in the interior, where until the war secret initiation societies played a central role in growing up, and even today still serve as an important repository of traditional knowledge and life skills.

The country's natural attractions are equally impressive. In contrast with its ravaged infrastructure, Liberia's dense, humid rainforests – some of the most extensive in West Africa – are alive with the screeching and twittering of hundreds of birds, who are kept company by forest elephants, pygmy hippos and other wildlife padding around the forest floor.

FAST FACTS

- **Area** 111,370 sq km
- **Capital** Monrovia
- **Country code** ☎ 231
- **Famous for** Rainforests, child soldiers, traditional masks, rubber plantations
- **Languages** English (official), plus Bassa, Kpelle, Kru, Grebo and other local languages
- **Money** Liberian dollar (L$); US$1 = L$66.50; €1 = L$88.45
- **Population** 3.3 million
- **Visas** Required by almost everyone, and must be arranged in advance

LIBERIA

HOW MUCH?

- **Sachet of water** US$0.07
- **Kilo of bananas** US$0.40
- **Fufu and soup** US$0.75
- **Short taxi ride** US$1
- **Soda** US$0.30

LONELY PLANET INDEX

- **Gallon of petrol** US$4.30
- **Litre of bottled water** US$0.20
- **Bottle of Club beer** US$1
- **Souvenir T-shirt** US$15
- **Cassava leaf snack** US$0.75

HIGHLIGHTS

- **Monrovia** (p460) Sidewalk vendors and the beat on the street.
- **Robertsport** (p466) Surfers and sun worshippers, and Liberia's coolest hotel at a little slice of African beach paradise.
- **Sapo National Park** (see the boxed text, p468) Lush, humid canopy of one of West Africa's last remaining rainforests.
- **Harper** (p467) Elegant reminder of Liberia's wealthy past.

ITINERARIES

- **One week** Spend several days in Monrovia (p460) getting to know the city and travelling to some of its nearby beaches before heading to Bomi Lake (p468) and on to gorgeous Robertsport (p466).
- **Two weeks** With an extra week you can add the journey to Sapo National Park (see the boxed text, p468) and on to charming Harper (p467) before heading into Côte d'Ivoire or flying back to Monrovia if you don't fancy the long, long drive!

CLIMATE & WHEN TO GO

Monrovia is one of the wettest capital cities in Africa, with rainfall averaging more than 4500mm per year here and elsewhere along the Liberian coast. Inland, it's less – in some areas only about 2000mm annually. Temperatures range from 23°C to 32°C in Monrovia, and are slightly higher inland. However, humidity levels of more than 85% in the dry season (November to April) and

more than 90% in the rainy season (May to October) often make it feel much warmer. There is little seasonal temperature variation. See also Climate Charts (p811).

The best time to visit Liberia is during the dry season, between November and April.

HISTORY

The area that is now Liberia has likely been populated for more than 2000 years, although little is known of its early history. Many present-day Liberians trace their ancestry to peoples who migrated southeast from the Sahel following the fall of the Empire of Mali in the 15th century. However, settlement of the area remained sparse because of the dense and inhospitable forests covering most of the country, and no great cities developed.

European contact with Liberia began in the 1460s with the arrival of Portuguese navigators, who named several coastal features, including Cape Mesurado (Monrovia) and Cape Palmas (Harper). Because of the trading success of a pepper grain, the area soon became known as the Grain Coast.

The Arrival of the Settlers

In the early 19th century, the Grain Coast rose to the forefront of discussions within the abolitionist movement in the USA as a suitable place to resettle freed American slaves. After several failed attempts at gaining the agreement of local chiefs, officials of the American Colonization Society (ACS) forced a treaty upon a local king at Cape Mesurado. Despite resistance by the indigenous people, settlement went ahead, and in April 1822, an expedition with the first group of Black American settlers arrived at Providence Island in present-day Monrovia. Within a short time, under the leadership of the American Jehudi Ashmun, the foundations for a country were established. Additional settlements were founded along the coast, notably at Greenville and Harper. Perhaps unsurprisingly, given their extremely brutal background, the former slaves' first action was to subjugate all the 'natives', forcing thousands to work as slaves for the ruling caste and laying the groundwork for decades of war a century and a half later.

A Shaky Independence

In 1846 the settlement at Cape Mesurado merged with others along the coast, and, settling on the name Liberia ('land of the

LIBERIA

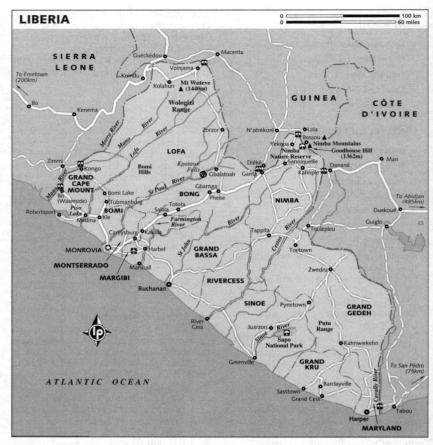

free'), made a declaration of independence the following year, becoming the first independent republic in Africa. Fatally for its future history, citizenship excluded indigenous peoples and was extended only to the tiny number of freed slaves, estimated to be about 3000 people. Joseph Roberts was elected the first president, and every successive president until 1980 was of American freed-slave ancestry.

By the mid-19th century, about half of the 3000 Black Americans who had originally migrated to Liberia had either died or returned to the USA. The remaining settlers, the citizens of the new republic, came to be known as Americo-Liberians. They saw themselves as part of a mission to bring civilisation and Christianity to Africa, and although constituting only a tiny fraction of Liberia's total population, they dominated the indigenous peoples. The Masonic Order, established in the country in 1851, came to be a symbol of Americo-Liberian solidarity, and five presidents, starting with Roberts, were grand masters.

For nearly a century, Liberia foundered economically and politically while indigenous populations continued to be repressed, suffering under a form of forced labour that anywhere else would have been called slavery. In 1930 Britain and the USA cut off diplomatic relations for five years because of the sale of human labour to Spanish colonialists in what was then Fernando Po (now Bioko in Equatorial Guinea).

The Golden Years?

The True Whig Party was the only legal political group for much of Liberia's history. Despite the country's labour-recruitment policies, the party was able to project an image of Liberia as Africa's most stable country. During William Tubman's presidency (1944–71), this led to massive foreign investment, and for several decades following WWII Liberia sustained sub-Saharan Africa's highest growth rate. Firestone and other American companies made major investments and Tubman earned praise as the 'maker of modern Liberia'. In the 1960s, iron ore–mining operations began near Yekepa by Lamco (Liberian-American Swedish Minerals Company), which became the largest private enterprise in sub-Saharan Africa.

The influx of foreign money soon began to distort the economy, resulting in exacerbation of social inequalities and increased hostility between Americo-Liberians and the indigenous population. Viewing this development with alarm, Tubman was forced to concede that the indigenous people would have to be granted some political and economic involvement in the country, including the franchise. Until this point (1963), 97% of the population had been denied voting rights.

William Tolbert succeeded Tubman as president in 1971. While Tolbert initiated a series of reforms, the government continued to be controlled by about a dozen related Americo-Liberian families and corruption was rampant. Tolbert established diplomatic relations with Communist countries such as the People's Republic of China, and at home clamped down on opposition.

Coup d'Etat & Years of Darkness

Resentment of these policies and of growing government corruption grew. In 1979 several demonstrators were shot in protests against a proposed increase in rice prices. Finally, in April 1980, Tolbert was overthrown in a coup led by a master sergeant, Samuel Doe. In the accompanying fighting, Tolbert and many high-ranking ministers were killed. For the first time, Liberia had a ruler who wasn't an Americo-Liberian, giving the indigenous population a taste of political power and an opportunity for vengeance. The 28-year-old Doe shocked the world by ordering 13 ex-ministers to be publicly executed on a beach in Monrovia. Despite the euphoria, Doe had no idea how to rule, surrounding himself with members of his own clan and accumulating vast sums of money at the population's expense.

Although the coup gave power to the indigenous population, it was condemned by most other African countries and by Liberia's other allies and trading partners. Over the next few years, relations with neighbouring African states gradually thawed. However, the post-coup flight of capital, coupled with ongoing corruption, caused Liberia's economy to rapidly decline. During the 1980s, real incomes fell by half, the unemployment rate in Monrovia rose to 50% and electricity blackouts became common.

Doe struggled to maintain his grip on power by any means available, including an election held in 1985 that was widely regarded as a sham, largely to appease his major creditor, the USA. By the late 1980s, however, it was clear that opposition forces had had enough. Following a foiled post-election coup attempt, members of Doe's Krahn tribe began killing and torturing rival tribespeople, particularly the Gio and Mano in Nimba County.

Civil War

On Christmas Eve 1989, several hundred rebels led by Charles Taylor (former head of the Doe government's procurement agency) invaded Nimba County from Côte d'Ivoire. Doe's troops arrived shortly thereafter and indiscriminately killed hundreds of unarmed civilians, raped women and burnt villages. Thousands fled into Côte d'Ivoire and Guinea.

Shortly after the invasion, Prince Johnson of the Gio tribe broke away from Taylor and formed his own rebel group. By mid-1990, Taylor's forces controlled most of the country, while Johnson's guerrillas had seized most of Monrovia; Doe was holed up with loyal troops in his mansion. Meanwhile, Liberia lay in ruins. Refugees were streaming into neighbouring countries, US warships were anchored off the coast and an Ecowas (Economic Community of West African States) peacekeeping force was despatched in an attempt to keep the warring factions apart.

It was all to no avail. Refusing to surrender or even step down as president, Doe and many of his supporters were finally wiped out by Johnson's forces, including Doe's brutal end (filmed for posterity) in which his ears were cut off as he knelt tied up before

LIBERIA

Johnson and refused to give up his private bank account number.

With both Johnson and Taylor claiming the presidency, Ecowas forces installed their own candidate, political-science professor Amos Sawyer, as head of the Interim Government of National Unity (IGNU). Meanwhile, Taylor's National Patriotic Front of Liberia (NPFL) forces continued to occupy about 90% of the country, while remnants of Doe's former army and Johnson's followers were encamped within Monrovia itself.

Peace Accords but No Peace

After a brutal assault by Taylor on Monrovia in October 1992, Ecowas increased its forces and in August 1993 the protagonists finally hammered out the Cotonou Agreement peace accord. This called for the installation of a six-month transitional government representing IGNU, NPFL and the third major player, Ulimo (United Liberation Movement for Democracy), Doe's former soldiers. When its mandate expired in September 1994 a new agreement, the Akosombo Amendment, was signed but then later rejected.

In August 1995, yet another peace agreement (the Abuja Accord) was signed by leaders of the main warring factions. This one lasted until April 1996, when fighting erupted in Monrovia between NPFL and Ulimo, resulting in widespread looting and damage.

August 1996 saw the negotiation of an amended Abuja Accord, providing for a ceasefire, disarmament and demobilisation, followed by elections. Despite serious ceasefire violations and an incomplete disarmament process, elections took place in July. Charles Taylor and his National Patriotic Party (NPP) won an overwhelming majority (75%).

Following the elections, life began to resume its normal rhythms, yet the political scene remained tenuous. By late 1998, all former faction leaders except Taylor were living in exile and power became increasingly consolidated in the presidency. In 1999 dissident groups led by the Liberians United for Reconciliation and Democracy (LURD) launched armed incursions in Lofa County near the Guinean border, setting off a new round of low-level fighting. The peace was further shattered with devastating outbreaks of fighting in 2002 and 2003. Finally, in August 2003, with LURD and other groups controlling much of the country, and under pressure from the inter-national community, Charles Taylor went into exile in Nigeria. A transitional government was established, headed by local businessman Charles Gyude Bryant and assisted by UN peacekeepers.

In late 2005 Liberians again went to the polls. In a hotly contested run-off vote between former World Bank economist Ellen Johnson-Sirleaf and international soccer star George Weah, Johnson-Sirleaf won the presidency, thereby also becoming the first woman to be elected president anywhere in Africa.

Liberia Today

Universally referred to as 'Ellen', President Johnson-Sirleaf remains an important national figurehead for the Liberian people to rally around, and although many are frustrated with the pace of change in the country, she remains a popular leader. The challenges that face Liberia are enormous, however, and many people are privately worried about the president's health (she is over 70 years old) and whether she'll be fit enough to see out her term, which doesn't end until 2012.

Many progressive measures have been taken in the past few years to overcome the wounds of the Civil War, including the introduction of free elementary schooling throughout the country. Perhaps most significant is the establishment of the Truth and Reconciliation Commission of Liberia, which, on the South African model, seeks to honestly and openly come to terms with the crimes committed over two decades of war.

Meanwhile, Charles Taylor was deported to the Hague in 2006, where he is currently on trial for 650 counts of war crimes and crimes against humanity – ironically, for his role in Sierra Leone's civil war rather than for any of the atrocities he is alleged to have committed in Liberia.

The UN, its military force UNMIL (UN Mission in Liberia) and a host of international NGOs run large parts of Liberia still, but change has been significant, and even though there's a huge distance still to go, Liberians are cautiously optimistic about the future.

THE CULTURE
The National Psyche

Liberians are a conservative and reserved people in comparison with their West African neighbours. Unlike elsewhere in the region, few people will initiate conversation with you or even smile at you initially, although don't mistake this for unfriendliness. Once you've said hello, the smiles and conversation begin to flow.

Most of all, Liberians are resilient. Despite all the suffering, there's a remarkable air of peppiness, especially on the streets of Monrovia, and a sense of cautious hope that the time has finally come to rise up from the ashes and start rebuilding.

One other defining factor in Liberia's national psyche is the longstanding division between Americo-Liberians ('Congos' in local parlance) and the indigenous population. The inequalities and sense of separateness that have existed since the country's earliest days (see p455) continue to shadow political and economic life.

Population

With about 30 persons per sq km, Liberia is one of the least densely populated of West Africa's coastal countries. Monrovia is the only real city, with other population centres elsewhere along the coast, in the centre near Gbarnga and Ganta, in the northwest near the Sierra Leone border and in the southeast near Harper. Elsewhere, large tracts of the country are completely uninhabited or have only very scattered populations.

The population of about 3.3 million consists overwhelmingly of people of indigenous origin belonging to more than a dozen major tribal groups. These include the Kpelle in the centre, the Bassa around Buchanan, the Krahn in the southeast, the Mandingo (also called Mandinka) in the north and the Kru along the coast. The Kpelle and the Bassa together make up just over one-third of the population, while Americo-Liberians account for barely 5% of the total. There's also a large Lebanese community in Monrovia, whose disproportionate economic power (they run many hotels, restaurants and other businesses) is often cause for resentment. In turn, there's resentment among the 4000-strong Lebanese community that they are banned from becoming citizens – almost uniquely in the world today, Liberia confers citizenship on the basis of race, extending it only to 'Negroes or persons of Negro descent', depriving the long-established Lebanese community of their rights to vote and to own land.

SPORT

Liberian soccer – long a national passion – gained worldwide attention with the rise of George Weah to become FIFA world player of the year in 1995. Since retiring, Weah has kept himself busy as coach and sponsor of Liberia's national team, the Lone Stars, as well as by campaigning for president and serving as a UN goodwill ambassador. His personal following in the country is almost as great as that for the sport itself.

RELIGION

Religious fervour is strong in Liberia. This is particularly evident on New Year's Eve, when many churches stay open throughout the night, filled with singing and praying Liberians, and on Sunday, when services are invariably packed. Close to half of the population is Christian and about 20% is Muslim, with the remainder following traditional religions.

ARTS
Film

Since peace a slew of films about Liberia have been produced. Most remarkable is *Johnny Mad Dog*, a 2008 Franco-Belgo-Liberian coproduction filmed in Liberia and starring former child combatants. The gruesome story of two children's struggle for survival during the Civil War is both gripping and deeply disturbing.

Two compelling 2008 documentaries include *Pray the Devil Back to Hell*, the story of the female-led peace movement in Liberia, and *Sliding Liberia*, an offbeat documentary about Liberia's first surfer. Both are excellent introductions to very different aspects of the country.

Sculpture

Liberia has long been famed for its masks, which hold religious as well as artistic significance, and were used for entertainment as well as to teach traditional values. The Gio in Nimba County in the northeast have some particularly rich traditions, including the *gunyege* mask, which shelters a power-giving spirit, and the *kagle* mask, which resembles a chimpanzee. The Bassa around Buchanan are renowned for their *gela* masks, which often have elaborately carved coiffures, always with an odd number of plaits.

LIBERIA

ENVIRONMENT
The Land

Liberia, which occupies a very wet 111,000-sq-km patch of the West African coastline, is just under half the size of the UK. Its humid and low-lying coastal plain is intersected by countless marshes and tidal lagoons, and bisected by at least nine major rivers, the largest of which is the St Paul. Inland is a densely forested plateau rising to low mountains in the northeast, in Lofa and Nimba counties. The highest point in the country is Mt Wuteve (1440m), near Voinjama. Mt Nimba (1752m), near Yekepa, is actually higher but is shared between Liberia, Guinea and Côte d'Ivoire.

Plants & Wildlife

Liberia's rainforests host an amazing diversity of birds, plants and other wildlife, including forest elephants, supremely rare pygmy hippos, various antelope species, and even leopards, as well as West African chimpanzees and numerous other primates. Sapo National Park alone is home to over 500 bird species.

National Parks

Liberia's only fully protected area is Sapo National Park (see the boxed text, p468) in the far southeast of the country. In 2003 the Nimba Nature Reserve was declared, near the borders with Guinea and Côte d'Ivoire, and contiguous with the Guinean-Côte d'Ivorian Mt Nimba Strict Nature Reserve (meaning no visitors are allowed). Sapo National Park is open to visitors, though there are no facilities operating at present.

Environmental Issues

Liberia is one of the last West African countries with significant areas of rainforest, although these now cover only about 40% of the land area, primarily near the Sierra Leone border and around Sapo National Park. Until recently, up to two dozen logging companies were operating in the country, primarily in the southeast, and large swaths of forest were cleared. The recent international timber trade sanctions have significantly halted this decimation, although only about 4% of Liberia's total forest cover is currently under protection, and effective regulation is weak.

On the brighter side, Liberia's forests are a critical part of the Guinean Forests of West Africa Hotspot – an exceptionally biodiverse area stretching across 11 countries in the region – and have attracted significant international attention, spearheaded by **Conservation International** (www.conservation.org), and its local partner, the **SCNL** (Society for the Conservation of Nature of Liberia; Map p461; ☎ 06 572 377; scnlib2001@yahoo.com; Monrovia Zoo, Larkpase). Among other endeavours, it has been working to bring at least 30% of Liberia's forest areas under protection, to curb poaching, and to protect endangered species, including the critically endangered Western chimpanzee.

FOOD & DRINK

Monrovia has an excellent array of dining options; elsewhere, you'll have to rely on rather basic shacks usually serving up one dish each day.

Traditional Liberian food consists of rice or a cassava-based staple (called *fufu, dumboy* or GB), which is eaten with a soup or sauce made with greens and palm oil, and sometimes also meat or fish. Other popular dishes include *togborgee* – a Lofa County speciality made with kittaly (a type of eggplant) or bitterbuoy (another local vegetable) and country soda – *palava* sauce (made with *plato* leaf, dried fish or meat and palm oil) and palm butter (a spicy sauce traditionally popular in the Maryland and Grand Kru counties, in the country's southern corner, and made from palm nuts).

MONROVIA

pop 1.01 million

Home to one in three Liberians, Monrovia in many ways *is* Liberia, a huge concatenation of villages, towns and slums that has grown and grown during decades of war to the point where it's the country's only true city and centre of almost all its economic and cultural life.

The centre of Monrovia retains a few elegant buildings, as well as its fair share of burnt-out shells and makeshift shops and housing. The overall impression is one of optimistic chaos, epitomised by the bustling Waterside Market, the city's mercantile heart. Here vast UN Land-Cruisers jostle with each other for space on the crowded streets and the colourful daily business of African life goes on just as it does anywhere else on the continent. Only sights such as the iconic Broken Bridge or the ruin of the

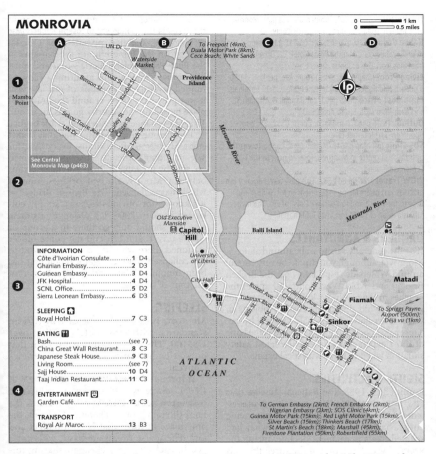

MONROVIA

0 ————— 1 km
0 ———— 0.5 miles

Mamba Point

UN Dr

Waterside Market

Benson St

Broad St

Randall St

To Freeport (4km);
Duala Motor Park (8km);
Cece Beach; White Sands

Providence Island

Sekou Toure Ave

UN Dr

Quiley St

Clinte St

Lynch St

Clay St

UN Dr

Camp Johnson Rd

Mesurado River

See Central
Monrovia Map (p463)

Old Executive
Mansion

Capitol
Hill

Balli Island

Mesurado River

University
of Liberia

Matadi

City Hall

Russel Ave

Coleman Ave
Cheeseman Ave

16th St

Fiamah

To Spriggs Payne
Airport (500m);
Déjà vu (1km)

Tubman Blvd

8

6

13

11

Warner Ave

Payne Ave

7

Sinkor

12

9

1

10

18th St

ATLANTIC
OCEAN

To German Embassy (2km); French Embassy (2km);
Nigerian Embassy (2km); SOS Clinic (4km);
Guinea Motor Park (15km); Red Light Motor Park (15km);
Silver Beach (15km); Thinkers Beach (17km);
St Martin's Beach (18km); Marshall (45km);
Firestone Plantation (50km); Robertsfield (55km)

INFORMATION
Côte d'Ivoirian Consulate...........1 D4
Ghanian Embassy......................2 D3
Guinean Embassy.....................3 D4
JFK Hospital..............................4 D4
SCNL Office..............................5 D4
Sierra Leonean Embassy...........6 D3

SLEEPING
Royal Hotel..............................7 C3

EATING
Bash.....................................(see 7)
China Great Wall Restaurant.......8 C3
Japanese Steak House................9 C3
Living Room...........................(see 7)
Sajj House..............................10 D4
Taaj Indian Restaurant.............11 C3

ENTERTAINMENT
Garden Café............................12 C3

TRANSPORT
Royal Air Maroc........................13 B3

Ducor Palace Hotel remind you that until recently this was a war zone.

ORIENTATION

The heart of town is Benson and Randall Sts, and along Broad St, all of which are busy with shoppers and hawkers from dusk till dawn. Southwest of here is Mamba Point is Monrovia's diplomatic enclave, and 1.5km to the southeast is Capitol Hill, where important ministries and the Capitol Building are located. Beyond that is Sinkor, which sprawls southeast until reaching Congo Town and Paynesville, home to Elwa Junction and Red Light Motor Park. On Monrovia's northern edge is Waterside Market, and beyond that, Freeport and Bushrod Island, home to the Duala Market. In the Mesurado River opposite Waterside Market is Providence Island, where the first expedition of freed American slaves landed in 1822.

INFORMATION

There's a reasonable selection of internet cafes in the town centre, including several on or around Broad St. This is also the best place to look for foreign-exchange bureaus and banks.

Charif Pharmacy (Map p463; ☎ 06 519 999; Randall St; ☼ 7.30am-7pm Mon-Sat) Has a good selection of European and US medicines.

EcoBank (Map p463; ☎ 06 553 915; Ashmun St; ☼ 8.30am-4pm Mon-Fri, 9am-2pm Sat) Foreign exchange and Western Union.

FedEx (Map p463; ☎ 06 975 284; Broad St) For anything important you need to send by mail.

JFK Hospital (Map p461; Tubman Blvd, Sinkor) Monrovia's main hospital, for dire emergencies only.

Karou Voyages (Map p463; ☎ 06 515 439; karou mlwkl@yahoo.com; Mamba Point Hotel, UN Drive) Flight bookings. Can also organise drivers.

Living Proof (Map p463; Sekou Toure Ave; per hr US$1.50; ✆ 9am-midnight Mon-Sat) Internet cafe with10 terminals.

Main post office (Map p463; cnr Randall & Ashmun Sts; ✆ 8am-4pm Mon-Fri, to noon Sat)

Outlook (Map p463; Randall St; per hr US$2; ✆ 8am-8pm Mon-Sat) Internet cafe.

SOS Clinic (off Map p461; Tubman Blvd, Congo Town) The best medical centre in Monrovia, located next to the No Lemon compound.

WOW Travel (☎ 06 841 582) This new travel agency (no office as yet) offers hiking expeditions to Mt Nimba, and trips to the beach and to Kpatawe Falls (p469). The owner, MD, is a mine of Liberia tourism information.

DANGERS & ANNOYANCES

It's now generally safe to walk around alone in Monrovia, although you should be very careful around Waterside (especially near the Broken Bridge) and avoid West Point and any of the beaches in town. Always keep your wits about you and avoid displaying cash or objects of value. After dark it's only safe to travel by car. This makes socialising difficult and is the bane of most expats' lives. Check the latest safety situation when in town with local expats.

SIGHTS & ACTIVITIES

Founded in 1958, the **National Museum** (Map p463; ☎ 06 498 488; Broad St; admission free, donation expected; ✆ 8am-4pm Mon-Fri) is a steadily improving entity, having been rescued from what had seemed like a permanent decline during the years of war. Only one of the three floors is currently open, but the display (including explanations sometimes stuck onto the exhibits with Post-it notes!) includes fetish objects from the Kru and Grebo peoples, local art, presidential paraphernalia, stone-hewn cult objects and traditional drums and masks. One display even contains fragments of a mortar that hit the building during the war.

The beautiful **Masonic Temple** (Map p463; Benson St) was once Monrovia's major landmark, and despite significant war damage it's still striking. Since most Masons were Americo-Liberian descendants of the original settlers, the Temple was a prominent symbol of previous regimes, and was vandalised after the 1980 coup, when the Masonic Order was banned. Today it's back in use as a Masonic lodge.

On the steep hill behind the Temple amid the trees is the **Monument to Joseph Roberts** (Map p463; Broad St), the first president of Liberia. Nearby on the same hill are the remains of the **Ducor Palace Hotel**, Liberia's first and most luxurious – now a ruin awaiting a Libyan-funded revamp. At the time of our last visit it was possible to look around the grand old place by asking the security guards for a tour. This may change as renovation work begins.

The chaotic and colourful **Waterside Market** (Map p463; Water St) offers almost everything for sale, including some attractive textiles (which are sold by the *lapa* or 2m). The market runs between Monrovia's two bridges, one of which has collapsed. The Broken Bridge, as it's known for obvious reasons, simply collapsed back in 2006. It's a dangerous area, and you should only go there in a group or with a driver, and befriend the police officer stationed there who will accompany you to the collapsed middle. Again, rebuilding has been announced, but work had yet to start at the time of writing.

SLEEPING

Monrovia is extremely expensive by African standards, with most hotels costing over US$100. The only real budget option that doesn't compromise safety is St Theresa's Convent.

St Theresa's Convent (Map p463; ☎ 06 784 276, 06 422 930; archdiocesanpastoralcenter@yahoo.com; Randall St; r with/without bathroom US$20/30, ste US$50) Thank the Lord (literally) for St Theresa's Convent, the only place in town that is both budget and safe. The sparse rooms are basic, with just a bed in each, the very cheapest sharing toilets and showers. Bring your own towels and mosquito nets, though sheets are provided. The most expensive room has air-con. Doors close for the night at 10.30pm, so this is not an option for revellers.

Metropolitan Hotel (Map p463; ☎ 06 472 977; Broad St; r/tw incl breakfast US$75/90; ✖) This place has a sleazy feel overall, but its 33 rooms are fine and good value by local standards, although they can be rather dark. Wi-fi is planned.

Tilda Guest House (Map p463; ☎ 06 699 232; www.tilda guesthouse.com; off UN Dr; s/d US$90/130; P ✖ ▢ �approx) This new, well-run compound is somewhere between a hotel and an apartment block. Each room has a private bathroom, TV and air-con, and shares a kitchen with neighbouring rooms as well as a comfortable communal sitting and

CENTRAL MONROVIA

0 — 300 m
0 — 0.2 miles

INFORMATION	
American Embassy	**1** A2
Bureau of Immigration	**2** C2
Charif Pharmacy	**3** C2
EcoBank	**4** C1
FedEx	**5** C2
Karou Voyages	(see 13)
Living Proof	**6** B3
Main Post Office	**7** C2
Outlook Internet	(see 29)

SIGHTS & ACTIVITIES	
Ducor Palace Hotel	(see 9)
Masonic Temple	**8** B1

Monument to Joseph	
Roberts	**9** B1
National Museum	**10** C2
Waterside Market	**11** C1

SLEEPING ⌂	
Cape Hotel	(see 13)
Krystal Oceanview	
Hotel	**12** B1
Mamba Point Hotel	**13** A2
Metropolitan Hotel	**14** C2
Palm Hotel	**15** C2
St Theresa's Convent	**16** B3
Tilda Guest House	**17** B3

EATING ⌂	
Abi Jaoudi	**18** B2
Bamboo Bar	(see 15)
Diana Restaurant	**19** C2
Evelyn's	**20** C2
First Food Center	**21** C2
Jamal's Pizza	**22** C2
La Pointe	**23** A1
Sidewalk Vendors	**24** B2
Stop & Shop	**25** B2
Sweet Lips	**26** B2

DRINKING	
Bamboo Bar	(see 15)

ENTERTAINMENT	
Metropolitan Hotel	
Disco	(see 14)

SHOPPING ⌂	
Craft Vendors	**27** A2
Craft Vendors	**28** A1
Waterside Market	(see 11)

TRANSPORT	
Aero	(see 29)
Brussels Airlines	**29** C2
Kenya Airways	**30** C2
Slok Air International	(see 30)

dining room. Wi-fi is an additional US$5 per day, and electricity comes on at 5pm.

ourpick Palm Hotel (Map p463; ☎ 06 535 177, 06 585 959; palmhotelmonrovia@yahoo.com; cnr Broad & Randall Sts; s/d incl breakfast US$91/139; ✂ ▢ 🗢) One of Monrovia's best-value options, the Palm is located in the very heart of the city, and the loud street-side rooms have balconies overlooking the bustle below. Despite this it's secure, clean and comfortable, with free in-room wi-fi and a great rooftop restaurant.

Royal Hotel (Map p461; ☎ 07 777 6925, 07 785 5333; www.royalhotelliberia.com; cnr 14th St & Tubman Blvd, Sinkor; s/d/ste incl breakfast US$150/175/190; ℗ ✂ ▢ 🗢) In the heart of bustling Sinkor, the Royal is another popular choice, especially with UN staff. The 30 small but pleasant rooms are fully

equipped. There are also apartments here for short-term let, and two excellent restaurants.

Cape Hotel (Map p463; ☎ 07 700 6633, 06 496 046; www.capehotel.com; UN Dr, Mamba Point; s/d incl breakfast US$150/200, ste US$175-250; ℗ ✂ ▢ 🗢) This newest addition to Monrovia's hotel scene is the city's best. Next door to the rather laurels-resting Mamba Point, the Cape offers up good breakfast espresso and sparkling-clean rooms, all with fridges, TV, phone and safe. Service is good, and the only disadvantage is that there's no pool. Reservations are essential.

Mamba Point Hotel (Map p463; ☎ 06 511 022, 06 544 544; www.mambapointhotel.com; UN Dr, Mamba Point; s/d/ste incl breakfast US$150/200/250; ℗ ✂ ▢ 🖳 🗢) This fortress-like establishment is home away from home to the business and diplomatic

LIBERIA

communities. Its 64 rooms are spacious and equipped with fridge, TV, phone and safe, although most are looking a bit tired these days. Recent refurbishments of the lobby and restaurant will, hopefully, now spread to the rooms. Sadly, while the food here is great, service is very lazy and the wi-fi is now charged (US$5 per day). On the plus side, there's a great free pool and tennis court across the road overlooking the beach. Reservations are recommended.

Krystal Oceanview Hotel (Map p463; ☎ 07 776 7676, 06 510 424; UN Dr, Mamba Point; r US$180, ste US$250-400; ⓟ ⌘ ⌨ ⌚) This 26-room Liberian-run hotel is well located near the sea and draws a loyal crowd for its spacious rooms and friendly service. The rates include internet access and laundry service – and there's a pricey but very pleasant restaurant-bar.

EATING

Due to its large and relatively well-paid expat community, Monrovia has some excellent eating options, all at a certain cost, of course.

Downtown

Sweet Lips (Map p463; Newport St; meals US$1.50-2.50; ⊗ 11am-9pm Mon-Sat) This firm favourite is said to serve up the very best Liberian food in town. Take a seat among the plastic flowers and try the excellent *fufu* rice and palm butter.

Jamal's Pizza (Map p463; ☎ 06 544 100; Center St; mains US$5-15; ⊗ breakfast, lunch & dinner) This place is great for brunch – its pancakes are Monrovia's best. Pies, pizza, burgers and sandwiches also feature. It also delivers.

Evelyn's (Map p463; 06 710 104; Broad St; mains US$7-12; ⊗ 7.30am-11pm Mon-Sat) This spotless oasis of air-conditioned calm is a great haven from the chaos of Broad St. The food is excellent, particularly the Liberian dishes, although there's a wide range of foreign classics as well.

Diana Restaurant (Map p463; ☎ 04 723 333, 05 623 333; Center St; meals US$8-20; ⊗ 7.30am-11pm) This small, no-frills place is a big favourite among locals and expats alike. The menu features Lebanese dishes, Asian food, sandwiches and pizza. Free delivery is available.

First Food Center (Map p463; ☎ 06 513 525; Gurley St; meals US$10-20) This gem of a place, known also as 'Mama Susu's', is thought by many to have some of the best food in town. Barracuda steak and garlic shrimps were both excellent when we visited. The air-conditioned space is

vibrantly decorated with local art, and service is friendly.

Bamboo Bar (Map p463; ☎ 05 618 618; Palm Hotel, cnr Broad & Randall Sts; mains US$10-25; ⊗ breakfast, lunch & dinner) This rooftop restaurant has a bird's-eye view over the chaos of downtown Monrovia, plus a convivial atmosphere and a good selection of Lebanese food, pizzas and grills. There's live music at the weekend.

La Pointe (Map p463; ☎ 06 510 587; UN Dr, Mamba Point; mains US$10-30; ⊗ noon-4pm & 6-10pm) The views over Mamba Point's dramatic drop-off to the sea are incredible, so La Pointe is well worth a detour for a cold drink on the terrace or for the excellent daily buffet lunch (US$20 per person).

Sinkor

Sajj House (Map p461; ☎ 06 830 888; Tubman Blvd; mains US$5-10; ⊗ 9am-10pm) Monrovia's most celebrated Lebanese restaurant is Sajj, where the zatar is famous but you can give the falafel a miss. The house specialities are the pies, which are delicious. Seating is under rattan thatch in the compound's front yard.

Taaj Indian Restaurant (Map p461; ☎ 07 777 6666, 06 510 078; 5th St; mains US$8-10; ⊗ noon-3pm & 6.30-11pm; Ⓥ) Another Monrovia mainstay, Taaj offers up delicious Indian food in a hangar-like building where live music is performed on Friday evening. Try the kadai chicken, the house speciality. There's also a large vegetarian selection, and the Sunday brunch buffet is very popular.

Bash (Map p461; ☎ 07 750 3930; Royal Hotel, Tubman Blvd, Sinkor; mains US$10-22) This smart place is a real charmer, housed in a large, blissfully cool, high-roofed barn behind the Royal Hotel. The mixed international menu includes shrimp tempura with ponzu sauce and *filet Cordon Bleu*, as well as Lebanese dishes and pizza.

China Great Wall Restaurant (Map p461; ☎ 05 888 778; Tubman Blvd, mains US$10-25; ⊗ 10am-10pm) Opposite the hotel of the same name, this is Monrovia's best Chinese eatery. While it feels rather sterile, the food is good.

Japanese Steak House (Map p461; ☎ 06 490 220; Tubman Blvd; mains US$14-20; ⊗ 10am-11.30pm) The menu at this bizarre place alone makes it worth a visit – the choice is meat, meat or meat, from 'flesh around the eyes' to 'brain of the cow' and nonspecific 'abdominal meat'. Get a private booth for full camp effect.

Living Room (Map p461; ☎ 06 850 333; Royal Hotel, cnr Tubman Blvd & 14th St; sushi US$3-10, mains from US$15;

ⓨ lunch & dinner) Celebrated by expats for its transcendent tuna salad, Monrovia's top sushi bar feels very glamorous, with smart leather chairs, sleek black tables and a gleaming sushi counter. Take away is available.

Self-Catering
Self-caterers can try the well-stocked **Abi Jaoudi** (Map p463; Randall St; ⓨ 8am-7pm Mon-Fri), between Sekou Touré Ave and Benson St, which sells everything from French cheese and croissants to wine and liquors, or **Stop & Shop** (Map p463; Randall St; ⓨ 8am-6pm), nearby, with a range of US products.

Sidewalk vendors along Benson St sell a colourful array of fruit, vegetables and freshwater prawns.

DRINKING & ENTERTAINMENT
For drinks, the Bamboo Bar (opposite) is a favourite at any hour, and has live music on Saturday evening.

Popular nightspots include the disco at the Metropolitan Hotel (p462), where entry to the bar is free, but there's a cover to go next door onto the dance floor. Go upstairs to find the 'secret' cocktail lounge – also free. For dancing, head to **Déjà vu** (Map p461; Airfield Bypass; ⓨ Wed-Sun), around midnight, which is the expat hangout of choice and offers free entry to UN and NGO personnel on Friday but charges US$15 on Saturday. There's also **Garden Café** (Map p461; 14th St; ⓨ Fri & Sat), where there's live music on Friday (the best night to go) and a host of prostitutes.

SHOPPING
Vendors near the US embassy sell everything from wooden masks to baskets and textiles. Other places to shop for crafts include the vendors opposite Mamba Point Hotel and in Waterside Market (near Gurley St; it also sells textiles).

For custom-made African clothes, try the tailors along Benson St near the Randall St junction.

GETTING THERE & AWAY
Air
Flights arrive at **Roberts International Airport** (Robertsfield), 60km southeast of Monrovia, as well as at the smaller Spriggs Payne Airport (Code: MLW) in Sinkor.

For details on flights to/from Monrovia see p473.

Bush Taxi & Minibus
Bush taxis for Tubmanburg and the Sierra Leone border leave from Duala Motor Park, 9km northeast of the town centre. Transport for most other domestic destinations leaves from Red Light Motor Park, Monrovia's main motor park, 15km northeast of the centre. Nearby Guinea Motor Park is where to head for buses to Guinea and Côte d'Ivoire.

GETTING AROUND
To/From the Airport
Roberts International Airport (Robertsfield) is 60km southeast of Monrovia. Going into Monrovia taxis charge around US$40, while taking a taxi from Monrovia to the airport should set you back around US$20. Note that there are sometimes no taxis at the airport and for safety as much as anything else, it's much better to arrange a pick-up in advance with your hotel. Some airlines operate a shuttle bus to their downtown offices – ask when you book.

Taxi
Shared taxis are the main public transport, and are generally safe to catch on the street. When doing private taxi hire it's best to get the number of a trusted driver - ask expats or at any hotel.

AROUND MONROVIA

BEACHES
There are some beautiful beaches stretching south and north of Monrovia, which fill up with locals and foreign residents on weekends. Before jumping in, get local advice, as currents can be quite dangerous. One of the most popular is **Silver Beach**, about 15km southeast of central Monrovia off the airport road. There's a restaurant here, a small volleyball court, craft vendors, shower and toilets, and chairs and umbrellas for hire. About 2km further south is **Thinkers Beach**, also with a small restaurant, shower and toilets. **St Martin's Beach**, just beyond Thinkers Beach, is quiet and isolated, with no facilities, and is good for getting away from the crowds.

About 45 minutes further southeast is **Marshall**, where the Junk, Farmington and Little Bassa Rivers meet the sea. It boasts a lagoon and a deserted stretch of beach.

Heading east out of Monrovia in the direction of the now ruined Hotel Africa, two more

LIBERIA

attractive beaches can be found – **Cece Beach** and **White Sands**.

FIRESTONE PLANTATION

Firestone – the world's largest rubber plantation – was established in 1926 when the Firestone tyre company secured one million acres of land in Liberia at an annual rent of only US$0.06 per acre. In its heyday, the company employed 20,000 workers, more than 10% of Liberia's labour force; Liberia was once known as the Firestone Republic.

After lying dormant during the war, Firestone is again operating, although at reduced capacity. There are no regular tours, but you can usually find employees on the grounds who can show you around and explain the tapping process. Stick to the beaten path, as Firestone is one of several areas in Liberia where land mines have been found.

The plantation is in Harbel, near Robertsfield International Airport. You'll need private transport to get here.

THE COAST

Liberia's wild and heavily vegetated coastline is broken only by occasional towns and fishing villages, and numerous major rivers. Infrastructure is nonexistent. The coastal road is passable as far as Greenville, from where you'll need to head up and around along the rugged inland route to Harper.

ROBERTSPORT

If you only visit one place outside Monrovia, make it lovely Robertsport, Liberia's closest thing to a beach resort, northwest of the capital. Don't come worried about package-tour crowds, though – with just two hotels and one restaurant, this idyllic spot is the last word in remote for surfers searching for the perfect break and beach lovers looking to chill out on golden sands. The drive here alone is quite lovely – the tarmac ends at the town of Medina, but a decent UNMIL-maintained dirt road wends its way gloriously through the wild countryside and down a long spit of land with Piso Lake on one side and the Atlantic on the other. During the rainy season, the road can be impassable due to flooding, so check in Monrovia before setting out.

Fantastic, eco-friendly **Nana Lodge** (☎ 06 668 332, 06 852 394; tent sleeping 4 incl breakfast US$100) is right on the beach and an excellent deal if you share your tent with a friend or two. Each tent has two double beds as well as its own beach-facing raised terrace and fan. There's a good restaurant (US$10 per meal) and bar right on the beach here. During the week it's usually empty, but it can often be booked weeks in advance for the weekend as it's a favourite spot for Monrovia's expats, so reserve in plenty of time. The other option in town is the decent **Wakolor Guest House** (☎ 06 925 259, 06 535 873; r US$35-40) opposite the UNMIL barracks, which has 10 comfortable double rooms with shared bathrooms. The town's only other restaurant is **Tata's Restaurant** (meals US$1.20; ☯ 10am-10pm), to one side of the Wakolor Guest House.

BUCHANAN

Lively, laid-back Buchanan is Liberia's second port and the capital of Grand Bassa County. There are some attractive beaches here and a colourful market but otherwise nothing to draw travellers in particular, although a large Fanti community, most of whom live in the lively Fanti Town fishing village, make this a surprisingly diverse place – a small piece of Ghana in Liberia.

Southeast of the port are some attractive (and cleaner) beaches. To reach them, follow the port road to the old Lamco Compound, then ask locals the way.

The town boasts the unusually excellent **Sparks Hotel** (☎ 06 452 781, 06 523 732; cnr Church & Gardner Sts; r US$75-125; ☒) near the beach, which boasts 15 large, well-equipped and clean rooms with electricity from 7pm to 7am. There's also a good but pricey restaurant (mains US$10 to US$20, open 6pm-midnight) and bar downstairs. The budget eating option is the popular EK Bar & Restaurant on Tubman Blvd (US$2 to US$4 for mains).

Getting There & Away

Bush taxis run daily to Monrovia (US$6.50, three hours). From Monrovia, it's better to get one at Elwa Junction than at the hectic Red Light Motor Park.

During the dry season, at least several vehicles travel weekly from Buchanan to River Cess. It's also possible to take a fishing boat, although these are notoriously unsafe. Boats leave from Fanti Town and from near the fish market just west of the town centre.

Bush taxis for all destinations depart from the main taxi stand near the market; some also

BUCHANAN

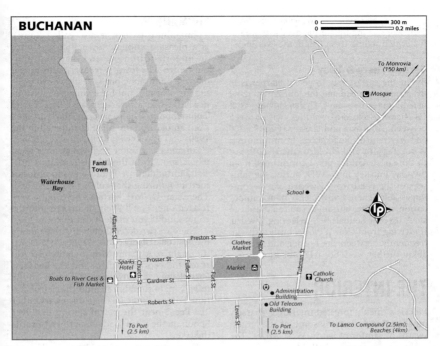

0 — 300 m
0 — 0.2 miles

To Monrovia (150 km)

Mosque

Fanti Town

Waterhouse Bay

School

Atlantic St

Preston St

Clothes Market

4th St

Sparks Hotel

Church St

Prosser St

Fuller St

Market

Tubman St

Catholic Church

Boats to River Cess & Fish Market

Gardner St

Fort St

Administration Building

Old Telecom Building

Roberts St

Lewis St

To Port (2.5 km)

To Port (2.5 km)

To Lamco Compound (2.5km); Beaches (4km)

leave from the junction on the Monrovia road several kilometres northeast of town.

GREENVILLE

Greenville (also known as Sinoe) is the capital of Sinoe County, and a former port and logging centre. On the edge of town is a beach, but to reach the open sea you'll need to cross a shallow lagoon.

Greenville is also the jumping-off point for excursions to Sapo National Park, though you'll need your own vehicle as there's no public transport; see the boxed text, p468.

The main route between Monrovia and Greenville is via Buchanan along the rough coastal road. Otherwise, the only route is via Zwedru. There's also an occasional boat service from Monrovia.

HARPER

Harper (sometimes referred to as Cape Palmas) is the capital of Maryland, which has long had a reputation as Liberia's most progressive county; until 1857 it was even a separate republic. In contrast with much of the rest of the country, where indigenous populations were severely repressed, settlers in Harper worked to cultivate a more cooperative relationship with the local residents. In the town centre is a monument commemorating the original accord between settlers and locals. Harper was also the seat of Liberia's first university (Cuttington, later transferred to Gbarnga), and the country's educational centre.

Now the town is just a shell of its former self. Only ruins remain of the many fine old houses that once graced Harper's streets, including former president William Tubman's mansion, but somehow Harper has managed to remain a charming, laid-back place, a large city now depopulated to feel more like a small town and a great introduction to Liberia if you're arriving from Côte d'Ivoire.

Adina's Guest House (☎ 06 620 005; r US$20) is the town's best-established hotel, which has several basic rooms with fans. A better option is to call local businessman **Jimmy Anderson** (☎ 06 685 913, 06 418 144), who rents out rooms of much better quality than Adina's. For food, head along Maryland Ave towards the main crossroads in the town centre known universally as 'the 18'. Here you'll find **Sophie's Spot** (mains US$1.50-2), serving up simple meals, as well as fishermen selling fresh fish in the evening.

Getting There & Away

By far the easiest way to get to Harper is to fly, as roads are bad and the journey overland usually takes two days. **Elysian Airlines** (☎ 06 444 747; www.elysianairlines.com) flies twice a week between Monrovia and Harper (US$175/200 one-way/return). Road access from Monrovia is via Tappita and Zwedru, then southeast to the coast. Under good conditions, it's a two-day journey in a 4WD; during the rainy season the road from Zwedru can become impassable. There's now plenty of accommodation en route, although you're advised to stock up on essentials before leaving Zwedru. If arriving from Côte d'Ivoire, bush taxis run frequently between the border and Harper, 20km further west. See p473 for more.

THE INTERIOR

Liberia's thickly forested interior is sparsely inhabited and contains some of the largest swaths of rainforest left in West Africa. The main transport route is the Ganta corridor, a largely tarmac road from Monrovia all the way to the Guinean border.

TUBMANBURG

Tubmanburg (which is also called Bomi), is a pleasant enough town that was once an important iron-ore and diamond mining centre. The town is recovering from war damage admirably, but is really worth visiting for nearby Bomi Lake, an absolute stunner in the hills a well-signposted 4km beyond Tubmanburg. The semi-crater lake, created from an old iron ore mine abandoned in the 1980s and also known as Blue Lake, has very clean and clear water and makes for a great picnic spot. Even though swimming is officially forbidden, we found a group of locals merrily ignoring that rule when we visited. There's an UNMIL barracks here, but a very relaxed one. You'll likely be invited into the compound if you make it out this way.

There are two decent hotels in Tubmanburg, the **Bomi Guest House** (☎ 06 452 679; r US$10-20), on the main road from Monrovia before you reach the centre of town, and the **Red Cross Guest House** (☎ 04 919 363; r US$10), right on the town's main junction behind the petrol station. For very basic Liberian dishes, try either Tee Pee 2 near the petrol station or Silver Spoon on the main road out of town towards the lake.

Bush taxis cost US$3 to Monrovia. There is also occasional transport to the Sierra Leone border, usually via Bo (Waterside).

SAPO NATIONAL PARK

Sapo, Liberia's only national park, is a lush 1808-sq-km tract containing some of West Africa's last remaining primary rainforest, as well as forest elephants, pygmy hippos, chimpanzees, antelopes and other wildlife, although these populations suffered greatly during the final years of fighting at the hands of both refugees and rebels who had moved into the park. Large swaths of nearby forest, as well as some forest areas within the park itself, were also felled.

There are still war refugees living in Sapo despite a big drive in recent years to totally clear the park. Work is now getting started on rebuilding infrastructure, including park headquarters, and on enforcing its protected status. Agro-forestry projects are slowly being recommenced in the 1.6km-wide buffer zone surrounding the park, and efforts are ongoing to increase community involvement in park management.

Currently, there are no commercial tours into Sapo, though it's still perfectly possible to visit. The best contact for updated information is SCNL (p460). Allow a full day to reach Sapo from Monrovia by 4WD along the road paralleling the coast, and at least two days going via Zwedru. Following the coastal road, once at Greenville, head 60km north to Juarzon and then 5km southeast to Jalay's Town in the park's buffer zone. From here it's 1.5km further on foot to the park boundary, on the opposite side of Pahneh Creek (a tributary of the Sinoe River). Once at the park, you can arrange guided hikes and canoe rides, but you'll have to bring all your own food and camping gear as there is nowhere onsite to stay.

In addition to SCNL, you can obtain information on Sapo through fpi@forestpartnersinter national.org.

SECRET SOCIETIES

Liberia is famous for its secret societies, called *poro* for men and *sande* for women. They are found throughout the country, except in the southeast, and they are especially strong in the northwest. Each society has a wealth of rites and ceremonies that are used to educate young people in tribal ways, folklore and general life skills, and they continue to be a major force in preserving Liberia's traditional culture.

Many rituals centre on initiations into adulthood, which traditionally involved up to four years of training, though these days the time is usually shorter. If you're lucky enough to spend time in the countryside, you may see initiates, who are easily recognised by their white-painted faces and bodies and shaved heads.

Within the societies, there's usually a strong pecking order, with lower-ranking members forbidden from sharing in the special knowledge of higher-ranking members or attending their secret meetings. The most extreme example of these hierarchies is the *poro* among the Vai, with up to 99 levels. Ascending in the ranks depends on a combination of birth (with leadership sometimes restricted to certain families), seniority and savvy in mastering traditional beliefs and rituals.

The secret societies shape not only religious rituals and education but also community life, with *zoes* (*poro* society leaders) wielding significant political influence. The societies also control the activities of traditional medicinal practitioners, and are used to settle disputes or to levy punishments. A village chief who doesn't have the support of the *poro* on important decisions can expect trouble enforcing them.

GBARNGA

During the war years, Gbarnga (pronounced 'Banga') gained notoriety as Charles Taylor's centre of operations, and became virtually the second capital of Liberia. Today its prominence has faded, but it remains a major town, and is easily reached on tarmac from Monrovia.

There's no real reason to stop in the town itself, but the must-see here is the Kpatawe Falls, 18km off the main road from the town of Phebe, 10km southwest of Gbarnga. Take the dirt road opposite Phebe Hospital to get here, where you can swim or hike up through the forest to the waterfalls higher up. It's well worth the detour and is one of Liberia's most picturesque spots.

Sleeping & Eating

SAT Guest House (☎ 06 439 651; r US$10-20) If you need to stay the night in Gbarnga, head for this large place at the entrance to town. There are 12 rooms, most with rudimentary bathrooms, and a nightclub, bar and restaurant onsite too.

CooCoo Nest (☎ 06 511 511; r US$60-90) This eccentric place is on the main road about 60km southwest of Gbarnga between Totota and Salala. It was former president Tubman's private residence and its name supposedly comes from Tubman's pet name for his young daughter. Rooms are reasonably spacious, and there's a restaurant run by the same management across the road.

Paulman's (fish meals US$2.50) At Gbarnga's main crossroads, delicious meals of spicy fish and ice-cold beers are served up to a crowd of loyal locals.

Getting There & Away

Bush taxis go frequently from Gbarnga to Monrovia (US$8, six hours). Taxis from Gbarnga to Phebe Junction (US$0.60) leave from the taxi union parking lot at the top of the hill just off the highway.

GANTA

Bustling and unassuming Ganta (officially called Gompa City) is just 2km from the Guinean border. For diversion, there's a busy **market**, and an intriguing, angular white **mosque** that boasts attractively decorated minarets made up of carved stars. Western Union transfers are available at EcoBank on the main road. There's nothing else to detain you.

Alvino Hotel (☎ 04 931 621; Guinea Rd; r with/without air-con US$35/50; ❄) is the best place in town, a secure hotel and restaurant with a recently built annexe at the back with air-conditioned rooms. This is also the best place in Ganta to eat (meals are US$5 to US$10). Look for the signpost to the hotel off the main road.

LIBERIA

TALKING DRUMS

One of Liberia's best-known traditional instruments – although it's not uniquely Liberian – is the 'talking drum'. It looks like an hourglass, with the upper and lower ends connected by tension strings. When the drummer compresses the strings while holding the drum under one arm next to his body, the pitch of the drum increases, producing a variable tone and giving the drum its name. Talking drums are generally beaten with a stick, rather than with the hands.

Getting There & Around

Bush taxis leave regularly from south of the market to Gbarnga (US$3, 1½ hours) and Monrovia (US$9, five hours). From north of the market bush taxis head to Sanniquellie (US$2.50, one hour) and to the Guinean border at Yekepa (US$5.50). Irregular bush taxis go to Tappita and Zwedru.

Bush taxis or motorbike rides from the centre to the Guinean border cost US$0.40; from the border there's daily transport to Diéké (US$1).

SANNIQUELLIE

The bustling market town of Sanniquellie has a disproportionately big place in history as the birthplace of the Organisation of African Unity. Along the main road into town you can see the building where William Tubman, Guinea's Sekou Touré and Ghana's Kwame Nkrumah met in 1957 to discuss a union of African states – an idea that was formalised the next year with the drafting of a preliminary charter. The compound is now used to house official visitors.

Ordinary folk should head for **Jackie's Guest House** (☎ 07 796 7474), signposted from the main road. At the time of writing it was only for employees of the mining company BHP Billiton but was shortly to reopen as a guest house.

The best eating option is the Club Universe Restaurant, on your right on the main street before you come to the market if you're entering the town from Monrovia.

Getting There & Away

For details of buses to Guinea and Côte d'Ivoire from here, see p473. Bush taxis and shared taxis heading south for Gbarnga

(US$3.50) and Monrovia (US$10) leave from Monrovia Parking on the main street at the other end of town.

YEKEPA

Beautiful Yekepa, about 350m above sea level and surrounded by lush mountains, has once again become a prosperous town since mining giant Arcelor Mittal moved in to develop it in 2007. Here some 2000 tidy white workers cottages stud the landscape, and there's something rather *Truman Show* about the whole place, with its prosperous workforce and tidy streets – whether this is your first or last stop in Liberia, you'll be surprised. Nearby is Guesthouse Hill (1362m), Liberia's highest peak.

There's nothing really to bring you here unless you're on your way through to Guinea, although the scenery is lovely. Accommodation is available at the **Noble House Motel** (☎ 07 728 5158; r US$10-15), which also serves basic meals. For a more gastronomic experience head to the Arcelor Mittal Canteen, which is open to anyone happy to pay US$22 for a meal.

Getting There & Away

The Guinean border is 2km away, traversed by foot or occasional moto-taxis. For Côte d'Ivoire, go first to Sanniquellie.

LIBERIA DIRECTORY

ACCOMMODATION

Monrovia has a wide selection of hotels, though almost all are upper midrange and top end. The city's only budget option offers rooms from US$20 to $50, while midrange options have prices around US$50 to $150, and from around US$150 for the top end. Outside Monrovia, small hotels and guest houses have sprung up all over the country, mainly aimed at the aid workers and other NGO and UN employees travelling in the country. Despite this they are generally reasonably priced – typically US$10 to $20 for a very simple bedroom with shared facilities. Many double as brothels, though, so security can be an issue.

BOOKS

The classic Liberia travel book is Graham Greene's *Journey Without Maps*, the tale of his adventures traversing the country on foot in the 1930s. While rich in cultural detail and a fascinating snapshot of a land that had yet to be fully mapped, it is no page-turner by Greene's standards.

More recent impressions of Liberia can be found in *The Mask of Anarchy: The Destruction of Liberia and the Religious Dimension of an African Civil War* by Stephen Ellis; it's one of the best factual accounts of the Civil War. *New York Times* journalist Helene Cooper's memoir *The House at Sugar Beach* gives a personal account of growing up privileged in prewar Liberia and the chaos and heartbreak that followed. A fictional, yet equally harrowing book about Liberia's wars is Russell Banks' *The Darling*.

BUSINESS HOURS

Government offices are open 8.30am to 4pm Monday to Friday. Most businesses operate 9am to 5pm Monday to Friday (often with a break between noon and 2pm) and 9am to 1pm Saturday. Banking hours are 9.30am to noon Monday to Thursday and until 12.30pm on Friday.

DANGERS & ANNOYANCES

Liberia, while finally peaceful, can still be a dangerous place. Going out after nightfall anywhere is currently not advisable – only travel by car when it's dark, and it's still best not to travel long distances at night. Monrovia is the most dangerous place in the country (see p462) and in general the countryside is much less problematic. Always exercise caution, use safes and money belts, keep car doors locked when travelling and keep up to date with local news. Before setting off, get a complete briefing from people who know the situation; embassies and resident expats are the best sources.

EMBASSIES & CONSULATES

Diplomatic representation in Monrovia includes the following. Canadians and Australians should contact their high commissions in Côte d'Ivoire (see p283) and Ghana (see p388), respectively.

Côte d'Ivoire (Map p461; ☎ 06 519 138; Warner Ave, btwn 17th & 18th Sts, Sinkor)
France (off Map p461; ☎ 031 235 576; German Compound, Congo Town)
Germany (off Map p461; ☎ 06 438 365; UNMIL Bldg, Tubman Blvd, Congo Town)

PRACTICALITIES

- Local dailies include the *Inquirer* and the *Monrovia Guardian*.
- Voltage is 110V, and most plugs are US-style (two flat pins).
- There's little power outside the capital except through generators. Power cuts are common in Monrovia.
- Liberia uses the imperial system for weights and measures.

Ghana (Map p461; ☎ 07 701 6920; cnr 15th St & Cheeseman Ave, Sinkor)
Guinea (Map p461; ☎ 06 573 049; Tubman Blvd, btwn 23rd & 24th Sts, Sinkor)
Nigeria (off Map p461; ☎ 06 261 148; Nigeria House, Tubman Blvd, Congo Town)
Sierra Leone (Map p461; ☎ 06 427 404; cnr 15th St & Coleman Ave, Sinkor)
UK (☎ 06 516 973; chalkleyroy@aol.com; Clara Town, UN Dr, Bushrod Island) Honorary consul; emergency assistance only. Otherwise, contact the British High Commission in Freetown (p764).
USA (Map p463; ☎ 07 705 4826; http://monrovia .usembassy.gov/; UN Dr, Mamba Point)

HOLIDAYS

Public holidays:
New Year's Day 1 January
Armed Forces Day 11 February
Decoration Day Second Wednesday in March
JJ Roberts' Birthday 15 March
Fast & Prayer Day 11 April
National Unification Day 14 May
Independence Day 26 July
Flag Day 24 August
Thanksgiving Day First Thursday in November
Tubman Day 29 November
Christmas Day 25 December

INTERNET ACCESS

Internet access is almost totally non-existent outside Monrovia. In Monrovia it can be found at better hotels and a few internet cafes downtown.

INTERNET RESOURCES

Analyst Newspaper (www.analystliberia.com) One of the best Liberian newspapers, with a free archive.
Friends of Liberia (www.fol.org) Started by former Peace Corps volunteers, with information on the activities and projects of the nonprofit Friends of Liberia group.

LIBERIA

Liberia Expats (groups.google.com/group/liberia-expats) An excellent group for anyone planning to live or work in Liberia.

Onliberia.org (www.onliberia.org/urls.htm) A comprehensive site with an excellent page of links.

UNMIL (www.unmil.org) The official site of the United Nations mission in Liberia, full of information and news about the current situation.

LANGUAGE

More than 20 African languages are spoken, including Kpelle in the north-central region, Bassa and Kru along the coast, and Grebo in the southeast. English is the official language. The following will help you begin to understand the local version:

dash	bribe
coal tar	tar road
waste	discard (waste the milk) or splash (waste water)
I beg you	please (with emphasis)
carry	give a ride to
wait small	just a moment please
kala kala	crooked, corrupt

MONEY

The unit of currency is the Liberian 'unity' dollar (L$). US dollars are accepted everywhere at a standard exchange of US$1 to L$60. Apart from at Monrovia hotels, you'll nearly always get change in Liberian dollars, though, meaning that you don't really need to change your dollars to get local money.

Bringing US dollars in a variety of denominations is the simplest way to travel. Euros are the only other easy-to-exchange currency, aside from neighbouring African currencies around border towns. Sterling can sometimes be exchanged in Monrovia. Foreign-exchange bureaus are generally called Forex. Travellers cheques and credit cards were still totally useless at the time of writing, although this may well change in the near future. In an emergency you can receive cash in Monrovia and other big towns through Western Union (and MoneyGram in Monrovia). The best plan is simply to carry plenty of cash and use safes and money belts.

TELEPHONE

The country code is ☎ 231, and the international access code is ☎ 00.

There are no area codes in Liberia, and almost everybody from individuals to businesses uses the far more reliable mobile networks rather than the landline system. Landline numbers are six digits, while mobile phones are six to seven digits preceded by 04, 05, 06 or 07 depending on the network.

Any GSM-compatible phone with roaming will automatically join the local network. To get a local SIM card and make cheap local calls, as long as your handset is unlocked, you can go to any mobile phone shop in Monrovia and buy a SIM card for around US$10.

VISAS

Visas are required by all (except nationals of Ecowas countries), with costs varying depending on where the visa is procured. In the US a three-month single-entry visa for US citizens costs US$131, or US$70 for all other nationals. The application process is simple: you submit your passport, the application form, two photos, a copy of your yellow-fever certificate (see p856) and proof of your financial resources (such as a bank statement).

Once in Liberia you can apply for an extension to your visa at the **Bureau of Immigration** (Map p463; Broad St; ◷ 9am-5pm Mon-Fri, to 3pm Sat) in Monrovia. Registration is no longer necessary.

Visas for Onward Travel

To obtain a visa for onward travel, you'll need to visit the embassy in question in Monrovia (see p471).

CÔTE D'IVOIRE

Bring one passport photo and leave your passport between 9am and 1pm or 2pm and 3pm Monday to Friday. A one-month single-entry visa costs US$75 for all nationals. Processing usually takes five working days but can be done faster at no extra cost if you're in a hurry.

GUINEA

Bring two passport photos and leave your passport between 9.30am and 4pm Monday to Friday. Single-entry, one-month visas cost US$65 for citizens of the EU, Australia and New Zealand, or US$100 for nationals of the US and Canada. Processing takes 24 hours.

SIERRA LEONE

You'll need two passport photos and a photocopy of your passport to get a visa. Applications are accepted only between 10am and 2pm on Monday, Wednesday and Friday. Single-entry visas valid for up to three months cost US$100 for citizens of the EU, Canada, Australia and New Zealand. US citizens are charged US$131.

TRANSPORT IN LIBERIA

GETTING THERE & AWAY

For information on getting to Liberia from outside West Africa, see p828.

Entering Liberia

You must have a valid passport, a Liberian visa and a yellow-fever certificate to enter the country. As tourists are still very rare, you'll usually be asked what organisation you're with and you can expect some questioning on arrival if you say you're a tourist! Despite this, entering the country is usually straightforward and hassle free.

Air

Nearly all international flights arrive and depart from **Roberts International Airport** (airline code ROB; Robertsfield), 60km southeast of Monrovia. The smaller Spriggs Payne Airport (airline code MLW) is far more conveniently located in Sinkor, a short drive from downtown Monrovia, and is currently served only by Elysian Airlines, connecting Liberia to numerous other West African destinations.

Aero (airline code AJ; Map p463; ☎ 06 877 866, 06 511 895; www.flyaero.com; Randall St) Hub: Lagos. Connects Monrovia with Lagos twice a week via Accra.

Brussels Airlines (airline code SN; Map p463; ☎ 06 520 777, 06 974 677; www.brusselsairlines.com; Randall St) Hub: Brussels. Two direct flights weekly between Brussels and Monrovia, and two further via Abidjan.

Delta Air Lines (airline code DL; www.delta.com) Hub: Atlanta. Launched an Atlanta–Monrovia service via Cape Verde in June 2009.

Elysian Airlines (☎ 06 444 747; www.elysianairlines .com) Hubs: Yaounde and Monrovia. Operates internal flights in Liberia from Monrovia to Harper, Greenville and Zwedru, as well as connecting to other West African cities.

Kenya Airways (airline code KO; Map p463; ☎ 06 556 693, 06 511 522; www.kenya-airways.com; KLM Bldg, Broad St) Hub: Nairobi. Three flights a week between Nairobi and Monrovia via Accra.

Royal Air Maroc (airline code AT; Map p461; ☎ 06 951 951, 06 956 956; www.royalairmaroc.com) Hub: Casablanca. Two flights weekly between Casablanca and Monrovia, via Freetown.

Slok Air International (airline code SO; Map p463; www.slok-air.com; ☎ 06 590 178; KLM House, Broad St) Hub: Banjul. Three flights weekly to/from Dakar via Freetown and Banjul.

SN Bellview Airlines (airline code B3; ☎ 07 727 3693, 06 463 409; www.flybellviewair.com) Hub: Lagos. Three flights weekly to/from Lagos via Accra and Abidjan.

Virgin Nigeria (airline code VK; ☎ 06 511 197; www .virginnigeria.com) Hub: Lagos. Connects Monrovia to Lagos via Accra.

Land

CÔTE D'IVOIRE

Border crossings with Côte d'Ivoire are just beyond Sanniquellie towards Danané, and east of Harper, towards Tabou.

There's a bus several times weekly from Monrovia to Abidjan and on to Accra via Sanniquellie (US$40 to Abidjan, US$60 to Accra, plus approximately US$20 for border fees).

Daily bush taxis go from Monrovia to Ganta and Sanniquellie, from where you can continue in stages to Danané and Man (12 to 15 hours).

In the south, a road connects Harper with Tabou, but you'll still need to cross the Cavally River in a ferry or canoe as there is no bridge. Once across, there are taxis to Tabou, from where there's transport to San Pédro and Abidjan.

GUINEA

For Guinea, the main crossing is just north of Ganta. From just north of Ganta's Public Market you can take a moto-taxi (50c) the 2km to the border and walk across. Once in Guinea, there are frequent taxis to N'zérékoré. From Sanniquellie's bush-taxi rank known as the 'meat packing' there are irregular bush taxis via Yekepa to the Guinean town of Lola (US$6.50). A place in a shared taxi is the same price. A moto-taxi from Yekepa to the border (if you can find one!) should cost only 50c, after which there are Guinean vehicles to Lola. There is also a border crossing at Voinjama to Macenta via a bad road from Gbarnga (often impassable in the wet season).

The Monrovia–Conakry bush taxi (US$50) takes two days and leaves from Monrovia's Guinea Park near the Red Light Motor Park in Paynesville. A place in a shared taxi on the same route is US$60.

For information on boats between Conakry (Guinea) and Monrovia (at least 36 hours), enquire at Monrovia's Freeport.

LIBERIA

lonelyplanet.com

Fishing boats run sporadically between Harper and San Pédro (Côte d'Ivoire).

SIERRA LEONE
The main Sierra Leone crossing is at Bo (Waterside). There are frequent daily bush taxis between Monrovia and the Bo (Waterside) border (three hours), from where it's easy to find onward transport to Kenema (about eight very rough hours further), and then on to Freetown.

GETTING AROUND
Air
Elysian Airlines (p473) connects Monrovia to Harper, Greenville and Zwedru and offers the only commercial internal flights at present.

Boat
Fishing boats link coastal cities and, while slow and often dangerous, are sometimes faster than road travel. There are also charter boats from Monrovia that sometimes have room for passengers. Ask locally for information.

Bush Taxi & Minibus
Public transport is still not considered safe for foreigners in Liberia, meaning your choice is: take risks with your security or pay for a driver. The main form of public transport is bush taxis, which go daily from Monrovia to Buchanan, Gbarnga, Ganta, Sanniquellie and the Sierra Leone border. Several weekly bush taxis link Monrovia with almost everywhere else, although many routes (especially those connecting Zwedru with Greenville and Harper) are restricted during the rainy season. Minivans (called 'buses') also ply most major routes, although they're more crowded and dangerous than bush taxis.

Car & Motorcycle
Vehicle hire can be arranged through better hotels and travel agencies in Monrovia; prices (including driver) average about US$100 per day for a 4WD. Petrol is usually paid for by the client – this is available everywhere, sold outside Monrovia in almost every small town from roadside stalls proffering glass jars of fuel.

ROAD CONDITIONS
Roads in and around Monrovia are surprisingly good, and there are also decent sealed roads all the way to Bo (Waterside) via Tubmanburg and to Gbarnga and Buchanan, although there are some deteriorated stretches on both the latter routes. Beyond Gbarnga to Yekepa the road is in bad condition, and becomes dirt north of Ganta. Most other roads are dirt and many are impassable during the rainy season, including the Zwedru–Harper road.

Driving is on the right. Road hazards here are similar to those elsewhere in West Africa; see the boxed text, p847. UNMIL guards still maintain a strong observational presence on the roads but rarely stop drivers. Liberian immigration officials tend to stop all traffic as it enters larger towns. They usually just want to know your name and organisation, and rarely cause problems. Ensure you carry your passport wherever you drive, however.

Mali

If you only visit one country in West Africa, make it Mali. This is a country as rich in historical significance as it is blessed by an extraordinary array of sights, not to mention being home to many of West Africa's major cultural groups.

Mali's natural wonders range from the deserts of the north to the fertile greenery of the south, with the Niger River weaving a path through the heart of the country. The lucrative trade routes of the Sahara once made the region the world's richest, and the Niger, one of the grand old rivers of Africa, still provides Mali's lifeblood. To journey along it (preferably on a slow boat) is one great journey.

Not far from the riverbank, the extraordinary Falaise de Bandiagara rises from the plains. It shelters one of West Africa's most intriguing peoples, the Dogon, whose villages and complex cultural rituals still cling to the rocky cliffs. A visit here is utterly unforgettable.

Some of Africa's greatest empires also rose from the Niger's hinterland and bequeathed to Mali some of its most dramatic attractions: the legendary city of Timbuktu – whose name has never lost its remote allure – and the gloriously improbable mosque at Djenné are merely two among many. Even in places where the landscape seems too barren to support life, you find Mali's famous elephants sharing the Sahelian soil with Tuareg and Fulani nomads.

There's almost as much to hear in Mali as there is to see, with a musical soundtrack provided by some of Africa's most celebrated stars. Whether you dive in to Bamako's wonderful live music scene or time your arrival to coincide with the country's two world-famous music festivals, Mali's diverse rhythms will soon have you on your feet.

FAST FACTS

- **Area** 1,240,140 sq km
- **Capital** Bamako
- **Country code** ☎ 223
- **Famous for** Timbuktu, Dogon Country, Festival in the Desert and the best in West African music
- **Languages** French, Bambara, Fula, Tamashek, Dogon, Bozo and Songhaï
- **Money** West African CFA franc; US$1 = CFA493; €1 = CFA656
- **Population** 13.1 million
- **Visa** Renewable five-day visa available at border (CFA15,000) or one-month visas at any Malian embassy

MALI

HOW MUCH?

- **Bamako-Mopti bus ride** CFA7500
- **4WD rental with driver** CFA45,000–50,000 per day, plus petrol
- **Sunset camel ride into Sahara** from CFA7500
- **Internet connection** CFA600–1500 per hour
- **Guide to Dogon Country** CFA12,500–22,500 per day

LONELY PLANET INDEX

- **1L of petrol** CFA530
- **1.5L of bottled water** CFA500
- **Bottle of Castel beer** small/large CFA500/1000
- **Souvenir T-shirt** CFA5000–6000
- **Portion of riz arachide (rice with peanut sauce)** CFA500

HIGHLIGHTS

- **Dogon Country** (p507) West Africa as it used to be, with timeless villages clinging to the Falaise de Bandiagara.
- **Djenné** (p497) Stunning mudbrick town with a fairytale mosque overlooking a clamorous Monday market.
- **Niger River** (see the boxed text, p504) One of Africa's epic rivers lined with fascinating villages, picturesque mosques and Mali's diverse cultures.
- **Timbuktu** (p516) City of Saharan legend and the gateway to the desert.
- **Réserve de Douentza** (p530) Home to the Sahel's last elephants and one of Africa's great wildlife-watching experiences.
- **Bamako** (p490) West Africa's live-music capital with weekend performances by Mali's musical superstars.

ITINERARIES

- **One Week** Stay Friday night in Bamako for a taste of Mali's live-music scene (p490) and make sure your Monday is spent at Djenné's weekly market (p498). Otherwise, we recommend a three-day trek in Dogon Country (p507), with one night in the lively port town of Mopti (p501) en route.

- **Two Weeks** An extra week will allow you to break up the long journey northeast by pausing for a couple of nights in languid Ségou (p493). From Mopti, you could also take a three-day slow-boat journey (see the boxed text, p504) up the Niger River to Timbuktu (p516) from where short desert excursions are possible.
- **One Month** In a one-month itinerary you could include an extra day in Djenné (p497) to enjoy its quiet postmarket charm, as well as a longer, one-week trek in the Dogon Country (p512). A couple of days in the Réserve de Douentza (p530) in search of Mali's elephants is a must, and factor in a half-day trek around La Main de Fatima (p530). Other possibilities include a visit to the remote outpost of Gao (p524), a longer Saharan camel trek (p521) from Timbuktu if the security situation allows, and a couple of nights in Teriya Bugu (p497) on your way back to Bamako.

CLIMATE & WHEN TO GO

The best time to visit Mali is from November to January, when you can expect generally fine weather, moderate temperatures and sufficient water levels on the Niger River to allow river trips. This is, however, Mali's tourist high season, so accommodation can be at a premium. Mali is wettest between July and August, although the rainy season runs from June to September. It's hottest between April and June, when temperatures frequently exceed 40°C. September and October are also extremely hot and Timbuktu in particular can be unpleasant. From January to June, the hot and dusty harmattan blows, irritating throats and reducing visibility. See also Climate Charts, p810.

Mali's most famous cultural event is the outstanding Festival in the Desert (p521) held in early January amid the sand dunes near Timbuktu. Fast catching up for quality and popularity is Ségou's Festival sur le Niger (p494), held late January to early February.

HISTORY
The Early Empires

Rock paintings and carvings in the Sahara suggest that northern Mali has been inhabited since 10,000 BC, when the Sahara was fertile and rich in wildlife. By 5000 BC farming was taking place, and the use of iron began around 500 BC. By 300 BC, large organised settlements had developed, most notably at

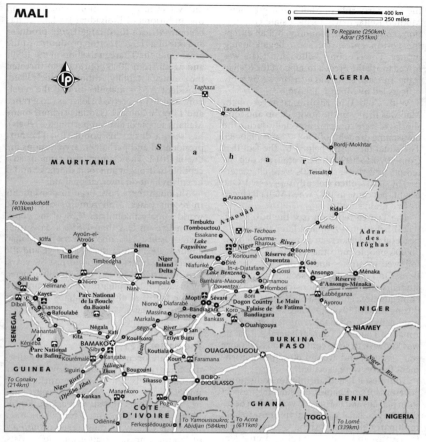

MALI

Djenné (see p500). By the 6th century AD, the lucrative trans-Saharan trade in gold, salt and slaves had begun.

From the 8th to the 16th centuries, Mali formed the centrepiece of the great empires of West African antiquity, most notably the Empires of Ghana, Mali and Songhaï (see p27). The arrival of European ships along the West African coast from the 15th century, however, broke the monopoly on power of the Sahel kingdoms and northern cities.

Later the Bambara kingdom of Ségou rose briefly to control huge swathes of Mali, before being usurped by two waves of Fula-led Islamic jihad, the second originating from the Tukulor Empire of northern Senegal. The Tukulor were still around when the French expanded east into Mali during the mid-19th century.

By the end of the 19th century, Mali was part of French West Africa. Remnants of this colonial era include the huge Office du Niger irrigation scheme near Ségou, and the 1200km Dakar–Bamako train line, the longest rail span in West Africa; both were built with forced labour. Such vast infrastructure projects notwithstanding, Mali remained the poor neighbour of Senegal and Côte d'Ivoire. France's chief interest was in 'developing' Mali as a source of cheap cash crops (rice and cotton) for export.

Independence
Mali became independent in 1960 (for a few months it was federated with Senegal). Under

the one-party rule of Mali's first president, Modibo Keita, newly formed state corporations controlled the economy, but all except the cotton enterprise soon began losing money. The economy wilted and Keita was forced to ask the French to support the Malian franc. In 1968, Keita was overthrown by army officers led by Moussa Traoré.

With Cold War rivalries at fever pitch, Mali was firmly in the Soviet camp and food shortages were constant, especially during the devastating droughts of 1968–74 and 1980–85. The situation wasn't helped by the fact that from 1970 to 1990 there were five coup attempts and the early 1980s were characterised by strikes, often violently suppressed. One bright spot came in 1987 when Mali produced its first grain surplus.

The Tuareg rebellion (see the boxed text, p525) began in 1990, and later that year a peaceful prodemocracy demonstration drew 30,000 people onto the streets of Bamako, followed by strikes and further demonstrations. On 17 March 1991, security forces met students and other demonstrators with machinegun fire. Three days of rioting followed, during which 150 people were killed. The unrest finally provoked the army, led by General Amadou Toumani Touré (General ATT as he was known), to seize control. Moussa Traoré was arrested, and around 60 senior government figures were executed.

Touré established an interim transitional government and gained considerable respect from Malians and the outside world when he resigned a year later, keeping his promise to hold multiparty elections. Alpha Oumar Konaré (a scientist and writer) was elected president in June 1992, and his party, the Alliance for Democracy in Mali (Adema), won a large majority of seats in the national assembly. Konaré oversaw political and economic liberalisation, but had to deal with a 50% devaluation of the CFA in 1994 (which resulted in rioting and protests) and an attempted coup.

Konaré stood down in 2002, as dictated by the new constitution he'd helped draft; he went on to become Chairman of the African Union. The former general, Amadou Touré, was rewarded for his patience and elected as president in April 2002.

Mali Today

On many fronts Mali is a model West African democracy, one in which the overall health of the system has proven more enduring than the ambitions of individual leaders. It has become Africa's third-largest gold producer and one of its largest cotton producers. At the same time, the Tuareg rebellion in the 1990s and again from 2006 continues to threaten the country's stability. Although widely liked, President ATT's inability to end the rebellion, and his perceived closeness to France and Libya's Colonel Gaddafi (whom many Malians accuse of also supporting the rebels), has seen a dip in his popularity. The next presidential and parliamentary elections are due in 2012. The country also remains susceptible to drought and food shortages and is heavily reliant on international aid.

Although there have been improvements in recent years, Mali remains one of the world's poorest countries: 72% of the population live on less than US$2 a day, adult literacy is just 24%, one in every five Malian children dies before the age of five and life expectancy hovers at around just 50 years. The country's economic growth is hampered by a rampant population growth rate and by the fact that 48% of Malians are under 15 years of age.

THE CULTURE
The National Psyche

Malians are open and tolerant. For centuries the country's diverse peoples have shared a country that is not always bountiful, and they've learned to do it pretty well (competing kingdoms and slavery aside). Ethnic identity is still important, but where once there was enmity, in most cases a *cousinage* or 'joking cousins' relationship now exists. People from different groups commonly tease and poke fun at ethnic stereotypes and past deeds to everyone's enjoyment. The only possible exception is the Tuareg, who remain a people apart.

In Mali, personal relationships are important, friendships are of great value, families are the glue that holds everything together, and hospitality and generosity seem to increase in inverse proportion to a person's means. Malians worry about the dire economic state of the country and a perceived loss of tradition, rail against corruption and long for a better life, but deep down they're a remarkably optimistic people who love to dance. They love it even more if you dance with them.

Daily Life

For many Malians, daily life is a struggle and those Malians with a steady job must support a large network of family and friends. People living in the burgeoning cities of Bamako and, to a lesser extent, Mopti are rushing headlong to embrace modern culture. As a result urban Malian society is becoming increasingly sophisticated, although its enjoyment is limited to a privileged few: UN figures suggest that more than 90% of Mali's urban population live in slums. At the same time, this rush to the cities comes at the cost of cultural alienation and, although people's roots and ethnic identity remain important, many Malians worry about the loss of traditions that occurs as young people leave behind the hardships of rural life. In rural areas, it's not unusual to find Malians who have never left their village or who continue to eke out a seminomadic existence. These Malians may hold fast to tradition, but their numbers are dwindling and their lives are made increasingly difficult by environmental degradation and a growing population competing for diminishing resources.

Greeting people in Mali is very important, and you'll often see highly formalised ritual greetings which last for minutes. People think it very impolite to ask for directions before saying hello or enquiring about their health.

Population

Mali's population is growing by almost 3% per year, which means that the number of Malians doubles every 20 years. Around two-thirds of Malians are tied to the land, directly or indirectly, so it's hardly surprising that most of the population lives in Mali's fertile south. The vast northern desert and semidesert (65% of Mali) contains just 10% of the population.

Concentrated in the centre and south of the country, the Bambara are Mali's largest ethnic group (33% of the population) and they hold much political power. Together with the Soninké and Malinké (who dominate western Mali) they make up 50% of Mali's population.

Fulani (17%) pastoralists are found wherever there is grazing for their livestock, particularly near Massina in the Niger Inland Delta. The farmlands of the Songhaï (6%) are concentrated along the 'Niger Bend', the stretch of river between Niafunké and Ansongo, while the Sénoufo (12%) live around Sikasso and Koutiala. The Dogon (7%) live on the Falaise de Bandiagara (Bandiagara Escarpment) in central Mali. The lighter-skinned Tuareg (6%), traditionally nomadic pastoralists and traders, inhabit the fringes of the Sahara. Other groups include the Bozo fisher people of the Niger River and the Bobo (2.5%) who live close to the border with Burkina Faso.

RELIGION

Between 80% and 90% of Malians are Muslim, and 2% Christian. The remainder retain animist beliefs, although these often overlap with Islamic and Christian practices, especially in rural areas.

Mali is a secular state, but Islam retains an influential hold over public life. In recent years some powerful imams have called for more Islamic influence in the running of the country and less Westernisation, although Malian Islam is generally tolerant and you'll encounter very little anti-Western sentiment in Mali.

ARTS
Music

The roots of Mali's now-famous musical tradition lie with the *griots* (also called *jelis*), a hereditary caste of musicians, and many of Mali's modern singers are members of the *griot* caste. The female *griots* of Mali are famed throughout West Africa for the beauty and power of their voices.

Lovers of the 21-string *kora* (a traditional *griot* instrument) will adore the work of the master, Toumani Diabaté, the 71st generation of *kora* players in his family, who has collaborated with everyone from Roswell Rudd and Taj Mahal to Spain's Ketama. Ballaké Sissoko and Mamadou Diabaté (who lives in America) are other fine *kora* players.

The much-loved Ali Farka Touré, who died in early 2006, was perhaps Africa's best-known modern musician. His blues-influenced sound highlights similarities between the music of Africa and the Mississippi Delta (some scholars believe that the roots of American blues lie with the Malian slaves who worked on US plantations). His portfolio is extensive, but we particularly like *The Source, The River, In the Heart of the Moon* (his Grammy Award–winning album with Toumani Diabaté) and his last album, *Savane*. Other much-loved blues performers include many from Ali Farka's stable, among

---

TOUMANI DIABATÉ

Toumani Diabaté is a Grammy Award–winning *kora* player. Read more about him at www
.toumani-diabate.com.

Why has Malian music taken the world by storm? First of all, we have quality. Secondly, each
ethnic group in Mali has deep cultural roots and long musical traditions. One of the most important things is our culture of the *griots*. Almost all of Mali's musicians come from *griot* families. As
griots, we learn the *kora*, the music in our families when we are growing up.

When did you start playing the kora? When I was five years old. The *kora* has been around for
700 years and I am the 71st generation to play the *kora*.

**Your father, Sidiki Diabaté, was considered one of the best kora players of his generation.
What did he think of your collaborations with Taj Mahal, Roswell Rudd, Ketama and others?** He liked the fact that I took the *kora* in a new direction, because he understood that every
generation has to find its own way.

Will there be a 72nd generation of kora players in your family? My son plays the *kora*, but he
likes more modern music and so he also plays the piano. He, too, has to find his own way.

Is it a difficult instrument to learn? Not at all. All you have to do is come to my school [see
p485]. Then it's easy!

As told to Anthony Ham

---

them Afel Bocoum, Ali Farka's son Vieux
Farka Touré, Baba Salah and Lobi Traoré.

A different take on the blues comes from
Tinariwen, a beguiling Tuareg group from
Kidal that has taken the world by storm
(see the boxed text, p62). Terakaft and
Toumast, whose members include former
Tinariwen performers, are also gaining
popularity for their desert blues style. For
more traditional Tuareg music, Tartit is the
best-known group.

Mali's wealth of talented female singers includes the hugely popular Oumou Sangaré,
whose songs deal with contemporary social
issues such as polygamy and arranged marriages. Her music is influenced by the musical
traditions of the Wassoulou region of southwestern Mali, and features the *kamelen-ngoni*,
a large six-stringed harp-lute. Other internationally renowned female singers to watch out
for include Ami Koita and Kandia Kouyaté.

After independence, Malian cultural and
artistic traditions were encouraged and several
state-sponsored 'orchestras' were founded.
The legendary Rail Band de Bamako (actual
employees of the Mali Railway Corporation)
was one of the greatest, and one of its ex-
members, the charismatic Salif Keita, has
become a superstar in his own right.

Other popular musicians to have made a big
splash beyond Mali's borders include Rokia
Traoré, Amadou et Mariam, Habib Koita and
Koita. Perhaps even more popular within
Mali, although rarely heard internationally,

are the female singers Nahawa Doumbia,
Adja Soumano, Amy Sacko, Dienaba Seck and
Khaira Arby; the balafon (xylophone) masters
Nemba Solo and Morobali Keita; Abdoulaye
Diabaté (who plays traditional Bambara and
Bobo music) and his son Iba, considered by
many to be the true heir to Ali Farka Touré;
and the rap/hip-hop star Amkoullel, the
grandson of Mali's finest novelist, Amadou
Hampaté Bâ.

To hear Mali's best musicians in action
in Bamako, see p490, while music lovers
shouldn't miss Essakane's Festival in the
Desert (p521) or Ségou's Festival Sur Le Niger
(p494). For a broader look at the West African
music scene, see p57.

Arts & Craftwork

The most famous exponents of Mali's famous sculptural and mask traditions are the
Bambara and Dogon; for more information
on Dogon masks, see the boxed text, p509.

Woodcarvings made by the Bambara people are noted for their angular forms. Bambara
masks are usually bold and solid, with cowrie
shells and human and animal features incorporated into the design; they're often used in
secret-society ceremonies. The best known is
the *chiwara*, a headpiece carved in the form of
an antelope, and used in ritualistic dances.

The Bambara also produce striking *bogolan*, or mud-cloth (p67). Djenné (p501) and
Ségou (p494) are the best places to find quality
bogolan pieces.

Literature

Mali's storytelling was once an almost exclusively oral tradition, but one of the few tales which has been committed to paper is that of one of ancient Mali's greatest kings, Sundiata (see the boxed text, p28), whose story delightfully blurs the lines between history and literature. An accessible version is *Sundiata: An Epic of Old Mali,* by DT Niane.

Mali's greatest writer of the modern era was the Bandiagara-born Amadou Hampaté Bâ, who died in 1991 (see also p49).

Cinema & Photography

Souleymane Cissé is perhaps the best known Malian director, especially for the masterful *Yeleen* (Brightness), which won the Special Jury Prize at the Cannes Film Festival in 1987. Other well-regarded Malian directors include Assane Kouyaté (whose *Kabala* won the Special Jury Prize at the 2003 Fespaco film festival), Abdoulaye Ascofaré, Adama Drabo, Falaba Issa Traoré, and Cheick Oumar Sissoko (whose *La Genése* and *Guimba, un Tyran, une Epoque* won prizes at Cannes (1999) and Fespaco (1995) respectively, and who has served as Mali's Minister of Culture.

Mali's photographers have also been attracting international acclaim in recent years, especially the self-taught Seydou Keita, whose eccentric but revealing portraits of his fellow Malians have been exhibited around the world. Malick Sidibe is best known for his stirring images from Bamako in the heady days surrounding Malian independence.

Books worth seeking out include *Seydou Keita;* the famous *You Look Beautiful Like That: The Portrait Photographs of Seydou Keita and Malick Sidibe;* and *Malick Sidibe: Photographs.*

ENVIRONMENT
The Land

Mali, one of the largest countries in West Africa with 1.24 million sq km, is home to five different environments. The north contains the Sahara; the south is relatively flat and well-watered agricultural land; the west is a hilly and well-wooded extension of the Futa Djalon highlands of Guinea; the central band is semi-arid scrub savannah (the Sahel) and the Niger Inland Delta is a maze of channels, swamps and lakes. The Niger River (see the boxed text, p80) flows for 1626km through the country.

National Parks

Mali has four national parks and reserves, but its wildlife has been devastated by centuries of human encroachment and the parks are not easily accessible.

Of most interest to visitors is the Réserve de Douentza (p530), a vast area of semidesert north of the main road between Douentza and Gossi inhabited by Africa's northernmost elephant populations.

Otherwise, the vast Parc National de la Boucle du Baoulé (p532), northwest of Bamako, reportedly has good bird-watching. Bordering the lake formed by Manantali dam, west of Kita, Parc National du Bafing (p531) protects a number of primate species, including chimpanzees.

The Réserve d'Ansongo-Ménaka (p529) lies southeast of Gao, next to the Niger River, and is extremely isolated. Much of the wildlife has gone but the Niger still has hippos.

Environmental Issues

Mali's most urgent environmental issues are deforestation (just 10.3% of Mali is covered by forest), overgrazing and desertification (an estimated 98% of Mali is at risk from desertification); between them, these three issues threaten much of the country. In the Sahel, trees are felled for cooking fuel and building materials. Elsewhere, overgrazing is stripping the land of ground cover and root systems, so that the soil has little to bind it together, and is unravelling and causing erosion.

FOOD & DRINK

Food in Mali is generally similar to that found in Senegal, with *poulet yassa* (grilled chicken in an onion and lemon sauce), *riz yollof* (rice with vegetables and/or meat) and *riz arachide* (rice with peanut sauce) featuring on many menus. All along the Niger River, restaurants also serve grilled or fried *capitaine* (Nile perch). Many tourist restaurants cater to more Western tastes with spaghetti and couscous. In Gao, look out for *wigila*, a local speciality of sun-dried dumplings dipped in a meat sauce.

Street food is usually excellent and widely available. Look out for beef brochettes (grilled on a stick), fried fish, fried bananas, omelette sandwiches, sweet-potato chips and plates of rice and sauce.

Soft drinks are omnipresent, but local drinks such as ginger juice, or red *bissap* or

GUIDES IN MALI

No matter where you find yourself in Mali, guides (many of them incredibly persistent) will sidle up and offer tours of the city where you are and further afield. You certainly don't need a constant companion or intermediary to enjoy Mali. That said, in many places, such as Djenné or Timbuktu, a knowledgeable local guide can greatly enhance your visit. Guides are also essential in Dogon Country.

So, how to choose a guide? In 2006, the Malian government instituted a scheme of guide accreditation. All accredited guides who passed the accreditation exams must now carry cards indicating whether they are accredited to guide nationally (blue) or only in their local district (yellow). The system is not foolproof: not every guide who has passed the exam is necessarily good and some who began guiding after 2006 have yet to sit the exam. We have also received unconfirmed reports of corruption allowing some budding guides to circumvent the exam process. In general, however, the system works. To find such a guide, ask at the local tourist office, guide association, hotel or tour operator, or ask other travellers for recommendations. For the Dogon Country, see the boxed text, p510.

For an interview with two of Mali's few female guides, see the boxed text, p493.

djablani juice (which is brewed from hibiscus petals then chilled) are sometimes available (but are not always sterile).

Although Mali is predominantly Muslim, most towns have at least one bar or hotel where you can buy Castel, a Malian lager. Flag, from Senegal, is also available.

BAMAKO

pop 1.73 million

Bamako grows on you and we don't just mean the pollution. Those who rush through will find Mali's capital a far cry from its origins as a small Bozo fishing village. Bamako today is sprawling and gritty, and can be a charmless place if you let the streets full of people, cars, buzzing flocks of *mobylettes* (mopeds) and clouds of pollution get to you. And yet, most expats who live here often end up loving the place; they're drawn in by great restaurants and a soundtrack provided by some of Africa's best music stars. Bamako's hotels are also excellent, while the National Museum is arguably the best in the region. If you're looking for a tranquil stay, you should probably look elsewhere. But if you like your markets colourful, clamorous and spilling into the surrounding streets, appreciate energy that illuminates the night and hanker for the opportunity to befriend open and friendly locals, Bamako might just get under your skin.

ORIENTATION

Bamako's city centre is on the north bank of the Niger River, focused on the triangle formed by Ave Kassa Keita, Blvd du Peuple and the train tracks. ACI2000, a new district west of the centre, will one day rival the downtown area as a commercial centre and many businesses and embassies are moving there. The Quinzambougou/Niaréla and Hippodrome districts, northeast of the centre, are great places to find hotels, restaurants and nightclubs. South of the centre, Pont des Martyrs leads across the river to Rte de Ségou (also called Ave de l'Unité Africaine; OUA), the main road out of town; the Sogoniko *gare routière* (bus station) is about 6km along this road. The Pont du Roi (west of Pont des Martyrs) carries a new highway that leads to Sénou International Airport (17km).

INFORMATION

Bookshops

For the occasional *International Herald Tribune* or *Newsweek,* as well as French-language material, try **Le Fourmi Superstore** (Map p483; ☎ 2021 6167; Rte de Koulikoro; ☒ 7.30am-1pm & 3.30-8.30pm Mon-Sat, 8.30am-1pm Sun).

The following two hotel bookshops have a good French-language selection, but very little in English:

Librairie Bah Grand Hôtel (Map p486; ☎ 2023 6705; Ave van Vollenhoven; ☒ 8.30am-1pm & 2.30-7pm Mon-Sat, 9am-12.30pm Sun)

Librairie Bah Hôtel Salam (Map p483; ☎ 2022 1200; next to Pont du Roi; ☒ 8.30am-1pm & 2.30-7pm Mon-Sat, 9am-12.30pm Sun)

Cultural Centres

Centre Culturel Français (Map p486; ☎ 2022 4019; www.ccfbamako.org; Ave de l'Indépendance;

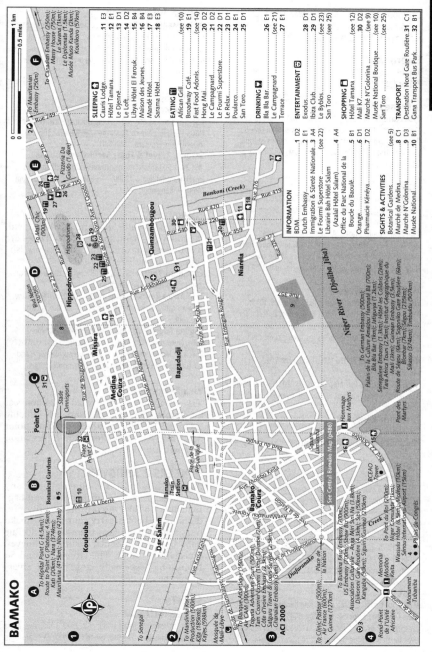

BAMAKO

INFORMATION
BDM..**1** D2
Dutch Embassy..................................**2** E1
Immigration & Sûreté Nationale........**3** A4
Le Fourmi Superstore.................(see 22)
Librairie Bah Hôtel Salam	
(Azalaï Hôtel Salam)..................**4** A4
Office du Parc National de la	
Boucle du Baoulé........................**5** B1
Orange...**6** D1
Pharmacie Kénéya.............................**7** D2

SIGHTS & ACTIVITIES
Botanical Gardens........................(see 5)
Marché de Medina...........................**8** C1
Marché N'Colonina...........................**9** D3
Musée National...............................**10** B1

SLEEPING
Cauris Lodge....................................**11** E3
Hôtel Tamana...................................**12** E1
Le Djenné..**13** D1
Le Loft...**14** D2
Libya Hôtel El Farouk......................**15** B4
Maison des Jeunes...........................**16** B4
Mandé Hôtel....................................**17** E3
Sarama Hôtel...................................**18** E3

EATING
African Grill.................................(see 10)
Broadway Café................................**19** E1
Fast Food Adonis........................(see 14)
Hong Mai...**20** D2
Le Campagnard................................**21** D2
Le Fourmi Superstore......................**22** D1
Le Relax...**23** E1
Poularco..**24** E1
San Toro..**25** D1

DRINKING
Bla Bla Bar......................................**26** E1
Le Campagnard...........................(see 21)
Terrace..**27** E1

ENTERTAINMENT
Exodus...**28** D1
Ibiza Club..**29** D1
Le Byblos...................................(see 23)
San Toro.....................................(see 25)

SHOPPING
Hôtel Tamana.............................(see 12)
Mall K7..**30** D2
Marché N'Colonina...........................(see 9)
Musée National Boutique...........(see 10)
San Toro.....................................(see 25)

TRANSPORT
Destination Nord Gare Routière.....**31** C1
Gana Transport Bus Park.................**32** B1

9.30am-1pm & 2-5.30pm Tue, Wed, Fri & Sat, 1.30-5.30pm Thu) Has a good library as well as a cinema and live performances (see p490).

Emergency
Ambulance (15)
Police (17)

Internet Access
Cybercafé HTM (Map p486; Place l'OMVS; per hr CFA500; 7.30am-10.30pm) Central but slower than Orange.
Orange (Map p483; Rte de Koulikoro; per hr CFA1000; 8am-10pm Mon-Fri, 9am-10pm Sat) Tech-savvy and fast connections.

Maps
Institut Géographique du Mali (off Map p483; 2020 2840; Rue 103, off Ave de l'OUA, Sogoniko; 8am-4pm Mon-Thu, to 5.30pm Fri) Go up to the 2nd floor to the room signed 'Atelier de Cartographie Numerique No.1 G21', where they'll print you out topographic maps (CFA5000 per sheet) of all corners of the country. They also do a detailed 2005 Bamako city map (CFA11,700).

Medical Services
Clinique Pasteur (off Map p483; 2029 1010; 24hr) West of town, this is Mali's best hospital for African diseases, emergencies and other consultations; it has its own labs and handles insurance claims with a minimum of fuss.
Hôpital Gabriel Touré (Map p486; 2022 2712; Ave van Vollenhoven)
Hôpital Point G (off Map p483; 2022 5002; Point G) Bamako's largest hospital, on the hill overlooking the city from the north.
Pharmacie Kénéya (Map p483; Rue Achkhabad, Quinzambougou)
Pharmacie Officine Coura (Map p486; Ave de la Nation)

Money
Banque Atlantique (off Map p483; Rte de Hamdalaye-Lafiabougou) *May* do cash advances on MasterCard.
BDM Ave Modibo Keita (**Map p486**); Rue de la Cathédrale (**Map p486**); Rue Achkhabad (**Map p483**) Can exchange cash and do cash advances on Visa card; most branches have a Visa-enabled ATM.
Ecobank cnr Blvd du Peuple & Rue Famolo Coulibaly (**Map p486**); Blvd 22 Octobre (**Map p486**) Changes euro and US dollars cash and travellers cheques.

Post
Main post office (Map p486; Rue Karamoko Diaby)
Tam Courrier Express (off Map p483; 2029 9152; yvesbko@yahoo.fr; Hamdallaye ACI2000) Local representatives for UPS and the best of the courier companies.

Tourist Information
Office Malien du Tourisme et de l'Hôtellerie (Map p486; Omatho; 2023 6450; www.tourisme.gov.ml, www.officetourisme-mali.com; Rue Mohammed V) Not all that useful for travellers, but has the occasional brochure and a list of guides.

Travel Agencies
AIR TICKETS
ESF (Map p486; 2022 5144; ankata@esftravel; Libya Hôtel L'Amitié, Ave de la Marne; 8am-12.30pm & 2-5pm Mon-Fri, 8am-noon Sat)
Satguru Travel & Tours Service (off Map p483; 2021 2613; stts@satgurutravel.com; Radisson SAS Hotel, Hamdallaye ACI2000; 8am-12.30pm & 2-5pm Mon-Fri, 8am-noon Sat)

TOURS
For tours around Mali and further afield, the following Bamako-based companies are recommended, and can arrange English-speaking guides:
Continent Tours (2022 7089; www.continenttours .com) Good region-wide company.
Tara Africa Tours (off Map p483; 2028 7091; www .tara-africatours.com) Dutch-Dogon-run agency in Baco Djicoroni.
Toguna Adventure Tours (off Map p483; /fax 2029 5366; www.geocities.com/toguna_adventure_tours; ACI2000) American-Malian-run Toguna is extremely professional and can arrange some ecotourism and volunteering options.

Visa Extensions
Visa extensions are processed in 24 hours at the Immigration & Sûreté Nationale building (Map p483), 200m northeast of Rond-point de l'Unité Africaine. For more information on costs, see p537.

DANGERS & ANNOYANCES
Bamako is largely safe, although, like any city, it has its share of pickpockets and bag-snatchers, so take the normal security precautions and never carry valuables. Bamako train station, the trains themselves and Rue Baba Diarra are popular haunts for thieves, especially at night. The streets around Sq Lumumba (especially close to the river) should be avoided after dark.

SIGHTS
Musée National
This **museum** (Map p483; 2022 3486; Ave de la Liberté; admission CFA2500, guide CFA3000; 9am-6pm

Tue-Sun), set in expansive grounds a 10-minute walk north of the centre, is outstanding. Its permanent collection consists of a stunning collection of textiles, masks, statues and archaeological artefacts that are well labelled (French only); it also hosts interesting contemporary art exhibitions in a separate building. The quiet, shady grounds are home to scale models of Mali's major architectural landmarks. There's an excellent French-language bookshop and boutique and a good restaurant (see p489).

Musée de Bamako

Occupying a pleasant garden this **museum** (Map p486; Place de la Liberté, admission CFA500; ⏰ 9am-6pm Tue-Sun) in the centre of Bamako. The museum itself has little to turn the head with some ethnographic exhibits from the Bamako area, but the enlarged postcards of colonial Bamako are what make the visit worthwhile. Look especially for the photo of Bamako train station awash in crinolines and pith helmets.

Musée Muso Kunda

This engaging **museum** (off Map p483; Rue 161, Korofina Nord) was closed for major rebuilding works at the time of writing. When it reopens, it should once again pay homage to Mali's women, with displays of traditional clothing and everyday household objects. Take a *sotrama* (battered green minibus; CFA150) or taxi (CFA1000) from the west end of Rte de Koulikoro and ask for Fagigula (the museum is signposted from there).

Markets

The mother of all Bamako markets is the **Grand Marché** (Map p486), which spreads over an ever-expanding postcode of city blocks in the heart of town. It's a claustrophobic warren of streets, overtaken by traders of food, clothing and household goods, and can easily submerge you in a crush of people and powerful smells. For those who've just arrived in Africa it can be overwhelming, but it's an essential part of the Bamako experience.

The **fetish stalls** (Map p486; Blvd du Peuple), near the Maison des Artisans (see p491), are not for the faint-hearted, offering up a stomach-turning array of bones, skins, dried chameleons and rotting monkey heads.

The **Marché de Medina** (Map p483), northwest of the Hippodrome, is a large bustling place where the locals do their shopping and traders

are too busy making a living to bother hassling tourists. **Marché N'Golonina** (Map p483), between Niaréla and the city centre, is another fascinating local market to visit.

Point G

On the escarpment north of the city, **Point G** (Map p483) promises a panoramic overview of Bamako (and, on a still day, its pollution). Apart from the Niger River, which bisects the city away to the south, you may be surprised by the city's sheer scope and the proliferation of trees across the city. To get there, take a shared taxi from Place Point G (CFA250). A few poorly marked trails lead between Point G and the leafy **botanical gardens** (Map p483) at the foot of the hill, just north of the Musée National on Ave de la Liberté, although it can be easier to find coming down.

COURSES

Want to learn how to play the *kora* from Toumani Diabaté, the world's undisputed king of the *kora*? His **Mandinka Kora Production** (Map p483; dtoumani@hotmail.com; Rue 506, Porte 322, Badialam III) organises classes (€10 per hour) that run for just a few hours or a few weeks. If Toumani's in town and not on tour (which he often is), he may be your teacher. If he's not, one of his well-trained professionals will take over. This is also the premier *kora*-making workshop in Mali. Serious musicians can also use his recently built recording studio – contact the studio in advance for rates.

FESTIVALS & EVENTS

For two weeks in February 2009, Bamako hosted the first **Bamako Jazz Festival**, with the big names including Oumou Sangaré, Bassekou Kouyate and Ballaké Sissoko. There are plans for it to become an annual event. In even years in September, the capital also hosts the **Biennal**, a sports and cultural festival with live music.

SLEEPING

Bamako has a good range of places to sleep, although a lot of it's overpriced. Most of the better midrange places have left behind the city centre to its chaos.

Budget

If none of the following places appeal, you might want to try the dorm at the excellent Hôtel Tamana (see p487), although it usually needs a minimum of four people.

MALI

CENTRAL BAMAKO

0 ————— 500 m
0 ————— 0.3 miles

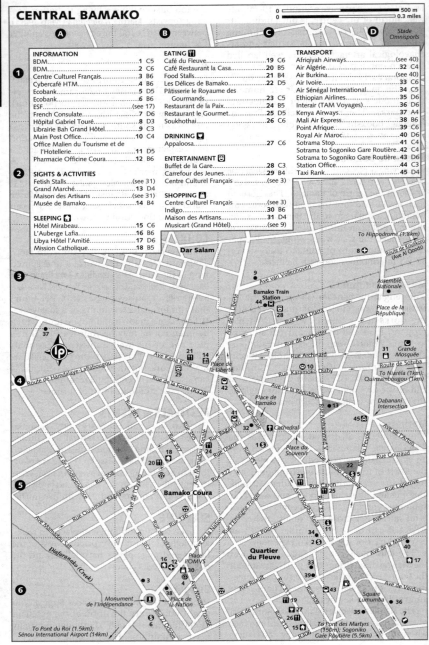

INFORMATION
BDM..................................1 C5
BDM..................................2 C6
Centre Culturel Français............3 B6
Cybercafé HTM.....................4 B6
Ecobank............................5 D5
Ecobank............................6 B6
ESF...............................(see 17)
French Consulate...................7 D6
Hôpital Gabriel Touré...............8 D3
Librairie Bah Grand Hôtel...........9 C3
Main Post Office...................10 C4
Office Malien du Tourisme et de
  l'Hôtellerie......................11 D5
Pharmacie Officine Coura...........12 B6

SIGHTS & ACTIVITIES
Fetish Stalls.......................(see 31)
Grand Marché......................13 D4
Maison des Artisans...............(see 31)
Musée de Bamako...................14 B4

SLEEPING
Hôtel Mirabeau.....................15 C6
L'Auberge Lafia....................16 B6
Libya Hôtel l'Amitié................17 D6
Mission Catholique.................18 B5

EATING
Café du Fleuve.....................19 C6
Café Restaurant la Casa............20 B5
Food Stalls........................21 B4
Les Délices de Bamako..............22 D5
Pâtisserie le Royaume des
  Gourmands.......................23 C5
Restaurant de la Paix..............24 B5
Restaurant le Gourmet.............25 D5
Soukhothai........................26 C6

DRINKING
Appaloosa.........................27 C6

ENTERTAINMENT
Buffet de la Gare..................28 C3
Carrefour des Jeunes..............29 B4
Centre Culturel Français ....(see 3)

SHOPPING
Centre Culturel Français ....(see 3)
Indigo............................30 B6
Maison des Artisans...............31 D4
Musicart (Grand Hôtel).............(see 9)

TRANSPORT
Afriqiyah Airways..................(see 40)
Air Algérie.........................32 C4
Air Burkina.......................(see 40)
Air Ivoire.........................33 C6
Air Sénégal International............34 C5
Ethiopian Airlines.................35 D6
Interair (TAM Voyages).............36 D6
Kenya Airways.....................37 A4
Mali Air Express...................38 B6
Point Afrique......................39 C6
Royal Air Maroc...................40 D6
Sotrama Stop......................41 C4
Sotrama to Sogoniko Gare Routière..42 C4
Sotrama to Sogoniko Gare Routière..43 D6
Station Office.....................44 C3
Taxi Rank.........................45 D4

Stade Omnisports

To Hippodrome (1.8km)

Route de Koulikoro (Ave Al Qoods)

Dar Salam

Assemblée Nationale

Place de la République

Bamako Train Station

Rue Baba Diarra

Rue de Rochester

Rue Archinard

Grande Mosquée

Route de Sotuba

To Niaréla (1km); Quinzambougou (1km)

Ave Kassa Keita

Place de la Liberté

Rue Karamoko Diaby

Ave de la République

Place de Bamako

Dabanani Intersection

Rue de la Fosse (R328)

Route de Hamdalaye-Lafiabougou

Rue 351

Place du Souvenir

Rue Gouraud

Cathedral

Rue Laperine

Ave de l'Indépendance

Bamako Coura

Rue Caron

Ave Pasteur

Quartier du Fleuve

Ave de la Marne

Ave Moussa Travelé

Place l'OMVS

Place de la Nation

Ave de Verdun

Square Lumumba

Monument de l'Indépendance

To Pont du Roi (1.5km); Sénou International Airport (14km)

Blvd 22 Octobre

Ave Rault

Ave de Tyser

To Pont des Martyrs (150m); Sogoniko Gare Routière (5.5km)

R306

Maison des Jeunes (Map p483; ☎ 2022 2320; mais jeunes@yahoo.fr; off Sq Lumumba; camping per person CFA1500, dm with fan CFA2500, d with air-con & without bathroom CFA8000; ✷) Maison des Jeunes is reasonable budget value. Rooms are so simple that the management calls them boxes, which is pretty accurate. Check the bed sheets for cleanliness in the larger dorms (ranging from two to 12 beds). Shared toilets are of the squat variety. Avoid walking the surrounding streets at night.

Mission Catholique (Foyer d'Accueil Bamako Coura; Map p486; ☎ 2022 7761; Rue Ousamane Bagayoko; dm CFA4000-5000, d with fan & without bathroom CFA10,000) This nun-run place gets high marks from travellers and could just be the best choice for those on a tight budget. It's a study in simplicity, but it's also clean, calm and secure, and a haven from hassles in one of Bamako's busiest areas (the courtyard is kept locked and guests are given a key, for a deposit of CFA5000). You'll need to bring your own sleeping bag/sheet and check-in is 7am to 1pm and 4pm to 10pm Monday to Saturday, 5pm to 10pm Sunday.

L'Auberge Lafia (Map p486; ☎ 7636 6894; bocoume@ yahoo.fr; Rue 367, Bamako Coura; dm CFA5000, d with fan from CFA10,000) As far as cheapies go, the simple, clean rooms here, with mosquito nets, are excellent. The sleeping quarters are ranged around a bare courtyard that has the feel of an African family compound. It's not sign-posted but ask around, as it's well known in the surrounding streets.

Massy House (off Map p483; ☎ 6676 3155; www .malifantasytours.com, in French; Rue 434, Porte 144, off Rte de Koulikoro, Boulkassoumbougou; roof mattress CFA2500, s/d with bathroom CFA7000/12,000, with air-con & bathroom CFA18,000/24,000, with fan & without bathroom CFA5000/8000) This place is hard to beat. Run by the super-friendly Massy who is a mine of information on all things Malian, this *maison d'hôte* is sparklingly clean, friendly and has a lovely African family atmosphere. Some may baulk at the distance from town – 2km beyond the Hippodrome – but we reckon it's one of the best budget places in Mali. Ring ahead for help in getting here.

Jatiguiya (off Map p483; ☎ 2023 9798; http://jatigu iya.free.fr, in French; Rue 108, off Rue Abdel Gamel Nasser, Badalabougou l'Ouest; dm CFA2500, d with fan & cold shower CFA10,500) This somnambulant place south of the river has spare rooms with thin mattresses and mosquito nets, and a better roof-terrace dorm with mosquito nets. You'll smell the shared toilets before you see them. Simple meals are also available (CFA1500).

Midrange

All the rooms at the following accommodations have private bathrooms, unless stated.

Cauris Lodge (Map p483; ☎ 6679 1438; hotelcaurislodge@ gmail.com; Rue 220, Niaréla; s/d with fan CFA10,000/13,000, with air-con CFA20,000/25,000; ✷ ▯ ⓦ ▣) Although not quite as good as Hôtel Tamana, Cauris Lodge is in a similar vein. The rooms are simple and nicely kept, but it's the overall atmosphere that wins plaudits from travellers. African art abounds in the lobby and the *paillote* (thatched awning) bar is chilled and quiet.

our pick **Hôtel Tamana** (Map p483; ☎ /fax 2021 3715; www.hoteltamana.com; Rue 216, Hippodrome; dm CFA8500, d with bathroom incl breakfast CFA26,000, without bathroom CFA24,000; ✷ ▯ ⓦ ▣) This charming French-run hotel out by the Hippodrome is easily our favourite in Bamako. The rooms have understated character (those with shared bathroom are overpriced), the local staff is among Bamako's friendliest, the bathrooms are immaculate and the leafy garden is a wonderful retreat after a long Bamako day. There's also a reasonably priced laundry service, a varied restaurant menu and the location is also one that you'll soon appreciate. The rooms in the annexe are quieter, especially on weekends. If you've spent any time researching Bamako hotels, you'll quickly realise what a great deal this is.

Sarama Hôtel (Map p483; ☎ 2021 0563; www.hotel sarama.com; Rue 220, Niaréla; s/d/ste CFA20,500/26,000/30,500; ✷ ⓦ ▣) Tucked away in the quiet streets of Niaréla, the Sarama is an interesting choice that sees fewer tourists than it deserves. Ever since it dropped its prices, it has been one of the best-value places in Bamako. Rooms are spacious, quiet and attractively furnished (apart from the carpet), and the friendly management is a plus. The only downside is the *tiny* swimming pool.

Hôtel les Colibris (off Map p483; ☎ 2022 6637; www .hotelcolibris.com, in French; off Ave de l'OUA, Sogoniko; s CFA20,000-30,000, d CFA25,000-35,000; ✷ ▯ ⓦ ▣) We love the swimming pool here, not to mention the expansive shady grounds. The cheaper rooms are actually better value, although the low ceilings make for a slightly claustrophobic feel. The bungalow-style rooms are better than the tired offerings in the main building. The location is either delightfully quiet or a fair hike into the centre, depending on your perspective.

MALI

Le Djenné (Map p483; ☎ 2021 3082; djenneart@afribone.net.ml; Rue 08, off Rte de Koulikoro; small s CFA21,000, larger s/d from CFA30,000/35,000; ✖ ◻ ☎) If you're tired of hotels that mimic European ambience, Le Djenné offers an antidote. Local and West African artists were given free rein to decorate this place: think masks, statues, African colour schemes and architectural flourishes. On the downside, some rooms are quite dark, maintenance is not what it could be and the service often goes missing.

Le Loft (Map p483; ☎ 2021 6690; leloft@orangemali.net; Rue Achkhabad, Niaréla; s/d/ste CFA32,500/36,500/50,500; ✖ ◻ ☎) This oasis of calm and sophistication is one place where you won't mind paying a little extra. Rooms are light, airy and spacious, with an attention to style that's lacking in many Bamako hotels. Wrought-iron furnishings and European-standard bathrooms set the tone, with the occasional nod to African themes. Good service, satellite TV, double-glazed windows and an excellent restaurant are among the other highlights.

Mandé Hôtel (Map p483; ☎ 2021 1993; www.mandehotel.com; Rue Niaréla, Cité du Niger; d/ste CFA47,500/53,000; ✖ ◻ ☎ ⛆) Yes, the Mandé is a long way from the city centre (a taxi should cost CFA1000), but its perch on a quiet stretch of the Niger River's bank is outstanding. The best views are reserved for the restaurant, while the bungalow-style rooms are set back behind the swimming pool. They're asking too much for the rooms, which are good if unspectacular, but prices are negotiable and we don't get too many complaints from travellers.

Hôtel Mirabeau (Map p486; ☎ 2023 5318; www.hotelmirabeaubko.net; Rue 311, Quartier du Fleuve; s/d/ste CFA44,000/48,500/60,000; ✖ ◻ ☎ ⛆) This place is terrific, with some of the most comfortable rooms in Bamako and a more intimate feel than the top-end places. Rooms are large and well appointed with satellite TV, there's a pleasant garden and pool and a business centre for those without laptops. Best of all, they readily admit that prices are negotiable.

Top End

Libya Hôtel El Farouk (Map p483; ☎ 2023 1830; www.laicohotels.com; Blvd 22 Octobre; s/d/ste from CFA89,000/99,000/139,000; ✖ ◻ ☎ ⛆) Opened in 2003, this is Bamako's most intimate and atmospheric top-end hotel. The public areas boast African art and the rooms are large, supremely comfortable and have all the bells and whistles. Unlike other riverbank hotels in Bamako,

every room has a river view, and the more you pay the better it is – the river suites have balconies overhanging the river. The service is also good.

Libya Hôtel L'Amitié (Map p486; ☎ 2021 4321; www.laicohotels.com; Ave de la Marne; s/d from CFA117,000/126,750; ✖ ◻ ☎ ⛆) One of Bamako's premier hotels, the recently renovated Amitié has a great location, rooms with a touch of class and incredible Bamako views from the roof. This is also a city in itself, with golf and tennis.

EATING
Quick Eats

Snacks like meat brochettes are cooked on small barbecues all around town. In the centre, try west of Place de la Liberté, across from Carrefour des Jeunes, where food stalls (Map p486) serve cheap rice and sauce.

Restaurant le Gourmet (Map p486; Rue Caron; meals from CFA750; ☽ 7am-6pm Mon-Sat) This small, simple place, just east of Ave Modibo Keita, offers only two or three dishes per day (often rice with a stew or sauce). The atmosphere is pleasant and the clientele predominantly African.

Restaurant de la Paix (Map p486; Rue Bagayoko; meals from CFA1000; ☽ lunch & dinner daily) Of the cheap and cheerful sit-down restaurants in Bamako Coura, this place is simplicity itself; it serves spicy Senegalese dishes and doesn't bother with printed menus.

Café Restaurant la Casa (Map p486; Rue Ousamane Bagayoko; meals from CFA1000; ☽ lunch & dinner daily) This chilled backpacker hang-out, opposite the Mission Catholique, dishes out spaghetti, couscous and ragout dishes with the freshest ingredients. If you want meat you'll need to order in advance.

Fast Food Adonis (Map p483; Rue Achkhabad; meals CFA2500-3000; ☽ 11am-midnight) In Niaréla east of the centre, Fast Food Adonis offers fast food (including shwarmas) and is one of the consistently reliable places in this part of town.

Broadway Café (Map p483; ☎ 2021 2618; Rue 224, Hippodrome; breakfast CFA1800-5000, hamburgers & salads CFA1200-3500, mains CFA2500-4000; ☽ breakfast, lunch & dinner daily) Run by two Malians who spent a decade in New York, the nonsmoking Broadway Café has mock American-diner decor, a laid-back vibe and a host of eating options that you won't find elsewhere in Bamako. Eggs Benedict or pancakes are a big breakfast hit among US expats, while the hamburgers, steaks, milkshakes, coke floats and desserts (including cheesecake) all have their admirers.

Poularco (Map p483; Rte de Bla Bla; paninis CFA1500-2300, pizza CFA3500-7000, mains CFA4500-7000; ☽ lunch & dinner) Out by the Hippodrome, this Lebanese-run place is terrific for snacks such as paninis (the *panini capt pané* – capitaine panini for CFA2000 is delicious), sandwiches, salads, shwarmas and hamburgers, as well as more substantial grilled dishes.

Restaurants

Le Relax (Map p483; ☎ 2021 7918; Rte de Koulikoro; starters CFA500-3000, mains CFA2500-5000, pastries CFA300-750; ☽ breakfast, lunch & dinner) Expats and wealthy locals rave about the food here, from the Lebanese and French specialities to the pasta, pizza and pastries. The atmosphere is informal and prices more reasonable than many places in Bamako.

Hong Mai (Map p483; ☎ 2021 7085; Rue 220, Niaréla; starters from CFA2000, mains from CFA3500; ☽ lunch & dinner Tue-Sun, dinner only Mon) This is one of our favourite Asian restaurants in Bamako, with predominantly Vietnamese cuisine served in a lovely oasis of a dining area; it also has plans for an outdoor terrace. You wouldn't think it's this good from the outside, but trust us: expats love this place, the food is terrific and the service attentive.

San Toro (Map p483; ☎ 2021 3082; djeneart@afribone .net.ml; Rte de Koulikoro; starters CFA2500, mains CFA4500; ☽ lunch & dinner) This original place has charmingly African decor and the specialities are quality Malian and regional West African dishes. There's no alcohol, but there are tasty fruit juices (CFA500) heavy on the ginger. Best of all, in the evenings from around 8pm (and occasionally at lunchtime), there's live *kora* music with djembe (type of drum) and balafon music sometimes thrown in.

Le Campagnard (Map p483; off Rte de Sotuba; starters CFA3200-6000, mains CFA4200-6250; ☽ 6am-11.30pm) Top marks for this place. High-quality French cooking, French wines and a switched-on ambience ensure plenty of regular customers among the expat community. The salad bar (CFA3100) is a nice touch and the wood-fired pizzas are good.

African Grill (Map p483; Musée National, Ave de la Liberté; starters from CFA2000, mains from CFA4500; ☽ lunch & dinner Tue-Sun) Within the tranquil grounds of the Musée National, this is a wonderful place to sample African specialities like *foutou* (sticky yam or plantain paste), *kedjenou* (slowly simmered chicken or fish with peppers and tomatoes) and *poulet yassa*. There's a different *plat du jour* (dish of the day) every day, a delightful dining area and friendly service. Also does sandwiches.

Pizzeria Da Guido (off Map p483; Rue 250, Porte 320, off Blvd Nelson Mandela, Hippodrome; starters CFA2000-3000, mains CFA4500-7500; ☽ lunch & dinner Fri-Wed) The friendly Italian owners produce what expats claim to be Bamako's best pasta and pizza, the salads are a delicious meal in themselves and the tiramisu has no peer south of the Mediterranean. The leafy courtyard out the back is a lovely place to enjoy it all. Serves wine and also does home/hotel delivery.

Soukhothai (Map p486; ☎ 6671 1051; Rue 311, Quartier du Fleuve; starters CFA4150-5950, mains from CFA6750; ☽ lunch & dinner Mon-Fri, dinner Sat) You won't find more authentic Thai cuisine in Africa, and expats swear by this place as one of Bamako's best restaurants. We're inclined to agree. If you order a bottle of wine, you'll easily pay CFA20,000 per person, so you may want to save it for a special occasion, but it's a classy place. Reservations are recommended.

Café du Fleuve (Map p486; ☎ 7918 9143; Rue 311, Quartier du Fleuve; starters CFA2800-4900, mains CFA6900-11,900; ☽ lunch & dinner) Styling itself as a brasserie, this elegant place is pricey but the quality and variety are high. The smoked *capitaine* and the duck brochettes with exotic fruits are among the highlights.

Cafes & Patisseries

If you're dreaming of flaky pastries and delicate cakes, Bamako doesn't have too much to get excited about. The following are the best of a fairly mediocre lot.

Pâtisserie le Royaume des Gourmands (Map p486; ☎ 2022 0725; Ave Modibo Keita; pastries & cakes CFA300-750; mains CFA1500-3000; ☽ 7am-11pm) It may not look much from the outside but this place is an air-con haven amid busy Bamako, with one of the nicest dining areas in downtown. More importantly, it serves decent croissants, cakes, coffee and fresh orange juice with a smile.

Les Délices de Bamako (Map p486; Immeuble Nimagala, Rue Famolo Coulibaly; pastries & cakes CFA300-700, meals from CFA2000; ☽ 7am-midnight Mon-Sat) This is a friendly and popular choice with cake eaters, although it's a bit down-at-heel.

Self-Catering

For imported food and wine, try **Le Fourmi Superstore** (Map p483; ☎ 2021 6167; Rte de Koulikoro; ☽ 7.30am-1pm & 3.30-8.30pm Mon-Sat, 8.30am-1pm Sun).

MALI

DRINKING

Bla Bla Bar (off Map p483; Rte de Bla Bla, Hippodrome; small beers CFA1500) This was once Mali's most sophisticated bar, and is so well known that the road on which it sits is now named after the bar. Regulars lament that it has lost something since being glassed in and blasted with air-con and that prices have soared, but it's still a Bamako institution filled with the bold and the beautiful at weekends.

Terrace (Map p483; Rte de Bla Bla, Hippodrome; small beers CFA1500; ☺ 8pm-late) Upstairs and open-air, Terrace is the place to gaze longingly into someone's eyes, if only because the high decibel music drowns out conversation streets away, let alone at the bar. It's a pretty upmarket crowd but the atmosphere, for all the noise, is agreeable.

If Bla Bla Bar and Terrace are too highbrow for you, there are plenty of earthy bars with an exclusively African clientele and outdoor tables between the Bla Bla and Rte de Koulikoro.

Le Campagnard (Map p483; ☎ 221 9296; www.lecampagnard.com, in French; off Rte de Sotuba; small beers CFA1000; ☺ 11am-late) This is the sort of place where South African gold miners rub shoulders with Peace Corps volunteers, which should give some idea of the breadth of its appeal, although it's mainly a foreign crowd. In 1995, *Newsweek* voted this one of the best bars in Africa – it's not *that* good but it is terrific.

Appaloosa (Map p486; Rue 311, Quartier du Fleuve; beers CFA1500-3000) This is the place to come for the evening frisson with long-legged, blonde-haired hostesses (who don't expect to pay for their drinks) rubbing shoulders and bottoms with rich Malian men and world-weary expats. Classily seedy, this is, for all its faults, a Bamako institution. Make of it what you will.

Apart from the above places, some of the nicest places for a drink are Bamako's live-music venues, even when no-one's playing. Our favourites include Le Diplomate (right) and Le Savana (opposite).

ENTERTAINMENT
Live Music

Bamako has some of the best live music in the world with many of Mali's international superstars performing most weekends. Venues change frequently and many of the artists spend much of the year touring outside Mali, so pay a visit to check who's on the bill. For more information on Mali's musicians, see p57 and p479.

Le Diplomate (off Map p483; ☎ 7678 1707; admission free; Rte de Koulikoro) This is one of the best venues in Bamako, with a classy crowd, sophisticated set-up and great music. Toumani Diabaté and his Symmetric Orchestra play here many Friday nights – the Friday night we were there, the orchestra started at 10pm, Toumani Diabaté took his place at 1.45am and even Habib Koita took the stage for a brief cameo. On nights like this, the whole world seems to be dancing. When Toumani's not in town, his band still plays.

Wassulu Hôtel (off Map p483; ☎ 2028 7373; Rte de l'Aéroport; admission CFA2500) Although she doesn't appear here as often as she used to, Oumou Sangaré sometimes takes to the stage at her hotel at 9pm on Saturday evenings. It's always worth a phone call in case you strike it lucky.

Centre Culturel Français (Map p486; ☎ 2022 4019; www.ccfbamako.org) The CCF's excellent regular program of events is always worth checking out because all the big names of the Malian music scene make an appearance here at some stage. Details are listed on its website.

Djembe (off Map p483; Lafiabougou; admission CFA2500) This live venue west of the centre may have a seedy feel and the sound system is terrible, but you'll see a fair sprinkling of expats among the shady characters and it remains one of the best places in Bamako for live music – mostly up-and-coming local bands with a few Guinean groups. There's live music most nights of the week, but this place really rocks on Friday and Saturday nights into the wee small hours.

Moffou (off Map p483), a nightclub 10km southwest of Pont du Roi, is owned by the legendary Salif Keita, but is really only worth it (and boy, is it worth it!) on the rare Saturday nights when he's playing. Otherwise you'll hear local bands of varying quality.

Other places where live music is on the program, usually Friday and Saturday nights:

Blonbar (off Map p483; Rte de Ségou) One of the 'in' places to be seen in Bamako with live music, comedians and occasional theatre.

Buffet de la Gare (Map p486; ☎ 2028 7373; off Rue Baba Diarra) Where the legendary Super Rail Band made its name. Now, you're more likely to hear a good but yet-to-be-famous local band on Friday and Saturday nights.

Carrefour des Jeunes (Map p486; Ave Kassa Keita) Under reconstruction when we were there, but good on weekends for local bands.

Exodus (Map p483; ☎ 7514 5528; off Rte de Koulikoro, Hippodrome) Casual outdoor venue with live music on Friday and Saturday nights from October to early March and a strong smell of horse from the surrounding stables…

Le Savana (off Map p483; Rte de Koulikoro, Korofina Nord) East of town, it attracts Bambara bands and a few Burkinabé groups.

San Toro (Map p483; Rte de Koulikoro) A restaurant with live *kora* music from 8pm nightly.

Nightclubs

Bamako comes into its own after dark, and on weekends it's a party town. Clubs don't get going before midnight and close around 6am. The only problem is that at most places you won't hear a whole lot of African music. Most clubs open every night of the week, but only really jump on Fridays and (even more so) Saturdays. Cover charges (CFA5000 to CFA7500) usually only apply on Friday and Saturday nights and include a drink; after that, drinks (ie small beers and soft drinks) start at CFA2000 and you'll pay around CFA5000 for spirits. There's not much to choose between them, but here are the most popular places:

Bla Bla Club (off Map p483; off Ave de l'OUA, Badala-bougou Est) South of the river and run by the people who brought you the famous Bla Bla Bar.

Ibiza Club (Map p483; Rte de Koulikoro, Hippodrome) A new megaclub providing serious competition to its more famous neighbour, Le Byblos.

Le Byblos (Map p483; Rte de Koulikoro, Hippodrome) The popularity of Bamako's first megaclub shows no sign of abating.

Show Biz (off Map p483; Rue 267, Porte 27, Djicoroni Para, ACI2000; Tue-Sun) This place bucks the trend with almost exclusively African music, and reasonable prices (Friday or Saturday admission CFA3000, drinks from CFA1000).

Theatre & Dance

Palais de la Culture Amadou Hampaté Bâ (off Map p483; 2022 3370; www.palaiscultureahb.net, in French; off Ave de l'OUA, Badalabougou Sema) Mali's national Palace of Culture, by the Niger River just south of the Pont des Martyrs, hosts Koteba (Mali's national theatre company), Le Ballet National and L'Ensemble National (for traditional Malian music), and generally provides support for local artists. Pop by for its three-monthly program *Kunnafoni*, which is also available in some hotels around town.

SHOPPING
Handicrafts

Mali Chic (off Map p483; 221 2442; malichic06@yahoo.fr; Rue 234, Porte 1528; 9am-5pm Mon-Sat) One of the most innovative and stylish boutiques in Mali, Mali Chic has reasonable prices and its commitment to working with over 140 artisans deserves to be supported. The array of items for sale – silver jewellery, masks, statues, textiles, artwork and home furnishings – is of the highest quality. To get here, head north along Rte de Bla Bla, turn right (east) on Rue 234, then look for the sign about 150m after you reach the mosque.

Indigo (Map p486; 2022 0893; www.indigo.com.ml; Place l'OMVS; 9am-6.30pm Mon-Sat) A charming, if small, boutique in the city centre, Indigo has reasonable prices for a well-chosen selection of textiles, masks, statues, musical instruments, crafts and home decorations.

Other places with fixed prices that are worth checking out include the boutique in the **Musée National** (Map p483; Ave de la Liberté; 9am-6pm Tue-Sun) and the boutique attached to San Toro (p489).

One local association worth supporting is **Association Culturelle – Anga Miri Sini Na** (off Map p483; 7643 9935, 7870 4409; www.kaderkeita.org; Rue 334, Porte 50, Lafiabougou). Run by renowned local artist Kader Keita and his partner Awa, it's a haven for the street kids of the Quartier. In addition to receiving shelter and food, the kids are taught artisan skills and most of what they produce is for sale. You can also do a tour of this small family-run project and donations are gratefully accepted. It's behind the cemetery in Lafiabougou, west of the town centre.

Traders drive a hard bargain at the **Maison des Artisans** (Map p486; Blvd du Peuple), where you'll find leather goods, jewellery and woodcarvings, as well as at Marché N'Golonina (Map p483). Local artisans also lay out their wares in the garden area of **Hôtel Tamana** (Map p483; Rue 216, Hippodrome).

Music

Mali K7 (Map p483; 2021 7508; www.mali-music.com; off Rue 540, Niaréla; 7.30am-4.45pm Mon-Fri, 8am-noon Sat) Set up by Ali Farka Touré to counter the rampant trade in pirated CDs, this is Mali's most reliable place for original CDs/cassettes, which cost CFA1600/1000. Not only can you be sure that your CDs will work when you get them home, but the proceeds also go to the artists. It also has an outlet in the **Centre Culturel Français** (Map p486; 2022 4019; Ave de l'Indépendance; 9.30am-1pm & 2-5.30pm Tue, Wed, Fri & Sat, 1.30-5.30pm Thu).

Musicart (Map p486; Grand Hôtel, Ave van Vollenhoven; 10am-8pm Mon-Sat) At this place in the Grand Hôtel, prices are on a par with Europe (up to CFA15,000 per CD), but buying here also means the musicians get royalties.

MALI

GETTING THERE & AWAY

Air

Bamako's **Sénou International Airport** (☎ 6600 7071) also serves a number of domestic routes. **MAE** (Map p486; ☎ 2023 1465; www.mae -mali.com; Ave de la Nation) has flights to Mopti/ Sévaré (CFA60,500, twice weekly), Timbuktu (CFA97,600, twice weekly) and Kayes (CFA69,000, three weekly). **Air CAM** (off Map p483; ☎ 2022 2424; www.camaero.com; Ave Cheick Zayed, Hamdallaye) is generally less reliable, but it does operate the only services between Bamako and Gao (CFA115,000, once weekly); it also runs three weekly flights to Mopti, Timbuktu and Kayes. For more on these two airlines, see p538.

Boat

The big boats leave from Koulikoro, some 50km downstream of Bamako. For details on the Niger River boat service, see p539.

Bus

Long-distance transport for destinations south of the Niger River leaves from the Sogoniko *gare routière* (off Map p483), 6km south of the city centre on the left-hand side of the road heading south (CFA2000 by taxi, CFA150 by *sotrama*). It's less a definable bus station than where all the major companies have their own compounds strung out along the road. This is home to **Bani** (☎ 2020 6081) and **Bittar** (☎ 2020 1205) among others with dozens of services heading north along the Bamako–Gao road.

Transport for destinations north of the Niger River leaves from **Destination Nord gare routière** (Map p483; near Place Point G) or around Marché de Medina (Map p483). Truck-buses to Kita leave at least three times a day, while occasional services to Nioro and Nara also leave from here. Transport to Koulikoro (CFA1250) leaves when full. **Gana Transport** (☎ 2021 0978) has its bus park at Place Point G.

Bamako to	Fare (CFA)	Duration (hr)
Bandiagara	8000	9-11
Douentza	10,000	10-12
Hombori	12,000	12-14
Gao	15,000	16-20
Mopti	7500	7-10
Ségou	3000	3
Sikasso	4500	3-4
Timbuktu	15,000	15

Train

Two companies operate services from Bamako's main train station, although both sell their tickets from the same **station office** (Map p486; ☎ 2022 8110). Beware of thieves amid the crowds.

Express operates international services to Dakar (see p539), which also stop in Kayes (2nd-class seat/couchette CFA7300/11,500, 1st-class seat/couchette CFA16,190/22,190). At the time of writing, trains were departing Bamako on Saturday and Wednesday, but this was subject to change.

Autorail also sends trains from Bamako to Kayes (seat only 2nd/1st class CFA7000/11,700) at 7am on Monday and Wednesday, and at 7.30pm Friday.

GETTING AROUND

The official rate from the airport to the city centre by private taxi is CFA7500, although it should cost CFA5000 going the other way.

Sotramas run (often out of control) from central Bamako to the *gares routières* and the outer suburbs for between CFA100 and CFA150. Important stops are marked on the Central Bamako map (Map p486).

Most taxis in Bamako are yellow. Those with a 'taxi' sign on the roof are shared, while those without signs are for *déplacement* (private hire) only. The longest journey (such as Sogoniko *gare routière* to Hippodrome) in a private taxi should never cost more than CFA2000, although most journeys should cost half that.

AROUND BAMAKO

KOULIKORO

Koulikoro was an important place in colonial days when the train from Dakar terminated here, but today most visitors only come here to catch the Comanav boat to Timbuktu. In November, there's an annual marionette festival at Diarabougou, 20km east of town.

Motel le Saloon (☎ 2126 2024; d from CFA12,500; 🕃) is the most pleasant place to stay.

Plenty of transport leaves from Koulikoro market for Bamako's Destination Nord *gare routière* (CFA1250, one to two hours). Gana Transport has four buses a day from Place Point G in Bamako. The **Comanav office** (☎ 2126 2095) is on the western outskirts of town. See the boxed text, p540, for more information.

AN INTERVIEW WITH TWO FEMALE GUIDES *Anthony Ham*

Guiding is an overwhelmingly male profession in Mali, and the number of female guides can be counted on one hand. In January 2009, I interviewed **Mariam Sow** (☎ 7637 2977; tenekounet@ yahoo.fr) and **Ramtou Koné** (☎ 7312 4580), two female Malian guides.

Anthony Ham (AH): What did your families think when you decided to become a guide?

Mariam Sow (MS): My mother accepted it, but my father and many of my aunts and uncles didn't like it. They told me I should get married and asked why I wanted to be a man.

Ramtou Koné (RK): My family has always encouraged me.

AH: Did they change their minds?

MS: My father died before he could change his mind, but now the rest of the family see that I bring more money into the family than they do, so they have learned to live with it.

AH: Is it difficult to be a female guide in Mali?

MS: At the beginning, yes. You have to be a very strong woman. Many people told me that I was trying to be a man, that guiding was a man's job. But they see that I can guide just like them, and so now they respect and help me.

RK: No-one has said anything to me directly, but I have heard that some other guides think that I must be a prostitute because I am doing this job. But most people encourage me.

AH: Why aren't there more female guides in Mali?

MS: In my opinion, it is because Malian women are lazy. Guiding is very hard work. I sat the guiding exam with a number of women, and they all stopped after their first trip. I am the only one left.

SIBY

The small town of Siby, 45km southwest of Bamako, lies in the heart of Mande country. The surrounding landscape is home to the beautiful Arch of Kamadjan, surrounded by hilly woodlands, and it is close to here that the Empire of Mali was born in the 13th century (see p27); traditional, small-scale gold mining is still carried on here. The best place to organise your exploration of the region (including rock climbing) is at **Hôtel Kamadjan** (☎ 7632 8033; www.hotelkamadjansiby.net; s/d/tr CFA3000/6000/7500, meals CFA2500-5000), which has simple but tidy bungalow-style accommodation and plenty of information about the local area. Saturday (market day) is a good day to be in town.

Occasional shared taxis leave from Bamako's Djikoroni *gare routière* (off Map p483) to Siby (CFA2000, two hours).

THE CENTRE

Central Mali is dominated by the Niger River and its tributary the Bani, and along the banks of these mighty rivers are some of Mali's most interesting towns. Ségou, just three hours from Bamako, is a pretty town with an outstanding music festival and travellers love Teriya Bugu, a pioneering ecotourism project on a quiet bend of the Bani River. The Great Mosque of Djenné and the town's Monday market are among Mali's most popular sights. Further to the northeast, Mopti is a lively river port where most travellers end up en route to Timbuktu or the Dogon Country.

SÉGOU
pop 104,987

Strung out lazily along the riverbank 230km east of Bamako, Ségou carries a wealth of historical associations for the Bambara people (Ségou was the capital of an important Bambara kingdom until the early 19th century) and it has enough sights to warrant at least a couple of nights' stay. For most of the year, its attractions include faded colonial buildings and a languid riverside charm, with easy excursions to nearby villages by pirogue, and to Ségou Koro, the old town of Ségou, 9km upstream from the modern town. If you're here in late January to early February, Ségou hosts the terrific Festival Sur Le Niger.

Information
EMERGENCY
Ambulance (☎ 15)
Hôpital Nianankoro Fomba (☎ 2132 0051; cnr Blvd de l'Indépendance & Rte de Mopti)
Pharmacie Officine Adam (☎ 2132 0643; Blvd de l'Indépendance)

MALI

INTERNET ACCESS
Cybercafé Sotelma (Blvd de l'Indépendance; per hr CFA1000; ⏲ 8am-9pm)
NTS Cyber Café (Rue 22; per hr CFA600; ⏲ 7.30am-midnight)

MONEY
BDM (Blvd de l'Indépendance) Changes euro cash and has a Visa-enabled ATM.
BNDA (Rte de Mopti) Changes cash and travellers cheques.
Ecobank (Rte de Mopti) Changes euro and US dollars cash and travellers cheques.

TOURIST INFORMATION & GUIDES
Association des Guides Segouvienne pour le Tourisme Solidaire (AGSTS; ☎ 7622 8609, 7302 4870; agstsmali@yahoo.fr; Rue 21) Local guides' association with fixed prices on the wall.
Centre d'Information AHRTS Quai des Arts
(☎ 2132 3206; www.tourisme-segou.com; Quai Ousmane Djiri; ⏲ 9am-12.30pm & 3-5.30pm Tue-Sun) Privately run tourist office with information on hotels, transport, restaurants and sights and finding guides.

Sights & Activities
Faded **French colonial buildings**, set just back from the road, line the western end of Ségou's Blvd de l'Indépendance. On the riverbank southwest of the centre, a small but interesting **pottery market** is a worthwhile finishing point for a pleasant riverside stroll. Quai Ousmane Djiri, also known as **Quai des Arts**, has some replica traditional buildings (including an artisan workshop and exhibition area). Market day in Ségou is Monday.

Espace Bajidala (☎ 2132 3437; www.bajidala.com; Rue 529, Quartier Administratif; admission CFA1000; ⏲ 10am-6pm) is a lovely contemporary art gallery 3km southwest of the centre.

PIROGUE TRIPS
From the waterfront, pirogues can take you on excursions to **Kalabougou**, where pottery is made (and fired at weekends), and **Farako**, a centre for mud-cloth making. A good place to organise these trips is AGSTS (see above). Three-hour guided trips to Kalabougou, for example, cost CFA22,500 per person, plus a CFA3500 tourist tax (per group, not per person). Opposite Ségou, the fishing village of **Kala Daka** can be reached by public pinasse (large pirogue; CFA250).

SÉGOU KORO
The historic and beautiful village of Ségou Koro lies 9km upstream, just off the main Ségou–Bamako road. In the 18th century it was the centre of Biton Mamary Coulibaly's Bambara kingdom; the great man is buried here and his former palace is being restored. Ségou Koro's crumbling mud buildings are interspersed with three pretty ancient mosques. Introduce yourself to the chief, who collects the CFA2500 tourist tax. A guided tour costs CFA15,000 per person, including transport from/to Ségou.

BOGOLAN WORKSHOPS
Ségou is home to two of Mali's most interesting *bogolan* workshops using all-natural products. In both places, it's free to wander around and visit the shop, while a guided tour costs CFA500 per person.

Ndomo (☎ 2132 2794; www.promali.org/ndomo; Rte de Mopti; guided tours CFA500; ⏲ guided tours 8am-2pm, shop 8am-5pm), around 5km south of the centre on the road to Mopti, runs guided tours that take you through the *bogolan* story, design techniques and staff members even let you try your hand at *bogolan* design. They also have a good shop (fixed price).

Galerie Soroble (☎ 2132 1367; soroblecentre@yahoo.fr; off Blvd El Hadj Omar Tall; guided tours CFA500; ⏲ guided tours 2-6pm, shop 8am-6pm), southwest of the centre and opposite the post office, is also outstanding, covering the entire *bogolan* process, from weaving and dyeing to the final design workmanship. The upstairs cafe serves delicious baobab or bissap juice (CFA750) with river views. It also has a small shop along Rue 21 in the centre of town.

Festivals & Events
First held in 2005, Ségou's **Festival Sur le Niger** (☎ 2132 1804; www.festivalsegou.org; 3-day festival pass €100), in late January or early February, has evolved into one of West Africa's premier music and cultural festivals. During the festival, the riverbank comes alive with exhibitions, dance, theatre and puppet performances, storytelling and craft displays. Headline acts in 2009 included Oumou Sangaré, Bassekou Kouyate, Vieux Farka Touré and Mamadou Diabaté.

Courses
Daouda Dembélé (☎ 6665 5095) is a local musician who organises private classes in djembe, *kora* or dance for CFA3500 per hour. Otherwise, **Motel Savane** (☎ 2132 0974; www.motelsavane.com; off Blvd de l'Indépendance) can

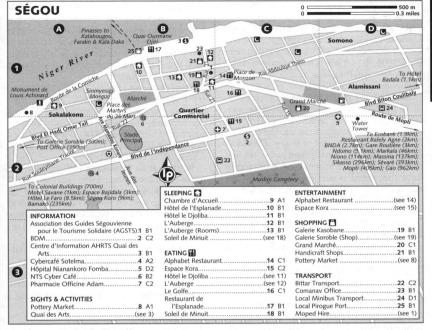

SÉGOU

arrange drumming classes with advance notice.

Sleeping

There aren't many options for budget travellers, but midrange choices are good.

If you'd like to arrange a home-stay with a local family (bed only CFA5000 per person), contact **Bala** (☎ 7603 0120) at Espace Kora (see p496).

Chambre d'Accueil (☎ 7608 5062; Rte de la Corniche; per person CFA2500) It doesn't get much more basic than this small, three-room guesthouse, but there's much to recommend it apart from the price: a riverside location and an African family atmosphere. The squat toilets are not Mali's cleanest and there are only bucket showers. Meals with the family cost CFA2500.

Hôtel Badala (☎ 2132 2486; Quartier Somono; roof mattress CFA2500, d with fan & without bathroom CFA10,000, s/d/ste with air-con & bathroom CFA18,000/20,000/50,000;) Good if you're keen to be away from the hassles of Ségou's port area but still by the river, Hôtel Badala has pleasant rooms in a quiet location, a 15-minute walk east of the centre. Prices include breakfast.

Soleil de Minuit (☎ 2132 1505; soleildeminuitsegou@ gmail.com; cnr Rue 21 & Blvd El Hadj Omar Tall; roof mattress CFA4000, s/d with fan from CFA12,500/15,000, d with air-con from CFA20,000;) Simple rooms are the order of the day at this place, but they're the cheapest beds you'll find in the heart of town.

Motel Savane (☎ 2132 0974; www.motelsavane .com; off Blvd de l'Indépendance; dm CFA3000, s/d with fan & without bathroom CFA10,000/13,000, with fan & bathroom CFA12,000/15,000, with air-con & bathroom CFA20,000/25,000, apt CFA39,000;) If you don't mind being a 10-minute walk from the riverbank, Motel Savane has spacious, sparkling rooms with splashes of colour and character. It's also wonderfully quiet with a shady garden area.

our pick Espace Bajidala (Chez Michel; ☎ 2132 3437; www.bajidala.com; Rue 529, Quartier Administratif; d with air-con & bathroom CFA24,000, breakfast CFA4000;) Although it's 3km southwest of the town centre, Espace Bajidala is wonderful. The rooms, arrayed around a verdant garden with contemporary art installations, are large and filled with character, and the riverside location is quiet and picturesque.

Hôtel de l'Esplanade (☎ 2132 0127; hotel.espla nade@hotmail.com; Quai Ousmane Djiri; s/d with fan & bathroom

CFA17,000/22,000, with air-con & bathroom CFA20,000/28,000; 🏠 💻 🛜 🍴) Position, position, position. Although most rooms don't take advantage of the riverside locale, walk out the door and there's the Niger in all its glory. Italian-run since 2006, the service is much improved and there's free wi-fi for guests, although the rooms are in need of an overhaul.

Hôtel Le Faro (☎ 7519 2006; www.lefaro.biz; s/d with air-con & bathroom incl breakfast CFA18,000/24,000, meals CFA5500; 🏠) Another terrific place, Hôtel Le Faro sits by the riverbank close to the entrance of Ségou Koro, 9km west of Ségou. There's an air of tranquillity here that you just don't find any more in Ségou proper, and most rooms have the added bonus of river views. The rooms, like the public areas, are attractive.

Hôtel le Djoliba (☎ /fax 2132 1572; www.segou-hotel-djoliba.com; cnr Rue 21 & Blvd El Hadj Omar Tall; s/d with fan & bathroom CFA21,500/24,500, with air-con & satellite TV CFA23,000/26,000, breakfast from CFA2000; 🏠) You can't get any more central than this well-run place not far from the riverbank. The rooms are large and attractive, the service is good and there is an ambience where European quality is wedded to African tranquillity.

L'Auberge (☎ 2132 1731; www.promali.org/aub-ind; Rue 21; s/d/ste CFA23,000/25,000,035,000; 🏠 🍴)L'Auberge is one of those African hotels where 4WDs park out the front and road-weary travellers fill the bar and restaurant. The garden (with swimming pool) is delightful, while the rooms (a short block away from the reception building) are nice if unspectacular.

Eating & Drinking

Restaurant Balely Agne (☎ 2132 1128; Rue 287, off Rte de Mopti; mains from CFA500; 🕐 6am-midnight) For cheap meals, it's hard to go past this place that serves hearty *riz sauce* (rice with sauce) and other local staples to hungry locals. It's signposted off Rte de Mopti 2km south of the centre.

Alphabet Restaurant (☎ 6676 2076; Place de Monzon; meals CFA1000-5000; 🕐 6pm-late) Alphabet gets rave reviews from travellers for its good food and friendly atmosphere, which is the work of Oumar Touré, the amiable owner and host. Dishes include some vegetarian choices and a host of river fish beyond the usual *capitaine*.

Espace Kora (☎ 2132 0950; Rue 21; mains CFA1500-5000; 🕐 7.30am-late) Although better known as a live-music venue (see right), Espace Kora serves reasonable food in a lovely garden setting. The atmosphere is great in the evening.

Le Golfe (☎ 7612 0555; Rte de Mopti; snacks from CFA1000, mains from CFA1800; 🕐 6am-late) This central place has gone ever-so-slightly upmarket since we were last here, which means you're more likely to see tourists than locals, but the food is still inexpensive, servings are well sized and the food's good.

Soleil de Minuit (☎ 2132 1505; cnr Rue 21 & Blvd El Hadj Omar Tall; meals from CFA3500; 🕐 7am-10.30pm) Highly regarded by travellers for its laid-back atmosphere, this place is warmly recommended. The *capitaine à la Bamakoise* (fried Nile perch with bananas and tomato sauce; CFA4000) is a highlight.

Restaurant de l'Esplanade (☎ 2132 0127; Quai Ousmane Djiri; starters from CFA1800, pizza from CFA5000, pasta from CFA4800) Excellent location right by the water's edge and an Italian host who knows his pizza make for a fantastic combination. It's not cheap, but there's no better pizza in Mali.

Of the other hotels, Hôtel le Djoliba (starters from CFA2500, mains from CFA2500) is excellent and also does a good pizza buffet (CFA4000) on the terrace on Saturday nights. L'Auberge also cooks up wood-fired pizzas.

Entertainment

For live music, **Espace Kora** (Rue 21; 🕐 7.30am-late) is the best venue in town with lively local bands and a terrific setting from 9pm Thursday to Sunday. Also good is **Alphabet Restaurant** (Place de Monzon; 🕐 6pm-late) with live acts most nights from 9pm. At both places, admission is free but you're expected to buy a drink.

Shopping

You can find Bambara pottery at the **pottery market** (Rte de la Corniche), 1km southwest. For Ségou strip cloth and blankets, try the **Grand Marché** (Rte de Mopti). A large group of curio sellers can be found opposite L'Auberge. Bargain hard.

For high-quality *bogolan* textiles, both Ndomo and Galerie Soroble (see p494) are hard to beat; the latter also has a small **boutique** (Rue 21) in the town centre. For a small but creative range of *bogolan* textiles, check out also **Galerie Kasobane** (☎ 2132 2168; Rue 21; 🕐 9am-6pm Mon-Sat).

Getting There & Away
BUS & MINIBUS
The only reputable bus company with a handy central location is **Bittar Transport** (☎ 7642

THE GREAT CROSSING

All across central Mali from November, you're likely to see vast Fula herds closing in on the Niger River, readying themselves for one of West Africa's most picturesque annual rituals. Every late December or early January (the exact date depends on water levels), the central Niger is transformed into a hive of activity, as hundreds of thousands of cows are driven southwards and across the Niger River to greener pastures. The crossing, known as *Dewgal,* dates back almost 200 years, and is a happy time for the Fula herders, who have been on the fringes of the Sahara for many months. The crossing means reunion with their families and a time to celebrate with music and dance. Fulani women adorn themselves in all their ritual gold-and-amber finery, while the men paint and decorate their favourite animal to see who owns the finest and fattest beast.

The first and most celebrated crossing takes place at Diafarabé, where massive crowds line the riverbanks. Competitions are held to reward the herdsmen with the fattest cattle, and there's even a booby prize of a single peanut for those deemed to have done the worst job. The herdsmen are usually young men between the ages of 10 and 16: this is an important Fulani rite of passage. It's also a chance for the young men to impress potential brides, as this is seen as an auspicious time for engagements.

1673; off Blvd de l'Indépendance) which has services to Bamako (CFA3000, six to seven daily, three hours), Mopti (CFA5000, two daily, five to six hours), as well as daily buses at 11.30am to Bobo-Dioulasso (CFA8000) and Ouagadougou (CFA15,000) in Burkina Faso. Otherwise, most other companies leave from the *gare routière,* 3km south of town. Other possible routes include Sikasso (CFA4500, four hours) and Gao (CFA14,000, 12 hours).

Minibuses to local destinations collect passengers on the dirt road behind the Elf petrol station.

BOAT

Comanav (☎ 2132 0204) has an office in Ségou; see p540 for details of boat services.

Getting Around

No journey around town should cost more than CFA300 in a shared taxi or CFA150 in a motor-rickshaw. Mopeds can be hired along Rue 21 for CFA6000 per day.

TERIYA BUGU

Ecotourism projects are pretty few and far between in Mali, but **Teriya Bugu** (☎ 2133 1000; www .tb-mali.com; guided visit CFA2500; dm CFA5000, d with fan/aircon CFA17,500/25,000, breakfast CFA1500, meals from CFA3000; 🍴) is a special place. Begun by the former French missionary Father Bernard Verspieren as a community development project, Teriya Bugu now employs 60 locals and supports 7000 people in 30 surrounding villages. The aim from the beginning was self-sufficiency and Teriya Bugu has for decades relied for most of its power on solar energy and the production of its own biofuels. As part of the project, which covers 450 hectares, 250,000 eucalyptus trees were planted, thousands of water pumps were created across the region, and schools, health clinics and microcredit schemes operate in numerous villages. Teriya Bugu also produces 80% of its own food.

After Father Bernard's death in 2003, the local custodians hit upon the idea of ecotourism to maintain the financial viability of the project, opening a number of delightful, large rooms and a restaurant just back from the riverbank. It's well worth taking the guided tour around the project; they also organise pinasse-and-picnic excursions (from CFA5000 per person) to neighbouring villages. More than that, at around 30km off the main highway and under the shade by the riverbank, you may wonder if you've wandered into a Malian paradise.

You'll need your own vehicle to get to Teriya Bugu. There are two roads from the main highway. If you're coming from Ségou, the well-signposted turn-off for Teriya Bugu is just after crossing the Bani River, although this 37km track is impassable during the rainy season. The other option is the 28km signposted track that leaves the main highway northeast of Bla, between the villages of Kemeni and Kotienso. This second route is passable year-round.

DJENNÉ
pop 23,790

Djenné's Unesco World Heritage–listed old town, which sits on an island in the Bani River,

MALI

is one of our favourite places in Mali, not to mention one of West Africa's oldest towns. Its incomparable mosque – the largest mud-built structure in the world – is like a fairy-tale apparition from a childlike imagination and provides the backdrop to Djenné's huge, lively and colourful Monday market. The market and mosque will turn your head, but stay after the traders and other tourists have gone home and you'll share the labyrinthine streets and sleepy atmosphere with just the locals: this is when many travellers really fall in love with Djenné.

Information

Visitors to Djenné must pay a CFA1000 tourist tax per person; it's collected at the checkpoint at the Djenné turn-off, soon after leaving the Bamako–Mopti road.

The only bank in Djenné at the time of research was BIM, opposite Restaurant Kita Kourou, which changes euros cash only. Otherwise, bring enough money for the duration of your stay.

To find an accredited guide, try the helpful **Omatho** (☎ 2142 1429; ☽ 8am-4pm Mon-Fri) office, where they also give out a good photocopy map (CFA100) of town, or the **Bureau de Guides** (☎ 7618 1698), next to Restaurant le Fleuve; the latter can be more hassle than it's worth. Standard rates for a two-hour city tour start at CFA5000 for one person, CFA2500 per person for two or more.

Other useful services:

Business Center BGS (per hr CFA1000; ☽ 8am-8pm) Internet access.

Centre de Sante de Reference Basic medical care west of the town centre.

Clic Internet (per hr CFA1500; ☽ 8am-1pm & 4-7pm)

Pharmacie Alafia Next to Restaurant Kita Kourou (p500).

Sights

A new city museum, expected to open in 2010, was being built north of the Great Mosque while we were there.

For information on visiting the various *bogolan* workshops, see p501.

MISSION CULTURELLE

Visiting the **Mission Culturelle** (☎ 2142 0535; ma madousamake@yahoo.fr; admission CFA500; ☽ 8am-6pm) gives an excellent background to Djenné. Apart from some photos and artefacts from Jenné-Jeno (p500), there are some fine old photos of Djenné, including one from 1893 showing the ruins of the previous Great Mosque of Djenné. The well-informed staff will accompany you to the archaeological site for a negotiable fee (around CFA2000). Staff services will, however, move to the new museum once the latter opens.

GRAND MOSQUÉE (GREAT MOSQUE)

Djenné's supremely elegant mosque was constructed in 1907, based on the design of an older Grande Mosquée that stood on the site. The Grande Mosquée was first built in 1280, after Koi Konboro (the 26th king of Djenné) converted to Islam. It remained intact until the early 19th century when the fundamentalist Islamic warrior-king, Cheikou Amadou, let it fall to ruin. The modern form – a sumptuous example of Sahel-style mudbrick architecture – is faithful to the original design, which served as a symbol of Djenné's wealth and cultural significance.

The wooden spars that jut out from the walls not only form part of the structure, but also support the ladders and planks used during the annual repairs to the mud-render. Overseen by specialist masons, this work takes place at the end of every rainy season, when up to 4000 people volunteer to help. At the time of writing, the mosque was undergoing restoration work by the Aga Khan Development Network.

Excellent views of the mosque are to be had from the roofs of surrounding houses (usually for CFA500) or the Petit Marché. Non-Muslim visitors cannot go inside, although some tourists pay large sums to do so, at great risk of offending local sensibilities.

MONDAY MARKET & PETIT MARCHÉ

Every Monday, the wide-open area in front of the mosque is transformed into a clamorous market, which has barely changed since the days when Saharan camel caravans brought salt to the gates of Djenné. Thousands of traders and customers come from miles around, and many of these itinerant traders follow the calendar of local market days in the region's villages. Most arrive late Sunday night or early Monday morning, by which time market-day traders are already staking out the best sites. By mid- to late morning (the best time to visit the market), the open square in front of the mosque is filled with traders selling everything from cloth to calabashes, spices to spaghetti and pottery to pungent

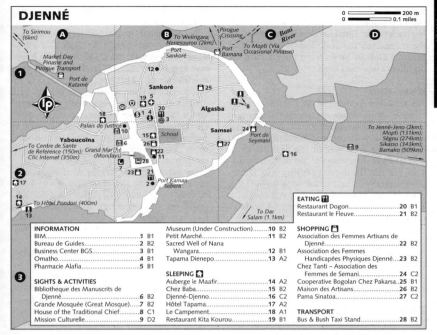

DJENNÉ

0 ——— 200 m
0 ——— 0.1 miles

To Sirimou (6km)

Market Day Pinasse and Pirogue Transport

Port de Katamé

To Welingara; Nenesourou (2km)

Pirogue Crossing

Port Sankoré

Port Bamana

Bani River

To Mopti (Via Occasional Pinasse)

Sankoré

Algasba

Palais de Justice

Yaboucoïna

To Centre de Sante de Reference (150m); Clic Internet (350m)

Grand Marché (Mondays)

School

Samsei

Port de Seymani

Port Kaman Sebera

To Hôtel Pondori (400m)

To Dar Salam (1.1km)

To Jenné-Jeno (2km); Mopti (131km); Ségou (274km); Sikasso (343km); Bamako (509km)

EATING 🍴
Restaurant Dogon....................**20** B1
Restaurant le Fleuve................**21** B2

INFORMATION
BIM...**1** B1
Bureau de Guides.......................**2** B2
Business Center BGS....................**3** B1
Omatho...**4** B1
Pharmacie Alafia.........................**5** B1

SIGHTS & ACTIVITIES
Bibliotheque des Manuscrits de
Djenné....................................**6** B2
Grande Mosquée (Great Mosque)....**7** B2
House of the Traditional Chief......**8** C1
Mission Culturelle.......................**9** D2

Museum (Under Construction)........**10** B2
Petit Marché................................**11** B2
Sacred Well of Nana
Wangara.................................**12** B1
Tapama Dienepo.........................**13** A2

SLEEPING 🛏️
Auberge le Maafir.......................**14** A2
Chez Baba...................................**15** B2
Djenné-Djenno...........................**16** C2
Hôtel Tapama.............................**17** A2
Le Campement............................**18** A1
Restaurant Kita Kourou...............**19** B1

SHOPPING 🛍️
Association des Femmes Artisans de
Djenné....................................**22** B2
Association des Femmes
Handicapées Physiques Djenné...**23** B2
Chez Tanti – Association des
Femmes de Semani...................**24** C2
Cooperative Bogolan Chez Pakarsa.**25** B1
Maison des Artisans.....................**26** B2
Pama Sinatoa..............................**27** C2

TRANSPORT
Bus & Bush Taxi Stand..................**28** B2

local foods and prize goats. The quintessentially African feel of the market, the stunning backdrop of the mosque and Djenné's island location add up to one of Mali's most memorable experiences.

If you can't be in Djenné on a Monday (and even if you can), don't miss the smaller-scale but daily Petit Marché.

ARCHITECTURE OF OLD DJENNÉ

You'll struggle to find a modern building anywhere in Djenné and the maze of dusty streets is lined with decrepit buildings and Moroccan- or Moorish-style structures with elaborate doors, windows and roofs. Unusually for Africa, many of the mudbrick houses are over a storey high; traditionally, the top part was for the masters, the middle floor for the slaves and the bottom floor for storage and selling. The porches of many houses are lined with wooden columns, and the window shutters and doors are painted and decorated with metal objects. You'll also see Fulani-style covered entrances. The oldest part of Djenné is west of the Great Mosque, known as Yaboucoïna.

On a stroll through Djenné you'll pass numerous **Quranic schools**; there are more such schools in Djenné than in any other Malian town as befits its history as a renowned centre of Islamic scholarship. With the help of a guide, you can also see the old **Sacred Well of Nana Wangara**; the facade and story (the Moroccan inhabitants of Djenné once believed that news from the river between Timbuktu and Djenné could be read in the well's waters) are more interesting than the well itself, for which the expected CFA1000 tip is way too much. The beautiful **house of the traditional chief**, at the eastern end of town, is also worth seeking out; René Caillié stayed here en route to Timbuktu in 1828. On the southern edge of town is **Tapama Dienepo**, the tomb of a young girl sacrificed here in the 9th century, after a local religious leader decided the town was corrupt.

BIBLIOTHEQUE DES MANUSCRITS DE DJENNÉ

This small **manuscript library** (admission CFA1000; ⏰ 9am-12.30pm & 4-6pm Mon-Sat), immediately north of the Great Mosque, will get better with age. Only a handful of its 2000 manuscripts (there are over 10,000 in Djenné, some dating back to the 13th century) is on display. In the meantime, the scale model of the Great Mosque and the views from the roof are the highlights of a visit here.

JENNÉ-JENO
About 2.5km southeast of Djenné are the ruins of Jenné-Jeno, an ancient settlement that dates back to about 300 BC. Implements and jewellery discovered here suggest that it may have been one of the first places in Africa where iron was used; for more information, see p26. In the 8th century AD, Jenné-Jeno was a fortified town with walls 3.7m thick (traces of which you can still see) with 15,000 inhabitants and covering 33 hectares (just under half the size of modern Djenné), but around 1300 it was abandoned. Today, there's nothing much to see – some mounds, millions of tiny pottery shards and even the occasional skeleton peeping up through the dust – so visiting is of greater historical than aesthetic interest.

Sleeping & Eating
Although the situation is improving, Djenné suffers from a severe shortage of hotel rooms on Sunday and Monday nights during the high season. Book ahead if you're coming on these days.

Restaurant Kita Kourou (☎ 7618 1811; roof mattress CFA2500, dm CFA3000, meals CFA3000) Rooms here are basic and cell-like, not entirely sealed off from their neighbours, and the mattresses sag prodigiously. But sleeping on the roof (mosquito nets are provided) is the most popular choice and it's a friendly place. The restaurant offers tasty, traditional Malian and European staples; it's a good place to try the local speciality of *tion-tion* (dried onions, tomato and local spices served with rice and chicken or meat; CFA2000).

Chez Baba (☎ 2142 0598; restauranbaba@yahoo.fr; camping or roof mattress CFA3000, dm CFA3500, meals from CFA3500) The large, open courtyard of Chez Bab could, at a stretch, resemble an old caravanserai, but it also has all the comings-and-goings of a bus station. The rooms with mattresses on the floor are swept clean, and the mattresses on the roof have good views (when things are busy, they often run out of mosquito nets). The food is reasonable and there's live music on Sunday

(djembe) and Monday (traditional Bambara groups) nights.

Le Campement (☎ 2142 0497; campdjenne@afribone.net.ml; roof mattress CFA4000, dm CFA5000, s/d with fan & bathroom from CFA10,000/12,500, with air-con & bathroom from CFA20,000/25,000, breakfast CFA2000, meals from CFA4000; ✷) This sprawling, handily located place is Djenné's tourism centre, with dozens of rooms across a wide price range and a large, if usually overcrowded, open-air restaurant. The generally clean and tidy rooms have the bare essentials and nothing more. Even with fan, some rooms can be *really* hot.

Dar Salam (☎ 2142 1423; darsalamdjenne@yahoo.fr; roof mattress CFA2500, dm CFA4000, s/d/tr with fan & bathroom CFA13,000/15,000/20,000) Although a fair hike southwest of Djenné, this new place will be terrific once its garden grows. The rooms are pleasant, the architecture gives a nod to traditional Djenné style and there are plans for a pirogue to transport travellers into town during the rainy season.

Hôtel Tapama (☎ 2142 0527; residencetapama@yahoo.fr; mattress on roof CFA2500, d with fan & bathroom CFA15,000, breakfast CFA1000) Hôtel Tapama is showing its age, with bare, neglected rooms, not averse to the occasional cockroach, and bathrooms that are slowly falling apart, although the Moroccan-style courtyard is really quite beautiful. Rather than spending money on renovations, it's building an extension which will have air-con rooms. Meals cost CFA2000.

Auberge le Maafir (☎ 2142 0541; sinintadiawoye@yahoo.fr; d with fan/air-con & bathroom incl breakfast CFA18,000/23,000; ✷) This pleasant place has attractively furnished rooms with some traditional design work (such as terracotta basins) and maintenance has improved since we were last here. It's an easy 10-minute walk from the mosque. No alcohol is served and dinner is CFA5000.

Hôtel Pondori (☎ 7621 3514; s/d with air-con & bathroom CFA20,000/25,000, meals CFA4000; ✷) Due to open not long after we were here, Hôtel Pondori is in Djenné's far east, although still only a 15-minute walk from the Great Mosque. Rooms are tidy and staff is friendly.

Djenné-Djenno (☎ 7933 1526; www.hoteldjennedjenno.com; d/ste with air-con & bathroom CFA25,000/35,000, breakfast CFA3000, meals CFA6500; ✷) Welcome to one of Mali's best hotels. Everything about this place carries a designer touch, from the beautifully decorated rooms to the traditional architectural features in the rooms and public areas. As its trees mature, it will become even more of an oasis, just beyond the city but close enough to get there on foot. There's also a *bogolan* studio where Sophie, the Swedish owner, runs classes; plus there's a horse-drawn carriage for organised excursions to surrounding villages, and proceeds from the small shop go to support local literacy and health projects.

Restaurant le Fleuve (dishes CFA1250-3000; ⏰ 6am-10pm) For simple Malian dishes such as *riz sauce*, this place is good; it also serves *tion-tion*, *wigila* and pigeon.

Restaurant Dogon (☎ 6659 0221; dishes CFA2000; ⏰ 6am-10pm) You'll find the usual suspects (*riz sauce*, couscous, spaghetti) here, but it's the grilled meat that the locals come for. It's ready around 1pm or 2pm, you choose the cut, and CFA1000 per person should see you well fed.

Shopping

Djenné is famous for *bogolan*, or mud-cloth (see p67). Three female artisan workshops, where *bogolan* techniques are explained and high-quality textiles are on sale, are the best places to start:

Chez Tanti – Association des Femmes de Semani (☎ 7928 3650; ⏰ 7am-10pm) On your left just after crossing the main bridge into Djenné, Chez Tanti is run by 'Tanti Bogolan', an exuberant, exceptionally warm host. She can arrange courses in *bogolan*.

Cooperative Bogolan Chez Pakarsa (☎ 7618 1836; Quartier Sankoré; ⏰ 6am-7pm) Here you can also try your hand at small-scale *bogolan* design.

Pama Sinatoa (☎ 7614 3259; almamydiaka@yahoo.fr; ⏰ 6am-9pm) The longest-established of the workshops and with perhaps the largest selection, Pama Sinatoa can arrange courses in *bogolan* design from a negotiable CFA12,5000/40,000 per day/week.

One shop worth stopping by is the **Association des Femmes Handicapées Physiques Djenné** (☎ 7312 1136; ⏰ 8am-8pm), a stone's throw from the Great Mosque. Its selection of predominantly jewellery and *bogolan* is made by local people with a disability.

For traditional Djenné clothing and embroidery, the small **Maison des Artisans** (⏰ 9am-6pm) is best, while the **Association des Femmes Artisans de Djenné** (⏰ 9am-6pm) also has a range of items.

Getting There & Away
BOAT

Djenné is away from the main river routes, but when the Bani River is high enough (usually from July to December), it's possible to arrive by public pinasse (CFA4000) from Mopti. There's a semiregular Sunday service as well as occasional departures on other days. For the rest of the year, everything goes by road.

BUS & BUSH TAXI

Apart from early Monday morning from Mopti (two hours), very little transport goes to Djenné, although there's usually one shared taxi (CFA2500) or minibus (CFA2250) a day from the Sévaré taxi park in Mopti; get there at 6am and be prepared to wait for transport to fill. Otherwise, you'll need to get transport to the Djenné–Mopti turn-off on the Bamako–Sévaré highway (ask for the 'Carrefour de Djenné'), 30km from Djenné, from where a shared/private taxi will cost CFA1500/15,000; this is your only real option if you're coming from Bamako. From Djenné all transport leaves from the open area immediately east of the mosque.

CAR & MOTORCYCLE

Just before Djenné there's a short ferry crossing which costs from CFA500 to CFA2000 depending on the vehicle size and the hour.

AROUND DJENNÉ

Welingara and Nenesourou are two of the most interesting Fula villages north of Djenné. Most travellers cross by the bridge on foot (to the west) or hire a moped; it costs CFA150 to cross by pirogue. Sirimou, a beautiful Bozo village with a stunning mud mosque, is approximately a 20-minute moped ride southwest from Djenné. Bicycles (CFA5000 per day), mopeds (CFA10,000 per day including fuel) and horse-drawn carts (from CFA12,500) are available for hire and can be arranged at most hotels in Djenné. Alternatively, make the arrangements through the Bureau de Guides (p498); prices start at CFA25,000 per person for one traveller, CFA12,500 if there's two or more of you.

MOPTI
pop 103,428

One of West Africa's largest river ports, Mopti is clamorous, competitive and can be a little overwhelming for first-time travellers. Boats

MALI

from here go to Timbuktu, and Mopti also serves as a gateway for the Dogon Country. As a result, the city swarms with guides and hangers-on and every conversation can seem to have an ulterior motive. But Mopti has its charms. Its port is Mali's most lively, its recently restored mosque is beautiful and there are a couple of terrific hotels here. But if it all gets too much, stay in Sévaré (p506), 12km away and with great hotels and transport options, and just come into Mopti when you have to.

Information

GUIDES

For guides to the Dogon Country and beyond, the Bureau Régional du Tourisme (below) has a list of accredited guides. It's also worth contacting the **Association des Guides Dogon de Mopti** (Dogon Vision; ☎ 7612 2387, 7622 5277; assodogonvision@yahoo.fr), whose president, Ogomono Saye, will make sure that you're well looked after.

INTERNET ACCESS

Cybercafé Guina (Ave de l'Indépendance; per hr CFA750; 8am-1pm & 4-8pm Mon-Sat)
Librairie & Cybercafé de la Venise (Ave de l'Indépendance; per hr CFA1000; 8am-1pm & 4-8pm Mon-Sat)

MEDICAL SERVICES

Hospital (☎ 2143 0441; Blvd de l'Indépendance) Basic health care.
Pharmacie Officine de La Venise (☎ 2143 0377; off Ave de l'Indépendance)
Pharmacie Officine du Carrefour (☎ 2143 0422; Ave de l'Indépendance)

MONEY

In addition to the banks, some hotels and shopkeepers will change cash. For travellers cheques, you'll need to head to the BNDA in Sévaré. Remember that banks in Mopti close at 11am on Friday and don't open again until Monday.
BCEAO (Rte de Sévaré) Changes euros.
BDM (off Ave de l'Indépendance) A visa-enabled ATM, but the bureau de change opposite the entrance is better for cash (euros and US dollars).

POST

Post office (Rue 68)

TOURIST INFORMATION

Bureau Régional du Tourisme (Omatho; ☎ 2143 0506; moptitourisme@hotmail.com; Blvd de l'Indépendance)

TRAVEL AGENCIES

The following companies can assist with hiring 4WDs and pinasses and arranging Dogon treks. With each, be scrupulous about double-checking everything:
Diatigui Travel (☎ /fax 2143 0273; www.diatigui travel.com in French; Rue de la Pâtisserie Dogon)
Mali Experience Tours (☎ 2143 1409; www.mali experience.com; off Blvd de l'Indépendance)
Satimbé Travel (☎ 2143 0791; www.satimbetravel .com, in French; Ave de l'Indépendance)

VISA EXTENSIONS

Comissariat de Police & Sûreté (Rte de Sévaré; 7.30am-5pm Mon-Fri, to noon Sat & Sun) One-month visa extensions cost CFA5000, you'll need two photos and extensions take about 15 minutes. It's best to come in the morning.

Sights & Activities

In Mopti's expansive **port** you'll see slabs of salt from Timbuktu, dried fish, firewood, pottery, goats, chickens and much more. You'll also encounter a wonderful cast of characters, from stylishly dressed local women taking a pirogue back home and small boys diving into the water, to grizzled fishermen who regard it all with the disdain of the ancients. Boat building happens next to Restaurant Bar Bozo.

The classic Sahel-style **Grande Mosquée de Mopti** (Great Mosque of Mopti; Ave de l'Indépendance) was built in 1933 and beautifully restored in 2007 by the Aga Khan Development Network's Historic Cities Programme (www.akdn.org/aktc_hcp_mali.asp?type=p). It towers over the old part of town and is easily the single-most beautiful structure in Mopti. The mosque is off limits to non-Muslims, but CFA500 to CFA1000 can buy you a view from a nearby rooftop.

Sleeping

The following three hotels have wi-fi access.
Hôtel Ya Pas de Probleme (☎ 2143 1041; www .yapasdeprobleme.com; off Blvd de l'Indépendance; roof mattress CFA4000, dm CFA5000, s/d with fan & without bathroom CFA10,000/13,000, with fan & shower CFA15,000/18,000, s/d/tr with air-con & bathroom CFA22,000/25,000/28,000, f CFA25,000-31,000; 🟦 🖥 🛜 🏊) A delightful French-Dogon-run place, Ya Pas de Probleme is Mopti's best place to stay with tastefully decorated rooms, an intimate and homely atmosphere and something for everyone regardless of budget. In addition to the spacious rooms, the swimming pool (free for guests,

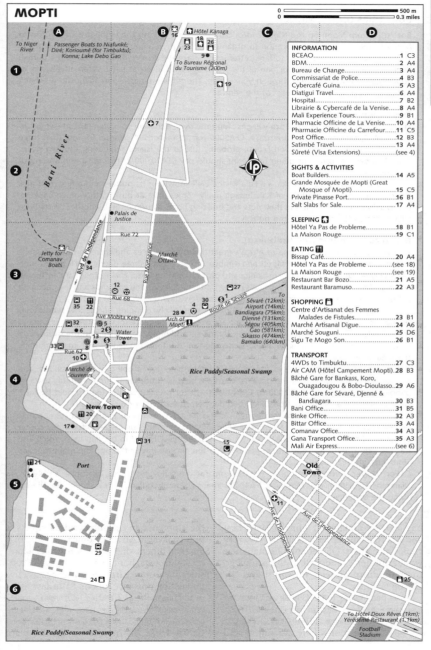

MOPTI

| 0 | 500 m |
| 0 | 0.3 miles |

INFORMATION

BCEAO	1 C3
BDM	2 A4
Bureau de Change	3 A4
Commissariat de Police	4 B3
Cybercafé Guina	5 A3
Diatigui Travel	6 A4
Hospital	7 B2
Librairie & Cybercafé de la Venise	8 A4
Mali Experience Tours	9 B1
Pharmacie Officine de La Venise	10 A4
Pharmacie Officine du Carrefour	11 C5
Post Office	12 B3
Satimbé Travel	13 A4
Sûreté (Visa Extensions)	(see 4)

SIGHTS & ACTIVITIES

Boat Builders	14 A5
Grande Mosquée de Mopti (Great Mosque of Mopti)	15 C5
Private Pinasse Port	16 B1
Salt Slabs for Sale	17 A4

SLEEPING

Hôtel Ya Pas de Probleme	18 B1
La Maison Rouge	19 C1

EATING

Bissap Café	20 A4
Hôtel Ya Pas de Probleme	(see 18)
La Maison Rouge	(see 19)
Restaurant Bar Bozo	21 A5
Restaurant Baramuso	22 A3

SHOPPING

Centre d'Artisanat des Femmes Malades de Fistules	23 B1
Marché Artisanal Digue	24 A6
Marché Souguni	25 D6
Sigu Te Mogo Son	26 B1

TRANSPORT

4WDs to Timbuktu	27 C3
Air CAM (Hôtel Campement Mopti)	28 B3
Bâché Gare for Bankass, Koro, Ouagadougou & Bobo-Dioulasso	29 A6
Bâché Gare for Sévaré, Djenné & Bandiagara	30 B3
Bani Office	31 B5
Binke Office	32 A3
Bittar Office	33 A4
Comanav Office	34 A3
Gana Transport Office	35 A3
Mali Air Express	(see 6)

MALI

BOAT TRIPS ON THE NIGER

Boat trips from Mopti on the Niger and/or Bani Rivers are among the highlights of any trip to Mali, but they can also be daunting to organise. Although you could try negotiating with the wily boat owners, you're likely to fare better if you make the arrangements through the Bureau Régional du Tourisme (p502) or one of the travel agencies listed at p502. Alternatively, ask at your hotel or organise a trip through your guide. The private pinasse port is on the riverbank opposite Hôtel Kanaga, northeast of the centre.

Day or Sunset Trips

There are numerous Fula and Bozo villages along the river, although your standard sunset excursion (CFA25,000 per motorised pinasse, CFA5000 for nonmotorised pirogue for less than three hours) won't get you far beyond Mopti, probably just to the island separating the two rivers. For a half-day excursion including food, you should pay CFA30,000/75,000 for a nonmotorised/motorised craft.

If you can spare a day, Kotaka is a Fula village well known for its pottery and a fine mudbrick mosque, and the Bozo village of Kakalodaga really comes alive at dusk, with women cooking, kids playing and men repairing their nets and building boats. Tongorongo is another pretty Bozo village known for its mosque and pottery.

Mopti to Korioumé (for Timbuktu)

A slow boat up the Niger is one of Africa's great travel experiences and travelling by pinasse is a terrific way to get between Mopti and Timbuktu (two nights, three days). You'll go through the low-lying wetlands of the inland delta and pass fascinating Bozo, Fulani, Songhaï and Tuareg villages. The elaborate riverside mosques of the Delta, the birds in the wetlands and the changing cultural landscape en route make for a memorable few days.

The first day includes sailing to Lake Debo and, most likely, camping on the low sand dunes by the shore. This enormous lake is an important overwintering place for migratory birds and has several Fula and Bozo villages on its shores. By the second night, you'll sleep on the riverbank a couple of hours before Niafunké. By late afternoon on the third day, you'll pull into Korioumé, the pinasse port of Timbuktu.

Before signing up to any river trip, check exactly where you're going, what's included, and the condition and comfort of the boat. To charter a boat to Timbuktu that comfortably seats 10 people, expect to pay CFA375,000 to CFA400,000; petrol is included and food should be for a small group. Otherwise, count on CFA15,000 per person for food for three days.

Getting a ride on a *pinasse transporteur* (cargo pinasse) or smaller *pinasse publique* (public pinasse) is an option between Mopti and Korioumé. Prices should be CFA5000 for a tiny corner of downstairs deck space, or CFA10,000 on the roof, but you'll need to bargain hard. You'll also need to bring your own food and remember that the pinasse travels through the night to reach Timbuktu in three days.

For shorter journeys by public pinasse, aim for the following prices: Niafunké (CFA4000), Diafarabé (CFA3000) and Massina (CFA4000). There's a semiregular Sunday service for Djenné along the Bani River.

CFA3500 for nonguests) is one of Mali's best and the rooftop bar-restaurant is very, very cool. The owners, Olivier and Ousmane, are wonderful hosts, and part of the profits go to community projects in Mopti and the Dogon Country.

Hôtel Doux Rêves (☎ 2143 0490; www.hoteldoux reves.com; Rue 540; s/d with fan from CFA11,000/14,000, s/d/tr with air-con & bathroom CFA20,000/23,000/26,000; ✕ 🖳 🛜) The rooms here are simple and

the ambience in the surrounding streets is unmistakeably African. Some rooms are bigger than others, there's free wi-fi and all have mosquito nets, but the drawback is the considerable distance from town. They have live percussion music at 7pm on Saturdays.

La Maison Rouge (☎ 2143 1402; www.lesmaisons dumali.com; off Blvd de l'Indépendance; s/d/ste with air-con & bathroom CFA30,000/35,000/60,000, breakfast CFA4000, dinner CFA9000; ✕ 🖳 🛜) Architecturally, this place is stunning and the rooms are some of the most beautiful in all Mali. The overall effect is of grace and cool elegance, with pleasing archways, mud-style walls and a designer's eye for detail. Our only complaint? Service could be friendlier and, as a result, the place lacks warmth.

Eating & Drinking

Restaurant Baramuso (Rue 68; meals from CFA500; ☺ lunch & dinner) This is the place for a hearty cheap meal (think rice in all its manifestations) in the centre of town.

Yérédémé Restaurant (☎ 2143 0492; starters CFA750-1250, mains CFA1500-2500) In the southeast of the Old Town, Yérédémé, opposite Hôtel Doux Rêves, offers reasonable food served on the pleasant covered rooftop. It does decent grilled *capitaine*, as well as *kedjenou poulet* (slowly simmered chicken or fish with peppers and tomatoes; CFA1500). There's a small shop run by a local women's cooperative.

Bissap Café (☎ 2143 1353; www.bissapcafe.com; Blvd de l'Indépendance; starters CFA1500-3500, mains CFA2800-5800; ☺ 7am-midnight) At last Mopti's port area has a place where you can eat great food, find a vantage point to watch all the comings-and-goings and enjoy a laid-back atmosphere that's a haven from Mopti's dull roar. The food (a mix of African dishes, pizza and fusion fare) is terrific and the back garden and salon (with salt slabs for lamps) is as agreeable as the roof.

Hotel Ya Pas de Probleme (☎ 2143 1041; www.ya pasdeprobleme.com; off Blvd de l'Indépendance; meals from CFA4000) The bar-restaurant atop the hotel of the same name serves terrific food (we especially enjoyed the *brochette de capitaine*), and the chilled atmosphere is terrific as much to eat as for a drink.

La Maison Rouge (☎ 2143 1402, 7623 5078; www .lesmaisonsdumali.com; off Blvd de l'Indépendance; dinner CFA9000) Serves sophisticated, predominantly French cuisine with a price tag to match.

Restaurant Bar Bozo (☎ 2143 0246; ☺ 6am-11pm) Bar Bozo is superbly located at the mouth of Mopti harbour, but the food here is best avoided (not least because it can take two hours to arrive), and it runs out of drinks on a regular basis. But this is *the* place to nurse whatever beverage it *does* have as the sun nears the horizon.

Shopping

Mopti's many salesmen are some of Mali's toughest traders. Mopti is famous for its blankets; ornate Fula wedding blankets can cost CFA50,000 or more.

There are numerous artisan stalls upstairs at **Marché Souguni** (Ave de l'Indépendance), while you could also try the Marché Artisanal Digue, southeast of the port; the newly built Marché des Souvenirs is largely empty, allegedly due to prohibitive rents – check it out in case that changes during the life of this book.

A couple of small handicrafts outlets run by people with a disability can be found north of the centre, off Blvd de l'Indépendance. They include **Sigu Te Mogo Son** (☺ 8am-1pm & 4-8pm Mon-Sat), just around the corner from the Hôtel Ya Pas de Probleme, and the **Centre d'Artisanat des Femmes Malades de Fistules** (☺ 8am-1pm & 4-8pm Mon-Sat).

Getting There & Away

AIR

The airport is about 2km southeast of Sévaré and 14km from Mopti. **Mali Air Express** (MAE; ☎ 2143 0273; www.mae-mali.com; Diatigui Travel, Rue de la Pâtisserie Dogon) has two weekly flights to/from Bamako (CFA60,500) and Timbuktu (CFA69,500). Less reliably, **Air CAM** (☎ 7631 7401; www.camaero.com; Hôtel Campement Mopti), next to Arch of Mopti, has three weekly flights to Bamako (CFA65,500) and Timbuktu (CFA69,560).

A private taxi from Mopti to the airport costs at least CFA6000.

BOAT

Comanav (☎ 2143 0006; Blvd de l'Indépendance) ferries head for Korioumé (Timbuktu's port) by boat from July or August to December, although tickets are scarce as this is the busiest sector on the boat's itinerary. For details, see p539.

For details on travelling by pirogue or pinasse, see the boxed text, opposite.

BUS & BUSH TAXI

Although some buses continue as far as (and originate in) Mopti, Sévaré is the main transport hub for the region. Bani, Binke, Bittar and Gana Transport all have offices in Mopti. For details on destinations and prices, see p507.

Bâchés (covered pick-ups used as basic bush taxis; CFA225) and Peugeot taxis (CFA275) cover the 12km between Mopti and Sévaré between 7am and 8pm daily (a private taxi costs CFA3000). They leave

MALI

from the bâché *gare* at the town entrance. Transport also leaves here every morning for Djenné (minibus/shared taxi CFA2250/2500) and Bandiagara (minibus/shared taxi CFA1500/1600). Bâchés and Peugeot taxis leave from near the port some mornings for Bankass (CFA3000, two hours) and Koro (CFA4000, three hours).

To Timbuktu, 4WDs (CFA12,500 to CFA15,000, six to eight hours on a good day) leave most mornings from 9am from behind the bâché *gare*. There are 11 or 12 people to a car; the uncomfortable seats at the back are the cheapest.

SÉVARÉ

This bustling town along the main highway has not a single sight worth seeing, but it's more relaxed than its more famous neighbour, has terrific places to stay, and ample transport connections. Bandiagara and the Dogon Country are just 63km away.

Information

BNDA (Rte de Mopti) Charges 2% commission on travellers cheques and cash.
Post office (Rte de Mopti)

Sleeping & Eating

All of the following places are either on or signposted off the main road through town.

Maison des Arts (☎ 2142 0853; www.maisondesarts .co.uk; Rue 106, Porte 377, Banguetaba Sect III; dm CFA8000, s/d without bathroom from CFA12,000/16,000, with bathroom CFA15,000/20,000, s/d/tr with air-con & bathroom from CFA20,000/25,000/30,000, meals CFA3000-4000; ❌) Style and simplicity are what it's all about here. Arrayed around a traditional mud-walled compound, and watched over by Kay and Amadou, the delightful Anglo-Dogon hosts, Maison des Arts is a lovely place. The spacious but unelaborated rooms all come with mosquito nets, comfy mattresses, occasional African handicrafts and cold showers.

Mon P'tit Repos (☎ 7859 0995; www.monptitrepos .com, in French; Rue 20, Village SOS, Socoura; camping CFA4000, s/d with fan & bathroom from CFA14,000/16,000, breakfast CFA1000, meals CFA2500; ❌ ▣ ▣) On Sévaré's northernmost tip, 3.5km north of the main roundabout, Mon P'tit Repos is a lovely place that opened in early 2009. The young French couple who run it are delightful, the bungalow-style rooms pleasant (there are plans for air-con) and it's won-

derfully quiet. Once the trees grow, it will be even better.

Mac's Refuge (☎ 2142 0621; malimacs@yahoo.com; Rue 124; camping without/with own equipment CFA6000/5000, dm CFA7000, s/d/tr with fan from CFA12,000/18,000/21,000, with air-con CFA21,000/25,000/30,000, breakfast CFA1800, meals CFA5000; ▣ ❌ ▣) Rooms here are individually styled to reflect the culture of Mali's many ethnic groups, the food here is legendary (there's a banquet meal of a different cuisine at 7pm every night) and Mac's buffet breakfasts are enough to make you want to stay longer. There's also a small pool, bicycle hire (CFA1000 per day), a small reference library on Malian culture and Mac's talents as a qualified masseur (CFA15,000 per hour).

Mankan Te Bed & Breakfast (☎ 2142 0193; www .mankan-te.de; off Rte de Bamako; s/d with air-con & without bathroom from CFA18,000/22,000, with bathroom CFA22,000/26,000; ❌) The intimate Mankan Te has lovingly maintained rooms with splashes of colour and superclean bathrooms. Jutta, the owner, is a fount of much practical knowledge on the region.

Mankan Te Restaurant (www.mankan-te.de; Rte de Bamako; starters CFA1000-2000, mains CFA2000-4000; ☽ lunch & dinner) A couple of blocks away from the B&B, Jutta of Mankan Te also runs this excellent restaurant with a garden setting and wide variety of dishes (vegetarian, pasta, African specialities); we especially liked the *soupe de capitaine* (CFA3500). It turns into a late-night bar after the kitchen closes, and local groups play here on weekends.

Hôtel Flandre (☎ 2142 0829; www.hotelflandre .com; off Rte de Bamako; s/d CFA24,000/28,000; ❌ ▣ ▣ ▣) While there are more stylish places in town, the well-run Flandre boasts superclean and spacious rooms that are well appointed and come with satellite TV (one of few Malian hotels in this price range to have this). There's also free wi-fi, a nice swimming pool and professional service.

Hôtel Ambedjele (☎ 2142 1031; www.ambedjele hotel.com; off Rte de Mopti; d/ste CFA39,500/55,000, meals CFA7500; ❌ ▣ ▣ ▣) Styled like a Dogon village, just off the road between Mopti and Sévaré, this charming Spanish-run place has expansive gardens, a rock pool for swimming and bungalows shaped like Dogon granaries. Rooms are not huge, but are beautifully decorated with terracotta basins, exposed stone walls and stylistic flourishes throughout; the suites are large and stunning. The restaurant (Spanish flair wedded to African flavours) is one of the best in Mali. There is free wi-fi for guests.

Shopping

Farafina Tigne (☎ 2142 0449; www.farafina-tigne.com; Rte de Bamako; ☻ 7am-8pm) Farafina Tigne has an extensive selection of quality Malian handicrafts, including *bogolan* cloth and Tuareg jewellery. There's zero sales pitch, and an interesting little bead museum upstairs.

Getting There & Away

AIR

For details about flights between Sévaré/Mopti and other Malian towns, see p505.

BUS

Sévaré is on a busy transport route with plenty of transport coming and going from the **gare routière** (Rte de Bandiagara). Represented here are **Bani Transport** (☎ 6672 6663), **Sonef** (☎ 6669 1149) and **Gana Transport** (☎ 7629 5076). Major destinations include Bamako (CFA7500, eight to 10 hours), Ségou (CFA5000, five to six hours), Douentza (CFA3000, three hours), Hombori (CFA5000, five to six hours) and Gao (CFA7500, nine to 12 hours); Gana Transport tends to be slightly cheaper, charging CFA7000 for Bamako. Along most major routes, most companies have two to five daily departures, except for Gao.

Transport to the Dogon Country leaves from outside the *gare routière,* along the Bandiagara–Sévaré road. Occasional minibuses go to Bandiagara (minibus/shared taxi CFA1500/1600, one hour), Bankass (CFA3000/3500, two hours) and, even less frequently, Koro (CFA3500/4000, three hours). There's more traffic on the market days in Bandiagara (Monday and Friday) and Bankass (Tuesday).

Bâchés head to/from Mopti (CFA225) between 7am and 8pm from close to the post office.

DOGON COUNTRY

Mali's Dogon Country (Pays Dogon) is a world apart. Partly its appeal lies in the Dogon landscape and architecture: here, unique houses and granaries cling to the massive escarpment known as the Falaise de Bandiagara, which extends some 150km to the east of Mopti and is 500m high around Tireli and Ireli. But more than this, a journey through Dogon Country takes you through a fascinating animist culture with traditions and cosmology as complex and elaborate as any in Africa.

The best way to see Dogon Country is on foot and in the company of a Dogon guide, and anything from one-day to three-week treks are possible. Ancient tracks link village with village and the plateau with the plains. In places, carefully laid stones create staircases up a fissure in the cliff face, while elsewhere ladders provide a route over a chasm or up to a higher ledge.

The best time to trek is from November to March, although the hotter months of April and May increase your chances of seeing a local festival. During the rainy season (June to August), the Dogon Country is wonderfully green, with waterfalls off the escarpment, although mosquitoes can be a problem.

History

Archaeological studies suggest that the Dogon arrived in the 13th or 14th centuries. As the Dogon tell it, their roots lie in Mande country in eastern Mali, close to the modern town of Kangaba. They lived alongside the Bambara, Songhaï and Bozo, but left due to overcrowding and approaching Islamic Fulani armies.

When they left Kangaba, there were five men and two women. By the time they arrived in what is now Dogon Country at Kani Bozon, there were four men and four women. With the Fulani still on their heels, the Dogon people dispersed throughout the plains, along the escarpment and atop the plateau. The man from the Arou family had been elected the spiritual leader of the Dogon and he chose Arou as the spiritual home of the Dogon people.

The Dogon found the Tellem living along the escarpment (the Dogon believe that before the Tellem, the escarpment was inhabited by Pygmies). The Tellem had managed to build dwellings and stores in the most inaccessible places high on the cliff – the Dogon believe the Tellem could fly, or otherwise possessed magic powers. The Tellem used the caves to bury their dead, and many still contain ancient human bones. According to Dogon tradition, the Tellem left of their own accord as the Dogon cleared the forests for agriculture at the foot of the escarpment and the Dogon claim that some Tellem still live on the plains.

MALI

DOGON CULTURE

For details of Dogon architecture, see the boxed text, p512.

Dogon Religion & Cosmology

The Dogon believe that the earth, moon and sun were created by a divine male being called Amma. The earth was formed in the shape of a woman, and by her Amma fathered twin snake-like creatures called the Nommo, which Dogon believe are present in streams and pools. Later, Amma made two humans – a man and a woman – who were circumcised by the Nommo and gave birth to eight children, who are regarded as the ancestors of all Dogon.

Amma is credited with creating the stars, and a feature of Dogon cosmology is the star known in Western countries as Sirius, or the Dog Star, which was also held to be auspicious by the ancient Egyptians. Modern astronomers knew Sirius to be two stars, but the Dogon long regarded it as three separate stars – two close together and a third invisible. In 1995, powerful radio telescopes detected a third body of superdense matter in the same area, confirming the Dogon version. The movements of these stars dictate the timing of the Sigui festival, which takes place every 60 years.

Aspects of Dogon religion readily seen by visitors are the *omolo* or fetishes, sacred objects that are dotted around most villages. Most are a simple dome of hard-packed mud, and their function is to protect the village against certain eventualities. To strengthen their power, sacrifices are made to these *omolo* once a year.

Watch out also for stones at the entry/exit points of the village which have turned white from decades of millet porridge being poured over them. Known as *punditouri,* which means 'the place to offer drinks to the ancestors', these stones are watched over by old women who perform a ceremony on behalf of villagers who wish to appease ancestors whom they have offended.

Dogon Villages – A Snapshot

Each Dogon village has its own special appeal and the following snapshots (from southwest to northeast) may help in choosing your route.

Kani-Kombolé Home to an interesting mosque

Djiguibombo Beautiful granary architecture and strongly animist

Teli Picturesque with waterfalls, a beautiful mosque and troglodyte Dogon cliff houses

Endé Pretty villages, nearby waterfalls, museum and famous for *bogolan* (mud-cloth) making

Begnimato Spectacular views of the plains, especially at sunset

Nombori Stunning setting, museum, lively market and troglodyte Dogon houses

Komokani Largely animist village with a fine *togu-na* (meeting place)

Idjeli-na Mango trees and nice place for a picnic

Tireli Known for its pottery, the best place to see a Dogon mask ceremony and a lively market

Amani Home to a sacred crocodile pool

Yaye Animist village still clinging to the cliff, and annual fishing ceremony (the first person to enter the village and given the first fish will die within a year...)

Ireli Classic Dogon village with cylindrical granary towers at the foot of the cliffs, and a mass of ancient Tellem houses (known locally as the 'capital of Tellem')

Banani Tellem buildings and a rainy season waterfall

Bongo Spectacular views of the plains and an enormous natural tunnel

Arou Home village of the only true *hogon* (person responsible for passing on traditions) in Dogon Country; the temple is marvellous

Kundu villages Stretch from top to the bottom of the escarpment making for an excellent walk; also home to sacred crocodiles

Youga villages Traditional animist villages on a separate hill on the plains; Youga-Piri still has a fetish inside the *togu-na,* and it's a beautiful walk to Youga-Dogourou (the home of the Sigui Festival) and with a stunning Tellem structure at the top

Damasongo Halfway up the cliff with good views
Kassa Numerous springs, mango trees and very attractive

Dogon Masks & Ceremonies

The most famous ceremony is the Sigui, performed every 60 years (most recently in 1967, with the next in 2027), which features a large mask and headdress called the *imina-tiou* (*imina-sirou* in Sanga) in the form of a prostrate serpent, sometimes almost 10m high. During the Sigui, the Dogon perform dances recounting the story of their origin. After the ceremony, the *imina-tiou* is stored in a cave high on the cliffs.

In Dogon tradition, when a person dies their spirit wanders about looking for a new residence. Fearful that the spirit might come to rest in another mortal, the Dogon bring out the *imina-tiou* when someone important dies and carry it to the deceased's house to entice the spirit to live in the mask. The accompanying ceremony lasts three days if the deceased is a man, four if a woman, and the bodies are interred in a cave high on the cliffs (sometimes appropriating a Tellem cave), usually on the same day or the day after they die. The body is wrapped in colourful cloth and paraded head-high through the village, then carefully lifted with ropes up to the cave.

Another important festival is Dama (which translates as 'forbidden') which serves to initiate young Dogon men into the mask dance; women may not touch the masks and men may only do so once initiated. The Dama ceremony, which occurs every 10 or 12 years, depending on the village, is the time when young people ask forgiveness from the ancestors.

Other masks used by the Dogon include the birdlike *kanaga*, which protects against vengeance (of a killed animal), and the houselike *sirige*, which represents the house of the *hogon*, who is responsible for passing on traditions. Most ceremonies, where you may see masks, take place from April to May. These include Boulo (a festival to ask the ancestors for rains), which takes place leading up to the first rains.

If it's not possible to be here at these times, at least four villages – Tireli, Sanga, Nombori and Begnimato – organise (with a day's advance notice) early-morning or late-afternoon re-enactments of the traditional mask ceremonies; for prices, see p510. The best places are Tireli and Sanga and the re-enactments provide a rare insight into an important aspect of Dogon culture. It's enjoyed as much by local women and children (who are forbidden from seeing the real thing) as by tourists. Female tourists are sometimes allowed to watch the real thing but it varies from village to village.

Weekdays & Markets

Traditional Dogon villages keep a five-day week, while those on the plateau tend to observe a seven-day week. Dogon markets are always lively affairs, although they don't get going until about noon and may last late into the night.

Five-day week	Dourou cluster	Sanga cluster	Others
1	Dourou	Tireli	Ibi
2	Gimini, Nombori	Banani, Tiogou	
3	Idjeli, Pelou, Amani	Yendouma	
4	Konsongo, Komokan	Sanga	
5	Doundjourou (near Begnimato)	Ireli, Kama	

Seven-day week	Village
Monday (big) & Friday (small)	Bandiagara
Tuesday	Bankass
Thursday	Kani Kombolé
Saturday	Bamba
Sunday	Douentza, Endé, Songo

MALI

The Dogon first came to the attention of the outside world through the work of French anthropologist Marcel Griaule, whose influential book *Dieu d'Eau: Entretiens avec Ogotemmêli* (Conversations with Ogotemmêli; published in 1948, in English in 1965) was the result of many years of living and studying near the village of Sanga. Griaule died in France in 1956. If the Dogon have a complaint about Griaule, it is that he extrapolated from what he learned in Sanga to apply to the entire Dogon Country, a generalisation that, the Dogon say, has led to many misunderstandings.

Guides

Guides are essential in the Dogon Country. Ideally a guide will be your translator, fixer (for accommodation and food) and verbal guidebook, not to mention a window into the Dogon world. Without one you'll miss many points of interest, and could genuinely offend the Dogon villagers by unwittingly stumbling across a sacred site. All guides speak French and some speak English.

Costs

We recommend negotiating an all-inclusive fee with your guide – such a fee will include everything except water, drinks, souvenirs and masked dance ceremonies. Standard costs include the following:

Breakfast (CFA1000)
Lunch or dinner (without/with meat CFA2000/3000)
Prices are generally CFA500 cheaper in the south.
Guide (per day per person all-inclusive 1-3 people CFA20,000-22,500, per person 4 people or more CFA15,000-17,500) Some guides will offer CFA12,500 per person, but make sure everything is included.
Porter (per porter per day CFA2500)
Village tourist tax (per person CFA500-1000) Nothing if you're just passing through.
Sleeping in village campement (per person per night on roof CFA1500-2000, r CFA4000)
Museums (per person CFA1000) There are small museums in Fombori, Nombori, Soroli and Endé.
Masked dance ceremony (per ceremony in Nombori or Begnimato CFA40,000, in Tireli CFA60,000, in Sanga CFA70,000)

The village tourist tax should allow you to take photos of houses and other buildings (but *not* people, unless you get their permission), and to visit nearby cliff dwellings.

You should always agree in advance with your guide on what's included in their fee. Make sure you discuss everything, from the above fees to who'll be paying for the guide's food and lodging (most get free food and lodging in the *campements,* ie guesthouses). The more people in the group and the longer the trek, the lower the per-person, per-day cost.

Your only other cost is reaching the escarpment, although most guides will include this in their price. From Bandiagara, a local taxi to any of the local trailheads will cost CFA15,000 to CFA20,000 one-way. If you're alone it might be cheaper to hire mopeds.

From Bankass to the escarpment at Endé or Kani-Kombolé (12km) by horse and cart costs around CFA5000 (the track is too sandy for mopeds).

FINDING A GOOD DOGON GUIDE

Finding a Dogon guide is easy, but finding a good one is more challenging. For a start, your guide to the Dogon Country should be a Dogon – non-Dogon guides are unlikely to speak Dogon or know anything about the culture or local paths, which can lead to problems. Your guide should also be an accredited guide able to produce the official blue or yellow official guiding card (see the boxed text, p482), and recommendations from other travellers. Choosing a guide can have a huge impact on your experience of the Dogon Country, so take your time and write down all the expenses, as this aids memory on both sides, and ask lots of questions about market days, history, festivals etc, to see if they know their stuff.

In addition to these general rules, places that we recommend for finding a good Dogon guide include the following:

- Bureau Régional du Tourisme (p502) in Mopti
- Association des Guides Dogon de Mopti (Dogon Vision; p502) in Mopti
- Association Tamakadi (p513) in Bandiagara

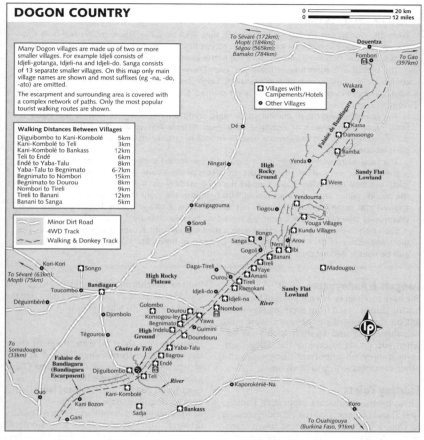

DOGON COUNTRY

From Douentza, a 4WD to Yendouma will cost CFA45,000 to CFA50,000 plus petrol.

An additional cost could be payments to visit the local representative of the *hogon* (spiritual leader); it's usual to give him a small gift of around CFA500 or kola nuts, which can be bought in Mopti or (more expensive) Bandiagara.

Equipment

The general rule is to travel as lightly as possible, because the paths are steep or sandy in places. Footwear should be sturdy, but boots are not essential. It is vital to have with you a sunhat, water bottle and plenty of water; heatstroke and serious dehydration are real possibilities. Reusable bottles can be bought in villages along the way and you can get water from village pumps (preferable to a well) en route, although it will need to be purified. Avoid carrying 'Western' products that have layers of packaging. Tents are not required, although a mosquito net is a good idea, especially after the rains. Nights are warm, although a lightweight sleeping bag will keep off the predawn chill from November to February. Dogon villages are dark at night, so a torch (flashlight) is useful, and you'll need toilet paper. Wearing shorts to below the knee for trekking is OK, although women will feel more comfortable wearing a skirt or long trousers when staying in a village. Women should not expose their shoulders.

DOGON ARCHITECTURE

When the Dogon first moved here, they took their lead from the Tellem (p507) and built their houses on the escarpment for protection. In recent times, many cliff dwellings have been abandoned, as more Dogon moved down to the better farmland on the plains.

The design of Dogon houses is unique. Each house is built of rock and mud, and set in a compound containing one or two granaries. Single-sex dormitories are constructed for those who have been circumcised, but are not yet married. Slight architectural variations occur across Dogon Country.

The granaries, with their conical straw roofs, stand on stone legs to protect the maize or other crops from vermin. At one time their most notable feature was the elaborately carved doors and shutters, but sadly, many have been sold to unscrupulous tourists and replaced with plain wooden doors.

The focal point of any village is the *togu-na,* a low-roofed shelter that serves as the meeting place for older men, where they discuss the affairs of the village or simply lounge, smoke, tell jokes and take naps. Nine pillars support the roof, made from eight layers of millet stalks, and the outside pillars are sometimes carved with figures of the eight Dogon ancestors. Women are allowed into some *togu-na,* although not all. The *taï* is a village's central square where most ceremonies take place; there's often an important *togu-na* close by.

Each clan in the village has a clan house, called a *guina,* which usually contains a shrine. The most impressive of these are characterised by rows of holes, like compartmentalised shelves, and geometric decoration.

Dangers & Annoyances

We have received isolated reports of travellers having things stolen from their luggage when left on the roofs of *campements*. Stow your valuables away and securely lock your bag when you go off to explore the village; and carry money, all important documents and other valuables with you at all times.

Starting Points

Three towns, Bandiagara (opposite), Bankass (p515) and Douentza (p516), provide gateways to Dogon Country. From these towns transport to the actual trailheads must be arranged. Of the numerous possible trailheads, Kani-Kombolé, Djiguibombo, Endé, Begnimato, Indelu, Dourou, Sanga and Yendouma are the most popular.

For horse safaris to the Dogon Country from Burkina Faso, see p139.

Trekking Routes

Time and money usually decide the length and starting point for a trek, but also consider how much energy you want to exert. Simple routes will take you along the bottom (or top) of the escarpment, while more interesting routes head up and down the cliff itself, often scrambling on all fours, leaping from boulder to boulder or using ladders carved from logs to cover the steepest sections. People with no

head for heights may feel shaky in places. You should also factor in local market days (see the boxed text, p509) when planning.

DAY TREKS

If you are very short on time, there are three circular walks from Sanga, aimed at tour groups on tight schedules. The **Petit Tour** (7km) goes to Gogoli, the **Moyen Tour** (10km) goes to Gogoli and Banani, and the **Grand Tour** (15km) goes to Gogoli, Banani and Ireli.

Another option in southern Dogon Country is to trek from Djiguibombo to Kani-Kombolé and on to Teli (8km), but you'll need transport from/to Bandiagara.

TWO DAYS

Spending a night in a Dogon village gives you a much better feel for Dogon life.

From Bandiagara, with a lift to Kani-Kombolé, you can walk through Teli, then sleep the night in Endé. The next day, hike to Yaba-Talu, climb to Begnimato, then hike 5km to meet a prearranged car back to Bandiagara. This trek covers 23km.

Another option (16km) is to start from Bankass, take a car or horse cart the 12km to Kani-Kombolé, then walk to Teli and sleep in Endé. The next morning, walk to Bagrou, then to Yaba-Talu to meet your transport back to Bankass. Another possibility from Bankass is a short, but rewarding, circuit to Kani-Kombolé, through Teli to Endé (spending the night at either) and then back (18km).

One final choice (23km) is to start in Sanga, climb down to Banani, and continue through Pege, Amani, Ireli and sleep in Tireli. The next morning climb up to Daga-Tireli to get your car back to Sanga.

THREE TO FOUR DAYS

A good three-day trek from Bandiagara starts with a lift to Djiguibombo. Visit the village and then continue by car to Kani-Kombolé to commence the trek. Continue on to Teli, then spend the night in Endé. The next day takes you to Yaba-Talu, then up to Indelu and sleep in Begnimato. On the third day, trek to Konsogou-ley for nice views of the plain, then on to Dourou to take a car back to Bandiagara. This trek covers 33km.

In the less-touristed northern Dogon Country, walk from Sanga to Yendouma (a gentle, 18km downhill walk). The next morning, hike the three Yougas, then sleep in Kundu. On your third day, hike up through the Yougas to the top of the escarpment, down through Arou and on to sleep in Ibi or Banani. On the fourth day, climb back up to Sanga (53km).

An excellent three- or four-day alternative (30km) is to start from Bandiagara, take transport to Dourou, then trek down the escarpment to Nombori (first night), head northeast to Ireli (second night), on to Tireli (third night), then up the escarpment to Sanga. This trek can also be done in reverse.

LONGER TREKS

If you have plenty of time, any of the routes described above can be extended or combined, and routes in from Douentza are possible. For example, from Douentza to Sanga takes at least seven days and takes in Gombori, Wakara, Kassa and Bamba. From Sanga and Banani you can head southwest via Tireli and Yawa to reach Dourou (after three days) or Djiguibombo (after another two or three days), and then end your trek at Bandiagara or Bankass. These treks can also be done in reverse.

Sleeping & Eating

These days almost every Dogon village has at least one *campement,* which invariably consists of one-storey buildings encircling a courtyard. Exceptions include Arou, Fombori,

Wakara, Gogoli, Ourou, Bongo and Kani-Bozon. Although some *campements* have rooms, sleeping on the flat roof under the stars is a wonderful experience: the sights and sounds of the village stirring in the early-morning light are unforgettable.

Evening meals are usually rice with a sauce of vegetables or meat (usually chicken). In the morning, you'll be given tea and bread with jam or processed cheese or, better still, deep-fried doughnuts. Small shops and restaurants catering for tourists have been set up in the most-visited Dogon villages, while beer, bottled water and soft drinks are available almost everywhere. Millet beer, an acquired taste, is also widely available.

BANDIAGARA
pop 9096

This small, dusty town, 63km east of Sévaré and about 20km from the edge of the Falaise de Bandiagara, was once a major administrative centre, but tourism is now the main show in town. Although not even remotely beautiful, Bandiagara is the most popular gateway town to the smaller and more beautiful Dogon towns and villages closer to the escarpment. As a result, the attention of numerous would-be guides as soon as you arrive will have you planning a rapid departure.

Information

In the heart of town is the market (market day is Monday, with a smaller version on Friday) where supplies can be purchased. When we were in Bandiagara, there were plans for a community-run tourist office (Syndicat d'Initiative) in the Palais Agibou Tall.

AGAT (☎ 2144 2905; babanapo@yahoo.fr; Rte de Sévaré) This private guide association is worth trying if Association Tamakadi can't help.

Association Tamakadi (☎ 2144 2053; http://tama kadi.wordpress.com; Rte de Sévaré; ☼ 7.30am-1pm & 4-8pm) The best and most reliable guide association in Bandiagara with 12 guides and fixed prices (all-inclusive trips CFA12,500 to CFA20,000 depending on the number of people). Next to Palais Agibou Tall.

Centre de Médecine Traditionnelle (☎ 2144 2006; crmt@afribone.net.ml) Known for its *maisons sans bois* (houses without wood) architecture and its work with medicinal plants.

Cybercafé Clic (Rte de Djiguibombo; per hr CFA1000; ☼ 8.30am-1pm & 3-6pm Mon-Fri, 9am-3pm Sat)

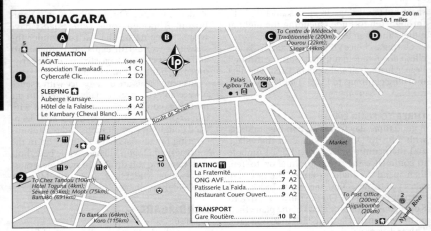

Festivals & Events

In late December, Bandiagara hosts the **Festival Culturel et Artistique de Bandiagara** with a small range of cultural activities. It's not a patch on the festivals in Ségou and Essakane, but may improve with age.

Sleeping & Eating

Auberge Kansaye (☎ 7322 9992, 6684 2456; kansaye bouba@yahoo.fr; roof mattress & dm CFA3000, s/d with fan & without bathroom CFA5000/8000, meals from CFA1500) We like this place. The rooms (bare, blue and concrete) are nothing special, but they come with mosquito net and there's a mellow atmosphere with reggae music a favourite of Bacar, the friendly owner. Its riverfront restaurant is a great place to pass an afternoon or evening.

Le Kambary (Cheval Blanc; ☎ /fax 2144 2388; www .kambary.com; s/d with fan & without bathroom CFA5000/8000, with fan & bathroom CFA19,000/20,500, with air-con from CFA25,000/27,000, breakfast CFA2800; 🍴 🖥 📶) Accommodation in this delightful Swiss-run place is in attractive stone igloos, with whitewashed and spacious interiors and portholes for natural light. If you've just arrived from Dogon, you may wonder if you've been transported to heaven. The restaurant (meals CFA5800) is outstanding (the food's great and the garden is beautifully designed) and there are sometimes musical evenings with buffet meals (CFA7500). There's also mini-golf.

Hôtel Toguna (☎ 2144 2159, 6688 7204; Rte de Sévaré; camping CFA2000, s/d with fan & bathroom CFA7500/10,000, breakfast CFA1500, meals CFA3500) Hôtel Toguna is outrageously good value, boasting tidy rooms with private (but outdoor) shower and toilet. The garden's pleasant, the *toguna*-style restaurant likewise, and it's superquiet. The downside is that it's 4km west of town with not a lot of passing public transport.

Hôtel de la Falaise (☎ 2144 2128; contact@hotel -lafalaise-mali.com; mattress on roof CFA1500, dm CFA4000, s/d with fan & bathroom CFA14,000/16,000, with air-con CFA22,500/25,000, breakfast CFA2500, meals CFA5500; 🍴) This new hotel in the centre of town has pleasant, comfortable rooms with splashes of Malian decoration and tiled floors, arrayed around a shady open area. It's also easily Bandiagara's friendliest place. Highly recommended.

Of the cheap restaurants, **La Fraternité** (☎ 7601 0779; Rte de Sévaré; snacks CFA1200, mains CFA1700-2750; 🕐 7am-midnight) has a friendly Nigerian owner and a range of dishes from sandwiches to grilled *capitaine*. It doesn't come much cheaper than the canteen at **ONG AVF** (☎ 2144 2505; off Rte de Sévaré; mains from CFA500; 🕐 7am-10pm), which serves up hearty rice dishes, *fonio* (traditional couscous) and brochettes. Also good is **Restaurant Couer Ouvert** (Chez Baba Dicko; Rte de Sévaré; mains CFA1000-1500; 🕐 6.30am-midnight) where they do steak, couscous, grilled chicken and spaghetti. Similar dishes are also on offer at **Patisserie La Faida** (off Rte de Sévaré; mains CFA1000-2500; 🕐 7am-midnight).

Getting There & Away

Most transport leaves Bandiagara around 7am or 5pm. There are around four daily departures to Sévaré/Mopti (minibus/shared taxi

MALI

CFA1500/1600). For Bankass (CFA1500), you'll be lucky to find more than one morning and one afternoon minibus departure. Koro (mini-bus/shared taxi CFA3000/3500) is even more difficult, with transport leaving when full, which is rarely more than once daily. You might also find the odd minibus between Bandiagara and Sanga on their respective market days (see the boxed text, p509). There are occasional Gana Transport buses from Bandiagara to Bamako (CFA8000, nine to 11 hours). The *gare routière* is in the centre of town, in the large open lot just south of the Route de Sévaré.

AROUND BANDIAGARA

Songo (also spelled Songho), around 5km off the main Bandiagara–Sévaré road northwest of Bandiagara, is a beautiful Dogon village. But its main claim to fame is as one of few Dogon villages to maintain its traditional animist circumcision ceremonies despite the village being almost entirely Islamic. The village is also an important weaving centre and freshly woven textiles line the main thoroughfares.

Every three years in March, young men be-tween the ages of 12 and 14 retreat to a rocky alcove overlooking the town where they are circumcised. The site is decorated with vivid rock paintings the like of which you won't see elsewhere; the paintings are hundreds of years old but have been touched up over the years. After the circumcision, the young men remain in seclusion under the rock wall for one month. Their return to village life as men is heralded with great celebration and the winner of a race earns free land and cow; second prize is a millet granary and cow, while the much-sought-after prize is the hand in marriage of the prettiest girl in the village.

All visitors to Songo must pay a CFA1000 village tax, while an obligatory guide to the circumcision site costs CFA1000 per group. The sunset views over the village are magnificent.

The only decent place to stay in Songo is the **Campement Hôtel de Songho** (☎ 6656 5681; roof mat-tress or camping CFA2000, d with fan & bathroom CFA10,000, meals CFA4000). The rooms are nice and big, but the staff really couldn't be bothered.

There's no public transport to Songo. It's a 5km walk from the main road.

SANGA

Sanga (also spelled Sangha), 44km north-east of Bandiagara and close to the top of the escarpment, is one of the largest Dogon villages and a good starting point for many treks. Although it has become quite tour-isty in recent years, it's a fascinating place to explore with a guide, in particular the strongly animist **Ogol Da** section, which is full of temples, fetishes and shrines. A few hundred metres southwest of the town, on the track to Ireli, watch out for the **fox tables**, a series of enclosed sand beds where local elders ask questions, and receive nightly an-swers, from the fox, an important spirit in Dogon cosmology.

Sleeping & Eating
Campement Gîte de la Femme Dogon (☎ 2144 2013; roof mattress CFA2500, d with fan & without bathroom CFA7000, breakfast CFA1000, meals from CFA2500) This friendly place looks and feels like a French refuge. It's a nice set-up, with a popular bar and restaurant and a small guides' office. Treks and 4WD hire can be arranged here, but you'll need to bargain hard.

Campement-Hôtel La Guina (☎ 2144 2028; hotel sangha@yahoo.fr; s/d/tr with fan & bathroom CFA15,000/20,000/25,000, with air-con CFA22,500/25,000/30,000, breakfast CFA2000, meals CFA2500-4000) This is a tour-group favourite and it's certainly the best-equipped place to stay. Rooms are spick-and-span and have good bathrooms. After a week's trekking the garden is lovely, the food good, and the hot showers and cold beer fantastic.

Getting There & Away
There's no regular public transport between Sanga and Bandiagara (CFA1500); chances are higher on Sanga's or Bandiagara's market day (see the boxed text, p509). Chartering a taxi costs at least CFA15,000, or getting a moped to drop you off costs CFA7500.

BANKASS
Bankass is 64km south of Bandiagara, along the dirt road to Burkina Faso. The Falaise de Bandiagara is about 12km away, which makes it a good gateway to southern Dogon Country, particularly if you're coming from Burkina Faso.

Information
There's a small and basic medical clinic in town.
Association Bandia (☎ 7448 0965) Represents Bankass' guides.

MALI

Sleeping & Eating

Campement & Hôtel Hogon (camping or roof mattress CFA2000, d CFA7000, mains CFA2500-3500) On the western edge of town, this is the best of the cheapies, although it's run-down and basic; you'll enjoy it more if you're camping rather than staying in the rooms. The best assets are the guys who run it: friendly and helpful with everything from finding guides to transport to Burkina Faso.

Hôtel Campement Le Nommo (☎ 7448 0965; mous saouedrago1@yahoo.fr; roof mattress CFA2500, s/d with fan & bathroom CFA12,500/16,000, with air-con CFA22,500/25,000; ✕) Easily the best place to stay in Bankass, Le Nommo opened in early 2008 and has pleasant rooms and public areas that will be wonderful once the trees grow. It's all watched over by Moussa, an agreeable host who can organise excursions to local sights, from little-known Dogon villages to hippos away to the southwest.

Getting There & Away

On most days, you'll find one morning and one afternoon minibus to Bandiagara (CFA1500), more on market days (Tuesday for Bankass, Monday and Friday for Bandiagara). There are also occasional minibuses/shared taxis to Sévaré (CFA3000/3500, two hours) and Koro (CFA1500/1600, one to two hours).

KORO

Koro has a nice mosque but little else to offer apart from the Saturday market and up to three daily buses along a soon-to-be-improved road to Ouahigouya (CFA3000, two to four hours) in Burkina Faso. Passport and customs formalities must be completed in Koro and Tiou (in Burkina Faso). Occasional minibuses/shared taxis ply the route between Koro and Sévaré (CFA3500/4000, three hours) with even fewer continuing on to Mopti for the same price. If you find yourself stuck here overnight, try **Aventure Dogon** (☎ 2144 2191; www .aventure-dogon.com; camping CFA4000, d from CFA8000, meals CFA4500), although its future is uncertain, or the local *campement*.

DOUENTZA
pop 9718

Douentza is where the track from Timbuktu joins the main highway and it's also possible to visit the Réserve de Douentza (p530) from here. Douentza is also the gateway to northern Dogon Country. Otherwise, Douentza has far more places to stay and eat than sights of

its own: a busy Sunday market is about all it can muster.

Sleeping & Eating

All of the following places are along the main Sévaré–Gao road and all can arrange guides to the Dogon Country and 4WD rental.

Auberge Gourma (☎ 2145 2054; roof mattress CFA2500, s/d with fan & without bathroom CFA4000/8000, meals CFA4500) is one of the most popular places to stay, with simple rooms and a reasonable restaurant. Its sister property next door, **Campement Dogon Adventures** (☎ 2145 2094; www .dogon-adventures-mali.com; roof mattress CFA3000, s/d with fan & without bathroom CFA8000/10,000, with air-con & bathroom CFA15,000/17,000; ✕) is marginally better. It rents out quad bikes for a highly negotiable €135/110 per day, with/without petrol.

Campement Hogon (☎ 7943 3104; hogondtza1@ yahoo.fr; camping CFA2500, Fulani tent CFA7500, d with fan/ air-con & without bathroom CFA7500/15,000; ✕) This Dogon-run place has a more intimate feel than many other places in Douentza, and we especially liked the Fulani tent.

Campement Chez Jérôme (☎ 2145 2052; half-board per person CFA15,000) With attractive, airy tents and wonderful food, this place wins plaudits from travellers.

Getting There & Away

Buses pass through Douentza en route between Sévaré (CFA3000, three hours) and Gao (CFA6000, seven hours), with an occasional service to Timbuktu (CFA8000, five to six hours).

THE NORTH & EAST

While much of northern Mali is off-limits due to the simmering Tuareg rebellion (see the boxed text p525), there are still plenty of stirring places that are safe to visit. Among these are the legendary frontier towns of Timbuktu (Tombouctou) and Gao, and the strange rock formations culminating in La Main de Fatima. An expedition in search of Mali's famous (and vulnerable) desert elephants in the Réserve de Douentza is one of Africa's most underrated wildlife-watching experiences.

TIMBUKTU (TOMBOUCTOU)
pop 35,638

Timbuktu, that most rhythmical of African names, has for centuries been synonymous with Africa's mysterious inaccessibility, with an end-of-the-earth allure that some travellers just have to reach. It's the name we all knew as kids, but never really knew where it was. More than just a name, Timbuktu's fame was derived from its strategic location, at once on the edge of the Sahara and close to the Niger, from its role as the fabulously wealthy terminus of a camel caravan route that has linked West Africa and the Mediterranean since medieval times, and from the vast universities of Islamic scholarship which flourished under the aegis of some of Africa's richest empires.

After it was 'discovered' by Western explorers, Timbuktu also became a byword for the West's disappointment with Africa. Even today, Timbuktu is a shadow of its former self, existing as a sprawl of low, often shabby, flat-roofed buildings that barely hint at its former grandeur and with streets filled with sand blown in from the desert. And yet, still the travellers come and you'll get the most from your visit here if you allow time to understand the significance of this town – its isolation, its history and its continuing importance as a trading post on the salt-trade route.

History

Timbuktu is said to have been founded around AD 1000 as a seasonal encampment for Tuareg nomads. An old woman was put in charge of the settlement while the men tended the animals. Her name was Bouctou, meaning 'large navel', possibly indicating a physical disorder. 'Tim' simply means 'well' and thus it was that one of Africa's most famous cities goes by a name that means 'the well of the woman with the large navel'…

Timbuktu was developed as a trading centre in the 11th century and went on to rival Gao to the east and Walata (in Mauritania) to the west. Gold, slaves and ivory were sent north and salt (from the mines of Taghaza and Taoudenni) came south.

Kankan Musa, the greatest king of the Empire of Mali (see p27), passed through in 1336, on his return from Mecca, and commanded the construction of the Dyingerey Ber mosque. Thereafter the city drew Islamic scholars, thus beginning a great tradition of Islamic education, which grew when Sonni Ali Ber and the Empire of Songhaï took the town in 1468. Timbuktu also began to get seriously rich. In 1494 Leo Africanus, a well-travelled Spanish Moor, recorded in his *History and*

BEST BOOKS ABOUT TIMBUKTU

- *Timbuktu: The Sahara's Fabled City of Gold*, by Marq de Villiers and Sheila Hirtle
- *The Hidden Treasures of Timbuktu: Rediscovering Africa's Literary Culture*, by John O Hunwick and Alida Jay Boye
- *The Meanings of Timbuktu*, by Shamil Jeppie and Souleymane Bachir Diagne (eds)
- *The Gates of Africa – Death, Discovery and the Search for Timbuktu*, by Anthony Sattin
- *The Race for Timbuktu – In Search of Africa's City of Gold*, by Frank T Kryza
- *Social History of Timbuktu*, by Elias N Saad

Description of Africa that Timbuktu had 'a great store of doctors, judges, priests and other learned men, that are bountifully maintained at the king's expense'.

In 1591 Moroccan armies sacked Timbuktu, killing many scholars and sending others to Fez (along with much of the city's riches). Fifty years later the remnants of the invading army had been assimilated into the local population, but their invasion signalled the start of the city's decline. Over the next 300 years Timbuktu fell to the Songhaï (1780–1826), Fula (1826–63) and Tuareg (1863–95). When the French explorer René Caillié became the first European to arrive in Timbuktu and live to tell the tale, he found 'a jumble of badly built mud houses, surrounded by arid plains of jaundiced white sand', and a city 'ruled over by a heavy silence'. The French marched in during 1894, and found the place pretty much how it looks today.

The Tuareg rebellion of the 1990s took a heavy toll on Timbuktu and it has only recently recovered. There was little fighting in the town itself, but Tuareg civilians and suspected sympathisers were arrested and imprisoned. Many were reportedly executed in the sand dunes.

Information

Officially every visitor to Timbuktu must pay a CFA2500 tourist tax, although if you don't visit the Musée Municipal (where the tax is collected), you're unlikely to pay.

MALI

INTERNET ACCESS

Bibliotheque Al-Imam Essayouti (per hr CFA1000; ☼ 8am-8pm) Situated next door to the Dyingerey Ber Mosque.

Internet cafe (Rte de Korioumé; per hr CFA1000; ☼ 7.30am-1pm & 4-7pm Mon-Fri, 7.30am-1pm Sat)

INTERNET RESOURCES

Explore Timbuktu (http://exploretimbuktu.com) An improving privately run website.

MEDICAL SERVICES

Centre de Sante de Residence (☎ 2192 1188) Hospital next to the Monument des Martyrs de l'Indépendance.

Hospital (☎ 2192 1169; off Rte de Korioumé) South of the centre.

Pharmacie Officine Jour et Nuit (☎ 2192 1333) Near the Sidi Yahiya Mosque.

MONEY

BDM (Rte de Korioumé) Changes cash (euros or US dollars) and does cash advances on Visa card.

BNDA (Rte de Korioumé) Changes cash and travellers cheques.

POST

Post office (Rte de Korioumé) For that all-important postmark.

TOURIST OFFICE & GUIDES

For arranging an accredited guide, and to get a free 'Tombouctou' stamp in your passport, visit the friendly **Bureau Régional du Tourisme** (☎ 2192 1779; Blvd Askia Mohamed; ☼ 8am-4pm). Two other places to try are the **Timbuktu Guide Service** (☎ 7602 3855; mali.guide@yahoo.fr), next to Hôtel Bouctou, and **Bureau Guides de Tourisme** (☎ 7604 2193; Blvd Askia Mohamed).

Azima Ag Mohamed Ali (☎ 7602 3547; azimaali@ hotmail.com) An experienced and much-in-demand guide whom we recommend wholeheartedly; he speaks French and English.

Commissariat de Police (☎ 2192 1007; Place de l'Indépendance) Will place a free 'Tombouctou' stamp in your passport.

Sights
MOSQUES

Timbuktu has three of the oldest mosques in West Africa and they represent classic examples of the Sudanese style of architecture which prevails throughout the Sahel. The mosques are closed to non-Muslims.

The oldest, dating from the early 14th century, is **Dyingerey Ber Mosque** and its mud minaret with wooden struts is one of the city's most enduring images. At the time of writing, the mosque was undergoing painstaking restoration work under the auspices of the Aga Khan Development Network's Historic Cities Programme (www.akdn .org/aktc_hcp_mali.asp?type=p). The use of a mud-cement mix will ensure that the mosque's mud walls no longer require regular replastering and will also change the mosque's appearance so that it more resembles the smooth facade of Djenné's mosque, rather than its former baked-mud appearance. Many locals grumble that it is considered good luck for a local to leave his imprint upon the mosque during replastering. For the best view of the mosque, you'll need to climb to the roof of the **Bibliotheque Al-Imam Essayouti** (admission CFA1000; ☼ 8am-8pm) located opposite the mosque's eastern entrance.

Sidi Yahiya Mosque, north of Place de l'Indépendance, is named after one of the city's saints (it's said that 333 saints have lived in Timbuktu) and was constructed in 1400. From the outside it's the least interesting of Timbuktu's mosques.

The **Sankoré Mosque**, northeast of the Grand Marché, was built (reportedly by a woman) a century later than Sidi Yahiya. It also functioned as a university, and by the 16th century was one of the largest schools of Arabic learning in the Muslim world, with some 25,000 students. Its pleasing minarets, historical significance and aesthetic harmony make it well worth a visit.

MANUSCRIPT LIBRARIES

Timbuktu's ancient manuscripts are like the keys to Timbuktu's past. There are countless priceless works, some dating from the 10th century and including some of the few written histories of Africa's great empires, as well as works of scholarship carried to Timbuktu from Granada after Muslims were expelled from Andalusia in 1492. For more information, see the boxed text, p29.

On 24 January 2004, the stunning new **Centre de Recherches Historiques Ahmed Baba** opened next to the Sankoré Mosque, on the site where Timbuktu's most famous scholar, Ahmed Baba, lived. The plan is for all the public and private manuscript libraries to

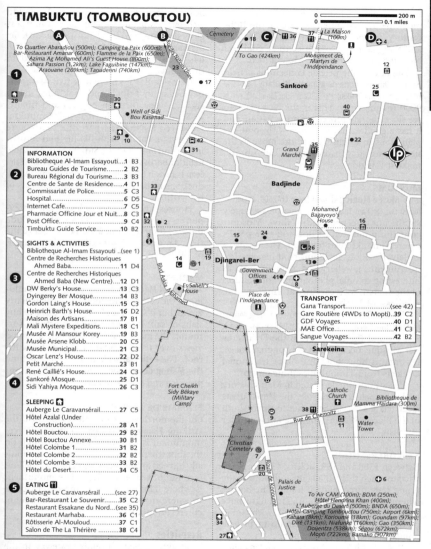

TIMBUKTU (TOMBOUCTOU)

INFORMATION
Bibliotheque Al-Imam Essayouti...1 B3
Bureau Guides de Tourisme.......2 B2
Bureau Régional du Tourisme......3 B3
Centre de Sante de Residence.....4 D1
Commissariat de Police...........5 C3
Hospital.........................6 D5
Internet Cafe....................7 C5
Pharmacie Officine Jour et Nuit..8 C3
Post Office......................9 C4
Timbuktu Guide Service..........10 B2

SIGHTS & ACTIVITIES
Bibliotheque Al-Imam Essayouti ..(see 1)
Centre de Recherches Historiques
  Ahmed Baba....................11 D4
Centre de Recherches Historiques
  Ahmed Baba (New Centre).......12 D1
DW Berky's House................13 C3
Dyingerey Ber Mosque............14 B3
Gordon Laing's House............15 C3
Heinrich Barth's House..........16 D2
Maison des Artisans.............17 B1
Mali Mystere Expeditions........18 C1
Musée Al Mansour Korey..........19 B3
Musée Arsene Klobb..............20 C3
Musée Municipal.................21 C3
Oscar Lenz's House..............22 D2
Petit Marché....................23 B1
René Caillié's House............24 C3
Sankoré Mosque..................25 D1
Sidi Yahiya Mosque..............26 C3

SLEEPING
Auberge Le Caravansérail........27 C5
Hôtel Azalaï (Under
  Construction).................28 A1
Hôtel Bouctou...................29 B2
Hôtel Bouctou Annexe............30 B1
Hôtel Colombe 1.................31 B2
Hôtel Colombe 2.................32 B2
Hôtel Colombe 3.................33 B2
Hôtel du Desert.................34 C5

EATING
Auberge Le Caravansérail ....(see 27)
Bar-Restaurant Le Souvenir......35 C2
Restaurant Essakane du Nord....(see 35)
Restaurant Marhaba..............36 C1
Rôtisserie Al-Mouloud...........37 C1
Salon de The La Thérière 38 C4

TRANSPORT
Gana Transport..................(see 42)
Gare Routière (4WDs to Mopti)...39 C2
GDF Voyages.....................40 D1
MAE Office......................41 C3
Sangue Voyages..................42 B2

move their collections here, although some of the private libraries are resisting the move. Until they do, there are two outstanding libraries to visit.

The largest collection of manuscripts is held at the **Centre de Recherches Historiques Ahmed Baba** (Cedrhab; ☎ 2192 1081; cedrhab@tombouctou.org.ml; Rue de Chemnitz; admission CFA1000;

⏱ 7.30am-12.30pm & 2-4.30pm Mon-Fri, 8am-1pm Sat). Home to (at last count) 23,000 Islamic religious, historical and scientific texts from all over the world, the centre is the focus of a South Africa–funded project to protect, translate and catalogue the manuscripts. Highlights among the few manuscripts on display include a letter of recommendation for the explorer Heinrich Barth, a treatise of medicine by Avicenne (980–1037), the 10th-century *Tarikh al-Soudan* (History of Sudan and Songhay) and a 17th-century gold-leaf biography of the Prophet Mohammed.

The best of the private collections is held by the **Bibliotheque de Mamma Haidara** (☎ 7942 7084; admission CFA1000; ☼ 7.30am-3pm Mon-Sat) with 9000 manuscripts. This is the best place to see the elaborate process of preservation, and it has a good exhibition room with some explanations in English. Until the move to the new centre, if you only go to one library, make it this one.

MUSEUMS

The **Musée Municipal** (admission CFA2500, as part of tourist tax; ☼ 8am-1pm & 3-6pm) occupies a hugely significant site near Sidi Yahiya Mosque, containing the well of Bouctou (see p517), where Timbuktu was founded. There's also a variety of exhibits including clothing, musical instruments, jewellery and games, as well as interesting colonial photographs and pictures of the ancient rock carvings at Tin-Techoun, northeast of Timbuktu.

The small and moderately interesting **Musée Al Mansour Korey** (admission CFA1500; ☼ 8am-8pm), just around the corner from the Dyingerey Ber Mosque, occupies an old Songhaï house. It contains household and other traditional artefacts from Timbuktu's ethnic groups.

A new museum dedicated to Mali's history under French colonial rule, the **Musée Arsene Klobb** (Rte de Korioumé), was due to open south of the Place de l'Indépendance not long after our visit.

EXPLORERS' HOUSES

Between 1588 and 1853 at least 43 Europeans tried to reach this fabled city; only four made it and only three made it home. The houses where they stayed while in Timbuktu have been preserved (and marked with small plaques) although most remain in private hands and not open to the public.

West of Sidi Yahiya Mosque, **Gordon Laing's house** (admission free; ☼ 8am-6pm), houses a small exhibition of manuscript copies, many of which are for sale. Only a couple of rooms are open to the public. Gordon Laing was the first European to reach Timbuktu, but was murdered shortly after leaving Timbuktu.

René Caillié was the first European to reach Timbuktu and live to tell the tale, even if his honest description of a careworn Timbuktu well past its prime initially earned him less glory than anger. West of Sidi Yahiya Mosque, the **house** where he did indeed stay in 1828 has been restored but remains closed to the public.

Heinrich Barth's incredible five-year journey began in Tripoli and took him first to Agadez, then through Nigeria and finally, in September 1853, he reached Timbuktu. He stayed for the best part of a year before narrowly escaping with his life and returning to Europe. East of Sidi Yahiya Mosque, **Heinrich Barth's house** (admission CFA1000; ☼ 8am-6pm) is now a tiny museum containing reproductions of Barth's drawings and extracts of his writings.

Houses where a host of lesser-known explorers stayed while in Timbuktu include those of **Oscar Lenz** and **DW Berky**, leader of the first American Trans-Saharan Expedition of 1912.

MARKETS

The **Grand Marché** is the large covered building in the centre of town. It's not particularly grand, but it's busy and not a bad place to buy slabs of salt. Its most colourful activity surrounds the main building and there are good views over the Timbuktu rooftops from the roof. The **Petit Marché** is further west, behind the **Maison des Artisans**, where local artisans produce and sell their wares.

FLAMME DE LA PAIX

On the northwestern outskirts of town, the striking **Flamme de la Paix** (Flame of Peace) monument is worth visiting. It was built on the spot where 3000 weapons were ceremonially burned at the end of the Tuareg rebellion (see the boxed text, p525). The monument is where Timbuktu meets the desert, close to where the salt caravans from Taoudenni enter Timbuktu.

Activities

Timbuktu is Mali's premier gateway to the Sahara, although for longer expeditions you should check the security situation before setting out.

Three operators we recommend for making the arrangements:

Azima Ag Mohamed Ali (☎ 7602 3547; azimaali@ hotmail.com) An English-speaking Tuareg guide and wonderful desert companion.

Mali Mystere Expeditions (☎ 7602 3239; www
.malimystereexpeditions.com; Blvd Askia Mohamed)
Shindouk Mohammed Lamine (☎ 7361 9145;
shindouk@yahoo.fr) A veteran French-speaking guide.

CAMEL RIDES & 4WD TOURS
Sunset or Overnight Trips
The most popular excursions include short
sunset trips to nearby dunes and/or Tuareg
encampments (from CFA7500 per person
per camel), and overnight trips that take you
to the dunes at sunset, followed by a night
under the stars, often at a Tuareg encampment (from CFA20,000 per person, including
a traditional meal).

Longer Expeditions
For extended trips, there are numer-
ous interesting options, including Lake
Faguibine (p524), Araouane (p524), and
even the salt mines at Taoudenni, deep in the
Sahara's heart.

Prices start at CFA20,000 per day by camel,
or it's at least CFA50,000 per day in a 4WD
(plus petrol), up to CFA90,000 including
guide, driver and food. No prices are cast in
stone and opening prices can be much higher
than these! Always agree on what's included
in the fee (food, sleeping bags etc) and write
it down before setting out. Never pay the full
amount until you return to Timbuktu.

SALT CARAVAN
Like a vestige from another age, salt caravans
of between 20 and 300 camels still travel between Timbuktu and Taoudenni, a return trip
that takes between 36 and 40 days. On arrival
in Timbuktu the salt is sold to merchants who
transport it upriver to Mopti, where it is sold
again and dispersed all over West Africa.

These are commercial operations and trips
are extremely gruelling; they're not to be taken
lightly: there's no escape if you find you can't
hack it or get sick. Expect to spend between
15 and 18 hours a day on the move, with no
rest days, and often with just four hours' sleep.
The food can be pretty grim (dates, peanuts,
dried goat meat and rice if you're lucky) and
not always sufficient. Most meals are taken
on the move.

Trip costs vary widely, but the daily rent
for one camel starts at CFA20,000 per camel
per day, to which must be added the cost of
a guide, interpreter (many guides and camel
drivers speak only Hasaniya, a Moorish dialect

of Arabic), food and water. November and
December are the ideal months to travel –
the desert is not too hot and the harmattan
has not begun.

For an evocative account of the journey and
of the salt mines themselves, read the excellent *Men of Salt: Across the Sahara with the
Caravan of White Gold* by Michael Benanav.

Festivals & Events
Every year in early January, Essakane, 50km
from Timbuktu, hosts the outstanding **Festival
in the Desert** (www.festival-au-desert.org; 3-day festival
pass €139) which attracts a host of Mali's best
musicians (especially Tuareg groups) and a
handful of international groups. The gravi-
tas of watching some of Africa's best musicians amid the sand dunes of the Sahara has
made this one of the world's most famous
(and exotic) music festivals and it really is a
once-in-a-lifetime experience.

Sleeping
Reaching Timbuktu can be pretty hard going
and many travellers dream of staying somewhere in an oasis of calm and cleanliness.
Finally there are a couple of places that fit
that description.

A word of warning: don't listen to local
would-be guides who tell you that your hotel
has closed. This is a particular problem for
those trying to reach Sahara Passion.

BUDGET
Sahara Passion (☎ 7942 6947; http//:hotelsaharapassion
.com; roof mattress CFA2000, dm CFA3000, s/d without bathroom CFA7500/10,000) On the northern outskirts
of Timbuktu, Sahara Passion is our favourite budget choice. It's run by the friendly
Canadian-Tuareg team of Miranda and
Shindouk and its attractions are many: the
quiet location, the rooftop views from where
you can sometimes see the arriving camel
caravans, a lovely entrance garden under a
Tuareg tent and a sense of being a part of
authentic Timbuktu life away from the tourist
scene. The only drawback in hot weather is the
lack of fans in the two rooms. It also provides
meals if given advance notice.

Hôtel Camping Tombouctou (☎ 7638 4900; chir
fiml@yahoo.fr; off Rte de Korioumé; roof mattress CFA4000, s/d
with fan from CFA7500/10,000, with air-con CFA15,000/18,000)
This place is simplicity itself, receives mixed
reviews from travellers and is a long hike into
town. The newer air-con rooms are quite

MALI

comfortable, but others won't have you rushing back here after a long Timbuktu day.

Camping La Paix (☎ 7604 1907, 7602 3575; camping or mattress on roof CFA3500, dm CFA5000, s/d with fan from CFA10,000/12,500, with air-con CFA17,500/20,000) Close to the Flamme de la Paix on Timbuktu's northern outskirts, Camping La Paix has good-sized, generally clean rooms with high ceilings. Some are a bit dark but it's in a quiet part of town.

Hôtel Bouctou (☎ /fax 2192 1012; dm, camping & roof mattress CFA6000, s/d with fan from CFA12,500/15,000, with air-con CFA19,000/22,500, meals CFA5000; ⊠) Arrive here at noon when things are quiet and you might find the place deserted, save for the staff sleeping in the restaurant. By sunset in high season, it swarms with tourists, guides and other hangers-on. The rooms are large and spacious with tiled floors, although they get mixed reviews from travellers. The central location is a plus and the rooms in the annexe are newer but even more bare.

MIDRANGE & TOP END
Auberge le Caravansérail (☎ 7541 4302; www.tom bouctoucaravanserail.com; off Rte de Korioumé; roof mattress CFA5000, roof tent CFA10,000, d with fan CFA10,000-25,000, ste with air-con & bathroom CFA28,000; ⊠) One of our favourite places in Timbuktu. This French-run place has large, high-ceilinged rooms brimful of rustic charm and the public areas are among the most agreeable in Mali. The laid-back garden bar (home to live music most weekend nights) is chilled and the large salon open to the stars and with a foot pool for dusty Timbuktu feet is a lovely touch. The tent rooms on the roof are wonderful.

Hôtel du Desert (☎ 2192 1199; hoteldudesert@hotmail .com; s/d with fan & bathroom CFA13,000/18,000, with air-con & bathroom CFA23,000/28,000; ⊠) A newish place with bland, large rooms that are already showing their age, Hôtel du Desert gets good reports from travellers. The air-con rooms are a touch overpriced, but it's a quiet place.

Auberge du Desert (☎ 2192 2025; alhous@hot mail.com; s/d with air-con, bathroom & breakfast CFA24,000/28,000; ⊠) A long way south of the centre, Auberge du Desert has tidy, modern rooms that are comfortable and quiet.

Hôtel Colombe 1 (☎ 2192 1435; fax 2192 1434; Blvd Askia Mohamed; s/d/tr from CFA24,500/26,500/42,000; ⊠ ⊠) If you like to be in the centre this place is ideal, with enormous rooms and a terrace overlooking the street where meals and drinks are served. Service can be woeful, however, and the plumbing is unreliable. The same

owners also run the nearby Hôtel Colombe 2 (☎ 2192 2132, with air-con) and Hôtel Colombe 3, which are newer but otherwise identical, and cost the same. The big plus is the outdoor swimming pool.

La Maison (☎ 2192 2179; www.lesmaisonsdumali.com; s/d with air-con & bathroom CFA30,000/35,000; ⊠) Timbuktu's best hotel, La Maison is a stunning oasis that incorporates traditional Timbuktu architectural features and a subtle designer touch in each room. The roof terrace is superb and the meals here are exceptional (see opposite). It's all watched over by Awa, the welcoming French owner. If you spoil yourself once while in Mali, this is a great place to do it.

Hôtel Hendrina Khan (☎ 2192 1681, 7602 3406; www.tomboctou.com; off Rte de Korioumé; s/d/ste CFA30,500/40,500/60,000; ⊠) Once Timbuktu's best hotel, the Hendrina Khan has been eclipsed by better places elsewhere. The rooms are large and comfortable with enormous beds, but they lack character and it's a long, hot walk into town.

The former Hôtel Azalaï, on a sand hill west of town, was being completely rebuilt at the time of writing. It promises luxury, but time will tell. Another accommodation option still in its early stages is the excellent, quiet guest house run by **Azima Ag Mohamed Ali** (☎ 7602 3547; azimaali@hotmail.com), with three well-kept rooms (CFA10,000) and options for camping and sleeping on the roof; it's close to the Flamme de la Paix monument.

Eating
Locals sometimes joke that there is one secret spice known only to people from Timbuktu: sand. Don't be surprised if it turns up in your food in cheaper places on windy days.

Our favourite place for a cheap meal is the unsigned place just west of the Monument des Martyrs de l'Indépendance. Known by every Timbuktu carnivore as **Rôtisserie Al-Mouloud** (meals from CFA1000; ⊙ 9am-10pm), it serves up terrific grilled meats and *luttre* (sausages; CFA500 each) for lunch and after sunset.

Restaurant Marhaba (☎ 7887 4946; mains from CFA600; ⊙ 6am-midnight) Perhaps the best sit-down budget restaurant, Restaurant Marhaba, just north of the centre, is a friendly place with hearty servings. Apart from spaghetti, couscous and rice, this is a good place to order (with five hours' notice) the local speciality of *toukassou* (CFA1250), a rather stodgy bread that you dip into a meat sauce.

MALI

Bar-Restaurant Amanar (mains CFA1250-2000; ☽ lunch & dinner) This mellow place opposite the Flamme de la Paix on Timbuktu's north-western outskirts is decent for the traveller staples of soup, spaghetti, couscous, steak and chicken. The music is usually Malian blues, except on Saturday and Sunday night when a DJ spins dance tracks until late.

Salon de The La Thérière (☎ 7524 0857; Rue de Chemnitz; meals from CFA1500; ☽ 7am-midnight) This languid place has reasonable food with all the usual suspects and a nice garden area in which to pass a warm Timbuktu night. There are sometimes local bands playing in the evening.

Other cheap meals are to be found on the roof of the Grand Marché where you'll find the pleasant **Bar-Restaurant Le Souvenir** (☽ 7am-midnight) and **Restaurant Essakane du Nord** (☽ 6am-midnight), both of which do couscous for CFA2000/15000 with/without meat.

La Maison (☎ 2192 2179; www.lesmaisonsdumali.com; breakfast/lunch/dinner CFA3500/5000/9000) The meals here are exquisite, if on the small side. The menu changes daily, but the French cook Gaetane brings subtlety, colour and flair to traditional and modern French cuisine. Although the ingredients are local, you won't eat another meal like this in Mali. On the roof of the hotel of the same name, the setting is as attractive as the food is special.

Of the other hotel restaurants, the best choice is **Auberge Le Caravansérail** (☎ 7541 4302; www.tombouctoucaravanserail.com; off Rte de Korioumé; meals CFA5000).

Getting There & Away

Getting out of Timbuktu is often harder than getting in. Start planning and negotiating your departure early.

AIR

Timbuktu's **airport** (☎ 2192 1320) is 6km south of town off Rte de Korioumé.

MAE (☎ 7602 3929; www.mae-mali.com; Place de l'Indépendance) has the most reliable flights to/from Bamako (CFA97,600, three weekly), Mopti (CFA65,000, three weekly) and Gao (CFA45,000, one weekly). The other option is **Air CAM** (☎ 7602 3548; www.camaero.com; Rte de Korioumé) with three weekly flights to Mopti (CFA69,500) and Bamako (CFA101,000).

BOAT

Between late July and late November (sometimes into February or March for the stretch between Gao and Timbuktu), the large Comanav passenger boats stop at Kabara (Timbuktu's old port), 18km south of town. For details on prices, see p539. The **Comanav ticket office** (☎ 2192 1206) is in Kabara.

Alternatively, you can travel between Mopti and Korioumé (the official port for Timbuktu) by public or private pinasse; for details see the boxed text, p504. You may be able to negotiate a cheaper rate if you find a private pinasse returning empty to Mopti. Public pinasses also go a few times a week to Niafunké (from CFA2500) and Mopti (CFA5000 to CFA10,000).

Apart from the Comanav ferry, there's very little transport to and from Gao, although an occasional pinasse goes to Gourma-Rharous, where you might find another pinasse going to Gao or (more likely) a place in a truck.

A Libya-funded canal from Korioumé to Timbuktu promises to provide the city with its first navigable link to the Niger River in centuries.

BUS & CAR

In the dry season, battered 4WDs carrying up to 12 passengers run between Mopti and Timbuktu (CFA12,500 in the back, CFA15,000 in the front for a seat, CFA60,000 for the car to yourself) most days. They leave from the open area around the Grand Marché and the journey takes six to eight hours.

Sangue Voyages (☎ 7638 2897; Blvd Askia Mohamed), **Gana Transport** (Blvd Askia Mohamed) and **GDF Transport** (☎ 7698 2771), near the Grand Marché, offer services between Timbuktu and Bamako (CFA15,000, at least 15 hours), via Sévaré (CFA10,000, seven to eight hours) and Ségou (CFA12,500, 13 to 14 hours). Departures are usually around 6am and tickets must be bought the day before. Most companies only offer two weekly services, on Thursday and Sunday.

At the time of writing, we don't recommend the land journey between Timbuktu and Gao along the north side of the river for safety reasons.

Getting Around

Most of Timbuktu can be managed on foot, but even the longest taxi ride within town shouldn't cost more than CFA1000. A private taxi/bâché to Kabara costs CFA9500/550 and to Korioumé CFA6000/350, but you may be asked for five times as much. A taxi to the airport will cost at least CFA3000.

MALI

AROUND TIMBUKTU

Niafunké

The sleepy town of Niafunké, on the west bank of the Niger River southwest of Timbuktu, is best known as the home city of master musician Ali Farka Touré (see p479) who named one of his albums after the town. Otherwise, it's a pleasant riverside settlement with shaded streets and friendly locals. The **campement** (r from CFA8000), which has pretty respectable rooms, was run by Ali Farka Touré until his death in 2006 and is close to the market (market day is Thursday).

Trucks leave each week to Timbuktu (CFA7500) and elsewhere, and you'll find plenty of river transport heading to Timbuktu (CFA2500) and Mopti (CFA4000), especially around market day.

Lake Faguibine

When the Empire of Ghana was at its height this lake, about 50km north of Goundam, was one of the most impressive in West Africa. However, it's in danger of disappearing entirely (for more information, see the boxed text, p90). Even so, the landscape and cliffs on the northern shore are very impressive, and cave paintings are found at Farach.

Tiboraghen

The small Tuareg settlement of Tiboraghen, 35km south of the Timbuktu ferry on the main track to Douentza, is a worthwhile place to rest from the road for a couple of nights. It's an untouristed spot that's home to the excellent, family-run **Campement Ténéré** (dm CFA4000, 2-person Tuareg tent CFA12,500, meals CFA5000). Apart from the lovingly maintained facilities, the friendly hosts can organise a range of visits and musical performances (CFA7500 to CFA30,000) in the village.

ARAOUANE

pop 100–200

There's nowhere on earth quite like Araouane, a remote, sand-drowned outpost 269km north of Timbuktu. It was once a place of great learning and an important staging post on the camel caravan route between the salt mines of Taoudenni and Timbuktu. Known for the sweet water from its many wells and for being the last watering hole for almost 500km on the barren route north, Araouane became a place of legend throughout the Sahara.

Araouane's unusual story took on a whole new dimension in 1988 when Ernst Aebi, a New York loft renovator, arrived in Araouane on a mission to make the town self-sufficient and prevent it disappearing under the Saharan sands. Using his own money, and in association with eager locals, he planted trees to keep the desert at bay, and gardens of fruits and vegetables, which he taught the villagers to tend. He even built a hotel, the Araouane Hilton. By the early 1990s, however, with the Tuareg rebellion brewing, Aebi left Araouane, after which his hotel fell apart and the gardens quickly died. Aebi's book, *Seasons of Sand,* tells the story in detail and is a great read.

Araouane is once again disappearing beneath the sand – in **Old Araouane**, 5km northeast of town, only the roofs of houses and a minaret remain above ground level – and only a few wells and tamarisk trees remain. The town survives on supplies trucked in from Timbuktu and most of the young men earn a backbreaking living in the mines of Taoudenni.

Sadly, until the latest rebellion dies down, we cannot recommend a visit here – the risk of banditry and kidnapping is simply too high. Although we visited here in January 2009, we did so in great secrecy and narrowly avoided an encounter with rebels.

Araouane is about seven days from Timbuktu by camel, or nine hours by 4WD.

GAO

pop 46,608

Although Gao never had the cachet of its more evocatively named cousin and rival, Timbuktu, it was once the capital of the Songhaï Empire (see p28) and was perhaps the greatest of Mali's historically illustrious centres of power. Modern Gao is a dusty, intriguing place, a largely mud-brick town encircled with semipermanent nomadic encampments and home to a largely Songhaï and Tuareg population. Apart from the delicious feeling of being 350km beyond Timbuktu in one of Africa's most forgotten corners and bordered by the Niger River on one side and the Sahara Desert on the other, Gao's attractions include a Unesco World Heritage–listed mosque-tomb complex and a stunning riverside dune just across the river.

History

Gao was probably founded in AD 650, and by 1000 (when Timbuktu was born) it was

---

MALI'S TUAREG REBELLION

Ever since Mali became independent in 1960, the Malian government (dominated by ethnic groups from southern Mali) has had an uneasy relationship with the Tuareg and twice in recent decades this has spilled over into open conflict.

In May 1990, a Tuareg rebellion broke out in Niger and quickly spread to Mali. In the six years that followed, Mali was in a state of near civil war and northern Mali was a no-go zone, with Timbuktu, Gao and Kidal virtually cut off from the outside world. A peace process begun in 1995 culminated in the ceremonial burning of 3000 weapons in Timbuktu on 27 March 1996 and the erection of the Flamme de la Paix monument (p520) on Timbuktu's outskirts. Aid money was pumped into the region and Tuareg refugees returned from Mauritania, Algeria and Libya (where many of the insurgents had been armed and trained).

Fast forward to May 2006 and fighting again broke out when Tuareg rebels briefly occupied the army garrison and town of Kidal in northeastern Mali. In the years since, incidents have been reported from Gao in the east to Nampala, close to the Mauritanian border in the west. After an apparent escalation throughout 2008, the signs in early 2009 were encouraging: in February 2009, the government announced that it had captured all rebel bases, that the main rebel leader Ibrahim Ag Bahanga had fled Mali and that 700 ex-rebels handed over their weapons at a ceremony in Kidal.

Although the prospects for peace appear stronger in Mali than in neighbouring Niger (see the boxed text, p606), it will be some time before it will be safe to travel anywhere north of Timbuktu or Gao (although both towns remain safe to visit), and north of the Niger River between these two towns. Mali's far east, between the Niger River and Niger border, is also extremely dangerous. Banditry remains rife, government control (always tenuous) over the open spaces of the Sahara is minimal and the threat of kidnappings remains high, especially close to the Niger border.

---

already a well-established city-state and gateway to eastern trans-Saharan trade routes. Gao would go on to become the capital of the Empire of Songhaï (see p28) and became one of the richest and most powerful cities in West Africa, with its heyday during the 15th century.

One of the greatest leaders of the Songhaï was Sunni Ali Ber, a ruthless military tactician more content with waging war than administering his empire, which soon included Djenné and Timbuktu. Alas, his son was not a patch on his father and was later overthrown by Askia Muhammad Touré. Askia was a devout Muslim and immediately set about restoring the prestige of Gao's Islamic institutions (he now lies in the Tomb of Askia in the north of the city). Then in 1591, 53 years after his death, Gao was smashed and looted by invading Moroccan armies. Gao subsequently fell into decline and has never recovered.

Information
INTERNET ACCESS
Internet cafe (Rte de l'Aéroport; per hr CFA500; 8am-2pm & 4-8pm Mon-Sat)

MEDICAL SERVICES
Hôpital de Gao (☎ 2182 0254; Rte de l'Aéroport) Staffed by predominantly Cuban doctors.
Pharmacie Attibey (☎ 2182 0441; Rue Aldousseini O Touré)
Pharmacie Populaire du Mali (Ave des Askia)

MONEY
BDM (Ave des Askia) Changes euro cash and has a Visa-enabled ATM that *usually* works.
BNDA (off Place de l'Indépendance; 7.30am-12.30pm Mon-Thu, to 11am Fri) Changes cash and travellers cheques.
Ecobank (Ave des Askia; 8am-4pm Mon-Fri, 9am-2pm Sat) Changes euros and US dollars cash and travellers cheques for hefty commissions.

POST
Main post office (Place de l'Indépendance; 8am-12.30pm & 2-3.30pm Mon-Thu, 8am-12.30pm & 2.30-5pm Fri)

TOURIST OFFICES
Omatho (☎ 2182 1182; Place de l'Indépendance; 7.30am-12.30pm & 2-4pm Mon-Fri) One of the best tourist offices in Mali. Its list of local sights, hotels, restaurants, accredited guides and other services (posted on the wall in French and English) may not always be updated, but it's extremely useful.

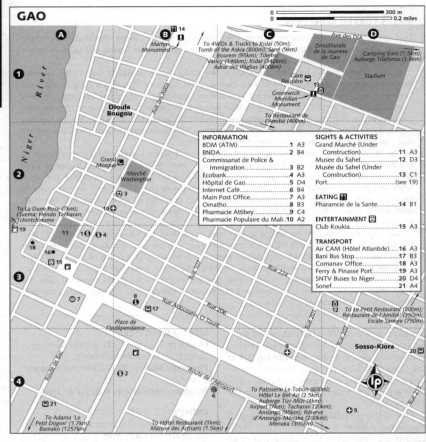

GAO

0 _____ 300 m
0 _____ 0.2 miles

INFORMATION		
BDM (ATM)	1	A3
BNDA	2	B4
Commissariat de Police &		
Immigration	3	B2
Ecobank	4	A3
Hôpital de Gao	5	D4
Internet Café	6	B4
Main Post Office	7	A3
Omatho	8	B3
Pharmacie Attibey	9	C4
Pharmacie Populaire du Mali	10	A2

SIGHTS & ACTIVITIES		
Grand Marché (Under		
Construction)	11	A3
Musee du Sahel	12	D3
Musée du Sahel (Under		
Construction)	13	C1
Port	(see 19)	

EATING		
Pharamcie de la Sante	14	B1

ENTERTAINMENT		
Club Koukia	15	A3

TRANSPORT		
Air CAM (Hôtel Atlantide)	16	A3
Bani Bus Stop	17	B3
Comanav Office	18	A3
Ferry & Pinasse Port	19	A3
SNTV Buses to Niger	20	D4
Sonef	21	A4

Map labels:
Martyrs Monument
To 4WDs & Trucks to Kidal (50m); Tomb of the Askia (800m); Sané (9km); Bourem (95km); Tilemsi Valley (146km); Kidal (342km); Adrar des Ifôghas (400km)
Directionale de la Jeunese de Gao
Camping Euro (1.5km); Auberge Tilafonso (1.8km)
Ave des DIA
Stadium
Gare Routière
Greenwich Meridian Monument
To Restaurant de l'Amitié (400m)
Dioula Bougou
Ave des Askia
Niger River
Grand Mosque
Marché Washington
To La Dune Rose (7km); Ouema; Hondo Tacharan; Tchintchinome
Rue 107
Rue 224
Rue 206
Rue 201
Rue 202
Place de l'Indépendance
Route de Bia
Route de l'Aéroport
Rue Aldoussehi O. Touré
Sosso-Kiora
To Le Petit Restaurant (200m); Restaurant de l'Amitié (350m); Escale Saneye (750m)
To Patisserie Le Tobon (600m); Hôtel Le Bel Air (2.5km); Auberge Tizi-Mizi (4km); Airport (7km); Tacharan (20km); Ansongo (95km); Réserve d'Ansongo-Menaka (200km); Menaka (306km)
To Adama 'Le Petit Dogon' (1.7km); Bamako (1257km)
To Hôtel Restaurant (1km); Maison des Artisans (1.5km)

Sights & Activities

It's worth checking out the town's bustling little **port** west of the town centre. After a devastating fire in May 2008, the **Grand Marché** is waiting for rebuilding to begin, until which time it spills colourfully into the surrounding streets; it's especially lively on Sunday (market day).

TOMB OF THE ASKIA

The Unesco World Heritage–listed **Tomb of the Askia** (admission CFA1500; ☼ daylight hours, closed from just before to just after Friday prayers), north of the centre, is an extraordinary mudbrick structure. Built in 1495 by Askia Muhammad Touré, one of the greatest rulers of the Songhaï Empire, the tomb now houses his remains, while those

of his descendants lie scattered in the cemetery surrounding the walls. The Tomb of the Askia is an evocative combination of mudbrick, wooden struts (including some wooden beams from Mecca used in the original 15th-century structure) and a tapering tower; local legend has it that the Askia was inspired by the Pyramids of Egypt during his pilgrimage to Mecca. The wooden struts are used by the Askia's surviving descendants who replaster the mosque over two days every second April or May (usually in even years). You can climb the 10m-high minaret for good views of the city and river. The tomb is flanked on two sides by the long prayer halls – the one to the northwest is for women and holds 200 people, while the men's prayer hall (southwest) holds

1400. The mosque/tomb still serves as Gao's main mosque.

LA DUNE ROSE & AROUND

For many travellers, Gao's premier tourist attraction is a sunset trip to **La Dune Rose** ('The Pink Dune', known locally as Koïma), a sand dune on the eastern bank of the Niger and visible from town 7km away. Local legends abound: it was once believed by locals to be the home of magicians and the local name (Koïma, which loosely translated means 'come and listen') derives from the days of the Songhaï Empire when drummers summoned the warriors from neighbouring regions in times of war from the dune's summit. The views are exceptional.

Upstream at **Quema** and **Hondo** (a three-hour trip) there are more stunning dunes, while you're almost guaranteed hippo sightings at **Tacharan**. One initiative worth supporting close to Tacharan is in the village of **Tchintchinome**, 20km from Gao, where the local **Zankai Aljanna** (Children's Paradise) organisation runs projects in experimental agriculture, traditional medicine and tree planting. You'll also be asked to plant a tree, and can enjoy traditional Songhaï dance and storytelling. Overnight stays in Songhaï huts can be arranged in advance – check with the Omatho office in Gao.

To get to La Dune Rose, you'll need to hire a motorised pinasse (the official price is CFA30,000, but we negotiated down to CFA22,500) or slower pirogue (CFA7500). For trips further afield, you'll probably want to rent a pinasse for the day (CFA75,000). Try your luck negotiating at the port, or call **Mohamed Traoré** (☎ 7605 1800) or **Ibrahim Maïga** (☎ 7901 8547). The best time for river trips is from September to February; at other times, you'll be at the mercy of variable water levels.

MUSÉE DU SAHEL

This dusty but engaging little **museum** (☎ 7603 9261; Rue 224, Sosso-Kiora; admission CFA1000; ⏲ 8am-noon & 3-6pm Sun-Fri) is devoted to the story of the Songhaï and Tuareg people, and the prehistoric sites in the surrounding region. It contains traditional artefacts, dress, jewellery and other items of interest. There are plans for the museum to move to new premises next to the Greenwich Meridian Monument.

Sleeping

Gao's accommodation is generally unexciting and don't expect hot showers anywhere.

The best places are a fair way from the town centre.

Camping Euro (☎ 7608 7827; shaolumese@yahoo.com; Rue 527, Porte 570, Aljanabandia; roof mattress CFA3500, s/d with fan & without bathroom CFA7500/10,500) Easily Gao's friendliest accommodation, Camping Euro is run by Shaka, a charming Nigerian who understands travellers' needs and keeps his place spotless. The rooms are simple but tidy and there's an attractive roof terrace and small but pleasant courtyard. Meals are available.

Auberge Tilafonso (☎ 7605 1350; Aljanabandia; roof mattress CFA2500, s/d with fan, half-board & without bathroom & CFA11,750/17,500, lunch CFA2500) This place sparkles from its regularly whitewashed walls to the superclean shared bathrooms. The rooms are simple but cleanly swept and spread around two pretty courtyards. The owner, Harbert N'Diaye, is a welcoming host.

Auberge Tizi-Mizi (☎ 2182 0194; camping or roof terrace CFA3500, d with fan CFA7500-12,500, with air-con CFA17,500; ❄) Probably the best of the many *campements* surrounding Gao, Auberge Tizi-Mizi, 4km southeast of the centre along Rte de l'Aéroport, is a pleasant place to stay. The rooms are nicely kept and are extremely quiet. The garden bar is a quiet place to pass an evening, but we'd avoid the food.

Hôtel le Bel Air (☎ 7605 2288; roof mattress CFA3000, dm CFA3500, s/d with fan & shower CFA12,500/15,000, d with bath & air-con CFA17,500-22,500, apt CFA30,000; ❄) It's a real mixed bag here. Some rooms are run-down, while others, especially in the annexe, are good value. But the real attraction is 'Joachim', the elderly African owner who loves to sit and chat with his guests. He gives such warmth to the place that you may forgive the less-than-sparkling rooms. The food here is reasonable and prices include breakfast.

Eating

Around the Grand Marché you can get coffee and bread in the mornings, and street food in the evenings (check out the excellent local sausages).

Le Petit Restaurant (off Rue 213, Sosso-Kiora; meals from CFA500; ⏲ 6am-11pm) This popular place may not win cleanliness awards, but the meals are cheap and hearty, including lentils, liver, couscous and macaroni. The kindly Algerian family who runs it is another plus.

Pharmacie de la Sante (Bellàh Rôtisserie; ☎ 7632 3513; Ave des Askia; ⏲ 6am-midnight) Known by everyone by the name of its exuberant owner Bellàh, this terrific place is the best of the rôtisserie found all across Gao. He does little else but delicious, lightly spiced grilled *mouton* (sheep or goat) and claims to open around the clock – as he says, you won't want to sleep once you've smelled his meat. A plate (CFA1500) should satisfy all but the hungriest of travellers.

Restaurant de l'Amitié (cnr Rues 234 & 213, Sosso-Kiora; starters from CFA1000, mains CFA1000-4000; 🕙 8am-4am) Here they do rice (CFA500), steak (CFA1000) and chicken (CFA2000) dishes, although it's better known as a bar and for live music.

Patisserie Le Tobon (Rte de l'Aéroport; pastries CFA250-300, meals CFA1500-3000; 🕙 7am-2am) The pastries and cakes here may be a little stodgy and the range is limited, but they do some local specialities such as *wigila* and *nêmes* (shredded beef in an egg roll) if you give them a couple of hours notice.

Adama 'Le Petit Dogon' (🕿 7627 1416; Rte de Bac; sandwiches CFA1000-2000, salads & soups CFA1000-3000, mains CFA2000-4500; 🕙 breakfast, lunch & dinner Mon-Sat, lunch & dinner only Sun) Thank God for this place, 2km south of Place l'Indépendance! Dogon-run and with the cleanest kitchen we had the privilege to inspect in Mali, Le Petit Dogon has excellent meals – which include couscous, pizza, pasta and *filet de chameau* (camel fillet; CFA2500) – and a delightful atmosphere to which the owner Adama contributes much warmth. It is easily the best place to eat or drink in town as long as you're not in a hurry – meals take a long time to prepare.

Drinking & Entertainment

Club Koukia (admission CFA1500; 🕙 8am-4am) Behind Hôtel Atlantide, this popular bar-cum-nightclub is the best place in the centre of town, but its opening hours vary with the whims of the owner.

Escale Saneye (Chez Michel; Rue 227, Sosso-Kiora) It's a fairly long trek out here, but this place east of the town centre has a garden bar and a real African ambience. Although it's probably true of most drinking options, lone women will feel especially uncomfortable here.

Restaurant de l'Amitié (above; admission free) This is probably our favourite place for a lively night-time atmosphere with a large courtyard and live music from 9pm Tuesday to Sunday.

Shopping

Five blocks east of the water tower, the **Maison des Artisans** (🕙 8am-dusk) has 60 artisan-owned shops and over 300 industrious resident artisans. The quality is high and the pressure to buy much lower than elsewhere in Mali.

Getting There & Away

AIR

Apart from occasional international flights operated by Point Afrique (see p538), **Air CAM** (🕿 7605 2555; Hôtel Atlantide) offers Gao's only air link with the outside world, with one flight per week (Saturday) to Bamako (CFA115,000) via Mopti (CFA81,000) and Timbuktu (CFA45,000).

BOAT

Pinasses go most Wednesdays to Ansongo (market day on Thursday), but the rapids at Labbe inhibit direct pinasse traffic to Niamey. Apart from the **Comanav ferry** (see p540; 🕿 2182 0466) there's no regular transport upstream to Timbuktu; chartering your own private pinasse is expensive (from CFA350,000).

BUS

Gao, on the north bank of the Niger River, is connected to the Bamako road by a new Chinese-built bridge (CFA500 for cars).

Of the many bus companies operating from Gao, the best are **Bani** (🕿 2182 0424; Place de l'Indépendance), **Binke** (🕿 2182 0558; Gare Routière) and **Sonef** (🕿 2182 0391; off Rte de Bac). Services include Bamako (CFA15,000, 16 to 20 hours) via Hombori (CFA4000, three to four hours), Douentza (CFA6000, seven hours), Sévaré (CFA7500, nine to 12 hours) and Ségou (CFA14,000, 15 to 20 hours) and scheduled departures are at 5am; Binke has an additional 1pm departure. Sonef has a daily 6am bus to Niamey (see p539) in Niger that stops in Ansongo (CFA2000).

Once travel to the north becomes safe, your best bet for Kidal is probably a 4WD (CFA12,500) or truck (CFA10,000) that leave when full from Ave des Askia, just north of the Martyrs Monument.

Getting Around

Gao has a handful of taxis and most trips around town cost CFA1000. Motorcycle taxis should never cost more than CFA500.

AROUND GAO

Most of Gao's hinterland was, at the time of writing, the most dangerous corner of Mali with banditry and kidnappings rife; the destinations covered here should be attempted only after peace has returned.

North of Gao lies some fascinating desert country, especially the beautiful **Tilemsi Valley**, while Neolithic rock paintings and carvings can be seen in the **Adrar des Ifôghas**, a remote desert massif around Kidal.

Southeast of Gao, the small border town of Andérramboukane hosts the **Festival of Andéramboukane** in late January, one of the most important Tuareg festivals. The **Réserve d'Ansongo-Ménaka**, next to the Niger River, is extremely isolated. Much of the wildlife has gone but with considerable luck you may see red-fronted gazelles or manatees, and the Niger River still contains hippos. You'll require a well-equipped 4WD and an informed guide.

GOSSI

Along the main highway around 160km southwest of Gao, Gossi is a possible gateway to the Réserve de Douentza (p530). In January or February, you may be lucky to see a few elephants in the vicinity of Gossi's lake, although only a few lone males still visit the lake. At the northern entrance to town is the region's only sleeping option, the Tuareg-run **Camping Le Ténéré** (☎ 7914 6164; camping or mattress CFA2000), which is simple but friendly.

HOMBORI

In the flatlands of the Sahel, the magnificent sandstone buttresses near Hombori, a large village on the main road between Mopti and Gao, can seem like an apparition – some people call the 80km stretch of road between Hombori and Douentza 'Mali's Monument Valley'. Hombori has a picturesque old town, the nearby Main de Fatima is West Africa's best climbing destination and Hombori serves as a gateway to the Réserve de Douentza, home to Mali's elephants.

Sights & Activities

For all of the following sights and activities, a local guide is recommended. Ask at any of the three *campements* in town. Expect to pay between CFA7500 and CFA10,000 per day, more if trekking, food and/or transport is involved.

Hombori's **weekly market** is on Tuesday and the animal market, at the eastern end of town, is famous throughout the region.

The stone-built village of **Old Hombori** overlooks the new town from the south. Its main attractions include the **chief's house**, the small **Maison des Arts** and a **13th-century door** brought from Timbuktu.

The easternmost tower of rock visible from Hombori is **Hombori Tondo** (1155m), Mali's highest point. To reach the wide summit plateau you'll need some climbing ability and equipment, but **La Clé de Hombori** ('Key to Hombori'), a separate jagged spire at the southwestern end of the massif, can be climbed without ropes in about four hours.

Southwest of town, four more buttresses rise, the largest of which, **Barkossi Tondo**, is the focal point of a little-known trekking route (five hours return from Hombori). It leaves from Old Hombori, passes through the small Songhaï village of Barkossi Tondo before climbing to a saddle and up onto the summit.

The best place to watch the sunset is near the verdant village of **Kobokire**, a Tuareg-Fulani-Songhaï settlement that sits beneath low sand dunes (Hondo Miyo), around 5km northeast of Hombori.

Sleeping & Eating

There's no electricity in Hombori, but the following three places have generators that are switched on at nightfall.

Campement Kaga Tondo (☎ 7635 1301; http://lelele .skyblog.com; camping or roof mattress CFA3000, dm CFA3000, r or Fulani tent CFA5000, meals CFA1500-3000) With vaguely traditional flourishes and along the main road, this place, run by the amiable Lélélé, is good for budget travellers. You may want to eat elsewhere.

Campement de Mangou Bagni (☎ 7543 0988; camping with/without mattress CFA2500/2000, s/d without bathroom CFA4000/6000, breakfast CFA1250, meals CFA1000-3000) The longest-established of Hombori's three *campements*, at the eastern end of town, this place has a pleasant atmosphere with plenty of through traffic. The owner's family lives onsite, lending it an agreeable African ambience.

Le Tondanko Campement (☎ 7515 6144; douncy@ gmail.com; camping or roof mattress CFA2000, s/d Fulani tent CFA3500/5000, s/d without bathroom CFA4000/7000, meals up to CFA3000) Set back from the main road at the northeastern end of town, this place is similar to Mangou Bagni: laid-back, simple and well run. It also offers three-day treks (CFA17,500 per person per day) through the villages around town, and has some climbing equipment.

Getting There & Away

Hombori lies along the main Sévaré–Gao road, and all transport between these two towns passes through Hombori. Departure times are one of Mali's least exact sciences. Destinations include Douentza (CFA2000, three hours), Gao (CFA4000, five hours) and Sévaré (CFA5000, five to seven hours).

AROUND HOMBORI

Climbers around the world may know nothing else about Mali, but they know about **La Main de Fatima** (The Hand of Fatima) whose narrow, fingerlike towers soar 600m from the plains and provide world-class technical rock climbing around 13km west of Hombori. Several routes have been established, most very high and of demanding standard (British grades around E4, French grades around 7A).

Anyone wanting to climb here should contact a Spanish climber called **Salvador Campillo** (http://avired.com/maindefatma, in French or Spanish), who lives in the area from October to March, and arranges climbing tours. One week's climbing starts at €430 per person.

A spectacular walking trail climbs up from the village of Daari, which lies beneath La Main de Fatima just off the Gao–Bamako road. The trail crosses a saddle between the rocks and onto a pretty plateau with an abandoned Songhaï village, whereafter the trail climbs down to the village of Garmi. The trek takes a minimum of three hours and you can flag down buses and bush taxis along the main road close to Garmi. To climb or trek in the area, there's a tourist tax of CFA1000 payable at Campement Bongujje in Daari.

There are two *campements* in the small Fulani village of Daari. Easily the best is **Campement Bongujje – Chez Manya** (bongujje@yahoo.fr; camping CFA1000, Fulani tent CFA2000, meals CFA1500-2000), which is run by Salvador's delightful Fulani wife and is clean and well kept. You can also rent bicycles (CFA2000 per day), climbing equipment (October to March) and 4WD vehicles (CFA30,000 to CFA45,000 per day plus petrol). The other place to stay is the more basic **Campement Au Pied de la Main de Fatima** (roof mattress CFA1500, dm or camping CFA2000).

RÉSERVE DE DOUENTZA

The Réserve de Douentza, which occupies the Sahelian wastelands north of Douentza and Hombori, west of Gossi and east of the main Douentza-Timbuktu piste, is home to an extraordinary relic of more fertile eras: the northernmost elephant herd in Africa and the last left in the Sahel. A recent study suggests that elephant numbers hover around 350.

The elephants occupy a range that extends beyond the reserve and is believed to encompass 30,000 sq km with an annual migration circuit of around 500km – the longest recorded elephant migration. Their annual journey in search of water and food takes them down towards Burkina Faso from June before they return north into the reserve around November or December. From January to April (the best time to see the elephants), the elephants move roughly west through the reserve, from waterhole to waterhole, with a particularly high concentration around In-a-Djatafane. As water levels drop and lakes dry out at the end of the dry season, usually around May, the elephants move west towards Lake Benzena, the region's only permanent body of water. At the first sign of rains (usually June), the elephants again head south, passing through a broad pass known as the Porte des Éléphants, just south of Boni.

The Réserve de Douentza is not your average wildlife reserve. The elephants share the 'reserve' with an estimated 100,000 Tuareg and Fulani herders and as many as 400,000 head of livestock. Villages and seasonal camps are dotted around the reserve. Although stories of the elephants raiding granary stores and crops are common, the elephants survive largely due to a remarkable culture of tolerance among the local population: they share the same water and pasture resources and there are countless tales of herders following the elephants to water sources. That said, a growing population of humans and domesticated cattle, coupled with diminishing rains, are placing untold pressure on the elephants and local inhabitants alike. Another devastating drought such as the ones in the 1970s and 1980s (when hundreds of elephants and people died for lack of water) could prove disastrous.

Given the elephants' vulnerability, they are the subject of an ongoing conservation project involving the Malian government, World Bank and the NGOs Save the Elephants (www.savetheelephants.org) and the WILD Foundation (www.wild.org). These groups are also involved in training local guides and planning strategies to ensure the elephants' long-term survival.

The main access to the reserve is from Douentza, Hombori, Gossi and Bambara-

Maoudé. To explore the reserve, you'll need to be self-sufficient in food and water, have a 4WD (around CFA50,000 per day including driver but not petrol) and a guide (from CFA15,000 per day). Your only additional cost should be the tourism tax (CFA5000) in In-a-Djatafane.

It's a major expedition to see the elephants and, given the extent of their range, there's no guarantee that you'll be lucky. But seeing the elephants on the barren soils of the Sahel remains Mali's finest wildlife-watching experience.

THE SOUTH

Southern Mali sees relatively few tourists, other than those making their way between Mali and Burkina Faso. There's not a whole lot to see, but you will experience a side to Mali entirely different from the more heavily touristed trails further north.

SIKASSO
pop 192,400

Agreeable, if unexciting, Sikasso stands at the heart of a relatively lush region known as the 'market garden of Mali'. Sikasso was the last Malian town to resist French colonialism, and King Babemba Traore chose to kill himself rather than surrender. The mudbrick *tata* (town wall) that fell to French cannons in 1898 is still visible (albeit barely) in places. The Palais du Dernier Roi still stands on the western side of town and in the centre is the Mamelon, a small hill that was sacred to the Kénédougou kings, and on which a French colonial tower now stands.

Information

BDM (Rond-Point Mamelon) Visa cash advances and changes euro cash.
Hospital (☎ 2162 0001; Ave du Gouverneur Jacques Fousset)
Pharmacie du Souvenir (☎ 2162 0119; Blvd Coiffet)

Sleeping & Eating

Hôtel Tata (☎ 2162 0411; Rte de Bamako; d with fan/air-con & bathroom CFA9000/15,000; 🕸) The pick of a fairly ordinary lot in Sikasso, Hôtel Tata has well-priced rooms that are better maintained than most in town. The attached restaurant, where they do all the usual traveller staples, is also reasonably priced.

Hôtel Lotio (☎ 2162 1001; Blvd Coiffet; s/d with fan & without bathroom CFA7500/10,000) If you're coming from Burkina Faso, basic rooms here can be a depressing introduction to Mali, but it's a friendly place.

Hôtel Mamelon (☎ 2162 0044; Ave Mamadou Konate; s/d with air-con & bathroom CFA17,500/20,000; 🕸) Like most people we encountered in Sikasso, the owners are a friendly lot, but their rooms are overpriced. Some of the air-con at this once-lovely hotel seems to date from the colonial era.

Blvd Coiffet has several cheap eateries serving good filling meals (heavy on the rice) for around CFA500 to CFA1500. **La Vieille Marmite** (Blvd Coiffet) and **Restaurant Kénédougou** (Blvd Coiffet) provide good Malian fare and the enormous Sunday market is a real bonus for street-food fans.

Getting There & Away

The *gare routière* is a 15-minute walk (CFA225 in a shared taxi) from the centre. There are daily buses to Bamako (CFA4500, three to four hours), Mopti (CFA6000, six hours) and Ségou (CFA4500, four hours).

AROUND SIKASSO

Riddled with chambers and tunnels, the fascinating **Grottes de Missirikoro**, a lump of limestone roughly 12km southwest of Sikasso, is important both to local animists and Muslims. One traveller described witnessing 'singing and praying people inside the caves and thousands of bats that dart through the rooms'. A taxi tour from Sikasso costs around CFA10,000.

THE WEST

Western Mali is hard work: transport is infrequent or nonexistent, as is tourist infrastructure, and most of the sights are few and very far between. The region's appeal lies, however, in these very facts. This is Mali largely untrammelled by tourists and the modern world and losing yourself here is about deep African immersion.

NATIONAL PARKS

Bordering the lake formed by Manantali dam, west of Kita, **Parc National du Bafing** protects a number of primate species, including chimpanzees, which are the focus of a small

MALI

RESPONSIBLE ELEPHANT-WATCHING

Visiting Mali's elephants is no East African safari. The Réserve de Douentza's infrastructure is rudimentary and the elephants are not accustomed to carloads of tourists. Indeed, unless you take extreme care, your attempts to see the elephants could increase the animals' stress levels and therefore contribute to their decline. Please take into account the following:

- Rapid visits under pressure of time are unlikely to yield elephant sightings and pursuing elephants in 4WDs dramatically increases the stress on the elephants, which can cause accidents to the tourist but also make the elephants jumpy and more likely to attack locals.

- Only use guides from within the reserve, especially from In-a-Djatafane and Dimamou, or from Boni, as this ensures that tourism revenues benefit the local communities. Although guides in Hombori, Douentza, Gossi and Bambara-Maoudé will claim to be elephant guides, they rarely have the requisite training. International NGOs and the Malian government have plans for a system of training and official accreditation for elephant guides, which, once implemented, should make it easier to find a good guide..

- Park your 4WD some distance away and proceed on foot. Apart from increasing your chances of seeing the elephants, approaching on foot reduces the distress caused by car engines.

- Use a long camera lens rather than trying to get too close.

- Be particularly careful of lone bull elephants and of female elephants with infants.

- Approach from downwind and leave before the elephants become aware of your presence.

- Make sure you pay the village tax in In-a-Djatafane.

NGO project. Access is from Kounjdan, 45km from Manantali on the route to Kéniéba. From Kounjdan, take the road south to Makandougou; the road is terrible. Manantali makes a good base for exploring the region.

Most of the large animals that once inhabited the vast **Parc National de la Boucle du Baoulé**, between two large bends on the Baoulé River northwest of Bamako, have been hunted to extinction; only a few hard-to-see lions reportedly remain. The park is mostly savannah with pockets of riverine forest with bird-watching the most rewarding experience. Access to the park is best via Négala, a small village 60km northwest of Bamako. You'll need a 4WD to be completely self-sufficient. Before setting out, contact the **Office du Parc National de la Boucle du Baoulé** (Map p483; ☎ 2022 2498) in Bamako.

KAYES
pop 133,101

The principal settlement in western Mali, Kayes (pronounced kai) is a convenient place to break up the long journey between Bamako and Dakar. Kayes is hot and dusty, and was the first place the French settled in Mali (several colonial buildings remain). There's a thriving, chaotic market, the town is largely hassle-free and a number of interesting excursions are possible.

Information
BDM Visa cash advances, and changes euros cash. Near the post office.
Hospital (☎ 2152 1232) Two kilometres south of town.
Pharmacie Niambélé (Ave du Capitaine Mamadou Sissoko)

Sleeping & Eating
Centre d'Accueil de Jeunesse (☎ 2152 1254; camping or mattress on roof CFA3000, s/d with fan & without bathroom CFA5000/7500) This hostel-style place is one of the most basic places to sleep in Mali. If you can pay more, do so.

Hôtel Le Khasso (☎ 2153 1666; s & d with air-con & bathroom from CFA17,500; 🞬) This is our choice for the best place to stay in town, with simple but well-kept bungalows and a lovely riverside location.

Hôtel du Rail (☎ 2152 1233; d with air-con CFA18,000-28,000; 🞬) Opposite the train station, Kayes' Rail Hotel is typical of such places across West Africa: always people coming and going and a lovely old colonial building slowly going to ruin. As such, the rooms are way overpriced, but the food here is good (three-course menu CFA6000), while the garden's an ideal place to wait for trains.

Cheap food stalls abound near the train station and in the market. **Restaurant Yankadi**

(Rue 122; meals CFA500-1000), near the junction with Rue Magdeburg, serves filling meals, while **Poulet Doré** (Ave du Capitaine Mamadou Sissoko) does roast chicken (whole chicken CFA3000). **Restaurant Chinois Shanghai** (meals CFA1500-3750), at the southern end of Ave du 22 Septembre, offers authentic Chinese cuisine (the portions are tasty, if a little small).

Getting There & Away

For cross-border transport to Senegal and Mauritania, see p539 and p539, respectively.

AIR

Air CAM (☎ 7615 3600; www.camaero.com) and **MAE** (☎ 7672 9396; www.mae-mali.com; Rue Soundiata Keita) each have three weekly flights between Kayes and Bamako (CFA69,000). Seats fill up fast with Malians on business. The airport is north of the Senegal River, on the road to Yélimané.

BOAT

Pinasses to the Senegal border at Goutioubé (from CFA3000) leave midafternoon. Some go on to Bakel (CFA11,000).

BUSH TAXI

Transport leaves daily from Kayes Ndi *gare routière,* on the north side of the river, to Nioro (CFA7000) and Yélimané (CFA5000).

TRAIN

There are five weekly train services between Kayes and Bamako. The three services operated by Autorail are the most reliable and cost CFA7000/11,700 for a seat in 2nd/1st class. You may also be able to take the weekly international Express service from Dakar to Bamako (2nd-class seat/couchette CFA7300/11,500, 1st-class seat/couchette CFA16,190/22,190), although getting tickets can be difficult. For more details on services to Senegal, see p539.

AROUND KAYES

The recently renovated **Fort de Médine**, 15km upstream from Kayes, was part of a chain of defence posts built along the Senegal River in French colonial times. Although something has been lost in the overhaul, the buildings here still hold a real sense of history and the old train station is particularly beautiful. You may be able to stay with a local family; ask either of the guides at Fort de Médine.

The **Chutes de Felou** are a set of rapids and waterfalls about 2km south from Médine.

Pinasses to Médine (CFA1500) leave from opposite the Total petrol station in Kayes around 6.30am and 1.30pm daily, and return the following morning. Pirogues to Médine (CFA1000) leave around 3pm and return to Kayes the following morning. A taxi there and back costs around CFA12,500.

KÉNIÉBA

This neglected town may be something of a dog's breakfast, but the surrounding escarpments and hills are dramatic and picturesque, ideal for trekking and wildlife-watching. The town was also once the centre of a gold-producing area and is the starting point for little-used routes into Guinea and Senegal.

The **Casa Ronde** (s/d CFA3500/5000) *campement* provides the only basic, grubby and rather depressing accommodation, but the simple food here is OK. **Restaurant Wassa** (meals from CFA1000), beside Pharmacie Abdoul Wahab and just up from the Total petrol station, has better grub.

Getting There & Away

There's usually one vehicle per day for Kayes (CFA7500) and other surrounding towns, with regular departures chalked up on a board in the square next to the mayor's office.

There are also cross-border options for Guinea (p539) and Senegal (p539).

MALI DIRECTORY

ACCOMMODATION

Mali has some outstanding hotels, although compared to other West African countries you pay a lot more for quality.

Everywhere, budget hotels (up to CFA10,000/12,500 for a single/double) vary from basic and depressing to simple and tidy, but rarely have any character; you won't get air-con for this price. Sleeping on flat roofs (mattresses are usually provided) is the cheapest accommodation option in Mali; prices range from CFA1500 in the Dogon Country (where it can be the only option) to CFA4000. Some hotels have dorms (from CFA2500 up to CFA8500 in better hotels). Elsewhere, the best you can hope for is a *campement,* which are simple and usually good value.

The standard of midrange hotels (from CFA12,500/15,000 for a single/double up to CFA45,000/55,000) is generally quite high across the country. There are excellent midrange hotels in Bamako, Ségou, Djenné, Mopti, Sévaré, Bandiagara and Timbuktu.

In Bamako there are dozens of top-end hotels (above CFA46,000/60,000 for a single/ double and up to CFA126,750 for a double) to choose from, but elsewhere there's nothing to speak of.

All hotels in Mali add CFA500 per-person per-night tourist tax to room costs, and this has been included in the prices in this chapter.

ACTIVITIES

Mali is one of the most active destinations in West Africa. Possibilities include exceptional trekking in the Dogon Country (p507); river journeys up the Niger between Mopti and Timbuktu (see the boxed text, p504); and world-class rock climbing near Hombori (p529). Desert expeditions by camel or 4WD in the Sahara around Timbuktu (p521) are also possible, although check the local security situation before setting out (for details, see the boxed text, p525).

BOOKS

Ségu, by Maryse Condé, is an epic and beautifully written generational novel about a late-18th-century family living in the Niger River trading town of Ségou.

Dogon – Africa's People of the Cliffs, by Stephenie Hollyman and Walter van Beek, is a beautifully photographed study of the Dogon, with informative anthropological text.

In Griot Time: An American Guitarist in Mali, by Banning Eyre, is a great read, offering up-close pen portraits of many of Mali's world-renowned artists and a meditation on the role of music in modern Malian society.

Banco: Adobe Mosques of the Inner Niger Delta, by Sebastian Schutyser, is a beautifully presented collection of black-and-white photographs of Mali's weird-and-wonderful mosques.

There are a host of travel literature titles set in Mali, most of which head for Timbuktu along the Niger River. They're all worth checking out and include *The Cruelest Journey: Six Hundred Miles to Timbuktu*, by Kira Salak; *The Road to Timbuktu*, by Tom Fremantle; *To Timbuktu*, by Mark Jenkins; and *Frail Dream of Timbuktu*, by Bettina Selby.

For a list of books about Timbuktu, see the boxed text p517, while other books are covered on p524 and p521.

BUSINESS HOURS

Banks open between 8am and noon, with sometimes shorter hours on Friday. Only some open in the afternoon. Ecobank is usually open longer hours (8am to 4pm Monday to Friday and 9am to 2pm Saturday). Bars normally serve from noon until late, while nightclubs hop between 10pm and the wee hours. You should be able to grab a bite in most restaurants between noon and 3pm, then 6.30pm to 11pm. Shops and businesses generally open from 8am to noon and 3pm to 5pm Monday until Friday, and 8am until noon on Saturday.

CHILDREN

Like most of West Africa, Mali can be a challenging destination for travellers with children, although bottled water is universally available, and baby-food products and nappies are available in pharmacies and supermarkets in larger cities, and in pharmacies in medium-sized towns. If you'll be spending your time in villages (including trekking in the Dogon Country), you'll need to carry everything you need. Children's car seats and high chairs are nonexistent.

While there are few sights or activities dedicated to kids, the improbable houses of the Dogon Country (p507), the sandcastle-like Great Mosque of Djenné (p498), a trip to see the elephants (p530), a slow boat up the Niger (see the boxed text, p504) and a Tuareg encampment amid the sand close to the legendary city of Timbuktu (p521) will be experiences your children will never forget.

COURSES

Mali's master *kora* player, Toumani Diabaté, runs Mandinka Kora Production (p485) in Bamako, where you can learn from the genius himself (when he's not on tour). This is a once-in-a-lifetime opportunity. Music courses are also possible in Ségou (p494).

If you'd like to try your hand at making *bogolan*, Mali's famous mud-cloth, there are numerous places to learn in Djenné (p497).

DANGERS & ANNOYANCES

Much of northern Mali is off-limits, especially the area north and east of the Niger River between Timbuktu and the Niger border. For more information, visit your government's travel advisory website (see the boxed text, p815) and read the boxed text, p525.

Other areas of concern are the road between Gao and Niamey in Niger: travel in private vehicles is not recommended. In the south, banditry is common after dark on the road between Koutiala and Kouri; most vehicles travelling between the two towns require a police escort.

Crime is not a big problem in Mali, although in Bamako you should be careful walking at night in some areas (see p484). People travelling by train should take extra care, especially between Kati and Bamako and before arriving at Kayes; the stations in Kayes and Bamako are targeted by thieves who enjoy the chaotic scenes when the train pulls in. Carry a torch (flashlight), keep nothing in your pockets and watch (and lock) your bags at all times. The main annoyance for visitors is the would-be guides and salesmen who lurk outside hotels where tourists congregate; for more information, see the boxed text, p482.

EMBASSIES & CONSULATES
Embassies & Consulates in Mali

The following embassies are in Bamako:

Burkina Faso (off Map p483; ☎ 2029 3171; off Rte de Guinée; ✆ 7.30am–noon & 2–4pm Mon-Thu, 7.30am–noon & 3.30-6pm Fri)

Canada (off Map p483; ☎ 2021 2236; www.bamako .gc.ca; Rte de Koulikoro) Assists Australian and UK nationals.

Côte d'Ivoire (off Map p483; ☎ 2021 2289; ACI2000 Hamdallaye; ✆ 8am-12.30pm Mon-Fri)

France (Map p486; ☎ 2021 3141; Sq Lumumba) Consulate; assists Austrian, Belgian, Spanish, Greek, Italian and Portuguese nationals.

Germany (off Map p483; ☎ 2022 3715; Ave de l'OUA, Rue 14, Porte 334, Badalabougou Est)

Ghana (off Map p483; ☎ 2029 6083; ACI2000; ✆ 8am-3pm Mon-Thu, 8.30am-12.30pm Fri)

Guinea (off Map p483; ☎ 2020 2036; Rue 37, off Ave de l'OUA, Faso-Kanu; ✆ 9am-4.30pm Mon-Thu, to 1.30pm Fri)

Mauritania (off Map p483; ☎ 2021 4815; Rue 213, off Rte de Koulikoro, Hippodrome; ✆ 8am-4pm Mon-Fri)

Netherlands (Map p483; ☎ 2021 5611; www.mfa .nl/bam; Rue 437, off Rte de Koulikoro, Hippodrome)

Niger (off Map p483; ☎ 2023 8868; Rue 136, Porte 739, Badalabougou Sema II; ✆ 8am-4.30pm Mon-Fri)

Senegal (off Map p483; ☎ 2023 8273; Rue 50, Badalabougou Sema; ✆ 7.30am-1pm & 1.30-4pm Mon-Fri)

USA (off Map p483; ☎ 2070 2300; http://mali.us embassy.gov/; Rue 243, Porte 297, ACI2000)

FESTIVALS & EVENTS

In addition to mask ceremonies in Dogon villages (April or May; see the boxed text, p509), Bozo fishing celebrations (February), marionette festivals in Diarabougou (November; p492) and the great cattle crossings of the Fulani (December to January; see the boxed text, p497), the following are worth checking out:

Bamako Jazz Festival (Bamako; February) First held in 2009. See p485

Biennal (Bamako; September in even years) A sport and cultural festival with live music groups from around Mali.

Festival in the Desert (www.festival-au-desert.org; January; Essakane, near Timbuktu) See p521

Festival of Andéramboukane (January; Andéramboukane)See p529

Festival Sur Le Niger (February; Ségou) See p494

Festival fever is very much catching on in Mali, with Bandiagara hosting the Festival Culturel et Artistique de Bandiagara (p514) in late December, and Mopti also has a festival although its place in the calendar is yet to be established. Neither festival is particularly well organised, but things may improve.

HOLIDAYS

Public holidays include the following:

New Year's Day 1 January
Army Day 20 January
For the Martyrs of the 1991 Revolution 26 March
Easter March/April
Labour Day 1 May
African Unity Day 25 May
Independence Day 22 September
Christmas Day 25 December

For Islamic holiday dates, see p816.

INTERNET ACCESS

Internet access is widely available throughout the country, even in smaller towns. Connections vary between reasonable and slow and access usually costs CFA1000 per hour, although a few places charge just CFA500. There's no internet access (and no electricity) in most of the Dogon Country.

Wi-fi access is almost universal in most midrange and top-end hotels in Bamako and Mopti, and you can expect more places to offer this service elsewhere during the life of this book. Connections are fast and it's either free for guests or there's a nominal one-off charge (up to CFA2000).

INTERNET RESOURCES

Dogon-Lobi (www.dogon-lobi.ch/index_1024.htm) Great photo site with an exceptional list of links.

Mali Pages (www.malipages.com) Yellow-pages listings for Mali.

Mali Photos (www.maliphotos.de) Excellent photos of Mali.

Maliweb (www.maliweb.net, in French) General information on Mali.

Ministère de l'Artisanat et du Tourisme (www.tourisme.gov.ml, in French) Government-tourist office site.

Musow (www.musow.com, in French) Online women's lifestyle magazine for African women with a Malian focus.

MAPS

For all your mapping needs, the Institut Géographique du Mali (p484) should be your first stop. Identify the region you want and they'll print you out detailed topographic maps (CFA5000 per sheet) of all corners of the country.

The French **IGN** (www.ign.fr) produces the excellent *Mali* (1:2,000,000), but it's not available in Mali itself. It also sells the Carte Internationale du Monde series (1:1,000,000), which is outdated for roads but good for physical geography. Michelin's 953 *Africa North and West* (1:4,000,000) is large scale, but shows Mali's minor roads accurately. For more information on maps and where to buy them, see p817.

MONEY

The unit of currency is the West African CFA franc.

Cash & Travellers Cheques

Most of Mali's banks change foreign cash. Euros are the best to carry. US dollars are OK, but commissions are usually higher and exchange rates grim. Both BNDA and Ecobank will change travellers cheques, although commissions can be prohibitive (between 2% and a flat CFA10,000, depending on the branch, depending on the day).

Changing money in a bank (even cash) can take up to an hour, but some Western-orientated businesses, such as supermarkets, hotels and big expensive cafes, will happily change cash. Moneychangers also deal openly outside the banks and at the airport. Most offer good rates with no commission and the process is quick. However, rip-offs do happen.

Western Union representatives (for international money transfers; see p818 for details) are found in most banks and post offices.

Credit Cards & ATMs

At the time of writing, only Banque de Développement du Mali (BDM) could be relied upon for cash advances for Visa cards; they usually only do it over the counter if the ATM outside isn't working. Take as much money out as you need in one hit, as some ATMs won't let you withdraw twice from the same bank in a week. Payment by Visa card is rarely possible, except in a few top-end hotels, restaurants and businesses.

For MasterCard, Banque Atlantique was promising cash advances from its ATMs, but our advice is not to rely on these for all your money in Mali – their relationship with MasterCard was uncertain at the time of research. Payment by MasterCard is almost nonexistent.

POST

Letter and parcel post from Mali's cities is reasonably reliable, but letters can still take weeks to arrive. Parcels do go missing, but usually only items sent from overseas. Anything of real value should be sent by TAM Courrier Express (p484).

TELEPHONE

Sotelma, the national telephone company, has installed cardphones, and phonecards are often sold nearby. That said, everyone in Mali seems to have a mobile and most public phones have fallen into disrepair. Most towns have privately owned *télécentres* or *cabines téléphonique,* which allow easy telephone and fax communication.

Mobile Phones

Malians love their mobile (cell) phones and costs are coming down. **Malitel** (www.malitel.com.ml) and **Orange Mali** (www.orangemali.com) are the two providers; coverage is expanding all the time, but generally works within 15km of any medium-sized town. Orange generally has the best coverage and a local prepaid Orange SIM card costs just CFA2000, including CFA1000 credit. Top-up cards are available from street vendors throughout the country.

Most GSM mobiles from European and other Western countries work in Mali.

TOURIST INFORMATION

Mali's **Office Malien du Tourisme et de Hôtellerie** (Omatho; www.tourisme.gov.ml) is something of a mixed bag, but is improving, thanks in part to a partnership with the US Peace Corps. Some local offices (Gao is a stand-out example) have really got their act together in recent years, whereas in other places their primary purpose is to provide a list of accredited guides. Otherwise, there's no real reason to visit the Omatho office (often called Bureau Régional du Tourisme), where you won't find much more than the odd brochure.

Most towns also have a guides' association office, which is useful for finding an accredited local guide.

VISAS

Visas are required by everyone. If there's no Malian embassy in your home country (and, usually, even if there is), it's possible to get your visa on arrival at the border. It costs CFA15,000 (€23) and you'll need three passport photos. The visa is valid for an initial period of five days and must then be extended (see right), whereafter it will be valid for one month. Obtaining a visa on arrival is generally a trouble-free process, unless you're flying with Air France, which won't let you on the plane to Bamako unless you have a valid visa in your passport.

Most Malian embassies in Europe charge €30 for a one-month visa, and €51 for the three-month multiple-entry variety. The Malian embassy in the USA (www.maliembassy.us) requires payment (US$131) by cashier's cheque or money order only (if paying by post), two copies of the application form, two photos, a yellow-fever vaccination certificate, printed flight itinerary and (sometimes) a hotel reservation.

At Malian embassies in West Africa, you'll usually pay CFA20,000 for a one-month single-entry visa.

Note that Mali has not yet signed up to the convenient Visa des Pays de l'Entente (see p826).

Visa Extensions

One-month visa extensions cost CFA5000, require two photos and are only available at the Immigration & Sûreté Nationale building in Bamako (p484) or at the Comissariat de Police & Sûreté office in Mopti (p502). There's a fine of CFA15,000 per day for every day you overstay, and border officials will delight in extracting this from you.

If you obtained your five-day visa at the border, the cost of a one-month extension is free in Bamako (where it usually takes 24 hours), but costs CFA5000 in Mopti (where they'll do it on the spot).

Visas for Onward Travel

BURKINA FASO

Single-/multiple-entry three-month visas cost CFA28,200/33,200 and require three identical photos. Leave your passport in the morning and pick it up in the afternoon.

CÔTE D'IVOIRE

The embassy will issue visas (one-month single-/multiple-entry CFA30,000/60,000, two photos) in three days. They'll ask you for an invitation from a Côte d'Ivoire company or a confirmed hotel reservation.

GHANA

For Ghanaian visas you'll require four photos and they're usually issued the same day, although can take 48 hours. Single-entry one-month/multiple-entry, nine-month visas cost CFA12,000/30,000.

GUINEA

The Guinean embassy issues visas in 24 hours, requires two photos and a photocopy of your passport, but fees are high: for European nationalities it's CFA46,500/60,000 for single-entry one-month/two-month visas, while multiple-entry three-month visas cost CFA76,500. US, UK, Canadian and Australian citizens pay CFA60,000/80,000 for single-/multiple-entry visas.

MAURITANIA

At the time of writing, the embassy was issuing visas (free; three photos with an extension required once in Mauritania for stays of no longer than 10 days). Expect that to change, however, and come with CFA16,000 just in case.

NIGER

The Niger consulate issues one-/two-/three-month multiple-entry visas for CFA30,000/45,000/60,000. You'll need two photos and the process takes at least three days.

SENEGAL

For those nationals requiring visas (including Australians and New Zealanders), one-month single-entry visas cost CFA5000, while three-month multiple-entry visas cost CFA10,000. You'll need two photos and visas are issued in 24 hours.

TRANSPORT IN MALI

GETTING THERE & AWAY

Entering Mali

Be scrupulous in ensuring that you have *all* your papers in order (visa, yellow-fever vaccination) whenever you enter (or leave) the country, because Malian border officials are adept at finding inconsistencies, whether real or invented. For more information on obtaining a Malian visa, see p537.

Air

Mali's main international airport is **Sénou International Airport** (☎ 2020 4626). Point-Afrique also flies into Mopti and Gao.

Numerous airlines fly into Bamako:

Afriqiyah (Map p486; ☎ 2023 1497; www.afriqiyah .aero; Ave de la Marne)

Air Algérie (Map p486; ☎ 2022 3159; www.airalgerie .dz; Rue de la Cathédrale)

Air Burkina (Map p486; ☎ 2021 0178; www.air -burkina.com; Ave de la Marne)

Air CAM (off Map p483; ☎ 2022 2424; www.camaero .com; Ave Cheick Zayed, Hamdallaye)

Air France (off Map p483; ☎ 2070 0330; www.air france.com; ACI2000) You can check-in your luggage at the office between 11am and 1pm on the day of departure.

Air Ivoire (Map p486; ☎ 2023 9558; www.airivoire.com; off Ave de l'Yser)

Air Sénégal International (Map p486; ☎ 2023 9811; www.air-senegal-international.com; Ave Modibo Keita)

Ethiopian Airlines (Map p486; ☎ 2022 2208; www .flyethiopian.com/et; Sq Lumumba)

Interair (Map p486; ☎ 2021 5693; www.interair.co.za; TAM Voyages, Sq Lumumba)

Kenya Airways (Map p483; ☎ 2022 1235; www.kenya -airways.com; cnr Ave Kassa Keita & Ave de l'Indépendance)

Mali Air Express (MAE; Map p486; ☎ 2023 1465; www .mae-mali.com; Ave de la Nation)

Point Afrique (Map p486; ☎ 2023 5470; www.point -afrique.com; Ave de l'Yser)

Royal Air Maroc (Map p486; ☎ 2021 6703; www .royalairmaroc.com; Ave de la Marne)

WEST AFRICA

Mali Air Express connects Bamako with Dakar (twice weekly) and Conakry (once weekly), while Air CAM operates on the same routes, with additional services to Lomé, Cotonou, Ouagadougou and Abidjan. Air Sénégal International also flies to most West African capitals, usually via Dakar, while Air Burkina connects Bamako with Ouagadougou.

Land

The Tanezrouft trans-Saharan route through Algeria is closed to travellers due to the Tuareg rebellion (see the boxed text, p525).

BURKINA FASO

You can cross into Burkina Faso (for Bobo-Dioulasso) just south of Kouri (southeast of Koutiala), although avoid travelling between Kouri and Koutiala after dark; see p535. Other possible routes include from Sikasso to Bobo-Dioulasso via the border post near Koloko, or between Koro and Ouahigouya; this latter route was being upgraded at the time of research.

Numerous buses leave Bamako's Sogoniko *gare routière* daily for Ouagadougou (CFA18,000, 20 hours) via Bobo-Dioulasso (CFA11,500, 15 hours), while you'll also find daily departures from Ségou to Bobo-Dioulasso (CFA8000, 12 hours) and Ouagadougou (CFA15,000, 17 hours). Three daily Sogebaf buses link Koro with Ouahigouya (CFA3000, up to four hours) from where there's onward transport to Ouagadougou.

CÔTE D'IVOIRE

The main route into Côte d'Ivoire is along the bitumen road through Zégoua, south of Sikasso. Daily buses leave Bamako's Sogoniko *gare routière* for Abidjan (CFA24,000, 36 to 48 hours). Bush taxis for towns in northern Côte d'Ivoire also leave from Sikasso.

GUINEA
Kourémalé is the main border crossing for Guinea, but some traffic takes the back roads via the border crossings at Bougouni, Sélingué or Kéniéba.

Peugeot taxis or minibuses run most days from Bamako's Djikoroni *gare routière* to the border at Kourémalé (CFA3500, three hours) and then on to Siguiri (CFA6500). There's occasionally transport to Kankan (CFA9000) and Kissidougou (CFA14,000), while a once-weekly bus continues all the way to Conakry (CFA25,000).

From Kéniéba, there's only intermittent cross-border traffic (usually a motorcycle or two) to Labé in Guinea via the border town of Kali.

MAURITANIA
The main access points to Mauritania are north of Nioro or Nara, but it's possible to travel direct to Sélibabi from Kayes.

Battered 4WDs and trucks are the usual transport. There are daily departures from Kayes' Ndi *gare routière* to Sélibabi (CFA11,500, eight hours) and from Nioro to Ayoûn el-Atroûs (CFA18,000). The latter option gets you onto the paved road leading to Nouakchott. All these routes are sandy from October to May, but extremely difficult in the rainy season from June to October. If you find yourself stuck in Nioro, the extremely basic rooms at **Wanda Chambres & Restaurant** (per person CFA4000), in the centre of town, are as good as it gets.

NIGER
Although bus routes between Gao and Niamey in Niger are generally considered safe, kidnappings have occurred of Western travellers in private vehicles. The border post is at Labbéganza, southeast of Gao.

Two companies operate services from Gao to Niamey (16 to 30 hours). Sonef has daily departures at 6am for Niamey (CFA8500) via Ayorou (CFA6000). The Nigerien company SNTV departs for Niamey (CFA7425) on Tuesdays and Fridays at 5am. The road between Ansongo and Gao is terrible. All passport formalities must be completed at the main police station in Gao the day before departure/upon arrival.

SENEGAL
The main crossing to/from Senegal is at Kidira/Diboli, west of Kayes, and the border crossing closes at 6pm. A new road which is planned between Kita and Saraya (via Kéniéba) will significantly cut travel time between the two countries. In the meantime, most travellers fly or take the train between Bamako and Dakar.

The train journey is one of Africa's great epics. In theory the train departs Bamako for Dakar (2nd-class seat/1st-class seat/1st-class couchette CFA25,500/34,620/53,145) on Saturday and Wednesday, although train schedules and reality are two different things. It could take forever but, if not, around 50 hours. Take care as theft is frequent (see p535).

There's regular road transport from Kayes (Blvd de l'Indépendance, about 2km west of the town centre) to Diboli (CFA3500, two hours); some transport continues over the bridge to Kidira in Senegal, from where there's transport to Tambacounda. Alternatively, there's an overnight bus direct to Dakar from Kayes (CFA15,000, 24 hours) twice a week. Gana Transport is the pick of the companies offering services between Bamako and Dakar (CFA20,000, around 36 hours).

GETTING AROUND
Air
Two airlines fly domestically in Mali:

Air CAM (off Map p483; ☎ 2022 2424; www.camaero .com; Ave Cheick Zayed, Hamdallaye)

Mali Air Express (MAE; Map p486; ☎ 2023 1465; www .mae-mali.com; Ave de la Nation)

Both airlines fly the same routes: Bamako–Kayes and Bamako–Mopti–Timbuktu. Air CAM also flies to Gao from Bamako (via Mopti and Timbuktu). For fares and frequency, see the Getting There & Away sections in the relevant city sections.

In general, Mali Air Express is more reliable, with Air CAM, which leases planes from other airlines for domestic flights, often plagued with flight cancellations, delays and overbooking.

Boat
Most boat journeys on the Niger River are only possible from August to December when water levels are high.

For information on travelling by pirogue and public or private pinasse, see the boxed text, p504.

PASSENGER BOAT

Large passenger boats operated by the Compagnie Malienne de Navigation (Comanav) ply the Niger River between Koulikoro (50km west of Bamako) and Gao, from August to November or December, stopping at Mopti and Korioumé (for Timbuktu) en route. One boat heads downstream from Koulikoro at 10pm Tuesday, arrives in Mopti at 3pm Thursday, in Timbuktu at 7am Saturday and Gao at midnight Sunday. Another boat heads upstream from Gao at 8pm every Monday, reaching Timbuktu at 6pm on Wednesday, Mopti at 4pm Friday and Koulikoro at midnight Sunday. The two-day section from Mopti to Korioumé (about 400km) is arguably the most interesting, although from Koulikoro to Mopti the boat is less crowded.

The journey is a fascinating insight into village life along the Niger, but it's not for everyone. The boats are like floating villages – people and cargo are everywhere, the cabins are sweltering, the toilets frequently flood and the food, well it ain't cordon bleu. But it *is* a quintessentially African experience.

The 'luxe' cabins have a bathroom and air-con, 1st-class cabins have two bunk beds, toilet and washbasin, and 2nd-class cabins are four-berth with a washbasin and shared toilets. Third class is an eight-berth cabin and in 4th class you get to fight for a space on deck.

Booze, food and water are all available (three meals per day are included in all except 4th class), but it's a good idea to take extra supplies as you may get stranded.

PIROGUE & PUBLIC PINASSE

Pirogues are small canoes, either paddled by hand or fitted with a small outboard motor. They're the slowest form of river transport.

Pinasses are larger motorised boats, carrying cargo and anything from 10 to 100 passengers. Public pinasse departures are unpredictable and the boats can be extremely crowded and overloaded. To avoid being seriously stranded, use the various market days (when there's more river transport).

Market day	Town
Monday	Danga, Diafarabé, Ségou
Tuesday	Diré
Wednesday	Gourma-Rharous
Thursday	Mopti, Niafunké, Ténenkou
Friday	Massina
Saturday	Youvarou
Sunday	Gao, Markala, Tonka

PRIVATE PINASSE

The only way to bend river schedules to your itinerary may be to hire a private pinasse. They come in a range of sizes but you can expect to pay between CFA375,000 and CFA400,000 (including petrol) for a boat that comfortably seats 10 people. If food is not included, count on CFA15,000 per person for food for three days. If you can get enough travellers together, per-person costs fall considerably.

Bus

Journey times vary hugely, depending on the gung-ho nature of the driver (most are pretty 'keen'), the fitness of the vehicle, and time taken at police and customs. As a rough guide, bank on at least 2¼ hours per 150km on sealed roads.

Sadly, no bus company consistently uses high-quality buses. One day you'll be on a seminew bus, only to find yourself the next day on a near-wreck that belongs to the same company. At departure, passengers are called by name: booking a ticket in advance puts you further up the list and thus ensures a good seat. In our experience, the better companies are **Bani** (☎ 2020 6081), **Bittar** (☎ 2020 1205) and

PASSENGER BOAT FARES (CFA)					
Route	Luxe	1st	2nd	3rd	4th
Koulikoro to Ségou	46,500	27,500	18,000	11,000	2750
Koulikoro to Mopti	120,500	65,500	46,000	27,000	6150
Koulikoro to Korioumé	210,000	112,000	79,500	47,000	10,350
Koulikoro to Gao	302,500	160,500	114,500	67,500	14,550
Mopti to Korioumé	95,500	51,500	36,500	21,500	5050
Mopti to Gao	188,500	101,000	71,500	42,000	9350

Gana Transport (☎ 2021 0978). For fares and frequency of departure, see the Getting There & Away entries in the relevant city sections.

Bush Taxi

Bush taxis and minibuses, which are slightly pricier than buses (you're likely to be charged a CFA500 luggage fee), are handy on shorter, less frequented routes, where they may be the only option. These are either Peugeot 504s, carrying nine people, bâchés (pick-ups) with about 16 passengers, or minibuses (25 to 30 passengers). Bâchés are slower, but about 25% cheaper than 504s, while minibuses can take an age to leave and much longer to arrive. General bus and bush-taxi stations in Mali are called *gares routières*.

Car & Motorcycle

Self-drive car rental is rare, and not recommended because accident insurance for foreigners can be ineffective and the correct roadblock/bribe etiquette takes a while to master. However, 4WDs with drivers are easy to arrange through tour operators and hotels in many places. Rates begin at CFA45,000 per day for a 4WD with unlimited mileage, plus petrol.

Tours

Although independent travel through Mali is easy, and the cheapest way to go, taking a tour will remove the hassle of guides and long waits for transport. For companies that we wholeheartedly recommend, see p484. For a list of international tour companies offering tours to Mali and elsewhere in West Africa, see p838.

You'll especially benefit from having a local guide in the Dogon Country (p510) and the desert around Timbuktu (p521).

Train

The train is the best way to travel between Bamako and Kayes, although it's never on time and is not without its insecurities (see p535). For details of prices and schedules, see the relevant sections for Bamako (p492) and Kayes (p533).

Second-class travel is cramped, chaotic and makes the journey seem eternal.

Mauritania

If West Africa is a playground for overlanders, then Mauritania often seems to be little more than a 'drive-through' country – less a destination in itself than somewhere to transit between the better-known attractions of Marrakesh, Dakar or Bamako. That's a shame because Mauritania has some tremendous secrets to reveal to those travellers prepared to stop and take a closer look.

Culturally, Mauritania is a place apart. The population is almost equally divided between Moors of Arab-Berber descent and black Africans. It's a Muslim country with a black African twist. It's a transition between the North African Arab world and black Africa, it doesn't really belong to either. This striking cultural combination is part of its appeal.

Just as striking is some of the grandest scenery the entire continent has to offer. The Adrar region offers up epic sand dunes, eye-popping plateaus, green oases and even the biggest monolith this side of central Australia. The Tagânt has similar charms, and both hide ancient (and World Heritage–listed) caravan towns – Chinguetti, Ouadâne and Oualâta. The World Heritage feast continues along the coast at Parc National du Banc d'Arguin, which attracts millions of migratory birds and is renowned as one of the best bird-watching sites on earth.

If you just breeze through, and stop at the (admittedly uninspiring) capital Nouakchott, you'll miss out on a truly incredible country. No one in Mauritania is in a rush, and you shouldn't be either.

FAST FACTS

- **Area** 1,030,700 sq km
- **Capital** Nouakchott
- **Country code** ☎ 222
- **Famous for** Desert landscapes; bird-watching; *zrig* (camel milk)
- **Languages** Hassaniya, French, Fula, Soninké and Wolof
- **Money** Ouguiya (UM); US$1 = UM264; €1 = UM351
- **Population** 3.36 million
- **Visa** In advance €35–45, at Moroccan border €20

HIGHLIGHTS

- **Chinguetti** (p561) Glorious sunrises from the labyrinthine lanes of the old city.
- **4WD tours or camel trips** (p558) The magic of the Sahara, sleeping beneath the star-studded skies at the saffron dunes in the Adrar region.
- **Banc d'Arguin** (p556) Vast flocks of birds to view from a traditional pirogue.
- **Oualâta** (p566) Admire the elaborate decorative paintings that grace traditional houses in one of Mauritania's best-kept secrets.
- **Iron-ore train** (p555) The world's longest train, and the most epic journey of your life!

ITINERARIES

- **One Week** For most travellers the lure of the desert is irresistible. **Atâr** (p557) is the best launching pad for exploring the mystifying Adrar region – a good combination of fantastic landscapes and stunning architecture. Spend two days exploring the ancient, earth-toned desert towns of **Chinguetti** (p561) and **Ouadâne** (p562), then laze some time away in the idyllic oasis *palmeraie* (palm grove) of **Terjît** (p560). Finish things off camping at the awesome monolith of **Ben Amira** (p560) with its unlikely sculpture park, before returning to Atar.
- **Two Weeks** Follow the one-week itinerary and, once you've had your fill of sand dunes, forge west to the Atlantic coast. From Atâr, take a bush taxi to Choûm where you'll hop on the iron-ore train that will bring you to **Nouâdhibou** (p554) the next day – an exciting, albeit arduous, ride. Seafood lovers will have a feast in Nouâdhibou. Consider taking a three-day tour to **Parc National du Banc d'Arguin** (p556), one of the best birdwatching areas in West Africa. Journey on to **Nouakchott** (p548), Mauritania's sprawling capital, with its striking melange of chaotic markets and modern buildings.
- **Three Weeks** Follow the two-week plan and then head to the far-flung corners of eastern Mauritania – it's a long drive but your patience will be amply rewarded. From Nouakchott, strike northeast to **Tidjikja** (p564). Stop en route at the crocodile-filled oasis of **Matmata** (p564). Get a

---

HOW MUCH?

- **Cup of tea in a nomad's tent** free
- **Taxi ride in Nouakchott** UM200
- **Camel ride in the desert** about UM6000 per day
- **Bush taxi fare Nouakchott–Nouâdhibou** UM4500
- **Auberge room** about UM2000 per person

LONELY PLANET INDEX

- **1L of petrol** UM240
- **1L of bottled water** UM200
- **Bottled beer** UM1000
- **Souvenir T-shirt** UM600
- **Plate of mafé (rice & fish)** UM300

---

decent eyeful of the panoramic Tagânt plateau before backtracking to the Route de l'Espoir and veer due east to rough-around-the-edges **Néma** (p566), not far from Mali. Striking north, it's an easy ride to **Oualâta** (p566), one of the most spellbinding desert towns in Mauritania.

CLIMATE & WHEN TO GO

In the Sahara region of the country, annual rainfall is usually less than 100mm. In the south, rainfall increases to about 600mm per year, mostly occurring during the short rainy season from July to September.

The most pleasant time to visit Mauritania is from November to March. Daytime temperatures hover in the mid-20°Cs with great regularity and the sky is invariably blue. Note that it can get quite cool at night, especially in the desert.

The heat is searing from April to October, especially from June to August when the *rifi* (hot winds) from the north send temperatures soaring to 45°C in the desert. However, along the coast, the *alizé* (trade winds) blow from the ocean, causing average highs to be 5°C lower. See also Climate Charts, p810.

HISTORY

From the 3rd century AD, the Berbers established trading routes all over the

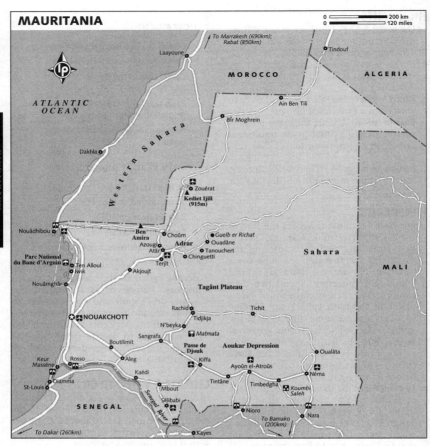

MAURITANIA

0 ————— 200 km
0 ————— 120 miles

ATLANTIC OCEAN

ALGERIA

MOROCCO

To Marrakesh (690km);
Rabat (850km)

Laayoune

Tindouf

Ain Ben Tili

Western Sahara

Bîr Moghrein

Dakhla

Zouérat
▲ Kediet Ijill (915m)

Nouâdhibou

Ben Amira

Choûm
Azougui Adrár
Atâr

Guelb er Richat
Ouadâne
Tanouchert

Sahara

Parc National
du Banc d'Arguin

Ten Alloul
Iwik

Terjît

Chinguetti

MALI

Nouâmghâr

Akjoujt

Tagânt Plateau

NOUAKCHOTT

Rachid
Tidjikja

Tichit

N'beyka

Matmata

Sangrafa

Passe de
Djouk

Aoukar Depression

Boutilimit

Aleg

Kiffa

Oualâta

Keur
Masséné

Rosso

Ayoûn el-Atroûs

Kaédi

Néma

St-Louis

Diamma

Mbout

Tintâne

Timbedgha
Koumbi Saleh

SENEGAL

Sélibabi

Nioro

Senegal River

Nara

To Dakar (260km)

Kayes

To Bamako
(200km)

Western Sahara, including Mauritania. By the 9th and 10th centuries the gold trade, as well as slavery, had given rise to the first great empire in West Africa, the Soninké Empire of Ghana (the capital of which is believed to have been at Koumbi Saleh in southeastern Mauritania).

After the spread of Islam in the 7th century, the Almoravids established their capital in Marrakesh (Morocco), from where they ruled the whole of northwest Africa, as well as southern Spain. In 1076 they pushed south and, with the assistance of Mauritanian Berber leaders, destroyed the Empire of Ghana. That victory led to the spread of Islam throughout Mauritania and the Western Sahara. The Mauritanian part of the empire

was subjugated by Arabs in 1674, after which virtually all Berbers adopted Hassaniya, the language of their conquerors.

The Colonial Period

As colonialism spread throughout Africa, France stationed troops in Mauritania to protect the rest of French West Africa from raids by neighbours and ambitious European powers, but did nothing to develop the area. They also used the region as a place of exile for political prisoners.

In 1814 the Treaty of Paris gave France the right to explore and control the Mauritanian coast, but it wasn't until 1904 that, having played one faction off against another, the French managed to make Mauritania a colonial territory; it took the French another 30 years to subjugate the Moors in the north.

Mauritania was a political backwater in the lead-up to independence, with her politicians resisting the anticolonial trend sweeping West Africa, siding instead with the French. In 1956, when an independent Morocco began claiming much of Mauritania as part of a 'greater Morocco', Mauritania's first political party, the Union Progressiste Mauritanienne (UPM), was formed and in 1957 won most of the seats in the territorial assembly elections.

Independence & Ould Daddah

When full independence came in 1960, Mokhtar Ould Daddah became the new president. The Moors declared Mauritania an Islamic republic and hastily set about building a new capital at Nouakchott.

During the late 1960s, Ould Daddah alienated the mainly black south (the Black Moors) by making both Hassaniya and French the country's official languages and by compelling all schoolchildren to study in Hassaniya. The government also joined the Arab League in a provocative assertion of the country's non-African aspirations. Mauritania withdrew from the franc zone and substituted the ouguiya for the CFA, and any opposition was brutally suppressed.

The issue of Western Sahara finally toppled the government. In 1975 Mauritania entered into an agreement with Morocco and Spain to divide the former Spanish colony: Mauritania would take a slab of desert in the south and Morocco would get the mineral-rich northern two-thirds. But the Polisario Front launched a guerrilla war to oust both Morocco and Mauritania and many towns in northern Mauritania came under attack; iron-ore exports plummeted.

A bloodless coup took place in Mauritania in 1978, bringing in a new military government that renounced all territorial claims to the Western Sahara.

Ould Taya & the 1980s

After a series of coups, the new government, ruled by a committee of high-ranking military officers, finally settled on the present ruler Colonel Maaouya Sid'Ahmed Ould Taya as leader in 1984.

Ould Taya immediately set about restructuring the economy, with an emphasis on agricultural development, fishing and tentative moves towards democratisation. However, it is for the persecution of the Black Moors that Ould Taya's early years of power will be remembered. In 1987 he jailed various prominent southerners and the subsequent rioting in Nouakchott and Nouâdhibou was partly quelled through the introduction of strict Islamic law. Later that year, the government dismissed some 500 Tukulor soldiers from the army and soon after, the jailed author of an antiracist manifesto died in prison. Ethnic tensions culminated in bloody riots between the Moors and Blacks Africans in 1989. More than 70,000 Black Moors were expelled to Senegal, a country most had never known.

Elections, Repression & Reforms

An unrepentant Taya spent the early 1990s continuing the persecution of Black Moors. By now, Mauritania had become an international pariah and Taya's closest ally became Iraq, which he supported during the 1991 Gulf War.

As a result of criticism, Taya attempted to moderate his approach, pushing through a new constitution that permitted opposition political parties. In early 1992, in the country's first presidential elections, Taya was re-elected with 63% of the vote, but electoral fraud was massive and the hotly contested election results won him little international respect. Opposition parties consequently boycotted the general elections later in the year.

Bread riots in 1995, stemming from a new tax on bread, led to the arrest of Taya's principal political opponents, Ould Daddah and Hamdi Ould Mouknass – another sign that the crossover to a civilian government had yet to materialise.

In late 2000 electoral reforms were introduced under which political parties were to receive funds according to their electoral performance, but the harassment and arrest of opposition figures meant that these changes were largely cosmetic. In October 2001 the ruling Parti Républicain Démocratique et Social (PRDS) won 64 out of the 81 National Assembly seats in elections.

In June 2003 there was an attempted coup and two days of violent riots in the capital. Rebels were led by disaffected army leaders. Although the coup was unsuccessful, two years later Taya was toppled by another (bloodless) coup, led by Colonel Ely Ould Mohamed Vall. Democratic elections were promised after a two-year transition period.

Vall was largely popular and stood by his word, as well as freeing up the press and formulating a new constitution. Elections were held as promised; in March 2007 Sidi Ould Cheikh Abdallahi was returned as Mauritania's first democratically elected president.

Mauritania Today

Unfortunately, Abdallahi had little over a year to enjoy his position. He openly condemned the 'dark years' of the late 1980s, and sought rapprochement with the expelled Black Moors. In doing so, he angered the traditional elites, including the army. His plan to dismiss several high-ranking officers backfired in August 2008, when on a trip to the UN, he was overthrown in a military coup. Claiming popular support, the junta installed General Mohamed Ould Abdel Aziz – a leading light of the 2005 coup – as head of state.

The coup was widely condemned, and the African Union applied sanctions against the country. Although new elections were promised for June 2009, the coup has again thrown Mauritania into political turmoil.

THE CULTURE
National Psyche

Mauritanian society is changing fast – with tourism developing in the heart of the desert, and internet and mobile phones playing a crucial role. You'll be surprised to see two parallel societies: the modern, Western-leaning society of Nouakchott and the main tourist areas, and the traditional society of the smaller towns and villages. But despite the profound social changes, the extended family, clan or tribe, remains the cornerstone of society, especially with the Moors. Deeply rooted traditional loyalties remain of the utmost importance.

As in many Muslim countries, religion continues to mark the important events of life. The 1991 constitution legalised political parties but prohibited them from being opposed to Islam. Although slavery was declared illegal in 1980, the caste system (see the boxed text, opposite) still impregnates society's mentality.

Daily Life

The iconic image of nomadic Moors sipping a cup of tea under a tent in the desert belongs to the past. Over the past three decades, drought has resulted in a mass exodus of traditionally nomadic Moors from the desert to Nouakchott. This doesn't mean that they have abandoned their cultural habits. Moors living in cities often feel the need to leave their concrete houses in Nouakchott for a couple of days spent under tents in the desert.

The men characteristically wear *draa* (long, light-blue robes). Many of them have the name Ould (son of), eg Ahmed Ould Mohamed. For women it's Mint (daughter of). Women are in a fairly disadvantaged position. Only a third as many women as men are literate and few are involved in commercial activities other than selling food and crafts. Female genital mutilation and the forced feeding of young brides are still practised in rural communities. However, Mauritanian women have the right to divorce and exert it routinely.

Population

Of Mauritania's estimated three million inhabitants, about 60% are Moors of Arab and Berber descent. Moors of purely Arab descent, called 'Bidan', account for 40%.

The other major group is Black Africans, ethnically split into two groups. The Haratin, or Black Moors, the descendants of people enslaved by the Moors, have assimilated the Moorish culture and speak Hassaniya, an Arabic dialect. Culturally, they have little affinity with the Black Mauritanians living in the south along the Senegal River, the 'Soudaniens'. The Soudaniens constitute 40% of the population and are mostly Fula (also known as Peul) or the closely related Tukulor. These groups speak Pulaar (Fula). There are Soninké and Wolof minorities.

ARTS

Mauritania has a strong tradition of arts and craftwork, especially silverwork. Most prized are wooden chests with silver inlay, but there are also silver daggers, silver and amber jewellery, earth-tone rugs of camel and goat hair from Boutilimit, Kiffa beads (see the boxed text, p565), hand-dyed leatherwork including colourful leather cushions and leather pipe pouches, camel saddles and sandals.

The traditional music of Mauritania is mostly Arabic in origin, although along its southern border there are influences from the Wolof, Tukulor and Bambara. One of the most popular Mauritanian musicians in Mauritania is Malouma. She has modernised the Moorish traditional music, blending it with more contemporary rhythms. She has

---

SLAVERY IN MAURITANIA?

Mauritania has one of the most stratified caste systems in Africa. The system is based on lineage, occupation and access to power, but colour has become a major determinant of status, splitting the population into Bidan and Haratin – White and Black Moors. At the bottom of the social pile are slaves and ex-slaves.

Chattel slavery has long been a part of Mauritanian culture, with the owning of slaves a sign of social status. Incredibly, it was only in 1980 that the government finally declared slavery illegal. Despite this, the head of Mauritania's Human Rights Commission has said that antislavery laws are rarely enforced, despite tougher punishments legislated for in 2007. Estimates vary, but it's thought that up to 100,000 Mauritanians may still be enslaved. The Mauritanian antislavery organisation SOS-Esclaves ('SOS-Slaves') continues to work with runaway slaves, helping to free nearly 50 slaves in 2008 alone.

---

created what is called the 'Saharan blues' and is to Mauritania what Cesária Évora is to Cape Verde.

Mauritanian cinema remains in its infancy, but Abderrahmane Sissoko's wonderful and haunting *En attendant le bonheur* ('Waiting for Happiness') won a prize at the Cannes Film Festival in 2002, and is well worth checking out.

There's superb traditional architecture in the ancient Saharan towns in the Adrar as well as in Oualâta. The adobe houses in Oualâta are enhanced with elaborate paintings.

ENVIRONMENT
The Land

Mauritania is about twice the size of France. About 75%, including Nouakchott, is desert, with huge expanses of flat plains broken by occasional ridges, rocky plateaus and sand dunes. Moreover, the desert is expanding southward. One of the highest plateau areas (over 500m) is the Adrar, 450km northeast of Nouakchott, with its towns of Chinguetti and Ouadâne. These plateaus are often rich in iron ore, and there are especially large deposits at Zouérat about 200km north of Chinguetti. The highest peak is Kediet Ijill (915m) near Zouérat. Mauritania has some 700km of shoreline, including the Banc d'Arguin. The south is mostly flat scrubland.

Wildlife

In the desert regions, the camel is the most common animal that visitors will come across. Giraffes and lions have long gone – victims of desertification and the bullet. One endangered species that you might see if you're lucky is the monk seal, off Cap Blanc near Nouâdhibou (see p554).

Mauritania is a paradise for twitchers. Between Nouâdhibou and Nouakchott is Parc National du Banc d'Arguin, where hundreds of thousands of birds migrate from Europe in the winter. It is one of the world's major bird-breeding grounds and is on Unesco's list of World Heritage sites.

Environmental Issues

Pollution, desertification, overgrazing – put them together and you have a glimpse of Mauritania's pressing environmental threats. Nearly 75% of Mauritania's land surface is desert or near-desert and this is increasing. Wood has become so scarce that most cooking is now done on kerosene stoves. Negligent garbage disposal is also a critical issue, but tourism development has fostered a growing awareness in the Adrar region.

Overfishing is another concern, with hundreds of tonnes of fish caught every day off the Mauritanian coastline due in large part to the Mauritanian government's sale of fishing rights to EU fleets, an action that has diminished the catches of local fishermen.

FOOD & DRINK

The desert cuisine of the Moors is rather unmemorable and lacks variety. Dishes are generally bland and limited to rice, mutton, goat, camel or dried fish. *Zrig* (unsweetened, curdled goat or camel milk) often accompanies meals served in private homes. Mauritanian couscous, similar to the Moroccan variety, is delicious. A real treat is to attend a *méchui* (traditional nomad's feast), where an entire lamb is roasted over a fire and stuffed with cooked rice.

Mauritania's Atlantic coastline is an abundant source of seafood, and this has influenced local cuisine, especially

MAURITANIA

MAURITANIAN MUSIC

Compared to its more famous neighbours, Mauritania isn't particularly known for its music. What brought you here?

I was in Smara in Western Sahara when I first heard [Mauritanian singer] Dimi Mint Abba. The mix of polyrhythmic and Arab scales, the call-and-response lyrics, and the bluesy pentatonic immediately captivated me. It sounded completely different yet somehow eerily familiar to American roots.

Can you give us a quick overview of the types of Mauritanian music?

The music of Mauritania is global, but it's an ancient globalism. It's the music of old empires stretching all the way to the Pyrenees and across sub-Saharan Africa, so can be reminiscent of everything from Andalucia to the blues. Hassaniya or 'Moorish' music is rich with discordant scales and sporadic hand clapping. The traditional guitar (*tidnit*) has been replaced by the electric guitar, which certainly gives it a more modern feel. There's also the Peul, especially in the south, who have a distinct music with melodic syncopation. Again, this Pulaar music has been modernised, with the *hoddu* (traditional banjo) exchanged for acoustic guitar. And finally, there is a massive diaspora of Africans from as far away as Congo, bringing more styles to the melting pot.

How did you go about finding musicians?

The music scene is very unorganised, very DIY. I started by simply heading out into the streets with my guitar and digital recorder and starting to play. In due course I found myself invited to houses, recording studios, playing in concerts with local musicians – and working my way up the musical food chain.

What's been your biggest revelation?

My most interesting moments have been finding those elements of universality. I'd been recording two amazing Peul musicians, and they asked me to play something from America. I played

---

in Nouakchott and Nouâdhibou. With negligible agriculture, fruit and vegetables are imported, and hard to find outside Nouakchott.

The cuisine of southern Mauritania, essentially Senegalese, may appeal more to your taste buds, with much more variety, spices and even a few vegetables. Two of the most popular dishes are rice with fish and Senegalese *mafé* (a peanut-based stew).

The restaurant scene is pretty dull, except in Nouakchott, where you'll find a good range of eateries serving a great variety of dishes.

There's not a lot of choice when it comes to beverages. Soft drinks and bottled water are available everywhere. Mauritanian tea is also ubiquitous, invariably strong and sweet and endlessly decanted between tiny glasses to produce a pleasing frothy head. It's polite to accept the first three glasses offered. Alcohol is technically forbidden, but in practice is widely (and expensively) available in Nouakchott, usually in restaurants catering to foreigners.

NOUAKCHOTT

pop 1 million

Barely 50 years old, Nouakchott has to be simultaneously one of Africa's strangest and most unassuming capital cities. Neither an ancient trading centre, colonial outpost or even holding a particularly strategic location, this is capital-building nomad style: a city simply plonked down as if on an overnight caravan stop and left to grow by accident.

Don't expect majestic monuments or cultural landmarks. Instead, prepare for plenty of dust. Despite having a busy port, Nouakchott deliberately turns its face from the freshening breath of the Atlantic, preferring to have a city centre in the desert. Major avenues are still populated by turbaned nomads and wandering goats (camels are usually parked on the outskirts), while the side streets turn quickly to sand dunes.

As capital of an Islamic republic, the city has a measured pace. However, with its phenomenal fish market (one of the most active in West Africa) and lively markets, Nouakchott has plenty of colour, and whether you're headed north to Morocco or deeper into West Africa, it makes a fascinating bridge between the Arab and black parts of the continent. It's also amazingly safe compared with many African capitals and has enough modern amenities, good restaurants and comfortable hotels in which to pamper yourself – bliss after the rigours of the desert.

Elizabeth Cotton's *Freight Train*, an old folk standard. They both listened politely, but when I'd finished one said, 'But that's African folk music – can't you play something American?'

And best musical find?
One of the most interesting groups I know is 'Dental' ('Union' in Pulaar) led by Sarr Abdoul. They play distinctly modern music – electric guitars and gourds, and sound like a fusion of Surf guitar and Rocksteady. But it's also deeply Mauritanian music, blending Hassaniya, Pulaar, Soninke and Wolof styles and lyrics. Unfortunately, like most of the musicians here they've yet to cut an album.

We were surprised to hear that there's even a small local hip hop scene in Nouakchott!
The hip hop scene is quite large here. All the young men are watching American rap videos! The resources for production are sparse – one friend's studio is also a barber and cell-phone repair shop – but the more interesting hip hop is forging a sound uniquely Mauritania, sampling traditional instruments. There was even a hip hop festival in 2008, and hopefully that will become an annual event (see www.assalamalekoum.com for more). But as an old Peul *griot* reminded me, 'Hip hop isn't new here, we've been doing rap for a long time.'

What's the best way for a traveller to hear live music here?
Aside from the French Cultural Centre, the Equinox Café now hosts Friday jam sessions. Otherwise, if you're feeling adventurous, your best bet is to wander the residential streets of Cinquième on a Friday or Saturday, where you'll undoubtedly find a wedding in progress under a big white tent – that's where the musicians will be!

Christopher Kirkley is an American musician living with and recording local musicians in Nouakchott. Musical samples can be downloaded from the website Sahel Sounds (www.sahelsounds.com).

ORIENTATION

The main streets are Ave Abdel Nasser running east to west and the parallel streets Ave du Général de Gaulle and Ave Kennedy running north to south. The more affluent Tavragh Zeina district is to the north while to the south, near where Ave Abdel Nasser and Ave du Général de Gaulle cross, is the Grand Marché and, 2km further south, the more traditionally African Cinquième Quartier, with its busy market. The ocean is 5km west along Ave Abdel Nasser, while Le Ksar district (old town) and airport are 3km northeast of the centre.

Apart from the main streets, side streets are unnamed, with blocks numbered and alphabetised, making taxi directions, well, a bit taxing. Navigating by local landmarks and road junctions is advised.

Librairie Vents du Sud (see below) sells a handy map, *Nouakchott – Centre-Ville*, for UM1500.

INFORMATION

Bookshops

Librairie Vents du Sud (☎ 525 2684; Ave Kennedy; ☒ 8am-1pm & 4-7pm Mon-Sat) Mostly French books and magazines, but also postcards and copies of *The Economist* and *Time*.

Emergency

Police (☎ 17)

Internet

There are plenty of internet cafes in Nouakchott. Speeds are reasonable, if not superfast, with UM200 per hour being the standard rate to get online.

Cyber Sahen (Ave du Général de Gaulle; per hr UM300; ☒ 8am-midnight)
Cyber Neja (Off Ave Kennedy; ☒ 8am-midnight)
Cybercafé Juxa (Rue Abu Bakr; ☒ 8am-11pm)

Medical Services

Hôpital National (Centre National l'Hospitalier; ☎ 525 2135; Ave Abdel Nasser)
Cabinet Médical Fabienne Sharif (☎ 525 1571) English-speaking doctor, recommended by expats.

Money

There are bureaus de change on Ave du Général de Gaulle, especially just below Rue Abu Bakr), where you can change CFA and Moroccan dirhams as well as euros and dollars, while in the Marché Capitale it's almost impossible to walk 25m without being approached by a street moneychanger. Banks are also an option but they keep shorter hours than bureaus de change.

MAURITANIA

NOUAKCHOTT

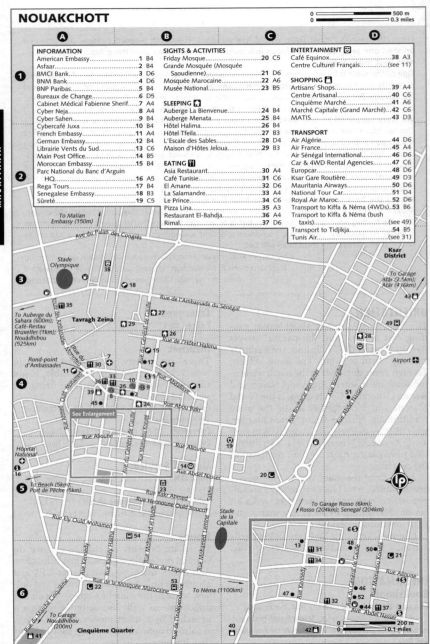

INFORMATION
American Embassy......................1 B4
Asfaar.......................................2 B4
BMCI Bank.................................3 D6
BNM Bank..................................4 D6
BNP Paribas...............................5 B4
Bureaux de Change......................6 D5
Cabinet Médical Fabienne Sherif...7 A4
Cyber Neja..................................8 A4
Cyber Sahen...............................9 B4
Cybercafé Juxa..........................10 B4
French Embassy.........................11 B4
German Embassy........................12 B4
Librairie Vents du Sud.................13 C6
Main Post Office........................14 B5
Moroccan Embassy.....................15 B4
Parc National du Banc d'Arguin
  HQ..16 A5
Rega Tours................................17 B4
Senegalese Embassy...................18 B3
Sûreté......................................19 C5

SIGHTS & ACTIVITIES
Friday Mosque...........................20 C5
Grande Mosquée (Mosquée
  Saoudienne)...........................21 D6
Mosquée Marocaine...................22 A6
Musée National.........................23 B5

SLEEPING
Auberge La Bienvenue.................24 B4
Auberge Menata........................25 B4
Hôtel Halima.............................26 B4
Hôtel Tfeila...............................27 B3
L'Escale des Sables.....................28 D4
Maison d'Hôtes Jeloua................29 B3

EATING
Asia Restaurant.........................30 A4
Café Tunisie..............................31 C6
El Amane...................................32 D6
La Salamandre...........................33 A4
Le Prince...................................34 C6
Pizza Lina..................................35 A3
Restaurant El-Bahdja..................36 B4
Rimal.......................................37 D6

ENTERTAINMENT
Café Equinox.............................38 A3
Centre Culturel Français..........(see 11)

SHOPPING
Artisans' Shops..........................39 A4
Centre Artisanal........................40 C6
Cinquième Marché.....................41 A6
Marché Capitale (Grand Marché)...42 C6
MATIS.......................................43 D3

TRANSPORT
Air Algérie.................................44 D6
Air France..................................45 A4
Air Sénégal International..............46 C6
Car & 4WD Rental Agencies.........47 C6
Europcar...................................48 D6
Ksar Gare Routière.....................49 D3
Mauritania Airways....................50 D6
National Tour Car.......................51 D4
Royal Air Maroc.........................52 D6
Transport to Kiffa & Néma (4WDs)..53 B6
Transport to Kiffa & Néma (bush
  taxis)................................(see 49)
Transport to Tidjikja...................54 B5
Tunis Air.............................(see 31)

There are no cash advances on credit cards either. If you need a money transfer, your best bet is to head to a Moneygram or a Western Union office.

Hopefully more international card-linked ATMs will open during the lifetime of this book (but then again, we said that last edition too).

BMCI (Ave Abdel Nasser) Agent for Western Union.

BNM (Rue Alioune) Agent for Moneygram.

BNP Paribas (Rue Mamadou Konaté) Has a Visa ATM – the only one in Mauritania.

Post

Main post office (Ave Abdel Nasser; 🕑 8am-3pm Mon-Thu, to noon Fri)

Telephone

There are heaps of private telephone offices in the centre where local and long-distance calls can be made. For local SIM cards, there are plenty of phone shops on Ave du Général de Gaulle, just below Rue Abu Bakr.

Travel Agencies

Rega Tours (☎ 524 0424; resa@regatours.com; Ave du Général de Gaulle) Reliable flight-booking agent.

Visa Extensions

Visa extensions can be obtained at the **Sûreté** (off Ave Abdel Nasser; 🕑 8am-3pm Mon-Thu).

DANGERS & ANNOYANCES

Nouakchott is a relatively safe city, especially compared with other capital cities in the region. It's also a late-night city, with many people walking around even at 11pm. Even at those hours walking is generally safe for men, but avoid the beach at night.

SIGHTS & ACTIVITIES
Port de Pêche

An absolute must-see, the fish market (locally called Port de Pêche or Plage des Pêcheurs), is by far Nouakchott's star attraction. It's incredibly lively and extremely colourful. You'll see hundreds of teams of men, mostly Wolof and Fula, dragging in heavy, handknotted fishing nets. Small boys hurry back and forth with trays of fish, which they sort, gut, fillet and lay out on large trestles to dry. The best time is between 4pm and 6pm, when the brightly painted fishing boats return and are hauled up through the surf onto the beach. It's a fantastic experience and not to be missed. It's pretty

safe as long as you're vigilant and sensible (wear a money belt).

Take a taxi to get there (around UM500 from the centre). Taxis pick up and drop off at the entrance to the market proper, with its stalls selling myriad species of fish. Walk through this to reach the beach, and the great lines of boats on the sand.

Musée National

The **Musée National** (Rue Mohammed Habib; admission UM300; 🕑 8am-3.30pm Mon-Fri) is mildly diverting for those with an interest in Moorish culture. On the first level is a prehistoric gallery with archaeological exhibits while the second level is taken up with more recent ethnographic displays from Moorish society. The building is labelled as the Ministry of Culture.

Mosques

Dominating the city's skyline, the Saudi-built **Grande Mosquée** (Rue Mamadou Konaté), better known as the Mosquée Saoudienne, is right in the centre. It's not exactly a model of architectural magnificence but it's worth a couple of pictures for its slender minarets.

South of Ave Abdel Nasser, towards the Cinquième Quartier, looms the large **Mosquée Marocaine** (Moroccan Mosque; Rue de la Mosquée Marocaine), another precious landmark in this bustling area. On the road to the airport, the **Friday Mosque** (Ave Abdel Nasser) is notable for its blindingly white facade. Visitors aren't allowed inside during prayer times.

SLEEPING
Budget

Auberge du Sahara (☎ 670 4383; www.auberge -sahara.com, in French; tents per person UM1500, dm UM2500, d UM4000; **P**) At this well-signed on the road to Nouâdhibou, your cordial hosts, Sidi, Hermann and Katia go the extra yards. Dorms and rooms are plain but functional and shared bathrooms are kept in good nick. The other pluses are the outdoor areas, a kitchen for guests' use and a rooftop terrace. You'll need a taxi, or your own vehicle to get to the centre.

Auberge Menata (☎ 636 9450; off Ave du Général de Gaulle; tents per person UM2000, dm UM2500, d UM5000, vehicle UM1500; **P**) A centrally located and perennially popular haunt for backpackers and overlanders, the laidback Menata is a decent option. Good meals are available on request or you can use the kitchen. The only drawback? It can be noisy, and shared bathrooms could be a lot better kept.

Auberge La Bienvenue (☎ /fax 525 1421; ☎ 676 7871; Ave du Général de Gaulle; s UM10,000-12,000, d UM12,000-14,000; ✂ 🖳) Although it's on the main drag, this auberge is surprisingly peaceful and there's a pleasant leafy garden at the front, ideal for breakfast. Rooms (all en suite) are good value for the price tag.

Midrange

Maison d'Hôtes Jeloua (☎ 636 9450, 643 2730, 525 0914; maison.jeloua@voila.fr; Tavragh Zeina; r UM10,000-12,000 or UM5000 with shared bathroom; P ✂ 🖳 🛜) Run by the same people as the Auberge Menata, this is a lovely *maison d'hôtes* (B&B). It's charmingly decorated and there's free wi-fi. Popular with business travellers.

L'Escale des Sables (☎ 525 23 75; www.escale-des-sables.com; Ksar District; d incl breakfast UM20,000-27,000; P ✂ 🖳 🛜) A bit out of the way, this gorgeous and welcoming place is certainly worth the detour. Rooms are seductively cosy and the garden is a great place to chill out after a hot day – there's even a pool. Meals are available on request.

Top End

Hôtel Tfeila (☎ 525 7400; www.hoteltfeila.com; Ave du Général de Gaulle; s/d from UM45,200/47,200; P ✂ 🖳 🛜 ✉). Forget the blinding orange-and-yellow facade of this former Novotel; the interior shows money and a classy eye bonded with impeccable service. From swish rooms to free wi-fi, a good restaurant and pool, this is by some degree Mauritania's best hotel.

Hôtel Halima (☎ 525 7920; fax 525 7922; Rue de l'Hôtel Halima; s/d UM30,500/34,000; P ✂ 🖳) Many hotels in this bracket could be plonked down anywhere in the world, but the Halima displays a definite Moorish charm. Fine value in the price bracket, it has well-presented rooms, good facilities and a tough-to-beat location.

EATING
Restaurants

Unless otherwise stated, all restaurants are open for lunch and dinner every day. In principle, alcohol is available at higher-end places.

Rimal (☎ 525 4832; Ave Abdel Nasser; mains about UM1000; ✆ closed lunch Sun) This place thoroughly lacks any pretensions, but is all the better for it. The surroundings might have seen better days, but the service is fast and the food piping hot. There are good salads, chicken dishes and a variety of tasty fishes straight from the Port de Pêche.

Pizza Lina (☎ 525 8662; Route des Ambassades; mains UM1500-3500; ✆ lunch & dinner) A long-established player on the Nouakchott dining scene, Pizza Lina now faces stiff competition from the many similar places along this stretch of Route des Ambassades. Whichever you go for though, you'll find decent crispy pizzas and a selection of pasta and meat dishes.

Restaurant El-Bahdja (☎ 630 5383; off Route des Ambassades; mains UM2500-3000; ✆ lunch & dinner) Mauritania imports plenty of produce from Morocco, so a restaurant serving *tajine* (Moroccan stew) and couscous should always do well. It doesn't disappoint – filling classics are served up in bright surroundings at very reasonable prices.

La Salamandre (☎ 524 2680; off Route des Ambassades; mains UM2000-4000; ✆ lunch, dinner, closed Sun) La Salamandre enjoys a deserved reputation for lip-smacking French cooking, but throws in a little Mexican and even Japanese for variety. Here you can fill yourself with salads, shrimps, pasta and *côte d'agneau grillée* (grilled lamb). The sleek setting, with lashings of bright colours splashed all over the walls, is another draw.

El Amane (☎ 525 2178; Ave Abdel Nasser; mains around UM1800; ✆ closed lunch Sat) Inside the hotel of the same name, this restaurant is popular with expats, and good for grilled meat, fish and salads.

Asia Restaurant (off Rond-point d'Ambassades; mains around UM3000; ✆ dinner) You can't miss this place with its grand entrance. Inside is a little more down at heel, but there's a comprehensive Chinese menu (half the clientele also seem to be Chinese), and a trickle of foreigners just coming here for the beer. Food is tasty but a bit pricey if you start adding side dishes.

Quick Eats

Rue Alioune between Ave Kennedy and Ave du Général de Gaulle is good for fast food, with most places open until 11pm or later; most have a Lebanese bent.

Le Prince (Rue Alioune; mains UM500-1300). A bit grander than most fast-food joints, Le Prince claims to be Nouakchott's oldest restaurant. Plonk yourself on a wobbly chair in the room at the back and tuck into a plate of well-prepared shwarma, sandwiches, salads and ice cream – all great value.

Café Tunisie (Ave Kennedy; breakfast UM1000; ☼ breakfast). On the corner next to Tunis Air, this cafe is fine for coffee and smoking a water pipe, but comes into its own with fantastic breakfasts – freshly squeezed orange juice, bread, jam, pastries, yoghurt, coffee and a bottle of mineral water. A fine way to start the day.

ENTERTAINMENT

Centre Culturel Français (☎ 529 96 31; www.ccf-nkc .com; next to French Embassy) You can pick up a program for the CCF at most hotels, and it's a good place to go for regular concerts by popular local musicians, as well as film screenings and art exhibitions.

Café Equinox (☎ 502 5238; www.equinoxecentre .com; btwn Ave du Palais des Congrés & Rue de l'Ambassade du Sénégal) Although mainly a cafe-restaurant (and a good one at that), the Equinox has started inviting local musicians to play on Friday evenings and has plans to expand into larger concerts.

SHOPPING

The slightly anarchic **Marché Capitale** (also called Grand Marché) offers a bit of everything. Potential souvenirs include brass teapots, silver jewellery, traditional wooden boxes with silver inlay, pipes, leather bags, sandals, cushions, beads and grigri. You'll find dress material, colourful Soninké tie-dyed material, Senegalese batiks and the inexpensive, crinkly *malafa* (fabric) that Moor women use as veils.

Cinquième Marché is full of migrants from across West Africa. It is good for browsing and people-watching, and has good vegetables, fish, tailors and music.

If you're after handwoven carpets, head to **MATIS** (☎ 525 5083; Ave Abdel Nasser, Ksar District; ☼ 8am-4pm Mon-Thu & Sun), a short hop from the airport.

For wooden boxes with silver inlay, daggers and jewellery, check the **artisans' shops** northeast of the corner of Ave Kennedy and Route des Ambassades. Also check the **Centre Artisanal** (silver market; Rte de Rosso), south on the highway to Rosso – it's beyond the roundabout intersection for Boutilimit and on your right.

GETTING THERE & AWAY
Air

Nouakchott's **airport** (☎ 525 8319) is on the eastern outskirts, about 2.5km from the centre. It has very few facilities. There's no formal currency exchange, but if you need

money to pay for the taxi ride, the shops will change dollars and euros, albeit for pretty poor rates.

For details of international flights to/from Nouakchott, see p569. For domestic flights see p570.

Bus

Although there is no formal bus station, there are a couple of private companies running luxury buses to Nouâdhibou. Most reliable of these is **Salam Transports** (☎ 501 9240; Rte des Ambassades), which runs a daily afternoon bus (UM5500, six hours). It also advertises a direct service to Dakar (UM10,000). This wasn't yet running when we visited, but it does have a daily morning bus to the border at Rosso (UM3000, 3½ hours).

Bush Taxi

There are specific garages for Mauritania's different regions. These are mostly on the outskirts of Nouakchott, so require a taxi ride to get there.

For Nouâdhibou (about UM4500, six hours), the Garage Nouâdhibou is close to Cinquième Marché; for Rosso (about UM2000, 3½ hours), the Garage Rosso is almost 10km south of the centre. For Atâr (UM3500, six hours), the Garage Atâr is on the road to Atâr, about 3km north of the airport. **Ksar Gare Routière** (nr the airport) serves destinations to the southeast: Kiffa (UM4500, 10 hours), Ayoûn el-Atroûs (UM6000, 14 hours) and Néma (UM7500, 24 hours). You should also be able to find bush taxis to Tidjikja (UM5600, 10 hours) from here.

Car Hire

If you want to hire a car with driver, try **Europcar** (☎ 525 24 08; Ave du Général de Gaulle) or **National Tour Car** (☎ 525 97 34; Rue Ghary), on the road to the airport.

The best place to start looking for 4WDs for hire is on the north side of Ave Abdel Nasser, about 50m west of the intersection with Ave Kennedy. Most hotels and auberges can also offer vehicles. The cheapest Toyota Corolla/Hilux (4WD) costs UM16,000/21,000 per day with driver, plus fuel.

GETTING AROUND
To/From the Airport

The airport is in the Ksar district. The standard taxi fare to the centre is about UM1000,

MAURITANIA

but it's cheaper to hail a taxi from the highway nearby (UM300).

Taxi
Green-and-yellow taxis are plentiful, although virtually any private car doubles as a taxi – stop at the roadside and you'll be honked at by prospective drivers. It costs UM200 for a ride within the centre, and about UM500 to Port de Pêche.

THE ATLANTIC COAST

With the new paved road from Nouâdhibou to the capital, travellers no longer have to travel along the beach, worrying about getting caught by the tide. While that'd good, it means that many people simply zip through without stopping. That's a shame – this is the place where wild coast meets Saharan dunes. This coastline, mostly occupied by Parc National du Banc d'Arguin – one of the world's greatest birdlife-viewing venues – is a rapturous place for tranquillity seekers, nature lovers and bird-watchers alike.

NOUÂDHIBOU
pop 80,000

For a port city, Nouâdhibou is a pretty relaxed sort of place, and an ideal stop to recharge the batteries on the long road between Western Sahara and Nouakchott or the Adrar. It's also the perfect base from which to head out to Banc d'Arguin.

The city sits on the Baie du Lévrier, in the middle of the narrow 35km-long Cap Blanc peninsula. The sea on both sides is chilled by the Canary current, and as a result is noted for its rich fishing. Foreign ships flock to the waters, and not just for the catch – lax local regulations means that Nouâdhibou has also become famous for its ships' graveyards, with dozens of boats scuppered around the peninsula – check out the Baie de Cansado, south of the main port for the watery wrecks.

Orientation
The city's main street, running north–south, is Blvd Médian. At the southern edge of town is the Port de Pêche Moderne (the container port) and 8km further south is Cansado. Port Minéralier, 3km further, is where the train line ends and ore is loaded

onto ships, while 4km beyond is Cap Blanc, the southern tip of the peninsula.

Information
If they have not bought it at the border, overland travellers with vehicles must buy insurance at any insurance company in town. The process is hassle-free. The camp-

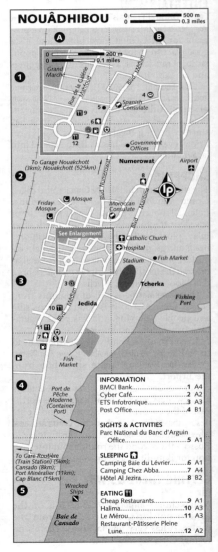

NOUÂDHIBOU

INFORMATION	
BMCI Bank	1 A4
Cyber Café	2 A2
ETS Infotronique	3 A3
Post Office	4 B1

SIGHTS & ACTIVITIES	
Parc National du Banc d'Arguin Office	5 A1

SLEEPING	
Camping Baie du Lévrier	6 A1
Camping Chez Abba	7 A4
Hôtel Al Jezira	8 B2

EATING	
Cheap Restaurants	9 A1
Halima	10 A3
Le Mérou	11 A3
Restaurant-Pâtisserie Pleine Lune	12 A2

MAURITANIA

AN EPIC JOURNEY ON THE IRON-ORE TRAIN

Africa offers some pretty wild train trips, but the train ferrying iron ore from the mines at Zouérat to Nouâdhibou might just be the wildest. One of the longest trains in the world (typically a staggering 2.3km long), when it arrives at the 'station' in Nouâdhibou, a decrepit building in the open desert, a seemingly endless number of ore wagons pass before the passenger carriage at the rear finally appears. The lucky ones find a place on one of the two long benches (UM2500); the rest stand or sit on the floor. There are also a dozen 'berths' (3000) that are so worn out that you can see the springs. It's almost brutally basic. It's also possible to clamber into the ore cars and travel for free. Dusty in the empty cars on the way into the interior, impossibly dusty on top of the ore heading to the coast, it's only for the really hardcore. Plastic sheets are essential to wrap your bags (and person), plus plenty of warm clothes – as the desert gets fearsomely cold at night – and food and drink.

The train leaves Nouâdhibou at around 2pm to 3pm daily. Most travellers get off at Choum, 12 hours later, where bush taxis wait to take passengers to Atâr, three hours away. In the other direction, the train leaves Zouérat around midday, and passes through Atâr at about 5.30pm.

It's possible to put a vehicle on the train, but this needs to be organised 72 hours in advance, and costs between UM23,000 and UM46,000 depending on the vehicle. Call the station in Nouâdhibou for more information (☎ 574 1754).

ing options listed below are good places for travel information and local guides.

There are several bureaus de change along Blvd Médian. Rates here are slightly lower than in Nouakchott, but you should be able to get Moroccan dirhams. **BMCI** (Blvd Médian; ☺ 8am-3pm Mon-Fri) has a branch here. The post office is east off Blvd Médian. Most internet outlets also double as telephone offices and Nouâdhibou has a number, including the following:

Cyber Café (Off Blvd Médian; per hr UM200; ☺ 8am-11pm)

ETS Infotronique (Blvd Médian; per hr UM200; ☺ 8am-midnight)

Sleeping

Camping Baie du Lévrier (☎ 574 6536, mobile 650 4356; Blvd Médian; s/d without bathroom UM3000/5000; P) Also known as Chez Ali, this auberge-style place has a good location and a welcoming and knowledgeable owner-manager. Rooms are a bit cell-like, but there is a tent to relax in and cooking facilities.

Camping Chez Abba (☎ 574 9896; fax 574 9887; Blvd Médian; tents per person UM1500, s/d UM3200/4400; P) A good overlanders' haunt, this has plenty of space to park and pitch a tent, and a few decent rooms with their own bathrooms and hot water. Recommended.

Hôtel Al Jezira (☎ 574 5317; Blvd Maritime; s/d incl breakfast UM13,000/15,000; P ✄) Nouâdhibou isn't overrun with topclass accommodation, but this midrange hotel slightly north of the centre just about works out. Rates are slightly high for what's on offer, but the rooms are fair, and occasionally border on the comfy.

Eating

In the centre, you'll find a slew of very cheap restaurants along Rue de la Galérie Mahfoud. They are nothing fancy, but they serve filling fare – fish and *mafé* – at unbeatable prices (around UM300 for a meal).

Restaurant-Pâtisserie Pleine Lune (☎ 574 9860; off Blvd Médian; mains UM1000-1500; ☺ breakfast, lunch & dinner) We like this place for its breakfasts – decent coffee and a good selection of pastries – but it's good at any time of day, with pizzas and sandwiches as quick fillers, or grilled fish and brochettes for something more filling.

Le Mérou (☎ 574 5980; Blvd Médian; mains UM1500-2500) This restaurant on the main drag is as upscale as Nouâdhibou's dining scene gets. Marine murals on the wall remind you that fish is always the dish of the day, from plates of tasty shrimp to some serious seafood steaks.

Halima (☎ 574 5428; Blvd Médian; mains UM1500-3000; ☺ closed lunch Fri) A blue-and-white frontage gives way to slight odd kitsch interior design at Halima. As with its main competitor, Le Mérou, it's all about the seafood. Meals are good, although at times the menu seems to be 'any way you like it, as long as it's fried'.

Getting There & Away

Mauritania Airways flies four times a week to Nouakchott (UM20,000, one hour).

MAURITANIA

There are plenty of bush taxis from the *gare routière* to Nouakchott (UM4500, six hours). You can also get transport from here to cross the border into Morocco (Western Sahara). Taxis go most days to Dakhla (UM11500, eight hours), and even Laâyoune (UM17,000, 16 hours). Try to get to the *gare routière* by 8am at the latest – any later and you'll be facing a long wait for the vehicles to fill and go.

For more information on the train from Nouâdhibou to Choum and Zouérat, see the boxed text, p555.

Getting Around

Chartered green-and-yellow taxis charge a cool UM500 to the centre from both the *gare routière* and airport. Within town, expect to pay about UM200.

PARC NATIONAL DU BANC D'ARGUIN

This World Heritage–listed **park** (www.mauritania .mr/pnba, in French; admission per person per day UM1200) is an important stopover and breeding ground for multitudes of birds migrating between Europe and Southern Africa, and as a result is one of the best bird-watching sites on the entire continent. Over two million broad-billed sandpipers *(limicoles)* have been recorded here in the winter. Other species include pink flamingos *(flamant rose)*, white pelicans *(pélican blanc)*, grey pelicans, royal terns *(sternes royales)*, gull-billed terns *(spatula blanche)*, black terns *(sterne bridée)*, white-breasted cormorants, spoonbills and several species of heron, egret and wader. For even the most casual birder it can be a spectacular place.

The park extends 200km north from Cape Timiris (155km north of Nouakchott). Most birds are found on sand islands in the shallow ocean. The best viewing time is December and January, which is also the mating season. The

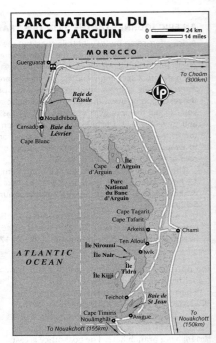

PARC NATIONAL DU BANC D'ARGUIN

0 — 24 km
0 — 14 miles

MOROCCO

Guerguarat

To Choûm (300km)

Baie de l'Étoile

Nouâdhibou
Cansado   Baie du Lévrier
Cape Blanc

Île d'Arguin

Cape d'Arguin

Parc National du Banc d'Arguin

Cape Tagarit
Cape Tafarit
Arkeiss   Chami

Île Niroumi   Ten Alloul
Île Nair   Iwik

ATLANTIC OCEAN

Île Tidra
Île Kijji

Teichot   Baie de St Jean

Cape Timiris
Nouâmghâr   Awgue   To Nouakchott (150km)

To Nouakchott (155km)

---

best way to see them is by traditional fishing boat, called a *lanche* – a recommended, ecofriendly excursion. The main island, 30km long, is **Tidra**, and just to the west of the northern tip are two tiny islands, **Niroumi** and **Nair**. The principal launching point is **Iwik**, a fishing village on the mainland 6km northeast of Tidra. You can find boats here; they cost UM15,000 (plus UM3000 for the guide) whether you stay out all day or only a few hours.

After, you could head to **Cape Tagarit**, 40km north of Tidra. The view from the cape is magnificent and the water is crystal clear.

Park permits are issued either at the entrance gates or in Nouâdhibou at the **park office** (☎ 574 67 44; Blvd Médian, Nouâdhibou; ☼ 8am-4pm Mon-Thu, to noon Fri). Both this office and the park's Nouakchott **headquarters** (☎ 525 8514; Ave Abdel Nasser, Nouakchott) sell an excellent foldout map and guide to the park, which includes comprehensive GPS waypoints.

Sleeping & Eating

Inside the park there are official **camp sites** (tents for up to 2/7 people UM3000/6000) equipped with

---

THE LAST MONK SEALS ON EARTH

The *phoque moine* (monk seals) near the lighthouse at the southern tip of Cap Blanc are a major attraction, although your chances of seeing these days these are pretty slim. Resembling elephant seals, these grey-skinned animals were hunted since the 15th century for their valuable skins and oil. The protected colony here of roughly 100 seals is one of the last on earth.

traditional tents at Arkeiss, Ten Alloul, Iwik and Nouâmghâr. Meals can also be ordered (about UM1000).

Getting There & Away

Your best bet to visit the park is to hire a 4WD with a knowledgeable driver, either in Nouakchott or in Nouâdhibou. You really need at least three days for the round-trip. Contact any travel or car-rental agency for more information.

If you want to cross the park with your own 4WD, the trip from Nouakchott to Nouâdhibou (525km) takes at least two days. The first 155km from Nouakchott north to Cape Timiris is along the beach and passable only during low tide. Thereafter you enter the worst section – dunes for 300km. There are poles every 5km between Nouâmghâr, the fishing village at Cape Timiris, and just before the railway track in the north, but they won't keep you from getting lost if you don't have a guide. The last 70km southwest along the railway tracks is flat and easy but don't stray from the track, as mines abound.

For safety reasons (it's easy to get lost) go with at least one other vehicle and a guide (typically UM50,000 for three days); in Nouâdhibou, ask at your hotel. Make sure you take sufficient food, water and warm clothes.

THE ADRAR

The Adrar is the undoubted jewel in Mauritania's crown. It's epic Saharan country, and shows the great desert in all its variety: ancient Saharan towns of Chinguetti and Ouadâne, mighty sand dunes that look sculpted by an artist, vast rocky plateaus and mellow oases fringed with date palms. For desert lovers, the Adrar is a must.

The region is easily accessed by road from Nouakchott, or by train from Nouâdhibou for the really tough. There's even a direct flight from France to Atâr. Once here though, camels and 4WDs are the order of the day – prepare for adventure.

ATÂR

pop 25,000

The unassuming town of Atâr is the commercial and tourist centre of the Adrar. There's nothing much to see, but it has a pleasant enough atmosphere, and everyone passes through to organise camel or 4WD forays in the Adrar. During the winter there are direct flights to Atâr from France, and when the plane touches down the town springs to life and the touts get to work picking up customers – the nearest thing that Mauritania gets to a tourist boom.

A large *rond-point* (roundabout) marks the centre of Atâr and the market is just north of it. You'll find several bureaus de change, banks (US dollars and euros) including the BMCI and telephone offices on or around the main drag. The small mazelike Ksar district, west of the market, is a good place to explore. It's the old residential quarter, with narrow winding streets, brick walls and carved doorways.

There are a couple of internet cafes at the time of writing: **Atar Internet** (per hr UM500)

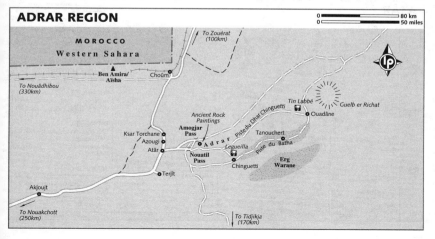

ADRAR REGION

0 ————— 80 km
0 ————— 50 miles

MOROCCO
Western Sahara

To Zouérat
(100km)

Ben Amira/
Aïsha

Choûm

To Nouâdhibou
(330km)

Tin Labbé

Guelb er Richat

Ancient Rock
Paintings

Piste du Dhar Chinguetti

Ouadâne

Ksar Torchane

Amogjar
Pass

Adrar

Tanouchert

Azougi

Atâr

Legueilla

Piste du Batha

Nouatil
Pass

Chinguetti

Erg
Warane

Terjît

Akjoujt

To Nouakchott
(250km)

To Tidjikja
(170km)

on the *rond-point,* and **Centre Internet** (per hr UM300).

Activities

There are over a dozen agencies in Atâr that can arrange **camel rides** or **4WD tours.** The most popular 4WD trip is a five-day circuit called 'tour de l'Adrar' (round the Adrar), taking in Chinguetti, Ouadâne, Tanouchert, Terjît and various other fine spots. But you can arrange custom itineraries.

The main costs are the vehicle and driver, so trips are cheaper if you're in a group. Four people is ideal. Count on paying up to UM21,000 per day for a Toyota Hilux plus petrol. Add about UM2000 per day per person for food.

Most travel agencies also organise custom camel rides in the Adrar but it's probably better to start your trip in either Chinguetti (p561) or Ouadâne (p562) where the most scenic dunes are almost on your doorstep. Prices start at UM12,000 per day with food and lodging.

The following agencies have been around for a few years and have good credentials:
Essafa Agence (☎ 529 5609; justusbuma@yahoo.com) At Auberge Bab Sahara.
Khatratty Voyages (☎ 664 6676, 662 3214; sidatty _medemin@yahoo.fr)
Salima Voyages (☎ 546 4611) At Auberge du Bonheur.
Tivoujar (☎ 678 1342, 625 5182; www.vuedenhaut .com) At Auberge Tivoujar.

Sleeping

our pick Auberge Bab Sahara (☎ 546 45 73, 647 39 66; justusbuma@yahoo.com; tents per person UM2000, stone

huts/caravans UM8000/5000, parking motorbike/car/truck UM200/400/1000; P) Off Route de Azougui, Bab Sahara has been a little slice of overlander's heaven for over a dozen years. There is a selection of *tikits* (stone huts, with AC), caravans and tents, set amid well-planted grounds, plus there's a campsite in another compound and a fully equipped mechanic's workshop. Meals are available on request and guests usually eat together, adding to the sociable atmosphere. The Dutch-German couple who run it are great sources of local information and travel advice.

Auberge du Bonheur (☎ 546 4537; fax 546 4347; tents or huts per person UM1500, r UM4000;) Those wanting a reliable base could do worse than checking in at this welcoming outfit, a five-minute stroll from the centre. It's nicely turned out, with simple but decent rooms and a large tent in the courtyard, and everything kept scrubbed pretty clean.

Auberge Avrah El Medina (☎ 671 2605; r UM2500, tents UM1500) Tucked in a side street not far from the hospital, this just about fits the bill for budget travellers, but the rooms are a bit dour and the mattresses wafer-thin.

Hôtel Monod (☎ 546 4236; Route de Chinguetti; r UM8000;) One of the few proper hotels in Atâr, the Monod offers the novelty of en suite rooms. It's all perfectly serviceable, although thoroughly lacking in personality.

Hôtel El Waha (☎ 546 4249; fax 546 4273; Route de l'Aéroport; r UM14,000-21,000, ste U38,000; P) Catering mainly to tour groups, this a reassuring choice with 26 well-equipped modern

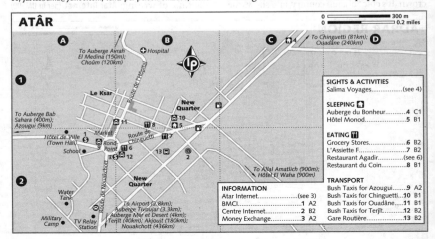

MAURITANIA

THE GUETNA SEASON

'You would be nuts to travel in the Adrar in summer.' Don't pay attention to this hackneyed cliché. Sure, from June to August the heat is muffling, with temperatures reaching 45°C, but this is the much-awaited Guetna season. The Guetna refers to the harvest of dates in the palm groves. In spite of the heat, it's a very festive season and all oases get very lively. During the Guetna, many Mauritanians from the cities return to their tribes and take part in the harvest – the population of oases like Azougi and Tanouchert swell by several thousand. There's a congenial, mellow atmosphere, with much socialising, tea and *zrig* drinking, game playing and dancing. Moreover, there are virtually no tourists – the perfect occasion to sample Mauritanian hospitality at its best.

---

tikits scattered around a well-tended garden. The facilities are good, but the price tag is correspondingly sharp.

Auberge Tivoujar (☎ 678 1342, 625 5182; www.vuedenhaut.com; tikits/r per person with half-board UM6000/10,000; P ✗ ☐) Opened in January 2006, this professionally run venture is the closest that Atâr comes to having a top-end hotel. It's popular with tour groups during the season, so don't expect much privacy, but it boasts excellent amenities, including wheelchair-accessible *tikits* and scrupulously clean bathrooms. Rooms are en suite, and services even run to hot-air balloon rides over the desert. The only drawback is the location, about 4km from the centre on the road to Nouakchott.

Auberge Mer et Desert (☎ 613 7576; www.aubergemeretdesert.com; tents/r per person with half-board UM4200/5200; P ✗ ☐ ☒) Another auberge out of town on the Nouakchott road, this new option has promise. Rooms and tents around the sandy compound are well appointed, management is keen, and also operates an agency running tours. The 'pool' is barely bigger than a hot tub, but refreshing enough for a plunge.

Eating

L'Assiette F (☎ 610 7150; Route de Chinguetti; set menu UM2500; ☽ breakfast, lunch & dinner, closed May-Aug) Formerly the Restaurant de l'Amitié, this French-run place brings a touch of culinary sophistication to down-at-heel Atâr. It has good fish, potato omelettes, *crêpes* (pancakes) and the occasional salad, as well as good breakfasts. There's shady outdoor seating at the rear.

Restaurant du Coin (Market, off Rte de Chinguetti; meals UM300) From the *rond-point* head down the Chinguetti road for a block, then turn left. This place is on the right-hand corner, marked by a tiny sign. It's as down-at-heel as you can get but serves great quantities of rice,

fish and Senegalese *mafé*. It's always busy, and the food piping hot and delicious.

Restaurant Agadir (Route de Chinguetti; mains UM500-700) Near the *rond-point*, this cheap and cheerful eatery rustles up some good couscous and *tajines* (Moroccan stews) as well as sandwiches and lighter bites.

There is a concentration of grocery stores in the streets leading out from the main roundabout, and most are pretty well stocked. Fresh produce is thin on the ground in Atâr.

Getting There & Away

From October to April **Point Afrique** (www.point-afrique.com) normally has a weekly flight from Paris to Atâr via Marseilles, although it was temporarily suspended at the time of going to press.

The main *gare routière*, in the heart of town, is where you can get vehicles for Nouakchott (UM3500, six hours) and Choum (UM1500, three hours). Choum transport tends to time its departures to meet the train heading to Nouâdhibou. Make sure they drop you where the passenger carriage is going to stop, as the train is over 2km long!

Vehicles for Chinguetti (car/4WD UM1500/2500, about two hours) leave once a day from near a shop located a block north of Hôtel Monod. Most days there is also transport to Ouadâne (bush taxi/4WD UM3000/4000; about four hours), leaving from a street north of the roundabout (ask for 'gare de Ouadâne'). For Azougui (UM500, 20 minutes), and Terjît (UM1000, one hour), infrequent 4WDs leave from near the roundabout. There are more services to all of these destinations during the Guetna season.

Getting Around

Most taxi fares weight in at around UM100, double that for farther destinations like the airport or the auberges on the edge of town.

BEN AMIRA

If you like big rocks, they don't come much more awesome than Ben Amira. Rising 633m out of the desert, it's Africa's biggest monolith, and in size is second only to Uluru (Ayers Rock) in Australia. It's clearly visible from the train between Nouâdhibou and Zouérat, but if you have a 4WD it makes a brilliant one-night camping trip from Atâr.

There are actually two granite monoliths. Ben Amira is the largest, with the slightly smaller Aïsha to the west. According to legend, they were once joined as 'man' and 'wife', but Aïsha was unfaithful and the two split apart. The smaller rocks between them are their children, keeping the couple forever separated.

Ben Amira is more massively spectacular, but Aïsha holds a delightful surprise of her own. In December 1999, a symposium of 16 international sculptors was held here to celebrate the millennium, and over a month turned many of the boulders at the base of Aïsha into art. The natural shapes of the rocks were reinterpreted as animals and birds, plus enigmatic faces and abstract creations. It's a wonderful spot, all the more so for being completely unheralded by its surroundings.

The monoliths are 4km north of the train track between Nouâdhibou and Choum, at Kilometre 395 (Ben Amira village sits next to the tracks here). The route is sand rather than piste. Aïsha is 5km west of Ben Amira. To find the sculptures, head for the eastern side of the Aïsha, it appears to join a lower mound made of giant 'melted' rocks: the sculptures are here. On the western side of Aïsha is the giant cleft that gives the rock her gender.

AZOUGI

An ancient imperial capital could hardly be more unassuming than the oasis of Azougi, 10km northwest of Atâr. It was from here in the 11th century that the Berber Almoravids launched their great expansion, attacking the Empire of Ghana, leading to the spread of Islam throughout West Africa, and then north into Morocco to establish their grand capital at Marrakesh. Now this small town with its spreading palm groves makes for an excellent retreat if you need some hush.

Auberge Oued Tillige (☎ 546 4343; r, tents or tikits per person UM2000) is an excellent, quiet alternative to staying in Atâr and has wonderful views down the valley. It's pretty well maintained and there are whitewashed huts with blue doors, tents or the traditional *tikits* in which to sleep.

Another worthy option is **Auberge de la Medina – Chez Khassem** (☎ 654 7784, 676 4794; tents or tikits per person UM1500), a more recent auberge further up, on the edge of the dunes. It's similar in standards to Auberge Oued Tillige and there's an hospitable feel, although it's a little bit out of the way.

There are bush taxis daily between Azougi and Atâr (UM500, 20 minutes).

TERJÎT

Terjît is another example of Mauritania's unerring ability to surprise. We've never seen an oasis quite like it. About 40km south of Atâr, a streak of palm groves is hemmed in by great red cliffs. The air gets cooler and greener and filled with the trickling of running water as the canyon narrows, until you reach its head, where two springs tumble out of the rocks. One is hot, the other cold, and by some small miracle they mix to form a natural swimming pool the perfect temperature for a dip. It's simply bliss.

You pay UM1000 to enter the site. On weekends in season, Terjît can be packed with tour groups, but at other times you'll have the place to yourself. The only drawback are the mosquitoes in the evening: bring repellent.

The main spring has been taken over by **Auberge Oasis de Terjît** (☎ 644 8967, 546 5020 in Atâr; tents or huts per person UM1500), where a mattress in a tent by the trickling stream is on offer. Service is erratic, and shared facilities middling at best, but the setting can hardly be beaten.

The only other place to stay is the **Auberge des Caravanes** (☎ 546 6180; r or tikits per person UM1500; P), at the entrance to the village. It's a 20 minute walk to the spring, but the set-up here is good, with six uncluttered yet clean *tikits*, four rooms (all with mosquito nets), well-maintained shared bathrooms and a pleasant tent for lounging, with a book swap and board games. Meals are available.

To get here by private car, drive 40km south of Atâr on the road to Nouakchott, then turn left at the checkpoint and follow a sandy track for 11km. The trip takes 1½ hours. By public transport, take anything headed out of Atâr towards Nouakchott and hitch a ride from the checkpoint. There's also a bush taxi that leaves every morning from near the roundabout in Atâr (UM1000).

CHINGUETTI
pop 4000

One of the more attractive of the ancient caravan towns in the Sahara, Chinguetti will appeal to spiritual seekers. The seventh-holiest city of Islam, it's shrouded with a palpable historic aura. The heavenly backdrop is another draw. You'll discover an outlandish landscape of mighty sand dunes upon which the light plays a daily show.

Once famous for its Islamic scholars, it was the ancient capital of the Moors, and some of the buildings date from the 13th century. In its heyday, Chinguetti had 12 mosques, 25 *madrassas* (Quranic schools) and was home to 20,000 people. Its wealth was drawn from the epic camel caravans laden with salt that travelled from Chinguetti, Marrakesh and Timbuktu.

The highlight of any visit is a wander through the labyrinthine lanes of Le Ksar (the old town). The modern town, which has a delightfully sleepy market (remarkable for how little produce is available), is separated from the old town by a broad, flat wadi where palm trees grow.

In February 2009, the town hosted the week-long *Festival Culturel Nomade de Chinguetti*, featuring camel races and traditional music, dancing and crafts. There are plans to make this an annual event.

Sights & Activities
LE KSAR

The old quarter's structures are mostly stone and most are in ruins and unoccupied. The principal attraction is the 16th-century stone mosque (no entry to non-Muslims). Also of great interest are the five old libraries, which house the fragile-as-dust ancient Islamic manuscripts of Chinguetti. In these libraries are the stories of Chinguetti's golden age. The libraries include the **Bibliothèque Ehel Hamoni** (admission UM1000), **Bibliothèque Moulaye** (admission UM1000), **Bibliothèque Habbot** (admission UM1000), and **Fondation Ahmed al Mahmoud** (admission UM1000) and each has an attached **museum** (admission

UM1000) containing items from the old caravans. None of the libraries keep regular opening hours and your best bet is to ask at your hotel for the man with the key.

DESERT TRIPS

The picture-postcard sand dunes around Chinguetti are the single most definitive image of Mauritania for many people. The eastern side of Chinguetti is bordered by the **Erg Warane**, Mauritania's biggest stretch of dunes, and more than enough to meet expectations of the great Saharan sand seas.

The best way to see this fascinating region is by camel. Numerous *méharées* (camel trips) are available. Plan on at least a full day's ride as you'll see little of the dunes in half a day. Possible trips include to the oases of Abeir (3km), Tendewalle (5km), Legueilla (12km) or a four-day return trip to Tanouchert (45km). With more time you could go as far as Ouadâne (five to six days), Terjît (six days) and even Tidjikja (13 to 15 days) in the Tagânt. Prices are reasonable – standard costs start from UM8000 per person per day for the camel, food and guide. Any reputable travel agency in Atâr (p558) or auberge owner in Chinguetti (Le Maure Bleu and Auberge La Rose des Sables are recommended) can arrange camel rides. You don't really have to haggle much, because everyone charges more or less the same price.

If you don't want to sweat it out, you can hire a 4WD and driver. It costs from UM17,000 (Toyota Hilux) to UM31,000 (Toyota GX) per day, petrol not included.

HOT-AIR BALLOONING

Fancy quietly sailing through desert skies at dawn? Auberge Tivoujar, a reputable outfit based in Atâr (see p558), can organise departures from Atâr or Chinguetti. It's not cheap (about €160 per person) but looking down on the dune fields and rock formations from the air is bound to be one of the highlights of your trip.

Sleeping & Eating

All the places listed here have shared shower and toilet unless stated otherwise. Breakfast and meals are available on request (usually about UM2000 per meal).

Auberge La Rose des Sables (☎ 540 0148; New Town; stone huts or tents per person UM1500) Stumbling distance from Auberge Abweir, this auberge is run by the amiable Cheikh Ould Amar. It is a touch more run-down than its competitors but still fits the bill for shoestringers, with adequate stone huts arranged in a compact compound.

Auberge Zarga (☎ 746 0628; New Town; r/tents per person UM1400/1700) At the entrance to the new town coming up from the wadi, the Zarga is a trifle grungy, with the price reflecting the facilities – basic, but fine.

Auberge des Caravanes (☎ 540 0022; fax 546 4272; New Town; r per person UM2000) With its eye-catching, traditional architecture, it's hard to miss this place right in the centre of town. Rooms are pretty simple, and it can feel a bit impersonal, but it's adequate for the price.

Auberge Abweir (☎ 540 0124; abweirauberge@yahoo .fr; New Town; stone huts or tents per person UM2500) Next door to Auberge des Caravanes, this welcoming place will appeal to a more sedate crowd, with a bunch of simple yet well-organised stone huts and small tents set around a plant-filled courtyard. The well-scrubbed ablution block is an added bonus.

L'Eden de Chinguetti (☎ 540 0014; New Town; r UM6000-8000) This impressive auberge is a great place to stay. It's neat, well tended and embellished with well-chosen knick-knacks and a nice garden. The English-speaking owner is a mine of information. There are only eight rooms, with proper beds and mosquito nets, and clean shared bathrooms. It's on the road to Atâr, not far from Auberge La Rose des Sables.

ourpick Le Maure Bleu (☎ 540 0154, 205 3819; www. maurebleu.com; Old Town; s/d with bathroom €30/40, without bathroom €24/34) One of Adrar's most appealing places to stay, this French-run peach of a place has oodles of rustic charm and features well-arranged rooms. It is trying to be green with its composting toilets (rooms with bathrooms only) and vegetable garden. The soothing courtyard is a great place to unwind over a cup of tea. Breakfast is included, while other meals are good enough to make a detour for.

Restaurant 7 Merveilles (☎ 609 7837; New Town; meals UM500-1500) Centrally located, with a pleasant roof terrace offering Saharan views, this new restaurant is a valuable addition to Chinguetti's scene. Meals range from simple sandwiches to pasta and couscous, plus it's a good place to nurse a cold drink or coffee.

Getting There & Away

There's at least one vehicle a day to/from Atâr (car/4WD UM1500/2500, about two hours).

They leave from just behind the market; you'll need to ask around as the driver often goes off looking for his full complement of passengers. There are no bush taxis between Chinguetti and Ouadâne – you'll have to go back to Atâr.

For those with their own vehicles, there are two routes to Atâr. The faster route (81km, two hours) is via the **Nouatil Pass** and the lunar-like Adrar plateau; while the other (91km, three to four hours) leads up to the breathtaking **Amogjar Pass**, which is slow going but offers spectacular views. If you're coming from Chinguetti, the turn-off for the Amogjar Pass is at the signpost to the faintly discernible Neolithic rock paintings. These paintings, of people, antelope and even giraffes, are at the top of the pass by a small campsite – the caretaker will show you the paintings. The pass is rocky and best attempted by 4WDs.

There are also two routes to Ouadâne – via the plateau or, more picturesque, across the **Erg Warane** to the east of town.

TANOUCHERT

This charming oasis, approximately half-way between Chinguetti and Ouadâne, is a popular stop for 4WD trips and camel treks. Deservedly so, as it's a classic set-up: nestled around a freshwater source, complete with palm trees and surrounded by superb dune fields, miles from anywhere.

Another attraction is the welcoming **Auberge Chez Chighaly Ould Bigue – Oasis Tanouchert** (☎ 654 1885; tents or tikits per person with half-board UM4200). Chighaly, your amiable host, is a local figure and will welcome you wholeheartedly in his unsophisticated but tidy auberge. The perfect *griot*, he is a pleasure to listen to if you can understand French. If there's a group, he'll organise a *méchui* feast (UM25,000 for five people) – the perfect meal to enjoy under desert stars.

Various camel rides can be organised in the area. Tanouchert is off the beaten track and you'll need to hire a 4WD with driver to get there. If you do a camel trek from Chinguetti to Ouadâne, you'll probably spend a night in Tanouchert.

OUADÂNE

After the flat sandiness of the surrounding landscape, the palm-fringed hill that Ouadâne sits astride seems most unexpected. The town itself is even more so – made from the same brown rocks as the hill, it seems organic and half-camouflaged until you get up close, and realise that the weird structures were built by people rather than giant ants.

Ouadâne was founded in 1147 by Berbers, and sits on the edge of the Adrar plateau, 120km northeast of Chinguetti. For 400 years, it was a prosperous caravan centre and a transit point for dates, salt and gold. It was the last stopover for caravans heading to Oualâta in the southeastern corner of the country. The decline began in the late 16th century when the powerful Moroccan prince Ahmed el Mansour gained control of this trans-Saharan route and diminished Ouadâne's commercial role.

Sights

As you arrive across the sands or plateau from Atâr or Chinguetti, the stone houses of **Ksar al Kiali** (Old Quarter; entrance UM1000) seem to tumble down the cliff like an apparition, and they change colour depending on the time of day. From the base of the town, the lush gardens of the oasis stretch out before the desert again takes hold. The top of the hill is dominated by the minaret of the **new mosque**, which is a mere 200 years old, while at the western end at the base of the town is the 14th-century **old mosque**. At the height of Ouadâne's power, the two mosques were connected by the **Street of 40 Scholars** *(savants)*, with houses occupied by the intelligentsia and families of the town's founders. In between, the crumbling structures seem to have been piled up higgledy-piggledy by some giant child playing with building blocks. From a distance, they can seem to blend to form a massive stone wall. Only 20 to 30 families still live in the old town.

Like Chinguetti, Ouadâne was a place of scholarship and is home to over 3000 manuscripts held in 23, mostly private, **libraries** (admission to each about UM1000). At the time of research, some of them were open to the public. There's also a **small museum** (admission UM1000) housing various artefacts from the ancient caravans.

The Ksar is fenced off, but there's a ticket office where you pay to enter; the fee includes a French-speaking guide.

Sleeping & Eating

Auberges here are listed in order as you drive into Ouadâne. All have shared bathrooms, and will prepare meals for their guests (about UM2000 for lunch or dinner). Try the *ksour,* a local thick pancake made of wheat. Dipped into a sauce, it makes a great accompaniment.

Auberge Warane 1 (☎ 546 4604 in Atâr; r or tents per person UM1500) The first place you'll encounter coming from Atâr, on the left. The rooms are a bit bunkerlike but serviceable enough.

Auberge Agoueidir – Chez Isselmou (☎ 525 0791; agoueidir@yahoo.fr; tikits/tents per person UM1200/2500, s/d UM5000/7000) Ouadâne's 'upscale' sleeping option, this auberge has helpful and friendly management offering orderly rooms (with proper beds) adorned with modest artistic touches, as well as a number of decent tents and *tikits*. It is at the entrance to town coming over the dunes from Chinguetti.

Auberge Vasque – Chez Zaida (☎ 681 7669; tikits or tents per person UM1700) This mellow auberge is run by Zaida, a congenial lady who goes out of her way to make your stay a happy one. There are five *tikits* and a couple of nomads tents – it's nothing particularly glam but the food is great.

Auberge El Ghalaouya (tents or tikits per person UM1500) Almost a carbon copy of the Vasque, and sitting just above it on the hill. There are pleasant stone huts and tents, as well as a clean ablutions block.

Auberge Mayateg (☎ 546 2094; tents or tikits per person UM2000) This is one of the few places to stay atop the rocky bluff and is an easy walk to the top of the old town. It won't win any style awards but it's salubrious enough and there's a homely feel.

Auberge Vareni (tikits per person UM1700) Next to the *gendarmerie* (police), this new auberge is probably the best option if you want to stay inside the town itself. The *tikits* are simple but nicely finished.

Getting There & Away

Without your own vehicle, getting to Ouadâne isn't always straightforward. Atâr is the place to look for transport, and vehicles run from between the two most days, usually in the mornings (bush taxi/4WD UM3000/4000; about four hours). Direct transport between Ouadâne and Chinguetti runs next to never.

If driving you have two alternatives: the southerly Piste du Batha, which passes through sand dunes and definitely requires a 4WD and guide, and the northerly Piste du Dhar Chinguetti along the plateau, which is in very good condition. The latter departs the Atâr-Chinguetti road 18km before Chinguetti.

MAURITANIA

AROUND OUADÂNE

The spectacular **Guelb er Richat** 'crater' is 40km to the northeast. A geological oddity, it's a series of vast concentric circular ridges 200m high and nearly 50km across. It looks like a giant meteorite crater, but is actually caused by natural erosion of ancient uplifted rocks. En route, stop at **Tin Labbé** (7km), a unique settlement where the large boulders prevalent in this area have been incorporated into the villagers' homes.

THE TAGÂNT

The Tagânt is probably Mauritania's least visited region. Poor road infrastructure has kept it isolated from the rest of the country, although this is now beginning to change. For the time being though, travellers are likely to have the place to themselves – visiting the crocodile-inhabited oasis of Matmata, or using the town of Tidjikja as a gateway for some really remote travelling. Whatever the option, the sense of adventure is ever palpable.

TIDJIKJA

pop 6000

Tidjikja is the capital of the Tagânt region and a major stopover for those who cross the Tagânt from Chinguetti down to Néma. Founded in 1680 and now surrounded by sand dunes, the town supports one of the country's more important palm groves (which dates from the 18th century), a busy market, a couple of eye-catching mosques, numerous shops and Fort Coppolani (an old French military fort used in subduing the Moors).

A good side trip can be made to Rachid, 35km north on the track to Atâr. High up a cliff, it's one of the most picturesque spots in Mauritania and was once used as a site for launching attacks on passing caravans.

Sleeping & Eating

Auberge Sahara Oudyan-Rive (☎ 641 4017; www .sahara-oudyan-riv.com; r UM3000, tikits 1500; ✕) Run by a French-Mauritanian couple, this auberge is Tidjikja's nicest accommodation option, with good rooms, tents, and great food (meals on request). The auberge can also organise tours across the Tagânt and up to the Adrar. It's on the road from Nouakchott, after the petrol station.

Auberge des Caravanes de Tidjikja (☎ 569 9225; r with full board UM7000, tikits s/d 9000/10,000; ✕) This reputable place is good value. In addition to plain rooms, a dozen comfortable *tikits* were under construction when we visited. It's in the north of the town, in the 'new' quarter.

Auberge Phare du Désert (☎ 563 2999; tikits UM5000-7000) Almost a carbon copy of Auberge des Caravanes, if a bit more intimate.

For food, there are also some small grocery shops and the market.

Getting There & Away

A good, sealed road connects Nouakchott with Tidjikja, and there are daily bush taxis between the two (UM5600, 10 hours).

It's possible to drive from Tidjikja to Atâr (470km) in two days. A guide is essential and attempting it with only one vehicle is inadvisable, as the piste frequently turns to sand.

MATMATA

Somehow, the words 'Sahara' and 'crocodile' just don't seem to fit comfortably together in the same sentence, but Matmata is home to this unlikely combination. Nestled in a rocky platform between impressive cliffs, this series of pools is home to a small population of Nile crocodiles, along with hyraxes and monkeys. It's a delightful place, fed by an impressive waterfall during the winter rains.

Getting to Matmata is easiest if you have a vehicle, but just about possible by public transport. Take a bush taxi from Nouakchott to Tidjikja, and get out at N'beyka (seven hours from Nouakchott). From here, you can hire a car to take you the short distance to Matmata – locals can show you the pools.

TICHIT

If you're adventurous and want to see a ghost town in the making, head for the isolated, ancient town of Tichit, 255km east of Tidjikja. Driving here, you'll pass through a barren landscape – the trees are bare, the scrub is twisted, and the ground is littered with the bleached bones of camels and goats. You should report to the police when you arrive.

The town once furnished water and precious supplies to desert caravans and boasted over 6000 people and 1500 houses. Today, fewer than 300 houses remain and only about half are inhabited. The main mosque is impressive, as are the old houses,

KIFFA BEADS

Made primarily by nomad women around Kiffa and Ayoûn el-Atroûs, Kiffa beads are one of Mauritania's loveliest craft items. Originally thought to be influenced by Venetian trade beads known in the region since medieval times, Kiffa beads are traditionally made of millefiori glass, shaped into bright mosaic patterns. Ground glass is made into a paste using the maker's saliva, and layered with a needle onto a core bead. The bead is then fired, and the process repeated to build up a series of bright layers. It's a slow process, and takes around half a day to make a single (usually triangular) bead of around 25mm in length.

It's still possible to track down old beads (known locally as *murakad* or *masnoura*) in Kiffa and Ayoûn el-Atroûs, although the art appears to be dying out in favour of modern imported beads. Old Kiffa beads can be expensive – over US$50 – but handpainted replicas can easily be found in shops in Nouakchott and elsewhere.

which are made of local stone of different hues. They have decorative motifs on the exterior and solid, ornate doors with wooden latches.

A guide is essential and you'll need your own transport. The tracks frequently disappear and there are few landmarks, so you'll need enough petrol (and food) for a return trip, including unplanned detours.

THE SOUTH

The south is mostly flat scrubland, with no great vistas and few remarkable towns. Most travellers with their own 4WDs head straight from Nouakchott to Ayoûn el-Atroûs or Néma and then journey on to Mali, or they go to Rosso and on to Senegal.

But there's Oualâta. This unique and unforgettable town is definitely worth the effort to get there and should be on every savvy traveller's itinerary. Check the security before heading to the far southeast, because banditry and overspill from Mali's Tuareg rebellion have been known to affect the region.

ROSSO
pop 30,000

Rosso is the main Mauritanian–Senegalese border crossing. It's a grubby, haphazard town with an air of hustle that prevents you from totally relaxing. Most travellers rush through, as there aren't really any worthwhile sights or attractions here. For more details, see p570.

The border means there are plenty of bush taxis zipping up and down from Nouakchott (UM2000, 3½ hours). From Rosso, you can also take a Peugeot bush taxi to Keur Masséne

(UM500) for the Diamma border post (which is named for the nearest Senegalese town, Diamma) to the west and cross into Senegal there.

THE ROAD TO MALI

The Route de l'Espoir (Road to Hope) from Nouakchott to Néma (around 1100km) is now entirely tarred, giving a smooth (if still very long) trip to the border.

The first major town on the road to the Malian border is **Kiffa**, an important regional trading centre and crossroads. Much of the activity of this vibrant place centres on the busy market. The best places to stay are **Hôtel Emel** (☎ 563 26 37; fax 563 26 38; s/d UM7000/10,000; ☒), 7km west of the centre, with fusty but spacious and well-equipped bungalows, and the more recent **Auberge Le Phare du Désert** (☎ 644 2421; pharerim@yahoo.fr; tikits UM10,000; ☒), a nicely laid-out auberge, also on the outskirts of Kiffa. Meals are available at both places.

There is daily transport to Nouakchott (UM4500, 10 hours) and Ayoûn el-Atroûs (UM3500, four hours) from Kiffa, and less frequently to Diamma (for the Senegal border).

Alternatively, head to **Ayoûn el-Atroûs**, which is a good place to spend your last ouguiyas before crossing into Mali. Although some way from the frontier, Ayoûn has the feel of a frontier town and has a lively African market that's a big contrast to the markets in the north. For accommodation, try the unpretentious **Hôtel Ayoûn** (☎ 515 14 62; s/d UM5000/8000; ☒), which is in the centre (rooms come with bathroom), or **Auberge Saada Tenzah** (☎ 515 1337, 641 1052; r UM2500-6000), about 3km east of the centre on the road to Néma. The beds in both places probably keep local chiropractors in business.

MAURITANIA

The tarred road ends at **Néma**, where you can already feel the flavour of neighbouring Mali. Néma doesn't have much to detain you but it's the main jumping-off point for Oualâta and the southern gateway to the Tagânt. You'll find several petrol pumps, a BMCI branch (euros only), a couple of modest stores and a police station at which you can get your passport stamped. You can base yourself at **Complexe Touristique N'Gady** (☎ 513 0900; bungalows s/d UM7000/9000, r 12,000/15,000; P ✗), a few kilometres west of the centre, or the simpler **Auberge Moulay Omar** (☎ 650 3489; r UM2500) near the market.

While there are daily bush taxis to Nouakchott (UM7500, 24 hours) via Ayoûn el-Atroûs, transport to Oualâta (UM2000, 2½ hours) is more spotty, so be prepared to wait patiently.

OUALÂTA

Dating from 1224, Oualâta used to be the last resting point for caravans heading to Timbuktu. These days it's one of Mauritania's better-kept secrets, and a look on the map shows you why: it's a long way from anywhere else in the country, and more easily accessed from Mali than Nouakchott. But it's high on atmosphere and personality and it's hard not to be touched by the end-of-the-world, forgotten-city feeling that emanates from this poignant place.

Sights & Activities

Entering the town you'll be struck by the red **mudbrick houses** adorned with decorative paintings on the exterior and interior. Many houses were restored with the help of a Spanish organisation. The women paint geometric designs with dyes, typically red or indigo, making use of all materials found in the region. If you're lucky, you may get invited inside one of them. A small donation is recommended (about UM500). There's also a small **museum** (UM500) and a **library**, which houses ancient Islamic manuscripts. If you're in for some souvenirs, Oualâta women are renowned for their original and fanciful clay carvings.

If you have plenty of time, you could easily spend several days pottering about in the town and the area – watching nomads bring vast herds of goats or camels down the hills to the river and enjoying the natural splendour. There are also several rock paintings and **archeological sites** in the vicinity. Various **camel trips** can also be organised (ask your hosts).

Eating & Sleeping

There is a clutch of decent sleeping options, all built in traditional style and decorated with murals. Bathrooms are shared. They all serve meals (about UM1800 for lunch or dinner, UM800 for breakfast). Try the local delicacy, *pigeon farci aux dattes* (pigeon stuffed with dates).

Auberge Tayib/Gamni – Auberge de l'Hôtel de Ville (r per person UM3000) is a great place with a very homely feel, as is the more basic but still welcoming **Auberge de l'Amitié** (r per person UM1500), not far from the old mosque. Moulaye Ahmed De, the chirpy owner, is used to dealing with travellers and will do his best to ensure a memorable stay. A notch up from these two, **Auberge Ksar Walata** (r per person UM5000) is tucked away in a lane in the old city. It features a lovely patio and attractive rooms.

Getting There & Away

There are two dirt tracks between Néma and Oualâta (approximately 110km). Land Rovers ply between the two towns (UM2000, 2½ hours) most days.

MAURITANIA DIRECTORY

ACCOMMODATION

In general, you can expect to spend less than US$15 per person in places we list as budget options; US$15 to US$50 in those we list as midrange; and more than US$50 in those we list as top end. Finding budget accommodation is easy in cities and major towns. There's also a sprinkle of air-conditioned hotels meeting international standards in Nouakchott and, to a lesser extent, Nouâdhibou and Atâr. In the desert, you'll find numerous basic auberges or *campements*. They consist of a series of *tikits* or *khaimas* that come equipped with mattresses on the floor.

The last couple of years has seen a gradual improvement in the choice on offer, with a growing number of tasteful, midrange *maisons d'hôtes*.

ACTIVITIES

Camel rides and 4WD expeditions in the desert are the most popular activities. Numerous tour companies can arrange custom trips in the desert (p558).

Alternatively, if bird-watching gets you in a flap, head for the Parc National du Banc d'Arguin (p556), along the Atlantic coast – this area is rated as one of the world's greatest birdlife-viewing venues.

BUSINESS HOURS

Although it's a Muslim country, for business purposes Mauritania adheres to the Monday to Friday working week. However, Friday is the main prayer day, so many businesses have an extended lunch break on Friday afternoon.

Many shops are open every day. Government offices, post offices and banks are usually open from 8am to 4pm Monday to Thursday and from 8am to 1pm on Friday.

CUSTOMS

It is illegal to bring any alcohol into the country and heavy fines are levied. There are no longer currency declaration forms and there is no restriction on the amount of foreign currency you can bring in. Local currency cannot be imported or exported.

DANGERS & ANNOYANCES

Despite the coup, you shouldn't let paranoia get the better of you. Mauritania is one of the safest countries in Africa, particularly the capital and the main tourist region of the Adrar.

In 2008, the Paris–Dakar Rally was cancelled due to threats against the Mauritanian leg by Islamist groups. Although there have subsequently been a small number of incidents, these have been restricted to remote areas unvisited by foreigners, such as around the Algerian border. In the southeast, however, insecurity from Mali has threatened to spill across the border. Coupled with periodic reports of banditry on the roads, travellers should take trusted advice before planning to travel in this region.

EMBASSIES & CONSULATES
Mauritanian Embassies & Consulates

In West Africa, Mauritania has embassies in Côte d'Ivoire, the Gambia, Mali, Nigeria and Senegal, and a consulate in Niger. For more details, see the relevant country chapter.

Embassies & Consulates in Mauritania

The following countries are represented in Nouakchott:

France (☎ 525 2337; Rue Ahmed Ould Mohamed)
Germany (☎ 525 1729; Rue Abdallaye)
Mali (☎ 525 4081, 525 4078; Tevragh Zeina)
Morocco (☎ 525 1411; Ave du Général de Gaulle)

> ### PRACTICALITIES
>
> ■ Mauritania uses the metric system for weights and measures.
>
> ■ Electrical current is 220V AC, 50Hz and most electrical plugs are of the European two-pin type.
>
> ■ Mauritania's only TV station is TVM, with programmes in Hassaniya and French, but top-end hotels have satellite TV.
>
> ■ For the news (in French), pick up *Le Calame* or *Horizons*.

Senegal (☎ 525 7290; Rue de l'Ambassade du Sénégal)
USA (☎ 525 2660; fax 525 1592; Rue Abdallaye)

HOLIDAYS

Public holidays include the following:
New Year's Day 1 January
National Reunification Day 26 February
Workers' Day 1 May
African Liberation Day 25 May
Army Day 10 July
Independence Day 28 November
Anniversary of the 1984 Coup 12 December

Mauritania also celebrates the usual Islamic holidays – see p816 for a table of estimated dates of these holidays.

INTERNET ACCESS

It's not a problem to get online in any reasonably-sized town, although outside of Nouakchott the connection speed can often be a little wanting. Expect to pay around UM200 for an hour.

LANGUAGE

Arabic is the official language, but French is still spoken in all government sectors and is widely used in business. The Arabic spoken is a dialect called Hassaniya, which includes many Berber loan-words. In the south, other languages are spoken, including Fula (Pulaar), Wolof and Soninké. See p860 for a list of useful phrases in French, Hassaniya, Fula and Wolof. English is not widely spoken.

MONEY

The unit of currency is the ouguiya (UM). Euros and US dollars are the cash to carry and

MAURITANIA

wads of cash it must be, as travellers cheques and credit cards are pretty useless.

Although you'll see ATMs in the larger towns, at the time of research only one machine in the entire country (at BNP Paribas in Nouakchott) accepted international bank cards. Only Visa cards are accepted, although it's hoped that this will change during the lifetime of this guide. No banks give cash advances on credit cards, but Western Union branches are everywhere if you need funds wired.

There are banks and bureaus de change in most cities, as well as street moneychangers, although there is no meaningful black market. Nouakchott has higher exchange rates than anywhere else; you can also exchange CFA and Moroccan dirhams here.

Credit cards are accepted only at top-end hotels in Nouakchott.

TELEPHONE

You can make international calls and send faxes at post offices. The innumerable privately run phone shops in the major cities and towns cost about the same and are open late. Mauritanian mobile (cell) phones use the GSM network, and a SIM card for the Mauritel and Mattel networks costs around UM2000.

There are no telephone area codes.

VISAS

Visas are required for all travellers, except nationals of Arab League countries and some African countries, although check that these exceptions haven't changed. The standard visa is valid for three months and good for a stay of one month from the date of entry.

In some places, Mauritanian embassies may require an onward air ticket (or at least an itinerary). This particularly used to be the case in Rabat, where the point of entry was marked on the visa as Nouakchott airport. However, this thankfully appears to have fallen out of practice, and travellers should be able to get visas for overland entry here within 24 hours (Dh340).

In countries where Mauritania has no diplomatic representation, including Australia and many countries in West Africa, French embassies will issue visas for around US$30.

Visa Extensions

Visa extensions can be obtained at the **Sûreté** (off Ave Abdel Nasser, Nouakchott; ☻ 8am-3pm Mon-Thu). It costs UM5000 for one month.

Visas for Onward Travel

In Mauritania you can get visas for the following neighbouring countries.

MALI

Visas are issued the same day (UM6500) and are valid for one month. You need two photos and a photocopy of the information pages of your passport.

MOROCCO

Most nationalities do not require visas, and simply get an entry stamp valid for 90 days on arrival. Nationalities that do (mostly Africans, including Mauritanians) must pay UM5800 and provide two photos and photocopies of your passport and (according to whim) an air ticket.

SENEGAL

One-month visas (UM1500) are issued in 24 hours. You need to supply four photos plus passport photocopies.

WOMEN TRAVELLERS

Mauritania is a conservative Muslim country but by no means the most extreme in this regard. It is not unusual to find women working in public offices and driving; headscarves are worn rather than a veil covering the face. The best way to meet local women is to hope for an invitation home from a family or to spend some time talking with stallholders, most of whom are women, in local markets.

Women travellers may be subjected to sexual harassment, especially when alone or with other women, although most women encounter no problems. It's a good idea for women to dress modestly. Cover the upper legs and arms and avoid shorts or skimpy T-shirts.

TRANSPORT IN MAURITANIA

GETTING THERE & AWAY

Most people from Western Europe or further abroad will fly to Mauritania, most probably to Nouakchott or Atâr. However, if you're doing a grand tour across West Africa, road border posts are open between Mauritania and neighbouring countries.

Entering Mauritania

Your passport must be valid for at least six months beyond your intended departure from Mauritania and stamped with a valid visa (see opposite). For travellers coming overland from Morocco, visas can also be issued at the border. You must also have proof of your vaccination against yellow fever.

Travellers arriving with the charter flight from Paris to Atâr from October to April don't need to bother about the visa; it's included in the price and is routinely issued upon arrival at Atâr airport.

Air

Nouakchott, Nouâdhibou and Atâr have international airports. Nouakchott's airport handles most traffic.

Mauritania's national carrier, Air Mauritania, went bust in 2007, and has been replaced by **Mauritania Airways** (MR; ☎ 524 7474, www.fly-mauritaniaairways.com; Rue Mamadou Konaté), a subsidiary of Tunis Air. The following airlines also fly to Mauritania:

Air Algérie (AH; ☎ 529 0992; www.airalgerie.dz; cnr Ave du Général de Gaulle & Ave Abdel Nasser) Hub: Algiers.

Air France (AF; ☎ 525 1808, 525 1802; www.airfrance .com; Ave Kennedy) Hub: Paris CDG.

Air Sénégal International (V7; ☎ 525 4852; www .air-senegal-international.com; Ave du Général de Gaulle) Hub: Dakar.

Point Afrique (BIE; ☎ 04 75 97 20 40, in France; www .point-afrique.com) Hub: Paris Orly.

Royal Air Maroc (AT; ☎ 525 3564, 525 3094; www .royalairmaroc.com; Ave Abdel Nasser) Hub: Casablanca.

Tunis Air (TU; ☎ 525 8762; www.tunisair.com.tr; Ave Kennedy) Hub: Tunis.

The only direct flights from Europe are through Paris, with Air France, Mauritania Airways and Point Afrique (although the latter was temporarily suspended at the time of going to press). For details on flying to Mauritania from outside Africa see p828.

AFRICA

Mauritania Airways flies five times a week between Nouakchott and Dakar, twice weekly to Bamako and four times to Abidjan. Air Senegal flies every day except Sunday. For other Saharan or sub-Saharan countries, you'll have to change in Dakar or Abidjan.

Mauritania is well connected to North Africa. Royal Air Maroc operates between Casablanca and Nouakchott five times a week, while Tunis Air connects Tunis with Nouakchott (three times a week). Air Algérie flies to Algiers twice a week.

Land

If driving into Mauritania, see p570.

MALI

At the time of research, the most straightforward route to Mali was from Ayoûn el-Atroûs to Nioro. This road is paved. You can also cross at Néma, Timbedgha (both connecting with Nara in Mali), Tintâne and Kiffa (both connecting with Nioro in Mali), although you should check local security before attempting these remote borders.

If crossing into Mali, have your passport stamped by police at the first town you reach after crossing the border. You must also clear customs, which is done in Néma or Ayoûn el-Atroûs.

From Nouakchott, you can catch bush taxis to Néma (about UM8000, two days) and Ayoûn el-Atroûs (about UM6400, 15 hours). From these places you can catch transport into Mali.

There are two routes between Nioro and Ayoûn el-Atroûs if you're travelling by car. The trip is roughly 230km and usually takes less than a day.

Petrol is available in Nioro, Nara, Néma, Ayoûn el-Atroûs and Kiffa.

MOROCCO (WESTERN SAHARA)

The trans-Sahara route via Mauritania is now a very popular route from North Africa into sub-Saharan Africa. This crosses the internationally disputed territory of Western Sahara, although the border itself is administered by Morocco.

The only border crossing between Morocco/Western Sahara and Mauritania is north of Nouâdhibou. Crossing this border is straightforward and the road is entirely tarred to Nouakchott, except for the 3km no-man's-land that separates the two border posts. Coming from Morocco, you can buy the Mauritanian visa at the border (€20), although border officials are unlikely to give the full 30-day visa issued by embassies. For more detailed information on crossing this border see p836.

There are direct bush taxis heading north from Nouâdhibou to Dakhla (Western

MAURITANIA

Sahara), but travelling in the opposite direction you'll need to change vehicles at the border. The 425km trip can easily be accomplished in a day.

SENEGAL
The main border crossing for Senegal is at Rosso but it's also possible to cross at Keur Massene (Diamma border post), west of Rosso. The latter is a much calmer experience, as Rosso is notorious for its hassles, although road conditions make Diamma largely a dry-season option. The border at both is marked by the Senegal River – at Rosso you catch a ferry, at Diamma there's a bridge.

When crossing into Senegal at Rosso, note that immigration is only open on the Mauritanian side from 9am to 11am and 3.30pm to 5pm. Be prepared for some confrontation with customs officials who usually ask for 'exit taxes'. If you're driving, make sure that your vehicle is properly organised (you must have a fire extinguisher and two warning triangles) and your paperwork ordered, although you should still expect much attention from greedy officials.

From Dakar to Nouakchott by public transport usually takes from 11 to 13 hours depending on the wait at the border. Most minibuses and bush taxis leave Dakar before 10am to be sure of arriving in Rosso well before the border closing time (6pm). At Rosso, most travellers without vehicles cross by pirogue (five minutes; UM200/CFA500) as the ferry crosses only four times daily. If you want to avoid the hassles at Rosso, you can take a bush taxi from Rosso to Diamma (Keur Masséne) and cross at Diamma. The border at Diamma is open 24 hours and the hassles are less problematic.

With your own vehicle, you can either cross the Senegal River at Rosso, which takes only 10 minutes by *bac* (ferry), or use the bridge at Diamma (open 24 hours). At Rosso, the ferry departs from the Mauritanian side at 9.30am, 11.15am, 3.30pm and 5pm, and from the Senegalese side some 45 minutes later. A car costs UM2000/CFA5000 (more for larger vehicles), and there are further police and customs fees on both sides: around UM1500 if you're entering Mauritania, CFA2000 for Senegal.

GETTING AROUND
Air
Mauritania Airways flies four times a week to Nouâdhibou (UM20,000, one hour), and three times a week to Zouerate (UM39,000, three hours). There are plans to extend services to the south.

Bush Taxi
The bush taxi (*taxi brousse*) is the main form of public transport in Mauritania, primarily Mercedes 190s, Peugeot 504s in that order of expense, followed by the occasional Land Rover and battered minibus when the roads are no longer tarmac but only gravel piste. Overcharging is rare except with the baggage fee, which is usually only levied for really hefty luggage. Bush taxis go to all the major towns daily, but finding one for small villages is challenging.

Mercedes or Peugeot bush taxis are uncomfortable because you're crammed in four to a row, so consider paying for two seats to avoid the misery. The front two seats are less cramped but they're also more expensive. Note that a *taxi course* is a taxi that you have all to yourself.

Car & Motorcycle
Mauritania's road network is mostly good, with tarred roads leading from the border with Western Sahara to Nouakchott, and on to the Senegalese and Malian borders at Rosso and Nioro respectively. The roads from the capital to Atâr and Tidjikja are also tarred. Elsewhere, piste is the order of the day, although great swath of the country are little more than sandy tracks (at best). Mauritania is heaven for off-roaders, and a 4WD is essential for exploring the Adrar (outside Atâr) and the Tagânt.

BRINGING YOUR OWN VEHICLE
You don't need a *carnet de passage en douane* in Mauritania (see p834 for more information). Mauritanian officials enter details of the car in your passport, which is then checked on departure from the country. An International Driving Permit (IDP) is not required, although on arrival you must buy a Mauritanian insurance policy at the border. Expect to pay around US$20 for 10 days. Petrol cost around UM240 per litre at the time of writing, slightly more in the Adrar and along the Route de l'Espoir. If crossing to/from Western Sahara, note that petrol is significantly cheaper on the northern side of the border.

If you're serious about off-roading in Mauritania with your 4WD (and can read

---

PAPERS PLEASE!

Mauritania is a country in love with police roadblocks, and you'll frequently be asked to produce ID, especially when entering or leaving a town. This is usually a straightforward procedure and nothing to worry about – police are generally polite. Your details are registered, so to speed things up we'd recommend you make your own form (*fiche*) to hand over. List all the personal details from your passport (including visa number), home address, occupation and parents' names. If you're driving, include your vehicle's make, colour and registration number. Make plenty of photocopies!

---

some French), get a copy of the essential *Pistes de Mauritanie* by Jacques Gandini, with comprehensive route and GPS information.

CAR HIRE

If you don't have a vehicle and you want more freedom than a tour can offer (most companies won't run tours for less than four people), consider renting a 4WD and driver.

The standard Toyota Hilux usually costs around UM21,000 per day for the vehicle, plus petrol.

Tours

There are numerous travel agencies in Nouakchott that offer tours around the country but it's not a bad idea to arrange a tour with a more regional-focused company – eg in Atâr, for the Adrar or the Tagânt. Travel is usually by 4WD. Standard tours include an eight-day tour to Atâr, Chinguetti, Ouadâne, Guelb er Richat and Terjît, the Tagânt plateau, or five-day excursions to the Banc d'Arguin. If there are at least four travellers, prices should average around UM17,000 up to UM21,000 per person per day.

Train

The Nouâdhibou–Zouérat train is certainly an epic adventure. It's an iron-ore train with no passenger terminals, but it has become a passenger train for lack of better alternatives. The trip takes 16 to 18 hours, but most travellers get off at Choûm (close to Atâr), 12 hours from Nouâdhibou. For detailed information see the boxed text, p555.

Niger

Niger is perhaps West Africa's most unfairly ignored country, and this is just the reason you should head here rather than one to give it a wide berth. True, Niger only seems to make the news for its Tuareg Rebellion, its uranium mines, famine and – incredibly in 2008 – for its ongoing slavery problem, but if you make the effort to visit this desert republic, you'll find a warm and generous Muslim population and some superb tout-free West African travel through ancient caravan cities at the edge of the Sahara.

Sadly, at the time of writing the country's greatest attractions, the Ténéré Desert and the Aïr Mountains in the north, were out of bounds due to the ongoing Tuareg Rebellion against the government in Niamey, but the fascinating trans-Saharan trade-route town of Agadez was still accessible, as well as a bevy of attractions in the peaceful south: the ancient sultanate of Zinder, the fantastic Parc Regional du W, West Africa's last herd of wild giraffe at Kouré and the impossibly romantic Sunday market of Ayorou. Add to this the laidback but cosmopolitan capital of Niamey and a trip down the mighty Niger River in a dugout pirogue (traditional canoe), and you've got yourself a West African adventure that can cheerfully rival any other in this book.

NIGER

FAST FACTS

- **Area** 1,267,000 sq km
- **Capital** Niamey
- **Country code** ☎ 227
- **Famous for** Slavery; *not* supplying uranium to Saddam; Cure Salée Festival
- **Languages** French, Hausa, Djerma, Fulfulde, Tamashek, Kanouri, Toubou and Gourman-chéma
- **Money** West African CFA Franc; US$1 = CFA493; €1 = CFA656
- **Population** 13.3 million
- **Visa** Required by almost everyone except West African citizens. Obtained easily in Algeria, Benin, Chad, Mali and Nigeria. Niger is covered by the Visa Entente.

HIGHLIGHTS

■ **Agadez** (p599) The view from the summit of the spiky mud mosque over the surrounding ancient caravan town and the Sahara beyond is majestic.

■ **Ayorou** (p589) The colours and aromas at the country's most exciting market are worth savouring, before a pirogue trip to see hippos in the Niger River.

■ **Kouré** (p589) A visit to the gregarious giraffes, the last wild herd of these beautiful animals in the Sahel region, is unforgettable.

■ **Zinder** (p596) The *banco* (clay or mud) houses of the Birni Quartier are well worth getting lost in, not to mention the sultan's palace with its brutal history.

■ **Parc Regional du W** (p592) Lions, monkeys, elephants and crocodiles can all be seen in one of West Africa's best and most diverse national parks.

ITINERARIES

■ **One Week** Base yourself in Niamey and make a series of day trips to Ayorou (p589), Filingué (p590) and to the giraffes near Kouré (p589) before spending two nights in the wonderful Parc Regional du W (p592) in the south.

■ **Two Weeks** After spending the first week in and around Niamey, travel up north to Agadez (p599) where you can see this glorious old Sahel city confident that few other tourists will be around, and then head south to Zinder (p596) where you can wander around the Birni Quartier and visit the sultan's palace before returning to Niamey, breaking the journey overnight in either Maradi (p595) or Birni N'Konni (p593)

CLIMATE & WHEN TO GO

October to February is the best time to visit, as temperatures are at their coolest and rainfall is nonexistent. From December the harmattan winds come into play, which can reduce visibility to less than 1km and spoil photographic opportunities.

The hottest part of the year is March to June, with April daytime temperatures reaching 45°C (113°F) or more, especially in the north, and heat so intense that rain evaporates before reaching the ground.

Rains dampen the south between late May and September, with August being the wettest time. The south's annual rainfall is usually 550mm, while the north is lucky to receive 150mm.

HISTORY

Early History

Some 6000 years ago, Niger's vast northern plateaus were verdant grasslands supporting hunters, herders and abundant wildlife. Around 2500 BC the Sahara began swallowing this region and its rivers whole, driving the population south. Little remains of this lush past, besides the splendid images captured in the Neolithic rock art of the Aïr Mountains. By the 1st millennium BC, the migrating peoples had learnt metalwork skills and developed complex social organisations and forms of trade.

Great West African Empires

Lying at the crossroads of the lucrative trans-Saharan trade route (in gold, salt and slaves), Niger's arid landscape once supported some of West Africa's great empires. One was the Kanem-Borno Empire, which flourished around Lake Chad between the 10th and 13th centuries AD. It survived the arrival of Islam during the 10th and 11th centuries, and remained a significant force until the 1800s. Between the 14th and 15th centuries, western Niger was controlled by the Islamic Empire of Mali before falling to the powerful Empire of Songhaï in the early 1500s, which subsequently controlled much of central Niger until the late 16th century.

HOW MUCH?

⌐ **Sachet of purified water** CFA50

⌐ **Croix d'Agadez** (historically stylised silver cross) CFA1500

⌐ **Simple Tuareg grigri (amulet)** CFA2000

⌐ **Street snack (beignet)** CFA25

⌐ **Moto-taxi across any town** CFA250

LONELY PLANET INDEX

⌐ **1L of petrol** CFA670

⌐ **1L of bottled water** CFA500

⌐ **Bottle of Bière Niger** CFA500

⌐ **Souvenir T-shirt** CFA1500

⌐ **Grilled beef brochettes** CFA100

NIGER

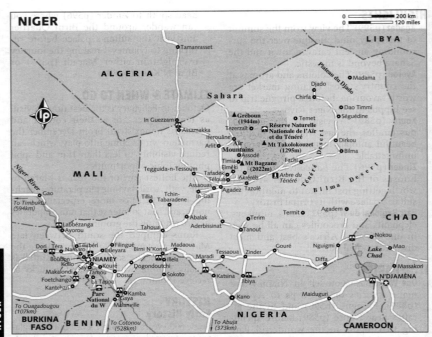

Also playing important roles before the arrival of Europeans were the Tuareg (who prefer to be known as Tamashek), who migrated south into the Aïr Mountains during the 11th century, and the Hausa and Kanouri peoples, who founded the mighty Damagaram state around Zinder having fled Nigeria in the 1600s.

Late Precolonial Niger

Although abolished in most of West Africa by the 1850s, the slave trade was still going strong in Niger and Chad. With 12,000 soldiers, the Sultan of Zinder had little trouble attacking villages in his own kingdom, capturing inhabitants and selling them as slaves to support his 300 wives and numerous children.

Agadez, once a great gold-trading centre, was hit as trade shifted from the Sahara to the Portuguese-controlled coastal ports; its population shrank from 30,000 in 1450 to less than 3000 by the early 20th century. As trade in gold declined, the value of salt rose. Mined at remote oases in the desert, salt deposits were the prerogative of the Tuareg nomads, and it was so rare that it was often traded

ounce for ounce for gold. Salt sustained the huge trans-Saharan camel caravans, and, as recently as 1906, a 20,000-camel caravan left Agadez to collect salt at Bilma, an oasis 610km to the east.

Colonial Era

The French strolled into the picture late in the 19th century and met stronger-than-expected local resistance. Decidedly unamused, they quickly dispatched the punitive Voulet-Chanoîne expedition, which laid waste to much of southern Niger in 1898–99. The Birni N'Konni massacre, numbering in the thousands, is one of the most shameful episodes in French colonial history. Although Tuareg revolts in the north continued, culminating in the siege of Agadez in 1916–17, French control over the territory was assured.

French rule wasn't kind to Niger. The colonial administration selectively cultivated the power of traditional chiefs, whose abuses were almost encouraged as a means of de facto control. The imposition of the French franc (in which taxes were paid) drove many agricultural workers to seek work in the cities.

The enforced shift from subsistence farming to cash crops further cemented French dominance, reorienting trade away from traditional trans-Saharan routes towards European-controlled coastal markets. Fallow periods, which previously preserved a fragile ecological balance, were replaced with high-density farming, the effects of which still contribute to the ongoing march of the Sahara.

Niger received less investment than other French colonies – by independence in 1960, the French had built 1032km of paved roads in West Africa, only 14km of them Nigerien.

Independence

In 1958 Charles de Gaulle offered France's 12 West African colonies a choice between self-government in a French union or immediate independence. Hundreds of thousands of votes conveniently disappeared, enabling the French to claim that Niger wished to remain within its sphere of influence.

Djibo Bakari and the radical Sawaba party campaigned for complete independence, and the infuriated colonial government banned the party, exiling Bakari. This left Hamani Diori, leader of the Parti Progressiste Nigérien (PPN), as the only presidential candidate when independence arrived in 1960.

Diori's repressive one-party state maintained close French ties. Diori survived several unsuccessful coups before the great Sahel drought of 1968–74, when food stocks were discovered in several ministerial homes. This was the final straw and Lieutenant Colonel Seyni Kountché overthrew Diori in a bloody coup. Kountché, then president, established a military ruling council.

Post-Independence Period

Kountché and Niger hit the proverbial jackpot in 1968 when uranium was discovered near Arlit. Between 1974 and 1979 uranium prices quintupled, permitting some ambitious projects, including the 'uranium highway' to Agadez and Arlit. Yet not everyone was smiling: the cost of living rose dramatically and the poorest were worse off.

In the early 1980s the price of uranium plummeted, halting the construction boom. Tragedy then struck with the drought of 1983. For the first time in recorded history the Niger River stopped flowing. Kountché's reputation for honesty helped him weather the unrest, which included an unsuccessful coup, but

in 1987 he died from brain cancer, and was replaced by his chosen successor, Ali Saïbou.

Saïbou immediately embarked on a process of constitution-making. In 1989 he formed a new political organisation called the Mouvement National pour une Société de Développement (MNSD), simultaneously enforcing Kountché's ban on political parties. He then stood as the sole candidate for presidential election (all in the name of national unity) and rather unsurprisingly, he won.

Nigeriens were keenly aware of the political changes sweeping West Africa and mass student demonstrations and worker strikes were held in 1990, protesting about Saïbou's fictitious democracy. After security forces killed several demonstrating at Niamey University, public outcry forced a reluctant Saïbou to convene a national conference in 1991. The resulting interim government ruled until the first multiparty elections in 1993, which made Mahamane Ousmane the country's first Hausa head of state.

His democratic reign was short-lived. A military junta, led by Colonel Ibrahim Bare Mainassara staged a successful coup in January 1996. Elections held in July were won by Mainassara – hardly surprising considering he'd dissolved the independent election commission and confined his main opponents to house arrest.

The Arrival of Democracy

In 1999, during widespread strikes and economic stagnation, the commander of the presidential guard assassinated Mainassara as he was boarding a helicopter. The prime minister described the death, without any apparent irony, as 'an unfortunate accident'. The coup leader, Major Daoud Mallam Wanké, quickly re-established democracy and peaceful elections were held in late 1999. Mamadou Tandja, a former minister of the interior and leader of the Mouvement National Pour La Société de Développement (MNSD), was elected with over 59% of the vote. In the 113-seat national assembly, Mamadou forged a coalition majority with supporters of former President Ousmane.

Niger inadvertently became dragged into the Iraq WMD debate when former US president George W Bush claimed in his 2003 State of the Union address that Saddam Hussein had attempted to procure uranium yellowcake from Niger. This theory was later debunked

TWENTY-FIRST–CENTURY SLAVES

In October 2008 an ECOWAS court ruling in Niamey sent shockwaves across West Africa and made headlines around the world. Hadijatou Mani, a 24-year-old woman who had been sold as a sex slave aged just 12 years old, won her case against the Nigerien government, who she claimed failed to protect her from slavery. Having been sold into slavery by her mother's master, Hadijatou was used throughout her childhood as a sexual slave as well as suffering brutal beatings and being made to work long hours for no pay as a domestic servant. The case was a significant victory for the antislavery lobby as it comprehensively undermined the Nigerien government's claims that slavery is now a thing of the past in Niger.

Perhaps the most astonishing thing about the case was that despite slavery being made illegal in Niger in 2003, when finally set free in 2005, Hadijatou was unable to leave her master, as local courts ruled that they were de facto married as a result of their previous master–sex slave relationship. Her attempts to escape were punished, with one local judge ruling that she was a 'disobedient girl'. When Hadijatou did finally escape and later married, her husband was jailed for bigamy rather than her former master. The case was taken up by Nigerien antislavery campaign group Timidria and Anti Slavery International, and was finally decided by judges from neighbouring Ecowas countries, proving to be an acute embarrassment to the Nigerien government when the verdict was recorded.

Throughout the Sahel slavery remains a tragic reality for thousands of people, yet Niger has a bigger problem than most, with slavery continuing to exist in rural areas through de facto hereditary ownership of a slave caste. Back in 2003 Timidria published a survey claiming that some 870,000 people live in conditions of forced labour in Niger, or some 7% of the population. For more information, or to donate money to help fight slavery in Niger, see www.antislavery.org.

after much intrigue in Washington, leading to the unmasking of CIA agent Valerie Plame and the imprisonment of former Vice President Dick Cheney's former head of staff.

The one bright spot in recent years is the impressive transition from military to democratic rule. In 2004 the first-ever successful municipal elections were held to select members of 265 local councils. The municipal elections were followed by a second presidential election in November 2004 in which President Mamadou was re-elected with 65% of the vote.

Niger Today

On the home front things a series of unpleasant events have defined Niger to the outside world. The devastating food crisis of 2005 saw the return of all-too-familiar scenes of hunger created by a mixture of desertification, climate change, the growing of cash crops instead of ones used to feed the local population and the crippling national debt. Another recurring theme returned in 2007 when the Tuareg Rebellion reignited after lying dormant for over a decade (see the boxed text, p606). A series of attacks against government troops, including a mine detonation in Niamey, meant that the entire of the northern region was closed to

tourists until late 2008, devastating the local economy that was largely reliant on foreign visitors. At the time of writing there was no prospect of resolution.

In 2008 Niger yet again made headlines around the world again for less-than-positive reasons when in a landmark case an Ecowas court found Niger guilty of not protecting a young woman from the continued practice of slavery in the country (see the boxed text, above), another piece of bad press for a country that appears to be a magnet for negative headlines.

The presidential elections in November 2009 will be an important test for Niger's fragile and imperfect democracy. While at the time of writing Mamadou is unable to seek a second term, apparently spontaneous demonstrations in Niamey in late 2008 demanded that his term be extended. Whether or not this happens remains to be seen, but going by the track records of other leaders in West Africa giving up power voluntarily, it seems a distinct possibility.

THE CULTURE
The National Psyche

Although arguably the poorest people in the world, Nigeriens are a proud bunch, quick with welcoming smiles and occasional spontaneous acts of generosity. Similarly refreshing is their willingness to stay and work to improve their nation, unlike citizens of some African countries, who admit they'd jump at the first chance to emigrate.

Although over 90% of the population is devoutly Muslim, the government is steadfastly secular and Islam takes on a more relaxed public persona here than in other countries with similar demographics. Women don't cover their faces, alcohol is quietly consumed by many and some Tuareg, recognising the harsh dictates of desert life, even ignore the annual Ramadan fast. The area around Maradi is the exception, where Muslims have long been calling for Islamic conservatism and the imposition of Islamic Sharia law.

Slavery has long been part of Niger's culture and remarkably it was only outlawed in May 2003. However, human rights groups believe that tens of thousands of Nigeriens still live in subjugation (see boxed text, opposite).

Daily Life

Above all, Islam plays the greatest role in Nigeriens' daily life, shaping beliefs and thoughts. Yet little of this is visible to the visitor. The one exception is at *salat* (prayer), when the country grinds to a halt at dawn, noon, afternoon, sunset and nightfall – buses and bush taxis will break their journeys to partake.

Religion aside, survival occupies the vast majority of Nigeriens' days. About 90% of the population make their tenuous living from agriculture and livestock, with the majority living on less than US$1 per day. Having numerous children to help with the burdening workload is a necessity for many families, a fact contributing to the rising population. For the majority of children, their youth is spent working and not studying – only 35% of boys and 21% of girls attend primary school, which leads to staggering adult illiteracy rates (only 7% of women and 21% of men are literate) and sentences further generations to a life in the fields.

Family life is further complicated by widespread polygamy and, more recently, urbanisation drawing men away from their families to seek work. The 2005 food crisis highlighted this phenomenon, when aid workers found numerous wives and children starving because their granaries, while stocked with sorghum and millet, were locked by long-

absent fathers and husbands. Traditionally in polygamist families the head of the household controls the family produce, while his wives must each fend for themselves and their children using only a small plot of land received at marriage.

The Tuareg, meanwhile, are effectively monogamous, and women enjoy greater independence, owning their own livestock and spending the income on themselves, while men must provide for the home.

Population

Niger boasts the highest birth rate in the world – women have a staggering average of eight children and the population is exploding, growing from 6.6 million in 1985 to 12.9 in 2007, and predicted to reach 21.4 million by 2025 – a time bomb in a country already hopelessly ill equipped as it is to look after its citizens. An astounding 49% of the population is less than 15 years of age. Currently, 23% of the population lives in urban areas, though this number is steadily rising and is expected to reach 35% by 2025.

More than 90% of the population lives in the south, mostly in the southwest. The south's population is dominated by the Hausa, who make up 56% of the country's populace, and the Songhaï-Djerma, who are centred on the Niger River and comprise 22% of Niger's population. The next-largest groups are the traditionally nomadic Fulani (8.5%) and Tuareg (8%), both found in Niger's north, and the Kanuri (4.3%), located between Zinder and Chad. The remaining 1.2% is made up of the Gourmantché in the south and the Toubou and Arabs in the north.

SPORT

Traditional wrestling, which intriguingly incorporates numerous Nigerien cultural elements like the use of prayers, poems and the wearing of grigri (charms), is overwhelmingly popular. Unfortunately it only occurs a few times a year.

Camel racing is a favourite Tuareg sport. The usual routine involves a champion riding off into the desert with a woman's indigo scarf. Competitors ride in hot pursuit and whoever is able to successfully grab the scarf wins. During the race, women decked out in their best silver jewellery cheer on the riders, singing and clapping to the sound of drums.

RELIGION

Over 90% of the population is Muslim and a small percentage of urban dwellers are Christian. A few rural communities still practise traditional animist religions.

Due to the strong influence of Nigeria's Islamic community in southern Niger, there's a minority of Muslims in areas like Maradi calling for Islamic conservatism and the imposition of Islamic Sharia law.

ARTS

The best-known artisans must be the Tuareg silversmiths, who produce a wide range of necklaces, striking square amulets and ornamental silver daggers, complete with leather hilts. In a Muslim country, the most unusual items are the stylised silver crosses, each with intricate filigree designs that represent towns and regions boasting significant Tuareg populations. The most famous cross is the *Croix d'Agadez*. Tuareg see the crosses as powerful talismans that protect against ill fortune and the evil eye.

The leatherwork of the *artisans du cuir*, found in Zinder, is also particularly well regarded. They produce traditional items such as saddle-bags, cushions and tasselled pouches (which hang from men's necks and carry tobacco or money), along with attractive modern items like sandals, backpacks and briefcases.

Beautifully unique to Niger are the vibrant Djerma blankets, or *kountas*, produced from patterns of bright cotton strips.

Although most Nigerien music remains traditional, there are some artists breaking moulds. Niger's first international album was 1994's *Niamey Twice*, by Saadou Bori and Moussa Poussy. Other bands to look out for are Mamar Kassey, an eight-piece band that combines Hausa, Djerma and Peul sounds, and Etran Finatawa, a Wodaabé-Tuareg band whose 2008 *Desert Crossroads* album is well worth a listen.

ENVIRONMENT
The Land

Niger is West Africa's second-largest country and is landlocked 650km from the sea. The Niger River, Africa's third-longest river, flows through 300km of the country's southwest.

While the south is largely flat and not particularly dramatic, the north's remarkable Aïr Mountains, which rise more than 2000m and culminate in the Bagzane peaks and the Ténéré Desert's spectacularly sweeping sand dunes, are by far the country's most impressive natural sights.

Wildlife

In desert regions, camels are the most common animal visitors will see, but gazelle herds still exist in remote areas (dorcas gazelles being the most common) and nocturnal fennecs (small foxes with large ears) are occasionally glimpsed. The Saharan cheetah is extremely rare.

Besides Kouré's graceful giraffes (p590) and the hippos bobbing in the Niger River, you also have the chance to see crocodiles, monkeys, buffalo and even lions in the Parc Regional du W (p592).

National Parks

Niger hosts part of one of West Africa's better national parks, Parc Regional du W (p592). Its dry savannah environment straddles the Niger River and welcomes an impressive array of bird and animal life.

The astounding Aïr Mountains (p603) and western section of the Ténéré Desert (p603) have also been designated as the Réserve Naturelle Nationale de l'Aïr et du Ténéré.

Environmental Issues

Today, two-thirds of Niger is desert and the rest is Sahel (the semidesert zone south of the Sahara). Desertification, Niger's greatest environmental problem, is primarily due to overgrazing and deforestation. Adding to the woes is the abundant quartz-rich sand, which is unsuitable for high-yield crops and prevents anchoring of topsoil, causing erosion.

Community-based projects continue, with limited success, to facilitate reafforestation by encouraging villagers to build windbreaks and establish nurseries. For more information, see the boxed text, p89. Irrigation projects in the north have also brought life back to once-barren soil, with the village of Azad now among those supplying Agadez with fruit. Other measures – such as the development of a new stove that burns less wood, and the introduction of coppicing rather than chopping down trees – are also helping combat the problem.

To help rebuild livestock herds (after they were decimated by the droughts in the early 1990s) and generate income, one aid scheme 'loans' young goats to farmers to tend until the animals mature and reproduce. The animals' offspring are then 'repaid' to the aid scheme. However, it's a fragile balancing act to prevent herds from growing beyond the land's carrying capacity.

FOOD & DRINK

Dates, yoghurt, rice and mutton are standard northern fare among the Tuareg, while rice with sauce and *capitaine* (Nile perch) are the most common southern dishes. Standard fare at restaurants is grilled fish or chicken with chips, or beef brochettes, rice and couscous. Niamey boasts Niger's best restaurants, with Chinese, French, Italian and Lebanese selections. Outside the capital, vegetarian options are very limited.

Tap water in the cities is generally safe, as are the bags of chilled water sold by children. If they don't float your boat, bottled water and soft drinks are everywhere. Sitting for a cup of Tuareg tea is as rewarding as it's thirst quenching.

Locally made Biére Niger and the slightly better Flag are both available in all restaurants, although outside Niamey they can be hard to find in shops.

NIAMEY

pop 795,000

Compared to many West African capitals, Niamey is a charmer, with the Niger River and its verdant banks providing a focal point to the city, more than its fair share of restaurants and far livelier nightlife than you'd expect in a devoutly Muslim country. Managing to be both bustling seat of government and relaxed backwater, the Nigerien capital is the kind of place where locals are rarely too busy to greet you with a friendly '*bonjour*' and pass the time of day with you in time-honoured West African fashion.

Since becoming the capital, Niamey has experienced fantastic growth – from around 2000 people in the 1930s to almost 800,000 today. Although once-smart government buildings from the '70s do rise from town's centre (a reminder of uranium's past sky-high prices), Niamey still has a traditional African ambience that gives the city its charm.

With a number of interesting trips possible from here, not to mention a good national museum and plenty of local markets in the city itself to keep you busy, you can comfortably spend several days here.

ORIENTATION

Niamey is quite spread out, which means a bit more walking than in other Sahel capitals. The street pattern can be confusing, but thankfully excellent street signs now aid navigation. If you're spending much time here, the excellent Editions Laure Kane map of the city is invaluable.

One of Niamey's major thoroughfares is Ave de l'Amitié/Route de l'Aéroport, which links Kennedy Bridge with the airport and Niger's only highway heading east across the country. Another is Blvd de l'Indépendance, which heads northwest out of town towards Tillabéri, Ayorou and Mali. A second bridge over the Niger a short distance west of the Kennedy Bridge was being built at the time of writing.

INFORMATION

Cultural Centres

American Cultural Center (☎ 20 73 31 69; Rue de la Tapoa; ☼ 8am-4.30pm Mon-Fri) You can use the library here, which has a selection of English-language newspapers and magazines. There are also regular film screenings.

Centre Culturel Franco-Nigérien Jean Rouch (☎ 20 73 48 34; Rue du Musée; ☼ 9am-12.30pm & 3.30pm-6.30pm Tue-Sat, 9am-noon Sun) Besides the library there's a busy schedule of lectures, exhibits, dance and theatre as well as a lovely garden bar perfect for a sundowner. Films are shown on Tuesdays at 8.30pm (CFA500).

Centre Culturel Oumarou Ganda (☎ 20 74 09 03; Blvd de Mali Béro; ☼ hours vary) Often closed, this centre sponsors a variety of African cultural activities that include traditional wrestling, dancing, local films, concerts and art exhibitions.

Internet Access

Cyber@Bebto (Blvd de l'Indépendance; per hr CFA500; ☼ 7.30am-11pm) A handy option for those staying in west Niamey.

Cybercafe Terminus (Rue du Sahel; per hr CFA500; ☼ 9am-11pm) A well-located option with lots of terminals.

Cybernet (Rue du Grand Hôtel; per hr CFA600; ☼ 8am-11pm) The best place in town, this central internet cafe has speedy connections and air con.

Centre Culturel Franco-Nigérien Jean Rouch (Rue du Musée; per hr CFA500; ☼ 9am-12.30pm & 3.30pm-6.30pm Tue-Sat, 9am-noon Sun) There's a small room for internet access inside the main building of the CCFN.

NIGER

NIAMEY

To Malian Consulate (1.2km);
Boubon (25km); Tillabéri (114km);
Ayorou (198km); Mali Border (237km)

To French
Embassy (150m);
American Embassy
(300m); Nigerian &
Algerian Embassies
(1.3km); Hôtel
les Rôniers (6.5km)

To Gare Routière for Burkina
Faso (1km); Say (56km);
Parc Regional du W (97km);
Ouagadougou (500km)

NIGER

Blvd de Syrte Maina

Blvd de Mali Béro

Ave de la jeunesse

Rond-
point Yantala

Yantala

Ave de la Gaulle
la republique

Blvd de la République

Corniche de Yantala

Ave du Palais

Blvd de l'Indépendance

Rue des Dallois

Ave du Général de Gaulle

Ave du Fleuve Niger

Rue de la Tapoa

Plateau

Presidential Palace

Pl Nelson Mandela

Ave des Ministères

Pl de la Republique

Ave du Counier 1ens

Blvd du Zarmaganda

Stade General
Seyni Kountche

Palais des Sports

Blvd de l'Indépendance

Ave Mamni Luther King

Ave du President Kah

Blvd de la Liberté

Rue de Kaleoua

Niger River

Ave Millerand

Palais du Congrès

Kennedy
Bridge

Rond-
point
Kennedy

See Enlargement

Rue de la Maire

Rue de Calweye

Rue du Souvenir

Rue de la Copro

Ave de

Blvd de la Liberté

Rue du Maroc

Corniche de Gambek

Niger River

Rond-point
Maourey

Ave de Maourey

Rue NB 29

Ave de la Maire

Ave du Commerce

Ave du President Heinrich Luebke

Rue de Calweye

Rue du Président

Rue Nasser

Grande Poste

Rue de Coulibaly Kalleye

Blvd du Stade

Rue du Stade

Rue de l'Ass

SV-26

Pl de la
Concertation

Assemblée
Nationale

Stadium

Pl
Monteil

Ave de l'Amitié

Rue du Souvenir

Rue du Maroc

Rue du Grand Hôtel

Rond-point
Grand Hôtel

Rue du Terminus

Rue de l'Afrique

0 —————— 200 m
0 —————— 0.1 miles

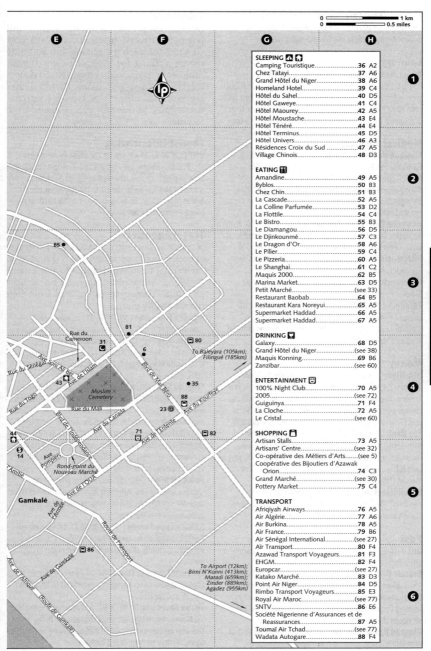

NIGER

Pl@anet Cyber Cafe (Blvd de Mali Béro; per hr CFA400; 8am-midnight) The cheapest access in town, albeit on ancient terminals near the Wadata Autogare.

Laundry

Most hotels offer a overnight laundry service at reasonable rates (CFA100 to CFA200 per item). Another option is **Pressing Top Net** (☎ 20 72 21 03; Ave du Château d'Eau) where you'll get a slower but very reasonably priced service.

Medical Services

Clinique de Gamkalé (☎ 20 73 20 33; Corniche de Gamkalé; 8.30am-12.30pm & 3.30-6.30pm Mon-Fri, 8.30am-12.30pm Sat) Consultations cost CFA11,000 during normal working hours, twice that at other times. Emergency services are open 24 hours, and the head doctor speaks English.

Nouvelle Poly-Clinic Pro-Santé (☎ 20 72 26 50, 20 72 50 50; Ave du Général de Gaulle; 24hr) A respected local clinic. Consultations cost between CFA3000 and CFA5000.

Pharmacie El Nasr (☎ 20 73 47 72; Rue du Président Heinrich Lubké)

Pharmacie du Terminus (☎ 20 73 58 38; Rue du Sahel; 9am-9pm)

Tafadeck (☎ 20 73 20 34; Rue du Président Heinrich Lubké; 8.30am-12.30pm & 2.30-6.30pm Mon-Fri, 8.30am-12.30pm Sat) This is the centrally located office of Niamey's best dentist.

Money

BIA-Niger (Rue du Commerce; 7.45am-12.30pm & 2.15pm-3.45pm Mon-Fri, 8-11.30am Sat) Charges 2% commission on travellers cheques in euros and dollars and can change most major currencies. Credit-card cash advances cost CFA10,000 per transaction and are available upstairs.

Eco Bank (Blvd de la Liberté; 8.30am-3.30 Mon-Fri, 9am-1pm Sat, to 3pm Sun) There's a painful CFA10,000 commission for changing travellers cheques, but changing cash is free. There's another handy branch by the Petit Marché (Ave de la Mairie).

Grand Hôtel du Niger (Rond-point du Grand Hôtel; 24hr) The hotel's front desk will change cash for free. There's also a Western Union office here.

Post

DHL (☎ 20 73 33 59; Blvd de la Liberté) has a helpful office for international express deliveries.

Grande Poste (☎ 20 73 31 44; Rue de la Grande Poste; 7.30am-12.15pm & 3.30-6.30pm Mon-Fri, 8am-noon Sat) Home to Niamey's poste restante service, as well as housing Chronopost, the most reliable international parcel service in the country.

Plateau Poste (Place de la République) Another central post office.

Telephone

Dozens of private telecentres now dot Niamey's streets. International calls cost CFA150 for each 10-second block. Some charge nothing for incoming calls. If your mobile is unlocked, consider buying a local SIM card and using that, as rates are low and competitive even for international calls. Skype calls can be made from internet cafes.

Tourist Information

ONT (☎ 20 73 24 47; Rue de Président Heinrich Lübke; 7.30am-4.30pm Sat-Thu, 7.30am-12.30pm Fri) Though little English is spoken, the staff at this government agency is helpful and has up-to-date information about travel within Niger. Latest updates on travel in the north of the country can also be got here.

Travel Agencies

Niamey is currently swamped with travel agencies, many of whom have relocated to the capital from Agadez due to the Tuareg Rebellion. Some of the agencies below have no formal Niamey offices, but work from their homes and by phone.

Agadez Tourisme (☎ 20 44 01 70; www.agadez -tourisme.com) Akly and Céline's much-loved company now operates from Niamey, even though their excellent hotel, l'Auberge d'Azel, remains open in Agadez. It currently offers Niger River tours, trips to Parc W and vehicle hire.

Croix du Sud (☎ 20 35 05 15; www.niger-croixdusud .com; Blvd Mali Béro) This well-run new agency has its own Niamey hotel, rents vehicles with drivers, sells plane tickets and offers a large program of tours throughout the country.

Expeditions Ténéré Voyages (☎ 20 73 54 12; www .agence-expeditionstenere.com; Rue du Parc W) Another northern travel agency now offering tours of the south, vehicle hire and tailor-made excursions.

Point Air Niger (PAN; ☎ 20 73 40 26; www.point -afrique.com; Rue du Sahel) The local office for French travel agency Point Afrique, PAN offers tours and excursions for independent travellers too.

Sahara Expeditions (☎ 96 98 58 71; sahara_expedi tions2000@yahoo.fr; Ave du Château d'Eau) This desert specialist currently offers car hire and excursions in the South.

Satguru Travel & Tours (☎ 20 73 69 31; Rue de la Copro) Satguru offers air tickets, excursions to Kouré and Parc W and car hire.

Turbo Tours (☎ 96 96 09 92; wallymamoudou@yahoo .fr) Mamoudou Wally, known to everyone as Turbo, heads this new venture renting 4WDs and organising all the usual tours. Warmly recommended by travellers.

Visa Extensions

Direction de la Surveillance du Territoire (☎ 20 73 37 43, ext 249; Rue de Président Heinrich Lübke). Niger visa extensions available, for further details see p608.

DANGERS & ANNOYANCES

Niamey is a safe city by regional standards. In the day, market pickpockets are your only worry. At night, as you would in most big cities, avoid carrying valuables openly and don't walk down dark and deserted streets. Take a taxi if you want to leave central, well-lit areas after dark. One area to avoid at night is Kennedy Bridge and the long, dark dirt roads along the riverbank, as these are home to slum areas and foreigners will be easy targets for opportunist muggers.

SIGHTS & ACTIVITIES
Musée National du Niger

This architecturally interesting **museum** (☎ 20 73 43 21; Rue du Musée; admission adult/student CFA1000/500, camera/video fee CFA1000/5000; ⏲ 9am-noon & 3.30-5.30pm Tue-Sun) is one of the better national exhibitions in West Africa. Numerous themed pavilions, each tipping their hat to Hausa architecture, give visitors a peek into Niger's history. The Pablo Toucet pavilion displays the dress of Niger's different ethnic groups – a quick way to train the eye for differentiating these groups as you travel in Niger. But it's the sprawling **zoo** (⏲ 8am-6.30pm Tue-Sun) that takes up most of the space. Crocs, hippos, monkeys, parrots and a selection of other indigenous unfortunates are crammed into unforgivably small cages and compounds.

At the museum's **artisans' centre** (⏲ 8am-6.30pm Tue-Sun), you can watch the creative process and purchase silver, leather and other items direct from artists, while opposite, the Boubou Hana pavilion's 100 million–year-old *Sarcosuchus imperator*, or 'Super Croc', and a host of other dinosaur skeletons are an awesome sight. Nearby, anchored in concrete, is the infamous Arbre de Ténéré (see p603).

Markets
GRANDE MARCHÉ

Wade through the chaos that is the exterior of the **Grand Marché** (Blvd de la Liberté; ⏲ 8am-6pm) and dive into the labyrinth of narrow lanes shaded by a kaleidoscope of tattered sheets. Although it's hard to ignore the heady aroma of spices, piles of colourful clothes, boisterous vendors and steady torrent of local shoppers,

if you manage to find a good hiding spot, the market is a wonderful place to observe Nigeriens interacting.

PETIT MARCHÉ

For our money the **Petit Marché** (Ave de la Mairie; ⏲ 8am-6pm), right in the centre of town, is even more picturesque and atmospheric than its bigger brother, with fewer imported goods and far more locally produced fruit, veg, spices and delicacies. As with any market, watch where your wallet is as pickpockets are rife.

Grande Mosquée

Rising above eastern Niamey is this impressive **mosque** (Ave de l'Islam), with its massive minaret and bulbous green dome. Everything from the elaborately carved exterior wooden doors to the interior's 16 ornate pillars and grand tiled dome were financed by CFA500 million of Libyan money. If you linger outside, someone will offer you a short tour (CFA2000 is fair). The view and breeze atop the minaret are well worth the dizzying 171 steps to get there.

Pirogue Trips

There's no better way to experience the Niger River than from aboard a peaceful pirogue skimming its surface at sunset. Although numerous 'guides' in town offer just such a trip, your cheapest option is to visit the piroguers themselves, on the riverfront between Palais du Congrés and La Flottile restaurant. After negotiating, four-passenger punted pirogues should cost about CFA2000 per person per hour – triple that if you want a motorised boat. If negotiating isn't your bag talk to one of the Niamey-based travel agencies, as they can all organise a trip (see opposite)

For more adventure, and some hippo action, you can hire a pirogue in Boubon for the two-hour trip downstream to Niamey (see p589 for more details).

Swimming

By the mid-afternoon the heat can be punishing and an hour or two by the pool can be in order. The best pool in town is the excellent **Piscine Olympique d'Etat** (Rue du Sahel; admission CFA1000; ⏲ 10am-5pm Sat-Thu, 6-10.30pm Fri) a superb 50m public pool by the Niger River. Other options include the pool at the **Hôtel Gaweye** (Ave Mitterrand; admission CFA2500), another large pool, complete with deck chairs to go with river views. The **Grand Hôtel du Niger** (Rond-point Grand

NIGER

SUPERSIZE ME!

During rare years of bountiful harvests, Niamey's Djerma population celebrates with the renowned Hangandi festival. Although the festivities are good fun, it's really the reputation of the festival's beauty contest that keeps on growing and growing, much like its competitors. For this is no ordinary beauty contest. You see, in the eye of the Djerma beholder, the larger a woman is the more magnificent she becomes. So in the months leading up to Hangandi, beautiful Djerma women who've been chosen to compete (some plucked right off buses!) train by ingesting as much millet, milk and water as they possibly can. The festival culminates with the heaviest, and thus most gorgeous, woman being crowned at the Palais du Congrés. Her reward? Much public admiration and...more food!

Hôtel; admission CFA2000) has a smaller pool with equally grand views.

Other Activities

To get a closer look at Niamey's massive bats in the daylight, head towards Place de la République where you'll find thousands hanging, snoozing and squeaking in the trees lining the compound of Banque Centrale de l'Afrique de l'Ouest. At sunset it's a hive of activity.

Other Niamey activities could include watching the cows wading and swimming across the Niger early in the morning or late in the evening, watching the sunset from the Kennedy Bridge and wandering along the corniches where you'll see clothes being washed in the river and see (and certainly smell) the work at the tanneries that line the riverbank.

FESTIVALS & EVENTS

Of Niger's many festivals, the only one centred in Niamey is Hangandi. See the boxed text, above for more weighty details.

SLEEPING

It's always best to reserve a room in advance – Niamey's hotels can be full when you least expect it.

Budget

Camping Touristique (☎ 20 75 44 89; Blvd des Sy et Mamar; camping per person CFA2000, plus per vehicle CFA1000;

P) This dusty site in western Niamey is the only option for campers. It's a long walk (or CFA200 in a shared taxi) to town. The site is run by the next-door Hôtel Univers.

Hôtel Moustache (☎ 96 59 66 65; Ave Soni Ali Ber; r with/without bathroom CFA7,500/5,000, r with bathroom & air con CFA10,000; X) Niamey's cheapest bed can be found at this memorable establishment. Its relatively attractive blue exterior belies the insalubrious 33 rooms that await you inside, where stinky bathrooms and mosquito-infested rooms are only slightly more welcoming than the crowd of hookers hanging out in the courtyard. It's well worth spending an extra CFA1000 to stay at Chez Tatayi.

our pick **Chez Tatayi** (☎ 20 74 12 81; www.tatayi .com; Rue de Président Heinrich Lubké; dm CFA6000, s/d without bathroom from CFA12,000/14,000; P X ⅁) Now in the heart of the city after a recent move, this charming hotel is stacked full of character and makes for the best budget option in Niamey. All rooms are spotless, share decent bathrooms and are set in shady courtyard with a small pool, communal kitchen and social area including a good library. For aircon add CFA4000.

Village Chinois (☎ 20 72 33 98; Blvd du Zarmaganda; s/d without bathroom CFA8500/9500; P X) In no way resembling a Chinese village, this sprawling place nevertheless offers passable chalet-style accommodation with basic bathrooms shared between two rooms. All rooms have air-con, although that's the extent of the frills here.

Midrange

Hôtel Univers (☎ 20 75 44 89; www.univers-isa-business .com; Blvd des Sy et Mamar; s/d/ste CFA22,500/25,500/33,500; X P) A relative newcomer to the local hotel scene, the Univers is located in a tidy, secure lot with individual circular cottages providing comfy accommodation. Each cottage has air-con, telephone and TV. Plans to build a swimming pool and install wi-fi are mooted for the future.

Hôtel du Sahel (☎ 20 73 24 31; hotel_sahel2006@ yahoo.fr; Rue du Sahel; s/d CFA25,550/28,500; P X ⅁) Having built a collection of spotless new bungalows in its large forecourt, the Sahel has rather rested on its laurels with its older rooms in the main building. These are fine, but dated, which is a shame, as many have superb river views. The terrace, where tasty *brochettes* are served up each evening, is still a great place for a sundowner. There's no pool or wi-fi, but the Piscine Olympique d'Etat is moments away and there's terminal access (CFA1000 per hour) from the lobby.

Hôtel Maourey (☎ 20 73 28 50; Rond-point Maourey; s/tw/ste CFA25,000/30,000/35,000; 🖳) Although this friendly establishment is located perfectly in the heart of town, rooms (all with air-con, TV and telephone) are on the dark side and some are musty thanks to the old carpeting and poor bathrooms – check out a few before you settle.

Résidences Croix du Sud (☎ 20 73 44 30; www.niger -croixdusud.com; Rue NB 29; s/d/ste CFA27,500/37,500/45,000; 🅿 🖳 🛜) A welcome addition to Niamey's midrange options is this professionally run guest house near the Petit Marché. The rooms are modern, clean and well equipped, while English-speaking staff is friendly and usually happy to give out the free wi-fi code if you ask nicely.

Hôtel Terminus (☎ 20 73 26 92; hotermi@intnet.ne; Rue du Sahel; s/d from CFA37,000-45,000/45,000-50,000, ste CFA60,000; 🅿 🖳 🛜 🛒) This large, centrally located complex is highly recommended for its friendly staff and pleasant atmosphere. The spacious bungalows are the cheapest option, many with African furnishings as well as TV, fridge and phone, while the newer, pricier rooms have better bathrooms, but feel a little sterile. Free wi-fi, a large pool and pleasant gardens sweeten the deal.

Hôtel Ténéré (☎ 20 73 20 20; contact@hotel-tenere -niger.com; Blvd de la Liberté; s/d CFA44,500/51,000, ste from CFA60,500-70,500; 🖳 🅿 🛜 🛒) Now gleaming (in its public areas, at least) after a recent revamp, somehow the rooms have missed out on the action and the ones we saw remained rather run down. Location isn't great either, and while free wi-fi is a boon, this is a poor deal overall.

Top End

Grand Hôtel du Niger (☎ 20 73 26 41; www.grand hotelniger.com; Rond-point du Grand Hôtel; s/d CFA49,500/59,500, ste from CFA60,000-87,000; 🅿 🖳 🛜 🛒) Niamey's top choice is without doubt the Grand, whose car park overflows with the vast Landcruisers of the NGO and diplomatic classes and whose gorgeous river-view terrace is the hang-out of choice for the expat community come sunset. Rooms are spotless, large and comfortable, with satellite TV, safe, fridge, phone and lovely river views from many. Our only gripe is that wi-fi is still charged and only available in the lobby.

Homeland Hotel (☎ 20 73 32 82; www.homelandhotel -niger.com; Ave du Général de Gaulle; r/ste CFA45,500/75,500; 🖳 🅿 🛜 🛒) A favourite with NGO workers,

this very comfortable option at the heart of Niamey's government quarter boasts clean rooms with decent bathrooms, satellite TV, phone, fridge and air con. Paid wi-fi is available in some rooms only (request this when you book) and the shady pool and terrace make for a pleasant communal area.

Hôtel Gaweye (☎ 20 72 27 10; www.hotel-gaweye.net; Ave Mitterrand; r with city/river view CFA70,000/75,000, ste from CFA100,000; 🅿 🖳 🛜 🛒) Begun next to the Palais du Congrés during the uranium boom, this towering riverside complex was once the jewel of Niamey's hotels. Its standards have slipped though, and the tired rooms appear to have been untouched since they were built, making them unsuitable for this price range. Free wi-fi and a superb pool and great river views do something to compensate, but arguably not enough.

EATING

Niamey enjoys the best culinary scene in the country, and after a long trek through the Sahel you'll enjoy splashing out at some of the places below, whether it be on fresh local *capitaine* (Nile perch) or on some of the city's more international options.

African & Middle Eastern

Byblos (☎ 20 72 44 05; Blvd de l'Indépendance; mains CFA1000-2000; 🕑 noon-11pm) This Niamey institution serves up superb Lebanese food: spicy baba ghanoush, fresh hummus and delicious falafels combine to make a perfect meal, all served up in a pleasant garden.

our pick Le Diamangou (☎ 96 29 14 17; Corniche de Gamkalé; meals CFA2000-4000; 🕑 9am-11pm) Hands-down the best place in town for an atmospheric setting, Le Diamangou is housed on a creaky boat moored on the Niger River (smother yourself if insect repellent) from where the views are gorgeous. The fresh *capitaine* here is divine, as are the *beignets de crevettes* (prawn fritters). Like La Flottile, this place isn't in the safest neck of the woods, so arrange a taxi after sunset. The staff can call you a taxi, or ask one of them to walk you to the main road (as we did).

Maquis 2000 (cnr St 19 & St 26; meals CFA2500-5800; 🕑 lunch Sun, dinner daily) This Ivorian-style open-air restaurant has a varied menu including *brochette de capitaine* and *crevettes grillées* (grilled prawns). It's a fun and friendly place on a sandy backstreet.

Le Djinkounmé (☎ 20 72 21 81; Ave du Fleuve Niger; meals CFA3000-7000; 🕑 lunch & dinner Mon-Sat) This unassuming restaurant is one of Niamey's best, offering a mouth-watering selection of African dishes from as far afield as Congo, Benin and Cameroon. The *yassa au poisson* (Nile perch in a lemon and onion sauce) was especially good on our last visit, although the manager warned us that the establishment is likely to change hands soon – hopefully its high standards will endure.

La Flottile (☎ 21 76 58 55; Corniche de Yantala; mains CFA3000-8500; ☺ 10am-2pm & 5-11pm Wed-Mon) The shady garden of this friendly restaurant is a perfect place to indulge in some of the River Niger's tastiest fish. The menu is all about *capitaine* – try the delicious fish soup, which is lightly curried and full of flavour, while for a main course choose the *capitaine braisé* over the *capitaine pané*; the latter is breaded and fried but tasteless, the former is sublime. It's not safe to walk here after sunset, so organise a taxi (either call a cab or organise to be picked up).

Asian

La Colline Parfumée (☎ 21 76 97 54; Blvd du Zarmaganda; mains CFA2000-3500; ☺ 10am-1.30pm & 6.30pm-midnight) This long-running Chinese restaurant has recently moved to the north of the city. It still serves up an authentic range of Chinese dishes, including excellent seafood meals.

Chez Chin (☎ 20 72 25 28; Blvd de l'Indépendance; meals CFA3000-4500; ☺ 10.30am-2.30pm, 6-11.30pm) Another excellent Chinese option set in a pleasant garden. The Chinese chef here cooks up a storm – try the fish with black mushroom and the pork with bamboo shoots.

Le Dragon d'Or (☎ 20 73 41 23; Rue de Grand Hôtel; mains CFA2500-7500; ☺ noon-2pm & 6.30-11.30pm) This charming Chinese-Vietnamese restaurant has a traditional interior and a more relaxed garden where unlucky diners are serenaded by a Casio-playing warbler of 1980s classics. In general the food is good, but in our experience the fish and veggie dishes score higher than the meat ones, which we've found to be tough and stringy. The *capitaine pho* (fish soup with noodles) is excellent, as is the Saturday night buffet (CFA8000).

Le Shanghai (☎ 20 75 38 29; Blvd de Mali Béro; meals CFA3500-8500; ☺ lunch & dinner) Run by the same people who brought you the Dragon d'Or, Le Shanghai's Chinese and Vietnamese cuisine is of a similarly high standard to that of Le Dragon d'Or, although it lacks the same garden ambience.

European

La Cascade (☎ 20 73 28 32; Rue NB 29; mains CFA2500-6000; ☺ lunch Tue-Sun, dinner daily; ☒) It may be sepulchrally dark in this popular establishment, complete with eponymous waterfall, but that doesn't stop patrons for coming here to taste the excellent pizza, and selection of other dishes from beef entrecôte to lamb curry.

Le Pilier (☎ 20 72 49 85; Rue de la Tapoa; mains CFA3000-6500; ☺ lunch & dinner Wed-Mon; ☒) One of Niamey's very best, Le Pilier is a favoured haunt of expats. You can choose between the courtyard terrace, the downstairs pizza taverna or the air-con-equipped main dining room. Food is excellent, from the large selection of pizza to the pasta and grills.

Le Pizzeria (☎ 20 74 12 40; Rue du Commerce; pizzas from CFA3100-4100; ☺ 6.30pm-midnight; ☒) The pizzas are excellent – a bit pricey, but they're much larger than what you'll get elsewhere. Le Pizzeria also the heart of Niamey's nightlife district and is a good place to line the stomach before dancing the night away.

Le Bistro (☎ 21 76 24 96; Rue du Fleuve Niger; mains CFA4500-7500; ☺ noon-10pm Tue-Sat, 6-10pm Sun) You'll find it hard to believe you're in Africa at this French-Breton place, which opened in late 2008. There's a sublime selection of Gallic cuisine from *épaule de mouton Bretonne* to *cassolette de mer*. The venture, run by French expats with decades of Africa experience between them, also contains Niger's only wine cellar and a gourmet sandwich bar for those without time for a four-course meal!

Quick Eats

Restaurant Baobab (Ave de Maourey; meals CFA500-3000; ☺ lunch & dinner) A short walk from the Grand Marché, this Senegalese place is a good spot for a simple but tasty lunch. It's usually packed with locals, so share a table and practise your French. We recommend the couscous.

Amandine (☎ 20 73 25 25; Ave de la Mairie; ☺ 5am-midnight) This invaluable addition to Niamey's eating scene is a great place for breakfast, with fresh croissants, good coffee and a host of other pastries. It's home from home to many foreign residents. Takeaway coffee is available, and it will even deliver.

Restaurant Kara Noreyui (Rue du Festival; meals CFA500-2000; ☺ lunch & dinner) This tiny eatery serves up some decent Senegalese dishes and is popular with locals.

The best place for really cheap food on the go is around the Petit Marché, where street stalls and basic eating houses serve *riz sauce* (rice with meat or chicken) for around CFA500. Until 9am they also serve up Nescafé, bread and fried-egg sandwiches for less than CFA500. The food stalls on Rond-point Yantala are similar.

In the late evening along the disco strip of Rue du Commerce, there are some great *suya* stalls (*suya* is Hausa for brochette) opposite the nightclubs; brochettes go for CFA100 a pop. There are also stalls selling Vietnamese snacks (*petit nêms, rouleaux de printemps*) around the city but particularly around the Petit Marché.

Self-Catering

Supermarket Haddad (Rue de Commerce) With two outlets close to each other near the Petit Marché, Haddad is the best and most centrally located supermarket in town.

Petit Marché (Ave de la Mairie) Cheap, fresh produce is available here. Especially good for fruit, veg and spices.

Marina Market (Ave de l'Amitié; 🕑 8am-1pm & 3.30-9pm Mon-Sat, 9am-1pm Sun) Further from the centre, Marina Market is another well-stocked supermarket, selling a good selection of wine among other things.

DRINKING

Grand Hôtel du Niger (Rond-point du Grand Hôtel) Few places can beat this hotel's poolside terrace for a sunset beer – the river views are tremendous, and it's well worth paying double for a bottle here given the setting.

Zanzibar (Rue de Commerce) With colourful flashing lights illuminating the otherwise dark interior, Zanzibar is a funky bar popular with a local preclubbing crowd. It also serves up pizza alongside the Congolese and Arab pop.

Galaxy (Rue du Sahel) Do not miss the absolutely stunning river views from this gem of a bar, hidden behind the Piscine Olympique d'Etat. The beers come with ice stuck to them – making this perfect for a break from the afternoon heat.

Maquis Konning (cnr St 24 & St 19) This open-air bar has a great vibe and is a top spot to meet locals.

ENTERTAINMENT
Nightclubs

Niamey swings in a most un-Muslim way after midnight. Head for the streets around Rue du Commerce for the action, although don't expect things to get moving until midnight.

Both the Hotel Sahel and the Hotel Gaweye have nightclubs that are popular with an expat and middle-class crowd at the weekends. The below are more local variants.

Guiguinya (Ave de l'Entente; admission free; 🕑 open nightly) Belting out African and European beats, this massive place is usually packed with locals (and the odd prostitute). Tear it up beneath the strobing red lights or stick your feet in the sand and chill out under the stars and trees in the courtyard.

2005 (Ave Luebké; cover CFA2500) Reverberating with Western and African tunes, this lively club remains the city's most popular and the best place to cut loose on the dance floor.

La Cloche (Ave Luebké; admission free) If you can get over the number of prostitutes and the glowing Christmas-light interior, this club (next to 2005) can be fun. There's a pool table and the music ranges from Arabic to Western, while the upstairs open-air terrace (complete with table football) is a great place to chill.

Le Cristal (Rue du Commerce; cover CFA5000; 🕑 Wed-Sun from 11pm) A smart option next to La Pizzeria, Le Cristal plays a heady mix of different music and attracts a glam party crowd.

100% Night Club (Ave de la Mairie; cover CFA1000; 🕑 weekends only) This is another Niamey favourite, whose more relaxed entry policy gives the place a laidback, local vibe.

Cinemas

Your only options for cinematic distraction are the **Centre Culturel Franco-Nigérien Jean Rouch** (Rue du Musée; admission CFA500; 🕑 8.30pm Tue), which screens excellent French, American and African films, and the **American Cultural Center** (Rue de la Tapoa; admission free), which plays Hollywood films.

Sport

You may be lucky enough to take in a traditional wrestling match at the **Stade de la Lutte Traditionelle** (Blvd de Mali Béro) or the **Centre Culturel Oumara Ganda** (☎ 20 74 09 03; Ave de l'Islam). Despite being quite the spectacle, they only happen a handful of times a year.

SHOPPING
Art & Craftwork

If you're patient and peruse the nether regions of the **Grand Marché** (Blvd de la Liberté) you'll find a fine selection of goods, including Tuareg and Hausa leatherwork, silver jewellery, *batiks* and tie-dyed cloth. Look out for *les couvertures*

NIGER

Djerma (known locally as a *kountas*) – large, bright strips of cotton sewn together into a blanket, which are truly spectacular and unique to Niger. The largest and most extraordinary *kountas* shouldn't cost more than CFA10,000 to CFA15,000 – as always, haggle within reason.

Also recommended is the museum's **artisans' centre** (Rue du Musée; ✆ closed Mon) and **Coopérative des Métiers d'Arts** (Rue du Musée), which is just up the road. Both of these also offer leather goods. The **artisan stalls** (Rue de Président Heinrich Lübke) south of Petit Marché are bursting with wares, but they are well used to foreigners and prices are higher. Better value is the small shop of the **Coopérative des Bijoutiers d'Azawak Orion** (Ave du Fleuve Niger), where exquisite Tuareg jewellery is for sale.

The handpainted pottery found at the informal **pottery market** (Ave de la Mairie) is bulky but beautiful, and limited leather goods are also sold here.

Music

Original and bootlegged CDs of local and Western music can be bought at the **Grand Marché** (Blvd de la Liberté) or from stalls along Ave Luebké adjacent to the Petit Marché.

GETTING THERE & AWAY
Air

For details of international flights to/from Niamey, see p609. At the time of writing there were no scheduled domestic flights within Niger.

Bus

Long-distance bus services within Niger run both ways along two main axes – the *Axe Arlit* (Niamey–Birni N'Konni–Tahoua–Agadez–Arlit) and the *Axe Zinder* (Niamey–Birni N'Konni–Maradi–Zinder). Services are offered by state-run **SNTV** (✆ 20 73 30 20; Ave de Gamkalé) and a host of private competitors, most notably **EHGM** (✆ 20 74 37 16; Blvd de Mali Béro), **Rimbo Transport Voyageurs** (RTV; ✆ 20 74 14 13; Blvd de Mali Béro), **Azawad Transport Voyageurs** (ATV; ✆ 20 73 93 57; Blvd de Mali Béro) and **Aïr Transport** (✆ 20 74 36 50; off Ave de l'Aïr)

All companies' buses leave Niamey between 4am and 6am, to ensure they reach their end destinations the same day. Due to early departures it's essential to book your ticket the day before and turn up at least 30 minutes before departure. One-way fares from Niamey are more or less standard across all the companies.

Destination	Fare (CFA)	Duration (hr)	Frequency
Agadez	4000	14	daily except Mon & Wed
Arlit	17,500	16	daily except Mon & Wed
Birni N'Konni	6800	6	daily
Dogondoutchi	4800	4	daily
Dosso	2400	2	daily
Gaya	5550	5	daily
Maradi	9300	11	daily
Tahoua	9000	8	daily
Zinder	12,400	15	daily

Bush Taxi

The **Wadata Autogare** (Ave du Kourfeye) is Niamey's main transport hub for bush taxis and several vehicles leave for each destination daily. The following is a list of one-way fares and their very approximate durations (always be prepared for break downs, prayer breaks, food breaks, breaks for the driver to drop goods off, to buy goods and even to visit friends!).

Destination	Fare (CFA)	Duration (hr)
Agadez	11,250	16½
Baleyara	2000	1¼
Birni N'Konni	4650	7½
Dogondoutchi	3200	4½
Dosso	2100	2½
Filingué	3000	2
Gaya	4250	5
Maradi	8250	11
Tahoua	6600	10
Zinder	11,250	14

Minibuses to Ayorou (CFA3500, five hours) via Tillabéri (CFA2000, 2½ hours) leave from **Katako Marché** (Blvd de l'Indépendance).

For details of getting to Burkina Faso, Benin, Mali and Nigeria, see p609.

Car

Hiring a car in Niger is only really possible (not to mention advisable) when hiring a driver too. This, combined with the terrible roads, can make car hire prohibitively expensive. Once you've taken into account paying the driver, for the car, insurance and petrol, you're looking at around CFA150,000 for a car, or CFA180,000 for a 4WD.

Nearly all Niamey travel agencies hire cars and 4WDs with drivers. Europcar (www.europcar-africa.com) is represented in Niamey by Satguru Travel (see p582).

GETTING AROUND
To/From the Airport
A private taxi from the airport to the city centre (12km) costs between CFA5000 and CFA10,000, depending on your bargaining powers and the time of day; going the other way costs about CFA2500. During daylight hours you could also walk from the terminal to the nearby highway and catch a shared taxi to town (CFA200). Most midrange and top-end hotels have a shuttle service to collect their guests and take them directly to their hotel.

Taxi
Taxis are abundant until about 10pm and most are shared. Share taxis simply head in the direction requested by the first passenger and troll for subsequent passengers en route. Simply hold out your arm or shout 'taximan!' and blurt your destination when the taxi slows. If it's going your way, you get the nod and you're only out CFA250, although check the price, as charging foreigners extra is common practice. A taxi to yourself (déplacement or location) costs about CFA1000 for a trip across town during the daytime.

AROUND NIAMEY

The busy Sahelian trading centres to the north of Niamey all have picturesque markets and make for fascinating day trips from the capital. While Boubon, Filingué and Baleyara are nearer and make for an easier round-trip, the stand-out attraction is wonderful Ayorou, whose vibrant Sunday market is complemented by its location on the chocolate waters of the Niger River and the possibility of staying overnight.

Elsewhere around the capital, don't miss your chance to marvel at the mighty giraffes of Kouré, the last remaining wild giraffes in West Africa.

BOUBON
This attractively set Niger River village, 25km northwest of Niamey, makes for an excellent day trip, especially if you come for its famous **Wednesday market**, where local pottery is the main draw. Potters from all over the neighbouring region converge here with a dazzling selection of jars, bowls and pots that make unique souvenirs. As well as the vibrant market, Boubon is a great place to take a pirogue excursion (around CFA5000) or pay about double that for an adventurous two-hour cruise down to Niamey's outskirts – the latter option almost guarantees you some up-close hippo action. There's no restaurant or hotel in Boubon, but it's easy to visit in a day. Buses to Tillabéri and Ayorou from the Katako Market can drop you here on their way through.

KOURÉ
An absolute must on even the shortest trip to Niamey is a half-day trip to Kouré, home to West Africa's last remaining **giraffe herd** (see p590), who quietly munch acacia trees and patrol the baking soils around the dusty village of Kouré, about 60km east of Niamey. The elegant long-necked beasts are rather tame and you can expect to get very close to them. Even if you don't have a vehicle, it's an easy half-day trip from the capital in a taxi (good natured negotiations should cut the taxi price to around CFA30,000). The turn-off to the giraffes is well marked with signs on the main highway, and there's a booth nearby where you must pick up your compulsory guide (CFA5000), entry ticket (CFA4000 per person), camera ticket (CFA500) and vehicle ticket (CFA10,000 per vehicle) – a combination that makes the whole experience rather pricey, but still totally worth it. Depending on the season, the giraffes can be right around the corner, or deep in the bush some 20km away. If possible, come on a Monday so you can visit Kouré's very picturesque market while you're here.

AYOROU
The undoubted highlight of this region is Ayorou on the River Niger's banks just 24km south of the Malian frontier. This otherwise sleepy town is renowned across the region for its multifaceted **Sunday market**. Head to the livestock portion, near the communications tower on the town's east side, and witness camels, cattle, mules, sheep and goats overrunning the place, along with their fascinating nomadic Bella, Fulani and Tuareg owners. It's especially frenetic between

NIGER

THE SAHEL'S LAST GIRAFFES

Don't let the gregarious giraffe herd wandering around Kouré fool you – most animal populations facing extinction are not so friendly or easy to find. Over the past few decades this herd has shrunk in size from more than 3000 giraffes down to an anaemic 50 in 1996. The threat to their existence has come from the destruction of their habitat through desertification and deforestation, as well as disease, poaching, road accidents and farmers killing them to protect their crops. It also didn't help that from April to August 1996, soldiers shot around a dozen of them while trying to carry out a presidential order to capture giraffes for presentation as gifts to friendly foreign leaders. In the late 1990s, the government of Niger and international conservation groups (the Association pour la Sauvegarde des Girafes du Niger is active in this, and has been supported by international wildlife groups such as The Wildlife Protection Foundation) finally launched a campaign to save the last wild giraffes left in the Sahel. Although the giraffe population today stands at around 175, vigilance and continued conservation efforts must continue to ensure these gorgeous and graceful giraffes live on another day. The money raised by charging visitors to see the giraffes (and supporting the rangers with whom you travel) goes to supporting local communities who have in recent years come to see the preservation giraffes as desirable, rather than resenting the animals for eating their crops.

November and April. The market's western section near the river is more subdued, but just as intoxicating. Songhaï-Djerma and Mauritanian Moors gather here between the crooked acacia supports and beneath the woven mat roofs to sell everything from fruit and veg to traditional medicines and slabs of Saharan salt. Keep an eye out for colourful *kountas* (Djerma blankets) and *sourgindis* (millet mats) as they are much cheaper here than in Niamey. The market warms up around noon, so if you arrive early watch cattle swimming across the Niger, or enjoy a pirogue trip on the Niger (CFA5000 for two hours) to see the local hippos. Although guides and piroguers can be persistent around town, it's not a bad idea to hire a guide (CFA5000 per day) as they'll help arrange photo permissions in the market.

Sleeping & Eating

Overnighters here have the choice of two very different establishments. In town itself is the much neglected **Hôtel Amenokal** (☎ 20 71 14 24; abdoulkatia@yahoo.fr; s/tw from CFA10,000/12,000; P ⊠), which has old rooms with cement floors, stained walls and sporadic running water in the bathrooms. Rooms with air-con cost CFA25000 more per night, though prices are negotiable considering the rooms, the lack of electricity during the daytime and the presence of crocodiles (little ones...) in the pool (really). There's also a restaurant (lunch/dinner CFA3500/5000) and a bar on the premises –

the only real plus is that it's on the river and centrally located for the market.

By far the best value is the new **Île aux Mangues** (☎ 96 11 21 98; bed per person CFA12,500), a charming camp site 3km south of the town where five well-appointed tents await you, each sleeping up to three. The price includes a pirogue transfer from Ayorou, dinner and breakfast, and there are toilets and showers for guests, not to mention a dreamy setting on the river. The project seeks to employ locals, encourages the preservation of local biodiversity by helping villagers and hippos live peacefully side by side, and even the tents are designed to blend in with the local environment.

Ask around for **Restaurant de l'Entente** (☎ 96 88 25 22; meals CFA1500-2800), a new venture in the dusty backstreets a short walk (with someone who knows the way!) from the market.

Getting There & Away

There are several daily bush taxis between Niamey's Katako Marché and Ayorou (CFA3500, five hours). Boats run north to Gao, Mali (CFA50,000 per seat, two days) on Mondays.

FILINGUÉ
pop 12,100

The 185km trip northeast to Filingué from Niamey is picturesque, with ochre mesas backdropping endless traditional villages. For a petite village, Filingué offers up a surprisingly dynamic **Sunday market**. Wander town looking for traditional architecture, or head up the small hill for a bird's-eye view of the action and a glimpse of the parched valley, Dallol Bosso.

If you come on a Sunday, don't fail to stop in **Baleyara** (meaning 'where the Bella meet'), halfway between Niamey and Filingué. Its **Sunday market**, heavenly shaded by a canopy of trees, is equally pleasing – the animal bartering, which takes place on the town side of the market, is particularly worth seeing.

In Filingué, the rudimentary **Kourfey Bar Restaurant** (☎ 20 77 10 58; d with shared toilets CFA5000) is your only sleeping option. The cement rooms are cell-like, but they are pretty clean and have fans and private showers. It's on your left as you enter town from Niamey – look for the sign across from the fortlike Red Cross building.

Regular bush taxis run to Niamey's Wadata Autogare (CFA3000, two hours) along good tarmac roads.

THE SOUTH

Niger's long, arid southern border stretches from Burkina Faso to Chad, a huge distance of over 1000km, taking in a diverse region of multiple ethnicities and cultures. It's also home to two of Niger's real highlights, the fantastic Parc Regional du W (one of West Africa's best national parks), and the beguiling Hausa city of Zinder, seat to a sultanate that once dominated the trans-Saharan trade in slaves, ivory and gold, and which is now notable for its Sultan's Palace and the traditional architecture of its Birni Quarter. A reasonable tarmac road links the entire region from west to east and makes transportation relatively painless. For details on getting into Burkina Faso, Benin, Nigeria and Chad, see p609.

DOSSO
pop 50,000

Named after 'Do-So', a Djerma spirit, Dosso is the first major settlement along the main southern road, 136km southeast of Niamey. Dosso was once an important Islamic centre and home to Djermakoye, Djerma's most important religious leader. Being at the crossroads of Niamey, Zinder, Benin and Nigeria, Dosso is an important trading centre and its **Grand Marché** is worth peeking at, although in general it's a fairly dusty and unimpressive place.

The **Musée Regional de Dosso** (☎ 20 65 03 21; Rte de Niamey; admission CFA500; ❂ 9am-5.30pm Tue-Sun) was inexplicably closed when we last visited, but thanks to the large open windows we were able to see the exhibits of local clothing and weaving nevertheless. More interesting is the surrounding **Centre Artisanal** (admission free), which offers guests the chance to see artisans in action, although 'artisans' in this case is not a particularly discerning term, including cobblers and seamstresses.

Sleeping & Eating
Auberge au Zenith (☎ 93 81 58 51; Rte de Niamey; r with shared toilet with fan/air-con CFA6300/12,600; ❄) The rooms here are very basic and the toilets are unpleasant, while the restaurant is home to more flies than we've ever seen in a place of food. However, it's the budget option and is fine for an overnight stay.

Hôtel Djerma (☎ 20 65 02 06; Rte de Gaya; d CFA12,500-25,000; ❄) This chaotic hotel hides behind an old petrol station just south of the *gare routière*. The rooms are fine, if old, and all have air-con. The magnificent mosaics on the empty pool are quite haunting. Staff was quite unfriendly when we were there.

Centre Artisanal (☎ 96 89 10 82, 94 67 77 87; r CFA18,000; ❄ P) This is by far the best place to stay in town. Four well-kept, clean and spacious rooms are housed within the Centre Artisanal. It's best to reserve ahead as they're very popular.

All three hotels have basic restaurants. Cheap street food can be found along the main road, particularly at the *gare routière*. Also, at night, the road running out from opposite Hôtel Djerma is alive with gas lanterns, diesel fumes and good street food.

Getting There & Away
There are always plenty of bush taxis to Niamey (CFA2100, 2½ hours), Gaya (CFA2000, three hours) and Dogondoutchi (CFA2000, 2½ hours).

GAYA
pop 33,300

Gaya is the only border town for Benin, and one of four for Nigeria – there's no reason to linger here. You'll find a **BIA-Niger** (Rte de Dosso) directly across from the *autogare* (bus

NIGER

or transport station) on the main drag, though it only changes euros and US dollars, and does not accept travellers cheques.

Hotel Dendi (Gaya Hwy; ☎ 20 68 03 40; d no fan/ fan/air-con CFA3000/5000, 12,000; ❄) sits on the main drag about a 15-minute walk south from the *autogare*. The father and son owners are delightful. **Hotel Hamdallah** (off Rte de Dosso; ☎ 20 68 04 68; s/d CFA12,500/13,500; ❄) is the most comfortable place to stay, but ask locals to help you find it, as it's located off the main road.

You can dine at your hotel or try **Station Bar** (Rte de Dosso; meals CFA1000-2000; ❍ lunch & dinner), which sits opposite Hotel Dendi.

Several bush taxis make daily runs to Niamey (CFA4250, five hours) via Dosso

(CFA2100, three hours). For information on getting to Benin and Nigeria, see p609.

PARC REGIONAL DU W

This excellent **national park** (www.parc-w.net; admission CFA6000) is named rather charmingly for the double bend in the Niger River at the park's northern border. Shared between Niger, Benin and Burkina Faso, the Parc Regional du W is a massive 9120 sq km, 2200 sq km of which is in Niger, and offers some of the most diverse wildlife-spotting opportunities in West Africa. Antelopes, buffalo, elephants, hippos, lions, leopards, cheetahs, baboons, crocodiles, hyenas, jackals, warthogs and over 300 species of migratory bird all call this unique environment home. The park rests on the west bank

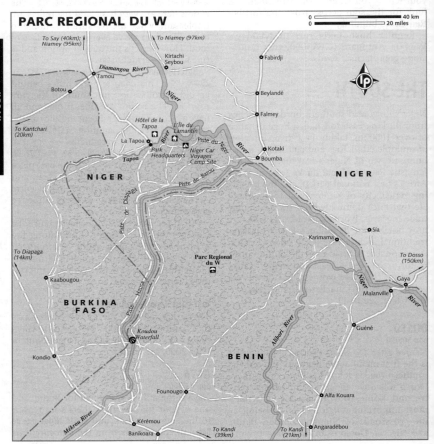

of the Niger River and is an area of dry savannah woodland, a transition zone between the Sahel and moister savannahs to the south.

While the park is now open year-round, the best wildlife viewing is March to May, when the migratory birds arrive and when the environment becomes incredibly barren, forcing animals to congregate around waterholes. A favoured haunt of the elephants is the river near the Hôtel de la Tapoa (the lodge).

The entrance to the park is at La Tapoa, 145km south of Niamey, where there's a small museum with sporadic opening times (and, when we last visited, the decaying decapitated heads of an elephant mother and child killed by poachers – a grim reminder that man remains the park residents' greatest threat). Your obligatory guide costs CFA10,000 per day. The park wardens in all three countries work hard to patrol the enormous park and encounters with poachers are not uncommon. However, on our last visit the wardens were complaining that despite their increased efforts poaching is still on the increase with rising demand, particularly from China, for various products.

Sleeping & Eating

Hôtel de la Tapoa (☎ 96 87 46 05, 96 28 81 83; www .hoteltapoa.com; s/d CFA15,000/20,000, with air-con CFA29,500/34,500; ☯ mid-Oct to mid-Jun; P ✗ ▣) This popular and friendly hotel is an unexpected luxury, with a great pool overlooking a stream in a dramatic setting. The 28 rooms are spacious and have air-con and private facilities. The cheaper bungalows are smaller and darker, and while they have their own bathrooms, they share toilets. Food is excellent, if on the pricey side (CFA6500 per set meal). Electricity is from a generator and comes on at 7pm.

A cheaper option is to stay at the Niger Car Voyages **camp site** (camping in your own tent CFA4000, in set up tents bed only/half board CFA6000/13,500) located right on the riverside with great views.

At the time of writing **Île du Lamantin** (☎ 96 32 03 44; www.iledulamantin.com), an exciting new ecolodge, was being constructed on a Niger River island, and is expected to give Hôtel de la Tapoa a run for its money.

Getting There & Away

Simply put, there's no point reaching the park independently without a vehicle. The journey from Niamey to Tapoa is about three hours by 4WD. Get a quote from a number of travel agencies for this trip (they usually include hotel, meals, guide and park fees, petrol and road tolls in the cost) as they vary hugely.

DOGONDOUTCHI
pop 32,200

'Doutchi' is a tiny village on the highway, about halfway between Dosso and Birni N'Konni. Everything but its **Friday market**, which swallows the *gare routière* whole, is outdone by the dramatic landscapes surrounding town. The ochre outcrops and rusty bluffs stand starkly out against the sky's blue backdrop and make for some interesting short hikes.

The well-signposted **Hôtel Magama** (☎ 20 65 42 82; s/d without bathroom CFA5000/6500, s/d bungalows from CFA10,000/11,500; P ✗) has pleasant rooms at a range of prices. Rooms are found in a basic block of bungalows and a series of missile silo–looking structures. Meals are available across the road in the hotel's pleasant garden-set **restaurant** (☎ 8am-11pm; mains CFA1000-3000). Another option is **Restaurant Saraounia Mangou** (mains CFA500-1250; ☯ 7.30am-9.30pm) on the main road as you come in from Niamey.

Bush taxis depart every few hours for Dosso (CFA2000, 2½ hours), Birni N'Konni (CFA1500, two hours) and Niamey (CFA3200, 3½ hours).

BIRNI N'KONNI
pop 50,000

Konni, as it's known to one and all, is the crossroads of Niger, where the country's two main roads diverge, one continuing east to Zinder and one heading north to Agadez. A short distance south is also one of Niger's four major border crossings with Nigeria. There's very little to see, but it makes a convenient place to break up a long journey.

Sleeping & Eating

Relais-Camping Touristique (☎ 20 64 06 00; Rte de Niamey; camping per person CFA1500, plus per vehicle CFA1000, d CFA10,000-12,500; P ✗) The spartan bungalows are large enough to make the sizeable double beds look lost inside. There's even some shade in the dusty yard for tents (bring your own if you want to camp).

Hôtel Kado (☎ 20 64 03 64; Rte de Nigeria; d with fan/air-con CFA6800/9800; ✗) This dirty, rundown place is poor value compared to the Nevada, but it's a reasonable budget option and handy

NIGER

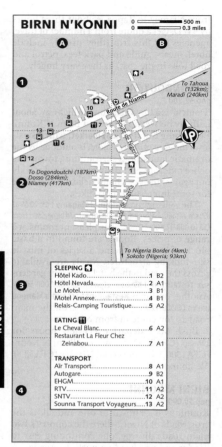

BIRNI N'KONNI

SLEEPING 🏠
Hôtel Kado......................................1 B2
Hotel Nevada...................................2 A1
Le Motel...3 B1
Motel Annexe..................................4 B1
Relais-Camping Touristique...........5 A2

EATING 🍴
Le Cheval Blanc..............................6 A2
Restaurant La Fleur Chez
  Zeinabou.....................................7 A1

TRANSPORT
Air Transport...................................8 A1
Autogare...9 B2
EHGM...10 A1
RTV..11 A2
SNTV..12 A2
Sounna Transport Voyageurs.....13 A2

for crossing into Nigeria. All rooms have bathrooms.

Hôtel Nevada (☎ 20 64 04 34; off Rte de Niamey; s/ d without bathroom CFA11,300/14,600 s/d with bathroom CFA12,300/15,600; 🔲) This modest and rather hidden-away option is great value. Rooms are well kept and all have TV and air-con. The hotel is signposted from the crossroads in the centre of town – walk down to the small thatched village and turn left.

Le Motel (☎ 20 64 06 50; Rte de Niamey; r CFA22,500– 37,500; 🅿 🔲) An oasis of calm on the busy main drag, Le Motel boasts friendly staff and spotless rooms all with TV, fridge, bathroom and air-con. If its main building is full, there's an annexe down the road that is just as good. Its restaurant (meals from CFA1000

to CFA4000, open for breakfast, lunch and dinner) is also by far the best in town. It's worth booking ahead.

The Route de Niamey is full of small restaurants. Try **Restaurant La Fleur Chez Zeinabou** (Rte de Niamey; mains CFA750-2000; 🕒 24hr) for tasty yams, rice and couscous, and **Le Cheval Blanc** (Rte de Niamey; mains CFA500; 🕒 1pm-midnight), for a basic dish of rice and sauce.

Getting There & Away
SNTV, EHGM, RTV and Aïr Transport (all on Route de Niamey) serve the same main routes from Konni. Daily buses go to Zinder (CFA6300–6600, six hours), Niamey (CFA6250– 6800, six hours) and Maradi (CFA3500, three hours), while buses to Tahoua (CFA2000, 1½ hours) and Agadez (CFA7750, 5½ hours) only run Tuesday and Thursday to Sunday. Most northbound and eastbound buses arrive around 11am. Westbound buses pull in around 1pm.

Sounna Transport Voyageurs (Rte de Niamey) has a daily 8am bus to Malanville in Benin (CFA7000, 12 hours). Bush taxis regularly leave the **autogare** (Rte de Nigeria) for Dogondoutchi (CFA1800, two hours), Maradi (CFA2800, four hours) and Tahoua (CFA1400, 1½ hours).

For transport to Nigeria, see p610.

TAHOUA
pop 999,000
This friendly Hausa town, about 130km north of Konni, is the country's fifth-largest. Although it's a slight detour off the Niamey to Agadez road, if you're riding public transport you'll end up stopping here. Besides enjoying the vibrant market day (Sunday) at the **Grand Marché** (Rte de Maternité), it's worthwhile visiting the **Centre Artisanal** (Rte de l'Artisanal; 🕒 9am-6pm) on the town's northwest edge. The leather bags in the Coopérative pour les Handicapés are lovely – don't forget prices are negotiable!

Information
BIA-Niger (Rte de l'Artisanal) Change travellers cheques (1.6% commission) and euros.
Pharmacie Populaire (☎ 20 61 05 43; Rte de l'Artisanal)

Sleeping & Eating
Hôtel les Bungalows (☎ 20 61 05 53; Jardin Publique; d with fan/air-con CFA7500/9500; 🔲) This budget option is friendly and slap-bang in the centre. However, you'll need a mozzie net and tolerance for unpleasant bathrooms.

Hôtel de L'Amitié (☎ 20 61 01 53; Rte de Maternité; d CFA12,000-14,500; ❄) Now eclipsed by the excellent Tarka, the Amitié is still a good option for lesser wallets. It's on the main drag, 400m east of the SNTV bus station – look for the wooden giraffes outside. There's also a friendly bar and reasonable restaurant.

Hôtel Tarka (☎ 20 61 07 35; hoteltarka@gmail.com; off Rte d'Agadez; r CFA35,500; P ❄ ☎) This new place is the swishest in town, with wi-fi (CFA3000 per day), 32 smart and clean rooms and a helpful staff. There's also a good restaurant and bar on the premises.

Restaurant Milana (Rte d'Arène; meals CFA1000-4000; ❄ breakfast, lunch & dinner) Just up the hill from the Centre Artisanal, this Italian place serves up delicious ravioli, lasagne, gnocchi, tagliatelle and does a mean range of pizza as well.

Getting There & Around

SNTV (Rte de Maternite) buses from Niamey stop here en route to Agadez (CFA7000, 4½ hours) daily except Monday and Wednesday, around noon. Southbound buses to Niamey (CFA8500, 7½ hours) arrive at a similar time daily save Monday and Wednesday. EHGM, RTV and Aïr Transport have similar services on a daily basis.

Minibuses frequently leave for Konni (CFA1500, 1½ hours) from the *autogare*, which sits just east of Place Tassaoungoum on Route de Maternite.

MARADI

pop 177,800

Maradi, the country's third-largest city, remains the administrative capital and commercial centre for agriculture. Its proximity to northern Nigeria has fostered staunchly conservative Islamic views and many Muslims here are calling for the introduction of Islamic Sharia law. It's not the most engaging place for visitors, but you can happily break up a journey here as there are two solid accommodation options.

Information

For changing naira (for Nigeria), try the *gare routière* 200m north of Sonibank.

BIA-Niger (1 SGI Rue 2) Change euros, US dollars and occasionally travellers cheques.

Pharmacie Populaire (39 SGI Rue 2)

Post office (off BRJ Rue 1)

Regional hospital (☎ 20 41 02 20; off Rue de l'Hôpital)

Sights

As you might imagine, sinking into Maradi's **Grande Marché** (BRJ Rue 1) on market days (Monday and Friday) is a pleasurable assault on the senses. Vending of an entirely different variety goes on at the **Centre Artisanal de Maradi** (BRJ Rue 1; ❄ 8am-10pm), 2km north of town.

Heading east to Place Dan Kasswa will bring you to the **Maison des Chefs**, which, though rather unimpressive, does possess traditional geometric designs and is a fine example of Hausa architecture. Nearby is the **Grande Mosquée** (Place Dan Kasswa), where you'll see children on the sidewalk studying the Quran and writing sections of it onto small wooden tablets.

Sleeping & Eating

Hôtel Larewa (☎ 96 87 01 44; d with fan/air-con from CFA6500/12,500; P ❄) Larewa is Maradi's best budget value and is found east of the EHGM station, north of town. Rooms are now in two complexes on opposite sides of the lane. The western side's rooms, with clean showers and shared toilets, are brighter and slightly less expensive than the eastern side's rooms, which have bathrooms.

our pick **Maradi Guest House** (☎ 20 41 07 31; s/d from CFA35,500/41,000; P ❄ ☎) This favourite of the NGO classes is a superb option for breaking a journey in style. The rooms are brilliant and massive, some even boasting king-size rod-iron canopy beds and verdant balconies. It's well signposted and is 2km southeast from the town centre. While more rooms are being built, there were only six functioning when we visited, so reservations are essential.

The best option in town is the **Maradi Guest House** (meals CFA1500-5000; ❄ breakfast, lunch & dinner; ❄), which serves up a very tasty selection of European food and even has some decent wine. A cheaper option is **Restaurant Marthaba** (43 SGI Rue 10; meals CFA500-1000; ❄ breakfast, lunch & dinner), a sleepy outdoor place that isn't bad for local dishes like *riz sauce* (rice with meat or chicken).

At night you can also find delicious grilled chicken and other snacks at **street stalls** (BRJ Rue 13) around the Jardin Publique.

Getting There & Around

All the main bus companies serve Maradi on the Niamey-Zinder 'Axis'. Buses depart Niamey usually around 6am heading east (CFA9000; nine hours).

From Maradi **SNTV** (81 BRJ Rue 1) has daily 5am buses to Zinder (CFA3000, three hours) and also Niamey (CFA9,000, nine hours). **RTV** (☎ 20 41 06 15; BRJ Rue 8) and **EHGM** (☎ 20 41 13 40; Rte de Niamey) have similar services. For onward buses to Diffa, or to get to Agadez, you'll need to change buses in Zinder.

Bush taxis regularly depart the *gare routière* for Zinder (costing CFA3000 and taking four hours) and Konni (CFA3500, five hours).

For transport to Nigeria, see p610.

ZINDER
pop 205,500

The last large town in Niger heading east from Niamey, Zinder feels like the last stopover before the middle of nowhere, a bustling place but also very much the end of the line. Yet it wasn't always so – Zinder was once the capital of the mighty Damagaram state, which thrived on the trans-Saharan trade in ivory, salt, slaves and gold. Today the Sultan of Zinder still rules, albeit nominally, from his fascinating palace complete with colourfully attired attendants. With its celebrated traditional Hausa houses, labyrinthine alleys of the old quarters, vestiges

of Birni's old fortifications, an infamous prison within the Palais du Sultan and the classic French fort, Zinder is by far the most interesting town in Southern Niger and well worth a day or two of your time.

Information

For Nigerian naira, look for moneychangers around the *gare routière*. Moneychangers in Kano give better rates for US dollars.

BIA-Niger (Ave des Banques) Change travellers cheques, euros and US dollars.

Centre Culturel Franco-Nigérien (☎ 20 51 05 35; Rue du Marché) French-language library and art gallery.

Cybercafé Kandarga (Rue du Marché; per hr CFA500; ☼ 8am-11pm)

Cybercafé Marhaba (Ave de la République; per hr CFA500; ☼ 8am-11pm)

National Hospital (☎ 20 51 00 50; Ave de Maradi)

Pharmacie Populaire (Ave des Banques)

Post office (Ave de la République)

Sights
BIRNI QUARTIER

The back alleys of Zinder's Birni Quartier may be strewn with rubbish and pungent with a se-

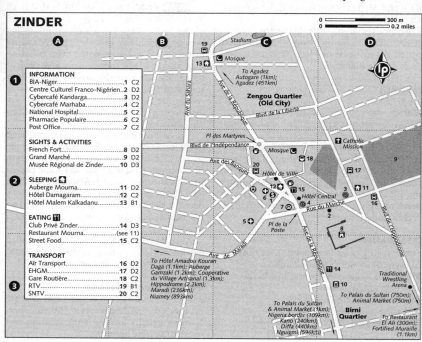

ZINDER

INFORMATION
BIA-Niger.................................1 C2
Centre Culturel Franco-Nigérien..2 D2
Cybercafé Kandarga...................3 D2
Cybercafé Marhaba....................4 C2
National Hospital.......................5 C2
Pharmacie Populaire..................6 C2
Post Office................................7 C2

SIGHTS & ACTIVITIES
French Fort...............................8 D2
Grand Marché............................9 D2
Musée Régional de Zinder.........10 D3

SLEEPING
Auberge Mourna........................11 D2
Hôtel Damagaram.....................12 C2
Hôtel Malem Kalkadanu.............13 B1

EATING
Club Privé Zinder......................14 D3
Restaurant Mourna..............(see 11)
Street Food..............................15 C2

TRANSPORT
Aïr Transport...........................16 D2
EHGM....................................17 D2
Gare Routière..........................18 C2
RTV.......................................19 B1
SNTV.....................................20 C2

lection of interesting odours, but they're also a fascinating must-see. The city's old fortified quarter grew up around the Sultan's Palace and is today an incredibly well-preserved maze of old *banco* (mud-brick) houses, many with colourfully painted geometric designs. The *quartier* is full of children playing and it's a real pleasure to get lost here while enjoying what is arguably the best traditional Hausa architecture in existence. Amazingly, a delicate sliver of Birni's massive original fortified *muraille* (tall wall) still stands at the southern section of the quarter.

PALAIS DU SULTAN
Originally constructed in the mid-19th century, the **Palais du Sultan** (Place de la Grande Mosquée, Birni Quartier) is now home to the 23rd sultan, Elhadj Mamadou Moustapha, along with his three wives and some of his 23 children – you'll see some of his guards out the front in their bright red-and-green garb. The original door still hangs in the entrance and is covered with countless metal plates, each tacked on by a different chief over the years as a sign of support for the sitting sultan. Behind the door is a courtyard that once contained a small prison for slaves. One of the cells, known as the *chambre des scorpions,* was scented with butter to lure the venomous creatures! If you linger outside the palace, you'll be offered a tour. The going rate is CFA2000, or more if you want a tour of the Birni Quartier too.

MUSÉE RÉGIONAL DE ZINDER
This **museum** (☎ 60 59 61 35; Ave de la République; admission CFA500; ☾ 8am–noon & 3-6pm) was in a dire state when we visited. Totally neglected, the few exhibits (a fanciful model of the museum, a hippo's skull, a bow and arrow and an old musket) were all covered in dust. A cold beer in the raucous beer hut outside may prove to be a better way to spend your CFA500.

ZENGOU QUARTIER
Although the Zengou Quartier predates the Birni Quartier, most of its present-day buildings are much younger, and cement structures outnumber classic *banco* homes. However, life within the quarter remains the same and a visit is still worthwhile.

OTHER SIGHTS
The **Grand Marché** (Blvd de l'Hippodrome; ☾ dawn to dusk) is one of the liveliest in Niger – the big day is Thursday. Look for leathergoods as Niger's best *artisans du cuir* are here. If you strike out, or just want to see goods being made, visit the **Cooperative du Village Artisanal** (Ave de Maradi; ☾ 8am-6.30pm), about 2km west of town. Thursday also brings the big **animal market** to Zinder's outskirts, near the Palais du Sultan. For something a bit less worthy, the horse races 3km west of town at the **Hippodrome** (Ave de Maradi; ☾ 4pm Sat & Sun) are a hotbed of healthy secular gambling. There's also a charming and stereotypical **French fort** that you'll see rising from a pile of massive rounded boulders just south of the town centre. Sadly, it and its surroundings, looking much like a giant's abandoned game of marbles, is currently used by the Nigerien military and is off-limits. A nearby viewpoint provides the best vista of the town.

Sleeping
Hôtel Malem Kalkadanu (☎ 96 66 66 53; Ave de la République; r CFA3400-6400; ℗) West of the Zengou Quartier, this rambling budget place has the cheapest rooms in town. Though it's a lot prettier inside the courtyard than you'd expect from the grotty exterior, the rooms are basic and cell-like.

Hôtel Amadou Kouran Daga (☎ 20 51 07 42; Ave de Maradi; s/d with fan from CFA7500/10,500, s/d with air-con CFA13,500/18,500; ℗ ✗) Opposite Gamzaki, this aging place has large, perfectly good rooms with could-do-better bathrooms.

Hôtel Damagaram (☎ 20 51 00 69; Ave des Banques; s/d/tw CFA16,500/20,000/20,000; ✗) Despite having a great location and being set around a pleasant courtyard, the Damagaram's rooms are very dated and musty, with mozzie-infested bathrooms and interesting smelling toilets.

Auberge Mourna (☎ 20 51 22 80, 96 95 03 06; off Rue du Marché; s/tw/d from CFA20,00/30,000/35,000; ℗ ✗) Right in the heart of town, the Mourna has eight large, clean rooms all with TVs, air-con and fridges, all in a safe courtyard setting with a great little restaurant attached. Reservations are usually essential.

ourpick **Auberge Gamzaki** (☎ 20 51 02 80, 96 98 83 31; www.gamzaki-voyages.com; Ave de Maradi; r CFA30,000-33,000; ℗ ✗) This fabulous new venture is quite unlike any other hotel in Zinder and it's a real treat to stay here. There are currently four rooms (although six more are planned), all furnished in Hausa style with pebble floors, stylish bathrooms and even a minibar. The only gripes are the location,

1.5km from the town centre (although it's a quick and easy with a CFA250 *moto-taxi*), and that while breakfast is served, there is currently no restaurant.

Eating & Drinking

Restaurant El Ali (meals CFA500-2000; ☺ breakfast, lunch & dinner) All your African favourites (especially rice and couscous with sauce) can be tasted underneath the pleasantly down-at-heel *paillotes* (thatched sun shelters). Follow Blvd de l'Hippodrome south and take the first left after the wrestling arena. There are no signs, but locals will point it out.

Club Privé Zinder (☎ 96 28 54 46; Ave de la République; meals CFA1000-2500; ☺ 6am-11pm Mon-Fri, 12.30pm-11pm Sat & Sun) This unlikely spot is popular with expats in Zinder for its pleasant bar and large pool. Nonmembers can use both (for a CFA1500 day membership) and enjoy the food here, which ranges from simple sandwiches to Chateaubriand.

Restaurant Mourna (off Rue du Marché; mains CFA1000-4500; ☺ breakfast, lunch & dinner) The best choice in town is this highly recommended Chinese-influenced establishment, whose charming courtyard restaurant's atmosphere is only marred by the TV usually being watched by the staff. Try the excellent *salade de maïs* (sweetcorn salad), or the Cantonese rice.

Some of the best **street food** (Ave de la République; brochettes CFA100, roast pigeons/chickens CFA900/1500) can be found in the square in front of the Hôtel Central in the evening. There are several supermarkets around town for self-caterers, particularly between Place des Martyres and Hôtel Central. For a beer try the fun local hang-out outside the Musée Regional.

Getting There & Away

SNTV (☎ 20 51 04 68; Ave des Banques) buses run to Niamey (CFA12,400, 14 hours, daily) and Agadez (CFA7600, eight hours, Tuesday and Saturday). **EHGM** (☎ 20 51 00 97) also serves Niamey (CFA12,000, 5am daily) via Maradi (CFA3000), Birni N'Konni (CFA6000) and Agadez (CFA7500, 6am Tuesday, Thursday and Saturday). **Aïr Transport** (☎ 51 02 47; Blvd de l'Hippodrome) and **RTV** (☎ 51 04 16; off Ave de la République) have similar services, including a bus to Diffa (CFA6500, 5am Monday, Wednesday, Friday, seven hours) from where it's possible to connect to Nguigmi and on to Chad. There are currently no direct services to Nguigmi from Zinder.

Bush taxis depart the *gare routière* daily for Diffa (CFA6000, nine hours) and Maradi (CFA3000, 4½ hours).

Bush taxis for Agadez (CFA7000, nine hours) depart on Tuesday, Thursday and Saturday from the Agadez *autogare*, which is 1km northeast of town on Ave de la République.

For transport to Nigeria, see p610.

Getting Around

Motos are everywhere, providing a fast and cheap way to get across town (CFA250).

DIFFA

pop 30,600

This diminutive and dusty town is only of interest to those travelling overland between Niger and Chad because it's the last place in Niger with decent facilities. Along the main drag you'll spot a Pharmacie Populaire, a BIA-Niger that changes cash (euros only) and a petrol station serving *essense* and *gasoil* out of the barrel. For recent arrivals from Chad, there's a branch of Société Nigerienne d'Assurances et de Reassurances that sells vehicle insurance.

Hôtel le Tal (☎ 20 56 03 32; off Rte de Nguigmi; d with fan/air-con CFA7500/13,500; ☒), behind the petrol station, is your only sleeping option. It's friendly and clean enough, but seriously overpriced. There's a passable restaurant here too.

If heading east, the market near the autogare is a good place to stock up on essentials – if you haven't already – and you should do as prices for whatever little you can find between here and Chad are very high.

Aïr Transport has a bus leaving Zinder at 6am to Diffa (CFA6500, Mon, Wed, Fri & Sat), returning the same afternoon. Rimbo runs the same route departing at 5am from Zinder, on Mondays, Wednesdays and Fridays. Irregular bush taxis run the potholed highway to Nguigmi (CFA3000, four hours).

NGUIGMI

pop 17,400

Nguigmi is a small town at the end of the sealed road, some 45km from the Chad border. It's the last Niger settlement of any size and it's where you must get your passport stamped. The town has no hotels or eateries, but there's is a lively market area to the south of town where you can buy brochettes.

There are a few bush taxis between Nguigmi and Diffa (CFA3000, four hours). For transport to/from Chad, see p610.

THE NORTH

Northern Niger has for years been the real draw of the country – the stunning scenery of the Aïr Mountains and the Sahara sea's most gargantuan dunes in the Ténéré Desert have long brought travellers here. However, at the time of writing in early 2009, almost the entire region was closed to tourism due to the Tuareg Rebellion that flared up in 2007 and was still ongoing. Check the latest information, but in early 2009 only the regional capital Agadez and the uranian-mining settlement of Arlit were open to travellers. Agadez merits a visit in its own right, even though it's frustrating to know that the country's most gob-smacking scenery is tantalisingly nearby yet totally out of reach.

AGADEZ
pop 88,569

Once Niger's tourism capital, Agadez has fallen on decidedly hard times since the Tuareg Rebellion reignited in 2007. Yet while the airport no longer sees scheduled flights and many restaurants and hotels are closed due to lack of travellers, the city remains open and this is a fascinating time to see an ancient Saharan trade town without the concomitant tour groups and touts that will be familiar to anyone who has travelled through northern Mali.

Despite the restrictions, Agadez itself is still the most fascinating of Niger's cities and should not be ignored. When standing in the porcupine shadow of the famous Grand Mosquée, or weaving through the sandy streets and distinctive mud-brick architecture, it's not hard to imagine what it was like at its zenith some four centuries ago. Back then its population of 30,000 flourished off the caravans *(azalai)* plying between Gao (Mali) and Tripoli (Libya), some as large as 20,000 camels, laden with gold, salt and slaves.

In terms of safety, check in Niamey before you travel, but at the time of writing foreigners were welcome to travel here. Annoyingly, on arrival at the town's checkpoint your passport is usually taken away overnight and can be collected from the town's police headquarters the next day – with the usual lazy attempt at a shake-down for the 'service'.

Information
INTERNET ACCESS

In addition to those below, there are two internet cafes outside Hôtel de la Paix.

Cybercafe le Dounya (off Place de la République; per hr CFA600; ☾ 8am-10pm) A central option handy for the bus stations.

Cybercafe Garmawa (off Rte de Bilma; per hr CFA600; ☾ 8.30am-10pm) Another central option.

MEDICAL SERVICES

Hospital (☎ 20 44 00 84; off Rte de l'Aéroport; ☾ 24hr)

MONEY

BIA-Niger (Rte de Bilma; ☾ 8.30am-12.45pm & 2-3.45pm Mon-Fri, 8-11.45am Sat) Changes travellers cheques, euros and US dollars and does cash advances on Visa cards (CFA10,000 charge).

BRS (Rte de Bilma; ☾ as BIA-Niger) Offers Western Union services.

VIP Bureau de Change (Rte de Bilma; ☾ 8am-11.30pm) Changes major currencies, with a 1% to 2% commission.

TELEPHONE

There are numerous private offices along Route de l'Aéroport offering international telephone. Calls to most nations cost CFA150 for each 10-second block. Conveniently, most offices charge nothing for incoming calls.

TOURIST INFORMATION
Centre National pour la Promotion Tourisme
(☎ 20 44 00 36; Rte de l'Aéroport; ☾ 8.30am-4.30pm Mon-Thu, to 1.30pm Fri) A good place for finding out the latest information about tourist facilities in the town.

TRAVEL AGENCIES

There were once over 70 travel agencies in Agadez, but the closure of the surrounding desert and mountains meant that at the time of writing all the agencies were either closed or had relocated to Niamey.

Sights & Activities
GRANDE MOSQUÉE

Agadez's focal point is its dazzling Grande Mosquée, which climbs spectacularly into the blue skies over the old town – it's a quite unforgettable sight. Although dating back to 1515, it was totally rebuilt in 1844. Its classic

NIGER

NIGER

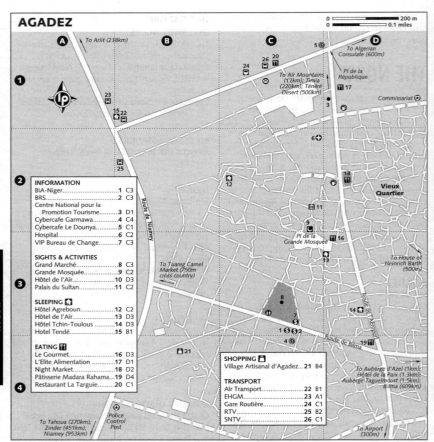

AGADEZ

0 — 200 m
0 — 0.1 miles

INFORMATION
BIA-Niger...........................1 C3
BRS...................................2 C3
Centre National pour la
  Promotion Tourisme........3 D1
Cybercafe Garmawa............4 C4
Cybercafe Le Dounya..........5 C1
Hospital.............................6 C2
VIP Bureau de Change.........7 C3

SIGHTS & ACTIVITIES
Grand Marché.....................8 C3
Grande Mosquée.................9 C2
Hôtel de l'Aïr....................10 D3
Palais du Sultan.................11 C2

SLEEPING
Hôtel Agreboun..................12 C2
Hôtel de l'Aïr....................13 D3
Hôtel Tchin-Toulous 14 D3
Hotel Tendé......................15 B1

EATING
Le Gourmet.......................16 D3
L'Elite Alimentation 17 D1
Night Market.....................18 D2
Pâtisserie Madara Rahama...19 D4
Restaurant La Targuie.........20 C1

SHOPPING
Village Artisanal d'Agadez...21 B4

TRANSPORT
Aïr Transport.....................22 B1
EHGM...............................23 A1
Gare Routière.....................24 C1
RTV..................................25 B2
SNTV................................26 C1

To Arlit (238km)
To Algerian Consulate (600m)
To Aïr Mountains (12km); Timia (220km); Ténéré Desert (500km)
Pl de la République
Commissariat
Vieux Quartier
To House of Heinrich Barth (500m)
Route de Niamey
To Tuareg Camel Market (750m cross country)
Pl de la Grande Mosquée
Route de l'Aéroport
Route de Bilma
To Auberge d'Azel (1km); Hôtel de la Paix (1.3km); Auberge Taguelmoust (1.5km); Bilma (609km)
To Tahoua (270km); Zinder (451km); Niamey (953km)
Police Control Post
To Airport (300m)

Sahel/Sudanic-style architecture was described by Bruce Chatwin as 'bristling with wooden spires like the vertebra of some defunct fauna'. Squeezing out of the ever-narrowing staircase to astounding views over Agadez and the surrounding Sahara will take your breath away. Knock at the door and ask the guardian politely if you can make the visit. A tip of CFA2000 per person is in order. If nobody is about, ask at one of the few remaining souvenir shops opposite the mosque entrance and someone will go and find him.

MARKETS

The **Grand Marché** (Rte de Bilma; dawn to dusk) is the most animated place in town. The variety of people, many dressed in traditional desert costumes, is at least as interesting as what's for sale. You can find a wide range of art and craftwork here, including rugs and Tuareg leatherwork.

The **Tuareg camel market** (dawn to dusk) on Agadez's western outskirts is as colourful as the Grande Marché, but even more odoriferous. Slobbering camels are joined by sheep, donkeys, goats, massive cattle and dozens of fascinating nomadic Tuareg traders. Photographs here usually require the market chief's permission, oh, and about CFA2500. Sunrise and sunset are the best times to visit.

VIEUX QUARTIER

This enchanting maze of small crooked alleys, tiny artisan shops, and fascinating mud-brick architecture of Tuareg and Hausa inspiration is as good a time machine as we've ever experienced – yes, hours just happily disappear within the Vieux Quartier. Some *banco* homes date back over 150 years, while others boast beautiful facades and the odd cattle horn. Definitely visit the **House of Heinrich Barth** (admission CFA1000; ☺ 8am-6pm), which is rather more interesting for the chance to see the interior of a traditional home than it is to see the rather paltry collection of the great Saharan explorer's belongings. He stayed here briefly in 1850 and was one of the first Europeans to witness the dramatic departure of the salt caravans from Agadez, describing it as 'a whole nation in motion'.

OTHER SIGHTS

Visible just north of the Grande Mosquée is the impressive **Palais du Sultan**, the courtyard of which it's possible to wander through, even though the palace itself – the current home of the city's traditional ruler – is not open to visitors. The residence of a previous Sultan, dating back to the late 19th century, also stands near the mosque and now houses **Hôtel de l'Aïr** (Place de la Grande Mosquée). Have a peek behind its 1m-thick walls into the large dining hall, where the Sultan's guests were entertained and where Tuareg rebels are believed to have been hanged by the French in 1917.

Festivals & Events

Islamic holidays are the best time to be in Agadez, especially Tabaski. Following the feast, you can see one of the desert's great spectacles – the 'cavalcade', a furious camel race through the crowded narrow streets to the square in front of the Palais du Sultan. Similar races take place during Eid al-Fitr. See p816 for more Islamic holiday details.

Sleeping

At the time of writing many of Agadez's hotels were shut due to lack of travellers. This may well change, however, so ask in Niamey for additional options before you set out. The following were open in early 2009.

BUDGET

Hôtel Agreboun (☎ 20 44 05 75, 96 98 63 32; s/tw/tr with shared toilet CFA4000/8000/12,000; 🅿) The cheapest hotel in town, the Agreboun is on the western edge of Agadez, a short walk from the bus stations. Rooms are rather rudimentary and bunkerlike, but they're cheap, clean and

surround two very pleasant and traditional courtyards for sitting out the day's heat. Call ahead, as its 13 rooms are often full.

MIDRANGE

Hotel Tendé (☎ 96 98 18 83; Rte de Niamey; s/tw without bathroom CFA11,000/14,000, s/tw with air-con & without bathroom CFA16,500/19,500, s/tw with air-con & with bathroom CFA20,500/26,000; 🍴) Slightly overpriced it may be, but this friendly hostelry is excellently located for those arriving late at night by bus. A pleasant and traditional courtyard garden leads into a block of rooms that have been enlivened by traditional arts and crafts. Rooms are charming and all are equipped with mosquito nets, although they can be stuffy – paying the extra for air-con is worth it. It's also possible to camp (CFA2000) or hire a simple Tuareg tent (CFA3000).

Hôtel de l'Aïr (☎ 96 55 67 44; Place de la Grande Mosquée; r CFA10,000-15,000; 🅿 🍴) This nine-room former sultan's palace makes up for in sheer charm and atmosphere what it may lack in terms of concierge service. Rooms can be dark and rather hit-and-miss, but with this courtyard space, history and location, who cares? Some toilets here are smelly, though – shop around and check your room isn't one of them before you settle in. Prices alter depending on your air-con and private bathroom needs.

Hôtel Tchin-Toulous (☎ 96 49 85 79; caravanevoyages@hotmail.com; Rte de l'Aéroport; r with/without bathroom CFA15,000/10,000; 🍴) Reopening when we visited, the charming Tchin-Toulous wins points for its quirky Tuareg style: pebble floors and traditional twig beds make this a charmer, and it's centrally located too, with air-con in the more expensive rooms alongside extremely makeshift bathroom facilities. CFA2500 gets you a mattress on the secure terrace here – quite possibly the best deal in town.

Hôtel de la Paix (☎ 20 44 02 34; hotel_dela_paix@yahoo.fr; Rte de Bilma; s/tw/d CFA25,000/25,000/35,000; 🅿 🍴 🛏) It's hard to imagine anything more incongruous in Agadez's old town than this modern Disney-esque place so totally out of keeping with the ancient settlement it adjoins. Rooms are of good standard, but can be dark. Its one standout feature – the only swimming pool in town – was empty when we visited. Overall it's a decidedly charmless affair.

TOP END

Auberge Taguelmoust (☎ 20 44 04 50, 96 97 31 39; off Rte de Bilma; r with fan/air-con CFA25,000/CFA30,000; 🍴) The

NIGER

latest addition to Agadez's hotel scene is the lovely Taguelmoust, a traditional affair with 12 charming rooms stuffed full of Tuareg furnishings and decoration. It's a fair walk from the old town at the edge of the desert.

ourpick **Auberge d'Azel** (☎ 20 44 01 70; www .agadez-tourisme.com; Rte de Bilma; tw/d CFA30,000/40,000; 🔀 🅿) Without doubt the most charming hotel in Agadez, the Auberge d'Azel is a boutique-style oasis of calm, bougainvillea-shaded courtyards and gorgeously attired rooms with domed brick ceilings and tonnes of character. Look no further for a place to kick back in style.

Eating

Most of the well-established restaurants of Agadez were closed at the time of research. The few that remained open are listed below, although things may well change in the near future.

Pâtisserie Madara Rahama (Rte de l'Aéroport; pastries from CFA250; 🕑 8am-midnight) This little place is favourite with locals who come for the freshly baked sticky buns and cold yoghurt. You can eat in or take away.

Le Gourmet (Place de la Grande Mosquée; meals CFA500-1500; 🕑 breakfast, lunch & dinner) Practically the only central dining option, this local haunt lies almost in the shadow of the Grande Mousquée and is fun and friendly, especially if you don't mind the satellite TV that stays on all day. Dishes are simple but fine – from salads to omelettes and couscous.

Restaurant la Targuie (meals CFA800-1500; 🕑 breakfast, lunch & dinner) Of all the restaurants in town, La Targuie has the most buzz and the biggest local clientele. It is well located for the buses, and you're guaranteed a good meal here. The salads are large and delicious, and the open-air atmosphere (when not ruined by the blaring TV) is superb, with great people-watching potential.

Restaurant Taguelmoust (☎ 20 44 04 50; off Rte de Bilma; mains CFA3000-4000; 🕑 breakfast, lunch & dinner) It may be a hotel restaurant, but it's worth a visit for its setting alone, the tranquil courtyard of a traditional-style house. The service was downright sloppy when we visited though, and while the food was freshly made it was pretty standard given the prices. However, as it's one of the few options in town, who are we to complain? There's one of the town's few bars here too.

Auberge D'Azel (Rte de Bilma; meals CFA3500-5500; 🕑 lunch & dinner) The *mouton targui* (Tuareg

mutton) is particularly recommended here – though prices are a little steep. If you aren't lucky enough to be staying here, then do come by for a meal at the very least.

The **night market** (Rte de l'Aéroport; 🕑 dinner) is great for ambience and a hearty selection of stews, *igname* (pounded yams baked in a doughy breadlike mix) and brochettes ensure you'll be stuffed for under CFA500. The daring can try goat's head. There's also a busy market on the strip around SNTV bus station, which operates from dawn well into the night and is a good place for a cheap breakfast of bread and omelette.

Besides perusing the Grand Marché, self-caterers can visit **L'Elite Alimentation** (Rte de l'Aéroport).

Shopping

For buying jewellery and seeing silversmiths at work, check out the **Village Artisanal D'Agadez** (off Rte de Niamey; 🕑 8am-6pm) in the town's southwest. Within the Vieux Quartier you'll also find silversmiths, leatherworkers producing Tuareg *samaras* (sandals), *coussins* (cushions) and magnificent *selles de chameau* (camel saddles), and bronzesmiths making a variety of objects, including jewellery. There are also some small Tuareg boutiques around Place du Grande Mosquée. Bargaining is always required.

If you're after a Tuareg turban expect to pay CFA500 per metre in the market (indigo costs more); 3m should suffice.

Getting There & Away
AIR

There are currently no scheduled flights to or from Agadez. Should the Tuareg Rebellion cease, then both **Point Afrique** (www.point-afrique.com) and **Go Voyages** (www.govoy ages.com) may start flying again from Paris.

BUS

At present bus is the only way to get to Agadez short of hiring a driver or chartering a plane. All road travel to the city needs to be in a military convoy to protect travellers, so timetables are restrictive, with convoys travelling once a day to/from Niamey (except Monday and Wednesday) and just three times a week to/from Zinder (Tuesday, Thursday and Saturday). Buses coming from Niamey and Zinder often continue to Arlit. **SNTV** (☎ 29 61 80) has a 6am daily bus to Niamey (CFA14,000, 12 hours, except Monday and Wednesday), as well as a 6am bus to Zinder (CFA7,500, 7½ hours, Tuesday, Thursday and Sunday).

Aïr Transport (off Rte de Niamey) has a daily departure to Niamey (CFA14,000, 12 hours, except Monday and Wednesday).

EHGM (Rte de Niamey) has a 6am departure to Niamey (CFA13,700, 12 hours, Thu-Sun) and a departure to Zinder (CFA7,500, 7½ hours, Tuesday, Thursday and Saturday).

RTV (Rte de Niamey) links Agadez with Niamey (CFA14,000, 12 hours, daily except Mon & Weds) leaving at 6am. Another 6am bus leaves for Zinder (CFA7600, 7½ hours, Tuesday, Thursday and Saturday).

There are daily bush taxis to Arlit (CFA3000, four hours), as well as bush taxis to Zinder (CFA7000/8000, nine hours, Tuesday, Thursday and Saturday). You can save a few thousand CFAs by taking a bush taxi all the way to Niamey, but you may lose the will to live at the same time.

Getting Around
As with most Niger towns, *motos* are ideal for getting across town quickly (CFA250 per ride).

AÏR MOUNTAINS & TÉNÉRÉ DESERT
Some of West Africa's most awesome scenery is located around Agadez, though at the time of writing it was totally inaccessible due to the Tuareg Rebellion and the government's closure of much of Northern Niger. In the hopes that the area will reopen in the future, we've retained the information below.

Aïr Mountains
Simply put, the Aïr Mountains are among the most spectacular sights in West Africa. Dark, volcanic masses dramatically rise from the Saharan surrounds and culminate in grand peaks, the highest being Mt Bagzane (2022m), 145km from Agadez. In some areas marvellous deep blue marble outcrops poke from rich red sands – just amazing. Lurking within this range – which covers an area the size of Switzerland – are some fascinating prehistoric sites.

Besides the Neolithic art and general jaw-dropping scenery, some specific highlights of Aïr include a dip in the thermal hot springs at **Tafadek** (a slight detour off the main route north, some 60km from Agadez), and the oasis of **Timia**, which sits about 110km north of Elméki and 225km north of Agadez. The village of Timia, with its Tuareg residents,

mud-brick homes, verdant gardens and wavering palms, is a sight indeed, as is the nearby waterfall during the rains. Almost 30km north of Timia are the intriguing vestiges of the former Tuareg capital, **Assodé**, founded around AD1000 – have a wander.

About 150km further north, or 160km east from Arlit, is the beautiful oasis of **Iferouâne**. Northeast of Iferouâne, on the eastern boundary of the Aïr, the sand dunes at **Temet** are also well worth the journey.

Ténéré Desert
The Ténéré, east of the Aïr Mountains, is the one of the world's most legendary deserts and plays home to some of the Sahara's most extraordinarily beautiful sand dunes. Other areas are rather harsh and bleak, monotonous miles of flat hard sand, but, much like the Aïr Mountains hide their Neolithic artwork, the Ténéré holds its fair share of sublime secrets too – massive dinosaur graveyards and evocative, deserted medieval settlements.

If you head east from Agadez towards Bilma, you'll come to Tazolé after 100km. To the south is one of the Ténéré's **dinosaur cemeteries**, believed to be one of the globe's most important. Its fossils are spread over a belt 150km long. Continually covered and uncovered by the sand, they are silent witness to the fact that the whole Sahara Desert was once green and fertile. You may see fossils of a number of species, maybe even the Super Croc (see p583 for more on this monster).

Another 179km east and you'll pass the *Mad Max*–looking metal **Monument to the Arbre du Ténéré**, the only tree to have been marked on Michelin's Africa map (see the boxed text, below).

AFRICA'S LUCKIEST AND UNLUCKIEST TREE
Why does the Arbre du Ténéré deserve such a title? Well, it was lucky to have been the last surviving acacia of the once-great Saharan forests – standing alone in the desert's core, some 400km from its nearest relative. Unlucky? Sitting in a sea of sand and open space, what were the odds of a collision with a truck? Oh to have been a fly on the wall when the Libyan truck driver explained the accident to his boss back in 1973!

LA CURE SALÉE

One of the most famous annual celebrations in West Africa is the Cure Salée (Salt Cure). It's held in the vicinity of In-Gall, particularly around Tegguidda-n-Tessoum.

Each group of herders has its own Cure Salée, but that of the Wodaabé people is famous throughout Africa. The festival lasts a week, usually during the first half of September, and the main event happens over two days.

The Wodaabé are a unique sect of nomadic Fulani herders. When the Fulani migrated to West Africa centuries ago, possibly from the Upper Nile, many converted to Islam. For the Fulani who remained nomads, cattle retained their pre-eminent position. Valuing their freedom, they despised their settled neighbours and resisted outside influences. Many called themselves 'Wodaabé', meaning 'people of the taboo' – those who adhere to the traditional code of the Fulani, particularly modesty. The sedentary Fulani called them 'Bororo', a name derived from their cattle and insinuating something like 'those who live in the bush and do not wash'.

Wodaabé men have long, elegant, feminine features, and believe they have been blessed with great beauty. To a married couple, it's important to have beautiful children. Men who are not good-looking have, on occasion, shared their wives with more handsome men to gain more attractive children. Wodaabé women have the same elegant features and enjoy sexual freedom before marriage. During the year, the nomadic Wodaabé are dispersed, tending to their animals. As the animals need salt to remain healthy, the nomads bring their animals to graze in the area around In-Gall (known for its high salt content) at the height of the rainy season, when the grass can support large herds. During the Cure Salée, you'll see men on camels trying to keep their herds in order and camel racing. The event serves, above all, as a social gathering – a time for wooing the opposite sex, marriage and seeing old friends.

For the Wodaabé, the Cure Salée is the time for their Gerewol festival. To win the attention of eligible women, single men participate in a 'beauty contest'. The main event is the Yaake, which is a late-afternoon performance when the men dance, displaying their beauty, charisma and charm. In preparation they'll spend long hours decorating themselves in front of small hand mirrors. They then form a long line, dressed to the hilt with blackened lips (to make the teeth seem whiter), lightened faces, white streaks down their foreheads and noses, starlike figures painted on their faces, braided hair, elaborate headwear, anklets, all kinds of jewellery, beads and shiny objects. Tall, lean bodies, long slender noses, white even teeth, and white eyes are what the women are looking for.

After taking special stimulating drinks, the men dance for hours. Their charm is revealed in their dancing. Eventually, the women, dressed less elaborately, timidly make their choices. If a marriage proposal results, the man takes a calabash full of milk to the woman's parents. If they accept, he then brings them the bride price, three cattle, which are slaughtered for the festivities that follow.

Rivalry between suitors can be fierce, and to show their virility the young men take part in the *Soro*, an event where they stand smiling while others try to knock them over with huge sticks. At the end of the festival, the men remove their jewellery, except for a simple talisman.

Sadly the Cure Salée has been disrupted in recent years – both by the government's attempts to sanitise and promote the festival as a tourist attraction and more significantly by the Tuareg Rebellion that has seen events in 2007 and 2008 cancelled. Check with travel agencies in Niamey to see if the Cure Salée will be back on when you visit.

Some 171km further east is the salt-producing oasis of **Fachi** and, 610km from Agadez, **Bilma** – which is truly the end of the earth. This town satisfies every thought you ever had of an exotic oasis in the middle of a forbidding desert. It's fortified and surrounded by palm trees and irrigated gardens – everywhere are piles of salt destined for the market towns of southern Niger and northern Nigeria. You'll see how it is purified and poured into moulds made from large palm trunks, giving the salt its loaflike form (in contrast, for example, to the doorlike slabs from Mali). Unlike most of the rest of the Ténéré region, Bilma was open to travellers at the time of writing, though only via the desert road from Nguigmi.

Amis du Kawar et Fils des Oasis (☎ 20 73 55 45; mattress CFA3000) is a fairly basic camp site and restaurant in Bilma. Meals cost CFA1000 and the owner can organise tours of the salt mines. To get here from Nguigmi you'll need to travel in two vehicles (obligatory on this desert route) and have an accredited guide with you.

If you go north to the **Plateau du Djado**, about 1000km from Agadez via Bilma, you'll see some of the prehistoric cave paintings of antelopes, giraffes and rhinos for which the area is noted – not to mention deserted old towns, medieval *ksars* atop rocky crags and forbidding mountain scenery. The honeycombed vestiges of Djado's citadel are truly stunning.

ARLIT
pop 90,700
If you really want to travel to the ends of the earth, head for Arlit, in Niger's far north. A boomtown creation of the uranium discovered here in 1965, this modern city is effectively run by Somaïr, the uranium-mining company that extracts the silver gold. Since the original boom, Arlit's prosperity has risen and fallen with the price of uranium but with several major governments (including France, the former colonists) leaning towards nuclear power, Arlit's future may be getting brighter again.

Very few travellers would bother passing through Arlit were it not for the fact that it's the first town of any size in Niger if crossing the Sahara from Tamanrasset (Algeria)

Hôtel l'Auberge la Caravane (☎ 20 89 29 49; d with fan/air-con CFA6000/14,000; 🌣) is just west of town centre and a short walk from the SNTV station. The rooms are spartan and all but six have shared, slightly stinky toilets. It's the best Arlit has to offer.

The only other option is the **Tamesna Club** (☎ 20 45 23 32; d CFA5000), which has large but rather dingy rooms above its loud bar and is also the best place for food. There's also a string of street stalls selling brochettes in front of the Tamesna Club.

SNTV buses run south to Agadez (CFA3000, three hours, 4am) and Niamey (CFA17,500, 15 hours, daily except Monday and Wednesday). RTV, Aïr Transport and EHGM all have similar services.

NIGER DIRECTORY

ACCOMMODATION
Accommodation in Niger is relatively expensive by West African standards, and prices have risen significantly in recent years. A government tax of CFA500 per room per night is added to most bills, and is not included in the prices given here. Breakfast is almost never included in a room price, even though most hotels offer food in the morning.

The cheapest single rooms range from CFA3000 (for a real fleapit) to CFA8000 (usually clean and decent enough). Camping (typically CFA2000 per person) is possible in Niamey, Birni N'Konni, Ayorou and Parc Regional du W, though if you have your own tent, all you need to do is find a sympathetic landowner. Many hotels are happy for you to pitch a tent in their courtyards for a minimal fee.

Midrange hotels usually offer more cleanliness and your own bathroom. Prices in smaller towns start from CFA12,000 for a double room with fan, and another CFA5000 if you want air-con. Expect to pay up to double that in Niamey and Agadez.

Niamey and Agadez have upmarket hotels, where rooms cost between CFA30,000 and CFA85,000.

PRACTICALITIES

- The only daily newspaper is the dry pro-government French-language *Le Sahel,* which is available from roadside stalls and bookshops in Niamey.
- Besides some local music stations in Niamey, the government-run La Voix du Sahel is the only national radio station. Other radio stations broadcast in Niamey include Saraounia and Anfani.
- Télé-Sahel, which broadcasts news and French-language films, is the only non-satellite TV channel available. Some of the TVs in Niamey's hotels and restaurants pick up French-based programs.
- Electricity supply is 220V and plugs are of the European two-round-pin variety.
- The metric system is used in Niger.

ACTIVITIES

Coasting in a pirogue through hippos and the Niger River's moist environments, and watching the animal and bird life in the Parc Regional du W are the most obvious activities on offer in Niger. Sadly, at the present time lumbering through the Sahara's beautifully barren expanse with a camel train is no longer an option. See below.

BOOKS

While rather limited in its scope, *Riding the Demon: On the Road in West Africa* by Peter Chilson is an interesting attempt at painting a portrait of Niger using information gleaned during the author's time in and around bush taxis. Another travelogue of note is Jeffrey Tayler's *The Lost Kingdoms of Africa*, a journey through the Sahel in the shadow of 9/11 that takes in Zinder and Ayorou.

Nomads of Niger by Carol Beckwith is a gorgeous picture book depicting the lives of the Wodaabé people. Despite being published in 1983, Marion Van Offelen's text and Carol's pictures still captivate most readers.

Kathleen Hill's semi-autobiographical novel *Still Waters in Niger* tells of an Irish-American returning to Niger after a 17-year absence to visit her daughter, who's working as an aid worker.

BUSINESS HOURS

Typical business hours are from 8am to noon and 3pm to 6pm Monday to Friday, and from 8am to noon Saturday, though large markets bustle daily between 8am to 6pm. Government offices are open from 8.30am to 12.15pm and

NIGER

NIGER'S TUAREG REBELLION

The current Tuareg Rebellion, which began in 2007, is a continuation of the Tuareg's long-standing grievances with the central government in Niamey, which have fuelled previous rebellions in the area, most recently in 1990–95. The Tuareg have long felt aggrieved at what they perceive as their unfair marginalisation both politically and economically within Niger. Despite the vast sums of money generated by the uranium mining at Arlit, The Niger Movement for Justice (MNJ) claims that the latest uprising is due to the Niamey government's failure to honour the terms of the 1995 peace treaty, in which the north was promised a larger share of the uranium mining profits. They claim there remains a massive disparity in government spending between the Agadez region and regions in the Hausa and Djerma south and that education, healthcare and other basics of life are unavailable to the large majority of Tuareg living here.

Further grievance has been caused by the government's sale of uranium-prospecting contracts in the region to large foreign corporations, most notably China's SinoU, some of whose employees were kidnapped and later released by the rebels.

Incidents of violence have been various – from targeted attacks on military installations in the Agadez Region to seemingly random acts of violence, most notably a landmine in Niamey that killed one bystander in 2008. Furthermore, the Front des Forces de Redressement (FFR), a breakaway faction of the MNJ, have been even more extreme in their activities, even allegedly kidnapping the UN special envoy to Niger just a short distance outside Niamey in late 2008.

Journalists and aid workers have been banned from travelling to the Agadez region, and there are claims from human-rights groups that local civilians have been arrested and detained for joining demonstrations in Agadez, and that some towns have even been emptied by government forces relocating entire populations. Most of all the rebellion has had a devastating effect on the north's thriving tourist industry, with Agadez like a ghost town at the time of writing, many hotels and restaurants closed and no more charter flights from Europe landing. In practical terms this means that tourist revenue (which unlike uranium mining actually benefits many local people directly) has dropped to just a tiny trickle of its former self. There is no sign of peace likely either, and the north remains closed to foreigners, with the exception of Agadez (see p599) and the uranium mining town of Arlit (p605). Check on the latest situation before you head north – at the time of writing all vehicles had to travel with a military convoy north of Tahoua.

3.30pm to 6pm Monday to Friday. Banking hours are from 8am to 11.30am and 3.45pm to 5pm Monday to Friday, and from 8.30am to noon on Saturday. Simple local eateries open around 6am and don't shut the doors until 10pm, while fancier options serve breakfast from 7am to 10am, lunch from noon to 2pm (usually closing on the dot at two) and dinner between 6pm and 10pm.

CUSTOMS

The thoroughness of searches by customs officials varies, though foreign travellers are rarely targeted for a total going-over. Ignore requests for 'special taxes'. There's no limit on the import or export of foreign currencies.

DANGERS & ANNOYANCES

Due to the ongoing Tuareg Rebellion the north of Niger was at the time of writing still under military control, with foreigners restricted to visiting Agadez and Arlit. Travel to and from these cities from the south is only possible in military convoys. If you do visit the north, follow the rules and do not attempt to leave the towns and explore the Aïr Mountains or the Ténéré Desert until the situation changes.

An alarming spate of foreigner kidnappings in late 2008 and early 2009, especially close to the border with Mali, means that all travellers in Niger should exercise precautions – namely never driving alone and ideally taking local advice on which areas are safe for travel. We do not currently advise travel along the road between Gao (Mali) and Ayorou (Niger).

EMBASSIES & CONSULATES
Embassies & Consulates in Niger

All embassies and consulates are in Niamey unless stated. There's no UK diplomatic representation in Niger – British citizens should contact their embassy in Accra, Ghana (see p388). In an emergency Australians should contact the Canadian representative office in Niamey.

Algeria Agadez (☎ 20 44 01 17; ☽ 8am-2.30pm Mon-Fri, 8.30am-noon Sat); Niamey (☎ 20 72 35 83; Blvd des Ambassades; ☽ 9-11.30am Tue-Fri)

Benin (☎ 20 72 28 60; Rue des Dallois; ☽ 9am-4pm Mon-Fri) A new embassy out by Blvd des Ambassades was being constructed at the time of writing.

Canada (☎ 20 75 36 86; off Blvd de Mali Béro)

Chad (☎ 20 75 34 64; Ave de Presidence; ☽ 8.30am-3.30pm Mon-Thu, 8am-noon Fri)

France (☎ 20 72 24 31/32/33; Blvd des Ambassades; ☽ 8am-12.30pm Mon-Fri).

Germany (☎ 20 72 35 10; Ave du Général de Gaulle; ☽ 9am-noon Mon-Fri)

Mali (☎ 20 75 42 90; off Blvd des Ambassades; ☽ 8am-noon Mon-Fri)

Nigeria (☎ 20 73 24 10; Blvd des Ambassades; ☽ 10am-1pm Mon-Fri).

USA (☎ 20 73 31 69, 20 72 39 41; niamey.usembassy .gov; Rue des Ambassades; ☽ 8am-5.30pm Mon-Thu, to 1pm Fri)

FESTIVALS & EVENTS

The largest festival in all of Niger is the annual **Cure Salée** (Salt Cure) celebration held by the nomadic Fula and Tuareg peoples during September. While each group of herders has its own Cure Salée, the Wodaabé's celebration is renowned throughout all of West Africa (see the boxed text, p604).

A beauty contest of a very different variety occurs at Niamey's **Hangandi festival** (p584).

The Muslim holiday of **Tabaski** (see p601) in Agadez is an event indeed, with the 'cavalcade' camel race passing through town's crooked and crowded streets.

The months of July and August are also rich ones for festivals in the Sahara, with a large feast being held in a different village almost every week. Unfortunately, though, it's impossible to travel in the Sahara at present.

HOLIDAYS

With over 90% of the population being Muslim, Islamic holidays dominate the calendar (see p815 for dates and details). Other public holidays include the following:

New Year's Day 1 January
Easter March/April
Labour Day 1 May
Independence Day 3 August
Settlers' Day 5 September
Republic Day 18 December
Christmas Day 25 December

INTERNET ACCESS

Internet is readily available in all large towns via web cafes. A few hotels in Niamey have wi-fi – we have mentioned this in the reviews. Prices for web-cafe access range from CFA500 per hour to CFA1000.

LANGUAGE

French is the official language. The principal African languages are Hausa, spoken mainly in the south, and Djerma (also spelt Zarma), spoken mostly in the west, including around Niamey. Other languages include Gourmanchéma in the south and Fulfulde, Tamashek, Toubou and Kanuri, the languages of the northern nomadic and seminomadic herders. See p860 for useful phrases in French, Hausa, Fulfulde and Tamashek, the language of the Tuareg.

MONEY

The unit of currency is the West African CFA franc. Carrying cash in euros is best, though you'll rarely have trouble with US dollars. The most convenient bank to change cash (no commission) or travellers cheques (1.6% commission) are the branches of Banque Internationale pour l'Afrique – Niger (BIA-Niger) in Niamey, Maradi, Tahoua, Zinder and Agadez. The branches of Ecobank can also be helpful, but they tend to have higher commission charges (especially for travellers cheques).

There are currently no ATMs that accept foreign cards in Niger and credit-card advances (Visa and MasterCard) are only a real option in Niamey and Agadez (though don't rely on it in Agadez, frankly).

PHOTOGRAPHY & VIDEO

A photo or video permit is not required, but you should avoid taking pictures of government buildings, military sites, checkpoints, bridges (especially Kennedy Bridge in Niamey) and people bathing in the river. For more details see p821.

POST

Postal services outside the capital are slow and unreliable, so you should send everything from Niamey.

TELEPHONE

Niger's benighted landline network is extremely unreliable and as a result the country runs on mobiles – the main providers are Telcel, Zain, Orange and Moov. Anyone with an unlocked GSM mobile phone can buy a Nigerien SIM card at any service provider and put it into their own handset. Top-up cards are sold by street hawkers everywhere.

For those unable to use their own handsets, calls can be made internationally from street-side booths all over the country.

VISAS

Visas are required by everyone who isn't a West African citizen. Requirements change all the time, however, so check with a Nigerien embassy. One requirement that never changes is having a valid yellow-fever certificate to show at immigration on arrival.

Getting a visa outside West Africa is generally straightforward. You usually have to provide three photos, proof of yellow-fever vaccination (and cholera vaccination if entering from a country with a recent outbreak), a recent bank statement proving you have at least US$500, and a copy of your airline ticket proving onward travel (although this can usually be a ticket for departing some months later from another African country). Your passport must also be valid for at least six months after your planned exit date from Niger. You can find up-to-date information and printable visa application forms from the websites of Niger's embassies in Paris and Washington DC (www.nigerembassyusa.org). If applying in person, embassies usually process visas within 24 hours. Costs vary depending where you apply.

If you're travelling overland you'll find Niger visa information for the following countries on the following pages: Benin (p126), Mali (p538) and Nigeria (p663). Note that Niger is one of the five countries covered by the Visa Entente scheme that covers Benin, Burkina Faso, Côte d'Ivoire and Togo as well (see p826)

Visas are also available in Chad at the **Niger Consulate** (off Ave Gourang, N'Djaména). There is currently no Niger representation in Burkina Faso, but there is a **Niger Consulate** (☎ 213-788921; 54 Rue du Vercors) in Algiers.

Visa Extensions

For a one- to three-month visa extension, take two photos, your passport and CFA20,000 to the **Direction de la Surveillance du Territoire** (☎ 20 73 37 43, ext 249; Rue du Président Heinrich Lubké, Niamey; ✆ 8am-12.30pm & 3.30-6.30pm Mon-Fri). Extensions are typically processed the same day.

Visas for Onward Travel

In Niger, you can get visas for the following neighbouring countries.

ALGERIA

Two passport photos, a photocopy of your passport and CFA22,500 gets you an Algerian visa. Lodge the documents any time between 9am and 11.30am Tuesday to Friday and collect at 11.30am on the dot on Friday. You can also get an Algerian visa from the consulate in Agadez if you have a letter from an Algerian travel agency (stating your plans with the agency), a photocopy of your vehicle's *carte grise* and three colour photos.

BENIN

Transit visas cost CFA10,000, three-month single-entry tourist visas are CFA12,000 and three-month multiple-entry visas go for CFA25,000. You'll need to bring two photos and your passport between 9am and 4pm Monday to Friday. Visas are issued within 48 hours.

CHAD

For a single-entry one-month visa you'll need two photos, CFA15,000 and a pleasant demeanour. Visas are usually ready the same day.

MALI

A one- or two-month single-entry visa costs CFA20,000, requires one photo and leaving your passport at the embassy for 24 hours. Unluckily for them, US citizens are singled out to pay an extraordinary US$131 for their visas.

NIGERIA

Two passport photos and a photocopy of your passport are required to get a visa here. Handily no other documents are required, and contrary to what the ancient sign at the entrance gate says, passports are taken daily between 10am and 1pm and visas issued within 48 hours. The drawback is that the embassy charges you what your own country charges Nigerians for visas – which can work out to be expensive!

WOMEN TRAVELLERS

Whether in a group or alone, women rarely face any different trouble than men when travelling in Niger. Solo travellers will face more than their fair share of suitors, but their advances are typically harmless and can be easily rebuked. Remember that dress is taken very seriously in Muslim countries and shorts or singlets are not advised as they show a lack of sensitivity. For more general information and advice, see p826.

TRANSPORT IN NIGER

GETTING THERE & AWAY
Entering Niger

Despite needing to provide a yellow-fever vaccination certificate to obtain a visa, you'll still need to show it when entering the country. Proof of cholera vaccination is also occasionally asked for if you're entering Niger from a country with a recent outbreak.

If you have your ducks in a row, arriving by air or overland on public transport is pretty routine. Those in their own vehicles usually face more scrutiny and officials usually do their best to find/create problems with your *carnet,* international drivers licence or insurance papers.

Air

Airlines with offices in Niamey include the following.

Afriqiyah Airways (8U; ☎ 20 73 65 68/72; www.fly afriqiyah.eu; Rue Nasser) Flies between Tripoli and Niamey twice a week.

Air Algérie (AH; ☎ 20 73 38 99; www.airalgerie.dz; Rue du Gaweye) Links Niamey to Algiers each Monday and Friday.

Air Burkina (2J; ☎ 20 73 90 55; www.air-burkina.com; Rue du Commerce) Flies to Ouagadougou.

Air France (AF; ☎ 20 73 31 21/22; www.airfrance.com; Rue du Grand Hôtel) A KLM code share flies four times a week to Paris Charles de Gaulle, continuing to Amsterdam.

Air Sénégal International (V7; www.air-senegal -international.com). Flies from Dakar. Satguru Travel is the local representative. See p582.

Royal Air Maroc (AT; ☎ 20 73 28 85; www.royalair maroc.com; Rue du Gaweye) Flies to/from Casablanca five times a week.

Toumaï Air Tchad (☎ 20 73 04 05; Rue du Gaweye) Flies between Niamey & N'Djaména on Thursdays.

Land
ALGERIA

The classic crossing from Assamakka (Niger) to In GuezzAm (Algeria) is still open despite the Tuareg Rebellion and the area's general instability. You'll need your visa and paperwork in advance, including a licensed desert guide and *feuille de route* (official itinerary) if entering Niger here. You'll also have to travel in an infrequent military convoy from here to Agadez. If you are entering Algeria here, you'll need to be met by an official guide on the Algerian side of the border.

BENIN
The Gaya/Malanville border is open 24 hours a day and few travellers have problems here. The road connecting Niamey and Cotonou is sealed all the way and **SNTV** (☎ 20 73 30 20; Ave de Gamkalé, Niamey) runs daily buses between the two cities (CFA17,500, 13 to 15 hours), continuing to Lomé (CFA18,500). **EHGM** (☎ 20 74 37 16; Blvd de Mali Béro, Niamey) runs a similar daily service to Cotonou for CFA18,700, as does **Rimbo** (☎ 20 74 14 13; Blvd de Mali Béro).

Bush taxis don't cross the border, so you'll have to use a *moto* (CFA500) to link Gaya and Malanville. See the Gaya (p591) and Malanville (p123) sections for further transport information.

BURKINA FASO
The main crossing linking Niger and Burkina Faso is Foetchango, southwest of Niamey. It's pretty straightforward and is open around the clock. SNTV and Rimbo buses cover the 500km between Niamey and Ouagadougou (CFA10,000, nine to 11 hours, daily).

Minibuses leave Niamey's *gare routière*, which is 1km west of Kennedy Bridge, for Makalondi (CFA2500, 1¼ hours), Kantchari (CFA3400, two hours) and Ouagadougou (CFA8500, 10 to 12 hours). Note that times to Kantchari and Ouagadougou don't include border festivities at Foetchango. Despite what drivers tell you, Peugeot taxis don't cross the border and you must change at Kantchari.

An alternative crossing for those with their own vehicles is the northwestern route via Téra. It involves a short but enjoyable ferry crossing (CFA1000) at Farié (62km northwest of Niamey).

Remember that there's an hour's time difference between Niger and Burkina Faso.

CHAD
Banditry is rife around the Niger–Chad border, so this is an adventurous route to take, and one you should only do in daylight. There's no scheduled public transport travelling across the border, but there are a couple of Landcruisers that make the dusty day-long journey from Nguigmi to Mao in Chad (CFA20,000) each week. From Mao you may have to wait several days before you find something to get you to N'Djaména.

Don't forget to get your passport stamped in Nguigmi and Mao, and remember that, in Chad, they use Central African CFA francs.

LIBYA
At present the border with Libya is closed.

MALI
Buses make the journey to Gao from Niamey every day. SNTV (CFA7225, daily except Sun) and Rimbo (CFA8500, daily) leave at 6am from their respective hubs in the capital and the journey can take between 24 and 30 hours. The road from Niamey to Ayorou is sealed; from the border at Labbézanga it's sandy to Gao. From July to September, the route is muddy and the journey has been described by one reader as 'a horrific journey of hassles, bureaucracy, time-wasting and general lunacy'. Take plenty of water.

It's also possible to take a slow-boat from Ayorou to Gao (CFA50,000, two days) on Monday. There's no shade, so a hat, or better yet an umbrella, is as crucial as a large supply of water.

NIGERIA
There are four border crossings between Niger and Nigeria: Gaya/Kamba, Birni N'Konni/Illela, Maradi/Katsina and Zinder/Jibiya. With Nigerian authorities having about five standard checks (customs, immigration, luggage, drugs and bribe), few travellers have a painless and timely crossing.

The quickest option from Niamey is the Gaya/Kamba crossing. Several buses/bush taxis make daily runs from Niamey to Gaya (CFA5500/4250, five hours), from where you can hop on a *moto* or grab a shared taxi to the Nigerian border (CFA100). From there you can get another *moto* to Kamba.

Crossing at Birni N'Konni/Illela is also straightforward. Take a *moto* from Birni N'Konni to the border (CFA150), where you'll find minibuses/Peugeots running to/from Sokoto (1½ hours).

Peugeots link Maradi with the Nigerian towns of Katsina (CFA1200, 1½ hours) and Kano (CFA3000, four hours).

Zinder is also connected to Kano via the Jibya crossing. Several Peugeots (CFA3000, 3½ hours) ply this route each day.

None of the transportation times mentioned above include border procedures/hold-ups.

GETTING AROUND
Air
There are no scheduled flights within Niger at present. If you're short on time and flush with cash, **Tamara Niger Aviation** (☎ 20 73 85 85/86; aklyjoulia@yahoo.fr) has a 10-seater plane for charter, and can even fly you to Agadez.

Bus
With decent tarmac roads stretching the breadth of the country, bus transport in Niger is fairly comprehensive, reliable and efficient. As well as the state-owned bus company SNTV, private companies EHGM, RTV and Aïr Transport are the major players, all offering very similar routes, prices and standards of service.

All companies have reserved seating, so there shouldn't be anyone in the aisles, though private companies sometimes bend this rule. It's best to book your ticket early to ensure a seat. Each company's buses leave from their respective offices in each town.

Bush Taxi
Bush taxis are cheaper and leave more frequently than buses, although they're always very crowded and can take twice as long for the same journey due to breakdowns, the driver stopping to buy or sell things, arguments and general chaos.

There are two types of bush taxi: Peugeot 504 seven-seater station wagons, which carry 10 people; and Japanese minibuses, which carry about 18 people. The Peugeots are preferable because they fill faster and stop less, though the most comfortable option is to pay about 10% more for the front window seat of a minibus (ask for cabin and point to the window). To get the same amount of room in a Peugeot you'd have to pay double.

Bush taxis cover all but the most remote villages, although there's next to no public transport in the Sahara. In rural areas you'll find converted trucks and pick-ups called *fula-fulas*, which are cheap, slow and terribly uncomfortable.

Car & Motorcycle
BRINGING YOUR OWN VEHICLE
While most information regarding bringing your own vehicle into West Africa is on p834, bear in mind that should the north reopen to independent travel, private vehicles are not allowed to drive north from Agadez or north from Nguigmi without a licensed Nigerien guide and *feuille de route* (official itinerary) – both normally available through Nigerien travel agencies. If you want to visit very remote areas, like the Plateau du Djado, you'll even have to hire a second vehicle to escort you.

HIRE
Car and 4WD hire can be organised in Niamey, though in general it's expensive. Shop around for the best deals. In general it's usually only possible to hire a car or 4WD with a driver, although some agencies may be flexible about this. See p588.

INSURANCE
To legally drive your vehicle in Niger, you must posses third-party insurance. This regulation is rigorously checked at roadside stops throughout the country and at the borders. While there's nowhere to buy insurance immediately upon entering Niger, officials will let you proceed to the first town that sells it. Société Nigérienne d'Assurances de Réassurances has offices in Niamey, Diffa, Maradi, Zinder and Birni N'Konni. Its insurance costs less than CFA2500 per day.

ROAD CONDITIONS.
Most main roads in Niger are tarmac and are in generally good condition, although some sections, like that between Zinder and Gouré, are rather cratered and dire indeed. Thanks to being engulfed by the desert, the Zinder-Agadez road is the only major road that isn't passable with a 2WD.

ROAD HAZARDS
While it's usually totally fine, you're best not driving at night. At the time of writing it was only possible to drive north of Tahoua towards Agadez as part of a military convoy.

ROAD RULES
Driving is done on the right side of the road in Niger. Private cars must pay a toll (*péage*) to use the main routes. You buy a ticket before travelling from a checkpoint on the edge of each town, either for a whole trip, eg Niamey to Agadez (CFA1000), or in sections, eg Niamey to Tahoua (CFA500), then Tahoua to Agadez (CFA500). If you don't have a ticket

when it's asked for at a checkpoint, you're fined on the spot.

As a courtesy while driving on the highway, you should always switch on your left-turn signal when you see a vehicle coming in the opposite direction. Don't turn it off until the vehicle has safely passed you. This routine is to simply let the approaching driver know that you've seen them and that it's safe to pass on your left.

Tours

Your only choice in order to visit Parc Regional du W may be to take an organised tour. Tours to Parc Regional du W are discussed on p582.

Nigeria

It's safe to say that Nigeria's reputation precedes it. Everyone seems to know the 'facts': it's big, crazy and dangerous, with email scams its most famous export. Enough to make you draw a big detour line on your travel map through West Africa? Think again, because we'd like to change your mind. Simply put: we love Nigeria.

Nigeria is superlative in every sense. It's the most populous country on the continent – every fifth African is a Nigerian – it dominates the region economically, and its cultural output ranges from literary masterpieces such as *Things Fall Apart* and *Purple Hibiscus* to the infectious grooves of Fela Kuti's Afrobeat.

Contrasts abound. The sprawling megalopolis of Lagos contrasts sharply with the ancient Muslim cities of the north and the river deltas and lush forests of the south and east. There's wildlife too, from pioneering conservation organisations in Calabar to Gashaka-Gumti National Park, recently reorganised to accept visitors.

Nigeria can feel like more than the sum of its parts – an unruly collection of regions and ethnicities pulling against each other with a centrifugal force that occasionally bursts into chaos. But against this, the hard work and proud smiles of Nigerians offer the perfect corrective for visitors.

We can't lie: getting around can sometimes be exhausting, and it's not a destination for first-timers to Africa. But put the scare stories to one side and you might be in for a pleasant surprise. If you don't visit Nigeria you can barely say that you've been to West Africa.

NIGERIA

FAST FACTS

- **Area** 924,000 sq km
- **Capital** Abuja
- **Country code** ☎ 234
- **Famous for** Corruption; email scams; writers Wole Soyinka and Chinua Achebe; Afrobeat
- **Language** English, Hausa, Igbo, Yoruba
- **Money** naira (N); US$1= N147; €1= N196
- **Population** 146 million
- **Visa** Get in advance, letter of invitation usually required

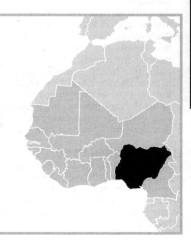

HIGHLIGHTS

- **Lagos** (p622) Plunge in and sample the adrenaline charge and social scene of Nigeria's wild beating heart.
- **Calabar** (p639) Take in colonial history and cutting-edge conservation in this easy-going old river port.
- **Kano** (p653) Find a trace of the old Saharan trade routes in the old city and the indigo dye pits.
- **Afi Mountain Drill Ranch** (p643) Head into the rainforest to spend time at a pioneering primate research centre, experiencing traditional village life and canopy walkways.
- **Gashaka-Gumti National Park** (p649) Head into the real wilds to explore this newly reorganised mountain-meets-savannah national park.

ITINERARIES

- **One to Two Weeks** No one should visit Nigeria without at least a few days in Lagos (p622), trying to navigate the city's mindset and traffic jams, and spending late nights in the bars and clubs. When Lagos gets too much, head east to Benin City (p635) to see the ancient craft of brass sculpture, before carrying on to the old port city of Calabar (p639), where you can check out some pioneering primate conservation work and the country's best museum, Calabar Museum. You could also stop off at Umuahia (p638) to see the National War Museum and learn about the Biafran conflict. Extend your time in the southeast in the lush forests of the Afi Mountain Drill Ranch (p643).
- **One Month** A longer trip allows you to further explore the south, but also to take in northern Nigeria. From Lagos, fly to Abuja (p643), and then continue by road to the old trading cities of Zaria (p651) and Kano (p653). An interesting detour would be via the cool plateau city of Jos (p646), with a side trip to the remote and exciting Gashaka-Gumit National Park (p649).

CLIMATE & WHEN TO GO

For travel to the south, March to August are the wettest months to visit, and best avoided if possible. Temperatures are hot year-round, peaking at about 35°C in the spring; the humidity is constant. Late spring to summer is the hottest part of the year in the north

> **HOW MUCH?**
>
> - **Okada (motocycle taxi) ride across town** N40
> - **Replica Benin brass sculpture** N12,000
> - **Afrobeat CD** N400
> - **Bribe at police roadblock** N20
> - **One-minute local phonecall** N20
>
> **LONELY PLANET INDEX**
>
> - **1L of petrol** N70
> - **1L of bottled water** N100
> - **Beer (bottle of Star)** N200
> - **Souvenir football shirt** N900
> - **Street snack (stick of suya)** N100

(sometimes topping out at an extreme 45°C). The mercury drops from October to January at the onset of the dusty harmattan winds. See also Climate Charts, p810.

As well as the weather, take note of political developments when planning your trip. Although the country is generally calm, local trouble can quickly flare up, so once you're in Nigeria keep an eye on the news and be prepared to change your plans at short notice if necessary.

HISTORY

The historical and cultural trajectories of northern and southern Nigeria followed vastly different paths up to their melding into one country under the British. The first recorded empire to flourish in this part of West Africa was that of the Kanem-Borno, in the north around Lake Chad. Its wealth was based on control of the important trans-Saharan trade routes from West Africa to the Mediterranean and the Middle East. Islam arrived in the 12th century and was adopted as the state religion in the empire. A number of Islamic Hausa kingdoms also flourished between the 11th and 14th centuries, based around the cities of Kano, Zaria and Nupe.

Islam made little headway in the south, and the southwest became a patchwork of small states, often dominated by the Yoruba. One of the earliest kingdoms, Ijebu, arose in the 10th century, and built the earthworks at Sungbo's Eredo. This was followed in the 14th and 15th

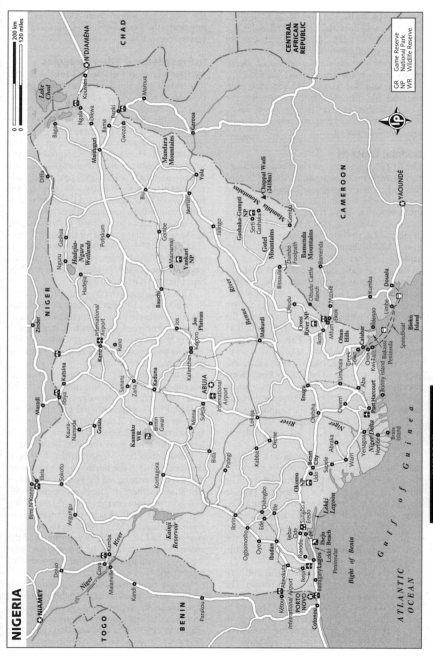

centuries by the Ife, Oyo and Benin Kingdoms, which became important centres of trade. The Benin, the most famous, produced some of the finest metal artwork in Africa. The political systems of these states rested on a sacred monarchy, with a strong court bureaucracy. The *obas* (chiefs or kings) of these states retain considerable influence. In the southeast, the Igbo and other agrarian peoples never developed any centralised empires, instead forming loose confederations.

Colonial Contacts

The first contact between the Yoruba empires and Europeans was made in the 15th century, when the Portuguese began trading in pepper – which was later supplanted by the more lucrative slave trade. In contrast, the northern Islamic states continued to trade principally across the Sahara, and remained untouched by European influence until well into the 19th century.

While the slave trade flourished until the early 19th century, the Portuguese were eventually pushed out by other European powers. As the abolition movement grew, the British took a lead in suppressing slavery along the Niger Delta, where conflicts with Yoruba slavers led to the annexation of Lagos port – their first colonial toehold.

At the same time, Islamic revivalism was sweeping the north. The Hausa kings were overthrown by their Fulani subjects who, in the 1820s, set up a caliphate based in Sokoto, led by Osman Dan Fodio. The caliphate eventually stretched from Senegal to Cameroon, with its religious fervour inspiring Islamic revolutions across the region.

The British grab for Nigeria was a classic piece of imperial buccaneering, inspired by the palm-oil trade that replaced slaving. The Royal Niger Company was formed in 1879, to cut out local middlemen and thwart the ambitions of the French, who were advancing along the Niger River. From here it was a short step to full annexation, and after the turn of the 20th century, British soldiers stormed Sokoto and Kano to create Nigeria.

Nigeria was divided in two – the southern Colony and the northern Protectorate. The British chose to rule indirectly through local kings and chiefs, a policy that worked well in the northern city-states, but much less so in the southwest, where none of the traditional Yoruba rulers had ever extracted taxes. In the southeast, where there had never been any centralised authority, the policy was even less successful.

Independence & Other Struggles

Indirect rule stored up trouble for the future. The north remained economically underdeveloped, while in the south, Western education and Christian missionaries were promoted. As cries for independence grew louder after WWII, the British struggled to balance the interests of the regions while drawing up a new constitution. The Hausa north feared that the southerners' educational advantage would allow them to dominate politics and commerce, while mistrust between the Yorubas and Igbos divided the south. The British divided the country into three regions between these ethnic groups.

Tensions arose over who was to dominate the federal parliament. After the hard-fought elections of 1959, Sir Abubakar Tafawa Balewa, a moderate northerner, was asked to form a government. Nigeria became an independent republic on 1 October 1960.

The coalition government of the First Republic was a disaster. Politics degenerated into regional self-interest, corruption became rampant and the elite accumulated wealth by any means possible. The elections of 1965 were so outrageously rigged that protesting groups went on a rampage.

By early 1966, the stage was set for a development that would dominate Nigeria for years: the army got involved in politics. A group of Igbo officers staged a coup. Balewa and the premiers of the north and west were assassinated, and General Ironsi, the Igbo head of the army, took the reins of power.

Ironsi barely lasted four months. Anti-Igbo riots broke out in the north, and he was overthrown by a regime led by Yakubu Gowon, a Christian northerner. The violence grew, with anti-Igbo pogroms in the north and attacks on Hausas in the south. A state of emergency was announced, but in May 1967 the east's military governor, Lt Colonel Ojukwu, announced the secession of Biafra, the Igbo homeland that was awash with newly found oil. A bloody civil war began.

Independent Biafra was recognised by only a handful of African countries, who were often insecure in their own postcolonial borders; most international powers supported the federal government. The civil war dragged on for nearly three years, as the Igbo forces fought tooth and claw for every inch of territory that the federal forces took back. By early 1970, as a result of a blockade imposed by the federal government, Biafra faced starvation – this was the world's first 'TV famine', reported by a largely pro-Biafra international media. Biafra's forces finally capitulated, and Ojukwu fled the country. Up to a million Igbos had died in the war, mainly from hunger.

Oil Boom & Bust

A policy of 'no victors, no vanquished' smoothed the path to reconciliation, which was aided in part by the sudden rocketing of world oil prices. Nigeria's oil production increased sevenfold between 1965 and 1973, and Gowon's military government became drunk on easy money. Foreign contractors chased oil dollars to Lagos, corruption exploded and crime was rampant. The chaos eventually became unbearable and, in July 1975, Gowon was overthrown in a bloodless coup led by General Murtala Mohammed.

The new government launched a cleanup of the civil service, the judiciary and the universities. However, despite his widespread popularity, Mohammed was assassinated by the army in early 1976. His successor, Biafra war hero Olusegun Obasanjo, drafted a US-style constitution and handed power back to a civilian government following elections in 1979. A northerner, Shehu Shagari, was sworn in as president.

Shagari followed earlier leaders by squandering Nigeria's wealth, a problem compounded when the price of oil crashed in the early 1980s and the country found itself in debt to the tune of US$18 billion. Foreign workers packed up and left, and those who didn't (three million West Africans) were expelled as convenient scapegoats for the economic crisis. Shagari's end came with a coup on New Year's Eve 1983.

The new general in charge, Mohammed Bahari, tried playing the autocrat, but didn't have much time to enjoy his position. As regular as clockwork, another coup – Nigeria's sixth since independence – toppled him from power, to be replaced by General Ibrahim Babangida in 1985.

Military Misrule

Babangida gained instant popularity by releasing political prisoners, and by lifting press controls. He also attempted something of an economic revolution, by devaluing the naira and privatising many public enterprises, but these measures bore little fruit. Oil revenues dropped again and the country's debt rose to US$20 billion. Crime and corruption increased, with those on government payrolls often the worst culprits. The country was broke.

Babangida promised to return Nigeria to democracy with his 1989 Abuja Declaration, announced from the new capital. Under this, political parties were allowed, but a return to civilian rule was twice postponed. A multibillion dollar oil windfall from rising oil prices on the back of the Gulf War disappeared before even reaching the government's coffers and, as the general population suffered fuel shortages, unrest spread.

The much-delayed presidential elections went ahead in June 1993. Chief Moshood Abiola, a wealthy Yoruba Muslim from the south, claimed victory, having gained unprecedented support across ethnic and religious lines. The result met with little favour among the Hausa-dominated military, and Babangida annulled the election result within a fortnight. Abiola fled the country and an announcement of new polls was greeted by widespread rioting. Babangida's army colleagues forced him out of power, to be replaced by the vice-president General Sani Abacha.

Abacha was a grotesque caricature of an African dictator. He offered no warm words about a return to democracy, abolished any institutions that might suggest otherwise and purged the army of potential coup plotters. Abiola was arrested and charged with treason. Intellectuals, labour leaders, politicians and prodemocracy leaders were also arrested.

Unrest in the oil-rich Delta brought a particularly tough clampdown. Ken Saro-Wiwa, an Ogoni activist and writer, was executed in November 1995 for allegedly plotting to overthrow the government – an action that led to Nigeria's expulsion from the Commonwealth and EU oil sanctions.

Abacha cared less about Nigeria's international isolation than siphoning off its wealth into foreign bank accounts. But in June 1998, Nigerians were finally rescued by the 'coup from heaven'. Aged 54, and worth somewhere between US$2 to US$5 billion in stolen money (figures from Transparency International reports) Abacha died of a heart attack while in the company of two prostitutes. His defence chief, Abdulsalam Abubakar, was sworn in as his successor and immediately promised reforms. In a strange echo of Abacha's fate, Abiola died of a heart attack within a month of the dictator, still claiming the presidency. While viewed as suspicious by many Nigerians, his death cleared the way for the military to hold elections, and many other political prisoners were subsequently released. In February 1999, Olusegun Obasanjo, the former military leader and southern Yoruba Christian, was elected as president, under the banner of the People's Democratic Party (PDP).

Nigeria Today

Nigeria was in tatters. Free from the military yoke, the deep political and cultural differences between the north and south of the country began to play themselves out in an unruly manner. A major test came in 2000, when several northern states introduced Sharia, or Islamic law, amid a climate of religious revivalism. Tensions between communities became inflamed and the federal government handled the situation badly, resulting in mass riots and bloodshed. Local and national politicians repeatedly used ethnic and religious differences to build power bases, sometimes stoking unrest for their own gain. During Obasanjo's first term as president, over 10,000 people were killed in communal violence.

Obasanjo brought Nigeria some muchneeded stability, and did much to restore the country's international image, making it a regional player economically and in African peacekeeping missions, as well as earning the country significant debt relief from Western financial institutions. But at the same time

infrastructure was allowed to further crumble, most notably the electricity and oil industries. Chronic power and petrol shortages proved a major brake on the economy, while longsimmering discontent over distribution of oil money blew into a full-scale insurgency in the Niger Delta region (see the boxed text, p639 for more).

Obasanjo's supporters sought unsuccessfully to amend the constitution to allow him to stand for a third presidential term. Despite party divisions, the PDP instead chose northern governor Umaru Yar'Adua as their presidential candidate for the April 2007 general election. Although he was duly returned, both election results and process were highly controversial. Violence at the ballot box and widespread allegations of vote-rigging led many local and international observers (including the US State Department and the Chief EU observer) to dispute the credibility of the results, prompting dozens of challenges against the results in the courts.

After the high-flying Obasanjo, Yar'Adua has proved a complete contrast. His quiet and deliberative style has earned him the nickname 'Baba Go-Slow'. He has declared the electricity shortages a national emergency, although electricity output (particularly for Lagos) has actually fallen slightly since he took office. At the same time, the increased audacity of the Niger Delta rebels has slashed oil production and cost the government billions in revenue. But governing as complicated a country as Nigeria is a balancing act that would tax the keenest of minds, and slow but steady progress is perhaps the best that the immediate future can offer.

419

Ever received an email offering you a share of untold riches in exchange for help repatriating a hidden fortune, quite possibly from the widow of an African dictator? Chances are it came from Lagos, spiritual home of the internet scam. Known locally as a 419 (from its classification in the Nigerian criminal code), so-called 'advance fee fraud' is rife in Nigeria. Successful scammers ('yahoo yahoos') can make thousands of dollars a month from 419. In Nigeria, there's often little sympathy for the *maghas* (Yoruba slang for fool) who lose their shirts – they're as often seen as victims of their own greed and gullibility, yet more foreigners hoping to make a cynical fortune out of Africa. Scams provide rich inspiration for local musicians, with songs like '419 State of Mind' by rapper Modenine and Osuofia's 'I Go Chop Your Dollar' both celebrating and satirising the hustle.

But foreigners aren't the only victims of fraud. Inside Nigeria, a popular scam is to break into an empty property and then sell it on to an unsuspecting buyer – watch out for painted signs everywhere announcing 'This house is not for sale: beware 419'.

THE CULTURE
National Psyche

The economy lumbers on, but is a long way from keeping up with the rapidly growing populace, let alone reaching the bright potential it showed at independence. Oil has proved to be a curse on the country, with politicians repeatedly pumping money straight out of the wells and into private bank accounts. In 2005, the government's anticorruption commission announced that over US$352 billion had been stolen or misused since the oil came on tap: four times the value of all Western aid given to the whole of Africa in the last 40 years.

Ordinary Nigerians have been the ones to pay the price. Infrastructure has been neglected and agriculture, the mainstay of most of the population, has been largely ignored. Once a food exporter, Nigeria now imports most of its food, meaning higher prices for the majority of Nigerians living on just a few dollars a day. Healthcare is also in crisis. Around 3.1 percent of adults ages 15–49 are living with HIV/AIDS, and Nigeria is one of the few African countries where polio is still endemic.

Corruption is probably the worst problem facing Nigeria, as its corrosive effects have permeated every aspect of society. While roadside billboards plead with people to pay their taxes, federal and state budgets are constantly skimmed by dodgy officials and ordinary people have to pay cash for everything from government services to getting through police roadblocks. No country in Africa has such a vast gap between its superrich and abject poor.

Against all this, it almost seems incredible that smiles come so readily to Nigerian faces. The important role that religion plays in everyday life is a major factor, along with the natural entrepreneurship of one of Africa's better-educated populations. Ill-served by repeated governments, Nigerians have had to learn to survive. As Fela Kuti sang, 'we suffer and we smile'. This resilience holds the best key to Nigeria's future.

Population

With 140 million people already, Nigeria has a huge and expanding population. By the middle of the 21st century it's thought that as many as one in three people on the African continent will be a Nigerian. The main ethnic groups are the Yoruba (in the southwest), Hausa (north) and Igbo (southeast), each making up around a fifth of the population, followed by the northern Fulani (around 10%). It's thought that up to 250 languages are spoken in Nigeria.

SPORT

Football is the only game that matters in Nigeria, and players regard themselves as virtually African footballing royalty. The country regularly produces fine players that make their way to Europe to play in the Premiership, La Liga and Serie A, and travellers should get used to being asked their opinions on the relative merits of Beckham and Ronaldinho. Unfortunately for Nigeria, their foreign-based players have a great tradition of being prima donnas, and of putting club before country. Used to good performances in successive World Cups since the mid-1990s, the 'Super Eagles' national side has largely disappointed in recent years. Nigeria hosted the FIFA Under-17 World Cup in 2009.

RELIGION

Nigeria may just be the most visibly religious country in Africa, but there's a very clear divide between the Christian south and the Muslim north.

In the south, everything stops on a Sunday, as the population goes to church en masse. The more traditional churches imported during colonial rule are now being upstaged by an explosion of evangelism. You'll constantly see them publicised on huge billboards, usually announcing 'miracle crusades' and faith healing. Large gatherings can attract tens of thousands of worshippers, but there's tight – and not always particularly faithful – competition between the churches for new souls. Older Nigerian faiths, such as those involving the rich pantheon of Yoruba gods, are also increasingly threatened, but some traditions have been carried over – look out for adverts for schnapps, used for libations at prayers: 'Don't offend your ancestors with fakes: insist on the Original Prayer Drink', reads one.

This 'good time' religion collides hard and fast with the mosques and minarets of the north. Cities such as Kano have long pedigrees as centres of Islamic learning, but they haven't been immune to the politicisation sweeping the Islamic world. Since the return to democracy in 1999, many northern states have enacted laws based on Islamic Sharia

NIGERIA

law. Alcohol bans have been enforced (with mixed success) and education is increasingly segregated. While Nigerian Muslims are tolerant and welcoming to foreign visitors, relations with Christians in the north are under increasing strain. The introduction of Sharia law – and the issue of its application to non-Muslims – is a political tinderbox, and one that has ignited with worrying frequency into communal violence.

ARTS

As befits its size, Nigeria is a major cultural player in West Africa.

Literature

Nigeria seems to have as many writers as the rest of the continent combined. Chinua Achebe is probably Nigeria's (and Africa's) most famous author; his *Things Fall Apart* is widely credited with opening the world's eyes to African literature. Equally acclaimed writers include Nobel laureate Wole Soyinka and Booker Prize winner Ben Okri. For more, see p47.

More recently, a new generation of young Nigerian writers has been claiming a seat at the literary table. Internationally acclaimed novels by Chimamanda Ngozi Adichie (*Purple Hibiscus* and *Half a Yellow Sun*), Helon Habila (*Waiting for an Angel*) and Sefi Atta (*Everything Good Will Come*)

have demonstrated that 'Naija Lit' is in rude health, with writers being broken by savvy Nigerian publishers like Cassava Republic and Kachifo/Farafina. Lagos and Abuja are both great places to pick up new African literature.

Music

Some of Africa's best-known musicians have been Nigerian. Two styles have traditionally been dominant, Afrobeat and *juju* (from the Yoruba word for dance), with their respective masters being the late Fela Kuti (see the boxed text, below) and King Sunny Ade. For more on these styles see p57.

Turn on the radio, and you're as likely to hear American influences on modern Nigeria, artists as much as traditional styles. Superstars like P-Square and D'Banj add R&B to the local mix, while Ruggedman and Modenine both fly the flag for Nigerian hip-hop. Thrown in folk-heroine Asa and Afrobeat stars like Lagbaja and Fela's son Femi Kuti, and Lagos is revealed as one of Africa's hottest musical destinations. In the 1970s, the likes of Paul McCartney and James Brown flocked to the city to pay tribute to Fela Kuti, but these days you're as likely to find 50-Cent, Beyoncé or Usher playing here, testament to the strength and influence of the contemporary Nigerian scene.

FELA KUTI – KING OF AFROBEAT

The figure of the late Fela Kuti stands like a colossus over modern Nigerian music. Born in 1938 in Abeokuta, he is celebrated as much for his political and social consciousness as much as his deliriously infectious music. Trained in both classical Western and African music, his personal style changed radically after a trip to the USA in the late 1960s, where he was profoundly influenced by the American civil rights struggle and the music of James Brown. Returning to Nigeria and teaming up musical virtuosos like drummer Tony Allen and trumpeter Tunde Williams, Fela mixed Brown's soul grooves with the many intricacies of Nigerian music to create Afrobeat. His bands Afrika 70 and Egypt 80 set the new gold standard for Nigerian music, with huge line-ups, massed dancers and epic concert lengths.

Using music to criticise Nigerian politics was key to Fela. During the 1970s, he formed the Kalakuta Republic, a commune for playing music and polygamy. Government forces burnt it down in 1977, an action that resulted in the death of Fela's mother. In response he continued to play music with lyrics critical of the military regime and simultaneously married 27 women. His views brought him repeated political trouble – briefly jailed on trumped-up currency-smuggling charges in 1985, he was later falsely accused of killing a man. Fela avoided the authorities throughout the 1990s and retired to a quiet life of performing twice a week at The Shrine, his Lagos nightclub. When he died of AIDS in 1997, his funeral prompted one of Lagos' greatest go-slows. Fela's essential recordings can be heard on *The Best Best of Fela Kuti* CD, and the documentary *Music is the Weapon*.

Cinema

Hidden from the eyes of most of the world, Nigeria has the third-biggest film industry on the planet, after the USA and India. With typical local brio it's dubbed 'Nollywood', and turns out over 45 movies *every week*. As cinemas are a rarity in Nigeria, films are shot to video and sold at shops and market stalls. They're great fun and hugely popular.

Nollywood's heartland is Surelere in Lagos. Movies are shot quickly and without fuss – it can take just two months to go from script to marketplace, with budgets typically around US$10,000. Plots are simple and melodramatic – family conflict and morality tales are staples. Nigeria's leading film-maker is Jeta Amata, whose films *The Amazing Grace* and *The Alexa Affair* have won international acclaim far beyond his Nollywood roots.

Visual Arts

Nigeria boasts some of the earliest and most acclaimed sculpture in Africa. The Jos Plateau's Nok Terracottas, featuring human figures 120cm tall and dating back over 2500 years, are the oldest sub-Saharan sculptures known. More famous still are the 16th-century Benin Brasses, ceremonial figures and masks produced for the court of the Benin Kingdom using the lost wax method, which were famously looted by the British army in 1897; most of those not in Lagos' National Museum are in the British Museum. Many tribal groups still produce fine sculptures and masks, most notably the wood carvings of the Yoruba.

Lagos is the home of Nigeria's busiest art scene, and contemporary artists display regularly at galleries such as Terra Kulture and Nimbus. Tola Wewe (sometimes dubbed the African Picasso) is one of Nigeria's most celebrated painters, while Nike Okundaye-Davies is internationally acclaimed for her batiks – see also her gallery and guesthouse in Oshogbo (p634), along with other galleries in that famous artists' city.

ENVIRONMENT

Nigeria occupies 15% of West Africa, but contains half of its people. In the north, the Sahel gives way to savannah and low hills, rising to a plateau in the centre of the country. From the west, the country is bisected by the Niger, Africa's third-longest river, which enters the Atlantic through a delta fringed with lagoons and swamps. Nigeria's second river is the Benue, which flows west from Cameroon and joins the Niger. Shared with Cameroon are Nigeria's mountains, the Adamawa Massif. Forest forms a thick line along the southern coast, inland from the delta.

Environmental Issues

Nigeria has extraordinary biological diversity, but the country's rapidly expanding population has put the environment under extreme pressure. An underfunded National Parks service does exist, but in practice very little land in Nigeria is protected. Deforestation is one of the largest problems, with Nigeria having logged around 95% of its original forests since independence. Where original forest exists, the local bushmeat trade threatens mammal species further.

In the Delta, the oil industry has created a host of problems to match the wealth it generates. Oil spills are commonplace, with few ever cleaned up adequately. The local fishing industry, a mainstay of the delta economy, has suffered grievously. Pollution caused by gas flaring (the burning of gas released during extraction) continues unabated, despite being declared illegal in 1984, as well as wasting a potential fuel source for electricity generation.

Wildlife

Despite the problems facing the Nigerian environment, it is possible to see wildlife in the country. **Yankari National Park** (p648) is the best-known area. It's home to elephants, lions, buffaloes, and several antelope species, plus has superb bird-watching. **Gashaka-Gumti National Park** (p649) is the largest national park in Nigeria and is very ecologically diverse, containing both savannah and forest species. Both Yankari and Gashaka-Gumti have newly improved facilities for visitors.

Nigeria's other national parks are largely devoid of game and infrastructure. A good bird-watching spot with facilities in the south is Okomu National Park near Benin City (p635).

Two organisations based in and around Calabar, **Cercopan** and **Pandrillus** are carrying out pioneering work in environmental education and primate rescue (see p639). The latter's Afi Drill Ranch, near Ikom (p643) is a real highlight, and has Africa's longest rainforest-canopy walkway.

NIGERIA

FOOD & DRINK

Nigerians like their food – known as 'chop' – hot and starchy. The classic dish is a fiery pepper stew (known as a soup) with a little meat or fish and accompanied by starch – usually pounded yam or cassava (*garri, eba,* or the slightly sour *fufu*). Beef, goat, chicken and fish are all eaten, along with bushmeat (mostly grasscutter – a rabbitlike rodent). Another popular dish is *jollof* – peppery rice cooked with palm oil and tomato. Cutlery isn't generally used – the yam or cassava is used to soak up the juices of the stew. As in most of Africa, you only eat with your right hand.

Specific dishes vary according to region. In the south, palm-nut soup – a thick stew made with meat, chilli, tomatoes, onions and palm-nut oil – is popular, along with draw soup (made with okra). Calabar cuisine is popular across Nigeria, with classics like *edikanikong* (soup with green leaves and smoked fish) available everywhere, along with *egusi,* flavoured with ground melon seeds. The Yoruba dish *isiewu,* or goat's head soup, is also popular countrywide. Northern cuisine is generally milder than in the south. Look out for *kuka* soup, and *tuwo shunkafa,* an especially delicious sort of pounded rice.

Chophouses serve food throughout the day, usually just cooking up one or two dishes and announcing when they're ready to eat by placing a sign saying 'food is ready' outside the door – look for these signs when you're hungry. Most hotels can rustle up 'tea bread eggs' for breakfast.

Street food is everywhere. *Suya,* simple kebabs served with a sprinkling of hot *pepe* spice, have spread beyond their northern roots to be found everywhere, although Kano remains the home of the best. *Kilishi* (dried spiced meat) is another popular northern speciality. *Moin-moin* are steamed bean cakes. Also on offer are fried yam chips, fried plantains, meat pies, *akara* (a puffy deep-fried cake made with black-eyed peas and eaten with chilli dip; known as *kosai* in the north), *kulikuli* (small deep-fried balls made of peanut paste), and lots of fresh fruit and nuts. Nigeria also has a few fast food chains, such as Mr Biggs, serving *jollof* and the like – they're worth noting for their clean toilets and air-con as much as for their food.

Nigerians drink a lot of beer. Star is the most popular but, as in much of West Africa, Guinness is drunk in vast quantities. In the north, Sharia law means that alcohol is often not available. Mineral water is widely available, although water is more commonly sold in sealed plastic bags – half a litre for N5. Labelled 'pure water', its provenance is not always guaranteed, so drink with care.

LAGOS

☎ 01 / pop 14 million

Like Nigeria itself it's fair to say that Lagos carries a certain unenviable reputation before it – crowded, polluted and dangerous; chaos theory made flesh and concrete. Exactly the kind of place you'd make a big detour to avoid. But we'd ask you hold on. While all these problems do exist to lesser or greater extents, Lagos is also vibrant and exciting, with a fantastic music and arts scene, great bars and restaurants, and all the raw energy of Nigeria distilled down into one buzzing city.

The city takes its name from the Portuguese word for lagoon. From the 16th century it was an important trading port between the Europeans and local Yorubas, before being subsumed into the Benin Kingdom. In 1861 the port became a British colony, later to become capital of the Nigerian Protectorate and, upon independence, of the new Nigerian nation. It lost the title to Abuja in 1991, but remains the economic and cultural powerhouse of the country, and the financial capital of West Africa itself.

Lagos' infrastructure has never kept pace with its growth. The modern city is an explosion of raised expressways hanging over mobbed streets of people and traffic. The electricity supply and garbage collection are hugely inadequate, and whole districts flood during the rainy season. Slums sit cheek-by-jowl with the richest addresses in Africa. The sprawl continues to grow irresistibly: already the biggest city in Africa, it's on course to become one of the world's largest in the next decade.

Lagos isn't going to be to everyone's taste (or pockets: it can be incredibly expensive), but its inhabitants frequently say they couldn't live anywhere else and if you're up for an urban adventure you'll begin to understand why. Unruly, exciting and compelling, Lagos is a true megacity, and the face of modern Africa as much as any picture-postcard national park. Jump right in.

ORIENTATION

Lagos is a series of islands, with Lagos Island the commercial heart of the city. The major road is Broad St, which passes Tinubu Sq, a major intersection near the centre of the island, and ends at Tafawa Balewa Sq. North of this is the market district, a warren of packed streets and shops. Running roughly parallel with Broad St is Marina St, which overlooks the harbour and is home to numerous large commercial establishments. The entire island is encircled by Ring Rd.

The island of Ikoyi to the east has now merged with Lagos Island; it's a mainly upscale residential area. Between the two areas is Obalende, with a useful motor park. On Ikoyi, the wide Kingsway Rd leads to the old Ikoyi Hotel. The liveliest street is Awolowo Rd, where there are many restaurants.

Most of the embassies and big houses are on Victoria Island (VI) to the southeast of Lagos Island – the most expensive part of Lagos. The towering 1004 Apartments building on the north of VI is a useful landmark. Ahmadu Bello Way skirts the south of VI, along sandy Bar Beach. VI is linked to Ikoyi by Falomo Bridge and to Lagos Island by Independence Bridge.

Most of the city's residential quarters are on the mainland, in the direction of the airport, and are connected to Lagos Island by three bridges. From east to west they are 3rd Mainland Bridge (an immense causeway), Carter Bridge and Eko Bridge. Heading north,

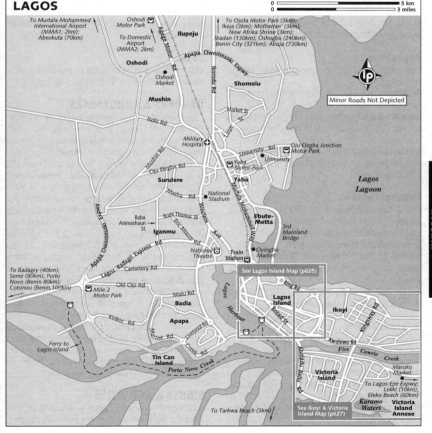

LAGOS

NIGERIA

Murtala Mohammed Way bisects the lively Yaba and Surulere districts. Two major expressways, Agege Motor Rd (leading to the airports) and Ikorodu Rd, intersect in Yaba. The latter passes through the major transport terminal of Ojota motor park in Ikeja. Ikorodu Rd eventually intersects with the Lagos–Ibadan Expressway, which leads to all points north.

Maps

Lagos Street Map (West African Books) is the best available, followed by the *Satod Street Guide to Lagos*. Both cost around N600 in bookshops.

INFORMATION

If you're spending any serious time in Lagos, pick up a copy of *Lagos Easy Access* (N2500), which is a great guide, albeit aimed primarily at expats. **Oyibos Online** (www.oyibosonline.com) is good for listings and events.

Bookshops

Lagos has Nigeria's best bookshops by a country mile.

Bookworm (Map p627; Eko Hotel Shopping Complex, Ajose Adeogun St, VI)

Glendora Bookshop (Map p627; Eko Hotel, Adetokumbo Ademola St, VI) Also good for international newspapers and magazines.

Jazz Hole (Map p627; Awolowo Rd, Ikoyi) With a coffee shop and great music, we think this must be one of Africa's coolest bookshops.

Cultural Centres

British Council (Map p627; ☎ 269 2188; 11 Kingsway Rd, Ikoyi; ☉ 9am-6pm) Day membership costs N500. Library, magazines, free internet access and cafe.

Centre Culturel Français (Map p627; ☎ 269 2365; Kingsway Rd, Ikoyi; ☉ 10am-7pm) This library and cafe opposite the Ikoyi Hotel also has live music several nights a week.

Goethe Institut (Map p627; ☎ 261 0717; Maroko Rd, VI; ☉ 10am-5pm) Has regular art exhibitions.

Internet Access

Internet places mushroom and then close on a weekly basis.

Cool Café (Map p627; Cool FM Bldg, Etim Inyang Crescent, VI; per hr N300) Expensive but fast.

Mega Plaza Internet (Map p627; Mega Plaza, Idowu Martin St, VI) On the top floor.

Staples Cybercafé (Map p625; King George V Rd, Lagos Island; per hr N150)

Medical Services

While the following places are recommended, if you do have a medical problem, consider contacting your diplomatic representatives for a list of reputable medical practitioners.

Chyzob Pharmacy (Map p627; ☎ 269 4545; Awolowo Rd, Ikoyi; ☉ 8am-8pm Mon-Sat)

Medicines Plus (Map p627; Mega Plaza, Idowu Martin St, VI; ☉ 10am-9pm Mon-Sat, 1-9pm Sun)

St Nicholas Hospital (Map p625; ☎ 260 0070; 57 Campbell St, Lagos Island) Has a 24-hour emergency clinic.

Money

There are exchange bureaus at Lagos airport. The following are convenient moneychangers; while on VI, ATMs (particularly for Zenith Bank) are everywhere.

Eko Hotel (Map p627; Adetokumbo Ademola St, VI) Find Hausa moneychangers at the craft shops by the gatehouse.

Ikoyi Hotel (Map p627; Kingsway Rd, Ikoyi) There's a *bureau de change* office and Hausa moneychangers outside the (closed) hotel.

Post

GPO Ikoyi (Map p627; Bourdillon Rd); Lagos Island (Map p625; Marina St; ☉ Mon-Fri); VI (Map p627; Adeola Odeku St)

DANGERS & ANNOYANCES

Contrary to popular perception, violent crime has decreased in Lagos in recent years. Most crime against foreigners targets expats in expensive cars, and travellers are unlikely to encounter any serious problems. That said, it always pays to take sensible precautions. Never carry any more money than is necessary and avoid flaunting valuables. Avoid walking at night where possible, particularly around hotels and restaurants frequented by foreigners, including on VI. Crowded areas carry a risk of pickpocketing. Listen out for the term Area Boy, Lagosian for a petty criminal or gang member, sometimes found holding up traffic or intimidating passengers or drivers in motor parks. The wide spaces under flyovers are common Area Boy hangouts, so give these a wide berth.

Rather than crime, the worst problem in Lagos is actually the traffic – the insane jams and drivers who treat the roads like a battleground. Take special care on the backs of *okadas* (motorcycle taxis; see p630).

SIGHTS & ACTIVITIES

In general principle, Lagos is a city to experience for itself rather than for particular sights.

Look out in Lagos Island, along Kakawa and Odunfa Sts, for examples of old Brazilian architecture – distinctive houses built by former slaves and descendants who returned from Brazil. Sadly most are in need of rescue and renovation.

National Museum

The **museum** (Map p625; Awolowo Rd, Lagos Island; admission N100; ⏰ 9am-5pm) is worth a look, but note no cameras are allowed. The stars are the brasses from Benin City, which get their own gallery. The Nok Terracottas are well represented. Another gallery dedicated to traditional symbols of power contains carved ivory and a royal host of crowns. A less fortunate symbol of power is the bullet-riddled car in which Murtala Mohammed was assassinated in 1976. The museum has a small crafts village with handicrafts for sale at fixed prices; you might also see a demonstration of *adire* – cloth-making from Abeokuta.

The museum is 150m southeast of Tafawa Balewa Sq, a huge arena adorned by statues of horses. In the square is Remembrance Arcade, with memorials to Nigeria's dead from two world wars and the Biafran conflict.

Markets

On Lagos Island the many markets are by far the best attractions, but consider getting

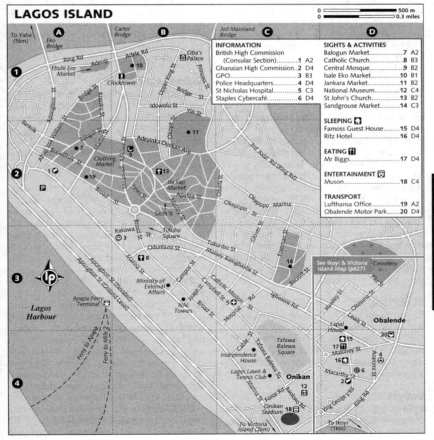

LAGOS ISLAND

INFORMATION	
British High Commission	
(Consular Section)..........**1** A2	
Ghanaian High Commission..**2** D4	
GPO.................................**3** B3	
Police Headquarters..........**4** D4	
St Nicholas Hospital..........**5** C3	
Staples Cybercafé.............**6** D4	

SIGHTS & ACTIVITIES	
Balogun Market..................**7** A2
Catholic Church..................**8** B3
Central Mosque..................**9** B2
Isale Eko Market................**10** B1
Jankara Market..................**11** B2
National Museum...............**12** C4
St John's Church................**13** B2
Sandgrouse Market............**14** C3

SLEEPING 🏠	
Famoss Guest House........**15** D4
Ritz Hotel.......................**16** D4

EATING 🍴	
Mr Biggs.........................**17** D4

ENTERTAINMENT 🎭	
Muson.............................**18** C4

TRANSPORT	
Lufthansa Office...............**19** A2
Obalende Motor Park........**20** D4

NIGERIA

a local to show you around. They're safe enough to get lost in during the day but be circumspect with your camera, as photography isn't usually appreciated. The main market area is north of Broad St, and is divided into several distinct districts.

Jankara Market (Map p625; off Adeyinka Oyekan Ave, Lagos Island) is a delight, with its closely packed stalls selling fabric and a witches' brew of *juju* ingredients. **Isale Eko Market** (Map p625; off Adeniji Adele Rd, Lagos Island) has plenty of food and household goods on offer. The rambling maze of **Balogun Market** (Map p625; off Breadfruit St, Lagos Island) is excellent for clothes and fabric from across West Africa. Finally, **Sandgrouse Market** (Map p625; off Lewis St, Lagos Island), slightly further east, is the place for interesting food, much of it sold live.

On VI, **Bar Beach Market** (Map p627; off Ahmadu Bello Way, VI) has fresh fish and a few handicrafts to attract the expats. Of course, thanks to the go-slow, every road in Lagos becomes an impromptu market, with hawkers making offerings to your vehicle as you wait in the stalled traffic.

Beaches

You'll need to travel slightly outside Lagos to reach the best beaches. **Tarkwa Beach** is popular, as there's no undertow and it's safe for swimming. There are sun lounges and umbrellas, and a few stalls selling *suya* and chop. It's accessible by launch from Tarzan Jetty in VI. The price is negotiable, with N800 per person (return) the maximum. Make arrangements to be picked back up in the afternoon.

A weekend favourite with fashionable Lagosians is **Eleko Beach**, a big 60km trip east of the city. You can rent a beach hut for the day here, and get someone to make a barbecue for you. There's also a small market selling interesting art. You'll need to hire a drop taxi to get there.

SLEEPING

Lagos has some of the best hotels in Nigeria – and some of the worst. Hotels either tend to be top of the range or at the grubbier end of the budget spectrum, with little middle ground. There's no real budget accommodation on Victoria Island.

Budget

YMCA (Map p627; ☎ 773 3599; lagosymca@yahoo.com; 77 Awolowo Rd, Ikoyi; dm N300, r N1500-2500; P) Exceedingly simple fare for men only, the YMCA is a busy hostel and is often full of African migrant workers. We'd really recommend getting a private room over the dorms, and some travellers have reported bad experiences here. Prices drop by N200 after the first night; all share bathroom facilities.

Ritz Hotel (Map p625; ☎ 263 0481; King George V Rd, Lagos Island; r with fan & without bathroom N2000, with air-con N2900-4000;) The name's a bit of a misnomer, but this hotel is a reasonably decent budget option. Rooms are fine in a grubby 'by the hour' sort of way (there's even an alternative price list at reception), but they're secure and management is friendly.

Famoss Guesthouse (Map p625; ☎ 0802 322 9172; 59 Lawson St, Lagos Island; r N3000-4000;) Another fairly basic outfit, with rooms priced according to size. All have bathrooms, none are spectacular, but it's secure and the management are surprisingly used to backpackers. It's opposite Lapal House if you need to ask directions; walk through the bar to get to reception.

Midrange & Top End

Hotel Victoria Palace (Map p627; ☎ 262 5901; victoria palace@gmail.com; 1623 Sake Jojo St, VI; s/d N12500-14000; P) The closest thing that VI gets to budget accommodation, the Victoria Palace is a good option down a reasonably quiet street. Rooms are fitted out well, and there's a brilliant Indian restaurant on the top floor.

Michael's (Map p627; ☎ 461 6802; michael@hyperia .com; Plot 411 Adetokumbo Ademola St, VI; r incl breakfast from N19,000; P) This hotel has two blocks – one overlooking a small pool (rooms are rather less generously proportioned than the mermaids on the pool mural), and slightly plusher rooms in the block with the hotel reception. With good and friendly service, it's a neat little choice.

Bogobiri House (Map p627; ☎ 270 7406; www.bogo birilagos.com; 9 Maitama Sule St, Ikoyi; r incl breakfast from N25,000;) A charming boutique hotel owned by the Nimbus Art Gallery opposite, Bogobiri House is an exhibition in itself. Beautifully decorated with paintings and sculptures by local artists, its side-street location provides a calm escape from the Lagos buzz. There are just 10 rooms, each exceedingly comfortable and more salon than sleeping place. Worth the budgetary blowout.

B-Jays Hotel (Map p627; ☎ 262 2902; www.bjayshotel .com; 24 Samuel Manuwa St, VI; r N25000-30000; P) A very comfortable guesthouse-cum-hotel.

IKOYI & VICTORIA ISLAND

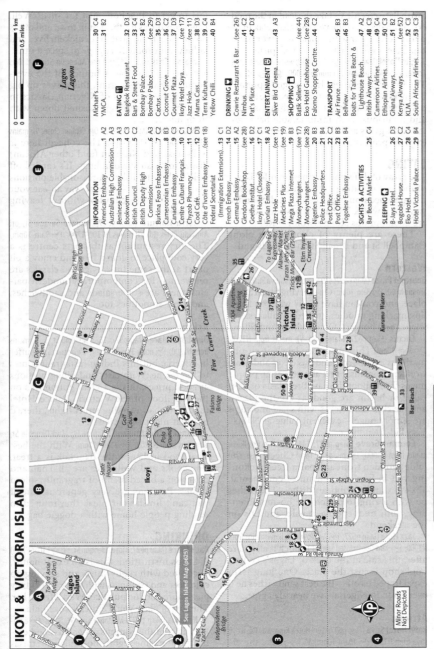

Swish flat-screen TVs take the lead in the modern room decor, while you can also relax in the plush Cowrie Bar with a pick-me-up or nightcap from a well-stocked range of spirits.

Eko Hotel (Map p627; ☎ 261 5118; www.ekohotels.com; Adetokumbo Ademola St, VI; r from N61,000; 🖥 🅿 🌀 🏊) The towering Eko has been Lagos's premier business hotel long enough to become a landmark in its own right. Everything is large and luxurious, with innumerable bars, restaurants, gyms and shops, all presented with extreme professionalism.

EATING

The array of different cuisines on offer is one of the joys of eating out in Lagos, especially if you've been on pepper soup and pounded yam for a while. VI has the best, while there are good options along Awolowo Rd.

There are plenty of chophouses along Campbell St and Broad St on Lagos Island.

Western

Gourmet Plaza (Map p627; 879 Samuel Manuwa St, VI; meals around N800; 🕙 8am-10pm) One serving fits all at this place, and you can have it any way you like – lip-smacking noodles, stuffed tortillas, sandwiches and burgers. Quick, cheap and filling.

Cactus (Map p627; Maroko Rd, VI; mains from N1200; 🕙 8am-10pm) This new place labels itself primarily as a patisserie, and has cakes and some wonderful breads, but it also serves up proper meals throughout the day. Breakfasts of pancakes or bacon are good, as are the pizzas, and the club sandwiches with salad and chips are simply huge – excellent value at N1800. Very kid-friendly.

Coconut Grove (Map p627; 144 Awolowo Rd, Ikoyi; mains from N3000; 🕙 midday-11pm) Check out the 'olde' wooden front and palm trees beckoning you in here, to a menu of continental, Tex-Mex and Caribbean dishes. The dishes go with a zing to match the up-tempo energy, with frequent live music, and DJs on the weekend.

Jazz Hole (Map p627; 168 Awolowo Rd, Ikoyi; mains from N3000; 🕙 9am-9pm, closed Sun) If brunch is all you're after, this cafe at the back of Lagos's coolest bookshop is just the place. One long-term expat tipped us off to the best sandwiches he'd ever eaten in Nigeria – we heartily agree.

African

Ikoyi Hotel Suya (Map p627; Ikoyi Hotel, Kingsway Rd, Ikoyi; suya from N100; 🕙 10am-10pm) Why make the effort to get to this hotel just for *suya*? Well, Lagosians do, as it's the best in town and offers not just beef and goat, but chicken, liver and kidney, plus some fiery *pepe* to spice it up.

Mama Cass (Map p627; Ajose Adeogun St, VI; dishes from N650; 🕙 7am-11pm) A branch of the ever-popular chain restaurant, this serves up big and healthy portions of Nigerian classics in pleasing surroundings, washed down with fresh juices.

Yellow Chilli (Map p627; 27 Ojo Olubun Close, VI; mains N1500-2500; 🕙 11am-10pm) The concept here is well-presented Nigerian (and other African) dishes in swish surroundings. It's carried off well, with tasty dishes in reasonable portions and good service – a great way to eat your way around the country without leaving your table.

Terra Kulture (Map p627; Tiamayu Savage St, off Ahmadu Bello Rd, VI; mains N1200-1700; 🕙 9am-10pm) The airy restaurant at this arts centre is a very cool place to grab a bite and enjoy a bit of art at the same time. Nigerian classics are reinvented for contemporary modern palates; there are some salads and sandwiches, and great smoothies too.

Asian

Bombay Palace (Map p627; 1623 Sakejojo St, Ikoyi; mains from N1200; 🕙 noon-3pm, 6-10pm) Vegetarians suffer in Nigeria, but this Indian restaurant comes to the rescue. With tasty and filling portions at good prices, this is a great option. It's on the top floor of the Victoria Palace Hotel (and if VI had working street lights, there'd be great night-time views).

Bangkok Restaurant (Map p627; Muri Okunola St, VI; mains from N1200; 🕙 11am-11pm) With the best Thai food in Lagos, the Bangkok is a treat. The cooks and waitresses are all Thai, and offer you a broad menu of fragrantly spiced dishes. Portions are very generous, and if you can't finish your meal, they're used to sending people home with a doggie bag.

DRINKING

Pat's Place (Map p627; Ajose Adeogun St, VI; 🕙 10am-late) A Lagos institution, this is an expat haunt, decorated with rugby shirts and serving up cold beer and Guinness with steak and kidney pie – more London pub than West African bar. The sort of place you'll either love or hate.

Nimbus (Map p627; Maitama Sule St, Ikoyi; 🕙 8am-11pm) Part of the Nimbus art gallery, and cultivating the same slightly Bohemian air, this is a lovely place for a drink – mellow in the day and happening at night. At weekends there's usually live music, so there's often a cover charge to get in.

Cowrie Restaurant & Bar (Map p627; Samuel Manuwa St, VI; ☯ 8am-11pm) Immaculately put together, the bar at B-Jays hotel is a classy place for a drink. It's very laid back, with squashy sofas and low lighting, all the better for sampling the good array of whiskies.

Tricks Music Bar (off Map p627; Tarzan Jetty, VI; ☯ 24hr) Right next to the ferry jetty, Tricks is a laid-back open-air bar that's a good place to unwind and sink a couple of cold ones with a plate of *suya*. Male patrons might get some attention, but a well-signed code of conduct for bar girls (including 'show respect' and 'don't rush the customers') ensures things never get too pushy.

The shacks along Bar Beach serve up cold beer throughout the day and into the small hours, with *suya* and other snacks on hand. They're authentically down at heel and enjoy a refreshing sea breeze, but keep to the well-lit areas after dark and don't carry valuables with you.

It's difficult to pick out bars on Lagos Island – every street has one or two local places serving drinks from early morning to late at night, and music blasting out – so follow your ears and dive right in.

ENTERTAINMENT
Nightclubs
The happening nightlife is on the mainland in Ikeja and Yaba, to the north of Lagos Island. There's usually a mix of live music and DJs, all blasting out the best Nigerian tunes. Don't even think of turning up before 11pm.

New Afrika Shrine (off Map p623; Pepple St, Ikeja; admission N500, ☯ Thu-Sun) The spiritual home of Afrobeat, Fela Kuti's original Shrine was burned down, but this replacement is run by his son Femi, who plays on Fridays and Sundays when he's in town (cover charge N1000). It's a huge shed, but the atmosphere is thick with palm wine and dope, and the music blows the roof off.

Motherlan' (off Map p623; Opebi Rd; Ikeja, admission N1000; ☯ Thu-Sun) This place is owned by Lagbaja (see p623, who mixes groovy jazz with African drums, and is always hidden under a traditional Yoruba mask (the name simultaneously means anybody and nobody). Lagbaja plays the last Friday of the month

(cover charge N1500). Motherlan' also hosts regular comedy nights, but the mix of pidgin English and Yoruba slang can be hard to follow. Stand-up comic Basketmouth is the current darling of the comedy scene.

Cinemas
Silver Bird Cinema (Map p627; Galleria Bldg, Ahmadu Bello Rd, VI) For Hollywood, rather than Nollywood, blockbusters.

Theatre
Muson (Musical Society of Nigeria; Map p625; ☎ 264 6670; 8-9 Marina, Onikan) Opposite the museum, this is Nigeria's home to high culture, with regular classical and folk music concerts, as well as the month-long Muson Festival every October.

GETTING THERE & AWAY
Air
Murtala Mohammed International Airport (MMA1) is the main gateway to Nigeria. The airport is roughly 10km north of Lagos Island. For international connections see p664.

Domestic flights depart from a new terminal 4km away (MMA2). Tickets are bought on departure. The most reliable domestic airlines are **Virgin Nigeria** (☎ 460 0505; www.virgin nigeria.com), **Bellview** (☎ 270 2700; www.flybellviewair .com) and **Aerocontractors** (☎ 764 7571; www.acn .aero). Flights to Abuja depart virtually hourly (N20,000, one hour); most domestic airlines operate this route. Every other major city in Nigeria is also connected to Lagos. Flights include Kano (N22,000, 90 minutes), Calabar (N16,000, one hour) and Port Harcourt (N20,000, one hour).

Bus, Minibus & Bush Taxi
ABC Transport (www.abctransport.com) is a good intercity 'luxury' bus company, serving many major cities, as well as destinations in Benin, Ghana and Togo. You can choose between day and night services, and although the depot is at Jibowu motor park (Map p623) there's a useful **booking office** (Map p627; ☎ 740 1010; Block D Falomo Shopping Centre, Awolowo Rd) inside a shoe shop in Ikoyi. Sample fares include Abuja (N4200, 10 hours) and Jos N4500, 13 hours).

Unsurprisingly, Lagos' motor parks are pictures of anarchy. Ojota motor park (off Map; p623, with Ojota New motor park next door) on Ikorodu Rd is the city's main transport hub. Minibuses and bush taxis leave to just about everywhere in the country from here, but you'll

NIGERIA

have to ask repeatedly to find the vehicle you want – it's a crazy place. Sample fares are Benin City (N1600, four hours), Ibadan (N500, 90 minutes), Oshogbo (N2000, three hours) and Abuja (N2600, 10 hours). You'll also find transport to most destinations north and east from Yaba motor park.

Mile 2 motor park (Map p623) serves destinations east of Lagos, including the Benin border at Seme (N400, 90 minutes). You'll also find a few minibuses going as far north as Ibadan from here.

Arriving in Lagos can be more complicated as, depending on your point of departure, you'll be dropped at various motor parks, but probably not Ojota itself. Oshodi (Map p623), Yaba (Map p623) and Oju Elegba (Map p623) motor parks are the likeliest candidates – minibuses run from these to more central points, such as Obalende motor park (Map p625) on Lagos Island.

GETTING AROUND

Might is right on the roads of Lagos, and driving is very much a contact sport. That's when it's moving: traffic jams, or go-slows, are an intrinsic part of travel in the city. Go-slows are worst at rush hours, or when you're trying to reach an important appointment.

To/From the Airport

Always allow more time than you think to get to the airport when catching a flight.

Licensed airport taxis can be booked from the arrivals hall of the international terminal, and from opposite the pick-up point at the domestic terminal. Fares should cost N2500–4000. Or most hotels can arrange to meet you on arrival for a premium. There are no airport buses.

From the domestic terminal it's just about possible to walk out of the airport toll road to get public transport (allow 15 minutes). Turn left out of the terminal, then right at the BP petrol station towards the flyover. There's public transport from the roundabout below this flyover. You'll almost need to change buses at least once to reach your final destination. If you flag a public taxi rather than a bus, agree the fare before getting in – not more than around N1000.

Public transport isn't particularly accessible from the international terminal.

Ferry

A pleasant way to get between VI and Ikoyi is the ferry from Tarzan Jetty (next

to Trick's Music Bar). You pay on the VI side (N50) and, amazingly for Nigeria, life-jackets are provided. There's also a car ferry here (N1000).

Minibus

Lagos is stitched together by an endless procession of battered yellow (or green and white on VI) minibuses, or *danfos,* each more beaten-up than the last. Short fares are around N50 while long trips involving crossing bridges ramp the price up considerably (for example, Obalende to Mile Two is twice the price of Obalende to Yaba.)

Taxi & Okada

Yellow taxis are everywhere. Fares start from N200, while crossing half of Lagos will easily beat N2000. For short distances, *okadas* (motorcycle taxis) are a better bet, but although nimbler in heavy traffic they're dangerous whenever they can pick up speed. Most trips will cost between N50–100, but you'll attract a hefty surcharge to persuade the driver to head out of his area and cross a bridge. If you're in a go-slow, jumping on an *okada* may be the only way out.

AROUND LAGOS

LEKKI CONSERVATION CENTRE

A 30-minute drive east from Lagos is **Lekki Conservation Centre** (Lagos-Epe Expressway; admission N200, camera fee from N700; ⊙ 8am-6pm). Run by the Nigerian Conservation Foundation, it has 78 hectares of wetlands which have been set aside for viewing wildlife. Raised walkways enable you to see monkeys, crocodiles and birds; early morning is the best time. There is a visitors centre, library and simple cafe. Make time to visit the market, which is good for all sorts of handicrafts, from metalwork and carvings to paintings and batiks.

The easiest way to get there is to flag down a passing bus on VI along Maroko Rd; the cost is around N100.

BADAGRY

On the road to the Benin border, Badagry was once Nigeria's busiest slave port, established in the 16th century. Thousands of people a year were shipped from here, mainly to Brazil, before slavery's abolition in the 1880s. Modern Badagry is worth visiting to see its slave heritage. The town is the site of Nigeria's first church.

Sights

Chief Obee Slave Relic Museum (admission N100, ☯ closed Sun) is run by the family of the local chief, descended from the area's slavers. It's a room full of interesting artefacts, including fearsome slave chains and shackles that you can try on. You'll need to find someone to open the display. A short walk from here is the **Heritage Museum** (admission N100, ☯ closed Sundays), which has similar displays, including a model of a slave ship with the captives crammed into every space. On the waterfront, you'll pass the **Brazilian Baracoons** (dash N50) once used to house slaves but now part of someone's house.

Near the barracoons, you can take a ferry (N20, 10 minutes) to the **Point of No Return**, on an island facing the Atlantic. It's a contemplative point, marked by a large arch, and the prettiness of the beach seems a shocking contrast to its dark history. The point is a well-marked (and very hot) 15-minute walk from the ferry. Halfway is a **Spirit Attentuation Well** – slaves were forced to drink from this to make them forget their homeland.

Getting There & Away

Minibuses to Badagry leave from Mile 2 motor park in Lagos (N200, one hour), returning from 'roundabout'. You can also catch transport to the Benin border at Seme (N100, 30 minutes)

ABEOKUTA

Abeokuta, 70km north of Lagos, translates as 'under the rock' in Yoruba. It's famous sons are a roll call of contemporary Nigeria – President Obasanjo was born here, along with Afrobeat superstar Fela Kuti and Nobel laureate Wole Soyinka.

The city is dominated by **Olumo Rock** (admission N50). This huge chunk of granite is sacred in Yoruba religion and is used in various celebrations and rituals. Climbing the rock (140m) affords commanding views of city and surrounding countryside. There are several traditional shrines on the rock. Guides will approach you, and can give interesting insights into Yoruba religion and history for a small dash (tip or bribe; N50 would be appropriate).

At the Itoku Market you can buy Abeokuta's renowned *adire* cloth and plenty of *juju* material.

Bush taxis leave from Ojota motor park in Lagos (N300, two hours).

THE SOUTH

The South is the most populous part of Nigeria. It is roughly bisected by the Niger River; to the west lie the lands of the Yoruba and to the east is Igboland, although many other ethnic groups also make the region home. It's green and fertile, most notably around the troubled Niger Delta (currently out of bounds), although there's a fair degree of urbanisation – towns and freeways cut through the bush, and a multitude of billboards advertise the explosion of evangelical churches.

Calabar, near the Cameroon border, is a big draw for travellers, as are the brass sculptures of Benin City, and the unexpected peace of Oshogbo's Sacred Forest. Those looking for 'wild' Nigeria will find it at Okomu National Park (near Benin City) and Afi Drill Ranch, north of Calabar.

IBADAN

☎ 02

Spread over a series of low hills, the word sprawling could have been invented to describe Ibadan. A century ago it was one of West Africa's largest cities, and it remains a major transport junction, but there's little else to detain you here before pushing on to more exciting destinations.

Orientation

Ibadan doesn't have a centre as such. Oyo Rd runs north–south, turning into Fajuyi Rd at the useful landmark of Mokola Roundabout (where it's bisected by Queen Elizabeth II Rd). Further south, it changes name again into Dugbe Rd around Dugbe Market – the high-rise Cocoa House here is another handy landmark – before changing name again to Iyaganku Rd.

Information

The moneychangers around Sabo Mosque on Racecourse Rd are reliable and friendly.
Booksellers (Iyanganku Rd; ☯ 9am-5.30pm) Most unexpected, an excellent bookshop rivalling the best of what Lagos can offer.
Tybom Cybercafé (cnr Ring Rd & Nihinlola St; per hr N150)
Periscope Internet (Mokola Roundabout; per hr N1500)
Post office (Dugbe Rd)
Zenco Supermarket (Magazine Rd) Useful supermarket with imported brands and international magazines.

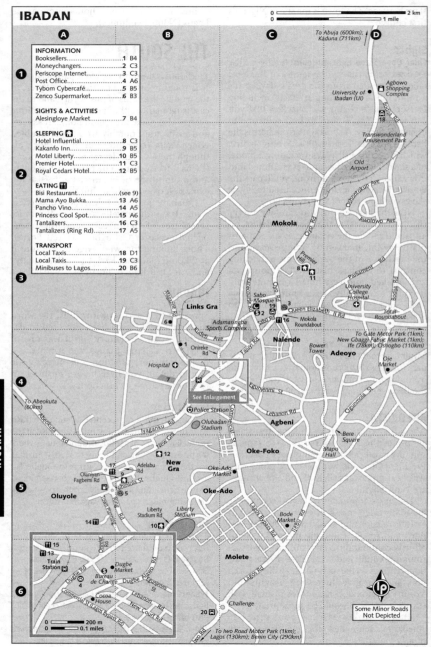

IBADAN

INFORMATION	
Booksellers.....................**1** B4	
Moneychangers...............**2** C3	
Periscope Internet............**3** C3	
Post Office.....................**4** A6	
Tybom Cybercafé..............**5** B5	
Zenco Supermarket............**6** B3	
SIGHTS & ACTIVITIES	
Alesingloye Market.............**7** B4	
SLEEPING	
Hotel Influential................**8** C3	
Kakanfo Inn....................**9** B5	
Motel Liberty..................**10** B5	
Premier Hotel..................**11** C3	
Royal Cedars Hotel............**12** B5	
EATING	
Bisi Restaurant...............(see 9)	
Mama Ayo Bukka..............**13** A6	
Pancho Vino...................**14** A5	
Princess Cool Spot............**15** A6	
Tantalizers....................**16** C3	
Tantalizers (Ring Rd)..........**17** A5	
TRANSPORT	
Local Taxis....................**18** D1	
Local Taxis....................**19** C3	
Minibuses to Lagos............**20** B6	

To Abuja (600km);
Kaduna (711km)

University of
Ibadan (UI)

Agbowo
Shopping
Complex

Transwonderland
Amusement Park

Old
Airport

Mokola

Premier
Hill

University
College
Hospital

Sabo
Mosque

Links Gra

Adamasingba
Sports Complex

Queen Elizabeth II Rd

Mokola
Roundabout

Nalende

Adeoyo

To Gate Motor Park (1km);
New Gbaggi Fabric Market (1km);
Ife (78km); Oshogbo (110km)

Oje
Market

Onireke
Rd

Hospital

See Enlargement

Police Station

Olubadan
Stadium

Agbeni

Lebanon Rd

Bere
Square

Mapo
Hall

New Gra

Oke-Foko

To Abeokuta
(60km)

Adelabu
Rd

Olaniyan
Fagbemi Rd

New
Gra

Oke-Ado
Market

Oke-Ado

Bode
Market

Liberty
Stadium Rd

Liberty
Stadium

Oluyole

Molete

Princess Cool Spot **15**
Mama Ayo Bukka **13**
Train Station

Dugbe
Market

Bureau
de Change

Cocoa
House

Dugbe Alawo St

Lebanon Rd

New Court Rd

0 ——— 200 m
0 ——— 0.1 miles

Challenge

To Iwo Road Motor Park (1km);
Lagos (130km); Benin City (290km)

Some Minor Roads
Not Depicted

NIGERIA

0 ——————— 2 km
0 ——————— 1 mile

Sights

New Gbaggi Fabric Market (Iwo Rd) is an excellent place to pick up traditional Nigerian fabrics, while you can buy anything and everything at **Alesingloye Market** (off Iyaganku Rd).

Sleeping

Motel Liberty (☎ 200 3418; Liberty Rd; r N3200-3800; P 🗙) This is budget Nigeria at its most stripped down – an adequate but basic hotel without restaurant, and the generator only runs at certain hours. There are plenty of chophouses in the area for eating, but also many prostitutes.

Hotel Influential (☎ 751 3588; Premier Hill, Mokola; 3418; r N5000-7000; P 🗙) Across the road from the Premier, this is a great midrange choice. Rooms aren't elaborate, but clean and comfortable enough, with fridge and satellite TV. If possible get a rooms with a view over Ibadan's hills.

Kakanfo Inn (☎ 751 8000; www.kakanfoinn.com; Nihinlola St; r from N15,000; P 🗙 💻 🛜 🍴) You know you've stepped up an accommodation bracket in Nigeria when the receptionist hands you an electricity-dependent keycard for your room and points you to the elevator. Rooms and service are good quality, and there's a good Indian restaurant attached.

Premier Hotel (☎ 8720 277; Premier Hill, Mokola; r from N12,0000; P 🗙 🍴) With a commanding view over Ibadan, the Premier tries to lord it over lesser establishments. It's not entirely successful, but rooms are comfy nonetheless, the Chinese restaurant is good, and you can burn off some calories in the pool.

Royal Cedars Hotel (☎ mobile 0806 280 4607; info@royalcedars.net; Alalubosa, New Gra; r N23,000-35,000 incl breakfast; P 🗙 💻 🛜 🍴) This swish new hotel is easily the classiest place to stay in town (and exclusive – there's no external sign, so look for the imposing buttermilk building with the tall gates). The well-finished rooms are an understated delight, and the service is excellent. There's a good restaurant and bar attached.

Eating

Tantalizers (Mokola Roundabout or Ring Rd, dishes from N200; 🕐 8am-10pm) Off-the-peg fast food. You might find yourself at either of these branches if you have a craving for genuine chips, a rarity in Nigeria. Otherwise, the toilets are nice and clean.

Bisi Restaurant (Kakanfo Inn, Nihinlola St; dishes from N700; 🕐 8am-10pm) Along with the usual suspects this hotel restaurant does a line in Indian cuisine, with a selection of vegetarian dishes.

Pancho Vino (Off Town Planning, Oluyole; pizzas around N1400; 🕐 noon-3pm, 6-11pm) Formerly 'All-in-One', Pancho Vino is a great option for pizzas and Lebanese food in clean modern surroundings.

For Yoruba food, try the chophouses off Dugbe Rd near the train station – we particularly enjoyed Princess Cool Spot and Mama Ayo Bukka.

Getting There & Around

Iwo Rd, to the south of the city, is Ibadan's major motor park; minibuses run to all points from here, including Lagos (N500, 90 minutes), Abuja (N2000, eight hours) and points north. The further you're travelling, the earlier you should get to the motor park. Transport to Lagos also leaves from Challenge motor park. For Oshogbo (N300, 90 minutes), go to Gate motor park in the east of the city.

Ibadan's sprawling nature makes *okada* trips more expensive than usual – around N50 for a typical ride. Pricier taxis are white with a thin blue stripe.

OSHOGBO
☎ 035

A quiet city sitting at the heart of Yorubaland, Oshogbo has a rich cultural tradition. It was at the forefront of an explosion of contemporary art in the 1960s, and still contains several thriving galleries. Oshogbo is also home to the Osun Sacred Forest, an important shrine to the ancient Yoruba religion, and a major drawcard for visitors.

At the start of August, the **Osun Oshogbo Festival** attracts thousands to celebrate the river goddess Osun, who legendarily founded the city. A frenetic affair, at its climax a virgin processes through the Sacred Forest to make offerings to Osun; visitors follow suit to ask for blessings of their own.

Information

There are moneychangers near the Central Mosque. For internet access try **Megatech Plaza Cybercafé** (Gbongan Rd; per hr N150).

Sights

Wander through the **Oja Oba Market** (cnr Station & Sabo Rds) across from the (slightly run-down) Oba's Palace. It's packed with stalls selling *juju* material.

NIGERIA

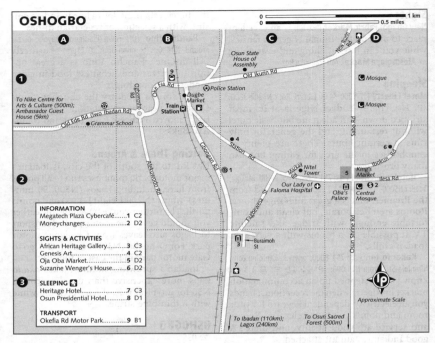

OSHOGBO

INFORMATION
Megatech Plaza Cybercafé......1 C2
Moneychangers......................2 D2

SIGHTS & ACTIVITIES
African Heritage Gallery...........3 C3
Genesis Art.............................4 C2
Oja Oba Market.......................5 D2
Suzanne Wenger's House........6 D2

SLEEPING
Heritage Hotel.........................7 C3
Osun Presidential Hotel...........8 D1

TRANSPORT
Okefia Rd Motor Park..............9 B1

OSUN SACRED FOREST & GROVES

This delightful **forest** (Osun Shrine Rd; admission N200, camera N500; 10am-6pm) is a cool green oasis away from the daily hustle of Nigerian life. An ancient centre for the Yoruba goddess Osun, the 'mother' of Oshogbo, its groves are filled with sculptures and shrines revering the traditional Yoruba gods – under increasing threat from the growth of evangelical Christianity. Many of the gods, some looking positively extraterrestrial, are overgrown and mossy, but somehow this adds further to their primal power.

Even without the shrines, the forest is a lovely place to walk, spotting monkeys and bright butterflies, with little more to disturb you than the sound of birdsong and running water. The forest was declared a World Heritage Site in 2006.

An *okada* from the centre of Oshogbo costs N50.

ART GALLERIES

In its heyday, Oshogbo was the flourishing centre of the Oshogbo School of Art, a movement that started in the 1960s. To see some of the artists' work, you'll have to visit individual studios.

Several galleries stand out: the **Nike Centre for Arts & Culture** (242 254; Old Ede Rd) run by Nike Davies-Okundaye, and strong on traditional and modern fabrics; the **African Heritage Gallery** (241 864; 1 Buraimoh St) run by Jimoh Buraimoh, selling abstract paintings and Buraimoh's trademark 'bead' paintings; and **Genesis Art** (242 826; 138 Station Rd), selling more reasonably priced paintings and woodcarvings.

Sleeping & Eating

Heritage Hotel (241 881; www.buraimoh.com; Gbongan Rd; r N2875-5100; P X) Next to the Coca Cola plant, and owned by local artist Jimoh Buraimoh, rooms here are fair-sized with huge beds, although the mustard walls make them seem gloomier than they should be. But electricity is 24 hours, and there's a decent restaurant-bar.

Osun Presidential Hotel (232 299; Old Ikurin Rd; r from N9800; P X) Once Oshogbo's grand old lady, this hotel is still adequate, but is almost ready to be pensioned off. Rooms are average for the price, which also sums up the restaurant.

Ambassador Guest House (☎ 242 254; Ido Osun Junction; r N15,000 P ❀) This place, in large leafy grounds on the edge of Oshogbo, is a real treat. More a home than a hotel, it's owned by artist Nike Davies-Okundaye and is decorated beautifully. Not all rooms have en suites, but otherwise the Ambassador does everything to treat you like a VIP. Reservations are must be made in advance.

Old Ede Rd is the main drag for chophouses serving 'food-is-ready' fare.

Getting There & Away

Okefia Rd is the main motor park. Minibuses leave pretty regularly for Ibadan (N300, 90 minutes), Lagos (N600, three hours). For other destinations, it's quicker to head to Ibadan and change there. Local taxis are blue with a yellow stripe, and there are plenty of *okadas*.

BENIN CITY
☎ 052

Until the end of the 19th century, Benin City was one of the great African cities. Its *obas* ruled much of southwest Nigeria and received embassies from the Portuguese, sending emissaries to Europe in return. The Bini people were particularly skilled at casting brass statues of superb quality, which were used to decorate the Oba's Palace. Their other great 'skill' was in human sacrifice, with hundreds of captives frequently dispatched to maintain the kingdom's good fortune.

In 1897, the killing of a British consul to Benin was met with a punitive military campaign. No amount of sacrifice could ward off modern weaponry, and when the British captured the city they promptly burned it to the ground. Nearly 5000 brass statues were collected, and then auctioned off in London to pay for the expedition. The Western world was astounded by their quality and the statues (often erroneously called the Benin Bronzes) became one of the first styles of African art to win worldwide recognition.

Today, Benin City, capital of Edo State, is a sprawling place. The art of brass statuary has been revived, and you can see craftsmen at work near the museum, and there are some good accommodation options.

A good time to visit is December, when the seven-day Igue (Ewere) Festival – featuring traditional dances, a mock battle and a procession to the palace – and the nine-day New Yams Festival, celebrated with parades and dancing, giving thanks for a productive harvest, takes place around Edo State.

Orientation

King's Sq is at the centre of town, circled by Ring Rd. Running northeast from here is the main artery of Akpakpava Rd, with Sapele and Sapoba Rds leading off to the southeast. You will find places to stay, plus restaurants, shops and local transport along these routes.

BLESSED SCULPTURE

Since the 1950s, Austrian sculptor Suzanne Wenger has been working in the Osun Sacred Forest outside Oshogbo to bring the Yoruba shrines a new lease of life through her imaginative restorations.

Called Aduni Olosa (meaning 'Adored One') by the local inhabitants, Wenger is so highly regarded that the local women have made her the priestess of two cults.

With the help of local artisans she has worked on restoring the shrines while adding her own touches. The result is a forest of spectacular, monumental and unique shrines. While they are different in style from what is traditionally associated with African art, the inspiration is still totally Yoruba.

The principal shrine is that of the river goddess Osun, in a grove enclosed by an intricately designed wall. By the sacred river, near the Lya Mapa grove where huge sculptures soar skywards, you can see a monumental and complex cement sculpture to Ifa, the divine Yoruba oracle. Another impressive sculpture, approximately 5m high, is the shrine to Onkoro, the mother goddess.

Now in her 90s, Wenger still lives in Oshogbo, and her four-storey **house** (Ibokun St) can be visited to see the extensive relief carvings that decorate the exterior – her staff is usually happy for you to take photos if you introduce yourself.

Information

Moneychangers (Sakponba Rd) Several offices are past St Matthew's Cathedral.

Post office (Airport Rd) Next to the hospital.

Vic-Biz Internet (Akpakpava Rd; per hr N150; ☷ 7.30am-6pm) Don't believe the signs that say 24-hour opening.

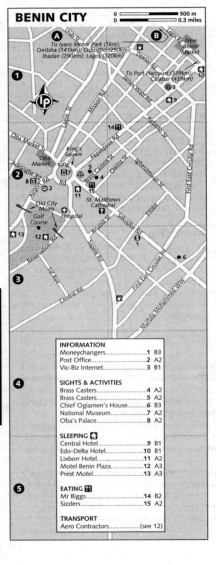

BENIN CITY

0 _____ 500 m
0 _____ 0.3 miles

INFORMATION		
Moneychangers	1	B3
Post Office	2	A2
Vic-Biz Internet	3	B1

SIGHTS & ACTIVITIES		
Brass Casters	4	A2
Brass Casters	5	A2
Chief Ogiamen's House	6	B3
National Museum	7	A2
Oba's Palace	8	A2

SLEEPING 🏠		
Central Hotel	9	B1
Edo-Delta Hotel	10	B1
Lixborr Hotel	11	A2
Motel Benin Plaza	12	A3
Prest Motel	13	A3

EATING 🍴		
Mr Biggs	14	B2
Sizzlers	15	A2

TRANSPORT		
Aero Contractors	(see 12)	

Sights

BRASS CASTERS

Part-funded by Unesco, **Brass Casters St**, near the centre, has been given over to reviving Benin brasswork. Craftsmen use the 'lost wax' technique, whereby a sculpture is made in wax, covered in clay and baked; the melted wax drains away, and the mould is poured with brass. As the mould must be smashed to retrieve the sculpture, every piece is unique (see the boxed text, opposite for more). The brassmakers are happy to show you their works, usually copies of the most famous Benin sculptures.

Everything is for sale – prices range from N300 for the smallest to over N50,000 for the big statues – and there's a blissful lack of sales pressure.

NATIONAL MUSEUM

The **museum** (King's Sq; admission N100; ☷ 9am-6pm), surrounded by the ferocious traffic of Ring Rd, is the city's main landmark. The ground floor is dedicated to the Benin Kingdom, with a display of beautiful brasses. Photos represent the more important pieces now overseas. The more bloodthirsty aspects of Benin culture are neatly glossed over, but look out for the representations of Portuguese traders. The upstairs galleries are more ethnological in nature, providing a good survey of traditional cultures from across Nigeria.

The museum is dark when there's no electricity, so a torch is a good idea.

OBA'S PALACE

The mud-walled **Oba's Palace** (cnr Adesogbe Rd & Airport Rd), a block southwest of the museum, is quite spectacular. The palace contains sculptures, brass relics and other art depicting historical events during Benin City's heyday. It also has an impressive array of traditional crafts and other works of art. It is still very much a working palace, and you'll see plenty of attendants and petitioners at the court.

You need the secretary's permission to visit, preferably arranged a day in advance; ask at the security post at the entrance. There's no fee but you'll be asked for a dash (N50 would be appropriate).

CHIEF OGIAMEN'S HOUSE

Ancient Benin was razed to the ground by the British in 1897, but this **ancient house** (97 Sakponba

Rd; dash requested N50; ☾ 8am-7pm) was one of the few to survive. Its red mud walls are decorated with shells, and topped with a tin roof. It's open to visitors, but parts are still lived in, so a dash is necessary. For other traces of royal Benin, look for the signs indicating the **old city walls and moat** on Reservation and Airport Rds.

Sleeping & Eating

Central Hotel (☎ 250 536; 7 Akpakpava Rd; r N2100/2625; **P** **X**) A bit knocked around the edges, and the sort of place you end up sharing a beer with the bar girls, but this is an otherwise serviceable budget option. Cheaper rooms have fan only.

Edo Delta Hotel (☎ 252 722; Akpakpava Rd; s/d N2500-3800; **P** **X**) This friendly option has a good selection of different rooms – cheaper motel-chalet style at the back, with nicer rooms in the new block at the front. There's a decent bar out front, and fast-food restaurant at the back.

HOW TO MAKE A BENIN BRASS

It takes a Benin craftsperson over a dozen years to become an expert in the art of lost wax casting. But if you've got ready access to clay, wax and molten brass, here's how you can start on your own path to metallic glory:

- Make a simple core of sand and water and leave to dry for a week in the sun.
- Cover the core with wax, and sculpt this into your preferred design.
- Cover the mould with more wet sand, adding a 'runner' to the bottom of the mould, and leave to dry. Bind with wire and cover with more sand and dry for three more days.
- Bake in the oven, melting the wax.
- Bury the mould in the ground with only the runner exposed, and carefully pour in melted brass. Leave for two days.
- Smash open the mould and hope the casting has worked. Clean and polish the piece to finish it.

Skilled artisans have approximately an 80% casting success rate: good luck!

Lixborr Hotel (☎ 256 699; Sakponba Rd; r N3000/3250-5000; **P** **X**) This is a great, well-run place with comfortable, tastefully decorated rooms. Look for the giant statue of the Benin woman outside; it's opposite Brass Casters St. There's a bar, restaurant, and small shop selling work by local artists.

Prest Motel (☎ 254 779; www.prestmotel.com; Airport Rd; r N4500-8000; **P** **X** **X**) In the GRA district, the Prest Motel would be a decent yet undistinguished hotel if it weren't for the idiosyncratic decorations. Art and photos adorn the walls, from African tribes to black historical figures from Toussaint Louverture to Miles Davis. There are plenty of eating options close at hand along Airport Rd.

Motel Benin Plaza (☎ 254 779; www.motelbeninplaza.org; Reservation Rd; r N5750-12,000; **P** **X** **X** **X**) Benin City's fanciest hotel, with lovely rooms, a restaurant, a couple of shops, moneychangers and a great bar next to the pool (with live music each evening).

Aside from hotel restaurant options, **Mr Biggs** (Akpakpava Rd, ☾ 8am-10pm) and **Sizzlers** (Sakopba Rd; ☾ 8am-10pm) both offer Nigerian fast food with bright lights and clean toilets. Mr Biggs has a 'Village Garden' counter with traditional Nigerian fare, while Sizzlers offers similar with its 'Foodies' counter, and also serves up some oddities like Jamaican beef with fries. The southern end of Akpakpava Rd has plenty of chophouses serving 'food-is-ready' fare.

Getting There & Away

Aero Contractors (☎ 271 512; Motel Benin Plaza, Reservation Rd) has a daily flight to Lagos (N12000, 40 minutes).

The main hub for motor transport is **Iyaro motor park** (Benin-Lagos Expressway). Transport to Lagos (usually to Yaba or Ojota motor park) leaves constantly throughout the day (N1600, six hours). The road is quite potholed. There are also plentiful minibuses to Port Harcourt (N1300, five hours) and Calabar (N1900, eight hours) as well as Ibadan and Abuja. Two convenient minibus lines are Faith Travel and Edo-Delta Travel, next to the Edo-Delta Hotel on Akpakpava Rd. They serve most destinations useful for travellers.

Okadas are everywhere in Benin City (N30 to N50 a ride), plus there are plenty of taxis, painted red with a yellow stripe. Visitors may also enjoy the novelty of working traffic lights.

NIGERIA

OKOMU NATIONAL PARK

Most of Nigeria's depleted rainforest runs close to the Cameroon border, but a small pocket remains at this national park, 40km from Benin City and threatened by outside farming and population pressures. The park is rich in birdlife and butterflies, as well as being home to the endangered white-throated guenon and other monkeys, buffalo and a tiny population of forest elephant. So close to the hustle of some of Nigeria's biggest cities, the quiet of the huge forest trees is a wonderful sensation.

The best way to visit Okomu is through the **Okomu Eco Resort** (☎ mobile 0808 468 0294; www.okomu ecoresort.com; near Udo village; chalets from N10,000). The resort can arrange transport from Benin City, and has guides who can lead you on nature trails, pointing out everything from termite colonies to the many medicinal plant species. A highlight is the viewing platform high in the rainforest canopy. There are well-appointed en-suite treehouse-chalets, and food on request.

PORT HARCOURT & THE NIGER DELTA

Built as a port for exporting the coal from Enugu, Port Harcourt now has another raison d'être: oil. Oil flares from the Delta light up the night, and you can taste the pollution. Although oil wealth washes through the city, it mostly ends up in Abuja, fuelling local grievances about corruption and underdevelopment, and giving the place a definite edge – many expat industry workers have relocated from here to Lagos on account of the security issues. As the oil capital of Nigeria, Port Harcourt is a major nexus for the social, environmental and corruption issues facing the country.

Orientation

Port Harcourt is all urban sprawl. Azikwe Rd runs north from Old Township by the docks, eventually turning into Aba Rd. On Azikwe Rd you'll find the (defunct) train station, major banks, and the post office. Aggrey Rd in Old Township is another commercial centre, with food stalls and shops. Northern Port Harcourt contains the GRA district, and is the traditional focus for many expats.

Sleeping & Eating

Security is the prime issue in choosing accommodation in Port Harcourt, and this comes at a cost. The following have all been recommended by regular visitors, and have facilities matching their price tags, including good restaurants and bars, and car hire:

Hotel Presidential (☎ 461 500; www.hotel-presidential .com; Aba Rd, GRA Phase II; r from N25000; 🅿 🖥)

Protea Hotel (☎ 465 700; www.proteahotels.com; Evo Crescent, GRA Phase II; r from N25000; 🅿 🖥)

Star King Hotel (☎ 461 280; Tombia St, GRA Junction; r from N15000; 🅿 🖥)

Getting There & Away

Overland travel to Port Harcourt is not recommended. There are plenty of flights from Lagos and Abuja with Virgin Nigeria, Aero Contractors and Arik. The main airport (40km north of the city) is currently closed, so flights go to and from Port Harcourt Military Airport (NAF Base). A trusted private driver is currently the only way for foreigners to get around in Port Harcourt.

AROUND PORT HARCOURT
The Niger Delta

The Niger Delta – Bayelsa, Rivers and Delta States – is one of Nigeria's most fascinating regions. A labyrinth of creeks, forests and mangrove, its history is one of great exploitation. Until the 19th century it was a major hub for the slave trade, which was eventually replaced by British palm-oil exportation and then, following independence, by the oil industry. Bonny Island in the Delta gives its name to Bonny Light, an important crude for making petrol.

In happier times, it was possible to take small boats to Bonny and Brass Islands in the Delta to visit fishing villages, but the increasingly violent insurgency (see the boxed text, opposite) means that the Delta is currently kidnap county, and firmly out of bounds to foreigners.

UMUHAIA

An otherwise unremarkable slice of urban Nigeria, Umuhaia (pronounced oh-*MOY*-ah) was the headquarters of the Biafran army dur-

---

WARNING

Political instability meant that we were unable to visit Port Harcourt or the Niger Delta during research. The threat of kidnap in the region remains extremely high, and we currently advise against travel here. For the most up-to-date information on travel and security risks in both Port Harcourt and the Delta, check the expat website **Oyibos Online** (www.oyibosonline.com).

OIL ON TROUBLED WATERS

Oil accounts for over 95% of Nigeria's exports, but despite being the source of the country's wealth, the Niger Delta remains one of the most underdeveloped parts of the country. Oil money simply flows out of the Delta into the deep pockets of central government – and secret overseas accounts – leaving the locals with a neglected infrastructure and massive environmental damage: oil spills, gas flaring and even acid rain.

The first major attempt to confront the state and the western oil companies was by the minority Ogoni people in the 1990s. Led by the writer and activist Ken Saro-Wiwa, the Movement for the Survival of the Ogoni People (Mosop) mounted a vigorous campaign in Rivers State that was met with extreme violence by the Nigerian government. Saro-Wiwa was executed for treason by the Abacha regime in 1995.

More than a decade on, the struggle for redistribution of oil wealth has been taken up by the group Movement for the Emancipation of the Niger Delta (MEND). It began a paramilitary campaign against oil installations, using arms paid for with the proceeds of smuggled oil. Further wrapped up in this are the oil-smuggling syndicates, who siphon off vast quantities of crude to sell on the black market. Such 'bunkering' and attacks led Nigeria to lose a quarter of its oil production in 2008, and allow Angola to knock it off its spot as Africa's biggest oil producer.

In recent years the federal government has allocated more of the oil revenues to the Delta region, but years of neglect have left a cruel legacy. The lines between militants, criminal gangs, ethnic rights and political and military manoeuvrings are frequently and unhappily blurred – gangs are pressed into service for security in political campaigns, governors are impeached for corruption and army officers have been caught selling arms to militants – while all the while the Delta's poorest inhabitants look on from the sidelines pondering the benefits of the vast wealth of Nigeria's black gold.

ing the civil war in the 1960s (see p616), and has the interesting **National War Museum** (Museum Rd; N100; 10am-6pm Mon-Fri), which commemorates the conflict.

The ingenuity of the blockaded Biafrans is on display in the grounds, with homemade armoured cars and the remains of their pitiful (but surprisingly effective) airforce, including a two-seater Cessna whose occupants literally dropped its bombs out of the window. There's also a 25m-long gunboat used by the Nigerian navy, now converted to a pleasant cafe serving drinks and simple meals. Inside the museum proper there's a fearsome array of traditional weapons, army uniforms and a photographic history of the Biafran war (inside the bunker that housed the Voice of Biafra radio station – you'll need to dash the staff to get electricity for this).

Umuhaia can be visited en route to other destinations, such as Calabar (N700, 2½ hours) or Enugu (N500, two hours). Travelling west, it's easier to head to Onitsha (N800, four hours) and change there.

CALABAR

☎ 087

Few travellers fail to enjoy Calabar, the capital of the verdant Cross River state. It sits high on a hill overlooking Cross River, and its port has historically made the town a prosperous place – Calabar was one of Nigeria's biggest slave ports, and later a major exporter of palm oil. Even its name seems the picture of an equatorial trading post.

It's one of the most rewarding Nigerian cities for visitors, with a good museum and two excellent primate-conservation centres. It's also surprisingly green and clean by Nigerian standards, with a civic pride extending to modern art statues on roundabouts and even signs exhorting road users not to use their mobile phones while driving. Many travellers pass through Calabar to or from Cameroon, and either way it is a great introduction or farewell to Nigeria.

Orientation

Calabar is surprisingly hilly. Calabar Rd runs high above the river. On the waterfront is the older colonial quarter of Duke Town, where you'll find the town's first church and the tomb of the still-revered Scottish missionary Mary Slessor. At the centre of Calabar Rd is the warrenlike Watt Market, where everything is for sale. To the east, Ndidan Usang Iso Rd runs north–south, which is where you'll find several of the better hotels and restaurants. The airport is 4km further to the east.

Information

Hausa moneychangers can be found in the area around the Central Mosque on Mary Slessor Ave, and change CFA for those heading to/from Cameroon.

Glorious Technologies Internet (Ndidan Usang Iso Rd; ⏰ 8am-8pm; per hr N150)

Molay Cyberworld (Atekong Rd; per hr N150)

Post office (Calabar Rd)

Sights

CALABAR MUSEUM

This **museum** (Court Rd; admission N100; ⏰ 9am-6pm) housed in the beautiful old British governor's building, is Nigeria's best by some distance. It has a fascinating and impressive collection covering Calabar's precolonial days as the Efik kingdom (and is quite frank about the local slave trade), the palm-oil trade, the British Oil Rivers Protectorate and Nigerian independence. Take a torch – the upstairs galleries are very dark when there's no NEPA. The museum also has great views of the river and a cafe.

South of the museum is Duke Town, the original colonial settlement. Duke Town Church is worth a visit (Mary Slessor is buried here), and the roads around Diamond Hill have several fine old colonial buildings.

OLD CALABAR & CREEK TOWN

An interesting day trip is a visit to Creek Town, on the opposite side of the river. A traditional fishing settlement, it has several very

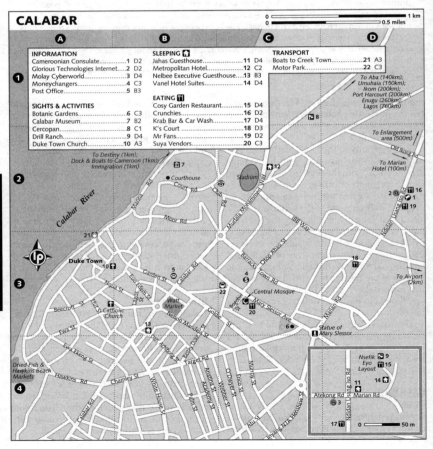

CALABAR

0 — 1 km
0 — 0.5 miles

INFORMATION	
Cameroonian Consulate	1 D2
Glorious Technologies Internet	2 D2
Molay Cyberworld	3 D4
Moneychangers	4 C3
Post Office	5 B3

SIGHTS & ACTIVITIES	
Botanic Gardens	6 C3
Calabar Museum	7 B2
Cercopan	8 C1
Drill Ranch	9 D4
Duke Town Church	10 A3

SLEEPING	
Jahas Guesthouse	11 D4
Metropolitan Hotel	12 C2
Nelbee Executive Guesthouse	13 B3
Vanel Hotel Suites	14 D4

EATING	
Cosy Garden Restaurant	15 D4
Crunchies	16 D2
Krab Bar & Car Wash	17 D4
K's Court	18 D3
Mr Fans	19 D2
Suya Vendors	20 C3

TRANSPORT	
Boats to Creek Town	21 A3
Motor Park	22 C3

To Aba (140km); Umuhaia (150km); Ikom (200km); Port Harcourt (200km); Enugu (260km); Lagos (760km)

To Enlargement area (500km)

To Marian Hotel (100m)

To Destiny (1km); Dock & Boats to Cameroon (1km); Immigration (1km)

Calabar River

Duke Town

Courthouse
Court Rd
Club Rd
Moor Rd
Murtala Mohammed Way
IBB Way

Barracks Town Rd
Otop Abasi St

To Airport (2km)

Garden St
Eto Edem St
Eto Eyo Rd
Ngua St
Beecroft St
St Catholic Church
Ewa St
Ewa Ekeng St

Watt Market
Nelson Mandela St
Dan Archibong St
Bedwell Duke St
Target Rd
Anantia St
White House St

Calabar Rd
Hawkins Rd
Chamley St
O'Dwyer St
Palm St
Murray St
Erica St
Webber St
Academy St
Atu St
Inyang NTA Henshaw St

Central Mosque
Mary Slessor Ave
Marian Rd
Statue of Mary Slessor

Dried Fish & Hawkins Beach Markets

Nsefik 9
Eyo 15
Layout
Ndidan Usang Iso Rd
11
14
Atekong Rd
Marian Rd
3
17
0 — 50 m

NIGERIA

old prefabricated buildings made in Liverpool or Glasgow and then shipped to Calabar, and a wonderful church from 1846. Boats to Creek Town (N150, 45 minutes) leave throughout the day from Calabar dock.

DRILL RANCH

Run by the pioneering NGO Pandrillus, this **primate rescue centre** (☎ 234 310; www.pandrillus .org; Nsefik Eyo Layout, off Atekong Rd; donations welcome; ☺ 9am-5pm) is home to a colony of drill monkeys and orphaned chimpanzees, both found in the forests east of Calabar but increasingly endangered. Pandrillus has been at the forefront of primate conservation in Nigeria and places great emphasis on local education to combat poaching and the bushmeat trade. The ranch runs the most successful drill captive-breeding program in the world, with groups eventually taken to Afi Mountain Drill Ranch (p643) near Cross River National Park – visits are arranged from here. Pandrillus also coruns the Limbe Wildlife Centre in Cameroon (p188).

CERCOPAN & BOTANIC GARDENS

The second of Calabar's primate charities, **Cercopan** (www.cercopan.org; Ishie Lane; donations welcome; ☺ 9am-5pm) works with smaller monkeys, such as guenons and mangabeys, and has a visitors centre with rescued primates. Cercopan works closely with schools in teaching conservation. Cercopan ultimately plans to relocate to the **Botanic Gardens** (www.irokofoundation.org; Mary Slessor Ave), which are under continuing redevelopment. The gardens will draw attention to the biodiversity of the area.

Sleeping

Jahas Guesthouse (Marian Rd; r N3500; 🖾) This clean and tidy budget option has a warm welcome, and is a pleasantly quiet option, off the main road. For those feeling weary from Nigeria's bustle, the health centre in the same compound offers restorative 'blood massages'.

Nelbee Executive Guesthouse (☎ 232 684; Dan Achibong St; r N3600-4650; P 🖾) Close to Watt Market is this handy budget option. Rooms are comfortable, the management friendly, and there's a terrifically formal dining room, but electricity can sometimes be a bit too reliant on NEPA.

Marian Hotel (☎ 220 233; Old Ikong Rd; r N7000-8000; P 🖾) The Marian has had a lick of paint and tidy-up since our last visit, and is all the bet-

ter for it. Rooms are spacious and tidy, and if the rates would be a couple of thousand naira lower in other cities, that's more a reflection of the general Calabar accommodation scene than the quality of the hotel itself.

Vanel Hotel Suites (☎ 0806 4355 511; info@vanel hotelsuites.com; Plot 1A Nsefik Eyo Layout; r N10,500-15,500; P 🖾 🖳) Despite the tragically broken paving laid in the forecourt, this brand-new, hotel has plush, bright rooms, with a warm welcome and competent service.

Metropolitan Hotel (☎ 230 911; www.metro politancalabar.com; Murtala Mohammed Way; r N35,000; P 🖾 🖳 🖳) The Metropolitan has been completely refitted recently, making it the swishest hotel in Calabar by some distance – the marble lobby is positively palatial. Rooms reflect the price tag with appropriate fixtures, fittings and amenities, and there's a great Chinese restaurant.

Eating

Cosy Garden Restaurant (Nsefik Eyo Layout, off Atekong Rd; mains from N300; ☺ 9am-8pm) If your mama was Nigerian, she'd cook like this. Choose hot and tasty pepper soup or delicately flavoured *egusi* with a mountain of pounded yam. It's poorly signed: look for the lime green building near the Drill Ranch.

K's Court (74 Ndidan Usang Iso Rd; dishes from N300; ☺ 11am-late) An open-air chophouse and bar, this place gets going better the later the day gets. It serves up fiery bowls of cow-leg soup with plantain, and once that's gone, pushes back the tables and cranks up the music to dance the weekend nights away.

Krab Bar & Car Wash (98 Ndidan Usang Iso Rd; dishes from N300; ☺ 10am-late) How Nigerian: drive to dinner, sink a few beers while your car gets washed and then drive home. During the day, meals don't run much past *jollof* rice, but in the evening the *suya* and grilled fish stands get going – there's cheap tasty food either way.

For filling sit-down fast-food from pies to *shwarmas*, try **Crunchies** (74 Ndidan Usang Iso Rd) or **Mr Fans** (30 Ndidan Usang Iso Rd) or the *suya* vendors near the mosque.

Getting There & Away

Virgin Nigeria (www.virginnigeria.com), **Aero Contractors** (www.acn.aero) and **Bellview** (www.flybellviewair.com) all fly daily to Lagos and Abuja (both around N16000, ticket desks at airport only). Calabar's

NIGERIA

PANDRILLUS

Liza Gadsby and Peter Jenkins set up Pandrillus to save the drill species.

When did you set up Pandrillus?

We arrived in Nigeria in 1988 as happy-go-lucky overlanders. We officially launched the project in 1991 when we leased the Calabar compound and stopped living exclusively in our Land Rover.

Why did you set up Pandrillus?

To save the drill as a species. There was no viable captive population of drills in the world and their situation in the wild was dismal – we'd been doing fieldwork from 1988–91 to ascertain this. We thought we could give a better life to drill orphans, establish a breeding population in captivity, and promote drill conservation generally.

What have been the challenges of running a conservation organisation in Nigeria?

Hardly anyone is doing conservation in Nigeria and it's not been a national priority as in many other African countries. Getting people and government to believe in the value of their wildlife and habitats, initiating the needed cultural shifts in thinking and behaviour to save it before it's gone, and getting government to make a meaningful commitment have all been challenges. Promoting the value of Nigeria's biodiversity has also been tough when the rest of world sees only the negative about the country.

The drill breeding program has been incredibly successful.

We simply took what we knew about drills in the wild and tried to see how we could replicate it in captivity, given our limited resources. This mean keeping drills in large, natural-sized social groups and giving them as many lifestyle choices (social, behavioural, diet etc). Our philosophy is to give the animals a role in their own management to the greatest extent possible.

What have been your other successes?

Our proudest achievement is probably the creation of the Afi Mountain Wildlife Sanctuary out of what was a production forest reserve. We started lobbying for that in 1993, it was legally gazetted in 2000, and is today the best-protected habitat for drills in the world, as well as the unique chimpanzees and gorillas endemic to the area.

How have the local communities accepted you?

Only they can answer that question but most people do now recognise that these animals – 'the Big Three' (gorilla, drill and chimpanzee) – are more valuable to them alive in the forest than as dead as bushmeat. It's become socially unacceptable to kill these species in our area and that's a huge step. People also respect the fact that we're the largest private employer in the Boki tribal area.

What are the key threat to primate populations in Nigeria?

The same as everywhere – habitat loss and hunting for the commercial bushmeat trade.

What does the immediate future for drills and Pandrillus look like?

I would say the outlook for drills as a species is brighter than it was 20 years ago. Over the border there are a couple of new national parks in Cameroon in drill habitat which is incredibly positive, but whether these entities succeed in providing a safe haven for their drill residents only time will tell. Overall we think they'll be lucky to survive in the wild in 100 years. As for the project, we hope to release our first group back to the wild in 2009 – four generations of drills!

Peter Jenkins and Liza Gadsby are the founders of Nigerian conservation organisation Pandrillus.

dark blue taxis will charge around N500 for an airport drop, while an *okada* should give change from N150.

Destiny (☎ mobile 085 514475; Calabar dock) sails every Tuesday and Friday to Limbe in Cameroon (N6000, 10–12 hours). For more information see p665.

The main motor park is tucked between Mary Slessor Ave and Goldie St. Sample minibus fares include Port Harcourt (N1000, four hours), Lagos (N3200, 10 hours), Umuahia (N700, 2½ hours) and Ikom (N700, three hours).

An average *okada* ride around town should cost around N40. Riders carry crash helmets, and a spare for passengers.

AROUND CALABAR

Cross River National Park dominates the landscape to the east of Calabar – hilly, rugged and spectacular. Park facilities are severely dilapidated, so the best way to appreciate the area is to visit the fantastic Afi ranch primate project on the edge of the park.

Afi Mountain Drill Ranch

Together with its base at Pandrillus in Calabar, the **Afi Mountain Drill Ranch** (community charge N200, hut N2000, camping N1000, car/motorbike N500/250) is one of Africa's most progressive and successful conservation organisations. In the lush forests north of Cross River National Park, it houses six large groups of captive bred and rehabilitated drills, plus a group of nearly 30 orphaned chimps. The monkeys and apes live in separate huge natural forest enclosures, in as close a state to the wild as possible. Long-term plans will involve releasing drills back into the wild, but it is impossible to release chimps that have been habituated to humans.

The camp consists of a series of simple screened huts, a kitchen hut, basic shower and drop toilets. The views over the mountains are gorgeous and wild, and well worth the effort of getting here. Nearby are the Bano Waterfalls, where it's possible to swim, and walking trails into the forest. There are also plenty of birds to spot, and a plant nursery – staff members are well-informed and eager to teach you about all aspects of the local environment. There's also a brilliant and vertigo-inducing rainforest-canopy walkway, reputedly the longest in Africa. Plan one more day than you anticipate for your stay here.

The N200 charge goes directly to the local Boki villages, towards community development projects; the ranch is the area's largest private employer. There is no food at the ranch; you'll need to bring tinned goods with you, while beans, rice, eggs etc can be bought at local villages. Bring insect repellent and cover up to avoid bites.

Visits to the ranch must be arranged in advance through Pandrillus in Calabar. A private taxi from Calabar should cost around N8500; the road is under improvement to allow all-year access. From Calabar, take transport to Ikom (N200, three hours). Afi is 90 minutes from here – either rent a car from Ikom or take a minibus to Ogbagante (near the junction for Afi, N100) and hire an *okada* for the final bumpy stretch.

THE CENTRE

Nigeria's centre is a transitional area, acting mainly as a hinterland between the north and south of the country. It's home to the Federal Capital Territory of Abuja, the modernist capital, and the city of Jos, which sits cool and high on a temperate plateau. There are also a couple of worthwhile national parks – Yankari and the rugged but newly-accessible Gashaka-Gumti.

ABUJA

☎ 09

Nigeria's made-to-measure capital, Abuja was founded in the booming 1970s. After the Biafran war, the decision was made to move the capital to the ethnically neutral centre of the country. Construction began as the price of oil crashed in the 1980s and, even today, it feels like a work in progress. The National Mosque, law courts and Presidential Palace are impressive, but the city has only slowly become the actual capital; many ministries and some embassies are still in Lagos. Clean, quiet and with good electricity, sometimes Abuja hardly feels like Nigeria at all. There's not much to do, but it's a good place to catch your breath and do some visa shopping.

Orientation

Abuja is criss-crossed by expressways and wide avenues – it's not built for pedestrians. Running parallel to each other southwest to northeast, the main roads are Constitution Ave, Independence Ave and Moshood Abiola

Rd. These surround the Central Business District, and are crossed by the expressways Olusegun Obasanjo Way and Shehu Shagari Way, with the latter running near the Presidential Palace and Supreme Court. Maitama is to the north, where there are many embassies. The National Mosque and large Sheraton Hotel are good for getting your bearings.

Information

The best place to change money is with the Hausa moneychangers outside the Sheraton Hotel.

Cool Cybercafé (Cool FM Tower, Independence Way; per hr N200; 🕑 24hr) Fast connection.

Area 1 Internet (Area 1 Shopping Centre, Moshood Abiola Way; per hr N150)

British Council (Plot 2395 Ibrahim Babangida Way; day membership N500; 🕑 10am-6pm) With a library, free internet and nice rooftop cafe.

Post office Garki (Moshood Abiola Way); Wuse Shopping Centre (Wuse Shopping Centre)

Sleeping

Abuja tends to empty at weekends, with people leaving for more exciting destinations, so many hotels offer discounts for Friday/Saturday nights – always ask if there's a deal when checking in. Budget hotels are thin on the ground.

BUDGET

African Safari Hotel (☎ 234 1881; Plot 11, Benue Crescent; r N3000-7000; 🔀 🖳) Just about squeezing into the budget bracket, with a range of rooms which increase in size as the price does – the cheapest are tucked away behind the kitchen, but the best are airy and spacious. Area 1 Shopping Centre is nearby for good street food.

Q Palace Hotel (☎ 413 3021; qpalacehotel@yahoo.com; Yedseram Crescent; r N3500-5000; 🔀) A rare budget option for this part of Abuja, this is a pleasant hotel, with a restaurant and handy shop onsite. Ask to see a few rooms – those facing inward are a little gloomy.

MIDRANGE

Algon Guesthouse (☎ 413 4798; Yedseram Crescent; r N6000-11,000; 🅿 🔀) Built in 'African modernist' style – lots of glass and marble – this is a good-value guesthouse with generously large rooms. Ask about weekend discounts here.

Pridemark Hotel (☎ 870 3405; Plot 1373, Borno St; r N5500-9100; 🔀) Formerly the Valley Pride, this

hotel has cosy rooms and friendly management, and is close to restaurants on Moshood Abiola. There's a church opposite, making for great Sunday spectacle as locals come out in their finery.

Afri Hotel (☎ 234 9723; 281 Herbert Macaulay Way; r N7000-12,000; 🔀) Good value in the price range, the Afri Hotel is all about plate glass and putting on a front. Luckily, things aren't just for show, and large comfortable rooms, and big bar and restaurant make this a good deal.

TOP-END

South African chain **Protea** (www.proteahotels.com) is expanding significantly into Abuja, and has a number of top-end hotels in the city aimed at the professional traveller.

Hilton Hotel (☎ 413 811; hilton.abuja@hilton.com; Aguiyi Ironsi; r from US$270; 🅿 🔀 🖳 🛎) Abuja's best hotel by far, this is one for the business account holder. All the top-flight facilities you'd expect are on offer – luxurious rooms, gym and tennis courts, shops, several restaurants and a poolside bar.

Eating

Abacha Barracks (Nassarawa Rd; fish around N500; 🕑 closes 10pm) Jump in a taxi to get to this great bar – it really is in an army barracks. Grab a beer and order from one of the women grilling fish, who will bring you your meal when it's cooked. Don't be put off by the military aspect – it's a popular place for locals.

Smi Msira Restaurant (Moshood Abiola Rd; dishes from N600; 🕑 9am-midnight) You can get all your favourite Nigerian dishes here, but the main draw is being able to sit in the pleasant leafy surroundings – a genuine beer garden. Claims they never close are exaggerated, but the food is still good (especially in the evenings).

Mama Cass (Aminu Kano Crescent; dishes from N650; 🕑 9am-10pm) This popular chain restaurant is a few doors up from Salamander Café, and serves up big and healthy portions of Nigerian classics in pleasing surroundings, washed down with fresh juices.

Salamander Café (☎ 708 4518; 72 Aminu Kano Crescent; mains around N2000, sandwiches N1000; 🕑 9am-9pm; 🛜) A very modern and funky place serving a mix of European and Nigerian dishes, and some great sandwiches and salads. The background music is cool, there's a film club every Sunday night and a gem of a bookshop in the back too.

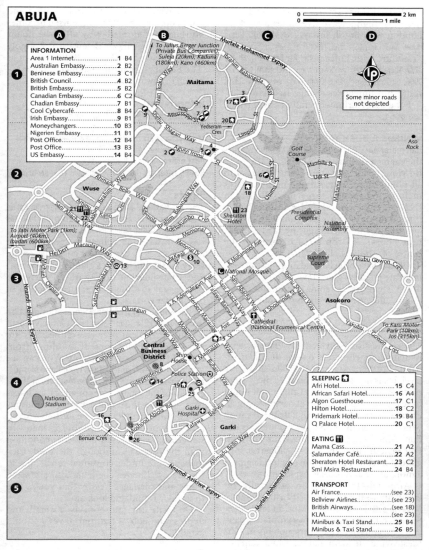

ABUJA

INFORMATION	
Area 1 Internet..................1	B4
Australian Embassy............2	B2
Beninese Embassy..............3	C1
British Council..................4	B2
British Embassy..................5	B2
Canadian Embassy.............6	C2
Chadian Embassy...............7	B1
Cool Cybercafé..................8	B4
Irish Embassy....................9	B1
Moneychangers...............10	B3
Nigerien Embassy.............11	B1
Post Office......................12	B4
Post Office......................13	B3
US Embassy.....................14	B4

Some minor roads not depicted

SLEEPING	
Afri Hotel.......................15	C4
African Safari Hotel..........16	A4
Algon Guesthouse............17	C1
Hilton Hotel....................18	C2
Pridemark Hotel...............19	B4
Q Palace Hotel................20	C1
EATING	
Mama Cass......................21	A2
Salamander Café..............22	A2
Sheraton Hotel Restaurant...23	C2
Smi Msira Restaurant........24	B4
TRANSPORT	
Air France......................(see 23)
Bellview Airlines...............(see 23)
British Airways...............(see 18)
KLM..............................(see 23)
Minibus & Taxi Stand.........25	B4
Minibus & Taxi Stand.........26	B5

NIGERIA

Both the **Hilton** (Aguiyi Ironsi) and **Sheraton** (Ladi Kwali Way) have restaurants worth a splurge.

Getting There & Away
AIR
The airport is 40km west of Abuja, a hefty N3500 taxi ride away (set fare). Flights depart constantly for Lagos with several air-

lines (N14,000, one hour), including **Virgin Nigeria** (☎ 460 0505; www.virginnigeria.com), with at least a dozen flights daily, and **Bellview** (☎ 270 2700; www.flybellviewair.com). From Abuja it's also possible to fly daily to Kano (N15,000, one hour), Calabar (N15,000, one hour) and Port Harcourt (N13,000, one hour), and many other state capitals.

Abuja also has several international connections: flights leave five times a week to London with **British Airways** (☎ 413 9610; Hilton Hotel, Aguiyi Ironsi); and three times a week to Frankfurt with Lufthansa. **Air France** (☎ 461 0777; Sheraton Hotel, Ladi Kwali Way) and **KLM** (☎ 523 9966; Sheraton Hotel, Ladi Kwali Way) also fly this route, but timetables change frequently.

For a list of airlines operating out of Abuja see p664.

MINIBUS & BUSH TAXI

Jabi motor park (Utoka; Nnamdi Azikiwe Expressway) is the main terminus for Abuja, on the Ring Rd close to the stadium. Transport goes to all points from here; sample minibus fares include Jos (N800, three hours), Ibadan (N2000, eight hours) and Kaduna (N600, three hours). Private cars from here are the quickest way to reach Lagos by road (N3600, nine hours). A drop taxi to Jabi from the centre of Abuja is N250.

Okadas have been banned in Abuja. Instead, there are plentiful green taxis (around N200 a drop). There are also some set minibus routes (N40), and even a few green rickshaws.

JOS
☎ 073

The scenic stone-covered Jos Plateau, with its temperate climes, is one of the older inhabited parts of Nigeria. At 1200m above sea level, Jos is noticeably cooler than most other parts of the country, and at night you might have the bracing sensation of having to put an extra layer on. Modern Jos is a British creation which grew on tin mining, and popular tradition claims its name is an abbreviation of 'Jesus Our Saviour', from the first missionaries. It's a good story, but a corruption of a local name is a more likely and prosaic explanation.

Although Jos seems an outwardly relaxed city to the visitor, it sits astride one of Nigeria's major Christian-Muslim fault-lines. Serious religious violence has erupted on several occasions in recent years, notably in 2002 (destroying the main market, which remains unrestored today) and in the summer of 2008 (when over 300 people were killed). It's essential to keep your ear to the ground before planning a visit.

Orientation

The city has two main north–south drags. One is Bauchi Rd, along which you'll find the large covered market, the train station and some commercial establishments; it becomes Murtala Mohammed Way after the major junction with Tafawa Balewa Rd. Roughly 1km to the west is Gromwalk Rd, known as 'The Beach', which runs parallel to the now-defunct railway line.

Information

Cyberhut Internet (Murtala Mohammed Way; per hr N200)

Moneychangers (cnr Museum Rd & Noad Ave) Several Hausa-run offices.

Post office (Ahmadu Bello Way)

Rabjib Internet (Murtala Mohammed Way; per hr N150)

Sights

The **Jos National Museum complex** (Museum Rd) is really four separate museums in one. The **Jos National Museum** (admission N50; ⏰ 8.30am-5.30pm) has an interesting collection ranging from old city gates to displays of costumes, some scary masks (including a giant sharklike fish) and a bewildering variety of old currency. At the rear is a huge open-air collection of traditional pottery.

The **Museum of Traditional Nigerian Architecture** (admission free; ⏰ 8.30am-5.30pm) is definitely worth a visit. Spread out over several hectares are full-scale reproductions of buildings from each of Nigeria's major regions. You can see a reconstruction of the **Kano Wall**, **Ilorin Mosque**, the hugely atmospheric **Zaria Mosque**, and examples of the major styles of village architecture – such as the circular *katanga* buildings of the Nupe people, with beautifully carved posts supporting a thatched roof. In many instances, these replicas are in better condition than the originals, although the mud-brick mosques are under continual repair due to Jos's rainy climate. There are also a few old trains and carriages nearby that you're free to wander round and look at.

Opposite the museum is a small and depressing zoo – animal lovers should avoid it.

Sleeping

Cocin Guesthouse (☎ 452 286; 6 Noad St; dm N350, r N800-1000; **P**) One of two church missions on this street. Accommodations is clean but spartan and bathroom facilities are shared, but it's hard to beat the price. Next door, **Tekan Guesthouse** (☎ 453 036; 5 Noad St; dm/r 350/1000) has more of the same.

NIGERIA

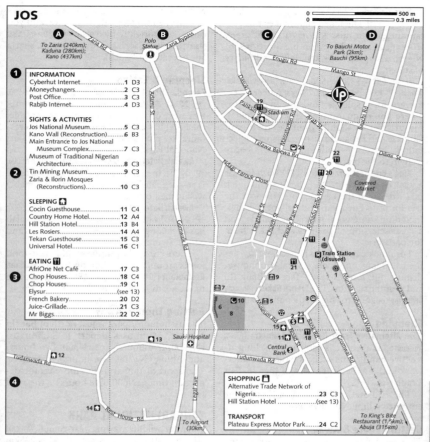

JOS

Universal Hotel (☎ 459 166; Pankshin St; r N1350-1850) A friendly budget option with a lively bar (and attendant bar girls). Cheaper rooms share a bathroom. Pankshin St is also known as Nziki Ave.

Country Home Hotel (☎ 462 479; Tudunwada Rd; r N4500-7000, ste from N9000; P 🗙 🖵) Smart green paint unifies this set of slightly sprawling blocks. Inside, rooms are cosy and all have water heaters. There's also a pleasant garden bar and a very helpful staff. Good value for the price.

Les Rosiers (☎ 0803 357 5233; 1 Rest House Rd; r from N6000; P 🗙) This bungalow bed and breakfast is a delightfully unexpected find. There are a couple of chalets amid pleasant gardens, and the French-Nigerian hosts are a good source of information. It lacks a proper sign, though – the entrance is opposite the Plateau Hotel.

Hill Station Hotel (☎ 455 300; joshillstationhotel@yahoo.com; Tudun Wada Rd; r from N7500, chalet N24,000; P 🗙 🖾) Set in huge grounds with shady trees and cacti, this hotel has two main blocks with fine rooms, and some nicer chalets set slightly further up in the hills.

Eating

AfriOne Net Café (24 Ahmadu Bello Way; dishes from N400; ⏱ 9am-10pm) Ignore the misleading name: this is a place to eat rather than surf. It's a reliable cafe-diner that's popular as a meeting place, with a kitchen quickly serving up generous plates of chicken, pasta, burgers and sandwiches, with cake and coffee for afters.

NIGERIA

Juice-Grillade (5 Ahmadu Bello Way; mains from N500; ☽10am-10pm) The faded sign makes this restaurant easy to miss – it has a bright green frontage. Come here for big portions of Nigerian staples – chicken, *jollof* and plenty of starch.

Elysur (☎ 455 300; Hill Station Hotel, Tudun Wada Rd; mains N950-1050; ☽noon-3pm, 7-10pm) A decent restaurant for a splurge (and one place in Jos where you're guaranteed spotting expats), Elysur offers a slightly unorthodox mix of Chinese and Lebanese dishes. Against expectations, it works – both food and service are well up to the mark.

King's Bite Restaurant (☎ 458 832; British-American Junction; mains around N1200; ☽9am-10pm) A quick taxi ride from the centre, this is worth the trip for tasty European and Lebanese dishes, including some good pastas and salads, and a great selection of pastries and cakes from the patisserie.

For quick eats, **Mr Biggs** (Ahmadu Bello Way) has the usual fare, and there several chophouses dishing out 'food-is-ready' fare on Bank Rd and near the stadium. The **French Bakery** (Ahmadu Bello Way) is good for bread, pies and pastries.

Shopping

The **Alternative Trade Network of Nigeria** (ATNN; Museum St) is a worker's cooperative selling attractive handicrafts such as baskets, leatherwork and jewellery. It's part of the UK Fair Trade Network.

The Hill Station Hotel has a shop at the entrance selling Nok-style pottery.

Getting There & Away

There is a daily afternoon flight between Jos and Lagos with **Arik Air** (☎ 01 2799 999 reservations; www.arikair.com). The airport is 30km south of Jos – N1800 by taxi.

Head for Bauchi motor park, northeast of town, if you're going north or east. Minibuses and bush taxis from here include to Kaduna (N800, four hours), Zaria (N700, four hours) and Kano (N900, five hours). From **Plateau Express motor park** (Tafawa Balewa Rd), minibuses leave for Abuja (N800, three hours) and points further south.

Okadas in Jos cost around N40 for a ride.

BAUCHI
☎ 077

Bauchi city, capital of Bauchi State, is a convenient stop on your way to or from Yankari

National Park. It was the home to Nigeria's first prime minister Tafewa Balewa, and you can visit his brightly-tiled **mausoleum** (near Central Market Roundabout; admission free; ☽7am-6pm). Sharia law operates in Bauchi.

Sleeping & Eating

Zaranda Hotel (☎ 543 814; Jos Rd; r N3500; P X □ ⊠) The Zaranda is several kilometres west of town. Rooms are comfortable; the hotel has a decent bar and two good restaurants, plus a booking office for Yankari National Park.

Awalah Hotel (☎ 542 444; Maiduguri Rd; r from N5000; P X) In the centre of Bauchi, the Horizontal is an adequate budget option, with reasonably well turned out facilities.

Awalah Hotel (☎ 542 444; Maiduguri Rd; r from N5000; P X ⊠) The best value in town, the Awalah has a relaxing environment, good rooms and a huge swimming pool.

There are chophouses and fast-food joints around the stadium on Jos Rd. **Sindaba Restaurant** (10 Himma Close, New GRA) is a great place to eat north Nigerian food.

Getting There & Away

The main motor park is just north of Bauchi Market. Minibuses depart to Maiduguri (N1200, five hours), Jos (N300, two hours) and Abuja (N1200, five hours) from here. Transport to Yankari is has more erratic departure times (N600, five hours) – the road is poor.

YANKARI NATIONAL PARK

Open for wildlife viewing year-round, **Yankari** (admission N300, car N500, photo permit N1250) is 225km east of Jos, and covers an area of 2244 sq km. It was once one of West Africa's best wildlife areas, but animal populations have suffered due to poaching. The park still holds reasonable numbers of buffalo, waterbucks, bushbucks and plenty of baboons. The biggest draw is the 500-strong population of elephants, but these can be hard to see and remain threatened. Hyenas and leopards can be found and it's possible that lions may also survive. The bird-watching is excellent.

The best time to see animals is from late December to late April, before the rains, when the thirsty animals congregate at the Gaji River. You're permitted to drive your own vehicle if you take a guide, otherwise the park has **game drives** (N300; ⏲ 7.30am & 3.30pm daily) in new 4WDs – these can also be hired separately for around N5000 a day.

Yankari's other great attraction is the incredibly picturesque **Wikki Warm Spring** (admission N200), near the park campsite. The crystal-clear mineral water is a constant 31°C, forming a lake 200m long and 10m wide. Bring your swimming gear – even if you don't see much wildlife, the spring is a real highlight and shouldn't be missed.

Sleeping & Eating

Wikki Warm Spring Camp (☎ 077 542 174; camping per person N600, bungalows N4200; ☒) Yankari's only accommodation is 40km inside the park. It has circular bungalows (currently under renovation, improving their quality no end), and a restaurant (meals around N800) and a bar. Campers will need their own tent. It's a short walk from the camp to the spring.

Getting There & Away

You can get to the park gate at Mainamaji by minibus from Bauchi (N600, five hours). After paying the entrance fee, you'll need to arrange transport to the camp – around N3000 in a taxi, or N1000 by *okada* (if you've got the stamina). Remember to arrange a pick-up from the camp for when you want to leave – you could be waiting days for a lift otherwise.

GASHAKA-GUMTI NATIONAL PARK

Nigeria's largest national park, **Gashaka-Gumti** (admission N1000, vehicle N500), is in also the remotest and least explored part of the country. Its 6700 sq km area contains rolling hills, savannah, montane forest and Nigeria's highest mountain, **Chappal Wadi** ('Mountain of Death'; 2418m). It's as wild and spectacular a corner of Africa as you could wish for.

It also holds incredible diversity and is one of West Africa's most important primate habitats. A new (to science) subspecies of chimpanzee was discovered here in 2003. The park also supports lions, elephants, hippos and buffalo. Much of the park is still being surveyed, although human encroachment presents a clear threat.

Recently, the UK-based **Gashaka Primate Project** (www.ucl.ac.uk/gashaka;) has been working with park authorities to radically improve access to the park, laying walking trails and training local rangers, as well as surveying

the wildlife. Anyone planning a visit is advised to get in touch beforehand for advice on logistics – accessing the park is not a casual affair.

The park entrance is at Serti, 10 hours from Jos (double by public transport) There is a small **tourist camp** (accommodation N750-2875) here, from where you can also hire excellent local guides (N500 per day). There are also 4WDs to rent (N3000 per day), although the real attractions of Gashaka-Gumti are the myriad walking trails. From Serti, you can head to the riverside park headquarters at **Gashaka** (camping N200, chalet N300) or take an *okada* to Kwano (a further 12km) where the primate researchers are mainly based. All accommodation is self-catering, so bring supplies. Exploring with a guide, you can go chimp tracking by foot (there are plentiful other monkeys to see too), or do a great two- or three-day hike to the mountains, via several Fulani villages. It's a truly magical place.

With your own vehicle, Gashaka-Gumti can be reached from Abuja, Jos or Bauchi in a day, but public transport takes two days as connections are sporadic and roads poor. From the north and centre, overnight in Jalingo, from where there are direct minibuses to Serti (via Mutum Biyo). From the south, you need to get to Wukari (a day from Calabar), from where you can get transport to Mutum Biyo and then Serti. Jalingo and Mutum Biyo both have several decent hotels and facilities for travellers.

The park is open year-round, although access is easiest during the dry season (December to March).

THE NORTH

The contrast between the green humidity of the south and the dry dust of northern Nigeria could hardly be starker. Here you're in the Sahel, and there's a taste of desert in the air that reminds you of the great sand ocean beckoning from beyond the border. Islam becomes more visible, and mosques and the call to prayer replace the south's profusion of churches.

Most northerners are Hausa or Fulani. The ancient trading cities of Kano, Zaria and Sokoto carry echoes of the old Sokoto Caliphate, and still have ties to the old trading routes across the Sahara. And, while many of

NIGERIA

the political and religious issues that divide Nigeria – such as the introduction of Sharia law – find their centre in the region, visitors to the north are likely to find nothing more than traditional Muslim hospitality welcoming them on their visit.

KADUNA
☎ 062

If you're travelling up from southern Nigeria, Kaduna is likely to be your first port of call. It was founded by Frederick Lugard, Nigeria's first colonial governor, in 1913 as a new political centre for the north, and named for the crocodiles found in the local river. It's a small, modern city and, as the capital of a Sharia state, finds itself on one of Nigeria's political and religious fault lines.

The equestrian traditions of both the British and local Hausa happily fused in Kaduna in the sport of polo. There are regular matches, culminating in the Ibrahim Isa Memorial Tournament (13 December) – a chukka that regularly attracts international players.

Kaduna's main artery is the wide Ahmadu Bello Way, running north to south.

Information

Al-Ameen Bureau de Change (Hamdala Hotel, Muhammed Buhari Way) Hausa moneychangers also congregate outside the hotel gate.

British Council (☎ 236 033; Yakubu Gowon Rd) Near the post office and banks.

Netpoint Internet (Leventis Bldg, Ahmadu Bello Way; per hr N200)

Post office (Yakubu Gowon Way)

Sights

The **national museum** (Ali Akilu Rd; admission N100; ⊙ 9am-4pm), at the northern end of the city, on the road to Kano and across from the Emir's Palace, has local masks, carvings, pottery, brasswork and woodcarvings. Better is the replica Hausa Village on site, with traditional huts and, in the late afternoon, drumming and dancing – worth making the trip for. Dash the staff to give you a guided tour.

Sleeping

Budget Master Hotel (☎ 372 915; 15 Abubakar Kigo Rd; r N1800-2500; ⊠) More than living up to its name, this hotel offers good quality, cheap lodgings. Rooms come with satellite TV and kettle, and there's a fast-food restaurant and bar off the lobby.

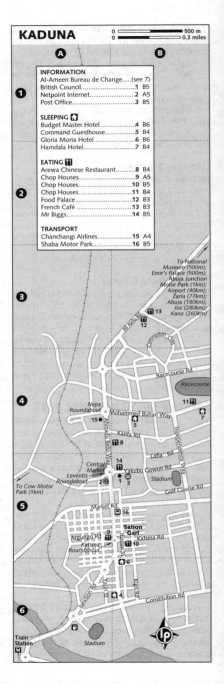

KADUNA

0 — 500 m
0 — 0.3 miles

INFORMATION
Al-Ameen Bureau de Change.....(see 7)
British Council...........................1 B5
Netpoint Internet.......................2 A5
Post Office.................................3 B5

SLEEPING 🏠
Budget Master Hotel...................4 B6
Command Guesthouse.................5 B4
Gloria Moria Hotel......................6 B6
Hamdala Hotel...........................7 B4

EATING 🍴
Arewa Chinese Restaurant..........8 B4
Chop Houses..............................9 A5
Chop Houses.............................10 B5
Chop Houses.............................11 B4
Food Palace..............................12 B3
French Café...............................13 B3
Mr Biggs...................................14 B5

TRANSPORT
Chanchangi Airlines...................15 A4
Shaba Motor Park......................16 B5

Gloria Moria Hotel (☎ 240 720; 2 Ahmadu Bello Way; r incl breakfast N3500; ☒) With cosy carpeted rooms, this is a tidy place to lay your head. All rooms have fridges and satellite TV, and staff is helpful, making this a great choice for the price.

Command Guesthouse (☎ 242 918; 10 Mohammed Buhari Way; r N8600-9200, ste N19,000; P ☒ ▣) Everything is prim and proper at this hotel complex, with bright modern rooms and pleasant gardens. There's a good restaurant with bar, and the internet cafe is open to guests 24 hours.

Hamdala Hotel (☎ 245 440; 26 Mohammed Buhari Way; r N11,000-14,000; P ☒ ▣ ☒) Kaduna's large upscale establishment, with good, if occasionally bland, rooms. There's a restaurant and pleasant garden bar, plus a well-stocked bookshop selling international press.

Eating

Food Palace (Alkali Rd; meals from N500; ☒ 12.30pm-9pm) If you've just arrived in the north, this is a good place to introduce yourself to the local cuisine. Staff will recommend dishes for you, but try *kuka* soup with *tuwo shunkafa*, (pounded rice), washed down with a glass of *zobo* (hibiscus).

Arewa Chinese Restaurant (☎ 240 088; Ahmadu Bello Way; mains N1000-1500; ☒ noon-3pm & 7-10pm) Decorated with red Chinese lanterns, this is a classy place for dinner. Meals come in small, medium or large servings, whichever the dish, and, notable for a restaurant in a Sharia state, both alcohol and pork feature on the menu.

French Café (☎ 246 154; 2 Ali Akilu Rd; mains N1800-1500; ☒ 8am-11pm) Lebanese, rather than French, this is a good place to treat yourself, either for a full meal with a bottle of wine, or with the large array of pastries, pies and filled sandwiches in the shop out the front. The all-you-can-eat Sunday buffet (N2000) is a real crowd-pleaser.

Mr Biggs (Yakubu Gowon Way; ☒ 8am-10pm) Kaduna has a branch of the reliable Nigerian fast -food outlet.

There are chophouses open all day on Ibrahim Talwo Rd and Ibadan St, and others serving up Nigerian dishes clustered around the Central Market, plus grilled fast food opposite the Hamdala Hotel.

Getting There & Away

AIR

Chanchangi Airlines (☎ 231 778, Ahmadu Bello Way) fly daily to Lagos (N18,000, one hour). The airport is 40km north of Kaduna; expect to pay N2500 for a taxi.

BUS & BUSH TAXI

The main motor park is at Abuja Junction on the northern edge of Kaduna. Minibuses and bush taxis go from here to Abuja (N600, four hours), Jos, (N700, four hours), Kano (N500, three hours) and Zaria (N200, one hour). Closer to the centre, Shaba motor park also has transport to Zaria.

ZARIA
☎ 069

While Kano is the north's biggest draw, it would be shame to miss this smaller walled city, just an hour from Kaduna. Another big player on the medieval Saharan trade routes, Zaria was one of the Hausa city states swept up by the tide of the Fulani jihad that formed the Sokoto Caliphate. Today, Zaria is a quiet and peaceful place, with its old walled centre surprisingly intact, sitting next to the tree-lined cantonments set up by the British in the early 20th century. Zaria's emir still lives in a grand palace, and leads the population in a grand ceremony at Friday prayers – an event worth seeing.

Sokoto Rd is the main road running through Zaria. At its northern end is Gra – the old British general residential area with hotels and restaurants (many around MTD Junction) and the main motor park. As it crosses the Kubani river to the south, it becomes Kaduna Rd, passing through Koko Dofa city gate and into the Old City.

Information

There are friendly moneychangers at the Zaria Hotel.

El-Hyatt Cybercafé (cnr Kaduna Rd & IBB Rd; ☒ 8am-8.30pm; per hr N170) Opposite Mr Biggs.

Ideal Cybercafé (Sokoto Rd, per hr N120) Opposite Aiffas Motel.

Sights

EMIR'S PALACE & CENTRAL MOSQUE

The Emir's Palace and Central Mosque form the spiritual centre of Zaria's old city. Both are modern affairs, built on the sites of much older constructions.

The palace has a brightly painted carved plaster facade, covered with abstract Hausa designs that somehow manage to look both traditional and very modern. They sit above the public gateway, with its shaded benches for those waiting for an audience with the emir. The emir's gate is actually the duller brown

NIGERIA

gate 20m to the right – look for the green flag that indicates if he is in residence. Outside the royal gate is a green-roofed round building that houses the emir's war drums. The head drummer (who's been in the position for over 55 years) will show you inside for a small dash.

Every Friday at around 2pm, the emir walks from his palace to the mosque opposite to lead prayers, surrounded by his splendidly dressed royal guards. The entire area surrounding the compounds fills with up to 10,000 (male) worshippers. It's an impressive sight, and it's worth getting there early to watch the street fill up and the prayer mats being unrolled. The actual prayers are over very quickly, but the silence during the ceremony is amazing. Unfortunately, women aren't likely to feel very comfortable here. Men are welcome, but don't take photos.

An *achaba* (motorcycle taxi) from Gra to the palace costs around N60.

ZARIA MARKET & DYE PITS

Zaria has a small area of dye pits in the south of the old city. They're tricky to find – ask around once you're in the main market. The cloth is dyed in much the same way as it is in Kano (opposite). The market is also well worth exploring, and gives a good taste of Zaria's history on the desert trading routes.

Sleeping

Beauty Guest Inn (☎ 334 038; MTD Junction, Sokoto Rd; r N2500; ✴) A low-slung hotel that's a cool and dark retreat from the blazing Zaria sun. Rooms are clean if not exactly bright, and water is supplied in drums in the bathrooms rather than via taps, but it's great value for the price tag.

Aiffas Motel (☎ 332 033; MTD Junction, Sokoto Rd; r N3450-5600; ✴) This Muslim-run establishment has cosy rooms with a homely feel, a point reinforced by the welcoming and chatty management. There's a shady garden and fast food out the front, while the breakfast menu even runs to cornflakes.

New Zaria Motel (☎ 332 451; Queen Elizabeth Rd; r N3150, bungalow N3650; P ✴) Set in large grounds, this motel is a series of colonial-style bungalows, each with huge rooms and large beds, plus smaller rooms in a separate block. With a decent restaurant also onsite, it's good value; but there's sometimes an issue with the water supply.

Teejay Palace Hotel (☎ 333 303; Western Way Close; r N6000-8000; P ✴) In a very secluded loca-

tion, well away from the thick of things, this is a well-maintained modern hotel, with tidy rooms around courtyards with neatly clipped hedges, just about tipping it into Zaria's top accommodation spot.

Zaria Hotel (☎ 333 092; Samura Rd; r N6095-8625; P ✴) Formerly the city's classiest hotel, the Zaria has fallen on harder times since Sharia law came in. The pool is now a stagnant puddle, and there's a slightly dusty, resigned air to the place. Rooms are fair, though, with extra cushions and tea-making facilities thrown in at the higher tariff.

Eating

La Reine (Queen Elizabeth Rd; dishes from N500; ✆ 7am-11pm) Just inside the main gate of New Zaria Motel, you can find large plates topped with the usual variations on meat/rice/pepper sauce here. It also does a good, if greasy, chips with baked beans – curiously only for breakfast though, not dinner.

Aminci Restaurant (MTD Junction, Sokoto Rd; dishes from N500; ✆ 9am-8pm) This is a reliable and well-located restaurant, serving up big plates of food-is-ready Nigerian standards. There is a handful of other restaurants and fast-food joints on this stretch of road.

Shagalinku Restaurant (Kongo Rd, Tudun Wada; meals from N1000; ✆ 10am-9pm) With an unmistakably grand frontage, Shagalinku is a popular place for Hausa food (you can even eat traditional-style sitting on the floor in the rooms upstairs). Some delicate soups balance the more fiery offerings; there's *tuwo shunkafa* (pounded rice), spiced lamb stew, yoghurt and eye-watering glasses of ginger juice.

For a fast-food fix, there's a **Mr Biggs** (Kaduna Rd), and **Chicken Republic** (Kaduna Rd) a few doors from each other just south of Gra. **Oasis Bakery** (Sokoto Rd) is a great stop for pies, bread and pastries. Heading from here towards the Zaria Motel, there are plenty of bars along IBB Way, where you can have a drink and chop and watch football.

Getting There & Away

Dadi motor park is on Sokoto Rd next to the Kano–Zaria Hwy flyover. Bush taxis and minibuses leave constantly for Kano (N300, two hours) and Kaduna (N200, one hour), as well as Sokoto (N700, four hours), Jos (N600, four hours), Abuja (N1000, six hours) and further destinations. Bush taxis fight here for the same custom.

KANO

☎ 064 / pop 4 million

Largest of the ancient Hausa city states (and now capital of Nigeria's most populous state), Kano is the oldest surviving city in West Africa, and was founded around 1400 years ago. It was a major crossroads in the trans-Saharan trade routes and, from the Middle Ages, an important centre for Islamic scholarship. Today, it is still the economic centre of northern Nigeria, and is the country's second-biggest city, with textiles and groundnuts the mainstay of its economy. Kano is also the major draw for travellers.

Kano's main attractions are found in the Old City. Indigo cloth has been made in dye pits here for hundreds of years, and the market remains atmospheric enough to evoke thoughts of Ibn Battuta and Mungo Park. There are several gems of traditional Hausa architecture, some good museums and one of one of Nigeria's grandest spectacles in the form of the Kano Durbar.

Modern Kano is a huge place, with notoriously bad traffic. Fumes, coupled with the scouring harmattan wind, mean that on a bad day you'll have grit in your teeth and the sky will turn a dusty brown. Kano is also at the forefront of the imposition of Sharia law, with issues such as alcohol, segregation of public transport cutting across community fault lines, and although these are unlikely to impact on foreign visitors, it's important to be aware of the issues.

Orientation

Murtala Mohammed Way is one of Kano's most important roads, running east–west through the city. Travellers often base themselves near here, particularly around Bompai Rd, where there are good restaurants and other facilities. North of Murtala Mohammed is Sabon Gari, where you'll find most of Kano's Christian population, along with the majority of bars and the some good budget hotels.

The Old City is to the southwest, surrounded by the decrepit old walls. Some of the gates in the wall, however, are still intact; the main gate is Kofar Mata, which leads to the central mosque and the Emir's Palace. The warren of Kurmi Market is in the centre of the Old City; for amazing views, climb Dala Hill just to the north.

Information

CULTURAL CENTRES

British Council (☎ 626 500; Emir Palace Rd) Built in traditional Hausa style.

INTERNET

Friends Internet (Murtala Mohammed Way; per hr N200) Also serves coffee, cakes and sandwiches.
See & Sweet Bakery Cybercafé (Bompai Rd; per hr N200)

MONEY

There are a number of moneychangers at the craft stalls outside the Central Hotel; they'll also exchange West African CFA. The tourist office has a bureau de change.

POST

Post office (Post Office Rd)

TOURIST INFORMATION

Kano State Tourist Board (☎ 646 309; Tourist Camp, Bompai Rd) A rarity in Nigeria – a working tourist office. Has pamphlets and can arrange guides to the Old City (per hour N1500).

Sights

KURMI MARKET & DYE PITS

With thousands of stalls in a 16-hectare area, Kurmi Market is one of the largest markets in Africa, and is the city's main attraction. It's a centre for African crafts, including gold-, bronze- and silverwork, and all types of fabrics – from ancient religious Hausa gowns and a huge selection of handpainted African cloth to the latest imported suits. It can be a bit overwhelming; you might want to take up the offer of a guide, who will no doubt approach you.

Away from the throng are the **Kofa Dye Pits** (Kofa Mata Gate; ☯ 7am-7pm daily), where indigo cloth has been dyed for hundreds of years. Each narrow pit is 6m deep, and is filled with 100kg of indigo, along with 30 buckets of ash and 5 buckets of potassium (usually from urine); the resulting mix lasts one year. The depth of colour varies according to the time the cloth is dipped – 90 minutes gives a pale blue, while the deepest indigo needs a six-hour soaking. Check out the room to one side where the finished cloth is hammered to give it a fashionable sheen. Finished cloth is for sale, starting from around N1500 for a couple of metres according to the design. A

NIGERIA

KANO

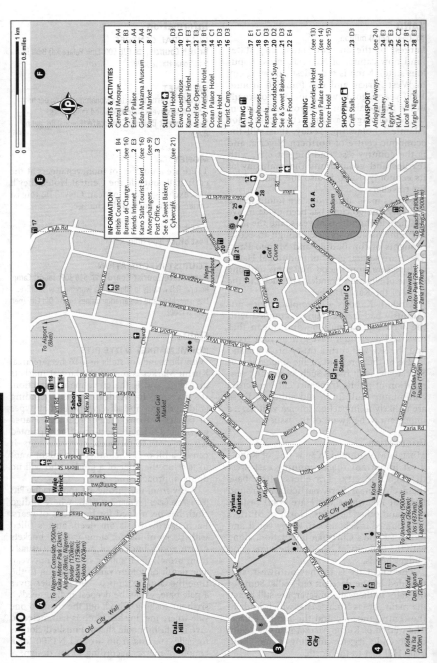

dash of around N100 is appropriate for a guided tour.

GIDAN MAKAMA MUSEUM

This **museum** (Emir Palace Rd; N100; ☺ 8am-6pm) is the best in northern Nigeria. It stands on the site of the original Emir's Palace (the oldest part is 15th century), and is a wonderful example of traditional Hausa architecture. In the entrance are two of Kano's original city gates, leading into a series of compounds. One of the first buildings is a mock-up of a Hausa bride's hut, followed by an interesting exhibition on the history of Islam (and particularly Sufism) in the region. Also on display is a fascinating photographic history of Kano, starting with the taking of the city by the British in 1902.

A guide is more or less compulsory, and with luck they'll also let you sit on the drumming and dancing practice sessions held at the museum (performances are held more weekend afternoons). A dash of N100 is appreciated.

EMIR'S PALACE & CENTRAL MOSQUE

The modern **central mosque** (Kofar Mata Rd) hosts Kano's main Friday prayers at around 1pm, attracting up to 50,000 worshippers – which is an amazing sight. The original Hausa mud-brick mosque was torn down in the 1960s after Kano's emir had been on the Haj to Mecca, to be replaced with a Saudi design. There are good photos of the original in the Gidan Makama museum.

The **Emir's Palace** (Emir Palace Rd), next door, has a parade ground outside which is used for the annual Durbar.

GIDAN DAN HAUSA

A great example of Kano's architecture is the **Gidan Dan Hausa** (Dan Hausa Rd; admission N50; ☺ 8am-4pm Mon-Thur, to 1pm Fri), blending Hausa and Arab styles. It's the former home of Hanns Vischer, the first British administrator, and was built in 1905. The house is now a museum, showing regional crafts and ceremonial costumes, but it's worth visiting for the building alone.

Festivals & Events

The Kano Durbar is held twice annually, marking the end of Ramadan (Eid al-Fitr) and Eid al-Kabir (also called Tabaski). Dates vary year on year (see p816). There is a cavalry procession featuring ornately dressed men mounted on colourfully bedecked horses. The horsemen wear breastplates and coats of flexible armour and, on their scarlet turbans, copper helmets topped with plumes. The emir, draped in white and protected by a heavy brocade parasol embroidered with silver, rides in the middle of the cavalry. The procession finishes outside the Emir's Palace, where there is drumming, singing, and massed cavalry charges.

Sleeping

BUDGET

Ecwa Guesthouse (☎ 631 410; 1 Mission Rd; r N1500-3500; ✷) A great budget option, this Christian mission guesthouse has been extensively renovated, adding a new block with excellent facilities. The cheapest rooms are in the old block and have fan only and some with shared facilities; the more expensive rooms in the new block have bathrooms, TV and air-con. Alcohol is forbidden onsite.

Tourist Camp (☎ 642 017; 11 Bompai Rd; r N2000) This state-run enterprise has a soporific air, and if you stay for too long you might end up as dusty and sleepy as the rooms and staff. Rooms are small and hot, but handy and cheap, and there's internet next door and a Lebanese restaurant about to open in the complex when we dropped in.

Ocean Palace Hotel (☎ 941 568; 35 Warri Rd; r N3500-4800; ✷) For the price, this Sabon Gari hotel is an absolute bargain. Some of the cheaper rooms are pretty compact, but you get satellite TV, a fridge and a generator that's run 24 hours – a rarity in this price bracket. Staff is friendly, food is available, and there's a good bar attached too.

Nordy Meridian Hotel (☎ 939 468; 26 Gold Coast Rd; r N3500-3700; ✷) Another good Sabon Gari deal, rooms here aren't quite as nicely finished as at the Ocean Palace, but the facilities easily match up – including a decent bar (with live music) and the all-important round-the-clock electricity.

MIDRANGE

Motel de Opera (☎ 316 347; 62 Hadejira Rd; r N5500-6500; ✷) On a busy main road, rooms here are small but functional, with a few decorated by someone with a clear Disney obsession. All have fridges. There's a pleasant courtyard cafe-bar, but no alcohol is served.

NIGERIA

Central Hotel (☎ 630 002; Bompai Rd; P ✗ ⚕)
A huge concrete confection in pink and blue,
with a crazy sci-fi dome in the courtyard, the
Central was closed for renovation when we
visited, and slated to reopen in late 2009 under
South African management. Its central location
makes this potentially a great deal – we expect
rooms to start at around N8000.

Kano Durbar Hotel (☎ 641 139; 116 Ahmadu Bello
Way; r N8500-12000; P ✗) This hotel has large
bright rooms, and bathrooms come with
water heaters. It's a decent choice, although
the acres of white tiles do much to preclude
any outbreak of personality.

TOP END

Tahir Guest Palace (☎ 317425; hwww.tahirguestpalace.com;
4 Ibrahim Natsugune Rd, off Ahmadu Bello Way; r from 14,000;
P ✗ ⚲) Naira for naira, this high-end establishment is a justifiable draw on the Kano hotel
scene. Front-of-house decor just about keeps on
the right side of opulent (the rooms are more
restrained) but facilities and service consistently
hit the mark. There's a decent restaurant, and
gym to burn off the acquired calories.

Prince Hotel (☎ 639402; Tamandu Rd; r N16,200-21,000;
P ✗ ⚲) Professionally understated, the Prince
is a classy operation in a quiet part of town.
Rooms are modern and exceedingly comfortable. Even nonguests should enjoy visiting the
very popular posh restaurant and bar.

Eating

Kano is the home of *suya*, so if you're looking
for a quick 'meat on a stick' eat, you'll be in
heaven here.

Nepa Roundabout Suya (Nepa Roundabout, Bompai
Rd; suya per stick N100; ⚙ evening) There's plenty of
suya in Kano, locals agreed that this otherwise nameless *suya* stand is one of the best in
town. The meat is top quality and wonderfully
tender, and flavoured with a mix of *pepe* and
crushed groundnuts, and served with plenty
of onion and tomato. Lip-smackingly good!
It's unlit at night, but the stand is about 50m
north of the Nepa roundabout under a tree.

See & Sweet Bakery (Nepa Roundabout, Bompai Rd;
suya per stick N100; ⚙ 8am-10.30pm) This Lebanese-
run place covers plenty of bases: the bakery
is great for cakes and breakfast pastries,
there's ice cream to cool you down, and
if you need something a little more substantial, then later in the day you can get
shwarma-style kebabs and selections from
the salad bar.

Al-Amir (12B Club Rd; dishes N250-400; ⚙ 11am-10pm)
If you want to eat as a local, head here. Food
is cheap and filling, and it's always full of
happy diners. The 'special plate' has a bit of
everything in a serving you'll be hard-pressed
to finish, but we'd also recommend northern
specialities like the fragrant *miyan taushe*
(pumpkin seed soup) and *tuwo shunkafa*
(pounded rice), washed down with a glass of
zobo (a drink made from hibiscus). There are
several branches of Al-Amir in Kano, so if you
jump on an *achaba*, the driver will probably
just take you to the nearest.

Spice Food (Magasin Rumfa Rd; dishes from N550; ⚙ 12-
3.30pm & 6-11pm) If you've been craving some vegetarian food in Nigeria, this fantastic Indian
restaurant will answer your prayers (meat
dishes are also served). The spices range from
delicate to lively, and the owner loves talking
to backpackers. The N750 buffet every Sunday
at 7.30pm is absolutely not to be missed.

Fasania (Bompai Rd; mains N680-1100; ⚙ noon-11pm)
This Chinese restaurant virtually opposite
the Tourist Camp has a better than average
selection of dishes, all cooked and served
confidently and efficiently. Alcohol is served.
Dishes are priced according to size, with medium or large servings.

The best 'food-is-ready' fare is found in
Sabon Gari, with plenty of pepper soup and
the like on offer. Enugu Rd has plenty of **chophouses** (dishes from N250, ⚙ 8am-late), most also
doubling up as bars.

Drinking

Sabon Gari has heaps of bars. There are plenty
around Enugu Rd and Ibo Rd – any chophouse with 'Cool Spot' in the name is also a
bar. We particularly enjoyed the bar in the
Ocean Palace Hotel (Warri Rd) for its icy air-con; its
slightly higher prices also keep away the bar
girls. Also good, the **Nordy Meridien Hotel bar**
(Gold Coast Rd) also has live music at weekends.
There are also plenty of tavern stores where
you can buy alcohol to take away. Don't drink
in public.

Outside Sabon Gari, many upscale and foreign restaurants also serve alcohol. The bar
at the **Prince Hotel** (Tamandu Rd) is a particularly
swish place to have a drink.

Shopping

Kurmi Market offers just about anything
under the sun for sale, but the indigo cloth and
leatherwork is particularly good. On Bompai

NIGERIA

Rd, opposite the Central Hotel, there's a small line of craft stalls, selling an interesting selection of goods and souvenirs from across north Nigeria. Beads, and wood or stone carvings are well represented.

Getting there & Away

AIR

Kano airport is 8km northwest of Sabon Gari – N150 on an *achaba,* three times that in a taxi. **Virgin Nigeria** (☎ 983 655; www.virginnigeria.com; cnr Murtala Mohammed Way & Racecourse Rd), **Bellview** (☎ 231 462; www.bellviewair.com; Kano Airport) and **IRS** (☎ 637939; Kano Airport) all fly daily to Lagos. The Virgin Nigeria flight stops at Abuja.

Kano also has good international connections: once a week to Niamey with **Air Niamey** (☎ 316 904; Murtala Mohammed Way), twice weekly to Cairo with **Egypt Air** (☎ 630 759; www.egyptair.com; Murtala Mohammed Way), and also weekly to both Tripoli and N'Djména with **Afriqiyah Airways** (☎ 977 255; Murtala Mohammed Way). There's also a useful European connection twice a week to Amsterdam with **KLM** (☎ 632 632; www.klm.com; Sani Abacha Way).

MINIBUS & BUSH TAXI

Kuka motor park, on the road to the airport on the west side of town, is the motor park for Sokoto and Katsina and to Maradi on the Nigerien border. Naiwaba motor park serves points south and west, including Zaria, Kaduna and Maiduguri, and is on Zaria Rd on the southern outskirts of town.

Sample fares and times include Zaria (N500, 90 minutes), Kaduna (N700, three hours), Maiduguri (N1300, six hours), Sokoto (N900, six hours) and Jos (N700, four hours). Stamina permitting, Lagos is reachable by bush taxi in 16 hours.

Getting Around

With no mass-transit options, Kano appears to have more *achabas* than the rest of Nigeria combined, charging N50 or thereabouts for a ride. Drivers tend to have bad English and worse driving skills, but there are also plenty of taxis for those wishing to skip the adrenaline rush.

A 2005 Sharia decree attempted to ban women from riding on *achabas,* a ruling that collapsed amid strikes and protests. As a compromise, modesty-protecting yellow rickshaws were introduced, but these are only used by devout Muslim women and families.

AROUND KANO

Katsina

Today, Katsina is best known as the birthplace of president Umaru Yar'Adua, but it has a venerable history as one of the Hausa city-states. Its Old City is still relatively intact, along with its city walls, and you can wander the back streets and markets getting a real taste of the Sahel. Camels and mud-brick architecture abound, making Katsina feel the closest of all the northern cities to its medieval roots as a Saharan trading centre.

The highlight of a trip to Katsina is the Gobarau Minaret, the best-preserved example of traditional religious architecture in the region. Standing 15m high, it has an unusual spiral design, with steps on the outside. This is thought to be a Fulani concept, brought by pilgrims who would have seen similar minarets in Cairo and Samarra (Iraq). The minaret is near Kangiwa Sq, Katsina's central point (off IBB Way), and home to the Central Mosque and Emir's Palace, built in old Hausa style and watched over by palace guards swathed in traditional robes. The square is also the focus for impressive open-air Friday prayers, and the impressive Emir's Durbar (similar to Kano's Durbar, see p655) held at Eid.

The best accommodation option in Katsina is the colonial-era **Katsina Motel** (☎ 065 430 017; Mohammed Bashir Rd; r N5000), with good rooms, and an adequate restaurant. Also good for eating is the **Katsina City Restaurant** (IBB Way; mains around N400), where you can eat your fill of Hausa specialities.

Katsina is an easy day trip from Kano (N500, two hours). It's also possible to travel from here to the Niger border at Maradi 30km away.

SOKOTO

☎ 060

Tucked away in the hottest and dustiest corner of Nigeria, Sokoto is a scruffy city with a grand past. One of the ancient Hausa city states, in the early 19th century it was the seat of the Sokoto Caliphate, its Fulani masters administering an empire which stretched from Senegal to Cameroon. While Sokoto is now a pale shadow of its former glorious self, and concentrates primarily on trade with Niger, its sultan remains the spiritual head of Nigeria's Muslims today.

At the Sultan's Palace, between 9pm and 11pm on Thursday, you can hear Hausa

---

ARGUNGU FISHING FESTIVAL

The Argungu Fishing Festival is one of West Africa's most exciting festivals. With ties stretching back to the 16th century, the modern festival was born in 1934 to commemorate the visit of the Sultan of Sokoto following a peace treaty between Sokoto and Kebbi.

The festival is held along the banks of the Sokoto River in Argungu. It lasts around four days, with traditional music, sports contests (including boxing and wrestling), horse and camel racing, and a huge bazaar. But the big draw is on the final day, when thousands of fishermen wait on the banks for the signal to plunge into the river, which is specially dammed for the event. Armed only with hand nets and gourds, they drive the fish into the shallow and wrestle them into their nets. With fish topping 50kg in weight, it's some spectacle. Prizes include cars, and free pilgrimages to Mecca, but there was scandal in 2008 when the winner was stripped of his title for allegedly smuggling in winning 70kg fish before the competition.

The festival is dependent on the height of the river, so dates aren't fixed (in 2006 it was cancelled due to drought), but it's generally held between the second half of February and the first half of March. Argungu is about 100km south of Sokoto, and there's plentiful transport during the festival.

---

musicians outside playing to welcome in the Holy Day, Friday. The Shehu Mosque is nearby. At the end of Ramadan, long processions of musicians and elaborately dressed men on horseback make their way from the prayer ground to the Sultan's Palace, a smaller version of Kano's Durbar.

The Central Market, well known for its handmade leather goods, is held daily except Sunday. Camels are sold just northeast of the market, near the old city gate.

Sokoto can be used as a base to visit the spectacular **Argungu Fishing Festival** (every February/March), for more details, see the box above.

Sleeping & Eating

Sokoto Guest Inn (☎ 233 205; Kalambaina Rd; r N2200) Rooms are slightly dreary, but it's still one of Sokoto's better budget options.

Shukura Hotel (☎ 230 006; Gusau Rd; r N5500; P ☒) This busy hotel, south of the centre on the road to Kano, is decent value, with good, spacious rooms.

Gingiya Hotel (☎ 231 262; Sokoto Bypass Rd; r from N7000; P ☒) Sokoto's classiest hotel by some distance, with excellent quality rooms and service, and a good restaurant and coffee bar.

Daddy Smart (Abdullahi Fodio Rd; meals from N600; ☯ 8am-11pm) A very popular and busy restaurant, with a takeaway section, serving a healthy mix of Nigerian staples.

Chophouses serving 'food-is-ready' are dotted about the main roads, along with lots of *suya* stalls. For meat pies, bread and cakes, try **Oasis Bakery** (Abdullah Fodio Rd), near the Central Market. Don't expect to find much alcohol.

Getting There & Away

Sokoto feels a long way from anywhere. **Virgin Nigeria** (www.virginnigeria.com; airport desk only) flies weekly to Lagos (via Abuja, N25,0000, one hour). Taxis to the airport (25 minutes) cost N1500.

The main motor park is next to the central market. Minibuses and bush taxis depart frequently to Kano (N800, six hours), Zaria (N600, four hours) and Kaduna (N650, five hours) and less frequently to further destinations. For Niger, transport also leaves from here to the border at Ilela (N500, 1½hours).

MAIDUGURI

☎ 076

Maiduguri is the capital of Borno State, and is close to the Chad and Cameroon borders. Once a British garrison town (its railway station marks the farthest reach of colonial influence in Nigeria), the city seems to be sleeping its time away. Even by Nigerian standards electricity is a problem here, so it's a case of early to bed, early to rise – not a bad idea given the scorching daytime temperatures.

Very few travellers make it to Maiduguri, and those who do are mostly on their way to or from Cameroon. The more adventurous might attempt a visit to Lake Chad.

City Internet (Shehidu Lamido Way; per hr N150) has internet access. For money, try **Barewu Bureau de Change** (Kashim Ibrahim Rd), near the Total petrol station.

Kashim Ibrahim Rd and Shehu Lamido Way, the main thoroughfares in Maiduguri, run north–south, roughly parallel to each other. There's a small, slightly dull museum off Bama Rd, 1km east of the centre.

Sleeping & Eating

Deribe Hotel (☎ 231 662; off Kashim Ibrahim Rd; r N3800; P ⬛ ⬛) Cavernous and gloomy, the Deribe has large rooms and friendly staff. Everything works too – when there's electricity. Ask how many guests there are when checking in, as it won't run the generator if the place is near empty.

Lake Chad Hotel (☎ 232 400; Kashim Ibrahim Rd; r N4650; P ⬛ ⬛) Another creaky but serviceable option, this hotel also has an adequate restaurant (but check what's available before planning dinner) and a shop selling old international newspapers.

Chez Frenchies (Kashim Ibrahim Rd; mains from N400; ⊗ 9am-8pm) Around the corner from the Deribe Hotel, this small restaurant serves pepper soup and *jollof*.

Further south, along Kashim Ibrahim Rd, you might also try Lizzy's Restaurant (next to Lake Chad Hotel) or, in a pinch, Mr Biggs.

Getting There & Away

Border transport to Cameroon is the main reason to find yourself in Maiduguri. Minibuses to the border at Bama (N400, 1½hours) leave from the busy Tishanbama motor park. Transport south also departs from here. Transport to Kano (N1400, six hours) leaves from Kano motor park, along with most other westbound vehicles.

Albarka Airlines fly to Abuja, but operations seem erratic – check at its desk at the Lake Chad hotel.

AROUND MAIDUGURI
Lake Chad

In recent years Lake Chad has receded northeast across the border, which means that Nigeria is no longer as good a vantage point for seeing the enormous lake as Chad or Cameroon. Given this, it is best to go when the water is at its highest, between December and February. Take a minibus to Baga (N700, two hours) from Baga motor park and arrange onward transport from there, most likely by *achaba*.

The bird-watching is excellent, and so is the people-watching – turbaned men leading camels and fisherman mending their nets by the water. It's incredibly remote, but well worth the effort of getting there. If you want to stay, you'll need to be self-sufficient.

NIGERIA DIRECTORY

ACCOMMODATION

Throughout this chapter, we've considered budget accommodation as costing up to N4000, midrange N4000 to N10,000 and top end beyond N10,000. Hotels are of a fair standard throughout Nigeria, although poor value compared to neighbouring countries. Most towns and cities have something to suit all pockets. The big exception to this is Lagos, where rooms are either very cheap and not particularly wonderful or very expensive; there's not much middle ground.

Even at the cheaper end of the scale, rooms come with air-con and attached bathroom – the shower is usually a bucket-and-scoop affair in the bathtub, unless you're paying top whack. Twin rooms are rare, with most rates varying according to the size of bed. Bathrooms often have water heaters (an interesting proposition given the frequency of power cuts), otherwise take promises of hot water with a pinch of salt. Rooms are subject to a hefty 15% tax, which has been included in all prices quoted in this chapter. When checking in, you'll also be asked to pay a deposit, which is usually somewhere between one and two night's room rate. This is refundable against your final bill. Many hotels, midrange and above, have a resident and nonresident rate; if you make it a habit of asking for the resident rate you can sometimes get lucky.

Camping isn't really an option anywhere in Nigeria.

PRACTICALITIES

- Privately owned English-language daily newspapers include the *Guardian*, *This Day*, *Punch* and *Vanguard*.

- There are over 30 national and state TV stations, broadcasting in English and all major local languages. South African satellite DSTV is hugely popular.

- Electricity supply is 220V. Plugs are square British three-pin, but most hotels have European two-pin adaptors.

NIGERIA

ACTIVITIES

As countries in the region go, Nigeria isn't a great destination for specific 'activities', lacking the wildlife, mountains or beaches of its neighbours. Visiting Nigeria should perhaps be seen as an activity in itself – travelling by public transport, people-watching in local bars, checking out the nightlife and talking to Nigerians themselves. Nigerians love to talk (and shout and laugh – often all at the same time) and are constantly delighted to see foreigners travelling outside the expat bubbles of the major cities – perhaps the best activity of all.

BOOKS

Although it really needs a new edition, *This House Has Fallen*, by Karl Maier, is an excellent primer on modern Nigeria, and is essential reading for anyone who wants to hold an informed conversation about the one topic everyone talks about: politics.

A Month and a Day, by Ken Saro-Wiwa – executed in 1995 – was written by the Ogoni activist in prison, and is part detention diary and part manifesto for a development in Nigeria. It is well recommended.

Lagos: A City at Work, by Olakunle Tejuouso, is an excellent Lagos-produced coffee-table book about the city.

A History of Nigeria, by Toyin Falola and Matthew Heaton is a great guide to how Nigeria got where it is today.

For more on Nigerian fiction, see p47.

BUSINESS HOURS

Business hours are from 8.30am to 5pm Monday to Friday. Government offices are open from 7.30am to 3.30pm Monday to Friday, and 7.30am to 1pm Saturday. Banking hours are from 8am to 3pm Monday to Thursday, and 8.30am to 1pm Friday. Sanitation days – when the streets are cleaned and rubbish collected – are held on the last Saturday of the month and traffic isn't allowed on the streets before 10.30am.

DANGERS & ANNOYANCES

There's no getting around the fact that Nigeria has a terrible reputation for safety. Corruption, fraud, civil unrest – it's all there in a big volatile mix. And yet, for the traveller, Nigeria really can seem like the friendliest and most welcoming country in West Africa. Navigating these apparently contradictory

---

POWER CUTS

An abiding memory of any trip to Nigeria is the lights going out, followed a minute later by the sound of generators striking up. Years of under-investment have left Nigeria with chronic power shortages. The country has a generating capacity of around 6000MW – a tenth of that of South Africa, in a country with three times the population, and demand outstrips supply 25-fold. The moribund National Electric Power Authority, Nepa, is more laughingly known as 'No Electricity Power Again' and has recently been broken up in anticipation of privatisation. Despite recent initiatives increased electricity-generating projects have been slow to come online. It's estimated that dependence on diesel generators costs Nigeria US$14 billion a year, acting as a huge brake on economic growth.

For travellers checking into hotels (particularly budget ones), ask when they 'on' and 'off' the 'gen'. That air-conditioning will be useless without it. Oh, and pack a torch.

---

states is the key to getting the most out of your visit.

It's a good idea to read the news before travelling; plenty of Nigerian newspapers have good websites (p662), while the expat website **Oyibos Online** (www.oyibosonline.com) carries excellent security updates on its forum, although you have to be a registered user (which is free) to access current information. Consistently the most troubled region is the Niger Delta – Bayelsa, Rivers and Delta states – due to the long-running grievances between the local population and the big oil companies (for more, see the boxed text, p639). Kidnapping of Westerners and oil employees is a continued threat here. In the north, communal disturbances between Muslims and Christians periodically spill over into bloody violence. Stay clear of demonstrations and areas where you suddenly see large numbers of police or army troops. Lagos has a terrible reputation for violent crime, not always undeserved.

Despite most preconceptions, as a traveller you are unlikely to have any trouble with corruption and bribery. Police roadblocks are common, but fines and bribes are paid by the driver. Some caution should be exercised on the major highways into Lagos, where armed robbery is a problem, although almost always at night. You should always travel in daylight – a good rule of thumb anyway, considering the terrible driving on Nigeria's roads.

Finally, while taking care to be sensible, it is still important not to get too hung up on Nigeria's bad name. Many travellers fear the worst and avoid the country; those who do make it here are more likely to come away with positive impressions than horror stories.

EMBASSIES & CONSULATES
Consulates in Nigeria

Some embassies have yet to relocate from Lagos to Abuja. Opening hours listed are for visa applications.

Australia (☎ 09 461 2780; www.nigeria.embassy.gov.au; 5th fl, Oakland Centre, 48 Aguyi Ironsi St, Maitama, Abuja)

Benin Abuja (☎ 09 413 8424; Yedseram Cres; ☣ 9am-4.30pm Mon-Fri); Lagos (Map p627; ☎ 01 261 4411; 4 Abudu Smith St, VI; ☣ 9am-11am Mon-Fri)

Burkina Faso (Map p627; ☎ 01 268 1001; 15 Norman Williams St, Ikoyi, Lagos)

Cameroon Calabar (☎ 087 222 782; 21 Ndidan Usang Iso Rd; ☣ 9am-3.30pm Mon-Fri); Lagos (Map p627; ☎ 261 2226; 5 Femi Pearse St, VI; ☣ 8am-11am Mon-Fri)

Canada Abuja (☎ 09 413 9910; 15 Bobo St, Maitama); Lagos (Map p627; ☎ 01 262 2616; 4 Anifowoshe St, VI)

Chad (☎ 09 413 0751; 53 Mississippi St, Abuja; ☣ 9am-3pm Mon-Fri)

Côte d'Ivoire (Map p627; ☎ 01 261 0963; 5 Abudu Smith St, VI, Lagos)

France (Map p627; ☎ 01 260 3430; 1 Oyinkan Abayomi Rd, Ikoyi, Lagos)

Germany (Map p627; ☎ 01 261 1011; 15 Walter Carrington Crescent, VI, Lagos)

Ghana (Map p625; ☎ 01 263 0015; 23 King George V St, Lagos Island, Lagos)

Holland (☎ 01 261 3005; 24 Ozumba Mbadiwe Ave, VI, Lagos)

Ireland (☎ 09 413 1751; Plot 415 Negro Crescent, off Aminu Kano, Maitama, Abuja)

Niger Abuja (☎ 01 413 6206; Pope John Paul II St; ☣ 9am-3pm Mon-Fri); Kano (☎ mobile 0806 548 1152; Airport Roundabout; ☣ 9am-3pm Mon-Fri); Lagos (Map p627; ☎ 01 261 2300; 15 Adeola Odeku St, VI; ☣ 9am-2.30pm Mon-Fri)

Spain (☎ 01 261 5215; 21c Kofo Abayomi St, VI, Lagos)

Togo (Map p627; ☎ 261 1762; Plot 976 Oju Olobun Cl, VI, Lagos)

UK Abuja (☎ 09 413 4559; www.ukinnigeria.fco.gov.uk; Dangote House, Aguyi Ironsi St, Maitama, Abuja); Lagos (Map

p627; ☎ 01 261 9541; 11 Walter Carrington Cres, VI); Port Harcourt (☎ 084 237173; 300 Olu Obasanjo Rd)

USA Abuja (☎ 09 461 4000; www.nigeria.usembassy.gov; Plot 1075, Diplomatic Drive, Central Business District); Lagos (Map p627; ☎ 01 261 0050; 2 Walter Carrington Cres, VI)

FESTIVALS & EVENTS

Of all the festivals in West Africa, the most elaborate are the celebrations in northern Nigeria (particularly in Kano, Zaria and Katsina) for two important Islamic holidays: the end of Ramadan, and Tabaski, 69 days later, which feature colourful processions of cavalry (see p655). Ramadan can be a tiring time to travel in the north – head for the Sabon Gari (foreigner quarter) in each town, where food is served throughout the day.

Around mid-February, the spectacular three-day Argungu Fishing & Cultural Festival takes place on the banks of the Sokoto River in Argungu, 100km southwest of Sokoto (see the boxed text, p658).

On the last Friday in August, the Osun Festival takes place in Oshogbo, 86km northeast of Ibadan. It has music, dancing and sacrifices, and is a centrepiece of the Yoruba cultural and spiritual year (see p633).

The Igue (Ewere) Festival, held in Benin City, usually in the first half of December, has traditional dances, a mock battle and a procession to the palace to reaffirm loyalty to the *oba*. It marks the harvest of the first new yams of the season (see p635).

If these are too culturally specific, a pan-Nigerian celebration held every November is the Abuja Carnival (see p643), with grand parades and music concerts.

HOLIDAYS

Public holidays include the following:
New Year's Day 1 January
Easter March or April
May Day 1 May
National Day 1 October
Christmas 25 December
Boxing Day 26 December

Islamic holidays are observed in Nigeria, even in the south – for a table of estimated dates for these holidays, see p816.

INTERNET ACCESS

Nigerians are great lovers of the internet. Cybercafés (as they are locally called) can be found in any town, usually prominently

NIGERIA

displaying requests that users don't send spam or scams. Costs average N150 per hour, but connections can sometimes be poor. Never use internet banking or online shopping in a Nigerian cybercafé.

INTERNET RESOURCES

www.nigeriaworld.com Huge portal site with news and current affairs, sport and business directory.

www.oyibosonline.com Expat guide to Nigeria, but with useful travel and security information, particularly for Lagos and Port Harcourt.

http://www.motherlandnigeria.com/arts.html All-round Nigerian arts resource.

www.nigeriavillagesquare.com Generic guide to Nigeria, strong on music, culture and politics.

LANGUAGE

English is the official language in Nigeria. The three principal African languages are Hausa in the north, Igbo in the southeast and Yoruba in the southwest, around Lagos. Nigerian English – pidgin – has its own cadences and vocabulary, which take a while to get your ear into.

MONEY

The unit of currency is the naira, divided into 100 kobo, with bills ranging from N5 to N1000 (with a N2000 note expected to be issued during the lifetime of this guide). There are N1, N2 and 50 kobo coins, but as only banks and some upmarket Lagos supermarkets accept them, they are effectively useless.

In Nigeria, cash is king, and you shouldn't really bring anything other than US dollars. It is estimated that around 60% of the nation's currency is currently held outside the banking system. Although the streets of towns are lined with banks, you are extremely unlikely ever to darken their doors, as none offer currency exchange. It is sometimes possible to find official exchange shops, otherwise you'll have to get used to changing on the street. Moneychanging areas are listed in the text – if you get caught short, head for an international hotel. They don't always let nonguests change money, but there are frequently moneychangers outside who will offer you business. Moneychangers are almost always Hausa, so if you're in the south, it's usually a safe bet to ask around at the town's mosque. In our experience, the moneychangers are among the most honest in Africa, but you should always be aware of potential scams (see p818). US$100

> ### DASH
>
> Used freely as both a noun and verb, dash is a word you'll hear a lot of in Nigeria. It can mean either a bribe or a tip. The most frequent form of dash you're likely to encounter is at roadblocks, where the driver pays. In large-scale corruption, money is referred to as 'chopped' (literally 'eaten'). Although you're actually unlikely to be asked for dash as a bribe, dashing someone who performs a service for you, such as a guide, is often appropriate.

and US$50 bills attract better rates. Travellers cheques are useless in Nigeria.

Credit cards aren't much use either, and given the high levels of financial fraud, trying to use one anywhere in the country should be avoided. If you're worried about carrying large amounts of cash, most towns have a Western Union branch for money transfers. ATMs are increasingly widespread, although many are not tied to international systems like MasterCard or Visa. However, some expats we spoke to registered concerns about the security of using international bank cards at Nigerian ATMs. At the very least you shouldn't rely on your card, but should advise your home bank if you might use it in Nigeria before travelling.

POST

The internal mail service in Nigeria has improved in the last few years, most letters taking just a few days, but you are still almost certain to beat your postcards home (N80 to most destinations worldwide). Sending packages by courier is far preferable to entrusting it to the post office; the international couriers have offices in most towns.

TELEPHONE

Nitel is the national phone company, but its poor connections and infrastructure have been greatly overtaken by the explosion in mobile-phone use. It's quicker and easier to make a call at a phone stand on the street than track down a Nitel office. Phone stands are run by women with a mobile phone, a table and sun umbrella, timing your call with a stop watch. Calls inside Nigeria cost around N20 per minute, depending on the network, and international calls around N60.

If you're taking your own phone, local GSM SIM cards cost from N300, according to the amount of credit purchased. Operators MTN and Glo are the market leaders and have the best coverage. Street vendors everywhere sell top-up scratch cards.

TOURIST INFORMATION

For all intents and purposes, the Nigerian Ministry of Tourism offers virtually nothing of use to the traveller, barring bland tourist promotional copy on embassy websites. One notable exception is the tourist office in Kano, which can offer guides for hire and a limited amount of tourist literature.

VISAS

Everyone needs a visa to visit Nigeria, and applications can be quite a process. Some Nigerian embassies issue visas only to residents and nationals of the country in which the embassy is located, so it's essential to put things in motion well before your trip. Exact requirements vary, but as a rule of thumb, forms are required in triplicate, along with proof of funds to cover your stay, a round-trip air ticket, and possibly confirmed hotel reservations.

You also need a letter of invitation from a resident of Nigeria, or a business in the country. This must explain the purpose of your visit and, preferably, take immigration and financial responsibility for you during your trip. If the invitee is an expat, the letter should also attach a copy of their residence permit and passport. Nigerian officialdom doesn't give the impression of encouraging tourism.

Fees vary. At the time of research, a one-month single-entry visa cost £70 in London and US$100 in Washington, or £110/$200 for a three-month multiple-entry visa. Applications at the High Commission in London were notably troublesome.

If you're travelling overland to Nigeria, the embassy in Accra (Ghana) is consistently rated as the best place in West Africa to apply for a visa, as no letter of introduction is required. The embassy in Niamey (Niger) also claims to issue visas the same way. The embassy in Cotonou (Benin) issues 48-hour transit visas only if you can provide an onward plane ticket.

On arrival in Nigeria, immigration will ask the length of your stay and write this on your entry stamp – if your visa is one month then

ask for this, even of you plan on staying for a shorter time. Several travellers have come unstuck having been stamped in for a week, then deciding they wanted to stay longer, but being unable to without either getting stuck in labyrinthine bureaucracy, or paying out lots of dash. Always check your passport stamp carefully before leaving immigration.

Visas for Onward Travel
BENIN
One-month visas cost CFA15,000, with one photo, and take 24 hours to issue. You can't pay in naira. The embassy in Lagos carries an uninviting reputation, and unexpected extra fees are not unknown.

CAMEROON
A one-month single-entry visa costs CFA50,000, with one photo, and is issued in a day. As well as Lagos and Abuja, there's a useful consulate in Calabar.

CHAD
Two photos and N5500 will get you a one-month single-entry visa, which you can pick up the next day.

NIGER
Best obtained in Abuja, a one-month single-entry visa costs N5300 with two photos, and is issued in 48 hours. The consulate in Kano (where the fee can also be paid in CFA) is also an excellent and speedy place to apply – take three photos.

Visa Extensions
Visas can reportedly be extended at the Federal Secretariat in Lagos, but it's a byzantine process of endless forms, frustration and dash, with no clear sense of success.

WOMEN TRAVELLERS
Nigeria is a nation where women have made more gains than in most African countries, but there is still a lot to achieve before any claims of gender equality can be made. Women shouldn't encounter any specific problems, although an effort should be made to dress modestly in the northern Sharia states, covering the shoulders and legs. Women generally aren't allowed in mosques, and will feel conspicuous at open-air prayers.

For more general information and advice, see p826.

TRANSPORT IN NIGERIA

GETTING THERE & AWAY

Air

The vast majority of flights to Nigeria arrive in Lagos, although there are also international airports in Abuja, Port Harcourt and Kano. Horror stories of arriving at Murtala Mohammed international airport in Lagos are a thing of the past. Nigerian airports have official porters, and notices urge passengers to ignore the services of touts. The three leading Nigerian carriers are Virgin Nigeria, Bellview and Aerocontractors, all of which have regional as well as domestic connections.

AIRLINES

Most domestic airlines just have desks at the airport. The following are airlines with service from Lagos (all offices are on Victoria Island unless stated):

Aero (AJ; ☎ 496 1340; www.acn.aero; Airport desk) Hub: Lagos

Air France (Map p627; AF; ☎ 461 0461; www.airfrance .com; Idejo Danmole St) Hub: Paris Charles De Gaulle.

Bellview (Map p627; B3; ☎ 791 9215; www.flybellview air.com; Ozumba Mbadiwe Ave) Hub: Lagos.

British Airways (Map p627; BA; ☎ 262 1225; www .britishairways.com; 1st fl, C&C Tower, Sanusi Fafunwa St) Hub: London Heathrow.

Cameroon Airlines (Map p627; UY; ☎ 261 6270; Oko-Awo Close) Hub: Douala.

Chanchangi Airlines (3U; ☎ 493 9744; www.chan changi.com Airport desk, Lagos Airport) Hub: Lagos.

Ethiopian (Map p627; ET; ☎ 263 1125; www.flyethio pian.com; Idowu Taylor St) Hub: Addis Ababa.

Ghana Airways (Map p627; GH; ☎ 266 1808; www.ghana-airways.com; 130 Awolowo Rd, Ikoyi) Hub: Accra.

Kenya Airways (Map p627; KQ; ☎ 461 2501; www .kenya-airways.com; Churchgate Tower, Badaru Abina St) Hub: Nairobi.

KLM (Map p627; KL; ☎ 461 2501; www.klm.com; Churchgate Tower, Badaru Abina St) Hub: Amsterdam.

Lufthansa (Map p625; LH; ☎ 266 4227, www .lufthansa.com; Broad St, Lagos Island) Hub: Frankfurt.

South African Airlines (Map p627; SA; ☎ 262 0607; www.flysaa.com; Adetokumbo Ademola St) Hub: Johannesburg.

Sosoliso (SO; ☎ 497 1492; www.sosolisoairline.com; airport desk, Lagos Airport) Hub: Lagos.

Virgin Nigeria (VK; ☎ 461 2747; www.virginnigeria .com; Sheraton Hotel, Ikeja, Lagos) Hub: Lagos.

The majority of international carriers have direct flights linking Lagos (and often Abuja) to European capitals, while South African Airways, Ethiopian, Royal Air Maroc and Kenya Airways link Lagos to their respective home hubs in wider Africa. From Kano it's possible to fly direct to Amsterdam (KLM), Cairo (Egypt Air) and Tripoli (Air Afriqiyah).

Across West Africa, Virgin Nigeria flies from Lagos to Abidjan, Accra, Cotonou, Dakar, Douala, Libreville and Monrovia. Bellview flies to Abidjan, Accra, Banjul Conakry, Douala, Freetown and Libreville, while Aero Contractors flies to Abidjan, Accra, Bamako, Libreville, Malabo and Sao Tomé.

Land

BENIN

The main border is on the Cotonou–Lagos highway. It's busy but slow, with lots of paper checks. Officials on both sides tend to have greedy eyes when they see foreigners. The border point is Kraké in Benin and Seme in Nigeria. Transport to either Cotonou or Lagos is plentiful on either side, as are police checkpoints – Seme to Lagos probably has the highest density in Nigeria. If you're in a rush, note that minibuses get stopped more frequently than taxis, or consider the direct Cotonou–Lagos bus service run by Nigerian bus company **ABC Transport** (☎ in Cotonou 21 33 33 77, in Lagos 740 1010; www.abctransport.com). If you're not in a rush, consider stopping at Badagry (p630), 30 minutes from Seme. Travelling from Lagos, border transport departs from Mile Two motor park.

An alternative border crossing is further north at Kétou. It can be a bit sleepy in terms of public transport, but hassle-free in terms of officialdom, and is recommended for those with their own vehicle. Transport connections in Nigeria take you through either Abeokuta or Ibadan.

CAMEROON

There are two main border crossings, in the north and south. The northern border post is at Bama, 2½ hours from Maiduguri. You'll have to ask to have the immigration office pointed out to you, as it's not immediately clear – it's a short hop on an *okada* from the bus stand. Leaving Nigeria, you have to walk through a small market to find the Cameroon border post (Banki). This is conveniently next to the minibus rank for transport on to Mora (two hours, CFA2000). Border facilities and customs are pretty relaxed here. A remote alternative crossing is at Ngala, used mainly for transiting to Chad (see below).

The southern border crossing is at Mfum, 30 minutes from Ikom. Arrangements are straightforward on the Nigerian side, but the road infrastructure collapses pretty much as soon as you cross to Ekok in Cameroon. From Ekok, minibuses struggle on terrible roads to Mamfe, 60km away (CFA1500). An alternative route to Mamfe is by pirogue, up the Cross River. This border is problematic during the rainy season, and you might consider taking the Calabar–Limbe ferry instead during the wettest months (see right).

CHAD

Although Nigeria and Chad share a short border, there are no official border crossings between the two countries. However, it is possible to make a quick transit across Cameroon, even without a Cameroonian visa. In Nigeria, the border crossing is at Ngala. You enter Cameroon here, but ask for a *laissez passer* to allow you to make the two-hour traverse to the Cameroon–Chad border point at Kousseri (see p225). Tell Nigerian immigration of your plan when getting stamped out. There's no fee for the paperwork on the Cameroon side, but this is a remote outpost with bored officials, so you're potentially a target for dash. We've also seen *laissez passers* for Chad being issued at the Nigeria–Cameroon border further south at Banki.

NIGER

There are four main entry points into Niger. From east to west they are Kano to Zinder, Katsina to Maradi, Sokoto to Birni N'Konni and Kamba to Gaya. Of these, the busiest is the Sokoto route, as this is the main road for trade between the two countries. Minibuses and bush taxis run daily to the border, just past Ilela. Crossing to Birni you can get on a bus heading straight for Niamey.

From Niger, it is easiest to cross at Gaya, four hours from Niamey. You'll probably have to hire a bush taxi to take you from the Nigerian side at Kamba on to Sokoto; beware the potholes.

Sea
CAMEROON

A ferry sails from Calabar to Limbe every Tuesday and Friday evening, very occasionally continuing on to Douala. The boat sails in the opposite direction on Monday and Thursday (see p641 for more details). It's an overnight trip in each direction. It's a very atmospheric way of entering Nigeria, sailing up the delta past grey-green trees under leaden skies to a tropical port: perfect for imagining that you're in a Graham Greene novel. Immigration at Calabar is straightforward – your passport is collected before boarding and returned on arrival – and there are moneychangers at the docks. Try to keep hold of your luggage – if it gets stowed in the hold you'll be waiting hours to get it back.

On a more ad hoc basis it's possible, if risky, to catch a speedboat to Limbe. These are fast, highly dangerous, and leave you open to paying lots of dash. They leave from Oron, a N100 boat ride across the river from Calabar port.

GETTING AROUND
Air

Internal flights are a quick and cheapish way of getting around Nigeria. Flights start from around N15,000. Most cities are linked by air to Lagos; you'll either have to change here or Abuja if you want to fly between two smaller cities (buying separate tickets for each leg if you need to change airlines).

Lagos–Abuja is the busiest route – Virgin Nigeria alone has seven flights a day – along with the Port Harcourt and (to a lesser extent) Kano routes. In most cases, passengers simply buy their tickets on departure, In these cases it's easy just to go straight to the airport, buy a ticket and be airborne pretty quickly. In some cities, airlines only have offices at the airport, or occasionally in the larger hotels.

The most reliable domestic airlines with the best connections are **Virgin Nigeria** (☎ 460 0505; www.virginnigeria.com), **Bellview** (☎ 270 2700; www.flybellviewair.com) and **Aero Contractors** (☎ 764 7571; www.acn.aero). Sample fares include Lagos to Abuja N20,000, Lagos to Calabar N16,000 and Lagos to Kano N22,000.

Following a number of fatal crashes, including one in October 2006 that killed the Sultan of Sokoto (Nigerian Muslims' spiritual head), airline safety was tightened, leading the closure of several small airlines, and the closure of Port Harcourt's main airport.

Bus & Bush Taxi

Each town has at least one motor park full of minibuses and bush taxis, which serves as the main transport depot. These places are Nigeria in microcosm – sprawling, chaotic and noisy. Vehicles have wooden signs on their roofs showing their destination, while touts shout out those that need filling. Minibuses don't run to any schedule – you pitch up at the motor park and wait until the vehicle is full. You'll do a lot of waiting during your trip. Luckily, motor parks are also huge markets, and there is a constant procession of hawkers and street-food vendors, so you won't go hungry.

Minibuses are either 'three across' or 'four across', referring to the number of passengers in each row. Prices listed in this guide are for 'three across'. Bush taxis – big old Peugeots – somehow manage to squeeze in nine passengers. Bush taxis are faster than minibuses and cost about 25% more. You'll also sometimes find private cars at motor parks – the comfiest, fastest and most expensive option. Slower minibuses have the edge on the danger front, and account for most traffic fatalities. Nigerians call them 'maulers' for good reason.

There are a few companies operating large buses from their own depots, usually on long-distance intercity routes. Best of the bunch is **ABC Transport** (www.abctransport.com), although it serves mostly cities in the south. Some services are overnight, and should be avoided for safety reasons.

The main roads are littered with road-blocks, allowing the Nigerian police to supplement their meagre income with highway robbery. An accomplished minibus driver can pass through and pay the standard N20 dash without stopping. There seems to be no system to decree whether a driver stops or speeds past – the extent to which the police are armed often seems a deciding factor. There are fewer roadblocks in the north.

Car & Motorcycle

Nigeria's road system is good, although for drivers this can bring problems in itself, as smooth tarmac allows Nigerians to exercise their latent talents as rally drivers. The accident rate is frighteningly high, and the only real road rule is survival of the fittest. Avoid driving at night at all costs.

Foreigners driving in Nigeria shouldn't get much hassle at roadblocks, particularly if your vehicle has foreign plates. If you get asked for a dash, a smile and some patience will often diffuse the request. Note however, that it's a legal requirement to wear a seatbelt; not doing so leaves you open to both official and unofficial fines. Petrol stations are everywhere, but keep your ear out for strikes that can cause fuel shortages. Diesel can sometimes be hard to come by, so keep your tank topped up.

Taxi & Okada

In towns and cities, the quickest way to get around is to hop on the back of a motorcycle taxi or *okada* (*achaba* in the north). In a Lagos go-slow they're the only practical option. A trip shouldn't cost more than N50, slightly more at night. *Okadas* are absolutely everywhere – just flag one down and hold on tight. Many drivers seem to have a fatalist's view of their own mortality, so don't be afraid to tell them to slow down (say 'small, small').

Taxis generally operate set routes, and you pay a similar price to an *okada*. If you want the car to yourself, ask for a 'drop'. Small change is essential for both taxis and *okadas*.

Train

Maps of Nigeria indicate that it has a rail network, but you'll be standing a long time on the platform waiting for a train – railway staff insists that passenger services still exist in the face of all available evidence. Should the decrepit locos ever run again, the main lines are Lagos–Kano (via Ibadan and Kaduna) and Port Harcourt–Maiduguri (via Jos). The latter line does run a semiregular service between Port Harcourt and Enugu, but the security situation in the former currently precludes taking it.

Senegal

Couched between the arid desert lands of the north and lush tropical forests in the south, Senegal boasts a stunning array of sights, sounds and flavours. The capital, Dakar, alone hands you the country in a capsule. Perched on the tip of a beach-lined peninsula, this dizzying city is composed elegance and street hustle rolled into one. Its busy streets, vibrant markets and glittering nightlife will easily draw you into their relentless rhythm, but the escape route is always open – be it to the meditative calm of the historical Île de Gorée or the sands of Yoff and N'Gor. And if Dakar's sensory overload really gets too much, the calm sway of architectural beauty Saint-Louis, the first French settlement in West Africa, boasts a vibrant urban culture without the inner-city bustle.

Most visitors head to Senegal for its beaches, and for good reason. North and south of Dakar, wide strips of white sand invite swimming and sunbathing, whether in the built-up resort zones, where a lazy day at the beach can be followed by a cocktail trail at night, or in one of the coast's charming fishing villages, whose beaches are dotted with hundreds of colourful wooden pirogues. At the wide deltas of the Casamance and Saloum Rivers, the straight coastline is broken up into a maze of thick mangroves, tiny creeks, wide lagoons and shimmering plains. A pirogue trip through these striking zones reveals hundreds of bird species, from the gleaming wings of tiny kingfishers to the proud poise of pink flamingos. Whether you want to mingle with the trendsetters of urban Africa or be alone with your thoughts and the sounds of nature, you'll find your place here.

FAST FACTS

- **Area** 196,192 sq km
- **Capital** Dakar
- **Country code** ☎ 221
- **Famous for** Its vibrant music scene, Dakar's urban culture, colonial houses
- **Languages** Wolof, Fula, Diola, Serer and French
- **Money** West African CFA franc; US$1 = CFA493; €1 = CFA656
- **Population** 11.1 million
- **Visa** Not needed for citizens of the EU, Ecowas (Economic Community of West African States), Canada, Norway, South Africa, Japan, Israel, the USA and some other (mainly African) countries. For all others, one- to three-month visas cost US$15 to US$20

SENEGAL

HOW MUCH?

- **Soft drink** CFA500
- **Newspaper** CFA200
- **Sandwich** CFA1200
- **French bread** CFA175
- **One hour's internet access** CFA300

LONELY PLANET INDEX

- **1L of petrol/gas** CFA600
- **1L of bottled water** CFA1000
- **Bottle of Flag beer** CFA1000
- **Souvenir T-shirt** CFA3000-5000
- **Shwarma** CFA1000

HIGHLIGHTS

- **The Casamance** (p725) Tiny villages dot the way to Senegal's best beaches in Cap Skiring.
- **Saint-Louis** (p707) West Africa's first French settlement.
- **Dakar** (p676) A vibrant nightclub, bar and concert scene in the capital.
- **Siné-Saloum** (p701) Pirogue rides through the mangroves of the Siné-Saloum Delta.
- **Bassari Country** (p717) Green hills and tiny villages.

ITINERARIES

- **One week** Spend a couple of days tasting the nightlife, arts and restaurant scene of Dakar (p676). From here, take day trips to the peaceful Île de Gorée (p693) and Îles de la Madeleine (p694). Head north to visit the historical town of Saint-Louis (p707). Put in a spot of bird watching at the Parc National des Oiseaux du Djoudj (p712) and Parc National de la Langue de Barbarie (p712). On your way back to Dakar, take in the Desert de Lompoul (p707).
- **Two weeks** Start as above, then head from Dakar south to the Petite Côte. Check out the community projects and beaches of Toubab Dialao (p696) and Popenguine (p697) before following the shoreline further south to Mbour (p700) and the unique seashell town of Joal-Fadiout (p701), if you like your beach life local, or Saly (p698), if you're more at home

in a holiday-resort zone. From Mbour, trace the coastal road beyond to Palmarin (p701), the stunning entry port to the region of the Siné-Saloum Delta, then head via Ndangane (p702) and Mar Lodj (p702) to Toubakouta (p703), one of the prettiest spots in the delta.

- **One month** Follow the two-week itinerary as described, then cross The Gambia from Toubakouta to reach the Casamance. Take the route towards Ziguinchor, with side trips to Affiniam (p729) and Koubalan (p729). Spend a couple of days in Ziguinchor (p721), the region's relaxed capital. Head west towards Oussouye (p725) and go kayaking, hiking and biking to places including Enampor (p725), with its stunning *campement villageois* (village 'camps' or guest houses). From Oussouye, pass via M'Lomp (p725) and visit its traditional *cases étages* (two-storey mud-brick houses), then carry on towards Elinkine (p726) and take a pirogue to Île de Karabane (p726). Take another pirogue to Cachouane (p729) and go on a long hike through tropical lands to Diembéring (p728). Cap Skiring (p727), with its stunning beaches, lies only a short stretch further south.
- **Six weeks** In six weeks, you can visit pretty much the entire country. Continue from the Casamance towards Tambacounda (p715) and the Parc National du Niokolo-Koba (p716). Keep going south towards Kedougou (p718) and the Bassari Country (p717). After visits to remote plateaus, waterfalls and forests, it's along the track back to Dakar. Stop at Kaolack (p706), Thiès (p704) or the holy town of Touba (p705) before re-entering the capital. Alternatively, if you have lots of time, the long river route via Bakel (p714), Matam (p714), Podor (p713) and the amazing Île à Morphil (p713) is Senegal's hidden treasure. Via Saint-Louis, you return to Dakar.

CLIMATE & WHEN TO GO

Senegal's main tourist season is from November to February, during the dry season and the 'coolest' months. Dakar's average daytime maximums are around 24°C (75°F) from January to March. It's also the best time to spot wildlife (particularly migratory birds). If you are the partying kind, the urban centre of Dakar is a great place to spend Christmas

SENEGAL

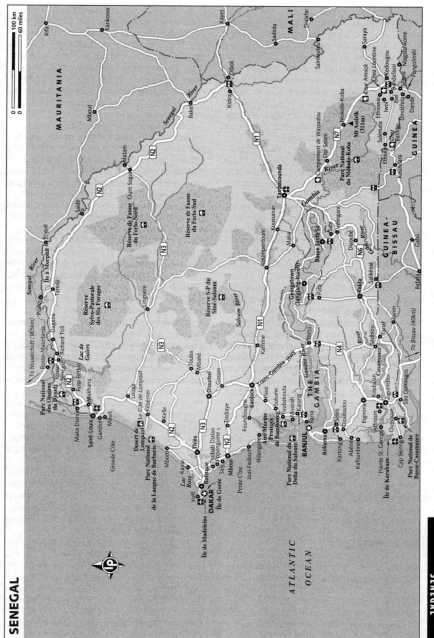

and New Year. Several of Senegal's famous dance and music festivals take place between March and June, when temperatures are higher, though the climate is still dry. See Climate Charts, p810, for more.

The wet months (late June to late September) see far fewer visitors, as some national parks become inaccessible or even close, malaria is a major problem, and heat and humidity presses down on the country. But it's also the time everything is green and beautiful, and many hotels reduce their prices by up to 50%.

Since you're travelling to a predominantly Muslim region, it's worth checking the lunar calendar, particularly for the dates of the fasting month Ramadan. Though it's perfectly possible to visit during Ramadan, and the month's special ambience is worth experiencing, many restaurants close and the entertainment scene is in hibernation. See p816 for more information on Islamic holidays.

HISTORY
The Age of Empires
The currents of many ancient African empires washed over Senegal, each adding a new influence, and often a new faith to the cultural make-up. The country's eastern regions were marked by the Empire of Ghana, which flourished between the 8th and 11th centuries and was brought to its knees by Almoravid warriors from north Africa, and their northern Senegal ally, the riverine Tekrur Empire. The mighty Mali Empire extended at its height over large areas of Senegal, and the coastal federation of kingdoms that formed the Jolof Empire (founded in 1360) used to be a vassal state to the central force. As Mali's power began to wane, Jolof – whose states spanned almost the entire Senegalese coast – became self-governing but soon split into its original entities of the Siné, Saloum, Kayor, Walo and Baol states, as the first influx of Portuguese trading wealth caused instability.

The Colonial Era
In 1443, Portuguese explorers reached the mouth of the Senegal River – a moment that marked medieval Europe's first direct contact with West Africa. The following year they landed at the Cap Vert peninsula, where today you find Dakar, and later settled on Île de Gorée, where they built the first trading station, soon to be followed by others.

By the 16th century other European powers had become increasingly active in West Africa. For the next two centuries the English and Dutch fought with the French over the islands of Gorée and Saint-Louis, and with it for control of the lucrative trade in gold, ivory and slaves. In 1659 the French developed a trading station in Saint-Louis at the mouth of the Senegal River, and in 1677 finally secured Gorée.

On the back of the trade, Saint-Louis grew throughout the 18th century in size and importance. When the slave trade was finally banned in 1815, the French turned their attention to new sources of wealth, and orders were given to gain control over the acacia gum trade along the Senegal River by establishing a string of forts. The task suited the expansionist zeal of governor Faidherbe (from 1845); with military force the river region was brought under control, and plantations, particularly groundnuts (peanuts), were established and expanded. Senegal became the gateway to the large territory of Afrique Occidentale Française (French West Africa), of which Saint-Louis was the capital (a title that was later transferred to the growing centre of Dakar).

Meanwhile, El Hajj Omar Tall, a marabout (Muslim holy man) from the Fouta Toro region in northern Senegal, was establishing a vast Muslim empire. His soldiers spread west into Senegal, where they clashed with French forces. El Hadj Omar Tall's forces were eventually defeated, yet his religious zeal inspired other leaders, including the illustrious Wolof King Lat Dior, who converted to Islam in order to build a united force against French expansion. His efforts at attempting the construction of the Saint-Louis–Dakar railway have become legendary.

Another thorn in the French side was a marabout called Cheikh Amadou Bamba (see the boxed text, p673), whose 1857 Islamic brotherhood of the Mourides became a hugely popular focal point of anticolonial sentiment.

At the Berlin Conference of 1884–85, following the 'scramble for Africa' (p33), the continent was divided between powerful European states. While Britain, Germany and Portugal got most of East and southern Africa, the greater part of West Africa was allocated to France. At the end of the 19th century, French West Africa stretched from the Atlantic to present-day Niger.

In the early 20th century, things began to change. In 1914, Senegal elected its first black African delegate, Blaise Diagne, to the French national assembly in Paris. After WWI, an increasing number of Senegalese studied in France. One of them was Léopold Sédar Senghor

Senghor was an astute politician and a gifted speaker, and when after WWII France granted each of its colonial territories the right to its own assembly, Senghor became the elected candidate for Senegal-Mauritania.

Independence

In the late 1950s, with independence movements on the increase, Senghor gained support from French Sudan (present-day Mali), Upper Volta (present-day Burkina Faso) and Dahomey (present-day Benin) to form a single union, the Mali Federation. Yet by the time independence was granted on 20 June 1960, only Senegal and Mali remained part of it – and then only for two months. On 20 August, Senegal was born in its current boundaries, with Senghor as first president.

Senghor was a popular leader, and despite challenges (such as the student riots of 1968), he consolidated his position. He was voted out of power a full 20 years later, and made history by stepping down from his seat voluntarily, making way for new president Abdou Diouf.

One of Diouf's first major acts as president was to help Gambian head of state Dawda Jawara regain power after he had been ousted in a coup, by sending in Senegalese military. Cooperation between the two countries was formalised by the establishment of the Senegambia Confederation later that year (a visionary effort at unifying the two areas that however crumbled a mere seven years later).

For Senegal, a union with Gambia would probably have been particularly useful. The fact that Gambia separates Senegal's northern regions from the southern Casamance has certainly heightened strong separatist feelings in the south. There had been periodic calls for independence in the Casamance for many years, but they came to a head in 1989, when rebels from the Mouvement des Forces Démocratiques de la Casamance (MFDC) started attacking government installations (see p721 for further details).

The Casamance problem was only one of Diouf's testing grounds. He also had to deal with a dispute with Mauritania and economic troubles. Calls for change become louder, and the most popular political candidate to address them was Abdoulaye Wade, who united opposition groups under the slogan *sopi* (meaning change). Attempts at stifling his force only rendered him more popular, and in 2000, on his third attempt, Wade finally won the election and became president, in Senegal's second peaceful change of government.

Senegal Today

In the early years of Wade's rule, things improved rapidly and visibly, with promising economic measures, strengthening of public services and a supportive climate of hope. But then things started to stagnate, and the government was felt to be lost in political infights. Though Wade (now 81) was re-elected in 2007, he no longer represented hope for change but quiet acceptance that there wasn't a strong alternative in the political arena.

Today, Senegal presents the paradoxical picture of a nation aiming for the skies yet troubled by severe economic problems. Dakar radiates new prosperity as well as deepening poverty and despair. While massive infrastructural investment is in progress, global price hikes of petrol and basic foodstocks have pushed large parts of the population deeper into poverty. Though Wade was quick to announce an ambitious plan to achieve self-sufficiency in food (GOANA) in 2008, the project was dismissed by many as being unrealistic. Against a background of increasing power cuts and rising frustrations (most visibly manifested in the number of youngsters seeking to emigrate aboard tiny wooden boats heading for Spain), Wade's government is seeking to boost the economy through stronger south-south investment (Iranian taxis, Kuwait-financed roads, and Indian gold mines are visible signs of this).

THE CULTURE
The National Psyche

Senegal takes great pride in being the 'Land of Teranga' – meaning 'hospitality'. The national football team is called 'Lions of Teranga', and plenty of hotels and restaurants have adopted the name. Much of this is promotional hype, but much of it is borne out in the national character: people tend to be open and welcoming towards visitors.

In the busy tourist areas, it can be hard to tell the difference between true hospitality and a 'con job' devised to trick you into some unplanned spending. The further you get away from the resort zones, the more 'real' society gets, and you can relax your shoulders and practise your rudimentary Wolof or French – people will be keen to teach you their language.

In Senegal, conversation is the key to local culture, and the key to conversation is a great sense of humour and a quick-witted tongue. The Senegalese love talking, teasing and testing you out, and the better you slide into the conversational game, the easier you'll get around. Someone mocks your habits? Don't tense up; retaliate with a clever remark, and you're likely to be on your way to an entertaining evening. People don't mean harm in laughing at you, and the ability to laugh at yourself is just as important an item in your luggage as your malaria pills and T-shirts.

Daily Life

The majority of Senegalese households are polygamous, the Quran allowing men to take up to four wives. Families are large and, as elsewhere in Africa, the extended family, with its clearly defined rules of interrelations, responsibilities and respect, plays a vital role. Unmarried children, particularly women, stay at their parents' home until they are wed, which is when men establish their own household, and women join their husband. In the case of a divorce, the woman usually rejoins her family, bringing her children with her. Single women, single-mother households (by choice) and even houses shared by young female students are virtually unheard of.

As is to be expected, traditional family relations tend to remain more deeply preserved in rural regions than in the cities. There are exceptions, however; as many young men leave their villages to seek work in the cities or abroad, some rural communities show a worrying absence of men, and women raising a large number of offspring on their own are becoming increasingly common.

A second factor that determines daily life is religious faith. In most Senegalese homes you'll notice the portraits of marabouts looking down earnestly from the walls. Men often join Senegal's influential Islamic brotherhoods for religious learning, while women tend to be the ones who mainly consult them for advice in mystic matters, such as protection for their children and ways of keeping a husband faithful.

Population

Senegal's population is young – around 42% of the people are under 14 years old. The greatest density is around the urban areas of Dakar – the rapidly growing, impoverished suburb of Pikine is a vivid example of the flight towards the cities and the problems this entails.

The main ethnic group of the country is the Wolof. They account for 43% of the population, and their language and culture is dominant. Smaller groups are the Fula (24%), Tukulor (a sub-branch of the Fula; 10%), Serer (14%) and Diola (5%). Geographical distribution of and cultural differences between these groups derive from Senegal's precolonial history of empires. With the exception of the Diola, these ethnic groups are structured in a hierarchical fashion: the free born (rulers and traders) are at the top, followed by professional occupational groups, including *griots* (traditional musicians and oral historians) and blacksmiths, and formerly the slaves. These structures still determine much of social life, though other aspects, such as economic success and education, are also important.

RELIGION

About 90% of the population is Muslim. What's distinctive about Islam in Senegal is the importance of Sufi brotherhoods, primarily that of the Mourides. Christian faith is most widespread among the Diola in the Casamance, and to a lesser extent the Serer in the Siné-Saloum region and the Bassari around Kedougou. Traditional religious forms (sometimes called animism) are most commonly practised in the Christian areas. Elements of animism have also found their way into the practice of Islam.

ARTS
Literature

Senegal has a prolific literary output, but most works are only published in French.

The most influential writer is probably Léopold Senghor, the country's first president. Studying in France during the 1930s, he coined the term 'negritude', which emphasised black African ideas and culture, countering the colonial policy of 'assimilation'. Naturally, these beliefs influenced Senghor's own political thought.

Great female authors include Aminata Sow-Fall and Mariama Ba, whose short novel *So Long a Letter* is one of the most sensitive,

---

MARABOUTS & BROTHERHOODS

Take a tour around Dakar, and you are bound to notice the images of two veiled men, one dressed in white and the other in black, painted on numerous walls, cars and shop signs. They are portraits of Cheikh Amadou Bamba , the 19th-century founder of the Mouride brotherhood, and Cheikh Ibra Fall , his illustrious follower and spiritual leader of the Baye Fall, a branch of Mouridism. *Télécentres* (telephone centres) and tailor shops are named after them, their names are written broadly across *cars rapides* (minibuses), and a vast number of pop songs, from *mbalax* (a mixture of Cuban beats and traditional, fiery *sabar* drumming) to hip-hop, praise the two revered personalities.

While orthodox Islam holds that every believer is directly in touch with Allah, Muslim faith in Senegal is more commonly channelled via saintly intermediaries who are ascribed divine powers and provide a link between God and the common populace. The concept of the marabout-led brotherhood was imported to Senegal from Morocco, where a spiritual leader is known as a *cheikh*, or khalif, terms that are also used in Senegal. The earliest brotherhood established south of the Sahara was the 16th-century Qadiriya. Today, most Qadiriya followers are Mandinkas, both in southern Senegal and in The Gambia.

The Moroccan-based Tijaniya brotherhood was introduced to Senegal by El Hajj Omar Tall in the mid-19th century, and remains powerful today, with large and important mosques in the towns of Tivaouane and Kaolack.

With over two million followers, the Mouridiya established by Cheikh Amadou Bamba is by far the most important brotherhood, and its power has consistently grown since the mid-19th century.

For many years, Cheikh Amadou Bamba was a humble marabout, not more, perhaps even less, renowned than any other religious leader of his time. Part of his rise to fame is due to the total adherence of his most famous *talibe* (student), Cheikh Ibra Fall. He was wholly devoted to the marabout, and demonstrated his commitment less through study than through hard, physical labour. 'Lamp' Fall, as he is often called, renounced Quranic study, and refused the Ramadan fast, stating that in order to serve God, he required all his time and bodily force to work hard. He soon gathered his own group of followers, the Baye Fall. Baye Fall adepts are traditionally recognisable by their long dreadlocks, heavy leather amulets containing pictures of their marabout, and patchwork clothing (not all follow the dress code), and to this day, the Baye Fall tend to be the hardest workers in the Touba region, building mosques and preparing fields for cultivation.

As the Mourides and Baye Fall gained immense popularity, the French began to fear their impact, and forced Cheikh Amadou Bamba into exile. His return in 1907 is still celebrated by the annual Magal pilgrimage (p706) to Touba.

---

intimate and beautiful contemplations of female lives in a polygamous society. Fatou Diome is a young author whose 2004 debut novel, *Le Ventre de l'Atlantique*, became an unexpected bestseller in France; it has since been translated into English.

The philosophical contemplation of religion and colonisation *An Ambiguous Adventure* by Cheikh Hamidou Kane has almost achieved the status of a Senegalese classic.

Cinema

Senegal is one of the most productive nations in African cinema. The doyen of Senegalese film is Ousmane Sembène, famous for the moving and critical insights into Senegalese society that marked his work from the 1962 production *Borom Sarret* to the 2006 release *Moolaade*, which treats the sensitive subject of female circumcision.

Other famous directors include the illustrious Djibril Diop Mambety; the younger Joseph Kamaka Gaye, whose acclaimed work *Karmen Geï* sets the classic story of Carmen in a Senegalese context; and Moussa Touré, with his hilarious *TGV Express*.

Music

Senegal is one of Africa's most musical nations, and names such as Youssou N'Dour, Baaba Maal and Ismael Lô are household names worldwide. The beat that moves the nation is *mbalax*. Created from a mixture of Cuban beats and traditional, fiery *sabar* drumming in the late 1970s, *mbalax* was made famous by Youssou N'Dour, still the unrivalled leader of the scene. Since its inception *mbalax* has evolved, always adapting to changing fashions without ever losing its essence. Today there's a whole new generation that causes havoc on the region's dance floors, including such excellent performers as Abdou Guité Seck, Ablaye Mbaye, Aliou Mbaye N'Der and Titi.

In the 1960s, Cuban music was the most prominent influence, and Senegal still has a vibrant salsa scene. The most famous salsa orchestra is Orchestra Baobab, who re-formed in 2001 and now tour regularly, luring audiences onto dance floors with their inimitable grandfather charm. The father of Senegalese music, however, is an artist that's lesser known today – Ibra Kasse, leader of the defunct Star Band de Dakar. In the line-up were Pape Seck and the illustrious Gambian-born singer Labah Sosseh. When the Star Band divided into glittering pieces, Etoile de Dakar emerged, which proved the rocket for Senegalese star Youssou N'Dour.

Influencing popular music are the *bbbb* (*gewel* in Wolof), West Africa's traditional praise singers, genealogists and oral historians (Youssou N'Dour is a griot through his mother's family lineage). The *griots'* soaring voice rings from modern recordings as well as traditional ceremonies, and their ancient repertoire forms the basis of many pop tunes.

Senegal has an exciting hip-hop scene, with leading names including Positive Black Soul (who emerged in the mid-1980s), Daara J, Pee Froiss, Carlou D, Chronik 2H and Sen Kumpe. On the quieter side, Afro-folk is represented by artists such as Xalam, the Frères Guisse and Cheikkh Lô.

Painting & Sculpture

Senegal has a vibrant contemporary arts scene. Well-known painters include Souleymane Keita and Ibra Ndiaye (leading artist of the '60s style Ecole de Dakar); leading sculptors are the world-famous Ousmane Sow and the emerging Gabriel Kemzo, who specialises in metal sculptures.

Senegal is particularly renowned for the unique art of *sous-verre* (reverse-glass painting). Outstanding artisans include Moussa Sakho (who has a workshop at l'Institut Français in Dakar), Babacar Lô, Andy Dolly, Séa Diallo, Mbida and Gora Mbengue.

And don't forget to keep your eyes open for the everyday art that gives Dakar its particular character. The city's *cars rapides* and taxis are draped in decorative writings and images. Reproductions of the portraits of Cheikh Amadou Bamba and Cheikh Ibra Fall adorn walls around town, and painted profiles add spots of colour to ragged barbe rshops.

ENVIRONMENT
The Land

Senegal is Africa's westernmost country; the continent's western tip, Le Point des Almadies, lies just north of Dakar. The nation comprises an area of just under 200,000 sq km, which compares in size to England and Scotland combined.

Senegal is largely flat, with a natural vegetation of dry savannah woodland. The country's western border, some 600km in length, is marked by the Atlantic Ocean.

Senegal has four major rivers, which flow east to west from the Fouta Jallon highlands in Guinea to the Atlantic. The Senegal River is the northernmost. The Gambia River flows through Senegal's only mountainous area (the lands surrounding Kedougou) before entering The Gambia itself. The Saloum River enters the ocean via a large delta to the south of the Petite Côte – this is a zone of labyrinthine mangrove swamps, salty plains, lagoons, small creeks and river islands. In the far south the Casamance River gives the surrounding region its name.

Wildlife
ANIMALS

Main areas for bird watching include the Parc National des Oiseaux du Djoudj, the world's third-largest bird sanctuary; the Parc National de la Langue de Barbarie; and the mangrove areas of the Casamance and the Siné-Saloum Delta.

Easily recognised mammal species include baboons, three types of monkey (vervets, patas and red colobuses) and warthogs. All of those can be seen in the Parc National de Niokolo-Koba. In the park's dry grasslands you'll find antelope species (including cobs, roans, waterbucks and Derby elands); hyenas and a couple of lions inhabit the lands, and crocodiles, hippos and manatees the waters. The best place to spot the latter is the manatee sanctuary at Pointe St George (p725).

PLANTS

Senegal lies in the Sahel zone, and in large areas only tall baobab trees, acacias and low scrub rise from the dry lands. Some northern areas come close to being desert, contrasting completely with the abundant greenery of the gallery forests in the Casamance and the mangrove deltas you find here as well as in the Siné-Saloum Delta and near Saint-Louis.

National Parks

Senegal has six national parks: Parc National du Niokolo-Koba (p716) in the southeast – the largest, with a wide range of habitat types; Parc National du Delta du Saloum (p704) with its coastal lagoons, mangroves, islands and dry woodland; the volcanic rocks of the Îles de la Madeleine (p694) near Dakar; and in northern Senegal, Parc National des Oiseaux du Djoudj (p712) and Parc National de la Langue de Barbarie (p712), both noted for their bird life. Parc National de Basse-Casamance has been closed for years because of rebel activity and suspected landmines.

Other protected areas include the Ferlo wildlife reserves, the Réserve de Bandia (p697), the small reserves of Popenguine (p697) and La Somone (p698), and the community-managed *aires marines protégéés* (marine protected areas) of Bamboung (p703) and Pointe St George (see p725).

Environmental Issues

Overfishing, coastal erosion and deforestation, which paves the way for the advancing Sahara, are the main environmental issues the country faces. Coastal erosion occurs naturally but is hugely aggravated by illegal sand mining conducted by construction companies, which has caused the disappearance of wide beaches in areas such as Malika, near Dakar.

Overfishing is a huge problem. Due to rising demands for fish in-country and abroad, Senegal's artisanal fishermen have increased dramatically in number (it's estimated that over 15,000 wooden pirogues work 700km of coast), and stocks are dwindling. The problem is compounded (though not primarily caused) by European and Asian boats fishing in the region. Species such as the iconic *thiof* (grouper) are already becoming rare, a decline that not only has dramatic environmental consequences but also increases poverty and despair among the fishing communities. The Dakar-based Océanium is doing amazing work in establishing *aires marines protégéés*, run in close conjunction with the resident communities.

Deforestation is partly caused by a growing demand for farmland, mainly to cultivate groundnuts, but trees are also felled for firewood and to make charcoal, much of which is used to smoke fish.

FOOD & DRINK
Staples & Specialities

Senegal's national dish is the *thiéboudieune* (spelt in different ways, and pronounced chey-bou-jen). The word means fish and rice, and refers to a delicious dish of rice cooked in tomato sauce and served with chunks of fried fish, often stuffed with parsley and garlic paste, carrots, cassava and other vegetables. The festive variation is *tiebouyapp* (or *yollof* rice), where fish is replaced by meat.

Another regional favourite is *yassa poulet*, grilled chicken marinated in a thick onion and lemon sauce. Occasionally chicken is replaced by fish or meat, changing the name to *yassa poisson* (fish) or *yassa bœuf* (beef).

Mafé, a meaty groundnut sauce served with rice, is another typical dish, and among the Fula and Tukulor, *lacciri* (millet couscous) is common, eaten with either a savoury sauce or *kosan* (milk).

Drinks

Locally produced juices include the hibiscus drink *bissap, gingembre* (ginger beer) and *bouyi*, made from the fruits of the baobab.

For a caffeine kick, try a *café touba*, a spicy brew served in small cups at roadside stalls, or *ataaya*, concentrated, bittersweet green tea that's the centrepiece of a social afternoon.

Palm wine is a popular home brew, particularly in the non-Muslim and palm tree–blessed Casamance.

Celebrations

The meals served for family celebrations are more refined versions of staples. For naming ceremonies *lakh* (millet porridge) is served with milk or yogurt, and for baptisms and weddings *beignet* (small doughnuts) are fried and given to the guests. At Tabaski (see p816), every Muslim family slaughters a sheep to commemorate Abraham's willingness to sacrifice his son on God's demand.

Where to Eat & Drink

Dakar's restaurant scene is excellent and varied, but meals in the best restaurants can be expensive. If you're on a budget, head for

SENEGAL

the *gargottes* (small, local eateries). Be careful, though – some are of rather dubious hygienic quality.

Also on the tiny side are the Senegalese *tanganas* (literally meaning 'hot stuff'), where you get your *café touba* and a sandwich with sauce. A *dibiterie* is a grilled-meat stall, usually only open in the evenings and the place people head to before a night out or before returning home in the wee hours. Dakar has fantastic patisseries, places to indulge in cakes and croissants, as well as a post-nightclub alternative to *dibiteries* for those who only leave at breakfast.

Vegetarians & Vegans

Outside of Dakar, vegetarian food is hard to find and there's little understanding of why someone who can afford it won't eat meat. This means that, when you order a dish without meat, you might still find that your rice is drowning in meat sauce, just without the chunks.

Dakar's varied restaurant scene has plenty of vegetarian options.

Habits & Customs

Meals are traditionally eaten squatting on the floor, grouped around a large platter of rice and sauce. People mostly eat the traditional rice dishes with a spoon or the hand. If you try the hand version, make sure you use your right only – the left is the hand you wipe your bum with and is strictly out at meal times.

It's usually polite to finish eating while there's still food in the bowl, to show you have had enough – comments along the lines of 'You haven't eaten anything!' aren't actually invitations to eat more.

DAKAR

pop 2.4 million

Once a tiny settlement in the south of the Cap Vert Peninsula, Dakar now spreads almost across its entire triangle, and keeps growing. This is a city made of furious drum beats, screeching traffic, exuberant nightlife, market shouting, street hustling and boundless creativity. It's also a city of contrasts, where you'll see horse-cart drivers chugging over swish highways and gleaming SUVs squeezing through tiny sand roads. Here impossibly elegant ladies dig skinny heels into dusty walkways and suit-clad businessmen kneel down for prayer in the middle of the street. It's a fascinating place – easily negotiated once you've learnt how to beat its scamsters, hustlers and traders at their own game.

ORIENTATION

The centre of Dakar, the historical Plateau sits right at the tip of the peninsula, opposite Île de Gorée. Its heart is the Place de l'Indépendance, from where Ave Pompidou heads west towards the sprawling Marché Sandaga. Ave Léopold Senghor leads south from here to the Hôpital Principal; a few blocks before it reaches the hospital, Ave Senghor connects via the wide Blvd de la République to the Rte de la Corniche Ouest – the modern main route out of the centre. The Corniche runs past Les Mamelles all the way to Les Almadies and N'Gor, where it turns into Rte de N'Gor and leads eastwards to Yoff.

A second main artery out of the Plateau is Ave Blaise Diagne, which passes through the old Senegalese *quartier* Médina before slicing as Ave Cheikh Anta Diop through fashionable Point E, with its bars and restaurants, Mermoz and the old Lebou neighbourhood Ouakam.

At the time of writing, the journey out of Dakar passed via Ave du Président Lamine Guèye and the autoroute to the huge interchange of Patte d'Oie, and from there through the *banlieues* (suburbs) of Pikine and Thiaroye to Rufisque, Diamnadio and finally anywhere else in the country. The construction of the new autoroute will change this – check progress when you're there.

Maps

By far the best city map is the colourful, detailed one by **Editions Laure Kane** (www.editions laurekane.com); you get it in bookshops and some hotels for CFA4000. Check the site, as the company has started developing virtual city tours.

INFORMATION

The excellent, pocket-sized, glossy *221* (CFA100) contains a comprehensive cultural calendar as well as interesting write-ups on music, arts and sport around the country. It's available at newsagents, shops, restaurants and hotels.

Bookshops

Librairie 4 Vents (Map p680; ☎ 33 821 8083; 55 Rue Félix Faure, Plateau; ⏰ 9am-1pm & 3-7pm Mon-Sat)

Librairie Clairafrique (Map p682; ☎ 33 864 4429; Ave Cheikh Anta Diop, university grounds; ☒ 8.30am-6.30pm Mon-Sat)

Cultural Centres

Centre Culturel Vivre et Apprendre (Map p685; ☎ 33 820 5484; culturevivreetapprendre@gmail.com; Ave Seydina Limmamou Laye, Yoff) Brand new in 2009, this initiative of the Global Ecovillage Network offers dance, percussion and Wolof courses, exhibitions, and exchanges in the urban village of Yoff.

Goethe Institut (Map p682; ☎ 33 869 8880; www .goethe.de/ins/sn/dak; cnr Rue de Diourbel & Piscine Olympique, Point E) The German cultural centre hosts frequent exhibitions, shows and films and has a great terrace cafe.

Institut Français Léopold Śedar Senghor (Map p680; ☎ 33 823 0320; www.institutfr-dakar.org; 89 Rue Joseph Gomis, Plateau) The French cultural centre is a hub of arts activity with a stage, workshops, shops and a great cafe.

Internet Access

You'll find small internet cafes in the town centre and near the university (around CFA300 to CFA500 per hour). Wi-fi is increasingly common, with plenty of hotels and restaurants offering a free service.

Cyber-Business Centre (Map p680; ☎ 33 823 3223; Ave Léopold Senghor; ☒ 8am-midnight)

Espacetel Plus (Map p680; ☎ 33 822 9062; Blvd de la République; ☒ 8am-midnight)

Medical Services

Compared to other West African countries, Senegal has a fairly good medical network, with several private clinics, emergency services and many pharmacies. The main emergency department is at Hôpital Principal.

Clinique de la Madeleine (Map p678; ☎ 33 821 9470; 18 Ave des Jambaars) General service and a maternity department.

Clinique du Cap (Map p678; ☎ 33 889 0202; Ave Pasteur) Private clinic; has an intensive care unit.

Hôpital Principal (Map p678; ☎ 33 839 5050; Ave Léopold Senghor) Main hospital.

SOS Medecin (Map p685; ☎ 33 889 1515; Baie de Soumbédioune, cnr Rues 62 & 64) Emergency service.

Suma Urgences (Map p682; ☎ 33 824 2418; Ave Cheikh Anta Diop, Fann) Emergency service.

Dakar has many pharmacies. Most open from 8am to 11pm, and there's a rotational 24-hour stand-by system; you'll find details of the current 24-hour place outside every pharmacy.

Pharmacie Guigon (Map p680; ☎ 33 823 0333; 1 Av du Président Lamine Guèye; ☒ 8am-11pm Mon-Sat) Dakar's best-stocked pharmacy.

Pharmacie Mandela (Map p678; ☎ 33 821 2172; Ave Nelson Mandela; ☒ 24hr) Near the Hôpital Principal.

Money

The main banks are CBAO, BICIS and SGBS, with branches across Dakar. They all have ATMs (Visa and MasterCard, withdrawal limit usually CFA250,000) and change cash, though not always travellers cheques. Below are the main branches; there are many, many more.

BICIS (Map p680; ☎ 33 839 0390; Pl de l'Indépendance)

CBAO (Map p680; ☎ 33 849 9300; www.cbao.sn; Immeuble SDIH 2, Place de l'Indépendance)

SGBS (Map p680; ☎ 33 842 5039; www.sgbs.sn; Av de la République)

Post

Main post office (Map p680; ☎ 33 839 3400; Blvd el Haji Djily Mbaye; ☒ 7am-7pm Mon-Fri, 8am-5pm Sat) Near Marché Kermel.

Post office (Map p680; ☎ 33 839 3400; Ave Pompidou) Smaller; has a small *télécentre* and a Western Union service.

Telephone

There are dozens of *télécentres*, mostly with similar rates. Post offices and internet cafes often also have telephone facilities.

Travel Agencies

Try the following for ticketing and charter flights, and see p739 for a listing of tour operators.

Dakar Voyages (Map p680; ☎ 33 823 3704; www .dakarvoyages.com; 29 Rue Amadou Assane Ndoye) Tends to have the best deals on charter flights.

Nouvelles Frontières (Map p685; ☎ 33 859 4447; www.nfsenegal.com; Rte des Almadies, Lot 1 Mamelles Aviation; ☒ 8.30am-6pm Mon-Fri, 9am-12.30pm Sat) Large French tour operator; can book seats on charter and regular flights.

Senegal Tours (Map p680; ☎ 33 839 9900; 5 Pl de l'Indépendance) Large tour operator that deals with ticketing as well as tours.

DANGERS & ANNOYANCES

Crime, especially muggings at knifepoint or from passing scooters were on the increase at the time of research, giving serious cause for concern about Dakar's safety. Avoid walking around after dark. Be particularly careful on the Petite Corniche (behind the presidential

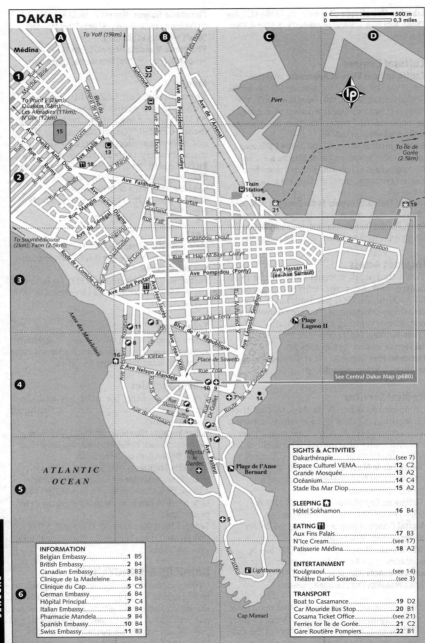

DAKAR

0 — 500 m
0 — 0.3 miles

SIGHTS & ACTIVITIES
Dakarthérapie......................................(see 7)
Espace Culturel VEMA.......................**12** C2
Grande Mosquée..................................**13** A2
Océanium...**14** C4
Stade Iba Mar Diop.............................**15** A2

SLEEPING 🏠
Hôtel Sokhamon...................................**16** B4

EATING 🍴
Aux Fins Palais.....................................**17** B3
N'Ice Cream..(see 17)
Patisserie Médina.................................**18** A2

ENTERTAINMENT
Koulgraoul...(see 14)
Théâtre Daniel Sorano.......................(see 3)

TRANSPORT
Boat to Casamance.............................**19** D2
Car Mouride Bus Stop.........................**20** B1
Cosama Ticket Office.........................(see 21)
Ferries for Île de Gorée.......................**21** C2
Gare Routière Pompiers......................**22** B1

INFORMATION
Belgian Embassy...................................**1** B5
British Embassy.....................................**2** B4
Canadian Embassy................................**3** B3
Clinique de la Madeleine....................**4** B4
Clinique du Cap....................................**5** C5
German Embassy...................................**6** B4
Hôpital Principal..................................**7** C4
Italian Embassy.....................................**8** B4
Pharmacie Mandela.............................**9** B4
Spanish Embassy...................................**10** B4
Swiss Embassy......................................**11** B3

ATLANTIC
OCEAN

SENEGAL

palace), the Rte de la Corniche-Ouest and the beaches.

Beware of pickpockets, especially at the markets and on Ave Pompidou. Less worrying, but very annoying, are street traders and hustlers. Be firm but friendly to shake them off. A confident *bakhna* (it's OK) or *après* (later) usually gets rid of them. Don't fall prey to the inner-city scams. The 'remember me?' scam is particularly popular. Someone might call out 'my friend, long time no see!', pretending they know you, then cheat you out of money. The remedy: don't respond to random calls. If someone doesn't know your name, chances are they don't know you.

SIGHTS

Strolling through Dakar means fighting a ninja struggle against parked cars, over-eager top-up-card touts and a nauseating network of open sewers. But the chaos is part of the charm – and there are some great buildings and urban scenes to take in.

PLATEAU

Start your tour from Place de l'Indépendance, with the majestic buildings of the **Gouvernance** (Map p680) and the **Chambre de Commerce** (Map p680). A few steps north you'll find the stately **Hôtel de Ville** (town hall; Map p680; Blvd el Hajj Djily Mbaye), and nearby the elegant facade of Dakar's famous **train station** (Map p678; Blvd de la Libération).

The nearby **Marché Kermel** (Map p680) is a pretty roundhouse and busy trading site, rebuilt in 1997 in its original 1860s beauty (the original building was destroyed in a fire).

Heading southwest, the awe-inspiring **Palais Présidentiel** (Map p680; Ave Léopold Senghor) is surrounded by sumptuous gardens and guards in colonial-style uniforms. The **Assemblée Nationale** (Parliament; Map p680; Pl de Soweto), with its modern glass facade, is easy to reach from here, as is Dakar's central **cathedral** (Map p680; Blvd de la République), a large 1920s building.

Museums & Art Galleries

A testament to former President Senghor's interest in promoting African art and culture, Dakar's **Musée Théodore Monod** (Map p680; ☎ 33 823 9268; Pl de Soweto; adult/child CFA2200/200; 🕙 9am-6pm Tue-Sun), formerly Musée IFAN, is a major centre of West African cultural studies, with interesting (if slightly dusty) historical exhibits as well as contemporary exhibitions.

The leafy garden of the **Institut Français Léopold Sédar Senghor** (Map p680; ☎ 33 823 0320; 89 Rue Joseph Gomis) houses the artistically messy workshop of *sous-verre* (reverse-glass painting) artist Moussa Sakho. Check out also the bird sculptures next door. The brilliant **Galerie Le Manège** (Map p680; ☎ 33 821 0822; 3 Rue Parchappe; 🕙 9am-5pm Tue-Sat), in a beautifully restored 19th-century building, is also part of the French cultural complex. The space of the **Galerie Nationale** (Map p680; ☎ 33 821 2511; 19 Ave Albert Sarraut; admission free; 🕙 9am-6pm) is a bit drab, but its frequently changing exhibitions of photography or paintings are usually very good. **Galerie Arte** (Map p680; ☎ 33 821 9556; www.arte.sn; 5 Rue Victor Hugo) displays its original selection of sculptures, paintings, jewellery and furniture like a shop, and while items are indeed for sale, there's no pressure to buy. At the **Galerie Antenna** (Map p680; ☎ 33 822 1751; 9 Rue Félix Faure; 🕙 9.30am-1pm & 4-7.30pm Mon-Sat), nearby, the commitment to African arts and antiques spills over even into the decoration of the gallery's impressive facade.

The warehouse of the **Espace Culturel VEMA** (Map p678; ☎ 33 821 7026; Embarcadère de Gorée; 🕙 8am-6pm) often houses excellent exhibitions (phone first), and at **Dakarthérapie** (Map p678; ☎ 33 839 5072; l'Hôpital Principal; 🕙 9am-1pm & 3-6pm Mon-Fri) you can see works by psychiatric patients at the hospital, created during artist-led workshops organised by the association Nit Nit Garabam.

SUBURBS: MÉDINA TO MAMELLES

Each of the suburbs that surround the town centre has its very own character and is worth visiting just to explore the many faces of the city. Closest to the Plateau is the bustling **Médina** (Map p678). Built as a township during colonial days, it is today a busy market and brims with life. Besides being a very real neighbourhood, where creative ideas and new trends grow between crammed, makeshift homes, it's also home to Dakar's **Grande Mosquée** (Map p678; Ave Malik Sy), built in 1964.

Following the Corniche northwards, you pass the large **Place du Souvenir** (Map p685). It was built in 2007 as a site of commemoration for the victims of the 2001 Joola ferry disaster, in which almost 2000 people perished. It houses occasional arts exhibitions with view across the Atlantic. Further along the Corniche, you'll see the tall **Mosquée de la Divinité** (Map p685; Rte de la Corniche-Ouest) perched on a calm

CENTRAL DAKAR

SENEGAL

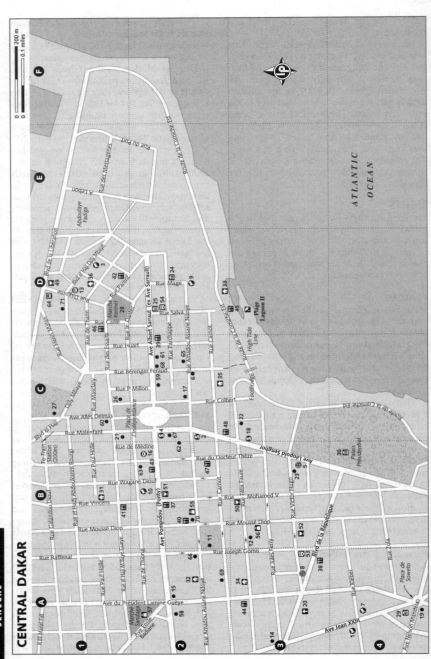

stretch of shore. The pretty **Mamelles lighthouse** (Map p685), off Rte de la Corniche-Ouest, sits on a small volcanic hill. To reach to the 1864 building, just follow the tarmac road up the hill. The leisurely 25-minute walk is rewarded with a great view across town. Eastwards from here, the neighbourhood **Ouakam** (Map p685) has retained the close-knit character of the Lebou village it used to be decades ago.

Museums & Art Galleries
In residential Point E, **Espace Agora** (Map p682; 33 864 1448; Rue D, Point E) has a tree-shaded patio where you can look at (and purchase) carefully selected Moroccan and Senegalese sculptures and paintings. A short walk from here, **Galerie Kemboury** (Map p682; 33 825 4843; Blvd Canal IV, Point E; 3.30-7pm Mon, 9.30am-1pm & 3.30-7pm Tue-Sat) has a reputation for tracking down new works by some of Senegal's most promising artists.

Beaches
The beaches along the Rte de la Corniche-Ouest are popular with local joggers and fitness fanatics but are unsuitable for swimming. The tiny spot of strand next to the Mosquée

de la Divinité (Map p685) is a popular surfing spot and grants great views over the Mamelles cliff.

LES ALMADIES, N'GOR & YOFF
Framed by beaches and brushed by strong winds, these three northwestern neighbourhoods each have their own, unique character. **Les Almadies** (Map p685) is Dakar's *quartier chic*, a plush neighbourhood where the polished villas of Senegal's richest look out onto private beaches. It's one of the fastest developing zones of the capital, with bars, restaurants and Dakar's best nightclubs. To dive into the popular ambience behind the luxurious facades, head along the coastal branch of the Rte des Almadies towards the westernmost point of the African continent – **La Pointe des Almadies** (Map p685), beautifully understated with its street-side food stalls, small cafes and secret surfer spots.

The small Lebou village of **N'Gor** (Map p685) is rarely visited by tourists, as their attention is entirely taken up by the area's wide beach and the small island across from it (see p683).

SENEGAL

In **Yoff** (Map p685), the situation is exactly inversed. The beaches close to the Lebou community are 'industrial' sands – launching pads for pirogues and garbage dumps for fish guts. Yoff is Dakar's most independent zone, where the Lebou village ties and traditions continue to dominate life and even local governance; the community is self-administering, with no government officials, and, apparently, no crime. The Lebou of Yoff are nearly all members of the Layen, one of the brotherhoods that dominate life in Senegal (see the boxed text, p673). The founder of the brotherhood, Saidi Limamou Laye, is buried here in the white-washed **Layen Mausoleum** (Map p685).

The Muslim faith of Yoff's residents strongly colours life in this community.

Smoking is not allowed here, there are no bars, and you have to wear long clothing while walking through the village streets.

Museums & Art Galleries

The **Village des Arts** (Map p685; ☎ 33 835 7160; www .vdesarts.com; Rte de l'Aeroport), near the stadium, is an amazing site, housing the busy workshops of over 30 photographers, painters and sculptors. An on-site gallery shows a selection of their work and the nearby restaurant is the place to have a drink and chat to the artists.

In the heart of Les Almadies, take a look at the **Céramiques Almadies** (Map p685; ☎ 77 533 0134), where Mauro Petroni displays his beautiful ceramics, and frequently the works of other artists, too. To get there, take the second left

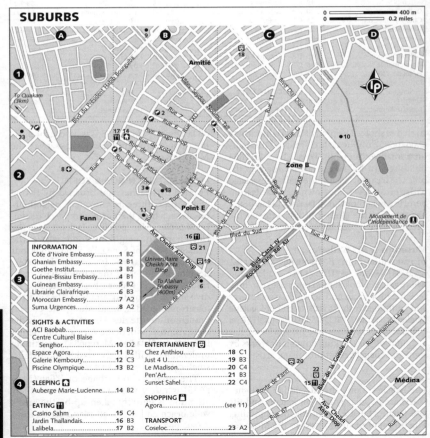

SUBURBS

0   400 m
0   0.2 miles

INFORMATION	
Côte d'Ivoire Embassy............1	B2
Ghanian Embassy....................2	B1
Goethe Institut.......................3	B2
Guinea-Bissau Embassy.........4	B1
Guinean Embassy...................5	B2
Librairie Clairafrique.............6	B3
Moroccan Embassy.................7	A2
Suma Urgences......................8	A2

SIGHTS & ACTIVITIES	
ACI Baobab............................9	B1
Centre Culturel Blaise	
Senghor.............................10	D2
Espace Agora.........................11	B2
Galerie Kemboury.................12	C3
Piscine Olympique................13	B2

SLEEPING 🏠	
Auberge Marie-Lucienne.......14	B2

EATING 🍴	
Casino Sahm 15	C4
Jardin Thaïlandais................16	B3
Lalibela................................17	B2

ENTERTAINMENT 🎭	
Chez Anthiou.......................18	C1
Just 4 U................................19	B3
Le Madison...........................20	C4
Pen'Art................................21	B3
Sunset Sahel........................22	C4

SHOPPING 🛍	
Agora...............................(see 11)	

TRANSPORT	
Coseloc...............................23	A2

Amitié

To Ouakam
(3km)

Zone B

Fann

Point E

Monument de
l'Indépendance

Médina

Universitaire
Cheikh Anta
Diop

To Malian
Embassy
(400m)

SENEGAL

off the Rte des Almadies. The **Centre Culturel Vivre et Apprendre** (Map p685; ☎ 33 820 5484; culture vivreetapprendre@gmail.com; Ave Seydina Limmamou Laye) in Yoff hosts occasional arts exhibitions and runs workshops.

Beaches
The sheltered **Plage N'Gor** (Map p685; admission CFA500) is the main escape spot for flirtatious youth and Dakarois families armed with picnic baskets. A short boat ride (CFA500 return) across the bay takes you to **Île de N'Gor** (Map p685), a tiny island with a couple of other beaches. As on Plage N'Gor, you can hire parasols and mats here for a small fee.

Winds and currents get stronger as you head towards Yoff, where the **Plage de Virage** (Map p685) is popular with surfers and bodyboarders, though swimming is also possible. Past the bustle and litter of Yoff's fishing beach (great for taking in the sights of pirogues rolling in on the surf), the sands of **Plage de Yoff** (Map p685) stretch out temptingly into the distance. The windy shore is great for mind-clearing walks, but strong currents make it unsuitable for bathing.

ACTIVITIES
Diving
To arrange diving courses, contact the **Océanium** (Map p678; ☎ 33 822 2441; www.oceanium.org; Rte de la Corniche-Est; ☣ Mon-Sat), where they come with an eco-edge. Ask about the ecotourism projects while you're at it (see p739).

Fishing
At Plage N'Gor, **Atlantic Evasion** (Map p685; ☎ 33 820 7675; www.atlantic-evasion.com) offers deep-sea fishing and angling excursions. The restaurant **Lagon I** (Map p680; ☎ 33 889 2525; Rte de la Corniche-Est) arranges deep-sea fishing trips and boasts several world-record catches.

Swimming & Sports
If the sea is too cold, try one of Dakar's pools. The 50m pool of the **Piscine Olympique** (Map p682; ☎ 33 869 0606; Tour de l'Œuf, Point E) is a training pool that's part of large fitness complex.

Club Olympique (Map p685; ☎ 33 864 5655; www.olympique-club.com; Rte de la Corniche-Ouest) is a state-of-the-art fitness centre with a large pool (admission CFA5000/4000 for adults/children), a tennis centre, a playground and a squash hall.

Most hotels open their pools to nonguests for a fee. Terrou Bi (admission CFA5000), Pullman Teranga (admission CFA8000) and

Le Méridien President (CFA10,000) all have good, though expensive pools.

Surfing
Dakar is growing into a surfing hot spot, thanks to its waves, and the following organisations, who have highly qualified trainers. **Pantcho Surf Trip** (Map p685; ☎ 77 534 6232; Plage N'Gor; 7 days CFA145,000) Courses available for adults and children on Senegal's two-time champion. Accommodation in N'Gor hotels.

Tribal Surf Shop (Map p685; ☎ 33 820 5400; www.tribalsurfshop.net; Plage de Virage; 2hr courses from CFA25,000) Board hire and repair, surfing classes for adults and children, and holidays. Also skateboarding, kayaking and accommodation in villas around Yoff.

Wrestling
Dakar's main arena for traditional wrestling is the **Stade Iba Mar Diop** (Map p678; Ave Cheikh Anta Diop). Fights of big-name wrestlers are national sports events, held in **Stade Léopold Sédar Senghor** (Map p685), Dakar's main stadium in Yoff. Senegal's entire population awaits the results of the traditional star match held on 1 January. Saturday and/or Sunday are the usual days for the fights, starting around 4.30pm or 5pm.

COURSES
Language
Recommended language courses are run at the following centres.
ACI Baobab (Map p682; ☎ 33 825 3637; Villa 509, Sicap Baobab) Small, friendly Wolof teaching centre set up by former Peace Corps volunteers.
Centre Culturel Vivre et Apprendre (Map p685; ☎ 33 820 5484; culturevivreetapprendre@gmail.com; Ave Seydina Limmamou Laye) Runs Wolof, French, English and Spanish courses.
Pôle Linguistique de l'Institut Français (Map p680; ☎ 33 823 84 83; 3 Rue Parchappe; ☣ Oct-May) Runs Wolof and French classes.

Dance
For dance courses or to watch rehearsals, try Yoff's Centre Culturel Vivre et Apprendre (see above) or the **Centre Culturel Blaise Senghor** (Map p682; 33 824 6600; Blvd Dial Diao). Its bleak facade doesn't do justice to the creative bustle going on inside.

FESTIVALS & EVENTS
Dakar's cultural calendar is packed, and outside the wettest months (July and August)

SENEGAL

you're almost bound to stumble across a festival.

Dak'Art Biennale (☎ 33 823 0918; www.dakart .org) May. Huge, biennial arts festival with great fringe exhibitions.

Kaay Fecc (☎ 33 824 51 54; www.kaayfecc.com) Early June. One of Africa's best contemporary-dance festivals.

SLEEPING

Dakar has a wide range of accommodation, from dodgy dosshouses to palatial hotels. This is a city that overcharges for most things – reasonably priced rooms can be hard to come by.

Budget

Dakar doesn't cater well for backpackers on a budget. Some of the cheapest hostels are of dubious cleanliness and clientele. If you're on a shoestring budget and on a tour around the country, try to save money in the regions and save up for something a little nicer when in the capital.

PLATEAU

Chez Nizar (Map p680; ☎ 77 319 1224; 25 Ave Pompidou; r CFA15,000) Just above the famous fast-food joint Ali Baba's, this hostel stretches an amazing 100 basic rooms into the Dakar skies. It's got all the charm of social housing, and it's just as cheap and useful as that.

Hôtel Saint-Louis Sun (Map p680; ☎ 33 822 2570; fax 822 4651; Rue Félix Faure; r CFA23,500-29,500; ☒ 및 ⑤) One of the few hotels to maintain reasonable prices, it hasn't exactly invested in its rooms either. Its greatest attribute is the central courtyard with huge palm trees, which turns the space into a calm oasis amid the crowds and fumes of central Dakar.

SUBURBS: MÉDINA TO MAMELLES

Espace Thially (Map p685; ☎ 33 855 0260; espace .thialy@orange.sn; Patte d'Oie, Impôts et Domaines; s/d incl breakfast CFA14,000/18,000; 및) Since it's far from the tourist bustle, this pretty guest house, with a leafy garden and a quiet terrace, can afford to charge very little for its homely, well-maintained rooms. It's not that close to the centre or the beach, but it's well-placed if you're planning to head for the regions.

Hôtel du Phare (Map p685; ☎ 33 860 3000; info@ lesmamelles.com; Les Mamelles; s with/without bathroom CFA22,000/15,000, d CFA28,000/20,000; ☒ 및) Tucked away in a side street off Rte de la Corniche-Ouest, this family-friendly guesthouse has a handful of rooms with simple charm and a homely ambience. The leafy patio provides quality relaxing space.

LES ALMADIES, N'GOR & YOFF

Keur Diame (Map p685; ☎ 33 855 8908; Parcelles Assainies; www.senegal.net.tf; s/d incl breakfast CFA13,000/21,300) Right in the strictly local neighbourhood Parcelles Assainies, you get immersion in Senegalese life on one side and the vastness that is Yoff beach a few steps in the opposite direction. Rooms here come with mosquito nets and fans, there's a roof terrace for sunbathing, and manager Ruth is fantastically friendly.

Hôtel Cap Ouest (Map p685; ☎ 33 820 2469; cap ouest@arc.sn; s/d from CFA19,500/23,000) This family hotel next to Plage Virage is the only address in Dakar where you get to dangle your feet in the ocean and lounge in a hammock on the shore for less than the rate of a downtown brothel. The newly decorated 1st-floor rooms with sea view cost CFA4000 more, an investment absolutely worth making.

GETTING UNDER DAKAR'S SKIN

A brilliant way of getting to know this city, its changeable moods and early-morning faces, is by staying with a local family, partaking in their lives for a few days and finding out what their Dakar looks like. There are now a couple of excellent organisations that can put you in touch with recommended families, and help you out should things go wrong. **Senegal Chez L'Habitant** (☎ 77 517 2666; www.senegalchezlhabitant.com) maintains a regularly updated register of families across the country who would like to open their houses. **L'Océanium** (☎ 33 822 2441; www.oceanium.org) has built an excellent database of private stays on Île de N'Gor. Both organisations have checked the places they recommend, and can put you in touch with someone who fits your profile, from the most basic to a more luxurious stay.

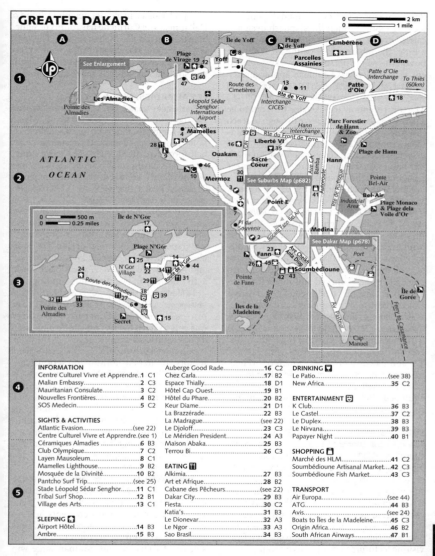

GREATER DAKAR

INFORMATION

Centre Culturel Vivre et Apprendre...**1**	C1
Malian Embassy...............................**2**	C2
Mauritanian Consulate.....................**3**	C2
Nouvelles Frontières........................**4**	B2
SOS Medecin..................................**5**	C2

SIGHTS & ACTIVITIES

Atlantic Evasion..........................(see 22)	
Centre Culturel Vivre et Apprendre.(see 1)	
Céramiques Almadies **6**	B3
Club Olympique.............................**7**	C2
Layen Mausoleum...........................**8**	C1
Mamelles Lighthouse......................**9**	B2
Mosquée de la Divinité..................**10**	B2
Pantcho Surf Trip.......................(see 25)	
Stade Léopold Sédar Senghor......**11**	B3
Tribal Surf Shop...........................**12**	B1
Village des Arts............................**13**	C1

SLEEPING

Airport Hôtel...............................**14**	B3
Ambre..**15**	B3

Auberge Good Rade.......................**16**	C2
Chez Carla..................................**17**	B2
Espace Thially.............................**18**	D1
Hôtel Cap Ouest..........................**19**	B1
Hôtel du Phare............................**20**	B2
Keur Diame.................................**21**	D1
La Brazzérade.............................**22**	B3
La Madrague............................(see 22)	
Le Méridien President...................**24**	A3
Maison Abaka..............................**25**	B3
Terrou Bi....................................**26**	C3

EATING

Alkimia......................................**27**	B3
Art et Afrique.............................**28**	B2
Cabane des Pêcheurs..................(see 22)	
Dakar City..................................**29**	B3
Fiesta..**30**	C2
Katia's.......................................**31**	B3
Le Dionevar................................**32**	A3
Le Ngor.....................................**33**	A3
Sao Brasil..................................**34**	B3

DRINKING

Le Patio.................................(see 38)	
New Africa..................................**35**	C2

ENTERTAINMENT

K Club.......................................**36**	B3
Le Castel....................................**37**	C2
Le Duplex...................................**38**	B3
Le Nirvana..................................**39**	B3
Papayer Night **40**	B1

SHOPPING

Marché des HLM...........................**41**	B3
Soumbédioune Artisanal Market......**42**	C3
Soumbédioune Fish Market............**43**	C3

TRANSPORT

Air Europa...............................(see 44)	
ATG..**44**	B3
Avis.......................................(see 24)	
Boats to Îles de la Madeleine.........**45**	C3
Origin Africa...............................**46**	B2
South African Airways...................**47**	B1

Chez Carla (Map p685; ☎ 33 820 1586; Île de N'Gor; d incl breakfast CFA20,000) Unless you stay with a N'Gor family, this is the place to spend the night on N'Gor island. You quickly become a member of Carla's honorary family of passing travellers. Simple rooms come with balcony or terrace, and the food served is good and adequately priced.

Midrange

All hotels in this price range have rooms with private bathrooms. Most offer free wi-fi and accept credit cards.

PLATEAU

Hôtel Ganalé (Map p680; ☎ 33 889 4444; hganale@orange .sn; 38 Rue Assane Ndoye; s/d CFA34,000/42,000; ✷ ▯ ◌)

Rooms are more welcoming than the sinister-looking lobby, though the slapdash design is carried over. Your air-conditioning might hum a little, the table wobble or the wi-fi stutter, but on the whole it's still the low-key, relaxed corner travellers have come to appreciate.

Hôtel Farid (Map p680; ☎ 33 821 6127; www.hotelfarid.com; 51 Rue Vincens; s/d from CFA36,100/41,200; ✿ 🖵) The tiny reception and elevator turn out to be a narrow gateway you squeeze through to reach three floors of spacious, clean and well-maintained rooms. It's by no means luxurious, but it's a valid, safe and comfortable option that's fair value for the city centre. The Lebanese restaurant on the ground floor is fabulous.

Hôtel Sokhamon (Map p678; ☎ 33 889 7100; www.sokhamon.com; cnr Aves Président Roosevelt & Nelson Mandela; s/d CFA48,000/53,000, with sea view CFA63,000/68,000; 🅿 ✿ 🖵) Like a slightly confused film set, this boutique hotel reminds you of Mali, the Middle East, the Caribbean and then a medieval wine cellar – and that's only the walk to the bar. All the furnishings of this hand-sculpted place have been sourced and made locally – as well as carefully designed. The terrace is Dakar's best spot for sipping sundowners.

Résidence Les Arcades (Map p680; ☎ 33 849 1500; www.arcades.sn; Blvd el Hajj Djily Mbaye; apt from CFA56,000; ✿ 🖵) Right in the centre of town, these discreetly decorated apartments with satellite TV and balcony provide a touch of homeliness many hotels can't match. Ideal for longer stays and self-caterers, they come with an equipped kitchen. There's no restaurant, but room cleaning is included in the rate.

SUBURBS: MÉDINA TO MAMELLES

Auberge Marie-Lucienne (Map p682; ☎ 33 864 37 56; Rue A, Point E; s/d CFA30,000/36,000; ✿ 🖵) A bit slow and a bit grumpy, this large guest house doesn't really try to charm its guests, and yet it's usually full. Rooms are much prettier than the dark corridors would have you expect, the unfussiness turns out to be quite pleasant, and proximity to the university and music clubs means that you often bump into interesting guests – from visiting lecturers to jazz bands on tour.

Auberge Good Rade (Map p685; ☎ 33 860 6030; goodrade@orange.sn; s/d CFA40,000/50,000) This is far less humble than the word *auberge* (hostel) suggests. With spacious rooms, welcoming staff and minimalist, modern decor, this rivals many of the more expensive hotels.

Le Djoloff (Map p685; ☎ 33 889 3630; www.hoteldjoloff.com; s/d CFA50,000/60,000; Fann Hock; ✿ 🖵) This

very pretty place in a quiet neighbourhood of Dakar near the Corniche has rooms designed to make you feel like Malian royalty. The space is a little dark, but the stunning roof terrace with view across the Corniche, sun roof, patio and smiling staff entirely make up for that.

LES ALMADIES, N'GOR & YOFF

La Brazzérade (Map p685; ☎ 33 820 0683; www.labrazzerade.com; Plage de N'Gor; d/ste CFA20,000/35,000; ✿ 🖵) Mainly known for its fabulous grill, this place also has a hotel floor, perched above the restaurant like a half-forgotten afterthought. The more expensive rooms have a small balcony and view over N'Gor island – an investment worth making.

Maison Abaka (Map p685; ☎ 33 820 6486; www.maison-abaka.com; r from CFA30,000; ✿ 🖵) Pool conversations here usually deal with waves and where to catch them – this family-style place is a favourite with surfers. Apparently watersports and interior design are more closely linked than expected – rooms are airy and lovingly decorated. A great place for an active holiday in beautiful surroundings.

La Madrague (Map p685; ☎ 33 820 0223; madrague-resa@orange.sn; Plage de N'Gor; r from CFA39,000; 🖵) This place is like one long bikini party where everyone gets to sleep over. With gaudy pink walls, a pool-centric set-up and, of course, the prime location on a private stretch of N'Gor beach, it tempts you to take nothing too seriously.

Ambre (Map p685; ☎ 33 820 6338; www.ambre.sn; Rte des Almadies; r from CFA42,000; 🖵 ✿ 🐾) Green, art-adorned and beautifully designed, this small guest house is as friendly as a smile. Each of the six rooms has its own subtle colour scheme, and the harmonious decor continues all the way through the downstairs lounge, garden and restaurant. A unique gem close to the city's best hotels and bars.

Airport Hôtel (Map p685; ☎ 33 869 7878; Rte de N'Gor; s/d CFA45,000/56,000; ✿ 🖵 🐾) Here's a hotel that does most things right without even trying very hard. No outlandish concepts here, no overblown identity. Just good-quality, practical and welcoming accommodation with satellite TV, fridge and minibar, large window with view across an inviting pool and the swish of palm trees to lull you to sleep.

Top End

At the time of writing the mighty hotel moguls Sheraton, Radisson and Kempinski, alongside a couple of other gold-endowed investors, were coming to the completion of six brand-new hotel complexes, all rumoured to become swanky five-star palaces. They're all perched close to the water along the Corniche-Ouest.

PLATEAU

Hôtel Lagon II (Map p680; ☎ 33 889 2525; www.lagon .sn; Rte de la Corniche-Est; s/d CFA106,000/110,000; 🞜 🖳) Careful. Behind the ginger-coloured cabin door lie the 1960s, when orange was all the rage and round-edged Formica tables every woman's dream. Lying back on the impressive 2m x 2m bed, thoughts of the sexual revolution prove a distraction from the fantastic view over Gorée island.

Pullman Teranga (Map p680; ☎ 33 889 2200; h0563@ accor.com; 10 Rue Colbert, behind Pl de l'Indépendance; r from CFA113,500; 🅿 🞜 🖳 🛋 🛜) Comfortable, practical and as smooth as a boardroom table, Dakar's most central hotel (formerly the Sofitel) is squarely aimed at business travellers and gets eight out of 10 on the post-seminar evaluation sheet for its conference rooms, business centre, dimly lit bars and hair salon. The breakfast buffet is fantastic (and pricey at CFA12,000).

SUBURBS: MÉDINA TO MAMELLES

Terrou Bi (Map p685; ☎ 33 839 9039; www.terroubi .com; r from CFA159,000; 🞜 🖳 🛋) Brand new in 2009, this business hotel with sea view has classy, comfortable rooms in minimalist red and white tones. It's part of a complex that houses one of Dakar's top restaurants and casinos, and a massage centre was still under construction. While the space is fantastic, it falls flat when it comes to service – in line with most of Dakar's top end places.

LES ALMADIES, N'GOR & YOFF

Le Méridien President (Map p685; ☎ 33 869 6969; www.starwoodhotels.com; r from CFA166,000) The drive through the abundant garden, the discreet politeness of the valets and the opulent lobby all make you feel like a very privileged person, until you float right off your plush carpet and into an almost ordinary bedroom. The theme is 'junior executive in provincial estate agency', rather than 'royalty on sojourn', and even the higher-bracket rooms are only set apart by their (admittedly very attractive) view.

EATING

Dakar's restaurant scene is definitely one of the capital's highlights. There are about 100 eateries in the town centre alone, and that's before you've even headed for the suburbs, where chic new restaurants open all the time.

French cuisine, a hangover from the colonial past, is a particular highlight, but there's more to Dakar than *entrecôte* (rib steak) and *crème brûlée* (cream dessert covered in caramelised sugar). The kitchen stretches from the Cape Verde islands over Vietnam, Thailand, Lebanon, Italy and India to Mexico.

Restaurants are usually open all day, though they'll only serve food from midday to 2pm and 7pm to midnight or later. (Many only close when the last guest has staggered out.) Note that most Dakar restaurants are closed on Sunday.

African

Almost every restaurant in Dakar has a couple of Senegalese dishes, but the following few either do a particularly mean *thiéboudieune* or offer other African flavours.

PLATEAU

Keur N'Deye (Map p680; ☎ 33 821 4973; 68 Rue Vincens; dishes from CFA2000; 🆅) The Senegalese dishes here are well prepared and vegetarians are looked after with large bowls of salad. The tinkling of a *kora* often accompanies the eager clattering of cutlery.

Chez Loutcha (Map p680; ☎ 33 821 0302; 101 Rue Moussé Diop; dishes CFA2500-4000; 🕑 noon-3pm & 7-11pm Mon-Sat) A restaurant like a bus stop, this always overflowing place serves huge portions of Cape Verdean and Senegalese cuisine. It has a real workman's vibe and gets busy during lunch hours.

Le Djembé (Map p680; ☎ 33 821 0666; 56 Rue St Michel; dishes CFA3000-5000; 🕑 11am-5pm Mon-Sat) Behind Place de l'Indépendance, this humble eatery is the whispered insider tip for anyone in search of a filling platter of *thiéboudieune* in a peaceful oasis right in the heart of town.

SUBURBS: MÉDINA TO MAMELLES

Lalibela (Map p682; ☎ 77 510 1569; Rue A, Point E; dishes around CFA6000; 🕑 11am-2am; 🆅) You sense the hosts' nostalgia for their Abyssinian homeland in every detail of the colourful decor, the rich Ethiopian coffee and the perfectly soured *injera* bread. It's open late, and there's occasional live music.

International
PLATEAU

Restaurant Farid (Map p680; ☎ 33 823 6123; 51 Rue Vincens; dishes CFA3500-6000; 🕑 6am-midnight; 🖳 🆅)

Squeezed between grey inner-city walls, this little oasis serves the best Lebanese mezze in town. It renders even a simple plate of grilled prawns outstanding by adding just the right touch of garlic and oil.

Le Bideew (Map p680; ☎ 33 823 1909; 89 Rue Joseph Gomis; dishes around CFA5000; 🕑 9am-11pm; **V**) In the cool shade of the Institut Français's mighty *fromager* tree, this colourful arts cafe is perfect for a break from the city. Little touches, like the drizzle of honey on the chicken and avocado salad or the fresh herbs sprinkled over the *brochettes de lotte*, make all the difference.

Cabane des Pêcheurs (Map p685; ☎ 33 820 7675; meals around CFA6000-9000; 🕑 11am-3pm & 7-11pm) Dakar's best fish restaurant serves you treats like amberjack and dolphinfish that you'll hardly find anywhere else in the city. Everything is absolutely fresh (it also runs a busy fishing centre) and served with style, and there's lovely decor and sea view to boot. It also has a couple of excellent rooms to rent (CFA30,000).

Lagon I (Map p680; ☎ 33 821 5322; Rte de la Corniche-Est; meals around CFA8000; 🕑 7am-midnight) This is very deservedly known as one of Dakar's best seafood places (just try the scrumptious seafood platter). It rather overstresses the point, though, by pursuing the nautical theme relentlessly from the cruise-ship decor and cabin-style toilets to the pontoon and uniformed waiters.

ourpick Le Cozy (Map p680; ☎ 33 823 0606; www .lecozy.com; 8 Rue Ramez Bourgi; dishes around CFA10,000; 🕑 noon-3pm & 7pm-midnight; **V**) Right behind the market streets of Marché Kermel, this food temple renders simple kitchen classics (like risotto) divine – it's a question of the right touch of everything. Presentation and service are as perfect as the classy restaurant and bar spaces.

La Fourchette (Map p680; ☎ 33 821 8887; 4 Rue Parent; meals around CFA10,000-15,000; 🕑 noon-2.30pm & 7.30-11pm Mon-Sat; **V**) This polished parlour does impeccable sushi and dishes from around the world. It's a favourite with Dakar's expats and the trendiest Senegalese folks. Don't leave without trying some of their fabulous desserts - possibly Dakar's best.

La Galette (Map p680; ☎ 33 823 1516; 16 Ave Pompidou; 🕑 teahouse 7am-11.30pm, restaurant noon-2.30pm & 7.30-11pm, closed Saturday morning; **V**) Past the excellent patisserie downstairs, the 1st-floor restaurant has creative French cuisine prepared with skill and served with a smile. The coffees are fantastic too.

Le Fuji (Map p680; ☎ 33 821 6000; mains CFA17,000; 🕑 noon-3pm & 7pm-1am Mon-Sat) Very new and very glamorous, this has to be one of the top sushi houses of West Africa. The fish is so fresh your tongue might be startled and the surroundings are pretty enough to while the evening away here. It's an investment, prices are sky-high, but justified.

SUBURBS: MÉDINA TO MAMELLES

Fiesta (Map p685; ☎ 77 587 3483; VDN Mermoz; dishes CFA4000; 🕑 10am-2am) It's thatch-roofed and cooled by busy ceiling fans, and yet it exudes subtle class. It does great pizzas and pints of draught too – particularly great when it also rolls out the big screen.

Jardin Thaïlandais (Map p682; ☎ 33 825 5833; 10 Blvd du Sud; meals around CFA8000; 🕑 10am-4pm & 6pm-1am Mon-Sat) There's no better Thai, perhaps no better Asian food altogether, in the whole of Senegal than that served at this understated place in Point E.

LES ALMADIES, N'GOR & YOFF

ourpick Le Ngor (Map p685; ☎ 77 504 3006; dishes CFA4000; 🕑 Tue-Sat) This quirky, seashell-adorned maze of a building, where waves lap at your feet, is where grilled prawns taste best. The mosaic-styled tapas bar next door is where you kiss a perfect day goodbye with a sundowner.

Art et Afrique (Map p685; ☎ 77 783 6686; Rte des Almadies; dishes CFA5000) The three-floor climb through an apparently infinite collection of African masks and sculptures is almost as enjoyable as the international cuisine you enjoy up on the straw-roofed terrace with view over the Mamelles lighthouse.

Sao Brasil (Map p685; ☎ 33 820 0941; behind Station Shell, Rte de N'Gor; pizza CFA5000; 🕑 noon-4pm & 6.30pm-midnight) Very confusingly named, this is one of Dakar's best Italian addresses. Pizzas come with a huge diameter, a thin base and a huge choice of toppings. The house cocktails (CFA4000) are equally impressive and can be consumed in peace while the kids get busy on the small playground.

Alkimia (Map p685; ☎ 33 820 6868; Rte du Méridien Président; tapas CFA6000; 🕑 noon-2.30pm & 7.30-11pm Tue-Sun) You might want to practise that nonchalant, carelessly affluent stroll before testing it by walking onto the select pebbles of this chic garden space. The size and quality of the tapas and sushi (prepared by a Japanese chef) almost justify the steep rates.

SENEGAL

Le Dionevar (Map p685; ☎ 33 820 0911; Pointe des Almadies; meals around CFA8000; ☷ 10.30am-2.30pm & 7.30-10.30pm) This solid seafood house does a staggering 23 fish dishes, each as tasty as the next. View from Africa's westernmost tip thrown in.

Quick Eats

You're never far from a corner with a streetfood stall, where you can get rice and sauce or greasy omelettes. A fast-food favourite is the shwarma (CFA1000), sold in snack bars and restaurants. Ave Pompidou in the town centre has lots of them.

PLATEAU

Ali Baba Snack Bar (Map p680; ☎ 33 822 5297; Ave Pompidou; ☷ 8am-5pm & 6pm-2am) Dakar's classic fast-food joint has always looked rough and smelt of hot oil. That hasn't deterred anyone yet from picking up their lunch-time kebab or shwarma here.

Caesar's (Map p680; ☎ 33 823 8400; 27 Blvd de la République) Sometimes only fried chicken wings, burgers and fries will do, and for those moments Caesar's is your place. Come here regularly and you'll gain precious insights into the complexities of teenage love lives.

LES ALMADIES, N'GOR & YOFF

Katia's (Map p685; ☎ 33 820 8082; 6 Rte de N'Gor; pizzas CFA4000) A strong contender for the top pizza place in town, this is equally great for takeouts or sipping Flag beers while watching hustlers and tourists, dressed-down locals and blinging babes drift in to quench that late-night hunger.

Cafés & Patisseries

In Dakar, a patisserie is not somewhere to buy your bread but a place to take your date if you really want to make an impression. There are plenty of places for guilty cake indulgence.

PLATEAU

La Royaltine (Map p680; ☎ 33 821 9994; Ave du Président Lamine Guèye) You know that a *mille-feuille* is perfect when the pastry is buttery but light and the vanilla cream rich without being too sweet. This is where you get to taste one. At this top address for sweet indulgence, cakes, *pralinés* and delicacies are fussed over like precious pearls.

Aux Fins Palais (Map p678; ☎ 33 823 4445; 97 Ave André Peytavin; ☷ 6.45am-8.30pm; Ⓥ) This is one of the very rare places to buy wholemeal bread, and in delicious varieties. With excellent coffees, pancakes and original creations, such as thyme-sprinkled puff pastries, it's a great place for breakfast.

N'Ice Cream (Map p678; ☎ 33 823 3545; 97 Ave André Peytavin; scoop CFA1000; ☷ 11am-10.30pm Mon-Fri, 10am-11pm Sat, 11am-9pm Sun) This is where you find Dakar's widest selection of ice creams, including flavours made from local fruit – we loved the *corossol* cream. Everything is made under rigorously hygienic conditions.

Time's Café (Map p680; ☎ 33 821 2168; snacks CFA4000; ☷ 7am-11pm; Ⓥ) New York was without a doubt the inspiration for this colourful breakfast parlour. It does the best latte in town – though you pay a staggering CFA2000 for the cup – and also has a tasty range of salads, snacks and light meals.

SUBURBS: MÉDINA TO MAMELLES

Pâtisserie Médina (Map p678; ☎ 33 823 1713; Ave Faidherbe; ☷ 24hr) Dakar's 'terminus'. Every night out ends here at 5am, with coffee, croissants and cream doughnuts. With some luck, you'll even see some of Senegal's biggest music and football stars huddled around cups of hot chocolate.

Self-Catering

Corner shops stacked sky high with basics are scattered across Dakar. For a wider selection, try the supermarkets **Casino Centre** (Map p680; 31 Ave Albert Sarraut), near the Place de l'Indépendance, **Casino Sahm** (Map p682; Blvd de la Gueule Tapeé), near Point E, or the gleaming **Dakar City** (p685; Rte de N'Gor), a large commercial centre.

If you can bear the bustle, get your fresh fruit and veg at Marché Kermel or Marché Tilène and your fish from Soumbédioune fish market.

DRINKING

Dakar by night can be almost as busy as Dakar by day. The glitziest, most pretentious and utterly good-looking party parlours are in Les Almadies.

PLATEAU

Ozio (Map p680; ☎ 33 823 8787; 21 Rue Victor Hugo) This ubertrendy bar-cum-club is a favourite with Dakar's glittering classes. Decor and attitude are ice cool, the air-conditioning too. Heavy electronic beats reduce conversation to gestures.

Le Viking (Map p680; ☎ 77 244 8056; 21 Ave Pompidou) While slick new R&B clubs with chilled champagne and skinny crowds open daily, this old-style pub is a beer-scented, slightly musty place where shirts are still allowed to crumple and draught pints are poured into glasses that are certainly not frosted. It's friendly and slightly tipsy, and women will feel better in a crowd.

Le Seven (Map p680; ☎ 33 842 6911; 25 Rue Mohamed V) This is the glittering queen of Dakar's bars. Think champagne bubbles, tiny tank tops, the latest hits. So *branché* (literally 'plugged in') that you risk electrocution, this is where the in-crowd parties.

Casino du Port (Map p680; ☎ 33 849 0649; Blvd de la Libération) One of several casinos in this money-burning capital, the Casino du Port doubles as a stylish bar and good restaurant, with live jazz on weekends. A good place to start the night out.

SUBURBS: MÉDINA TO MAMELLES
New Africa (Map p685; ☎ 33 827 5371; newafrica@orange.sn; ☺ 7pm-2am Mon-Sat) Possibly Dakar's most relaxed bar (the meals are great too), this fills the gap between the chic 'in-bars' and the dodgy drinking holes. On Friday nights the courtyard explodes with couples dancing superbly to contemporary Latin beats. Unmissable.

LES ALMADIES, N'GOR & YOFF
Le Patio (Map p685; ☎ 33 820 5823; Rte de N'Gor) Past the broad-shouldered bouncers and across the red carpet, this large outdoor place looks like a private garden party. Cocktails here are divine, and it's only a short stumble to the next club.

ENTERTAINMENT
Everything from cafes to bars and nightclubs seems to put on live gigs. In restaurants and bars admission is often free, while clubs charge between CFA3000 and CFA10,000. The Cultural Agenda in the journal *221* or online at www.ausenegal.com has the best listings.

For a fun night out, don't even get your kit on before midnight. Leaving the house around 1am is impeccable timing, returning home before 4am a sign of weakness. Now go party.

Live Music
Pen'Art (Map p682; ☎ 33 864 5131; Blvd du Sud, Point E) Around the corner from Just 4 U, this is a cosy jazz club with good bands in a relaxed atmosphere. Come here when a reggae outfit like Timshell is playing and the place turns into a sweaty, swaying cave of excitement.

Just 4 U (Map p682; ☎ 33 824 3250; www.just4udakar.com; Ave Cheikh Anta Diop; ☺ 11am-3am) The small stage of this outdoor restaurant has been graced by the greatest Senegalese and international stars. There's a concert on every day, and you often get to catch the big names, including Orchestra Baobab, Omar Pene and occasionally even Youssou N'Dour.

Papayer Night (Map p685; ☎ 77 513 1841; Rte de l'Aéroport) Some of Dakar's best parties happen here, at this nightclub with live music. Upstairs, you warm up to the whispering guitars and moaning voices of folk stars like Pape & Cheikh, before you head downstairs for *mbalax* fever, spread by the big masters, such as Mbaye Ndiaye Faye or Thione Seck.

Chez Anthiou (Map p682; ☎ 77 634 0290; Rue 10, Amitié 2) A visit here is like an invitation to a house party by a greying salsa lover. Couples contemplate their marriages while sweeping elegantly across a dance floor that trembles to the classic sounds of Pape Fall and his band.

Sunset Sahel (Map p682; ☎ 33 821 2118; Centre Commercial Sahm) As streetwise as its surrounding Médina neighbourhood, the Sahel is great for a Senegalese party, with dizzying *mbalax* vibes and occasional live music by Thione Seck.

Nightclubs
PLATEAU
Koulgraoul (Map p678; ☎ 77 532 2648; Rte de la Corniche-Est; admission CFA3000) Every first Saturday of the month, Dakar's most dressed-down party happens in the sea-bordering backyard of the Oceánium. It reliably attracts everyone, from hustling rasta boys to glammed-up Lebanese ladies and most of the expat community.

Café de Rome (Map p680; ☎ 33 849 0200; 32 Blvd de la République) Everyone congregates in this cushy basement club, from shady businessmen to the ambassadors of various nations. You could put on a suit, pose in a leather armchair and suck on cigar, and no one would even flinch at the glamour cliché.

SUBURBS: MÉDINA TO MAMELLES
Le Madison (Map p682; ☎ 77 738 7308; km1, Ave Cheikh Anta Diop) Once all the lights are plugged in, this place glitters like a department store at Christmas. From Monday to Wednesday, you can practise your *mbalax* moves at the Senegalese nights.

LES ALMADIES, N'GOR & YOFF
K Club (Map p685; ☎ 33 820 6467; Rte des Almadies; ☺ 8pm-3am) With a shimmering pool in the middle

and VIP sections that you purchase with a CFA100,000 bottle, Akon's favourite club is modelled on an R&B clip. The crowd is very young and slightly too serious about having fun.

Le Duplex (Map p685; ☎ 77 354 2954; Rte de N'Gor) Dakar's most renowned DJs play here to a select crowd. Dress smart, look cool and practise the lines 'Normally I only drink Cristal' and 'My cousin lives right next door to Diddy. Apparently he's a really nice guy.'

Le Nirvana (Map p685; ☎ 77 366 8814; Rte de N'Gor) This is the grown-up version of the kids' clubs across the road. Still super-smart and polished, it has several intimate seating areas for those that can buy privacy with precious liquor bottles.

Le Castel (Map p685; ☎ 33 860 6030; VDN, Sacré Coeur 3 ext) Finally, a club where you're allowed to be an adult, listen to your favourite old-school tracks and swig champagne not to be cool but because you can pay for it yourself.

Theatre & Cinema

In the absence of a regular cinema, the national **Théâtre Daniel Sorano** (Map p678; ☎ 33 822 1715; Blvd de la République) has screenings (as well as plays and dance shows). At **Kadjinol Station** (Map p680; ☎ 33 842 8662; www.kadjinol-edu.com), off Ave Albert Sarraut, you can watch DVD versions of world cinema and Hollywood blockbusters.

SHOPPING
Markets

You need plenty of energy and a safe place to hide your purse for a Dakar market tour. **Marché Sandaga** (Map p680) in the centre is the largest, with rickety stalls that claim most of the area around Ave Pompidou. In Médina, **Marché Tilène** (Map p678) sells mainly fruit, veg and household items. The **Soumbédioune artisanal market** (Map p685), on Rte de la Corniche-Ouest, is popular place for buying wood carvings, metalwork and batiks. Less touristy, the fabulous **Marché des HLM** (Map p685) is stacked with dazzling African fabrics.

Shops

On the Plateau, the 'Moroccan mile' on Rue Mohamed V, between Ave Pompidou and Rue Assane Ndoye, has a line of small shops with masks and carvings and Maghreb shoe-makers that can produce made-to-measure footwear, even copying your designer originals. At the Institut Français, **Maam Samba** (Map p680; ☎ 33 973 3040; www.ong-ndem.org; Institut Français, 89 Rue Joseph Gomis) has amazing woven items, all made from stun-

ningly coloured, biological cottons in a fantastic local-development project at Ndem village. For a wide selection of funky souvenirs, try **Cocktail du Sénégal** (Map p680; ☎ 33 823 5315; 108 Rue Moussé Diop), or pick up some original glass-painted tableware at **Naaj** (p680; ☎ 33 825 7546; 66 Rue Michel). **Cajou** (Map p680; Rue Assane Ndoye) has lovely, handmade children's clothes and toys. In Point E, the airy patio of **Agora** (Map p682; ☎ 33 864 1448; Rue D) has Moroccan artwork, homeware and locally made craftwork, and opposite the Soumbédioune market you'll find a row of shops selling quirky items made from recycled cans.

GETTING THERE & AWAY
Air

Léopold Sédar Senghor International Airport is in Yoff. See p828 for information on flights between Dakar and destinations outside Senegal. Within Senegal, the only regular flight connection is between Dakar and Ziguinchor. Flights to Cap Skiring are limited to high season (October to May), and Tambacounda can only be reached by plane from January to March. See p738 for further information.

For airline offices in Dakar see p736.

Boat

The excellent ferry *Aline Sitoé Diatta* travels between Dakar and Ziguinchor twice weekly in each direction; see p724.

Car Mouride

This bus service financed by the Mouride brotherhood offers a fairly reliable, though

---

PUBLIC TRANSPORT FROM DAKAR

Note that these prices are indications only; you may encounter minor variations, luggage charges, and increases due to the rising cost of petrol.

Destination	Sept-Place (CFA)
Bakel	13,500
Karang (The Gambia)	6000
Kaolack	3000
Mbour	1500
Saint-Louis	4500
Tambacounda	9000
Thiès	1500
Touba	3000
Ziguinchor	9000

SENEGAL

LA MAISON DES ESCLAVES

Île de Gorée was a busy trading centre during the 18th and 19th centuries, and many merchants built houses in which they would live or work in the upper storey and store their wares on the lower floor. La Maison des Esclaves is one of the last remaining 18th-century buildings of this type on Gorée. It was built in 1786 and renovated in 1990 with French assistance. With its famous doorway opening directly from the storeroom onto the sea, this building has enormous spiritual significance for some visitors, particularly African-Americans whose ancestors were brought from Africa as slaves.

Walking around the dimly lit dungeons, particularly after a visit to the historical museum, you will begin to imagine the suffering of the people held here, reinforced by the gruesome details provided by the curator. La Maison des Esclaves is a significant symbol and reminder of the horrors of the slave trade. Although an important slaving culture existed in Gorée, the island's role as a major slave-shipment point is sometimes overstated. Of the 20 million slaves that were taken from Africa, only 300 per year may have gone through Gorée, and even then, the famous doorway would not have been used – a ship could not get near the dangerous rocks and the town had a jetty a short distance away.

But the number of slaves transported from here isn't necessarily what matters in the debate around Gorée. The island, and particularly La Maison des Esclaves, stands as a terrible reminder of the immense suffering inflicted on African people through the Atlantic slave trade.

Written with assistance from Chris de Wilde (specialist in 19th-century West African history)

---

slow and uncomfortable connection to major towns in Senegal.

You book your seat ahead of travel, best in person, at **Gare Routière Pompiers** (Map p678; ☎ 33 821 8585), at the junction between the *autoroute* and Ave Malik Sy. The *car mouride* bus stop is near the petrol station, close to the *gare routière*.

Sept-Place Taxi & Ndiaga Ndiaye

Most Ndiaga Ndiayes (large minibuses) and *sept-place* (seven-seater) taxis for long-distance destinations leave from Gare Routière Pompiers (Map p678). It's best to get there early. The only chance to avoid the gridlock of neighbouring Rufisque is by getting out of town before 7.30am.

Train

Talks about improving Senegal's train network have gone on for years. In the meantime, the classic Dakar–Bamako service keeps getting worse. If it runs, you can travel on it to Thiès, Diourbel and Tambacounda, as well as Kayes and Bamako. For details, see p737.

GETTING AROUND
To/From the Airport

Taxis wait outside the airport, hidden behind throngs of touts, hustlers and thieves. Be brave, and firm in negotiating your rate – the ride into town is supposed to cost CFA4000.

Bus

Dakar's **DDD** (www.demdikk.com) bus service is surprisingly good. DDD stands for Dakar Dem Dikk (meaning Dakar going and returning), and the large, blue DDD buses do go and come back with astonishing regularity – avoid rush hours, though, when they do get delayed and very, very full. They have fixed stops and go about every 10 minutes. Rates are between CFA150 and CFA250. You pay at the conductor's booth on the bus. You can view the full network on the website. The main DDD terminal (Map p680) is near the port, on Blvd de la Libération.

Car

Car-hire agencies in Dakar include the following (among many, many others).

Avis (Map p685; ☎ 33 849 7757; www.cfaogroup.com) Branches at Le Meridien President hotel and the airport.

Coseloc (Map p682; ☎ 33 869 2525; www.coseloc.sn; km 5.5, Ave Cheikh Anta Diop, Fann) Tends to get good deals.

Dakar Location (Map p680; ☎ 33 823 8610; 7 Rue de Thiong)

Hertz (Map p680; ☎ 33 822 2016; www.hertz.sn; 64 Rue Joseph Gomis) Has branches at the airport and on the Plateau.

Senecartours (Map p682; ☎ 33 889 7777; www .senecartours.sn; 64 Rue Carnot) One of Senegal's biggest operators; also has branches in Almadies.

Car Rapide

These colourfully decorated, blue-and-yellow minibuses are Dakar's postcard symbols, and while travelling in those pretty (though battered) vehicles is certainly an experience, you won't get anywhere fast with them. Their routes aren't marked (you need to listen to the touts' shouting until you know the city well), they stop randomly and frequently, and they drive off as though rear mirrors had never been invented.

Ndiaga Ndiaye

These privately owned, white, 30-seater minibuses (most of them have 'Alhamdoulilai' written across the front) roughly follow the same routes as the DDD buses. Fares are between CFA100 and CFA150 depending on the length of your trip. Destinations and routes are not marked, so you'll have to ask or listen for the call from the apprentice.

Senbus

These white minibuses are assembled in Senegal. They are a bit more comfortable and user-friendly than *cars rapides* but do very few routes.

Taxi

Going by taxi is the easiest way to get around Dakar. Fares need to be negotiated, sometimes quite fiercely. A short ride across the town centre should cost around CFA750. Plateau to Point E is around CFA2000, Plateau to N'Gor between CFA3000 and CFA4000.

Taxi Sister is an enterprise worth supporting – see the boxed text, p738.

CAP VERT PENINSULA

Before Dakar really fades out into open savannah lands, it first puts on the street culture really thickly, via the huge *banlieues* (suburbs) Pikine, Guediewaye and Thiaroye. These sprawling conurbations are where many hopeful rural emigrants en route to the city's fame and fortune get stranded. They're poor, and not entirely safe, but they're also hugely exciting if you're interested in urban youth culture. Further eastwards, fishing villages and a tranquil monastery announce the city's exits – you have now officially escaped Dakar's grip.

ÎLE DE GORÉE

The historical Île de Gorée is enveloped by an almost eerie calm. There are no sealed roads and no cars on this island, just narrow alleyways with trailing bougainvillea and colonial brick buildings with wrought-iron balconies. But Gorée's calm is not so much romantic as meditative, as the ancient buildings bear witness to the island's role in the Atlantic slave trade.

Information

Any tourist entering Gorée needs to pay a tax of CFA500. You pay this at the tourist information booth near the ferry landing. You can also hire tourist guides here but Gorée is tiny and can easily be explored independently. You can check your mail at **Espace Multimedia** (per hr CFA500; ☺ 10am-1pm & 3-10pm).

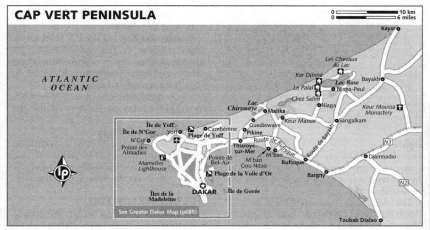

CAP VERT PENINSULA

0 _____ 10 km
0 _____ 6 miles

ATLANTIC OCEAN

Kayar

Les Chevaux du Lac

Ker Djinné
Le Palal
Bayakh
Lac Rose
Niaga-Peul

Chez Salim

Lac Chirouaye
Malika
Niaga
Keur Moussa Monastery

Île de Yoff
Île de N'Gor
Yoff
Cambérène
Guediewaye
Keur Massar
Sangalkam

N'Gor
Plage de Yoff
Pikine

Pointe des Almadies
Route de Rufisque
Thiaroye-sur-Mer
M'bao
Route de Bayakh
N3

Mamelles Lighthouse
Pointe de Bel-Air
M'bao Gou Ndao
Rufisque
Diámnadio

Îles de la Madeleine
DAKAR
Île de Gorée
Plage de la Voile d'Or
Bargny
N2

See Greater Dakar Map (p685)

Toubab Dialao

SENEGAL

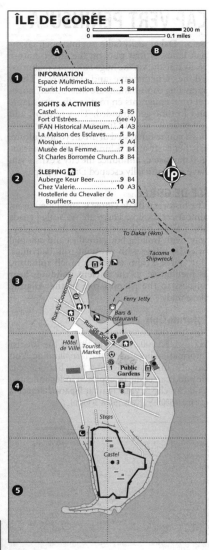

ÎLE DE GORÉE

```
0            200 m
0            0.1 miles
```

INFORMATION
Espace Multimedia...............1 B4
Tourist Information Booth....2 B4

SIGHTS & ACTIVITIES
Castel...................................3 B5
Fort d'Estrées....................(see 4)
IFAN Historical Museum......4 A3
La Maison des Esclaves.......5 B4
Mosque...............................6 A4
Musée de la Femme.............7 B4
St Charles Borromée Church.8 B4

SLEEPING
Auberge Keur Beer...............9 B4
Chez Valerie.......................10 A3
Hostellerie du Chevalier de
  Boufflers.........................11 A3

To Dakar (4km)

Tacoma Shipwreck

Ferry Jetty

Bars & Restaurants

Rue du Govenrment

Rue de Port

Hôtel de Ville

Tourist Market

Public Gardens

Steps

Castel

Sights

There's plenty to see on the island to fill a day, but don't come on a Monday, as all the museums and historical buildings will be closed.

The island's most famous house is the 1776 Dutch building **La Maison des Esclaves** (admission CFA500; 10.30am-noon & 2.30-6pm Tue-Sun), a pow-

erful symbol of the horrors of slavery, with its famous arched staircase opening onto the ocean (see the boxed text, p692.)

The **Castel** at the southern tip of the island was erected in the 17th century, with other fortifications, including massive WWII guns, added over time. You get excellent views over the island from the top of the rocky plateaus. On the other end of the island, the ancient French **Fort d'Estrées** (1850) houses the **IFAN Historical Museum** (33 822 2003; admission CFA500; 10am-1pm & 2.30-6pm Tue-Sat) and affords views across to Dakar from its roof.

Gorée's 1830 **St Charles Borromée Church** is usually open to visitors, and the **mosque**, built slightly later in 1892, is one of the oldest stone mosques in Senegal. The most interesting museum is the **Musée de la Femme** (admission CFA500; 10am-5pm Tue-Sun), dedicated to the role of Senegalese women throughout history.

Each of Gorée's historical houses is a little sight in itself. Come here in May, during the festival **Regards sur Courts** (33 842 1622; www .goree-regards-sur-cours.org), and you get to peek into their beautiful courtyards, adorned with spontaneous exhibitions for the occasions.

Sleeping & Eating

Many Gorée residents keep a spare room for unexpected (and paying) visitors.

Chez Valerie (33 821 8195; 7 Rue St Joseph; csao dakar@orange.sn; r from CFA15,000) One of the prettiest private options is this old Goréen house, with a shaded patio and artful decor.

Hostellerie du Chevalier de Boufflers (33 822 5364; www.boufflers.com; r from CFA18,000-23,000) Gorée's classic hostelry is mainly famous for its garden restaurant but also has good rooms.

Auberge Keur Beer (/fax 33 821 3801; keurbeer gie@yahoo.fr; Rue du Port; s/d CFA20,000/25,000) Accommodation here is simpler (some rooms have shared bathrooms), though you can ask for private accommodation as well.

For cheaper food options than the Hostellerie, try any of the many eateries opposite the jetty.

Getting There & Away

A **ferry** (33 849 7961, 24hr infoline 77 628 1111) runs regularly from the wharf in Dakar to Gorée (CFA5000 return for nonresidents, 20 minutes). See the boxed text, opposite, for the timetable.

ÎLES DE LA MADELEINE

From Dakar's shores, the **Îles de la Madeleine** (admission CFA1000, guide CFA5000, pirogue CFA4000) look like

SENEGAL

GORÉE FERRY TIMETABLE

Departing from Gorée		Departing from Dakar	
Mon-Sat	Sun & holidays	Mon-Sat	Sun & holidays
6.45am	7.30am	6.15am	7am
8am	9.30am	7.30am	9am
10.30am	10.30am	10am	10am
noon	12.30pm	11am	noon
2pm	2.30pm	12.30pm	2pm
3pm	4.30pm	2.30pm	4pm
4.30pm	5.30pm	4pm	5pm
6.30pm	7pm	5pm*	6.30pm
7pm	8pm	6.30pm	7pm
8.30pm	9pm	8pm	8.30pm
11pm	11pm	10.30pm	10.30pm
11.30pm	midnight		

*except Saturday

a couple of bare, hostile rocks. The beauty of their volcanic formations reveals itself only as the waves carry your pirogue into the natural harbour of Sarpan, the main island.

The site was declared a national park in 1985 to protect the rare bird species that live here and the unusual vegetation of dwarf baobabs. If small trees and big birds don't make your heart beat faster, you can come here for some snorkelling, diving or swimming in the clear rock pool.

Pirogues to Îles de la Madeleine go from Dakar's **National Park Office** (☎ 77 113 2108) on the Rte de la Corniche-Ouest, south of Magic Land. It's obligatory to take a guide with you (CFA5000) and there's a minimum group size of four people per boat. If you are a lone traveller, contact the office and see if you can join another group.

LAC ROSE

Also known as Lac Retba, this shallow lagoon surrounded by dunes is a popular day-trip destination for Dakarois and tourists, all coming to enjoy the calm and catch the lake's magic trick – the subtle pink shimmer that sometimes colours its waves. The spectacle is caused by the water's high salt content: 10 times that of your regular ocean. It's a beautiful sight but can only be enjoyed when the light is right. Your best chances are in dry season, when the sun is high. But even if nature refuses to put on her show, a day out here is enjoyable. You can swim in the lake, buoyed by the salt, or look at the small-scale salt-collecting industry on its shores. Better still,

venture out on horseback with the excellent hosts at Les Chevaux du Lac (see below).

Sleeping & Eating

Most hotels here are clustered near the Village Artisanal, a spot that's rather plagued by touts and hustlers.

ourpick Les Chevaux du Lac (☎ 77 630 0241; www .leschevauxdulac.com; half/full board CFA14,000/19,000) On the other side of the lake is our favourite place. Friendly and secluded, it not only has welcoming rooms but also offers brilliant horseback tours around the lake (1½/three hours CFA10,000/20,000).

Ker Djinné (☎ 77 634 0468; r with/without air-con CFA19,000/14,000; ⌗ ⌗) The cheapest option in the Village Artisanal is this relaxed place with accommodation in well-maintained round-huts and *kora* music in the restaurant.

Chez Salim (☎ 33 836 2466; www.chez-salim.com; d CFA20,000; P ⌗ ⌗) More upmarket, Chez Salim has spacious bungalows and a vast garden. Ask about its bivouac excursions.

Le Palal (☎ 33 836 2651; www.lac-rose-palal.com; s/d CFA33,000/48,000; ⌗ ⌗) Also more upscale than Ker Djinné, Le Palel feels most like a resort hotel for large tour groups.

Getting There & Away

It's best to get here by hire taxi from Dakar (return trip with some waiting time around CFA20,000). Otherwise, take public transport to Keur Massar (bus 11, Ndiaga Ndiayes and cars rapides all go there from Dakar) and hire a taxi from there (around CFA5000). You can also join an organised excursion (see p677).

SENEGAL

RUFISQUE

Rufisque was one of the first and most important French colonial settlements, but unlike Saint-Louis or Gorée, it hasn't managed to preserve many of its old buildings, nor much of its cosmopolitan character. If you want to check out the place and its surroundings, you can stay comfortably at **Oustal de l'Agenais** (☎ 33 836 1648; Rte de Rufisque; r CFA15,000; 💻), a good option with clean, comfortable rooms, a cosy restaurant and friendly management.

Rufisque is on the main road out of Dakar, and until the new autoroute is completed every vehicle out of town squeezes through here, including DDD bus 15.

KEUR MOUSSA MONASTERY

About 12km southeast of Lac Rose and 50km from Dakar on the road to Kayar, Keur Moussa Monastery is a great place to spend a reflective Sunday morning. The 10am mass is famous for its unique music – a stunning mixture of African music and Gregorian chants in Wolof.

You can buy CDs (CFA10,000) of this beautiful sound after the service, and even have a *kora* made to learn yourself. Most locals come here to purchase the monks' famously delicious goat's cheese.

Take bus 15 to Rufisque and change for a minibus to Bayakh or Kayar (CFA150). Tell the driver where you're headed and you'll be dropped off at a junction, from where it's a 1.5km walk to the monastery. It's signposted and all the drivers know it.

KAYAR

The pretty Lebou village of Kayar marks the point where the coast swings from the east towards the north – the beginning of Senegal's Grande Côte. It's one of the largest fishing centres in Senegal, and on its wide beach you can watch the whole cycle of a fisherman's day, from the rolling out to sea in the morning, to the gutting and selling of the glistening catch right on the beach.

The northern beaches aren't particularly recommended for swimming, as the current here is very strong. But the coastline is an impressive sight and a great place to relax. Pirogue trips, as well as walks to the sand dune behind the village, fill a day nicely, and watching pirogue makers at work is fascinating. Kayar isn't far from Lac Rose,

and the two destinations can easily be combined in a weekend excursion.

You can sometimes get direct transport from Dakar; otherwise, jump off at Rufisque and change for a Kayar taxi or minibus.

PETITE CÔTE

South of Dakar, the Petite Côte is where Senegal greets the Atlantic with 70km of sandy coast. Safe swimming beaches attract large numbers of tourists and cause the flashy holiday village Saly to spill over its boundaries. If you like your holiday more low-key and your beach body slightly less exposed, small villages have white strands that still swing to the local rhythm.

TOUBAB DIALAO & NDAYANE

The calm fishing village **Toubab Dialao** is an excellent hideout from the bustle of Dakar – a great place for walking, swimming and horse riding. **Les Cavaliers de la Savane** (☎ 77 569 0365) takes beginners and advanced riders on tailor-made excursions (two hours CFA12,500).

Perched on a cliff, the seashell-decorated **Sobo-Bade** (☎ /fax 33 836 0356; www.espacesobobade .com; dm per person CFA4000, r from CFA12,000) looks like the cutest of all the hobbit homes, and has enough activities on offer to keep you here for a week. Its design has inspired two other places: **La Source Ndiambalane** (☎ 33 836 1703; ndiambalan@orange.sn; d/tr CFA12,000/15,000), which has a great airy terrace for meals, and **La Mimosa** (☎ /fax 33 836 0015; lamimosa@ gmail.com; s/d CFA10,000/12,000; 🍽 💻), with its sculpture-sprouting garden.

A short dirt track takes you from Toubab Dialao to **Ndayane**, where Baba Mbengue has opened one of the most comfortable, child-friendly and tranquil places on the Petite Côte – **La Pierre de Lisse** (☎ 33 957 7148; www.itin erairelisse.net; per person from CFA33,500; 🍽 💻 🏊). Also highly recommended is **Centre Mampuya** (☎ 77 569 3773; www.mampuya.org; s/d incl breakfast CFA18,000/28,000), with its beautiful, community-run gardens and dance courses. It's stunningly located but reclusive; you need to phone to arrange pick-up from Toubab Dialao.

To get here from Dakar, take any transport headed for Mbour and get off at the Diamniadio junction. Minibuses run from here to Toubab Dialao (CFA300). A taxi from Dakar should cost around CFA15,000.

SENEGAL

RÉSERVE DE BANDIA & ACCROBAOBAB

This private **wildlife reserve** (☎ 33 958 2024; adult/child CFA10,000/5000, guide CFA3500; ☺ 8am-6pm) sits 65km from Dakar on the road to Mbour, about 5km south of Sindia. It's well managed and crowded with wildlife, including species indigenous to Senegal as well as rhinos, giraffes, buffaloes, ostriches and other mammals that have never inhabited West Africa or been long extinct here. In that sense it's more like an amazingly beautiful zoo with no cages, and you're guaranteed animal sightings. There are also a couple of Serer burial mounds and a giant baobab, once used to bury **griots**, to visit.

Walking isn't allowed here. You can normally enter with any vehicle, unless the roads have been washed away by rains, when you'll need a 4WD. You can hire one at the entrance (CFA40,000). Hiring a guide is obligatory.

A visit to Bandia's **restaurant** (☎ 33 958 2024; dishes from CFA6000) is highly recommended. You can usually spot buffaloes, crocodiles, monkeys and plenty of birds at the pond below the terrace.

A trip here is easily combined with a climbing adventure at **Accrobaobab** (☎ 77 637 1428; www .accro-baobab.com; adult/child CFA17,500/12,500). At this ingenious theme park, you can climb, glide and clamber through mighty baobab trees – there are kids' circuits too.

POPENGUINE

This tranquil, friendly village has a multi-ethnic community and is famous for its

PETITE CÔTE & SINÉ-SALOUM DELTA

0   20 km
0   12 miles

ATLANTIC OCEAN

THE GAMBIA

WOMEN IN ENVIRONMENT: TOUBAB DIALAO & RÉSERVE DE POPENGUINE

While the fishermen of the villages along the Petite Côte struggle to preserve their traditional way of life in the face of dwindling stocks, the women of those communities have often been quick to adapt, and seek out new projects in cooperative efforts. In Popenguine a collective of energetic ladies took on the task of looking after the local community reserve, setting an impressive precedent in the region. With only 1000 hectares of protected savannah woodland stretching over gentle hills, the Réserve de Popenguine is tiny – small enough to be managed locally. To support preservation efforts, the local women's group conducts tours (including bird watching with a trained guide) and runs the Campement Keur Cupaam (see below), whose revenue is partly invested in the mini-park and partly used to support other enterprises run by the women.

The small, but significant success of this project inspired the female community of neighbouring Toubab Dialao to imitate the ladies. They obtained a modest environmental grant to start working on the sustainable management of local resources, and have so far reforested small areas, and started working on preserving Toubab Dialao's lagoon, carrying heavy stones to create protective barriers. As the project also includes training in irrigation, planting, accounting and other skills, the women look set to surprise their men with projects to come. To find out more, or arrange a visit, contact the collective on ☎ 77 564 0180.

---

annual Pentecostal pilgrimage (check www .sanctuaire-popenguine.sn for details) and a modern church that commemorates the apparition of the black Madonna in 1986.

Bird-watchers love it for its small nature reserve and the adjacent community reserve of La Somone – a beautiful lagoon. More than 150 species of birds can be spotted in the two protected areas.

The basic **Campement Ker Cupaam** (☎ 33 956 4951; rnpopenguine@gmail.com; dm/d CFA6000/12,000) sits right at the edge of the reserve, and the boisterous women's cooperative that runs it also organises recommended ornithological tours. Across the road, **Keur de Sable** (☎ 33 957 7164; s/d CFA7500/12,000, houses CFA25,000-60,000) rents houses in varying sizes – but all with sea view. Food and homemade cocktails are good here too. There are plenty of little eateries in the main village and on the beach. **L'écho-Côtier** (☎ 33 637 8772; meals CFA5000) on the wave-kissed shore and **Chez Fatou** (village centre; dishes around CFA4000) in town are recommended.

From Dakar, head for Mbour and get off at Sindia, from where infrequent bush taxis run to Popenguine for CFA350.

LA SOMONE & NGAPAROU

Eighty kilometres from Dakar, La Somone is the gentle medium between the mass tourism of Saly and the village intimacy of Toubab Dialao. The hotel-lined main road takes you through to the lagoon, great for bird watching and pirogue tours.

Under the easygoing management of party joker, coffee importer and dressed-down busi-

nessman Formica, **Le Tamarin** (Chez Formica; ☎ 77 570 9674; tamarinformica@yahoo.fr; r incl breakfast CFA17,000; 🗶 🍽) has turned into the soul and open arms of La Somone. Rooms and meals follow the same concept: simple but solid. **Le Phenix** (☎ 33 957 7517; www.lephenix.net; villas CFA40,000; 🍽) rents two-bedroom villas that aren't exactly sparkling but sit directly on the beach. There's also the resort hotel **Lookea Club Baobab** (www.de cameron.com; 🗶 🖴 🍽), beautifully located on the lagoon, but only interested in tour groups – come here for a meal.

The most attractive option in the area is Ngaparou's **Africa Lodge** (☎ 33 958 5330; www.africa lodge-senegal.com; Ngaparou; per person incl breakfast from CFA16,000; 🅿 🗶 🖴 🍽) a fabulous, family-friendly guesthouse with striking decor and welcoming hosts.

For food and drinks try **Café Creole** (☎ 33 958 5191; dishes CFA2500-3000; 🕒 lunch & dinner), at the main junction, or the much calmer **Le Vivier** (☎ 77 656 6581; dishes around CFA4000; 🍽) where meals are served under straw roofs between pool and beach.

To get to La Somone take a Mbour-bound taxi; get off at Nguékokh, where taxis leave for Ngaparou and La Somone (CFA350).

SALY

Saly is the hedonistic queen among the coastal villages – a buzzing centre of beach tourism, home to a multitude of hotels, sandy shores and packed nightclubs. But the spook is over only a few metres of beach towards Mbour, where Saly-Niakhniakhal tempts with intimate hotels and local-style bars that allow you to enjoy the luxuries of beach life without the hassle.

BICIS (☎ 33 957 3331) and **SGBS** (☎ 33 957 3703) have branches in Saly, and there are several internet cafes.

Activities

Fishing and watersports are popular. Lamantin Beach and Espadon hotels also have highly rated fishing clubs; at Lamantin Beach you also get to hire watersports equipment.

Aqua Passion Plongée (☎ 33 958 5049; www.aqua passion-plongee.com) Dives for beginners and advanced divers and children.

Blue Marlin Fishing (☎ 77 442 2025; Plage Centre Commercial) Fishing club and booking point for Saly–Gorée–Dakar boat tours.

Marlin Club (☎ 33 957 2477; marlinclub@arc.sn) Popular fishing club in the heart of Saly's tourist zone; you can taste the fresh catch in the restaurant downstairs.

Senegal Loisirs (☎ 77 638 7626; contact@senegal -loisirs.com; Plage Saly-Sud) Next to Habana Café, a good address for watersports including jet skis and catamarans.

Sleeping

This is a tiny selection of the dozens of hotels and self-catering apartments in Saly.

La Medina (☎ 33 957 4993; s/d 15,000/20,000; Saly Village, Terrain de Football; ❒❒❒) This Mediterranean-style place has simple rooms on three balcony-adorned floors surrounding a leafy patio. An unexpected oasis of peace in the heart of Saly.

our pick **Ferme de Saly & Les Amazones** (☎ 77 638 4790; www.farmsaly.com; half board Ferme/Amazones CFA16,500/30,200; ❒) Jean-Paul, a man like a bear hug, was already receiving travellers on his organic farm and horse stable when Saly was still a tiny fishing village of 300 souls. The original backpackers' haunts are still there (and still good), but the jewel of this beachside farm is the Résidence les Amazones, with great apartments, sea views and the best pool on the coast.

L'Eden du Pescadou (☎ 33 957 5158; www.eden dupescadou.com; s/d from CFA18,000/20,000; ❒❒) In the kitchen, the chef experiments with great results with the marriage of European and African flavours (dishes around CFA4000). Rooms are bright and spotless.

Au Petit Jura (☎ 33 957 3767; www.aupetitjura.ch; d CFA23,000; ❒❒❒❒) This pretty, Swiss-owned retreat has huts so spotless you can't help but be reminded of the best clichés about

Switzerland. It's a hard choice between the central swimming pool and the quiet beach that's only steps away from your bed.

Auberge Treizeguy (☎ 33 957 0509; www.autre izeguy.com; r incl breakfast CFA26,000; ❒) The lovely couple that runs this intimate place rents out a handful of rooms in the main house. They've got kids and welcome other parents with children. The beach is right outside the front door.

Savana Saly (☎ 33 939 5800; www.savana.sn; s/d CFA45,000/55,000; ❒❒❒❒) What the rooms and family apartments lack in style, the hotel makes up for with its vast garden space, enormous pool and utterly forthcoming service. There are plenty of activities on offer, and children are very welcome.

Espadon (☎ 33 939 7099; www.espadon-hotel .com; s/d incl breakfast CFA67,000/107,000; ❒❒❒) The double-storey bungalows are bright and classy and have private, sunny terraces. The restaurant is one of the best in the country, and there's a wellness centre for relaxation.

Lamantin Beach Hotel (☎ 33 957 0777; www .lelamantin.com; s/d incl breakfast from CFA85,000/130,000; ❒❒❒) This glitzy establishment calls itself paradise on earth, and if your idea of heaven involves being pampered in a spa and relaxing in a *hammam* or on a private beach, than you'll probably agree with it. Service and food are outstanding.

Eating & Drinking

Saly's restaurant scene leaves you spoilt for choice, and the kitchens of Lamantin Beach and Espadon hotels are among the best.

Chez Poulo (☎ 77 659 6331; Saly-Niakhniakhal; dishes around CFA1000; ⏰ 11am-midnight) No one seems to be able to remember a time before Chez Poulo. This is where you get the best Senegalese food in the area, as well as tasty local juices and rustic European meals.

Le Tam Tam (☎ 33 957 8813; Saly main street; ice creams CFA2000) For an afternoon coffee and a trip through the endless possibilities of flavouring homemade ice cream this arty, green-walled cafe is unbeatable.

Escale Jappo (☎ 33 957 2222; Saly-Niakhniakhal; ⏰ 7am-11pm) Jappo is a local NGO that helps young people get an education and employment. Its restaurants are one way of doing that – the young staff are all locals that have been trained under the scheme. With its wood and brick decor, leafy patio and frequent live music, it's great for simple meals, snacks or a relaxed drink.

Le Soleil (☎ 77 541 2526; dishes CFA5000; ❤ 9pm-4am) Opposite Village Artisanal, this boisterous restaurant-cum–live venue gets so packed with tables that even the model-aspiring waitresses are barely able to squeeze through. Great for party vibes – the food is unspectacular.

Habana Café (☎ 33 957 1730; Plage de Saly-Sud; dishes around CFA5000; ❤ 11am-1am Mon-Sat) The skilled chef here shapes dishes from fresh ingredients, and friendly waiters serve them to you on the beach-view terrace. That's why Saly locals keep coming back.

Le Sapoti (☎ 77 575 4076; Centre Commerciale; meals from CFA5000; ❤ Wed-Mon) This large and friendly place gets busy on Sunday night, when tango and waltz, mussels and white wine turn back time for punters. If you don't remember when Clark Gable died, the Sunday crowd isn't yours, but the food is good here on any day.

Les Tables du Marlin (☎ 33 957 2477; marlinclub@arc.sn; dishes CFA6000; ❤ 10am-7pm) Part of a fishing club, this cosy, wood-floored restaurant on the beach near the Centre Commerciale serves gigantic seafood platters heaving under lobster, gambas skewers, and a selection of grilled fish (CFA16,000).

MBOUR

Five kilometres south of Saly, Mbour is a big fishing centre. The 200m-long fish market on the beach, the colourful dots of pirogues and the surrounding marine-related commerce are exciting, if slightly nauseating, to watch.

The *gare routière* (bus station) is near the exit towards Dakar. Mbour has a **BICIS** (☎ 33 957 1086) with ATM, several internet cafes and a post office. Mbour hospital is on the route towards the beach and Tama Lodge.

Sleeping

Ndaali (☎ 33 957 4724; www.ndaali.com; Zone résidentielle; r CFA15,000; ❎ ▣) Made and maintained with love, this small, impeccable *campement* is brilliantly run by young hotelier Aziz, who's not only a perfect host but also a great chef.

Hôtel Club Safari (☎ 33 957 1991; www.hotelclubsafari .com; s/d incl breakfast CFA16,000/22,000; ❎ ▣ ▣) This intimate, seashell-adorned hotel has comfy rooms set around a pool and boasts a range of facilities (including a massage centre) and activities that put larger hotels to shame.

Keur Marakiss (☎ 33 954 7454; www.marakiss.com; Mbour Serere-Souf; s/d incl breakfast CFA22,750/26,000

❎ ▣ ▣ ❖) This homely cottage with white-washed walls, wooden beams, country kitchen and thatched roof is family friendly and offers excellent tours to community projects.

New Blue Africa (☎ 33 957 0993; Rte de Niakhniakhal; s/d CFA23,000/28,000) What it lacks in style, this small hotel makes up for in location – it sits right behind a fine dune on the finest stretch of beach in the area. Rooms are fine, if unspectacular, and young manager Fode is not only a great host but also mixes a mean house cocktail.

Tama Lodge (☎ /fax 33 957 0040; www.tamalodge .com; s/d from CFA33,000/46,000) Right on the Plage des Cocotiers, Tama Lodge is more of a piece of art than a hotel. The sublime mud bungalows look like the homes of a West African king and the beach restaurant is fantastic.

Eating & Drinking

Chez Paolo (☎ 33 957 1310; dishes from CFA2500; ❤ 11am-11pm) Mbour's unbeatable address for food is this local-style place on the main road (everybody knows it).

Liqueur de Warang (☎ 77 524 5416; gambanar@yahoo.com; ❤ 11am-1pm & 3-7pm) In Warang, a short drive from Mbour, you can enjoy a very persuasive tasting session of local-fruit liqueurs here.

Check whether **Les Jardins Plage** (☎ 77 527 8963; Rte Saly-Niakhniakhal-Mbour) has opened near New Blue Africa – at writing time it looked set to become the prime music venue of the Petite Côte.

Getting There & Away

There's frequent public transport between Mbour and Dakar (minibus CFA950, *sept-place* CFA1300).

NIANING

Nianing is quieter and more local in character than Saly, though the wide beach continues its flawless sway down to here.

The place to stay is Nicole Diop's **Le Ben'Tenier** (☎ 33 957 1420; www.lebentenier.org; s/d incl breakfast CFA15,000/23,000; ❎ ▣ ▣), welcoming with its spacious bungalows and well-kept gardens, and dedicated to improving local education standards through the association Tchekanam. Nicole also runs brilliant, women-aimed tour agency **Afrika Touki Voyages** (☎ 33 957 1420; www.afrika touki.com).

For food, seek out **Le Coco Diop** (☎ 77 570 9404; meals around CFA4000; ❤ 11.30am-3pm & 6.30pm-midnight Tue-Sun; ▣), which serves excellent food (including a great range of salads) in stylish surroundings.

Nianing is on the main road between Mbour and Joal; public transport is frequent. Hiring a taxi from Mbour costs around CFA1000.

JOAL-FADIOUT

Joal, on the mainland, and its offshore sister Fadiout are tied together by a long, wooden bridge. Fadiout is no ordinary island. It's entirely made of oyster and clam shells, thrown here on a pile ages ago. The shells find their way everywhere – on house walls, car-free roads and the shared Muslim and Christian cemetery.

Joal and Fadiout are often cited as examples of religious tolerance – not only the cemetery but also the coexistence of Fadiout's impressive church, Catholic shrines and mosque tells that story.

Pirogue trips to the cemetery, a nearby oyster cultivation and a set of stilt-balanced granaries make for a great day out. To find a boat, head for the boat owners' association at the Joal end of the bridge. Like a taxi park, it's got a strict order of departure and fixed prices.

Sleeping & Eating

Le Thiouraye (☎ 77 515 6064; s/d incl breakfast CFA10,000/12,000; 🍴) This tiny *auberge* on the riverside is a great budget option. Rooms are basic but good value, and the terrace restaurant sits right on the water. The menu (composed by one of Senegal's top chefs) is fantastically varied: try the pork in coconut sauce or house-style prawn salad.

Keur Seynabou (☎ 33 957 6744; www.keurseynabou.com; r CFA35,000 🍴 🛒 💻) If your budget stretches just an inch further, try Keur Seynabou, whose three 1st-floor rooms are magazine-perfect lodgings. It's a place like a beauty bath, where every detail has been taken care of, from the atmospheric lighting to the hand-stitched bed covers, the home-made lamps and the lush garden.

Getting There & Away

A minibus to/from Mbour is CFA700. If you're heading on down the coast, it costs CFA1300 from Joal to Palmarin. A *sept-place* taxi goes directly to Dakar most mornings (without changing at Mbour) for CFA2000.

THE SINÉ-SALOUM DELTA

From Palmarin southwards, an area of otherworldly beauty opens up. Endless salt and sand plains stretch into the distance, and singular baobabs rise from the glistening lands like watchful giants. This is the gateway to the Siné-Saloum Delta, a 180,000-hectare zone of shimmering flats, small palm groves, mangrove creeks and lagoons where the Saloum River spills artfully into the Atlantic.

PALMARIN

Some 25km south of Joal, Palmarin sits where the beaches of the Petite Côte merge with the myriad landscapes of the Siné-Saloum Delta. Encompassing four small villages, Palmarin is a breathtaking spot with tall palm groves, salty plains and patches of gleaming water.

Sleeping & Eating

Palmarin seems to attract original *campements*. The most original are both found on adjacent islands.

Djidjack (☎ 33 949 9619; www.djidjack.com; d/q CFA25,000/35,000, camping CFA2500) This place has bungalows, but the centrepiece is a giant *case à impluvium* (large, round traditional house) that offers a good restaurant and the slightly eccentric company of the Swiss hosts.

Yokam (☎ 77 567 0113; www.au-senegal.com/pages/yokam; Palmarin Facao; per person incl breakfast CFA8000) The cheapest bed is at the always-smiling Yokam, where you stay in a lightweight straw hut close to the beach.

Lodge de Diakhamor (☎ 33 957 1256; www.lesenegal.info; half board s/d CFA23,000/41,000) The red, mud-walled bungalows here look like a cross between a medieval fort and a Fula village. Pirogue excursions, horse riding, bicycle and fishing trips are included in the room rate.

Lodge des Collines de Niassam (☎ 77 639 0639; www.niassam.com; half board per person CFA52,000; 🍴 🛒) Palmarin's top spot is this quirky and very romantic lodge, with swish log cabins wedged between the mighty branches of baobabs, or suspended over the shallow waters of the delta. The views are breathtaking and the home-mixed fruity rums tempting.

Rêve Nomade (☎ 77 727 5717; www.revedenomade.com; luxury lobster lunch per person CFA72,000, enquire for weekend rates) Here fantastic French chef Thomas

SENEGAL

Morin puts out crystal glasses, silver cutlery and an old gramophone in the shade of a huge tent on a small, sandy island. For the real 'nomad's dream', you can spend the night here, on the beach or in large Mauritanian tents.

M'boss-Dor (☎ Nov-Jun 77 541 9683, Jul-Oct in France (33) 5 58 77 91 89; www.mboss-dor.com; full board per person CFA53,800) At this mangrove-hidden retreat you get to stay in a classy log cabin so lovingly decorated that even a bucket shower feels somewhat glamorous. Best of all – on the ULM tours (20 minutes CFA25,000) on offer you get an amazing bird's-eye view over the delta. You won't find this place on your own – arrange pick-up from either Dakar (CFA40,000 to CFA50,000) or the mosque at Palmarin Ngallou.

Getting There & Away
Palmarin is most easily reached from Mbour, via Joal-Fadiout and Sambadia (where you may have to change). The fare from Joal to Sambadia is CFA500 in a Ndiaga Ndiaye, and from Sambadia to Palmarin it's CFA400.

Dionewar & Surroundings
Dionewar is one of the larger islands in the Delta, a great base for pirogue excursions through narrow *bolongs* (small rivers) and creeks. This can be arranged through the helpful staff at the plush **Delta Niominka** (☎ 33 948 9935; www.deltaniominka.com; s/d incl breakfast CFA45,000/60,000; 🗙 🗷). Nestling among the lush greenery of Dionewar, it has stylish accommodation in two-storey bungalows that hide under massive straw roofs. Pick-up and drop-off can be arranged from Djifer, south of Palmarin (one way CFA6000). Otherwise, jump on a crammed public pirogue that leaves Djifer around 3pm every day and returns from Dionewar the day after (CFA1000 per person).

NDANGANE & MAR LODJ
Ndangane is a thriving tourist centre on the northern side of the Siné-Saloum Delta. From here you can get boats across the river to the village of Mar Lodj, on a peaceful island cut off from the mainland by the delta. There's no bank here, but internet connections are available at a couple of places.

Sleeping & Eating
NDANGANE
For food outside your hotel, try **La Maroise** (☎ 33 949 9320; dishes from CFA3000) or the more local-style **Le Picbœuf** (☎ 77 638 7601; dishes CFA1500).

Le Barracuda (Chez Mbacke; ☎ 33 949 9815; r per person CFA6000) Rooms here are cheap and the ambiance cheerful. The restaurant terrace grants great views across the pirogue landing.

Le Cormoran (☎ /fax 33 949 9316; www.lecormoran .net; r per person CFA12,000; 🗙 🗷) Decent bungalows in a garden setting, and a tiny square of a pool have kept the guests coming here for years.

Auberge Bouffe (☎ 33 949 9313; info@aubergebouffe .com; s/d incl breakfast CFA16,000/24,000; 🗷) So colourful it reminds you of a playgroup, this auberge brings out the kid in you. Or the food fanatic – the Italian cuisine here is great.

Les Cordons Bleus (☎ 33 949 9312; www.lescordons bleus.com; s/d/tr CFA34,000/46,000/58,000; 🅿 🗙 🗓 🗷) Here, right on the river, with views over the mangroves to Mar Lodj, you find Ndangane's most stylish rooms. Indulge in massages and minigolf sessions.

Le Pélican du Saloum (☎ 33 949 9320; resapeli can@senegal-hotels.com; half/full board CFA40,000/60,000; 🗙 🗓 🗷) A typical resort hotel, this place offers plenty of activities though limited character. Try the terrace for sunset gazing.

MAR LODJ
Le Marsetal (☎ 77 637 2531; s/d half board CFA16,000/ 21,000) Kurt, the Austrian host and soul of this utterly relaxed place, has a talent for making you feel at home, and great taste in food – everything here is clean, fresh and wholesome. Bring your own mosquito net.

Essamaye (☎ 77 555 3667; www.senegalia.com; Marfafako; full board per person CFA17,500) On the other side of the island is this place like a hug from a loved one – highly recommended for family vibes and its impressive Casamance-style *case à l'impluvium*.

Le Bazouk (☎ 77 633 4894; www.bazoukdusaloum .com; half board per person CFA18,000) On the island's main stretch, Le Bazouk has spacious bungalows scattered over a vast, sand-covered garden where bougainvilleas lend shade and palm trees carry hammocks. A great place for families.

La Nouvelle Vague (☎ 77 566 2648; khadynv@gmail .com; r CFA20,000) A short walk further on, at La Nouvelle Vague dedicated Khady keeps a close eye on the preparation of the recommended meals and the tidying of the brightly tiled rooms.

Getting There & Away
Take any bus between Kaolack and Mbour, and get off at Ndiosomone, from where bush

taxis shuttle back and forth to Ndangane. For Mar Lodj, contact your *campement* for pirogue pick-up or hire a boat at the **GIE des Piroguiers** (☎ 77 213 7497, 77 226 6168), the boat owners' association at the jetty. Prices are fixed.

FIMELA & SIMAL

Just north of Ndangane, these tiny villages are fabulously located at the edge of the mangrove. At the rootsy **Gîte de Simal** (☎ 77 957 1256; www.lesenegal.info; half board s/d CFA21,000/37,000) you stay in traditional-style thatched huts and experience the pleasure of an open-air shower. Pirogue and fishing trips are included in the half-board rate. Fimela's **Souimanga Lodge** (☎ 77 638 7601; www.souimanga -lodge.com; s/d CFA80,000/120,000; ❷ 🖳 🖳) is one of Senegal's best hotels – with luxury log cabins nestled between tropical gardens and bird-rich mangroves, it's honeymoon romantic.

There are fairly frequent *sept-places* from Ndangane to Fimela (CFA400), from where you can hire a taxi to either hotel for about CFA2000 to CFA3000. Taxis from Fimela to Ndiosomone cost CFA600.

FOUNDIOUGNE

Once a French colonial outpost, the expansive village of Foundiougne now mainly attracts keen anglers. This area has notoriously bad drinking water – stick to bottled. The place to stay is **Le Baobab sur Mer** (Chez Anne Marie; ☎ 33 948 1262; s/d incl breakfast CFA10,000/17,000) – your address for generous meals on the terrace, lively drink-ups, sparkling company and simple accommodation. In town, the small Senegalese eatery **Bingo-Bingo** (☎ 77 565 4400; dishes CFA1500) serves a mean *thiéboudieune*.

The only really important thing about Foundiougne is that it's a ferry point. The large boat (per person/car CFA100/1500) leaves the departure jetty at Dakhonga at 8.30am, 10.30am, 12.30pm, 3.30pm and 6.30pm. From Foundiougne, departure times are 7.30am, 9.30am and 11.30am, as well as 3pm and 5pm. There's no ferry on Wednesday afternoons.

To get here from Dakar, jump on a *sept-place* to Fatick (CFA2500), where you change for a bush taxi to Dakhonga. Coming from the south, you reach Foundiougne from Passi, on the potholed tarmac road between Kaolack and Sokone.

SOKONE

This village on the way from Kaolack to Toubakouta often gets passed over. It's worth putting in a day stop to visit the eco-tourism initiative **Fadidi Niombato** (☎ 77 215 6860; www.niombato.com; s/d CFA15,000/20,000). Run in association with the village, it organises village encounters, proffers meals made from fresh, locally grown ingredients and arranges excursions to the delta and Forêt de Fathala. Ask one of the camp staff to take you to try some fresh or grilled oysters – they're delicious.

Gambia-bound *sept-places* from Dakar (CFA7500) or Kaolack pass by.

TOUBAKOUTA & BAMBOUNG

Nestled among mazes of mangroves, the tiny town of Toubakouta is one of the most beautiful spots of the Siné-Saloum Delta. It's an excellent base for excursions to the nearby Parc National du Delta du Saloum and the stunning Aire Marine Protégéé de Bamboung, both of which teem with wildlife, including pelicans, flamingos, herons and egrets.

Toubakouta has a couple of cybercafes and *télécentres* and a post office, but no bank.

Sleeping & Eating

Keur Youssou (☎ 33 948 7728; s/d CFA6250/12,500; ❷) This budget choice has rhun-palm-scented and nicely furnished rooms.

Keur Thierry (Brasserie de Toubakouta; ☎ 77 439 8605; d incl breakfast CFA12,500; ❷) Another budget option, Thierry has a handful of white-tiled lodgings, a great kitchen and Belgian beers.

Hôtel Keur Saloum (☎ 33 948 7715; www.keur saloum.com; s/d incl breakfast CFA34,200/55,000; 🅿 ❷ 🖳 🖳 🕭) If you book here, go for a suite with view across the river. Families might prefer the double-bungalows in the back of the large garden.

Keur Bamboung (☎ 77 510 8013; www.oceanium.org; half/full board CFA17,000/22,000) Sitting right in the *aire marine protégéé*, Keur Bamboung is the camp that protects the reserve – profits go towards financing the guards on the lookout for illegal fisherpeople. Accommodation is simple, green and stunningly located. Phone to arrange pick-up from Toubakouta – the place is a pirogue and donkey-cart ride away from the mainland.

Getting There & Away

Toubakouta is just off the main road between Kaolack and Karang. Kaolack to Toubakouta is CFA3000 by *sept-place* taxi.

PARC NATIONAL DU DELTA DU SALOUM

The 76,000 hectares of the **Parc National du Delta du Saloum** (admission CFA2000) encompass the savannah woodland of the Forêt de Fathala, wide stretches of mangrove swamp, and a maritime section that extends from the islands of Bétanti to the Pointe de Sangomar. Wildlife in the forest section includes (a few) red colobus and patas monkeys, warthogs and hyenas. The sea sections allow for bird watching, though sea turtles and dolphins can occasionally be spotted.

The forest sections are best explored from Missirah (south of Toubakouta), where the **Gîte de Bandiala** (☎ 33 948 7735; www.gite-bandiala. com; half/full board per person CFA16,300/22,600) organises tours. The camp itself sits among all the greenery and a water hole attracts plenty of wildlife.

Hire a taxi from Toubakouta to get here (around CFA5000).

CENTRAL & NORTHERN SENEGAL

This region covers a vast area, from the windy Atlantic coast with its desertlike dunes in Lompoul to the far east of the country. Some of this zone is barely inhabited, such as the eastern Ferlo plains, but it's also home to a few of Senegal's largest cities. Some of them, such as Saint-Louis and Thiès, developed into cosmopolitan communities during colonial days. The town of Touba, by contrast, is the fastest-growing city today, a head-spinning clash of religion and commerce.

THIÈS

When the French colonial administration laid out its planning for West Africa's railways, it fixed the crossing point of the two major lines (Dakar–Niger and Dakar–Saint-Louis) at Thiès, inadvertently creating a vibrant new urban centre. Today it's still called the 'railway town'. As that, it has a lot more atmosphere than the dusty centres that evolved around road junctions. Tall

trees line some of the central streets, the rhythm is relaxed, and there are a handful of good places to stay.

CBAO (☎ 33 952 0505; Rue Nationale 2), **SGBS** (☎ 33 951 8225; Ave Léopold Sédar Senghor) and **BICIS** (☎ 33 951 8339; Pl de France; ☒ 7.45am-12.15pm & 1.40-3.45pm) all have branches with withdrawal facilities. Thiès is wi-fi central – almost every hotel and restaurant offers the service.

The town is famous for the quality of the tapestries made at the **Manufactures Sénégalaises des Arts Décoratifs** (☎ /fax 33 951 1131; admission CFA1000; ☒ 8am-12.30pm & 3-6.30pm Mon-Fri, 8am-12.30pm Sat & Sun). Created in the 1960s, this factory and crafts centre has produced motifs sought after across the world. On a visit, you can see the artisans at work.

Sleeping

New guest houses are springing up here all the time.

Domaine Kalao (☎ 77 277 8893; Rte de St-Louis; r CFA12,500) This tiny place offers simpler accommodation than Massa Massa, but the setting, still in the sticks, just outside town, is infinitely more attractive. The food is divine.

Massa Massa (☎ 33 952 1244; Cité Malik Sy; r with/without air-con CFA26,000/16,000; ☒ ☐) A perennially popular choice, Massa Massa has a fabulous restaurant and clean, welcoming rooms.

Bidew Bi (☎ 33 952 2717; bidewbi@orange.sn; Ave Houphouët-Boigny; s/d CFA25,000/30,000; ☒ ☐) Party people find their hotel of choice here, where good-quality rooms are part of a huge entertainment complex.

Résidence de Lat-Dior (☎ 33 952 0777; www.resi dencelatdior.com; s/d CFA27,600/35,200; ☐ ☐ ☐) For a place with a pool and sports centre, head for the grand hotel of town.

Eating

Eating well is not a problem here.

Big Faim (☎ 33 952 0622; Ave Léopold Sédar Senghor, Escale; meals CFA1000-5000; ☒ 6am-2am; ☐) This place fills hungry tummies around the clock, mainly with the globally understood cuisine of chips, chicken, pizza and coffee.

Croissant Magique (☎ 33 951 1878; Ave Lamine Guèye; dishes around CFA2000) Fast food and excellent pizzas are the enticing offer of this enduring place, in a quiet, central location.

Les Vieilles Marmites (☎ 33 951 4440; dishes around CFA3000; ☒ 11am-2pm & 6pm-midnight) If you don't mind waiting a little while (in good

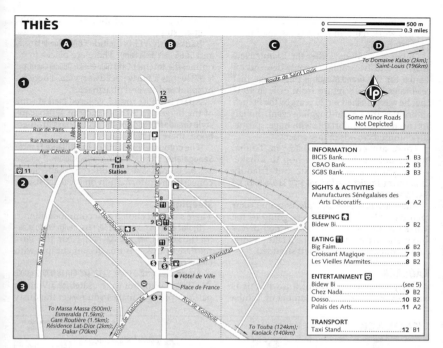

THIÈS

company), this is a brilliant little corner for Senegalese rice and sauce.

Esmeralda (☎ 33 951 0248; Cité Malik Sy; 💻) Near the *gare routière*, the classy Esmeralda has a space for every client – there's the lover's corridor, the VIP space and, well, that wide area for common folk. The menu's main message is on visible display outside: French, Italian and Senegalese flags tell you what the food choice is.

Entertainment

There are two good nightclubs: **Dosso** (☎ 33 951 2640; Rue Sans Soleil; ☷ Tue-Sun; 🍸), the 'grandfather' of Thiès nightlife, and the glitzy **Bidew Bi** (☎ 33 952 2717; ☷ 7pm-4am).

Palais des Arts (☎ 33 951 7010; Sounoumakane; ☷ 6pm-3am) Since Senegalese star Ma Sane, who hails from Thiès, invested her cash in the creation of this magnificent venue, Thiès has a stage and exhibition space to rival Dakar's best.

Chez Nada (☎ 33 951 0700; Av Lamine Gueye; ☷ 9pm-2am) For something more intimate, try Chez Nada, where good acoustic bands perform every Friday and Saturday.

Getting There & Around

Bush taxis and minibuses leave from the *gare routière,* 1.5km from the centre, on the southern outskirts. There are frequent *sept-place* taxis to Dakar (CFA1500, one hour, 70km), Kaolack (CFA2300, two hours, 140km) and Saint-Louis (CFA3000, four hours, 196km). Any taxi trip around town should cost you CFA500; there's a taxi stand at the roundabout on Rte de Saint-Louis

TOUBA

Touba is the sacred focus of the Mouride Sufi brotherhood, where their spiritual leader, Cheikh Amadou Bamba, lived, preached and died. He is buried in the Grand Mosque of Touba, an awe-inspiring structure whose minaret dominates the town. The always expanding building has an impressive library containing the complete works of Bamba.

But Touba is not only about spirituality; it's also about big business. The Mouride brotherhood is an influential economic and political force in the country, and much of Senegal's money is concentrated in Touba. Touba market is a huge sprawl of tax-free activity. Seeing the combined forces of religion, economy and politics work hand in hand is fascinating, if a bit confusing.

Once a year, 48 days after the Islamic New Year, around two million people descend on Touba for the **Grand Magal**, a pilgrimage that celebrates Bamba's return from exile in 1907 after he was banished for 20 years by the French authorities. It's a mind-boggling event, though you need to be comfortable with huge, spiritually enthused crowds in tiny spaces.

There are no places to stay in Touba, but it's only a short, 10km hop to Mbaké, where you'll find the basic but friendly **Campement Touristique le Baol** (☎ 33 976 5505; s/d CFA13,800/15,800; 🛏).

There are plenty of *sept-places* from Dakar each day (CFA3000). If you're going to the Mbaké *campement* first, let the taxi driver know, and insist; otherwise, he'll take a shortcut to Touba and you'll be left stranded.

KAOLACK

A dusty, polluted sprawl of a town, this is where every vehicle from Gambia or Tamba to Dakar puts in a food and, more commonly, a repair stop.

Banks with ATMs include **CBAO** (Rue de la Gare) and **SGBS** (Rue de la Gare). There are places to go online; the **Internet Café** (Rue Cheikh Tidiane Cherif; per hr CFA150) has a fairly speedy service. There's a hospital and several pharmacies.

Apart from its round, covered **market** (one of the biggest in Africa) and the Moroccan-style **Grande Mosquée** of the Baye Niass brotherhood, there's little to see.

The colourful building of the **Alliance Franco-Senegalaise** (☎ 33 941 1061; www.kaolack.af-senegal .org; Rue Galliène) is a spot offering shade, good concerts and information on local artists.

Sleeping

There's a good choice of accommodation.

Djolof Inn (☎ 33 941 9360; Fass; r with/without aircon CFA15,000/11,000; 🛏 🖥 🛜) Near the *gare routière* to Dakar is this decent cheapie with clean rooms.

Arc en Ciel (☎ 33 941 1212; s/d CFA18,000/21,000; 🛏 🖥 🛜) With hot water, satellite TV and a patio so pretty it makes you forget the dusty

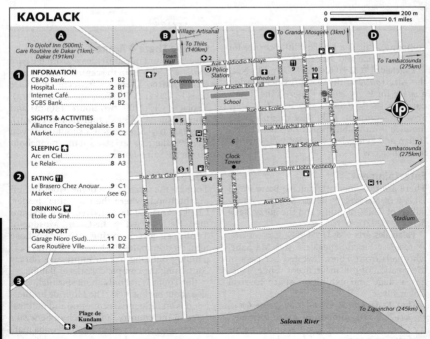

KAOLACK

0 ————— 200 m
0 ————— 0.1 miles

INFORMATION		
CBAO Bank	1	B2
Hospital	2	B1
Internet Café	3	D1
SGBS Bank	4	B2

SIGHTS & ACTIVITIES		
Alliance Franco-Senegalaise	5	B1
Market	6	C2

SLEEPING 🏠		
Arc en Ciel	7	B1
Le Relais	8	A3

EATING 🍽		
Le Brasero Chez Anouar	9	C1
Market	(see 6)	

| DRINKING 🍸 | | |
| Etoile du Siné | 10 | C1 |

TRANSPORT		
Garage Nioro (Sud)	11	D2
Gare Routière Ville	12	B2

To Djolof Inn (500m);
Gare Routière Dakar (1km);
Dakar (191km)

Village Artisanal

To Thiès (140km)

Town Hall

To Grande Mosquée (3km)

To Tambacounda (275km)

Ave Valdiodio Ndiaye

Police Station

Gouvernance

Cathedral

Ave Cheikh Ibra Fall

School

Rue des Ecoles

Rue Marechal Joffre

Rue Maréchal Bugeaud

Rue Cheikh Tidiane Cherif

Ave Nobel

To Tambacounda (275km)

Rue Paul Seignet

Clock Tower

Ave Filiatre (John Kennedy)

Rue de la Gare

Ave Délois

Rue de Faidherbe

Rue la Mare

Stadium

Rue Médoud-Fam

Plage de Kundam

Saloum River

To Ziguinchor (245km)

SENEGAL

town, Arc en Ciel is far more upmarket than the humble exterior suggests.

Le Relais (☎ 33 941 1000; Plage de Kundam; s/d CFA25,000/30,000; 🅿 🖵 🖳 🛜) Run by the same management as Arc en Ciel, Le Relais is Kaolack's most sparkling choice, with all the amenities of a quality hotel (bar, restaurant, TV) and a great location – hard to find in this town.

Eating & Drinking

All listed hotels have good restaurants – the variety and quality reflects the standing of each place.

Self-caterers have the whole, huge market at their disposal and several good corner shops.

Le Brasero Chez Anouar (☎ 33 941 1608; Ave Valdiodio Ndiaye; meals about CFA3000; ⊙ 7am-11pm) Make the pilgrimage that almost every passing traveller undertakes. Laidback Le Brasero serves a different *plat du jour* every day, and is the kind of place to head to for advice on anything from car repairs to party spots.

Etoile du Siné (Ave Cheikh Ibra Fall) The busiest bar in town is this indefatigable place.

Getting There & Away

The town has three *gares routières*: Gare Routière de Dakar, on the northwestern side of town, for western and northern destinations; Garage Nioro (Sud), on the southeastern side of the city centre, for Ziguinchor, Gambia and Tambacounda; and Gare Routière Ville for local taxis.

There are frequent *sept-place* taxis to Dakar (CFA3000, three hours), Karang on the Gambian border (CFA2500, two hours), and Tambacounda (CFA6000). Shared taxis around town cost CFA500.

DESERT DE LOMPOUL

Near the Grande Côte, west of Kébémer, Lompoul surprises with huge sand dunes that stretch from the coast far into the country's interior, forming a veritable desert. You can pick from two *campements*, both offering accommodation in huge, Mauritanian tents, as well as campfires and dromedary tours through the dunes. **Le Gîte de Lompoul** (☎ 33 957 1256; www.lesenegal.info; half board s/d CFA21,000/37,000) has the rootsier set-up, while the **Lodge de Lompoul** (☎ 33 869 7900; www.africatravel-group.com; half board s/d CFA50,000/70,000) makes you feel like the chief of the bedouins (or the lead actor in *Out of Africa*; views differ), with tents raised on wooden platforms, artfully scattered earthen- and metal-wares, and stylish outdoor wash corners. The first desert festival was in planning when we visited the Lodge – keep checking the site; it sounded impressive.

To get here, contact the relevant travel agency – TPA for the Gîte, ATG or Sahel Découverte for the Lodge (see p739).

SAINT-LOUIS
pop 147,100

Like a monument to colonial aspiration, Saint-Louis impresses its sense of the past on you with every step you take along its narrow streets. The madness of European expansionism in Africa, the beauty of its 19th-century architecture and the unique culture born from the difficult encounter between different civilisations – Saint-Louis' historical buildings speak of all of that and more.

Founded in 1659 by Louis Caullier on the strategic Île de Ndar, Saint-Louis was the first French settlement in Africa. The trading station soon grew into a major urban centre, with a unique cosmopolitan culture defined by its growing *métis* (mixed-race) elite. The most striking expression of this are the *signares* – *métis* women who married wealthy European merchants temporarily based in the city, thereby attaining bourgeois status and wealth. *Signare* traditions, like the *fanals* (lantern) processions are kept alive for events such as New Year's Eve. The unique make-up of Saint-Louis' population impresses itself onto you as soon as you step onto the island.

In 1958, Saint-Louis become the capital of the vast territory that was l'Afrique Occidentale Française (French West Africa), a status it lost (along with the glory that came with it) 44 years later to Dakar. Today, the town has long grown beyond the confines of the island. Its historical part has been protected as a Unesco World Heritage Site since 2000.

Orientation

The city of Saint-Louis (the ancient European quarter with its grand houses) straddles part of the Langue de Barbarie Peninsula, Île de N'Dar and the mainland. From the mainland you reach the island via the 500m-long Pont Faidherbe; Pont Mustapha Malick Gaye links the island to the peninsula, where the thriving fishing community of Guet N'Dar inhabits the old African quarter.

MAPS

The map *Saint-Louis et la Region du Fleuve Senegal* (CFA3000), a cross between a cartoon and an aerial photograph, is available from the Syndicat d'Initiative (see below).

Information

Both **BICIS** (☎ 33 961 1053; Rue de France; ☿ 7.45am-12.15pm & 1.40-3.45pm Mon-Thu, 7.45am-1pm & 2.40-3.45pm Fri) and **CBAO** (☎ 33 938 2552; Rue Khalifa Ababacar Sy; ☿ 8.15am-5.15pm Mon-Fri) change money and have ATMs; CBAO also has a Western Union office.

Institut Jean Mermoz (☎ 33 938 2626; www.ccfsl .net; Ave Jean Mermoz; ☿ 8.30am-12.30pm & 3-6.30pm Tue-Fri, 8.30am-4pm Sat) Has a library and cafe and hosts films, concerts and art exhibitions.

Internet Café (Ave de Gaulle; per hr CFA500; ☿ 8am-11pm) Has decent terminals and several phone booths.

Post office (Ave de Gaulle) Art Deco–style building opposite the Hôtel de la Poste.

Sahel Découverte (☎ 33 961 4263; www.sahelde couverte.com; Ave Blaise Diagne) This travel agency is quite simply the best address for exploring the northern region.

Syndicat d'Initiative (☎ 33 961 2455; sltourisme@ orange.sn; Gouvernance; ☿ 9am-noon & 2.30-5pm) A haven of regional information with excellent tours.

www.saintlouisdusenegal.com This website contains plenty of useful of information and has links to all major hotels and restaurants.

Sights

The metal arches of the low-lying **Pont Faidherbe** (1897) are the city's most significant landmark, and you'll cross its clicking steel planks when driving into town. A grand piece of 19th-century engineering, it has a rotating middle section.

Across the bridge, you see the **Gouvernance** and **Hôtel de la Poste**, where the colonial air-mail pilots used to stay. Opposite the **Governor's Palace**, Pl Faidherbe is flanked north and south by the 1837 **Rognât Casernes** (one crumbling, the other one a modern hotel). The nearby **Cathedral** (Rue Scholcher), built in 1828, is one of the oldest churches in Senegal. The **Grand Mosque** in the north was constructed in 1847 and features the oddity of an attached clock tower.

Saint-Louis is made of historical buildings, remarkable with their patios and balconies, and while some are largely in ruins, some have been beautifully restored, notably the **Maison Yves Lamour**, **La Maison Rose**, **La Résidence** and **Sunu Keur**, all of which house hotels.

At the southern tip of the island, the **Musée de CRDS** (☎ 33 961 1050; Quai Henri Jay; adult/ child CFA500/250; ☿ 9am-noon & 3-6pm) has historical artefacts and photographs. **Galerie Mame Thioub** (☎ 33 961 3611; Ave Blaise Diagne; ☿ 8am-7pm) sometimes has good arts exhibitions, and **Les Ateliers Tèsss** (☎ 33 961 6860; Rue Khalifa Ababacar Sy) displays beautiful woven products (you can see the artisans at work).

Guet N'Dar on the mainland is a fantastically busy fishing town, where the focus changes from historical architecture to contemporary life.

Festivals & Events

The **Saint-Louis Jazz Festival**, held every May, attracts jazz greats and music lovers from around the world. If you pass through town in October, you might catch the impressive **Regatta of Guet-Ndar**, a lively boat race that passes through the river arm between Saint-Louis and Sor. **Les Fanals** can usually be seen around Christmas and sometimes during the jazz festival.

There's much more to cultural life here, including a festival of Fula music and regular concerts. Consult the Institut Jean Mermoz and www.saintlouisdusenegal.com for events calendars.

Sleeping

Saint-Louis offers accommodation for all budgets, of all types, and in any surrounding. You can either stay on the island within walking distance to all bars and restaurants and the town's historic architecture, or try the beach-lined places on the Langue de Barbarie Peninsula.

ISLAND

L'Atlantide Auberge de Jeunesse (☎ 33 961 2409; pisdi allo@yahoo.fr; Rue Bouet; s/d CFA5750/11,500) Behind the scrubbed white walls and blue shutters hides a typical youth hostel: cheap, mosquito netted, ventilated, clean, slightly rough around the edges and full of travellers with stories to tell.

La Louisiane (☎ 33 961 4221; www.aubergelalouisiane .com; r from 14,500; ✂ ▯) An enviable river-view location, a great restaurant and the engaging company of owner Marcel make this a travellers' favourite. The outdoor verandah shields you from the chilly river wind while

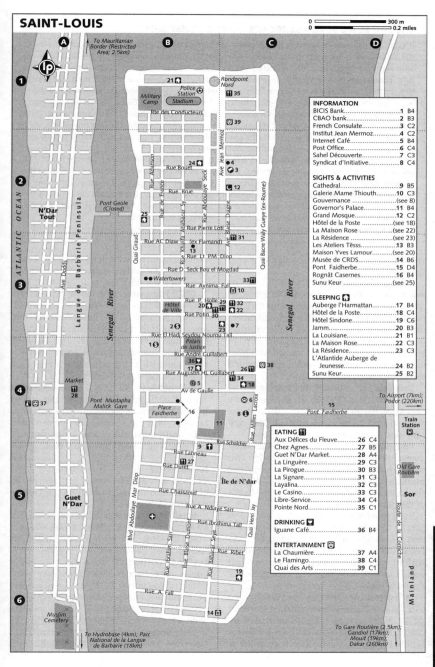

SAINT-LOUIS

0 ____ 300 m
0 ____ 0.2 miles

INFORMATION
BICIS Bank.................................1 B4
CBAO bank...............................2 B3
French Consulate.......................3 C2
Institut Jean Mermoz.................4 C2
Internet Café.............................5 B4
Post Office.................................6 C3
Sahel Découverte......................7 C3
Syndicat d'Initiative..................8 C4

SIGHTS & ACTIVITIES
Cathedral..................................9 B5
Galerie Mame Thiouth.............10 C3
Gouvernance.....................(see 8)
Governor's Palace....................11 B4
Grand Mosque.........................12 C2
Hôtel de la Poste................(see 18)
La Maison Rose...................(see 22)
La Résidence.......................(see 23)
Les Ateliers Tèsss....................13 B3
Maison Yves Lamour.........(see 20)
Musée de CRDS.......................14 B6
Pont Faidherbe........................15 D4
Rognât Casernes......................16 B4
Sunu Keur...........................(see 25)

SLEEPING 🏠
Auberge l'Harmattan...............17 B4
Hôtel de la Poste.....................18 C4
Hôtel Sindone..........................19 C6
Jamm.......................................20 B3
La Louisiane.............................21 B1
La Maison Rose........................22 C3
La Résidence............................23 C3
L'Atlantide Auberge de
  Jeunesse...............................24 B2
Sunu Keur................................25 B2

EATING 🍴
Aux Délices du Fleuve.............26 C4
Chez Agnes..............................27 B5
Guet N'Dar Market..................28 A4
La Linguère.............................29 C3
La Pirogue...............................30 B3
La Signare...............................31 C3
Layalina...................................32 C3
Le Casino.................................33 C3
Libre-Service...........................34 C4
Pointe Nord.............................35 C1

DRINKING 🍷
Iguane Café.............................36 B4

ENTERTAINMENT 🎭
La Chaumière...........................37 A4
Le Flamingo.............................38 C4
Quai des Arts...........................39 C1

SENEGAL

THE BOU EL MOGDAD – SENEGAL'S CLASSIC CRUISE SHIP

It's hard to estimate how much the presence of the historic cruise liner *Bou El Mogdad* means to the communities living along the Senegal River. But the moved expressions on the faces of those who watched its glorious return in 2005 tell a story of fond reminiscence. Built in the 1950s, the boat chugged regularly up and down the river, connecting villages and facilitating trade. With the construction of the Maka Diama Dam in the mid-'80s it left the northern waters, but it didn't leave the mind of Jean-Jacques Bancal, head of Sahel Découverte Bassari travel agency, who's grown up here as part of Saint-Louis' oldest *métis* families. He decided to bring the vessel back home. In November 2005, the boat returned in its former glory, and for the first time in decades, the classic Pont Faidherbe was creaked open, while onlookers watched with bated breath and sweaty palms, fearing for Saint-Louis' symbolic iron construction.

A trip on this classic ship feels like an adventure straight out of an Agatha Christie novel. The planks creak, the bars are wood panelled, the furniture exudes old-time elegance, and even the clinking of the ice cubes in your rum glass makes you feel like a spy on a mission. But if any of the guests mysteriously disappear, rest assured – they've probably just hopped off at one of the stops. You can join the journey along small northern villages and the historical town of Podor for a weekend or a week, whatever your schedule and budget permit.

See www.saheldecouverte.com and www.compagniedufleuve.com for details on the cruise.

you dig into a fantastic meal with a view over the waves.

Auberge l'Harmattan (☎ 33 961 8253; mimi-saint louis@hotmail.com; Rue Abdoulaye Seck; d/tr CFA15,000/20,000; 🔀) With huge rooms packed with trinkets, paintings of topless beauties and odd bits of old furniture, this looks like the illegal sublet of a naughty grandmother. The glamour piece is the glass-paned top floor, packed with heirlooms and a double bedroom directly behind the private bar.

Sunu Keur (☎ 33 961 8800; www.sunu-keur.com; Quai Giraud; s/d from CFA18,000/23,000; 🔀 💻) Based in a completely rebuilt historical house, this is a place for good food, homely ambience and a magnificent view across town from the terrace.

Hôtel Sindone (☎ 33 961 4245; www.hotelsindone .com; Quai Henri Jay; s/d from CFA30,000/36,000; 🔀) This narrow historical building houses a surprising number of rooms, all decked out in discreet shades and classy fabrics. It's also home to one of the best restaurants in town.

Hôtel de la Poste (☎ 33 961 1118; www.hotel-poste .com; Ave de Gaulle; s/d CFA30,000/36,000; 🔀 💻) The best rooms offered by this grandma of Saint-Louis' hotels are on the 2nd floor, beautiful with its bare-brick arches, tiled floors, white walls and view onto the hotel's centrepiece – the leafy patio.

La Résidence (☎ 33 961 1260; www.hoteldelaresidence .com; Ave Blaise Diagne; s/d/ste CFA30,000/36,000/40,000; 🔀 💻 ♿) This is one of Saint-Louis' most ancient hotels, and the old Saint-Louisian Bancal family that owns it has done a great job of evoking history. Invest in a suite; they've got a lot more space and are quieter. The restaurant is one of the town's very best.

our pick Jamm (Maison Yves Lamour; ☎ 77 443 4765; http://jamm-saintlouis.com; Rue Paul Holle; s/d incl breakfast CFA50,000/55,000; 🔀 💻) One of Saint-Louis' most beautifully restored buildings, this guesthouse has the tallest ceilings in town, beautiful rooms and a sunny terrace. Every tiny detail is renovated with loving care, and there's a good range of excursions on offer.

La Maison Rose (☎ 33 938 2222; www.lamaisonrose .net; Ave Blaise Diagne; s/d from CFA53,000/65,000, ste from CFA91,500) Discreetly glamorous, this old Saint-Louisian villa has stylish suites personalised with antique furniture and contemporary paintings and a *hammam* in the back.

HYDROBASE

These hotels are all located on Hydrobase, 4km from Saint-Louis island on the Langue de Barbarie Peninsula.

Hotel Dior & Camping Océan (☎ 33 961 3118; www.hotel-dior.com; camping CFA3500, s CFA24,100-32,000, d CFA31,200-40,000; 🛜) With Mauritanian tents tucked away behind sand dunes, this overlander favourite feels like a desert home. If you've just crossed the Sahara that may be the last thing you want – in this case, rent a classy bungalow with hot water and minibar.

Résid Hôtel Diamarek (☎ 33 961 5781; www.hotel diamarek.com; d from CFA25,000; 🔀 💻 🖴 🛜) Like a guest house on the beach, this garden-set hotel has a well-stocked library (with wi-fi point) and plenty of personal touches (such as hand-embroidered blankets). The double bungalows are great for families.

Hôtel Cap Saint-Louis (☎ 33 961 3939; www.hotelcap saintlouis.com; s/d CFA28,000/35,000; P ⓧ ▢ ▣) This family-run place has a fantastic sea-view restaurant, vast sand beaches and one of the best swimming pools around. It's also child friendly all the way down to the kids' menu.

Also recommended:

Hôtel Mermoz (☎ 33 961 3668; www.hotel mermoz.com; s/d/tr from CFA15,500/20,950/26,500; P ⓧ ▢ ▣) The largest place on Hydrobase, with a range of activities and an excellent beauty and massage centre.

Oasis Fishing (☎ 33 961 4232; oasisnico@arc.sn; s/d CFA15,000/21,000; ⓧ ▣) The cheapest of the Hydro-base choices is an overlander favourite with simple huts (shared toilets) and large bungalows.

Eating & Drinking

Many of Saint-Louis' hotels double as fantastic restaurants – the kitchens of Hôtel Sindone, La Louisiane and La Résidence are rated among the best places to eat in town.

Self-caterers can shop at Guet N'Dar market and try the **Libre-Service** (Ave Blaise Diagne) for packaged food and good French wine.

BUDGET

Chez Agnes (Complexe Aldiana; ☎ 33 961 4044; Rue Duret; meals around CFA2000) In this pretty, tree-lined patio-restaurant, lovely Agnes serves portions of Senegalese rice and sauce that are so generous the word generosity itself ought to be redefined. The best lunch break in town.

Pointe Nord (☎ 33 961 8716; Ave Jean Mermoz; dishes around CFA3000; ⓨ 11am-4pm & 7pm-midnight Mon-Sat) Nowhere else in Saint-Louis but in this laughter-filled greasy spoon do you get half a juicy chicken of such quality for CFA3000 or grilled fish served Cote d'Ivoire–style with *athieke* and *aloko*.

For simple Senegalese and European meals (around CFA2000), try **La Pirogue** (☎ 77 376 8104; Rue Potin) or **La Linguère** (☎ 33 961 3949; Ave Blaise Diagne). There are quite a few rice-and-sauce places across town that all open for lunch and dinner.

MIDRANGE & TOP END

Aux Délices du Fleuve (☎ 33 961 4251; Quai Bacre Waly Gueye; pastries around CFA500; ⓨ 7.30am-1pm & 3pm-midnight) For a relaxed continental breakfast

or some afternoon espresso-and-cake indulgence, this is the best address. It's also great for pre-nightclub aperitifs.

Layalina (☎ 33 961 8102; Ave Blaise Diagne; meals around CFA4000) A breakfast place in the mornings, Layalina serves fast food during the day and turns into a cosy dinner parlour at night.

Le Casino (La Terrasse; ☎ 33 961 5398; Quai Bacre Waly Gueye; mains around CFA5000; ⓨ 7pm-midnight Wed-Mon) Forget about the poker games – this place serves the best pizzas in town, and also offers gems such as goat's cheese salad with local honey and homemade bread, or artichokes baked in Roquefort.

La Signare (☎ 33 961 1932; www.lasignare.com; Ave Blaise Diagne; mains CFA5000) Management may have changed, but not the list of refined starters (try the hot goat's cheese salad, or squid in garlic butter) and the excellent selection of main courses that made this diner one of Saint-Louis' most popular addresses.

Entertainment

Le Flamingo (☎ 33 961 1118; Quai Bacre Waly Gueye; ⓨ 11am-2am) Any night out here starts safely at this pool-adorned riverside bar. Always packed, it's Saint-Louis' best place for live music.

Iguane Café (☎ 77 633 4956; Rue Abdoulaye Seck) The Cuban-styled Iguane is good for warming up for the clubs.

La Chaumière (☎ 77 495 6086, Pointe à Pitre; admission from CFA2000; ⓨ from 10pm) Smart and glittering, La Chaumière is the best club. Pick the right night: it's a Senegalese soirée on Wednesday and Friday, global beats on weekends.

Le Papayer (☎ 77 566 8382; Carrefour de l'Hydrobase; ⓨ 10am-5am) On Hydrobase, this is the party place of choice.

Quai des Arts (☎ 33 961 5656; Ave Jean Mermoz) The biggest concerts in town (including the main acts of the jazz festival) happen at this vast complex.

Getting There & Away

AIR

Saint-Louis has an airport, but at writing, there were no more regular flights.

TAXI

The *gare routière* sits on the mainland 4.5km from town, south of the Pont Faidherbe.

A taxi from here to the city centre on the island costs CFA500. The fare to or from Dakar is CFA4500 by *sept-place* taxi.

Getting Around
TAXI
Taxi prices in Saint-Louis are fixed (CFA500 at the time of writing). Prices to any destination in the surrounding regions depend on your negotiating skills.

AROUND SAINT-LOUIS
Gandiol & Mouit
Gandiol is a small village on the mainland, about 17km south of Saint-Louis. From the lighthouse north of the village, pirogues cross the estuary to the two *campements* on the southern end of the Langue de Barbarie.

About 2km south of Gandiol is Mouit, where you'll find the national park office and, on the edge of the river, the brilliant **Zebrabar** (☎ 77 638 1862, 33 962 0019; www.zebrabar .net; Mouit; camping per person CFA2500, s CFA4000-20,000, d CFA7000-25,000). This spacious *campement* is a longstanding favourite with overlanders (perfect for trading travel stories), as well as families. Accommodation ranges from very simple to royal comfort, and it's a great place for kayaking, pirogue tours or bird watching. Close by, the family-run **Auberge Teranga** (☎ 33 962 5853; www.gandiole-teranga.com; Gandiol; r CFA17,000; 🖭) is a homely place between lagoon and lush garden. The coco-punch here is delicious and the massages come with river view.

Hiring a taxi from Saint-Louis to Mouit and Zebrabar should cost you around CFA5000. The hotel owners can arrange pick-up if you call them from Saint-Louis.

Parc National de la Langue de Barbarie
This stunning **park** (admission CFA2000, pirogue for 1 or 2 people CFA9000, extra person CFA2500; 🕑 7am-7pm) includes the far southern tip of the Langue de Barbarie Peninsula, the estuary of the Senegal River and a section of the mainland on the other side of the estuary. Its 2000 hectares are home to numerous birds – notably flamingos, pelicans, cormorants, herons, egrets and ducks. From November to April these numbers are swelled by the arrival of migrants from Europe.

The park is best explored by pirogue, which can cruise slowly past the mud flats, inlets and islands where the birds feed and roost.

If you come to the park independently, go first to the park office at Mouit to pay

your entrance fee. Pirogues can be hired at Gandiol lighthouse.

SLEEPING
In a paradise spot, you'll find two *campements*. Even if you don't stay, a day out here is easily the most relaxing thing you'll do from Saint-Louis.

Campement Océan et Savane (☎ 77 637 4790; www .oceanetsavane.com; tent per person CFA10,000, bungalows from CFA30,000) This relaxed *campement* is run by La Résidence in Saint-Louis (see p710). You can stay in low-roofed Mauritanian tents or choose the comfort of a log cabin right on the river featuring the attraction of a river-view bathtub.

El Faro (☎ 33 961 1118; per person CFA15,000) Just under new management when we passed, and still closed, El Faro looked promising, with pretty yellow bungalows surrounded by greenery. Contact the Hôtel de la Poste for the latest information.

GETTING THERE & AWAY
Make a booking with the hotels running the *campements*, or take a taxi to Gandiol lighthouse (around CFA4000), from where you can cross with the free pirogue at noon, 4pm and 5pm, or phone **Jules** (☎ 77 656 4633) to book his boat outside those hours for CFA2500.

Parc National des Oiseaux du Djoudj
This 16,000-hectare **park** (☎ 33 968 8708; admission CFA2000, pirogue CFA3500, car CFA5000; 🕑 7am-dusk Nov-Apr) 60km north of Saint-Louis is one of the best places on earth to view migratory birds from Europe. It is a bird sanctuary of global significance: its myriad channels, creeks, lakes and mud flats are a recognised Ramsar site (wetland of global significance) and it appears on the World Heritage list.

Even if you're not a keen ornithologist, it's hard to escape the impact of seeing vast colonies of pelicans and flamingos in such stunning surroundings. Experienced bird-watchers will recognise many of the European species, impressive by their sheer numbers. Around three million birds pass through the park annually, and more than 350 species have been recorded.

There are also a few mammals and reptiles in the park, most notably populations of warthogs and mongooses, snakes and crocodiles. Other mammals include jackals, hyenas, monkeys and gazelles.

Trips around the park are usually done by pirogue. The best time for bird-watching is from December to January, when the migrants have arrived.

SLEEPING

Hôtel du Djoudj (☎ 33 963 8702; www.hotel-djoudj.com; r 27,000; ⌚ accommodation 1 Nov-31 May; ⚑) The main hotel on site is near the park headquarters. Naturally, it arranges pirogue rides around the park, and also hires out bicycles (CFA3000/6000 per half/full day).

Station Biologique (☎ Ibrahima Camara 77 524 0105, Ibrahima Diop 77 656 7038; full board per person CFA16,000) At the park headquarters, this station is really intended for researchers but sometimes puts up budget travellers if there's room. You can camp here.

GETTING THERE & AWAY

There's no public transport to Djoudj, so you have to negotiate a hire taxi (around CFA25,000) or join an organised tour, which might work out cheaper. If you're driving from Saint-Louis, take the paved highway towards Rosso for about 25km. Near Ross-Béthio you'll see a sign pointing to the park, from where it's another 25km along a dirt road. You can also book a night on the *Bou El Mogdad* (see p738), which puts in a stop here.

SENEGAL RIVER ROUTE

From Saint-Louis, the route along the valley of the Senegal River traces the French conquest of the interior, as well as the signs of its opposition. Along the river, which marks Senegal's northern and eastern borders, you'll find a string of mid-19th-century forts, two of which (Dagana and Podor) have now been restored – the Podor site is particularly beautiful. The French fortifications were military and administrative centres and battle stations in the enduring clashes with the army of El Hadj Omar Tall, who put up fierce resistance to the colonial efforts.

The historical leader had plenty to defend – at its height his expansive Islamic empire reached all across West Africa to Timbuktu (in today's Mali). Tucked away on the Île à Morphil are some of the 18th-century mosques Omar Tall used to pray in.

Rosso-Senegal

The fly-blown frontier town of Rosso-Senegal, around 100km northeast of Saint-Louis, is the main ferry crossing point between Senegal and Mauritania. The boat service is also about the only reason you might want to visit this hustler-ridden town.

If you get stuck, there's a small hostel that also prepares meals. The journey from Rosso-Senegal to Dakar costs CFA5500 by *sept-place* taxi; to Saint-Louis the fare is CFA2000. For information on crossing the border, see p737.

Richard Toll

Richard Toll was once a colonial administrative centre and home to a French agricultural experiment that tested the tropical adaptability of European plants (hence the name Richard Toll, meaning 'Richard's Garden').

CBAO (☎ 963 32 89; Rte de Matam) and **BICIS** (☎ 963 3499; Rte de Matam) have ATM-equipped branches here, and there are a couple of internet cafes.

The town is now the centre of Senegal's sugar industry. Take a stroll (or, better, a horse-cart ride) to the crumbling colonial villa **Château de Baron Roger**, and find out how Senegal's only local dairy gets this fabulous yogurt into the packs on a visit to the **Laiterie de Berger** – the boulangerie in the market sells its excellent products.

The best place to stay is the river-bound **Gîte d'Étape** (☎ /fax 33 963 3240; s/d CFA29,400/32,800; ⚑ ⚑), with clean rooms and a pontoon that's made for sundowners. Cheaper food options include the Auberge de la Cité on the main road and a few roadside cafes near the petrol stations.

A direct *sept-place* from Dakar to Richard Toll costs CFA7500.

Podor & Île à Morphil

The ancient town of Podor has been a busy trading centre since the first encounters between the Arabs and the Tukulor of Fouta Toro. It's home to an ancient fort, first built in 1744, then reconstructed by Faidherbe in 1854, and now beautifully restored. Renovation has also touched the large colonial warehouses along Podor's famous quay, rendering this slow-moving, historical town more attractive than ever.

Podor is the gateway to excursions along the **Île à Morphil**, which stretches for 100km between the Senegal River and a parallel channel. Rugged landscape, scenic Tukulor villages and the historical Omarian mosques of Guédé and Alwar, beautiful examples of the Sudanese architectural style, make this a great off-the-beaten-track diversion. Nearby is Wouro Madiyou, home to the unique, mosaic-ornamented mausoleum of Cheikh Ahmadou Madiyou.

Maison Guillaume Foy (☎ 33 965 1682; r incl breakfast CFA15,000; 🔀 🖳), the first house on the quay, has been carefullly restored. You could watch the river forever from your window or the lovely terrace, unless you're too busy finding out about the restoration work, community investment and excursions at the office of **Daande Mayo** (☎ 77 526 5200) downstairs. There are only three rooms. If you find it full, try the **Catholic Mission** (☎ 33 965 1125; Ave El Hajj Oumar Tall; r CFA5000) next door, where the chatty Père Mohiss will be glad to receive you. In the nearby Quartier Thioffy, the **Centre de Formation** (☎ 33 965 1222; d/tr CFA10,000/15,000; 🔀) has a few clean, well-maintained rooms where you'll be looked after by hospitality students from the college.

Sept-place taxis travel fairly regularly between Podor and Saint-Louis (CFA4500, four hours, 262km) sometimes continuing all the way to Dakar (CFA9000). Coming from Saint-Louis, you will have to get off at Taredji and jump on a minibus to Podor from there (CFA500). Hiring a taxi from Saint-Louis to Podor costs around CFA50,000.

Matam & Ouro Sogui

Once a proud administrative centre, Matam, 230km southeast of Podor, has over the years lost in status to its neighbour Ouro Sogui, which is now a busy trading centre and transport hub for the Ferlo plains. Apart from the remains of Matam's old warehouses and the beautiful river, there isn't much to see here, though the tranquil village is worth taking in, and intrepid travellers can explore the hinterland. Ouro Sogui is the kind of place you need to fill the tank, get cash from the ATM (if it's working) and maybe spend a night. The town's two hotels face one

another. **Oasis du Fouta** (☎ 33 966 1294; s/d incl breakfast CFA15,000/17,000; 🔀) has decent rooms around a small courtyard and a lively bar. **Hôtel Sôgui** (☎ 33 966 1536; s/d CFA18,500/23,000; 🔀) is the larger, with similar rooms but less atmosphere.

Battered *sept-place* taxis run to Dakar (CFA10,500, 10 hours, 690km) and Bakel (CFA2000, two hours, 148km).

Bakel & Kidira

A backdrop of gentle hills and the fascinating, crumpled earth mounds of the Falémé tributary lend Bakel a unique charm. In town, an 1854 **fort**, another ambitious Faidherbe endeavour and now site of the Governance, and the **Pavilion René Caillé**, once a temporary home to the famous French voyager, point to the past, when this remote town was right on the explorer route.

To spend the night, travel 60km south to Kidira, where you'll find **Etoile de Boundou** (☎ 33 983 1248; r with/without air-con CFA18,600/15,000; 🔀) at the entrance to town. Spotless rooms and smiles all round make it the best hotel for miles.

If you're headed for Mali, a fast way of getting your passport stamped is to hire a taxi for a quick round trip (CFA2000) to the Senegalese and Malian border posts and finally to the long-distance bus to Bamako. See also p737.

There are daily bush taxis from Bakel to Kidira (CFA2000).

EASTERN SENEGAL

It takes some courage to brave the distance from Dakar to the east, but the rewards are sweet. The remote Bassari lands, with their tucked-away waterfalls, green hillsides and unique culture are a strikingly beautiful hiking area, and you get to visit Senegal's main wild-

---

PODOR RIVE GAUCHE

Only a few years ago, Podor used to be far off the tourist trail, a small northern town only of interest to intrepid travellers and fans of dry Sahel landscapes. Today, the place is climbing out of its forgotten corner – and it's doing so with style. The restoration of the old fort was a first crucial step, and the efforts of the association **Podor Rive Gauche** (☎ 33 965 1682; maison-guillaumefoy@podor-rivegauche.com; Maison Guillaume Foy, Podor) are building interest in the town in the most beautiful way. The most visible aspect of its work is the renovated waterfront on Podor's historical quay. Other projects include cultural exchanges, the promotion of local creative talent and the publication of historical and artistic materials. Visit it at the Maison Guillaume Foy to find out more.

life reserve, the gigantic Parc National du Niokolo-Koba, on the way.

TAMBACOUNDA

Tambacounda is all about dust, sand and sizzling temperatures. This junction town is a tough gateway to Bassari country, but it reveals its charming soul on an early-evening stroll when the traffic fumes subside, the dust settles, and the roadsides turn into improvised cinemas, as people carry their TV sets into the road to watch the latest series together.

Information

Tambacounda has a small hospital, pharmacies and a health centre. There's wi-fi access in the better hotels. Ask your hotel reception about 4WD hire to Niokolo-Koba (CFA80,000 to CFA100,000).

Agence de Voyage (☎ 33 981 0084; Quartier Abattoir) Arranges tours.

CBAO (☎ 33 939 9900; Blvd Demba Diop) Unreliable ATM.

Cyber Misat (☎ 33 981 5444; Ave Léopold Senghor; per hr CFA250; ☼ 8am-9pm) Internet access.

Hôtel Niji (☎ 33 981 1250; nijihotel@orange.sn) Has a Syndicat d'Initiative tourist-information representative.

National Park Office (☎ 33 981 1097; ☼ 7.30am-5pm) Can help with enquiries about Niokolo-Koba.

SGBS (☎ 33 981 1530; Ave Léopold Senghor) Has an unreliable ATM.

Sleeping

Bloc Gadec (☎ 77 531 8931; dm CFA3000; r CFA8000) Rooms here are bare apart from a bed and a fan but are very clean, and that includes the shared bathrooms.

Hôtel Niji (☎ 33 981 1250; www.hotelniji.com; s/d CFA18,500/22,000; P ✷ ▯ ▣) has everything from very simple bungalows to lush (but soulless) quarters.

Le Relais de Tamba (☎ 33 981 1000; www.horizons-bleus-senegal.com; Rte National; s/d/tr incl breakfast CFA25,000/30,000/37,000; P ✷ ▯ ▣ ☎) This pretty place is one of the two top picks in town. Relaxing gardens, good service.

Oasis Oriental Club (☎ 33 981 1824; www.oasisoriental .com; Rte de Kaolack; s/d incl breakfast CFA27,500/34,500; P ✷ ▯ ▣) The other prime choice, the Oasis is near Le Relais at the entry to town, with similar setting, service and facilities.

Eating & Drinking

There are a few simple eateries. Self-caterers can get fresh food at the market and packaged stuff at **Azur Commercial** (☼ 9am-1am), opposite

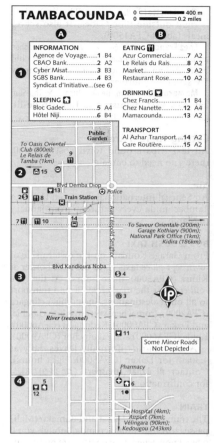

Relais du Rais, where you'll find a bakery next door.

Being a truck stop, Tamba also abounds with small drinking holes that can get pretty sleazy.

Restaurant Rose (☎ 77 554 6542; dishes from CFA1000; ☼ noon-2.30pm & 6-11pm) Here you'll be treated to Ada's engaging company as well as her decent steak.

Le Relais du Rais (☎ 77 552 7096; dishes from CFA2000; ☼ noon-2.30pm & 6-11pm) Next door to Rose, Le Relais du Rais serves solid portions of rice and sauce.

Saveur Orientale (☎ 77 322 5619; Garage Kothiary; meals CFA2500; ☼ 11am-1am) This neon-lit place further from the centre does good pizzas and snacks.

SENEGAL

Chez Nanette (☺ 8am-midnight) This lively place is right outside Bloc Gadec. It also serves meals (about CFA1500).

Chez Francis (☎ 77 643 1231; Ave Léopold Senghor; snacks CFA2000; ☺ 11am-2am) Chez Francis has cold beers and an ambience defined by the noisy TV set in the courtyard.

Mamacounda (Blvd Demba Diop; ☺ Thu-Sun) Tamba's best nightspot is this strobe-lit, glitterball-adorned place.

Getting There & Around

All taxi trips around town cost CFA500; there's no need to bargain.

AIR

Air Sénégal International flies from Dakar to Tambacounda every Saturday from January to March.

BUS & BUSH TAXI

From Garage Kothiary on the eastern side of town *sept-place* taxis go to the Mali border at Kidira (CFA5000, three hours). At the *gare routière* near the market you'll find transport to all other destinations, including Vélingara (CFA2000), from where you cross into Gambia, and Dakar (CFA9000), Kedougou (CFA6000), Kolda (CFA6000) and Ziguinchor (CFA9000).

A *car mouride* normally leaves daily at 4.30am for Dakar (CFA5000, eight hours). Contact **Al Azhar Transport** (☎ 33 937 8125) for confirmation.

TRAIN

The train between Dakar and Bamako (Mali) passes through Tambacounda, though you'll never know when, as schedules are pretty random (see p737).

WASSADOU & MAKO

About 50km south of Tambacounda, **Campement de Wassadou** (☎ 33 982 3602; wassadou@niokolo.com; s/d CFA17,000/24,200) tempts with well-equipped thatched huts and fabulous river views. Overlanders and families come here to go on bivouac, campfire and hippo-viewing boat trips through Niokolo-Koba.

Mako lies another 150km further south, at the entry to the Pays Bassari. **Keur Annick** (☎ 77 405 1941; half board CFA12,500) overlooks the tranquil flow of the Gambia River from its vast terrain. There are plenty of tours on offer, and profits support the adjacent village.

PARC NATIONAL DU NIOKOLO-KOBA

The World Heritage site of Niokolo-Koba, a vast biosphere reserve spanning about 9000 sq km, is Senegal's major national park. The landscape is relatively flat, with savannah woodland, plains, marshes and a few hills – the highest being Mt Assirik (311m) in the southeast.

The Gambia River and its two tributaries, the Niokolo-Koba and the Koulountou, cross the vast wilderness and are crucial sources of water for the 80 species of mammals and 350 bird species that inhabit the park. On a tour through its vast woodlands, you may however be forgiven for thinking that there's little but wild boar, a few antelopes and baboons. Sadly, many species have today been hunted down and the few remaining lions are very rarely spotted. You can have a great day out here – just don't expect anything like the wildlife parks in east or southern Africa.

The most stunning spots in the park are the banks of the Gambia River, from where you often see hippos and Nile, slender-snouted and dwarf crocodiles. Commonly viewed animals include waterbucks, bushbucks, kobs, duikers, roan antelopes, giant derby elands, hartebeests, baboons, monkeys (green and patas) and warthogs. Chimpanzee troops inhabit parts of the eastern areas, though they're as rarely seen as the few leopards that still exist here.

The best part for animal spotting is Simenti, with its hide overlooking a waterhole where animals regularly come to drink, and a lovely river bend that's great for crocodile sightings. A boat tour on the Gambia River (CFA6500) is highly recommended – far more exciting than hours of driving around the park's dry woods.

Your guide will be able to point out other drinking holes, as well as the picture-perfect rope bridge.

Information

The park is officially open from 15 December to 30 April, though you can visit any time. You enter the park at Dar Salam, where you find a *campement* and hire your obligatory guide. An hour's drive further on is Simenti, the park's main focus, where many animals are concentrated. There's also a park office, a visitor information centre and the large Hôtel de Simenti.

You must have a vehicle to enter the park. Walking is only allowed near accommodation sites or in the company of a park ranger. If you don't have a car, you're

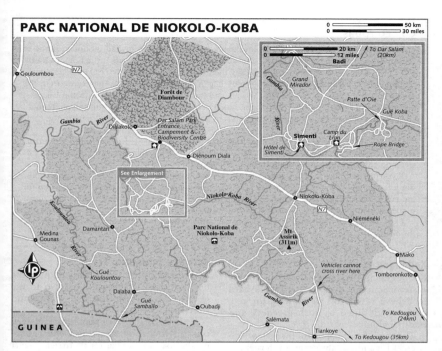

PARC NATIONAL DE NIOKOLO-KOBA

best off hiring a 4WD for a day trip in Tambacounda (CFA80,000 to CFA100,000 including fuel, driver and admission for the car). Ask at your hotel or the **National Park Office** (☎ 33 981 2454; ⌚ 7.30am-5pm).

All other options, such as getting to the park by public transport or hiring a taxi end up costing about the same. In Tambacounda you'll usually meet other park-bound travellers, and there are often opportunities to hitch or share a car.

The entrance fee (adults/children under 10 CFA2000/free, vehicles CFA5000) gives you access for 24 hours. It's obligatory to hire a guide (CFA8000 per day), even if you've got one already.

Pirogue tours along the river (per person CFA6500) are a great thing to do. They can be arranged from Simenti.

Sleeping & Eating

Camp du Lion (☎ 33 981 2454; park headquarters; camping CFA4000, s/d CFA8000/12,000) The Camp du Lion has flimsy huts but the attraction of hippo spotting nearby.

Dar Salam Campement (☎ 33 984 4275; Dar Salam; camping per tent CFA5000, s/d/tr CFA5000/8000/9500) At the park entrance, the *campement* has clean bungalows and a simple restaurant, great for a post-park beer.

Hôtel de Simenti (☎ 33 982 3650; Simenti; s/d CFA15,000/25,000; P ✖ ▣) Sitting in the heart of the park on a prime spot above the river, the Simenti has rooms that are far less spectacular than its location, next to a waterhole that attracts many animals.

BASSARI COUNTRY

Bassari Country, characterised by the unique and reclusive culture of its inhabitants, is the only mountainous region of Senegal and a fabulous area for hiking through green hillsides and tiny, traditional villages. It's advisable to walk with an experienced guide who knows the area and local people well.

Exploitation of the region's iron and gold mines is becoming increasingly important, causing social and economic shifts in the area.

SENEGAL

GUIDED TOURS

The company of a clued-up guide is invaluable for exploring the myriad mountain paths of Bassari Country. The best place to find a reliable and knowledgeable guide is the hotel **Le Bédik** (☎ 33 985 1000). Two recommended guides there are **Alpha Diallo** (☎ 77 652 6450; alphaguia.blogspot.com) and **Doba Diallo** (☎ 77 360 6401; http://dobadiallo.mi-website.es). They come from the area, know the best routes through the hills and have a good relationship with the villagers, which will make you, the visiting stranger, much more welcome. It remains up to you, though, to show the proper respect and perhaps present kola nuts, money and small gifts to the *chefs de village* (village chiefs).

Guides can arrange anything from leisurely day trips to strenuous hikes of up to eight days through the forests, mountains and tiny Bédik, Bassari and Fula villages, with the possibility of sleeping either in the homes of locals or in *campements*.

If you're after more far-flung destinations, take the guides up on their offer to cross the border into Guinea. You need a valid visa before setting out and a 4WD (hire can be arranged for around CFA100,000 per day including petrol and driver). The rocky trip via Fongolimbi (220km) is spectacular, passing through almost-mountainous terrain and thick forest.

Both guides charge CFA10,000 per day to accompany you on 4WD tours, CFA15,000 per day for hikes.

Kedougou

Kedougou is the largest town in southeastern Senegal, though this seems hard to believe when you walk along the red, dusty roads lined by lush greenery and traditional huts.

The town has a colourful market, which is great for indigo fabrics, and internet access can be had from the sluggish computers of **Netekoto Cyber** (☎ 33 985 1512; Daande Maayo Kedougou; per hr CFA300) or by wi-fi from Le Bédik and Relais de Kedougou. There's a large health centre.

SLEEPING

Le Nieriko (☎ 33 985 1459; Togoro; r CFA8000; 🞨) At the end of the dusty road to the neighbourhood Togoro, this small *campement* is managed with a smile but also a minimum of energy expenditure – rooms are slightly dark and dusty.

Le Soninke (☎ 33 985 1107; Daande Maayo, Kedougou; s/d incl breakfast CFA16,000/24,000; 🞨 🞩) Location (on the river) and rooms (with hot water) are better here, but the vibes aren't as good.

Relais de Kedougou (☎ 33 985 1062; lerelais@orange.sn; s/d from CFA17,000/21,000; 🅟 🞨 🖥 🞩 🛜) This more upmarket choice caters mainly to hunters.

our pick **Le Bédik** (☎ 33 985 1000; s/d incl breakfast 25,000/30,000; 🅟 🞨 🖥 🞩 🛜) By far the best option, Le Bédik is pricier, but the great location on the river, the friendly staff and the impeccable rooms are all worth it.

EATING & DRINKING

Le Bédik and Relais de Kedougou have the best kitchens. Otherwise it's down to the cheap eateries near the market (around CFA1500).

Mussolia (☎ 77 355 6500; mussolia@yahoo.fr) Seek out this tiny shop, near the Gendarmerie on the road to Tamba, for its frozen yogurt (CFA150 to CFA300).

Black & White (town centre; meals CFA2000-3500; ☽ 8pm-2am) Try this place for dinner and a dance.

GETTING THERE & AWAY

There's plenty of traffic between Tambacounda and Kedougou (*sept-place* CFA6000, four hours). At the time of writing, work had been started on the road connecting Saraya in Senegal to Kita in Mali. Supposedly to be finished in late 2009, this will open a brilliant new route to connect the two countries. Friday is the best day to find a public pickup or 4WDs to Labé in Guinea (CFA20,000, two days) – the ride along the treacherous dirt roads is extremely rough.

GETTING AROUND

Try your hotel for car hire, or Doba and Alpha, the guides at Le Bédik. You'll pay around CFA55,000 per day for a 4WD (fuel not included), CFA15,000 a day for a motorbike (not including fuel) and CFA5000 for a good mountain bike.

Around Kedougou

The best way of exploring Kedougou's stunning surroundings is a combination of driving (in a 4WD) and hiking – best under the care of a good guide; see the boxed text, opposite.

THE KEDOUGOU–SALÉMATA ROUTE

One of the nearest villages is **Bandafassi** (15km from Kedougou), where you'll find the wonderfully welcoming campement **Chez Léontine** (☎ 77 554 9915; d CFA7500), with solar-powered lights and delicious meals prepared by the charming owner. It's a great base for hikes up the hill to the Bédik village of **Ethiowar**, from where there are fabulous views over the surrounding savannah.

Ibel, a Fula village, lies another 7km up the road from Bandafassi. Visits here are usually combined with a steep hike up to **Iwol**, a pretty village stretched out between a giant *fromager* (kapok tree) and a sacred baobab. The teacher can tell you about the village's history (CFA1000), and the local women make beautiful pottery statues (CFA300 per piece).

The regional hub of **Salémata**, 83km west of Kedougou, is still rarely visited. You can stay at the friendly campement **Chez Gilbert** (☎ 77 107 4584; r CFA6000). Gilbert can arrange the famous masked dances of the Bassari, modelled on the annual initiation ceremonies (April and May). Content yourself with the 'tourist version' – or if you're there for the 'real thing', keep a respectful distance and don't start snapping away. The 15km trip to **Ethiolo** leads through mainly thick forest and bush grass, and there's a good chance of spotting chimpanzees in the trees (some of the few wild chimps left in Senegal). **Chez Balingo** (☎ 33 835 1570; r CFA7000) has accommodation in traditional Bassari stone huts, and is run by the enthusiastic and knowledgeable Balingo, who can feed you morsels of local lore while taking you on exciting tours of Ethiolo's surroundings.

Getting There & Away

Public transport along this route is sporadic, and the road is rough. A 4WD is recommended. You can also jump on the Nenefecha minibus, which takes patients and visitors to Nenefecha hospital. It leaves Kedougou Monday to Friday at 9am and 3pm, returning from Nenefecha at 1pm and 7pm. Tuesday is market day in Salémata, so chances for transport are better.

DINDEFELO & SEGOU

One of the most popular destinations from Kedougou is Dindéfelo, famous for its impressive 100m **waterfall**, with a deep, green pool suitable for swimming. You start the 2km hike there from the **Campement Villageois** (☎ 77 354 8911; per person CFA2500), where you'll also pay your CFA1000 waterfall admission. Accommodation and ambience are nicer at the adjacent **Dogon du Fouta** (☎ 77 552 3831; moktardiallo@hotmail.com; per person stone/stilted huts CFA2500/7000); the thatched huts on stilts are a quirky touch. If you love steep climbs, hike up to **Dande**, where you can stand scarily close to the edge of the waterfall (don't go here without a guide – the deep drop is hidden by some innocent-looking shrubs). Your guide can also point out other sights, including a large cave, and point you to the basic campement **Chez Doba** (☎ 77 360 6401; http://auberge chezdoba.blogspot.com; per person CFA2500).

Much less visited are the falls of **Segou**, a 7km hike from Segou village through stunning woodlands and rarely visited hills. There's a small **campement** (r per person CFA3000).

If you rely on public transport, go to Dindefelo and Segou on Sunday, market day. The minibus costs CFA1000 and takes at least two hours. Again, the road is so bad that a hired 4WD is recommended.

CASAMANCE

With its lush tropical landscapes, watered by the graceful wind of the Casamance River, and the unique culture of the Diola, this area seems far from Dakar and its surroundings, in every sense. That's what many locals feel as well, so strongly that separatist rebellions have troubled the region for years. Things have largely calmed down, but the rebellions have left a destabilising legacy of banditism.

Forget the region's worries for a few seconds – there isn't a more fascinating area in the whole country. On one end there's Ziguinchor, an atmospheric regional capital, where fading colonial houses line majestic, tree-shaded avenues. On the other is Cap Skiring, which greets the Atlantic with some of West Africa's finest beaches. And along the Casamance River that connects the two, tiny community *campements* nestle

SENEGAL

CASAMANCE

0 — 10 km
0 — 6 miles

THE GAMBIA

To Serekunda (30km);
Banjul (45km)

Darsilami

Séléti

Néma

Kartong

Niafourang

Diouloulou

Kabadio

Bankikaki

Marigot de Baïla

Sindian

Kagnarou

ATLANTIC OCEAN

Abéné

Diannah

N5

Baïla

Kafountine

Sanctuaire
Ornithologique
de Kassel

Tiobon

Kagnobon

Diégoune

Tendième

Bignona

N4

Casamance Nord

To Dakar (425km)

Presqu'île
des Oiseaux

Tionk-Essil

Sanctuaire
Ornithologique de la
Pointe de Kalissaye

Kalissaye

Marigot

Dioulou

de

Tendouk

N4

Mangagoulak

Marigot

Koubalan

Tobor

Niomoune

Pointe St
George

Affiniam

Barrage

Djilapao

Île des
Oiseaux

To Dakar
(500km)

Diogué

Casamance River

Manatee
Sanctuary

Bandial

Ziguinchor

N6

Karabane

M'Lomp

Etama

Brin

To Sédhiou;
Kolda (188km)

Nikine

Île de
Karabane

Kagnout

Séleki

Essil

N4

Cachouane

Elinkine

Loudia
Ouolof

Enampor

Kamoubeul

Toubacouta

Diembéring

Oussouye

Edioungou

Oukout

Diohère

Nyassia

Mpak

Diakène
Ouolof

Niambalang

Boucotte

Diakène
Diola

Basse Casamance

Kaguite

São Domingos

Cap Skiring

Parc National
de Basse-
Casamance
(Closed)

Santiaba
Mandjak

Youtou

To Ingore (40km);
Bissau (120km);
Diaoubé (226km)

Kabrousse

GUINEA-BISSAU

SENEGAL

Campements Villageois
4WD Only

between its mangrove-lined creeks and lagoons and on tucked-away islands, offering plenty of choice for those seeking out routes of responsible travel.

History

The Diola people of Casamance have a long history of resisting the rule of outsiders. It's a sentiment that underlined their outright rejection of slavery, their refusal to accept France's colonial administration and enduring secessionist wars.

In the 19th and early 20th centuries, the French colonial authorities controlled their colonies through local chiefs, and frequently installed leaders from other ethnic groups to administer Diola territories. This increased the resentment that colonisation itself had provoked. Diola resistance against foreign interference remained strong into the 1930s.

The last Diola rebellion against the French was led in 1943 by a traditional priestess from Kabrousse called Aline Sitoé Diatta. The rebellion was stopped and Aline Sitoé was imprisoned in Timbuktu (Mali), where she eventually died.

The conflicts that have plagued the region for the last 20 years originated from a pro-independence demonstration held in Ziguinchor in 1982, after which the leaders of the Mouvement des Forces Démocratiques de la Casamance (MFDC) were arrested and jailed. As the government clamped down on separatist sentiments with increasing severity, the north-south divide only increased, and the secessionist movement gained in strength.

Throughout the '90s, periods of civil war alternated with fragile ceasefire agreements, causing destruction and a rising death toll among the civilian communities. When the disappearance of four French tourists in 1995 was blamed on the MFDC, its leader, Father Diamacoune Senghor, accused the army of trying to turn international opinion against the rebels. Peace talks continued but, following the government's refusal to consider independence for Casamance, a group of hardliners broke away from the MFDC and resumed fighting.

Against a background of ongoing clashes causing the death of over 500 people in the late 1990s, Father Diamacoune urged his supporters to continue to pursue reconciliation with the government. Several peace deals were made and broken until the final one in 2004 was largely adhered to. Still, up to this day, violence erupts occasionally (see the boxed text, below).

ZIGUINCHOR
pop 217,000

Depending on your state of mind, Ziguinchor can either be a slowly swinging, charming town, or a gradually crumbling provincial capital. True, the roads are increasingly dented by potholes, and most buildings haven't seen a lick of paint in years. But huge mango trees, old colonial houses and a decidedly friendly

---

TO GO OR NOT TO GO?

It's the nature of the news that you hear more about killing than about living, and in the case of the Casamance good news is rarely broadcast. You hear about separatist struggles and armed bandits, road blocks and gunfire. And yet the stories told by local residents differ widely. Following the years of conflict, people are once again opening small businesses and planning for the future – stuff that's based on hope that things are going to get better.

A strong feeling of independence certainly reigns in this region, but the fact is that the street robberies and road blocks that still occur occasionally are often the work of common criminals – rather than rebels with a goal – who profit from the availability of guns in the area.

You're probably not going to encounter any major problems on your journey – on the whole, the Casamance is far more peaceful than, let's say, London or Lagos. Still, be vigilant on your trip. Don't travel the roads after dark – if there's going to be trouble, that's when it'll occur. And don't venture out on your own in areas you're not familiar with. People here are incredibly helpful, and they love showing strangers their beautiful region – take them up on their offers. The Casamance used to be one of Senegal's major tourist destinations, and for most people the suffering is greater for the lack of tourists and their dollars than for any direct confrontation with separatist fighters.

The only real permanent no-go zone is the Parc National de Basse-Casamance, which has been closed for years because of suspected landmines.

vibe provide real atmosphere worth exploring for a couple of days.

Information

BOOKSHOPS

The **bookshop** (9am-noon & 2.30-6pm) on the northern end of Rue Javelier has a good selection of titles on Senegal and the Casamance (mostly in French).

CULTURAL CENTRES

Alliance Franco-Sénégalaise (☎ 33 991 2823; Ave Lycée Guignabo; 9.15am-noon & 3-7.15pm Mon-Sat) Giant, beautifully decorated *case à impluvium* with a large concert hall and a cafe. There's a visiting fee of CFA1000.

INTERNET ACCESS

Most hotels have free wi-fi and there's a speedy internet cafe at the Alliance Franco-Sénégalaise.

Sud-Informatique (☎ 33 991 1573; www.sudinfo.sn; Rue Javelier; per hr CFA1000; 9am-midnight)

MEDICAL SERVICES

Véronique Chiche at Le Flamboyant hotel can recommend reliable doctors in town.

Hospital (☎ 33 991 1154) Has an emergency department but is not well equipped.

MONEY

The following banks change money and have ATMs taking Visa and MasterCard.

ZIGUINCHOR

0   500 m
0   0.3 miles

Some Minor Roads Not Depicted

INFORMATION
Alliance Franco-Sénégalaise ....(see 10)	
Bookshop....................................**1** C1	
Casamance Voyages Tourisme....**2** C1	
CBAO Bank.................................**3** C1	
Conseil Régional.....................(see 11)	
Diambone Voyages....................**4** C1	
Diatta Tour International..........**5** C1	
French Consul.........................(see 18)	
Guinea-Bissau Consul............(see 21)	
Main Post Office.......................**6** B1	
SGBS Bank................................**7** C1	
Sud-Informatique....................**8** C1	

SIGHTS & ACTIVITIES
Africa Batik..............................**9** C2	
Alliance Franco-Sénégalaise...**10** B4	
Conseil Régional....................**11** C1	
Diatta Tour International ....(see 5)	
Marché Artisanal....................**12** B3	
Marché St-Maur......................**13** B3	
Mission..................................(see 21)	
Pirogue Jetty...........................**14** B1	
Post Office...............................(see 6)	

SLEEPING
Auberge Casafrique.................**15** C2	
Hôtel Aubert...........................**16** B1	
Hôtel Kadiandoumagne...........**17** B1	
Le Flamboyant........................**18** C1	
Le Nema Kadior......................**19** B4	
Le Perroquet..........................**20** B1	

EATING
Hôtel Tourisme........................**21** C1	
L'Abondance...........................**22** B1	
Le Erobon...............................**23** B1	
Le Kassa.................................**24** C1	
Le Tamarinier.........................**25** C2	
Marché Escale.........................**26** C1	
Pâtisserie...............................**27** C1	
Superette...............................**28** C1	
Walkunda Bar.........................**29** C1	

ENTERTAINMENT
Le Bombolong.........................**30** C1	
Le Rubis.................................**31** C1	

SHOPPING
Massoumé...............................**32** C1	

TRANSPORT
Cosama Ticket Office................**33** C1	
Gare Routière.........................**34** D2	
Taxi Rank...............................**35** C1	

SENEGAL

CBAO (Rue de France; ☿ 7.45am-noon & 1.15-2.30pm Mon-Thu, 7.45am-1pm & 2.45-3.45pm Fri)
SGBS (Rue du Général de Gaulle; ☿ 7.45am-noon & 1.15-2.30pm Mon-Thu, 7.45am-1pm & 2.45-3.45pm Fri)

POST
Main post office (Rue du Général de Gaulle)

TOURIST INFORMATION
Check whether the planned information centre on touring the *campements villageois* has opened at the **Conseil Régional** (Rue Javelier).

TRAVEL AGENCIES
Casamance Voyages Tourisme (☎ 33 991 4362; cvtzig@orange.sn; Rue Javelier) Ticketing, tours and car hire.
Diambone Voyages (☎ 77 641 5132; www.diambone voyages.com; Rue de France) Flight bookings, tours, car hire and more.
Diatta Tour International (☎ 33 991 2781; aessibye@yahoo.fr; Rue du Général de Gaulle) Tours and hotel reservations. Also has a subsidiary branch in Cap Skiring.

Sights & Activities
Ziguinchor has some colourful historical buildings, including the central **post office**, the office of **Diatta Tour International** and the old **Conseil Régional** on the corner of Rue Javelier. The huge *case à impluvium* of the **Alliance Franco-Sénégalaise** (☎ 33 991 2823; ☿ 9.15am-noon & 3-7.15pm Mon-Sat) is architecturally interesting and also hosts fine exhibitions and events.

Not far from there, the **Marché Artisanal** and the **Marché Saint-Maur**, both on Ave Lycée Guignabo, tempt with wood carvings, fabrics, fresh fruit and atmosphere.

Along Rue du Commerce in the north, you can see dozens of pirogue makers and painters at work and watch women cleaning mussels.

Heading 5km west out of town, you can walk through the garden and crocodile farm of **Ferme de Djibelor** (☎ 33 991 1701; admission CFA2000; ☿ 9am-6pm). At **Africa Batik** (☎ 77 653 4936) you can try your hand at making batiks.

For pirogue excursions, ask your hotel or speak to the boat owners at the pirogue jetty near Hôtel Kadiandoumagne.

Sleeping
BUDGET
Auberge Aw-Bay (☎ 33 936 8096; Kolobane; per person CFA3600) For the price of a camping spot, you can get a real roof over your head in this clean *auberge* with its sky-blue doors and hammock-adorned garden. The shared toilets are kept spotless.

Le Perroquet (☎ 33 991 2329; perroquet@orange .sn; Rue du Commerce; s/d CFA11,000/13,000) Dozens of yellow-billed storks attract you with their noisy chatter to Zig's favourite budget place. For 1st-floor rooms with balcony you pay an extra CFA1000, a small investment for stunning river views.

Auberge Casafrique (☎ 33 991 4122; Santhiaba; s/d with air-con CFA17,000/19,000, without air-con CFA11,000/13,000; ⌘) Rooms are well maintained and set in bungalows surrounded by a leafy garden. There are several chill-out spaces, and for a cover charge of CFA3000 you can camp here.

MIDRANGE & TOP END
Ferme de Djibelor (☎ 33 991 1701; s/d CFA15,000/22,000) With their kitchen corner, fold-down beds and timber walls, the three log cabins on the croc farm are strangely reminiscent of ski chalets, until the lush gardens remind you where you are.

Le Flamboyant (☎ 33 991 2223; www.casamance .info; Rue de France; s/d CFA16,000/18,000; ⌘ ▯ ▣ ⌂) With their red-brick floors, quality mattresses, minibar and satellite TV, rooms here offer comfort way above the price you pay. The setting is pretty, the service friendly and manager Veronique Chiche is not only an excellent host but also the honorary French consul in Ziguinchor. Add CFA4000 for air-con.

Le Nema Kadior (☎ 33 991 1052; nemakadior@orange .sn; Ave Lycée Guignabo; s/d incl breakfast CFA20,000/26,000; ⌘ ▯ ▣) It's no longer glorious, but it does fading with style. Rooms are well maintained and the garden setting is lovely. There's a tennis court and a pool that outsiders can use for a cover charge of CFA2000.

Hôtel Aubert (☎ 33 938 8020; hotelaubert@orange .sn; Rue Fargues; d/tr CFA22,000/25,000; ⌘ ▯ ▣) Ziguinchor's oldest hotel is not quite the luxury haven you first expect, though it's a valid option. The central setting and sports centre across the road are a bonus.

Hôtel Kadiandoumagne (☎ 33 938 8000; www .hotel-kadiandoumagne.com; Rue du Commerce; s/d from CFA25,000/30,000; ⌘ ▯ ▣ ☗ ⌂) The tongue-twisting Kadiandoumagne (kaj-an-dou-man-ye) has picked the prime spot on the Casamance River. The garden and views are fabulous and almost worth the cost of the slightly unspectacular rooms (they do have satellite TV and minibar).

Eating

Le Erobon (☎ 33 991 2788; Rue du Commerce; meals CFA2000; ☸ 10am-1am) This very simple place sells grilled fish on the edge of the river. Every Wednesday night a local musician entertains beer drinkers with guitar tunes.

Le Tamarinier (☎ 33 992 0022; Ave Carvalho; meals around CFA2000-4000) Manager Marie-Agnès runs this lively, local-style bar-cum-restaurant with the cunning and strength of a judoka (which she is, black belt) and the smiles of an air hostess. The grilled prawns here taste even better to the live music on weekends.

Le Kassa (☎ 33 991 1311; Rond-Point Jean-Paul II; mains around CFA2500-4000; ☸ 8am-2am) It's proven itself for years, this patio-pretty place on the Ziguinchor roundabout. It's spacious and relaxed and, best of all, the good kitchen stays open late. The live shows on weekends are often great.

Walkunda Bar (☎ 33 991 1845 ; mains CFA3000-5000; ☸ 9am-1am) A popular haunt for affluent locals and localised expats, the Walkunda is often referred to as Zig's classy place. Don't dress up too smartly, though: the ambience is still healthily relaxed. The garden tables are the best.

L'Abondance (Rue du Général de Gaulle; 1kg grilled meat CFA4000; ☸ 5pm-3am) This small, local *dibiterie* (grilled-meat place) serves pork and lamb skewers and cold beers to night owls.

Hôtel Tourisme (☎ 33 991 2223; Rue de France; mains CFA4000; ☸ noon-2.30pm & 7-10pm) Across the road from the Flamboyant and managed by the same couple, this is a great place to wind down over a plate of seafood or the usually excellent Senegalese *plats du jour*.

Ferme de Djibelor (☎ 33 991 6855; dishes around CFA5000) If the thought of crocodile on skewer is too much, you can pick from a good range of standard meats (and even a vegetarian option). The surrounding garden is as attractive as the menu is unusual.

There are lots of small eateries, though they're hardly spectacular. Self-caterers can buy all the fresh fruit, vegetables and fresh prawns they can carry at **Marché Escale** (Rue Javelier), right in the heart of town. There's also a small **superette** (Rue Lemoine), as well as a good **pâtisserie** (Rue Javelier) in the centre of town.

Entertainment

Le Rubis (Rue de Santhiaba; admission CFA1000-2000) is the trendy choice, while **Le Bombolong** (☎ 33 938 8001; Rue du Commerce; admission CFA1500-3000) has the most raucous party.

Shopping

Massoumé (☎ 77 573 3388; ☸ 9am-7pm Mon-Sat, 10am-1pm Sun) For original craftwork, there's no better place than Massoumé, behind Marché Escale.

Keur Boutesse (☎ 33 991 6620; jofettweis@gmail .com; Grand Dakar) For beautifully printed handwoven fabrics, seek out Keur Boutesse. Call her before you visit and she'll pick you up at the hospital nearby.

Getting There & Away

AIR

Air Sénégal International (☎ 81 804 0404) has an office at the airport.

BOAT

Cheaper than the plane and far more comfortable, safe and reliable, the boat is a great way of travelling between Dakar and Ziguinchor. The overnight trip takes 16 hours, and you arrive in the Casamance just in time for brilliant views as you start moving up the Casamance River.

The German-built 500-passenger boat *Aline Sitoé Diatta* that travels the route has a variety of price classes, ranging from two-bed cabins (CFA30,500 per person) to seats (CFA15,500). It leaves Dakar every Tuesday and Friday at 8pm (check-in opens from 2.30pm to 5.30pm) and returns from Ziguinchor every Thursday and Sunday (departure 2pm, check-in from 11.30am to 1pm). You have to book your place on the overnight trip in advance in person – seats frequently fill up. Contact the **Cosama ticket office** (☎ in Ziguinchor 33 991 7200, in Dakar 33 821 2900; casama@orange.sn) for more information. Its Dakar offices (Map p678) are located next to the Gorée ferry pier; in Ziguinchor they're at the port.

SEPT PLACE & NDIAGA NDIAYE

Ziguinchor's comparatively well-organised *gare routière* is 1km east of the centre. If you want to get all the way to Dakar (CFA9000, eight to 10 hours), get there at around 6am or 7am. Other *sept-place* destinations include Bissau (CFA5000, three to five hours), Cap Skiring (CFA1500, two hours), Kafountine (CFA3500), Kolda (CFA4500) and Tambacounda (CFA9000).

SENEGAL

Getting Around

TAXI

The official rate for a taxi around town or to the *gare routière* (1km) is CFA500. The main taxi rank is at Rond-Point Jean-Paul II.

BASSE CASAMANCE

Enampor

The **Campement Villageois** (☎ 77 563 3801; per person CFA4000) is a huge *case à impluvium*, a typical Casamance architectural style, where rainwater is funnelled into a large tank in the centre of the house through a hole in the roof. This is a particularly beautiful one, and the displays grant insights into Diola culture.

There's an unreliable Ndiaga Ndiaye from Ziguinchor to Enampor (CFA600). Hiring a private taxi will set you back CFA8000 to CFA10,000 and a pirogue from Ziguinchor is CFA20,000.

Oussouye

Roughly halfway between Ziguinchor and Cap Skiring, relaxed Oussouye is a beautiful base for exploring the Basse Casamance region. For the local Diola population this town is of significance, as it's home to the animist king.

At **Casamance VTT** (Chez Benjamin; ☎ /fax 33 993 1004; www.casamancevtt.com) you can hire mountain bikes (half/full day CFA6500/13,000) and book bike and kayak tours.

SLEEPING & EATING

Aljowe (Chez François; ☎ 77 517 0267; s/apt per person CFA4000/7000) At this red-brick *case à l'impluvium* the cute apartments, with private bathrooms, are recommended.

Campement Villageois d'Oussouye (☎ 33 993 0015; http://campement.oussouye.org; s/d CFA4500/6000) The impressive *case à étage* (tw-storey mud house) at this beautifully restored *campement villageois*, in the region's typical mud-architecture, has small rooms with shared bathrooms and good Senegalese food. Rooms can get hot in the summer months.

Campement Emanaye (☎ 77 573 6334; emanaye@ yahoo.fr; s/d CFA4500/7000) In a similar building to d'Oussouye, Emanaye grants great views over the local rice fields from the 1st floor. But, really, it's young manager Maxim that brings the place to life.

Le Kassa (Chez Odette; ☎ 563 7186; dishes around CFA1000) The best option for a quiet lunch,

and you can get delicious fresh *bissap* from the women's community project next door.

Le Passager (☎ 77 512 0243; meals around CFA2000) If you like your meals in a boisterous atmosphere, go for this place next to the *gare routière*.

GETTING THERE & AWAY

All bush taxis between Ziguinchor and Cap Skiring pass through Oussouye, the halfway point. Rates are usually around CFA1500.

M'Lomp

Famous for its *cases à étages*, this is a tranquil spot in the shade of an enormous kapok tree. The **Small Museum of Diola Culture** (☎ 77 563 3833; donations welcome) has a few interesting artefacts. Yannick, who runs it, is also a reliable guide. For food, drop in to **Les Six Palmiers** (meals CFA500-1000; ⊙ 8am-11pm).

Oussouye to M'lomp is CFA300 by Ndiaga Ndiaye and CFA500 by *sept-place*.

Pointe St George & Petit Kassa

Sitting between rice fields, forest and the Casamance River, Pointe St George boasts perhaps the most stunning surroundings in the whole region. The river zone is also an *aire marine protégée* and manatee sanctuary – one of the very few places in West Africa where you reliably get to see the fascinating creatures. It's a rich bird-watching area to boot. The protection project is largely managed by the local community and partly financed through the small village *campement*.

A short boat ride from here takes you to the Petit Kassa, another protected area, with a slightly different landscape. Contact **Océanium** (☎ 33 822 2441; www.oceanium.org; Dakar) to arrange your trip – either a return from Cap Skiring or Elinkine, or a hop over several islands in the vicinity.

Niomoune

Only accessible via a long, picturesque pirogue journey, Niomoune is far off the classic trail. At the lovely **Campement Alouga** (☎ 77 576 0977; www.alouga.com; half board per person CFA8500) you get to stay village style, and that includes taking open-air showers, tasting locally grown and made food (the oysters in lemon sauce beat the food of any of the restaurants on Cap Skiring) and an

CAMPEMENTS VILLAGEOIS

At a time when hardly anyone spoke about responsible or sustainable travel, two inspired thinkers – Adama Goudiaby and Christian Saglio – came up with a model of using tourism as a way of counteracting rural exodus and offering perspectives to young people in the village. In the mid-1970s they initiated the *campements villageois*, traditional-style lodgings that allowed travellers to explore life the rural way, and were built, owned and run by the local community. Very successful for the first years, the *campements* ran into a variety of problems. Some of the original 10 camps were destroyed during the years of conflict, others were abandoned as tourists deserted the region. And even the ones that lasted during those hard days or were renovated often suffer from problems of maintenance and management – with responsibility spread across a whole community, the potential for conflict is huge.

Even if the great era of the *campements villageois* has perhaps fizzled out along with platform shoes and Afro haircuts, one thing is certain: this early initiative at handling tourism responsibly has inspired similar thinking all across the region. Today the French cooperative in Ziguinchor is investing time and money in reigniting activity in some *campements*, including Enampore, Coubalan and Affiniam, and an increasing number of private hoteliers are looking at ways of marrying village benefits with the advantages of private management. From Kafountine to Niomoune and Oussouye, you can today go village-hopping across the Casamance region knowing that the money you've spent will be invested in the community you just got to know a little bit better.

introduction to village life by Hyacinthe, who created this lovely mini-lodge.

There's a public pirogue from Ziguinchor every day except Tuesday and Saturday that returns daily except Monday and Thursday (CFA1400, four hours). Chartering a boat from Elinkine is CFA35,000 (one hour).

Elinkine

The busy fishing village Elinkine is the best jumping-off point for Île de Karabane and other places. The **Campement Villageois d'Elinkine** (☎ 77 376 9659; campementelinkine@free.fr; per person CFA8000) had just been beautifully restored when we visited, and looked enticing, with pretty rooms and a river-facing restaurant. It's managed privately today, but in the spirit of a true village camp, meaning profits flow back into the community.

There are normally several Ndiaga Ndiayes each day from Ziguinchor to Elinkine (CFA1400) or from Oussouye for CFA700.

Île de Karabane

Île de Karabane was the first French trading station in the region (1836 to 1900). The French legacy is now in ruins, but you can still see the crumbling remains of a tall Breton-style church and a school. Further along the beach lies the so-called Catholic cemetery, with the graves of French settlers

and sailors. The beach is good for swimming (and occasionally dolphin spotting), and the mangroves surrounding the island are great for bird-watching tours.

SLEEPING & EATING

There are no landline phones on Karabane and mobile coverage isn't great. Always leave a message if you don't get an answer on any of the numbers given – you will be called back. All places mentioned can arrange pick-up from Elinkine (around CFA15,000).

Badji Kunda (☎ 77 556 2856; s/d CFA4000/6000) Artfully scattered with small statues and colourful wall paintings, the hotel is the extension of sculptor Malang Badji's busy workshop. It has great atmosphere and adequate rooms and you can try your hand at glass painting or pottery.

Campement Le Barracuda (☎ 77 659 6001; half/full board CFA7300/9800) Many travellers, aspiring anglers and day-time tourists wouldn't consider going anywhere else, not because the accommodation is anything special, but because Amath the manager is a generous host whom you trust to sort out any minor request and organise the best fishing trips.

Hôtel Carabane (☎ 77 569 0284; hotelcarabane@yahoo.fr; half board CFA16,500/25,000) You'll have the honour of staying in what used to be the colonial governance, and enjoying your drink in the former Catholic mission. Plenty of pirogue excursions can be arranged.

DRINKING
Africando (☎ 77 533 3842) Following the beach from Barracuda towards Hôtel Carabane, you'll pass this fabulous bar, where Nicolas, the entertaining and inspiring host, serves drinks between the roots of a giant *fromager* tree.

GETTING THERE & AWAY
Île de Karabane is best reached by motorised pirogue from Elinkine. A fairly regular boat *(navette)* leaves Elinkine daily at 2.30pm and 5pm, reaching Île de Karabane half an hour later before continuing to the village of Diogé on the northern bank of the Casamance River. It returns at 10am the next day. The fare for each stretch is CFA1500. Chartering a pirogue costs around CFA15,000 to 20,000 each way – just ask at the harbour or arrange pick-up with your hotel.

Cap Skiring
Cap Skiring's beaches are rumoured to be among the finest in West Africa. They're certainly Senegal's best, and considering their awesome beauty the tourism industry here is enticingly low-key. Even in high season, you get a few hundred metres of white sand to yourself, and there are plenty of intimate guesthouses and small *campements*.

INFORMATION
Cap Skiring has a (very basic) health centre, a post office and internet access at **Net's Cap** (☎ 77 245 5380; net-s-cap@orange.sn; per hr CFA300; ☀ 9am-10pm). The **CBAO** (☎ 33 938 8111; Pl du Marché) in the village has an ATM that accepts Visa cards. For tour bookings, contact **Diatta Tours** (☎ 33 991 2781; aessibye@yahoo.fr) and try **Casa Loisirs** (☎ 33 993 5393; clpassion@orange.sn; village centre) for kayak, beach buggy and car hire. Pirogue excursions along the river are easily negotiated at Pont Katakalousse, opposite the hotel of the same name (3km south of Cap Skiring on the main road).

SLEEPING
Unless otherwise stated, places are situated on the beach from the Cap to Kabrousse (about 5km and CFA1000 by taxi from the village). There are many more budget *campements* there than listed here, but we found most in a deplorable state – check if things have changed.

Budget
Auberge Le Palmier (☎ 33 993 5109; Cap Skiring village; d with/without hot water & air-con CFA10,000/CFA5000; ⊠) Opposite Club Med, this small family hotel has well-maintained, if slightly dark, rooms with comfortable beds and a terrace overlooking the village square.

Campement Chez M'Ballo (☎ 33 936 9102; r with/without bathroom CFA12,000/6000) Rooms are just about passable (forget about the cheap ones, though), the setting fantastic. Palm trees fight for space in this pretty plot of green, and the restaurant gives great views across the beach.

Le Paradise (☎ 33 993 5303; r CFA14,000; ⊠) Among the string of rootsy *campements* that line the beach near the Cap, we found this in the best condition. Accommodation ranges from basic options with shared toilets to one air-conditioned room with sea view. The lush gardens are stunning.

Midrange & Top End
Kaloa les Paletuviers (☎ 33 993 5210; www.hotel-kaloa.com; Cap Skiring village; s/d incl breakfast CFA15,000/26,000; ⊠ ⚑) This Senegalese-owned hotel is fantastic value, with clean rooms around a pool and a setting on the mangroves (kayak tours available).

Villa des Pêcheurs (☎ 33 993 5253; www.villadespecheurs.com; s/d incl breakfast CFA19,000/23,500; ⊠) Made with love, this wood-pannelled, garden-enhanced place on the beach is far too beautiful to leave to the sports fishermen that flock here. The restaurant is fantastic – there's even an in-house bakery and cookery courses on offer.

Hôtel Katakalousse (☎ 33 993 5282; www.katakalousse.com; Pont de Katakalousse; r CFA25,000) During fishing season, this is all about catch sizes and fishing equipment; otherwise it's a clean and friendly spot for excursions, watersports, and Jacuzzi luxury.

Mansa Lodge (☎ 33 993 5147; www.capsafari.com; s/d CFA30,000/44,000; ⊠ ⚑) The lovely couple that runs this beautiful family guesthouse effortlessly makes you feel at home. They're experienced hoteliers and have lived in the Casamance for 30 years, so you get treated like a king and benefit from their vast local knowledge.

La Mer (☎ 33 993 52 80; Kabrousse beach; d from CFA30,000) The waves lap at your toes at this beach bar turned mini-guesthouse. The pretty studios come with a hammock-adorned terrace, sound system and DVD player.

Fromager Lodge (☎ 33 993 5421; www.fromagerlodge .com; Kabrousse village; s/d incl breakfast CFA35,000/56,000; ☒ ☚) The design of the bungalows is as colourful as the homemade punch is potent. The restaurant serves excellent Italian food, and the beach is a short walk from its village setting.

La Maison Bleue (☎ 33 993 5161; www.lamaisonbleu .org; r per person CFA43,000/66,000) This is the supermodel among the hotels at the Cap – a designer's skilled hand has lent the airy rooms, inviting outdoor garden and lounge corners a personal touch. Most people come here to jump on the light plane to Guinea-Bissau's Bijagos archipelago (see p445).

La Paillote (☎ 33 993 5151; www.paillote.sn; s/d incl breakfast CFA71,000/84,000; ☒ ▢ ☚) The charming grandmother of Cap Skiring's hotels spoils visitors the most. Having been here longest, it's grabbed the best location, and offers a supreme variety of activities.

EATING

Among the hotel kitchens, Fromager Lodge stands out for its Italian food, La Maison Bleue has a recommended Oriental menu, and the Villa des Pêcheurs is best for seafood.

Chez Les Copains (☎ 77 548 15 93; Allée du Palétuvier; dishes around CFA2000) For generous portions of *thiéboudieune* and other Senegalese dishes, pick a vinyl-clad table here, behind the Palétuvier Hôtel.

Bar de la Mer (☎ 33 993 52 80; Kabrousse beach; dishes around CFA4000) In Kabrousse, this place does excellent seafood right on the beach.

Le Djembé (Chez Nadine & Patrick; ☎ 77 533 7692; mains CFA4000-6000) In the village, Le Djembé has long held down a well-deserved reputation for serving the most imaginative dishes in a relaxed atmosphere.

Le Kassala (☎ 33 653 0382; Cap Skiring village; roast meat per kg CFA5000; ☯ 8pm-4am) In the village, Le Kassala buzzes in the evenings, when the party folk come for grilled meat and gossip.

Case Bambou (☎ 33 993 5178; mains CFA5000-7000) Across the road, Case Bambou serves excellent international cuisine during the day and turns into the Cap's hottest nightclub after 11pm.

ENTERTAINMENT

Bakine (☎ 33 641 5124; Croisement du Cap; ☯ 10pm-3am) A rootsier party than Case Bambou's happens here, where the drumbeats are pounding and the dancing gets wilder as the night wears on.

GETTING THERE & AWAY

Air

Air Sénégal International operates daily flights between Dakar and **Airport Cap Skiring** (☎ 33 993 5194) from October to May, and also connects to Paris. **Air CM** (www.aircm.com) is one of several charters.

Bush Taxi & Minibus

Sept-place taxis (CFA1500) and minibuses (CFA1000) run regularly throughout the day between Ziguinchor and Cap Skiring.

GETTING AROUND

A taxi from the main *campement* area to Cap Skiring village is around CFA1000, as is the trip from the Cap to Katakalousse.

Ask at your hotel for bike hire. For car hire, try Casa Loisirs (see p727).

Boucotte

The beach at Cap Skiring will seem unremarkable compared with the seemingly endless stretch of white sand and blue waves at Boucotte beach, 7km from the Cap. In the village, take a look at the Diola exhibits of **Boucotte Museum**, spread out among the roots of a kapok treee. Further north, walks through a **tropical garden** (☎ contact Diatta Tours 33 992 0648) are enjoyable, with great views over the rice fields from a small hill.

There are two places to stay. **Oudja Hôtel** (☎ 33 992 0648; diattatour@yahoo.fr; s/d incl breakfast CFA11,000/14,000) has simple, ventilated rooms on vast terrain right behind the beach. **Hôtel Maya** (☎ 77 575 6177; www.hotel-maya.com; s/d incl breakfast 23,000/36,000; ☒ ☚ ⬤) is more upmarket, with 20 spacious rooms overlooking sea and pool. Communicating family rooms and a babysitting service allow stressed parents to mind their kids while catching up on couple time.

Both hotels can pick you up from Cap Skiring; otherwise, hire a taxi (CFA2000 to CFA3000).

Diembéring

With its giant kapok trees and gentle hill, Diembéring is so pretty that a chart-topping ballad has been devoted to it. It's still quieter than the Cap, though *campements* are springing up fast. Right on the village square, **Campement Asseb** (☎ 77 541 3472; sembesene@yahoo.fr; per person incl breakfast CFA5500) is run by a Diembéring native, who has turned this once-neglected space around with an investment in paint and simple repairs. The tiny five-room affair that is the **Auberge Les Rizières** (☎ 77 721 3281; www.casamance-les-rizieres.com; per person CFA10,000) is mainly geared towards djembe, dance and batik lovers. You can camp here and hire bicycles.

Diembéring is great for excursions to Cachouane and Île de Karabane, as well as for beach lounging and a taste of village life. For the latter, ask about the crafts workshops of the local women's collective.

The route from Cap Skiring to Diembéring is a bouncy, dusty dirt track – unless the promise of paving has really been kept. A seat on a minibus or *sept-place* costs CFA800. You're best off phoning your *campement* for pick-up options, or hiring a taxi (around CFA7000) or 4WD.

Cachouane
A spectacular hike from Diembéring or pirogue trip from Elinkine (CFA8000) takes you to this remote spot with white sands, palm trees, mangrove-lined creeks and dolphins close by. **Campement Sounka** (☎ 77 645 3707; half board per person CFA 8500) allows you to explore all of this, as well as the small Diola village. You're well looked after by Papis and his team, who prepare tasty meals to order and sweep the simple rooms of the large *case à l'impluvium* (bathrooms shared) daily.

CASAMANCE NORD
Koubalan & Dioubour
About 22km northeast of Ziguinchor, east of Tobor, Koubalan's large **campement villageois** (☎ 77 527 7130) was being beautifully restored when we passed. In the neighbouring village the banco-brick building of the **Gîte de Dioubor** (☎ 33 957 1256; infotpa@orange.sn; per person CFA10,000) is a typical *campement* of the TPA chain – privately managed, dedicated to training local staff and to putting a percentage of profits back into the community (see the boxed text, p726).

A hire taxi from Ziguinchor is CFA7000 (45 minutes), a hire pirogue around CFA35,000 (two hours).

Affiniam
A few kilometres north of the river, Affiniam is stunningly located between forest and river, and easily reached from Ziguinchor by boat. The **campement villageois** (☎ 77 567 0044; r CFA4000) is in a beautiful *case à impluvium* on the edge of the village, shaded by giant *fromager* trees, and in close proximity to the pirogue point.

Its village and nature excursions (including pirogue trips) are fantastic.

The *campement* can pick you up by pirogue from Ziguinchor (around CFA25,000). There's a daily public pirogue from Zig, except Thursday and Sunday (CFA600, two hours). Hiring a taxi from Ziguinchor costs CFA15,000 (one hour).

Bignona
With crumbling colonial buildings, Bignona is a sleepy crossroads town where the main route to/from Banjul joins the Trans-Gambia Hwy 30km north of Ziguinchor.

The best place to stay is the cosy **Auberge Kayanior** (☎ 33 994 3014; kayanior@yahoo.fr; Quartier Château d'Eau; s/d CFA10,000/12,000; 🖳 🛜), with clean, pretty rooms in a family house, and a garden to relax in. If Rosalie the manager isn't available to share her passion for the region (including excursions to nearby villages and forests) with you, she'll find someone who is.

Kafountine & Abéné
A number of illegal marijuana plantations near the town have spawned the kind of holiday centre where the tie-dye-sporting 'baba cool' swing their dreadlocks to the all-pervasive djembe beat. Spread out near the end of the tarred road leading in from Diouloulou, Kafountine is reasonably well equipped, with a *télécentre*, a slowish cybercafe, a hospital and a post office but no bank.

KAFOUNTINE
The typical Kafountine tourist does as the locals do – very little. A day fills nicely with relaxing swims, some hammock lounging and a spell of djembe drumming in the evening. But don't get sucked into Kafountinian apathy before taking a bird-watching tour to Kassel. The trips organised by Esperanto Lodge are particularly recommended.

The **fishing village** is great to visit at high tide, when boats are launched into the sea. A completely different attraction is the **Village d'Outouka** (Chez Joachim; ☎ 77 633 9418), a world of stunning creation and carnival-mask making on the beach near Campement Sitokoto.

Sleeping
Unless otherwise stated, places are situated along the beach.

Le Bolonga (☎ 33 994 8515; per person incl breakfast CFA7500) This quality place really is as warm and welcoming as the bar-reception in the wide brick building at the entrance suggests. Rooms are pretty, but the absence of fans means sweaty summer nights.

Le Paradise (☎ 77 327 2123; awa@club-internet.fr; r per person CFA9000) In one swift clearing of the smoke, this former rasta-paradise near Le Flamant Rose has been turned into an arty *campement* with hand-sculpted chairs, a whiff of red wine hanging over the restaurant and world music drifting from the speakers. The restaurant serves a good selection of salads.

Le Kelediang (☎ 77 542 5385; www.senegam.net; full board CFA10,000) Sitting in a 3-hectare forest, this nature-bound *campement* is designed to be rootsy – as basic as a bucket shower and outdoor long-drop. Everything is very clean and the restaurant serves delicious three-course meals (using local ingredients; what else?) on a large terrace behind the sea.

Le Mampato (Chez Kiné Basse; ☎ 77 575 1684; btwn village & beach; s/d CFA12,000/15,000) Kiné Basse is something of a local institution, renowned for her love of parties – making you wonder how she keeps this pretty little place together so well. Her very good restaurant has gradually grown into a small hostel with four bright and tiled rooms.

our pick **Esperanto Lodge** (Chez Eric; ☎ 33 936 9519; www.esperantolodge.com; per person incl breakfast CFA13,500; 🔒 💻) This relaxed place on the river is a real gem, with attractive, family-sized bungalows and a landscaped palm-tree garden. The location between river and sea (and the bird life this attracts) is the envy of the whole village, and the restaurant wakes you with pancakes and fresh orange juice and puts you to sleep with local-juice cocktails.

Mama Maria (☎ 33 994 8541; www.hotelmamamaria .com; s/d incl breakfast CFA14,400/23,000) This Spanish-run lodge looks like a country mansion on the beach. There's a fantastic lounge with library, and after your first omelette-coffee-prawns-fresh-fruit breakfast on the sunny terrace you'll definitely feel at home.

Le Fouta Djalon (☎ 77 503 9922; lefoutadjalon@ yahoo.fr; r CFA15,000; 🔒) The slope of a large dune shades the lodge's red-brick huts from the sea winds, and gently whispers 'beach' until you succumb and climb up, then down and into the sea. This is one of the most reliably managed and maintained places in Kafountine, with a clean beach.

Hôtel Le Karone (☎ 33 994 8525; www.lekarone.net; s/d CFA16,500/27,000; 🔒 🍽) This very nice place

with a pool (the only one in Kafountine) and a welcoming garden setting had just been put up for sale when we passed. Could it have been improved further, or has it been turned into a car park? Worth phoning to find out. It's a great place to stay.

Eating

Kafountine isn't a gourmet's paradise, and the hotel restaurants are still your safest bet. Esperanto, Fouta Djalon and Le Mampato are all recommended.

Mama Africa (dishes CFA1500) Ask anyone about where to eat and you'll probably be taken straight here, where the whole village enjoys generous portions of Senegalese food and welcoming smiles.

Couleur Café (☎ 33 994 8555; dishes CFA4000) In the village, Couleur offers excellent grilled fish, good prawn dishes and homemade desserts in a low-key setting.

Le Bissap (☎ 33 994 8512; dishes CFA3000-4000; 🕓 8am-midnight) Here you don't only eat well but can check your mail and buy groceries at the same time.

Le Flamant Rose (☎ 77 541 2504) This place only really wakes up in the evenings, when the bar doubles as favourite pick-up joint.

Self-caterers can stock up at the **Mini Marché** (🕓 9am-11pm).

Entertainment

This is a town full of party-ready inhabitants. The nightclubs are usually packed with dreadlocked youngsters and fuelled with smoke and liqueur. There's always a drumming party on somewhere in the village.

Farafina (admission CFA1500-2000) Kafountine's most upmarket place sparkles from the disco balls to the sequins on the ladies' tops.

Chez Pablo (admission CFA500-1000) More local-style, Chez Pablo plays mainly Guinean and Senegalese music to a very young crowd.

Getting There & Away

From Ziguinchor, *sept-place* taxis (CFA2200) run directly to Kafountine. You can also get bush taxis from Serekunda or Brikama in The Gambia (around CFA1500). Traffic sometimes goes via the back roads and the sleepy Darsilami border rather than the main crossing at Séléti, causing difficulties for your entry stamp.

VILLAGE D'OUTOUKA

'If a child loves drawing and you step in his way, you'll disturb his life forever,' explains Joachim while spreading out dozens of brightly painted canvases on the large tables outside the main house of his very special community. Along the walls children's paintings in various stages of completion shout colours at you. Enter the building, and sculptures from recycled materials, masks and giant carnival figures eye you up lazily. Every day, dozens of kids come running to Joachim's village and spend their free hours drawing, painting and modelling. When the storm of daily creativity passes, Joachim carefully traces the figures in each work with a thin black line, giving them the typical 'Outouka look'. 'I've seen children deal with issues here they haven't been able to express elsewhere,' he says, 'many of these kids have seen violence, sometimes war.' But mainly, this is a place of laughter and creative overflow. You can visit any day. Paintings can be purchased – the profits are used to keep the village going, buy new paints and brushes, and organise exhibitions.

Getting Around

It's quite a walk from the hotel-lined beach-front to the village centre. You can hope for a ride with a friendly local, ask your hotel to call you a cab (CFA1000 to CFA2000), or hire a bicycle at the **Spanish Adult Education Centre** (Kafountine village) – tracks are sandy, though.

ABÉNÉ

As smoke hazy as Kafountine, Abéné (6km north) only really comes to life over New Year, when the Dutch-run **Abéné Festivalo** (www.alnaniking.co.uk/senegal/festival) attracts djembe drummers from across the world. Anyone is welcome – whether budding percussionist or professional – this event is all about the community spirit rather than the big names. For details see the website.

Sleeping

La Belle Danielle (☎ 77 936 9542; r per person CFA3500) If the rooms were anything as great as the helpful and well-connected manager Mamadou Konta, this would be a star-studded place. Accommodation here is as basic as it's cheap – a mattress, a roof and shared toilets.

Le Kossey (☎ 77 223 8052; r per person CFA6000) The vast tropical garden is luxuriously large for the 10 roundhuts it contains. Rooms are impeccable and only a few metres away from the beach. Lighting is by candles and petrol lamps.

Maison Sunjata (☎ /fax 33 994 8610; info@senegambia .de; s/d CFA10,000/16,000) Staying here is like a visit to grandma's. There's a nicely tended garden, the spacious guest rooms are brushed to shine and you'll get fussed over a fair bit. The communicating rooms with shared bathroom are great for families.

Le Casamar (☎ 77 565 8939; per person CFA10,000) With its large garden, spacious bungalows in bright blue-yellow and beach proximity, this is an attractive option. The large, straw-roofed restaurant gets good reviews.

Le Kalissai (☎ 33 994 8600; www.kalissai.com; s/d CFA28,000/32,000; 🏊 🖫) Abéné's most polished hotel has large bungalows in a vast, tended garden. The closure of its private flight path caused worry about possible closure – if it's open it's Abéné's most luxurious choice.

Eating

Bistro Café (☎ 77 229 2649; pizzas CFA2000-3000) A good option, Bistro has decent pizzas, a well-stocked boutique selling batiks and clothes, bicycle hire and the occasional drumming soiree.

Chez Vero (☎ 77 617 1714; meals around CFA3000; ⏰ 10am-10pm) This is the much-loved auntie of Abéné's restaurant scene. The consistently good food is served on a terrace, under the watchful eyes of gaudy Madonnas and *griots* painted on the wall.

Getting There & Away

All public transport to and from Kafountine stops at the turnoff to Abéné, near Diannah. The village is 2km off the main road and the beach is a further 2km that you can walk or taxi (CFA1000). A private taxi from Kafountine is CFA3000 to CFA4000.

Niafourang

Here, where the djembe drumming makes way for the chatter of hundreds of birds, you find the utterly friendly **Tilibo Horizons** (☎ 77 501 3879; half board CFA11,000), wedged between the river and the sea. Ousmane Sané, who runs

SENEGAL

the simple place like a *campement villageois*, can indicate walking routes, arrange for meals cooked to your taste and pirogue excursions along the mangroves. Longer tours are organised by Casamance Horizons (see also p739), devoted to community tourism.

Phone Tilibo Horizons to pick you up from Ziguinchor or Bandikaki, where the *sept-place* from Ziguinchor to Kafountine can drop you off.

HAUTE CASAMANCE
Sédhiou
Some 100km east of Ziguinchor, river-lined Sédhiou is the largest town in this part of Casamance, a tranquil place that sleepwalks through an existence rarely disturbed by visitors. From 1900 to 1909, this was the main trading post of the French colonial administration, though this moment in the political spotlight has left few marks.

The **Hôtel La Palmeraie** (☎ 33 995 1102; philippe .bertrand@apicus.net; s/d CFA20,000/28,000; 🔀 🖭) is Sédhiou's main address. It generally caters to hunters, though the beautiful setting in a large, palm grove makes it a great place to unwind even if you're not into chasing wild boar.

A short diversion off the smooth tarmac road from Kolda to Carrefour Diaroumé takes you to Sédhiou (bush taxi CFA3500); the turnoff is signposted.

Kolda & Diaoubé
Kolda looks back on a glorious past as the capital of a 19th-century Fula kingdom. Today it's an unspectacular place, though the area surrounding the Casamance River is lovely, with small river islands, birds and monkeys. On Wednesday, a day trip (Ndiaga Ndiaye CFA1000) to the famous market of **Diaoubé** (38km from Kolda on the route to Vélingara) is a must, when traders from as far as Mali come here to peddle their wares.

To spend a night in Kolda, head for **Le Firdou** (☎ 33 996 1780; www.lefirdou.com; s/d CFA16,000/19,000; 🅿 🖭 🖭), a pretty oasis with bungalows in a palm-shaded garden that lies a short walk from the centre. Another option is the impressively sized **Hôtel Hobbe** (☎ 33 996 1170; www.hobbe-kolda.com; s/d CFA20,000/25,000; 🔀 🖭 🖭), where black-crowned cranes stalk around the swimming pool and hunters like to take photographs with prey at their feet.

Kolda lies on the route from Ziguinchor to Tambacounda, and there's regular transport in both directions (*sept-place* to Zig CFA4500, six hours), to Tambacounda CFA4000, six hours). To travel from here to The Gambia, go first to Vélingara (CFA2500, 3½ hours), where you'll find Gambia-bound vehicles.

Diaoubé is Senegal's transport hub for Guinea. The market day is best, but there are *sept-place* taxis every day.

SENEGAL DIRECTORY

ACCOMMODATION
In this chapter, rates are quoted exclusive of tourist tax (CFA600 per person per night). For larger towns, places are organised according to price range: budget hotels (less than US$30 per night), midrange (between US$40 and US$100 per night) and top end (more than US$100 per night). Dakar has the biggest range of accommodation, though everything is expensive and there are few budget options. Inland, there are several good rural *campements*, where accommodation is usually in roundhuts or bungalows. Many of those are run for the benefit of the local community, including the *campements villageois* in the Casamance (see the boxed text, p726), and there are several upmarket options.

Some hotels charge by the room, so it makes no difference whether you're alone or sharing, but many have favourable rates for two people sharing. The high season is from around October to May, with extra hikes around Christmas and New Year. During the low season, rates can drop by up to 50%.

ACTIVITIES
Most tourists head to Senegal for the beaches, particularly those of the Petite Côte (p696) and Cap Skiring (p727). The main tourist centres have a range of sea-related activities on offer, including sailboarding, kayaking and so on. Pirogue journeys are popular, particularly around the mangrove creeks of the Siné-Saloum Delta (p701) and the Casamance (p725). The boat journeys are often combined with bird watching. Unfortunately, there's no equivalent in Senegal to The Gambia's well-organised network of ornithologists, but Gambian guides and tour operators often organise trips to Siné-Saloum and the Casamance.

Sport fishing is popular in Dakar (p683), Saly (p698) and Cap Skiring (p727); the same areas are also the most popular for watersports, though Dakar is the only place where you can go surfing.

Some cautious wildlife spotting can be done in Senegal's national parks.

BOOKS

Most books about Senegal are in French; if you can read the language you should pick up *Sénégal*, musings on the country by Christian Saglio, former head of Dakar's Institut Français.

The stunning *Senegal Behind Glass* by Anne-Marie Bouttianaux-Ndiaye contains reproductions of *sous-verre* paintings, including historical and contemporary examples, giving artistic insights into the country's religion and culture (as well as the arts scene).

Music lovers should read the amusing *The Music in My Head* by Mark Hudson, which describes the power, influence and everyday realities of modern African music. It's set in a mythical city that is instantly recognisable as Dakar.

BUSINESS HOURS

Government offices are open from 8am to 1pm and 2pm to 5pm Monday to Friday.

Banks usually open from 7.45am to noon and 1.30pm to 4.45pm from Monday to Thursday, and from 7.45am to 12.30pm and 2.45pm to 4pm on Friday. Some key branches open from 8.45am to 12.30pm on Saturday morning, and upcountry branches often close in the early afternoon.

Shops are usually open from 9am to 1pm and from 2.30pm to 7pm Monday to Saturday, and 9am to 12.30 on Sunday. Some shops are open all day. Supermarkets open all day from 8am to 8pm and are closed on Sunday.

Most restaurants offer lunch (noon to 3pm) and dinner (7pm to 11pm), but stay open for drinks outside those hours. Most restaurants in Dakar are closed on Sunday.

For a night out in Dakar, don't even think of leaving the house before midnight; most places only get going around 1am.

CHILDREN

There's little in the way of child-centred activities, though Dakar has a few playgrounds and some children's entertainment (Reserve de Bandia and Accrobaobab are particularly good; see p697). Safe, child-friendly beaches are indicated in individual sections.

PRACTICALITIES

- *Focus on Africa* (BBC) often has excellent news stories on Senegal, and is sold in the country.

- If you read French, *Jeune Afrique* and *l'Intelligent* are good sources of political and cultural news.

- The electricity supply in Senegal is 220V. Plugs have two round pins, as in France and continental Europe.

- Senegal uses the metric system.

Children are generally welcome, and hotels and restaurants are usually accommodating, rustling up a kids' meal and arranging extra beds (at an extra cost). Babysitting services are rare, and only available in the more upmarket places.

Disposable nappies and baby food are found in the supermarkets and many smaller shops in the larger towns around the country; stock up before heading to the more remote regions. Babies are best carried in a baby rucksack – it's near impossible to push a pram around anywhere in the country.

DANGERS & ANNOYANCES

Dakar, particularly its inner city, markets and beaches, is a hot spot for pickpocketing and scams, and muggings have increased (see p677). It's still nowhere on the scale of Lagos. Another risk is civil unrest in the Casamance (see the boxed text, p721).

EMBASSIES & CONSULATES

If you need to find an embassy that is not listed here, phone directory enquiries from Senegal (☎ 1212). The following embassies are all located in Dakar.

Belgium (Map p678; ☎ 33 889 4390; www.diplomatie.be; Ave des Jambaars, Plateau)

Canada (Map p678; ☎ 33 889 4700; Immeuble Sorano, 3rd fl, 45-47 Blvd de la République, Plateau)

Cape Verde (Map p680; ☎ 33 821 3936; 3 Blvd el Haji Djily Mbaye, Plateau)

Côte d'Ivoire (Map p682; ☎ 33 869 02 70; www.ambaci-dakar.org; Allées Seydou Nourou Tall, Point E)

France (Map p680; ☎ 33 839 5100; www.ambafrance-sn.org) There's also a consular service in Saint-Louis (Map p709; www.arc.sn/consulatstlouis) and an honorary consul in Ziguinchor (Map p722).

Gambia (Map p680; ☎ 33 821 7230; 11 Rue de Thiong)

Germany (Map p678; ☎ 33 889 4884; www.dakar.diplo .de; 20 Ave Pasteur)

Ghana (Map p682; ☎ 33 869 4053; Rue 6, Point E)

Guinea (Map p682; ☎ 33 824 8606; Rue de Dioubel, Point E)

Guinea-Bissau (Map p682; ☎ 33 824 5922; Rue 6, Point E) There's also a mission in Ziguinchor (☎ 33 991 1046).

Italy (Map p678; ☎ 33 889 2636; www.ambdakar.esteri .it/Ambasciata_Dakar; Rue Alpha Hachamiyou Tall)

Mali (Map p685; ☎ 33 824 6252; 23 Rte de la Corniche-Ouest)

Mauritania (Map p685; ☎ 33 823 5344; Fann Mermoz)

Morocco (Map p682; ☎ 33 824 3836; Ave Cheikh Anta Diop, Mermoz)

Netherlands (Map p680; ☎ 33 849 0360; 37 Rue Kléber)

Spain (Map p678; ☎ 33 821 3081; 18-20 Ave Nelson Mandela)

Switzerland (Map p678; ☎ 33 823 0590; Rue René Ndiaye)

UK (Map p678; ☎ 33 823 7392; 20 Rue du Dr Guillet) One block north of Hôpital Le Dantec.

USA (Map p680; ☎ 33 823 4296; Av Jean XXIII)

FESTIVALS & EVENTS

There's always a festival on somewhere in Senegal; some so small and informal that you'll hardly hear about them, others huge, international events.

Abéné Festivalo (☎ 33 994 8615; www.alnaniking .co.uk) Annual New Year's djembe fiesta.

Dak'Art Biennale (☎ 33 823 0918; www.dakart.org) Huge contemporary-arts fair with great fringe shows. It usually takes place in May.

Les Blues du Fleuve (☎ 33 868 2126; www.festival lesbluesdufleuve.com) Dates vary. Sahel sounds in Podor.

Kaay Fecc (☎ 33 824 51 54; www.kaayfecc.com) Late May or early June; Dakar. Large contemporary-dance festival.

Regards sur Courts (☎ 33 842 1622; www.goree -regards-sur-cours.org) May. Gorée's old houses open their doors to the public.

Saint-Louis International Jazz Festival (☎ 33 961 2455; www.saintlouisjazz.com) Late May; Saint-Louis. Renowned international jazz festival.

Festival de Sahel (☎ 33 869 7900; www.africatravel -group.com; Rte du Méridien Président, Dakar) Sahel music amid Lompoul's dunes; first edition in November 2009.

GAY & LESBIAN TRAVELLERS

Homosexuality is illegal and punishable with fines or imprisonment of up to five years. It's a cultural taboo for most people. The fact that a group of nine men was charged with eight years' prison in 2008 (for 'indecent conduct and unnatural acts' as well as for 'forming a criminal group') has lead human rights groups to deplore the extremity of the sentence and rapidness of the trial.

At the time of writing, aggression against homosexuals was on the increase, after a magazine article talked about a gay marriage, causing even moderate people to express strong anti-gay sentiments. Of course there are still thriving scenes, especially in Dakar and Saly, but discretion is advised. Note that public expressions of affection are even frowned upon among heterosexual couples.

ILGA (www.ilga.org) The site of the International Lesbian, Gay, Bisexual, Trans and Intersex Association features regular updates on the situation for homosexuals worldwide.

MASK (www.mask.org.za) South Africa–based organisation Behind the Mask has dedicated pages for individual African countries, containing legal and social information that's regularly updated.

HOLIDAYS

Both Christian and Islamic events are celebrated. The Muslim holidays, such as Korité, Tabaski, Tamkharit and Moulid, are determined by the lunar calendar and occur on different dates each year. Forty-eight days after Islamic New Year, Senegal celebrates the Grand Magal pilgrimage in Touba (p706).

The exact dates of Islamic holidays are only announced just before they occur, as they depend on the sightings of the moon. See p816 for more information.

Other holidays:

New Year's Day 1 January
Independence Day 4 April
Easter Monday March/April
Whit Sunday/Pentecost Seventh Sunday after Easter
Whit Monday Day after Whit Sunday
Ascension Fortieth day after Easter
Workers Day 1 May
Assumption 15 August
Christmas Day 25 December

INTERNET ACCESS

Web services are excellent in most parts of the country. The growth of wi-fi and mobile phone access has caused many internet cafes to close. Wi-fi is available at many hotels and restaurants in the main urban centres and is usually free of charge. The 💻 symbol in the reviews refers to internet access from computers; the 🛜 symbol refers to wi-fi connections.

INTERNET RESOURCES

Au Senegal (www.au-senegal.com) A fantastically packed information site, with hotel booking facilities and up-to-date cultural and political information. The English version is software translated.

Senegalaisement (www.senegalaisement.com) Quite disorganised and very opinionated French site with very detailed historical, cultural and practical information.

MAPS

There's no huge difference between any of the internationally available maps. In Senegal, the **DTGC** (Direction des Travaux Géographiques et Cartographiques; www.dtgc.au-senegal.com) produces very detailed regional maps that are on sale in Dakar bookstores. For Dakar, the colourful street map by **Editions Laure Kane** (www.editionslaurekane.com) is a must have (last updated in 2008).

MONEY

The currency of Senegal is the West African CFA franc. CFA stands for Communauté Financière Africaine; the CFA franc is also the official currency of Benin, Burkina Faso, Côte d'Ivoire, Guinea-Bissau, Mali, Niger and Togo.

There are notes for CFA500, CFA1000, CFA5000 and CFA10,000. The value of the CFA is tied to the euro at a fixed rate of one euro to CFA655.967.

ATMs

Banks with ATMs exist in most major towns throughout the country. Visa is the most widely accepted plastic. The withdrawal limit is supposed to be CFA300,000, though some bank branches only allow up to CFA150,000.

Cash

Euros, US dollars, UK pounds and other major currencies can be changed in banks, bureaux de change and hotels. Euros are most widely accepted and are the only currency dealt with outside Dakar. It's best to do all your changing in Dakar before heading into the country.

Credit Cards

The use of Visa cards is limited to top-end hotels, some restaurants, car hire and a few shops, and there's a risk of fraud.

Moneychangers

All major bank branches change money, and there are a few exchange bureaus in the tourist zones.

Tipping

You're expected to tip in restaurants, but not in taxis. People offering services from cleaning rooms to carrying bags and indicating routes will often expect a tip.

Travellers Cheques

Only the central CBAO branch reliably accepted travellers cheques at the time of writing. The best currency is the euro.

POST

Senegal's postal service is slow, and anything containing more than a letter is likely to get stuck in customs, and sometimes lost. Letters to and from Europe usually take about a week, up to 15 days for Australasia. For speedier mail, there are DHL offices in Dakar and other major towns.

SMOKING

Smoking is allowed in most places. Note that it's forbidden in the village of Yoff, (near Dakar), which is governed by the Islamic principles of the Layen community.

TELEPHONE & FAX

Good mobile-phone coverage means that many of the public *télécentres* have now closed. You'll still find one in most towns, but it's much easier to bring an unlocked phone (or buy a cheap one) and insert either an Orange, a Tigo or an Expresso SIM card. Top-up credit for all is available absolutely anywhere. They all charge similar rates: around CFA90 per minute for local and CFA180 per minute for international calls. Network coverage is excellent across the country.

The country code is ☎ 221. For directory assistance dial ☎ 12.

TIME

Senegal is on GMT/UTC, which for most European visitors means there is no or very little time difference. There is no daylight-saving time.

TOURIST INFORMATION

Senegal's Syndicat d'Initiative has an office in each of the regions. The main and best branch is in Saint-Louis.

Gorée (☎ 33 823 9177; methiourseye@hotmail.com; Mairie de Gorée)

Saint-Louis (☎ 33 961 2455; sltourisme@orange.sn; Gouvernance)

Tambacounda (☎ 33 981 1250; nijihotel@orange.sn; Niji Hôtel)

An excellent online source for travelling to Senegal is **Au Senegal** (www.au-senegal.com).

VISAS

Visas are not needed by citizens of the EU, Ecowas, Canada, Norway, South Africa, Japan, Israel, USA and some other (mainly African) countries. Tourist visas which last for one to three months cost about US$15 to US$20.

Visa Extensions

Most people wishing to stay beyond the initial three-month period granted when entering simply take a quick trip to The Gambia, and on returning earn another three months. Otherwise, submit a request to the **Ministère de l'Interieur** (Map p680; Pl de l'Indépendance, Dakar), who will explain the (tedious) procedure to you.

Visas for Onward Travel

For Mali and Mauritania you can get visas at the border. For Guinea-Bissau, you should arrange your visa beforehand, at the consulate in Dakar or Ziguinchor (see p733). For The Gambia, it's also better to get a visa beforehand, as the availability at the border largely depends on the whims of the officials you encounter.

WOMEN TRAVELLERS

While it's not exactly dangerous to travel on your own as a woman, you'll have to put up with low-key hassle and constant advances. If you travel on your own, inventing a husband is a good strategy, and you should also refer to your boyfriend as your husband, to gain respect for your relationship.

It's always better to dress modestly, especially in rural areas. Short skirts don't do anything to keep trouble away.

Downtown Dakar is a prime 'hunting ground' for guys out to chat up women, either to get you into bed or to cheat you out of money and most probably both. Shake them off with a firm but polite *bakhna* (meaning OK, it's all right) or by simply ignoring them. Use your good judgment. If you wouldn't give your phone number to a random stranger in a supermarket at home, you shouldn't do it here.

Beaches are prime hassle zones; don't walk them alone in the evenings. Very few women become the victims of physical harm or rape.

TRANSPORT IN SENEGAL

GETTING THERE & AWAY
Entering Senegal

A full passport is essential for entering Senegal. If you enter from within the region, you might need to show a yellow fever vaccination certificate. Border checks are usually pain free, and the Dakar airport is pretty organised (until you step outside).

Air

Senegal's main airport is **Aéroport International Léopold Sédar Senghor** (DKR; ☎ 33 869 50 50, 24hr information line 77 628 1010; www.aeroportdakar.com) in Yoff, 30 minutes from central Dakar. **Cap Skiring Airport** (☎ 33 993 51 77) has connections to Dakar and Paris.

The national carrier, Air Sénégal International, is one of Africa's most reliable airlines, with good connections throughout West Africa and to Europe.

Airlines servicing Senegal and with offices in Dakar include the following.

Afriqiyah Airways (airline code 8U; Map p680; ☎ in Dakar 33 849 4930; www.afriqiyah.be) Hub: Tripoli, Libya.

Air Europa (airline code UX; Map p685; ☎ in Dakar 33 822 0299; www.air-europa.com) Hub: Madrid, Spain.

Air France (airline code AF; Map p680; ☎ in Dakar 33 839 7777; www.airfrance.fr) Hub: Paris, France.

Air Ivoire (airline code VU; Map p680; ☎ in Dakar 33 889 0280; www.airivoire.com) Hub: Abidjan, Côte d'Ivoire.

Air Sénégal International (airline code V7; Map p680; ☎ in Dakar 81 804 0404; www.air-senegal-international .com) Hub: Dakar, Senegal.

Brussels Airlines (airline code SN; Map p680; ☎ in Dakar 33 823 0460; www.brusselsairlines.com) Hub: Brussels, Belgium.

Delta Airlines (airline code DL; Map p680; ☎ in Dakar 33 849 6955; www.delta.com) Hub: Atlanta, USA.

Ethiopian Airlines (airline code ET; Map p680; ☎ in Senegal 33 823 5552; www.flyethiopian.com) Hub: Addis Ababa, Ethiopia.

Iberia (airline code IB; Map p680; ☎ in Dakar 33 889 0050; www.iberia.com) Hub: Madrid, Spain.

Kenya Airways (airline code KQ; Map p680; ☎ in Dakar 33 823 0070; www.kenya-airways.com) Hub: Nairobi, Kenya.

Royal Air Maroc (airline code AT; Map p680; ☎ in Dakar 33 849 4748; www.royalairmaroc.com) Hub: Casablanca, Morocco.

SENEGAL

South African Airways (airline code SA; Map p685; ☎ in Dakar 33 869 4000; www.flysaa.com) Hub: Johannesburg, South Africa.

TACV Cabo Verde Airlines (airline code VR; Map p680; ☎ in Dakar 33 821 3968; www.flytacv.com) Hub: Praia, Cape Verde.

TAP Air Portugal (airline code TP; Map p680; ☎ in Dakar 33 821 5460; www.tap.pt) Hub: Lisbon, Portugal.

Virgin Nigeria (airline code VK; Map p680; ☎ in Dakar 33 889 9010; www.virginnigeria.com) Hub: Lagos, Nigeria.

Land

GAMBIA

See p321 for details.

GUINEA

Nearly all traffic between Senegal and Guinea goes to/from Labé, a large town in northwestern Guinea, to Diaoubé, a busy market town near Kolda in the Casamance. From there, you can catch connections to other places in Senegal. There are also regular cars via Koundara and Mali-Diembering in Guinea to Kedougou, Senegal. The Diaoubé route has the better roads, and the trip should take around 24 hours (CFA20,000). The Kedougou–Mali route is so bad that even public transport is by 4WD (CFA20,000). From Kedougou, your best chance for public transport to Guinea is on Friday. Diaoubé is best served on Wednesday, when traders and buyers head there for the weekly *lumo* (market).

GUINEA-BISSAU

Bush taxis run several times daily between Ziguinchor and Bissau (CFA6000, 147km) via São Domingos (the border) and Ingore. The road is in good condition and border crossings usually swift. At the time of research, the toll bridge across the wide Cacheu River on the Guinea-Bissau side was nearing completion (July 2009 was the intended opening date). Once it's open, Ziguinchor–Bissau should take no longer than two to three hours (depending on the border). As long as the ferry remains in operation, you can spend anything from four to seven hours on the road.

MALI

You can take the train or a *sept-place* from Dakar via Tambacounda (CFA9000, 12 hours, 467km) to Kidira/Diboli (CFA5000, three hours, 184km). Border crossings are swift and hassle free. From Diboli, most people continue with long-distance buses to Kayes and Bamako (CFA13,000). Direct long-distance buses from Dakar to Bamako (CFA22,000) and beyond leave the Pompiers station in Dakar several times a week. Most transporters are Malian, Ghanaian or Nigerian. Ask at Pompiers for more information – rates, departure spots and so on change very frequently.

Note that the Dakar–Tambacounda route was still in terrible condition at research, though roadworks had started (temporarily making things even worse, with transport rerouted through the bush).

Roadworks had also started along the track from Saraya in Senegal to Kita in Mali. Once completed (expected in late 2010), this will be an attractive option to enter Mali from the Bassari lands.

MAURITANIA

The main border point is at exhausting Rosso, where a ferry (CFA2000/3000 per passenger/car) crosses the river four times daily. The town is full of hustlers and garbage, and the immigration post on the Mauritanian side is only open from 8am to noon and 3pm to 6pm.

If you have your own wheels you can cross at the Maka Diama dam, situated 97km southwest of Rosso and just north of Saint-Louis. The route is graded dirt track and can be washed out during and just after the rainy season. The border crossing here is usually swift.

Dakar–Rosso by *sept-place* is CFA6000 (six hours, 384km), from Saint-Louis it's CFA2000 (two hours, 106km).

Train

The Dakar–Bamako train is something of a traveller's classic. In theory, trains run between Dakar and Bamako twice a week in each direction and the trip takes about 35 hours. In practice, this almost never happens – one train is often out of action, the trip usually takes 40 hours or longer, and derailments are frequent. Enquire about the situation at Dakar **train station** (Map p678; ☎ 33 849 4646) for the latest information or check the train travellers' cult site **Seat 61** (www.seat61.com/senegal.htm). Once on the train, watch out for pickpockets.

SENEGAL

GETTING AROUND
Air
Air Sénégal International (☎ 81 804 0404; www
.air-senegal-international.com) has a connection to
Ziguinchor, with two or three flights in low
season (May to October) and a daily serv-
ice in high season (November to April).
In high season only, there are three flights
(Friday, Saturday and Sunday) to Cap Skiring
(CFA55,000). Weekly flights from Dakar to
Tambacounda (one way CFA80,000) only
operate from January to March.

Check all details with the airline, as internal flights are often subject to changes of
route, price and departure time and date at
short notice. At the time of writing, there
were no longer any flights between Dakar
and Saint-Louis.

Bicycle
Senegal's flat savannah landscape is great for
cycling, but roads are in poor condition and
often sandy. The bigger problem, however,
is that drivers aren't used to cyclists, which
makes city cycling in particular a risk. The
best place to hire bikes is Casamance VTT in
Oussouye (see p725).

Boat
In some areas, including Ndangane, N'Gor,
Elinkine and Affiniam, pirogues are used as
public transport. It's always possible to hire
a pirogue for an excursion (particularly in
the Casamance and Siné-Saloum regions). If
you go to Île de Gorée or Foundiougne, you
need to cross by ferry – these services are safe
and reliable.
Africa Queen (☎ 33 957 7435; Saly) Contact
Saly's Espadon hotel to see if the boat is in Senegal
during your stay (usually it is from around May to
October).

Aline Sitoé Diatta (☎ in Ziguinchor 33 991 7200, in
Dakar 33 849 4893) Departs from Dakar every Tuesday and
Friday around 8pm, returns from Ziguinchor every Sunday
and Thursday around 2pm. By far the most important boat
service in Senegal; see p724.
Bou El Mogdad (☎ 33 961 5689; www.saheldecou
verte.com, www.compagniedufleuve.com) One- to four-
day trips from Saint-Louis to Podor on the '50s ship *Bou
El Mogdad* can be booked through Sahel Découverte in
Saint-Louis (see p708).
Gorée Ferry (☎ 33 849 7961, 24hr info line 77 628
1111) Provides several daily boat connections between
Dakar and Île de Gorée (see p694) and organises recommended mini-cruises between Île de Gorée and Îles de la
Madeleine, as well as between Gorée and Saly.

Bus, Bush Taxi & Minibus
Senegal has a pretty good and cheap long-
distance bus network. Owned by the Mouride
brotherhood, it's usually called *cars mourides*.
In Dakar they go from the Shell station at Ave
Malik Sy near *gare routière* Sapeurs-Pompiers
(just referred to as Pompiers), usually in the
middle of the night to most major destinations in the country. Dakar is also connected
to long-distance buses from Niger, Mali and
Ghana that do unbelievably long journeys
across West Africa (ask at Pompiers for information; operators, departure points and prices
vary too much to warrant inclusion here).

'Bush taxi' is the generic term for all public
transport smaller than a big bus. The most
common forms include Ndiaga Ndiayes or
grands cars, large white Mercedes with
'Alhamdoulilai' printed across the front;
minibuses (usually Nissan Urvans) carrying
20 people; and *sept-place* taxis. These seven-
seaters, usually Peugeot 504s, are always the
most comfortable and fastest option. They
cost around 20% more than Ndiaga Ndiayes.
In some remote areas, however, Ndiaga

TAXI SISTER

Among the mass of clapped-out taxis that ply Dakar's roads, the bright-yellow Chinese Cherys
jump out like flowers in a field. Not only because the tiny model is unusual, or because they're
in polished condition, but mainly because they are the only public vehicles in town driven by
women. Under a government scheme designed to get women working, a handful of female drivers
were given cars to start their own one-woman taxi business. They now gradually pay them off,
carrying clients through the city's hectic streets, defying all the male prejudice raining down on
them from the competition. For women passengers, this is an obvious way of travelling safely,
and without the constant marriage offers male taxi drivers tend to weave into conversations. You
find the Taxi Sisters parked outside Novotel near the French embassy. Or you can ring them to
pick you up on ☎ 88 408 4084.

Ndiayes, minibuses, or even pick-up trucks might be your only option.

Bush taxis leave when they're full, which is why travelling in larger vehicles is such a pain. They fill up fastest in the morning, from 6.30am or earlier to 8.30am. In remote locations, your best chance for transport is on market days, when people will be heading to the market town in the early morning and returning in the evening.

Car & Motorcycle

No cars older than five years may be imported to Senegal. You need an international driving licence to drive or hire a car. Most hire companies request a minimum age of 23.

Car hire is generally expensive. By the time you've added up the costs, you can easily end up paying over US$1000 per week. In Senegal all the international names (Hertz, Avis, Budget) are represented, and there are also smaller independent operators. Dakar is the best place for car hire (see p692 for contact details).

It usually works out better to hire a *sept-place* with its driver. To work out the cost of a journey, multiply the number of seats by the fare and add some extra, particularly for waiting times, and you've got your estimated price.

To take a car across to other countries you need an Ecowas permit, which you can sometimes get at the border, or in Dakar, Ziguinchor or Tambacounda.

Tours

Most places of interest in Senegal can be reached by public transport or car, but if you're short of time you could get around the country on an organised tour. A small selection of recommended operators is included here.

Africa Dream (☎ 33 957 0328; www.africadream.org; Ngaparou) This tiny, French-run agency proposes personalised circuits even to the most unlikely corner. Can cater to tiny groups. French speaking.

ATG (Map p685; ☎ 33 869 7900; www.africatravel -group.com; Rte de N'Gor, Dakar) A big player with a vast range of quality excursions to all regions, a number of lodges and excellent partners across the country. Particularly good for Spanish, Portuguese and French clients. Also organises festivals and plenty more.

Casamance Horizons (☎ 77 709 3241; www .casamance-horizons.com) Excellent local initiative devoted to responsible tourism in Casamance, supporting the communities you visit. Based at Tilibo Horzons at Niafourang.

Origin Africa (Map p685; ☎ 33 860 1578; www.origin -africa.sn; Cité Africa, Ouakam) This small tour operator has a good selection of tours around even remote regions.

Sahel Découverte (Map p709; ☎ 33 961 4263; www .saheldecouverte.com; Saint-Louis) Quite simply the very best way of exploring northern Senegal.

Senegal Experience (☎ in UK 0845 330 2080; www .senegal.co.uk) The Senegal branch of Serenity holidays specialises in tours to Siné-Saloum for travellers from the UK. Visits are arranged from The Gambia.

Touki Voyages (☎ 33 957 1420; www.afrikatouki.com) Has excellent tours, and invests a percentage of profits in local education and development projects. Particularly great are the women's tours, aimed at making travel for individual female tourists more comfortable.

our pick **TPA** (☎ 33 957 1256; www.lesenegal.info) A tour operator with a difference, TPA is the leading agency for rural tourism, offering unique tours to less-travelled routes, typically with its original tourist trucks. Its *campements* are built in local architectural styles and run in the spirit of community *campements* – a percentage of earnings is locally invested, and staff are locally recruited and trained.

Sierra Leone

Sierra Leone has largely stayed out of the news lately, which, considering how it earned most of its press in the 1990s, is a good thing. The decade-long civil war garnered regular media coverage thanks to widespread atrocities committed by rebel soldiers, many of them not yet in their teens.

But oh, how things have changed. Peace was declared in 2002, and it has blossomed. Life has largely returned to normal and today Sierra Leone is one of West Africa's safest destinations. Reconstruction continues apace, investors are arriving in droves and travellers are trickling in. A cruise ship even made a port call in Freetown in January 2009. And the one recent event that did make headlines was a free and fair election.

With some of the most perfect palm-lined sands on the African continent, it won't be long before Sierra Leone takes its place in Europe's packaged beach-holiday scene; but for now, visitors can have the surf outside the capital pretty much, and often completely, to themselves. Travel to the provinces, where roads are often abysmal and facilities usually basic (but getting better), remains in the realm of the adventurous, but with cheerful people and wonderful parks, the rewards are many.

To be sure, Sierra Leone still has problems. For the past two years it ranked last in the UN's Human Development Index, unemployment remains high and corruption is worsening, but most locals hang onto their optimism.

FAST FACTS

- **Area** 72,325 sq km
- **Capital** Freetown
- **Telephone code** ☎ 232
- **Famous for** Diamonds
- **Languages** English, Krio, Mende and Temne
- **Money** leone (Le); US$1 = Le3050; €1 = Le3960
- **Population** 6.4 million
- **Visa** Officially, must be arranged before arrival

HIGHLIGHTS

- **Beach bumming** Freetown Peninsula (p753) and Banana Islands (p755).
- **Tiwai Island** The relaxed Wildlife Sanctuary (p757); Pygmy hippos and primates at the famous wildlife sanctuary.
- **Outamba-Kilimi National Park** (p762) Wildlife-spotting on foot or from a canoe.
- **Freetown** (p747) Minor historic sites painting a vivid history.
- **Tacugama Chimpanzee Sanctuary** (p756) Rehabitation for humanity's closest relative.

ITINERARIES

- **One week** Many people spend their whole week at the beaches. Although it might be hard to pull yourself off the sand, it's worth taking some days up-country to visit Tiwai Island Wildlife Sanctuary (p757) and a town or two. If you're here for wildlife you can get to both Tiwai Island and Outamba-Kilimi National Park (p762) and still sneak a little beach time.
- **Two weeks** In two weeks you can see most of the country without travelling too fast.
- **One month** A month is enough time to see and do just about everything in this chapter.

CLIMATE & WHEN TO GO

Sierra Leone is one of West Africa's wettest and hottest countries, with an average annual rainfall of 3150mm and temperature of 27°C (see Climate Charts, p810). The rainy season stretches from mid-May to mid-November, with July and August the wettest months. The humidity can be oppressive along the coast, although sea breezes afford some relief. Inland, the days are even hotter, but it cools down much more at night, especially in the northwest.

The best time to visit is November, after the rains and before the dusty harmattan winds blow in and paint the skies grey. The further you go into the dry season the more heat you'll have to endure and the less green you'll see in the countryside. During the rainy season, washed-out roads make travel to some destinations difficult or impossible.

HISTORY

The region now called Sierra Leone was on the southern edge of the great Empire of Mali, which flourished between the 13th and 15th

---

HOW MUCH?

- **Small Temne basket** Le5000
- **100km bush taxi ride** Le15,000
- **Bottle of palm wine** Le1500
- **2 lapa (about 4 sq yd of gara cloth** Le20,000
- **A night at a music show** Free

LONELY PLANET INDEX

- **1L of petrol** Le2500
- **1.5L of bottled water** Le2500
- **Bottle of Star beer** Le2000
- **Souvenir T-shirt** Le10,000
- **Fry-fry with egg** Le1200

---

centuries (for more details on the early history of the region, see p27). Early inhabitants included the Temne, Sherbro and Limba, who were organised into independent chiefdoms. Mandingo/Malinké traders had also entered the region early on and integrated with indigenous peoples.

European Contact

Contact with Europeans began in 1462 with the arrival of Portuguese navigators who called the area Serra Lyoa (Lion Mountain), which was later modified to Sierra Leone. Around 120 years later, Sir Francis Drake stopped here during his voyage around the world; however, the British didn't control the area until the 18th century when they began to dominate the slave trade along the West African coast.

The American War of Independence in the 1770s provided an opportunity for thousands of slaves to gain freedom by fighting for Britain. When the war ended, over 15,000 ex-slaves made their way to London, where they suffered unemployment and poverty. In 1787 a group of philanthropists purchased 52 sq km of land in present-day Sierra Leone from a local chief for the purpose of founding a 'Province of Freedom' for ex-slaves. This became Freetown. That same year, the first group of about 400 men and women (300 ex-slaves and 100 Europeans, mainly prostitutes) arrived.

Within three years all but 48 settlers had deserted or died either from disease or in fights with the local inhabitants. But in 1792

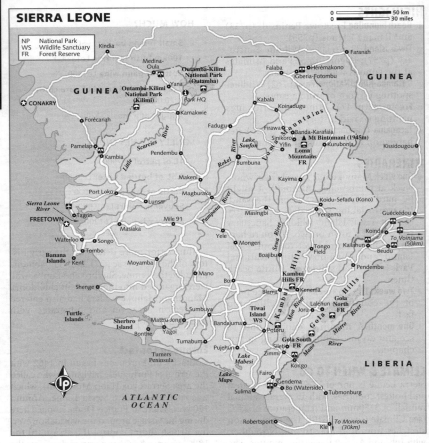

the determined philanthropists sent a second band, this time 1200 ex-slaves who had fled the USA bound for Nova Scotia. Later, they sent 550 more from Jamaica. To the chagrin of the philanthropists, some settlers, both white and black, joined in the slave trade. In 1808 the British government took over the Freetown settlement and declared it a colony.

The Colonial Period

By the early 1800s, slavery had been abolished in Britain. Over the next 60 years British ships plied the West African coast, intercepting slave ships. Freetown became the depot for thousands of 'recaptives' from West Africa, as well as many migrants from the hinterland.

By 1850 over 100 ethnic groups were represented in the colony. They lived in relative harmony, each group in a different section of town.

Like the previous settlers, the recaptives became successful traders and intermarried. All nonindigenous blacks became collectively known as Krios. British administrators favoured the Krios and appointed many to senior posts in the civil service.

Near the end of the 19th century, the tide began to turn against the Krios, who were outnumbered 50 to one by indigenous people, and in 1924 the British administrators established a legislative council with elected representatives, to the advantage of the more numerous indigenous people.

Independence

At independence in 1961, it seemed that Western-style democracy would work. There were two parties of equal strength, but they became divided along ethnic lines. The Sierra Leone People's Party (SLPP) was the party of the Mendes. The All People's Congress (APC), formed by trade unionist Siaka Stevens, became identified with the Temnes and voiced the dissatisfaction of the small modernising elite. The Krio community threw its support behind the SLPP, whose leader, Milton Margai, became the first prime minister.

Following Margai's death in 1964, his brother Albert took over and set about replacing the Krios in the bureaucracy with Mendes. The Krios took revenge in the 1967 elections by supporting the APC, which won a one-seat majority. Hours after the results were announced, a Mende military officer led a coup, placing Siaka Stevens under house arrest. Two days later fellow officers staged a second coup, vowing to end the corruption that was so widespread under the Margai brothers.

Stevens went into exile in Guinea and with a group of Sierra Leoneans began training in guerrilla warfare techniques for an invasion. This became unnecessary when a group of soldiers mutinied and staged a third coup 13 months later: an African record for the number of coups in such a short period.

The Downward Spiral

Stevens returned and formed a new government, but his first decade in office was turbulent. He declared a state of emergency, banned breakaway parties from the APC and put a number of SLPP members on trial for treason. Meanwhile, the economy deteriorated. The iron-ore mine closed, diamond revenues dropped, living costs increased, students rioted and Stevens again declared a state of emergency. The 1978 election campaign almost became a civil war, and the death toll topped 100. Stevens won, and Sierra Leone became a one-party state.

Despite the one-party system, the 1982 elections were the most violent ever. Stevens was forced to give Mendes and Temnes equal representation in the cabinet, although this didn't stop the deterioration of economic and social conditions. With virtually no support left, Stevens finally stepped down in 1985 at the age of 80, naming as his successor Major General Joseph Momoh, head of the army since 1970.

Under Momoh, the economy continued its downward spiral. By 1987 the inflation rate was one of the highest in Africa, budget deficits were astronomical, and smugglers continued to rob Sierra Leone of up to 90% of its diamond revenue.

Things worsened in late 1989 when civil war broke out in neighbouring Liberia. By early 1990, thousands of Liberian refugees had fled into Sierra Leone. The following year, fighting spilled across the border and the Revolutionary United Front (RUF), Sierra Leonean rebels who were opposed to Momoh, took over much of eastern Sierra Leone, beginning a vicious campaign against the population (see boxed text, p761).

The Difficult Decade

The Momoh government used the war in the east as an excuse to postpone elections, but finally, in September 1991, a new constitution was adopted that allowed a multiparty system. Before an election date could be announced, though, a group of young military officers overthrew Momoh in April 1992. The National Provisional Ruling Council (NPRC) was set up, and 27-year-old Captain Valentine Strasser was sworn in as head of state. Elections and a return to civilian rule were promised for 1995.

Soon, though, optimism began to fade. A major drain on resources was the continuing fighting in the east against the RUF, which expanded its control over the diamond-producing areas, robbing the government of revenue. They were bolstered after the coup by supporters of the Momoh regime and by escaping rebels from Liberia. It soon became apparent that none of these groups was fighting for a political objective, but rather their goal was to control the diamond and gold fields. By late 1994 northern and eastern parts of the country had descended into near anarchy, with private armies led by local warlords, government soldiers, rebel soldiers and deserters from the Sierra Leonean and Liberian armies roaming the area at will and terrorising local communities.

In January 1996 Brigadier General Julius Maada Bio overthrew Strasser in a coup. Despite NPRC efforts to postpone them, previously scheduled elections went ahead and in March, Ahmed Tejan Kabbah , the leader of the SLPP, was elected president. Kabbah's government continued peace talks with the

RUF, which had been initiated by the previous military government, but his efforts bore little fruit.

The Rise of the RUF

On 25 May 1997, a group of junior military officers sympathetic to the RUF staged a coup in Freetown. President Kabbah fled to neighbouring Guinea, and the wave of looting, terror and brutality that had ravaged the provinces engulfed the capital. By early 1998 food and fuel supplies were scarce almost everywhere, and thousands of Sierra Leoneans had fled the country.

In February 1998 a Nigerian-led West African peacekeeping force, Ecomog (Ecowas Monitoring Group), succeeded in ousting the junta and in taking control of Freetown and many up-country areas; although not before fleeing rebels had looted and destroyed much in their path. President Kabbah was reinstated in March, but the situation failed to stabilise. On 6 January 1999, with nearly a quarter of the entire Nigerian military serving in Sierra Leone, the RUF staged its boldest assault yet on Freetown: code-named Operation No Living Thing. In the ensuing weeks the city was virtually destroyed and over 6000 people killed before Ecomog again forced the rebels from the capital.

The bloody battle prompted the government to sign the Lomé Peace Agreement with the RUF in July. Under the agreement, RUF leader Foday Sankoh was to become the country's vice-president and the cabinet minister in charge of diamond production, but over the next year the RUF repeatedly violated the agreement. In May, shortly after his soldiers shot and killed 19 anti-RUF demonstrators, Sankoh was arrested for plotting a coup. He suffered a stroke and later died in prison.

As part of the Lomé Peace Agreement, the UN deployed a peacekeeping mission, Unamsil, in Sierra Leone that became the largest and most expensive ever deployed by the body. Unamsil's disarmament of the RUF (over 40,000 firearms were destroyed) finished in February 2002, officially ending the war. Elections held that May garnered an 80% turnout and were deemed Sierra Leone's fairest in years. Kabbah was re-elected to a five-year term, while the RUF's political party didn't win a single seat in parliament. That summer a Truth and Reconciliation Commission (read the final report at www .trcsierraleone.org) began work.

In 2003 the Special Court for Sierra Leone issued its first indictments against leaders from all sides of the conflict, including former Liberian president Charles Taylor, who was arrested in Nigeria in 2006. The last of the 17,500 Unamsil soldiers left Sierra Leone in December 2005 and were replaced by Uniosl, the UN Integrated Office for Sierra Leone, which promotes government accountability, reinforces human rights and oversees development.

Sierra Leone Today

September 2007 brought about a peaceful change of government via the ballot box. With President Kabbah stepping down after serving his constitutionally permitted second term, Sierra Leoneans gave power back to the APC with insurance broker Ernest Bai Koroma winning 55% of the vote in a run-off against Vice-President Solomon Berewa. The APC also netted a parliamentary majority. There was sporadic violence before and after the voting, but both candidates denounced it and international observers declared the vote 'free, fair and credible'. Sierra Leoneans are already gripped by party posturing in the run-up to the 2012 elections.

THE CULTURE
National Psyche

When Sierra Leoneans get together, whether they're the best of friends or strangers thrown together in a *poda-poda* (minibus), talk usually turns to politics, development and corruption: the three largely being one and the same in Sierra Leone. Nobody can deny there's been progress since the war, but most feel the pace is inexcusably slow. Though people will argue their points vigorously, they can still share a laugh with those taking the other side. But, while the war did much to foster nationalism, the elections showed that a significant north–south/Temne–Mende divide remains; and political parties worked to exploit it. Some people worry about how this will play out in coming years.

Daily Life

The Mendes and Temnes operate a system of secret societies responsible for maintaining culture and tradition. If you see young girls with their faces painted white, you'll know they're in the process of being initiated. They wear coloured beads when finished. Masks are an important feature of many ceremonies.

Population

The two largest of the 18 indigenous tribal groups, the Temnes of the north and Mendes of the south, each comprise about one-third of the population. Other groups include the Limba and Koranko in the north, the Kissi in the east and the Sherbro in the southwest. Krios, most living in Freetown, constitute about 1.5% of the population, but are a large percentage of the country's intellectuals and professionals. About 4000 Lebanese, 500 Indians and 2000 Europeans reside in Sierra Leone permanently.

SPORT

English Premier League football is far more popular than the local club scene, though people are working to revive it. Parasports, naturally, have come to Sierra Leone and the Single-leg Amputee Sports Club plays in many international football tournaments.

RELIGION

Muslims, who are concentrated in the north and east, comprise about 76% of the population. Christians, mainly Anglican, Methodist and a growing number of evangelicals, make up most of the rest. Sierra Leoneans are very tolerant of other faiths, and mixed marriages are common.

ARTS
Textiles & Craftwork

Sierra Leone is known for its fabrics, especially country cloth and *gara*. Country cloth is a coarse material woven from cotton into narrow strips that are joined to make blankets and clothing. *Gara* is a thin cotton material, tie-dyed or stamp-printed, with bright colours and bold patterns. As you'll see it in most hotels, it makes attractive bedding.

The Mendes produce the country's best-known masks, which are used in initiation ceremonies of the women's *bondo* (secret societies). Sierra Leone is one of the few places in Africa where women perform masked dances during sacred ceremonies. Another distinctive traditional craft is Temne basketry.

Music & Dance

Sierra Leone's main contribution to the world of music is palm-wine music, known locally as *maringa,* which merged the acoustic guitars introduced by Portuguese sailors with Caribbean Calypso brought back by freed slaves. *Maringa* strongly influenced other West African music, but has been on the decline since its best-known exponent, SE Rogie, who crooned with a country twang even before moving to the US, died in 1994. For more about the music scene, see p57.

Visitors are welcome to stop by the wishfully named Freetown Cultural Village (Map pp748–9) in Aberdeen, Freetown to watch the Sierra Leone National Dance Troupe practise; usually on weekday mornings about 8.30am to 10.30am.

Literature

The narrator of *Moses, Citizen & Me* (2005), by Delia Jarrett-Macauley, must deal with the fact that her cousin is an eight-year-old child soldier. Uzodinma Iweala's *Beasts of No Nation* (2005) takes a more visceral look at child soldiers. Graham Greene's classic *The Heart of the Matter* (1948) goes back to colonial times, with Freetown as the setting for a tale of human weakness, waste and frustration. Richard Dooling's *White Man's Grave* (1994), the story of the search for a missing Peace Corps worker, was a National Book Award finalist.

On the local scene it's very difficult to find books by Sierra Leonean authors. Freetown book vendors on Garrison and Lightfoot Boston Sts (Map p750) usually have a few in stock, as might Diaspora Café (p752). Dozens of poets share their work at www.sierra-leone.org/poetry.html.

Cinema

Leonardo DiCaprio put Sierra Leone on the movie map as a smuggler in *Blood Diamond* (2006), a thriller set in 1999 Sierra Leone, though mostly filmed in Mozambique. Steven Spielberg's *Amistad* (1997) tells the story of Mende slaves, led by Sengby Pieh, who in 1839 revolted to obtain their freedom while being shipped from one Cuban port to another. The Amistad case so fuelled anti-slavery feelings in the USA that it became one of the catalysts of the American Civil War and, later, Sierra Leone's drive for independence.

Two documentaries worth seeking out are *The Refugee All Stars* (2005), an inspiring story of the eponymous band, and the harrowing *Cry Freetown* (2000), featuring first-hand footage from Operation No Living Thing (see p744).

ENVIRONMENT

The Land

The coastal zone, consisting of mangrove swamps, beaches and islands, is flat except for the Freetown Peninsula (one of the few places in West Africa where mountains rise near the sea), where some peaks top 600m. Inland is an undulating, forested and extensively cultivated plateau. There are many mountains in the northeast, including Mt Bintumani (1945m), one of the tallest peaks in West Africa.

Wildlife

Much of the country's wildlife was killed during the war, but crocodiles, chimpanzees, bongos, buffaloes, hippopotamuses, elephants and leopards all hung on and are slowly recovering. Birdlife is much richer and great blue turacos, brown-cheeked hornbills and rufous fishing-owls are among the 628 recorded species. Between September and January, humpback whales swim off the Freetown Peninsula. See p753 for information on how best to see the whales around Freetown.

National Parks

The government has established 21 parks and reserves, covering 4% of the country, though most are protected more by proclamation than practice. The new government, however, has improved things. Tiwai Island Wildlife Sanctuary (p757) is one of the world's best places to see primates, while Outamba-Kilimi National Park (p762) has some large mammals and good birding. Sierra Leone's last significant remaining lowland rainforest covers the Gola Hills in the southeast, and the Gola Forest Reserve (p760) is primed to become the nation's second national park. Protected by its remoteness, the highland rainforest of the Loma Mountains Forest Reserve, surrounding Mt Bintumani, is also quite pristine.

Environmental Issues

Most of Sierra Leone's original forest cover has been destroyed by logging, mining and unsustainable agricultural practices. Less than 4% remains today, and even that remains under threat, especially with a fast-growing population. In a rare positive development, however, timber exports were banned in 2008 due to what the government called 'indiscriminate destruction' caused mostly by Chinese-owned companies.

According to the Conservation Society of Sierra Leone, rapid development in the hills above Freetown now causes floods down below. Also, diamond mining is polluting the Sewa River and gold mining is draining sacred Lake Sonfon.

FOOD & DRINK

Rice is the staple and *plasas* (pounded potato or cassava leaves, cooked with palm oil and fish or beef) is the most common sauce. Other typical dishes are okra sauce, palm-oil stew, groundnut (peanut) stew, pepper soup and, for special occasions, *jollof rice*. Street-food favourites include roasted groundnuts and corn; fried chicken, and plantain; *suya* sticks (spiced beef or chicken on a kebab skewer); and fry-fry (simple sandwiches, usually with a pepper sauce). Even little villages will have at least one *cookery* (simple restaurant) serving tasty, filling *chop* (food), while Freetown has restaurants serving cuisine from around the globe. Most cities will also have a little Lebanese food available. Seafood, often bought right off the boat, is a real treat on the coast.

Vegetarians might want to pick up *Sweet Salone: A Guide for the Vegetarian Wanderer*, a cookbook by Kate Press sold for Le10,000 at Freetown's Diaspora Café (p752).

Star is the top-selling beer, though Star Draft, Holsten and Heineken are preferred by those who can spend a little extra. *Poyo* (palm wine) is light and fruity, but getting used to the smell and the life forms floating in your cup takes a while.

FREETOWN

☎ 022 / pop 1 million

Reminders of the recent violence have largely disappeared in the capital, but evidence of its growing pains is never far away. The city is still crammed with war victims and refugees who have chosen not to return to their up-country homes, traffic jams last from morning until night, and there hasn't been reliable electricity since the 1980s.

But, despite the difficulties, Freetown feels less threatening than many other large West African cities and the beautiful setting and stunning beaches nearby compensate for the chaos. Besides, if you spend all your time in the tourist-friendly Lumley and Aberdeen areas you'll encounter few of these problems anyway. But if you do head into the heart of town to explore the historical sights and markets, you'll soon find there's more to the city than first meets the eye. Freetown is filthy and frantic, but you can't help loving it.

ORIENTATION

Central Freetown is set out on a grid pattern with Siaka Stevens St as the main thoroughfare. Halfway along is the huge Cotton Tree, a good landmark by which to orient yourself. Budget hotels are clustered near PZ Turntable, which stays busy (and thus generally safe) late into the night.

The main route to the east is Kissy Rd, although many drivers snake through the hills to avoid the horrible traffic on this street. Going west, the main route follows Sanders St and Main Motor Rd towards Aberdeen and Lumley, where most visitors spend their time. Note that Sir Samuel Lewis Rd is often called Aberdeen Rd because it ends there. Wilkinson Rd, with many good restaurants, goes south all the way to Lumley Village.

INFORMATION
Cultural Centres
British Council (Map p750; ☎ 224683; www.british council.org; Tower Hill; ☼ 8.30am-4.30pm Mon-Thu, 8.30am-2pm Fri) Hosts monthly artistic events.

Emergency
☎ 999

Internet Access
Lumley Beach Dot Com (off Map pp748-9; Lumley Turntable; per hr Le4000; ☼ 24hr)
Sylvia Blyden Dot Com (Map p750; 24 Garrison St; per hr Le3000; ☼ 24hr)

Medical Services
Central Pharmacy (Map p750; ☎ 076-615503; 30 Wallace Johnson St; ☼ 8.15am-7.30pm Mon-Sat)
Choithram Memorial Hospital (off Map pp748-9; ☎ 232598; Hill Station) Freetown's best hospital, though for serious problems you'll need to go to Dakar or Europe.
Kono Care Pharmacy (Map p750; ☎ 076-625000; 11 Siaka Stevens St; ☼ 9am-6pm Mon-Fri, 9am-5pm Sat)

Money
Forex bureaus can be found throughout the city: Rawdon and Wilberforce Sts have several.

Rates at the airport's exchange bureau aren't horrible, though you'll do better in town.
ProCredit Bank Central (Map p750; 11 Rawdon St; ☼ 8.30am-6pm Mon-Fri, 9am-1pm Sat); Lumley (off Map pp748-9; 157 Wilkinson Rd; ☼ 8.30am-6pm Mon-Fri)
Rokel Commercial Bank (Map p750; 25 Siaka Stevens St; ☼ 8.30am-3.30pm Mon-Fri)
Sierra Leone Commercial Bank (Map p750; 29 Siaka Stevens St; ☼ 8.30am-3.30pm Mon-Fri, 9.30am-1.30pm Sat)

Post
DHL Central (Map p750; ☎ 033-315299; 15 Rawdon St; ☼ 8am-5pm Mon-Fri, 8am-2pm Sat); Greater (Map pp748-9; ☎ 236156; 30 Main Motor Rd; ☼ 8am-6pm Mon-Fri, 9am-5pm Sat)
Post office (Map p750; 27 Siaka Stevens St; ☼ 8am-4.45pm Mon-Fri, 9am-1pm Sat)

Tourist Information
Conservation Society of Sierra Leone (Map pp748-9; ☎ 033-470043; cssl_03@yahoo.com; 2 Pike St; ☼ 9am-5pm Mon-Fri) Very helpful for travellers to Sierra Leone's natural reserves including the Turtle Islands.
Tourist Information Office (Map pp748-9; ☎ 236620; Lumley Beach Rd; ☼ 8am-6.30pm Mon-Fri) Run by the National Tourist Board, staff sell postcards and try to answer questions.

Travel Agencies
IPC Travel Central (Map p750; ☎ 221481; info@ipc travel.com; 22 Siaka Stevens St); Greater (Map pp748-9; ☎ 231543; 10 Sir Samuel Lewis Rd)
Visit Sierra Leone (Map pp748-9; ☎ 076-877618; www.visitsierraleone.org; 28 Main Motor Rd) Doesn't sell flights out of Freetown, but handles everything else visitors might need, including transport guides and landing visas.

DANGERS & ANNOYANCES

Freetown is a reasonably safe city, but heed all usual big-city precautions. Crime in the East End isn't as bad as the stories suggest, but it's still best to watch your back in the day and stay out of the area at night. Most of downtown (except the PZ area where the recommended hotels are) is deserted by 7pm. Don't stroll empty stretches of Lumley Beach alone, even in the daytime. Also, watch your valuables in the markets, especially Victoria Park, and on the ferry to/from Tagrin.

SIGHTS & ACTIVITIES
Downtown
The massive **Cotton Tree** (Map p750), perhaps 500 years old, in the heart of town, is the city's

SIERRA LEONE

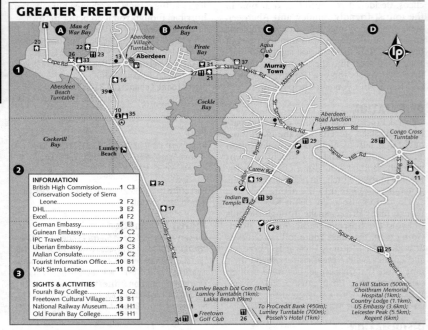

GREATER FREETOWN

principal landmark and most beloved resident. Thousands of bats fly out en masse at dusk. It casts its shadow on the **Sierra Leone National Museum** (Map p750; ☎ 223555; Siaka Stevens St; admission free; ☼ 10.30am-4pm Mon-Fri), which has a small but interesting collection of drums, masks, household goods and other historical artefacts, including Temne guerrilla leader Bai Bureh's clothes, drum and sword. The ornate 1915 **Law Courts** (Map p750; Siaka Steven St) are immediately east of the tree, while the **State House** (Map p750; Independence Ave), incorporating the bastions and lion gate from Fort Thornton (built at the turn of the 19th century), is just up the hill.

The ancestors of nearly all present-day Krios passed through **King's Yard Gate** (Map p750; Wallace Johnson St). Now the site of Connaught Hospital, this is where the British housed and treated rescued slaves before they set out to start their new lives. Most of these new arrivals climbed the **Old Wharf Steps** (Map p750), sometimes erroneously called the Portuguese Steps, that lead up from Government Wharf. The stones were set in 1818.

St John's Maroon Church (Map p750; Siaka Stevens St), a squat white building with big windows, was built around 1820 by former Jamaicans. The much larger **St George's Cathedral** (Map p750; Wallace Johnson St) was completed in 1828.

Many wood-framed **Krio houses** are scattered west of Tower Hill (Map p750). A walk down Pademba Rd presents many good examples. Most date from the late 19th century, but some are older.

Up the Hills

Freetown's beauty and potential show clearly when seen from above. The views are especially good from **Leicester Peak** (Map p754), the big hill with the transmission towers. It's 1.7km up a good paved road starting opposite the US embassy.

On Mt Aureol is **Fourah Bay College** (Map pp748-9; Barham Rd), founded in 1827. It later became the first Western-style university in sub-Saharan Africa. On the edge of campus is a botanical garden and you can follow walking paths down to the waterfall you passed on the drive up.

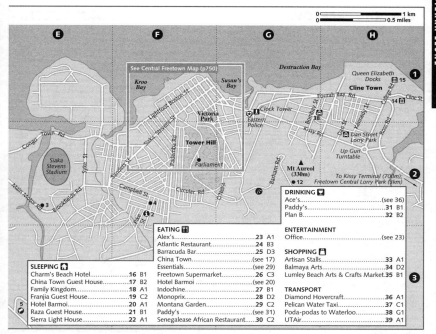

Sierra Leone's **Parliament** (Map p750) building sits atop Tower Hill, near downtown. If MPs are in session (usually Tuesday and Thursday) the police will take you in for a look. Next to the entrance is the foundation of **Martello Tower**, built in 1805 to defend Freetown against Temne attacks.

Lumley Beach

With every patch of beachfront property purchased and many construction projects under way, it's all too easy to imagine what Lumley Beach will look like in coming years, but for now development is fairly scattered and there are far more fishermen and football players on the sands than sunbathers. Lifeguards and beach wardens are usually on duty, though the beach isn't very clean. It's a better location for dinner and drinks than swimming.

Cline Town

Visitors to the **National Railway Museum** (Map pp748-9; ☎ 076-468880; Cline St; admission free; 🕐 9.30am-5pm Mon-Sat) are rare, but the short tour around these restored engines and cars is fairly interesting.

Gutted by fire in 1999, only the laterite shell of the **Old Fourah Bay College** (Map pp748-9; College Rd) building remains, but this 1848 structure is graceful even in its decay.

FESTIVALS & EVENTS

The nation goes kite crazy on Easter Monday, and Lumley Beach is packed with free-flying families. Freetown's recently revived **Lantern Parade** is a procession of illuminated floats on 26 April, the night before Independence Day.

SLEEPING
Budget

Generators run all night at these places.

Place Guest House (Map p750; ☎ 076-662358; 42 Rawdon St; s with shared bathroom Le35,750; r Le41,800-59,400) The best budget hotel in Freetown, the Place is simple but reasonably clean.

Andy's Hotel (Map p750; ☎ 076-622002; 31 Wilberforce St; r with fan/air-con Le50,000/90,000; ❄) A block over from the Place, rooms at this

SIERRA LEONE

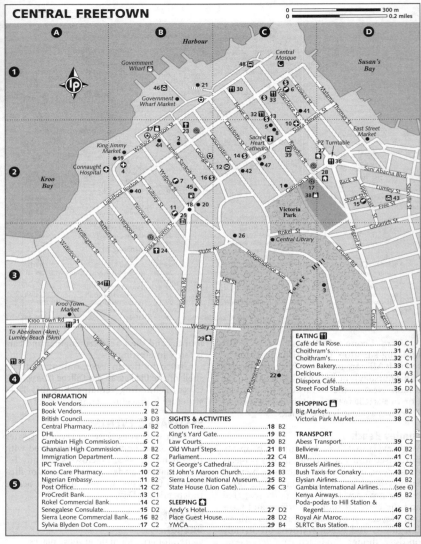

CENTRAL FREETOWN

0 — 300 m
0 — 0.2 miles

friendly spot are scruffier, but have mini-fridges and two-channel satellite TV.

YMCA (Map p750; ☎ 223608; www.ymca-sl.org; 32 Fort St; s with shared bathroom Le35,000, d & tr with shared/private bathroom Le70,000/120,000; P 💻) Rooms at the revamped Y are now pretty decent, though ambitiously priced. The views over the city are a nice bonus, however. There's a restau-rant serving local meals (Le5000) and an internet cafe.

Charm's Beach Hotel (Map pp748-9; ☎ 033-366080; 29 off Cape Rd; r with fan Le75,000-150,000, with air-con Le150,000-225,000; P 🌊) Straddling the budget-midrange divide, this peculiar pink place on a quiet backstreet isn't on the beach, but the surf and sand are just a short walk away.

Rooms come in a mix of styles and standards, but generally those in the new building are better.

Franjia Guest House (Map pp748-9; ☎ 030-240426; 9K Carlton Carew Rd; r with fan & shared bathroom Le70,000, r with fan/air-con Le100,000/150,000; P ⅃) The simple Franjia, in a quiet neighbourhood just off Wilkinson Rd, is kind of homey, and the staff is eager to please. Prices are rather high (try to negotiate), but include breakfast.

Midrange & Top End
There aren't many choices on this side of the price scale, so hotels are often fully booked. Making reservations would be wise. The following, all on the west side of the city, have refrigerators (except Raza's standard rooms), satellite TV, hot water and 24-hour power.

Posseh's Hotel (off Map pp748-9; ☎ 076-750240; 11 Babadorie Rd; s/d Le180,000/330,000; P ⅃ 🖵) This small, out-of-the-way place is as homey as it gets in Freetown, and the restaurant is good enough to attract locals. The singles offer the best value in the midrange, but the doubles definitely don't.

Raza Guest House (Map pp748-9; ☎ 076-956389; 62 Sir Samuel Lewis Rd; r Le210,000-300,000, ste Le450,000; P ⅃ 🖵 ⓢ) This newish property in an oddly attractive building has good-value rooms (by Freetown standards), some with nice views of Cockle Bay. Wi-fi reaches some rooms.

China Town Guest House (Map pp748-9; ☎ 076-625239; 84 Lumley Beach Rd; r Le225,000-255,000; P ⅃) The priced-right rooms at the back of this Oriental-themed complex (which also includes massage and a supermarket) lie just across the road from a quiet stretch of Lumley Beach.

Family Kingdom (Map pp748-9; ☎ 076-777949; www.familykingdomresort.net; Lumley Beach Rd; r Le225,000-375,000, ste Le420,000-540,000, villas Le540,000-750,000; P ⅃ 🖵 ⓢ) Freetown's most colourful lodging has ordinary rooms, and the cheapest are tiny and could use a touch-up. But the real attractions are inside the compound, which has enough playground equipment for several schools' worth of children, a wading pool, and duikers roaming the grounds. Most rooms have kitchenettes.

Sierra Light House (Map pp748-9; ☎ 076-706036; 5 Man of War Bay; s/d Le285,000/315,000; P ⅃ 🖵 ⓢ) Though the building is profoundly ugly from the outside, all 38 of the large rooms have a balcony sticking right out over the bay and a separate sitting area.

Hotel Barmoi (Map pp748-9; ☎ 076-603556; www.hotelbarmoi.com; 75C Cape Rd; s Le324,000-399,000, d Le456,000-486,000, s/d with kitchenette Le384,000/510,000; P ⅃ 🖵 ⓢ) This recently expanded lodge has fine rooms and a great seaside location near the lighthouse. Sea views cost extra, and sometimes it's worth it. There's a good restaurant and two swimming pools.

Country Lodge (off Map pp748-9; ☎ 076-691000; www.countrylodgesl.com; Hill Station; r Le420,000-565,000, ste Le710,000-870,000; P ⅃ 🖵 ⓢ) The first choice for Freetown's most discerning visitors, Country Lodge has lovely rooms with big views. (Some lack the views; be sure to request one.) Plus, its ridge-top spot keeps it cooler than the oceanside competition. The rooms have all the expected mod cons and the complex features a tennis court, gym and a pool large enough for a real swim. You'll pass a row of stilted wooden houses, the former homes of the British colonial leaders, on the way up.

EATING
Aberdeen & Lumley
China Town (Map pp748-9; ☎ 076-625239; 84 Lumley Beach Rd; meals Le9000-80,000; ⓨ dinner; ⓧ) Arguably Freetown's best Chinese food; served with views of the beach. A cheaper fast-food version downstairs opens all day.

Barracuda Bar (Map pp748-9; ☎ 076-618240; Wilberforce Junction; meals Le9500-60,000; ⓨ lunch Mon-Sat, dinner daily; ⓧ) Uphill from Lumley, this stylish spot at Mamba Point Guest House is Freetown's first sushi bar. You can listen to live jazz on Friday nights.

Atlantic Restaurant (Map pp748-9; ☎ 076-667677; 30 Lumley Beach Rd; meals Le15,000-62,000; ⓨ lunch Sun, dinner Tue-Sun) This restaurant-bar on the southern half of Lumley Beach has good fish dishes and a terrace, which is great for drinks at sunset.

Alex's (Map pp748-9; off Cape Rd; ☎ 076-679272; meals Le15,000-70,000; ⓨ lunch Sat & Sun, dinner Tue-Sun) From under the palm trees you have a great view west over Man of War Bay, making this Freetown's loveliest dining spot. The large global menu includes enchiladas, lasagne, *jollof rice* and Cajun chicken. The adjacent sports bar has projection TVs and a pool table.

Indochine (Map pp748-9; ☎ 076-661768; 64 Sir Samuel Lewis Rd; meals Le18,000-60,000; ⓨ lunch Tue-Sun, dinner daily) This classy, Vietnamese-owned spot with a patio overlooking Cockle Bay serves decent Vietnamese, Chinese and Thai food.

Hotel Barmoi (above) serves food that's as good as the views, and Paddy's (p752) also makes very good meals, especially from the Chinese and Indian lists.

Wilkinson Rd

Senegalease African Restaurant (Map pp748-9; ☎ 033-666559; 68 Wilkinson Rd; meals Le8000-43,000; ☺ lunch & dinner; ☒ ☒) Mention this simple spot as your dining destination to a local, and their eyes will light up and they'll give you a nod of approval.

Montana Garden (Map pp748-9; ☎ 033-666608; 38 Wilkinson Rd; meals Le10,000-45,000; ☺ breakfast, lunch & dinner; ☒) This Lebanese restaurant makes one of Freetown's best pizzas. You can sample some delicious sweets or huff a hookah (Le12,000 to Le15,000) for dessert.

Downtown

ourpick Diaspora Café (Map p750; ☎ 076-411144; 2 Priscilla St; meals Le8000-30,000; ☺ lunch daily, dinner Mon-Sat; ☒ ☎) This wonderful little oasis is a sliver of sophistication in central Freetown. The food, a mix of local and beyond (Western breakfasts to Eastern curries to southern fried calamari), is excellent, and it's got the best vegetarian selection around. Although it encompasses only a few shelves, this is also Sierra Leone's best bookstore. You can sometimes use their wi-fi.

Café de la Rose (Map p750; ☎ 076-772919; 2 Howe St; meals Le10,000-25,000; ☺ lunch & dinner Mon-Sat; ☒) Popular with bankers and business people, Rose serves tasty local dishes like cassava leaves and pepper soup (plus more substantial meat and seafood choices) indoors and on a breezy 1st-floor patio.

Crown Bakery (Map p750; ☎ 030-160081; 5 Wilberforce St; meals Le12,000-50,000; ☺ breakfast & lunch Mon-Sat; ☒) Besides being a delicious bakery, this favourite of expats and local bigwigs has a broad menu spanning pancakes to pastas and chicken cordon bleu to fajita wraps.

Delicious (Map p750; ☎ 076-610797; 67 Siaka Stevens St; meals Le25,000-50,000; ☺ lunch & dinner Mon-Sat; ☒ ☒) Freetown's first Indian restaurant is also one of the most pleasant sitting spots downtown. The food, mostly north Indian but also various international options like pizza, stroganoff and grilled *kofte* (Middle Eastern meatballs), generally lives up to the name. They deliver to Aberdeen and are considering opening another branch out there.

Like just about all downtown diners, the above establishments are closed by 7pm.

Street-food vendors, however, work their lantern-lit stalls around PZ Turntable late into the night.

Self-Catering

The flock of well-heeled UN and NGO workers living in Freetown keep many supermarkets, all full of expensive imported goods, in business. **Freetown Supermarket** (Map pp748-9; 137 Wilkinson Rd) is the biggest, but **Choithram's** (Map p750; 7 Rawdon St & 1 Kroo Town Rd), at two locations, **Essentials** (Map pp748-9; 34 Wilkinson Rd) and **Monoprix** (Map pp748-9; 4 Wilkinson Rd) are also good.

DRINKING & ENTERTAINMENT

No place really gets hopping until midnight.

Paddy's (Map pp748-9; 63 Sir Samuel Lewis Rd; ☺ 24hr) No longer the den of iniquity it once was, Paddy's is still Freetown's most famous nightspot and the only place were everyone, no matter what their stripe, can really let their hair down at the bar or on the dance floor. Drink prices are low and the food (Le9000 to Le43,000) can be very good.

Ace's (Map pp748-9; 74 Cape Rd; ☺ 7pm-late) The Refugee All Stars (see also p745) play this large, multifaceted venue on Thursday nights.

Plan B (Map pp748-9; ☎ 076-619650; Lumley Beach Rd; ☺ 5pm-late Mon-Sat, 1pm-late Sun) Unusually tranquil for Freetown, Plan B is a jazz-infused wine bar.

Office (Map pp748-9; off Cape Rd; ☺ 6pm-late) Freetown's hot spot of the moment is just an upscale bar, but it's so popular that on weekends it's packed like a club and the crowd can't resist dancing to the hip hop and R&B.

SHOPPING

The **Lumley Beach Arts & Crafts Market** (Map pp748-9; ☺ 8am-7pm) and the artisan stalls (Map pp748–9) near Aberdeen Beach Turntable are the main places people pick up woodcarvings, baskets and other tourist bric-a-brac.

The top floor of the **Big Market** (Map p750; Wallace Johnson St; ☺ 8am-6pm Mon-Sat), AKA Basket Market, downtown has a larger selection and lower prices than Lumley, though what really makes this the best place to shop for souvenirs are the traditional household goods on the ground floor. This market, along with the hectic Victoria Park Market (Map p750), is the best place to buy *gara*, and is also tops for country cloth. Clothing can be custom made, usually the same day.

Balmaya Arts (Map pp748-9; 32 Main Motor Rd) has top-quality stuff from across West Africa (plus good sandwiches and salads).

GETTING THERE & AWAY
Air
For details of international flights, see p766.

Bus, Bush Taxi & Minibus
SLRTC buses leave from the downtown **bus station** (Map p750; Wallace Johnson St), though not every day to every town, so check the schedule before making plans. The queue starts around 5am, the ticket office opens at 6am and the buses leave when full (and they're always full), usually 7am to 7.30am. Cities served include Bo, Kabala, Kenema, Kono, Makeni and Conakry, Guinea. An air-conditioned express service to Bo (Le20,000) and Kenema (Le22,000) leaves at 6am and tickets are sold up to 24 hours in advance.

Abess Transport (Map p750; ☎ 033-350003) buses park on Rawdon St and begin departing around 6am. Competition for tickets isn't as fierce as for SLRTC. There are a couple of departures daily to Bo and Kenema and one to Kono.

Most bush taxis leave from **Freetown Central Lorry Park** (off Map pp748-9; Bai Bureh Rd), AKA Clay Factory, at Texaco Junction on the far east side of town. From downtown catch a taxi on Goderich St. *Okada* (motorcycle taxis) cost Le5000 for the very exciting ride.

GETTING AROUND
To/From the Airport
Lungi International Airport (Map p754) is inconveniently located across the Sierra Leone River from Freetown, but there are many options for getting to the city.

The fastest ways are **UTAir** (Map pp748-9; ☎ 033-807420; one way Le210,000) helicopters, followed by **Diamond** (Map pp748-9; ☎ 076-614888; one way Le150,000) hovercraft. Both drop and depart at Aberdeen, but they don't meet every flight. **Pelican Water Taxi** (Map pp748-9; ☎ 033-111118; www.pelicanwatertaxi.com; one-way Le120,000) runs slower, smaller boats to Aberdeen Bridge for every flight.

The slowest, cheapest option is the ferry (passengers 2nd-class/1st-class/ VIP Le2000/5000/30,000, car/4WD Le25,000/30,000) that crosses from Tagrin to Kissy Terminal (Map p754; service may shift to the more convenient Government Wharf)

five times a day between 8am and 9pm. **Abess Transport** (Map p750; ☎ 033-350003; one-way Le75,000) uses the ferry for its door-to-door shuttle. You can speed things up on the ferry route by taking a shared taxi (Le2000) to Tagrin and then either one of the *pam-pahs* (large cargo/passenger boats) for Le2000 or the less overcrowded speedboats for Le5000 (plus extra if you have lots of luggage). These are wet landings, but men wait to carry passengers to the boats for a small tip. If you're in a real rush you can charter a speedboat from Man of War Bay for Le300,000.

Taxis stake out all the landing sites.

Okada
Okada have finally caught on in Freetown because they can wind through the traffic jams, but drivers can be astoundingly reckless: don't hesitate to tell them to slow down. Short rides (up to about 1.5km) cost Le1000 and anything beyond that depends on your negotiating skills. Just wave down any passing motorcycle whose driver isn't wearing a backpack and odds are it's an *okada*.

Shared Taxi & Poda-Poda
Shared taxis and *poda-podas* cost Le700. Taxis make short hops between major road junctions while *poda-podas* run long distance, including going from downtown (Regent Rd at Circular Rd) to Lumley and Aberdeen. *Poda-podas* have their routes painted on the front (but still ask about the destination since drivers sometimes change their minds). For taxis, just call out your destination to each passing vehicle. There are few vehicles after 10pm.

Taxi
Freetown doesn't have private-hire taxis; just bargain with the shared taxi drivers to get where you want to go. A trip from downtown to Aberdeen during bad traffic will cost about Le15,000, while a short hop won't be less than Le3000.

AROUND FREETOWN

BEACHES
Some of Africa's best beaches lie along the mountainous, 40km-long Freetown Peninsula, and on weekdays you can have many of them to yourself. Fishing and,

between September and January, whale-watching trips are available and fresh fish meals cost a standard Le25,000 virtually everywhere. A parking icon below indicates parking inside a fence, but there's a place for a car everywhere.

It's infrequent, but transport runs down the coast from Freetown to River No 2 (Le3000, one hour) and Tokeh (Le3500, 1½ hours). Start the journey at Lumley Bridge, 250m south of Lumley Turntable, taking a *poda-poda* to Funkia (Le700, 20 minutes) and changing vehicles there. Transport is better the other way around, with taxis running all day from Waterloo round to Kent (Le3000, 45 minutes) and Tokeh (Le3000, one hour). Get to Waterloo (Le1200, 30 to 60 minutes) by *poda-poda* from Bombay St in the East End. There's also an SLRTC bus to Tokeh (Le3500, Monday to Saturday).

Six kilometres after **Goderich** and its animated afternoon fish market is **Lakka Beach**, the first good beach out of Freetown, and thus a popular place on weekends. The best of several places to sleep, eat and drink is ourpick **Hard Rock** (☎ 033-464908; r Le130,000) with three rooms on a lovely little peninsula. The far side of the same bay is so-so **Hamilton Beach** where **Samso's** (☎ 030-212393; r Le120,000, 2-bedroom villa Le300,000) is quieter on weekends than anything on Lakka.

About halfway down the peninsula is gorgeous **Sussex Beach** where you'll find **Franco Diving Centre** (☎ 076-744406; r Le198,000; P 🏊). Besides leading scuba trips to shipwrecks, Italian-born Franco offers seven large, well-equipped rooms and a restaurant with seafood and Italian dishes for Le15,000 to Le30,000. He says internet is coming soon. **Julcy's** (☎ 033-871649; julcyholidayresort@yahoo.com; s/d Le120,000/135,000; P), in a colourful compound on a rocky point, is a cheaper alternative.

Sussex is followed by little **Bawbaw Beach** (rooms were under construction at the time of writing) where you can camp, though the guys here make a ridiculously high first offer. Ask for directions to the natural rock pool.

Many people rank **River No 2** as the choicest beach in the country, and scenery-wise it's clearly a contender, but it's also one of the busiest. The community-run **Sankofa Entertainment Complex** (☎ 033-457012; camping per tent Le60,000, r Le150,000; P) offers large but overpriced rooms right on the beach. Entry for the day (Le5000) gets you use of thatch huts and showers. Be sure to let them paddle you up to the waterfall

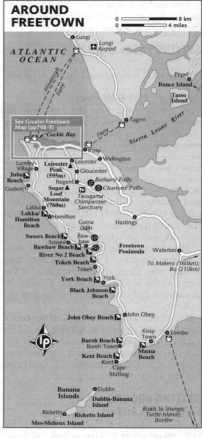

AROUND FREETOWN

on River No 2, passing monkeys and crocodiles on the way. The nearby **Guma Dam** is a popular picnic spot. You can either drive there or walk along the overgrown **Guma-No 2 Nature Trail**, passing a waterfall on the way.

Around the bend is **Tokeh Beach** (you can walk here from River No 2, using a boat over the river at high tide) where the guys running **Africana Tokeh Beach** (☎ 077-934243) will set up a mattress and mossie net under a thatch roof for Le30,000, or let you pitch a tent for less. They'll also build bonfires and cook dinner. The spot is well outside the village behind the large luxury resort that has been under construction for many years.

York is an interesting Krio village, with seldom-visited **York Beach** down below. From

York's seaside cave, where slaves supposedly stayed before being loaded onto ships, you can look across Whale Bay to deserted **Black Johnson Beach**. It may be possible to walk here in the dry season; otherwise get a boat in York or follow the unmarked 1.5km-long dirt road (veer right at the first junction) that begins just after the Whale River Bridge.

Next up is stunning **John Obey Beach** where **ourpick** John Obey Beach Boys (☎ 076-896669; s/d Le40,000/60,000) has a similar but superior sleeping set-up to that available at Tokeh. They'll cook meals, but bring your own drinks.

Arguably the loveliest stretch of sand in West Africa is **Bureh Beach**, where the Crocodile River feeds the ocean and frames the mountain views. There's one simple room available through **Bureh Beach Boys** (☎ 077-721899) who also have tents for hire and have built toilets. All prices are negotiable. It's not *Endless Summer*-worthy, but in the rainy season the six-to eight-foot right-handed break here offers Sierra Leone's best surfing. A hotel is under construction, but it's not going to ruin the views.

At the tip of the peninsula is **Kent** with its ruined fort and yet another beach.

BANANA ISLANDS

Dangling off the southern tip of the peninsula like an emerald pendant, the Banana Islands provide an easy, comfortable journey to a world seemingly far away. Occupied at times by the Portuguese and British, who used this as a base to fight piracy, its current Krio residents put down roots in the late 18th century. Dublin (*doo*-blin) on the northern tip of the main island has several minor historic sites including some cannon, decorative street lights (but no longer any proper streets), the jungle-encased remains of 1881 **St Luke's Church**, and a cemetery with a tombstone dated 1712. Further afield there's a bat cave and decent snorkelling. A boat ride around the island is lovely, but a better option is to stop at **Ricketts Island** and then walk the easy, topical trail back to Dublin, crossing the rock bridge between the two isles.

While you can still do Banana Island day trips from any peninsular beach, there are now two great places to sleep in Dublin (with more on the way), both on little beaches. Friendly, family-run **ourpick** Dalton's **Banana Guest House** (☎ 076-570208; r with shared/private bathroom Le40,000/50,000) faces the loveliest (though not cleanest) beach. It has the best budget rooms (cheaper ones are planned) on any beach in Sierra Leone and probably the largest thatch roof too, under which are served simple local meals. The community-run **ourpick** Banana **Island Guest House** (☎ 076-989906; www.bananaisland guesthouse-biya.org; s/d/tr Le165,000/190,000/225,000) is pricier and correspondingly better in quality.

BUNCE ISLAND

Tiny Bunce (rhymes with dunce) Island, 32km up the Sierra Leone River from the ocean, was home to the largest and one of the most profitable slave castles in West Africa. Slave traders operated here beginning around 1670, and before the British outlawed the trade in 1807 some 30,000 men, women and children were shipped into exile.

The British-controlled island was attacked many times by competitors, pirates and the French (including once in 1779 during the American Revolution), and the fortress was levelled at least six times. The jungle-encrusted ruins you'll see today were built following the last French attack in 1794. Though in poor condition (the World Monuments Fund lists it as one of the world's 100 most-endangered historic sites), the isolated location makes visits very evocative. The self-appointed caretaker, who'll join you on the island from Pepel, tells interesting, though sometimes erroneous tales in Krio, so taking a guide from Freetown is highly recommended.

Though, as elsewhere in Africa, the vast majority of human cargo was destined for the West Indies, Bunce Island sent more slaves than most other trading centres to Britain's North American colonies, where they fetched premium prices due to their knowledge of rice planting. The Gullah people of South Carolina and Georgia trace their unique heritage directly to Sierra Leone. For this reason and others, Bunce is considered the most important historic site in Africa connected to the US.

Any travel agency in town can take you there, though costs are high. Doing it yourself is cheapest from Kissy Terminal where a *pam-pah* (large cargo/passenger boat) will cost Le200,000 (plus 12 gallons of fuel and one gallon of oil) and take two hours to reach Bunce. A speedboat can do it in under one hour from Man of War Bay. This will cost about Le600,000 all-inclusive.

Solar cells provide the power and the fairly large menu (Le24,000 to Le43,000) even has wine.

Dalton's charges Le90,000 for the round-trip ride to the island, while the Banana Island Guest House charges Le120,000. You can also do what most islanders do; just wait around Kent until a boat is going. Locals pay Le2000 for this option, but travellers end up paying Le5000.

REGENT & AROUND

The village of **Regent** still has many interesting Krio houses, some dating from the early 19th century. Simple **St Charles Church**, begun in 1809 and completed seven years later, is the third-oldest stone church built by Europeans on the continent, and the oldest south of the Sahara.

Three kilometres past Regent, **Tacugama Chimpanzee Sanctuary** (☎ 076-611211; www.tacugama .com; adult/child Le30,000/10,000; ☺ tours by appointment at 10.30am & 4pm) is home to nearly 100 abandoned and confiscated chimps who are being prepared for eventual release. Most live semiwild inside large fenced enclosures. If you want to trade Freetown's car horns for the call of the wild, Tacugama has three excellent, solar-powered **our pick** cottages (Le240,000-360,000; P): the two-storey Augusta is the most popular. Price includes breakfast and tours, and soon they will be offering lunch and dinner, but for now you need to cook your own. Taxis run regularly from Government Wharf to Regent (Le1000), from where you'll have to walk (up-hill the whole way) or charter a taxi for around Le5000. The last 100m need 4WD.

There are several waterfalls in the area, including little **Bathurst Falls**, visible from the road just past the bridge, and, further on, lovely **Charlotte Falls** (pay Le2000 at the chief's colourful house), which is a good spot for a swim. Tacugama has printed a detailed guide-map (Le5000) to Charlotte and other scenic spots.

THE SOUTH & EAST

Bo, Kenema and Kono are the largest and busiest towns outside the capital, but the region is still principally pastoral with some fantastic wildlife-watching opportunities, plus remote islands and beaches ripe for exploration. This country's major diamond-mining areas also lie here.

BO
pop 149,000

Sierra Leone's second-largest city, the former capital of the Protectorate of Sierra Leone, is a lively town in the heart of Mende country. Bo's large downtown is evidence of its former prosperity, and a strong local militia group ensured that the city suffered less than most others during the war. Despite this, there isn't really anything to see or do except stroll the market or have a tailor sew you a smart shirt using kola-nut *gara*.

Crime is on the rise in Bo. It's still safe to walk around the city centre into the early

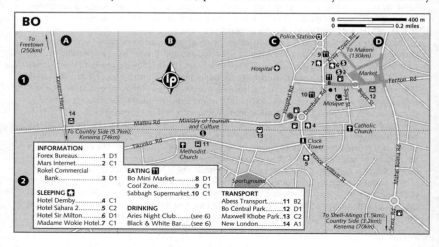

BO

INFORMATION		
Forex Bureaus	1	D1
Mars Internet	2	C1
Rokel Commercial		
Bank	3	D1
SLEEPING		
Hotel Demby	4	C1
Hotel Sahara 2	5	C2
Hotel Sir Milton	6	D1
Madame Wokie Hotel	7	C1

EATING		
Bo Mini Market	8	D1
Cool Zone	9	C1
Sabbagh Supermarket	10	C1
DRINKING		
Aries Night Club	(see 6)	
Black & White Bar	(see 6)	

TRANSPORT		
Abess Transport	11	B2
Bo Central Park	12	D1
Maxwell Khobe Park	13	C2
New London	14	A1

evening, but if you're heading further afield, have someone at your hotel recommend an *okada* driver.

Information

Banks are clustered along Bojon St, including **Rokel Commercial Bank** (10 Bojon St), which does cash advances on Visa cards, though the two forex bureaus on Fenton St offer better exchange rates.

Mars Internet (1 Dambala Rd; per hr Le8000; ⏱ 9am-9pm Mon-Fri, 10am-8pm Sat, noon-6pm Sun) When it has a connection, it's pretty fast.

Sleeping

Hotel Demby (☎ 076-379503; 3 Tikonko Rd; r Le10,000-25,000) You get what you pay for at this crumbling place, but the no-nonsense owners keep the riff-raff away. There's no generator and all rooms share bucket-shower bathrooms.

Hotel Sir Milton (☎ 076-921774; 6 Kissy Town Rd; s/d Le50,000/55,000, r with air-con Le70,000-110,000; Ⓟ ▨) This centrally located hotel is rather rough around the edges, but fair for the price, and renovations were under way when we last slept there. Most rooms have a couple of satellite TV channels and an internet cafe is planned. The same friendly owner operates the Madame Wokie Hotel. around the corner.

Hotel Sahara 2 (☎ 076-871251; 2 Fatu Rd; r with shared/private bathroom Le50,000/60,000, s with air-con Le70,000-90,000, d/tr with air-con Le100,000/120,000; Ⓟ ▨) Rooms are much newer, and thus better than the Milton, but it lacks that old-timer's congeniality and central location.

Country Side (☎ 076-883527; s/d Le100,000/150,000; Ⓟ ▨ ▣ ▤) Outside town on the Kenema Hwy, Country Side is nothing too fancy, but it's pleasant enough and has a swimming pool and tennis court.

Eating & Drinking

Cheap local and Lebanese food can be found at several downtown restaurants including **Cool Zone** (34 Dambala Rd; meals around Le7000; ⏱ lunch & dinner). Try the hotels for more substantial meat and seafood dishes (around Le10,000 to Le20,000) of both African and continental origin.

Imported groceries can be bought at the **Bo Mini Market** (26 Dambala Rd) and **Sabbagh Supermarket** (7 Dambala Rd).

After dusk most visitors camp out at their hotel and watch the passing crowds. People-

watching is also good from the 2nd-storey **Black & White Bar** (8 Kissy Town Rd), which has fewer prostitutes than most of the watering holes. Combine B&W with the nearby **Aries Night Club** (2 Kissy Town Rd), and you've almost got a mini-Paddy's.

Getting There & Away

Early in the morning you can catch bush taxis (Le18,000, four hours) and SLRTC buses (regular/express Le16,000/20,000) to Freetown outside Maxwell Khobe Park. After 7.30am, head out to New London for the Freetown service. Maxwell Khobe is also the spot for Mattru Jong (Le12,000, three hours) and the Liberian border (see p767 for full details). Abess Transport buses (Le19,000) leave from Tikonko Rd around midnight.

Poda-podas for Kenema (Le4000, 1½ hours), Potoru (Le10,000, two hours) and Makeni (Le15,000, four hours) depart from Bo Central Park by the market. The quickest way to Kenema is usually to go out to Shell-Mingo on the highway and jump in a taxi there.

TIWAI ISLAND WILDLIFE SANCTUARY

Tiwai Island (☎ in Freetown 076-755146, in Potoru 076-748542; www.tiwaiisland.org; day trip/overnight Le30,000/60,000, children half-price) is a beautiful reserve on a fairly pristine 12-sq-km island in the Moa River. Many animals that are rare elsewhere thrive here, including pygmy hippos, river otters and white-breasted guinea fowl, but it's most famous for its world-class abundance and concentration of primates. It's not unusual to see a majority of the island's 11 primate species (which include chimps and Diana monkeys) on a two-hour walk. And the 135 avian species make for good birding too.

Besides strolling the web of trails or taking a river trip, community tours are available and small beaches emerge in the dry season. Guided excursions range from Le20,000 to Le30,000. Overnight visitors sleep in tents perched on covered platforms (bedding provided) and local meals (Le6000 to Le10,000) are available, or you can do your own cooking.

The nearest town with transport is Potoru. Generally three taxis make the trip from Bo (Le10,000, two hours), but just one comes from Kenema (Le15,000, three hours, 2pm). *Okada* drivers in Potoru hold out for Le15,000 for the final 16km to Kambama village, where

SIERRA LEONE

you take a boat to the island. Tiwai staff will arrange taxi charters to/from Bo. Visitors are requested to call before arrival.

SULIMA

It's hard to believe when you see it, but Sulima was once a busy port town. Today this shady spot at the mouth of the Moa River consists of mostly mud-and-thatch houses and a few crumbling colonial buildings. Siaka Stevens' old vacation home, a victim of the war, lies along the metal track leading to the lagoon, and Fanti fishermen, originally from Ghana, repair their nets down by the steep beach. It's a great place to chill a while: and you'll need to after roughing it over the road that brings you here. But, it's also a great destination if you're looking for adventure as the area is full of rivers and footpaths to explore. One hour's walk down the beach, you can get a dugout to look for crocodiles on the Mano River. It's an all-day walk, with several river crossings, to beautiful Lake Mape and back. Locals can offer advice and find guides.

The only hotel is the spartan **Mamie Sambo Guest House** (☎ in Liberia 00-231-682 9495; r Le20,000), but the equally simple **pastor's house** (admission by donation) by the naval base makes for a more pleasant night.

There are many taxis to Gendema (Le10,000) and Fairo (Le14,000) – they sometimes go to Gendema first and sometimes to Fairo first – Thursday to Saturday (market days), but only one or two on other days. *Okada* cost Le15,000 from Fairo.

BONTHE
pop 9800

Bonthe, the only notable town on Sherbro Island, was used by the British as an anti-slaving post from 1861; later it grew into a prosperous port. Old colonial buildings, including several large churches, still dot the sandy streets, and despite a pervasive decrepitude, the car-free town has genuine charm. Though small and remote, Bonthe is a district headquarters so there's a hospital and college, and shops are pretty well stocked.

There are no sights per se, but don't miss the **boat** with a tree growing inside it near the naval base. You can walk past the airstrip (and its rotting airplane) to visit some villages or hire a boat to explore the surrounding mangrove forests, outlying beaches and the **Turtle Islands** (see boxed text, below).

Homey **John Cole Guest House** (☎ 076-441653; 46 Medina St; r with shared bathroom Le30,000), on the clock tower road, is the best of the three simple guesthouses. Rooms are very good for the price, and the generator is reliable. Primarily the domain of fanatical fishermen, **Bonthe Holiday Village** (☎ 076-532544; www .bontheholidayvillage.com; r Le450,000; 🖥 🐾) is a very utilitarian place, but on the comfort scale it's as good as anything Freetown has, minus in-room TVs and air-conditioners. Locals call it 'Complex'.

Eating in Bonthe is all about seafood, and wherever you're staying will prepare what you request, as long as someone caught it that day.

Bush taxis go from Bo to Mattru Jong (Le13,000, 2½ hours, Monday to Saturday) early in the morning, and there you catch the 1pm boat (Le12,000, four to five hours) for a beautiful ride down the Jong River to Bonthe. The return boat leaves Bonthe at 8am. On Sundays, boats only connect Bonthe with Yagoi, but there are *usually* enough passengers travelling that you can reach Yagoi by taxi from Mattru Jong

---

TURTLE ISLANDS

Perched off Cape St Ann at the far tip of Sherbro Island, the idyllic Turtle Islands are often talked about but rarely visited. The Conservation Society of Sierra Leone (p747) is opening a small lodge on Baki Island; or find the local chief who'll give you permission to camp on the beach or find a family to put you up for the night.

Bonthe Holiday Village charges Le900,000-and-up for trips to the Turtles in top-notch boats. The Bonthe fisheries office charges Le100,000 for their speedboat, plus 40 gallons of fuel and two gallons of oil. There's also a public *pam-pah* (large cargo/passenger boat) to the islands on Tuesday, returning a week later with other stops on the way. If you'd prefer to come direct from the Freetown Peninsula, see p767 for boat hire information. We can't vouch for the safety of the trip, but a *pam-pah* runs from Tombo to the Turtles (Le15,000, six hours) on Friday night or very early Saturday morning.

(Le7000, one hour) in time for the afternoon boat. Returning from Bonthe on Sundays, you can easily make it to Bo or Freetown.

KENEMA
pop 127,000

Kenema, the province's most prosperous town, is a busy trade centre for coffee, cacao, timber and, most visibly, diamonds. The main artery, Hangha Rd, is a crush of Lebanese diamond merchants, and, as in Kono, you can visit area mines if you wish.

Birdwatchers come to the not-so-unspoiled **Kambui Hills Forest Reserve** just outside Kenema for the near-guaranteed sightings of white-necked rockfowl. Stop by the District Forestry Office before visiting.

Information

There are several banks, including **Rokel Commercial Bank** (12 Dama Rd) for credit card advances, though for changing money use the forex bureaus on Hangha Rd.

Kenema gets online at **Infinity** (51 Hangha Rd; per hr Le8000; ☽ 8.30am-9pm Mon-Fri, 9am-7pm Sat & Sun).

Sleeping

Makasa Guest House (☎ 088-947199; 27 Humonya Ave; r with shared bathroom Le25,000-45,000, with private bathroom Le60,000; ⬛) A simple but clean place with five rooms and a good central location.

Lambayama Motel (☎ 076-976872; 2 Aruna St; s with shared/private bathroom Le35,000/45,000, d Le60,000-75,000; ⓟⓧ) This friendly place, down many back-streets south of town, has good-value rooms and a village-like setting.

Pastoral Centre (☎ 033-126399; Dama Rd; r with shared/private bathroom Le40,000/50,000; ⓟ) The Catholic Mission offers decent rooms 600m off the road in a peaceful, palm-filled compound. Other than a simple breakfast, food is unavailable.

Capitol Hotel (☎ 033-161616; 51 Hangha Rd; s/d Le155,000/255,000, ste Le415,000; ⓟⓧⓡ) Capitol is Kenema's best hotel, though it's overpriced for what you get.

Eating

SLRA Canteen (Hangha Rd; meals Le4000-10,000; ☽ lunch & dinner) This surprise, hidden behind the Sierra Leone Roads Authority's metal gate, is the cosiest restaurant in town. They make about half-a-dozen local dishes daily, and will take requests if you make them early.

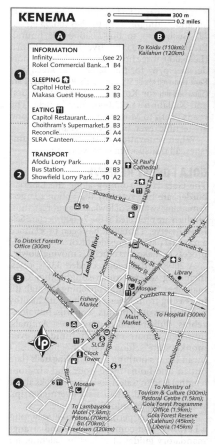

Reconcile (Blama Rd; meals around Le10,000; ☽ lunch & dinner) Popular for basic fish-and-rice and chicken-and-rice dishes and, at night, drinks.

Capitol Restaurant (☎ 033-618888; 51 Hangha Rd; sandwiches Le6000-10,000, meals Le10,000-30,000; ☽ lunch & dinner) This old stand-by has the biggest menu in the provinces, though the service and the food are more ordinary. Stick to African or Lebanese and it'll probably be good. There's a disco in the back on Wednesday and Saturday nights.

Choithram's Supermarket (4 Hangha Rd) Well-stocked with imported goods.

Getting There & Away

To Freetown, SLRTC (regular/express Le20,000/22,000) buses run mornings and

Abess Transport (Le23,000) buses depart around midnight from the **bus station** (Hangha Rd). Bush taxis to Bo (Le4000, 1½ hours), Freetown (Le23,000, five hours), Potoru (Le15,000, three hours) and the Liberian border (see p767 for full details) use **Afodu Lorry Park** (Maxwell Khobe St). Go to **Showfield Lorry Park** (Showfield Rd) for Kono (Le30,000, five hours) and Kailahun (Le25,000, four hours). The roads south to Monrovia and north to Kono are terrible, even in the dry season.

When renovation of the bus station finishes, all transport may move there.

GOLA FOREST RESERVE

The Gola Hills, running along the Liberian border, are blanketed by the nation's largest remaining swathes of lowland rainforest, most of which are protected as the 75,000-hectare **Gola Forest Reserve**. Though it has been proclaimed a national park by President Koroma, the legal process to make this official is moving slowly.

A 2008 bird survey recorded 333 species, including several much-sought-after Gola malimbes. There's little poaching (though it's increasing from Liberia) so there are healthy populations of elephants, leopards, buffaloes, zebras, duikers and chimpanzees. Animals, however, remain extremely timid, so even monkeys are seldom spotted. That doesn't mean there's nothing to see. **Hiking trails** (laid out in one-hour, three-hour and six-hour lengths) lead to waterfalls and overlooks above the canopy. And, if you make overnight trips, you can get deep into virgin jungle.

You can buy permits (Le15,000/day, plus a Le15,000/visit community fee) and arrange mandatory guides at offices in Lalehun, for the larger and more pristine Gola North unit, and Sileti, for the more accessible Gola South. The best source of information is the **Gola Forest Programme** (☎ 076-420218; golaforest@yahoo.com; 164 Dama Rd, Kenema) with offices currently in Kenema, but soon to relocate to Lalehun. Following the move, the **Ministry of Tourism & Culture** (☎ 033-548793; 44 Dama Rd; ☒ 8am–3pm Mon-Fri) will distribute Gola information in Kenema.

Tourism development is taking a very community-focused approach and community-run **guesthouses** (r with shared bathroom Le30,000) have opened in towns on the periphery of park. The Gola Forest Programme can make reservations and also hires camping equipment.

Lalehun is 45km southeast of Kenema: take a *poda-poda* to Joru (Le10,000, 1½ hours) and

from there hire an *okada* for the final 15km. Sileti (Le20,000, four to five hours) is on the Monrovia road, just before Zimmi.

KOIDU-SEFADU (KONO)

pop 80,000

Sprawling Kono, as this dusty town is usually called, is one of Sierra Leone's largest cities, but it has a transient feel, and you half suspect that its populace might pack up and leave at any time. Kono suffered more during the war than anywhere else, and it clearly hasn't earned a fair share of the peace dividend despite being the centre of the diamond-mining industry. Fortune seekers have come from across the country and even inside the city limits you'll see denuded swathes of land where eager prospectors are trying to strike it rich. Any *okada* driver can take you to see a mine, but you'll get more out of the experience if you ask someone at your hotel to come along and explain the process.

There are several banks, including **Rokel Commercial Bank** (6 New Sembehun Rd), and **Network Movement for Justice & Development** (2 Suku Tamba St; per hr Le5000; ☒ 9.30am–6.30pm Mon-Fri) provides internet access. Both are located south of Cotton Tree Roundabout.

Sleeping & Eating

Kono is flush with diamond dealers, but short on lodges. The cheapest is **Cool Jay's Guesthouse** (☎ 088-909134; 5 Maraka Corner; r Le30,000-40,000) with simple, shared-bathroom quarters. Though inconveniently located at 555 Spot outside the centre, spic-and-span **Uncle Ben's Guesthouse** (☎ 077-210976; s/d Le50,000/70,000; P ☒) presents a huge leap in quality. **D&S VIP Guest House** (☎ 077-923868; 36 Kainkordu Rd; r Le90,000; P ☒) is a little better still (and good value if the air-conditioner, TV and refrigerator are working; but don't bet on it) and located right in the heart of the city. **Kono Hotel** (☎ 078-666618; Mile 210 Kenema Hwy; s/d Le150,000/190,000; P ☒), well west of town, is the top of the heap, and the only property that runs the generator all night.

Dining is pretty much limited to some cheap *cookery* and Kono Hotel's expensive Lebanese and pizza. If you crave some flavours from home, **Unique Supermarket** (43 Kainkordu Rd) may have them.

Getting There & Away

There are daily SLRTC (Le21,000) and Abess Transport (Le24,000) buses to Freetown,

DIAMONDS FROM SIERRA LEONE

One of the tragedies of Sierra Leone is that despite being one of the earth's poorest countries (annual per capita income is US$700 and life expectancy is 42 years) it possesses abundant wealth, including diamonds. Most mines have been dug around Kenema, Bo, Kono and, most famously, Tongo Field, but new finds are being uncovered elsewhere and for the first time since independence, Sierra Leone is able to harness the wealth of its diamonds for the benefit of its citizens.

When the Revolutionary United Front (RUF) began its war in 1991, its core strategy was to control the country's diamond mines. It used forced labour to extract the wealth, and the receptive government of Charles Taylor in Liberia and ask-no-questions Western diamond dealers to put the gems on the world market. The money the RUF reaped from this enterprise (estimated at between US$25 million and US$125 million per year) was used to buy weapons to continue the brutal war. In the end, two million people (about one-third of the population) were displaced and at least 50,000 killed, while another 30,000 had their hands, lips, ears, or other body parts amputated by the rebels.

Diamonds are one of the most portable forms of wealth, making smuggling them across borders very easy. They're also readily resold into the world market and practically impossible to trace. Osama bin Laden's Al-Qaeda terrorist network reportedly bought millions of dollars' worth of Sierra Leone diamonds prior to the 11 September 2001 attacks on the USA.

Although Sierra Leone's was not the only African war fuelled by 'blood diamonds' (they still play a role in Côte d'Ivoire's current crisis; see p258) it was largely the atrocities committed by the RUF that brought the issue to international attention. In 2003 industry leaders worked with the UN to adopt the Kimberly Process Certification Scheme to regulate the trade in rough diamonds. The breakthrough deal, two years in the making, is a weakened version of the original proposal (monitoring is voluntary rather than mandatory) but proponents have claimed that it covers up to 99% of exported diamonds. It's impossible to know if this is the case, however, because rough-cut diamonds are still smuggled across borders to legitimate markets in neighbouring countries; and buyers in these places have little incentive to care. Yet, though far from perfect, the Kimberly Process is a significant silver lining on Sierra Leone's recent dark cloud.

poda-podas to Makeni (Le13,000, four hours) and 4WDs to Kenema (Le30,000, five hours).

THE NORTH

Northern Sierra Leone is the homeland of the Temne people. The landscape is higher and drier than the southeast and the largest towns feel more like overgrown villages than cities. Where they haven't been cultivated, the undulating hills are covered in light bush or savannah woodland, although ribbons of dense forest run along rivers. The hills become mountains in several places, with many peaks rising above 1500m.

MAKENI
pop 82,000

Makeni, the quiet, tree-filled capital of Northern Province and birthplace of President Koroma, is a market town for the surrounding villages. Despite being the RUF headquarters for the final three years of the war, Makeni suffered little physical damage: there was horrible human suffering though.

Nothing really warrants a stop, but if you do find yourself here you can kill an hour wandering the crowded **market**, which is chock-full with fish. **Wusum Hill**, rising behind the town, can be climbed in 30 minutes. The longer route up the back is less steep, but also less fun. The views from the quicker climb up **Mena Hill** to the south are also pretty good, haze permitting. Other peaks north of town, along the road to Kabala, are just begging for rock hounds to break out the ropes.

There are some banks and forex bureaus on the main square (by the uncompleted arch) and Wusum Hotel has an **internet cafe** (per hr Le5000; ☉ 8.30am-5pm Mon-Sat, 7-10pm daily) with fast connections.

Sleeping & Eating

There's no lodging in the city centre, so get ready to ride some *okada*.

Thinka Hotel (☎ 076-805542; 24 Loya St; s/d with shared bathroom Le20,000/30,000, r with private bathroom Le40,000; P) It's cheaper but better than most of Makeni's other bottom-end lodging. The generator runs all night, at least most of the time. The pricier hotel across the street advertises internet service, but don't get your hopes up.

MJ Motel (☎ 076-713945; 14 Azzolini Hwy; s/d Le100,000/130,000; P ⊠) Though no longer Makeni's best, the aging MJ still provides reasonable-value rooms. It has one-channel satellite TV and power all night, though the air-con is only switched on from 9pm to 2am. David Beckham slept in room 204 during his January 2008 tour of the country on behalf of Unicef.

Wusum Hotel (☎ 076-341079; wusum.hotel@yahoo .co.uk; 65 Teko Rd; s/d Le264,000/330,000, chalet Le350,000; P ⊠ ⌨ ⌨) Known to locals as Apex, the name of the nightclub that predates the hotel, the pale-green Wusum is a genuine four-star facility; as good as similarly (over)priced places in Freetown. Anyone can use the pool for Le10,000.

Ab-Zain's (2 Station Rd; meals Le3500-10,000; ☯ lunch Mon-Sat, dinner daily) Our vote for the best restaurant goes to this place in the centre, just south of the arch, which prepares about six meals a day; perhaps fried fish or beans and rice.

Highway Restaurant (Azzolini Hwy; meals Le7000-20,000; ☯ lunch & dinner) Many foreign aid workers are regulars at this Lebanese-owned eatery, which has a slightly larger menu than Ab-Zain's and lots of liquor.

Getting There & Away

Bush taxis run frequently to Freetown (Le12,000, three hours) plus the SLRTC buses (Le9000) to Kono and Kabala will drop passengers here. There are also *poda-podas* to Kabala (Le12,000, 2½ hours), Kamakwie (Le12,000, four hours), Bo (Le15,000, four hours) and Kono (Le13,000, four hours).

OUTAMBA-KILIMI NATIONAL PARK

This remote **national park** (admission Le7500) protects some healthy populations of big-name wildlife, but don't come expecting an East African–style safari. Except for near-guaranteed sightings of hippos in the dry season, encounters with the leopards, elephants, buffaloes, bushbucks, waterbucks, crocodiles and chimpanzees are rare. But OKNP is still worth a visit as it's a beautiful, peaceful place.

The 74,000-hectare Outamba section is covered by savannah woodland and grass-

land plus patches of closed-canopy rainforest. The headquarters is here. The 36,800-hectare Kilimi section is flatter, grassier, less ecologically intact and has no facilities.

The Wilderness Camp, as the park is known locally, has no roads, so visitors need to explore on foot or by canoe. Two seldom-used (ie overgrown) **hiking trails** cross deep into the park. It's 14.5km to Yombo Waterfall, which is usually the place to head if you're looking for elephants, though between November and January they might be seen along the 6.5km loop trail that climbs Karangia Mountain. By canoe you can go down the Little Scarcies River to **Lake Idrisa**, where in the dry season you can roam around at will. Staff are hoping to get funds to fix the wildlife-watching tower here. Excursions cost Le10,000 per person plus Le5000 for the guide.

There are simple thatch **huts** (per person Le10,000) near the river, and if you bring your own tent you can camp in the bush. Come prepared for cold nights. You also need to bring your own food, though someone will cook it for Le2000.

Expect all park prices to rise during the lifetime of this book, but probably not too much.

Without your own transport you'll need to hire an *okada* (try for Le30,000) or 4WD (much more) in Kamakwie, the nearest sizeable town, for the 26km trip: the entrance road is too rough for taxis. Alternatively, you can try to catch a northbound vehicle (but they're rare) and walk the 6km from the main road. Motorcycles are the only option if the Little Scarcies River is running so high that ferry service is suspended (this can last a day or two) or if the ferry breaks down (this might last a week). In these instances, you and the motorcycles cross in a dugout canoe.

There's usually only one *poda-poda* per day to Makeni, leaving around 8am to 9am. Hitching is sometimes possible, but expect long waits. If you're continuing to Guinea (see p767), *okada* drivers will pick you up at the park.

If you get stuck in Kamakwie, there are two simple guesthouses to choose from. Rooms at **Sella Guest House** (☎ 076-810087; r with shared bathroom Le20,000), on the hill by the phone towers, aren't as nice as those at **IK Guest House** (☎ 076-997227; 8 Sella St; r with shared/private bathroom Le20,000/30,000), but Sella runs a generator until midnight as part of the price while you'll get no electricity at IK unless you pony up for the fuel.

KABALA
pop 19,000

Kabala is at the end of the sealed road and the last place of any size en route to Guinea. It's quiet and friendly and well worth a visit despite the meagre facilities and lack of attractions. Gbawuria (*bow*-ree-ah) Hill provides a dramatic backdrop and is easily climbed. A colourful New Year celebration is held at the top. Any *okada* driver can take you to see the women who dye *ronko*, a rust-coloured country cloth that the Koinadugu district and the local Kuranko people are known for.

Kabala Community Bank (Makeni Rd) is a Western Union agent, and **Manans Foreign Exchange Bureau** (⊗ Mon-Sat) inside the main market changes dollars at a reasonable rate.

Weyone Guest House (28 Yagala Rd; r Le 35,000, with shared bathroom Le25,000; [P]) and the louder **Paygay's Pub** (☎ 076-994625; 2 Moneh St; r Le35,000, with shared bathroom Le25,000) are the best places to stay in the town proper. The generators run all night; ensure your room has a fan. At the most popular *cookery*, **Choice's Bar & Restaurant** (17 Barrier Rd; meals Le2500-5000; ⊗ breakfast, lunch & dinner), get the cassava leaves or special and a genuinely cold beer.

Bush taxis travel to Freetown (Le24,000, 5½ hours) and Makeni (Le12,000, 2½ hours). There's also an SLRTC bus (Le18,000) to Freetown daily except Sunday. Both leave from the taxi park. 4WDs for Faranah, Guinea wait at Gbini Park near the mosque. See p767 for full travel details to Guinea.

MT BINTUMANI

Loma Mansa, as Sierra Leone's highest peak is also known, rises 1945m, the highest mountain in West Africa between Mt Cameroon and Mt Fogo. In clear weather views from the summit are excellent, but it's really the journey more than the destination that draws intrepid travellers here. The Loma Mountains Forest Reserve protects the highland rainforest covering the lower slopes, home to leopards, elephants, bongos and chimpanzees. Above 1500m the forest gives way to savannah grassland where you can spot baboons, warthogs, duikers and buffaloes.

The most scenic and wildlife-rich approach to the summit is from the west, typically through Banda-Karafaia, which can be reached by riding on the occasional cargo truck from Kabala. In the dry season, 4WDs or *okada* (best arranged in Kabala or Koinadugu) can reach Sinikoro, from where the summit could be reached in a very rushed day, but it's better to allow three days for the round-trip. The eastern route from Kurubonla, north of Kono, can reach the summit in two days if you move fast. A 4WD usually heads to Kurubonla (Le25,000, five hours) from Kono on Thursday afternoon, returning Friday. The ideal trip is to cross the mountain from one gateway to the other.

Pay your respects to the chief in either Sinikoro or Sokurela (along the eastern route) and he'll find you a guide (expect to pay around Le10,000 to Le15,000 per day), which is necessary because many paths are overgrown. The climb isn't technical, but you need to be self-sufficient with camping gear, food and a water filter. Contact the Conservation Society of Sierra Leone in Freetown (p747) for the latest advice.

SIERRA LEONE DIRECTORY

ACCOMMODATION

Thanks to the abundance of aid workers, Freetown has a choice of comfortable and

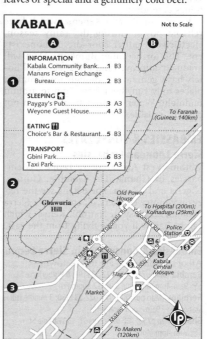

KABALA   Not to Scale

INFORMATION	
Kabala Community Bank.....1	B3
Manans Foreign Exchange	
Bureau............................2	B3
SLEEPING 🛏	
Paygay's Pub...................3	A3
Weyone Guest House........4	A3
EATING 🍴	
Choice's Bar & Restaurant...5	B3
TRANSPORT	
Gbini Park......................6	B3
Taxi Park........................7	A3

To Faranah (Guinea; 140km)

Gbawuria Hill

Old Power House

To Hospital (200m); Koinadugu (25km)

Police Station

Kabala Central Mosque

Flag

Market

To Makeni (120km)

SIERRA LEONE

costly hotels. In Freetown, budget quality lasts until around Le150,000 for a double, while out in the provinces, this usually gets you the top hotel in town, but it's unlikely to satisfy those needing plenty of creature comforts. Don't expect good mattresses in anything but truly top-end places. Always request discounts for stays of more than one night, as you'll usually get them. The 10% room tax is almost always included in the prices posted at reception, but some top-end places add it at check-out.

ACTIVITIES

Hiking is excellent on the remote southern beaches and northern mountains. Climbers can scale Mt Bintumani (p763) and several other peaks, though getting to the mountains is more challenging than getting to the top. The deep-sea fishing is some of Africa's best: the world record tarpon (128.5kg) was snagged off Sherbro Island and many individual line-class records were set here. For information on boat hire, see p767.

BOOKS

The war spawned numerous harrowing books including Ishmael Beah's controversial A Long Way Gone: Memoirs of a Boy Soldier (2008) and Daniel Bergner's In the Land of Magic Soldiers (2004). Fishing in Rivers of Sierra Leone (1987), edited by Heribert Hinzen, is a collection of local folk tales and songs. In the first half of The Devil that Danced on Water (2003) Aminatta Forna recounts her childhood in Freetown, during which her dissident father was executed, and then returns as a journalist 25 years later to investigate his death.

BUSINESS HOURS

General business and office hours are 9am to 5.30pm Monday to Saturday, though some places close at 1pm on Saturday. Banking hours are usually 8.30am to 3.30pm Monday to Friday with a select few also open 9am to 1pm Saturday.

CUSTOMS REGULATIONS

Exporting gold and diamonds without a licence is illegal.

DANGERS & ANNOYANCES

These days Guinea's uncertain political future presents a bigger challenge to Sierra Leone than anything internal. Check on conditions near the border if things deteriorate.

Except for Bo and Kenema, which have reliable power during the rainy season, electricity is either sporadic or nonexistent. The forthcoming Bumbuna Dam will gradually improve things. Just about all hotels have generators, though most budget places only run them from 7pm to around midnight. Water supplies are more, but not entirely, reliable.

EMBASSIES & CONSULATES

Sierra Leonean Embassies

Within West Africa, Sierra Leone has embassies in Ghana, The Gambia, Guinea, Nigeria and Liberia. For details see the relevant country chapters. There's also a Sierra Leonian embassy in Nairobi, Kenya, which can be handy if you're flying from the east.

Embassies & Consulates in Sierra Leone

All of the following are in Freetown:
Gambia (Map p750; ☎ 022-225191; 6 Wilberforce St; ✆ 9am-4pm Mon-Thu, 9am-12.30pm Fri)
Germany (Map pp748-9; ☎ 022-231350; 3 Middle Hill Station; ✆ 9am-noon Mon-Fri)
Ghana (Map p750; ☎ 022-223461; 13 Walpole St; ✆ 9am-4pm Mon-Fri)

PRACTICALITIES

- Awoko and Concord Times are the most respected newspapers, though the satirical Peep is more popular.

- Magazines like Newsweek and BBC Focus On Africa are sold at supermarkets.

- Sierra Leone's two TV stations are the government-owned SLBS and the private ABC, both of whose most popular programming is Nigerian soap operas.

- The BBC World Service is heard on 94.3FM and Voice of America on 102.4FM. SKYY (106.6FM) plays the most local music.

- Sierra Leone uses British metric weights and measures.

- Electricity is 220V/50Hz and plugs have three large pins, like the UK.

Guinea (Map pp748-9; ☎ 022-232496; ambagui_sl@yahoo.fr; 6 Carlton Carew Rd; ☒ 9am-3.30pm Mon-Thu, 9am-1pm Fri)

Liberia (Map pp748-9; ☎ 022-230991; 2 Spur Rd; ☒ 9am-5pm Mon-Thu, 9am-3pm Fri)

Mali (Map pp748-9; ☎ 033-422994; 40 Wilkinson Rd; ☒ 9am-4pm Mon-Thu, 9am-noon & 2-3.30pm Fri)

Nigeria (Map p750; ☎ 022-224229; 37 Siaka Stevens St; ☒ 10am-2pm Mon-Fri)

Senegal (Map p750; ☎ 030-230666; 2nd fl, 7 Short St; ☒ 8am-5pm Mon-Sat)

UK (Map pp748-9; ☎ 022-232961; http://ukinsierraleone.fco.gov.uk; 6 Spur Rd; ☒ 8am-4.30pm Mon-Thu, 8am-1pm Fri) British High Commission; assists French nationals.

USA (off Map pp748-9; ☎ 076-515000; http://freetown.usembassy.gov; Leicester Rd; ☒ 8am-5pm Mon-Thu, 8am-1pm Fri)

HOLIDAYS

Public holidays include the following:
New Year's Day 1 January
Easter March/April
Independence Day 27 April
Christmas Day 25 December
Boxing Day 26 December

Sierra Leone also celebrates Islamic holidays; see p816 for details.

INTERNET ACCESS

It can be hit or miss, but internet cafes in Freetown usually have reasonable speeds for around Le3000 per hour. Access in the provinces, when you can find it, is more expensive and usually less swift.

INTERNET RESOURCES

National Tourist Board (www.welcometosierraleone.org)
Sierra Leone Web (www.sierra-leone.org) Lots of good background information.
Visit Sierra Leone (www.visitsierraleone.org) Tonnes of travel advice and an active discussion forum where, no matter how obscure your inquiry, someone will probably have an answer.

LANGUAGE

The most common tribal languages are Mende and Temne. English is the official language, though Krio is the most widely spoken. See p860 for a list of useful Krio phrases.

MAPS

The best map of both Sierra Leone and Freetown is the *International Travel Map* (2009; 1:500,000/1:13,000) produced by the National Tourist Board. At the time of research it was sold (Le35,000 to Le45,000) exclusively in Sierra Leone at places such as hotels and travel agencies. A 2008 edition minus the detailed Freetown coverage is available for purchase before arrival.

MONEY

The most easily exchangeable currencies are US dollars, UK pounds and euros, in that order. Forex bureaus (and street traders, though avoid them unless somebody you trust makes the introduction) invariably offer better rates than banks.

You can't pay with a credit card in Sierra Leone, but some Rokel Commercial Bank branches give cash advances (up to US$2000) on Visa cards, and ProCredit Bank has ATMs in Freetown that spit out up to Le300,000 per day for Visa credit and debit cards: but don't rely on them too heavily as they don't always work. Rokel and Sierra Leone Commercial Banks, plus some forex bureaus, cash travellers cheques, but with high charges.

One hundred Leones is a 'block' and one thousand is a 'grand'.

POST

Sierra Leone's regular post is reasonably reliable if you send something from Freetown, though it's still recommended to use the separate express service for anything important.

TELEPHONE

Mobile phone service is good and so popular that landlines are disappearing. SIM cards cost around Le5000. Mobile prefixes are Africel ☎ 077/088, Comium ☎ 033, Tigo ☎ 030 and Zain (still called Celtel by nearly everyone) ☎ 076/078. The latter has the widest coverage. You can't call landlines with these mobile companies, but a new Sierratel mobile service, available from mid-2009, will allow this.

Without a mobile, the easiest way to make a call is at the countless small *télécentres* (telephone centres), which generally charge Le500 per minute for most calls except Le1000 to a Zain number. Calls to the USA/UK/Australia cost Le1000 to Le2000 per minute at telecentres and some internet cafes.

VISAS

All visitors, except those from Ecowas countries, need visas, and they're supposed to be

SIERRA LEONE

obtained before arrival. It's possible to show up at land borders (and perhaps even the airport) and finagle a visa, but this is completely unofficial, and you run the risk of not succeeding.

Visa prices and rules vary widely by nationality of applicant and embassy of issuance. Generally you'll be expected to show a plane ticket and a letter of invitation (a hotel reservation will suffice) and your passport should have one year of validity rather than the typical six months.

Freetown travel agents can arrange 30-day, single-entry landing visas; present these at immigration. Prices vary: Singaporeans and many African nationals pay nothing; most Asians pay Le145,000; Australians, New Zealanders and most EU residents pay Le236,000; Canadians pay Le247,000; British pay Le275,000; and those from the USA get socked for Le630,000 (nearly double what they pay for one-year multiple-entry visas at the Washington, DC embassy). Visit Sierra Leone (p747) charges US$40 for this service, and everything can be done online in a couple of days with payment through PayPal.

Visa Extensions

To get a free extra 30 days, submit a letter to the Chief Immigration Officer at the **Immigration Department** (Map p750; ☎ 022-223220; 15 Siaka Stevens St; ⏱ 10am-3.30pm Mon-Fri). Enter on Rawdon St.

Visas for Onward Travel

GUINEA

Three-month multiple-entry visas cost US$50 for most Westerners and US$100 for Americans. You need two photos and the visa should be ready right away.

LIBERIA

Two-month single-entry visas cost US$75 and six-month multiple-entry visas are US$100. You need one photo and the visa is issued promptly.

VOLUNTEERING

Whether you want to settle in for a few months or just drop by for an hour, the kids at **Excel** (Map pp748-9; ☎ 033-789293; www.excelschool ars.org; 9 Dillet St, Freetown; ⏱ 9am-5pm), an after-school program, will appreciate your time.

Tacugama Chimpanzee Sanctuary (p756) can always use people with marketing, ad-

ministration, IT and community development experience, as long as they can offer a three-month commitment. Housing is provided. The Conservation Society of Sierra Leone (p747) can also find ways to put people to work.

WOMEN TRAVELLERS

Sierra Leone presents no specific problems for women travellers other than a handful of beach boys, though they're tame compared to The Gambia. For general information, see p826.

TRANSPORT IN SIERRA LEONE

GETTING THERE & AWAY

Entering Sierra Leone

You're required to show proof of vaccination for yellow fever.

Air

Return London–Freetown flights can be had for around UK£600, while Brussels Airlines charges less for better service from Brussels. Kenya Airlines connects Nairobi to Freetown for around US$1300.

Airlines flying to and from Sierra Leone, with offices based in Freetown, are:

Bellview Airlines (Map p750; B3; ☎ 022-227311; www .flybellviewair.com; 31 Lightfoot Boston St) Hub: Lagos.

BMI (Map p750; BD; ☎ 076-541230; www.flybmi.com; 14 Wilberforce St) Hub: London.

Brussels Airlines (Map p750; SN; ☎ 076-333777; www .brusselsairlines.com; 30 Siaka Stevens St) Hub: Brussels.

Elysian Airlines (Map p750; GIE; ☎ 022-228857; www .elysianairlines.com; 22 Wallace Johnson St) Hub: Douala.

Gambia International Airlines (Map p750; VR; ☎ 022-220013; www.gia.gm; 6 Wilberforce St) Hub: Banjul.

Kenya Airways (Map p750; KQ; ☎ 076-536899; www .kenya-airways.com; 13 Lamina Sankoh St) Hub: Nairobi.

DEPARTURE TAX

The airport departure tax is Le120,000, payable in dollars, pounds or leones. Some airlines (generally those flying beyond West Africa) include it in the price of the ticket, but most don't.

REGIONAL FLIGHTS FROM FREETOWN			
Destination	**No of flights per week**	**Airline**	**Approx Fare One-way/return (US$)**
Abidjan (Côte d'Ivoire)	1	Bellview	313/545
Accra (Ghana)	4	Kenya	373/580
Banjul (The Gambia)	6	Bellview, Elysian, Gambia International	180/236
Conakry (Guinea)	1	Elysian	100/200
Dakar (Senegal)	6	Bellview, Brussels, Elysian, Gambia International	220/400
Lagos (Nigeria)	3	Bellview	396/590
Monrovia (Liberia)	3	Elysian	250/300
Praia (Cape Verde)	2	Gambia International	459/676

Royal Air Maroc (Map p750; AT; ☎ 022-221015; www .royalairmaroc.com; 19 Charlotte St) Hub: Casablanca.

Land
GUINEA
The main border crossing is at Pamelap. Bush taxis run frequently between Freetown and Conakry (Le48,000) and there's an SLRTC bus (Le40,000) on Monday and Thursday. The road between Port Loko and the border is a mess (though could be paved by 2010) and the journey usually takes eight to 10 hours. You can also get to Pamelap from most large towns and easily continue to Conakry from there and some taxis even go all the way to Conakry.

From Kamakwie to Kindia there's little transport on the Sierra Leone side, where the road is quite bad; 4WDs usually leave Kamakwie every two to three days, take eight to 10 hours and charge Le30,000. Alternatively, hire an *okada* driver to the border (they'll ask for Le60,000) where it's about a 1.5km walk to Medina-Oula in Guinea, which has plenty of transport. Motorcycles are the only option when the Little Scarcies River ferry stops running: see Outamba-Kilimi National Park (p762) for details.

The road from Kabala to Faranah, Guinea, is also in bad shape and only has transport a couple of times a week, or less. A seat in the battered and crammed 4WDs departing Kabala costs Le50,000. Drivers insist that in the dry season, if there are no breakdowns, the 140km journey can be made in four to five hours, but seven to eight is much more likely and we've heard of trips lasting 16 hours. *Okada* drivers will take you to Faranah for Le150,000 in four hours. A better *okada* option might be to go only as far as Hérémakono just inside Guinea

where you should be able to get an afternoon taxi the final 40km to Faranah.

In the far east, the most common crossing is between Koindu and Guéckédou. First get a taxi from Kailahun to Koindu (Le15,000, three hours) and then an *okada* (Le5000) to the border, where there's a ferry over the Moa River; but you'll likely end up in a dugout canoe. Then at Nongowa you can get a taxi or motorcycle taxi the rest of the way.

LIBERIA
The only practical and frequently travelled crossing to Liberia is at Bo (Waterside), in the far south. There are daily taxis (Le40,000) and sometimes *poda-podas* (Le35,000) from both Bo and Kenema, taking six to eight hours in the dry season and 10 to 12 hours in the wet. It's usually a little quicker from Bo when drivers head straight south, but in the rains they run round through Kenema. All taxis stop at Gendema at the border, where you walk over and continue in another car. If you arrive after the border has closed, there are some grubby guesthouses and plenty of *cookery*.

Check the security situation before attempting any other crossing.

Sea
There's talk of reviving the ferry service between Freetown and Conakry, Guinea; inquire at Government Wharf for details.

GETTING AROUND
Boat
Pam-pahs (large cargo/passenger boats) run to several towns, most notably between Mattru Jong and Bonthe (see p758).

Hiring a boat isn't cheap, though using one to travel to/from beaches can be competitive with 4WD hire. Speedboats start at around Le850,000/day plus fuel and oil (and boats burn plenty of both) while slower *pam-pahs* (that can hold 20 people) cost around Le500,000.

In Freetown you can find boats for hire at Man of War Bay, Government Wharf and Kissy Terminal. Pelican Water Taxi (p753) does charters and the Conservation Society of Sierra Leone (p747) can also connect you with boats, or maybe hire you theirs.

Most beach resorts have their own boats.

Bus, Bush Taxi & Minibus

Taxis and *poda-podas* (minibuses) link all major and many minor towns, though, except for departures to/from Freetown (and between Bo and Kenema), traffic is usually pretty sparse, especially on Sundays. Note that travel times are just approximations given the bad roads and frequent breakdowns.

Government-run Sierra Leone Road Transport Corporation (SLRTC) buses are cheaper and more comfortable than taxis, but slower. Abess Transport buses are faster than SLRTC, but not as comfortable. See p753 for full details.

Car

Car hire is expensive (starting at around Le240,000 for Freetown, excluding fuel; much more for up-country), but don't choose a company only on price; ask about the terms too. Kilometres will always be unlimited and a driver included, but after-hours charges vary, and ask if drivers' food and lodging are your responsibility or his. The travel agencies listed under Freetown (p747) have good cars and service.

You could also just charter ('chatah') a taxi. By the hour in Freetown you can usually negotiate Le15,000 for one hour and Le12,000 per hour for several hours.

ROAD CONDITIONS

The highways from Freetown to Kenema and Makeni are paved and in excellent condition. After Makeni, the road to Kono has deteriorated and is now only about half paved while the stretch from Makeni to Kabala is also paved, but deteriorating fast. Also surfaced and still smooth is the peninsular highway between Waterloo and Tokeh. South from Freetown this road is very rough and paving isn't likely to happen anytime soon. Paving of the highway to the Guinean border at Pamelap could be finished in 2010. The rutted dirt road between Kenema and the Liberian border is terrible; and though the route straight south from Bo is better, don't head this way before ensuring the Moa River car ferry is working.

Okada

Okada (motorcycle taxis) rule the roads in many towns. Outside Freetown a ride costs Le1000 no matter how far you're going. It's sometimes convenient to hire *okada* for long journeys because on really bad roads they travel faster than shared taxis and *poda-podas* plus they depart when you're ready, not when the vehicle is full.

Togo

Once regarded as the pearl of West Africa for its scenic landscapes, elegant capital and affluent markets, Togo fell by the tourism wayside following the political turmoil of the 1990s and mid-2000s.

Two decades of visitors' neglect have taken their toll: national parks have been reclaimed by desperate farmers, information for travellers is virtually nonexistent, roads are in an appalling condition and getting around without your own transport requires the patience of a saint and the determination of a fighter.

But for those fond of travelling off the beaten track, Togo will prove a rewarding destination. It is as beautiful as ever, with a great diversity of landscapes, and wildlife that has clung on against all odds. Elephants, crocs, monkeys and antelopes can be found in Fazao-Malfakassa, and the coast remains a favourite mating area for whales and nesting ground for marine turtles.

The end of mass tourism has also given small, independent outfits a chance to make their mark: great little guesthouses are stealing the show from the once-grand hotels of the 1970s; passionate guides are working the ecotourism trend, and an outstanding West African art collection can now be seen at a gallery in Lomé.

Culturally, Togo is a melting pot. The fortified compounds of Koutammakou and the vertigo-inducing caves of Nano are a reminder that the country's ethnically diverse population didn't always get along. Nowadays however, voodoo, Muslim, Christian and traditional festivals crowd the calendar and are often joyful and colourful celebrations for all. And if one thing can definitely bring all five million Togolese together, it is their conquering football team, Les Éperviers.

FAST FACTS

- **Area** 56,790 sq km
- **Capital** Lomé
- **Country code** ☎ 228
- **Famous for** Emmanuel Adebayor, Les Éperviers, the ruling Eyadéma family
- **Languages** French (official), Ewe, Mina, Kabyé
- **Money** West African CFA franc; US$1 = CFA493; €1 = CFA656
- **Population** 5.1 million
- **Visa** CFA10,000 seven-day visa at border; one-month extension free; CFA10,000 for second month

HOW MUCH?

- **Pagne Ewe kente cloth** CFA8000
- **Butterfly walk** CFA5000
- **Koutammakou access** CFA1500
- **Taxi-moto** CFA200
- **National park entry** CFA13000

LONELY PLANET INDEX

- **1L of gas/petrol** CFA550
- **1L of bottled water** CFA500
- **Bottle of Flag beer** CFA350
- **Souvenir T-shirt** CFA2500
- **Street treat (cake/fruit)** CFA100

HIGHLIGHTS

- **Lomé** (p774) The bars and restaurants show off the coastal capital in all its decaying glory.
- **Musée International du Golfe de Guinée** (p776) Wxquisite West African art is displayed at this unique gallery.
- **Kpalimé** (p785) Lush forested hills for hiking and taking in the chilled vibe of coffee country.
- **Togolese gastronomy** (p774) Any of Togo's numerous maquis offer a chance to enjoy *fufu sauce arachide, aloko, koliko* or grilled Nile perch, best washed down with a shot of *sodabe*.
- **Koutammakou** (p795) Northern Togo's remote clay-and-straw fortresses, the *tata* compounds, are set amidst stunning scenery.

ITINERARIES

- **One Week** Allow at least a week for exploring Lomé (p774) and its surrounds. Within easy reach of the coastal capital, the Friday market in Vogan (p784) is particularly interesting. Combine this trip with one to Lake Togo (p783).
- **Two Weeks** After investigating all that Lomé has to offer, head for Kpalimé (p785) at the heart of coffee country – a great place to go hiking. From there, you could head to the Akloa waterfalls outside Badou (p790), then to Parc National de Fazao-Malfakassa (p790) and as far as the vibrant Kabyé town of Kara (p792).

- **Three Weeks** For those with more time on their hands, Koutammakou (p795), home to the fascinating Tamberma people and their fortress-like *tatas,* is well worth a visit. And if Koutammakou piqued your curiosity, head to the once-inhabited caves in the cliffs of Mount Semoo (p799) close to the northern town of Dapaong (p797) on the Burkinabé border.

CLIMATE & WHEN TO GO

This long, thin country stretches across six geographic zones and its climate ranges from tropical in the south to savannah in the north. Rain falls from May to October. In the south there's a dry spell from mid-July to mid-September. In the north there is no such interlude, but on the whole the north is more arid than the south. Mid-February (after the harmattan wind lifts) to mid-April is the hottest period; November to February is the driest.

The two dry seasons are the best time to visit, although the November-February season coincides with the harmattan and is a rotten time for photographers. Major roads are dependable throughout the year, but unsealed roads can be unpassable during and after the rains. See climate charts, p810.

HISTORY

Togo's name comes from *togodo,* which means 'behind the lake' in Ewe – a reference to the body of water now called Lake Togo. The region was once at the edge of several empires, including the Dahomey and Akan-Ashanti kingdoms in present-day Benin and Ghana respectively. It played a few bit parts in the Dahomey story: the Alladahanou from Tado, southeast of Sokodé, established kingdoms in what would become known as Dahomey; and Togo was the toppled Dahomeyan kings' refuge of choice.

With the arrival of Europeans in the 16th century, the power vacuum in Togo allowed the slave-traders to use the country as a conduit. The Mina – who had immigrated from the west along with the Guin (while the Ewe had arrived from the east) – became ruthless agents for the slave-traders.

Germans in Togoland

With the abolition of slavery, the Europeans turned their attention to trade in commodities – palm and coconut oils, cocoa, coffee

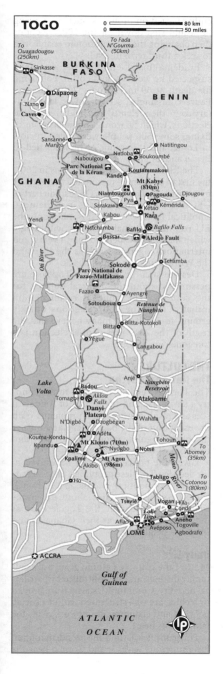

TOGO

0   80 km
0   50 miles

and cotton. In 1884, Germany surprised its colonial rivals Britain and France, when it signed a treaty in Togoville with the local king, Mlapa, agreeing to 'protect' the inhabitants in return for German sovereignty.

Togoland, as the Germans called the area, underwent considerable economic development before WWI. The Togolese, however, didn't appreciate the Germans' forced labour, direct taxes and 'pacification' campaigns, in which thousands of locals were killed. So they welcomed British forces during WWI. Encircled by British and French troops, the Germans surrendered at Kamina – the Allies' first victory in the war.

After the war, the League of Nations split Togoland, with France acquiring the eastern two-thirds of the country and Britain the remainder. This controversial move divided the populous Ewe, and political groups were still agitating for reunification following WWII.

Independence & the Coup

Following a 1956 plebiscite, hopes of reunification were dashed when British Togoland was incorporated into the Gold Coast (present-day Ghana). The division is still a source of discontent.

French Togoland became an autonomous republic and in 1960 gained full independence under the leadership of Sylvanus Olympio, who became the first president.

In 1963, Togo became the first African country to have a military coup after independence. Sylvanus Olympio, an Ewe from the south, disregarded the northerners, whom he called *petits nordiques* (small northerners); when he refused to integrate 600 soldiers returning from the Algerian War (predominantly Kabyé northerners) into his army, they rebelled. Olympio was killed at the gates of the US embassy as he sought refuge.

His replacement, Nicolas Grunitzky, was deposed in turn – in a bloodless coup led by Kabyé sergeant Gnassingbé Eyadéma. The new leader set out to unify the country's tribal groups, insisting on one trade union and one political party, the Rassemblement du Peuple Togolais (RPT). But the unifying process soon gave way to a different regime style: an authoritarian, despotic rule with alleged widespread electoral fraud and a personality cult.

TOGO

Struggling for a Multiparty System

In 1990, France began pressuring Eyadéma to adopt a multiparty system. He resisted, and portrayed African multiparty systems negatively through TV broadcasts of scenes of violence and unrest in nearby countries. Early 1991 saw riots and strikes by pro-democracy forces, many of whom were killed in clashes with the army. In April 1991, 28 bodies were dragged out of Lomé-Bé Lagoon and dumped on the steps of the US embassy, drawing attention to the repressive nature of Eyadéma's dictatorship.

Finally bowing to international pressure, Eyadéma agreed to a conference in 1991, to decide the country's future. Delegates there stripped him of his powers and installed an interim government, headed by Joseph Koffigoh, pending democratic elections. Months later, however, troops loyal to Eyadéma attacked Koffigoh's residence and detained him, leaving Eyadéma, once again, in full control of the government.

Eyadéma now postponed the promised elections, prompting the trade unions to call a general strike in November 1992. This continued for months, paralysing Togo's economy – banks and businesses closed, exports lay stranded in Lomé port, tourism collapsed. In the ensuing violence, some 250,000 southerners fled the country.

In a contest boycotted by the opposition and denounced by international observers, Eyadéma won the August 1993 presidential elections. A coalition of opposition parties – the Committee for Renewed Action (CAR) and the Union Togolaise Démocratique (UTD) – won the 1994 parliamentary elections, which were boycotted by the Union des Forces du Changement (UFC) and marred by the killing of three opposition members.

In the 1998 presidential elections Eyadéma triumphed again, although international observers criticised the conduct of the election. Fearing government manipulation, the opposition then boycotted the 1999 legislative elections, allowing the RPT to win 77 of the 81 seats in the national assembly.

Togo Today

International pressure on Eyadéma increased at the same rate as aid from donors decreased. Amnesty International made allegations about executions and torture taking place around the 1998 elections, and Eyadéma consist-

ently reneged on promises, such as assuring he would step down for the 2003 elections then changing the constitution to enable him to seek a third term instead.

Eyadéma finally left office the way many suspected he would – in a coffin. Following his death at 69 in February 2005, his son, Faure Gnassingbé, seized power in a military coup, then relented and held presidential elections, which he won. Amid allegations of fixing, some 500 people were killed in riots in Lomé, and thousands of refugees fled to Benin and Ghana.

The RPT won legislative elections in 2007, the first to be deemed reasonably free and fair by international observers. Opposition parties UFC and CAR also won seats in parliament, a political first. Following this milestone, the EU resumed normal relations with Togo, which had been suspended for 14 years, and international agencies such as the IMF and the World Bank are coming back.

Despite such progress, the Togolese are pessimistic about the political outlook for the country. The political reconciliation initiated after the 2007 elections quickly ground to a halt and many believe that the result of the 2010 presidential election is a foregone conclusion.

THE CULTURE
The National Psyche

The Togolese ego corresponds to the country's small size and the dearth of tourists it sees as a result of its political problems. With the exception of the odd official and hustler in Lomé, Togolese people are friendly and easy to deal with.

Given the police state they have lived in for decades, Togolese people are understandably wary of political discussions. Although some pessimism remains about the country's political situation, the Togolese are as outgoing and vibrant as their Ghanaian and Beninese neighbours.

Daily Life

Most of the country's ethnic groups are culturally distinct, and are controlled by patrilineal heredity. Communities, which are headed by a chief, are well structured within a social, political and economic framework, with the family at its heart.

Polygamy is still rife – the president himself has numerous wives – and women bear the brunt of daily chores, looking after children, fetching water, buying, preparing and selling foodstuff and cooking.

Overall, the country is young, with more than 40% of the population under the age of 14. Life expectancy at birth is 58, but literacy is better than in many neighbouring countries, with more than half the population able to read and write, one of the positive legacies of the Eyadéma years. Officially, HIV's prevalence is 3.2% but since the disease remains a major taboo, it is thought the actual figure is much higher.

Population

With about 40 ethnic groups in a population of some five million people, Togo has one of Africa's more heterogeneous populations. The three largest groups are the southern Ewe and Mina, and the northern Kabyé; the latter count President Gnassingbé among their number and are concentrated around Kara. Other significant groups include the Kotokoli, who live around Bassar and Bafilo, and the Tamberma, who live in fortified compounds east of Kara.

The Ewe- and Mina-related people – including the Guin, Anlo, Adja and Pla-Peda – are concentrated on the plantations in the southwest. Although they call themselves Ewe, some of these groups are not ethnic Ewe. The Mina and the Guin are Fanti and Ga people respectively, both from the Ghanaian coast.

ECONOMY

Togo's economy is reliant on agriculture, which contributes 40% of the GDP and is the livelihood of 65% of the population. Cocoa, coffee, and cotton form 40% of exports, with the industrial sector dominated by phosphate mining – Togo is the world's fourth-largest producer of phosphate.

Severely damaged by two decades of political unrest, the economy is now picking up. The international donors and businesses that deserted Togo are returning and Lomé's port is expanding. It's not without its challenges: food and oil prices increased sharply in 2008–9 and the floods of August 2008 left considerable infrastructural damage (to roads and bridges) and affected food crops.

SPORT

Togo's football team, Les Éperviers (the Sparrow Hawks), has been successful given Togo's tiny size, having qualified for the 2006 World Cup. Qualifying for the 2010 World Cup was still a possibility at the time this book was going to press, but with fierce competition from Cameroon, Gabon and Morocco in their group. Striker Emmanuel Adebayor (who currently plays for the English team Arsenal) is a national icon, and the team's victories prompt street parties and public holidays.

RELIGION

Christianity and Islam are the most evident religions in Togo – in the south and north respectively. However, a majority of the population have animist beliefs, which are harder to spot. Voodoo is strongest in the southeast but there are traces of it throughout the country.

ARTS
Architecture

The country is well known for its French and German colonial buildings, and the fortified Tamberma compounds in Koutammakou are some of the most striking structures in West Africa.

Arts & Craftwork

Togo's traditional arts and crafts are as varied as its people. Ironwork, pottery and weaving predominate in the northeast, while decorative wood burning (marking wood or calabashes with intricate geometric designs) is common in the northwest.

Batik and wax printing is popular throughout Togo, but the most well-known textile is the Ewe kente cloth, which is less brilliantly coloured than the Ashanti version. Cloth is sold by the *pagne* (2m strip).

Music & Dance

Music and dance play an important part in Togolese daily life. Dances revolve around traditional life, incorporating subjects such as hunting, fishing, warfare, harvesting and love.

While drums play a pivotal role in all festivities, there are diverse musical styles. In the south you'll find percussion instruments, such as bells and gongs; in the central region, *lithophones* (stone percussion instruments); and in the north, flutes and the musical bow – played while holding an arrow.

Today, traditional music has fused with contemporary West African, Caribbean and

South American sounds, creating a hybrid that includes highlife, reggae and soukous. Togo's most famous singing export was Bella Bellow, who, before her death in 1973, ruled the local music scene, toured internationally and released an album, *Album Souvenir.*

Literature

The country's best-known author is Tété-Michel Kpomassie. His unlikely sounding autobiography, *An African in Greenland,* contains his unique perspective on life in the chilly land.

ENVIRONMENT
The Land

Togo's coastline measures only 56km, but the country stretches inland for over 600km. Lagoons stretch intermittently along the sandy coast, and further inland are rolling hills covered with forest, yielding to savannah plains in the north.

National Parks

Togo's national parks are disappointing because the larger mammals have largely been killed or scared off. The country's remaining mammals, which include monkeys, buffaloes and antelopes, are limited to the north, while crocodiles and hippos are found in some rivers.

Since 1995, the Swiss Fondation Franz Weber has been working, with some success, to resurrect Parc National de Fazao-Malfakassa (see p790), but the other parks have been more or less abandoned.

Environmental Issues

Pressure for land, combined with lack a of government commitment to conservation, a lack of financial resources, and traditional practices such as slash-and-burn agriculture, have taken their toll on the environment. Conservationists are now attempting to involve communities in preservation efforts.

The coastline is also in a precarious state. Since the construction of a second pier at Lomé's port, several beaches have disappeared. Pollution compounds the situation.

FOOD & DRINK

Togolese dishes, some of the best in West Africa, are typically based, as in much of the region, on a starch staple such as *pâte* (a dough-like substance made of corn, manioc or yam) accompanied by sauce. Sauces include *arachide* (peanut and sesame), *boeuf* (beef stew), *rouge* (literally red, from palm nut oil) and *gombo* (okra, also aptly named *sauce gluante* because of its frightening alien slobber-like texture). Some Togolese specialities are *fufu* (pounded yam served with vegetables and meat), *djenkoumé* (a *pâte* made with corn-flour and cooked with chicken stock, spices, onions and tomato and served with fried chicken) and *pintade* (guinea fowl).

Common snacks include: roasted peanuts and cashews (often sold in old whisky or gin bottles – recycling at its best), *aloko* (fried plantain, served with a fiery chilli sauce), *koliko* (yam chips), *gaou* (bean flour fritters) and *wagasi* (a mild cheese fried in hot spice). You'll also find fresh fruit everywhere you go, including wonderfully sweet oranges (green is their normal colour) that women sell partly-peeled so that you can just slice the top off and suck the juice out (watch and learn from the locals!).

Togo has its fair share of generic (Flag, Castel, Lager) and local brews. *Tchoukoutou* (fermented millet) is the preferred tipple in the north, often found in the market areas. Elsewhere, beware of *sodabe,* a terrifyingly potent, clear-coloured moonshine distilled from palm wine. Best enjoyed with plenty of lime.

LOMÉ

pop 675,000

Locals joke that it used to be *Lomé la plus belle* (Lomé the most beautiful) but that it's now *Lomé la poubelle* (Lomé the dump). It's true that Togo's capital is a shadow of its former self, but it retains a charm and nonchalance that is unique among West African capitals. Recent investment into its thriving port and the construction of Ecobank's new headquarters on Blvd du Mono might restore some its lost grandeur, but in the mean time, you'll probably appreciate its human scale and unexpected treats and gems: from tasty *maquis* to palm-fringed beaches, stunning galleries and colourful markets.

ORIENTATION

Street names are not Lomé's forte: many streets have several names or no name at all, and even when they do, people often don't know them. Landmarks are a more reliable bet. Most places of interest are in the D-shaped central area within the coastal highway and the semicircular Blvd du 13 Janvier (often called Blvd Circulaire).

The heart of town is around the intersection of Rue de la Gare and Rue du Commerce, which becomes Rue du Lac Togo east of the market. The Grand Marché is a few blocks to the east of the intersection. Ave Maman N'Danida leads north from the centre to meet Blvd de la Paix – which runs northeast to the airport – and turns into Blvd Gnassingbé Eyadéma.

Maps

The best map of Lomé is the *Lomé* city map (1998) but it was out-of-print at the time of our last visit. The excellent *Guide Lomé* has a detailed street directory, and is written in English and French, but again, copies are hard to come by.

INFORMATION
Bookshops

Librairie Bon Pasteur (☎ 221 36 28; cnr Rue du Commerce & Ave de la Libération; ☼ 8am-12.15pm & 3-6pm Mon-Fri, 9am-1pm Sat) Lomé's only bookshop, a block west of the cathedral. It sells maps and, occasionally, English publications like the *International Herald Tribune* and *Time*.

Cultural Centres

Centre Culturel Français (☎ 223 07 60; www.ccf-lome.org; 19 Ave du 24 Janvier; ☼ 10am-8pm Tue-Sat, 5-8pm Sun) Regular films, concerts and exhibitions, and has a good selection of books and up-to-date newspapers.

Espace Culturel Africain Le 54 (☎ 220 62 20; Blvd du 13 Janvier; ☼ 10am-midnight Tue-Sun) A nice blend of exhibition space, affordable craft and jewellery, and a vibrant restaurant-bar.

Emergency

Centre Hospitalier Universitaire de Tokoin (☎ 221 25 01; Route de Kpalimé) The main hospital, 1.5km northwest of the city.

Internet Access

There are numerous internet cafes in Lomé. Expect to pay CFA300 to CFA500 per hour.
Cybercafé MZ (☎ 236 90 08; Place Anani Santos; per hr CFA350; ☼ 7am-10pm Mon-Sat, 1-10pm Sun) A little cramped but friendly and open on Sunday.

Cyber Poste (Rue Kponvene; per hr CFA400; ☼ 7am-9pm Mon-Fri, 8am-6pm Sat) Reliable connection.

Media

Newspaper racks at major road intersections stock newspapers.

Medical Services

If you need a doctor or a dentist, contact your embassy for a list of recommended practitioners. Out of hours, ring ☎ 242 to find out which pharmacy is on call.
Dr Noël Akouvi (☎ 221 32 46; Cabinet Dentaire NIFA 10, Rue Amouzou) For dental emergencies.
Pharmacie Bel Air (☎ 221 03 21; Rue du Commerce; ☼ 8am-7pm Mon-Fri, 8am-1pm Sat)

Money

Banks listed below all change cash but only Ecobank and the BIA change travellers cheques. All are open without a lunch break and on Saturday too, albeit for shorter hours.

Moneychangers congregate on Rue du Commerce, but there is a good chance of being ripped off.
Banque Atlantique (☎ 220 88 92; Place du Petit Marché; ☼ 8am-4pm Mon-Fri, 9am-2pm Sat) The only place that accepts MasterCard in Togo; also accepts Visa.
BIA (☎ 221 32 86; 13 Rue du Commerce; ☼ 7.30am-4pm Mon-Fri, 9am-1pm Sat)
BTCI (☎ 221 46 45; Rue du Commerce; ☼ 7.45am-4.30pm Mon-Fri, 9am-3pm Sat) Has a Visa ATM, which issues up to CFA400,000 per transaction.
Ecobank (☼ 7.45am-5pm Mon-Fri & 8am-4pm Sat) Rue de Chemin de Fer (☎ 222 65 74; 1 Rue de Chemin de Fer); Rue du Commerce (☎ 221 71 14; 20 Rue du Commerce) Both equipped with Visa cash machines.

Post

Post office (☎ 221 31 95; Ave de la Libération; ☼ 7.30am-5pm Mon-Fri, 7.30am-12.30pm Sat) Has an efficient poste restante service.

Telephone

Local and international calls can be made from any of the multitude of private telephone agencies around the city.
Cyber Poste (Rue Kponvene; ☼ 7am-6pm Mon-Fri, 8am-noon Sat) Just behind the post office, offers private phone booths, fax services and sells mobile phone SIM cards and vouchers.

Tourist Information

Direction de la Promotion Touristique (☎ 221 43 13; www.togo-tourisme.com; Rue du Lac Togo) Located in a rundown building near Marox Supermarché. Staff are helpful, if surprised to see tourists, and can give you a reasonable road map of Togo as well as information on traditional festivals, which they are keen to promote.

TOGO

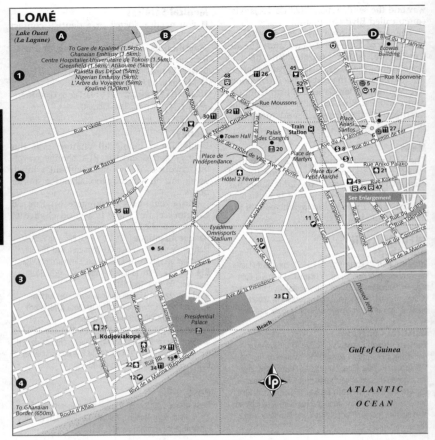

Travel Agencies

Lomé's many travel agencies are mostly in and around the Immeuble Taba on Ave Georges Pompidou. They can help with flight bookings and organise excursions.

Jossika Voyages (☎ 221 41 21; 25 bis Rue de la Gare)
Togo Voyages (☎ 221 12 77; Rue du Grand Marché)

DANGERS & ANNOYANCES

There are pickpockets around the Grand Marché and along Rue du Commerce, and muggings are frequent, some at knife-point. The worst thing you could do is walk on the beach alone, especially at night.

There are occasionally violent riots in Lomé. If this happens, locals will generally suggest that you avoid certain districts – sound advice.

Even in a street party, carry as little as possible with you, as muggers may take advantage of the general chaos.

If swimming, be aware of a very dangerous undertow (see opposite).

SIGHTS

Lomé's cultural highlight is the outstanding our pick **Musée International du Golfe de Guinée** (☎ 220 57 90; www.musee-igg.com; 1603 Blvd du Mono; admission & guide CFA1000; ☼ 10am-5.30pm Wed-Sat, from 2.30pm Tue). Founded in 2007, it is the brainchild of a Swiss ethnologist and art dealer who decided to open his private collection to the public in a bid to 'give African culture back to Africans'. The 400 artefacts exhibited in the small villa on the

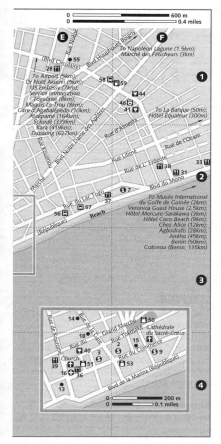

TOGO

seafront are all stunning and some of them extremely rare. Check out the 18th-century sculpted elephant tusk depicting the history of the kings of the Benin Kingdom (from Nigeria), the 2000-year old terracotta Nok statues (again from Nigeria) and the beautiful Yoruba wooden gates carved with intricate bas-reliefs. You'll also find an amazing array of gold Ashanti jewellery.

Another good place to admire art, of the contemporary variety this time, is the small and privately-run **Arte Viva** gallery (☎ 220 47 27; www.assafo.com; cnr Blvd de La Marina & Blvd du 13 Janvier; admission free; ☺ 10am-noon & 3-6pm Tue-Sat). Michelle Brunet, the owner, is hugely knowledgeable about contemporary West African art – Ghana, Togo and Nigeria in particular –

and can talk you through the nuances of these different schools. The works exhibited are for sale.

The small and rundown **Musée National** (National Museum; ☎ 221 68 07; Palais des Congrès; admission CFA1000; ☺ 8am-noon & 2.30-5.30pm Mon-Fri, 9am-5pm Sat & Sun) pales in comparison but displays historical artefacts such as cowries, the former currency.

Southwest of the Palais des Congrès, spanning a few blocks along the seafront are the old Presidential Palaces (the ugly concrete one and beautiful colonial mansion). Don't get too close as the guards don't like it (see p801). The new palace is about 7km north of the centre.

The **Marché des Féticheurs** (fetish market; ☎ 227 20 96; Quartier Akodessewa; admission & guide CFA3000, plus per camera/video CFA5000/10,000; ☺ 8.30am-6pm), 4km northeast of the centre, stocks all the ingredients for traditional tonics and fetishes – porcupine skin, warthog teeth, donkey skull, serpent head and more. It's all a bit grisly and some visitors will feel uncomfortable at the sight (and stench) of this traditional pharmacy, some of it protected species (turtle, elephant etc). It's important to remember however, that despite the tourist spin, a vast majority of Togolese retain animist beliefs and that fetishes are an integral part of local culture. To get there charter a taxi (CFA1000) or a taxi-moto (CFA500).

The labyrinthine **Grand Marché** (Rue du Grand Marché; ☺ to 4pm Mon-Sat), home to the once famous and fabulously rich 'Mama Benz' (who'd made their fortunes selling the beautiful Dutch wax materials and were nicknamed after their favourite cars), is Togo at its most colourful and entrepreneurial. You'll find anything from Togolese football tops to cheap cosmetics, roasted peanuts and cloth (see our tips in the boxed text, p782).

ACTIVITIES

The surf in Lomé is very dangerous because of a strong undertow, and drownings are common – be careful. Many of the beaches are also used as the local toilet. The beaches east of Lomé are better and more secluded (see p783).

Nonguests can use the swimming pools at **Hôtel Ibis** in the centre (see p779), and – bigger and better – **Hôtel Mercure-Sarakawa** (see p779), which also has tennis courts and organises horse riding.

TOGO

LOMÉ FOR CHILDREN

Greenfield restaurant (p780) screens kids' films in its outdoor cinema on Saturday at 4pm.

TOURS

Run by French couple Loïc and Paule Henry, biologists by trade, adventurers by nature, **our pick** **1001 Pistes** (1001 rough tracks; ☎ 927 52 03; africatoy1001pistes@yahoo.fr) offers fantastic excursions across the country: from easy day walks (€75) from Lomé, to several-day treks and 4WD adventures with bivouacs (€150 per chauffeured vehicle per day, for up to three people, plus €45 per person, including food and camping equipment) to whale-watching outings along the Atlantic coast (€75). The trips are great fun and Loïc and Paule bring invaluable knowledge to their tours having lived in the country for nearly 20 years.

FESTIVALS & EVENTS

Lomé grabs any excuse to take a day off and party. Street parties are awesomely anarchistic events, but embassies normally advise against attending them: pickpockets and muggers often use the chaos to their advantage and Togo's already dangerous roads turn truly wild.

SLEEPING

The following entries cover accommodation options that are within 5km of the centre of town. You should know that most budget hotels in Lomé, like in much of Africa, double as brothels during the day. The options we've listed below don't – to the best of our knowledge!

Budget

My Diana Guesthouse (☎ 995 46 20, 983 45 82; Rue des Jonquilles; r CFA6000-8000; ⚄) A family affair, this lovely guesthouse is a simple but proudly maintained establishment. You'll have to pay more for air-con (CFA500-1000 per night, depending on electricity consumption) but considering you get use of the kitchen, garden terrace and TV lounge, it's an absolute bargain.

Hôtel Le Galion (☎ 222 00 30; www.hotel-galion.com; 12 Rue des Camomilles; s/d with fan CFA6000/8000, with air-con CFA12,000/14,000; ⚄) Spread across three colonial style white-washed villas, this Swiss-owned hotel is the stalwart of budget accommodation in Lomé: the 24 rooms are basic but clean and the restaurant and bar popular with locals and travellers alike, particularly on Friday nights for the live music sessions.

Midrange

our pick L'Arbre du Voyageur (☎ 933 62 64; lpen naneach@yahoo.fr; r with fan/air-con incl breakfast CFA10,000/15,000; P ⊠) Run by a friendly young French-Togolese couple, this laid-back, comfortable guesthouse located 5km north of town just off the road to Kpalimé, is a breezy retreat from central Lomé. The villa peaks out from a lush garden and rooms are equipped with balconies and DVD. To find it, ask for directions to the IAEC business school in Atikoumé; the guesthouse is the (unmarked) villa on its left.

Hôtel Équateur (☎ /fax 221 99 92; www.hotelequateur.com; 102 Rue Litimé; d CFA17,000-25,000; ⊠ ⌨) Friendly, young and funky, Équateur is an attractive choice in the Ocam district, east of the Blvd de 13 Janvier. The 11 rooms are spacious, with all mod-cons, and the *paillote* (straw awning) bar-restaurant (meals around CFA4000) is a prime spot to enjoy the sweet nights of the tropics. The helpful staff can also arrange car rental and find you a chauffeur/guide.

Napoléon Lagune (☎ 227 56 66; www.woezon.com/napotogo; Blvd de l'Oti; s/d CFA22,800/24,800; P ⊠ ⌨) Poised on the edge of the Bê lagoon, and just a couple of kilometres northeast of the centre, this is an unexpected oasis: tropical garden, swimming pool, plush rooms, and a very lively restaurant-bar (meals CFA6000) that uses any excuse for a party.

Hôtel Belle-Vue (☎ 220 22 40; fax 220 76 28; www.hotel-togo-bellevue.com; Kodjoviakopé; s/d/tw from CFA23,000/27,000/32,000; P ⊠ ⌨ ⏅) In the leafy district of Kodjoviakopé, right behind the German embassy, the Belle-Vue is a stylish option that won't break the bank. Rooms are spotless and elegantly decorated with African print curtains and dark wood furniture. It is also home to one of Lomé's best restaurants, La Belle Époque (see p780), and has a great *paillote*-bar in a lush garden. There is wi-fi throughout.

Top End

Hôtel Aristos (☎ 222 97 20; fax 221 13 65; hotelaristos@yahoo.fr; Rue Aniko Palako; small/big d CFA35,000/45,000; P ⊠) Smack bang in the centre of town, the raspberry-coloured Aristos sports impeccable little rooms with all mod-cons and balconies to soak in the surroundings. The atmospheric roof-terrace, where you can sip a cold beer and dine on wood-fired pizzas or good African and European fare (mains CFA3000 to CFA5000), is a great perk.

Veronica Guest House (☎ 222 69 07; veronicagh@bibway.com; Blvd du Mono; r CFA35,000-50,000; ⊠ ⌨ ⏅ ⏅) This charming 10-room hotel with friendly staff, beautiful mahogany fittings and a pint-sized pool is a more Togolese alternative to the upmarket chain hotels. Although it is on the busy highway, the rooms have thick double-glazing and views across the road to the beach. Meals are available for CFA9000 and there is free wi-fi as well as an internet terminal.

Hôtel Ibis (☎ 221 24 85; fax 221 61 25; www.accorhotels.com; Blvd de la Marina; r with city/sea view CFA49,000/57,000; P ⊠ ⌨ ⏅) Another establishment from the Accor chain: it lacks charm both inside and outside, but the lovely sea views definitely make up for it. It also has the best city centre swimming pool (open to nonguests for CFA3000).

Hôtel Mercure-Sarakawa (☎ 227 65 90; www.accor-hotels.com; Blvd du Mono; r with city/sea view CFA84,000/94,000; P ⊠ ⏅) Despite its concrete bunker exterior, this is one of West Africa's most exclusive hotels. Located 3km east of the centre on the coastal road to Benin, the 164 rooms are comfortable but the Sarakawa's main draw is its stunning Olympic-sized pool set in acres of coconut grove (nonguests over/under 13 CFA4000/2000, CFA6000/3000 on Sunday). As well as bars, a nightclub (entry CFA4500) and two restaurants, the hotel also offers horse riding (per hour adult/child CFA4000/3000) and tennis courts.

EATING

Most restaurants in Lomé are open for lunch and dinner unless otherwise noted. Many of the more informal joints are also open throughout the day.

Restaurants
AFRICAN

Brochettes de la Capitale (Blvd du 13 Janvier; kebabs CFA200; ☻ 5pm-1am) This Lomé institution is suffering somewhat from its popularity and location on the increasingly polluted Blvd Circulaire, but it's still a cool place to devour lip-smacking and cheap as chips kebabs washed down with a CFA300 beer.

Maquis Le Trou (☎ 988 98 99; Route d'Atakpamé) Also affectionately referred to as Les Pintades by those in the know, this little *maquis* behind the Texaco garage in the GTA area specialises in guinea fowls. Slow cooked for hours, they

TOGO

are so tender they melt in your mouth. Local women are on hand to provide side dishes (*pâte*, rice or fries) and the tiny bar generally has beer and wine (although it can run out after a busy weekend!).

Nopégali (☎ 222 80 62; Blvd du 13 Janvier; meals around CFA2500) Another classic Lomé establishment, hugely popular, particularly for lunch. It's very much a canteen, but a good one, with friendly service and an outdoor terrace.

La Barque (☎ 221 40 97; off Rue de l'Ocam; meals CFA3000-4500) Service is rather slow at La Barque but the food reliably good and surprisingly innovative. Try the *agouti* (a tasty rodent called grasscutter in English) for local fare or go for tasty European dishes with an African twist such as the lemon-grass and *crème fraîche* chicken with saffron rice. To find it, take Rue de l'Ocam from Blvd du 13 Janvier and turn left when you get to Pharmacie de l'Ocam. La Barque will be on your right hand side.

ASIAN

China Town (☎ 222 30 06; 67 Blvd du 13 Janvier; meals around CFA8000; 🕑 lunch & dinner Wed-Mon) Fresh-looking, reliable and in a good location at the Kodjoviakopé end of the Blvd Circulaire, you'll find a great selection of steamed dumplings and meat dishes.

Golden Crown (☎ 221 03 36; cnr Blvd du 13 Janvier & Blvd du Mono; mains around CFA5000; 🕑 lunch & dinner) This long-standing place, easily spotted at night by its row of red lanterns, offers Vietnamese and Chinese dishes such as crab and lobster cooked with lashings of ginger and garlic.

Koh Samui (☎ 336 64 11; Rue Moussons; mains from CFA6000; 🕑 dinner Mon-Sat) Opened in 2008, this new upmarket Japanese and Thai restaurant has raised the bar of Asian cuisine in Lomé: the food is excellent, if pricey, and the decor infused with Southeast Asian influences. It's off Ave Nicolas Grunitzky, just down the road from the Hôtel de Ville.

EUROPEAN

Greenfield (☎ 222 21 55; Rue Akati; mains CFA2500-4500, pizza & tortillas from CFA2000; 🕑 6pm-midnight) Tucked away off Route de Kpalimé, near Tokoin Hospital, this great French-owned garden bar-restaurant is decorated with dancing Keith Haring figures, colourful lanterns and super funky colonial seats with retro faux-leather cushions. It is family-friendly, with a menu for children, and films screened for youngsters at 4pm on Saturday, in addition to the

adult films at 8.30pm on Tuesday (in French with English subtitles, CFA2500 including a margherita).

our pick La Savane (☎ 906 17 48; Blvd du Mono; mains CFA3000-4500; 🕑 lunch Mon-Fri & dinner Mon-Sat) This Swiss-owned haunt is hugely popular with expats and well-off Togolese. Regulars prop up the bar for an *apéritif* before settling down for delicious French staples such as *blanquette de veau* (creamy veal stew with mushrooms and rice) or their African counterparts such as *poulet Yassa*.

Le Triskell (☎ 220 95 57; Blvd du 13 Janvier; meals CFA3500-8000; 🕑 lunch & dinner, closed Sun lunch) Close to the Air France office, Le Triskell has an exotic pleasure garden full of cackling birds and fountains. The food is resolutely French (with amazing *crêpes* on Sunday night) with the exception of the pizzas (equally good, evenings only).

Le Barakouda (☎ 220 17 54; Blvd de la Marina, Kodjoviakopé; mains CFA6000-10,000; 🕑 lunch & dinner Tue-Sat, dinner Sun) The name gives it away: this is a fantastic seafood place where you'll enjoy succulent lemon sole, gambas *à la plancha* and red mullet filets. Portions are generous and the atmosphere jovial. The owner also organises fishing trips.

La Belle Époque (☎ 220 22 40; Kodjoviakopé; menu du jour CFA6500, mains CFA6000-12,000) Lomé's finest table, La Belle Époque, all crisp white table-cloths and dimmed lighting, serves wonderfully refined cuisine such as grilled sole with spiced red wine or turbot in vanilla butter. The *menu du jour* is a bargain considering the quality, and you can then blow your budget on one of the 50-odd wines on offer.

LEBANESE

El Mahata (Blvd du 13 Janvier; meals CFA3000) Flame-grilled chicken, flatbread and mounds of hou-mous make a brisk trade at this great Lebanese establishment. It's packed at lunchtime but you'll be able to grab a bite at any time of the day.

Quick Eats

Lomé is awash with cafeterias: good places to grab a cheap coffee with an omelette or spa-ghetti. They're typically open from 7am until midnight, and Rue de la Gare or Blvd du 13 Janvier are where you're sure to find them.

Al Donald's (Blvd du 13 Janvier) Just for fun try the cheeky rip-off of the American fast-food giant (it even has a single golden arch…).

Boston Maquis (☎ 222 26 06; Ave du 24 Janvier; mains from CFA1500) Sit in battered garden chairs and enjoy an ice-cold Flag with grilled chicken and tasty *pommes frites* (fries), the lot for less than CFA3000. Bargain.

Bena Grill (☎ 222 41 38; Rue du Lac Togo; meals CFA2000-4700) Under two huge *paillotes* and a battery of fans, this informal joint serves inexpensive grilled meats and salads. It's tucked back from the main street, next to the Marox supermarket.

L'Abeille d'Or (☎ 904 07 77; Rue de Kouromé; mains from CFA6000; ☺ Tue-Sun) Lurid luminescent lights and pricey mains, but the teashop is very good for Lebanese pastries and coffee. You can also smoke hookah, and there is live jazz Thursday to Sunday.

Self-Catering

You'll find fruit and vegetable stalls at every street corner. For groceries, the following supermarkets are stocked with everything you'd expect from a Western supermarket:

Leader Price Supermarché (Rue du Commerce; ☺ 8.30am-1pm & 3-6.30pm Mon-Sat, 9am-1pm Sun)

Marox Supermarché (Rue du Lac Togo; ☺ 8am-12.20pm & 1-6.30pm Mon-Fri, 8am-1pm Sat)

Ramco Supermarché (☎ 221 46 10; Rue de Kouromé; ☺ 8.30am-12.30pm & 2.30-7.30pm Mon-Sat, 9am-1pm Sun)

DRINKING

Lomé's nightlife can be seedy; prostitutes are a fixture at many bars along the northern and eastern part of the Blvd du 13 Janvier, but the atmosphere can be good fun. Just leave valuables at the hotel.

our pick **Bar Le Mondial** (Rue Tokmaké; ☺ 11am-1am) With African football shirts decorating the walls, Le Mondial has a great international chilled-out vibe and conversations tend to flow as fast as the beer. Located at the end of the Rue des Artisans, it's a great place to recover from hectic haggling.

Domino (665 Rue de la Gare; ☺ from 6pm) Den-like but funky and very popular, Domino houses Lomé's biggest selection of beers (50 or so) as well as a dozen whiskies and last but not least, vodka and Red Bull. Punters get going on the dance floor on Friday and Saturday night.

Koh Samui (☎ 336 64 11; Rue Moussons; ☺ from 7pm Mon-Sat) The rooftop bar of this restaurant is simply stunning and a fabulous place for sundowners. You'll find all the usual beers as well as elaborate cocktails. This really wouldn't

be out of place in an expensive resort in Mauritius or Bali.

Le Rézo (☎ 338 21 38; 21 Ave de la Nouvelle Marche; ☺ 10am-1am) Inside, it's like a 1980s disco with its blacked-out windows, VIP corner and heavy velvet fabric, but Le Rézo is more contemporary than it looks: wi-fi access, giant screens showing Champions League football games, karaoke nights and live jazz on Thursday.

Espace Culturel Africain Le 54 (☎ 220 62 20; Blvd du 13 Janvier; ☺ 10am-midnight Tue-Sun) Great live music and themed nights Thursday to Sunday catering for all musical tastes. As for food tastes, it's grill galore (dishes CFA3500 to CFA5000).

Café Panini (☎ 904 00 56; Blvd du 13 Janvier; ☺ from 5pm) Heaving, loud and seedy – the gloriously sleazy epicentre of Lomé's nightlife. There's a likelihood that men may be hustled by multilingual prostitutes.

La Terrasse (☎ 906 60 66; Blvd du 13 Janvier; ☺ 8am-3am, from 5pm Mon) This lively bar, with pool tables at the back and a big terrace at the front, is a less hectic haunt than many of its rivals nearby on the boulevard. The Lebanese owners are friendly and quick meals are available throughout the day (CFA2500 to CFA3800).

ENTERTAINMENT

Nightclubs

As in Europe, nightclubs are pricey and have cover charges, typically CFA3000 to CFA5000, including a drink.

Z Nightclub (Rue de la Gare; ☺ from 5pm) This jazzy nightclub, owned by Frenchman Philip, has been around for eons and enjoys a solid reputation. The music really gets going at the weekend after 11pm.

Byblos (Blvd du 13 Janvier; admission CFA5000; ☺ from 10pm Wed-Sun) Next to Café Panini is Byblos, a trendy nightclub that is a favourite haunt of rich young Togolese.

Ozone Discothèque (☎ 920 20 00; cnr Ave de Calais & Blvd du 13 Janvier; ☺ from 10pm Tue-Sat) You can't miss this bright-yellow hip hangout at the northern edge of town; cool features include a beer garden with a barbecue.

Le Privilège (☎ 221 85 11; Rue de Kouromé; admission CFA3000; ☺ 10pm-4am) One of the biggest nightclubs in West Africa, and recently refurbished, the crowd is quite young and the drinks rather expensive.

Live Music

Hôtel Le Galion (p778), Espace Culturel Africain Le 54 (above), Le Rézo (above)

TOGO

and L'Abeille d'Or (p781) all feature regular live music.

ourpick **Le Mandingue** (Rue Koketi; ☾ from 9pm Tue-Sat) One of Lomé's classier venues, this is a great piano-bar with a good mix of jazz, Latin vibes and blues. Drinks are pricey though.

Chez Alice (☎ /fax 227 91 72; chezalicetogo@hot mail.com; admission CFA6000) To party long into the night, take a bush taxi to Chez Alice in the village of Avéposo, about 12km from the heart of Lomé on the coastal highway to Aného. This Swiss-owned joint, popular with overlanders, hosts barbecues or fondue feasts with traditional music and dancing on Wednesday from 8pm. Meals are available for CFA5000.

Cinemas
Greenfield restaurant (p780) and the CCF (p775) both show films weekly.

SHOPPING
The Grand Marché (see p777) is perfect for browsing and purchasing bric-a-brac. If you can't face haggling over cloth, **Woodin** (☎ 221 28 00; 16 Rue du Commerce; ☾ 10.30am-6pm Tue-Fri, 9am-noon Sat, 12.30-6pm Mon,) provides air-conditioned and fixed (but reasonable) price respite just down the road.

Rue des Artisans (☾ 7.30am-6.30pm Mon-Sat) A relatively low-pressure place to buy wood-carvings, leather bags and sandals as well as jewellery (some of it made from semi-precious stones such as malachite) from across West Africa. The short street is east of the Leaderprice supermarket. Come with your haggling cap firmly on.

Village Artisanal (☎ 221 68 07; Ave de la Nouvelle Marche; ☾ 8am-5pm Mon-Sat) At this centre you'll see Togolese artisans weaving cloth, carving statues, making baskets, lampshades, cane chairs and tables, sewing leather shoes – all for sale at reasonable fixed prices. Lomé is famous for leather sandals; they were originally all made at the Village Artisanal, but you can also buy them around the Grand Marché for about CFA3000.

GETTING THERE & AWAY
Air
The international airport is 5km northeast of central Lomé. For details on flights to and from Lomé see p801.

Bus
Rakiéta (☎ 923 25 38) runs a daily service between Lomé and Kara (CFA6000, 6½ hours). It leaves at 7.30am from its depot in Atikoumé opposite the Lycée Klikamé, and stops in Sokodé (CFA5200, five hours) on the way. Bags are CFA500. Book ahead or arrive early (6am) on the day. This service is more reliable, less squashed and about the same price as bush taxis, ie a better option.

There are also a number of coach services between Lomé and many other major West African cities – see p802. Because of the lack of a bus station, each company has its own 'stop', subject to regular changes depending on the mood of the authorities.

Bush Taxi & Minibus
Bush taxis and minibuses travelling east to Aného (CFA900, one hour), Cotonou

---

HELLO TAILOR

Fabric is sold by the *pièce* (12 yards), the amount needed for a complete outfit (skirt, top and headscarf for women) or the *demi-pièce* (6 yards, generally enough for a shirt and trousers for men). Traders often refuse to sell less than this as it's not always easy to shift the rest. Prices vary enormously, courtesy of the recent flood of Chinese imports, but quality Dutch wax (which is colour-fast and very durable) *is* expensive: a *pièce* will cost about CFA35,000 whereas a Chinese *demi-pièce* could be bargained down to as little as CFA6000.

There are some very skilled tailors in the region and most will be able to copy whatever design you throw at them. Many will also have posters or little books of patterns and models you can choose from. Take your cue from the swishier hotels too where the colourful materials are used to make curtains, bed and table linen. Again tailors will happily oblige provided you have the measurements.

(CFA3500, three hours) and Lake Togo/Agbodrafo (CFA600, 45 minutes) leave from **Gare de Cotonou** (Blvd de la Marina), just west of the STIF bus station.

If you're going to Ghana it's best to catch a taxi (CFA500 shared, CFA1500 chartered) or *taxi-moto* (CFA500) to the border and cross on foot. Buses for Accra leave from just across the Ghanaian border in Aflao.

Gare d'Agbalépédo (Quartier Agbalépédo), 10km north of central Lomé, serves all northern destinations. Services include: Atakpamé (CFA2700, two hours), Dapaong (CFA8800, 10 hours), Kara (CFA6000, five hours), Sokodé (CFA5200, four hours) and Ouagadougou (CFA16,000, 24 hours). Helpfully, taxis congregate per destination and fares have been written on the wall. The earlier you get to a *gare* (station), the more chance you stand of finding a bush taxi without too long a wait.

Minibuses to Kpalimé (CFA1900 plus CFA500 baggage charge, two hours) leave from **Gare de Kpalimé** (Rue Moyana), 1.5km north of the centre on Route de Kpalimé.

GETTING AROUND
To/From the Airport
To the airport the taxi fare is about CFA1500 (but count on CFA2000 from the airport into the city).

Car
Avis (☎ 221 05 82; avis_togo@yahoo.fr; 252 Blvd du 13 Janvier; ⏰ 7.30am-12.30pm & 2.30-7pm Mon-Sat) Also has a branch at Hôtel Mercure-Sarakawa.

Taxi & Taxi-Moto
Taxis are abundant, even at night, and have no meters. Fares are CFA250 for a shared taxi (CFA350 after 6pm, more to the outlying areas) and CFA1000 non-shared. A taxi by the hour should cost CFA2500 if you bargain well.

Zippy little *taxi-motos* (motorcycle taxis) are also popular, if rather dangerous. You should be able to go anywhere in the centre for CFA200 to CFA300.

AROUND LOMÉ

BEACHES
Past the Nioto oil plant, and the port and customs east of Lomé, is another world – a mellow land of beachfront auberges which are far preferable to similarly priced hotels in the city centre.

The first one you come to, 9km from the city centre on the highway to Aného, is Hôtel Coco Beach. The well-marked turn-off is 1km east of the large roundabout at the port. A private taxi from the Gare de Cotonou costs about CFA1700.

our pick **Hôtel Coco Beach** (☎ 271 49 37; www.hotel-togo-cocobeach.com; s/d with air-con CFA30,000/32,000, s/d with air-con & sea view CFA34,000/36,000, bungalows from CFA32,000; ⧉ ⧉) is the swishest hotel on this part of the coast, with boardwalks leading to a great restaurant (meals CFA2500 to CFA4800), a seafront bar, a tip-top Jacuzzi-like swimming-pool and a private beach with deckchairs and *paillotes* (shaded seats) for hire. It's the safest beach to swim from thanks to a reef that blocks the strong undertow. Rooms are bright and cheerful with colourful bedspreads; great value for the level of comfort.

The parties on Wednesday night at **Chez Alice** (☎ 227 91 72; chezalicetogo@hotmail.com; camping per person CFA750, d/tr with fan & shared bucket shower CFA3500/4500, beachfront bungalows CFA7000) may be legendary (see opposite) but the sleeping quarters are less memorable: spartan rooms offering little more than a mattress, bed net and fan, with al fresco bucket showers and shared toilets. Rooms with ensuite in the annexe down the road are better. You can also pitch your own tent.

AGBODRAFO & LAC TOGO
On the southern shores of Lac Togo – part of the inland lagoon that stretches all the way from Lomé to Aného – Agbodrafo is a popular weekend getaway for frazzled Lomé residents. Swimming in the lake – croc and bug-free – is blissful and a great consolation prize for not being able to swim in the sea. It's also a good place to find a pirogue to Togoville.

On a secluded lakeside spot just a few kilometres west of Agbodrafo, you'll find the basic **Auberge du Lac** (☎ 904 72 29; bungalow with fan CFA8000). It's very low-key but the staff are friendly and will rustle up a tasty meal for you. You can also camp for CFA2000.

East of Agbodrafo is **Hôtel Le Lac** (☎ 320 65 79; www.hotellelactogo.com; r/ste CFA44,000/68,000; meals from CFA4200; ⧉ ⧉), a breezy retreat in an idyllic location on the shore of Lac Togo. The recently renovated rooms are spacious and well-appointed, with private patios and

TOGO

sweeping lake views. It has jet skis (per 10 minutes CFA15000), pedal-boats (per 30 minutes CFA4000), tennis, table tennis, guided pirogue trips to Togoville (CFA1500 return), a pool (CFA2000 for nonguests) and, separately, some crocodiles. Meals are available from CFA4200. The popular Sunday buffet (adult/child CFA10,000/5000) is an all-you-can-eat African and European cuisine extravaganza. The price includes use of the swimming-pool: perfect for a daytrip from Lomé.

A little further east, clearly marked down a dirt road heading towards the sea, **Hôtel Safari** (☎ 339 48 20; chez-hotel-safari@hotmail.com; d with fan CFA8000-12,000, with air-con CFA11,000-25,000; ❄) is a delightful place: run by a Swiss lady who's been in Togo for more than four decades, it sports impeccable rooms at unbeatable prices, beautiful surroundings and an excellent garden restaurant (mains CFA4000) that does a roaring trade at the weekend.

From the Gare de Cotonou in Lomé, bush taxis frequently travel along the coastal road to Aného, via Agbodrafo (CFA600).

TOGOVILLE

On Lake Togo's northern shore is Togoville, a village whose sleepy appearance belies its historical importance. It was here in 1884 that Chief Mlapa III signed a peace treaty with the German explorer Gustav Nachtigal that gave the Germans rights over all of Togoland. It is also a voodoo stronghold, with an important sacred forest nearby.

Having disembarked at the jetty, you'll come to the tiny **Centre Artisanal** and the German-built **cathedral**. A shrine to the Virgin commemorates her reported appearance on the lake, which attracted Pope John Paul II to visit. Fetishes in the streets attest to the practice of voodoo here.

Inside the **Maison Royale**, 100m west of the church, a one-room museum houses the now-toppled Mlapa dynasty's throne and some interesting old photos of the former chiefs. A *cadeau* (gift) is expected

Hôtel Nachtigal (☎ 339 48 53; r with fan/air-con CFA7800/14,800; Ⓟ ❄ ❄), a surprisingly good hotel 100m west of the market, has clean, pleasant rooms and bungalows with a pretty patio featuring two giant travellers' trees. There's also a pool and a large *paillote* bar-restaurant (mains CFA4000).

To get there, catch a bush taxi to Agbodrafo and take a pirogue (CFA1500 return) across the lake.

THE SOUTH

The cocoa and coffee triangle between Kpalimé, Badou and Atakpamé is an alluring area in this part of West Africa. With its rolling forested hills, numerous waterfalls and profusion of butterflies, it is a hiker's paradise. If you could only see one place in Togo, this would surely be it.

As you head a little further north, the landscape leaves its mantle of lush forest green for the light green and yellowy tinges of wooded savannah land. This is where the vestiges of Togo's wildlife cling to their ancestral land, in the Parc National de Fazao-Malfakassa.

ANÉHO

pop 28,100

Aného is a little like Togoville in the sense that what is left to see doesn't do justice to its history. All that remains of its days as colonial capital in the late 19th century are crumbling pastel buildings. And there is little Afro-Brazilian heritage to speak of, despite decades spent as a Portuguese slave-trade port.

Voodoo is strong here and most obvious at **Vogan's Friday market**, 20km northwest of Aného, one of the biggest and most colourful in Togo. Taxis from Aného (CFA600, 30 minutes) leave from the junction on Route de Lomé.

Aného also plays host to the **Festival des Divinités Noires** (Festival of Black Divinities), held in October each year since 2006, an attempt at celebrating and demystifying voodoo.

Sleeping & Eating

La Becca Hôtel (☎ 331 05 13; Route de Lomé-Cotonou; r with fan/air-con CFA8800/12,800; ❄) The cheap and cheerful La Becca, southwest of the market, is a good budget option, with an excellent restaurant that serves hearty portions of grilled fish and *koliko* for just CFA3000.

Hôtel Oasis (☎ 331 01 25; oasisaneh@hotmail.com; Route de Lomé-Cotonou; d with fan/air-con CFA10,000/14,000; ❄) An unbeatable location east of the bridge, looking across the lagoon and the beach to the sea. Rooms are well maintained, the management is friendly, and the terrace is a prime place for a sunset drink. The restaurant serves fine cuisine and charges for it (mains around CFA5000).

Drinking
Le Jardin d'Eden, close to La Becca at the southwest end of town, is good for a drink in an outdoor setting. Anastasia is another busy spot in this part of town, with tables scattered under a big tree and a roaring BBQ at night.

Further east, Bar Marigot is a great bar on the river mouth, just before the bridge.

Getting There & Away
From the *gare routière,* at the northeastern end of town, bush taxis and minibuses head to Lomé (CFA900, one hour) as well as to the Beninese border and Cotonou (CFA2500, 2½ hours).

KPALIMÉ
pop 48,300
Kpalimé (pah-lee-may) is only 120km from Lomé, but feels like another world, hidden among the forested hills of the cocoa and coffee region, which offer some of Togo's best scenery and hiking (see the boxed text, p786). It's also a busy place thanks to its proximity to the Ghana border and important market.

Although many of Kpalimé's hotels are outside the centre, most commercial activity takes place between the Grand Marché and Rond-point Texaco. There are four major sealed roads out of town: northwest to Klouto, northeast to Atakpamé, southwest to Ho (Ghana) and southeast to Lomé.

Information
Cifaid (☎ 441 07 38; Rue Kuma; per hr CFA350; ☼ 8am-8pm Mon-Sat), southwest of the church, is the only internet cafe in town.

Ecobank (☎ 441 03 29; Rue du Marché; ☼ 4.45am-5pm Mon-Fri, 8am-4pm Sat), opposite the Total Garage, and **BTCI** (☎ 441 01 27; ☼ 7.30am-noon & 2.30-6pm Mon-Fri, 9.30am-3pm Sat), north of the market, are your best options to change money. If you want to buy or sell Ghanaian cedis, money-changers can be found at the *gare routière* – but make sure you get an idea of the going rate first.

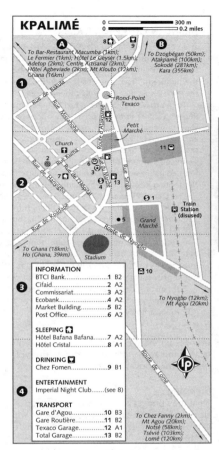

KPALIMÉ

INFORMATION	
BTCI Bank	1 B2
Cifaid	2 A2
Commissariat	3 A2
Ecobank	4 A2
Market Building	5 B2
Post Office	6 A2

SLEEPING 🏠	
Hôtel Bafana Bafana	7 A2
Hôtel Cristal	8 A1

DRINKING 🍷	
Chez Fomen	9 B1

ENTERTAINMENT	
Imperial Night Club	(see 8)

TRANSPORT	
Gare d'Agou	10 B3
Gare Routière	11 B2
Texaco Garage	12 A1
Total Garage	13 B2

Sights
Kpalimé's main attraction is its natural beauty. There are excellent **trekking** opportunities around Klouto, home to a wonderful variety of butterflies, and Mt Agou, Togo's highest peak at 986m (see the boxed text, p786). The area is also well-known for its waterfalls (Wli, Womé), many of which feature natural swimming pools too good to resist after a long walk.

The area is Togo's fruit basket and the colourful and thriving **Grand Marché** (☼ Tue & Sat) is an attraction in its own right; thousands of people from the surrounding hills descend on Kpalimé to trade their goods. For miles around you'll see mounds of mangoes or

---

HIKING IN THE KPALIMÉ AREA

The heartiest walk is up **Mt Agou** (986m), 20km southeast of Kpalimé. The path climbs between backyards, through cocoa and coffee plantations and luxuriant forests bristling with life. Small terraced mountain villages pepper the slopes and provide fabulous views of the area. In fact, the panorama from the village of **Akibo**, one hour from the peak, is as good as the view from the top. On a clear day, you can even see Lake Volta in Ghana.

To get to Mt Agou, catch a taxi from Kpalimé to the village of **Nyogbo**. The track can be hard to find so it's best to take a guide (see opposite). As well as showing you the way, a good guide will show you cool plants (such as the 'tattoo fern'), unusual fruit and veg, weird and wonderful creepy-crawlies and fill you in on local culture and history. The walk takes four hours return. Alternatively, there is a road to the top so you could walk one way and arrange a taxi for the other.

The area around **Mt Klouto** (741m), 12km northwest of Kpalimé, is another walking heaven, with forested hills, waterfalls and a myriad of butterflies. Early morning is the best time to search for them. Net-touting kids will offer to guide you; most local guides also offer butterfly walks (see opposite).

The **Danyi Plateau** on the road between Kpalimé and Atakpamé is another jewel of a landscape. At Adéta, 30km north of Kpalimé, turn left on a tar road in the direction of Ghana. When you reach **N'Digbé**, turn right (north) to **Dzogbégan** where you'll find a **Benedictine monastery** (☎ 221 55 12) and **convent** (☎ 929 80 17) famous for their plantations and wonderful products. You can tour the monastery's huge domain and find out more about the many plants grown here. Take a look at the monastery's chapel too, which was made exclusively of local materials (mahogany, teak, iroko etc). In the shops, you'll find all sorts of goodies (exotic fruit jams, biscuits, home-grown coffee) as well as lotions and potions for ailments from asthma to colds.

Both institutions offer simple but impeccable rooms (CFA7000, full-board). Curfew is at 8.30pm though, and you will need to book ahead as the monastery is often full. You can also order lunch (CFA2500) if you've come for a day trip.

---

oranges bobbing up and down on women's heads, and *taxi-motos* overladen with pyramids of maniocs and yams.

Sleeping

Kpalimé's budget accommodation is not particularly inspired. The auberges in Klouto will get you better value for money if you're watching the pennies.

Hôtel Bafana Bafana (Rue de l'Hôpital; s with/without bathroom CFA5000/4000) The terminally laid-back Bafana Bafana has stuffy rooms with fan but a good central location near the church. The whitewashed courtyard bar is great for a drink and you have plenty of choices nearby to keep the night going.

Hôtel Le Geyser (☎ 441 04 67; www.hotellegeyser .com; r with fan/air-con CFA10,000/14,500; 🅿 🅡) You'll find the tranquil Hôtel Le Geyser 2km from the centre on the road to Klouto. With its pretty garden and swimming pool, it's a great and affordable choice. Rooms are clean and airy, and the restaurant (mains CFA3000 to CFA4000) serves good food.

Hôtel Agbeviade (☎ 441 05 11; www.berezny .com/hotelagbeviade; r with fan/air-con/air-con & balcony CFA7500/14,500/17,500; 🅡) Signposted off the road to Klouto 1.5km northwest of town, the Agbeviade is super-friendly, comfy and spotless. The views of the surrounding hills from the rooftop terrace are stunning; a couple of rooms even have balconies. Meals are CFA2500 to CFA4000.

ourpick Chez Fanny (☎ /fax 441 00 99; hotelchez fanny@yahoo.fr; Route de Lomé; r CFA15,000; 🅿 🅡) Run by a delightful French-Togolese couple, this charming guesthouse in a villa 2km south of town is a homely retreat. The six rooms are huge and impeccable, and the patio and first-floor terrace are lovely spots to while away the time with a book or a drink. The restaurant (mains CFA3000 to CFA5000) is hands-down the best in town, and Fanny and Jean-René can offer invaluable advice on the area.

Hôtel Cristal (☎ /fax 441 05 79; www.hotelcristaltogo .com; Rue de Bakula; small r CFA9800-13,800, big r 16,000-26,000; 🅡) A fine example of Stalinist grace, with its concrete facade, green neon-lit hallway and functional but soulless rooms, the Cristal's only redeeming feature is the rather kitsch but amply proportioned pool (nonguests CFA1500) complete with spa-like archways and diving boards.

Eating

Le Geyser, Chez Fanny and Hôtel Agbeviade all have good restaurants if you prefer to stay in. For street food, head towards the Grand Marché and Rue Singa, south of Rond-point Texaco.

Le Fermier (☎ 902 98 30; meals CFA3000-4000; ☺ lunch & dinner Tue-Sun) For excellent European and African food, with a side of nostalgic 1970s rock band hits, try this low-roofed, intimate spot on the northwestern outskirts of town. Didier, the self-effacing but delightful owner, is a mine of information.

Bar-Restaurant Macumba (☎ 441 09 68; meals from CFA3000; ☺ 8am-midnight) For the usual suspects of grilled chicken and braised guinea fowl in rowdy ambiance, you can't beat the open-air Macumba on the northern outskirts of town, signposted from the road to Klouto. It's quite hard to find but its popularity ensures everyone knows its whereabouts so ask the locals if you get lost.

Drinking & Entertainment

Restaurants Le Fermier and the Macumba are popular for drinking, and the *buvettes* (small bars) near the Petit Marché are guaranteed to quench your thirst at any time, day or night.

Chez Fomen (☎ 916 10 17; Rue de Bakula; ☺ 11am-late) Just down the road from Hôtel Cristal, this cheerful and easy-going bar is a fun place for a drink. It also shows regular football games (African and European).

Imperial Night Club (Rue de Bakula; admission CFA3000; ☺ Fri & Sat) In Hôtel Cristal, very popular at the weekend among Kpalimé's golden youth.

Shopping

Centre Artisanal (☎ 441 00 77; ☺ 8am-6pm) Touristy but tasteful, this is a good place to watch craftsmen at work and buy their products, anything from beautiful mahogany salad bowls to ebony figurines, colourful batiks and masks of all shapes and sizes.

Getting There & Away

The *gare routière* is in the heart of town, two blocks east of the Shell petrol station. Northbound bush taxis leave from Rond-point Texaco. The road between Kpalimé and Atakpamé is the worst in the country and it can take up to four hours to drive. This means few taxis from Kpalimé travel further north than Atakpamé (CFA1700, two to four hours) and you'll have to change there for services to Sokodé or Kara.

You can get minibuses direct to Lomé (CFA1900, two hours), Notsé (CFA1700, 1½ hours), Tsévié (CFA1800, two hours), to the Ghanaian border (CFA1000, 30 minutes) and to Ho in Ghana (CFA1500, 1½ hours).

MT KLOUTO

The village of Kouma-Konda, 12km northwest of Kpalimé, is at the heart of the forested slopes of Mt Klouto. The winding mountain road to get there, a feat of early 20th-century German engineering, alternates between scenic views, dense forests and seasonal waterfalls.

The **Dzawuwu-Za harvest festival** takes place in Kouma-Konda in early August, featuring markets, feasts, traditional Apkesse music and dancing.

Sights & Activities

In addition to the eccentric **Château Viale**, a state property that can be visited with any of the accredited guides listed here, the big attraction in Klouto are the masses of colourful butterflies in the surrounding forests. **Guided butterfly walks** as well as **treks** in the area can be arranged with the following places:

Adetop (☎ 441 08 17; www.adetop-togo.org; Route de Klouto; ☺ 7.30am-noon & 3-5pm Mon-Fri) Also offers walks to nearby waterfalls (CFA5000), as well the option of spending the night in a local village with evening lessons in singing and drumming for CFA15,000.

our pick ARPV (☎ 989 20 27; afelete2002@yahoo.fr) Set up by the dynamic and highly-recommended Guillaume, this local guides' association will accommodate most requests, from cultural tours to treks, in Togo as well as neighbouring Ghana and Benin. Day trips cost CFA8000 per person, including food. Transport costs extra unless you have your own.

Auberge des Papillons (☎ 335 61 05) Run by the legendary Prosper, a keen lepidopterist, it offers half-day excursions including picnic for CFA7500, or shorter walks for CFA1500 per hour. Staff are very knowledgeable and can show you plants used to make natural dye such as indigo.

Sleeping & Eating

Auberge Nectar (☎ 449 16 43; aubergenectar@yahoo.fr; r CFA7000) On the quiet road leading to Mt Klouto, this auberge is a bargain: rooms are bright, clean, with decent ensuite bathrooms and TV. There is no need for air-con as the nights are blissfully cool on these forested hills, and you can count on chef David to rustle up some tasty grub.

Campement de Klouto (☎ 913 17 69; s/d CFA6000/8000; P) This former German hospital will make you feel like you've reached the last outpost of civilisation. At the start of the path to Mount Klouto's summit, it sees few customers. The 14 large, breezy rooms are immaculate though, with crisp sheets and welcome blankets for the cool nights. The restaurant serves unpretentious but decent food and even if you don't stay there, you could come for a drink and revel in the views and silence.

Getting There & Away

Taxis from Kpalimé to Kouma-Konda cost about CFA300 and your best chance to find one is on Kpalimé's market days (Tuesday and Saturday). A moto-taxi will cost about CFA600. From the Kouma-Konda checkpoint it's an easy walk to Auberge Nectar (10 minutes), Campement de Klouto (30 minutes) and then to the summit (1½ hours). To return to Kpalimé, go to the checkpoint and wait for a taxi or a bike.

ATAKPAMÉ
pop 41,300

Once the favourite residence of the German colonial administrators, Atakpamé today is a commercial centre that lacks the charm of other parts of the coffee country. Located at a major crossroads and strategically perched on a hill, its situation has defined its history as a place of refuge and commerce.

There are no sights in town, but it is still a pleasant enough stopover on long journeys (ever more relevant with the worsening state of the roads). You could also visit the **Akloa Falls** (see p790) as a daytrip from Atakpamé.

The town's layout is confusing, but it effectively has two main areas: the town centre, with the market, banks and post office at the northwest end of town, and the 'transport centre' in the southeast where most of the hotels and transport congregate. The road linking both areas is called Rue de la Station de Lomé.

Information

There is slow internet access at the two branches of **CIB-Inta** (☎ 440 03 07; per hr CFA300) Ave de la Libération (⊙ 7.30am-12.30pm & 2.30-7pm Mon-Fri, 7.30am-12.30pm Sat, 9am-8pm Sun); Rue de la Station de Lomé (⊙ 7.30am-8pm Mon-Fri).

Banks close on Sunday and Monday and only change cash. Try **BTCI** (☎ 440 01 74; Rue du Commerce) or **BIA-Togo** (☎ 440 01 92; Rue du Commerce).

There is a basic **hospital** (☎ 440 01 91; Rue de l'Hôpital) uphill northwest of the centre.

Sleeping

Hôtel California (☎ 335 85 44; resto_california@yahoo.fr; Route Internationale; r with fan & shared bathroom CFA2500, r with air-con & bathroom CFA8000;) Run by the inimitable Jeanne, this lovely hotel-restaurant is a gem of a place: the rooms are spotless, the food delicious and beautifully presented (mains CFA3000), and the welcome so warm you'll feel like you're hanging out with old friends. Find Hôtel California right at the back of the Total petrol station (Total Agbonou).

Hôtel de l'Amitié (☎ 440 06 25; Agbonou, off Route Internationale; r with fan/air-con CFA4000/7800;) Colourful rooms, good views and atmosphere but bad location up a dirt track from the Route Internationale with no street lighting. Service is a little lacklustre too. Meals are available for CFA2000 to CFA3000.

Hôtel Kapokier (☎ 440 02 84; Rue de l'Hôpital; r with fan/air-con CFA5000/7000;) Kapokier's bare rooms are nothing to write home about but the hotel is in a good location, overlooking the football pitch behind the post office. If you can afford it, take an air-con room: the building is west-facing and turns into a sauna at sunset.

Hôtel Le Sahélien (☎ 440 12 44; htelsahlien@yahoo.fr; Route Internationale; r CFA8800, with hot water CFA10,800, deluxe CFA14,300;) This once swish hotel has been resting on its laurels: the staff look blasé and rooms are noisy and in need of a good clean. Its two restaurants however, don't seem to have suffered the same service meltdown.

Roc Hôtel (☎ 440 02 37; fax 440 00 33; off Rue de la Station de Lomé; s/d/tr CFA10,000/12,000/13,000;) The government-owned Roc Hôtel has been here 30 years and looks it. It's a shame because a new coat of paint and a good airing would help make the best of those dreamy views. For the time being though, it's not a particularly enticing place.

Eating

There are plenty of cheap food stalls lining Route Internationale between the Total Garage and Le Sahélien. They are mainly there for the coach services that plough the Lomé-Ouaga route; service therefore tends to be expedient.

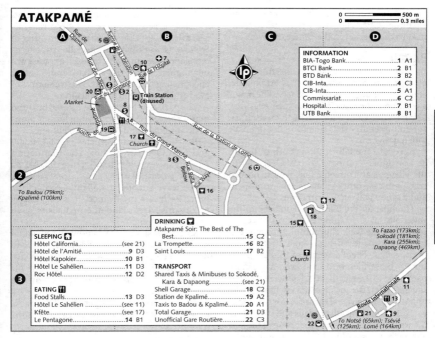

ATAKPAMÉ

INFORMATION
BIA-Togo Bank	1 A1
BTCI Bank	2 B1
BTD Bank	3 B2
CIB-Inta	4 C3
CIB-Inta	5 A1
Commissariat	6 C2
Hospital	7 B1
UTB Bank	8 B1

SLEEPING
Hôtel California	(see 21)
Hôtel de l'Amitié	9 D3
Hôtel Kapokier	10 B1
Hôtel Le Sahélien	11 D3
Roc Hôtel	12 D2

EATING
Food Stalls	13 D3
Hôtel Le Sahélien	(see 11)
Kfête	(see 17)
Le Pentagone	14 B1

DRINKING
Atakpamé Soir: The Best of The Best	15 C2
La Trompette	16 B2
Saint Louis	17 B2

TRANSPORT
Shared Taxis & Minibuses to Sokodé, Kara & Dapaong	(see 21)
Shell Garage	18 C2
Station de Kpalimé	19 A2
Taxis to Badou & Kpalimé	20 A1
Total Garage	21 D3
Unofficial Gare Routière	22 C3

Kfête (☎ 440 03 57; dishes from CFA500; ☼ 24 hr) Whether at the street-side counter or in the patio at the back, this is a good place to tuck into omelettes or grilled chicken at any time of the day or night.

Le Pentagone (☎ 440 09 06; Rue du Grand Marché; meals CFA2500-3500; ☼ 8am-10pm) Low-key but very pleasant first-floor restaurant serving tasty dishes such as *poularde à la cocote* (chicken stew) or grilled seabream.

Hôtel Le Sahélien (☎ 440 12 44; Route Internationale; meals CFA2800-5000; ☼ lunch & dinner) The downstairs restaurant does a brisk trade with the town's *taxi-motos*: it's very much *maquis*-like with its enormous grill and informal atmosphere. Upstairs is a favourite among the few organised tours that still visit Togo, and the roof terrace is a nice spot to catch the evening breeze and watch the world go by.

Drinking

Saint-Louis (Rue du Grand Marché; ☼ 8am-11pm) The music is quite loud at this roof-top *paillote* bar but it's the perfect place to sink a beer and watch the clouds of bats spanning the sky at sunset.

La Trompette (☎ 442 10 25; Rue Bella Bellow; ☼ 7am-dawn) The place to be on a Friday or Saturday night if you want to show off your moves, but make sure they're good ones because the standards are high! Pretty low-key the rest of the week.

Atakpamé Soir: The Best of the Best (☎ 440 07 11; Rue de la Station de Lomé; ☼ 5-10pm Mon-Thu, later Fri & Sat) With its ultraviolet lights and psychedelic decor, this cavernous place near the Shell garage has the feel of a hangar awaiting an illegal rave.

Getting There & Away

The T-junction between Rue de la Station de Lomé and Route Internationale serves as the unofficial terminal for most public transport. Wait south of the junction for taxis to Lomé (CFA2700, two hours); and east of the junction on Route Internationale, outside the Total garage, for taxis to Sokodé (CFA3050, four hours), Kara (CFA4200, five hours) and Dapaong (CFA8500, eight hours).

Taxis to Badou (CFA1800, 2½ hours) and Kpalimé (CFA1700, two hours) leave from next to the market in the centre of town.

BADOU

Badou is lost somewhere in the northwest of coffee country, 88km west of Atakpamé, amidst stunning mountain scenery. The major attraction is the **Akloa Falls** (also spelt Akrowa), 11km southeast of Badou. The town itself, an agricultural outpost, is small and doesn't have much going on.

Access to the falls is 9km south of Badou at Tomagbé. You have to pay CFA1500 to the villagers at Tomagbé (ask for the official receipt in case other villagers ask for money) and a guide will accompany you.

The hike up the hill from Tomagbé to the waterfalls takes 40 minutes. It's very steep in places but the walk is beautiful, through lush forests and paddy fields, across streams and over bridges. There is plenty of wildlife to observe – butterflies, birds and even monkeys – partly due to the fact that the falls were a sacred site until a few decades ago and off-limits to the uninitiated. It's an ideal excursion for a picnic as you can swim beneath the falls and stop along the way. You can also walk to the top of the falls although you should add another hour and a half to do that. Accessing the site is practically impossible during the wet season.

Hôtel Abuta (☎ 449 00 08; r with fan/ air-con/bathroom CFA6500/10,500/16,500; 🛏), past the post office on the road to Ghana, doesn't see many customers but has decent rooms with slightly surreal faux-leather 1970s furniture. Dinner (CFA3500) has to be ordered in advance.

Cascade Plus (☎ 443 00 71), on the main street, will see you right for a drink and a snack while you wait for a bush taxi back to Atakpamé.

Bush taxis head to Badou (CFA1800, 2½ hours) from the market area in Atakpamé. Get there early (6am) if you don't want to wait all day. The road there is in poor condition but the landscape is breathtaking. Taxis (shared/ hired CFA300/1000) and *taxi-motos* (CFA500) go from Badou to the waterfalls.

PARC NATIONAL DE FAZAO-MALFAKASSA

This 192,000-hectare **National Park** (🕑 Dec-May), in central Togo's beautiful Malfakassa Mountains, is one of the most diverse West African parks in terms of landscape – with forest, savannah, rocky cliffs and waterfalls.

The Swiss **Fondation Franz Weber** (☎ 550 02 96; www.ffw.ch; Route de Kara, Sokodé; 🕑 7.30am-12pm & 2.30-5.30pm Mon-Fri, 7.30-12pm Sat), which has an office in Sokodé, is working to protect the park from population pressure. This has seen a crackdown on poachers, Peul (Fula) nomads and villagers, encouraging them to find alternative sources of food and income, such as apiculture.

The park now boasts 203 species of bird and many species of mammal – including monkeys, antelopes and 60 elusive elephants.

Entry for private vehicles is CFA10,000 and CFA3000 per person. The foundation also organises **guided trips** (1 person CFA18,000, 2-3 people per person CFA13,000, 4-6 people per person CFA9000), which leave Sokodé at 4.30am – contact the office 24 hours in advance. It is also happy to organise treks and themed visits such as bird-watching.

Since the park's hotel is now closed, you'll have to base yourself in Sokodé. The drive to the park takes about one hour: drive south on the Route Internationale and turn off at Adjengré, 38km south of Sokodé on the main highway.

The park occasionally opens late if the tracks have suffered badly during the rainy season.

THE NORTH

As you head north, Islam takes over from Christianity as the dominant religion, and the Kabyé replace the Ewe as the main ethnic group. Sokodé, Kara and Dapaong are short on sights but are good spots to watch the world splutter past on a dysfunctional *taxi-moto*.

For those with their own vehicle however, or the determination to have a showdown with local bush taxis, fabulous highlights await in the castellated shapes of the Tamberma compounds in Koutammakou or the heady heights of the Nano caves.

SOKODÉ
pop 120,400

Sokodé is Togo's second-biggest city but it doesn't feel like it, with no major sites beyond the odd colonial building. Predominantly Muslim, the city echoes with the sound of prayer calls five times a day, and the Kotokolis, the main ethnic group, wear clothes reminiscent of those worn in North Africa.

The **Grand Marché** is the usual random assortment of plastic goods, live animals and street food. The T-junction between the Kara–Lomé highway and the Route de Bassar, is where the **Adoss ceremony** takes place, on the second day after the Prophet's birthday (for details see p816). During this spectacle, men engage in a series of violent, knife-flashing dances after drinking a special potion that supposedly makes their skin impenetrable.

Sokodé is the best base for trips to the Parc National Fazao-Malfakassa; head to the office of **Fondation Franz Weber** (☎ 550 02 96; www .ffw.ch; Route de Kara; ❧ 7.30am-12pm & 2.30-5.30pm Mon-Fri, 7.30-12pm Sat) for more information (see also opposite).

Information

There are two branches of the cybercafe **CIB-Inta** (per hr CFA300) Route de Bassar (❧ 7am-9pm); Route de Kara (❧ 7am-8pm Mon-Fri).

UTB (☎ 550 01 62; Route de Lomé) and **BTCI** (☎ 550 01 07; Route de Kara) change money.

Sleeping

Campement Tchaoudjo (☎ 445 19 09; Rue de la Préfecture; r with fan & shared/private bathroom CFA2500/4500; **P**) The austere *campement* is up the hill from the

douane (customs post) on the southern edge of town, a fair walk from the centre. Its dark but spacious rooms have sheets and fans, and some have private bathrooms.

Hôtel Essofa (☎ 550 09 89; off Route de Bassar; r with fan/air-con CFA4800/8800, with air-con & TV CFA10,800; **✖**) With its pleasant bar-restaurant and well-maintained garden, this is one of the better options in Sokodé. Rooms are clean and relatively comfortable although the bathrooms could do better (lack of toilet seat and paper). Meals are available from CFA1600.

Hôtel Ave Kedia (☎ 550 05 34; off Route de Kara; r with fan/air-con CFA13,000/24,000, ste CFA28,000; **✖**) Fan rooms are a rip-off but the air-con rooms are very clean and guaranteed to stay cool as it's the only hotel in town with a generator (power cuts are all too frequent). Suites in the gleaming new annexe feature the most surreal decor with huge flat-screen TVs and back-to-the-future furniture. Meals are available from CFA3000.

Hôtel Central (☎ 550 01 23; Route de Lomé; s/d/ bungalow CFA13,000/15,000/25,000; **P ✖**) Like all state hotels in Togo, it's rather institutional and lacks both character and customers, but

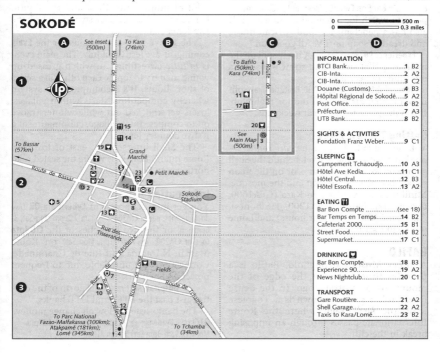

SOKODÉ

0 _____ 500 m
0 _____ 0.3 miles

INFORMATION	
BTCI Bank	**1** B2
CIB-Inta	**2** A2
CIB-Inta	**3** C2
Douane (Customs)	**4** B3
Hôpital Régional de Sokodé	**5** A2
Post Office	**6** B2
Préfecture	**7** A3
UTB Bank	**8** B2

SIGHTS & ACTIVITIES	
Fondation Franz Weber	**9** C1

SLEEPING 🏠	
Campement Tchaoudjo	**10** A3
Hôtel Ave Kedia	**11** C1
Hôtel Central	**12** B3
Hôtel Essofa	**13** A2

EATING 🍴	
Bar Bon Compte	(see 18)
Bar Temps en Temps	**14** B2
Cafeteriat 2000	**15** B1
Street Food	**16** B2
Supermarket	**17** C1

DRINKING 🍸	
Bar Bon Compte	**18** B3
Experience 90	**19** A2
News Nightclub	**20** C1

TRANSPORT	
Gare Routière	**21** A2
Shell Garage	**22** A2
Taxis to Kara/Lomé	**23** B2

the staff are lovely and the bungalows in the unkempt garden have a slight holiday feel about them. The restaurant serves a *menu complet* for CFA7500.

Eating

Sokodé is not well set up for eating out. Your hotel's restaurant is probably your best bet, otherwise try the teetotal (BYO beer) **Cafeteria 2000** (off Route de Kara; mains from CFA1000; 24 hr) whose menu spells out every possible combination of meat and side dish. **Bar Temps en Temps** (Route de Kara; kebabs from CFA200; dinner) with its massive BBQ and candle-lit tables is a nice joint, as is the friendly **Bar Bon Compte** (Route de Lomé; mains from CFA1000; 7am-11pm), which sports the same comedy menu as Cafeteria 2000 but does serve beer.

There's a small and erratically-supplied **supermarket** (8am-1pm & 3-11pm) at the back of Hôtel Ave Kedia.

You'll find plenty of street food around the market.

Drinking

With the local football pitch at the back, the open-air **Bar Bon Compte** (Route de Lomé) is a great place to watch local schoolkids in action. It also has a penchant for loud African music and dreadful soap on TV. All good fun.

Experience 90 (Route de Kara) A lively spot on the main drag that sits behind straw walls and a multitude of beer flags.

News Nightclub (550 11 30; Route de Kara) Split into an open-air bar and indoor nightclub, this is the place to boogie at weekends.

Getting There & Away

You can catch taxis from the *gare routière* – one block west of the market, behind the Shell garage on Route de Bassar – or on the main square between the market and the mosque. Minibuses go regularly to Kara (CFA1600, two hours), Bafilo (CFA1200, 1½ hours), Atakpamé (CFA3050, four hours) and Lomé (CFA5200, six hours).

BAFILO

Another Muslim stronghold, Bafilo is a peaceful little town on the edge of the mountains of central Togo. In the dense forest 10km south of town is a Togolese icon, the **Aledjo Fault**, where the Route Internationale passes through an imposing break in the cliff.

Visit the **Bafilo falls**, 5km east of town, for a panoramic view of the surrounds. The falls themselves are a bit of a let-down but the walk there, through maize and manioc fields surrounded by imposing cliffs, is very scenic. Visit the chief in his compound, past the first mosque (there are several), to get permission (CFA500).

At the **Groupement Artisanal des Tisserands** (660 02 26; 7am-5pm Mon-Sat), you can see weavers in action and buy *pagnes* of cloth. You'll be able to hear the rhythmic clicking of their looms as you walk up the hill.

Stay if you must at the dilapidated **Hôtel Maza Esso** (976 01 24; Route de Kara; r with/without bathroom CFA5000/2500). You'll have to rely on food stalls for sustenance.

KARA

pop 34,900

Laid out by the Germans on a spacious scale, Kara is the relaxed capital of northern Togo and a good base for trips to Koutammakou (p795) and the Mt Kabyé (p795) area. Because Eyadéma was from Pya, a Kabyé village about 20km to the north, he pumped a lot of money into Kara and the region has remained a political stronghold of the Eyadéma clan.

The Kabyé region is famous for the **Evala** coming-of-age festival in July. The main event is *la lutte* (wrestling), in which greased-up young men try to topple each other in a series of short bouts. It's a championship system whereby competition starts within villages; losers get knocked out while winners move on to compete inter-village, culminating at a Kabyé country level.

The Shell intersection, east of town on Route Internationale, is where the sealed road northeast to Benin begins.

Information

You get internet access at **Cyber Kara-OK** (Ave du 13 Janvier; per hr CFA300; 8am-7.30pm Mon-Sat, 3-6pm Sun) or the two branches of the **CIB-Inta** (per hr CFA200; 7am-11pm Mon-Sat) on Route Maman N'Danida and Rue de Chaminade. Connections are unreliable due to frequent power and network cuts.

The **hospital** (Ave Eyadéma) is north of the centre, just past the BTCI and UTB banks.

The banks listed below all change money: **BTCI** (Ave Eyadéma; 7.30am-noon & 2.30-4.30pm Mon-Fri, 9am-3pm Sat) Has an ATM.

KARA

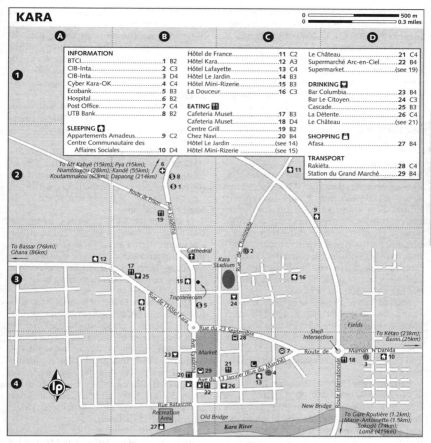

INFORMATION		
BTCI	**1**	B2
CIB-Inta	**2**	C3
CIB-Inta	**3**	D4
Cyber Kara-OK	**4**	C4
Ecobank	**5**	B3
Hospital	**6**	B2
Post Office	**7**	C4
UTB Bank	**8**	B2

SLEEPING		
Appartements Amadeus	**9**	C2
Centre Communautaire des Affaires Sociales	**10**	D4

Hôtel de France	**11**	C2
Hôtel Kara	**12**	A3
Hôtel Lafayette	**13**	C4
Hôtel Le Jardin	**14**	B3
Hôtel Mini-Rizerie	**15**	B3
La Douceur	**16**	C3

EATING		
Cafeteria Muset	**17**	B3
Cafeteria Muset	**18**	D4
Centre Grill	**19**	B2
Chez Navi	**20**	B4
Hôtel Le Jardin	(see 14)	
Hôtel Mini-Rizerie	(see 15)	

Le Château	**21**	C4
Supermarché Arc-en-Ciel	**22**	B4
Supermarket	(see 19)	

DRINKING		
Bar Columbia	**23**	B4
Bar Le Citoyen	**24**	C3
Cascade	**25**	B3
La Détente	**26**	C4
Le Château	(see 21)	

SHOPPING		
Afasa	**27**	B4

TRANSPORT		
Rakiéta	**28**	C4
Station du Grand Marché	**29**	B4

Ecobank (Ave Eyadéma; 7.45am-5pm Mon-Fri, 8am-4pm Sat) One of only two banks outside Lomé to change travellers cheques.

UTB (Ave Eyadéma; 7.45-11.30am & 2.45-4.30pm Tue-Fri, 7.30am-12.30pm Sat)

Sleeping
BUDGET
Centre Communautaire des Affaires Sociales (660 61 18; Route de Maman N'Danida; dm shared/solo CFA1500/2000, s/d/tr with fan CFA2500/3500/5000, d with air-con CFA4500;) This large centre has a ghostly feel and cleanliness is borderline, but the staff are friendly and it's a good place to meet young Togolese. The cafeteria-style restaurant (meals CFA1500 to CFA3000) is also popular.

Hôtel Mini-Rizerie (660 17 44; Ave Eyadéma; r with fan/air-con CFA5600/7600;) Run by the affable Ali, the basic rooms were being repainted at the time of our visit. Facilities are shared and leave something to be desired, but the bar-restaurant and patio are very pleasant (meals CFA3000). It's opposite the Togo Telecom building.

our pick La Douceur (660 11 64; douceurkara@yahoo.fr; off Rue de Chaminade; r with fan/air-con CFA5000/8000, ste CFA12,000;) Don't be put off by the bumpy ride down a dirt track in the stadium's neighbourhood: this is a hidden gem and by far the best place to stay in town. There is indeed a certain *douceur de vivre* inside the proudly maintained and flowered little compound. Rooms are spotless with simple decor, the well-stocked bar serves the coldest beer in town, and the *paillote* restaurant (mains CFA1500 to CFA4000) does great food including tasty salads.

Hôtel Le Jardin (☎ 660 01 34; off Rue de l'Hôtel Kara r CFA8500; 🐕) This delightful hotel is aptly named: it's all about the tumbling purple bougainvilleas, yellow hibiscus and beautifully tended garden. Rooms are small but attractive, with ensuite bathrooms that include an outside toilet. It is also one of Kara's top restaurants, with mains costing around CFA2500.

MIDRANGE

Marie-Antoinette (☎ 660 15 04; http://ma.kara-tg.com; Route Internationale; s/d with fan CFA7500/8500, s/d with air-con from CFA9500/12,500; ℗ 🐕) In a pretty house, 2km south of Kara on the Route Internationale, Marie-Antoinette is a little oasis of greenery. Rooms at the back share a pleasant patio while those in the main buildings have access to small balconies. The restaurant cooks up decent meals for CFA2500 and you can camp in the annexe (CFA1000 per car, CFA1500 per person).

Hôtel de France (☎ 660 03 42; off Rue de Chaminade; r with fan/air-con CFA5500/11,000; ℗ 🐕) The quiet Hôtel de France, north of town, has large, attractive rooms and a peaceful rooftop terrace where you can watch the sun set over the town and the hills. Meals are available for CFA900 to CFA2500.

Hôtel Lafayette (☎ 660 13 51; alcortogo@yahoo.fr; Ave du 13 Janvier; r CFA12,000-15,000; 🐕) Located above a bright green mobile phone shop, Lafayette is a reliable address, with clean, plush rooms and staff who'll go out of their way to make you feel at home. There is also a huge roof terrace, perfect for sundowners and preparing the next day's plans.

TOP END

Appartements Amadeus (☎ 445 30 73; Route Internationale; 2-/6-person apt CFA20,000/60,000; ℗ 🐕) An excellent option for groups of friends and families. The studio flats are effectively king-size double rooms but the three-double-bedroom flats are huge, with a big living-room, flat screen TV and ace views of the city.

Hôtel Kara (☎ 660 05 16; fax 660 62 42; Rue de l'Hôtel Kara; s/d from CFA18,500/21,500, s/d bungalow CFA25,000/28,500; ℗ 🐕 🐕) Kara's only top-end hotel has seen better days but its claims to fame include the only (working) lift outside

Lomé and the only swimming pool north of Kpalimé (nonguests CFA1000). The stone bungalows are the most appealing with little patios and TVs, although rooms on the 3rd floor have great views of the area. The restaurant serves meals for CFA6000.

Eating

Chez Navi (☎ 660 19 02; Ave Eyadéma; meals CFA500; 🕑 7am-11pm) A traditional Togolese eatery where you'll get a blob of *pâte* and ladle of sauce for next to nothin'.

Cafeteria Muset (Rue de l'Hôtel Kara; mains from CFA1500; 🕑 lunch & dinner) Good for cheap, filling and not particularly creative meals (think omelette or grilled chicken with rice). Another branch is found just south of the Shell roundabout.

Le Château (☎ 660 60 27; Ave du 13 Janvier; meals CFA775-1975; 🕑 11am-2am Tue-Sun) This fun bar-restaurant with a street-facing balcony, yellow paint and wooden decor is a perennial favourite. It serves draught beer, plays loud Togolese pop and offers anything from pepper steak to yam chips.

our pick **Centre Grill** (cnr Route de Prison & Ave Eyadéma; meals CFA4000; 🕑 lunch & dinner) An attractive place with its straw roof, wicker light shades and blackboard menus, Centre Grill (also known as Marox) serves divine Togolese food and good Western dishes such as pizzas. Try their *fufu sauce arachide* with grilled fish, or guinea fowl with *koliko*, wash the lot down with a Castel or Lager and polish it off with banana fritters. African gastronomy at its finest.

Also worth investigating are the bar-restaurants at **Hôtel Mini-Rizerie** (☎ 660 17 44; Ave Eyadéma; 🕑 dinner) and **Hôtel Le Jardin** (☎ 660 01 34; off Rue de l'Hôtel Kara; 🕑 lunch & dinner).

In addition to the large Tuesday market, there is a small **supermarket** (cnr Route de Prison & Ave Eyadéma; 🕑 6.30am-12.30pm & 3-6.30pm Mon-Sat, 6.30am-noon Sun) next to Centre Grill and the well-stocked **Supermarché Arc-en-Ciel** (Ave du 13 Janvier; 🕑 8am-8pm Mon-Sat).

Drinking

The small, tumbledown **Bar Columbia** (off Ave Eyadéma), close to the market, always has something going on. Also good in the centre is La Détente (just south of Ave du 13 Janvier) all white and blue and pumping music night and day. **Le Château** (Ave du 13 Janvier) is popular with Peace Corps volunteers.

For more *maquis*-like atmosphere, try **Cascade** (Rue de l'Hôtel Kara), or the mellow, beach-like **Bar Le Citoyen** (Rue de Chaminade), perfect to sit under the trees or watch the stars with a (cheap) beer.

Shopping

Afasa (Rue Batascon; ☉ 8am-12.30pm & 2.30-5pm Mon-Fri) Across the football pitch at the southern end of town, this women's group sells fabulous bags (CFA1200 to CFA2000), blankets (CFA20,000), exfoliating gloves made of natural fibres (CFA2000) and beautiful batiks (CFA3000 to CFA20,000). The money finances literacy classes, training in income-generating activities and basic health and hygiene skills for women from local villages.

Getting There & Away

From the main *gare routière*, about 2km south of the town centre on Route Internationale, minibuses regularly head south to Sokodé (CFA1200, 1½ hours), Atakpamé (CFA4200, four hours) and Lomé (CFA4600, seven hours). For some inexplicable reason, taxis heading north to Dapaong (CFA3800, four hours) and beyond are few and far between and it's not rare to have to wait half a day for one to fill up.

For buses heading to Lomé, **Rakiéta** (Rue du 23 Septembre) has a daily departure at 7.30am (CFA6000, six hours) from its depot. To get to the border with Benin via Kétao (CFA600, 30 minutes) and to local towns such as Bassar (CFA1700, 1½ hours) and Niamtougou (CFA750, 45 minutes), get a minibus or bush taxi from **Station du Grand Marché** (Ave Eyadéma) next to the market.

AROUND KARA

One of Kara's main draws is the surrounding scenery, a mix of rocky outcrops interwoven with grassland, tropical forests and fields.

Mt Kabyé & Around

Mt Kabyé (810m), 15km north of Kara and the area's culminating point, rises among picturesque villages such as Pya, birthplace of the late Gnassingbé Eyadéma and famous for its blacksmith, Pita where potters use ancient firing techniques (sun-dried pots are covered with grass and then set fire to) or Tcharé, nestled in a valley amid terraced fields. Unfortunately you'll need your own transport

to get there. A chartered taxi (CFA20,000 for the day) could take you to some areas; others are only accessible by 4WD.

The only village that is easily accessed by bush taxi is Kétao, on the main northern border crossing with Benin. Its busy Wednesday market features *tchoukoutou* stands and fetish stalls.

Niamtougou

This sleepy town, 28km north of Kara on Route Internationale, has a Sunday market, where you'll find a selection of baskets and ceramic bowls, and **Codhani** (☎ 665 00 30; codhani .niamtougou@yahoo.fr; ☉ 8am-1pm & 3-5.30pm, from 8.30am Sat & 9am Sun). This centre, 2km south, sells good-quality T-shirts (CFA2500), tablecloths (CFA8000), kids' clothes (from CFA4000) and batik murals, all made by artisans with a disability. You can tour the workshop and watch them weaving, hammering, painting and boiling up wax. Prices are fixed but reasonable and you can be certain it will support a good cause: many of the people there would struggle to find employment elsewhere.

Codhani also has five basic bungalows (shared bathroom CFA2500, or private bathroom CFA4000) and a bar-restaurant serving Togolese grub (CFA500 to CFA2400).

KOUTAMMAKOU

Also known as Tamberma Valley or Land of the Batammariba after the people who live here, Koutammakou has a unique collection of fortress-like mud houses, founded in the 17th century by people fleeing the slave-grabbing forays of Benin's Dahomeyan kings (see the boxed text, p797). The site was listed as World Heritage by Unesco in 2004 and it's the closest thing Togo has to a tourist hotspot. The area is one of the most scenic in the country, with stunning mountain scenery and intense light.

You can visit Koutammakou as a daytrip from Kara or **Kandé** (also spelt Kanté). Either way, turn eastward off the highway near the garage in Kandé and follow the track in the direction of **Nadoba**, the area's main village. About 2km down the road, you'll have to pay CFA1500 at the **police post** (☎ 909 08 14; ☉ 7am-7pm) to enter the site. If you haven't arranged a guide before setting off, it's a good place to pick one up.

The *piste* is in good condition and crosses the valley all the way to Boukoumbé and

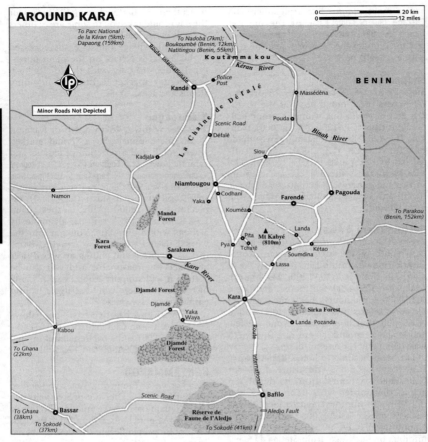

AROUND KARA

0 ——— 20 km
0 ——— 12 miles

TOGO

Minor Roads Not Depicted

To Parc National
de la Kéran (5km);
Dapaong (159km)

Route Internationale

To Nadoba (7km);
Boukoumbé (Benin, 12km);
Natitingou (Benin, 55km)

Koutammakou

Kéran River

Police Post

Kandé

BENIN

Massédéna

Pouda

Binah River

La Chaîne de Défalé

Scenic Road

Défalé

Siou

Kadjala

Niamtougou

Codhani

Farendé

Pagouda

Namon

Yaka

Kouméa

To Parakou
(Benin, 152km)

Manda Forest

Landa

Kara Forest

Pita
Pya

Mt Kabyé
(810m)

Tcharé

Kétao

Sarakawa

Lassa

Soumdina

Kara River

Djamdé Forest

Djamdé

Yaka Waya

Kara

Sirka Forest

Landa Pozanda

Kabou

To Ghana
(22km)

Djamdé Forest

Route Internationale

Scenic Road

To Ghana
(38km)

Bassar

Bafilo

Aledjo Fault

To Sokodé
(37km)

**Réserve de
Faune de l'Aledjo**

To Sokodé (41km)

Natitingou in Benin (see also p802). The drive to Natitingou actually ranks as one of this author's favourites for the breathtaking beauty of the landscape; set off early in the morning when the light is still soft and the air dust-free.

If you don't have your own transport, chartering a taxi for the day will cost around CFA20,000. If you're based in Kandé, you could rent a bike for a lot less (CFA3500 to CFA4000). Alternatively, if you happen to be there on a Wednesday, it's market day in Nadoba and taxis then plough the route between the valley and Kandé (CFA500). Nadoba's market is as much a *tchoukoutou*-fuelled gathering as a commercial event, and worth a visit in itself.

The best guide in the valley is the articulate and super-friendly **Jacques** (☎ 996 20 29). He runs the small souvenir shop in Nadoba and organises walking and cycling tours. You can also contact the local association **Ajvdc** (☎ 667 20 11), which as well as tours, runs a very basic *tata*-style **auberge** (r CFA2000) in Nadoba, with meals from CFA1500. Expect to pay about CFA5000 for a guide, including all *tata* entrance fees.

In Kandé **Auberge La Cloche** (☎ 916 78 02; r with fan/air-con CFA4500/7500; ❄) is without pretension but it is reassuringly clean and the Fetna family are a friendly lot (and they cook a mean *fufu sauce boeuf* for just CFA1200). It's about 500m from the main road, close to the water tower.

TOGO

TAMBERMA COMPOUNDS

A typical Tamberma compound, called a *tata*, consists of a series of towers connected by a thick wall with a single entrance chamber, used to trap enemies so they can be showered with arrows. The castlelike nature of these extraordinary structures helped ward off invasions by neighbouring tribes and, in the late 19th century, the Germans. As in the Somba people's *tata somba* nearby in Benin (see the boxed text, p120), life in a *tata* revolves around an elevated terrace of clay-covered logs, where the inhabitants cook, dry their millet and corn, and spend most of their leisure time.

Skilled builders (that's what Tamberma means), the Batammariba only use clay, wood and straw – and no tools. The walls are banco (a mixture of unfired clay and straw, which is used as a binder), waterproofed with a mixture of cow-dung and sand. The towers, capped by picturesque conical roofs, are used for storing corn and millet. The other rooms are used for sleeping, bathing and, during the rainy season, cooking. Entrances tend to be very narrow, and meant to be entered backwards to always face the enemy. The animals are kept under the terrace, protected from the rain.

There may be a fetish shrine in front of the compound, as well as animal skulls on the walls inside.

Traditionally, when a man is old enough to start his own family, he shoots an arrow and, where it lands, builds his own *tata*.

PARC NATIONAL DE LA KÉRAN

Once a thriving wildlife sanctuary, a visit to La Kéran will probably leave you wanting these days. People re-appropriated the land following the troubles of the 1990s and all the animals fled; the highway from Kandé to Dapaong goes through the park, and none of the tracks have been maintained.

DAPAONG

pop 31,800

This lively little town is a West African melting pot, with the Burkinabé and Ghanaian borders both within 30km. It sits in the middle of Togo's most arid landscape and gets the full force of the harmattan (p770) between November and February when visibility is sometimes reduced to just 100m or so.

There's a busy Saturday market and you can visit the small **Coopérative de Tissage** (☎ 770 86 05; 8am-5pm Mon-Sat) next to Radio Maria. It sells beautifully woven bags, tablecloths and purses made by local women using Burkinabé and Beninese cotton. They're a friendly bunch and might even get you to try your hand at weaving!

But Northern Togo's most remarkable sight, and an amazing hike, is the **cliffside caves** of Mt Semoo (see boxed text, p799).

For Western goods, go to **Hope** store at the market. **Ecobank** (Route de Nasablé; 7.45am-5pm Mon-Fri, 8am-4pm Sat) changes travellers cheques but only in the morning and not on Saturday.

Internet access is available at **CIB-Inta** (Route de Nasablé; per hr CFA300; 7.30am-8pm Mon-Fri, from 8am Sat & 9am Sun).

Sleeping & Eating

Hôtel La Colombe (☎ 770 81 84; Rue du Marché; r with fan CFA5000) The only central option, next to the market, La Colombe has basic rooms and a bar. It's fairly quiet except on Saturday when the market kicks off at dawn and funeral processions (funerals are generally held on Saturday so that a maximum number of relatives can attend) parade through town.

Hôtel La Princesse (☎ 445 44 04; Route Internationale; r with fan CFA5000-6000) There's not much to say about the rooms except that they're clean but the restaurant cooks up a storm from its African (read open-air) kitchen at the back of the yard. It also gets the thumbs up from LP readers.

Auberge Idriss (☎ 770 83 49; off Route Internationale; r with shared facilities & fan/air-con CFA4000/6500, r with bathroom & air-con CFA11,500-13,000;) A tidy little guest house in a quiet neighbourhood 2km north of town. Rooms in the main building are spacious; those in the annexe have shared facilities but are cosier. Idriss also serves food but if you don't fancy eating in, Maquis Bethel across the road is excellent.

Hôtel Le Campement (☎ 770 80 55; Route de la Station de Lomé; r with fan/air-con CFA9800/14,800;) Dapaong's only plush hotel, but it's overpriced. However, rooms are pleasant and

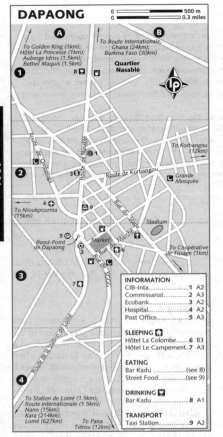

DAPAONG

0 — 500 m
0 — 0.3 miles

To Golden King (1km);
Hôtel La Princesse (1km);
Auberge Idriss (1.5km);
Bethel Maquis (1.5km)

To Route Internationale,
Ghana (24km);
Burkina Faso (30km)

Quartier
Nasablé

To Korbangou
(12km)

Route de Korbangou

Grande
Mosquée

To Nioukpourma
(15km)

Stadium

Rond-Point
de Dapaong

Market

To Coopérative
de Tissage (1km)

To Station de Lomé (1.5km);
Route Internationale (1.5km);
Nano (15km);
Kara (214km);
Lomé (627km)

To Pana
Tiérou (12km)

INFORMATION
CIB-Inta...................1 A2
Commissariat..............2 A3
Ecobank...................3 A2
Hospital..................4 A2
Post Office...............5 A3

SLEEPING
Hôtel La Colombe..........6 B3
Hôtel Le Campement........7 A3

EATING
Bar Kadu...............(see 8)
Street Food............(see 9)

DRINKING
Bar Kadu..................8 A1

TRANSPORT
Taxi Station..............9 A2

spacious, and the overgrown garden filled with oversized sculptures is a cool place to laze around. The staff seemed pushy and generally clueless but the French bar-restaurant (mains CFA4000) serves extravagant desserts, an unusual and rather luxurious treat if you happen to have a sweet tooth.

Bethel Maquis (☎ 770 88 38; ☾ noon-11pm) Behind Auberge Idriss north of the centre, this place serves delicious African and Western food (meals from CFA2000) in a tranquil garden.

Bar Kadu (Route de Nasablé; ☾ 7am-11pm) For a brilliant insight into local life, join the punters at this typical canteen. Pick and choose your meal from the cauldrons in the kitchen and tuck in while watching Ivorian soaps:

they're so popular kids will sneak under the tables or stand at the back to share the fun.

There are plenty of informal food stalls on Route de Nasablé and by the market.

Drinking

All *maquis* such as **Bethel** (off Route Internationale) and **Bar Kadu** (Route de Nasablé) offer cheap beer as well as food. Otherwise, get down to the glitzy **Golden King** (☾ 10pm-dawn Fri & Sat), near Auberge Idriss.

Getting There & Away

Taxis leave the station on Route de Nasablé for Sinkasse on the Burkinabé border (CFA1000), from where transport heads to Ouagadougou.

From Station de Lomé on Route Internationale, 2km south of the centre, bush taxis head to Kara (CFA3800, four hours) and Lomé (CFA8000, 12 hours).

TOGO DIRECTORY

ACCOMMODATION

Owing perhaps to its undeveloped tourist industry, Togolese accommodation is generally cheap. Expect to pay less than CFA8000 for budget rooms, CFA8000 to CFA15,000 for midrange and CFA15,000 to CFA25,000 for top end. In Lomé, prices are quite a lot higher, and you can stay in (ie not a brothel) budget rooms costing up to CFA12,000, and top end hotels upwards of CFA35,000.

Top-end hotels with swimming pools and other amenities can be found in Lomé, at Lake Togo and in Kara.

ACTIVITIES

There are plenty of hiking opportunities in Togo, particularly in the Kpalimé region (see the boxed text, p786).

For swimming, there are some good beaches near Lomé and you can swim in Lake Togo. Several of the top-end hotels have swimming pools and tennis courts. Water sports can be arranged at Hôtel Le Lac (p783), and horse riding at the Mercure-Sarakawa (p779) in Lomé.

BOOKS

The Village of Waiting, by George Packer, is an interesting observation on life in Togo.

TOGO

CASTLE IN THE CLIFF

Halfway up a cliff in the remote mountain ranges about 30km southwest of Dapaong is an amazing **cave settlement**.

During the 19th century the Chokossi Empire, revolving around Sansanné-Mango, established a feudal empire over much of northern Togo. The Moba people, who lived on and around the plateau, resented this, and built cliff-side stores on Mt Semoo to hide their possessions – and themselves – from Chokossi soldiers and tax collectors. The cliff's ledge provided perfect natural protection.

While the Moba people had to scale the cliff using tree roots and rocky ledges, there is now a protected steel ladder. At the long-since abandoned site you'll find a series of large conical clay containers, which were used to store food supplies, as well as the sleeping and cooking areas.

To reach the escarpment, which is known locally as **Grottes de Nano** (Nano Caves), follow Route Internationale south of Dapaong for about 15km. At the sign for Croix Rouge Togolaise Dispensaire de Nano, turn right onto a dirt road and follow it 10km west to the village of Nano. From Nano, ask for direction to the village of Kpierik, another 5km southwest, from where the walk to the cliff and back will take about three hours.

The walk passes through cotton fields and tall grass, climbs up the ledge and then crosses the plateau, all amid beautifully rugged scenery. When you arrive at the village of Nago, you must ask the chief permission to visit the caves. Entrance is CFA2000; you'll also have to pay for a local guide (CFA500) and the chief will ask for baksheesh.

The site is dramatic (not good for people scared of heights) and proffers miles of breathtaking views. Gawping at this panorama, it's obvious why the Moba decided to hide in such a strategic spot.

You should be able to get a guide (often a child) either in Nano or Kpierik, but make sure you agree a price before setting off (CFA1500 to CFA2000 should be adequate) and beware of any hangers on who will want to accompany you and then demand to be paid.

If you don't have your own vehicle, getting there will involve chartering a taxi (CFA12,000) who will drive you there and wait for you while you walk. Otherwise, you'll find taxis on Thursday, Nano's market day (CFA700, 30 minutes).

It is one of the best books yet on the Peace Corps experience, covering a volunteer's two years in Lavié, and it's quite candid about the country's autocratic politics.

Do They Hear You When You Cry? is Fauziya Kassindja's harrowing account of her flight from Togo, where she was facing female circumcision, to more Western forms of brutality in detention centres and prisons in Germany and the USA.

Hustling is not Stealing: Stories of an African Bar Girl follows the adventures of Hawa, a feisty hustler and 'pay-as-you-go wife', whose tales of Togo and Ghana were transcribed by musicologist John M Chernoff in the late '70s.

BUSINESS HOURS

In general, you will find that information places are open from 7am to noon and from 2.30pm to 5.30pm Monday to Friday. Eating out is normally possible for lunch (12.30pm to 2.30pm) and dinner (6pm to 9pm), Monday to Sunday, while you can usually get a drink between 11am and midnight Monday to Saturday. Many of the smaller *maquis*-style eateries/*buvettes* serve food and drink continuously from about 11am until 11pm. Nightclubs are commonly open from 10pm until late Friday and Saturday. As a rule shops keep the following hours: 7.30am to 12.30pm and 2.30pm to 6pm Monday through to Friday, and until 12.30pm Saturday.

CHILDREN

In Lomé, activities such as horse riding are available through the top-end hotels, and Greenfield restaurant screens children's films in its outdoor cinema (see p780).

DANGERS & ANNOYANCES

Petty theft and muggings, sometimes violent, are rife in Lomé, especially on the beach and near the Grand Marché (see p776). *Taxi-motos* in the city may be convenient, but are dangerous. Avoid large groups of people, and seek advice if you're planning to attend a street party.

Because of the dearth of street lighting at night, muggings and accidents (falling into

TOGO

a ditch or tripping over a pothole) are common; bring a torch or better, take a taxi.

People will endlessly try to attract your attention, either by making a 'psssst' or kissing sound. It's tiresome, irritating at worst, but harmless.

Driving in Togo is hair-raising: take care on the road, particularly at night.

EMBASSIES & CONSULATES

Angola, the Democratic Republic of the Congo, Egypt, Gabon, Libya and Senegal have representation in Lomé. For more details, check out www.republicoftogo.com.

France Embassy (☎ 223 46 00; www.ambafrance-tg.org; 13 Ave du Golfe); Consulate (☎ 223 46 40; www.ambafrance-tg.org; Ave Général de Gaulle; ☽ 8am-12pm)

Germany (☎ 221 23 38; fax 222 18 88; Blvd de la Marina)

Ghana (☎ 221 31 94; 8 Rue Paulin Eklou, Tokoin; ☽ 8am-2pm Mon-Fri)

Nigeria (☎ 221 34 55; Atikoumé)

UK British Nationals should contact the British High Commission in Accra (p388).

USA (☎ 261 54 70; www.togo.usembassy.gov; Blvd Eyadéma; ☽ 8am-5pm Mon-Thu, 8am-12.30pm Fri)

FESTIVALS & EVENTS

Special events include: Evala, the coming-of-age and wrestling festival in the Kabyé region around Kara, in July (p792); and the country's harvest festivals, notably

Dzawuwu-Za in Klouto (p787). There are many others; contact the tourist office in Lomé for details.

HOLIDAYS

Public holidays include the following:

New Year's Day 1 January
Meditation Day 13 January
Easter March/April
National Day 27 April
Labour Day 1 May
Ascension May
Pentecost May/June
Day of the Martyrs 21 June
Assumption 15 August
All Saints 1 November
Christmas Day 25 December

See p816 for a table of dates of Islamic holidays.

INTERNET RESOURCES

Republic of Togo (www.republicoftogo.com) The best site, with plenty of country information as well as news and travel links.

Togo Globe (www.togodaily.com) A useful English-language newspaper online.

Togo Tourisme (www.togo-tourisme.com) Not the freshest looking but offers a good overview of the country's main sites and practicalities.

LANGUAGE

French is the official language. The main African languages are Ewe, Mina and Kabyé; the latter being the language of the current president.

MAPS

The 1:500,000 *Carte Touristique du Togo* (Institut Géographique National) is the best country map but can't always be found in Lomé's bookshops (try buying it at home before you go). However, its 1977 predecessor, the *Carte Routière et Touristique du Togo* is available for about CFA3000. The Direction de la Promotion Touristique in Lomé also gives out dated but free road maps.

MONEY

Travellers cheques can be exchanged in Lomé, Kara and Dapaong, but you'll pay a commission. Make sure to bring your receipt (*preuve d'achat*) as well as your passport and a good dose of patience. Ecobank offers the best services for travellers throughout the country with long opening hours (no lunch time closure), cash advances and Western Union money transfers. You'll find Visa cash machines in Lomé and Kara. Only Banque Atlantique in Lomé accepts MasterCard.

Money changers can be found in most border towns.

PHOTOGRAPHY & VIDEO

Do not photograph or film government buildings – travellers have been beaten by the police for photographing the presidential palace. See also p821.

POST

Postcards and letters cost CFA550 to Europe and CFA650 to Australasia and North America. The poste restante service at the main post office in Lomé is reliable.

TELEPHONE & FAX

Make international calls (and faxes) at Telecom offices, or the private telephone agencies in every town. The latter charge from CFA200 per minute to North America and Europe, and CFA300 to Australasia.

The Togocel and Telecel networks, owned by the same company, cover 80% of Togo. It costs CFA3000 to get a pay-as-you-go SIM card; top-up vouchers range from CFA450 to CFA45,000. It costs CFA20 to send a local SMS, and CFA90 to send one internationally. International calls cost CFA300 per minute.

There are no telephone area codes in Togo.

TIME

Togo is on GMT – one hour behind Benin, Niger, Nigeria and Cameroon, and the same as the rest of mainland West Africa.

VISAS

Visas are required for everyone except nationals of the Economic Community of West African States (Ecowas) countries. One-week extendable visas (CFA10,000) are issued at major border crossings with Ghana (Aflao/Lomé), Benin (Hilakondji) and Burkina Faso (Sinkasse) and at the airport.

The **Service Immigration Togolaise** (☎ 250 78 56; Route d'Atakpamé; ⏲ 7.30am-noon & 2.30-6pm), near the GTA building 8km north of Lomé centre, issues 30-day visa extensions in two days, though it may be possible to speed up this process. They're normally free when you extend the seven-day visa, or cost CFA10,000

if you're extending a one-month visa. Four photos are required. It's worth having a certified photocopy of your passport while your application is being processed, in case you encounter any awkward policemen.

The French consulate in Lomé (see opposite) issues visas for Burkina Faso and Côte d'Ivoire.

You can get a 48-hour transit visas (CFA10,000) for Benin at the Hilakondji border and extend it in Cotonou.

The Ghanaian embassy in Lomé (see opposite) issues one-month visas within three days for CFA12,000 (CFA10,000 for Commonwealth citizens); four photos are needed.

Unfortunately the Visa des Pays de l'Entente (p826), despite including Togo, appears to be unobtainable in the country, and travellers have reported being denied access to the country with it, having to buy the normal seven-day visa at the border.

WOMEN TRAVELLERS

The Togolese are rather conservative when it comes to marriage: it is therefore incomprehensible to them that women past their 20s might not be married, and if married, not be with their husband and children. This will lead to many questions, but it is generally harmless. To avoid attracting any more attention, dress conservatively (legs in particular) and don't hang around bars on your own. For more information and advice, see p826.

TRANSPORT IN TOGO

GETTING THERE & AWAY
Entering Togo

Getting into Togo is a breeze. You need a yellow fever certificate, but it's rarely asked for, except at the airport.

Air

Togo's international airport is 7km northeast of the centre of Lomé. **Air France** (AF; ☎ 223 23 23; www.airfrance.com/tg; Immeuble UAT, Lomé; Hub: Paris) has the most frequent and reliable services between Togo and Europe.

The following airlines also operate in Togo and have offices in Lomé:

Afriqiyah Airways (8U; ☎ 220 88 51; www.afriqi yah99.eu; Immeuble Taba) Hub: Tripoli.

Air Ivoire (VU; ☎ 221 67 13; Immeuble Taba) Hub: Abidjan.

Ethiopian Airlines (ET; ☎ 221 70 74; Immeuble Taba) Hub: Addis Ababa.

Royal Air Maroc (AT; ☎ 223 48 48; www.royalairmaroc .com; Immeuble Taba) Hub: Casablanca.

Land

Benin

Bush taxis regularly ply the road between Gare de Cotonou in Lomé and Cotonou (CFA3500, three hours) via Hilakondji (CFA800, one hour), while **STIF** (☎ 221 38 48; Gare de STIF) has buses to Cotonou (CFA3000, three hours) every other day.

The main northern crossing is at Kétao (northeast of Kara). You can also cross at Tohoun (east of Notsé) or Nadoba (in Koutammakou country), but public transport is infrequent and Beninese visas are not readily available. Numerous *pistes* also cross the border in remote areas. If you decide to take those roads-less-travelled, don't forget to get your passport stamped at the nearest police post on each side as you won't find a border check-point.

Burkina Faso & Mali

The best way to get to Ouagadougou from Lomé is by bus (CFA15,000, 22 hours). **SKV** (☎ 220 03 01; Blvd du 13 Janvier) has two weekly departures, on Tuesday and Friday at 5pm, and is reliable. The service goes on to Bamako (CFA33,000, 48 hours).

Minibuses to Ouagadougou go daily from Gare d'Agbalépédo in northern Lomé (CFA12,000, 24 hours). Given that it's 627km from Lomé to Dapaong, Togo's northern-most town, you may want to break up the journey. From Dapaong, you'll easily find a taxi to Sinkasse (CFA1000, 45 minutes), which straddles the border. From there it's CFA5000 to Ouagadougou by bus. The border is open from 6am to 6pm.

Ghana & Côte d'Ivoire

From central Lomé it is only 2km – CFA500/1500 in a shared/hired taxi – to the chaotic border crossing (open 6am to 10pm) with Aflao in Ghana. From there, you can pick up minibuses to Accra. **STIF** (☎ 221 38 48; Gare de STIF) runs a bus service from Lomé to Abidjan (CFA24,000, 24 hours) via Accra (CFA6000, four hours), with an armed escort in Côte d'Ivoire. In addition to the black marketeers, Global Forex in Aflao buys and sells cedis and CFA.

There are quieter crossings from Kpalimé, Klouto and Yikpa-Djigbé on the Danyi Plateau to eastern Ghana, and many visitors travelling with their own vehicle tend to prefer these, but you'll need to have visas and currency sorted out beforehand. Further north, you can cross at Badou, Natchamba (accessible from Sokodé and Kara) and northwest of Dapaong at Sinkasse, although all of these are subject to road conditions.

Nigeria

ABC Transport (☎ 234 9 670 2078; www.abctransport .com) runs daily services between Lagos and Lomé (CFA6,300, seven hours).

GETTING AROUND

Road safety is not Togo's forte. Accidents are a daily occurrence, a combination of bad road conditions, poor driving skills and the appalling state of the vehicles (Togo is home to a flourishing second-hand car trade, with many of Europe's wrecks ending up here).

If you can avoid it at all, don't drive at night: many vehicles don't have lights, so the risks of collision are high. Other issues to contend with include wildlife, cattle, people using the road as a path and the frightening and genuinely dangerous 'titans' – huge lorries that plough the main Togo–Mali axis at neck-breaking speed.

Bush Taxi & Minibus

Togo has an extensive network of dilapidated nine- and 15-place bush taxis and minibuses (which respectively carry 16 and 22 passengers, not including children) held together with rope, sticky tape and the divine intervention of the African god of transport. Travel is often agonisingly slow; unfortunately, they're generally the only way to get around.

Fares are fixed-ish but there is always room to negotiate. Paying for two places gives you the front seat to yourself, as well as shortening the time you have to wait for the taxi to fill. There is occasionally a surcharge for luggage, generally about CFA500.

Car & Motorcycle

The are parts of the sealed Route Internationale that are still in good condition, but they're few and far between. The roads linking Kpalimé, Badou and Bassar with the Route

Internationale used to be sealed but have deteriorated to the point where it's hard to call them so now.

Cars can be rented from Avis in Lomé (p783). If you're driving, you need an International Driving Permit. Police checkpoints are common but rarely nasty or obstructive.

Petrol stations are plentiful in major towns and you'll find numerous clandestine roadside stalls everywhere in the bush selling smuggled Nigerian fuel of varying quality.

Local Transport
TAXI
Taxis are abundant in Lomé, even at night, and have no meters. Fares in the city centre are CFA300 for a shared taxi and CFA100 nonshared (more after 6pm). A taxi by the hour should cost CFA3000.

TAXI-MOTOS
Taxi-motos, also called *zemi-johns,* are everywhere. A journey across town costs about CFA200 – more in Lomé. They are also a handy way to get to remote locations in the bush, but tell your driver to go slowly – particularly in busy Lomé, where there are daily *taxi-moto* crashes.

Tours
1001 Pistes (p778) organise excellent trips across the country.

TOGO

West Africa Directory

CONTENTS

This chapter provides a general overview of the essential things you need to know about West Africa, covering, in alphabetical order, everything from accommodation to women travellers. Each individual country chapter also has a directory that includes more specific information about these headings as they relate to each country. Please consult both when searching for information.

ACCOMMODATION

In the countries covered in this book, there's almost always some sort of accommodation available in midsized and larger towns, although quality and price vary widely. For details of accommodation in each country, see individual country chapters. For general

---

> **BOOK ACCOMMODATION ONLINE**
>
> For more accommodation reviews and recommendations by Lonely Planet authors, check out the online booking service at www.lonelyplanet.com. You'll find the true, insider lowdown on the best places to stay. Reviews are thorough and independent. Best of all, you can book online.

advice on the costs of travelling in the region, see p16.

Throughout this book, accommodation is divided into budget, midrange and top-end places. Within each category, listings are ordered according to price, from the cheapest to most expensive. The prices we give are for rooms with a bathroom; exceptions are noted in specific listings.

In general, Mali and Senegal are the most expensive countries, while neither Nigeria nor Niger offer outstanding value for money when it comes to accommodation. Togo is one of the region's cheapest countries. In some countries, including Guinea, Mali, Burkina Faso and Nigeria, establishments charge a government tourist tax on top of the price they'll quote you. Sometimes (such as in Burkina Faso) this is a one-off payment regardless of the number of nights you stay, while in Nigeria or Mali it's a nightly surcharge added on to the quoted price.

In many parts of West Africa, particularly in the Sahel during the hot season, people often sleep outside their hut or on the flat roof of their house as it's much cooler. In some hotels this is also possible, and carrying a mattress onto the roof – where you'll have some breeze and views of the stars – is usually allowed if you ask.

One other thing to note is that in Guinea, Sierra Leone and some other countries, a man and a woman may share a room with no questions asked, but a same-sex couple, regardless of whether they are a couple, usually cannot.

B&Bs

Burkina Faso is leading the way with smaller, more intimate alternatives to in with a range of excellent B&Bs. Prices are usually cheaper than hotels; they are the sort of places where the warmth and personality of the owners (often a French-Burkinabé couple) is a big drawcard. They're also known as *chambres d'hôtes* or *maisons d'hôtes*. The innovation is catching on, with a handful of similar places appearing in Mali and Mauritania.

Campements

Most towns and many villages in Francophone countries have a *campement* whose primary purpose is not as a camp site in the traditional sense (ie a place for tents), although some do provide areas where you can pitch a tent and have access to shower facilities. *Campements* offer cheap and simple accommodation that is far less elaborate than a hotel, containing the bare necessities, shared facilities and little else, but some are very good quality, with prices on a par with midrange hotels. Either way, they're often the best (and sometimes only) option in small towns. They're the sort of places where 4WDs fill the compound, and overlanders with their vehicles mingle with backpackers who've just arrived on the latest bush taxi.

In trekking areas such as Mali's Dogon Country (p507), it is established practice for visitors to sleep on the roof of the *campements* in each village, as it's usually preferable to the stifling rooms.

Camping

There are few dedicated camp sites in West Africa, and those that do exist cater mainly for overlanders in their own vehicle. However, some hotels and *campements* allow camping or provide an area where tents can be pitched. Grassy knolls on which to pitch your tent are rare – you often have to force pegs through hard-packed gravel. Camping in the wild is a risky business in most countries as theft can be a problem; if you do decide to camp, always seek permission from the local village chief before setting up.

Hotels

Most hotels charge for a bed only, with all meals extra. If breakfast is included it's usually on a par with the standard of accommodation: a full buffet in more-expensive places, instant coffee and bread further down the scale. Hotels are often called auberges.

Independent travellers on tight budgets are fairly well catered for, although there are almost no backpacker lodges. Although you will come across some gems, most of what's on offer is basic, devoid of any discernible character, and ranges from the recently swept to downright grubby. The showers and toilets are usually shared and often of the squat variety. Some hotels in this price range double as brothels.

Midrange hotels tend to be at their best in the capitals or major towns where you're likely to find at least one place with lovingly maintained rooms, private bathrooms, splashes of local colour, satellite TV and even a swimming pool. Most midrange places, however, fall somewhat short of this ideal and, though fine, will hardly have you rushing back to your room at the end of the day. Most offer a choice between a fan and air-con.

At the luxury end of the scale, West Africa has very few top-end hotels outside the capitals and offers little in the way of exclusive wildlife lodges or tented camps as found in East or Southern Africa.

Missions

If you're travelling on a tight budget, mission accommodation can be a good alternative to cheap and nasty budget hotels, although rooms are usually reserved for mission or aid workers and are open to others only on a space-available basis. Usually called *missions catholique,* they're invariably clean, safe and good value, although these are not places to stagger home drunk at 4am – at many missions travellers are only allowed to stay if they respect the rules.

Resorts

You'll find European-style resorts all along the West African coast, but the best facilities are at those that cater to Europeans looking for a two-week beach holiday without really having to look Africa in the eye. These are especially popular in Senegal, The Gambia and, to a lesser extent, Cape Verde, where you'll find all-inclusive packages of meals, accommodation and airport transfers. Although it's occasionally possible to get a room by simply walking in off the street, most rooms (and the best deals) are reserved for those who book the whole package through a travel agency in Europe.

ACTIVITIES

If the region's natural beauty stirs not just your soul but also your body into action, West Africa has some world-class activities to get involved in. Desert expeditions, diving and snorkelling, deep-sea fishing, hiking, rock climbing, surfing and windsurfing are all possible. Adding to the allure is the fact that, unlike elsewhere in the world, you may be the only traveller taking part. Remember, however, that infrastructure can be rudimentary, so be prepared to be self-sufficient. West Africa is home to some outstanding guides and even more young men ready to drop everything and take you out into the wilderness or on a limb: choose carefully.

Cycling

In several parts of West Africa, bicycles can be hired by the hour, day or week, and can be a good way to tour a town or area. Your choice may range from a new, imported mountain bike (*vélo tout terrain* in French, or VTT) to ancient, single-gear, steel roadsters.

Away from tourist areas, it's almost always possible to find locals willing to rent their bicycles for the day; good places to enquire include the market or your hotel. Costs range from US$1 to US$10 per day, depending on the bicycle and the area. Remember to always check the roadworthiness of your bicycle, especially if you're heading off-road.

The flat roads of Burkina Faso are particularly good for cycling, especially around Banfora in the country's southwest; cycling tours are possible around the otherworldly Sindou Peaks (p158).

For information on cycling in West Africa and on bringing your own bicycle to the region, see p841.

Desert Expeditions

For many travellers, West Africa means the Sahara, and deep desert expeditions used to be among the region's most rewarding activities. Sadly, the security situation (see p812) means that most such expeditions were not possible at the time of research.

In the meantime, short camel expeditions around Gorom Gorom (p164) in the Sahel region of Burkina Faso are a terrific way to get a taste of what you're missing further north. Overnight camel trips to Tuareg encampments surrounding Timbuktu (p521) are also considered safe at the time of research.

The following information is included for when the situation stabilises sufficiently for travel in northern Mali, Mauritania and Niger.

The main gateway towns to the Sahara, and hence the best places to organise Saharan

expeditions, are Timbuktu and Gao (Mali), Atâr (Mauritania) and Agadez (Niger). In the Malian Sahara, the main drawcards are the end-of-the-earth feel of Araouane (p524), either as part of an epic camel salt caravan en route to the salt mines of Taoudenni (p521) or for its own sake, and the Tilemsi Valley and Adrar des Ifoghâs massif (p528) north of Gao. In Mauritania, the remote outposts of Ouadâne (p562), Tidjikja (p564) and Tichit (p564) exist in splendid Saharan isolation, while the crater of Guelb er Richat (p564), near Ouadâne, is stunning. In Niger, home to perhaps West Africa's best desert scenery, the Aïr Mountains (p603) and Ténéré Desert (p603) are simply extraordinary.

The main choice you'll have to make for your expedition is whether to travel by camel or 4WD. You'll obviously cover far more territory if you rent a 4WD, but costs can be prohibitive (up to CFA60,000 per day, plus petrol). Travelling by camel is more economical, environmentally friendly and allows you to experience the desert at a more leisurely pace, although you'll cover less territory.

Diving & Snorkelling

Cape Verde is the best place in West Africa to go diving and snorkelling amid the dolphins, sharks and even whales, especially off the islands of Boa Vista (p247) and Sal (p246). It's possible to take open-water PADI dive courses at both places, although remember that Cape Verde has no decompression chambers. March to November are the best months.

Other places where diving and/or snorkelling are possible include off Busua (p360) in Ghana, and Dakar (p683) and Saly (p699) in Senegal.

Fishing

The Atlantic waters off West Africa are some of the world's richest fishing grounds. Sierra Leone (see p764) in particular is one of the world's most underrated deep-sea fishing destinations, especially off Freetown and Sherbro Island where many individual line-class records were set.

Other deep-sea fishing possibilities exist off the island of Sal (p246) in Cape Verde, in The Gambia (p302), Guinea-Bissau's Arquipélago dos Bijagós (p451), and Dakar (p683) and Saly (p699) in Senegal.

Less serious anglers could try a fishing course in Cape Coast (p353) in Ghana, while Lake Ahémé (p111) in Benin offers a fascinating insight into traditional fishing techniques.

Hiking

There are so many spectacular hiking trails in West Africa that it's hard to know where to start. For a list of our favourite hiking destinations in the region, see the boxed text that follows this section.

The set-up in this region is very different from that in East or Southern Africa and the experience is often less wilderness than a stirring combination of cultural and natural landscapes. There's little in the way of good walking infrastructure, such as detailed maps, marked trails or trail accommodation, and much of the hiking is through populated areas. All of which means that, as long as you don't mind roughing it, hiking can be a great way to interact with the locals: on foot you can meet on more equal terms than staring at each other through the windows of a bush taxi.

As there's very little formal organisation, expect to arrange everything yourself (eg bring a good water filter/purifier). Hiring a local guide (either for the entire expedition or to lead you from village to village) is usually a good idea. In some places, because of the distances involved, it may also be necessary to use donkeys, hitching or public transport to get around.

Horse Riding

There aren't many places where you can explore the countryside on horseback, but those close to Ouagadougou (see p139) in Burkina Faso are outstanding. Everything from one-hour excursions to multi-day expeditions into the Sahel, and even as far as Mali's Dogon Country, provide a terrific alternative way of seeing West Africa.

Less far-ranging rides can also be arranged in Grand Bassam (p276) in Côte d'Ivoire, Lomé (p779) in Togo, and Lac Rose (p695) and Toubab Dialao (p696) in Senegal.

Rock Climbing

West Africa has one world-class climbing destination: the area around Hombori (p529) in Mali, where some spectacular rock formations rise above the Sahel and attract a small but growing number of serious rock climbers from Europe. The most famous of the climbs are those centred on La Main de Fatima (p530) where the renowned Spanish climber Salvador Campillo organises climbs from October to March.

Another area with rock-climbing potential is Mali's Falaise de Bandiagara (p507). The famous French climber Catherine Destiville

---

WEST AFRICA'S TOP HIKING TRAILS

- Sindou Peaks, southwestern Burkina Faso (p158)
- Climbing Mt Cameroon, Cameroon (p191)
- Mandara Mountains, northern Cameroon (p210)
- Santo Antão, Cape Verde (see the boxed text, p242)
- Climbing Mt Fogo, Cape Verde (see the boxed text, p245)
- Parque Natural Serra Malagueta, Cape Verde (p238)
- Tongo Hills, Ghana (p385)
- Around Ho, Ghana (p367)
- Fouta Djalon, Guinea (see the boxed text, p414)
- Mt Nimba, Guinea (see the boxed text, p425)
- Dogon Country, Mali (p507)
- Bassari Country, Senegal (see the boxed text, p718)
- Gola Forest Reserve, Sierra Leone (p760)
- Climbing Mt Bintumani, Sierra Leone (p763)
- Kpalimé, Togo (see the boxed text, p786)

established some routes here (she featured prominently in a TV film, *Solo in Mali*, about climbing in Dogon Country) some years ago, and groups from Europe occasionally follow her footsteps (and handholds).

Otherwise, well-known 'climbing' destinations such as Mt Cameroon (p191), Cape Verde's Mt Fogo (see the boxed text, p245) and Sierra Leone's Mt Bintumani (p763) are actually strenuous hikes that involve no technical climbing.

Surfing, Windsurfing & Kitesurfing

West Africa may not be the world's most famous surfing destination, but discerning surfers are rapidly discovering the region's Atlantic coastline, partly for its waves and partly because you may just have the breaks to yourself.

In general terms, the waves off Mauritania, Cape Verde, Senegal and Gambia are best during the European winter, while the coast from Sierra Leone to Cameroon offers the best conditions during the European summer.

Ghana has at least two beaches that surfers rave about: Busua (p360) and Cape Three Points (p363), while the Cape Verdean island of Sal (p246) is also popular. Even less-known, Bureh Beach (p753), close to Freetown in Sierra Leone, has a fine right-handed break during the rainy season, while Robertsport (p466) in Liberia has that unmistakeable call of the remote that hard-core surfers love; *Sliding Liberia*, an award-winning documentary on surfing in Liberia, is definitely worth tracking down. Côte d'Ivoire (p276 and p278) and Dakar (p683) in Senegal are other options.

For wider coverage of surfing in the region, check out **Low Pressure** (www.lowpressure .co.uk), while **Ocean Surf Productions** (www.oceansurf productions.co.uk) is great for first-hand accounts of surfing in the region.

Cape Verde is rightly famous for offering some of the best windsurfing in the world. Most of the buzz surrounds the island of Sal (p246) but Boa Vista (p247) is also fantastic. Kitesurfing is possible at both places.

Other windsurfing possibilities exist in Senegal (see p732).

Swimming & Water Sports

You could, of course, follow the sun-starved European hordes and head for a beach resort in Senegal, The Gambia or Cape Verde, but West Africa's beaches can be so much more appealing than this. In fact, the West African coast has everything you dream of in a tropical beach, with pristine sand, swaying palm trees and, in some cases, not another tourist in sight. You just need to know where to look. For our pick of West Africa's best beaches, see the boxed text that follows this section. For the potential dangers of swimming at many West African beaches, see p812.

There are plenty of water-borne activities (including sailing and other boat hire) in tourist area such as The Gambia's Atlantic Coast (p298) or Senegal's Petite Côte (p696). For a less-touristy feel, Busua (p360), in Ghana, offers both jet-skiing and sea-kayaking, while jet-skiing can also be arranged on the more placid waters of Lake Bosumtwe (p376).

BUSINESS HOURS

Business hours vary across the region; check each individual country's Directory for details there.

WEST AFRICA'S TOP BEACHES

- Ebodje, Cameroon (p219)
- Kribi, Cameroon (p216)
- Maio, Cape Verde (p250)
- Praia de Santa Monica, Cape Verde (p247)
- Santa Maria, Cape Verde (p246)
- Tarrafal, Cape Verde (p238)
- Niega, Côte d'Ivoire (p278)
- Sanyang, The Gambia (p308)
- Akwidaa Beach, Ghana (p362)
- Anomabu, Ghana (p351)
- Busua, Ghana (p360)
- Kokrobite Beach, Ghana (p348)
- Îles de Los, Guinea (p410)
- Arquipélago dos Bijagós, Guinea-Bissau (p442)
- Varela, Guinea-Bissau (p447)
- Robertsport, Liberia (p466)
- Cap Skiring, Senegal (p727)
- Bureh Beach, Sierra Leone (p753)

TEN WEST AFRICA BOOKS FOR KIDS

Start searching for children's books on West Africa and you'll quickly discover a whole library of everything from folk tales to simply told histories that you never knew existed. Aimed at children learning about the diverse peoples of the region, the *Heritage Library of African Peoples: West Africa* is an excellent series. Otherwise, here are some of our favourites:

- *The Adventures of Spider: West African Folktales* by Joyce Cooper Arkhurst (suitable for 4–8 years)
- *The Fire Children: A West African Folk Tale* by Eric Maddern (four to eight years)
- *Why Mosquitoes Buzz in People's Ears: A West African Tale* by Verna Aardema (four to eight years)
- *The Hatseller and the Monkeys* by Baba Wague Diakite (four to eight years)
- *Sundiata: The Lion King of Mali* by David Wisniewski (four to eight years)
- *Traditional Stories from West Africa* by Robert Hull (seven to 11 years)
- *The Cow-Tail Switch and Other West African Stories* by Harold Courlander (nine to 12 years)
- *Indigenous Peoples of Africa – West Africa* by Tony Zurlo (nine to 12 years)
- *Ancient West African Kingdoms: Ghana, Mali and Songhai* by Mary Quigley (10 to 14 years)
- *Tales from West Africa* by Martin Bennett (mixed ages)

CHILDREN

Your children have a big advantage over the rest of us – having yet to acquire the stereotypes about Africa to which the rest of us are exposed, their first impression of the continent is likely to be the warmth and friendliness of the people. Indeed, many West Africans have grown up in large families and children help open doors to closer contact with local people, who are generally friendly, helpful and protective towards children. In short, travelling with children in West Africa adds a whole new dimension to your journey.

Practicalities

In West African countries with a mainstream tourism industry (eg Senegal and The Gambia), some package-tour hotels cater for families with children and, in large cities, top-end hotels usually have rooms with three or four beds for only slightly more than a double. Alternatively, arranging an extra bed or mattress is generally easy and inexpensive. You'll almost certainly want something with a private bathroom and hot water, thereby precluding most budget accommodation.

Despite such exceptions, there are very few child-oriented facilities in the region. In most hotels there are generally no discounts for children. Likewise, on public transport, if you want a seat it has to be paid for. Most local children travel for free on buses but spend the whole journey on their parent's lap.

In addition to the length and discomfort involved in road journeys, possible concerns include the scarcity of medical facilities, especially outside major cities, and the difficulty of finding clean, decent bathrooms outside of midrange and top-end hotels. Canned baby food, powdered milk and sometimes also baby cereal (usually with sugar in it), disposable nappies, wipes and other items are available in most capitals, but not everywhere, and they are expensive. It's best to avoid feeding your children street food.

There are other factors to bear in mind when travelling with kids. The rainy season may mean that temperatures are lower, but the risks of malaria and other mosquito-borne diseases are higher. At all times, bring mosquito nets along for your children and ensure that they sleep under them. Bring child-friendly mosquito repellent and long-sleeved shirts and trousers.

For more information and hints on travelling with children, Lonely Planet's *Travel with Children* is highly recommended.

Sights & Activities

The specific highlights kids are sure to enjoy include the otherworldly villages and festivals of the Dogon Country (Mali; p507) and Koutammakou (the Tamberma Valley, Togo; p795), the chance to tell their friends that they've been to Timbuktu (p516), the stilt villages of Ganvié (p104), a trip down the

---

TRAVELLING WITH CHILDREN: A POSITIVE EXPERIENCE

We received the following letter from a Canadian family who travelled for six weeks in Senegal, Guinea and Guinea-Bissau with a one-year-old:

In West Africa, travelling with a baby was not too difficult, even though life is different. People constantly wanted to touch him, and even though this bothered us on occasion, it was not serious. Most of the time we enjoyed the contact. We learned to travel light and went with one 50L backpack and a baby carrier, which also carried another 10L of luggage. Clothes could be washed every day and dried while wearing them.

We used small chlorine pills to clean unbottled water – apparently iodine may be harmful to children. In every capital we found nappies at grocery stores selling imported items. Sometimes the quality was poor so we secured them with strong sticky tape. Baby cereal and powdered milk were available in most towns, even small villages, and prices were similar to those at home.

In Senegal our baby got a rash caused by the heat and humidity. This was not dangerous, and with soothing powder it was gone in two days.

Gino Bergeron, Julie Morin & 'little Thomas'

Niger River (see the boxed text, p504) and the beaches, castles and markets all along the West African coast.

The thrill of a West African 'safari' to see elephants, monkeys, turtles or other mammals will surely be another highlight. See p24 for a tailored wildlife itinerary, while other possibilities are covered on p81.

CLIMATE CHARTS

For more information on the climate in the region, see p15 and the charts, (opposite).

COURSES
Music & Dance

There are numerous places where you can take your passion for West African music to a whole new level.

Perhaps the most enticing opportunity is the chance to learn the *kora* from West Africa's finest exponent of the art, Toumani Diabaté, when he's in Bamako – see p485 for information. Almost as enticing is the chance to learn the *kora* at the school run by Ba Cissoko, Guinea's premier living *kora* player, in Conakry (p405). Another outstanding opportunity to learn the *kora*, this time from one of Gambia's most prestigious *griot* families is to be found in Brikama (see the boxed text, p313); they also teach other traditional instruments including djembe, *bolon*, balafon and *sabar*. Similar possibilities exist in the village of Tabato (see the boxed text, p448) in Guinea-Bissau, where *kora*, balafon, drumming and singing are all taught. Guinea's respected djembe drummer,

Fadoua Oularé, also offers djembe classes in Faranah (p420). Private classes in *kora*, djembe, dance and drumming are also possible in Ségou (p494), in Mali.

Burkina Faso is another terrific place to learn with a smorgasbord of choices (including dance, drumming and other instruments, including the Malinké flute) around Ouagadougou, Bobo-Dioulasso and around Banfora – see the boxed text, p154 for a full list.

Batafon Arts (www.batafonarts.co.uk) organises dance and percussion courses in Conakry (p405) in Guinea, and Serekunda in The Gambia (p302); they can also arrange accommodation. Dance classes are also possible in Dakar (p683) in Senegal.

Ghana also has a handful of highly recommended places to learn drumming, dance and balafon (see p348 and p353 for details). Drumming and singing lessons can also be arranged around Mt Klouto in Togo (p787).

Other Courses

For a region so diverse in languages, West Africa has few places where you can take a crash course in local languages. Two exceptions are Dakar in Senegal, where you can learn Wolof (p683), and Cotonou in Benin, where you can organise Fon-language courses (p100). Benin is also home to one of West Africa's more unusual learning opportunities – traditional fishing techniques along the shores of Lake Ahémé (p111).

In Ghana, fishing and cookery courses are available in Cape Coast (p353), while cooking

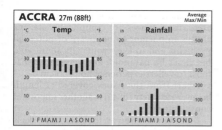

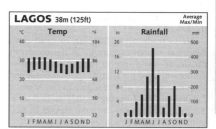

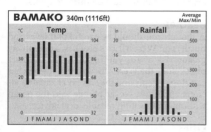

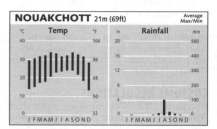

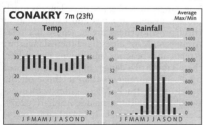

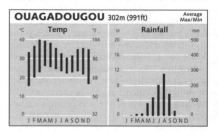

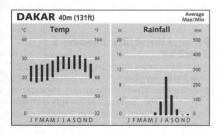

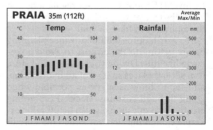

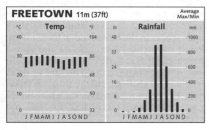

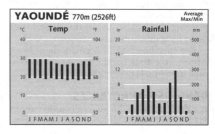

classes are also possible in The Gambia (see the boxed text, p312).

Mali's tradition of Bogolan or mud-cloth design is almost as famous as the country's music. If you'd like to learn how to make your own, head for Djenné (p501). Batik and yoga courses are also available in the Atlantic Resorts of The Gambia (p302) as well as at Kartong, where you can take classes in sustainable tourism practices (p310).

For something considerably more energetic, windsurfing, kitesurfing and diving courses are available in Cape Verde on the islands of Boa Vista (p247) and Sal (p246). Also guaranteed to get the blood flowing are acrobatics and trapeze classes (p405) in Conakry, Guinea.

CUSTOMS REGULATIONS

Except in CFA (Communuaté Financière Afficaine)-zone countries, the import and export of local currency is either prohibited or severely restricted to negligible amounts, although enforcement of this regulation is fairly lax. As part of their fiscal control, some countries use currency declaration forms. More commonly, control consists simply of asking how much currency you have. Or, you may occasionally be asked to open your wallet or show the contents of your pockets – a wallet bulging with cash is likely to prompt underpaid and ever-hopeful airport agents (ie police and customs officials) to suddenly discover (ie invent) fictitious currency regulations that you've just violated by a sizeable proportion of the amount you have in your wallet.

It's worth doing a bit of advance planning before getting to the airport to avoid a scenario like this. Divide your money and store it in several places so it's not all in one lump, and try to look as savvy as possible when going through customs checks. Responding creatively to questions is also helpful, for example explaining that you relied on a credit card for the majority of your expenses (be prepared to show a card), or (if it's true) explaining that you're just in transit and thus don't have much money with you.

For specific customs regulations of West African countries, see the Customs section in each individual country chapter.

DANGERS & ANNOYANCES

It's difficult to make generalisations about the personal-safety situation in West Africa. While there may be considerable risk in some areas, most places are completely safe. It's always important to be aware of potential problems and to keep your wits about you, but don't be paranoid, and remember that most travellers experience no problems.

Apart from the issues covered at length below, road safety (p845) is another important consideration.

More information on the potential risks is given in the individual country chapters.

Beaches

Although you should be careful of thieves and hustlers on West Africa's beaches, a potentially greater risk awaits you in the water. In many places along the West African coast, the beaches can slope steeply and the waves can create a vicious undertow. Never plunge into the ocean without first seeking reliable local advice.

Cities

The danger of robbery with violence is much more prevalent in cities and towns than in rural or wilderness areas, where it's relatively rare. Most cities have their dangerous streets and beaches, but towns can differ; there's more of a danger in places frequented by wealthy foreigners than in those off the usual tourist track. Major cities with questionable reputations include Abidjan (p267), Dakar (p677), Douala (p184), Lagos (p624) and Yaoundé (p180). Muggings do occur, although pickpocketing and bag-snatching are more frequent.

Political Instability, Banditry & Rebellion

Apart from areas prone to political instability (especially northern Côte d'Ivoire, Guinea and Guinea-Bissau), the major concern at present is the Sahara. Although our authors visited Saharan gateway towns such as Timbuktu and Gao (Mali), Chinguetti and Ouadâne (Mauritania) and Agadez (Niger), and these towns remain largely safe, rebellion and banditry continues to haunt the Sahara's open spaces in the hinterland of these towns. While researching this book, we also visited Araouane (269km north of Timbuktu in Mali) and, although we lived to tell the tale, we don't recommend visiting until the situation stabilises. For more information on where not to visit, see the boxed text on p525 for Mali, and p606 for Niger.

Safety Tips

Most travellers to West Africa experience no problems at all and some simple precautions should ensure that you have a trouble-free trip. The recommendations listed here are particularly relevant to cities, although some may also apply to other places (especially popular tourist areas).

- Carry as little as possible. Thieves will be less interested if you're not carrying a daypack, camera and personal stereo. Consider leaving them in your room if your hotel is secure. Even passports, travellers cheques and credit cards can be left behind if the hotel has a reliable safe or security box, preferably in some sort of lockable pouch or at least in a signature-sealed envelope so that any tampering will be clear. Never take valuables to beaches, which are often hotspots for thieves. (In many countries you're required to carry your passport at all times, although you're unlikely to be stopped in the street by police and asked for it. It may be possible to carry a photocopy of your relevant passport pages instead.)
- Be discreet. Don't wear jewellery or watches. Use a separate wallet for day-to-day purchases, and keep the bulk of your cash out of sight, hidden in a pouch under loose-fitting clothing. Your money should be divided into several stashes and stored in various places on your body.
- When walking about town, keep a small amount of cash, including ready change and small bills, separate from your other money, so that you don't need to pull out large wads of bills for paying taxi fares or making purchases.
- Try not to look lost. Walk purposefully and confidently, and don't obviously refer to this guidebook or a map. Photocopy or tear out the pages you need, or duck into a shop or cafe to have a look at the map and get your bearings.
- Avoid back streets and risky areas at night. Take a taxi. A dollar or two for the fare might save you a lot of pain and trouble.
- Avoid getting in taxis with two or more men inside – especially at night and especially if you're female – even (or especially) if the driver says they are his 'friends'.
- Consider hiring somebody locally to accompany you when walking around a risky area. It's usually not too difficult to find someone who wouldn't mind earning a few dollars for warding off potential molesters – ask at your hotel for a reliable recommendation.
- If possible, keep your backpack or suitcase locked whenever you leave it anywhere, whether it be the roof of a bush taxi or your hotel room.

Scams

The main annoyance you'll come across in West Africa are the hustlers, touts and con men who prey on tourists, and most are either good or numbingly persistent. Scams are only likely to be tried in tourist areas and remember that, on most occasions, especially in remote or rural areas, you're more likely to come across genuine hospitality.

A NICE WELCOME

You may be invited to stay in someone's house in exchange for a meal and drinks, but your new friend's appetite for food and beer may make this an expensive deal. More seriously, while you are dining, someone else will be back at the house going through your bag. This scam is only likely to be tried in tourist areas and would-be dance and drumming teachers are among the decoys. Most offers of hospitality are, however, genuine.

DUD CASSETTES

Street sellers walk around with boxes of cassettes by local musicians. You browse, you choose, you pay. And then when you get back to your hotel and open the box, it's got a cheap blank tape inside. Or the tape itself is missing, or the music is by a completely different artist. Tapes sealed in cellophane are normally fine, but look at, or try to listen to, tapes before buying them.

POLICE & THIEVES

If you're unwise enough to sample local narcotics, don't be surprised if the dealers are in cahoots with the local police, who then come to your hotel or stop you in the street and find you 'in possession'. We've received reports of travellers being stung by con men claiming to know somebody living in Bamako/Dakar/Conakry (or wherever you are) from Sydney/Washington/Manchester/Berlin (or wherever you're from). They're having a party tonight and there'll be music, beer and good times. By the time you arrive, other local guests are already there, and you're assured the Aussie/American/Brit/ German you've come to meet will be here soon. In the meantime how about smoking some grass? You decline, but some of the other guests light up, at which point, enter the police stage left.

REMEMBER ME?
A popular trick in the tourist areas is for local lads to approach you in the street pretending to be a hotel employee or 'son of the owner'. There's been a mix-up at the shop. Can you lend him some money? You can take it off the hotel bill later. He'll know your name and room number, and even give you a receipt. But back at the hotel they've never heard of him.

SMOKESCREENS
Some travellers warn of hustlers who begin talking to you, meeting any resistance with a loud and obscene argument and an apparent potential for violence. Don't rise to it. If necessary, go into a shop or restaurant and ask for help. Your 'assailant' will soon be chased off.

SOCK SELLERS
A youth approaches you in the street with socks for sale. You say no, but he follows, whereupon his buddy approaches from the other side and also tries to persuade you to buy the socks. He bends down to show you how well the socks would go with your outfit. Irritated and distracted, you bend down to fend him off and, whoosh, the other guy relieves you of your wallet. The solution? Be firm, walk purposefully, and never buy socks in the street. Why socks? We have no idea…

SPIKED DRINKS
It doesn't happen frequently but often enough that you need to watch out: don't accept drinks from newly found acquaintances on buses or trains, or you may soon find yourself asleep while your 'acquaintance' runs off with your wallet.

EMBASSIES & CONSULATES
It's important to realise what your own embassy can and can't do to help if you get into trouble. Generally speaking, embassy staff have mastered the sympathetic look but remain representatives of governments who aren't in the least sympathetic in emergencies if the trouble is remotely your own fault. Remember that you are bound by the laws of the country you are in and this is very much the approach your embassy will take. Your embassy will not be sympathetic if you end up in jail after committing a crime locally, even if such actions are legal in your own country.

In genuine emergencies you might get some assistance, but only if other channels have been exhausted. For example, if you need to get home urgently, a free ticket home is extremely unlikely – the embassy would expect you to have insurance. If you have all your money and documents stolen, it might assist with getting a new passport, but a loan for onward travel will be out of the question.

Some embassies used to keep letters for travellers or have a small reading room with newspapers and magazines from home, but few provide these services any more.

For the addresses and contact details of embassies and consulates in West Africa, see the Directory sections in the individual country chapters. Note that in some parts of

---

PRESERVING WEST AFRICA'S HERITAGE
After the plundering of African artefacts by colonial officials and, later, by private collectors, most West African countries prohibit the export of antiquities (from tribal masks to archaeological finds). In Mali, Nigeria and Ghana in particular – countries with a rich tradition of highly prized and beautiful artworks and handicrafts – you must obtain an export permit from the Department of Antiquities or from the national museums in Bamako, Lagos or Accra if you want to take anything over 100 years old out of the country. Even then, expect to explain why you're taking Africa's heritage off the continent and to pay very high export duties.

Very little art purchased by non-experts fits this description. Most art that is 'very old' in the words of many a trader is actually recently made, but traders realise that tourists prefer dusty, more authentic-looking pieces than shiny, new mass-produced 'art'. In such cases, it's more a matter of being hassled by customs than doing something illegal. To avoid difficulties later, if the piece looks old, it might be worth having it checked before you purchase.

LATEST TRAVEL ADVICE

Lonely Planet's website (www.lonelyplanet.com) contains information on what's new, and any new safety reports, as well as reports from other travellers recounting their experiences while on the road.

Most governments have travel advisory services detailing terrorism updates, potential pitfalls and areas to avoid. Remember, however, that some government travel advisories overstate the risks somewhat and you should read carefully through the reports to see when actual incidents occurred. Some of the government services are:

Australian Department of Foreign Affairs & Trade (☎ 1300 139 281; www.smartraveller.gov.au)
Canadian Department of Foreign Affairs & International Trade (☎ 1-800-267-6788; www.voyage .gc.ca)
French Ministere des Affaires Etrangeres Europeennes (www.diplomatie.gouv.fr/fr/conseils-aux -voyageurs_909/index.html)
New Zealand Ministry of Foreign Affairs & Trade (☎ 04-439 8000; www.mft.govt.nz/travel)
UK Foreign & Commonwealth Office (☎ 0845 850 2829 www.fco.gov.uk)
US Department of State (☎ 202-647-4000; www.travel.state.gov)

Africa, countries are represented by an 'honorary consul' who is not a full-time diplomat but usually an expatriate with limited (and rarely visa- or passport-issuing) duties. If your country does not have an embassy in a particular country, another embassy will likely be designated to look after your interests (eg Canadian embassies often have an 'Australian interests' section).

FOOD

For an overview of West African cuisine see p51; see also the Food & Drink sections of each country chapter for country-specific information. Throughout this book places to eat are divided into types of cuisine. Within each category, listings are ordered according to price, from the cheapest to most expensive.

GAY & LESBIAN TRAVELLERS

Homosexuality is explicitly illegal in 12 out of the 17 countries covered in this book; the exceptions are Burkina Faso, Cape Verde, Côte d'Ivoire, Mali and Niger, although remember that even in these countries laws relating to 'offending public morals' may serve a similar purpose. Maximum legal penalties for homosexual acts range from the death penalty in Mauritania and possibly Nigeria, to labour camps in Guinea-Bissau and 14 years' imprisonment in The Gambia. In 2009, nine gay men in Senegal were sentenced to eight years each in prison for 'indecent conduct and unnatural acts', although these convictions were later overturned on appeal.

Regardless of the legality, however, all countries covered in this book are conservative in their attitudes towards gays and lesbians, and gay sexual relationships are taboo and are either extremely rare or conducted in the utmost secrecy. In most places, discretion is key and public displays of affection should be avoided as a means of showing sensitivity to local feelings, advice that applies to homosexual and heterosexual couples.

In the hotels of some countries (eg Guinea and Sierra Leone), same-sex couples, regardless of whether they are indeed a 'couple', will most likely be refused permission to share a room.

An excellent website to get the low-down on local laws and attitudes to homosexuality is the South African-based **Behind the Mask** (www .mask.org.za), which has detailed information on each country. **Global Gayz** (www.globalgayz.com) and **ILGA** (www.ilga.org) are also good resources with information for many West African countries. **Afriboyz** (www.afriboyz.com/Homosexuality-in-Africa.html) is also worth checking out.

A US-based tour company offering specialist tours for gay men and women, including to West Africa, is **David Travel** (☎ 949-723 0699; www.davidtravel.com; 310 Dahlia Pl, Suite A, Corona del Mar, CA 92625-2821, USA).

HOLIDAYS

You should always keep an eye out for the timing of local holidays – these can be wonderful occasions with countrywide parties or a day when everything grinds to a halt. One highlight of any trip to West Africa is witnessing one of the many ceremonies that

---

TABASKI

Two weeks before Tabaski, sheep prices steeply rise, as every family is expected to provide one during the celebrations. Those who cannot afford a sheep are socially embarrassed and most will do anything to scrape together the money. One-third of the slaughtered animal is supposed to be given to the poor, one-third to friends, and one-third is left for the family. If you can manage to get an invitation to a Tabaski meal (it usually takes place after prayers at the mosque), you'll be participating in Muslim West Africa's most important and festive day of the year. It's celebrated with particular colour (and cavalry processions) in Kano, Nigeria (p653), but is also a festive time in Senegal and Mali. Here and elsewhere during Tabaski (and during Eid al-Fitr and the other Islamic holidays), you'll see entire families dressed in their finest clothes, strolling in the streets or visiting the mosque.

---

are an integral part of traditional culture in the region. For the best of these, see the boxed text, p19.

For specific information on holidays celebrated in each country, see the Holidays section of the Directory in each country chapter.

Islamic Holidays

Important Islamic holidays, when much of West Africa's commercial life grinds to a halt, include the following:

Tabaski Also called Eid al-Kebir; it commemorates Abraham's readiness to sacrifice his son on God's command, and the last-minute substitution of a ram. It also coincides with the end of the pilgrimage to Mecca, and is the most important Muslim event, marked in most countries by great feasts with roasted sheep and a two-day public holiday.

Eid al-Fitr The second major Islamic holiday; it marks the end of Ramadan, the annual fasting month when Muslims do not eat or drink during daylight hours, but break their fast after sundown. Offices usually grind to a halt in the afternoon throughout Ramadan.

Eid al-Moulid Celebrates the birthday of the Prophet Mohammed. It occurs about three months after Tabaski.

Since the Islamic calendar is based on 12 lunar months totalling 354 or 355 days, these holidays are always about 11 days earlier than the previous year. The exact dates depend on the moon and are announced for certain only about a day in advance. Estimated dates for these events are:

Event	2009	2010	2011	2012	2013
Ramadan begins	22 Aug	11 Aug	31 Jul	20 Jul	9 Jul
Eid al-Fitr	20 Sep	9 Sep	30 Aug	19 Aug	8 Aug
Tabaski	28 Nov	17 Nov	6 Nov	26 Oct	15 Oct
Eid al-Moulid	9 Mar	27 Feb	16 Feb	5 Feb	25 Jan

PUBLIC HOLIDAYS

In addition to the Islamic ceremonies, there are many public holidays – either government or religious – when businesses and government offices are closed. Public holidays vary from country to country, but some – including Christmas and New Year's Day – are observed throughout the region. Government holidays are often marked with parades, dancing and other such events, while the Christian religious holidays invariably centre on beautiful church services and singing.

See the Directory in individual country chapters for country-specific listings.

INSURANCE

A travel insurance policy to cover theft and loss is recommended, and some sort of medical insurance is essential. Always check the small print when shopping around. Some policies specifically exclude 'dangerous activities', which can include scuba diving, off-road driving, motorcycling and even trekking, and a locally acquired motorcycle licence may not be valid under some policies. Also, some policies offer lower and higher medical-expense options, with the higher ones chiefly for countries such as the USA, which have extremely high medical costs.

Hospitals in Africa are not free, and the good ones are not cheap. If your policy requires you to pay on the spot and claim later, make sure you keep all documentation. Some policies ask you to call collect (reverse charges) to a centre in your home country where an immediate assessment of your problem is made.

Check in particular that the policy covers an emergency flight home, as emergency air evacuations can be extremely expensive.

Worldwide cover to travellers from many countries is available online at www.lonely planet.com/travel_services.

For further information on health insurance see p850, and for car insurance, see p835.

INTERNET ACCESS

Internet cafes are found throughout West Africa and there's usually at least one in every large or medium-sized town. Rates vary but you'll rarely pay more than €1 or US$1 for an hour online. Connection speeds are generally better in larger towns; some places still use dial-up connections, but services are improving all the time. For things like burning photo CDs, you're better off using internet cafes in capital and other large cities. If you'll be primarily using internet cafes, consider setting up a trip-specific email address as viruses and keystroke-capturing software are small but significant risks.

High-speed wireless access, or wi-fi, for those toting laptops is increasingly the norm in top-end and many midrange hotels across the region; expect the number of places offering this service to grow rapidly during the life of this book. Wi-fi access in such places is sometimes (but not always) free. In some countries, it may also be possible to obtain internet access through your mobile. See the individual country chapters for more information on the internet access situation there.

The 🖳 icon that appears in hotel and some restaurant reviews throughout this book indicates that a place has internet accessvia a communal internet-enabled computer. The 🛜 icon indicates places where wireless internet (ie wi-fi) access is available for those carrying their laptop.

For a list of useful West Africa–wide websites, see p18, while useful country-specific websites are covered in the Internet Resources section of each country's Directory.

FRENCH KEYBOARDS *Amy Karafin*

Many internet cafes in Francophone West Africa have 'French' keyboards, which can slow you down when typing if you're not used to them. Happily, though, some are loaded with English-language settings. To 'Anglicise' a keyboard, look for a 'Fr' icon on the bottom right of the screen, and scroll up to click on 'En'.

LAUNDRY

Outside of top-end hotels, laundry is washed by hand, often with brushes or on cement or rocks, which will cause your clothes to wear quickly if you spend much time in the region. Everything is usually impeccably pressed (included in the price). Places charge per piece: at budget hotels it may be as low as US$0.10 or US$0.20 per piece, and rates are sometimes negotiable. Rates are higher at top-end and midrange hotels, sometimes several dollars per piece. In the rainy season it may take longer to get your clothes back, as drying time depends on the sun. Dry-cleaning services are limited to major cities. In most West African countries, it's a good idea to wash your own 'smalls' (socks and underwear) as it's considered impolite in many places if you ask someone else to do this.

MAPS

The regularly updated Michelin map *Africa: North and West* (sheet No 741, formerly No 153, then 953; scale 1:4,000,000) is one of the best and most detailed, and something of a classic. It's lent its name to the **153 Club** (www .the153club.org) whose members have travelled through the regions covered by this map. Whether you join the club or not, the map – together with this guide – is something no overland traveller should be without. Even so, if you're driving don't rely solely on the Michelin map as its scale makes it insufficiently detailed for most desert navigation; expect a few discrepancies between the map and reality, especially regarding road information, as old tracks get upgraded and once-smooth highways become potholed disasters. The map excludes the southernmost portion of Cameroon.

Other maps include *Westafrika Sahelländer* (*Africa West: the Sahara;* 1:2,200,000) put out by RV Reise-und Verkehrsverlag in Germany; it also excludes southern Cameroon. The Bartholemew *Africa West* (1:3,500,000) has the advantage of contour shading but lacks the route accuracy of the Michelin and hasn't been updated since 1993.

Maps of individual countries are described in detail in the relevant chapters, but worth noting are the maps produced by the Institut Géographique National (IGN). The *Pays et Villes du Monde* series (1:1,000,000) and the more recent IGN *Carte Touristique* (1:2,000,000) have country maps, which are excellent and available for most countries in West Africa.

If you're likely to be driving off-road (or simply love maps), you really must get hold of as many of the IGN-produced sheets as part of the *Carte Internationale du Monde* series (1:1,000,000) as possible. Devoted to West Africa, they're noted for their almost peerless topographical detail. Their drawback is an important one: they were surveyed in the 1960s and don't seem to have been updated since, meaning that road detail is not to be trusted and even a few natural features (such as the extents of Lake Chad or Mali's Lake Faguibine) are no longer accurate.

Another alternative is the *Worldwide Topographic Map Series – TPC* (1:500,000), which is also good for topographical detail, less so for roads and towns.

To try and track down these and other West Africa maps, your first stop should be **Stanfords** (☎ 020-7836 1321; www.stanfords.co.uk; 12-14 Long Acre, Covent Garden, London WC2E 9LP, UK), the world's largest supplier of maps. They also have stores in Manchester and Bristol in the UK.

In France, **IGN** (☎ 01 43 98 80 00; www.ign.fr; 107 rue de La Boétie, 75008 Paris) sells its sheet maps at stores in Paris and Dijon.

MONEY

Although ATMs are changing things a little, cash remains king in West Africa. And not just any cash: don't bring anything except euros in former French or Portuguese colonies, while US dollars and, to a lesser extent, UK pounds are preferred in Anglophone countries. Using a credit/debit card to withdraw from ATMs is increasingly possible, thereby allowing you to rely on this in combination with cash; Visa remains more widely accepted than MasterCard.

For a full list of exchange rates, see the table inside the front cover of this book, while advice on how best to carry your money is covered in each individual country chapter.

ATMs

ATMs are found in most major West African towns and cities. In theory they accept credit and debit cards from banks with reciprocal agreements. In almost all cases, Visa is the most widely accepted credit/debit card at most ATMs, with MasterCard increasingly (but far from universally) possible.

At the time of writing it was impossible to extract money from your MasterCard in most countries, including Burkina Faso, Cameroon, Cape Verde, Mauritania, Nigeria and Sierra Leone. In some Francophone countries (eg Mali, Benin and Togo), Banque Atlantique usually has MasterCard-enabled ATMs, although sometimes only in capital cities. For security reasons, we also advise against withdrawing money from an international account from a Nigerian ATM, while ATMs in Guinea-Bissau are yet to be integrated into international networks. Ghana is the most ATM-friendly country in the region for both Visa and MasterCard, while some Côte d'Ivoire ATMs also handle Maestro.

Whenever you do use an ATM, expect to be slugged with prohibitive bank fees from your bank back home (€15 is not unusual for a CFA200,000 transaction). For this reason, always take out the maximum the ATM allows.

Black Market

It can sometimes be best to change your money through unofficial sources such as moneychangers, supermarkets and other businesses, either for convenience (they keep longer hours than banks) or to get a better-than-official exchange rate. In CFA-zone countries, exchange rate considerations rarely apply because local currency is easily converted and the rate is pegged to the euro, although Abidjan in Côte d'Ivoire has a thriving US-dollar black market. Unofficial moneychangers are also tolerated by the authorities in some border areas, where there are rarely banks.

Although you may have no choice at a border crossing, the general rule throughout West Africa is to only change money on the street when absolutely necessary. The chances of getting ripped off are high, and even if the moneychanger is honest, you don't know who's watching from the other side of the street. Even at borders, be alert, as changers are notorious for pulling all sorts of stunts with bad rates and folded notes.

In countries with a real black market (eg Guinea and Nigeria), where you can considerably more for your money, don't forget that this is against the law. What's more, dealers often work with corrupt police officers and can trap you in a set-up where you may be 'arrested', shaken down and eventually lose all your money.

Cash & Travellers Cheques

Cash is easily the most convenient way to carry your money as it's always the easiest to change. Remember, however, that it cannot be replaced if lost or stolen, even by insurance companies.

Travellers cheques are refundable if lost or stolen, but they're usually difficult to change (sometimes only one bank will do it and sometimes only in capital cities) and almost always attract high commissions. As a result, few travellers use them in West Africa. The best countries for travellers cheques are Cape Verde and Ghana; they're not worth the paper they're printed on in Nigeria, Liberia, Guinea and Guinea-Bissau.

Well-known brands of travellers cheques are better as they're more likely to be recognised by bank staff. Amex, followed by Visa and Thomas Cook/MasterCard, are the most widely accepted, and some banks will take only one of these three. Most banks require you to show your original purchase receipts in order to change travellers cheques, so it's essential to bring these. Carry them with you (separately from your cheques), but also leave a copy at home, as well as elsewhere in your luggage, in case the original receipts or the cheques themselves are stolen.

For both cash and travellers cheques, take a mixture of high and low denominations. Rates are better for high denominations (ie €50, €100, US$50 or US$100). Note that the USA changed the design of the US$100 bill in the mid-1990s and old-style US$100 notes are not accepted at some places, especially those that don't have a light machine for checking watermarks.

You may also need some small amounts if you're about to leave the region, or a certain country, and only need to change a small amount. Also, a supply of small denomination cash notes (eg US$1 and US$5 or the euro equivalent) can come in handy for cases when change is unavailable.

In addition to your main travel funds, carry an additional stash of cash with you, preferably kept separate from the rest of your cash and travellers cheques. This will serve as a contingency fund for emergencies.

Unless you're relying on ATMs, try to anticipate your needs and change enough in advance to cover yourself on weekends and during non-banking hours. If you do get stuck outside banking hours, you can try changing money at top-end hotels or tour companies, although rates are likely to be poor. Another option, and much better than changing on the street, is to ask discreetly at a shop selling imported items. 'The banks are closed, do you know anyone who can help me…?' is a better approach than 'Do you want to change money?'.

Credit Cards

You can rarely use a credit card to pay for items, and such occasions are limited to top-end hotels and restaurants, car-rental companies and air tickets; an extra commission is often attached, usually ranging from 3% to 15%. Visa is the most widely accepted card, followed a distant second by MasterCard; Amex is accepted at some places in The Gambia. Credit cards are useless in Sierra Leone, Guinea-Bissau and Liberia, and we advise against using them in Nigeria. Cape Verde probably offers the widest choice of paying by credit card.

Watching a person put your card through the electronic credit-card machine (as opposed to letting them do it out of sight) is a good idea to ensure you don't receive unwanted bills back home.

For advice on obtaining cash advances from your credit/debit card, see opposite.

International Transfers

Western Union Money Transfer has representatives in just about every West African country, usually as part of local banks or post offices.

International bank-to-bank money transfers may save you from carrying large amounts of money, but it's best used only as a last resort. Transfers can take three to four days, and sometimes several weeks, to clear. If you do need to transfer money, ask your forwarding bank to send you separate confirmation with full details, including the routing or transfer number, account and branch numbers, and address and telephone contacts. With this, you can then go to the recipient bank with proof that your money has been sent. Most countries will only give you cash in local currency.

Moneychangers

In CFA-zone countries, the best currency to travel with is definitely the euro. Other major international currencies such as the US dollar and the UK pound can be changed in capital

---

17 COUNTRIES, 10 CURRENCIES

The difficulties of juggling the currencies of the 17 countries in this book is ameliorated by the fact that eight countries (Benin, Burkina Faso, Côte d'Ivoire, Guinea-Bissau, Mali, Niger, Senegal and Togo) use the West African CFA (Communauté Financière Africaine) franc, which can be used (or exchanged for local currency) in some other countries, such as The Gambia and Ghana. Many people will also accept it as valid currency, especially in taxis or at market stalls in The Gambia and Guinea.

The CFA is fixed against (and supported by) the euro at a rate of 655.967:1, making it a 'hard' currency. One result of this arrangement is that most banks change euros into CFA without charging a fee or commission. At hotels and foreign exchange bureaus, expect rates of 650 or lower, and plan on paying commissions when changing euro (or any other currency) travellers cheques into CFA.

In recent years, the political leaders of The Gambia, Ghana, Guinea, Nigeria and Sierra Leone – the majority of West Africa's non-CFA block – have spoken of moving towards their own common currency, to be known as the 'eco', which would later merge with the CFA and thereby create a single currency throughout most of West Africa. In the meantime, countries outside the CFA zone each have their own individual currencies.

Cameroon, as well as neighbouring Central African countries, uses the Central African CFA franc, which is linked to the euro at the same rate as the West African CFA franc. However, you can't make payments with Central African CFA in the West African CFA zone or vice versa.

---

cities and tourist areas, but at less-favourable rates. In the non-CFA countries, the best currency to travel with is US dollars, with euros and UK pounds sometimes accepted in larger cities.

The main places to change money are banks and forex bureaus. Where they exist, forex bureaus are often more efficient than banks, usually offer slightly higher rates and are open longer hours, though many don't accept travellers cheques. Charges and commissions vary, with some banks and forex bureaus charging a flat fee, and others a percentage commission; some charge both a fee and a commission. The bank or forex bureau with the higher commission may also offer a higher exchange rate though, so you could still be better off.

Apart from export restrictions, exchanging CFA francs in countries outside the region is nearly impossible, except in France. In most countries in the CFA zone, it's relatively easy to change remaining CFA francs into euros, but difficult to change CFA francs to dollars. On leaving non-CFA countries, it's usually not possible to reconvert local currency into foreign currency, though you can usually change back to CFA francs in The Gambia and Guinea, where it's relatively straightforward, although rates are low. Try and come to an arrangement with other travellers if you think you're going to be caught with a surfeit of local cash.

Also, note that if you're travelling between the West African and Central African CFA zones (eg from Niger to Cameroon), it's easy to change CFA notes of one zone for those of the other at banks, but more difficult to change coins.

Tipping

There are few clear rules on tipping in West Africa. In general, only the wealthy (ie well-to-do locals and nearly all foreign visitors) are expected to tip. Anyone staying in a fancy hotel would be expected to tip porters and other staff, but there would not be the same expectation from a backpacker in a cheap hotel.

Everyone – locals and foreigners – is expected to tip 10% at the better restaurants, although check whether service is included in the bill. At more basic restaurants and eating houses no tips are expected. There's a grey area between these two classes of restaurants, where tipping is rarely expected from locals but may be expected of foreigners. Even wealthier West Africans will sometimes tip at smaller restaurants – not so much because it's expected, but as a show of status.

Locals seldom tip in privately hired taxis, but some drivers expect well-heeled travellers to tip about 10%, especially if you have hired the vehicle for a lengthy trip. On most short trips, however, loose change is normally appreciated. In shared taxis around cities tipping is almost unheard of. If you rent a car with driver, a tip is always expected, usually about 10% of the total rental cost, and more if it is a multi-day rental or if your driver has been exceptionally good. The same applies to guides.

PHOTOGRAPHY & VIDEO

You'll find plenty of subjects in West Africa for photography (with a video or camera), but if this is a primary reason for your visit try to avoid the harmattan season, which is at its height in many areas of the region from January through to May. The region's extremes of climate, such as heat, humidity and very fine sand, can also take their toll on your camera, so always take appropriate precautions; changing lenses in a dust-laden wind is, for example, a recipe for disaster. See p15 for general information on climate conditions.

For more advice, Lonely Planet's *Travel Photography: A Guide to Taking Better Pictures* by Richard I'Anson is an excellent resource, full of helpful tips for photography while on the road. For more specific advice, Lonely Planet also publishes *Landscape Photography* by Peter Eastway, and *People Photography* by Michael Coyne.

Equipment

Memory cards are available in major cities of most West African countries, although you won't have much choice when it comes to the brand. Expect prices to be broadly similar to what you'd pay back home. The situation for batteries is similar, although for more professional cameras you're better off bringing your own supply. Most (but not all) internet cafes in major cities will let you burn photos onto CDs, although the equipment may not be up to scratch in more out-of-the-way places.

Print film in West Africa is imported and expensive and, increasingly, difficult to find outside major cities, while slide film is almost non-existent. Also, even if the expiry date is still good, film may have been damaged by the heat. It's best to bring all you need with you.

For charging batteries, remember to bring the necessary charger, plugs (see the Practicalities box in the Directory section of each country chapter) and transformer for the country you are visiting.

Lens paper and cleaners can be difficult to find in some countries, so bring your own. A dust brush is also useful.

Photographing People

As a matter of courtesy, don't photograph (or video) people without first asking their permission. Digital cameras have the advantage of being able to show people their photo immediately after you've taken it, which is usually temptation enough for most people to say yes. That said, while some West Africans may like being photographed, many don't. They may be superstitious about your camera, suspicious of your motives, or simply interested in whatever economic advantage they can gain from your desire to photograph them and demand a fee. Other locals maintain their pride and never want to be photographed, money or not. In more conservative areas, including in many rural areas, men should never photograph women and in most circumstances should never even ask.

Restrictions

Avoid taking pictures of bridges, dams, airports, military equipment, government buildings, border posts and anything else that could be considered strategic. You may be arrested or have your camera and/or memory card confiscated. The definition of what is 'strategic' differs from one country to the next, and signs are rarely posted, so err on the side of caution and ask your friendly neighbouring police officer for permission if in doubt.

Photography is usually allowed inside religious and archaeological sites, unless there are signs indicating otherwise. As a rule, however, do not photograph inside mosques during a service and dress conservatively. You should also exercise caution around sacred sites.

Many West Africans are sensitive about the negative aspects of their country, so exercise discretion when taking photos in poorer areas.

POST

Postal services are moderately reliable in most West African capitals and cities. In rural areas, though, service can range from slow to nonexistent. For details on rates and prices, see the Directory in individual country chapters.

Letters sent from a major capital take about a week to 10 days to reach most of Europe, and at least two weeks to reach North America or Australasia, although it's sometimes much longer. For more speed and certainty, a few countries have 'express' services, but the main alternative (though expensive) is a courier service. DHL, for example, has offices in most West African capitals.

If you're only going to be in West Africa for a few weeks, it's unlikely it'll be worth arranging for mail to be sent to you, if only because in such a short time frame the margin of error is small. However, if you're planning on spending months travelling through the region, there are a handful of ways that you can receive mail.

The most common way to receive mail is the poste restante service offered by post offices, where letters are held for your collection. Although some smaller post offices may offer this service, using the main post office in a capital or large city is strongly advised. Letters should be addressed clearly to you, with your family name in capitals and underlined, at Poste Restante, General Post Office (English-speaking countries) or PTT (Francophone countries), then the town and country where you want to collect the mail.

To collect your mail, you generally need to show your passport or other identification. Letters sometimes take a few weeks to work their way through the system, so have them sent to a place where you're going to be for a while, or will be passing through more than once. Some poste restante services levy a nominal charge when you collect mail, and many limit the length of time they will hold letters (usually one month).

Some hotels and tour companies operate mail-holding services, and Amex customers can sometimes have mail sent to company branches.

SHOPPING

Making items for sale is nothing new to West Africa: among the oldest 'tourist' art in sub-Saharan Africa was that produced by the Sapi people of Sierra Leone in the 15th century – they sold ivory salt pots and trumpets to the Portuguese traders.

West Africa's range of art and craftwork will have you dreaming of decorating your home with masks, statues and other wood-carvings, and textiles with a fantastic variety of colours and patterns. Other popular purchases include glass beads and jewellery made from gold and silver, as well as a fascinating assortment of urns, stools, weapons, musical instruments and more. You'll also find baskets and pottery with intricate designs, which are almost always produced by women.

Leatherwork, with colourful incised patterns, mostly made from goat hide, is a specialty of the Sahel and Sahara region. For a rundown on the signature items that you're likely to come across, see p65.

Whether you're a serious collector or looking for a souvenir from your trip, you'll find plenty to choose from, and prices are more reasonable than they are at home. Of course, many items you'll see in shops and markets are made expressly for the tourist trade, although they are often copies of traditional items. Even contemporary pieces of art are usually based on traditional designs.

Cassettes of local music are also a good buy. However, remember that the trade in pirated music is devastating for often-struggling musicians who receive no royalties from the tape you buy for a pittance. For more details see p57, as well as the Shopping sections of individual town entries.

Bargaining

In many West African countries, bargaining over prices is a way of life. Visitors often have difficulty with this idea, as they're used to things having a fixed value, whereas in West Africa, commodities are considered to be worth whatever their seller can get for them. It really is no different to the concept of an auction.

BASICS

In markets selling items such as fruit and vegetables, traders will sometimes put their price higher when they see you, a wealthy foreigner. If you pay this – whether out of ignorance or guilt about how much you have compared with most locals – you may be considered foolish, but you'll also be doing fellow travellers a disservice by creating the impression that all foreigners are willing to pay any price. You may also harm the local economy: by paying these high prices you put some items out of the locals' reach. And who can blame the traders – why sell something to a local when foreigners will pay twice as much? The best advice is to discreetly ask locals the correct price or to watch and listen in on other transactions before buying.

Having said that, don't go around expecting everybody to charge high prices: many traders will quote you the same price that locals pay, particularly away from cities or tourist areas. It's also wise to keep things in perspective and not haggle over a few cents. After the first few days in a country (when you'll inevitably pay over the odds a few times) you'll soon get to learn the standard prices for basic items. Remember though that prices can change depending on where you buy. For example, a soft drink in a city may be one-third the price you'll pay in a remote rural area, where transport costs have to be paid. Conversely, fruit and vegetables are cheaper in the areas where they're actually grown.

SOUVENIRS

At craft stalls, where items are specifically for tourists, bargaining is very much expected. The trader's aim is to identify the highest price you're willing to pay. Your aim is to find the price below which the vendor will not sell. People have all sorts of formulae for working out what this should be, but there are no hard-and-fast rules. Some traders may initially ask a price four (or more) times higher than what they're prepared to accept, although it's usually lower than this. Decide what you want to pay or what others have told you they've paid; your first offer should be about half this. At this stage, the vendor may laugh or feign outrage, while you plead abject poverty. The trader's price then starts to drop from the original quote to a more realistic level. When it does, you begin making better offers until you arrive at a mutually agreeable price.

And that's the crux – mutually agreeable. Travellers often moan about how they were 'overcharged' by souvenir traders. But, when things have no fixed price, nobody really gets overcharged. If you don't like the price, then don't pay it.

The best results when bargaining come from a friendly and spirited exchange. Better still, take the time to sit with the trader, drink tea with him, ask about his family or get him to explain the history of the piece you're wanting to buy. Bargaining is so much more fun for both sides if you take the time to get to know who you're dealing with. It won't necessarily mean that you make a purchase but you could just make a new friend and, at the very least, you'll counter the impression that all tourists arrive loaded up with cash and little time to engage with locals.

There's never any point in losing your temper. If the effort seems a waste of time, politely take your leave. Sometimes traders will call

you back if they think their stubbornness may be counterproductive. Very few will pass up the chance of making a sale, however thin the profit.

If traders won't come down to a price you feel is fair (or if you can't afford the asking price), it either means they really aren't making a profit, or that if you don't pay their prices, they know somebody else will.

Bringing Items Home

When you buy a new woodcarving you may find it has cracked by the time you get home. New wood must be dried slowly. Wrapping the carvings in plastic bags with a small water tray enclosed is one technique. If you see tiny bore marks with white powder, it means the powder-post beetle (often confused with termites) is having a fiesta. There are three remedies – zap the beasts in a microwave, stick the piece in the freezer for a week, or drench it with lighter fluid. You could try fumigating items. Be warned that if you have wooden objects with insect damage, the items may be seized by customs on your return home (Australia is very strict on this) and you will have to pay to have them fumigated.

If you buy textiles, note that some dyes, including indigo, may not be colour-fast. Soaking cloth in vinegar or very salty water may stop the dye running, but this method should only be used on cloth of one colour. Adinkra cloth is not meant to be washed.

For advice on preserving West Africa's heritage by not purchasing antiquities, and thereby avoiding the ire of customs officials, see the boxed text, p814.

SOLO TRAVELLERS

You're watching the sunrise in the Sahara or sunset under the palms of the Atlantic Coast. Do you wish there was someone alongside to share it with, or do you try to find a quiet spot to enjoy the view in peace and solitude? How you answer that question should give you a pretty good idea as to whether travelling solo is for you.

Logistically, travelling on your own in West Africa is as easy as travelling with others – you don't need two people to buy a bus ticket or arrange accommodation. More importantly, you wake up in the morning and the day is yours and yours alone. The opportunity to meet locals is greatly enhanced by travelling on your own rather than in a larger group. Few people like to travel alone 24/7, but solo travellers who want to come into the fold or simply a few hours' company can easily meet other travellers wherever there's a travellers' scene.

The downside of travelling alone is that it can prove to be a little more expensive, not least because hotel rooms generally cost more for individual travellers (a single room is rarely half the price of a double room). Although many hotels organise tours to surrounding sights, organising your own taxi will invariably prove pricey unless you can find other travellers to share costs.

If you don't speak the local language, you may also find yourself frustrated in having little more than broken conversations with locals and, in countries where few tourists are found (eg Guinea), you may end up feeling pretty isolated. If you want to travel in Francophone countries and think you may end up pining for a new travel buddy, head for those countries with more well-worn travellers' paths (eg Mali, Senegal or Burkina Faso).

Women travellers often travel alone through West Africa without any problem, although we'd only recommend it for seasoned travellers or those of you who have visited the region before. A woman travelling solo is still rare enough for it to draw attention and, although most of that will be benign, you'll almost certainly attract a following of male admirers. For more advice for women travellers, turn to p826.

TELEPHONE & FAX

Telephone and fax connections to places outside West Africa are reasonably good, as the transmission is usually via satellite, though it's generally much easier and less expensive to call in the other direction – from the USA, Europe or Australasia to West Africa. Calls between African countries, however, are often relayed on landlines or through Europe, which means the reception is frequently bad – assuming you can get a call through in the first place. Things are improving, but slowly. The best places to make international calls (unless you have a fast internet connection and telephone through Skype or other software from your laptop or, less privately, at an internet cafe) are at government telephone offices or private telecentres, which you'll find in most towns. International calls using local mobile SIM cards (see right) can also work out cheaper than landlines.

Costs for international calls and faxes to Europe, the USA or Australasia start at about US$1 per minute, with a few countries offering reduced rates at night and on weekends.

Dial-direct or 'home-direct' numbers are available from a few countries. With these, you dial an operator in your home country who can reverse the charges, or charge the call to a phone-company charge card or your home number. These home-direct numbers are toll free, but if you are using a phone booth you may need a coin or phonecard to connect. Check with your phone company for access numbers and a list of countries where they have home-direct numbers.

Country codes for dialling West African countries are given inside the front cover of this book.

Fax

Most cities and large towns have public telephone offices at the post office where you can make international calls and send faxes. There are also private telecommunications centres in major towns and cities throughout the region. Sending a fax from a hotel is much more expensive.

Mobile Phones

Mobile (cell) phones are everywhere in West Africa, to such an extent that many privately run telephone offices have closed down. In most countries, local SIM cards are readily available from street vendors in any town reached by mobile coverage; top-up cards are similarly widely available. If you prefer not to use your own phone, or your mobile hasn't been 'unlocked' as is the case with many US cell phones, cheap mobile phones (as little as €15) can be purchased in capital cities and most larger towns. International calls using a local SIM card often work out cheaper than calling from landlines. Although mobile coverage is usually restricted to urban settlements, coverage is expanding all the time. See the Directory in individual country chapters for details on the situation in the country you'll be visiting.

A European or North American mobile phone will probably have reception in most West African countries, whereby your carrier's local partner will allow you to receive and send text messages, as well as phone calls, although making calls can be extremely expensive. Remember that if someone calls your mobile phone while you're in West Africa, you may pay the bulk of the charge. In some cases, a local SIM card purchased in one country may also work in other West African countries where that carrier operates; Orange is one carrier that operates in a number of countries in the region and may offer such a service.

TIME
Burkina Faso, Côte d'Ivoire, The Gambia, Ghana, Guinea, Guinea-Bissau, Liberia, Mali, Mauritania, Senegal, Sierra Leone and Togo are on GMT/UTC. Cape Verde is one hour behind. Benin, Cameroon, Niger and Nigeria are one hour ahead. None of the West African countries in this book observe daylight saving.

TOILETS
There are two main types of toilet: Western sit-down, with a bowl and seat; and African squat, with a hole in the ground. Standards vary tremendously, from pristine to those that leave little to the imagination as to the health or otherwise of the previous occupant.

In rural areas, squat toilets are built over a deep hole in the ground. These are called 'long drops', and the waste matter just fades away naturally, as long as the hole isn't filled with too much other rubbish (such as paper or synthetic materials, including tampons). Even some Western toilets aren't plumbed in, but just balanced over a long drop. In our experience, a non-contact hole in the ground is better than a filthy bowl to hover over any day.

TOURIST INFORMATION
With just a handful of exceptions, West Africa's tourism authorities are not geared up for tourism, and there are few tourist offices abroad. Some countries run small tourist offices at their embassies, which may be helpful for getting moderately useful brochures or general travel information.

Once in West Africa, some countries have Ministry of Tourism information offices but, apart from offering a few old brochures, they're unlikely to be of much assistance. Notable exceptions, where a town or city may have a genuinely useful tourist office, are listed in individual country chapters; in Mali for example, Peace Corps Volunteers have been attached to regional tourist offices and services are improving all the time. Otherwise, you'll usually have more success enquiring with staff at tour companies or hotels.

TRAVELLERS WITH DISABILITIES
West Africa has very few facilities for the disabled. This, combined with weak infrastructure in the region, can make travel difficult, although it's not impossible. Few hotels have lifts (and those that do are generally expensive), streets may be either badly potholed or else unpaved, footpaths are few and far between, and ramps and other things to ease access are often non-existent. While accommodation at many budget hotels is on the ground floor, bathroom access can be difficult, and doors are not always wide enough for wheelchairs. Such difficulties are only partly counterbalanced by the fact that West Africans are usually very accommodating and willing to offer whatever assistance they can, as long as they understand what you need.

As for transport, most taxis in the region are small sedans, and buses are not wheelchair equipped. Minibuses and larger 4WD vehicles can usually be arranged through car-rental agencies in major towns and cities, although this will be pricey.

In general, travel and access will probably be easiest in places with relatively good tourism infrastructure, such as some of the coastal areas of Senegal and The Gambia or, to a lesser extent, Mali. As far as we are aware, there are no facilities in the region specifically aimed at blind travellers.

Before setting out for West Africa, travellers with disabilities should consider contacting any of the following organisations who may be able to help with advice and assistance:
Access-able Travel Source (☎ 303-232 2979; www.access-able.com; PO Box 1796, Wheatridge, CO, USA)
Accessible Travel & Leisure (☎ 01452-729739; www.accessibletravel.co.uk) Claims to be the biggest UK travel agent dealing with travel for the disabled. The company encourages disabled people to travel independently.
Holiday Care (☎ 0845 124 9971; www.holidaycare.org.uk; The Hawkins Suite, Enham Place, Enham Alamein, Andover SP11 6JS, UK)
Mobility International USA (☎ 541-343 1284; www.miusa.org; 132 East Broadway, Suite 343, Eugene, Oregon 97401, USA)
Royal Association for Disability & Rehabilitation (RADAR; ☎ 020-7250 3222; www.radar.org.uk; 12 City Forum, 250 City Rd, London, EC1V 8AF, UK) Publishes a useful guide called *Holidays & Travel Abroad: A Guide for Disabled People.*
Society for Accessible Travel and Hospitality (☎ 212-447 7284; www.sath.org; 347 5th Ave, Suite 610, New York, NY 10016, USA)

VISAS

This section contains general information about visas. For country-specific visa information, see the Directory sections of individual country chapters.

The general rule for West Africa is to get your visas before leaving home. They are rarely issued at land borders and only occasionally at airports. Also, if you're flying from outside Africa, many airlines won't let you on board without a visa anyway.

Visa agencies are worth considering if you need visas to several countries before you leave or if there's no relevant embassy in your country. For longer trips or more flexibility, it's possible to get most of your visas in the region as you go, although this requires some advance planning and careful checking of the location of embassies for the countries in question – most West African countries have insufficient resources to maintain expensive embassies in many countries.

Visa fees average between US$20 and US$50, with prices depending on where you apply, your nationality and whether you're asking for multiple- or single-entry visas. Always check the visa's validity length and its start date when deciding where to make your application. When applying for a visa, you may have to show proof that you intend to leave the country (eg an air ticket) or that you have enough funds to support yourself during your visit.

Most visa applications require between two and four identical passport photos, either black and white or colour. Inexpensive photo shops are found throughout the region, and rural areas sometimes have a village photographer who can do the job for you.

Visa des Pays de l'Entente

The Visa des Pays de l'Entente is a multi-country visa that covers travel in Benin, Burkina Faso, Côte d'Ivoire, Niger and Togo. If you've never heard of it, don't be surprised – it's so poorly publicised that most travellers never learn of its existence. Implementation of this relatively new visa is also still patchy, which significantly diminishes its appeal – border officials in both Benin and Togo have, in some cases, refused to recognise the Visa des Pays de l'Entente and have forced travellers to purchase a new Beninese or Togolese visa. At the time of writing, it was also not possible to buy this visa inside Togo.

Before you go rushing off to your nearest West African embassy to ask for this visa, you need to learn how it works. For a start, it is only obtainable *within* these five West African countries, which means that first you must obtain a visa for the first of these countries and, once there, apply at the immigration or visa extension office in the capital city. To get the Visa des Pays de l'Entente, which is valid for two months, you'll need to take along CFA25,000 and up to two passport photos. It usually takes a couple of days for the visa to be issued.

Although the Visa des Pays de l'Entente may work out to be more convenient in some cases, it's worth remembering that it's only valid for one entry into each country: ideal for overlanders, less so for those who plan to visit countries more than once. The visa's appeal is also limited by the fact that Mali and Senegal are yet to sign up for the visa.

WOMEN TRAVELLERS

When travelling in West Africa – solo or with other women – you're unlikely to encounter any more difficulties than you would elsewhere in the world. The female authors of this book have travelled for extended periods (including solo travel) and/or lived in West Africa, usually without incident, and most did their research for this book travelling alone.

For more information on the situation for women travellers in specific countries, see the Women Travellers section in the Directory of the relevant country chapter.

Hints

Although women will undoubtedly attract more attention than men, more often than not you'll meet only warmth and hospitality, and find that you receive kindness and special treatment that you wouldn't be shown if you were a man. While you're likely to hear some horror stories (sometimes of dubious accuracy) from expats who may be appalled at the idea of solo female travel, it's worth remembering that the incidence of rape or other real harm is extremely rare.

With that in mind, it's important to not let these concerns ruin your trip. Remember that some sections of the region, such as parts of the Sahel, are wonderfully hassle free. You'll also have the opportunity to meet local women, something that few male travellers have the chance to do on the same terms.

'C'EST MADAME? OU BIEN, MADEMOISELLE?'

Women travelling on their own through Francophone West Africa will undoubtedly hear these words ad nauseam: translated, the phrase means 'are you married or not?' Sometimes, for example when you're filling out forms or registering at a hotel, it's not ill-intentioned. But, all too often, it's a leering soldier or border official who's a little too eager for company. Although there's not much you can do to prevent the question, having at least a fictitious husband – ideally one who will be arriving imminently at that very place – can help in avoiding further advances. If you're travelling with a male companion, a good way to avoid unwanted interest is to introduce him as your husband. If you're questioned as to why your husband/children aren't with you, explain that you'll be meeting them later.

Good places to try include tourist offices, government departments or even your hotel, where at least some of the staff are likely to be formally educated young to middle-aged women. In rural areas, starting points include female teachers at a local school, or staff at a health centre where language barriers are less likely to be a problem.

That said, it's inevitable that you'll attract some unwanted attention. Here are a few tips:

- Dress modestly. This is the most successful strategy for minimising unasked-for male attention. Wear trousers or a long skirt, and a conservative top with sleeves. Tucking your hair under a cap or tying it back, especially if it's blonde, sometimes helps. Exposing your midriff is rarely a good idea.
- Use common sense: trust your instincts and take the usual precautions when out. For example, if possible, avoid going out alone in the evenings, particularly on foot. Avoid isolated areas, roadways and beaches during both day and evening hours, and be cautious on beaches, many of which can become deserted very quickly. Throughout the region, hitching alone is not recommended.
- Don't worry about being rude, and don't feel the need to explain yourself. If you try to start explaining why you don't want to meet for a drink/go to a nightclub/get married on the spot, it may be interpreted as flirting. The more you try to explain,

the more you'll see your hopeful suitor's eyes light up with that pleased, knowing look – 'ah, she's just playing hard to get, but really, she wants me…'.

- Ignore hissing, calls of '*chérie*', or whatever – if you respond, it may be interpreted as a lead on.
- Wear a wedding ring or carry photos of 'your' children, which will make you appear less 'available'.
- Avoid direct eye contact with local men; dark sunglasses help. There are, however, times when a cold glare is an effective riposte to an unwanted suitor.
- On public transport, sit next to a woman if possible.
- If you need help (eg directions), ask a woman first. That said, local women are less likely than men to have had an education that included learning English. You'll also find this to be a major drawback in getting to meet and talk with them.
- Going to the nearest public place, such as the lobby of a hotel, usually works in getting rid of any hangers-on. If they still persist however, asking the receptionist to call the police usually frightens them off.

Tampons & Sanitary Pads

Tampons (imported from Europe) are available from pharmacies or large supermarkets in capital cities throughout West Africa, and occasionally in other large towns. Elsewhere, the only choice is likely to be sanitary pads so you may want to bring an emergency supply.

Transport in West Africa

CONTENTS

GETTING THERE & AWAY

This chapter tells you how to reach West Africa by air, land and sea from other parts of the world and outlines the routes for onward travel from the region. For general details of travel once you are in the region, turn to p840. For more specific information on getting between one country and its neighbours see the Getting There & Away section in the relevant country chapter. Flights, tours and rail tickets can be booked online at www.lonelyplanet.com/travel_services.

ENTERING WEST AFRICA

Entering West Africa varies from country to country but is generally hassle free, provided you have all your documents in order. For details of the visa requirements for each country covered in this guide, see the Directory section of each individual country chapter.

AIR

There are direct flights from Europe into every West African capital, although very few airlines fly into Bissau (Guinea-Bissau), Freetown (Sierra Leone) and Monrovia (Liberia). European cities offering the widest range of choices are London, Paris, Brussels and Amsterdam. It's also relatively easy to fly into West Africa from North Africa and the Middle East, with a handful of airlines offering services from elsewhere in Africa. If you're travelling from Australia, Canada or the USA, you'll usually need to connect to a flight from Europe, the Middle East, Morocco or South Africa.

Airports & Airlines

International airports with the greatest number of incoming flights (and the best onward connections) include Dakar (Senegal), Abidjan (Côte d'Ivoire), Accra (Ghana), Bamako (Mali), Lagos (Nigeria) and Douala (Cameroon). There are also international airports at: Cotonou (Benin); Ouagadougou and Bobo-Dioulasso (Burkina Faso);

THINGS CHANGE

The information in this chapter is particularly vulnerable to change. International air fares are volatile, schedules change, special deals come and go, and rules are amended. Airlines and governments seem to take a perverse pleasure in making fare structures and regulations as complicated as possible. In addition, the travel industry is highly competitive and agents' prices vary considerably.

Fares quoted in this book are approximate and based on the rates advertised by travel agents at the time of going to press. Airlines and travel agents mentioned in this chapter do not necessarily constitute a recommendation.

Ensure that you get quotes and advice from as many airlines and travel agents as possible – and make sure you understand how fares and tickets work – before you part with your hard-earned cash. The details given in this chapter should be regarded as pointers and are not a substitute for your own careful, up-to-date research.

DON'T FORGET...

There are a few essential things that you must have when you arrive at your first West African border:

- Valid entry visa, unless you are entering a country where the visa is available on arrival.

- Your up-to-date international vaccination booklet *(livre jeune)*, which contains proof of yellow fever vaccination.

- Enough empty pages in your passport for visas, entry and exit stamps, and registration with police within some countries – make sure you have at least two pages per country.

- A passport that expires at least six months after your trip ends – it's not mandatory in all cases but some officials will cause problems if your passport is about to run out.

- The patience of a saint: bureaucracy can be epic in its obsession with minutiae.

- An awareness that some officials will assure you that your perfectly valid visa has expired – unless it has, they're just asking for a bribe.

Yaoundé and Garoua (Cameroon); Conakry (Guinea); Monrovia (Liberia); Mopti and Gao (Mali); Nouakchott, Nouâdhibou and Atâr (Mauritania); Niamey (Niger); Kano and Port Harcourt (Nigeria); Praia and Sal (Cape Verde); Banjul (The Gambia); Freetown (Sierra Leone) and Bissau (Guinea-Bissau).

AIRLINES FLYING TO/FROM WEST AFRICA

Aero (airline code AJ; www.flyaero.com)
Afriqiyah Airways (airline code 8U; www.afriqiyah.be)
Air Algérie (airline code AH; www.airalgerie.dz)
Air Burkina (airline code 2J; www.air-burkina.com)
Air CM (www.capcasamance.com, in French)
Air France (airline code AF; www.airfrance.com)
Air Ivoire (airline code VU; www.airivoire.com, in French)
Air Sénégal International (airline code V7; www.air-senegal-international.com, in French)
Alitalia (airline code AZ; www.alitalia.com)
Bellview Air (airline code B3; www.flybellviewair.com)
British Airways (airline code BA; www.britishairways.com)
British Midland Airways (airline code BD; www.flybmi.com)
Brussels Airlines (airline code SN; www.brusselsairlines.com)
Delta (airline code DL; www.delta.com)
Egyptair (airline code MS; www.egyptair.com)
Emirates (airline code EK; www.emirates.com)
Ethiopian Airlines (airline code ET; www.ethiopianairlines.com)
First Choice (airline code DP; www.firstchoice.co.uk)
Gambia International Airlines (airline code GC; www.gia.gm)
Ghana International Airlines (airline code G0; www.fly-ghana.com)
Go-Voyages (www.govoyages.com)

Iberia (airline code IB; www.iberia.com)
Interair (airline code D6; www.interair.co.za)
Kenya Airways (airline code KQ; www.kenya-airways.com)
KLM-Royal Dutch Airlines (airline code KL; www.klm.com)
Lufthansa (airline code LH; www.lufthansa.com)
Mauritania Airways (airline code MR; www.fly-mauritaniaairways.com)
Middle East Airlines (airline code ME; www.mea.com.lb)
Monarch Airlines (airline code ZB; www.flymonarch.com)
Point Afrique (www.point-afrique.com, in French)
Royal Air Maroc (airline code AT; www.royalairmaroc.com)
South African Airways (airline code SA; www.flysaa.com)
Swiss International Airlines (airline code LX; www.swiss.com)
TACV (airline code VR; www.flytacv.com)
TAP Air Portugal (airline code TP; www.flytap.com)
Thomas Cook (airline code MT; www.flythomascook.com)
Thomson (airline code BY; www.thomsonfly.com)
Toumaï Air Tchad (airline code XX; www.toumaiair.com)
Tunis Air (airline code TU; www.tunisair.com, in French)
Virgin Atlantic (airline code VS; www.virgin-atlantic.com)
Virgin Nigeria (airline code VK; www.virginnigeria.com)

Tickets

Buying cheap air tickets in West Africa is a challenge. Usually the best deal you can get is an airline's official excursion fare, and there's no discount on single tickets unless you qualify for a 'youth' (under 26, sometimes 23) or 'student' rate. In cities that handle plenty of international traffic, such as Dakar or Abidjan, cheaper tickets are easier to come by from

CHECKING IN

In some West African cities, check-in procedures are as much of an adventure as the flight itself. Conakry and Lagos win our vote as the airports with the most disorganised and chaotic check-in procedures, but every traveller probably has their own 'favourites'. The fun starts from the moment you enter the airport building. Underpaid security personnel, in an effort to subsidise their meagre incomes, may view the baggage check procedures as a chance to elicit bribes from tourists. After searching your bag, they might ask what you have for them or, alternatively, try to convince you that you've violated some regulation. Be compliant with requests to open your baggage, be friendly and respectful, smile a lot, and you should soon be on your way. Also remember that, in some cases, officials may search your bag out of genuine curiosity, so put your dirty underwear on top and watch their interest evaporate.

After getting past the initial baggage check, wade into the fray by the check-in counter. While some places have lines, many don't – just a sweaty mass of people, all waving their tickets and talking loudly to a rather beleaguered-looking check-in clerk. Although everyone with a confirmed ticket usually gets on the flight, confirmed passengers are 'bumped' just frequently enough to cause many people, locals and foreigners alike, to panic and lose all sense and civility when it seems there may not be enough seats to go around. The West African answer to this situation is the 'fixer' – enterprising locals who make their living by getting people smoothly checked in and through other formalities such as customs and airport tax, all for fees ranging from a dollar or two up to about US$10. If you don't have a confirmed booking, the fee may be more, as some money has to go to the boarding pass clerk.

Without the services of a fixer, the best strategy for avoiding the chaotic scene is to arrive early at the airport – ideally no later than the official reporting time, preferably earlier. This way, you also have a better chance of getting a confirmed seat if too many 'confirmed' tickets have been sold.

Once you have your boarding pass in hand, there's usually a second luggage inspection as you pass from the check-in terminal to the waiting area. Then it's just a matter of waiting, and often waiting far longer than you planned. Don't schedule any other critical plans for the day (especially connecting flights), and try to calm any frustration you may feel by remembering that your journey would be several days to several weeks longer via bush taxi, and much more uncomfortable.

There is one exception to the general chaos of checking in, at least if you're flying Air France. In most West African capitals where Air France has late-night departures for Paris, the airline allows a morning check-in (either at a central Air France office or, less conveniently, at the airport itself), thereby allowing you to check out of your hotel and pass the day unencumbered by luggage.

travel agents; in Bissau or Monrovia you won't have much choice about fares or airlines.

Charter flights are worth considering as they're generally direct and cheaper than scheduled flights. Some charter flights come as part of a package that includes accommodation and other services, but most charter companies sell 'flight only' tickets.

Once you have your ticket, keep a note of the number, flight numbers, dates, times and other details, and keep the information somewhere separate from your money and valuables. If the ticket is lost or stolen, this will help you get a replacement.

It's sensible to buy travel insurance early. If you get it the week before you fly, you may find, for example, that you're not covered

for delays to your flight caused by industrial action. For more details see p816.

A few hours surfing the web can help give you an idea of what you can expect in the way of good fares as well as be a useful source of information on routes and timetables, although not all online agencies offer flights to West Africa. Reputable online agencies for scheduled carriers include:

Atrapalo (www.atrapalo.com, in Spanish)
eBookers (www.ebookers.com)
Expedia (www.expedia.com)
Kayak (www.kayak.com)
Opodo (www.opodo.com)
PlaneSimple (www.planesimple.co.uk)
Rumbo.es (www.rumbo.es, in Spanish)
STA Travel (www.statravel.com)

Travel.com.au (www.travel.com.au)
Travelocity (www.travelocity.com)

For airline websites, see p828, while some recommended travel agencies are listed in the sections that follow. See p838 for more information on tours.

Travellers with Special Needs

If you have special needs of any sort – you've broken a leg, you're vegetarian, travelling in a wheelchair, taking the baby, terrified of flying – you should let the airline know as soon as possible so that they can make arrangements.

Airports in West Africa can be pretty basic and services such as escorts, ramps, lifts, accessible toilets and reachable phones are generally scarce and basic. Deaf travellers can ask for airport and in-flight announcements to be written down for them.

Children aged under two travel for 10% of the standard fare (or free on some airlines) as long as they don't occupy a seat. They don't get a baggage allowance either. 'Skycots' should be provided by the airline if requested in advance; these will take a child weighing up to about 10kg. Children aged between two and 12 can usually occupy a seat for half to two-thirds of the full fare, and do get a baggage allowance.

Africa

EAST OR SOUTHERN AFRICA

For travellers going to/from East or Southern Africa, there aren't a whole lot of choices, but there are direct connections to West Africa from Nairobi (Kenya), Addis Ababa (Ethiopia), and Johannesburg (South Africa). Apart from direct flights, more circuitous routes (eg, Johannesburg to Abidjan via Addis Ababa on Ethiopian Airlines) are possible, although remember that flying across Africa – and particularly between East and West Africa – can be slow and subject to delays and cancellations. If you have connecting flights, allow yourself plenty of time.

From Kenya, Kenya Airways flies from Nairobi into Abidjan, Accra, Douala, Lagos, Yaoundé and (sometimes) Monrovia. One good agency for buying tickets is **Let's Go Travel** (☎ 20-4447151; www.lets-go-travel.net).

From Addis Ababa, Ethiopian Airlines, that enduring (if not always reliable) workhorse of the African skies flies to Abidjan, Accra, Bamako, Dakar, Douala, Lagos, Lomé and Ouagadougou.

A greater range of airlines heading for West Africa is to be found in Johannesburg: South African Airways (Abidjan, Accra, Dakar and Lagos) and Interair (Cotonou and Ouagadougou) fly into the region. Air Sénégal International also flies between Dakar and Johannesburg and Bellview Air flies Johannesburg–Douala. **STA** (☎ 0861 781 781; www.statravel.co.za) has several branches in South Africa and is a good place to start for arranging discounted fairs.

CENTRAL AFRICA

Not many travellers fly from Central to West Africa, but there is an array of options for those that do, albeit on less well-known airlines.

Toumaï Air Tchad connects N'Djaména (Chad), Bangui (Central African Republic) and Brazzaville (Congo) with Douala, Lomé and Cotonou, although few flights are direct. For buying tickets in N'Djaména, try **Tchad Evasion** (☎ 252 65 94; tchad.evasion@intnet.td).

The Nigerian airline Aero flies into Abidjan, Accra and Lagos from Libreville (Gabon) and Malabo (Equatorial Guinea), with an additional service between Lagos and São Tomé (São Tomé & Príncipe).

Virgin Nigeria also connects Lagos with Libreville, Bellview Air flies from Gabon to Cameroon and Nigeria, and Air Ivoire flies Abidjan–Brazzaville.

NORTH AFRICA

The best connections from North Africa are on Royal Air Maroc, which has flights

---

STARTING YOUR JOURNEY IN PARIS

To an extent far greater than other colonial powers in Africa, France retains strong links with its former colonies. One of the benefits of this is that Paris has the best transport links (both in terms of coverage and price) to West Africa and is, therefore, the best starting point for your West African journey. Starting your journey in Paris also enables you to pick up hard-to-get visas as most Francophone West African countries, who have few embassies around the world, certainly have one in Paris. And besides, there are worse places to wait for your passport to be returned or for your flight to leave.

from Casablanca (Morocco) to 15 West African airports. The best deals are to the region's Francophone countries where Royal Air Maroc has taken on Air France's traditional hegemony by undercutting the French carrier's prices.

From Tunisia, Tunis Air flies between Tunis and Abidjan, Bamako, Dakar and Nouakchott. If you happen to find yourself in Algeria, you'll have little choice but to take Air Algérie, which connects Algiers with Bamako, Dakar, Niamey, Nouakchott and Ouagadougou. Egyptair flies into Lagos and Accra from Cairo.

An interesting alternative is Afriqiyah Airways, which flies to Abidjan, Accra, Bamako, Cotonou, Douala, Kano, Lagos, Lomé, Niamey and Ouagadougou from Tripoli (Libya).

Australasia & the Middle East

There are no direct flights to West Africa from Australia, New Zealand or Asia. Although many travellers fly into the UK and Europe and take a flight from there, the most direct option is to fly with Emirates to Dubai, from where there are onward Emirates flights to Abidjan, Accra and Lagos. Another option from the Middle East is Middle East Airlines, which connects Beirut with Abidjan, Accra, Kano and Lagos.

Another option from Australia or New Zealand is to fly South African Airways to Johannesburg, with onward connections to Abidjan, Accra, Dakar and Lagos.

Both **STA Travel** (☎ 134 782; www.statravel.com.au) and **Flight Centre** (☎ 133 133; www.flightcentre.com.au) have offices throughout Australia.

In New Zealand, both **Flight Centre** (☎ 0800 243 544; www.flightcentre.co.nz) and **STA Travel** (☎ 0800 474 400; www.statravel.co.nz) have branches throughout the country.

Continental Europe

The easiest way to reach West Africa by air is from Western Europe, with a range of flights from most European capital cities.

Air France has dozens of direct flights into the region, reaching 15 West African cities from Paris. KLM-Royal Dutch Airlines has a similarly broad network, flying to 11 West African countries from its Amsterdam base. Breadth of coverage by established national airlines doesn't always equate to the most reasonable fares, however, so it pays to shop around.

Airlines that may prove competitive on price but with a wide range of destination choices include Brussels Airlines (which connects the Belgian capital with eight West African cities) and Point-Afrique (a semi-charter airline that flies from Paris and Marseilles to Dakar, Bamako, Gao, Mopti and Ouagadougou.

If you don't mind a non-direct flight, your range of choices grows considerably. Afriqiyah Airways is usually a reasonably priced possibility – they fly from London, Paris, Geneva, Brussels and Amsterdam to Abidjan, Accra, Bamako, Cotonou, Douala, Kano, Lagos, Lomé, Niamey and Ouagadougou, all via Tripoli (Libya). The same applies to Royal Air Maroc, which flies from numerous European capitals to 15 West African cities, with a stopover in Casablanca en route.

Other European-based airlines also serve West Africa. They include: Alitalia (which connects Italy with Ghana, Nigeria and Senegal), Iberia (Madrid to Dakar and Lagos), Ghana and Nigeria); Swiss International Airlines (Zurich to Douala and Yaoundé); and Tap Air Portugal (Lisbon to Bissau, Dakar, Praia and Sal).

And then there are the national airlines of various West African countries, which generally fly between their capitals and Paris. Standards of service and punctuality vary, and they include: Air Burkina (Ouagadougou–Paris); Air Ivoire (Abidjan–Paris); Mauritania Airways (Nouakchott–Paris, as well as a service from Spain's Canary Islands to Nouakchott or Nouâdhibou); Air Sénégal International (Dakar to Paris, Brussels or Madrid) and TACV (Sal in Cape Verde to Paris, Munich and four Italian cities). Of these, Air Sénégal International has easily the best reputation.

Last, and by no means least, numerous charter airlines fly sun-seekers into cities along the West African coast, especially The Gambia, Senegal and Cape Verde. Unless you're looking for an all-inclusive by-the-beach holiday, these generally only work if you can get a flight-only fare and use it as a jumping-off point for the region. This could be a problem if you're planning to remain in West Africa for a while. Charter airlines operating mostly from France include Go-Voyages and Air CM.

In addition to the online agencies listed on p829, and the websites of the airlines themselves (see p828), recommended travel agencies in continental Europe include:

Airfair (☎ 0900 7 717 717; www.airfair.nl, in Dutch; The Netherlands)

Barcelo Viajes (www.barceloviajes.com, in Spanish; Spain)

Connections (☎ 070 23 33 13; www.connections.be; Belgium)

CTS Viaggi (☎ 06-4411166; www.cts.it, in Italian; Italy)

Nouvelles Frontières (☎ 01 49 20 65 87; www .nouvelles-frontieres.fr, in French; France) Also in Belgium and Switzerland.

Voyageurs du Monde (www.vdm.com, in French; France)

If you're buying your ticket in West Africa, the best places to try are Dakar and Abidjan, followed by Accra, Lagos and possibly Bamako. See the individual country chapters for recommended travel agents.

North America

There's only a handful of direct flights between the US and West Africa. These include Delta, which flies from New York to Accra, and TACV, which flies from Boston to Praia and Sal in Cape Verde.

If you're looking to fly anywhere else in the region, your best bet is with Royal Air Maroc from New York or Montreal to Casablanca, from where the airline flies into 15 West African cities. Otherwise, most travellers go via Europe, usually London or Paris. If you can find a good deal on the transatlantic leg of the trip, it can be cheaper to buy one ticket to London and then a separate, discounted ticket onwards from there.

In the USA, **STA Travel** (☎ 800-781 4040; www .statravel.com) has offices in many major US cities; call the toll-free 800 number for office locations or visit its website. Some of the tour companies listed on p839 also sell flights.

There are no direct flights to West Africa from Canada. You'll need to go via New York, Boston, Casablanca or a major European capital. **Travel CUTS** (☎ 1-866 246 9762; www.travelcuts.com) is Canada's national student travel agency and has offices in all major cities.

UK

London is another good place for West African flights (especially to Ghana and Nigeria), although British Airways doesn't match Air France in its breadth of choices and the only direct flights generally go to Nigeria, Ghana and, less often, Freetown.

British Airways flies into Accra, Freetown, Lagos and Abuja (in case you want to avoid Lagos) from London Heathrow. Another direct option is Ghana International Airlines, which flies between London Gatwick and Accra. Bellview Air connects Lagos with London, as does Virgin Atlantic. KLM-Royal Dutch Airlines is also worth considering for direct flights into the region.

For connections to Francophone countries, Afriqiyah Airways flies into 10 West African cities (via Tripoli), and Royal Air Maroc rack up an even better tally with 15 West African destinations if you're willing to fly via Casablanca. TAP Air Portugal solves the problem of getting to Cape Verde and Guinea-Bissau, travelling there (via Lisbon) from London.

The UK is easily the most popular place to start if you're looking for a charter airline and/or flight-accommodation package. If you can get a flight-only fare, prices are often cheaper than you'll find elsewhere. The Gambia in particular is big business in the UK, with dozens of flights heading to Banjul from London, Manchester and Birmingham among other cities. The leading charter flight and tour operator is **The Gambia Experience** (☎ 0845-3302060; www.gambia.co.uk), while other charter airlines include First Choice, Go-Voyages, Monarch Airlines, My Travel, Thomas Cook and Thomson. During popular periods (peak tourist seasons or busy holiday times such as Christmas or the end of Ramadan), prices inevitably rise.

London is usually the most competitive place to buy a ticket through a travel agency, although there are specialist travel agents around the country. (Some of the agencies listed on p839 also sell tickets.) It's worth checking the ads in weekend newspapers or travel magazines, or in *Time Out*, but the following places, with branches around the country, are a starting point for discounted tickets:

STA Travel (☎ 0871-230 0040; www.statravel.co.uk) Has offices throughout the country.

Trailfinders (☎ 0845-058 5858; www.trailfinders.co.uk)

LAND
Border Crossings

If you're travelling independently overland to West Africa – whether cycling, driving your own car or taking public transport – you can approach the region from three main directions: from the north, across the Sahara; from the south and southeast, through the countries bordering southern and eastern Cameroon; or from the east, through Chad.

DRIVING TO WEST AFRICA – FURTHER READING

Driving your own car or motorbike to West Africa, and driving off-road within the region, are vast subjects beyond the scope of this book. Two specialist guides that we recommend:

- *Adventure Motorcycling Handbook*, by Chris Scott, covers all parts of the world where tar roads end. It contains stacks of good information on the Sahara and West Africa, all combined with humour and personal insights.

- *Sahara Overland (2nd Edition)*, by Chris Scott, is the best, most recent and most comprehensive book on all aspects of Saharan travel by two or four wheels, with information on established and newer Saharan routes, and more than 100 maps. Chris Scott's highly recommended website, www.sahara-overland.com, has updates of the book, as well as a useful forum.

These books cover matters such as equipment, carnets, insurance, recommended routes, driving techniques, maintenance, repairs, navigation and survival.

If you're coming from the north, the main border-crossing point into West Africa is just north of Nouâdhibou, via Morocco and the Western Sahara. In theory, there are also crossings at Bordj-Mokhtar (Algeria/Mali), Assamakka (Algeria/Niger) and Tumu (Libya/ Niger) but these were either closed or not recommended at the time of writing. For more information, see p836.

If you come into West Africa from the south or east, the border-crossing points are at Garoua-Boulaï or Kenzou (for the Central African Republic); at Kousséri, Bongor or Léré (for Chad); Moloundou, in Cameroon's far southeastern corner (for Congo); Kye Ossi (for Gabon); and Ebebiyin or Campo (for Equatorial Guinea). Another option is to take the 'long way around', crossing the border on the northern side of Lake Chad on the route to Nguigmi (Niger). Remember that very few travellers use these routes. For more information on these routes, see p837 and p836.

More details on the various border crossings are given in the Getting There & Away sections of the relevant country chapters.

Car & Motorcycle

Anyone planning to take their own vehicle to West Africa should check in advance what spare parts and petrol are likely to be available (see opposite for general advice). Further information on driving in the region is covered on p845.

A number of documents are also required:
Carnet See the boxed text, opposite.
Green card Issued by insurers. Insurance for some countries is only obtainable at the border. Check with your insurance company or automobile association before leaving home. See opposite for further advice.
International Driving Permit (IDP) Although most foreign licences are acceptable in West African countries, an IDP issued by your local automobile association is highly recommended. For more information, see opposite.
Vehicle registration documents Carrying all ownership papers is a must.

For some more tips on driving in the region in general, see the boxed text, p847.

BRING YOUR OWN VEHICLE

If you want to travel in West Africa using your own car or motorbike, but don't fancy the Saharan crossing, another option is to ship it. The usual way of doing this is to load the car onto a ship in Europe and take it off again at either Dakar or Banjul (Abidjan and Tema, in Ghana, are other options).

Costs vary depending on the size of the vehicle and the final destination, but generally start from around US$1000. Apart from cost, your biggest problem is likely to be security – many drivers report theft of items from the inside and outside (such as lights and mirrors) of their car. Vehicles are usually left unlocked for the crossing and when in storage at the destination port, so chain or lock all equipment into fixed boxes inside the vehicle. Getting a vehicle out of port is frequently a nightmare, requiring visits to several different offices where stamps must be obtained and mysterious fees paid at every turn. You could consider using an official handling agent or an unofficial 'fixer' to take your vehicle through all this.

One possibility is **Grimaldi Lines** (☎ 081-496 203; www.grimaldi-freightercruises.com, in Italian; Via Marchese Campodisola 13, 80133 Naples, Italy), which ships accompanied vehicles to Dakar from a number of European ports.

DRIVING LICENCE

To drive a car or ride a motorbike in West Africa you'll need a driving licence and, ideally, an International Driving Permit (IDP). If you intend to hire a car, you will usually need both. IDPs are easy and cheap to get in your home country – they're usually issued by major motoring associations, such as the AA in Britain – and are useful if you're driving in countries where your own licence may not be recognised (officially or unofficially). They have the added advantage of being written in several languages, with a photo and many stamps, and so look more impressive when presented to car-rental clerks or policemen at road blocks.

FUEL & SPARE PARTS

The quality, availability and price of fuel (petrol and diesel – called *essence* and *gasoil,* respectively, in the Francophone countries, *gasolina* and *diesel,* or sometimes *gasóleo,* in former Portuguese colonies) varies greatly throughout the region. Where taxation, subsidies or currency rates make petrol cheaper in one country than its neighbour, you'll inevitably find traders who've carried large drums across the border to sell 'black market' fuel at the roadside. However, watch out for fuel sold in plastic bags or small containers along the roadside. While sometimes it's fine, it's often diluted with water or kerosene. Don't expect to find unleaded petrol beyond major cities and even there it may be scarce.

African mechanics are masters of ingenuity, using endlessly recycled parts to coax life out of ageing machines that would have long ago been consigned to the scrap heap in the West. That said, they're often unable to help with newer-model vehicles – for these, either bring your own spare parts, or check with your manufacturer for a list of accredited parts suppliers in West Africa. Be warned, however, there may be very few (or none at all) of the latter.

INSURANCE

Insurance is compulsory in most West African countries. Given the large number of minor accidents, not to mention major ones, fully comprehensive insurance is strongly advised, both for your own and any rental vehicle. Always check with your insurer whether you're covered for the countries you intend to visit and whether third-party cover is included. Car-hire companies customarily supply insurance, but check the cover and conditions carefully.

Make certain that you're covered for off-piste travel, as well as travel between countries (if you're planning cross-border excursions). A locally acquired motorcycle licence is not valid under some policies.

CARNETS

A *carnet de passage* is like a passport for your car, a booklet that is stamped on arrival and departure from a country to ensure that you export the vehicle again after you've imported it. It's usually issued by an automobile association in the country where the vehicle is registered. Most countries of West Africa require a carnet although rules change frequently.

The sting in the tail with a carnet is that you usually have to lodge a deposit to secure it. If you default on the carnet – that is, you don't have an export stamp to match the import one – then the country in question can claim your deposit, which can be up to 300% of the new value of the vehicle. You can get around this problem with bank guarantees or carnet insurance, but you still have to fork out in the end if you default.

Should the worst occur and your vehicle is irretrievably damaged in an accident or catastrophic breakdown, you'll have to argue it out with customs officials. Having a vehicle stolen can be even worse, as you may be suspected of having sold it.

The carnet may need to specify any pricey spare parts that you're planning to carry, such as a gearbox, which is designed to prevent any spare-part importation rackets. Contact your local automobile association for details about necessary documentation at least three months in advance.

In the event of an accident, make sure you submit the accident report as soon as possible to the insurance company or, if hiring, the car-hire company.

From Chad

Between Cameroon and Chad, the main border crossing is between Maroua (Cameroon) and Kousséri, although the actual border is at Nguelé. Corrupt officials abound here. For more adventure, try the crossings further south to the towns of Bongor or Léré; the former requires a pirogue (dugout canoe) across the Logone River. For details see p224.

For hard-core travellers, a more arduous (and adventurous) route into West Africa from Chad runs around the top of what's left of Lake Chad between Nguigmi in Niger and the Chadian capital N'Djaména. Be warned: banditry is common along this route. Unless you have your own vehicle, finding public transport on the Chadian side of the border requires extreme patience. From Nguigmi, twice-weekly landcruisers sometimes make the dusty day-long journey from Nguigmi to Mao in Chad; onward transport to N'Djaména is infrequent. For more information, see p610.

There are no official border crossings between Nigeria and Chad although the countries do share a short border. For transiting through Cameroon without the need for a visa, see p665).

From the North – Crossing the Sahara

With rebellion and banditry plaguing northern Mali and northern Niger at the time of writing, most trans-Saharan routes have fallen quiet. Apart from entering Mauritania via Morocco and Western Sahara, we are unable to recommend any of the other routes across the Sahara into West Africa; we have covered these routes below in case the situation changes during the life of this book. There is no public transport along any of the routes covered here. For more information see the boxed texts, p525 and p606.

Whichever route you take, you'll need to get a thorough update on the security situation before setting off. Anybody planning to travel in the Sahara should check out the excellent website put together by Chris Scott, www.sahara-overland.com; its forum is particularly useful on which routes are open. Be sure to bring sufficient food, water and warm clothes for the journey.

WESTERN SAHARA ROUTE

Travel through Morocco is straightforward (see Lonely Planet's *Morocco* guide). About 500km south of Agadir you enter the disputed territory of Western Sahara, where the main road continues along the coast to Dakhla, from where it's another 425km to Nouâdhibou in Mauritania. The road is now entirely sealed from Dakhla to Nouakchott, except for the 3km no man's land that separates the two border posts. The border area is littered with landmines, so don't stray from the road.

A grand taxi from Dakhla to the Mauritanian border costs Dh250 to Dh400, although make sure that you ask the driver to ferry you across no man's land to the Mauritanian border post – otherwise, it's a hot, 3km walk along a road lined with minefields unless you can hitch with lurking moneychangers (for a fee). From the Mauritanian border post to Nouâdhibou costs UM1800 in a grand taxi.

If you're hitching, Hôtel Sahara and Camping Moussafir in Dakhla are where most of the overlanders stay and are good places to find other travellers to team up with or to look for a lift. There's a thriving trade in second-hand cars being driven from Europe to sell in West Africa and plenty of vacationing French travellers in campervans; remember that sharing costs is expected. On the Moroccan side of the border, there's the basic Hôtel Frontière if you get stranded.

If you're driving your own car, fill your tank up in Western Sahara (the last petrol station is 80km before the border) as petrol is much cheaper here than in Mauritania.

Moneychangers will flag you down as you cross no man's land; their rates for ouguiya are poor. At the Mauritanian border post, you can buy the Mauritanian visa (€20), while those with their own vehicles will need to buy a temporary import form (*engagement sur honneur;* €10) and Mauritanian insurance (around €30 for two weeks). Expect searches for alcohol by Mauritanian customs. After Mauritanian border formalities it's approximately 45km further to Nouâdhibou.

If you're travelling from south to north, shared Mercedes taxis travel the entire route from Nouâdhibou's motor park to Dakhla (UM11,500) with some continuing on to Laayoune (UM17,000). Arrive at the motor park no later than 8am on the day you wish to travel.

In whichever direction you travel, expect to take a minimum of eight hours between Dakhla and Nouâdhibou, including two hours completing border formalities.

For more details on this route, see p569.

ROUTE DU HOGGAR

Although only for hard-core Saharan travellers in these troubled times, the Route du Hoggar, through Algeria and Niger, remains open provided you stick to the main highway and don't stray into the Aïr Mountains. The border crossing is between Assamakka (Niger) and In Guezzem (Algeria); make sure you have your visa and other paperwork in order in advance. If you're entering Niger here, you'll need a licensed desert guide and *feuille de route* (official itinerary). From Assamakka to Agadez, you must travel as part of an infrequent military convoy. If you are entering Algeria here, you'll need to be met by an official guide on the Algerian side of the border.

The Route du Hoggar is sealed, except for the 600km section between Tamanrasset ('Tam') and Arlit, although the road is in poor condition on many sections. Unless you have your own vehicle, you'll need to hitch a ride in trucks between Tamanrasset and Agadez. Very few travellers head south, but even fewer travellers make the journey in reverse, due in large part to the difficulty of getting an Algerian visa in Niger – Algerian visas and arrangements with an Algerian travel agency must have been made prior to reaching the border.

Southern Algeria is generally considered safe for travel although remember that things can change: more than 30 Western tourists were kidnapped in the Algerian Sahara in 2003 and not released until months later in Mali; one woman died while held hostage. Apart from official sources (such as Western embassies in Algiers or Niamey), the latest security situation is widely publicised in Agadez and, to a lesser extent, Tamanrasset, so keep your ear to the ground. Also, check in with the police before setting out and, where possible, avoid travelling at night.

OTHER ROUTES

The Route du Tanezrouft – which runs through Algeria and Mali, via Adrar and the border at Bordj-Mokhtar, ending in Gao – has always been one of the most romantic (for its sheer remoteness) and most dangerous trans-Saharan routes. Although it's technically easier than the Route du Hoggar, with a sand section more than 1300km long, northern Mali is currently a no-go area, the domain of a shadowy crowd of bandits, rebels and Islamic militants. In short, it has become one of the Sahara's most dangerous corners.

The other trans-Saharan route into West Africa – from Libya into northeastern Niger, via Bilma – was not an option at the time of writing. Quite apart from the complications of obtaining a Libyan visa and the dangerous unrest across northern Niger, the Libya–Niger border has been closed to independent travellers for years.

From Central Africa

There are two main crossing points between Cameroon and the Central African Republic, but roads that are dire at the best of times are catastrophic in the rainy season. The standard route is via Garoua-Boulaï, which straddles the border. Buses and trucks go to Bangui, taking two days with an overnight in Bouar. An equally rough alternative is to go to Batouri further south and cross via Kenzou to Berbérati. For information on routes into the Central African Republic, see p224.

The overland route to Congo is an epic journey traversing long, rutted tracks (which are probably impassable in the rainy season) through dense rainforest. The route goes

---

TOUAREG TRAIL

The Dakar Rally may have abandoned West Africa (see the boxed text, p39), but there is an alternative and, best of all, it's for non-professional drivers. The **Touareg Trail** (www.touareg-trail .be) is a four-week, 8500km rally with a difference, beginning in Brussels and ending up in Grand Popo in Benin, crossing the Sahara en route. The cars are all Citroën 2CVs and there's an emphasis on getting to know the countries you travel through. As such, it's all about adventure, rather than seriously competitive rally-driving. In addition to the full course, it's also possible to join the rally for the last 10 days for a road-trip known as 'Meet & Greet'. Check out their website for further details.

via Yokadouma, Moloundou and on to the border crossing at Sokambo on the Ngoko River. After crossing the river, there's onward transport to Pokola, where you must register with the Congolese police, and Brazzaville. For more details, see p224.

The main border crossings into Equatorial Guinea and Gabon are a few kilometres from each other, accessible from the Cameroonian town of Amban. In Ambam the road splits, the easterly route heading for Bitam and Libreville (Gabon) and the westerly route heading for Ebebiyin and Bata (Equatorial Guinea). There's also a border crossing into Equatorial Guinea on the coast near Campo but it's frequently closed and should not be relied on. See p225 for more detailed information.

SEA

Very occasionally, we hear from a lucky traveller who manages to hitch a ride on a private yacht sailing from Spain, Morocco or the Canary Islands to Senegal, The Gambia and beyond. Otherwise, the only sea-going option is to take a comfortable office-style cabin in a cargo ship. The main operator is **Grimaldi Freighter Cruises** (☎ 081-496 203; www.grimaldi-freightercruises .com, in Italian; Via Marchese Campodisola 13, 80133 Naples, Italy), which has weekly boats from Hamburg (Germany), Amsterdam (The Netherlands), Tilbury (London) and Antwerp (Belgium) to Dakar (Senegal), Lomé (Togo), Tema (Ghana) and Lagos (Nigeria).

Prices vary depending on the quality of the ship and on the cabin (inside cabins are cheaper; check the website for the latest prices). A typical voyage from London takes about nine days to Dakar and 16 days to Lagos. There's a full list of worldwide ticket agents on the Grimaldi website.

Ad hoc sea-going transport can sometimes be arranged to Malabo (Equatorial Guinea) from Limbe (Cameroon); see p225.

TOURS

First-time travellers to West Africa may want to consider taking a tour – what you sacrifice in the freedom to go when and where you want, you gain in having someone else take care of all those logistics (such as visas, dealing with officialdom, organising transport and accommodation) that can drive independent travellers to distraction.

Two main options are available: inclusive tours (where you fly to your destination and spend two to three weeks in one or more countries) and overland tours (two- to six-month tours that begin in Europe and travel by land to and around West Africa). Some overland tours allow you to join for a short section (usually three to five weeks), flying out and back at either end. In addition to the tours listed here, some of the specialist travel agents listed on p831 also organise tours, as do numerous West African–based agencies (p848), although with the latter you'll usually need to arrange your own flight into and out of the region.

Inclusive Tours

This type of tour includes your international flight, transport around the country, food, accommodation, excursions, local guide and so on. The number of inclusive tour companies operating in West Africa is much smaller than in East or Southern Africa, but there's still a fair selection. As with flights and overland tours, a good place to look is the advertisements in the weekend newspapers and travel magazines; the print edition of **Travel Africa** (www.travelafricamag.com) usually has some West Africa–specific advertisements. The following list is not exhaustive. Australian travellers will find that tours with many UK-based companies are sold through local agencies.

FRANCE

Explorator (☎ 01 53 45 85 85; www.explorator.fr, in French) Experienced company with tours in 11 West African countries.

Nouvelles Frontières (☎ 01 49 20 65 87; www .nouvelles-frontieres.fr, in French) Mainstream French agency with tours to Senegal and Mali.

Point Afrique (☎ 0820 830 255; www.point-afrique .com, in French) West Africa specialist agency offering excellent tours to Benin, Burkina Faso, Mali, Mauritania, Niger, Senegal and Togo.

Terres d'Aventure (☎ 0825 700 825; www.terdav.com, in French) Adventurous trips to at least seven West African countries with a specialty in the Sahara.

Voyageurs en Afrique (☎ 0892 235 656; www.vdm .com, in French) Worldwide tour company with tours across West Africa, including Cameroon, Cape Verde, Mali and Senegal.

GERMANY & BELGIUM

Anders Reizen (☎ 013-33 40 40; www.andersreizen .be, in Flemish; Belgium) Belgium-based operator with tours to Benin, Cape Verde, Guinea and Mali.

Blue Planet Reisen (☎ 040-386 123 11; www.blue -planet-reisen.de, in German; Germany) Tours to Ghana.

Djoser (☎ 0221-920 15 80; www.djoser.de, in German; Germany) Köln-based operator that goes to Mali, Togo, Benin and Burkina Faso.

ITALY
Antichi Splendori Viaggi (☎ 011-8126715; www .antichisplendori.it, in Italian) Trips to Mali, Mauritania, Ghana, Togo and Benin.
Harmattan Tours (☎ 041-5420654; www.harmattan .it) Experienced Africa hand covering eight West African countries.

NETHERLANDS
Baobab Reizen (☎ 020-627 51 29; www.baobab.nl, in Dutch) Tours to Mali.
Sawadee Reizen (☎ 020-420 22 20; www.sawadee.nl, in Dutch) Covers Benin, Cameroon, Mali and Togo.
Timbuktu Travel (☎ 06-23 80 53 91; www.timbuktu travel.nl, in Dutch) Small company with tours to Mali.

SPAIN
Montañas del Mundo (☎ 963 730 067; www.mont anasdelmundo.es, in Spanish) Valencia-based adventure company that offers an 11-day tour to Mali.
Viajes Tembo (☎ 91 447 0474; www.taranna.com, in Spanish) Offices in Madrid and Barcelona with tours to Benin, Burkina Faso, Cameroon, Mali, Mauritania, Niger, Senegal and Togo.
Viatges Tuareg (☎ 932 652 391; www.tuareg.com, in Spanish) Respected Barcelona agency with tours to Cameroon, Mali, Burkina Faso, Niger, Senegal, Togo and Benin.

UK
Batafon Arts (☎ 01273-605791; www.batafonarts .co.uk) Dance and percussion courses/tours in The Gambia.
Birdfinders (☎ 01258-839066; www.birdfinders.co.uk) Birdwatching tours to The Gambia, Ghana and Cameroon.
Explore Worldwide (☎ 0845-013 1537; www .explore.co.uk) Well-established company offering a wide range of adventurous tours and treks in nine West African countries.
From Here 2 Timbuktu (www.fromhere2timbuktu .com) Wonderful tours to Mali, Senegal and Cameroon, with a focus on wildlife, music, culture and getting away from the tourist hordes.
Fulani Travel (☎ 01341-421969; www.fulanitravel .co.uk) Excellent African specialist agency with tours to Mali, Ghana, Senegal, Benin, Togo and elsewhere.
Hidden Gambia (☎ 0121-288 4100; www.hidden gambia.com) Gambia-specialist that avoids the package-tour resorts and heads upcountry.
Imaginative Traveller (☎ 01473-667337; www .imaginative-traveller.com) Adventure tours to Benin, The Gambia, Ghana, Mali, Senegal and Togo.

Limosa Holidays (☎ 01263-578143; www.limosa holidays.co.uk) Specialist birding trips, including The Gambia and Ghana.
Naturetrek (☎ 01962-733051; www.naturetrek.co.uk) Bird and wildlife specialists offering tours in Mali and The Gambia.
Peregrine Adventures (☎ 0844-736 0170; www.pere grineadventures.com) Five-country tour to Benin, Burkina Faso, Ghana, Mali and Togo, with additional tours to Mali.
Rainbow Tours (☎ 020-7226 1004; www.rainbow tours.co.uk) Trips to Sierra Leone.
Responsible Travel (☎ 01273-600030; www.respon sibletravel.com) Serves as a clearing house for eco-tours and sustainable travel operators with 10 West African countries covered.
Songlines Music Travel (☎ 020-8505 2582; www .songlines.co.uk/musictravel) Music-centred tours to Mali, Senegal and Cape Verde.
Tim Best Travel (☎ 020-7591 0300; www.timbest travel.co.uk) Recommended and experienced company that can take you to Senegal, Niger and Mali (including Mali's music festivals).
Undiscovered Destinations (☎ 0191-296 2674; www.undiscovered-destinations.com) Off-the-beaten-track agency that goes to Sierra Leone.

USA
Access Africa (☎ 212-368 6561; www.accessafrica.com) Tours to nine West African countries including, unusually, Nigeria and Côte d'Ivoire.
Adventure Center (☎ 800 228 8747; www.adventure center.com) Multi-country tours covering 10 countries as well as those tailored to Mali, Mauritania, The Gambia, Senegal and Ghana.
Adventures Abroad (☎ 800 665 3998; www .adventures-abroad.com) Small-group tours to a range of countries.
Alken Tours (☎ 800 221 6686; www.alkentours.com) A range of tours to eight West African countries.
Born Free Safaris (☎ 800 472 3274; www.bornfree safaris.com) Tours to Ghana, Senegal, The Gambia, Mali and Benin.
Elder Treks (☎ 800 741 7956; www.eldertreks.com) Tours for the over-50s to Mali, Burkina Faso, Niger, Togo, Ghana and Benin.
Journeys International (☎ 800 255 8735; www .journeys-intl.com) Small-group or customised tours to a handful of West African countries.
Mountain Travel-Sobek (☎ 510-549 6000; www .mtsobek.com) Two- to three-week tours in Mali, Burkina Faso and Mauritania.
Museum for African Art (☎ 718-784 7700; www .africanart.org) Cultural tours to Mali.
Palace Travel (☎ 800 683 7731; www.palacetravel .com) West Africa specialist with tours to eight countries.

Spector Travel (☎ 617-351 0111; www.spectortravel
.com) An Africa specialist with tours to Mali, The Gambia,
Senegal, Togo and Benin.
Turtle Tours (☎ 888-299 1439; www.turtletours.com)
Tours for small groups in Mauritania, Mali and Niger, and
customised tours to seven West African countries.
Wilderness Travel (☎ 800 368 2794; www.wilder
nesstravel.com) Trips to Burkina Faso, The Gambia, Ghana,
Mali and Senegal.

Overland Tours

For these trips, you travel in an 'overland
truck' with about 15 to 28 other people, a
couple of drivers/leaders, plus tents and
other equipment. Food is bought along the
way and the group cooks and eats together.
Most of the hassles (such as border crossings)
are taken care of by the leader. Disadvantages
include a fixed itinerary and the possibility of
spending a long time with other people in
relatively close confines. That said, overland
truck tours are extremely popular.

The overland-tour market is dominated
by British companies, although passengers
come from many parts of the world. Most
tours start in London and travel to West
Africa via Europe and Morocco. For those
with plenty of time, there's also the option
to do the West Africa trip as part of a longer
trans-Africa trip.

Among the UK-based overland tour
companies offering trips in West Africa are
the following:
African Trails (☎ 01580-761171; www.africantrails
.co.uk)
Keystone Journeys (www.keystonejourneys.com)
Dragoman (☎ 01728-861133; www.dragoman.com)

GETTING AROUND

This section outlines the various ways of
travelling around West Africa. For more
details see the Getting There & Away and
Getting Around sections of the Transport
section in each individual country chapter.

AIR

Travelling by bus, bush taxi and even train
are essential parts of the West African experience, but so vast are the distances that
a few flights around the region can widen
your options considerably if your time is
limited. The region has a reasonable network of air routes, although, bizarrely, if

you're heading a long way off the beaten
track (eg Monrovia or Bissau) it can occasionally work out cheaper or easier to fly
to Europe and then back into the region.
The best connections are generally between
Francophone countries.

Air safety is a major concern in West
Africa and a spate of accidents (especially
in Nigeria) means that you should always be
wary of the region's local airlines, particularly smaller operators. For more details on
the air safety record of individual airlines,
visit www.airsafe.com/index.html.

Although the airports in some capital cities are large and cavernous (and occasionally
even modern), some smaller West African
airports are little more than single-shed terminals. Regardless of the size, don't be surprised
if you spend half a day at check-in – see the
boxed text, p830 for more on the potential
hassles of checking in.

Airlines in West Africa

For a list of major airlines that fly to West
Africa, see p828. Of these, Air Sénégal
International has excellent connections across
the region to Francophone and Lusophone
countries, as well as a few domestic services
within Senegal, although nothing to Ghana
or Nigeria. Air Burkina also has a reasonably
extensive West African service as well as a domestic Ouagadougou–Bobo-Dioulasso service. Air Ivoire, Bellview Air, Virgin Nigeria
and Aero also cross national boundaries and
sometimes span the Franco-Anglo divide
with extensive regional networks; Bellview
Air, Virgin Nigeria and Aero also operate
domestic Nigerian routes. TACV connects
Praia (Cape Verde) to Dakar on the mainland,
from where they also operate a small range of
services to neighbouring countries.

Other airlines that also operate 'domestic'
West African services (again, either within or
between West African countries) include:
Antrak Air (www.antrakair.com) Ghanaian airline that
flies domestically between Accra, Kumasi and Tamale, as
well as from Accra to Cotonou and Ouagadougou.
Benin Golf Air (www.benin-golf-air.com) Good regional
network encompassing Abidjan, Bamako, Conakry,
Cotonou, Dakar, Douala and Lomé.
Chanchangi Airlines (www.chanchangi.com) Domestic
Nigerian airline.
Compagnie Aerienne du Mali (Air CAM; www
.camaero.com) Domestic Malian airline that also flies to
Lomé, Cotonou, Ouagadougou and Abidjan.

Elysian Airlines (www.elysianairlines.com) Domestic Liberian, Cameroonian and some wider West African routes.
Halcyon Air (www.halcyonair.com) Domestic Cape Verde airline.
Mali Air Express (MAE; www.mae-mali.com) Private Malian airline that flies within Mali.
Slok Air International (www.slok-air.com) Gambian airline that connects Banjul with Dakar, Freetown, Monrovia, Accra, Conakry, Abidjan and Bamako.
Sosoliso (www.sosolisoairline.com) Domestic Nigerian airline.

Reputable travel agents throughout the region (see the individual country chapters) can also sometimes find tickets for international airlines as they hop between West African cities as part of their intercontinental routes.

Tickets

Long distances, high fuel costs and a state of budgetary crisis among most regional airlines ensure that fares within West Africa don't come cheap. Flying from Dakar (Senegal) to Abidjan (Côte d'Ivoire), for example, can cost the equivalent to flying halfway across the USA. Return fares are usually double the one-way fares, though less expensive excursion fares are occasionally available, as are youth or student fares. For comprehensive information on flying from specific West African cities see the Transport sections in the individual country chapters.

Once you've bought your ticket, reconfirm your reservation several times at least, especially if the airline you're flying with has a less-than-stellar reputation for reliability. After the flight, if you checked-in luggage, hold on to your baggage claim ticket until you've exited the baggage claim area at your destination, as you'll often be required to show it.

BICYCLE

A small but steady number of travellers visit West Africa on bicycle. As long as you have sufficient time, a sturdy bike, are ready to be self-sufficient and possess a willingness to rough it, cycling is an excellent way to get to know the region. You'll end up staying in small towns and villages, interact more with the local people without vehicle windows and other barriers between you, and eat West African food more frequently.

Because of the distances involved, you'll need to plan your food and water needs in advance, and pay careful attention to choosing a route in order to avoid long stretches of semidesert, areas with no villages or heavily travelled roads. In general, cycling is best well away from urban areas, and in the early morning and late afternoon hours. When calculating your daily distances, plan on taking a break during the hottest, midday period, and don't count on covering as much territory each day as you might in a northern European climate. Countries that are particularly good for cycling include southern Senegal, The Gambia, southern Ghana, Togo and Benin.

The best time to cycle is in the cooler, dry period from mid-October to February. Even so, you'll need to work out a way to carry at least 4L of water, and you'll also need to carry a water filter and purifier. If you get tired, or simply want to cut out the boring bits, bikes can easily be carried on bush taxis, though you'll want to carry some rags to wrap around the gearing for protection. You'll need to pay a luggage fee for this, but it shouldn't be more than one-third to one-half the price of the passenger fare.

Mountain bikes are most suitable for cycling in West Africa and will give you the greatest flexibility in setting your route. While heavy, single-speed bicycles can be rented in many towns (and occasionally mountain bikes), they're not good for anything other than short, local rides, so you should bring your own bicycle into the country if you plan on riding extended distances. To rent a bike locally, ask staff at hotels, or enquire at bicycle-repair stands (every town market has one).

Apart from water, your main concern will be motorists. Cyclists are regarded as 3rd-class citizens in West Africa, even more than they are in Western countries, so make sure you know what's coming up behind you and be prepared to take evasive action, as local cyclists are often forced to do. A small rear-view mirror is well worth considering.

Wherever you go, you'll be met with great local curiosity (as well as much goodwill). As in most places in the world, don't leave your bike unattended for any lengthy period of time unless it's locked, and try to secure the main removable pieces. Taking your bike into your hotel room, should you decide to take a break from camping, is generally no problem. If you're camping near settlements in rural areas, ask the village headman each night

TRANSPORT IN WEST AFRICA

where you can stay. Even if you don't have a tent, he'll find you somewhere to sleep.

You'll need to carry sufficient spare parts and be proficient at repairs; punctures, in particular, will be frequent. Take at least four spare inner tubes, some tyre repair material and a spare tyre. Consider the number of tube patches you might need, square it, and pack those too. Some people don't like them but we've found inner-tube protectors indispensable for minimising punctures.

A highly recommended contact is **Bicycle Africa** (☎ /fax 206-767 0848; www.ibike.org/bikeafrica; 4887 Columbia Drive South, Seattle, WA98108-1919, USA), which is part of the International Bicycle Fund, a low-budget, socially conscious organisation that arranges tours in some West African countries, provides fact sheets and posts letters from travellers who've travelled by bike in the area. Another useful resource is the **Cyclists' Touring Club** (CTC; ☎ 01483-238337; www.ctc.org.uk), a UK-based organisation which offers tips and information sheets on cycling in different parts of the world.

Transporting Your Bicycle

If you're planning to bring your bike with you on the plane to West Africa, some airlines ask that you partially dismantle it and put the pieces in a large bag or box. Bike boxes are available at some airports. Otherwise, you can arrange one in advance with your local bicycle shop. To fit it in the box, you'll usually need to take off (or turn) the handlebars, pedals and seat, and will need to deflate the tyres. Some airlines don't charge, while others (including many charter airlines) levy an extra fee – usually around US$50 to US$100 – because bike boxes are not standard size. Some airlines are willing to take your bike 'as is' – you can just wheel it to the check-in desk – although you'll still need to partially deflate the tyres and tie the handlebars into the frame. Check with the airline in advance about their regulations.

BOAT

At several points along the West African coast you can travel by boat, either on a large passenger vessel or by local canoe. Some of the local canoe trips are definitely of the informal variety, and many are dangerous. Countries where ferries provide an important means of coastal transport include Cape Verde (p253), Senegal (p738), Sierra Leone (p767), Liberia (p474) and Guinea-Bissau (p453).

There are two ferries a week between Limbe (Cameroon) and Calabar (Nigeria). Decidedly dodgy speed boats also make the trip, see p665). Other places where you can cross international borders by boat are by barge from Guinea to Mali (p430) and, possibly, by ferry between Conakry (Guinea; p430) and Freetown (Sierra Leone; p767).

On most major rivers in the region, pirogues, *pinasses* (larger motorised boats, carrying cargo and anything from 10 to 100 passengers) and/or public ferries serve towns and villages along the way, and can be an excellent way to see the country. Some involve a simple river crossing, others can be a longer expedition where you sleep by the riverbank. One of the most popular boat trips for travellers is along the Niger River in Mali, especially between Mopti and Timbuktu. For more information on Niger River trips, see p539, and the boxed text, p504. Other riverboat options exist, for example along the Gambia and Senegal Rivers. Remember that many such journeys are only possible at certain times of the year (usually August to December) when water levels are still high enough after the rains.

Whether you're renting a pirogue or *pinasse*, or taking a public ferry, check what food and water is included in the price you pay and it's always worth taking more just in case. On some journeys you'll be able to buy snacks and fruit along the way. Also, bring something to protect yourself from the sun, as few boats have any shade, and something to waterproof your gear. Avoid getting on boats that are overloaded, or setting off when the weather is bad, especially on sea routes in coastal areas.

BUS & BUSH TAXI

The most common forms of public transport in West Africa are bus (*car* in some Francophone countries) and bush taxi (*taxi brousse*). Buses may be run by state-owned or private companies; bush taxis are always private, although the driver is rarely the owner of the vehicle. Vehicles are usually located at a bus and bush taxi park, called *gare routière* or sometimes *autogare* in Francophone countries, 'garage', 'lorry park' or 'motor park' in English-speaking countries, and *paragem* in Portuguese-speaking countries. Most large cities have several *gares routières*, one for each main direction or destination, often located on the road out of town headed in that direction.

In some countries, buses are common for intercity routes and bush taxis are hard to find; in other countries it's the reverse. Either way, travel generally costs between US$1.50 and US$2 per 100km, although fares depend on the quality of the vehicle and the route. On routes between countries (eg between Ouagadougou in Burkina Faso and Bamako in Mali), costs can be more because drivers have to pay additional fees (official and unofficial) to cross the border. You can save a bit of money by taking one vehicle to the border and then another on the other side, but this prolongs the trip considerably.

In many countries, transport fares are fixed by the government, so the only way the bush taxi drivers can earn a bit more is to charge for luggage. Local people accept this, so travellers should too, unless of course it's unreasonable. The fee for a medium-sized rucksack is around 10% of the fare. Small bags will be less and are often not charged at all. If you think you're being overcharged, ask other passengers, out of earshot of the driver. Once you know the proper rate, bargaining will be easy and the price should soon fall.

Bus

Long-distance buses (sometimes called a 'big bus' or *grand car*, to distinguish it from a minibus) vary in size – from 35 to 70 seats – and services vary between countries and areas. On the main routes buses are good quality, with a reliable service and fixed departure times (although arrival times may be more fluid depending on anything from checkpoints and breakdowns to the number of towns they stop in along the way).

On quiet roads in rural areas, buses may be decrepit, and may frequently break down, and stop regularly. These buses have no timetable and usually go when full or when the driver feels like it. They are usually overcrowded, in contrast with some of the better lines on major routes, where the one-person-per-seat rule is usually respected. Generally, bus fares are cheaper than bush taxi fares for a comparable route and are usually quicker.

You may arrange a long ride by bus (or bush taxi) and find yourself transferring to another vehicle somewhere along the way. There's no need to pay more – your driver pays your fare directly to the driver of the next vehicle – but unfortunately it can mean long waits while the arrangements are made.

RESERVATIONS

You can reserve in advance on some main-route buses, which is advisable. In some countries you book a place but not a specific seat. Just before the bus leaves, names get called out in the order that tickets were bought, and you get on and choose the seat you want. Seats to the front tend to be better ventilated and more comfortable. If you suffer from motion sickness, try to get a seat towards the front or in the middle. Whichever end of the bus you sit in, it's worth trying to get a seat on the side that will be away from direct sunlight for most of the journey.

Bush Taxi

A bush taxi (known as a tro-tro in Ghana) is effectively a small bus. Almost without exception, bush taxis leave when full, not according to any recognisable timetable. As soon as one car leaves, the next one starts to fill. Depending on the popularity of the route, the car may take half an hour or several days to fill. Either way, drivers jealously guard their car's place in the queue.

Early customers can choose where to sit. Latecomers get no choice and are assigned to the least comfortable seats – usually at the back, where the seating is cramped and stuffy, seat springs work their way into any orifice and window-winders jam into knees. If you have a choice, the best seats are those in the front, near the window. Some travellers prefer the very front, though you're first in line if there's a collision. Better is the row behind the driver, near a window (ideally one that works), and preferably on the side with more shade during the journey.

If a group of passengers has been waiting a long time, and there are only two or three seats to fill, they may club together and pay extra so as to get moving. If you do this, don't expect a discount because you're saving the driver the hassle of looking for other passengers – time ain't money in Africa. If you pick up someone along the way, however, the fare they pay goes to the passengers who bought the seats, not to the driver.

By far the best time to catch bush taxis is early in the morning; after that, you may have difficulty finding vehicles on many routes. Sometimes, however, departures are

---

TOUTS AT THE GARE ROUTIÈRE

At most gares routières (motor parks), bush taxis leave on a fill-up-and-go basis, but problems arise when you get more than one vehicle covering the same route. This is when a tout (sometimes called a *coti-man*) can earn money by persuading you to take 'his' car. Most will tell you anything to get you on board: 'this one is very fast', 'this minibus is leaving now', 'this bus is a good, cheap price' etc. Another trick involves putting your bags on the roof rack as a 'deposit' against you taking another car (which means you shouldn't give up your bags until you're sure you'll go with them).

Don't think that you're being targeted because you're a wealthy foreigner – the touts hassle everybody. In the end, it's always somewhat of a gamble, but the vehicle that has the most passengers will usually be the one to depart first.

---

determined by market days, in which case afternoon may be best.

If a bush taxi looks like it's going to get uncomfortably full, you can always buy two seats for yourself – it's simply double the price. Likewise, if you want to charter the whole car, take the price of one seat and multiply it by the number available. Occasionally you may also need to add a bit more for luggage, although in our experience this is rarely requested for charters. You can either hire a city taxi or a bush taxi (although in most places, city taxis won't have the necessary paperwork for long-distance routes) or, alternatively, ask around at your hotel and arrange something privately.

Whatever vehicle you go with, make sure it's mechanically sound before agreeing anything. Even if you know nothing about cars, just looking at the bodywork or listening to the engine will give you an idea. Also, don't forget to check the tyres. If they're completely bald or badly out of alignment, it's probably better to look for another vehicle. If you're going on a longer trip, it's also worth checking that there's a spare (and the tools to change it). Hiring a car for a short test run in town is a good way to check out both vehicle and driver before finalising arrangements for a longer trip.

The price you pay will have to be worth the driver taking it out of public service for the day. If you want a deal including petrol, he'll reduce the speed to a slow trot and complain every time you take a detour. A fixed daily rate for the car, while you pay extra for fuel, is easier to arrange. Finding a car with a working petrol gauge may be tricky, but you can work on the theory that the tank will be empty when you start and, if you allow for 10km per litre on reasonable roads (more on bad roads), you should be OK.

There are three main types of bush taxi in West Africa, as follows.

MINIBUS

Some routes are served by minibuses (*minicars*) – usually seating about 12 to 20 passengers. They're typically about 25% cheaper than Peugeot 504s, and sometimes more comfortable, depending on how full they are. They're also slower, take longer to fill, tend to stop more, and police checks at roadblocks take longer because there are more passengers to search.

PEUGEOT TAXI

Peugeot 504s, assembled in Nigeria or imported from Europe, are used all over West Africa and are also called *cinq-cent-quatre*, Peugeot taxi, *sept place* and *brake*. With three rows of seats, they're built to take the driver plus seven passengers. In some countries this limit is observed, in others it's flagrantly flaunted. All 504s in Mali, for example, take the driver plus nine passengers. In Guinea you might be jammed in with at least a dozen adults, plus children, the odd goat and bags, with more luggage and a couple of extra passengers riding on the roof. That these cars do hundreds of thousands of kilometres on some of the worst roads in the world is a credit to the manufacturer and the ingenuity of local mechanics.

While some drivers are safe and considerate, others verge on insanity. Some cars are relatively new (there are quite a few Peugeot 505s, the later model, around these days) and well maintained, with comfortable seats. Others are very old, reduced to nothing more than chassis, body and engine: there's more weld than original metal, the tyres are bald, most of the upholstery is missing and little extras like windows, door handles and even exhaust pipes fell by the roadside long ago.

PICK-UP

With wooden seats down the sides, covered pick-ups (bâchés) are definitely 2nd class, but are sometimes the only kind of bush taxi available. They take around 16 passengers but are invariably stuffed with people and baggage, plus a few chickens, and your feet may be higher than your waist from resting on a sack of millet. Up on the roof go more bags, bunches of bananas, extra passengers and goats (also live). Bâché rides are often very slow, and police checks at roadblocks are interminable as drivers or passengers frequently lack vital papers. The ride is guaranteed to be unpleasant unless you adopt an African attitude, which means each time your head hits the roof as the vehicle descends into yet another big pothole, you roar with laughter. There's nothing like local humour to change an otherwise miserable trip into a tolerable, even enjoyable, experience.

CAR & MOTORCYCLE

For advice on the necessary documentation and insurance that you'll need if you're bringing your own vehicle to West Africa, general information on shipping your vehicle to West Africa and the availability of fuel and spare parts in the region, see p834.

Hire

There are car-rental agencies in most capital cities and tourist areas. Most international companies (Hertz, Avis, etc) are represented, plus smaller independent operators, but renting is invariably expensive – you can easily spend in one day what you'd pay for a week's rental in Europe or the USA. If the small operators charge less, it's usually because the vehicles are older and sometimes not well maintained, and corners can be cut on insurance, but it can also simply be because their costs are lower and they can do a better deal. If you have the time, check around for bargains. You will need to put down a large deposit (credit cards are usually, but not always, good for this).

It's very unlikely you'll be allowed to take a rental car across a border but, if you are (for example from The Gambia into Senegal), make sure the paperwork is valid. If you're uncertain about driving, most companies provide a chauffeur at very little extra cost and, with many, a chauffeur is mandatory. In many cases it's cheaper to go with a chauffeur as you will pay less for insurance. It's also prudent, as getting stuck on your own is no fun and chauffeurs generally know the intricacies of checkpoint etiquette.

In tourist areas, such as The Gambia and Senegal, and in some parts of Mali and Burkina Faso, it's possible to hire mopeds and motorbikes. In most other countries there is no formal rental available, but if you want to hire a motorbike (and know how to ride one) you can arrange something by asking at an auto parts shop or repair yard, or by asking at the reception of your hotel. You can often be put in touch with someone who doesn't mind

---

ROAD SAFETY

Road safety is probably your biggest safety risk in West Africa. Bush taxi drivers, in particular, race along at hair-raising speeds and overtake blind to reach their destination before another car can get in front of them in the queue for the return journey. Drivers can be sleepy from a long day, and drink-driving is a problem. Travelling early in the morning is one step you can take to cut the risk, as drivers are fresher and roads less travelled. Avoid night travel at all costs. If you are in a vehicle and feel unsafe, if it's a heavily travelled route, you can take your chances and get out at a major station to switch to another car (though don't expect a refund, and the second vehicle may not be much better). You can complain about dangerous driving, but this usually doesn't have any effect and, unless things are really out of control, you'll seldom get support from other passengers. Saying that you're feeling sick seems to get better results. Drivers are often quite considerate to ill or infirm passengers and, in any case, seem to care more about keeping vomit off their seats than about dying under the wheels of an oncoming lorry. You might be able to rally other passengers to your side this way as well. Most locals take a stoic approach to the situation, with many viewing accidents as a matter of the will of God or Allah. (This explains slogans such as 'Allahu Akhbar' painted on vehicles – probably in the belief that a bit of extra help from above might see the vehicle through the day's runs.) Drivers seem to discredit the idea that accidents are in any way related to vehicle speed or condition, or to wild driving practices.

ROAD DISTANCES (KM)

	Abidjan (Côte d'Ivoire)	Accra (Ghana)	Bamako (Mali)	Banjul (The Gambia)	Bissau (Guinea-Bissau)	Conakry (Guinea)	Cotonou (Benin)	Dakar (Senegal)	Freetown (Sierra Leone)	Lagos (Nigeria)	Lomé (Togo)	Monrovia (Liberia)	Niamey (Niger)	Nouakchott (Mauritania)	Ouagadougou (Burkina Faso)
Accra (Ghana)	560														
Bamako (Mali)	1160	1710													
Banjul (The Gambia)	2490	3210	1340												
Bissau (Guinea-Bissau)	2180	2900	1460	310											
Conakry (Guinea)	1700	2260	920	1230	980										
Cotonou (Benin)	910	360	2020	3360	3110	2610									
Dakar (Senegal)	2790	3350	1420	300	585	1530	3360								
Freetown (Sierra Leone)	1590	2090	1210	1440	1190	320	2440	1740							
Lagos (Nigeria)	1030	480	2140	3480	3230	2730	120	3560	2560						
Lomé (Togo)	760	200	1870	3220	2970	2460	160	3290	2290	280					
Monrovia (Liberia)	1020	1520	1040	1860	1610	740	1870	2160	570	1990	1720				
Niamey (Niger)	1570	1390	1410	2750	2880	2320	1040	2740	2900	1160	1190	2330			
Nouakchott (Mauritania)	2800	3360	1650	870	1180	2100	3670	570	2320	3790	3560	2730	3050		
Ouagadougou (Burkina Faso)	1070	970	900	2240	2360	1820	1120	2240	2400	1240	1240	1830	500	2550	
Yaoundé (Cameroon)	2650	2100	3760	4410	4160	4350	1740	4670	4120	1620	1620	3610	2090	5240	2860

CAR HIRE, CHICKENS & OTHER HAZARDS OF THE ROAD

If you've never driven in a developing country before, hiring a self-drive car is not to be undertaken lightly and nor is it for the faint-hearted. Road conditions outside capitals are bad and, apart from potholes and the inevitable chickens, dangers include people and camels, cows and other animals moving into your path. Keep in mind that many locals have not driven themselves, and are thus not aware of braking distances and similar concepts. Smaller roads are not sealed, so you need to be able to drive on dirt (and sometimes on sand). One of the biggest hazards is overtaking blind or on curves. Moderate your speed accordingly and, when going around curves or blind spots, be prepared to react to oncoming vehicles in your lane. If you see some branches in the road, it's usually a sign that there's a problem or a stopped vehicle in the road ahead, so you'll need to go slow.

There are very few signposts, so you should take a map and be able to read it. Remember, however, that roads get washed away in the rainy seasons and what looks like a fine piece of tarmac on paper may not correspond with reality. Also, outside capital cities, phones are few and far between, should you need to contact your rental company in case of a breakdown, and cellular telephone networks often don't reach rural areas.

Throughout the region, driving at night is unsafe; try to avoid doing so. If you do need to drive in the dark, be particularly alert for vehicles stopped in the roadway with no lights or hazard warnings. Basic mechanical knowledge – at the very least being able to change a wheel – is very useful.

If this litany of potential hazards hasn't put you off, remember that many adventurous travellers do drive in West Africa and live to tell the tale. For everyone else, we recommend renting a car with a local driver as part of the package. In addition to having mechanical knowledge, and (usually) knowledge of the route, they can often be helpful as translators.

earning some extra cash by renting out their wheels for a day or two. Remember, though, that matters such as insurance will be easily overlooked, which is fine until you have an accident and find yourself liable for all bills. Also, if you do this, be sure to check out the motorbike in advance to ensure it's in acceptable mechanical condition.

Road Rules

Traffic drives on the right throughout West Africa (as in continental Europe and the USA), even in countries that have a British colonial heritage (such as The Gambia).

HITCHING

As in any other part of the world, hitching or accepting lifts in West Africa is never entirely safe, and we don't recommend it. Travellers who decide to hitch should understand that they are taking a small but potentially serious risk. If you're planning to travel this way, take advice from other hitchers (locals or travellers) first. Hitching in pairs is obviously safer, and hitching through less-salubrious suburbs, especially at night, is asking for trouble. Throughout most of the region, women should avoid hitching alone.

In many countries, as you venture further into rural areas, however, the frequency of buses or bush taxis drops, sometimes to nothing. Then the only way around is to ride on local trucks, as the locals do. A 'fare' is payable to the driver, so in cases like this the line between hitching and public transport is blurred – but if it's the only way to get around, you don't have a choice anyway. Usually you'll be riding on top of the cargo – it may be cotton or rice in sacks, which are quite comfy, but it might be logs or oil drums, which aren't.

If you want to hitch because there's no public transport leaving imminently from the *gare routière*, you'll normally have to go well beyond the town limits, as bush taxi drivers may take umbrage at other vehicles 'stealing' their customers. Even so, you'll probably still have to pay for your lift – but at least you'll get moving more quickly.

Hitching in the Western sense (ie because you don't want to get the bus or, more specifically, because you don't want to pay) is also possible but may take a long time. The only people giving free lifts are likely to be foreign expatriates or the occasional well-off local (very few West Africans own a car). Remember, however, that most people with space in their car want payment – usually on a par with what a bus would have cost.

LOCAL TRANSPORT

For getting around cities and larger towns, you'll generally have a choice of bus (capital cities only) and a range of taxis.

Bus

Within some capital cities, you may find well-developed city bus and minibus networks connecting the city centre and suburbs. In most other cities, it's minibuses only. In general, city buses travel along set routes, while minibuses may detour a little more.

Taxi

MOTORCYCLE TAXI

In many countries, motorcycle taxis (*moto-taxis* or *motos*) are used. While they're often cheaper than shared taxis and handy for zipping around, safety can be an issue. If you have a choice, it's usually better to pay slightly more and go with a regular shared taxi.

PRIVATE TAXI

Only in the bigger cities, such as Dakar, Abidjan and Ouagadougou, do taxis have meters (*compteurs*). Otherwise, bargaining is required or you'll be given the legally fixed rate. In any case, determine the fare before getting into the taxi. The fare from most airports into town is fixed, but some drivers (in Dakar, for example) will try to charge at least double this. In places like Bamako, it costs up to 50% more to go into town from the airport than it does to go the other way. The price always includes luggage unless you have a particularly bulky item. Also, fares invariably go up at night, and sometimes even in rainy weather.

If the city you're exploring is spread out and you've limited time, or if you're likely to be jumping in and out of taxis, consider renting a taxi by the hour or day. It will probably cost you less (anywhere from about US$20 to US$50 per day), and if the car breaks down it will be the driver's problem.

SHARED TAXI

Many cities have shared taxis that will stop and pick up more passengers even if they already have somebody inside; you pay just for one seat. Some run on fixed routes and are effectively a bus, only quicker and more comfortable. Others go wherever the first

passenger wants to go, and other people will only be picked up if they're going in the same direction. They normally shout the name of the suburb or a landmark they're heading for as the taxi goes past. In some places, it's common for the waiting passengers to call out the name of their destination or point in the desired direction as the taxi passes by. Once you've got the hang of the shared taxi system, it's quick and inexpensive, and an excellent way to get around cities – and also a good way to experience local life. It's also one of West Africa's great bargains, as fares seldom exceed US$0.35. It's always worth checking the fare before you get in the car though, as they're not always fixed, and meters don't apply to shared trips. If you're the first person in the taxi, make it clear that you're expecting the driver to pick up others and that you don't want a private hire (*déplacement*, *depo*, 'charter' or 'town trip') all to yourself.

TOURS

Compared with most areas of the world, West Africa has few tour operators. There are exceptions – such as heavily touristed areas like Mali and Senegal – but not many. Tour companies are usually based in the capital cities and typically offer excursions for groups (rather than individuals) from one-day to one-week trips, or longer. Good West African companies, many of whom organise tours beyond the borders of their own country, include the following:

Benin

Bénin Adventure (www.beninaventure.com, in French)
Eco-Bénin (www.ecobenin.org)

Burkina Faso

Couleurs d'Afrique (www.couleurs-afrique.com, in French)
L'Agence Tourisme (www.agence-tourisme.com, in French)

Cameroon

Safar Tours (www.safartours.com, in French)

The Gambia

Gambia Experience (Map pp300–1; ☎ 4461104; www.gambia.co.uk; Senegambia Beach Hotel, Kololi) Gambia's biggest tour operator. Does everything from charter flights and all-inclusive holidays to in-country tours. Good Senegal-Gambia tours can be organised through its Senegal Experience branch.

WEST AFRICA'S TOP TRAIN RIDES

Taking a long-distance West African train is the ultimate road movie with all the region's colours, smells and improbabilities of life writ large. More than a form of transport, West African trains are like moving cities, a stage for street performers, marketplaces, and prayer halls. And, like most forms of transport in West Africa, you'll have plenty of time to contemplate the experience, whether waiting on a platform for your train to appear a mere 12 hours late or stopped on remote rails in the middle of nowhere for no apparent reason. But for all their faults (and there are many) the trains work and are an essential part of the West African experience. Our three favourites:

- Zouérat to Nouâdhibou, Mauritania (see the boxed text, p555) – one of the great train experiences of the world on the longest train in the world.
- Dakar to Bamako (p737 and p541) – another of Africa's great epics, at once endlessly fascinating and interminable (up to 40 hours).
- Yaoundé to N'Gaoundéré, Cameroon (p226) – like crossing a continent, from the arid north to the steamy south, with glorious rainforests en route.

Guinea
Mondial Tours (www.mondialtours.net, in French)

Mali
Continent Tours (www.continenttours.com)
Geo Tours (www.geotours.org, in French)
Tara Africa Tours (www.tara-africatours.com)
Toguna Adventure Tours (www.geocities.com/toguna_adventure_tours)

Niger
Agadez Tourisme (www.agadez-tourisme.com)
Turbo Tours (wallymamoudou@yahoo.fr)

Senegal
Sahel Découverte Bassari (www.saheldecouverte.com, in French)
Senegal Experience (☎ in UK 0845 330 2080; www.senegal.co.uk) The Senegal branch of Serenity holidays specialises in tours to Siné-Saloum for travellers from the UK. Visits are arranged from The Gambia.

Togo
1001 Pistes (1001 'rough tracks'; ☎ 927 52 03; africatoy1001pistes@yahoo.fr)

A more complete list appears in the Transport section of each individual country chapter, while international companies offering tours to West Africa are listed on p838.

There are also plenty of hotels or guides who offer less professional tours that may be little more than a man with an underutilised car. On most tours, the larger the group, the lower the cost per person.

TRAIN

There are railways in Mauritania, Senegal, Mali, Côte d'Ivoire, Ghana, Burkina Faso, Togo, Nigeria and Cameroon. Most services run only within the country of operation, but there are international services, notably between Dakar and Bamako, and, depending on the security situation in Côte d'Ivoire, between Ouagadougou and Abidjan.

Some trains are relatively comfortable, with 1st-class coaches that may have air-conditioning. Some also have sleeping compartments with two or four bunks. Other services are 2nd or 3rd class only and conditions can be uncomfortable, with no lights, no toilets and no glass in the windows (equals no fun on long night journeys). Some trains have a restaurant on board, but you can usually buy things to eat and drink at stations along the way.

Health

CONTENTS

As long as you stay up-to-date with your vaccinations and take basic preventive measures, you'd have to be pretty unlucky to succumb to most of the health hazards covered in this chapter. Africa certainly has an impressive selection of tropical diseases on offer, but you're more likely to get a bout of diarrhoea (in fact, you should bank on it), a cold or an infected mosquito bite than an exotic disease such as sleeping sickness. When it comes to injuries (as opposed to illness), the most likely reason for needing medical help in Africa is as a result of road accidents – vehicles are rarely well maintained, the roads are potholed and poorly lit, and drink driving is common.

BEFORE YOU GO

A little planning before departure, particularly for pre-existing illnesses, will save you a lot of trouble later. Before a long trip get a check-up from your dentist, and from your doctor if you have any regular medication or chronic illness, such as high blood pressure or asthma. You should also organise spare contact lenses and glasses (and take your optical prescription with you), get a first aid and medical kit together, and arrange necessary vaccinations.

It's tempting to leave it all to the last minute – don't! Many vaccines don't take effect until two weeks after you've been immunised, so visit a doctor four to eight weeks before departure. Ask your doctor for an International Certificate of Vaccination (otherwise known as the yellow booklet or *livre jeune*), which will list all the vaccinations you've received. This is mandatory for the African countries that require proof of yellow-fever vaccination upon entry (see the boxed text, p857), but it's a good idea to carry it anyway wherever you travel in case you require medical treatment or encounter troublesome border officials.

Travellers can register with the **International Association for Medical Advice to Travellers** (IAMAT; www.iamat.org). Its website can help travellers find a doctor who has recognised training. Those heading off to very remote areas might like to do a first-aid course (contact the Red Cross or St John Ambulance) or attend a remote medicine first aid course, such as that offered by the **Royal Geographical Society** (www.wildernessmedicaltraining.co.uk).

If you are bringing medications with you, carry them in their original containers, clearly labelled. A signed and dated letter from your physician describing all medical conditions and medications, including generic names, is also a good idea. If carrying syringes or needles, be sure to have a physician's letter documenting their medical necessity.

How do you go about getting the best possible medical help? It really depends on the severity of your illness or injury and the availability of local help. If malaria is suspected, seek medical help as soon as possible or begin self-medicating if you are off the beaten track (see p854).

INSURANCE

Find out in advance whether your insurance plan will make payments to providers or will reimburse you later for overseas health expenditures (in many countries doctors expect payment in cash). It's vital to ensure that your travel insurance will cover the emergency transport required to get you to a hospital in a major city, to better facilities elsewhere in Africa, or all the way home by air and with a medical attendant if necessary. Not all insurance covers this, so check the contract carefully. If you need medical help, your insurance company might be able to help locate the nearest hospital or clinic, or you can ask at your hotel. In an emergency, contact your embassy or consulate.

The **African Medical and Research Foundation** (Amref; www.amref.org) provides an air-evacuation service in medical emergencies in some African countries, as well as air-ambulance transfers between medical facilities. Money paid by members for this service goes into providing grass-roots medical assistance for local people.

RECOMMENDED VACCINATIONS

The **World Health Organization** (www.who.int/en/) recommends that all travellers be covered for diphtheria, tetanus, measles, mumps, rubella and polio, as well as for hepatitis B, regardless of their destination. Planning to travel is a great time to ensure that all routine vaccination cover is complete. The consequences of these diseases can be severe, and outbreaks do occur.

According to the **Centers for Disease Control and Prevention** (www.cdc.gov), the following vaccinations are recommended for all parts of Africa: hepatitis A, hepatitis B, meningococcal meningitis, rabies and typhoid, and boosters for tetanus, diphtheria and measles. Yellow-fever vaccination is not necessarily recommended for all parts of West Africa, although the certificate is an entry requirement for many countries (see p857).

MEDICAL CHECKLIST

It is a very good idea to carry a medical and first aid kit with you, to help yourself in the case of minor illness or injury. Following is a list of items you should consider packing.

- Acetaminophen (paracetamol) or aspirin
- Acetazolamide (Diamox) for altitude sickness (prescription only)
- Adhesive or paper tape
- Antibacterial ointment (prescription only) for cuts and abrasions (eg Bactroban)
- Antibiotics (prescription only), eg ciprofloxacin (Ciproxin) or norfloxacin (Utinor)
- Anti-diarrhoeal drugs (eg loperamide)

- Antihistamines (for hay fever and allergic reactions)
- Anti-inflammatory drugs (eg ibuprofen)
- Anti-malaria pills
- Bandages, gauze, gauze rolls
- DEET-containing insect repellent for the skin
- Digital thermometer
- Iodine tablets (for water purification)
- Oral rehydration salts
- Permethrin-containing insect spray for clothing, tents and bed nets
- Pocket knife
- Prickly-heat powder for heat rashes
- Scissors, safety pins, tweezers
- Sterile needles, syringes and fluids if travelling to remote areas
- Steroid cream or hydrocortisone cream (for allergic rashes)
- Sun block
- Syringes and sterile needles

If you are travelling through a malarial area – particularly an area where falciparum malaria predominates – consider taking a self-diagnostic kit that can identify malaria in the blood from a finger prick.

INTERNET RESOURCES

There is a wealth of travel-health advice available on the internet. For further information, the **Lonely Planet website** (www.lonelyplanet.com) is a good place to start. The WHO publishes a superb book called *International Travel and Health,* which is revised annually and is available online at no cost. Other websites of general interest in this area are **MD Travel Health** (www.mdtravelhealth.com), which provides complete travel-health recommendations for every country, is updated daily and is also available at no cost; the **Centers for Disease Control and Prevention** (www.cdc.gov); and **Fit for Travel** (www.fitfortravel.scot.nhs.uk), which has up-to-date information about outbreaks and is very user-friendly.

It's also a good idea to consult your government's travel-health website before departure, if one is available:

Australia (www.smarttraveller.gov.au/tips/travelwell.html)

Canada (www.hc-sc.gc.ca/english/index.html)

UK (www.nhs.uk/Healthcareabroad/Pages/Healthcareabroad.aspx)

USA (www.cdc.gov/travel)

HEALTH

FURTHER READING

- *A Comprehensive Guide to Wilderness and Travel Medicine* by Eric A Weiss (1998)
- *Healthy Travel* by Jane Wilson-Howarth (1999)
- *Healthy Travel Africa* by Isabelle Young (2000)
- *How to Stay Healthy Abroad* by Richard Dawood (2002)
- *Travel in Health* by Graham Fry (1994)
- *Travel with Children* by Cathy Lanigan (2009)

IN TRANSIT

DEEP VEIN THROMBOSIS (DVT)

Blood clots can form in the legs during flights, chiefly because of prolonged immobility. This formation of clots is known as deep vein thrombosis (DVT), and the longer the flight, the greater the risk. Although most blood clots are reabsorbed uneventfully, some might break off and travel through the blood vessels to the lungs, where they could cause life-threatening complications.

The chief symptom of DVT is swelling or pain of the foot, ankle or calf, usually but not always on just one side. When a blood clot travels to the lungs, it could cause chest pain and breathing difficulty. Travellers with any of these symptoms should immediately seek medical attention.

To prevent the development of DVT on flights you should walk about the cabin, perform isometric compressions of the leg muscles (ie contract the leg muscles while sitting), drink plenty of fluids, and avoid alcohol.

JET LAG & MOTION SICKNESS

If you're crossing more than five time zones you could suffer jet lag, resulting in insomnia, fatigue, malaise or nausea. To avoid jet lag drink plenty of (nonalcoholic) fluids and eat light meals. Upon arrival, get exposure to natural sunlight and readjust your schedule (for meals, sleep, etc) as soon as possible.

Antihistamines such as dimenhydrinate (Dramamine) and meclizine (Antivert, Bonine) are usually the first choice for treating motion sickness. The main side effect of these drugs is drowsiness. A herbal alternative is ginger (in the form of ginger tea, ginger biscuits or crystallized ginger), which works like a charm for some people.

IN WEST AFRICA

AVAILABILITY & COST OF HEALTH CARE

Health care in West Africa is varied: it can be excellent in the major cities, which generally have well-trained doctors and nurses, but it is often patchy off the beaten track. Medicine and even sterile dressings and intravenous fluids might need to be purchased from a local pharmacy by patients or their relatives. The standard of dental care is equally variable, and there is an increased risk of hepatitis B and HIV transmission via poorly sterilised equipment. By and large, public hospitals in Africa offer the cheapest service, but will have the least up-to-date equipment and medications; mission hospitals (where donations are the usual form of payment) often have more reasonable facilities; and private hospitals and clinics are more expensive but tend to have more advanced drugs and equipment and better-trained medical staff.

Most drugs can be purchased over the counter in West Africa, without a prescription. Many drugs for sale in West Africa might be ineffective: they might be counterfeit or might not have been stored under the right conditions. The most common examples of counterfeit drugs are malaria tablets and expensive antibiotics, such as ciprofloxacin. Most drugs are available in capital cities, but remote villages will be lucky to have a couple of paracetamol tablets. It is recommended that all drugs for chronic diseases be brought from home. Also, the availability and efficacy of condoms cannot be relied on – bring contraception. Condoms bought in West Africa might not be of the same quality as in Europe or Australia, and they might not have been correctly stored.

There is a high risk of contracting HIV from infected blood if you receive a blood transfusion in West Africa. To minimise this, seek out treatment in reputable clinics, such as those recommended in the country chapters of this book. If you have any doubts, the **BloodCare Foundation** (www.blood care.org.uk) is a useful source of safe, screened blood, which can be transported to any part of the world within 24 hours.

The cost of health care might seem cheap compared to its cost in first-world countries, but good care and drugs might not be available. Evacuation to good medical care (within West Africa or to your own country) can be very expensive. Unfortunately, adequate health care is available only to very few West Africans.

INFECTIOUS DISEASES

It's a formidable list but, as we say, a few precautions go a long way…

Cholera

Although small outbreaks can occur, cholera is usually only a problem during natural or humanmade disasters. Travellers are rarely affected. It is caused by a bacteria and spread via contaminated drinking water. The main symptom is profuse, watery diarrhoea, which causes debilitation if fluids are not replaced quickly. An oral cholera vaccine is available, but it is not particularly effective. Most cases of cholera could be avoided by making sure you drink clean water and by avoiding potentially contaminated food. Treatment is by fluid replacement (orally or via a drip), but sometimes antibiotics are needed. Self-treatment is not advised.

Dengue Fever

Found in Senegal, Burkina Faso, Guinea, and some parts of East and Southern Africa, dengue fever (also called 'breakbone fever') is spread by mosquito bites. It causes a feverish illness with headache and muscle pains similar to those experienced with a bad, prolonged attack of influenza. There might be a rash. Self-treatment: paracetamol and rest.

Diphtheria

Spread through close respiratory contact, diphtheria is found in all of Africa. It usually causes a temperature and a severe sore throat. Sometimes a membrane forms across the throat, and a tracheostomy is needed to prevent suffocation. Vaccination is recommended for those likely to be in close contact with the local population in infected areas. More important for long stays than for short-term trips, the vaccine is given as an injection alone or with tetanus, and lasts 10 years.

Filariasis

Tiny worms migrating in the lymphatic system cause filariasis. It is found in most of West, Central, East and Southern Africa, and in Sudan in North Africa. A bite from an infected mosquito spreads the infection. Symptoms include itching and swelling of the legs and/or genitalia. Treatment is available.

Hepatitis A

Found in all of Africa, Hepatitis A is spread through contaminated food (particularly shellfish) and water. It causes jaundice and is rarely fatal, but can cause prolonged lethargy and delayed recovery. If you've had hepatitis A, you shouldn't drink alcohol for up to six months after, but once you've recovered, there won't be any long-term problems. The first symptoms include dark urine and a yellow colour to the whites of the eyes. Sometimes a fever and abdominal pain might occur. Hepatitis A vaccine (Avaxim, VAQTA, Havrix) is given as an injection: a single dose will give protection for a year, and a booster after a year gives 10-year protection. Hepatitis A and typhoid vaccines can also be given as a single-dose vaccine (Hepatyrix or Viatim).

Hepatitis B

Spread through infected blood, contaminated needles and sexual intercourse, Hepatitis B is found in Africa. It can be spread from an infected mother to the baby in childbirth. It affects the liver, causing jaundice and occasionally liver failure. Most people recover completely, but some might be chronic carriers of the virus, which can lead eventually to cirrhosis or liver cancer. Those visiting high-risk areas for long periods or with increased social or occupational risk should be immunised. Many countries now give Hepatitis B as part of the routine childhood vaccination. It is given singly or can be given at the same time as Hepatitis A (Hepatyrix).

A course of vaccinations will give protection for at least five years. It can be given over four weeks or six months.

HIV

Human immunodeficiency virus (HIV), the virus that causes acquired immune deficiency syndrome (AIDS), is a huge problem in Africa but is most acutely felt in sub-Saharan Africa. The virus is spread through infected blood and blood products, by sexual intercourse with an infected partner, and from an infected mother to her baby during childbirth and breastfeeding. It can be spread through 'blood to blood' contacts, such as with contaminated instruments during medical, dental, acupuncture and other body-piercing procedures, and through sharing intravenous needles. At present there is no cure; medication that might keep the disease under control is available, but these drugs are too expensive for the overwhelming majority of Africans, and are not readily available for travellers either. If you think you might have been infected with HIV, a blood test is necessary; a three-month gap after exposure and before testing is required to allow antibodies to appear in the blood.

Leptospirosis

This is found in West and Southern Africa; in Chad, Congo and Democratic Republic of the Congo in Central Africa; in Algeria, Morocco and Sudan in North Africa; and in Ethiopia and Somalia in East Africa. It is spread through the excreta of infected rodents, especially rats. It can cause hepatitis and renal failure, which might be fatal. It is unusual for travellers to be affected unless they're living in poor sanitary conditions. It causes a fever and sometimes jaundice.

Malaria

One million children die annually from malaria in Africa. The risk of malarial transmission at altitudes higher than 2000m is rare. The disease is caused by a parasite in the bloodstream spread via the bite of the female Anopheles mosquito. There are several types of malaria, falciparum malaria being the most dangerous and the predominant form in Africa. Infection rates vary with season and climate, so check out the situation before departure. Unlike most other diseases regularly encountered by travellers, there is no vaccination against malaria (yet). However, several different drugs are used to prevent malaria, and new ones are in the pipeline. Up-to-date advice from a travel-health clinic is essential, as some medication is more suitable for some travellers than for others. The pattern of drug-resistant malaria is changing rapidly, so what was advised several years ago might no longer be the case.

Malaria can present in several ways. The early stages include headache, fever, general aches and pains, and malaise, which could

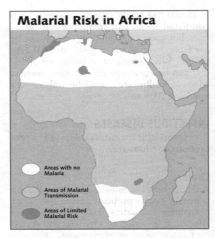

Malarial Risk in Africa

Areas with no Malaria

Areas of Malarial Transmission

Areas of Limited Malarial Risk

be mistaken for flu. Other symptoms include abdominal pain, diarrhoea and a cough. Anyone who gets a fever in a malarial area should assume infection until a blood test proves negative, even if you have been taking antimalarial medication. If not treated, the next stage could develop within 24 hours, particularly if falciparum malaria is the parasite: jaundice, then reduced consciousness and coma (known as cerebral malaria), followed by death. Treatment in hospital is essential, and the death rate can still be as high as 10% even in the best intensive-care facilities.

Many travellers are under the impression that malaria is a mild illness, that treatment is always easy and successful, and that taking antimalarial drugs causes more illness through side effects than actually getting malaria. In Africa, this is unfortunately not true. Side effects of the medication depend on the drug being taken. Doxycycline can cause heartburn and indigestion; mefloquine (Larium) can cause anxiety attacks, insomnia, nightmares and (rarely) severe psychiatric disorders; chloroquine can cause nausea and hair loss; and proguanil can cause mouth ulcers. These side effects are not universal and can be minimized by taking medication correctly, eg with food. Also, some people should not take a particular antimalarial drug, eg people with epilepsy should avoid mefloquine, and doxycycline should not be taken by pregnant women or children younger than 12.

If you decide that you really do not wish to take antimalarial drugs, you must understand

---

THE ANTIMALARIAL A TO D

A – Awareness of the risk. No medication is totally effective, but protection of up to 95% is achievable with most drugs, as long as other measures have been taken.

B – Bites – avoid at all costs. Sleep in a screened room, use a mosquito spray or coils, sleep under a permethrin-impregnated net. Cover up at night with long trousers and long sleeves, preferably with permethrin-treated clothing. Apply appropriate repellent to all areas of exposed skin in the evenings.

C – Chemical prevention (ie antimalarial drugs) is usually needed in malarial areas. Expert advice is needed as resistance patterns can change, and new drugs are in development. Not all antimalarial drugs are suitable for everyone. Most antimalarial drugs need to be started at least a week in advance and continued for four weeks after the last possible exposure to malaria.

D – Diagnosis. If you have a fever or flu-like illness within a year of travel to a malarial area, malaria is a possibility, and immediate medical attention is necessary.

---

the risks and be obsessive about avoiding mosquito bites. Use nets and insect repellent, and report any fever or flu-like symptoms to a doctor as soon as possible. Some people advocate homeopathic preparations against malaria, such as Demal200, but as yet there is no conclusive evidence that this is effective, and many homeopaths do not recommend their use.

People of all ages can contract malaria, and falciparum causes the most severe illness. Repeated infections might result eventually in less serious illness. Malaria in pregnancy frequently results in miscarriage or premature labour. Adults who have survived childhood malaria have developed immunity and usually only develop mild cases of malaria; most Western travellers have no immunity at all. Immunity wanes after 18 months of nonexposure, so even if you've had malaria in the past and used to live in a malaria-prone area, you might no longer be immune.

If you are planning a journey in a malarial area, particularly where falciparum malaria predominates, consider taking standby treatment. Standby treatment should be seen as emergency treatment aimed at saving the patient's life and not as routine self-medication. It should be used only if you will be far from medical facilities and have been advised about the symptoms of malaria and how to use the medication. Medical advice should be sought as soon as possible to confirm whether the treatment has been successful. The type of standby treatment used will depend on local conditions, such as drug resistance, and on what antimalarial drugs were being used before standby treatment. This is worthwhile, because you want to avoid contracting a particularly serious form such as cerebral malaria, which affects the brain and central nervous system and can be fatal in 24 hours. Self-diagnostic kits, which can identify malaria in the blood from a finger prick, are also available in the West (see p851).

The risks from malaria to both mother and foetus during pregnancy are considerable. Unless good medical care can be guaranteed, travel throughout Africa when pregnant – particularly to malarial areas – should be discouraged unless essential.

Meningococcal Meningitis

Meningococcal infection is spread through close respiratory contact and is more likely in crowded situations, such as dormitories, buses and clubs. Infection is uncommon in travellers. Vaccination is recommended for long stays and is especially important towards the end of the dry season, which varies across the continent (see p15). Symptoms include a fever, severe headache, neck stiffness and a red rash. Immediate medical treatment is necessary.

The ACWY vaccine is recommended for all travellers in sub-Saharan Africa. This vaccine is different from the meningococcal meningitis C vaccine given to children and adolescents in some countries; it is safe to be given both types of vaccine.

Onchocerciasis

Also known as 'river blindness', this is caused by the larvae of a tiny worm, which is spread by the bite of a small fly. The earliest sign of infection is intensely itchy, red, sore eyes. Travellers are rarely severely affected. Treatment in a specialised clinic is curative.

Poliomyelitis

Polio is generally spread through contaminated food and water. The vaccine is one of those given in childhood and should be boosted every 10 years, either orally (a drop on the tongue) or as an injection. Polio can be carried asymptomatically (ie showing no symptoms) and could cause a transient fever. In rare cases it causes weakness or paralysis of one or more muscles, which might be permanent. The WHO states that Nigeria and Niger are polio hotspots following recent outbreaks.

Rabies

Rabies is spread by receiving the bites or licks of an infected animal on broken skin. It's fatal once the clinical symptoms start (which might be up to several months after the injury), so post-bite vaccination should be given as soon as possible. Post-bite vaccination (whether or not you've been vaccinated before the bite) prevents the virus from spreading to the central nervous system. Animal handlers should be vaccinated, as should those travelling to remote areas where a source of post-bite vaccine is not available within 24 hours. Three preventative injections are needed in a month. If you have not been vaccinated you will need a course of five injections starting 24 hours or as soon as possible after the injury. If you have been vaccinated, you will need fewer post-bite injections and will have more time to seek medical aid.

Schistosomiasis

Also called bilharzia, this disease is spread by flukes that are carried by a species of freshwater snail. The flukes are carried inside the snail, which then sheds them into slow-moving or still water. The parasites penetrate human skin during paddling or swimming and then migrate to the bladder or bowel. They are passed out via stools or urine and can contaminate fresh water, where the cycle starts again. Avoid paddling or swimming in suspect freshwater lakes or slow-running rivers. There may be no symptoms or there may be a transient fever and rash, and advanced cases can have blood in the stool or in the urine. A blood test can detect antibodies if you have been exposed, and treatment is then possible in travel- or infectious-disease clinics. If not treated, the infection can cause kidney failure or permanent bowel damage. It isn't possible for you to infect others.

Tuberculosis (TB)

TB is spread through close respiratory contact and occasionally through infected milk or milk products. BCG (Bacille Calmette-Guérin) vaccination is recommended for those likely to be mixing closely with the local population, although it gives only moderate protection against TB. It is more important for long stays than for short-term stays. Inoculation with the BCG vaccine is not available in all countries. It is given routinely to many children in developing countries. The vaccination causes a small, permanent scar at the injection site and is usually given in a specialised chest clinic. It is a live vaccine and should not be given to pregnant women or immunocompromised individuals.

TB can be asymptomatic, only being picked up on a routine chest X-ray. Alternatively, it can cause a cough, weight loss or fever, sometimes months or even years after exposure.

Typhoid

This is spread through food or water contaminated by infected human faeces. The first symptom is usually a fever or a pink rash on the abdomen. Sometimes septicaemia (blood poisoning) can occur. A typhoid vaccine (typhim Vi, typherix) will give protection for three years. In some countries, the oral vaccine Vivotif is also available. Antibiotics are usually given as treatment, and death is rare unless septicaemia occurs.

Trypanosomiasis

Spread via the bite of the tsetse fly, trypanosomiasis, also called 'sleeping sickness', causes a headache, fever and eventually coma. There is an effective treatment.

Yellow Fever

Travellers should carry a certificate as evidence of vaccination if they have recently been in an infected country, to avoid any possible difficulties with immigration. For a full list of these countries visit the **WHO website** (www .who.int/en) or the **Centers for Disease Control and Prevention website** (www.cdc.gov/travel). There is always the possibility that a traveller without a legally required, up-to-date certificate will be vaccinated and detained in isolation at the port of arrival for up to 10 days or possibly repatriated.

Yellow fever is spread by infected mosquitoes. Symptoms range from a flu-like illness to severe hepatitis (liver inflammation), jaundice and death. The yellow-fever vaccination must be given at a designated clinic and is

Yellow Fever Risk in Africa

Areas with no
Yellow Fever

Endemic Zones

valid for 10 years. It is a live vaccine and must not be given to immunocompromised or pregnant travellers.

TRAVELLER'S DIARRHOEA

It's not inevitable that you will get diarrhoea while travelling in Africa, but it's certainly likely. Diarrhoea is the most common travel-related illness – figures suggest that at least half of all travellers to Africa will get diarrhoea at some stage. Sometimes dietary changes, such as increased spices or oils, are the cause. To help prevent diarrhoea, avoid tap water unless you're sure it's safe to drink (see p858). You should only eat cooked or peeled fresh fruits or vegetables, and be wary of dairy products that might contain unpas-

teurised milk. Although freshly cooked food can often be a safe option, plates or serving utensils might be dirty, so you should be very selective when eating food from street vendors (make sure that cooked food is piping hot all the way through). If you develop diarrhoea, be sure to drink plenty of fluids, preferably an oral rehydration solution containing water, and some salt and sugar. A few loose stools don't require treatment, but if you start having more than four or five a day you should start taking an antibiotic (often a quinoline drug, such as ciprofloxacin or norfloxacin) and an antidiarrhoeal agent (such as loperamide) if you are not within easy reach of a toilet. If diarrhoea is bloody, persists for over 72 hours or is accompanied by fever, shaking, chills or severe abdominal pain, you should seek medical attention.

Amoebic Dysentery

Contracted by eating contaminated food and water, amoebic dysentery causes blood and mucus in the faeces. It can be relatively mild and tends to come on gradually, but seek medical advice if you think you have the illness, as it won't clear up without treatment (which is with specific antibiotics).

Giardiasis

Like amoebic dysentery, this caused by ingesting contaminated food or water. The illness appears a week or more after you have been exposed to the parasite. Giardiasis might cause only a short-lived bout of traveller's diarrhoea, but it can cause persistent diarrhoea. Seek medical advice if you suspect you have

---

MANDATORY YELLOW-FEVER VACCINATION

▪ North Africa – Not mandatory for any of North Africa, but Algeria, Libya and Tunisia require evidence of yellow-fever vaccination if entering from an infected country. It is recommended for travellers to Sudan, and might be given to unvaccinated travellers leaving the country.

▪ Central Africa – Mandatory in Central African Republic (CAR), Congo, Democratic Republic of the Congo, Equatorial Guinea and Gabon, and recommended in Chad.

▪ West Africa – Mandatory in Benin, Burkina Faso, Cameroon, Côte d'Ivoire, Ghana, Liberia, Mali, Niger, Sao Tome & Principe and Togo, and recommended for The Gambia, Guinea, Guinea-Bissau, Mauritania, Nigeria, Senegal and Sierra Leone.

▪ East Africa – Mandatory in Rwanda; it is advised for Burundi, Ethiopia, Kenya, Somalia, Tanzania and Uganda.

▪ Southern Africa – Not mandatory for entry into any countries of Southern Africa, although it is necessary if entering from an infected country.

giardiasis, but if you are in a remote area you could start a course of antibiotics.

ENVIRONMENTAL HAZARDS
Heat Exhaustion

This condition occurs following heavy sweating and excessive fluid loss with inadequate replacement of fluids and salt, and is common in hot climates when taking exercise before full acclimatisation. Symptoms include headache, dizziness and tiredness. Dehydration is happening by the time you feel thirsty – aim to drink sufficient water to produce pale, diluted urine. Treatment: fluid replacement with water and/or fruit juice, and cooling by cold water and fans. The treatment of the salt-loss component consists of consuming salty fluids, as in soup, and adding a bit more salt to food than usual.

Heatstroke

Heat exhaustion is a precursor to the much more serious heatstroke. In this case there is damage to the sweating mechanism, with an excessive rise in body temperature; irrational and hyperactive behaviour; and eventually loss of consciousness and death. Rapid cooling by spraying the body with water and fanning is best. Emergency fluid and electrolyte replacement is required by intravenous drip.

Insect Bites & Stings

Mosquitoes might not always carry malaria or dengue fever, but they (and other insects) can cause irritation and infected bites. To avoid these, take the same precautions as you would for avoiding malaria (see p854). Use DEET-based insect repellents. Excellent clothing treatments are also available; mosquitos that land on treated clothing will die.

Bee and wasp stings cause real problems only to those who have a severe allergy to the stings (anaphylaxis). If you are one of these people, carry an EpiPen – an adrenaline (epinephrine) injection, which you can give yourself. This could save your life.

Sandflies are found around the beaches. They usually only cause a nasty, itchy bite but can carry a rare skin disorder called cutaneous leishmaniasis. Prevention of bites with DEET-based repellents is sensible.

Scorpions are frequently found in arid or dry climates. They have a painful sting that is sometimes life-threatening. If stung by a scorpion, seek immediate medical assistance.

Bed bugs are found in hostels and cheap hotels and lead to itchy, lumpy bites. Spraying the mattress with crawling-insect killer after changing bedding will get rid of them.

Scabies are also found in cheap accommodation. These tiny mites live in the skin, often between the fingers, and they cause an intensely itchy rash. The itch is easily treated with malathion and permethrin lotion from a pharmacy; other members of the household also need treating to avoid spreading scabies, even if they do not show any symptoms.

Snake Bites

Avoid getting bitten! Don't walk barefoot, or stick your hand into holes or cracks. However, 50% of those bitten by venomous snakes are not actually injected with poison. If bitten by a snake, do not panic. Immobilise the bitten limb with a splint (such as a stick) and apply a bandage over the site, with firm pressure (similar to bandaging a sprain). Do not apply a tourniquet, or cut or suck the bite. Get medical help as soon as possible so antivenom can be given if needed. It will help get you the correct antivenin if you can identify the snake, so try to take note of its appearance.

Water

Never drink tap water unless it has been boiled, filtered or chemically disinfected (eg with iodine tablets). Never drink from streams, rivers or lakes. It's best to avoid drinking from pumps and wells – some do bring pure water to the surface, but the presence of animals can contaminate supplies.

TRADITIONAL MEDICINE

At least 80% of the African population relies on traditional medicine, often because conventional Western-style medicine is too expensive, because of prevailing cultural attitudes and beliefs, or simply because in some cases it works. It might also be because there's no other choice: a WHO survey found that, although there was only one medical doctor for every 50,000 people in Mozambique, there was a traditional healer for every 200 people.

Although some African remedies seem to work on malaria, sickle cell anaemia, high blood pressure and some AIDS symptoms, most African healers learn their art by apprenticeship, so education (and consequently application of knowledge) is inconsistent and unregulated. Conventionally trained physicians in South Africa, for example, angrily describe how their AIDS patients die of kidney failure because a *sangoma* (traditional healer) has given them an enema containing an essence made from powerful roots. Likewise, when traditional healers administer 'injections' with porcupine quills, knives or dirty razor blades, diseases are often spread or created rather than cured.

Rather than attempting to stamp out traditional practices, or pretend they aren't happening, a positive step taken by some African countries is the regulation of traditional medicine by creating healers' associations and offering courses on such topics as sanitary practices. It remains unlikely in the short term that even a basic level of conventional Western-style medicine will be made available to all the people of Africa (even though the cost of doing so is less than the annual military budget of some Western countries). Traditional medicine, on the other hand, will almost certainly continue to be practised widely throughout the continent.

HEALTH

Language

CONTENTS

West Africa's myriad ethnic groups speak several hundred local languages, many subdivided into numerous distinct dialects. The people of Nigeria – West Africa's most populous country – speak at least 350 languages and dialects, while even tiny Guinea-Bissau (population just over one million) has around 20 languages.

Consequently, common languages are absolutely essential, and several are used. These may be the language of the largest group in a particular area or country. For example, Hausa has spread out from its northern Nigerian heartland to become widely understood as a trading language in the eastern parts of West Africa. Similarly, Dioula has become a common tongue in markets over much of the western part of the region. Also widespread are the former colonial languages of French, English and Portuguese. In some areas, the common tongue is a creole – a combination of native African and imported European languages.

EUROPEAN LANGUAGES

FRENCH

Although we have generally only included the polite form of address with the following phrases – *vous* (you) – the informal mode *tu* is more commonly used in West Africa; you'll hear less *s'il vous plaît* and more *s'il te plaît* (which in France may be considered impolite unless spoken between good friends). If in doubt in Africa (when dealing with border officials or older people) it's always safer to use the polite *vous* form. The pronunciation guides included with each French phrase should help you in getting your message across.

If you fancy getting stuck into your *français* to a greater extent than is possible with what we include here, Lonely Planet's compact *French* phrasebook offers a handy, pocket-sized guide to the language that will cover all your travel needs and more.

Accommodation

I'm looking for a ...	*Je cherche ...*	zher shersh ...
campground	*un camping*	un kom·peeng
hotel	*un hôtel*	un o·tel

Where is a cheap hotel?
Où est-ce qu'on peut trouver un hôtel pas cher?
oo es·kon per troo·vay un o·tel pa shair

Could you write the address, please?
Est-ce que vous pourriez écrire l'adresse, s'il vous plaît?
ay·kreer la·dres seel voo play

Do you have any rooms available?
Est-ce que vous avez   e·sker voo·za·vay
des chambres libres?   day shom·brer lee·brer

How much is it per night/person?
Quel est le prix par   kel e ler pree par
nuit/personne?   nwee/par per·son

May I see it?
Est-ce que je peux voir   es·ker zher per vwa
la chambre?   la shom·brer

Where is the bathroom?
Où est la salle de bains?   oo e la sal der bun

I'd like (a) ...	*Je voudrais ...*	zher voo·dray ...
single room	*une chambre à un lit*	ewn shom·brer a un lee
double-bed room	*une chambre avec un grand lit*	ewn shom·brer a·vek un gron lee
room with two beds	*une chambre avec des lits jumeaux*	ewn shom·brer a·vek day lee zhew·mo

air-conditioning	*climatisation*	klee·ma·tee·za·syon
hot water	*eau chaude*	leeo shod
key	*clef/clé*	klay
sheet	*drap*	drap
shower	*douche*	doosh
toilet	*les toilettes*	lay twa·let

Conversation & Essentials
Hello.	*Bonjour.*	bon·zhoor
Hi.	*Salut.* (inf)	sa·loo
Goodbye.	*Au revoir.*	o·rer·vwa
Yes.	*Oui.*	wee
No.	*Non.*	no
Please.	*S'il vous plaît.*	seel voo play
	S'il te plaît. (inf)	seel ter play
Thank you.	*Merci.*	mair·see
You're welcome.	*Je vous en prie.*	zher voo·zon pree
	De rien. (inf)	der ree·en
Excuse me.	*Excusez-moi.*	ek·skew·zay·mwa
Sorry. (forgive me)	*Pardon.*	par·don

(Have a) good evening.
Bonne soirée.   bon swa·ray

What's your name?
Comment vous   ko·mon voo·za·pay·lay voo
appelez-vous?
Comment tu   ko·mon tew ta·pel
t'appelles? (inf)

My name is ...
Je m'appelle ...   zher ma·pel ...

Where are you from?
De quel pays êtes-vous?   der kel pay·ee et·voo
De quel pays es-tu? (inf)   der kel pay·ee e·tew

I'm from ...
Je viens de ...   zher vyen der ...

I like ...
J'aime ...   zhem ...

I don't like ...
Je n'aime pas ...   zher nem pa ...

Directions
Where is ...?
Où est ...?   oo e ...

Go straight ahead.
Continuez tout droit.   kon·teen·way too drwa

DON'T BE LOST FOR WORDS IN ...

Country	Official Language	Principal African Languages (in this guide)
Benin	French	Fon, Hausa, Yoruba
Burkina Faso	French	Dioula, Fon, Hausa, Moré, Senoufo
Cape Verde	Portuguese	Crioulo
Côte d'Ivoire	French	Dan (Yacouba), Dioula, Hausa, Senoufo
Gambia	English	Diola (Jola), Mandinka, Wolof
Ghana	English	Ewe, Ga, Hausa, Twi
Guinea	French	Fula (Futa Djalon), Malinké, Susu
Guinea-Bissau	Portuguese	Crioulo
Liberia	English	Dan (Yacouba)
Mali	French	Bambara, Malinké, Sangha dialect, Senoufo, Tamashek
Mauritania	Arabic (French also still in common use)	Dioula, Fula (Fulfulde), Hassaniya, Wolof
Niger	French	Djerma, Fon, Hausa, Tamashek
Nigeria	English	Hausa, Igbo, Yoruba
Senegal	French	Crioulo, Diola, Fula (Fulfulde), Malinké, Mandinka, Wolof
Sierra Leone	English	Krio
Togo	French	Ewe, Fon, Kabyé, Mina

LANGUAGE

Turn left.
Tournez à gauche.   toor·nay a gosh
Turn right.
Tournez à droite.   toor·nay a drwat
How many kilometres is …?
À combien de kilomètres   a kom·byun der kee·lo·me·trer
est …?   e …

Health
I'm ill.   *Je suis malade.*   zher swee ma·lad
antiseptic   *l'antiseptique*   lon·tee·sep·teek
condoms   *des préservatifs*   day pray·zair·va·teef
contraceptive   *le contraceptif*   ler kon·tra·sep·teef
diarrhoea   *la diarrhée*   la dya·ray
medicine   *le médicament*   ler may·dee·ka·mon
nausea   *la nausée*   la no·zay
sunblock cream   *la crème solaire*   la krem so·lair
tampons   *des tampons*   day tom·pon
                      hygiéniques   ee·zhen·eek

I'm …   *Je suis …*   zher swee …
  asthmatic   *asthmatique*   (z)as·ma·teek
  diabetic   *diabétique*   dee·a·bay·teek
  epileptic   *épileptique*   (z)ay·pee·lep·teek

I'm allergic   *Je suis*   zher swee
to …   *allergique …*   za·lair·zheek …
  antibiotics   *aux antibiotiques*   o zon·tee·byo·teek
  nuts   *aux noix*   o nwa
  peanuts   *aux cacahuètes*   o ka·ka·wet

Language Difficulties
Do you speak English?
Parlez-vous anglais?   par·lay·voo zong·lay
Does anyone here speak English?
Y a-t-il quelqu'un qui   ya·teel kel·kung kee
parle anglais?   parl ong·glay
I don't understand.
Je ne comprends pas.   zher ner kom·pron pa
Could you write it down, please?
Est-ce que vous pourriez   es·ker voo poo·ryay
l'écrire, s'il vous plaît?   lay·kreer seel voo play
Can you show me (on the map)?
Pouvez-vous m'indiquer   poo·vay·voo mun·dee·kay
(sur la carte)?   (sewr la kart)

Numbers
0	*zéro*	zay·ro
1	*un*	un
2	*deux*	der
3	*trois*	trwa
4	*quatre*	ka·trer
5	*cinq*	sungk
6	*six*	sees
7	*sept*	set

EMERGENCIES

Help!
Au secours!   o skoor
There's been an accident!
Il y a eu un accident!   eel ya ew un ak·see·don
I'm lost.
Je me suis égaré/e. (m/f) zhe me swee·zay·ga·ray
Leave me alone!
Fichez-moi la paix!   fee·shay·mwa la pay

Call …!   *Appelez …!*   a·play …
  a doctor *un médecin*   un mayd·sun
  the police *la police*   la po·lees

8	*huit*	weet
9	*neuf*	nerf
10	*dix*	dees
11	*onze*	onz
12	*douze*	dooz
13	*treize*	trez
14	*quatorze*	ka·torz
15	*quinze*	kunz
16	*seize*	sez
17	*dix-sept*	dee·set
18	*dix-huit*	dee·zweet
19	*dix-neuf*	deez·nerf
20	*vingt*	vung
21	*vingt et un*	vung tay un
22	*vingt-deux*	vung·der
30	*trente*	tront
40	*quarante*	ka·ront
50	*cinquante*	sung·kont
60	*soixante*	swa·sont
70	*soixante-dix*	swa·son·dees
80	*quatre-vingts*	ka·trer·vung
90	*quatre-vingt-dix*	ka·trer·vung·dees
100	*cent*	son
1000	*mille*	meel

Shopping & Services
I'd like to buy …
Je voudrais acheter …   zher voo·dray ash·tay …
How much is it?
C'est combien?   say kom·byun
It's cheap.
Ce n'est pas cher.   ser nay pa shair
It's too expensive.
C'est trop cher.   say tro shair

Can I pay by …? *Est-ce que je peux*   es·ker zher per
                     payer avec …?   pay·yay a·vek …
  credit card   *ma carte de*   ma kart der
                     crédit   kray·dee
  travellers   *des chèques*   day shek
  cheques   *de voyage*   der vwa·yazh

LANGUAGE

I'm just looking.
Je regarde. zher rer·gard
May I look at it?
Est-ce que je peux le voir? es·ker zher per ler vwar

I want to	*Je voudrais*	zher voo·dray
change …	*changer …*	shon·zhay …
(cash) money	*de l'argent*	der lar·zhon
travellers	*des chèques*	day shek
cheques	*de voyage*	der vwa·yazh

more	*plus*	plew
less	*moins*	mwa
smaller	*plus petit*	plew per·tee
bigger	*plus grand*	plew gron

I'm looking for …	*Je cherche …*	zhe shersh …
a bank	*une banque*	ewn bonk
the … embassy	*l'ambassade de …*	lam·ba·sahd der …
the hospital	*l'hôpital*	lo·pee·tal
the market	*le marché*	ler mar·shay
the police	*la police*	la po·lees
the post office	*le bureau de poste*	ler bew·ro der post
a public phone	*une cabine téléphonique*	ewn ka·been tay·lay·fo·neek
a public toilet	*les toilettes*	lay twa·let
the telephone centre	*la centrale téléphonique*	la san·tral tay·lay·fo·neek
the tourist office	*l'office de tourisme*	lo·fees der too·rees·mer

What time does it open/close?
Quelle est l'heure d'ouverture/ de fermeture? kel ay lur doo·ver·tewr/ der fair·mer·tewr

Time & Dates
What time is it?
Quelle heure est-il? kel er e til
It's (8) o'clock.
Il est (huit) heures. il e (weet) er
It's half past …
Il est (…) heures et demie. il e (…) er e day·mee

When?	*Quand?*	kon
in the morning	*du matin*	dew ma·tun
in the afternoon	*de l'après-midi*	der la·pray·mee·dee
in the evening	*du soir*	dew swar
today	*aujourd'hui*	o·zhoor·dwee
tomorrow	*demain*	der·mun
yesterday	*hier*	yair

Monday	*lundi*	lun·dee
Tuesday	*mardi*	mar·dee
Wednesday	*mercredi*	mair·krer·dee
Thursday	*jeudi*	zher·dee
Friday	*vendredi*	von·drer·dee
Saturday	*samedi*	sam·dee
Sunday	*dimanche*	dee·monsh

January	*janvier*	zhon·vyay
February	*février*	fayv·ryay
March	*mars*	mars
April	*avril*	a·vreel
May	*mai*	may
June	*juin*	zhwun
July	*juillet*	zhwee·yay
August	*août*	oot
September	*septembre*	sep·tom·brer
October	*octobre*	ok·to·brer
November	*novembre*	no·vom·brer
December	*décembre*	day·som·brer

Transport
What time does … leave/arrive?	*À quelle heure part/arrive …?*	a kel er par/a·reev …
boat	*le bateau*	ler ba·to
bus	*le bus*	ler bews
train	*le train*	ler trun

I want to go to …
Je voudrais aller à … zher voo·dray a·lay a …
Which bus goes to …?
Quel autobus/car part pour …? kel o·to·boos/ka par poor …
Does this bus go to …?
Ce car là va-t-il à …? ser ka la va·til a …
Please tell me when we arrive in …
Dites-moi quand on arrive à … s'il vous plaît. deet·mwa kon·don a·reev a … seel voo play
Stop here, please.
Arrêtez ici, s'il vous plaît. a·ray·tay ee·see seel voo play

the first	*le premier* (m)	ler prer·myay
	la première (f)	la prer·myair
the last	*le dernier* (m)	ler dair·nyay
	la dernière (f)	la dair·nyair
ticket	*billet*	bee·yay
ticket office	*le guichet*	ler gee·shay
timetable	*l'horaire*	lo·rair
train station	*la gare*	la gar
daily	*chaque jour*	shak zhoor
early	*tôt*	to
late	*tard*	tar
petrol/gas	*essence*	ay·sons
diesel	*diesel*	dyay·zel

I'd like to hire	Je voudrais	zher voo·dray
a/an ...	louer ...	loo·way ...
car	une voiture	ewn vwa·tewr
4WD	un quatre-quatre	un kat·kat
motorbike	une moto	ewn mo·to
bicycle	un vélo	un vay·lo

Is this the road to ...?
C'est la route pour ...?   say la root poor ...
Where's a service station?
Où est-ce qu'il y a   oo es·keel ya
une station-service?   ewn sta·syon·ser·vees
Please fill it up.
Le plein, s'il vous plaît.   ler plun seel voo play
I need a mechanic.
J'ai besoin d'un   zhay ber·zwun dun
mécanicien.   may·ka·nee·syun

PORTUGUESE

Like French, Portuguese is a Romance language (ie one closely derived from Latin). In West Africa it's the official language in Cape Verde and Guinea-Bissau.

Note that Portuguese uses masculine and feminine word endings, usually '-o' and '-a' respectively – to say 'thank you', a man will therefore say *obrigado*, a woman, *obrigada*.

Accommodation

I'm looking for	Procuro ...	proo·koo·roo·...
a ...		
campground	um parque de	oong park·de
	campismo	kang·peezh·moo
hotel	um hotel	oong oo·tel

I'd like a ...	Queria um	kree·a oong
room.	quarto de ...	kwarr·too de ...
double	casal	ka·zal
single	individual	ing·dee·vee·dwal
twin	duplo	doo·ploo

How much is it	Quanto custa	kwang·too koos·ta
per ...?	por ...?	porr ...
night	uma noite	oo·ma noyt
person	pessoa	pso·a

Conversation & Essentials

Hello.	Bom dia.	bong dee·a
Hi.	Olá/Chao.	o·la/chow
Good day.	Bom dia.	bong dee·a
Goodbye.	Adeus/Chao.	a·dyoos/chow
See you later.	Até logo.	a·te lo·goo
How are you?	Como está?	ko·moo shta
Fine, and you?	Tudo bem, e tu?	too·doo beng e too

Yes.	Sim.	seeng
No.	Não.	nowng
Please.	Faz favor.	fash fa·vorr
Thank you (very	(Muito)	(mweeng·too)
much).	Obrigado/a. (m/f)	o·bree·ga·doo/da
You're welcome.	De nada.	de na·da
Excuse me.	Desculpe.	des·koolp
(before asking a question/making a request)		

What's your name?
Como se chama?   ko·moo se sha·ma
My name is ...
Chamo-me ...   sha·moo·me ...
Where are you from?
De onde é?   de ong·de e
I'm from ...
Sou (da/do/de) ...   so (da/do/de) ...

Directions

Where is ...?
Onde fica ...?   ongd fee·ka ...
Can you show me (on the map)?
Pode mostrar-me   pod moos·trarrm
(no mapa)?   (noo ma·pa)
How far is it?
Qual a distância daqui?   kwal a dees·tan·see·a da·kee

Turn ...	Vire ...	veer ...
left	à esquerda	a skerr·da
right	à direita	a dee·ray·ta

straight ahead	em frente	eng frengt
north	norte	nort
south	sul	sool
east	este	esht
west	oeste	oo·esht

Health

I'm ill.
Estou doente.   shto doo·engt
I need a doctor (who speaks English).
Preciso de um médico   pre·see·zoo de oong me·dee·koo
(que fale inglês).   (ke fal eeng·glesh)

antiseptic	antiséptico	an·tee·sep·tee·koo
asthma	asma	azh·ma
condoms	preservativo	pre·zer·va·tee·voo
diarrhoea	diarréia	dee·a·ray·a
fever	febre	febr
painkillers	analgésicos	a·nal·zhe·zee·koos
sanitary napkins	pensos higiénicos	peng·soosh ee·zhee·
		e·nee·koosh
tampons	tampões	tang·poyngsh

I'm allergic   Sou alérgico/a   so a·lerr·zhee·koo/ka
to …   à …   a …
  antibiotics antibióticos   ang·tee·byo
                                   ·tee·koos
  peanuts   amendoins   a·meng·doyngs
  penicillin   penicilina   pnee·see·lee·na

Language Difficulties
Do you speak English?
  Fala inglês?   fa·la eeng·glesh
Does anyone here speak English?
  Alguém aqui fala inglês?   al·geng a·kee fa·la eeng·glesh
I (don't) understand.
  (Não) Entendo.   (nowng) eng·teng·doo
Could you please write it down?
  Pode por favor escrever   po·de·porr fa·vorr es·kre·verr
  num papel?   noom pa·pel

Numbers
0	zero	ze·roo
1	um/uma (m/f)	oong/oo·ma
2	dois/duas (m/f)	doys/dwash
3	três	tresh
4	quatro	kwa·troo
5	cinco	seeng·koo
6	seis	saysh
7	sete	set
8	oito	oy·too
9	nove	nov
10	dez	desh
11	onze	ongz
12	doze	doz
13	treze	trez
14	quatorze	ka·torrz
15	quinze	keengz
16	dezesseis	dze·saysh
17	dezesete	dze·set
18	dezoito	dzoy·too
19	dezenove	dze·nov
20	vinte	veengt
21	vinte e um	veengt e oong
22	vinte e dois	veengt e doysh
30	trinta	treeng·ta
40	quarenta	kwa·reng·ta
50	cinquenta	seeng·kweng·ta
60	sessenta	se·seng·ta
70	setenta	steng·ta
80	oitenta	oy·teng·ta
90	noventa	noo·veng·ta
100	cem	sang
200	duzentos	doo·zeng·toosh
1000	mil	meel

Shopping & Services
What time does … open?
  A que horas abre …?   a ke o·ras abr …
I'd like to buy …
  Queria comprar …   kree·rya kom·prarr …
How much is it?
  Quanto é?   kwang·too e
That's too expensive.
  É muito caro.   e mweeng·too ka·roo

Where is …?   Onde fica …?   ong·de fee·ka …
  a bank   o banco   oo ban·koo
  the … embassy a embaixada   a eng·bai·sha·da
                   do/da …   doo/da …
  a market   o mercado   oo merr·ka·doo
  a pharmacy   uma   oo·ma
   (chemist)   farmácia   far·ma·sya
  the police   o posto de   oo pos·too·de
   station   polícia   poo·lee·see·a
  the post office o correio   oo coo·ray·oo

Can I pay …?   Posso pagar   po·soo pa·garr
                   com …?   kom …
  by credit card cartão de   karr·towng de
                   crédito   kre·dee·too
  by travellers traveler cheque tra·ve·ler she·kee
   cheque

less	menos	me·noos
more	mais	maizh
big	grande	grangd
small	pequeno/a (m/f)	pke·noo/na

Where can I …? Onde posso …?   on·de po·soo …
  change a   trocar traveler troo·karr tra·ve·ler
  travellers cheque cheques   she·kes
  change money trocar   troo·kar
                    dinheiro   dee·nyay·roo

LANGUAGE

Time & Dates

What time is it?

Que horas são?		ke *o*·ras sowng

It's (ten) o'clock.

São (dez) horas.		sowng (desh) *o*·ras

When?

Quando?		kwang·doo

now	*agora*	a·*go*·ra
today	*hoje*	ozh
tomorrow	*amanhã*	a·ma·*nyang*
Monday	*segunda-feira*	sgoon·da·*fay*·ra
Tuesday	*terça-feira*	terr·sa·*fay*·ra
Wednesday	*quarta-feira*	kwarr·ta·*fay*·ra
Thursday	*quinta-feira*	keeng·ta·*fay*·ra
Friday	*sexta-feira*	saysh·ta·*fay*·ra
Saturday	*sábado*	*sa*·ba·doo
Sunday	*domingo*	doo·*meeng*·goo

Transport

Which ... goes	*Qual o ... que*	kwal oo ... ke
to ...?	*vai para ...?*	vai *pa*·ra ...
boat	*barco*	barr·koo
local bus	*autocarro*	ow·too·*ka*·rroo
train	*comboio*	kom·*boy*·oo

Is this the (bus) to ...?

Este (autocarro)		esht (ow·to·*ka*·rroo)
vai para ...?		vai *pa*·ra ...?

What time does it leave?

Que horas sai?		ke *o*·ras sai

What time does it get to ...?

Que horas chega a ...?		ke *o*·ras *she*·ga a ...

A ticket to ...

Um bilhete para ...		oong bee·*lyet pa*·ra ...

I'd like to hire	*Queria alugar ...*	ke·rya a·loo·*garr* ...
a/an ...		
4WD	*um quatro por*	oom *kwa*·troo por
	quatro	*kwa*·troo
bicycle	*uma*	*oo*·ma
	bicicleta	bee·see·*kle*·ta
car	*um carro*	oong *ka*·rroo
motorbike	*uma*	*oo*·ma
	motocicleta	mo·too·see·*kle*·ta

Is this the road to ...?

Esta é a estrada para ...?		esh·ta e a es·*tra*·da *pa*·ra ...

Where's a gas/petrol station?

Onde fica um posto de		on·de *fee*·ka oong *pos*·too de
gasolina?		ga·zoo·*lee*·na

Please fill it up.

Enche o depósito, por		en·she oo de·*po*·see·too porr
favor.		fa·*vorr*

I need a mechanic.

Preciso de um		pre·*see*·soo de oong
mecânico.		me·*ka*·nee·koo

diesel	*diesel*	dee·sel
petrol/gas	*gasolina*	ga·zoo·*lee*·na

AFRICAN LANGUAGES

Representing many African languages in the Roman alphabet is a difficult task, as many of Africa's languages don't have an official written form. In our written representations, italics indicate which syllable takes the stress within a word. Syllables themselves are separated by dots.

BAMBARA & DIOULA

Differences between Bambara and Dioula (also known as Jula) are relatively minor and the two languages share much of their vocabulary, eg 'Goodbye' in Bambara is *kan·bay,* in Dioula it is *an·bay.*

Bambara (called *bamanakan* in Bambara) is the predominant indigenous language of Mali, while Dioula is widely spoken as a first language in Côte d'Ivoire and Burkina Faso. Dioula is one of West Africa's major lingua francas (a common language used for communication between groups with different mother tongues) so the words and phrases included here can be used not only in Burkina Faso, Côte d'Ivoire and Mali but also in southeastern Mauritania (Néma and the south), eastern Senegal, and parts of Gambia. In addition, there are distinct similarities between Bambara/Dioula and the Mandinka of northern Gambia and parts of southern Senegal, and most Senoufo speakers in southern Mali (Sikasso region), southwestern Burkina Faso, and northern Côte d'Ivoire (Korhogo region) can speak Bambara/Dioula. It's not hard to see that some knowledge of it will prove very useful in this part of West Africa!

Bambara and Dioula are normally written using a phonetic alphabet; in this guide we've mostly used letters common to English. Some specific pronunciations you need to be aware of are:

a	as in 'far'
e	as in 'bet'
i	as in 'marine'

o	as in 'hot'
u	between the 'u' in 'pull' and the 'oo' in 'boot'
g	always hard, as in 'get'
j	as in 'jet'
ñ	as in the 'ni' in 'onion'
ng	as the 'ng' in 'sing' – indicates that the preceding vowel is nasal
r	almost a 'd' sound

In the following phrase lists variation in vocabulary is indicated by (B) for Bambara and (D) for Dioula.

Greetings

The response to any of the following greetings (beginning with i·ni· …) is n·ba (for men) and n·seh (for women).

Hello.	i·ni·*che*
Hello. (to someone working)	i·ni·*baa*·ra (literally 'to you and your work')
Good morning.	i·ni·*so*·go·ma (sunrise to midday)
Good afternoon.	i·ni·*ti*·le (12 noon to 3 pm)
Good evening.	i·ni·*wu*·la (3 pm to sunset)
Good night.	i·ni·*su* (sunset to sunrise)
Goodbye.	kan·beng (B) an·beng (D)
Please.	S'il vous plaît. (French)
Thank you.	i·ni·*che/ba*·si·tay (lit: no problem)
Sorry/Pardon.	ha·ke·to
Yes.	a·wo
No.	a·yee (B)/*uh*·uh (D)
How are you?	i·ka·kéné
I'm fine.	tu·*ro*·te
And you?	e·dung?

Can you help me please?
 ha·ke·to, i·*bay*·say·ka nn de·me wa?
Do you speak English?
 i·be·say·ka *aang*·gi·li·*kaang* meng wa?
Do you speak French?
 i·be·se·ka tu·*ba*·bu·*kan* meng wa?
I only speak English.
 nn·be·se·ka *aang*·gi·li·kaang meng do·ron
I speak a little French.
 nn·be·se·ka tu·*ba*·bu·*kan* meng *do*·nee

I understand.	nn·*y'a*·fa·mu
I don't understand.	nn·*m'a*·fa·mu
What's your (first) name?	i·to·go?
My name is …	nn·to·go …
Where are you from?	i·be·bo·*ming*?

I'm from …	nn·be·bo …
Where is …?	… be·*ming*?
Is it far?	a·ka·*jang*·wa?
straight ahead	a·be·ti·*leng*
left	nu·man·bo·lo·fe (lit: nose-picking hand)
right	ki·ni·bo·lo·fe (lit: rice-eating hand)
How much is this?	ni·*ñe*·jo·li·ye?
That's too much.	a·*ka*·ge·leng—*ba*·ri·ka! (lit: lower the price)
Leave me alone!	bo'i·sa!

1	ke·leng
2	fi·*la* (or fla)
3	saab·ba
4	na·ni
5	du·ru
6	wo·ro
7	wo·lon·fla
8	shay·ging
9	ko·nong·taang
10	taang
11	taang·ni·kay·len
12	taang·ni·*fla*
13	taang·ni·sa·ba
14	taang·ni·*na*·ni
15	taang·ni·*doo*·ru
16	taang·ni·wo·ro
17	taang·ni·wo·lon·fla
18	taang·ni·*shay*·ging
19	taang·ni ko·non·*taang*
20	mu·*gang*
30	bi·saab·ba
31	bi·saab·ba·ni·*ke*·leng
40	bi·na·ni
50	bi·du·ru
60	bi·wo·ro
70	bi·wo·lon·*fla*
80	bi·shay·ging
90	bie·ko·non·taang
100	ke·me
1000	wa
5000	wa·du·ru

LANGUAGE

CRIOULO

Crioulo is a Portuguese-based creole spoken (with more or less mutual intelligibility) in the Cape Verde islands, Guinea-Bissau (where it's the lingua franca and 'market language') and parts of Senegal and Gambia. Nearly half the Crioulo speakers of Cape Verde are literate in Portuguese, but since independence in 1975, Crioulo has become increasingly dominant; upwards of 70% of the country's population speak Crioulo. Even allowing for regional differences, the phrases listed below should be understood in both Cape Verde and Guinea-Bissau.

Good morning.	bom·*dee*·a
Good evening.	bow·a *no*·tay
Goodbye.	*na*·buy
How are you?	ou·*kor*·po ees·ta·*bon?*
I'm fine.	ta·*bon*
Please.	pur·fa·*bor*
Thank you.	ob·ree·*ga*·do
How much is it?	kal e *pre*·su

1	aan
2	dos
3	tres
4	*kwa*·tu
5	*sin*·ku
6	*say*·es
7	se·tee
8	*oy*·tu
9	*no*·vee
10	des
11	*oan*·zee
12	*do*·zee
13	*tre*·zee
14	ka·*to*·zee
15	*kin*·zee
16	dee·za·*say*·es
17	dee·za·*se*·tee
18	dee·*zoy*·tu
19	dee·za·*no*·vee
20	*vin*·tee
30	*trin*·ta
100	sen
1000	meel

DAN (YACOUBA)

Dan (also known as Yacouba) is one of the principal African languages spoken in Côte d'Ivoire (in and around Man). There are also a significant number of Dan speakers in Liberia (where it's referred to as 'Gio').

There are a couple of major dialects and more than 20 subdialects; as a result most communication between different language groups in the region is carried out in Dioula (see the Bambara/Dioula section on p867 for a comprehensive list of Dioula words and phrases).

Good morning. (to a man)	un·*zhoo*·ba·bo
Good morning. (to a woman)	*na*·ba·bo
Good evening. (to a man)	un·*zhoo*·attoir
Good evening. (to a woman)	*na*·attoir
How are you?	bwee·*aar*·way
Thank you.	*ba*·lee·ka

DIOLA (JOLA)

The Diola people inhabit the Casamance region of Senegal, and also the south-western parts of Gambia, where their name is spelt Jola. Their language is Diola, also known as Jola, which should not be confused with the Dioula/Jula spoken widely in other parts of West Africa.

Diola society is segmented and very flexible, so several dialects have developed which may not be mutually intelligible between different groups even though the area inhabited by the Diola is relatively small.

Hello/Welcome.	*ka·sou·mai·kep*
(response)	*ka·sou·mai·kep*
Goodbye.	*ou·ka·to·rra*

DIOULA (JULA)

See Bambara/Dioula (p867).

DJERMA (ZARMA)

After Hausa, Djerma (pronounced 'jer·ma', also known as Zarma) is Niger's most common African language (people with Djerma as their first language make up around a quarter of the country's population). It's spoken mostly in the western regions including around Niamey, and it is one of the official national languages used for radio broadcasts.

Good morning.	ma·teen·ke·*nee*
Good evening.	ma·teen·*hee*·ree
How are you?	*bar*·ka?
Thank you.	fo·fo
Goodbye.	ka·*la* ton·ton

EWE

Ewe (pronounced 'ev-vay') is the major indigenous language of southern Togo. It is also an official language of instruction in primary and secondary schools in Ghana where it's spoken mainly in the east of the country. You'll find that Twi (the language of the Ashanti and the Fanti, see p876) is the more universally spoken language of Ghana. There are also several closely related languages and dialects of Ewe spoken in Benin.

Good morning/	nee-*lye*-nee-aa
Good evening.	
(response)	*mee*-lay
What's your name?	n-ko-*wo*-day?
My name is ...	nk-nee-*n*-yay ...
How are you?	nee-*fo*-a?
I'm fine.	*mee*-fo
Thank you.	mou-*do*, ack-pay-*now*
Goodbye.	mee-*a* do-go

FON (FONGBE)

Fon (called *Fongbe* in the language itself) belongs to the Kwa group of the Gbe language family, *gbe* being the Fon word for 'language'. It is another of the major lingua francas of West Africa, spoken for the most part in Nigeria and Benin, but also used widely in Côte d'Ivoire, Burkina Faso, Niger and Togo. While Fon is subject to clear dialectal variation depending on the region, you should find that the list of words and phrases below will be universally understood.

The Fon language is written using the IPA (International Phonetic Alphabet); for the sake of simplicity we've used a pronunciation system that uses letters common to English. Fon is a tone language (ie intended meaning is dependent upon changes in pitch within the normal range of a speaker's voice) with a standard system of five tones. In this guide we have simplified things by using only two written accents for tones: an acute accent (eg **á**) for a high tone; a grave accent (eg **à**) for a low tone; an unmarked vowel has a mid-tone.

Pronounce letters as you would in English, keeping the following points in mind:

a	as in 'far'
e	as in 'met'
i	as in 'marine'
o	either as in 'hot' or as in 'for'
u	as in 'put'
g	as in 'go'
h	silent
ng	indicates that the preceding vowel is nasalised, eg the 'ing' sound in 'sing'
ñ	as the 'ni' in 'onion'

Hello.	ò-*kú*
Goodbye.	é-*dà*-bò
Please.	kèng-*kéng*-lèng
Thank you.	à-*wà*-nu
You're welcome.	é-*sù*-kpé-a
Sorry/Pardon.	kèng-*kéng*-lèng
Yes.	*eng*
No.	é-*wo*
How are you?	ne-à-*dè*-gbòng?
I'm fine.	ùn-*dò*-gàng-jí
And you?	*hwe*-lo?
Can you help	kèng-*kéng*-lèng-
me please?	dá-lò-mì?

Do you speak ...?	à-*sè* ... à?
English	glèng-*síng*-gbè
French	flàng-*sé*-gbè

I only speak English.
glèng-*síng*-gbè ké-dé-wè-ùn-sè
I speak a little French.
ùn-sè flàng-*sé*-gbè kpè-dè

I understand.	ùn-*mò*-nu-jé-mè
I don't understand.	ùn-*mò*-nu-jé-mè-a
What's your name?	ne-à-*nò*-ñí?
My name is ...	ùn-*nò*-ñí ...
Where are you from?	tò-té-mè-nù-wé-ñí-wè?
I'm from ...	... nù-wé-ñí-mì
Where is ...?	fi-té-wé ...?
Is it far?	e-ling-wé-a?
straight ahead	tre-le-le
left	à-*myò*
right	à-*dì*-sí
How much is this?	nà-bí-wè-ñí-é-lò?
That's too much.	é-vá-khì-*díng*
Leave me alone!	jo-mí-*dó*!

1	ò-*de*
2	ò-*wè*
3	à-*tòng*
4	e-*nè*
5	à-*tóng*
6	à-yì-*zéng*
7	te-*we*
8	ta-*to*
9	téng-*nè*
10	*wo*
11	wo-dò-*kpó*

12	*we·wè*
13	*wa·tòng*
14	*we·nè*
15	*à·fò·tòn*
16	*à·fò·tòng·nù·kúng·dò·pó*
17	*à·fò·tóng·nu·kúng·wè*
18	*à·fò·tóng·nu·kúng·à·tòng*
19	*à·fò·tóng·nu·kúng·è·ne*
20	*kò*
30	*gbàng*
40	*kàng·dé*
50	*kàng·dé·wo*
60	*kàng·dé·ko*
70	*kàng·dé·gbàng*
80	*kàng·wè*
90	*kàng·wè·wo*
100	*kàng·wè·kò*
1000	*à·fà·tóng*

FULA (PULAAR)

Fula (which is also known as Pulaar) is one of the languages of the Fula people found across West Africa, from northern Senegal to Sudan in the east, and as far south as Ghana and Nigeria. The Fula are known as Peul in Senegal (they are also called Fulani and Fulbe).

There are two main languages in the Fulani group: Fulfulde, spoken mainly in northern and southern Senegal (includes the dialects known as Tukulor and Fulakunda); Futa Fula (also known as Futa Djalon), the main indigenous language of Guinea, also spoken in eastern Senegal.

It's worth noting that these far-flung languages have many regional dialects which aren't always mutually intelligible between different groups.

FULFULDE

The following words and phrases should be understood through most parts of Senegal. Note that **ng** should be pronounced as one sound (like the 'ng' in 'sing'); practise iso lating this sound and using it at the beginning of a word. The letter **ñ** represents the 'ni' sound in 'onion'.

Hello.	*no ngoolu daa* (sg)
	no ngoolu dong (pl)
Goodbye.	*ñalleen e jamm* (lit: Have a good day)
	mbaaleen e jamm (lit: Have a good night)
Please.	*njaafodaa*

Thank you.	*a jaaraama* (sg)
	on jaaraama (pl)
You're welcome.	*enen ndendidum*
Sorry/Pardon.	*yaafo* or *achanam hakke*
Yes.	*eey*
No.	*alaa*
How are you?	*no mbaddaa?*
I'm fine.	*mbe de sellee*
... and you?	*... an nene?*

Can you help me please?	
ada waawi wallude mi, njaafodaa?	
Do you speak English/French?	
ada faama engale/faranse?	
I only speak English.	
ko engale tan kaala mi	
I speak a little French.	
mi nani faranse seeda	

I understand.	*mi faami*
I don't understand.	*mi faamaani*
What's your name?	*no mbiyeteedaa?*
My name is ...	*ko ... mbiyetee mi*
Where are you from?	*to njeyedaa?*
I'm from ...	*ko ... njeyaa mi*
Where is ...?	*hoto woni?*
Is it far?	*no woddi?*
straight ahead	*ko yeesu*
left	*nano bang·ge*
right	*nano ñaamo*
How much is this?	*dum no foti jarata?*
That's too much.	*e ne tiidi no feewu*
Leave me alone!	*accam!/oppam mi deeja!*

1	*go·o*
2	*didi*
3	*tati*
4	*nayi*
5	*joyi*
6	*jeego*
7	*jeedidi*
8	*jeetati*
9	*jeenayi*
10	*sappo*
11	*sappoygoo*
12	*sappoydidi*
13	*sappoytati*
20	*noogaas*
30	*chappantati*
100	*temedere*
1000	*wujenere*

FUTA FULA (FUTA DJALON)

This variety of Fula known as Futa Fula or Futa Djalon is predominant in the Futa

Djalon region of Guinea. It is named after the people who speak it, and is distinct from the variety known as Fulfulde that is spoken in northern and southern Senegal.

Good morning/Good evening.	on·*jaa*·ra·ma
How are you?	ta·na·la·*ton*?
I'm fine.	ta·na·*o*·ala
Where is ...?	ko·hon·to wo·nee?
Thank you.	on·*jaa*·ra·ma
Goodbye.	on·ount·tou·ma

GA & ADANGME

Ga (and its very close relative Adangme) is one of the major indigenous languages of Ghana, spoken mostly around Accra.

Good morning/ Good evening.	meeng·ga·bou
How are you?	tey·yo·tain?
I'm fine.	ee·o·jo·baan
What's your name?	to·cho·bo·tain?
My name is ...	a·cho·mee ...
Thank you.	o·ye·ra·don
Goodbye.	bye·bye

HASSANIYA

Hassaniya is a Berber-Arabic dialect which is spoken by the Moors of Mauritania. It's also the official language of Mauritania.

Good morning.	sa·*la*·ma a·*lay*·koum
Good evening.	ma·sa el·*hair*
How are you?	ish·*ta*·ree?
Thank you.	shu·kraan
Goodbye.	ma·sa·*laam*

HAUSA

Hausa is spoken and understood in a vast area of West Africa and beyond. Dialectal variation is not extreme in Hausa so the phrases included in this language guide will be widely understood, and will prove useful in Benin, Burkina Faso, Côte d'Ivoire, Niger, Nigeria and northern Ghana (where it is the principal language of trade).

Hausa is a tone language (where variations in the pitch of a speaker's voice have a direct influence on the intended meaning) with three basic tones assigned to vowels: low, high and rising-falling. Standard written Hausa isn't marked for tones and the pronunciation guide for the words and phrases

included below doesn't show them either. Your best bet is to learn with your ears by noting the inflection of local speakers.

The consonants **b**, **d** and **k** have 'glottalised' equivalents where air is exhaled forcefully from the larynx (the voice box); these glottal consonants are represented in this guide by **B**, **D** and **K** respectively.

Distinctions in vowel length are also overlooked in standard written Hausa. In this guide long vowels are represented by double vowels, eg *aa'aa* (no).

Hello.	*sannu*
(response)	*yauwaa sannu*
Good morning.	*eenaa kwanaa*
Good morning.	*lapeeyaloh* (response)
Good evening.	*eenaa eenee*
Good evening.	*lapeeyalo* (response)
Goodbye.	*sai wani lookachi*
Please.	*don allaa*
Thank you.	*naa goodee*
Don't mention it/ It's nothing.	*baa koomi*
Sorry/Pardon.	*yi haKurii, ban ji ba*
Yes.	*ii*
No.	*aa'aa*
How are you?	*inaa gajiyaa?*
I'm fine.	*baa gajiyaa*
And you?	*kai fa?*
What's your name?	*yaayaa suunanka?*
My name is ...	*suunaanaa ...*
Where are you from?	*daga inaa ka fitoo?*
I'm from ...	*naa fitoo daga ...*

Can you help me please?
  don allaah, koo zaa ka taimakee ni?
Do you speak English/French?
  kanaa jin ingiliishii/faransancii?
I speak only English.
  inaa jin ingiliishii kawai
I speak a little French.
  inaa jin faransancii kaDan

I understand.	*naa gaanee*
I don't understand.	*ban gaanee ba*
Where is ...?	*inaa ...?*
Is it far ...?	*da niisaa ...?*
straight ahead	*miiKee sambal*
left	*hagu*
right	*daama*
How much is this?	*nawa nee wannan?*
That's too much.	*akwai tsaadaa ga wannan*
Leave me alone!	*tafi can!*

1	d'aya
2	biyu
3	uku
4	hud'u
5	biyar
6	shida
7	bakwai
8	takwas
9	tara
10	gooma
11	gooma shaa d'aya
12	gooma shaa biyu
13	gooma shaa uku
14	goma shaa hud'u
15	goma shaa biyar
16	gooma shaa shida
17	gooma shaa bakwai
18	gooma shaa takwas
19	gooma shaa tara
20	ashirin
30	talaatin
40	arba'in
50	hamsin
60	sittin
70	saba'in
80	tamaanin
90	casa'in
100	d'arii
1000	dubuu

IGBO (IBO)

Igbo, also known as Ibo, is the predominant indigenous language of Nigeria's southeast, where it is afforded the status of official language. It's used in the media and in government, and is the main lingua franca of the region. There are over 30 dialects of Igbo, each with varying degrees of mutual intelligibility.

Good morning.	ee-bow-la-chee
Good evening.	na-no-na
How are you?	ee-may-na aan-ghan?
Thank you.	ee-may-na
Goodbye.	kay-may-see-a

KABYÉ

After Ewe, Kabyé is Togo's most common African language, predominant in the Kara region. One Kabyé word you'll always hear is *yovo* (white person).

Good morning	un-la-wa-lay
How are you?	be-ja-un-sema
I'm fine.	a-la-fia

Thank you.	un-la-ba-lay
Goodbye.	be-la-bee-ta-si

KRIO

Krio is Sierra Leone's most common non-European language. Its major ingredient is English, but its sound system and grammar have been enriched by various West African languages. Because Krio was imported by different slave groups, there are strong differences between the Krio spoken in various regions, so strong in fact that some people find it easier to understand the Krio of Nigeria than the Krio spoken in other parts of Sierra Leone.

Hello.	kou-sheh
How are you?	ow-dee bo-dee?
I'm fine.	bo-dee fine/ no bad (more common)
Thank you.	tenk-kee
Please.	dou-ya (a-beg; added for emphasis)
Goodbye.	we go see back
How much?	ow mus?
Can I get a discount?	dou-ya les me?
food	chop
Where is ...?	oos e-ye ...?
Sierra Leone	salone

MALINKÉ

Malinké is spoken in the region around the borders between Senegal, Mali and Guinea. It's one of Senegal's six national languages. While it's very similar in some respects to the Mandinka spoken in Gambia and Senegal (they share much of their vocabulary), the two are classed as separate languages.

Good morning.	nee-so-ma
Good evening.	nee-woo-la
How are you?	tan-aas-te?
Thank you.	nee-kay
Goodbye.	m-ba-ra-wa

MANDINKA

Mandinka is the language of the Mandinka people found largely in central and northern Gambia, and in parts of southern Senegal. The people and their language are also called Mandingo and they're closely related to other Mande-speaking groups such as the Bambara of Mali, where they originate. Mandinka is classed as one of Senegal's national languages.

In this guide, **ng** should be pronounced as the 'ng' in 'sing' and **ñ** represents the 'ni' sound in 'onion'.

Hello.	*i/al be ñaading* (sg/pl)
Good bye.	*fo tuma doo*
Please.	*dukare*
Thank you.	*i/al ning bara* (sg/pl)
You're welcome.	*mbee le dentaala/wo teng fengti* (lit: It's nothing)
Sorry/Pardon.	*hakko tuñe*
Yes.	*haa*
No.	*hani*
How are you?	*i/al be kayrato?* (sg/pl)
I'm fine.	*tana tenna* (lit: I'm out of trouble)
	kayra dorong (lit: Peace only)
And you?	*ite fanang?*
What's your name?	*i too dung?*
My name is ...	*ntoo mu ... leti*
Where are you from?	*i/al bota munto?* (sg/pl)
I'm from ...	*mbota ...*

Can you help me please?
i/al seng maakoy noo, dukare? (sg/pl)
Do you speak English/French?
ye angkale/faranse kango moyle?
I speak only English.
nga angkale kango damma le moy
I speak a little French.
nga faranse kango domonding le moy
I understand.
ngaa kalamuta le/ngaa fahaam le
I don't understand.
mmaa kalamuta/mmaa fahaam

Where is ...?	*... be munto?*
Is it far?	*faa jamfata?*
Go straight ahead.	*sila tiling jan kilingo*
left	*maraa*
right	*bulu baa*
How much is this?	*ñing mu jelu leti?*
That's too much.	*a daa koleyaata baake*
Leave me alone!	*mbula!*

1	*kiling*
2	*fula*
3	*saba*
4	*naani*
5	*luulu*
6	*wooro*
7	*woorowula*
8	*sey*
9	*kononto*
10	*tang*
11	*tang ning kiling*
12	*tang ning fula*
13	*tang ning saba*
20	*muwaa*
30	*tang saba*
100	*keme*
1000	*wili kiling*

MINA (GENGBE)

Mina, also known as Gengbe, is the language of trade in southern Togo, especially along the coast. It belongs to the Gbe (*gbe* meaning 'language') subgroup of the vast Kwa language family. Other Gbe languages of Togo include Ajagbe, Fongbe, Maxigbe and Wacigbe.

Good morning.	*so*·bay·do
(response)	dosso
How are you?	*o*·foin?
I'm fine.	aaaa ('a' as in 'bat')
Thank you.	*ack*·pay
Goodbye.	*so*·day·lo

MORÉ

Moré (the language of the Mossi) is spoken by more than half the population of Burkina Faso – with over 4½ million speakers it's the country's principal indigenous language.

Good morning.	*yee*·bay·ro
Good evening.	nay·*za*·bree
How are you?	la·*fee*·bay·may?
I'm fine.	la·*fee*·bay·la
Thank you.	un·*pus*·da *bar*·ka
Goodbye.	wen·a·*ta*·say

SANGHA DIALECT

Sangha is one of the main dialects (from around 48 others!) spoken by the Dogon people who inhabit the Falaise de Bandiagara in central Mali. Dialectal variation can be so marked that mutual intelligibility between the many Dogon groups is not always assured.

Good morning.	a·*ga*·po
Good evening.	dee·*ga*·po
How are you?	ou *say*·yo?
I'm fine.	*say*·o
Thank you.	bee·ray·*po*
Goodbye.	ee·eye·*ee* way·dang
Safe journey!	day·gay·day·*ya*

LANGUAGE

SENOUFO

The Senoufo words and phrases following will prove useful if you're travelling through southern Mali, southwestern Burkina Faso and northern Côte d'Ivoire.

Senoufo pronunciation can be a very difficult prospect for foreigners, and with no official written form the task of matching the sounds of the language with letters on a page presents quite a challenge. The pronunciation system used in this guide provides rough approximations only. Try to pick up the sounds and inflections of the language by listening to fluent Senoufo speakers.

a	as in 'far'
e	as in 'bet'
é	as the 'ay' in 'bay'
i	as in 'marine'
o	as in 'hot'
u	between the 'u' in 'pull' and the 'oo' in 'boot'
g	always hard, as in 'get'
ñ	as in the 'ni' in 'onion'
ng	as the 'ng' in 'sing' – indicates that the preceding vowel is nasal

Hello.	kéné
Goodbye.	wu·ñe·té·re
Thank you.	fa·na
Sorry/Pardon.	ya·hé·ya
Yes.	huu or mi·lo·go
No.	mé·tye
How are you?	ma·cho·lo·go·la?
I'm fine.	min·bé·gé·ba·mén
And you?	mohn·dohn?
What's your name?	men·ma·mi·in·ye?
My name is …	men·min·ye …

Do you speak …?	mun·na … chi·yé·ré·lu·gu·la?
English	aan·gi·li·kan
French	tu·ba·bu·kan

I only speak English.
min·na aan·gi·li·kan chi·yé·re·ye·ké·né
I speak a little French.
min·na tu·ba·bu·kan chi·yé·re tye·ri·ye
Can you help me please?
na·pu·gu?

I don't understand.	min·nay·chi·men
Where are you from?	shi·mo·na yi·ri·ré?
I'm from …	min·na·yi·ri …

Where is …?	shi·ong·ye …?
Is it far?	ka·lé·li·la?
left	ka·mohn
right	kin·yi·ka·ni·gi·he·ye·ré
How much is this?	jur·gi·na·de·le?
That's too much!	ka·la·ra·wa·a, de!
Leave me alone!	yi·ri·wa! or me·ya·ba!

Numbers

Numbers in Senoufo can be a very complicated affair. For example, the number 'one hundred' translates literally as 'two-times-five-times-two-times-four-plus-two-times-ten' – use the numbers in the Bambara/Dioula section (p867) and you'll have no trouble being understood.

SUSU

Susu is Guinea's third most commonly spoken indigenous language. It's spoken mainly in the south around Conakry.

Good morning.	tay·na ma·ree
Good evening.	tay·na ma·fay·yen
How are you?	o·ree to·na·mo?
Thank you.	ee·no·wa·lee
Goodbye.	oo·ne·gay·say·gay

TAMASHEK

Tamashek (spelt variously 'Tamasheq', 'Tamachek', 'Tamajeq' and more) is the language of the Tuareg. There are two main dialects: Eastern, spoken in western Niger and eastern Mali; Western, spoken in western Niger, the Gao region of Mali, and northern Nigeria.

How do you do?	met·al·ee·kha? (pol)/o·yeek? (inf)
I'm fine.	eel·kha·rass
How's the heat?	min·ee·twi·xe? (a traditional greeting)
Good/Fine.	ee·zott
How much?	min·ee·kit?
Thank you.	tan·oo·mert
Goodbye.	harr·sad

TWI

Twi (pronounced 'chwee'), the language of the Ashanti, is the most widely spoken African language in Ghana, where it's the official language of education and literature. Along with Fanti it belongs to the large Akan language family. Most of the dialects within this group are mutually intelligible.

Hello.	a·*kwa*·ba
(response)	yaa
Good morning.	ma·*cheeng*
Good evening.	ma·jo
Are you going to ...	ya·co ...?
Goodbye.	ma·*krow*
Safe journey.	nan·tee yee·yay
Let's go.	yen·co
How are you?	ay·ta·sein?
I'm fine.	ay·ya
Please.	me·*pa*·wo·che·o
Thank you.	may·*da*·say
Yes.	aan
No.	da·be
Do you speak English?	wo·te *bro*·fo aan·na
I don't understand.	um·*ta* se
I'd like ...	me·*pay* ...

1	bee·*a*·ko
2	a·bee·*eng*
3	a·bee·*e*·sa
4	a·*nang*
5	a·*nuhm*
6	a·*see*·ya
7	a·*song*
8	a·*wo*·twe
9	a·*kruhng*
10	du
11	du·bee·*a*·ko
20	*a*·dwo·nu
100	o·*ha*
1000	a·*pem*

WOLOF

Wolof (spelt *Ouolof* in French) is the language of the Wolof people, who are found in Senegal, particularly in the central area north and east of Dakar, along the coast, and in the western regions of Gambia. The Wolof spoken in Gambia is slightly different to the Wolof spoken in Senegal; the Gambian Wolof people living on the north bank of the Gambia River speak the Senegalese variety. Wolof is used as a common language in many parts of Senegal and Gambia, often instead of either French or English, and some smaller groups complain about the increasing 'Wolofisation' of their culture.

For some traditional Arabic Islamic greetings which are used in Muslim West Africa, see p867.

Most consonants are pronounced as they are in English; when they are doubled they are pronounced with greater emphasis. Some vowels have accented variants.

a	as in 'at'
à	as in 'far'
e	as in 'bet'
é	as in 'whey'
ë	as the 'u' in 'but'
i	as in 'it'
o	as in 'hot'
ó	as in 'so'
u	as in 'put'
g	as in 'go'
ñ	as the 'ni' in 'onion'
ng	as in 'sing'; practise making this sound at the beginning of a word
r	always rolled
s	as in 'so', not as in 'as'
w	as in 'we'
x	as the 'ch' in Scottish loch

Hello.	*Na nga def.* (sg)
	Na ngeen def. (pl)
Good morning.	*Jàmm nga fanaane.*
Good afternoon.	*Jàmm nga yendoo.*
Goodnight.	*Fanaanal jàmm.*
Goodbye.	*Ba beneen.*
Please.	*Su la nexee.*
Thank you.	*Jërëjëf.*
You're welcome.	*Agsil/agsileen ak jàmm .* (sg/pl)
Sorry/Pardon.	*Baal ma.*
Yes.	*Waaw.*
No.	*Déedéet.*
How are you?	*Jàmm nga/ngeen am?* (sg/pl)
	(lit: Have you peace?)
I'm fine.	*Jàmm rekk.*
And you?	*Yow nag?*
How is your family?	*Naka waa kër ga?*
Where do you live?	*Fan nga dëkk?*
Where are you from?	*Fan nga/ngeen jòge?* (sg/pl)
I'm from ...	*Maa ngi jòge ...*

What's your first name?
  Naka nga/ngeen tudd? (sg/pl)
What's your last name?
  Naka nga sant?
My name is ...
  Maa ngi tudd ...
Do you speak English/French?
  Dégg nga Angale/Faranse? (sg/pl)
I speak only English.
  Angale rekk laa dégg.
I speak a little French.
  Dégg naa tuuti Faranse.

I don't speak Wolof/French.	Màn dégguma Wolof/Faranse.
I understand.	Dégg naa.
I don't understand.	Dégguma.
I'd like ...	Dama bëggoon ...
Where is ...?	Fan la ...?
Is it far?	Sore na?
straight ahead	cha kanam
left	cammooñ
right	ndeyjoor
Get in!	Dugghal waay!
How much is this?	Lii ñaata?
It's too much.	Seer na torob.
Leave me alone!	May ma jàmm!

Monday	altine
Tuesday	talaata
Wednesday	àllarba
Thursday	alxames
Friday	àjjuma
Saturday	gaawu
Sunday	dibéer

0	tus
1	benn
2	ñaar
3	ñett
4	ñeent
5	juróom
6	juróom-benn
7	juróom- ñaar
8	juróom- ñett
9	juróom- ñeent
10	fukk
11	fukk-ak-benn
12	fukk-ak-ñaar
13	fukk-ak-ñett
14	fukk-ak-ñeent
15	fukk-ak-juróom
16	fukk-ak-juróom benn (lit: ten-and-five one)
17	fukk-ak-juróom ñaar
18	fukk-ak-juróom ñett
19	fukk-ak-juróom ñeent
20	ñaar-fukk (lit: two-ten)
30	fanweer
40	ñeent-fukk (lit: four-ten)
50	juróom-fukk (lit: five-ten)
60	juróom-benn-fukk (lit: five-one-ten)
70	juróom-ñaar-fukk (lit: five two-ten)
80	juróom-ñett-fukk
90	juróom-ñeent-fukk
100	téeméer
1000	junne

YORUBA

Yoruba belongs to the Kwa group of the Ede language family (ede is the Yoruba word for 'language'). Along with Fon it is one of the main lingua francas in much of the eastern part of West Africa but it is principally spoken as a first language in Benin and Nigeria. As with the majority of indigenous West African languages, Yoruba is subject to a degree of dialectal variation, which is not surprising given the broad geographical area its speakers are found in. Fortunately, the majority of these variants are mutually intelligible.

Yoruba is normally written using the IPA (International Phonetic Alphabet). It is a tone language, (ie changes in voice-pitch are important in giving words their intended meaning). To give a comprehensive description of the five-tone Yoruba vowel system goes beyond the scope of this chapter. For simplicity we've used an acute accent (eg á) to represent a high tone, a grave accent (eg à) to represent a low tone; unmarked vowels take a mid-tone.

The pronunciations we give for the words and phrases below are approximations only. Pronounce letters as you would in English, keeping the following points in mind:

a	as in 'far'
e	as in 'met'
i	as in 'marine'
o	as in 'hot'; as in 'or'
u	as in 'put'
g	as in 'go'
h	not pronounced
ng	indicates that the preceding vowel is nasalised, eg the 'ing' in 'sing'

Hello.	bá·o
Goodbye.	ó·dà·bò
Please.	e·dá·kuhn
Thank you.	e·she·wu
You're welcome.	e·wo·lè
Sorry/Pardon.	e·dá·kuhn
Yes.	e
No.	è·ré·wo
How are you?	shé·wà·dá·da?
I'm fine. (And you?)	à·dú·kpé (è·nyi·na·nkó?)
What's your name?	bá·wo·le·má·jé?
My name is ...	mo·má·jé ...
Where are you from?	à·rá·ibo·lo·jé?
I'm from ...	à·rá ... ni mi

Can you help me please?	*e·dá·kuhn e·ràang· mí·ló·wó?*	7	*è·je*
Do you speak English?	*she·gbó ge·sì?*	8	*è·jo*
Do you speak French?	*she·gbó fraang·sé?*	9	*e·saang*
I only speak English.	*ge·sì ni·kaang nì·mo·gbó*	10	*e·wa*
I speak a little French.	*mo·gbó fraang·sé dí·è*	11	*mó·kàang·la*
		12	*mé·ji·la*
I don't understand.	*kò·yé·mi·sí*	13	*mé·tà·la*
Where is ...?	*ibo ni ...?*	14	*mé·ri·la*
Is it far?	*o jin·ni?*	15	*má·rùhng·la*
straight ahead	*tro·lo·lo*	16	*mé·ring·dó·gúhng*
left	*ò·túhng*	17	*mé·tá·dó·gúhng*
right	*ò·sìng*	18	*mé·jì·dó·gúhng*
How much is this?	*é·lo·lè·yi?*	19	*ò·kaang·dó·gúhng*
That's too much.	*ó·wáang·jù*	20	*ò·gúhng*
Leave me alone!	*fi·mí·nlè!*	30	*mé·wa·lé·ló·gbòng*
		40	*ò·gbòng*
1	*e·ní*	50	*mé·wà·lé·ló·gbòng*
2	*è·ji*	60	*ò·góng·lé·ló·gbòng*
3	*e·ta*	70	*ò·gúhng·mé·wa·lé·ló·gbòng*
4	*e·ring*	80	*ò·gbòng·mé·jì*
5	*à·rúng*	90	*mé·wa·lé·ló·gbong·mé·jì*
6	*è·fà*	100	*ò·gúhng·lé·ló·gbong·mé·jì*

Glossary

The following is a list of words and acronyms used in this book that you are likely to come across in West Africa. For a detailed food and drink glossary, see p55.

abusua – clan or organisation of the Akan
achaba – motorcycle taxi (northern Nigeria); see also *okada*
adinkra – handmade printed cloth from Ghana worn primarily by the Ashanti
Afrique Occidentale Française – see *French West Africa*
Afro-beat – a fusion of African music, jazz and soul originated and popularised by Fela Kuti of Nigeria; along with *juju* it's the most popular music in Nigeria
Akan – a major group of peoples along the south coast of West Africa; includes the Ashanti and Fanti peoples
akuaba – Ashanti carved figure
aluguer – for hire (sign in minibus)
animism – the base of virtually all traditional religions in Africa; the belief that there is a spirit in all natural things and that human spirits (ancestors) bestow protection
asantehene – the king or supreme ruler of the Ashanti people
Ashanti – the largest tribal group in Ghana, concentrated around Kumasi
aso adire – a broad term for dyed cloth, a common handicraft found in many markets in Nigeria
auberge – used in West Africa to mean any small hotel
autogare – see *gare routière*
autoroute – major road or highway

bâché – covered pick-up ('ute') used as a basic bush taxi
balafon – xylophone
Bambara – Mali's major ethnic group found in the centre and south and famous for its wooden carvings
banco – bank; clay or mud used for building
Baoulé – an Akan-speaking people from Côte d'Ivoire with strong animist beliefs
barco – large boat
bar-dancing – term widely used throughout the region for a bar which also has music (sometimes live) and dancing in the evening
barrage – dam across river, or roadblock
bidon – large bottle, container or jerry can
bidonville – shantytown
Bobo – animist people of western Burkina Faso and southern Mali, famous for their mask traditions
bogolan cloth – often simply called mud-cloth, this is cotton cloth with designs painted on using various types of mud for colour; made by the Bambara of Mali but found throughout the region

boîte – small nightclub (literally 'box')
bolong – literally 'river' in Mandinka, but when used in an English context it means creek or small river
boubou – the common name for the elaborate robe-like outfit worn by men and women
boukarous – open-sided, circular mud huts
BP – Boîte Postale (PO Box)
brake – see *Peugeot taxi*
Bundu – Krio word for 'secret society'; used in Liberia and in certain parts of Sierra Leone and Côte d'Ivoire; includes the Poro society for men and the Sande for women; in Sierra Leone, the women's secret society is spelled Bondo
Burkinabé – adjective for Burkina Faso
bush taxi – along with buses, this is the most common form of public transport in West Africa; there are three main types of bush taxi: Peugeot taxi, minibus and pick-up (bâché)
buvette – refreshment stall

cadeau – gift, tip, bribe or handout, see also *dash*
campement – loosely translated as 'hostel', 'inn' or 'lodge', but it's not a camping ground (ie a place for tents, although some *campements* allow you to pitch tents); traditionally, *campements* offer simple accommodation
canoa – motor-canoe
car – large bus, see also *petit car*
carnet – document required if you are bringing a car into most countries of the region
car rapide – minibus, usually used in cities; often decrepit, may be fast or very slow
carrefour – literally 'crossroads', but also used to mean meeting place
carrefour des jeunes – youth centre
carte jaune – vaccination certificate
cascata – waterfall
case – hut
case à étage – two-storey mud house
case à impluvium – huge round hut with a hole in the roof to collect rainwater
case de passage – very basic place to sleep (often near bus stations) with a bed or mat on the floor and little else, and nearly always doubling as a brothel; also called 'chambre de passage' or 'maison de passage'
CFA – the West African franc (used in Benin, Burkina Faso, Côte d'Ivoire, Guinea-Bissau, Mali, Niger, Senegal and Togo) or Central African franc (Cameroon)
chambre de passage – see *case de passage*
chasée submersible – see *pont submersible*
chèche – light cotton cloth in white or indigo blue that Tuareg men wear to cover their head and face

chiwara – a headpiece carved in the form of an antelope and used in ritualistic dances by the Bambara
cidade – city
cinq-cent-quatre – 504; see *Peugeot taxi*
climatisée – air-conditioned; often shortened to 'clim'
coladeiras – old-style music; romantic, typically sentimental upbeat love songs
commissariat – police station
compteur – meter in taxi
correios – post office
couchette – sleeping berth on a train
CRI – Campements Rurals Integrés; system of village-run campements in the Casamance region of Senegal
croix d'Agadez – Tuareg talisman that protects its wearer from the 'evil eye'

Dan – an animist people living in western Côte d'Ivoire and Liberia with strong mask traditions
Dahomey – pre-independence name of Benin
dash – bribe or tip (noun); also used as a verb, 'You dash me something...'
demi-pension – half board (dinner, bed and breakfast)
déplacement – a taxi or boat that you 'charter' for yourself
djembe – type of drum
Dogon – people found in Mali, east of Mopti; famous for their cliff dwellings, cosmology and arts
durbar – ceremony or celebration, usually involving a cavalry parade, found, for example, in the Muslim northern Nigerian states
dournis – minibus

Ecowas – Economic Community of West African States
Eid al-Fitr – feast to celebrate the end of Ramadan
Eid al-Kabir – see *Tabaski*
Empire of Ghana – one of the great Sahel empires that flourished in the 8th to 11th centuries AD and covered much of present-day Mali and parts of Senegal
Empire of Mali – Islamic Sahel empire that was at its peak in the 14th century, covering the region between present-day Senegal and Niger
essence – petrol (gas) for car
Ewe – Forest-dwelling people of Ghana and Togo

fado – haunting melancholy blues-style Portuguese music
fanals – large lanterns; also the processions during which the lanterns are carried through the streets
fanicos – laundry men
Fanti – part of the Akan group of people based along the coast in southwest Ghana and Côte d'Ivoire; traditionally fishing people and farmers
fête – festival
fêtes des masques – ceremony with masks
fetish – sacred objects or talismans in traditional religions, sometimes called 'charms'

fiche – form (to complete)
Foulbé – see *Fula*
French West Africa – area of West and Central Africa acquired by France at the Berlin Conference in 1884–85 which divided Africa up between the European powers; 'Afrique Occidentale Française' in French
Fula – a people spread widely through West Africa, mostly nomadic cattle herders; also known as 'Fulani', 'Peul' or 'Foulbé'
fula-fula – converted truck or pick-up; rural public transport
funaná – distinctive fast-paced music with a Latin rhythm that's great for dancing; usually features players on the accordion and tapping with metal

gara – a thin cotton material, tie-dyed or stamp-printed, with bright colours and bold patterns
garage – bush taxi and bus park
gare lagunaire – lagoon ferry terminal
gare maritime – ferry terminal
gare routière – bus and bush-taxi station, also called 'gare voiture' or 'autogare'
gare voiture – see *gare routière*
gargotte – small, local eatery
gasoil – diesel fuel
gelli-gelli – minibusl in The Gambia
gendarmerie – police station/post
girba – water bag
gîte – used interchangeably in West Africa with *auberge* and *campement*
Gold Coast – pre-independence name for modern state of Ghana
goudron – tar (road)
Grain Coast – old name for Liberia
griot – traditional caste of musicians or praise singers; many of West Africa's music stars come from *griot* families
gué – ford or low causeway across river

Hausa – people originally from northern Nigeria and southern Niger, mostly farmers and traders
highlife – a style of music, originating in Ghana, combining West African and Western influences
hôtel de ville – town hall

ibeji – Yoruba carved twin figures
IDP – International Driving Permit
Igbo – one of the three major peoples in Nigeria, concentrated predominantly in the southeast
IGN – Institute Géographique National
IMF – International Monetary Fund
immeuble – large building, for example, office block
impluvium – large round traditional house with roof constructed to collect rain water in central tank or bowl
insha'allah – God willing, ie hopefully (Arabic, but used by Muslims in Africa)

jardim – garden
jeli – see *griot*
juju – the music style characterised by tight vocal harmonies and sophisticated guitar work, backed by traditional drums and percussion; very popular in southern Nigeria, especially with the Yoruba; see also *voodoo*

kandab – a large belt used to climb trees to collect palm wine
kandonga – truck or pick-up
kente cloth – made with finely woven cotton, and sometimes silk, by Ghana's Ashanti people
Kingdom of Benin – one of the great West African kingdoms (13th to 19th centuries); based in Nigeria around Benin City and famous for its bronze or brass
kola nuts – extremely bitter nuts sold everywhere on the streets and known for their mildly hallucinogenic and caffeine-like effects; they are offered as gifts at weddings and other ceremonies
kora – harp-like musical instrument with over 20 strings
kwotenai kanye – earrings

lapa – four square yards (used in Sierra Leone for measuring cloth)
line – fixed-route shared taxi
Lobi – people based in southwest Burkina Faso and northern Côte d'Ivoire, famous for their figurative sculpture and compounds known as *soukala*
lorry park – see *motor park*
lumo – weekly market, usually in border areas
luttes – traditional wrestling matches
lycée – secondary school

macaco – monkey; a popular meat dish in upcountry Guinea-Bissau
mairie – town hall; mayor's office
maison de passage – see *case de passage*
maison d'hôte – small hotel or guesthouse
makossa – Cameroonian musical form that fuses Highlife and soul
malafa – crinkly voile material worn as a veil by women in Mauritania
Malinké – Guinea's major ethnic group, the people are also found in southern Mali, northwestern Côte d'Ivoire and eastern Senegal; closely related to the Bambara and famous for founding the Empire of Mali; also related to the Mandinka
Mandinka – people based in central and northern Gambia and Senegal; also the name of their language, which is closely related to Malinké; both Malinké and Mandinka are part of the wider Manding group
maquis – rustic open-air restaurant; traditionally open only at night
marché – market
marigot – creek

mbalax – percussion-driven, Senegalese dance music
mercado – market
mestizos – people of mixed European and African descent
mobylette – moped
Moors – also called 'Maurs'; the predominant nomadic people of Mauritania, now also well known as merchants and found scattered over French-speaking West Africa
mornas – old-style music; mournful and sad, similar to the Portuguese *fado* style from whence they may have originated
Moro-Naba – the king of the Mossi people
Mossi – the people who occupy the central area of Burkina Faso and comprise about half the population of that country
motor park – bus and bush-taxi park (English-speaking countries); also called 'lorry park'
moto-taxi – motorcycle taxi
Mourides – the most powerful of the Islamic brotherhoods in Senegal
mud-cloth – see *bogolan cloth*

NEPA – National Electric Power Authority in Nigeria; supplier of the highly erratic electricity
nomalies – sandstone ancestor figures

OAU – Organisation of African Unity
oba – a Yoruba chief or king
occasion – a lift or place in a car or bus (often shortened to 'occas')
okada – motorcycle taxi
orchestra – in West Africa, this means a group playing popular music

pagne – a length of colourful cloth worn around the waist as a skirt
paillote – a thatched sun shelter (usually on a beach or around an open-air bar-restaurant)
palava – meeting place
paletuviers – mangroves
pam-pah – large cargo/passenger boats (Sierra Leone)
papelaria – newsagency
paragem – bus and bush-taxi park
patron – owner, boss
péage – toll
peintures rupestres – rock paintings
pensão – hotel or guesthouse
pension – simple hotel or hostel, or 'board'; see also *demi-pension*
pension complet – full board (lunch, dinner, bed and breakfast)
pension simple – bed and breakfast
petit car – minibus
pétrole – kerosene

Peugeot taxi – one of the main types of bush taxi; also called 'brake', 'cinq-cent-quatre', 'Peugeot 504' or *sept place*
Peul – see *Fula*
pinasse – large *pirogue*, usually used on rivers, for hauling people and cargo
pirogue – traditional canoe, either a small dugout or large, narrow sea-going wooden fishing boat
pharmacie de garde – all-night pharmacy
piste – track or dirt road
poda-poda – minibus
pont submersible – bridge or causeway across a river which is covered when the water is high
posuban – ensemble of statues representing a proverb or event in Fanti culture
pousada – guesthouse
pousada municipal – town guesthouse
praça – park or square
praia – beach
préfecture – police headquarters
PTT – post (and often telephone) office in Francophone countries

quatre-quatre – 4WD or 4x4, a four-wheel drive vehicle

Ramadan – Muslim month of fasting
residencial – guest house
rond-point – roundabout
rua – street

Sahel – dry semi-desert and savannah area south of the Sahara desert; most of Senegal, The Gambia, Mali, Burkina Faso and Niger; the name means 'coast' in Arabic
Scramble for Africa – term used for the land-grabbing frenzy in the 1880s by the European powers in which France, Britain and Germany laid claim to various parts of the continent
Senoufo – a strongly animist people straddling Côte d'Ivoire, Burkina Faso and Mali
sept place – Peugeot taxi seven-seater (usually carrying up to 12 people)
serviette – towel (in bathroom)
serviette de table – table napkin, serviette
serviette hygiénique – sanitary pad (feminine pad, feminine towel)
sharia – Muslim law
Songhaï – ethnic group located primarily in northeastern Mali and western Niger along the Niger River; also Empire of Songhaï which ruled the Sahel with its heyday in the 15th century

soukala – a castle-like housing compound of the Lobi tribe found in the Bouna area of southern Burkina Faso
spirale antimostique – mosquito coil
sûreté – police station
syndicat d'initiative – tourist information office

Tabaski – Eid al-Kabir; also known as the Great Feast, this is the most important celebration throughout West Africa
taguelmoust – shawl or scarf worn as headgear by Tuareg men
tama – hand-held drum
tampon – stamp (eg, in passport)
tampon hygiénique – tampon; see also *serviette hygiénique*
tampon periodique – see *tampon hygiénique*
tata somba – a castle-like house of the Batammariba tribe who live in northwestern Benin and Togo
taxi brousse – bush taxi
taxi-course – shared taxi (in cities)
taxi-moto – see *moto-taxi*
télécentre – privately run telecommunications centres
tikit – traditional thatched stone hut used as accommodation in Mauritania
toca-toca – small minibus in Bissau
toguna – traditional Dogon shelter where men sit and socialise
totem – used in traditional religions, similar to a fetish
toubab – white person
town trip – private hire (taxi)
tro-tro – a minibus or pick-up
Tuareg – nomadic descendants of the North African Berbers; found all over the Sahara, especially in Mali, Niger and southern Algeria

voodoo – the worship of spirits with supernatural powers widely practised in southern Benin and Togo; also called *juju*

wassoulou – singing style made famous by Mali's Oumou Sangaré
WHO – World Health Organization
Wolof – Senegal's major ethnic group; also found in The Gambia
woro-woro – minibus

Yoruba – a major ethnic group concentrated in southwestern Nigeria

zemi-john – motorcycle-taxi

The Authors

ANTHONY HAM
Coordinating Author, Mali

Anthony's love affair with West Africa began on his first trip to Niger when he fell irretrievably in love with the people and landscapes of the Sahel and Sahara. Since then, he has returned many times, visiting every Sahelian and Saharan country as he seeks out stories about the people and wildlife of the region. He loves nothing better than finding a remote corner of the Sahara and spending nights around the campfire with his Tuareg friends. In addition to Lonely Planet's *West Africa, Africa, Libya* and *Algeria* guides, Anthony writes for numerous newspapers and magazines around the world. When he's not in West Africa, Anthony lives in Madrid with his wife and daughter.

TIM BEWER
Sierra Leone

While growing up, Tim didn't travel much except for the obligatory pilgrimage to Disney World and an annual summer week at the lake. He's spent most of his adult life making up for this and has since visited over 50 countries. After university he worked briefly as a legislative assistant before quitting capitol life in 1994 to backpack around West Africa. It was during this trip that the idea of becoming a freelance travel writer and photographer was hatched, and he's been at it ever since, returning to Africa many times for work and pleasure. The half of the year he isn't shouldering a backpack somewhere he lives in Khon Kaen, Thailand.

STUART BUTLER
Cape Verde

English-born Stuart Butler has travelled widely throughout West Africa. His first experience of Cape Verde was on a surf trip a few years ago. The winds blew offshore day after day, the swell was perfect, the line-ups empty, the people great, the lifestyle idyllic and he quickly decided he'd stumbled upon paradise. In addition to West Africa his travels have taken him from the desert beaches of Pakistan to the coastal jungles of Colombia. He now calls the beautiful beaches of southwest France home, but whenever it rains he tries to talk his wife into moving to Cape Verde.

JEAN-BERNARD CARILLET
Burkina Faso

A Paris-based journalist and photographer, Jean-Bernard is a die-hard Africa lover. He has travelled the length and breadth of the continent for nearly 20 years now, from Djibuti to Ziguinchor and Tunis to Jo'burg. This assignment in Burkina Faso was something of a revelation – Jean-Bernard was thrilled by the largely underrated local arts scene, and he took the opportunity to meet emerging and leading Burkinabé artists, from djembe (drum) masters and bronze sculptors to choreographers and painters. He also got his much-needed adrenaline fix in the desolate expanses of the Sahel and the national parks of the South. Jean-Bernard has also co-authored Lonely Planet's *Ethiopia & Eritrea*. He also writes for various travel magazines.

PAUL CLAMMER Mauritania, Nigeria

Once a molecular biologist, Paul has long since traded his test tubes for a rucksack, and the vicarious life of a travel writer. Overlanding in Africa was his first significant travel experience, and he has returned to the continent many times since. For the last edition of *West Africa,* Paul was swept away by the buzz of Nigeria, that most maligned of African countries, and was eager to return, this time twinning the adrenaline rush of Lagos with the empty desert spaces of Mauritania.

EMILIE FILOU Benin, Togo

Emilie first travelled to West Africa aged 8 to visit her grandparents who had taken up a late career opportunity in Mali. More visits ensued, including an epic family holiday in Togo and Benin, the highlight of which was the beautiful and amusingly-named Grand Popo ('big poo' in French – simply hilarious when you're aged 10). Emilie pursued her interest in Africa at university where she studied geography and did her dissertation on health care provision for no-madic people in Niger. For this book she has crossed borders, visited national parks and zoomed across the cities of Benin and Togo all aboard the dreaded *zemi-johns* (motorcycle taxis) – she is glad to be alive to tell the tale.

KATHARINA KANE The Gambia, Guinea, Guinea-Bissau, Senegal

Katharina Lobeck Kane has earned enough bush taxi miles to tour the entire continent at least a dozen times. A year of PhD research in Guinea was fol-lowed by work visits to dozens of countries on the continent, usually with clutched camera and voice recorder, to dig up gems of the local music scenes. In 2005, she moved to Senegal where she discovered a peaceful, paradoxical and puzzling place with a rampant capitalism and *dirianké* style, and her relaxed negotiation of societal and linguistic labyrinths convinced her that she was meant to be living on the world's cultural crossroads. Katharina cur-rently works as a writer, radio producer and presenter and projects manager. Unless Berlin or Cologne has embraced her, you'll find her in Dakar.

LONELY PLANET AUTHORS

Why is our travel information the best in the world? It's simple: our authors are passionate, dedicated travellers. They don't take freebies in exchange for positive coverage so you can be sure the advice you're given is impartial. They travel widely to all the popular spots, and off the beaten track. They don't research using just the internet or phone. They discover new places not included in any other guidebook. They personally visit thousands of hotels, restaurants, palaces, trails, galleries, temples and more. They speak with dozens of locals every day to make sure you get the kind of insider knowledge only a local could tell you. They take pride in getting all the details right, and in telling it how it is. Think you can do it? Find out how at **lonelyplanet.com**.

THE AUTHORS

ADAM KARLIN
Cameroon

Adam has contributed to over a dozen Lonely Planet guides ranging from the Americas to Asia to Africa. On this research trip to Cameroon he was mugged in Yaounde, where he engaged in probably the most amusing one-handed fight (trying to keep his wallet in his pocket) in that city's history, was almost arrested by police with a Cameroonian friend in Wum (situation averted by CFA3000 bribe) and road a horse 50km bareback across the Extreme North frontier into Nigeria. It was, to say the least, a hell of a trip.

TOM MASTERS
Liberia, Niger

Long a fan of countries most people go out of their way to avoid, Tom was a natural choice for both Liberia and Niger, two of West Africa's least travelled destinations. In newly safe Liberia Tom did the first on-the-ground update in years and was both heartened to see how far the shattered country has come in getting back on its feet and genuinely amazed at the scale of the international effort to help. In Niger, despite the Tuareg rebellion Tom was able to make it to the far north of the country, even if for now the stunning landscapes of the Aïr Mountains and the Ténéré Desert remain closed. When not travelling in Africa, Tom is a freelance writer living in Berlin. More of his work can be found at www.mastersmafia.com.

KATE THOMAS
Ghana, Côte d'Ivoire

Growing up in an English seaside town, Kate would sit on the pebbly beach contemplating life on the other side of the sea. After finishing her studies in Paris and London, she flew to Melbourne, returning by cargo ship, road and rail. When she took a job on the foreign desk of a British newspaper, she pinned a map of Africa above her desk. It soon became torn and tattered and she knew she had to see the real thing. For the past few years she's been writing from Africa, notably Cote d'Ivoire, Liberia, Ghana, Guinea and DR Congo.

Behind the Scenes

THIS BOOK

The first two editions of West Africa were written and researched by Alex Newton. Alex was joined by David Else for the 3rd edition while the 4th edition was updated by David Else, Alex Newton, Jeff Williams, Mary Fitzpatrick and Miles Roddis. For the 5th edition Mary Fitzpatrick was the coordinating author; she was ably assisted by Andrew Burke, Greg Campbell, Bethune Carmichael, Matthew Fletcher, Anthony Ham, Amy Karafin, Frances Linzee Gordon, Kim Wildman and Isabelle Young. Anthony Ham assumed the mantle as coordinating author and also researched Burkina Faso and Mali for the 6th edition. His intrepid cohorts included James Bainbridge, Tim Bewer, Jean-Bernard Carillet, Paul Clammer, Mary Fitzpatrick, Michael Grosberg, Robert Landon, Katharina Kane and Matt Phillips. Jane Cornwell wrote the Music chapter and Michael Benanav contributed to the 'Timbuktu Salt Trade' boxed text. This 7th edition was again coordinated by Anthony Ham, who was assisted in authoring by Stuart Butler, Emilie Filou, Adam Karlin, Katharina Kane, Kate Thomas, Tom Masters, Tim Bewer, Paul Clammer and Jean-Bernard Carillet. This guidebook was commissioned in Lonely Planet's Melbourne office, and produced by the following:

Commissioning Editors Stefanie Di Trocchio, Holly Alexander & Lucy Monie
Coordinating Editor Jeanette Wall
Coordinating Cartographer Mark Griffiths
Coordinating Layout Designer Carol Jackson
Managing Editors Brigitte Ellemor, Geoff Howard
Managing Cartographers Hunor Csutoros, Corey Hutchison, Alison Lyall
Managing Layout Designer Sally Darmody
Assisting Editors Sarah Bailey, Monique Choy, Jackey Coyle, Michala Green, Jocelyn Harewood, Anne Mulvaney
Assisting Cartographers Mick Garrett, David Kemp, Kanh Luu
Cover Image research provided by lonelyplanetimages.com
Project Manager Craig Kilburn

Thanks to Glenn Beanland, David Carroll, Nicholas Colicchia, Daniel Corbett, Bruce Evans, Ryan Evans, Trent Holden, Lisa Knights, John Mazzocchi, Annelies Mertens, Maryanne Netto, Darren O' Connell, Kirsten Rawlings, Averil Robertson, John Taufa, Juan Winata

THANKS
ANTHONY HAM

Ogomono Saye was a terrific guide, wonderful travel companion and a valued friend who taught

---

me so much about Mali – *manga tao*! The same applies to Azima Ag Mohamed Ali who took me to Araouane at considerable personal risk. Baba Mahamane was an outstanding driver and great company, while Karen Crabbs of Toguna Adventure Tours was also extraordinarily helpful. Special thanks also to: El-Mehdi Doumbia and Shitta al-Mohktar (In-a-Djatafane); Moussa Dicko (Dimamou); Mohammed Bashir (Araouane); Amassomou M Saye (Dogon Country); and Mamadou Keita (Djenné). I'm especially grateful to my interviewees, especially Toumani Diabaté (Bamako), Colonel Biramou Sissoko of PCVBG-E (Bamako), Dr Inamoud Ibny Yattara of Temedt (Bamako), Menidou Keita (Ibi), Ramtou Koné (Bandiagara) and Mariam Sow (Ségou). Thanks also to Sarah Castle, Susan Canney, Birgit Snitker, Kim Nooyens, Olivier, Mohammed Traoré, Mamatou, Draba, Yves, Sidibé, Modibo Koné, Sindefing Demble, Julie Dupars, Vieux Traoré and all my editors and co-authors at Lonely Planet. Mali just wasn't the same this time around without my wife and best friend, Marina: *te quiero mi amor*. And to my daughter Carlota who really is the most wonderful little person in all the world: next time we'll go to see the elephants together.

My work on this book is dedicated to Rebecca, who did so much to better the lives of West African women but died in tragic circumstances during the writing of this book. Her work with the Physicians for Human Rights Asylum Network (www.physicians forhumanrights.org/asylum) will be remembered.

TIM BEWER

A hearty *tenki* to the wonderful people of Sierra Leone who rarely failed to live up to their reputation for friendliness and hospitality when faced with my incessant questions. In particular Edward Aruna, Bimbola Carrol, Edleen Elba, Alieya Kargbo, Alhaji Siaka and David Zeller all provided good help and good company. And to Holly Alexander, Stefanie Di Trocchio, Anthony Ham and everybody else in Lonely Planet–land, it was a pleasure as always.

STUART BUTLER

I'd like to thank the handful of Cape Verdean surfers for their smiling acceptance of me on their waves, in particular Claudio Pretelli on Boa Vista. I'd also like to thank Laurent at the Casa Café Mindelo for his patience, the staff at all the airline and ferry offices for theirs, the man in the cowboy hat for the black market tickets and the man in the travel agency who told me about him, the receptionist at the Por de Sol Arte for the super strength Deep Heat and, as always, Heather for her patience and understanding.

JEAN-BERNARD CARILLET

Heaps of thanks to Lonely Planet's Holly and Stef for their confidence. In Burkina Faso and in France, a heartfelt *merci beaucoup* to Guillaume, Maurice, Alain, Christophe, Xav', Gerard, Dominique, Simon, Mickael, Nicolas, Laure, Salifou and Hama for their good company, Princess Abiba, Olivia, Kader, Jerome, Lucien, Irene, Moko, Fernand, Bassirou, Rosalie and all the Burkinabé people I met on the road – you're all so very charming.

Anthony, coordinating author extraordinaire, deserves the thumbs up for his courage and stamina.

And how could I forget my daughter Eva, who hopefully will share some of my African experiences sooner or later…

PAUL CLAMMER

Number one thanks – for myriad reasons – to Mal and Awoba (and BB!) in Lagos. It literally couldn't have happened without you both. In Ibadan, thanks to Summer and Nazih for their warm hospitality, to Ridwan Siddiqi and David Ehrhardt (Kano), and to Peter Jenkins of Pandrillus (Calabar and Afi). Thanks also to Giora Moss for his brilliant readers' letter. In Mauritania, particular thanks to Just and Cora in Atar, Christine and Sven for the brilliant trip to Ben Amira, and Chris Kirkley in Nouakchott. Finally, thanks as always to Jo, especially for her patience when visas were looking dubious.

EMILIE FILOU

In Togo, I am hugely indebted to Ram Shriyan and his family for their heartfelt welcome. Thanks also to Jean-Marie Lascaux, Eric Miens and the Henrys for their insight. In Benin, thank you to Rikke Offenberg, Sarah Christoffersen, Marie Heuts and Mireia Idiaquez for their hospitality. Thanks also to Hélène Verwaerde in Nati for her friendship and useful introductions. Back home, I'd like to thank Adolfo for his daily calls and apologise for the grey hair I've given him. And finally, thank you to my grandparents Pauline and Gilbert Tanguy for being such an inspiration: *ce livre est pour vous*.

KATHARINA KANE

Hard to squeeze in the helping hands and minds of four countries into a few lines. First of all, apologies to Jules and Ishema for travelling on my own so much that I'm now too tired for family holidays. Coming home after each long trip has been fabulous. In Senegal, special thanks go to Cherif Bodian, PJ, Haidar, Elise, Marcel, Ursula, Jean-Jacques Bancal & Muriel, Ines Gontek, Alpha & Doba, Mwana, Julien, Romuald, Laure, Jean-Paul, Clara & Jean Pierrot, Stef & Baba. In Gambia: Geri & Maurice, Tomm, Lamine, Mark & Jayne, James, Peter & Malang, Deepa and Jess Tyrell. In Guinea-Bissau: Miguel, Solange & team, Diego, Joseph & Martha. In Guinea: Telivel & Billy, Gerhard, Lama Foutah, Boubacar, Soundioulou, Cellou, Stefan & Mamadi, Marie-Claude, Diams Diallo, Solo, Peter, El Hadj Dioulde Ba & Salimatou.

ADAM KARLIN

Mbouombouo Aramiyahou: my guide, friend and brother. I am indebted to the kindness shown by you and your family throughout Cameroon. Give Abdu a hug, tell your daughter to smile, thank Adamou with all my heart and send all my best to your father, mother, siblings and cousins. Also: shout outs to Agnes and friends in Kumba and my fellow passengers in the Kribi-Campo taxi we pushed uphill so many times. Thanks Holly for getting me on this book, Anthony Ham for being understanding and Kate for storytelling – both listening to mine and letting me listen to hers.

TOM MASTERS

In Niger a huge shout out to Douglas de Carvalho, my companion whose company made those long bus rides fly by – Obama night in Niamey will not be forgotten anytime soon! Thanks also to Céline at Agadez Tourisme, Turbo at Turbo Tours and Moussa my reliable taximan. In Liberia a big thank you to Meg Riggs at the US Embassy in Monrovia, to Adam Kybird, Meredith Safer, Dana Rosen, Cristy Lewis, Callista Chen and the many other expats who helped me out with advice and information. Much gratitude also to Bacchus, my fearless driver, and to Jeffrey Austin and Soso Gaye in Harper. I'm extremely grateful to Lucy Monie and Holly Alexander at Lonely Planet for sending me to Africa, to fellow authors Tim Bewer, Kate Thomas, Paul Clammer and Emilie Filou for various bits of shared information and to coordinating author Anthony Ham for all his help and advice.

KATE THOMAS

In Côte d'Ivoire, special thanks to Aminata Soumahoro, Hortense Gnonogo and Franck Kodjo, who helped shape the chapter more than they realised. Thanks also to Ben Mpeck, everyone at Côte d'Ivoire Tourisme and Alain. John James, Jeff

Simpson, Nico Colombant, Emmanuel and the antenne guys were also helpful. In Ghana, I owe so much to Ben Clayton. In and around Accra, thanks to Key Tugbe Toe, Angeline, Daniel Oblie, McKenzie, Carly, Tristan, Tiggy, Olivier and everyone who shared thoughts. To Christian and Linda, I'm grateful. Also to Adam. In England, enormous thanks to Sam Thomas, Michele McIntyre, Fiona Thomas and Gordon Vincent, for their constant faith. In the US, very special thanks to Art and Helen Thomas. Lani, the McGatheys, Andre and so many others also brightened that summer. At Lonely Planet, big thanks to Holly, Stefanie and Anthony. Lastly, to my good friends in Liberia.

OUR READERS

Many thanks to the travellers who used the last edition and wrote to us with helpful hints, useful advice and interesting anecdotes:

A Nasir Abubakar, Sue Adams, Gary Adams, Ronnie Allebrandi, Miriam Alvarado, Olga Avila **B** Humphrey Barclay, James Barr, Laurie Barrett, Gili Bassan, Jean-Marc Baudot, Jacob Betz, Deborah Binder, Domi Bischops, Sabine Bleuel, Hazel Bober, Auke Boere, Jo Busby **C** Michael Carney, Georg Caspary, Adam Casselden, Antoine Chamussy, Michael Chapman, Suzanne Charkas, Marianne Christensen, Rachael Clapson, Tristan Clements, Adam David Cohn,

---

SEND US YOUR FEEDBACK

We love to hear from travellers – your comments keep us on our toes and help make our books better. Our well-travelled team reads every word on what you loved or loathed about this book. Although we cannot reply individually to postal submissions, we always guarantee that your feedback goes straight to the appropriate authors, in time for the next edition. Each person who sends us information is thanked in the next edition – and the most useful submissions are rewarded with a free book.

To send us your updates – and find out about Lonely Planet events, newsletters and travel news – visit our award-winning website: **lonelyplanet.com/contact.**

Note: we may edit, reproduce and incorporate your comments in Lonely Planet products such as guidebooks, websites and digital products, so let us know if you don't want your comments reproduced or your name acknowledged. For a copy of our privacy policy visit lonelyplanet.com/privacy.

BEHIND THE SCENES

Bob Cone, Christine Cooper **D** Antonello Decortes, Grigorios Delichristos, Seanan Denizot, Sumudu Dhanapala, Nathan Dhillon, Miranda Dodd, Colin Doyle **E** Roland Ehrat, Joumana El-Khoury, Beth Elder, Mohamed Elmeshad, Susanne Elsas, Brett Emerson, Abbette Evertzen **F** Clarence Fahnbulleh, Eva Farago, Mariella Fourli, David Furnival **G** Jeff Geipel, Christos Georgalas, Uwe Gesierich, Sam Godding, Peter Goltermann, Ann-Marie Grant **H** Lauren Hall, Matthew Hall, Patricia Hartlief, Celine Heinbecker, Brian Hermon, Yuri Horowitz, Petr Hruska **J** Bradwell Jackson **K** David Kerkhoff, Kerstin Koch, Kevin Krol, Jonas Kubitscheck, Deepak Kumar, Michiel Kupers **L** Ruud Leijtens, Stefano Lena **M** Tamara Mack, Megan Malachi, Roger McMeans, Ian Merkel, Angela Michalek, Mary Milton, Ian Morley, Trish Morrow, Giora Moss, Anthony Murray **N** Mike Newby, Steve Newcomer, Nanjala Nyabola **O** Sofie Op De Beeck, Sally Overton **P** Aspa Plakantonaki, Tatjana Proske **R** Sanjay Ranchod, Julie Ranger, Jean Francois Reynaud, Jessica Reynolds, Christian Riedke, Thomas Roger, Anne Rogiers **S** Franklin S, Gonzalo Scanferla, Andreas Schoenherr, Sylvia Schubert, Federica Seymandi, Joanne Shirley, Paul Smith, Danielle Steenman, Luluk Suhada, Corinna & Immanuel Sy Hick **T** Wright Thompson, Tajan Tober, Eva Tombs, Charlotte Torp Møller, Jess Tyrrell **V** Robert Van Den Bos, J Van Der Kolk, Robin Van Oosterhout **W** M'Basen Wazir, Tony Wheeler, George Wolf **Z** Daniel Ziegler, Rachel Zuback

ACKNOWLEDGMENTS
Many thanks to the following for the use of their content:

Globe on title page ©Mountain High Maps 1993 Digital Wisdom, Inc.

Index

INDEX

INDEX

INDEX

INDEX

GreenDex

The following attractions, activities, tours, accommodation and restaurants have been selected by Lonely Planet authors because they demonstrate a commitment to sustainability. Our criteria for inclusion in the GreenDex covers environmental (minimising negative environmental impacts and, where possible, making positive contributions), social or cultural (respecting culture and traditions and fostering authentic interaction and greater understanding between travellers and hosts) and economic (providing financial benefits for the host community and operating on the principles of fair trade) issues. For more tips about travelling sustainably in West Africa, turn to the Getting Started chapter (p15). We want to keep developing our sustainable-travel content. If you think we've omitted someone who should be listed here, email us at www.lonelyplanet.com/contact. For more information about sustainable tourism and Lonely Planet, see www.lonelyplanet.com/responsibletravel.

912

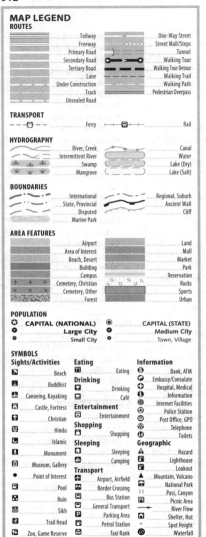

MAP LEGEND

ROUTES
Tollway
Freeway
Primary Road
Secondary Road
Tertiary Road
Lane
Under Construction
Track
Unsealed Road
One-Way Street
Street Mall/Steps
Tunnel
Walking Tour
Walking Tour Detour
Walking Trail
Walking Path
Pedestrian Overpass

TRANSPORT
Ferry
Rail

HYDROGRAPHY
River, Creek
Intermittent River
Swamp
Mangrove
Canal
Water
Lake (Dry)
Lake (Salt)

BOUNDARIES
International
State, Provincial
Disputed
Marine Park
Regional, Suburb
Ancient Wall
Cliff

AREA FEATURES
Airport
Area of Interest
Beach, Desert
Building
Campus
Cemetery, Christian
Cemetery, Other
Forest
Land
Mall
Market
Park
Reservation
Rocks
Sports
Urban

POPULATION
○ CAPITAL (NATIONAL)
● Large City
● Small City
◉ CAPITAL (STATE)
● Medium City
○ Town, Village

SYMBOLS
Sights/Activities
Beach
Buddhist
Canoeing, Kayaking
Castle, Fortress
Christian
Hindu
Islamic
Monument
Museum, Gallery
Point of Interest
Pool
Ruin
Sikh
Trail Head
Zoo, Game Reserve

Eating
Eating

Drinking
Drinking
Café

Entertainment
Entertainment

Shopping
Shopping

Sleeping
Sleeping
Camping

Transport
Airport, Airfield
Border Crossing
Bus Station
General Transport
Parking Area
Petrol Station
Taxi Rank

Information
Bank, ATM
Embassy/Consulate
Hospital, Medical
Information
Internet Facilities
Police Station
Post Office, GPO
Telephone
Toilets

Geographic
Hazard
Lighthouse
Lookout
Mountain, Volcano
National Park
Pass, Canyon
Picnic Area
River Flow
Shelter, Hut
Spot Height
Waterfall

LONELY PLANET OFFICES

Australia
Head Office
Locked Bag 1, Footscray, Victoria 3011
☎ 03 8379 8000, fax 03 8379 8111
talk2us@lonelyplanet.com.au

USA
150 Linden St, Oakland, CA 94607
☎ 510 250 6400, toll free 800 275 8555
fax 510 893 8572
info@lonelyplanet.com

UK
2nd fl, 186 City Rd,
London EC1V 2NT
☎ 020 7106 2100, fax 020 7106 2101
go@lonelyplanet.co.uk

Published by Lonely Planet Publications Pty Ltd
ABN 36 005 607 983

© Lonely Planet Publications Pty Ltd 2009

© photographers as indicated 2009

Cover photograph: Sudanese-style Muslim mosque (16th century), Nakoui, Ghana, Kevin O'Hara/Age Fotostock. Many of the images in this guide are available for licensing from Lonely Planet Images: www.lonelyplanetimages.com.

Mixed Sources
Product group from well-managed forests and other controlled sources
www.fsc.org Cert no. SGS-COC-005002
© 1996 Forest Stewardship Council